THE
FACTS ON FILE
ENCYCLOPEDIA OF
WORD AND
PHRASE ORIGINS

THE
FACTS ON FILE
ENCYCLOPEDIA OF
WORD AND PHRASE
ORIGINS

Robert Hendrickson

Facts On File Publications
New York, New York ● Oxford, England

For my son
Robert Laurence Hendrickson

To make dictionaries is hard work.
—DR. SAMUEL JOHNSON

The Facts On File Encyclopedia of Word and Phrase Origins

Copyright © 1987 by Robert Hendrickson

Library of Congress Cataloging-in-Publication Data

Hendrickson, Robert, 1933-
   The Facts on File encyclopedia of word and phrase origins.

   Bibliography: p.
   Includes index.
   1. English language—Terms and phrases. 2. English language—Etymology—Dictionaries. I. Facts on File, Inc. II. Title.
PE1689.H47 1987   422'.03   86-2067
ISBN 0-8160-1012-9

Printed in the United States of America

BOMC offers recordings and compact discs, cassettes and records. For information and catalog write to BOMR, Camp Hill, PA 17012.

PREFACE

Covering some 7500 words and phrases, in the space of about one million words, this book is, I believe, the longest collection of word and phrase origins in print.

In any case, I've tried to make all the selections as accurate and entertaining as possible and tried to use words illustrating all of the many ways words and phrases are born (words deriving from the numerous languages and dialects that have enriched English, echoic words, coined words, slang, words from the names of places, people, animals, occupations, leisure activities, mispronunciations, etc.). Yet in the final analysis any selection from such a vast semantic treasure house (the 5-10 million or so general and technical English words) must be highly subjective. Perhaps I have erred in devoting too much space to fascinating but speculative stories about word origins, but I don't think so, for the wildest theories often later turn out to be the correct ones. In any case, while no good tale is omitted merely because it isn't true, where stories are apocryphal or doubtful, they are clearly labeled so. I've tried to include as many plausible theories about the origins of each expression as possible and also attempted to show the first recorded use of a word or phrase wherever possible, something lacking in many word books but a great, sometimes indispensable help to anyone using the work as a linguistic or historical reference. The only limitations I have imposed are those of importance and interest. Some expressions, no matter how prosaic the stories behind them, have been included because they are commonly used; on the other hand, interesting and unusual expressions have often been treated even if obscure or obsolete. No word or phrase has been eliminated because it might offend someone's sensibilities, and you will find all the famous four-letter words here (and then some!). I consider myself no judge of what is or is not obscene, and such self-appointed lobotomizers of language remind me of Kurt Vonnegut's dictator who eliminated noses in order to eliminate odors. Though there has been a renewed general interest in word origins recently—thanks mainly to magazines like *Verbatim*, the work of Stuart Berg Flexner, Professor Frederic Cassidy's monumental *Dictionary of American Regional English*, or *DARE* (the first volume, A-C, of which was published this year), and William Safire's excellent and entertaining syndicated column "On Language"—etymology remains something less than an exact science. Devoted scholars like Professor Gerald Cohen of the University of Missouri-Rolla do devote years and pages enough for a book in scientifically tracking down the origins of a single word, but a great number of the word derivations on record amount to little more than educated guesswork. I agree, however, with the late, great and "always game" word detective Eric Partridge that even a guess is better than nothing—even if it's just inspired fun, or if it merely stimulates thinking that leads eventually to the expression's true origin.

The debts for a work of this nature and length are so numerous that specific thanks must be confined to the many sources noted in the text, and due to space limitations even these are only a relative handful of the works I have consulted. On a personal note, however, I would like to thank my editor, Gerard Helferich, for all his herculean labors (just toting the manuscript about was a herculean labor), and of course my wife, Marilyn—this book, like every line I write, being as much hers as mine. Nevertheless, despite all the help I've gotten, any errors in these pages result from my own wide-ranging ignorance and are solely my responsiblity. They cannot even be blamed on a committee or a computer.

—R.H.

ABBREVIATIONS FOR THE MOST FREQUENTLY CITED AUTHORITIES

BARTLETT—John Bartlett, *Dictionary of Americanisms* (1877)

BREWER—Rev. Ebenezer Cobham Brewer, *Brewer's Dictionary of Fact and Fable* (1870)

DARE—Frederic Cassidy, ed. *Dictionary of American Regional English*, v.1, 1986

FARMER AND HURLEY—John S. Farmer and W.E. Hurley, *Slang and Its Analogues* (1890-1904)

FOWLER—H.W. Fowler, *Modern English Usage* (1926)

GRANVILLE—Wilfred Granville, *A Dictionary of Sailor's Slang* (1962)

GROSE—Captain Francis Grose, *Dictionary of the Vulgar Tongue* (1785, 1788, 1796, 1811, 1823 editions)

MATHEWS—Mitford M. Mathews, *A Dictionary of Americanisms* (1951)

MENCKEN—H.L. Mencken, *The American Language* (1936)

O.E.D.—*The Oxford English Dictionary*

ONIONS—C.T. Onions, *The Oxford Dictionary of English Etymology* (1966)

PARTRIDGE—Eric Partridge, *A Dictionary of Slang and Unconventional English* (1950)

PARTRIDGE'S ORIGINS—Eric Partridge, *Origins, A Short Etymological Dictionary of Modern English* (1958)

PEPYS—Henry Wheatley, ed., *The Diary of Samuel Pepys* (1954)

RANDOM HOUSE—*The Random House Dictionary of the English Language* (1966)

ROSTEN—Leo Rosten, *The Joys of Yiddish* (1968)

SHIPLEY—Joseph T. Shipley, *Dictionary of Word Origins* (1967)

SKEAT—W.W. Skeat, *An Etymological Dictionary of the English Language* (1963)

STEVENSON—Burton Stevenson, *Home Book of Quotations* (1947)

STEWART—George R. Stewart, *American Place Names* (1971)

WALSH—W.S. Walsh, *Handbook of Literary Curiousities* (1892)

WEBSTER'S—*Webster's Third New International Dictionary of the English Language* (1981)

WEEKLEY—Ernest Weekley, *Etymological Dictionary of Modern English* (1967)

WENTWORTH AND FLEXNER—Harold Wentworth and Stuart Berg Flexner, *Dictionary of American Slang* (1975)

WESEEN—Maurice H. Weseen, *Dictionary of American Slang* (1934)

WRIGHT—Joseph Wright, *English Dialect Dictionary* (1900)

Many different works by the same authors, and additional works by other writers, are cited in the text.

THE
FACTS ON FILE
ENCYCLOPEDIA OF
WORD AND
PHRASE ORIGINS

A

A. Like Chinese characters today, each letter in our alphabet began with a picture or drawing of an animal, person, or object that eventually became a symbol with little resemblance to the original object depicted. No one is sure what these pictographs represented originally, but scholars have made some educated guesses. *A* probably represented the horns of an ox, drawn first as a *V* with a bar across it like the bar in *A*. This may have been suggested by early plowmen guiding oxen by lines attached to a bar strapped across the animal's horns.

aa. *Aa* for rough porous lava, similar to coal clinkers, is an Americanism used chiefly in Hawaii, but has currency on the mainland, too, especially among geologists, or where there has been recent volcanic activity, mainly because there is no comparable English term to describe the jagged rocks. The word *aa* is first recorded in 1859, but is much older, coming from the Hawaiian *'a'a*, meaning the same, which, in turn comes from the Hawaiian *a*, for "fiery, burning."

A & P. These familiar initials have become the common name of the supermarket chain they were once an abbreviation for. The Great Atlantic *and* Pacific Tea Company began life in 1859 as a partnership between George Huntington Hartford and George Gilman. The new company originally bought tea directly off ships bringing it to America and sold it to consumers, eliminating the middleman. Within twenty years the company became the first American grocery chain.

aardvark; aardwolf. Both these animals dig in the earth for termites and ants, the former somewhat resembling a pig, the latter looking a little like a striped wolf. Thus the Boers in South Africa named them, respectively, the *aardvark* (from the Dutch *aard*, "earth," plus *vark*, "pig") or "earthpig," and *aardwolf*, or "earth wolf."

Aaron lily; Aaron's beard; Aaron's rod; Aaron's serpent. Numerous plants are named for the patriarch Aaron. Mention in Psalms, 133, of "the beard of Aaron" led to *Aaron's beard* becoming the common name of the rose of Sharon (which in the Bible is really a crocus), icy-leaved toadflax, meadowsweet, *Aaron's-beard* cactus, and the Jerusalem star, among others, in reference to their beard-like flowers. *Aaron's rod* comes from the sacred rod that Aaron placed before the ark in Num., 17:8, a rod that Jehovah caused to bud, blossom, and bear ripe

almonds. Many tall-stemmed, flowering plants that resemble rods, such as mullein, goldenrod, and garden orpine, are called *Aaron's rod*, and the term is used in architecture to describe an ornamental moulding entwined with sprouting leaves, a serpent, or scrollwork. The *Aaron lily* also honors Aaron, but the name derives from the folk etymology of arum lily. *Aaron's serpent*, denoting a force so powerful as to eliminate all other powers, alludes to the miracle in Exod. 7:11-12, when the Lord commanded that Aaron cast down his rod before Pharaoh: "Then Pharaoh also called the wise men and the sorcerers: now the magicians of Egypt, they also did in like manner with their enchantments. For they cast down every man his rod, and they became serpents, but Aaron's rod swallowed up their rods." Linguists have found that the word *tannen* given in the Exodus sources really means "reptile," but there is little chance that "Aaron's reptile" will replace *Aaron's serpent* in the language.

AB; able-bodied seaman. *AB* stands for an *able-bodied seaman*, a first-class sailor who is a skilled seaman and has passed his training as an ordinary seaman. The expression *able-bodied* dates back to 17th-century England, when apprentices or boys formed the other, inexperienced class among the crews on sailing ships.

abacus. Our name for this incredibly efficient instrument, which a skilled person can operate as fast and as accurately as an adding machine, is from the Greek *abax*, meaning a tablet for ciphering. The *abacus* was invented by the Chinese, but they call the beaded ciphering machine a suan pan.

abash. (*See* **bah!**)

abassi. Though of interest primarily to collectors, the *abassi* is the first of many coins named after famous persons. It is a silver piece worth about twenty-nine cents that was formerly used in Persia, and it honors Shah Abas II.

abbreviation. Deriving from a Latin word meaning the same and spelled the same, *abbreviation* was first recorded in the early 16th century. Unlike acronyms, abbreviations aren't usually pronounced as words, but they do serve the same purpose as time and space savers. They have been popular since Roman times, a good example being SPQR, the abbreviation for *Senatus Popu-*

lusque Romanus (the Senate and People of Rome), the famous insignia of Rome. Most abbreviations merely suggest the whole word they represent to the reader (as *Dr.*), but many have become almost words themselves, with the letters spoken, as in *IQ* for intelligence quotient. A few are even spoken as words, such as *vet* for veterinarian or armed forces veteran, *ad* for advertisement, and *ad lib*. There are entire dictionaries devoted to the tens of thousands of abbreviations we use, and a complete list of abbreviations of government agencies can be found in the *U.S. Government Organization Manual*.

Abderian laughter. Inhabitants of Ancient Abdera were known as rural simpletons who foolishly derided people and things they didn't understand. Thus these Thracians saw their name become a synonym for foolish, scoffing laughter or mockery. Though proverbially known for their stupidity, the Abderites included some of the wisest men in Greece, Democritus and Protagoras among them.

abedecedarian hymns. (*See* **acrostic**.)

Abe Lincoln bug. Anti-Lincoln feelings died hard in the South after the Civil War, as the name of this little bug shows. Even as late as 1901 this foul-smelling insect, also known as the harlequin cabbage bug, was commonly called the *Abe-Lincoln bug* in Georgia and other Southern states. (*See also* **Lincoln**.)

to abet. *Abet* means to incite, instigate, or encourage someone to act, often wrongfully. The word derives from an old command for a dog to "sic 'em" or "go get 'em," and owes its life to the "sport" of bearbaiting, which was as popular as cricket in 14th- and 15th-century England. In bearbaiting, a recently trapped bear, starved to make it unnaturally vicious, was chained to a stake or put in a pit, and a pack of dogs was set loose upon it in a fight to the death, which the bear always lost, after inflicting great punishment on the dogs. Spectators who urged the dogs on were said to *abet* them, *abet* here being the contraction of the Old French *abeter*, "to bait, to hound on," which in turn derived from the Norse *beita*, "to cause to bite." Bearbaiting was virtually a Sunday institution in England for eight hundred years, until it was banned in 1835; Queen Elizabeth I once attended a "Bayting" at which 13 bears were killed.

abeyance. (*See* **bah!**)

abigail. A lady's maid or servant is sometimes called an *abigail*, which means "source of joy" in Hebrew. Several real Abigails contributed their names to the word. The term originates in the Bible (Sam. I:25) when Nabal's wife, Abigail, apologizes for her wealthy husband's selfishness in denying David food for his followers—humbly

referring to herself as David's "handmaid" six times in the course of eight short chapters. David must have appreciated this, for when Nabal died he made Abigail one of his wives. The name and occupation were further associated when Francis Beaumont and John Fletcher's *The Scornful Lady*, written about five years after the King James version of the Bible (1611), gave the name Abigail to a spirited "waiting gentlewoman," one of the play's leading characters. *Abigail* was thereafter used by many writers, including Congreve, Swift, Fielding, and Smollett, but only came to be spelled without a capital when popularized by the notoriety of Abigail Hill, one of Queen Anne's ladies-in-waiting, 1704-14.

able-bodied seaman. (*See* **AB**.)

A-bomb; H-bomb; the bomb. The atomic bomb was first called the *atom bomb* or *A-bomb* within a few months after it was dropped on Hiroshima on August 6, 1945. People were also calling it simply *the bomb* by then. Soon after the far more powerful thermonuclear hydrogen bomb or *H-bomb* was tested, in 1952, it was commonly called *the bomb*, too.

aborigine. William Hone, in his *Table Book* (1827-28) says that *aborigine* "is explained in every dictionary . . . as a general name for the indigenous inhabitants of a country. In reality, it is the proper name of a peculiar people of Italy, who were not indigenous but were supposed to be a colony of Arcadians." Nevertheless, these people of Latium were thought by some Romans to have been residents of Italy from the beginning, *ab originie*, which gave us the Latin word *aborigines* for the original inhabitants of a country.

Aboriginal Australian words. English words that come to us from Aboriginal Australian include *boomerang*, *kangaroo*, *dingo*, *koala*, *wallaby*, *wombat*, and *bellycan* (water can).

aboveboard; under the table. *Aboveboard* means "honest." The expression, first recorded in the late 16th century, derives from card-playing, in which cheating is much more difficult and honesty more likely if all the hands of cards are kept above the board, or table. *Under the table*, a later expression, means dishonest, and refers to cards manipulated under the playing surface.

above the salt. (*See* **salt**.)

abracadabra. One of the few words entirely without meaning, this confusing term is still used in a joking way by those making "magic." It was first mentioned in a poem by Quintus Severus Sammonicus in the second century. A cabalistic word intended to suggest infinity, abracadabra was believed to be a charm with the power to cure toothaches, fevers, and other ills, especially if written on parchment in a triangular arrangement and suspended from the neck by a linen thread. *Abracadabra* is of unknown origin, though tradition says it is composed of the initials of the Hebrew words *Ab* (Father), *Ben* (Son), and Ruach Acadsch (Holy Spirit). When toothache strikes, inscribe the parchment amulet in the following triangular form:

```
ABRACADABRA
 ABRACADABR
  ABRACADAB
   ABRACADA
    ABRACAD
     ABRAC
      ABRA
       ABR
        AB
         A
```

Abram; Abraham man; Abraham's bosom.   *Abram* or *Abraham man*, a synonym for beggar, can be traced to the parable in Luke 16:19-31, where "the beggar [Lazarus] died and was carried into Abraham's bosom." But it may actually derive from the Abraham Ward in England's Bedlam asylum, whose inmates were allowed out on certain days to go begging. *In Abraham's bosom* is an expression for the happy repose of death, deriving from the same source.

absence make the heart grow fonder; out of sight, out of mind.   Whether you believe this proverb or the contradictory saying *out of sight, out of mind*, the phrase does not come from the poem "Isle of Beauty" by Thomas Haynes Bayly (1797-1839), as Dr. Brewer, Bartlett, and other sources say. Bayly did write "Absence makes the heart grow fonder,/Isle of Beauty, Fare thee well!," but the same phrase was recorded in Francis Davison's "Poetical Rapsody" in 1602. *Out of sight, out of mind* comes from the poem "That Out of Sight" by Arthur Hugh Clough (1819-1861):

That out of sight is out of mind
Is true of most we leave behind.

the absent are always wrong.   This saying is a translation of the old French proverb *Les absents ont toujours tort*, which dates back to the 17th century. The words suggest that it is easy to blame or accuse someone not present to defend himself.

absolutism tempered by assassination; despotism by dynamite.   Count Ernst F. Munster (1766-1839), the German envoy at St. Petersburg, was referring to the Russian Constitution when he said this in 1800, but he claimed that a Russian noble really invented the phrase.

Gilbert and Sullivan altered the phrase to *despotism by dynamite.*

abyss.   *Abyss* is one of the few English words that derive from Sumerian, the world's first written language, which evolved some 5,000 years ago in the lower Tigris and Euphrates Valley of what is now called Iraq. The word came into English in the late 14th century from the Latin word *abyssus*, meaning "bottomless, the deep," but has been traced ultimately to the primordial sea that the Sumerians called the Abzu. Another word with Sumerian roots is *Eden*, the word for the lost paradise that came into English from a Hebrew word.

academy, academic.   (*See* **groves of academe.**)

Acapulco gold.   First recorded in 1967, *Acapulco gold* supposedly means a strong variety of marijuana grown near Acapulco, Mexico. But no one is even sure whether it is really a special variety of marijuana grown there or just any premium pot that dealers ask high prices for. Hawaiian *Maui wowie* is another well-known kind.

accidentally on purpose.   Someone who does something *accidentally on purpose* does it purposely and only apparently accidentally—often maliciously, in fact. The expression is not an Americanism, originating in England in the early 1880s before it became popular here.

according to Cocker.   *According to Cocker*, an English proverb similar to the four *According* entries following, means very accurate or correct, according to the rules. *According to Cocker* could just as well mean "all wrong"; however, few authorities bother to mention this. The phrase honors Edward Cocker (1631-75), a London engraver who also taught penmanship and arithmetic. Cocker wrote a number of popular books on these subjects, and reputedly authored *Cocker's Arithmetick*, which went through 112 editions, its authority giving rise to the proverb. Then in the late 19th century, documented proof was offered showing that Cocker did not write the famous book at all, that it was a forgery of his editor and publisher, so poorly done in fact that it set back rather than advanced the cause of elementary arithmetic.

according to Fowler.   Many disputes about proper English usage are settled with the words, "according to Fowler . . . ." The authority cited is Henry Watson Fowler (1858-1933), author of *A Dictionary of Modern English Usage* (1926). Fowler, a noted classicist and lexicographer, and his brother, F. G. Fowler, collaborated on a number of important books, including a one-volume abridgement of the *Oxford English Dictionary* (1911). But *Modern English Usage* is his alone. The book remains a standard reference work, though some of the old schoolmaster's opinions are debatable. Margaret Nicholson's *A*

Dictionary of American English Usage, Based on Fowler, is its American counterpart.

according to Guinness.   Arthur Guinness, Son & Co., Ltd., of St. James Gate, Brewery, Dublin, has published *The Guinness Book of World Records* since 1955. Many arguments have been settled by this umpire of record performance, which has inspired the contemporary expression *according to Guinness.* Few business firms become factual authorities like the Guinness family, which has brewed its famous stout since 1820, its registered name becoming synonymous with stout itself for over a century.

according to Gunter, etc.   Many practical inventions still in use were invented by the English mathematician and astronomer Edmund Gunter nearly four centuries ago. Gunter, a Welshman, was professor of astronomy at London's Gresham College from 1619 until his death five years later when only forty-five. In his short life he invented Gunter's chain, the 22-yard-long, 100-link chain used by surveyors in England and the United States; Gunter's line, the forerunner of the modern slide rule; the small portable Gunter's quadrant; and Gunter's scale, commonly used by seamen to solve navigation problems. Gunter, among other accomplishments, introduced the words *cosine* and *cotangent* and discovered the variation of the magnetic compass. His genius inspired the phrase *according to Gunter,* once as familiar in America as "According to Hoyle" is today.

according to Hoyle.   *A Short Treatise on the Game of Whist* by Englishman Edmond Hoyle, apparently a barrister and minor legal official in Ireland, was published in 1742. This was the first book to systemize the rules of whist and remained the absolute authority for the game until its rules were changed in 1864. The author also wrote *Hoyle's Standard Games,* which extended his range, has been republished hundreds of times, and is available in paperback today. The weight of his authority through these works led to the phrase *according to Hoyle* becoming not only a proverbial synonym for the accuracy of game rules but an idiom for correctness in general. History tells us little about Hoyle, but he enjoyed his eponymous fame for many years, living until 1769, when he died at age ninety-seven or so. Hoyle is responsible for popularizing the term *score* as a record of winning points in games, a relatively recent innovation. "When in doubt, win the trick," is his most memorable phrase.

accumulate.   *Accumulate* means literally "to heap up," from the Latin *accumulare.* (We also find the idea in "cumulus" clouds, billowing clouds heaped up in the sky.) One who accumulates wealth piles it up by adding money to the figurative pile.

ace; aces.   *Aces* has been American slang for the best at least since the first years of this century, deriving from *aces,* the highest cards in poker and other card games. But *ace* for an expert combat flier who has shot down five or more enemy planes appears to have been borrowed from the French *as,* "ace," during World War I. From there *ace* was extended to include an expert at anything. The card name *ace* comes ultimately from the Greek *ás,* one.

Achilles' heel.   When he was a baby, Achilles' mother, the goddess Thetis, dipped him into the magic waters of the river Styx to coat his body with a magic shield that no weapon could penetrate. However, she held him by the heel, so that this part of his body remained vulnerable. Paris learned of his secret during the Trojan War, shooting an arrow into his heel and killing him. *Achilles' heel* has since come to mean the weak part of anything.

acid test.   This expression dates back to frontier days in America, when peddlers determined the gold content of objects by scratching them and applying nitric acid. Since gold, which is chemically inactive, resists acids that corrode other metals, the (nitric) *acid test* distinguished it from copper, iron, or similar substances someone might be trying to palm off on the peddlers. People were so dishonest, or peddlers so paranoid, that the term quickly became part of the language, coming to mean a severe test of reliability.

to acknowledge the corn.   Much used in the 19th century as a synonym for our "copping a plea," this phrase is said to have arisen when a man was arrested and charged with stealing four horses and the corn (grain) to feed them. "I acknowledge [admit to] the corn," he declared.

aconite; monkshood; wolfsbane.   *Aconite (aconticius Napellus),* a deadly poisonous plant, is also known as *wolfsbane,* because it was once used to poison wolves, and *monkshood,* because the plant resembles a monk's head. *Aconite* itself derives from an ancient Greek word meaning "wolfsbane." Ancient legend says the showy perennial herb is of the buttercup family and that it became poisonous from the foam that dropped from the mouth of the monstrous hound Cerberus, who guarded the gates of Hell, when Hercules dragged him up from the nether regions. Some authorities say *aconite* derives from the Greek *akon,* "dart," because it was once used as an arrow poison.

acre.   The Sumerian *agar* meant a watered field, a word the first farmers in Babylonia formed from their word *a* for water and applied to fertile watered land in the river valleys. *Agar*—related to the Sanskrit *ajras,* an open plain—entered Latin as *ager,* "fertile field," and finally came into English as *acre* or *acras* in the tenth century. At first the word meant any unoccupied land. It then came to mean the amount of land a yoke of oxen could plow from sunup to sundown, and finally in the reign of Edward I was more fairly and accurately defined as a parcel of land four rods in width and forty rods in length (a rod measuring 16 1/2 feet). It remains the same today, except that the land does not have to be rectangular, that is, 4 x 40 rods.

acrobat; neurobat. *Acrobat* comes from the Greek *akros*, "aloft," plus *batos*, "climbing or walking," referring of course to the stunts early acrobats performed in the air, which included ropewalking. The greatest of the ancient Greek acrobats were called *neurobats*, from the Greek *neuron*, "sinew." These men performed on sinewy rope that was only as thick as the catgut or plastic used for fishing line today, appearing from the ground as if they were walking on air.

acrolect; basilect; idiolect. The *acrolect* (from the Greek *acro*, "topmost") is the best English spoken, *the King's English* (*q.v.*), while the *basilect* means the lowest level of poor speech. Another unusual word patterned on *dialect* is *idiolect*, meaning the language or speech of an individual, which always differs slightly from person to person. These words were apparently coined toward the end of the 19th century. (*See* **dialect**.)

acrostic; telestich; abedecedarian hymns. *Acrostics* can be any composition (poems, puzzles, etc.) in which certain letters of the lines, taken in order, form a word, phrase, or sentence that is the subject of the composition. When the last letters of lines do this, the acrostic is sometimes called a *telestich* (from the Greek *tele*, "far," and *stichos*, "row"). Acrostic derives from the Greek *akros*, "extreme," and *stichos*, "row or line of verse." The term was first applied to the prophecies of the Greek Erythraean sibyl, which were written on separate pages, the initial letters forming a word when the pages were arranged in order. Another famous early acrostic was made from the Greek for "Jesus Christ, God's Son, Savior": *Jesus Christos, Theou, Uios, Soter.* The first letters of each word (and the first two letters of *Christos*) taken in order spell *ichthus*, Greek for "fish," which became a Christian symbol for Jesus. There are even earlier examples of acrostics in the Bible. In Hebrew, for instance, Psalm 119 is an acrostic in which the first letters of each of the twenty-two stanzas descend in alphabetical order. Such alphabetical acrostics are usually called *abedecedarian hymns*, or *abecedarius*, and there are more complicated species of them in which each word in every line begins with the same letter:

An Austrian army, awfully array'd
Boldly by battery besieged Belgrade, etc.

actuary. An *actuary* is a highly skilled statistician who calculates and states insurance risks and premiums, but his or her title derives from the Latin for clerk, *acturarius*, for in the Roman army during Caesar's time, an *actuary* was no more than a payroll clerk.

act your age. Perhaps *act your age!* originated as a reproof to children, but it is directed at both children and adults today, meaning, of course, don't act more immature than you are, or don't try to keep up with the younger generation. The expression originated in the U.S., probably during the late 19th century, as did the synonymous *be your age!*

Adam; human. Adam, the name of the first man in the Bible, is the Hebrew word for man, deriving from *adama*, "earth," just as the Latin *humanus*, "human," is related to the Latin *humus*, "earth." For his sins, according to the Talmud, Adam was evicted from Paradise after only twelve hours. In addition to entries following, his name is represented by *Adam's wine*, or ale, a humorous expression for water; *Adamic*, naked, free like Adam; *Adamite*, a human being or descendant of Adam; *the second Adam*, a biblical reference to Christ; *the old Adam in us*, a reference to man's disposition to evil; and *I don't know him from Adam. I wouldn't know him from Adam's off ox* is an attempted improvement on the last, referring to the ox in the yoke farthest away from the driver. Neither expression is very accurate. Hardly anyone drives oxen these days, and as more than one humorist has observed, Adam had no navel, wore only a fig leaf, and shouldn't have been hard to identify at all.

Adamastor. Vasco da Gama is said to have seen a hideous sea phantom called the *Adamastor*, the spirit of the stormy Cape of Good Hope, which warned him not to undertake his third voyage to India. Da Gama made the voyage anyway and died soon after reaching his destination. The Adamastor is first mentioned in the epic poem the *Lusiads* by Portuguese adventurer and poet Luis de Camoens (1524–80), which was translated into English by Sir Richard Burton in 1881. The word *Adamastor* is probably Portuguese in origin, but its exact derivation is unknown.

Adam's apple. Adam never ate an apple, at least not in the biblical account of his transgressions, which refers only to unspecified forbidden fruit on the tree in the Garden of Eden. The forbidden fruit of which the Lord said "Ye shall not eat of the fruit which is in the midst of the garden, neither shall ye touch it, lest ye die" (Gen. 3:3) was probably an apricot or pomegranate, and the Muslims—intending no joke—believe it was a banana. Many fruits and vegetables have been called apples. Even in medieval times, pomegranates were "apples of

Carthage"; tomatoes, "love apples," aphrodisiacs; dates, "finger apples"; and potatoes, "apples of the earth." At any rate, tradition has it that Adam succumbed to Eve's wiles and ate of an apple from which she took the first bite, that a piece stuck in his throat forming the lump we call the *Adam's apple*, and that all of us, particularly males, inherited this mark of his "fall." Modern scientific physiology, as opposed to folk anatomy, explains this projection of the neck, most prominent in adolescents, as being anterior thyroid cartilage of the larynx. But pioneer anatomists honored the superstition in the mid-18th century by calling it *pomum Adami*, or *Adam's apple*. They simply could find no other explanation for this evasive lump in the throat that even seemed to move up and down.

Adam's apple tree. This particular tree is popularly named for Adam and the entire genus containing it was named by Linnaeus in honor of German botanist Dr. J.T. Tabernaemontanus (d. 1590), a celebrated Heidelberg botanist and physician who—despite the length of his patronym—also has species in two other plant genera commemorating him. Why the folkname *Adam's apple tree?* Clearly still another case of a claim on Eden. I quote from the *Encyclopedia of Gardening* (1838) by J.C. Loudon: "The inhabitants of Ceylon say that Paradise was a place in their country . . . They also point out as the tree which bore the forbidden fruit, the *Devi Ladner* or *Tabernaemontana alternifoxlia* [the species name has since been changed to *coronaria*] . . . In confirmation of the tradition they refer to the beauty of the fruit, and the fine scent of the flowers, both of which are most tempting. The shape of the fruit gives the idea of a piece having been bitten off; and the inhabitants say it was excellent before Eve ate of it, though it is now poisonous." *T. coronaria*, a five-to-eight-foot-high tropical shrub with white fragrant flowers, is also called the East Indian rosebay, crape jasmine, and *Nero's crown*, after the Roman emperor.

Adam's profession. "There is no ancient gentlemen but gardeners, ditchers, and grave-makers; they hold up Adam's profession," Shakespeare wrote in *Hamlet*. The bard also said "And Adam was a gardener" in *King Henry VI, Part III*. Much later, Kipling wrote: "Oh Adam was a gardener, and God who made him sees/That half a proper gardener's work is done upon his knees." The phrase *Adam's profession* was proverbial for gardening long before both poets lived. No one has called it "Eve's profession," even though she picked the first apple. (*See also* **fiacre**.)

adder; auger. Many English words have changed over the years because of lazy or quick pronunciation—depending on how you look at it. *Adder*, is an example. *Adder* was originally "nadder," but starting in the 14th century its *n* began to become part of the article *a*, making *an adder* out of "a nadder." Much the same hap-

pened to the tool, an *auger*, during the same time, the auger having originally been "a nauger."

to add insult to injury. One of the oldest of expressions, this goes back to an early fable of Aesop, in which a bald man tried to kill a fly on his head and missed the fly, smacking himself instead. Said the fly: "You wanted to kill me for a mere touch. What will you do to yourself, now that you have added insult to injury."

addisonian termination. (*See* **preposition**.)

adieu. *Je vous recommande à Dieu*, "I commend you to God," was in times past said to Frenchmen who were going on a long journey and would not be seen for some time. Eventually the *à Dieu* detached itself (merged to *adieu*) from the phrase and came to mean the same kind of good-bye.

Adirondacks. The Mohawk Indians contemptuously dubbed a tribe of Algonquin Indians *Adirondack*, meaning "they eat bark," and the tribe's nickname came to be applied to the mountain region in northeastern New York that these Indians inhabited. The insulting name gives us, literally, "they eat bark" chairs, pack baskets, and even grapes, among many other items characteristic of the *Adirondacks*.

ad lib. Deriving from the Latin *ad libitum*, at will, *ad lib* means to speak words or perform actions not in a script or speech being used. *Ad libitum* is first recorded in 1705.

the Admirable Crichton. The perfect man, the perfect servant. James Crichton, born in 1560, was an English prodigy who while still in his teens earned his Master of Arts degree, mastered over a dozen languages, all the sciences, and achieved some fame as a poet and theologian. The fabled prodigy was also said to be handsome and without peer as a swordsman—"All perfect, finish'd to the fingernail," Tennyson wrote of him. Unfortunately, this ideal man proved either unwise or human enough to steal the heart of a prince's lady while traveling in Italy and was assassinated by three men in the prince's hire. Crichton was only twenty-five or so when he died. His name, in the form of *The Admirable Crichton*, was long used as a synonym for the perfect man, and when playwright James M. Barrie used it as the name of his butler hero in *The Admirable Crichton* (1902) it became synonymous for a perfect servant.

admiral. Technically, all *admirals* come from the Arabian desert, for the word can be traced to the title of Abu Bakr, who was called *Amir-al-muninin*, "commander of the faithful," before he succeeded Muhammad as caliph in A.D. 632. The title *Amir*, or "commander," became popular soon after, and naval chiefs were designated *Amir-al-ma*, "commander of commanders." Western seamen who came in contact with the Arabs assumed that *Amir-al* was one word, and believed this was a distinguished title. By the early 13th century, officers were calling themselves *amiral*, which merely means "commander of." The *d* was probably added to the word through a common mispronunciation.

Admiral of the Red.   An old term for a drunkard whose face and nose are always red. The expression is a play on the naval term *Admiral of the Red*, one of the three classes of admirals in early times named from the color of their flags. In British naval engagements prior to 1864 the *Admiral of the Red* held the center of the line, while the "Admiral of the White" held the vanguard and the "Admiral of the Blue" held the rear.

Adonis.   During the *Adonia*, an annual feast held in Greece, women wept eight days over Adonis's death, finally rejoicing in his resurrection. In classic mythology Adonis was the handsome lover of Aphrodite, goddess of love and beauty, and thus any man called an *Adonis* is among the most handsome of men.

Adonis flower.   This is the name of several flowers that were anciently believed to have sprung from the blood of Adonis, the handsome youth loved by the goddess Venus, after a wild boar killed him. Among other flowers, the anemone, the poppy, and the rose have been called the *Adonis flower*.

Adonis garden.   Any worthless or very perishable thing is called an *Adonis garden* in reference to the baskets of earth in which quick-growing plants were sown during the ancient feast of Adonis, the *Adonia*, in which the death and resurrection of Adonis (*see* **Adonis flower**) were celebrated. The plants were tended only for eight days, then allowed to wither and thrown into the sea along with images of Adonis.

adroit.   (*See* **right**.)

Aegean Sea.   King Aegeus of Greek mythology gives his name to the Aegean Sea. The king's son Theseus promised to hoist a white sail on his voyage home to Athens from Crete, to signal that he was alive. Theseus neglected to do so and Aegeus, thinking his son had been killed, committed suicide by throwing himself into the sea that came to be named for him.

aegis.   (*See* **under the umbrella of**.)

aerial.   *Aerial*, formed from the Latin word for "airy," wasn't introduced during the age of aviation, nor does it have its origins in circus aerial acts. The word is first recorded by Shakespeare, who may have coined it, in *Othello* (1604).

aerugo.   (*See* **Verdigris**.)

affiliate.   "Adopted" is the meaning of the Latin *affileatus*, composed of *ad*, "to," and *filius*, "son," from which the word *affiliate* derives. Thus a smaller company affiliated with a larger one could be said to have been adopted by the parent corporation. The word is first recorded by Smollett in *Gil Blas* (1761).

Afghan hound.   Bred in Afghanistan since at least 3000 B.C., this large, slender, heavy-coated dog, related to the greyhound, was used by the Egyptians for hunting.

Africa.   The Romans named this continent *Aprika*, meaning "sunny," which became the English *Africa*.

Afrikaans words.   English words that came to us from Afrikaans (the Taal) include: *veldt, trek, commando, wildebeest,* and *aardvark*.

African language words.   English words and phrases that possibly came to us from African languages include: *banjo, bad mouth, boogie-woogie, to bug, buckra, chigger, cooter, goober, hip, jazz, jitterbug, jukebox, mumbo jumbo, okra, poor Joe* (great blue heron), *speak softly and carry a big stick, sweet talk, tote, voodoo, yam,* and *zombie*.

Afro.   The bushy hairstyle called the *Afro* became popular in the early 1960s. The term *Afro* originated at the time, along with its synonyms *fro* and *natural*.

aftermath.   The *after mowth*, which later came to be pronounced *aftermath*, is the second or later mowing, the crop of grass that springs up after the first hay mowing in early summer when the grass is best for hay. This term was used as early as the 15th century, and within a century *aftermath* was being applied figuratively to anything that results or follows from an event.

afterward.   The Saxons called the stern of a boat the *aft* and their word *ward* meant "in the direction of." Thus *aftward* meant "toward the rear of a ship," or "behind." Over the years, the word *aftward* changed in spelling to *afterward* and came to mean "behind in time," "later on," or "later."

againbite [agenbite] of inwit.   James Joyce revived the expression *agenbite* [againbite] of *inwit* in *Ulysses*. It is a good example of Anglo-Saxon replacements of foreign words, meaning the "remorse of conscience" and originally being the prose translation of a French moral treatise (*The Ayenbite of Ynwit*) made by Dan Michel in 1340.

agate; agate type; aggie.   In ancient times colored stones were often found near the Achates River in Sicily.

The river gave its name to these pretty stones, or gems, as they were called. Because they were small, the stones also gave their name to a small printing type, *agate type*, that is still used widely today. This type is called *ruby* in England but has been *agate type* in America since 1871. The marbles called *aggies* are so named because their coloring resembles agate.

agave. Named for Agave, daughter of the legendary Cadmus, who introduced the Greek alphabet, the large *Agave* genus includes the remarkable century plant (*Agave americana*), which blooms once and dies (though anytime after fifteen years, not in one hundred years, as was once believed). Introduced to Europe from America in the 16th century, this big agave is often used there for fences. It is regarded as a religious charm by pilgrims to Mecca, who hang a leaf of it over their doors to ward off evil spirits and indicate that they have made a pilgrimage.

age before beauty. One still hears this facetious expression, which seems to have originated in late 19th-century England. Clare Booth Luce reputedly said this to Dorothy Parker, who retorted as she went on ahead, "Yes, and pearls before swine."

agelast; agelasta. An *agelast*, from the Greek for "not laughing," is a person who never laughs. The term for a non-laugher is first recorded in 1877, but *agelastic*, also meaning a morose, severe person who never laughs, is recorded in English as early as 1626. Rabelais was the first writer to use the word, fashioning it from the Greek. The *agelasta*, coming from the same Greek root for "joyless," is the stone upon which the fatigued Ceres sat when worn down in searching for her daughter Persephone.

Agent Orange. This herbicidal spray, used in Vietnam for purposes of jungle defoliation and crop destruction, has great toxicity, and many former U.S. soldiers claim to have suffered terribly because of it. Tens of thousands of tons of 2,4,5,-T, as it is called more scientifically, were used on over five million acres in South Vietnam during the 1960s. The term *Agent Orange* is first recorded in 1970 and derives from the color code stripe on the side of the herbicide's container—to distinguish it from the toxic herbicides Agent Blue, Agent Purple, and Agent White, which had their own appropriately colored stripes.

ageratum. "The flower that never grows old" translates the name of this flower, from the Greek *a*, "not," and *geras*, "old age." Actually, the Greeks were probably referring to another flower than our garden annual the *ageratum*, but it seemed a good name for this little, long-lasting, lavender-blue bedding plant, also known as the "everlasting flower."

aggie. (*See* **agate**.)

agit-prop drama. *Agit-prop* plays were commonly performed in the 1930s. They are plays that convey very emphatic social protest, the word *agit-prop* being a combination of *agit*ation and *prop*aganda. The word has its roots in the early U.S.S.R. *Agitpropbyuro*, "Agitation and Propaganda Bureau."

agonizing reappraisal. Secretary of State John Foster Dulles coined the phrase *agonizing reappraisal* and used it at a NATO meeting in December 1954. The term was so overworked and applied to so many piddling matters everywhere that it became a cliché, as did "massive retaliation," which the Secretary had coined several months earlier. *Agony* itself derives from the Greek *agonia*, a contest between wrestlers, boxers, or even dramatists that took place at an *agon*, or meeting. The physical or mental struggles of these contestants gave rise to our word *agony*. *Agony* was first used in English by the translators of the Bible in describing Christ's intense mental suffering or anguish in the Garden of Gethsemane. Thus in the true spirit of the word, any *agonizing reappraisal* would be best made regarding matters of great consequence, if used at all.

agony. The Greek word from which *agony* derives first meant an athletic contest, next came to mean a struggle for victory in an athletic contest, then any struggle, and finally mental struggle or anguish like Christ's in Gethsemane. The idea of physical pain and suffering isn't recorded for *agony* until about the 17th century, but its hard not to think of an athletic contest when contemplating this meaning. As one writer notes: "You only have to look at a photograph of anybody running the 100-yard dash to understand how it [the athletic contest] came in its English version to have the sense of 'agony.'"

agree to disagree. To *agree to disagree*, to remain friendly while holding differing opinions, is considered an Americanism by many writers. But in 1948 a writer in *Notes and Queries* reported finding the expression in a 1770 sermon of English theologian John Wesley, founder of Methodism. What's more, he found the phrase in quotation marks, suggesting that Wesley hadn't invented it but had heard it elsewhere.

agronomist. *Agronomists* are today's scientifically trained farmers, taking their name from the Greek *agros*, "field," and *nomis*, "to manage." The word only recently came into the language—in the early 19th century.

ahoy. Sailors had been saying *ahoy* for "hello" or "hey" at least a few years prior to 1751, when Tobias Smollett first recorded it in his novel *The Adventures of Peregrine Pickle*: "Ho! the house a hoy." The word is a combination of the interjection *a* and *hoy*, a natural exclamation used to attract attention that is first recorded as a cry for calling hogs and which in nautical language was also spelled "hoay." Incidentally, *ahoy* was suggested by Alexander Graham Bell as the salutation for telephone calls when he invented the telephone, but the term never caught on, phone users opting for "hello" and depriving *ahoy* of a more prominent place in the language.

ain't. *Ain't*, first recorded in 1706, began life in England as a contraction of "am not" (an't). Once widely used among all classes and quite proper, it became socially unacceptable in the early 19th century, when people began to use it improperly as a contraction for "is not" and "are not" as well as "am not." But "proper" or not, *ain't* is still widely used wherever English is spoken.

ain't hay. *Hay* has meant a small amount of money in American slang since at least the late 1930s, which is about the same time that this expression is first recorded. Little more is known about the very common *and that ain't hay* for a lot of money, a saying that I would suspect is older than currently supposed.

Airedale terrier. First called a *Bingley terrier* after the Bingley district in Yorkshire, England, the dog's name was officially changed to *Airedale* in 1886 (the Aire River runs through Bingley). *Terrier*, from the Latin *terra* ("earth"), means a dog that "takes to earth," a reference to the terrier digging into burrows for badgers and other prey.

airtights. Canned food was called *airtights* by cowboys in the American West during the latter part of the 19th century. Canned beef was specifically *meat biscuit* and *beef biscuit*.

aisle. *Aisle* strictly means a section of a church or auditorium, deriving from the Latin *ala*, "wing," and that is how the word has been used by the British until relatively recently. But Americans have long used *aisle* to mean a passageway in a church, auditorium, or elsewhere, and this usage is becoming universal.

akimbo. *In kene bowe* meant "in a sharp bend" in Middle English. It is believed that *akimbo*, for a hand resting on the hip, comes from the mispronunciation of this phrase, the shape of the arm in this position resembling "a sharp bend."

Alabama. "The Cotton State," our 22nd, took the name *Alabama* when admitted to the Union in 1819. *Alabama* is from the Choctaw *alba ayamule*, which means "I open the thicket," that is, "I am one who works the land, harvests food from it."

alabaster. *Albastron*, a town in the Thebais region of ancient Egypt, is supposed to be the basis of the word *alabaster*, according to Pliny's *Natural History*, perhaps because the very white sulphate of calcium was mined or traded there. The word comes to us from the Greek *alabastros*, via the Latin *alabaster* and the Old French *alabastre*. The word also means "smooth and white," like the gypsum.

alarm; to arms! *As armes! As armes!* was the old French military call when a sentry spotted the enemy coming. This became the English *At arms! At arms!* and finally the more recent *To arms! To arms!* Though these were all signals indicating danger, it was, strangely enough, the Italian expression *all' arme!* meaning the same thing, that passed into English as *allarme* and became the English word *alarm*, "a warning."

alas. Our *alas*, expressing grief or unhappiness, is recorded as early as 1260. It derives from the Old French *ah, las!*, "oh weary [me]!"

Alaska. *Seward's folly, Seaward's icebox* (qq.v.), Seward's iceberg, Icebergia, and Walrussia were all epithets for the 600,000 square miles now known as Alaska. All of these denunciations today honor one of the great visionaries of American history, William Henry Seward. Seward's most important work in Andrew Johnson's administration was the purchase of Alaska, then known as Russian America, from the Russians in 1867. Negotiating with Russian Ambassador Baron Stoeckl, the shrewd lawyer managed to talk the Russians down from their asking price of $10 million to $7.2 million, and got them to throw in a profitable fur-trading corporation. The treaty was negotiated and drafted in the course of a single night and because Alaska was purchased almost solely due to his determination—he even managed to have the treaty signed before the House voted the necessary appropriation—it was widely called *Seward's folly* by irate politicians and journalists. Seward himself named the new territory Alaska, from the Aleut *A-la-as-ka*, "the great country."

Albany beef. Sturgeon was once so plentiful in New York's Hudson River that it was humorously called *Albany beef*. The term is first recorded in 1791 and was in use through the 19th century; sturgeon caviar was so cheap in those days that it was part of the free lunch served in bars. Cod was similarly called *Cape Cod turkey* in Massachusetts.

albatross. Probably the subject of more legends than any other seabird, the albatross takes its name from a corruption of the Portuguese *alcatraz*, meaning "large pelican." Dubbed "gooney birds" because of their clumsy behavior, the big albatrosses—whose wingspans often reach twelve feet, greater than that of any other bird—frequently lumber about the decks of ships, unable to take off after they land because of the cramped space, and actually get as seasick as any landlubber. Another name for them is "mollymawks" or "mollyhawks," from the Dutch *mollemok*, "stupid gulls." Despite their apparent stupidity and stubbornness—nothing can force them to abandon their nesting sites, as the U.S. Navy learned at Midway Island—and their poor flying ability when there is no wind current, albatrosses have managed to thrive. They are also called Cape Hope sheep.

album.   The Romans called the white tablet on which edicts were written an *album*, from the Latin *albus*, "white." In English *album* came to mean any empty book for entering or storing things, especially photographs, only the wedding album still being traditionally white. A record album, a collection of songs, derives from the same root.

alchemilla; Lady's mantle.   Grown for their silvery leaves, these plants derive their name from the Arabic word *alkemelych*, which refers to their use in the past by alchemists who collected dew from their leaves for operations. They are also called *Lady's mantle*, after the Virgin Mary, to whom the plant was dedicated.

alcinoo poma dare.   Alcinous, legendary king of Phaeacians on the island of Scheria, who entertained Odysseus, had the most renowned and prolific orchards of ancient time. *Alcinoo poma dare*, to give apples to Alcinous, was long proverbial for to do what is superfluous, as to carry coals to Newcastle.

alewife.   One early traveler in America, John Josselyn, seems to have thought that this plentiful fish was called the *alewife* because it had "a bigger bellie" than the herring, a belly like a wife who drank a lot of ale. More likely the word is a mispronunciation of some forgotten Indian word.

Alexandria, Alexander cocktail.   Whether the Alexander cocktail celebrates Alexander the Great is a matter of dispute, though the conqueror was certainly a drinking man. There is no doubt, however, that ancient *Alexandria* in the Nile delta was founded in 332 B.C. by the king of Macedonia, that the *Alexandrine verse* or line of poetry derives from a French poem written about him, and that even the *Alexandrine rat*, or roof rat, indirectly comes from his name, via the Egyptian city. Great though he was in war and statecraft, Alexander's personal life was a loss. It would be fitting if the Alexander, a cocktail made with creme de cacao, gin or brandy, and cream, was named for the conqueror. For, excluding the Sicilian ruler Dionysus, he is probably the only king to die from overindulging in drink. One story has it that a six-day drinking bout led to his death, while another claims that his wife, Roxana, persuaded him to plunge intoxicated into an ice-cold pool, causing the conqueror of Persia to die of a high fever at the tender age of thirty-three. Robert Graves, however, points out that Alexander may have died from poisoning after a mushroom orgy rather than a drunken one.

alga.   Snow in Arctic and Alpine regions that appears red has often been regarded as a supernatural portent of evil. It is actually caused by the presence of large numbers of the minute *alga Protococcus nivalis*. *Alga*, from the Latin *alga*, "seaweed," are flowerless plants of very simple microscopic organisms, ranging from those that coat ponds with green scum to giant seaweeds one hundred feet long.

alibi.   "We the jury, find that the accused was *alibi*," was the verdict in one 18th-century criminal trial. This simply meant that the defendant was "elsewhere" when the crime was committed, and therefore innocent. Over the centuries, the Latin *alibi*, for elsewhere, was used so often in the courts in this sense that it entered everyday speech as both the synonym for an accused criminal's "story" and an excuse, often a spurious one, in general.

Alice; Alice in Wonderland.   For over a century Lewis Carroll's *Alice in Wonderland* (1865) has been the most famous and possibly the most widely read children's book. That there is an *Alice* cult even among adults is witnessed by the numerous works of criticism devoted to the book, which has been translated into Latin. The model for the fictional Alice was Alice Liddell, daughter of Dean Henry George Liddell, noted coauthor of *Liddell & Scott's Greek Lexicon*, still the standard Greek-English Dictionary. Carroll, his real name being Charles Lutwidge Dodgson, wrote *Alice* for his friend's daughter, who later became Mrs. Reginald Hargreaves. The author apparently made up the story while on a picnic with Alice and his sisters, actually improvising the classic tale as the group rowed about a lake. Incidentally, Carroll is regarded as the greatest 19th-century photographer of children and his best pictures were of Alice Liddell. An *Alice*, in allusion to *Alice in Wonderland*, is sometimes used to refer to a person newly arrived in strange, fantastic surroundings.

Alice blue.   *Alice blue* is one of several colors named for real people. The shade signalizes Alice Roosevelt Longworth, daughter of President Theodore Roosevelt, who favored the pale greenish or grayish-blue. Mrs. Longworth is the witty lady who said of Calvin Coolidge: "He looks as if he had been weaned on a pickle." Princess Alice, as she was called, was born on February 12, 1884; her mother Alice died from Bright's disease, a kidney inflammation, two days after her birth, on the same day that Theodore Roosevelt's mother died of typhoid fever. On February 17, 1906, Alice married Congressman Nicolas

Longworth of Ohio in an elegant East Room wedding in the White House. Mrs. Longworth long remained a leader of Washington society, her name and the color *Alice blue* rendered familiar by the tune "Alice Blue Gown," which she inspired.

alien corn. (*See* **corn.**)

alive and kicking. Though it is a cliché by now, this expression has an interesting history. Meaning alert and active, *alive and kicking* apparently goes back to the 18th century, when it was first used by London fishmongers in reference to their fresh fish.

alkahest. The *alkahest* was the universal solvent of alchemy that supposedly dissolved anything, the word being coined from Arabic by the Swiss alchemist Theophrastus Bombastus von Hohenheim (1490-1541), who also coined his own pseudonym. This charlatan called himself Paracelsus, from the Greek *para*, "beyond," plus *Celsus*, the name of a prominent first century physician—thus advertising himself as beyond or better than the much esteemed Celsus!

alkali. Arab chemists in medieval times extracted sodium carbonate from the marine saltwort plant, calling the substance *al-qaliy*, "ashes of salt wort." Later chemists applied the term *alkali*, a transliteration of the Arab word, to all salts with properties similar to sodium carbonate.

all aboard! This common train conductor's call is an Americanism, first recorded in 1837, and is nautical in origin. Wrote Joshua T. Smith in his *Journal in America* (1837): "They [the Americans] describe a situation by the compass 'talk of the voyage' of being 'all aboard' & etc.; this doubtless arises from *all* their ancestors having come hither over ocean & having in the voyage acquired nautical language." The call *all aboard!* was used on riverboats here before it was used on trains.

all at sea. Early mariners hugged the coastlines because their navigational aids were crude and inaccurate. But often they were blown far out to sea where they had no landmarks to guide them. The expression *all at sea* described their plight perfectly, as anyone ever caught in rough, open seas will testify, and the term was soon used to describe the condition of any helpless, bewildered person.

all chiefs and no Indians. Many businesses have experienced trouble because they had all chiefs and no Indians, that is, too many officers who want to do nothing but give orders to others. The origin of this common worker's complaint has been traced to about 1940 in Australia, where the expression was first *all chiefs and no*

Indians, like the University Regiment. Yet the first half of the expression has an American ring, and one suspects that some determined word sleuth might turn up an earlier printed use in the U.S.

all ears. *I'm all ears*, I'm listening attentively, is hardly modern slang, being at least three centuries old. Its first recorded use in this precise form is by Anthony Trollope in 1865. But over two centuries before this Milton wrote in *Comus* (1634): "I was all ear,/And took in strains that might create a soul/Under the ribs of death."

all gussied up. A *gusset*, (probably from the French *gousset*, "pod, or shell of nuts") is a triangular piece of material inserted into a garment to make it more comfortable, and perhaps more fashionable because it fits better. *Gusseted* means to have a gusset or gussets in clothing and may have become corrupted in everyday speech to *gussied*. Someone with many gussets in her dress, many improvements in it, might have been called *all gussied up*, which could have come to mean "to be dressed in one's best clothes." This is all guesswork, but it is the best explanation we have for the phrase, which dates back to the 17th century.

all hands and the cook! *All hands and the cook on deck!* was a cry probably first heard on New England whalers in the early 19th century when everyone aboard was called topside to cut in on a whale, work that had to be done quickly. Fishermen also used the expression, and still do, and it had currency among American cowboys to indicate a dangerous situation—when, for example, even the cook was needed to keep the herd under control.

alligator. The biggest lizard that the Romans knew was about the size of the forearm and was thus named *lacertus* ("forearm"), which eventually came into Spanish use as *lagarto*. When the Spaniards encountered a huge New World saurian that resembled a lizard, they called it *el lagarto*, "the lizard," putting the definite article before the noun as they are accustomed to doing. Englishmen assumed this to be a single word, *elagarto*, which in time became corrupted in speech to *alligator*. This is probably the way the word was born, but much better is an old story about an early explorer sighting the creature and exclaiming, "There's a lagarto!" Less dangerous than the crocodile, the alligator does have a worse "bark": it is the only reptile capable of making a loud sound. (*See also* **crocodile tears.**)

all I know is what I read in the papers. This saying has become a popular American expression since Will Rogers invented it in his 1927 *The Letters of a Self-Made Diplomat to His President* (1927). It has various shades of meaning, but is commonly used to mean: "I'm not an expert, I'm just an ordinary person and what I've told you is true to the best of my knowledge." It implies one may be wrong because one's sources are nothing exceptional.

all in the same boat. Just more than a century old, this saying means that two or more people are sharing the same risks or living under similar conditions. It may derive from some unknown situation when two or more people were adrift in the same lifeboat, or it may even come from the earlier expression "to stick" or "have an oar in another's boat"; that is, to meddle in someone else's affairs, which dates back to the 16th century.

all is lost save honor. After Francis I of France was defeated by Spain's Charles V at Pavia, Italy in 1525, captured, and forced to sign a humiliating treaty, he sat down and wrote to his mother. His actual words were not so eloquent, but the most memorable phrase in his letter was translated into English as *All is lost save honor.* Despite the fact that Francis soon lost his honor by breaking the treaty, the sentiments of this patron of Rabelais and creator of Fontainebleau became proverbial.

all my eye and Betty Martin. This saying may have originated when a British sailor, looking into a church in an Italian port, heard a beggar praying "*An mihi, beate Martine*" ("Ah, grant me, Blessed Martin") and later told his shipmates that this was nonsense that sounded to him like "All my eye and Betty Martin." Most authorities dismiss this theory summarily, especially because *Joe Miller's Jests* included the story, but St. Martin *was* the patron saint of beggars. One etymologist tells us that "no such Latin prayer is to be found in the formulary of the Catholic Church" and another claims to have in his possession "a book of old Italian cosmopolitan life . . . [that] mentions this prayer to St. Francis by beggars." It seems likely that beggars would have recited such a prayer and so the story has some basis in fact, more at least than linguists have been willing to admit. Meanwhile, there is no better identification of "Betty Martin."

the all-overs. An American Southernism that goes back to at least the early 19th century, the *all-overs* describes a general state of nervousness. Something close to it is first recorded in an 1820 song entitled "Oh, What a Row": "I'm seized with an all-overness, I faint, I die!"

all roads lead to Rome. The ancient Romans built such an excellent system of roads that the saying arose *all roads lead to Rome*, that is, no matter which road one starts a journey on, he will finally reach Rome if he keeps on traveling. The popular saying came to mean that all ways or methods of doing something end in the same result, no one method being better than another.

all's right with the world! This saying is frequently misquoted as "all's *well* with the world." The words are from

Robert Browning's dramatic poem "Pippa Passes" (1841) and is one of the songs of Pippa, a young girl who passes through town on her yearly holiday. Unknown to her, each of her songs affects and changes the lives of people who hear them, the best known one filling a murderer with remorse for what he has done:

> The year's at the spring,
> And day's at the morn;
> Morning's at seven;
> The hill-side's dew-pearled;
> The lark's on the wing;
> The snail's on the thorn:
> God's in his heaven—
> All's right with the world!

all systems go. All preparations have been made and the operation is ready to start. Widely used today, the expression originated with American ground controllers during the launching of rockets into space in the early 1970s.

all the tea in China. *All the tea in China* would be 369,000 tons or so, according to the 1977 *Food and Agricultural Organization of the United Nations Yearbook.* It may be an Americanism, but this expression denoting a great sum probably is of British origin and over a century old; the trouble is that no one has been able to authoritatively pin it down.

all the traffic will bear. *Partridge*'s definition of this catchphrase is "The situation, whether financial or other, precludes anything more." Because it literally relates to railroad fares and freights, the expression, which is first recorded in the U.S. circa 1945, may originally be the cynical words of a railway magnate.

all this for a song. The phrase, reflecting an often prevalent attitude toward poetry, was spoken by William Cecil, Lord Burleigh, England's Lord Treasurer under Queen Elizabeth, when the Queen ordered him to give 100 pounds to Edmund Spenser as a royal gratuity for writing *The Faerie Queene.* Burleigh was later satirized in Richard Sheridan's *The Critic*, in which he comes on stage but never talks, just nodding because he is much too busy with affairs of state to do more. This inspired the expression "Burleigh's nod" and "as significant as a shake of Burleigh's head."

all thumbs. *All thumbs* for a clumsy person, or someone with no dexterity has its roots in an old English saying first recorded in John Heywood's *Proverbs* (1562): "Whan he should get ought, eche fynger a thumbe."

all washed up. At the end of a day's work a factory worker usually washes his hands. From this notion of washing hands after finishing a job came the expression *all washed up*, finished with anything, which led to its later meaning of a business failure, finished with everything, or anything that has become obsolete and unfashionable. The expression dates back to the early 1920s.

almanac.

> Early to bed and early to rise
> Makes a man healthy, wealthy and wise.

The above is just one sample of the shrewd maxims and proverbs almost all of which became part of America's business ethic, that Benjamin Franklin wrote or collected in his *Poor Richard's Almanac.* This was by no means the first almanac issued in America, that distinction belonging to *An Almanack for New England for the Year 1639,* issued by William Peirce, a shipowner who hoped to attract more paying English passengers to the colonies and whose almanac was (except for a broadside) the first work printed in America. *Poor Richard's* was written and published by Franklin at Philadelphia from 1733 to 1758 and no doubt takes its name from the earlier English *Poor Robin's Almanac,* first published in 1663 by Robert ("Robin") and William Winstanley. *Almanacs,* which take their name from a medieval Latin word for a calendar with astronomical data, were issued as early as 1150, before the invention of printing, and were compendiums of information, jokes, and proverbs.

almighty dollar. Washington Irving coined the phrase *the almighty dollar* in his sketch called "The Creole Village," first published in 1836: "The almighty dollar, that great object of universal devotion throughout the land, seems to have no genuine devotees in these peculiar villages." But Ben Jonson had used "almighty gold" in a similar sense more than two hundred years before him: "that for which all virtue now is sold, / And almost every vice—almighty gold."

almond; Jordan almond. *Almond* has its roots in the medieval Latin word *amandola* for the nut. The famed *Jordan almond* comes not from the River Jordan but from a corruption of the French *jardin* almond: the garden or cultivated almond.

aloha. Both a greeting and farewell, the Hawaiian *aloha* means, simply and sweetly, "love." It has been called "the world's loveliest greeting or farewell." Hawaii is of course the *Aloha State,* its unofficial anthem "Aloha Oe" (Farewell to Thee) written by Queen Liliuokalani. *Mi loa aloha* means "I love you" in Hawaiian.

aloof. To *stand aloof* was originally a nautical term meaning "to bear to windward," or luff, which derives from the Dutch *loef,* meaning "windward." Since a ship cannot sail to windward except by keeping the bow of the ship pointed slightly away from the wind, the term took on the general meaning of "to keep away from," "to keep at a distance," "to be reserved or reticent."

alpha and omega. Everything, the most important part. The expression has its origins in the Greek alphabet, where *alpha* and *omega* are the first and last letters respectively, as well as in the biblical phrase (Rev. 1:7): "I am the Alpha and Omega, the beginning and the ending, saith the Lord."

alphabet. *Alphabet, Brewer* notes, is our "only word of more than one syllable compounded solely of the names of letters"—the Greek *alpha* (*a*) and *beta* (*b*). He goes on to say that the English alphabet "will combine into 29 thousand quadrillion combinations [possible words]," that is, 29 followed by 27 zeros (29,000,000,000,000,000,000,000,000,000). Others dispute this figure, saying the number of combinations of words possible is "only" 1096 followed by 25 zeros. In any case, remember that these figures were arrived at by using each of the 26 letters of the alphabet *only once* in each combination or word—and they do not include possible compound words, homonyms, etc.! I'd guess that there are now at least ten times as many English words as the half million or so recorded in the most complete dictionary, there being over one million scientific words for organic and inorganic chemical compounds alone.

Alphard, and other star names. *Alphard,* the only bright star in the constellation Hydra, was named by Bedouin tribesmen traveling through the desert thousands of years ago. The word comes to us from the Arabic *Fard ash-Shuja,* meaning "the lone one." Surprisingly, most star names are of Arabic origin. Of 183 star names listed in one study, 125 are Arabic (Vega, Algol, etc.), 14 are Latin (Capella, Spica), 9 are Arabic-Latin combinations (Yed Prior), and three are Persian (Alcor). A good number of Arabic star names were bestowed by tribesmen who named the more prominent stars after camels, sheep, birds, jackals, hyenas, frogs, and other animals, but most were named by Arabian astronomers.

also-ran. The joy may be in playing, not winning, but an *also-ran* means a loser, someone who competed but didn't come near winning. The term is an Americanism first recorded (as *also ran*) with political reference in 1904, and derives from horse racing. The newspaper racing results once listed win, place, and show horses before listing under the heading "Also Ran", all other horses that finished out of the money.

aluminum. The English word *aluminum* for the metal is the same or very similar in many languages: Italian, *alluminio;* Spanish, *aluminio;* French, *aluminum;* Dutch, *aluminium;* Danish, *aluminium;* Hungarian, *aluminium;* Polish, *aluminjum;* Indonesian, *aluminium;* Arabic, *alaminyoum*; and Japanese, *aruminyuumu*. The words are so alike simply because British scientist Sir Humphrey Davy named the metal *aluminium* when he discovered it in 1812, from the Latin *Alumina*, for "a white earth," which he used in his experiments.

always be nice to people on your way up—you may meet them on your way down.   Not comic Jimmy Durante but humorist Wilson Mizner invented this catchphrase coined in the 1920s, when Mizner served the Muse in Hollywood and invented dozens of well-known, usually caustic expressions. The phrase is now heard almost everywhere English is spoken.

"always scribble, scribble, scribble! eh! Mr. Gibbon?"   Henry Digby Beste, in his *Personal and Literary Memorials* (1829), tells the full story of this famous remark made to English historian Edward Gibbon: "The Duke of Gloucester, brother of King George III, permitted Mr. Gibbon to present him with the first volume of *The History of the Decline and Fall of the Roman Empire*. When the second volume of that work appeared, it was quite in order that it should be presented to His Royal Highness in like manner. The prince received the author with much good nature and affability, saying to him, as he laid the quarto on the table, 'Another damn'd thick, square book! Always scribble, scribble, scribble! Eh! Mr. Gibbon?' " This insulting remark about the greatest historical work in English (though Gibbon generally saw history as "little more than the crimes, follies and misfortunes of men") has also been attributed to the Duke of Cumberland.

alyssum.   The Greek word for madness is the chief component of this delicate plant's name, for the Greeks believed it cured madness and named it *alysson*, from *lysa*, "madness," and *a*, "not." The popular garden plant with its clusters of fragrant white or golden flowers is called "madwort" for the same reason. "Wort," from the Old English *wyrt*, "root, plant," means a plant, herb, or vegetable and is usually used in combinations like "madwort."

A.M.; P.M.   *A.M.* is the abbreviation of the Latin *ante meridiem*, "before noon or midday", not ante meridian, even though *meridian* also means noon. *P.M.* is the abbreviation of *post meridiem*, "after noon."

amalgamationist.   "Blending of the two races by amalgamation is just what is needed for the perfection of both," a white Boston clergyman wrote in 1845. Few American abolitionists were proponents of *amalgamation*, but many were called *amalgamationists* by pro-slaveryites in the two decades or so before the Civil War. This Americanism for one who favors a social and genetic mixture of whites and blacks is first recorded in 1838, when Harriet Martineau complained that people were calling her an *amalgamationist* when she didn't know what the word meant.

amaranth.   The Greeks believed this flower never died and gave it the name *amarantos*, "everlasting." It was said to be a symbol of immortality because the flowers keep their deep blood-red color to the last. Milton wrote in *Paradise Lost*:

> Immortal amarant, a flower which once
> In Paradise, fast by the Tree of Life,
> Began to bloom, but, soon for man's offence
> To heaven removed where first it grew, there grows
> And flowers aloft, shading the Fount of Life . . .

amaretti.   A lovesick baker daydreamed so long about his lady while baking a special kind of almond cookie for her that he left the cookie in the oven too long and the light, dry *amaretti* cookie resulted. Such is the legend, though all we know for sure is that the delicious cookies, often served with wine, take their name from the Italian *amaretti*, "little loves." *Amaretto* liqueur comes from the same source, the Italian word for love, probably because the liqueur was thought to predispose one to love.

Amazon.   The first *Amazons*, from the Greek *a* ("without") plus *mazos* ("breast"), were said to be a tribe of fierce warrior women who cut or burned off their right breasts so as not to impede the drawing of their bows. *Amazons* have been reported in Africa and South America as well as in Greece. The Amazon River, which had been named Rio Santa Maria de la Mar Dulce by its discoverer, is said to have been rechristened by the Spanish explorer Francisco de Orellana in 1541 after he was attacked by the Tapuyas, a tribe in which he believed women fought alongside men.

ambidextrous.   (*See* **right**.)

ambition.   Politicians are still among the most ambitious men, but the Romans thought them so much more so than others that they confined their word *ambito* (from *ambi*, "around," and *eo*, "go"), meaning "ardent striving for pomp and power," to politicians alone. In fact it took centuries before *ambition*, the English derivative of *ambito*, took on a more positive meaning and was applied to any person striving for wealth, power, skill, or recognition.

ambulance chaser.   It is said that ambulance chasers in days past had cards like the following:

SAMUEL SHARP
THE HONEST LAWYER
CAN GET YOU

$5000
for a leg

$10,000
for a liver

Ambulance chaser is a thoroughly American term that originally described (and still does) a lawyer who seeks out victims immediately after an accident and tries to persuade them to let him represent them in a suit for damages. The expression probably originated in New York City during the late 1890s, a time when disreputable lawyers frequently commissioned ambulance drivers and policemen to inform them of accidents and sometimes rode with victims to the hospital to proffer their services.

ambush. In the mid-16th century the Old French *embusche* became through mispronunciation the English *ambush*. Appropriately, the French word derived from *embuscher*, "to hide in the woods."

an Ameche. Though not much used anymore, *an Ameche* has been American slang for a telephone since 1939 when actor Don Ameche played the lead role in *The Story of Alexander Graham Bell*, the inventor of the telephone.

amen corner. A group of fervent believers or ardent followers is called an *amen corner*, after the similarly named place near the pulpit in churches occupied by those who lead the responsive "amens" to the preacher's prayers. The term may come from the Amen Corner of London's Paternoster Row, but it is an almost exclusively American expression today.

America. Many writers have assumed that the Italian navigator Amerigo Vespucci (whom Ralph Waldo Emerson called "a thief" and "pickle dealer at Seville") was a con man who never explored the New World and doesn't deserve to be mentioned in the same breath as Christopher Columbus, much less have his name honored in the continent's name. Deeper investigation reveals that Vespucci, born in Florence in 1454, did indeed sail to the New World with the expedition of Alonso de Ojeda in 1499, parting with him even before land was sighted in the West Indies. Vespucci, sailing in his own ship, then discovered and explored the mouth of the Amazon, subsequently sailing along the northern shores of South America. Returning to Spain in 1500, he entered the service of the Portuguese and the following year explored 6,000 miles along the southern coast of South America. He was eventually made Spain's pilot major and died at the age of fifty-eight of malaria contracted on one of his voyages. Vespucci not only explored unknown regions but also invented a system of computing exact longitude and arrived at a figure computing the earth's equatorial circumference only fifty miles short of the correct measurement. It was, however, not his many solid accomplishments but a mistake made by a German mapmaker that led America to be named after him—and this is probably why his reputation suffers even today. Vespucci (who had Latinized his name to Americus

Vespucci) wrote many letters about his voyages, including one to the notorious Italian ruler Lorenzo de' Medici in which he described "the New World." But several of his letters were rewritten and sensationalized by an unknown author, who published these forgeries as *Four Voyages* in 1507. One of the forged Letters was read by the brilliant young German cartographer Martin Waldseemüller, who was so impressed with Vespucci's account that he included a map of the New World in an appendix to his book *Cosmographiae Introductio*, boldly labeling the land "America." Wrote Waldseemüller in his Latin text, which also included the forged letter: "By now, since these parts have been more extensively explored and and another 4th part has been discovered by Americus Vespucius (as will appear from what follows); I see no reason why it should not be called Amerigo, after Americus, the discoverer, or indeed America, since both Europe and Asia have a feminine form from the names of women." Waldseemüller's map roughly represented South America and when cartographers finally added North America, they retained the original name; the great geographer Gerhardus Mercator finally gave the name "America" to all of the western hemisphere. Vespucci never tried to have the New World named after him or to belittle his friend Columbus, who once called him "a very worthy man." The appellation *America* gained in usage because Columbus refused all his life to admit that he had discovered a new continent, wanting instead to believe that he had come upon an unexplored region in Asia. Spain stubbornly refused to call the New World anything but *Columbia* until the 18th century, but to no avail. Today Columbus is credited for his precedence only in story and song ("Columbia, the Gem of the Ocean"), while Amerigo Vespucci is honored by hundreds of words ranging from *American know-how* to *American cheese*.

the American dream. *The American dream* is almost impossible to define, meaning as it does so many different things to so many different people. These words go back at least to de Tocqueville's *Democracy in America* (1835) and are usually associated with the dreams of people new to these shores of freedom, material prosperity, and hope for the future.

American Indian language words. English words that come to us from American Indian languages include: *chocolate, tomato, potato, llama, puma, totem, papoose, squaw, caucus, Tammany, mugwump, podunk, chinook, chautauqua, tomahawk, wampum, mackinaw, moccasin, sachem, pot latch, manitou, kayak, hogan, teepee, toboggan, wigwam, igloo, porgy, menhaden, quahog, catalpa, catawba, hickory, pecan, persimmon, pokeweed, scuppernong* (grapes), *sequoia, squash, tamarack, hominy, hooch, firewater, pone, bayou, pemmican, succotash, cayuse, wapiti, chipmunk, caribou, moose, muskrat, opossum, raccoon, skunk, terrapin,* and *woodchuck.*

Americanism. In 1781 Dr. John Witherspoon, president of the College of New Jersey (now Princeton), wrote a series of essays on "the general state of the English language in America." He listed a number of "chief improprieties" such as Americans using "mad" for "angry," etc., and coined the word *Americanism* to define them.

America's Cup. This racing trophy was originally called the Hundred Guinea Cup when it was offered by the British Royal Yacht Squadron to the winner of an international yacht race around the Isle of Wight. The U.S. schooner *America* won the first race in 1875, defeating fourteen British yachts, and the cup, still the greatest prize in yachting, was renamed in her honor. American yachts won the cup in every competition until 1983, when the Australians took it home to Perth, ending the longest winning streak in sport.

Ameslan. *Ameslan* is the acronym for *American Sign Language*, the shorter term being first recorded in 1974. American Sign Language, a system of communication by manual signs used by the deaf, is more efficient than finger spelling and closer to being a natural language. Finger spelling is just "a means of transposing any alphabetized language into a gestural mode."

amethyst. This bluish-violet gem was once regarded as a great charm against drunkenness, leading the ancient Greeks to name the variety of quartz *amethystos*, from *a*, "not," and *methystos*, "drunk." *Amethystos* eventually became our *amethyst*.

amicus curiae. Latin for "friend of the courts," *amicus curiae* in law applies to "any person, not a party to the litigation, who volunteers or is invited by the court to give advice on some matter pending before it." Its second word is pronounced "kyoor-ee-eye" and its plural is *amici curiae*.

Amish; Mennonites. The Amish people, located mainly in Pennsylvania, Ohio, Iowa, Indiana, and Canada, are descended from the followers of Jakob Amman, a 17th-century Swiss Mennonite bishop. The Mennonites are an evangelical Protestant sect that practices baptism of believers only, restricts marriage to members of the denomination, and is noted for simplicity of living and plain dress. They, in turn, were named for the religious leader Menno Simons (1496-1556). The Amish still cling to a rural, simple way of life, but many of their young have begun to rebel against seemingly restrictive conventions and to yield to the attractions and conveniences of 20th-century life.

ammonia. While camel riders worshipped at the Egyptian temple of the god Ammon, near Thebes, enterprising men and women extracted urine from the sand where their camels were hitched, later using it for bleaching or whitening clothes. The agent was called "sal ammoniac," salt of Ammon, by the Romans, and when the gas obtained from this salt (NH_3) was first extracted in 1782 it was named *ammonia*.

amok. (*See* **run amuck**.)

among. *Among* comes from the Old English *on*, "in" and *gemang*, "crowd." These terms made up the Old English *onmang*, "in a crowd," which eventually became *among*.

amortize. You gradually kill a debt (in the sense of resolving it) when you amortize it, for *amortize*, once more generally used than it is today, has its roots in the Latin *mors*, "death." Chaucer wrote: "The goods werkes that men don whil they ben in good lif ben al amortised by synne folwying." The word *mortgage* comes from the same source.

& (ampersand). The symbol *&* was invented by Marcus Tullius Tiro, who introduced it about 63 B.C. as part of the first system of shorthand of which there is any record. A learned Roman freedman & amanuensis to Cicero, Tiro invented his "Tironian notes" to take down his friend's fluent dictation, but he also used it to write works of his own, including some of the great orator's speeches & even some of Cicero's letters to Tiro! His system was based on the orthographic principle & made abundant use of initials, the *&* sign that was part of it being a contraction for the Latin *et* or "and." Tiro's shorthand system was taught in Roman schools, used to record speeches in the Senate, & saw wide use among his businessmen in Europe for almost a thousand years.

ampere. (*See* **moron**.)

amphigory. *Amphigory* derives from the Greek for "circle on both sides" and means a burlesque or parody, usually a kind of nonsense verse that seems to make sense but doesn't. Swinburne's *Nephelidia*, a parody of his own style, is an example.

amscray. (*See* **pig latin**.)

anachronism.

> Cecil B. De Mille
> Was feeling ill
> Because he couldn't put Moses
> In the War of the Roses.

This famous clerihew by Nicholas Bentley, the son of the inventor of the *clerihew* (*q.v.*), comments on filmmakers who don't often get ill about the *anachronisms* in their epics. If Moses was put in the War of the Roses, or if Cleopatra's barge was depicted as powered by an outboard motor, these would be *anachronisms*. The word derives from the Greek *ana chronos*, "out of time," to be late, or "back-timing," and means an error in chronology, putting a person, event, or thing in the wrong time period. Some classic examples are Shakespeare's reference to billiards in *Antony and Cleopatra*, to cannon in *King John*, and to turkeys in *Henry IV, Part I*. Famous American anachronisms include George Washington throwing a silver dollar across the Potomac (there were no silver dollars at the time) and the flying of the Stars and Stripes in paintings of major Revolutionary War battles (the flag wasn't used until 1783). Sometimes *anachronism* is used to describe an institution or a person who lives in the past.

anaconda. This is one of the few English words, if not the only, that comes to us from Singhalese. *Anaconda* probably derives from the Singhalese *henakandayā*, although this word means "lightning stem" and refers to Ceylon's whip snake, not the large snake we know as the *anaconda*. Weekley notes that "the mistake may have been due to a confusion of labels in the Leyden museum."

Anadama bread. Anadama bread, a Yankee cornmeal recipe, offers one of the most humorous stories connected with any foodstuff. Tradition has it that a Yankee farmer or fisherman, whose wife Anna was too lazy to cook for him, concocted the recipe. On tasting the result of his efforts a neighbor asked him what he called the bread, the crusty Yankee replying, "Anna, damn her!" Another version claims that the husband was a Yankee sea captain who endearingly referred to his wife as "Anna, damn 'er." Anna's bread was much loved by his crew because it was delicious and would not spoil on long sea voyages. The captain is said to have written the following epitaph for his wife: "Anna was a lovely bride,/ but Anna, damn'er, up and died."

anagram. An *anagram* is the rearrangement of the letters of a word or group of words to make another word or group of words, the word anagram itself deriving from the Greek *ana graphein*, "to write over again." Popular as wordplay since the earliest times, anagrams were possibly invented by the ancient Jews, and the cabalists, constantly looking for "secret mysteries . . . woven in the numbers of letters," always favored them, as did the Greeks and Romans. A famous Latin anagram was an answer made out of the question Pontius Pilate asked in the trial of Jesus. *Quid est veritas?* ("What is truth") was the question, the answer being *Est vir qui adest* ("It is the man who is here"). Though poet John Dryden called anagrams the "torturing of one poor word ten thousand ways," the English are among the best and most accurate anagrammatists. Samuel Butler's novel *Erewhon* derives its title from the word *nowhere*, almost spelled backward, and a tribe in the book is called the Sumarongi, which is *ignoramus* spelled backward. Among the many interchangeable words that can form *anagrams* in English are *evil* and *live*, and *eros* and *rose*, but the longest are two sixteen-letter pairs: *conservationists* and *conversationists*; and *internationalism* and *interlaminations*. A recent apt anagram suggested by Martin Gardner is *moon starers*, an anagram for *astronomer*.

Ananias. The word *Ananias*, for a liar, refers to the New Testament's Ananias (Acts 5:1-10), who with his wife, Sapphira, tried to cheat the church at Jerusalem by withholding part of the money he made from a sale of land. Ananias was struck dead after the apostle Peter declared that he had "not lied unto men, but unto God." His wife shared his fate later that day when she maintained his deception and was told of his demise. *Ananias* was popularized by President Theodore Roosevelt, who referred to those he suspected of deceit as members of the *Ananias Club*, especially members of the working press who published confidential information they had promised not to reveal. Roosevelt did not coin the phrase, but as H. L. Mencken observed, he popularized or originated scores of other expressions, including "walk softly and carry a big stick," "to pussyfoot," "the strenuous life," "one hundred percent American," and "muckraker," all of which are still in use today.

Andalusia. The region of Andalusia in southern Spain is named for the Vandals who invaded and occupied it some fifteen centuries ago. The region was first called *Vandalusia*, the word dropping the *V* over the centuries.

and don't you forget it! An intensive recorded in England as early as 1898 and adopted in the U.S. soon after, *and don't you forget it!* remains a popular expression often used to reinforce one's anger, especially anger in chastising children. For close to a century experts have inveighed against it as "vulgar and senseless," but it is alive and thriving nonetheless.

Andes Mountains. The name for these mountains derives from the Quecha *andi*, meaning "high crest." The similarity of *andi* to the Egyptian *andi* for "high valley," along with the similarity of other Egyptian and Quecha words, has led some observers to suggest that Egyptian explorers may have traveled to South America in ancient times.

and how! Indicating "intensive emphasis of what someone else has just said," *and how!* is a long-popular catchphrase first recorded in 1924. The Americanism possibly derives from the German *und wie!* or the Italian *e come!*, meaning the same thing, and once very common among Americans of German and Italian extraction, respectively.

andirons. Andirons are pairs of metal stands used to hold logs above the floor in a fireplace. One theory holds that the word derives from the Gaulish *andera*, "heifer," cows' heads once commonly used as decorations on the supports.

Andrea Ferrara. Many Scotsmen will know that an *Andrea Ferrara* is the Scottish broadsword frequently mentioned in Elizabethan literature, and more than a few will proudly claim that the original sword maker was a Scottish drill sergeant named Andrea Ferras or Ferrier. However, it is more likely that the real Andrea Ferrara was a 16th-century Italian sword maker who lived in Belluno and whose correct name was *Andrea dei Ferrari*, "Andrew of the armorers." How his swords got to Scotland is something of a mystery; either he was an exile, or as Sir Walter Scott suggests in the notes on *Waverley*, he was brought over by James IV or V to instruct the Scots in the manufacture of his blades. In any event, he left us with many references in literature to *Andrea Ferraras*, *Ferraras*, and even *Andrews*, all deriving from his name.

the Andrew. Since at least 1860 *The Andrew* has been British slang for the Royal Navy, and *The Andrew Miller* was used long before that. The expression derives from the name of Andrew Miller, a notorious press-gang leader of Lord Nelson's day who *shanghaied* many men into the British Navy.

andromeda. Linnaeus named this early blooming shrub with white blossoms for the mythological maiden Andromeda, who was chained to a rock as an offering to a sea monster but was rescued by Perseus.

Andromeda strain. Any strain of bacteria or other microorganism "whose accidental release from a laboratory might have catastrophic effects because of its unknown biochemical makeup" is called an *Andromeda strain*. The term comes from American author Michael Crichton's 1971 novel of that title, in which an unknown type of bacteria escapes accidentally from a returning space probe and threatens to contaminate the planet Earth.

and then some! *and then some!* is an Americanism dating back to about 1910. But its roots probably go deeper than this in history, some investigators believing it is an elaboration of the Scots *and some*, meaning "and much more so," which is recorded about two centuries earlier. One British professor claimed he found a parallel expression in the *Aeneid* (Book viii, line 487)!

anecdote; anecdotage. We owe the word *anecdote* to Justinian, Byzantine emperor from A.D. 527 to 565, who wrote a book of brief tales about life in his court. These true stories were satirical, scandalous, and sometimes off-color. Justinian—better known for the Justinian legal code—probably didn't intend them for publication, but they were published by Procopius, a secretary to one of Justinian's generals, as a supplement to his history of the times. Procopius entitled the book *Anekdota*, a Greek word meaning "unpublished, secret." The title of the book later became the term *anecdote*, meaning a brief factual story like the ones *Anekdota* contained. *Anecdotage*, "the state of being advanced in age and strongly inclined to tell reminiscent anecdotes," is probably a happy coinage of John Wilkes in about 1835.

anemone. Also called the windflower, the dainty *anemone* takes its name from the Greek *anemos*, "wind," and *mone*, "habitation," the Greeks having observed that it often grew in windy places. A Greek legend says that the *anemone* was born after the handsome Greek youth Adonis, beloved by Aphrodite, goddess of love and beauty, was killed in the forest on a wild boar hunt. Aphrodite was so grief-stricken that the gods took pity on her and allowed Adonis to spend each spring with her in the form of a flower, the *anemone* rising from his blood.

angel dust. So called because of its white color, *angel dust*, or PCP (phencyclipine), is used as a narcotic, being mixed with barbiturates or sprinkled on marijuana and smoked. The potent, dangerous depressant goes by many street names, including "white powder," "peace pills," "superjoint," "green tea," "busy bee," "hog elephant," "tranquilizer," and "killer weed"—all first recorded in the early 1970s.

angelica. According to one story, the Archangel Raphael assured a pious hermit that this plant was a remedy against the plague. This may account for the name *angelica*, which comes from the Latin *herba angelica*, "the angelic root," or "root of the Holy Ghost," and is first recorded in English in 1570. A confection called candied angelica was made from its roots in early times.

angels on horseback. One of the more colorfully named foods of the world, *angels on horseback* are oysters rolled in bacon, cooked (often on skewers over a fire) and served on points of toast. They are recorded under this name early in this century, but the name is probably a translation of the earlier French *anges a cheval*.

angel teat. Down in the holler, in mountain country, moonshiners call particularly good mellow whiskey with a good bouquet *angel teat*, or *angel's teat*. The term is first recorded in 1946 but is probably much older.

Angelus; Angelic Hymn; Angelic Doctor. The Angelus is a Roman Catholic devotion, so named for its initial word. The prayer, which is said three times a day (at 6

A.M., noon, and 6 P.M.) commences at the sound of a bell called the *Angelus* and begins "Angelus Domini . . . (The Angel of the Lord . . .)." The *Angelic Hymn* isn't a synonym for the *Angelus*. It is the hymn beginning "Glory be to God in the highest" that was sung by the angels to the shepherds of Bethlehem after they brought tidings of the birth of Christ the Lord that day. St. Thomas Aquinas (ca. 1225-74) is traditionally called the *Angelic Doctor* because of the purity of his thought, regarded as the result of more than human intelligence. His schoolmates had called him the "Dumb Ox," and his teacher Albertus Magnus had predicted, "This dumb ox will one day fill the world with his lowing." Followers of the scholastic philosopher are called *Thomists*.

angle with a silver hook. An unlucky fisherman who fails to catch anything doesn't want to go home empty-handed. Thus when he buys fish (with silver coin, in past times) to conceal his abject failure, he is said to *angle with a silver hook*.

Angora cat; Angora goat. *Angora cats* probably originated in Ancyra or Angora, Turkey (now Ankara), where their long, silky hair may have been used like wool. Bred in Angora two thousand years ago for its hair, sometimes called mohair, the *Angora goat* is now raised throughout the world.

angstrom. A unit of length equal to one ten-millionth of an inch is known as an *angstrom unit*, or *angstrom*. It is used primarily to measure wavelengths of light and was named for Anders Jonas Angstrom (1814-74), Swedish astronomer and physicist, as was the *Angstrom crater* in the moon. Anders Angstrom taught physics at Uppsala University, his most important research work undertaken in heat conduction and light, and he is considered one of the founders of spectrum analysis. In 1867 he became the first man to examine the spectrum of the aurora borealis; the characteristic bright line in its yellow-green region is often called the *Angstrom line* in his honor.

Annie Oakley. Annie Oakley was the stage name of Ohio-born Phoebe Annie Oakley Mozee (1860-1926), star rifle shot with Buffalo Bill's wild west show. Married at sixteen, Annie joined Buffalo Bill at twenty-five and amazed audiences for more than forty years with her expert marksmanship and trick shooting. Annie once broke 942 glass balls thrown into the air with only 1,000 shots. Her most famous trick was to toss a playing card, usually a five of hearts, into the air and shoot holes through all its pips. The riddled card reminded circus performers of their punched meal tickets, which they began to call *Annie Oakleys*, and the name was soon transferred to free railroad and press passes, both of which were customarily punched with a hole in the center. Today all complimentary passes, punched or not, are called *Annie Oak-*

leys, and the expression is also used in yacht racing for a ventilated spinnaker or head sail.

Annuit Coeptis. The mottoes on the reverse side of the Great Seal of the U.S. are *Annuit Coeptis* ("He [God] has favored our undertakings") and *Novus Ordo Seclorum* ("a new order of the ages"). These were condensed by William Barton, designer of the Great Seal, from a line in Virgil's *Eclogues* (line 5).

anode. (*See* **farad**.)

another nail in my coffin. (*See* **coffin nails**.)

another Richmond in the field. Henry of Richmond, afterwards England's King Henry VII, is honored by this expression, which means that still another, unexpected opponent has shown up to do battle. The phrase is from a speech made by the king in Shakespeare's *Richard III*, though the last line is more famous than the first:

> I think there be six Richmonds in the
> field;
> Five have I slain today, instead of him—
> A horse! a horse! my kingdom for a horse!

Anstie's limit. Nineteenth-century English physician Edward Anstie advised his patients that more than one-and-a-half ounces of pure alcohol a day, consumed day in and day out, will eventually cause physical damage to the body. Stay under this limit, Anstie said, and drinking won't harm you. One-and-a-half ounces of pure alcohol translates roughly into three one-ounce drinks of 100-proof whiskey, or four beers, or half a bottle of wine. Some experts still agree with Anstie, but most refuse to generalize. Dr. Charles S. Lieber, who specializes in the effects of alcohol on health, does set a "danger level." He says that anything over eight ounces of whiskey a day regularly "is the cause of complications in most individuals. Anyone who drinks above that level is high risk." Judging by this, *Anstie's limit* is very cautious.

antenna. The Romans originally applied *antenna* to a ship's wooden horizontal yard, from which sails were hung. Centuries later, in the 1600s, the word was borrowed to describe the "horns" of various insects, such as the snail. In the early 20th century the term was finally applied to radio and television receptors.

anthology. *Anthology* derives from the Greek word meaning "a collection of flowers"—the first recorded one, in fact, is the Greek *Garland of Meleager* (ca. 90 B.C.). Two of many historically famous ones include the *Anthologia Palatina*, called the *Greek Anthology* (ca. 925), and Palgrave's *Golden Treasury* (1861), the most noted of English anthologies. Tens of thousands of anthologies have been compiled since. Bennett Cerf told the story of a book called *The Ten Commandments* that was to be published for the armed services but was too long. "How about using only five of them," quipped editor Philip Van Doren Stern, "and calling it 'A Treasury of the World's Best Commandments'?"

antibiotic. *Antibiotic*, a relatively new word, literally means "against life," a reminder that, while the drugs may save human lives, they act to end the life of germs. In fact, the first recorded use of *antibiotic* is in 1860, when its definition was "opposed to a belief in the presence or possibility of life." Not for thirty years or so would the word begin to take on its modern meaning.

anticlimax. Dr. Johnson seems to have invented or at least been the first to record the word *anticlimax*, which he defines as "a sentence in which the last part expresses something lower than the first." Pope used the anticlimax humorously in his line "Men, monkeys, lap-dogs, parrots, perish all." Everyone has a favorite anticlimax, but one of the best is the last line of Tennyson's poem "Enoch Arden" (1864), in which Enoch Arden, thought dead at sea, returns home after some years to find his wife happily married, and resolves that she won't know of his return until his death. The poem ends this way:

So past the strong heroic soul away.
And when they buried him, the little port
Had seldom seen a costlier funeral.

antifogmatic. An *antifogmatic* is any alcoholic drink taken in the morning to brace one against the fog or dampness outside, or taken with that as the excuse. This amusing Americanism is first recorded in 1789.

antimacassar. Macassar oil, a trademarked product originally made in Makassar, Indonesia, was a highly popular men's hair dressing in Victorian times. The oil stained chair backs and housewives used *antimacassars*, small cloths that they pinned to the backs of armchairs, to protect their fabric.

ants in one's pants. (*See* **antsy**.)

antsy. Originating in the late 1960s, *antsy* means jittery, restless, nervous. The expression derives from the earlier phrase *to have ants in one's pants*, which dates back to World War II America and seems to have first been recorded in humorist H. Allen Smith's book *Putty Knife* (1943): "She dilates her nostrils a lot, the way Valentino used to do it in the silent movies to indicate that he had ants in his pants." The quotation shows that *to have ants in one's pants* can suggest lust, but to my knowledge *antsy* never has this sexual meaning.

Antwerp. *Antwerp*, Belgium got its name, legend says, because a giant who lived there used to hack off the hand (*handt*) of any traveler who couldn't or wouldn't pay a toll on entering the area, throwing (*werpen*) each hand into the water. But the city really is so named because it is "the city at the wharf," Antwerp, composed of the Dutch *aan*, "at," and *werf*, "wharf."

anvil chorus. When the opposition, especially in politics, joins collectively in condemning an action or proposal, the criticism is called *an anvil chorus*. The reference is to the famous "Anvil Chorus" based on the "Gypsy Song" in Giuseppe Verdi's opera *Il Trovatore*, complete with the sound of many loud anvils and cymbals.

the anxious seat. Front seats at religious revivalist meetings in the American West during the nineteenth century were called *anxious seats*, because their occupants were so eager to be saved.

any man who hates dogs and children can't be all bad. W. C. Fields didn't coin this expression. It was adlibbed by the admirable Leo Rosten, author of *The Joys of Yiddish*, among many marvelous books, at a Friars Club testimonial banquet given to honor the comedian in 1938, which marked Field's 40th year in show business.

anything for a quiet life. Though Dickens's Sam Weller immortalized this phrase in *The Pickwick Papers*, referring to a man who took a "situation" at a lighthouse, the expression dates back to the 17th century and a play by Thomas Middleton. A jocular variation, dating only to about 1968, is the catchphrase *Anything for a quiet wife*.

A-O.K. An accidental coinage, *A-O.K.* was not used by American astronaut Alan Shepard while making the first suborbital space flight, as was widely reported. The term is actually the result of a mistake by NASA public relations officer Colonel "Shorty" Powers, who thought he heard Shepard say "A-O.K." when the astronaut, in fact, uttered a rousing "O.K." Powers liked the sound of *A-O.K.* so much that he reported it several times to newsmen before he learned of his mistake. By then it was too late, for the term became part of the language practically overnight. Speech purists insist that *A-O.K.* is a repetition, increasing O.K. 50 percent in size, but in spoken communication redundancy is not necessarily bad—in fact, it is often essential to clarity and understanding, especially in emergencies. And in every day conversation *A-O.K.* usually means "better than O.K.," "great," "near perfect"—not, repeat *not*, just "all right." (*See* **O.K.**)

A-1. *A-1*, for anything excellent, first class, originated with the expression *A-1 at Lloyd's*, referring to the rating of ships in *Lloyd's Register*. Lloyd's of London, the world-famous insurance association, has insured everything from the first airplane to Hollywood sex symbols, but the company wrote only marine insurance at its inception. Lloyd's takes its name from a coffeehouse operated by Edward Lloyd, of whom the earliest record is in 1688 and who died in 1713. For travelers, Lloyd served as a sort of one-man tourist bureau, and there is even evidence that he would fix the press gang who shanghaied men into the naval service—for a price. Virtually nothing else is known about the elusive, enterprising Lloyd except that businessmen willing to insure against sea risks congregated at his coffeehouse on Lombard Street and issued marine policies to shipowners. Here *Lloyd's List*, a paper devoted to shipping news, was published in 1734, making it the oldest London newspaper, except for the *London Gazette*. By 1760 the precursor of *Lloyd's Register of Shipping* had been printed, and only fifteen years later the phrase *A-1* was used in its pages to denote the highest class of ship; Charles Dickens first applied *A-1* to people and things in 1837. Lloyd's, now international in scope, eventually moved to the Royal Exchange and finally to its present $15-million headquarters on Lime Street. It adopted its name legally when incorporated a century ago, not long before writing the first burglary insurance (1889). Lloyd's also wrote the first policy covering loss of profits resulting from fire and pioneered in automobile and workman's compensation insurance. The corporation can issue anything but long-term life insurance. Not actually an insurance company, Lloyd's is a corporate group of some 300 syndicates composed of about 5,500 strictly supervised individual underwriters, each of whom must deposit large sums—about $35,000—as security against default on the risks each accepts. Some interesting Lloyd's policies and losses in its risky history include:

- A $100,000 "love insurance" policy that provided payment if a certain photographer's model married (she did, after the policy expired).
- A "happiness policy" that insured against "worry lines" developing on a model's face.
- Losses paid of $3,019,400 after the Lutine Bell rang over the rostrum announcing the *Titanic* disaster; more than $5.6 million on the sinking of the *Andrea Doria*; $1,463,400 on the 1906 San Francisco earthquake damage; and $110 million on Hurricane Carol in 1954.

Apache. An *apache* is a Parisian criminal or ruffian and an *apache dance* is a violent dance originated by the Parisian *apaches*. The word, in this sense, was coined by French newspaper reporter Emile Darsy, who is said to have read of bloodthirsty Apache Indians in the works of American authors and thought that their name would aptly fit denizens of the underworld. The Apache Indians, perhaps not deserving this reputation, derive their name from a Zuni word meaning enemy, and the name was applied to many nomadic bands of Indians roaming the southwestern United States. The Apaches called themseves *dene*, an Athabascan word for "human being."

A-per-se. This common expression for the best, something or someone unbeatable, goes all the way back to Chaucer, who calls Cressida "the floure and A-per-se of Troi and Greek."

Apicius. Apicius might be called the world's first gourmand and bon vivant as well as the author of the earliest cookbook. His *Of Culinary Matters*, has gone through countless editions since first written about fifteen hundred years ago. Some historians claim that Apicius was a rich Roman merchant who collected recipes wherever he traveled, others that his name is a nom de plume deriving from the word "epicure," but most authorities believe that he was the Roman nobleman Marcus Gavius Apicius, who lived under Tiberius in the first century A.D. Whatever his identity, an *Apicius* still brings to mind a chef and gastronome without peer, one who went to such lengths as spraying his garden lettuce with mead in the evening so that it would taste like "green cheesecakes" the next morning, one who concocted *Apician* dishes that remain, in the words of Mark Twain, "as delicious as the less conventional forms of sin."

an appeal from Philip drunk to Philip sober. A woman petitioned King Philip of Macedon for justice for her husband and was refused. "I shall appeal against this judgment!" she exclaimed, and Philip—while still in his cups—roared: "Appeal—and to whom will you appeal?" "To Philip sober," the woman replied, and according to Valerius Maximus, who tells the tale, she won her case.

apple; apple hawk; apple orchard. *Apple* for a baseball dates back to the early 1920s; before that the ball had been called a "pea," a term heard no more. A good fielder was called an *apple hawk* at the time; this term is obsolete now, and the ball park was called an *apple orchard*, an expression still occasionally used. *Apple* itself comes from the Old English *appel* for the fruit.

apple cart. (*See* **to upset the apple cart**.)

appleknocker. An abusive term meaning a stupid person, especially a rustic stupid person, that is still used by city dwellers. The term is first recorded in this sense in a 1939 *New Yorker* story: "I had a reform-school technique, whereas them other sailors was apple-knockers. They were so dumb they couldn't find their nose with both hands." *Appleknocker* first meant a fruit picker, deriving from the mistaken urban belief that fruit is harvested by being knocked from trees with long sticks.

apple of discord. This legendary golden apple was thrown on the table by the god Eris (Discord) at the wedding of Thetis and Peleus, to which all the Greek gods but Eris had been invited. The apple was said to be "for the most beautiful woman" present, and Paris judged between Hera (Juno), Aphrodite (Venus), and Athene (Minerva), who offered him, respectively, bribes of power, sex, and martial glory. He chose Aphrodite, and the vengeance of Hera and Athene supposedly led to the fall of Troy. The *apple of discord* still means the cause of a dispute, or something to be disputed.

apple of one's eye. That which one holds dearest, as in "You're the apple of my eye." The phrase is from the Bible (Deut. 32:10), which says the Lord kept Israel "as the apple of his eye." *Pupillam*, or pupil, is actually the Latin for the "apple" of the phrase, but English translators of the Bible used "apple" because this was the early word for the pupil of the eye, which was thought to be a solid apple-shaped body. Because it is essential to sight, the eye's apple, or pupil, is to be cherished and protected, and *the apple of one's eye* came to mean anything extremely precious. The literal translation of the Hebrew phrase, incidentally, is "You are as the little man in the eye" (one's own reflection in the pupil of another's eye).

apple orchard. (*See* **apple.**)

apple-pie order. One old story holds that New England housewives were so meticulous and tidy when making their apple pies—carefully cutting thin slices of apples, methodically arranging them in rows inside the pie, making sure that the pinches joining the top and bottom crusts were perfectly even, etc.—that the expression *apple-pie order* arose for prim and precise orderliness. A variant on the yarn has an early American housewife baking seven pies every Monday and arranging them neatly on shelves, one for every day of the week in strict order. Nice stories, but the term *apple-pie order* is probably British in origin, dating back to at least the early 17th century. It may be a corruption of the French *nappes-pliees*, folded linen (neatly folded) or *cap-a-pie*, which means "from head to foot" in English usage. Yet no use of either *nappes-pliees* order or *cap-a-pie* order appears in English. "Alpha beta order" has also been suggested, but seems unlikely. The true source of the term must still be considered a mystery, the matter far from *in apple-pie order*.

apple-polisher. The traditional practice of a student giving teacher a bright, shiny apple is the source for this expression for a sycophant, the Americanism being first recorded in 1928. The synonym *sycophant* (*q.v.*) interestingly has its origins in another fruit, figs.

applesauce. The expression *applesauce* for disguised flattery dates to the early 20th century and may derive from "the boarding-house trick of serving plenty of this cheap comestible when richer fare is scanty," according to a magazine of the time. The term also came to mean lies and exaggerations. As a word for a sauce made from stewed, sweetened apples, *applesauce* is an Americanism dating back at least to the mid-18th century. *Applesauce* as a term for insincere flattery may also have been invented by American cartoonist Thomas Aloysius Dorgan (1877-1929), "Tad" having been the most prolific word coiner of his day. No one knows for sure.

apples of paradise. According to tradition, each of the apples in the Garden of Eden had a bite taken from it after Eve took a bite of the forbidden fruit. Over the years *apples of paradise*, referring to the apples in Eden, has come to mean forbidden fruit.

apples of perpetual youth. These were golden apples of Scandinavian mythology that were in the care of Idhunn, daughter of Svald the dwarf. By eating them, the gods preserved their youth.

apples of Sodom. An old legend says that apple trees grown near the Dead Sea, "where Sodom and Gomorrah stood," bear beautiful red fruit that fall to soot and ashes in the mouth. The gallnuts produced on apples by the insect *Cynips insana* are said to be scientific fact behind the legend, but the expression still means anything disappointing.

apricot. The Romans called this fruit *praecoquum*, or "early ripe." From there the word entered Arabic as *al-burquq* and went into Portuguese as *albricoque*, whence it come into English as *apricock*. By the 18th century the shears of prudery had pruned the word from apri*cock* to apri*cot*.

April. The romantic Romans named *April* after the flower buds that open in this month, basing their *Aprilis* on the Latin *aperia*, meaning "open."

April fool! All Fool's Day, when childish pranks are played and their victims are taunted with cries of *April fool!*, seems to have been brought from France to England in about 1700. But its origins and the reason it is celebrated on April first remain unknown. There are several explanations. The oldest says All Fool's Day is a relic of the Roman "Cerealia," held at the beginning of April to honor Ceres, the goddess of Agriculture. It seems that Ceres's daughter Proserpina was carried off by Pluto, the King of Hades, and when Ceres heard the echo of her screams, she followed the echo—a fool's errand. Other theories hold that April Fool's Day falls in April because of the tricky weather at the time; because April is the first month of spring, when people are half awake from their winter hibernation and easily hoaxed; and because of the mock trial of Christ held in April. Still another explanation is that New Year's Day fell on March 25 under the old Julian calendar (used until the Gregorian calendar was adopted in 1756) and that people capped a week of festivities with April Fool's Day on April first. The French call an April Fool a *poisson d'Avril* (an "April fish"), in reference to a newly spawned, naive, and easily caught fish.

apron strings. (*See* **tied to his mother's apron string**.)

aptronyms. American columnist Franklin P. Adams (F.P.A.) coined the term *aptronym*, but writers have used aptronyms—"label names" that fit the nature or occupation of a character—at least since the time of Spenser's allegorical *Faerie Queene* and Bunyan's *Pilgrim's Progress*. It is said that Plato's real name was Aristocles and that he was called Plato ("broad") because of his broad shoulders. Mr. Gradgrind, Mr. Worldly Wiseman, Lord Easy (a careless husband), William Congreve's gossipy character Scandal, Scott's Dr. Dryasdust, and many of Dickens's characters are famous fictional examples of aptronyms.

aquanaut; oceanaut. Based on the Greek *nautes*, sailor, these words were coined in recent times to describe scientist-explorers who work and live at sea for long periods. Jacques Cousteau coined *oceanaut*.

aqua tofana. *Aqua Tofana*, a favorite potion of young wives in 17th-century Italy who wanted to get rid of their rich, elderly, or ineffectual husbands, recalls a woman who peddled her deadly home brew on such a large scale that she has achieved immortality of a kind. Her first name is unknown, but Miss or Mrs. Tofana was either a Greek or Italian lady who died in Naples or Palermo, Sicily about the year 1690. Apparently she died a natural death, although five others headed by an old hag named Spara, who had bought her secret formula, were arrested and hanged in 1659. Tofana's poison was a strong, transparent and odorless solution of arsenic that she sold in vials labeled *Manna di S. Nicolas di Bari* (the "Manna of St. Nicholas of Bari"), in honor of the miraculous oil that was said to flow from the tomb of the saint. (*See* **brucine**.)

Arabic words. English words that come to us from Arabic include: *saffron, mattress, admiral, hazard, cotton, henna, camphor, alembic, alchemy, elixir, alkali, zenith, almanac, azimuth, cipher, gismo, syrup, antimony, alcoran, mosque, sumac, bedouin, rebec, sash, algebra, monsoon, arsenal, assassin, jar, alcohol, apricot, giraffe, hashish, coffee, sirocco, fakir, emir, sherbet, alcove, sofa, harem, gazelle, minaret, zero, albatross, Allah, houri, magazine, genie, ghoul, candy, jehad, safari, tariff, coffee, cafe* and, possibly, *so long* (from *salaam*).

arachnida. *Arachnida*, the class of spiders (plus scorpions and mites), takes its name from the Lydian maiden Arachne, so skilled at weaving that she challenged Athena, goddess of the household arts, to a contest. Athena won the contest, weaving perfect tapestries that told glorious stories about the gods, while Arachne's excellent but imperfect efforts were unflattering to the gods. The proud Arachne, frightened when Athena tore her impious work to pieces, tried to hang herself, but the goddess interceded, changing her into a spider (from the Greek *arachne*) so that she would forever weave her beautiful designs. Yet she really wants no more of her weaving, legend says, and keeps trying to hang herself—the reason spiders hang on threads from their webs.

Arbor Day. "Tree Day" is the exact meaning of *Arbor Day*, for *arbor* is a Latin word for "tree." Arbor Day was first celebrated in 1872, when Nebraskan J. Sterling Morton and his supporters persuaded their state to set aside April 10th for tree planting, to compensate for all the trees Americans had destroyed over the years in clearing the land for settlements. More than a million trees were planted on that first Arbor Day alone, and today the holiday is celebrated in every state.

arbor vitae. The white cedar was named *arborvitae*, Latin for the "tree of life," by French explorers in Canada during the early 17th century. Champlain's men had observed that Indians drank a medicinal tea made from the bark and needles of the white cedar (*Thuja occidentalis*) and so named the tree because it saved lives.

arcades ambo. (*See* **six of one and half dozen of another**.)

Archaeopteryx. One of the world's most famous fossils, the 150 million-year-old *Archaeopteryx* has the body and teeth of a small dinosaur and the feathered wings of a bird. When found in a German limestone quarry in 1861 it was hailed as a missing evolutionary link between reptiles and birds. Since that time five similar specimens have been found. *Archaeopteryx* is, appropriately, the Greek for "ancient wing."

Archimedean principle. The Greek mathematician and inventor Archimedes, supposedly born at Syracuse in Sicily in 287 B.C., was both the Albert Einstein and Thomas Edison of his day. He devised the *Archimedean drill, pulley*, and *windlass*, and the *screw of Archimedes*, a machine for raising water, among many other inventions. Archimedes, however, thought little of these ingenious contrivances, even declining to leave written records of most of them. He preferred to be remembered for his great work in mathematics, or for his founding of the science of hydrostatics, which his *Archimedean*

Principle made possible. As fate would have it, Archimedes is best remembered for his coining of an expression. One day he was asked to determine the amount of silver an allegedly dishonest goldsmith had used for the king's crown, which was supposed to have been made of pure gold. While pondering the solution to the problem in his bath, he observed that the quantity of water displaced by a body will equal in bulk the bulk of the immersed body (the *Archimedean Principle*). All he had to do then was to weigh an amount of gold equal in weight to the crown, put crown and gold in separate basins of water, and weigh the overflow to determine how much gold the crown really contained. According to one story, he was so overjoyed with his discovery that he forgot his clothes and ran out into the streets naked, astonishing passersby with his shouts of *"Eureka, eureka!"* ("I have found it, I have found it!")

archipelago. *Archipelago* first referred only to the Aegean Sea, the Italians giving the Aegean this name in the 13th century from their word *arcipelago,* "chief sea." *Archipelago* later came to mean any group of islands.

architecture is frozen music. Goethe did not coin the above phrase which we owe to the German poet Friedrich von Schelling (1775-1864). Von Schelling used the term several times in his *Philosophy of Art*: "Since it [architecture] is music in space, as it were a frozen music . . . . If architecture in general is frozen music . . ." Soon after, in 1830, Goethe said *Die Bakunst ist eine estarrete Music,* the form usually quoted today.

Arctic. *Arctic* for the far north derives from *arctos,* the Greek word for bear. The Greeks referred to the north as *arctos* because the Great Bear constellation (Ursa Major) is the most prominent one in the northern skies.

arena. The floors of the amphitheaters of ancient Rome had to be covered with absorbent sand because so much blood was spilled in the gladiatorial contests held there. The Latin word for sand is *arena,* and this became the name for the structure itself.

are you a man or a mouse? American slang probably dating back to the early days of the century, *Are you a man or a mouse?* is used to disparage or spur on a timorous person. The reply is often: "A man; my wife's afraid of mice."

argosy. An *argosy* was originally a merchant ship built at Ragusa, Dalmatia (now Dubrovnik, Yugoslavia) in the 16th century. English sailors called this type of ship a *ragusa* after the port city and this word was corrupted to *ragusy* and then to *argosy.* The name was finally applied to any richly laden merchant vessel.

argus-eyed. In Greek mythology the hundred-eyed Argus was chosen by the jealous Zeus to guard over the nymph Io, even though he had turned his love into an unattractive cow. Apparently he grew jealous of Argus, too, for he had him killed and transferred his eyes to the peacock's tail—which is, according to tradition, why it looks the way it does. Argus managed to live on in name only; *argus-eyed* still meaning vigilant.

argyle. The original pattern for argyle socks was the traditional green and white pattern of the Scottish Campbell clan of Argyle, or Argyll. The Duke of Argyle, head of the clan, was famous among Highlanders for the posts he erected in his pastures to enable his cows to rub their backs and ease the itching caused by insects. Perhaps the posts were only erected to indicate a trail covered with snow, but nevertheless "God bless the Duke of Argyle!" became a common humorous remark whenever a Scotsman scratched himself. The clan found new popularity when mentioned in several of Sir Walter Scott's novels. Not long after, its tartan was adapted by fabric manufacturers as the *argyle plaid,* and socks knitted in such a pattern were called *argyle socks.* Nowadays, argyle socks are any two or more bright colors, retaining only the diamond-shaped pattern of the original adaptation.

aria. *Aria,* for an air or melody, or a melody for a single voice with accompaniment, is an Italian word (*aria,* "air," "music") that entered English in the first half of the 18th century. It is said that three-quarters of our musical terms are Italian in origin, including, to name only a few, *violin, mandolin, pianoforte, orchestra* (from Greek), and *opera.*

Aristotelian logic. A number of words are named after Aristotle (384-322 B.C.), the Greek philosopher who was the pupil of Plato and tutor to Alexander the Great. These include *Aristotelianism,* a philosophy emphasizing deduction and investigation of concrete, particular things and situations; *Aristotelian logic,* traditional formal logic; *Aristotle's lantern,* a zoological term so called from a reference by Aristotle to a sea urchin that resembled certain lanterns; and the *Aristotelian* or dramatic *unities,* the necessity for unit of action, time, and place in drama. One of the greatest thinkers of all time, Aristotle's habit of giving his lectures in the peripatos, or walking place, of the Athenian Lyceum gave his school of philosophy the name Peripatetic, which yielded the English word *peripatetic,* "walking about or carried on while walking about from place to place."

Arizona. Our 48th state, admitted to the Union in 1912, is nicknamed "the Grand Canyon State." *Arizona* derives from the Papago Indian word *Arizonac,* "the place of the small spring."

Arizona strawberries.   American cowboys and lumberjacks used this term as a humorous synonym for beans, also employing the variations *Arkansas strawberries*, *Mexican strawberries*, and *prairie strawberries*. Dried beans *were* pink in color like strawberries. One wit noted that the only way these beans could be digested was for the consumer to break wild horses.

Arkansas.   Originally spelled *Arkansaw*, our 25th state, nicknamed "the Wonder State," was admitted to the Union in 1925. *Arkansas* is the Sioux word for "land of the south wind people."

Arkansas toothpick.   (*See* **bowie knife.**)

armadillo.   *Armadillo* is Spanish diminutive of "the armed one" and is related to words like armor, this obviously in reference to the little porkilotherm's being encased by bony armor and by its habit of rolling itself, when threatened, into an impregnable ball. The Mexican native, which cannot survive north of Texas, was a source of food to Americans during the Great Depression, when it was known as "Hoover hog" or "Texas turkey." Darwin was fascinated by the little *armadillo* and its ancient prehistoric predecessor, the *glyptodont*, which was about the size of a Volkswagen Beetle. A children's poem has it that a peccadillo of the armadillo is that it must be washed with Brillo.

Armageddon.   Today *Armageddon* usually refers to a nuclear war that marks the end of the world. It derives from the biblical prophecy that the final battle between good and evil on Judgment Day would be fought on the battlefield of Armageddon (Rev. 16:14-16), which is now Megiddo, near Samaria in Israel. The Hebrew *har Megiddo*, from which *Armageddon* derives, means the *har* or mountain of Megiddo.

armed to the teeth.   Some real or imaginary pirate swinging aboard a prize, one hand on a rope, the other hand wielding a cutlass or a pistol, with a knife clamped between his teeth, suggested this expression. The phrase, still used if mostly in a humorous way, seems to have originated in the first half of the last century. English politician Richard Cobden used it in 1849, perhaps inspired by an adventure writer of the day.

armoire.   These large wardrobes or cupboards started off as places to store weapons, deriving from the Roman *armarium*, "closet," which derives from the Latin *arma*, "arms."

around the horn.   In the days of the tall ships any sailor who had sailed around Cape Horn was entitled to spit to windward; otherwise, it was a serious infraction of nautical rules of conduct. Thus, the permissible practice of spitting to windward was called *around the horn*. Cape Horn isn't so named because it is shaped like a horn. Captain Schouten, the Dutch navigator who first doubled it in 1616, named it after Hoorn, his birthplace in northern Holland.

arrant thief; knight errant.   *Arrant* was at first just a variation of *errant*, nomadic or vagabond, the word best known in *knight errant*, a knight who roamed the country performing good deeds. But from its persistent use in expressions such as an *arrant thief*, a thief who roamed the countryside holding up victims, *arrant* came to mean thorough, downright, or out-and-out. Expressions such as *an arrant thief, an arrant coward*, etc., have been common since the late 14th century.

arras.   This richly woven tapestry with scenes and figures takes its name from the town of Arrasin, in Artois, France, where it was first woven in medieval times. The French call it a *tapisserie*.

artesian wells.   *Artesian wells*, wells whose shafts penetrate through an impervious layer into a water-bearing stratum from which water runs under pressure, take their name from Arteseum, now Artois, in northern France, where such wells were worked as early as the 17th century.

artichoke; Jerusalem artichoke.   As Richard Armour observed, the *artichoke* is the one vegetable you have more of when you finish eating it, due to its compact leaves, which are scraped with the teeth and discarded. Often called the *globe* or *French artichoke*, it is the flower bud of a thistle picked before it blooms. At one time it was seriously suggested that the plant was so named because some *artist* had *choked* on the inedible "needles" covering its delicious base, or "heart." Actually *artichoke* has more prosaic and complicated origins. The Arabians called it *al* ("the") *kharshuf*, which became *alcachofa* in Spanish. Northern Italians corrupted the Spanish version to *articiocco* and this entered French as *artichaut*, from which our *artichoke* evolved. It is true that the English *choke* in the word replacing the French *chaut* may have been influenced by the sensation one gets from eating the wrong part of the vegetable. As for the *Jerusalem artichoke*, it neither comes from Jerusalem, is an artichoke, nor tastes anything like an artichoke. The starchy underground tuber (a good potato substitute) was called *girasole articiocco*, "sunflower artichoke," by northern Italians because it is a member of the sunflower family and resembles a sunflower in leaf and stem. To Englishmen hearing the word *girasole* sounded like *Jerusalem*, and they mistakenly translated the name as *Jerusalem artichoke*.

ascham. This tall narrow locker for arrows takes its name from Roger Ascham, an English scholar who would otherwise not be remembered for his 16th-century treatise on archery.

as every schoolboy knows. Jonathan Swift used this expression, which has been traced back as early as 1621. It is generally associated with the British historian Macaulay because of his frequent references to somewhat abstruse subjects as subjects that any public schoolboy should know.

Asiatic hordes. This expression is so distasteful to Orientals that they have officially asked on several occasions to be called Asians instead of Asiatics in all cases, so as to avoid any association with the term *Asiatic hordes*. "Hordes" itself, however, is clearly associated with Asians. The word first described the tent of Batu Khan, Genghis Khan's grandson, who crossed the Volga in 1235 leading the savage Mongol invasion of Europe that left massacred people and leveled cities in its path. Batu's magnificent tent, made mostly of embroidered silk, was called the *sira ordu*, the "silken camp." Conquered Poles called it the *horda* and soon the name "Golden Horde" was applied to both Batu's tent and his army. In time "horde" came to describe any large, savage army, especially as in the phrase *Asiatic hordes*.

ask a silly question and you'll get a silly answer. Still a common expression, the above probably dates to the late 19th century. It possibly evolved from the old proverb "ask no questions and you'll be told no lies."

as one man. Unanimously, with one accord. The expression is an ancient one, coming from the Bible (Judges, 20:8): "So all the people got them up as one man."

asparagus. There is a story that *asparagus* takes its name from the Greek *aspharagos*, meaning according to this theory, "as long as one's throat," because diners often swallowed the spears whole. But the meaning of the word *aspharagos* from which our *asparagus* derives is unclear and more likely meant "sprout or shoot" in Greek. (See **quicker than you can cook asparagus**.)

aspen; trembling poplar. The *trembling* or *quaking poplar*, as the *aspen* is also known, is said to have trembling leaves because it began shaking in shame and horror when Christ's cross was made from its wood. *Populus tremula* and its related species have long, compressed, twisted leafstalks that cause the leaves to tremble in even the slightest wind.

asphodel; Jacob's rod. The asphodel of the ancients so frequently encountered in poetry is *Asphodeline luta*, a perennial yellow-flowered herb sometimes called *Jacob's rod*. In ancient times the dead were thought to sustain themselves on the roots of asphodels, and the flowers were often planted on graves. Interestingly, the much better known daffodil bears a name that is a corruption of *asphodel*.

aspic. A tasty meat jelly, *aspic* is supposed to have been named for the asp (the same hooded venomous snake that Cleopatra used to kill herself), because French gourmets said it was "cold as an asp." The word came into English late in the 18th century and there is no better explanation for its origin.

aspidistra. This foliage plant takes its name from the Greek *aspis*, a small round shield in reference to the shape of its stigma. It is often called the cast-iron plant because it withstands all kinds of ill-treatment. Widely used in bars, movie houses, and other public places, it is also called the beerplant—because bartenders often water it with beer left on the bar at the end of the evening!

assembly line. The term *assembly line* was first recorded in 1914 in connection with Henry Ford's car company, but the practice in America goes back at least to the 18th century, when muskets were made from several standard parts in one factory. Among automobile manufacturers, Henry Ford is generally credited with the idea for an assembly line, but Ford actually improved upon a method the Olds Motor Vehicle Company, maker of the Oldsmobile, used long before him in 1902, although he did introduce the electric conveyer belt.

ass in a sling. The *Dictionary of American Slang* says that *to have one's ass in in a sling* means "to be or appear to be sad, rejected, or defeated." Originating in the South perhaps a century ago, the now national expression was probably suggested by someone with his arm in a sling, that image being greatly and humorously exaggerated. A good story claims that this ass is really a donkey, that the expression comes from a practice of blacksmiths rigging slings for donkeys, or asses, because they can't stand on three feet while being shoed. But the good story isn't a true story. Donkeys *can* stand on three feet and so far as is known, no blacksmith ever shoed a donkey in a sling.

aster. This daisy takes its name from the Latin *aster*, "a star," in reference to the shape of its flower. However, when *aster* occurs at the end of other plant names, as in *Cotoneaster*, it doesn't have anything to do with this root but instead indicates inferiority.

asterisk. *Asterisk*, from the Greek word for "star," can mean "little star" in English, but much more frequently refers to the star that writers use after a word to indicate a footnote at the bottom of the page. Stoddard King wrote about one in "The Writer and the Asterisk" (1913), showing another function of the star:

A writer owned an Asterisk,
and kept it in his den,
Where he wrote tales (which had large sales)
Of frail and erring men
And always, when he reached the point
Where carping censors lurk,
He called upon the Asterisk
To do his dirty work.

asteroid. An *asteroid*, from the Greek *aster*, "star," and *eidos*, "form," is also called a minor planet, being one of the thousands of small planets, the largest less than 500 miles in diameter, that circle the sun mainly between the orbits of Jupiter and Mars. *Asteroid* was coined in 1804 by British astronomer Sir William Herschel, who so named the minor planets for their star-shaped form. (*See* **earthlight** for a word Herschel's son coined.)

astrology. *Astrology* means "speaking of the stars" in Greek, and an astrologist is "one who speaks of the stars." The word did not come into English, through Latin, until the late 14th century. Prior to that *astronomy* (*q.v.*) had been used in its place.

astronomy. *Astronomy* comes from a Greek word meaning "star arranging, or arrangement of the stars," and was first applied to the work of men charting the heavens. It came into English, via Latin, early in the 13th century, meaning at first the whole field of astrology (*q.v.*), not the modern science of *astronomy*.

Athanasian wench. Though it's rarely used anymore in everyday speech, this 18th-century slang for "a forward girl, ready to oblige any man that shall ask her" has an amusing origin. It alludes to the Ecumenical *Athanasian Creed*, which takes its name from St. Athanasius, an exiled third-century Alexandrian bishop who was a pioneer in scientific theology. The *English Book of Common Prayer* includes the *Athanasian Creed*, and the term *Athanasian wench* arose when some wit pointed out that the familiar first words of the creed read *quicunque vult*, "Whosoever desires . . ."

Athens. According to the myth, when Cecrops founded a great city in Attica, the Greeks offered to name it for the god who gave them the most valuable gift. Poseidon gave them the horse, but Athena stuck her spear in the ground and an olive tree rose from the earth. Because she gave them this greatest gift of all, the city was named in her honor. In any event, the city is assuredly named for the goddess.

athlete. Athlete comes to us from the Greek *athlon*, meaning literally "the winning of an *athlon*, or prize." Entering English early in the 16th century, the word described anyone who competed in the physical activities—running, jumping, boxing, wrestling, etc.—that formed part of the public games in ancient Greece.

athlete's foot. An advertising copywriter coined this term in 1928 when Absorbine Jr., a remedy for this disease often caught in gyms and locker rooms, popularized the euphemism. For over four hundred years before that, *athlete's foot* had been called "ringworm." *Jock itch*, the term for a condition caused by the same fungus, was coined in the 1970s.

Atlantic Ocean. The Atlantic may take its name from the fabled kingdom of Atlantis that is said to have existed in its domain, or from the Atlas Mountains in northwest Africa, which the ancients thought overlooked the entire ocean. It is interesting to note that the Atlantic Ocean is widening an inch every year, while the Pacific Ocean is shrinking.

Atlantis; Lemuria; Lyonesse. First mentioned by Plato and said to have existed in the Atlantic Ocean, *Atlantis* was supposed to have been destroyed by an earthquake and sunk beneath the bottom of the sea more than ten thousand years ago, which hasn't stopped legions of adventurers from searching for it over the ages. *Lemuria*, said to be near Madagascar, is another famous lost island in history, as is *Lyonesse*, a mythical country "forty fathoms down" stretching off England from Lands End to the Scilly Isles.

atlas. In Greek mythology Atlas stood on a mountain peak in what is now Africa holding the heavens apart from the earth. This myth inspired the great geographer Gerardus Mercator (1515-94) to use a drawing of Atlas holding a globe on his shoulders for the cover of a collection of maps he published in the 16th century. The picture was used on so many similar books to follow that *atlas* became synonymous for any book of maps.

atom. The *atom* takes its name from the Greek *atomos*, undivided or indivisible, being to the Greeks something that could not be cut up or divided anymore. More poetically, the Greek word *atomos* is closely related to the Greek for "the twinkling of an eye," a charming way to express minuteness. *Atom* came into English in the 15th century from the Latin *atomus*, which derives from the Greek word.

atomic bomb. This term was apparently first used in a science fiction story—H. G. Wells's "The World Set Free," written in 1914. Thirty years later it became a reality.

to atone. *Atone* strictly means "to be at one with." As early as the 13th century religious sermons often implored worshippers "to be at one with God" ("one" pronounced "own" at the time), so often, in fact, that the phrase came to be written *atone* within a century or so. *To atone* meant at first to be reconciled with, to be at one with, but since reconciliation often came after parties to a dispute made amends, the word took on its present meaning of expiation.

at one fell swoop. The first use of this phrase in English appears to be by Shakespeare in *Macbeth*, where he describes a Hell-Kite killing chickens. But the word *swoop*, referring to a bird of prey pouncing suddenly on its victim, occurs in an earlier reference to a fabled bird of Madagascar that could swoop down and carry off "a horse and his rider, or an elephant." *One fell swoop* means a sudden single strike or blow, fierce and often brutal. The *fell* in the phrase has nothing to do with the verb "fall," as might be suspected, deriving instead from the old English adjective *fell* meaning "fierce, savage, ruthless," which is the basis for the word *felon*. *Swoop* comes from a Scandinavian word that meant to move in a stately manner, to sweep along as with trailing garments.

atropidae. *Atropidae* are book lice that feed on the bindings and paper of books, eventually destroying them. They are named for *Atropos*, one of the three Fates in Greek mythology, the Fate that finally cut the thread of life. Why were the Atropidae or book lice named for someone who destroyed life? In ancient times the ticking sound they made was said to forebode a death.

attest. (See **testify**.)

attic; attic salt. Both the *attic* in one's house and *attic salt*, pointed wit, came to us from the same source, the Greek word *Attikos*, an Athenian, or citizen of Athens. Salt was a common term for wit and the Athenians were noted for their elegant turns of thought, which inspired the Romans to coin the expression *sal atticus* ("attic salt"). The Athenians had no *attics* in their houses as we know them, but the Attic (Athenian) style of architecture featured decorative walls at the tops of buildings. When storage rooms were built behind such decorative walls centuries later, they were called *attics*, after the walls.

attorney. (See **lawyer**.)

Aubry's dog. The dog Dragon's French master, Aubry of Montdidier, was murdered in 1371 by Richard of Macaire. Thereafter, whenever Richard appeared, Dragon attacked him. This excited suspicion of Richard, and he was ordered into judicial combat with the dog. Dragon killed him, and in his last moments Richard confessed the murder of Aubry. An *Aubry's dog* is thus a very loyal, faithful dog.

auction; augment. When an item is auctioned, bids on it keep going up, of course, until there is no more bidding and the highest bidder makes the purchase. The word *auction*, widely used by the Romans, reflects the process, deriving as it does from the Latin *augere*, to increase, which also gives us *augment*.

auger. (See **adder**.)

auger in. Pilots superstitiously avoid the use of the word *crash*, using many euphemisms, including *buy the farm* (*q.v.*) and *auger in*. *Auger in* dates back to the day of the prop plane, planes with props resembling an auger as they crashed into the earth.

August; Augustan age. Augustus Caesar stole a day from February to give *August* thirty-one days—simply because he did not want July, named after his great uncle and adopted father, to be longer than his own name-month. History is made up of such petty jealousies, but Augustus and Julius Caesar really got along very well; there is no evidence of any generation gap. Born Gaius Octavianus, his mother the daughter of Julius Caesar's sister, Augustus was eventually chosen by the Roman ruler as his heir, adopting the name Caesar. Octavius, as he was commonly known, was only nineteen at the time of his uncle's assassination in 44 B.C. On returning to Rome from Spain, he found that Caesar had secretly adopted him and willed him all his property. It was then that he changed his name and embarked on a celebrated military career that included the conquest of Egypt. In 29 B.C., already immensely popular among the people, he was chosen first emperor of Rome, and two years later the Senate bestowed upon him the title *Augustus*, or "imperial majesty." Finally, what was the sixth month of the year (*Sextillus*) before the Julian calendar was renamed "Augustus" in his honor—complete with an extra day at his insistence. *August* wasn't chosen because it was his birth month (September), but because it happened to be his "lucky" month of the year—the one in which he first became a consul, reduced Egypt, put an end to civil wars, received the oath of allegiance from his legions at Janiculum, and scored his greatest military triumphs. Octavius Augustus ruled wisely until his death at the age of seventy-five, his reign marked by great progress and a flowering of literature that is today known as the *Augustan age*.

Aunt May. An *Aunt May* is British naval slang for a person generous to sailors. It is aptly named for Mrs. May Hanrahan, the widow of a United States naval captain, who "adopted" sixteen British destroyers during World War II and spent almost a quarter of a million dollars on their crews in the form of presents and comforts. *Aunt May* Hanrahan was received by the queen when she visited England after the war and was piped on board the destroyer *Tartar* while a naval band on the jetty played in her honor.

aurora borealis; auroral. *Aurora borealis* means "northern dawn" in Latin and is used to describe the electrical streams of light sometimes seen at night in the northern sky. The phenomenon is so named because the Greek goddess Aurora was said to begin her day's travels before the sun rose. Aurora's name is also remembered in *auroral*, "dawnlike."

auspicious, auger, augury. The Roman auspex was a man appointed to foretell the future by observing the flight of birds, listening to their songs, observing the food they ate, or examining their entrails. The name comes from the Latin *avis*, "bird," and *specere*, "to look at." No important enterprise was begun without the auspex's consulting the birds to see if omens were favorable; favorable omens came to be called *auspicious* ones. In later Roman times the *augur* replaced the auspex as the observer and interpreter of bird signs, his name deriving from the Latin *avis*, "bird," and *garrire*, "to talk or tell." His interpretation was called an augurism, which became the English word *augury*, an omen, while the Latin *inaugurare*, "to install an official after consulting the birds," became our word *inaugurate*.

Aussie. Australians have been called *Aussies* since about 1895, when the term seems to have been coined by Australians. *Aussie* became popular worldwide during the Great War (1914-18), as did *digger* for an Australian soldier, though this last term may have originated during the Australian gold rush in the 1850s. Australia, of course, has long been called *the land down under* (along with New Zealand). In contrast, Alaska is sometimes jokingly called *the land up over*.

Australian crawl. Pacific Island natives probably invented this fastest of all swimming strokes—the one used by all freestyle swimmers today—but it was introduced into Europe (where the breaststroke was the favored stroke) from Australia at the turn of the century, and thus dubbed the *Australian crawl*.

Austrian lip. The British historian Macaulay wrote that Charles II of Spain, last of the Austrian Hapsburgs, had a jaw so malformed that he couldn't chew his food. Another Hapsburg, Emperor Charles V, possessed a lower jaw that protruded so far beyond his upper jaw that he could not speak an intelligible sentence. This inherited genetic defect, one of the most curious in history, is common to all the Hapsburgs, and can be seen in many of their portraits. It was probably inherited through marriage with the Polish princely family of Jagellon and perpetuated by intermarriage among the Hapsburgs themselves. The term *Austrian lip* describes the deformity far better than "severely protruding lower jaw."

autantonym. An *autantonym* (from the Greek for "self" + "antonym") is a word that has come to mean its opposite. An example is the word *fast*, which in the case of a fast runner means a runner who runs rapidly, but in the case of a *fast* color means a color that doesn't run at all. The word seems to have been coined in the last half century or so.

auto-da-fé. A public judgment against someone tried by the Spanish Inquisition was called an *auto-da-fé*, the judgment usually followed by burning condemned heretics at the stake, burning employed because the Catholic Church forbade the shedding of blood. *Auto-da-fé* is Portuguese for "act of the faith."

automatic writing. *Automatic writing* is writing performed without the will or control of the writer, sometimes without the writer being conscious of the words written. The phenomenon first appeared in mid-19th-century America as a tool of spiritualism, and the writer was sometimes (but not always) hypnotized or drugged and aided by instruments including a planchette, "a little heart-shaped board running on wheels," that was supplemented by a Ouija board containing the alphabet and other signs.

automation. *Automation* was coined in 1936 by D. S. Harder, a General Motors employee, but it didn't come into popular use until the 1950s. Harder defined *automation* as the "automatic handling of parts between progressive production processes," but it is more commonly defined today as "the technique or system of operating a mechanical or productive device by highly automatic means, as by electronic devices."

autumn; fall. *Autumn* is used much more in England, *fall* in America. Both are lovely old words. *Autumn*, from the Latin *autumn* for the season, dating back to the early 14th century, and *fall*, first recorded in 1545, is short for the season of *leaf-fall*. In the 1850s *autumn* was British slang for a hanging through a drop door, the grim joke showing that the British did use *fall* as a synonym for *autumn*.

average. *Average* has an unusual rather than average derivation. The word derives from the French *avarie*, a word of Arabic origin that meant "less than total damage to a ship or its cargo." Since average damage was a mean between the extremes of total damage and no damage, the word average ultimately came to take its current meaning.

avocado. When Montezuma served the *avocado*, or alligator pear, to Cortez and his conquistadores, the Aztecs explained that their *ahucatl* was so named from their word meaning "testicle," not only because the fruit resembled a testicle but because it supposedly excited sexual passion. The Aztecs even drew their guests pictures to illustrate their story, but to the Spaniards *ahucatl* sounded like *avocado*, their word for "advocate," and they named it so when they brought it back to Spain. In Europe the *avocado* became a great favorite, and France's Sun King called it *la bonne poire* (the good pear) because it seemed to get a rise out of his setting libido. Aphrodisiac or not, the fruit remains an important meat substitute in parts of the world today and a delicious dessert in others.

avoid extremes.   Common to many languages, *avoid extremes* has been traced back as far as the writings of Pittacus of Mitylene (652-569 B.C.), one of the Seven Wise Men of Greece. Ovid has it "You will go more safely in the middle," and Aristotle, "Moderation in all things."

axel.   In ice skating an *axel* is a graceful leap consisting of one-and-a-half turns in the air, among other qualifications. Having nothing to do with the axle of a wheel, it is named for its inventor, Norwegian skater Axel Paulsen, who perfected it in the late 19th century.

Axis Sally.   (*See* **Tokyo Rose.**)

an ax to grind.   In the tale "Who'll Turn Grindstones" a man carrying a dull ax compliments a boy on his intelligence and good looks and then asks him if he can borrow his father's grindstone. Flattered, the boy says yes, and then the man proceeds to tell him how strong he looks for

his age. The boy falls for all this flattery, and to demonstrate his strength keeps turning the grindstone until the dull ax is as sharp as a razor. Then the man goes off without so much as thanking the boy. The author concludes his story with the observation: "When I see a merchant overpolite to his customers, begging them to taste a little brandy and throwing half his goods on the counter—thinks I, that man has *an axe to grind*." Ben Franklin is frequently credited with this yarn, thought responsible for the expression meaning to flatter a person while seeking a favor from him, but perhaps the credit should go to Charles Miner (1780-1865), who related this incident from his childhood in the columns of the *Wilkes-Barre Gleaner* (1811). The phrase *an ax to grind* has since the publication of his story become widely synonymous for an ulterior motive.

azalea.   The ancient Greeks had the erroneous idea that this shrub required a dry, sandy soil and named it after their word for dry, *azalea*. Technically, azaleas are not different from rhododendrons, but they are kept distinct from that genus by gardeners.

Aztec two-step.   More commonly known as *Montezuma's revenge*, a term recorded much earlier, the *Aztec two-step* is a humorous designation for diarrhea, usually diarrhea suffered by travelers in Mexico, and refers, of course, to the ancient Aztecs of Mexico. The term is first recorded as the title of a book in 1953, but is probably older.

B

B. Our capital *B* can be traced back to the Phoenician alphabet; the lower-case *b* derived from the cursive form of the capital. *B* was called *Beth*, "a house," in Hebrew.

baaad. *Bad*, when slowly pronounced *baaad*, has long been black slang for something or someone good, and recently this meaning has come into general usage to a limited extent. The variation is so old that it is found in the American Creole language Gullah three centuries ago, when *baaad* was used by slaves as an expression of admiration for another slave who successfully flaunted "Ole Massa's" rules.

babbitt. Congress deemed the invention of *babbitt* or *babbitt metal* so important to the development of the industrial age that it awarded inventor Isaac Babbitt (1799-1862) a $20,000 grant. Babbitt is a soft, silver-white alloy of copper, tin, and antimony used to reduce friction in machine bearings. It was discovered as a result of the inventor's experiments in turning out the first Britannia metal tableware ever produced in America. After the Taunton, Massachusetts goldsmith successfully manufactured Britannia in 1824, he experimented further with the same three metals and ultimately invented *babbitt*, which he used to line a patented journal box in 1839. The metal proved far better than any other substance used for reducing friction and is still widely used for machine bearings today. *Babbitt soap*, no longer marketed, also bore the inventor's name. Babbitt wasn't the prototype for Sinclair Lewis's ambitious, uncultured, and smugly satisfied American businessman in his novel of the same name, but the character's name was probably suggested by Lewis's early memories of advertisements for the soap.

babble; babel. *Babel*, for a confused turbulent medley of sounds ("a babel of sounds"), or a scene of utter confusion, takes its name from the biblical city of Babel described in *Genesis*, where as punishment for the people's attempt to build a tower to reach heaven itself, God confused their speech and, where there was previously one universal language, created the many tongues that we know today. *Babel* comes to us from the ancient Assyrian *bab-ili*, "gate of the gods." *Babel* and Babylon are the same city, the latter word passing to us from the Greek *Babulon*. Babylon stands for any corrupt, luxury-loving place of riotous living, owing much of its reputation to the Babylon of the Revelation of St. John the Divine—"Babylon the Great, the Mother of Harlots and Abominations of the Earth." In days past, and in rare instances today, Protestants have called Rome, seat of the Catholic Church, "the Woman of Babylon." *Babel* is of no relation to *babble*, a word probably suggested by the sounds made by infants, though the *OED* says that *babble*'s association with *babel* may have affected some of the former word's meaning.

Babcock test. Though not as famous as Pasteur, the agricultural chemist Stephen Moulton Babcock played an important role in the development of the modern dairy industry. While chief chemist at the Wisconsin Agricultural Experiment Station in 1890, Babcock invented a process for determining the butterfat content of milk. The *Babcock test* makes possible rapid, accurate milk grading and helps farmers develop better dairy herds by enabling them to test milk from their stock. Babcock taught for twenty-five years at the University of Wisconsin, from 1887 to 1913. He died in 1931, at age eighty-eight, having spent the last twenty years of his life researching the nature of matter.

babe; baby. *Babe* was once the standard English word for child, deriving from the Middle English *baban*, an imitative nursery word in origin—that is, similar to the cries of an infant. Infant sounds also give us "mamma" and "poppa" and the Latin *mamma*, breast, from which all we *mammals* take our name. *Baby* is just a diminutive of *babe* and was once used as a word for doll. *Baby* as a term of endearment for a sweetheart, male or female, doesn't seem to go back further than 1901 in America, though it may have arisen a little earlier in fast English sporting circles, and *baby* for a tough guy ("That baby packed some punch") dates back only to the Roaring Twenties.

babe in the woods. The old ballad "Children in the Wood" (1595), gives us the still-common expression *a babe in the woods*, for someone easily gulled because he is simple and trustful, inexperienced in life or some aspect of life. The ballad probably predates a tragedy by Robert Harrington on the same theme that was written in about 1601. Both play and ballad tell the story of two children left by their dying father to the care of his wife's brother. The brother, wanting their inheritance, hires two men to kill the children, but one of them repents and kills his companion, abandoning the children in the wood, where they die. The wicked uncle is arrested and dies in jail and the hired killer is sentenced to death. The ballad was vastly popular, and no doubt became a nursery story, too.

Babel. (*See* babble.)

babe of love. (*See* love child.)

babushka. One of the few Russian words widely used in English, *babushka*, for a woman's scarf, derives from the Russian *baba*, "grandmother," plus the diminutive suffix *ushka*—because scarves have long been worn hoodlike by old women in Russia.

baby boom. According to *New York Times* columnist William Safire, *baby boom*, the sharp increase in the birth rate after World War II, hasn't been traced back further than 1953, when it appeared in a report to President Truman by the Commissioner on Immigration and Naturalization. Attorney Harry Rosenfield wrote the report, but he doesn't claim to have coined the expression.

baby-kisser. Politicians have been baby-kissing since the first election, but the term doesn't seem to have been used before the U.S. presidential election of 1884. The words were applied to Benjamin Butler, who ran on the independent Greenback-Labor ticket and came in a poor third behind Democrat Grover Cleveland and Republican James Blaine. "As a baby-kisser," a contemporary newspaper observed, "Ben Butler is not a success." One theory has it that the idea for the term appears in the Eatanswill election episode of Dickens's *Pickwick Papers* (1837), although *baby-kisser* doesn't appear there.

bachelor. It wasn't until relatively recent times that the word *bachelor* was used exclusively for unmarried males. In the past the word was applied without distinction of sex, Ben Jonson using it to mean an unmarried woman in his play *The Magnetic Lady* (1632). *Bachelor* derives ultimately from the medieval Latin *baccalaris*, which became the Old French *bacheler*.

bachelor's buttons. In his *Herbal*, Gerard wrote that "The similitude these flowers have to the jagged cloath buttons anciently worne . . . gave occasion . . . to call them Bachelor's Buttons." But *bachelor's buttons*, a name now applied mainly to *Centaurea cyanus*, or the common cornflower, but also to the red campion, the upright crowfoot, and the white ranunculus, may take their name from the old custom of bachelors carrying the flower in their pockets to determine how they stood with their sweethearts. If the flowers stayed fresh in the pocket, it was a good omen; if they shriveled up "she loves me not." Other colorful names for the cornflower include bluebottle, blue bonnets, and ragged sailor.

bacitracin. This antibiotic used to treat bacterial skin infections takes its unusual name from *baci*(llus) plus the first four letters of the last name of Margaret *Tracy* (b. 1936), a child in whose tissues *Bacillus subtilis* was found.

back and fill. Hardly any progress is made when you *back and fill* a sailing ship; that is, when you are tacking the craft while the tide is running with her and the wind is against her. The sails are alternately backed and filled and the ship seems to remain in roughly the same place, going back and then forward. The term was a natural for sailors, and then landlubbers, to apply to any vacillating or irresolute action—to *hemming and hawing* (*q.v.*).

Back Bay. The Back Bay area has been since the mid-19th century a fashionable residential district in Boston, Massachusetts. So much so, in fact, that *Back Bay* has been synonymous almost as long for the culture of Boston.

to backbite. This expression was formed from the noun *back* and the verb *bite*, almost certainly as an obvious description of someone slandering another person in his absence, or behind his back. An old chestnut connects the words with the medieval "sport" of bearbaiting, where the bear was fastened to a post by a short chain, some of the dogs that fought him holding him at bay face to face while others attacked him from the back. There are no known old quotations to support this theory, the oldest one recorded (1175) referring to "Cursunge [cursing] backbitunge [backbiting] and fikelunge [deceit]." There is a legend that Diogenes, when asked what beasts "bit sorest," answered: "Of wilde beasts, the Back-biter; of tame, the Flatterer." Wrote Tennyson of the secret calumniator, "Face-flatterers and back-biters are the same."

backhand. One of our oldest technical sport's terms, *backhand* can be traced to at least the early 18th century, when Sir John Van Brugh recorded it in his play *The Mistake* (1706). Van Brugh uses the term figuratively in the play, but there seems no doubt that he borrowed it from the tennis court.

backseat driver; backseat necker. Automobiles have introduced many general terms into the language. "Step on the gas," "detour," "hitchhiker," "hit-and-run," "streamlined," and "joyride" are only a few of the automobile expressions that are now widely applied. *Backseat driver*, describing species *Autokibitzer accidentus*, an indomitable breed that does more harm than good on the road (and often occupies the *front* seat next to the driver) has considerably weakened the meaning of "to take a back seat"—that is, to be humble, to take an inconspicuous position in the background. The newer expression, coined in the 1920s, applies to all those who have pinned humility to the mat for their lifetime, particularly critics of the incumbent administration in politics. *Backseat necking*, making love in the backseat of a car, dates to 1922, and "necker's knob," the suicide knob on a car's steering wheel that allows for one-armed driving, was first recorded in the early 1940s.

back to the drawing board. (*See* **well, back to the old drawing board.**)

to back water. When a steamboat's paddle wheel is reversed it is said *to back water*, or move backward. The expression came into use with the rise of the steamboat in the early 1800s and was soon being used figuratively to mean "to reverse one's position on a subject, withdraw from a situation, or retract a statement."

bad. Most major dictionaries, including the *O.E.D.*, hold that *bad* derives from the Middle English *badde*, meaning the same, which, in turn, most probably derived as a back formation (altering a word by dropping rear syllables, *e.g.*, "zoo" from "zoological garden") from the Old English *baeddel*, "hermaphrodite," and *baeddling*, "effeminate man" or "sodomite." This would explain why there aren't many early written examples of the word, which is first recorded circa 1300 ("good" is recorded circa 800, with many early examples). By that time *bad* had almost entirely lost its sexual connotation, but it still retains the sense of "evil misbehavior" that was then the dominant attitude about homosexuality—though *bad* of course means many things today, including "of poor quality," "invalid," "spoiled or rotten," "dejected (feeling bad)," and even (in black slang) "good" (especially in the sense of very stylish or sharp). (*See* **good**.)

bad cess to you. Many of us on hearing the Irish expression *bad cess to you* have assumed that the *cess* in the term is a corruption of the word success. This, however, isn't the case. The expression originated in Ireland, where *cess* meant an assessment or land tax. The words thus mean "May your taxes be raised."

bad egg; good egg. Shakespeare used the word *egg* to contemptuously describe a young person in *Macbeth*, when the murderers of Macduff's son cry, "What you egg! Young fry of treachery!" But the expression *bad egg* for a disreputable, thoroughly rotten person doesn't seem to have been coined until the mid-18th century in America, no matter how obvious the analogy might seem. "American criminal Thomas Egg" isn't in any way responsible for the expression; it derives from just the odor of a bad egg itself. *Good egg*, for a "nice guy," came along about fifty years later, probably originating as Oxford University slang.

badger; badger game. Badger baiting consisted of putting a badger in a barrel or hole and setting dogs on him to "worry him out"; the cruel process was repeated several times until the animal died. The ancient "sport" gave us the word *to badger*, to worry or tease, even though the dogs, not the badger, did the badgering. Centuries later *badger* was applied to the *badger game* by American confidence men and women. Commonly the woman member of the team in this con game pretends to fall for her victim and goes to bed with him. While they are having sex, the male member of the team surprises them, playing the part of the outraged husband. The victim is badgered by the "husband," who finally agrees to accept money as compensation for the wrong done him. It is sometimes months before the victim realizes he is being blackmailed, and even then he often keeps on making payments to avoid publicity. Figuratively, the expression *badger game* is used to indicate any deception for personal or political gain.

badminton. The racket game, really the Indian game of *poona* adopted by the British, is named for the eighth Duke of Beaufort's estate, Badminton, in Gloucestershire, where it was introduced in 1783.

Baedeker; Fielding guide. A *Baedeker* once referred to a specific guidebook published by the German printer and bookseller Karl Baedeker (1801-1859), but the word is now used loosely to mean any travel guide. *Baedeker's* guides were so authoritative and comprehensive that they were eventually printed in numerous languages and became almost a necessity for travelers of the time. Similar to the contemporary *Fielding guides*, named for travel writer Temple Hornaday Fielding (b. 1914), the books covered every aspect of travel, from historic questions to cuisine, and started the practice of rating places with one to four stars. *Baedeker* became synonymous for an exhaustive guide, the word adopted in many countries.

bafflegab. (*See* **gobbledygook**.)

bagel; bialy. "Bagels, begorrah!" Macy's bakery once advertised on St. Patrick's Day in our word-rich land. *Bagel* derives from the Middle High German *bouc*, "bracelet," which became the Yiddish *beggel*—the *bagel*, of course, resembling a bracelet in shape. The roll topped with onion flakes called a *bialy* (plural *bialys*, not *bialies*) takes its name from Bialystok, Poland, where it was first made. Bialystok, played by Zero Mostel in *The Producers*, is one of the great comic characters in movie history.

bag lady; old bag; bag. Short for "shopping bag lady," *bag lady* entered the language in the 1960s. It has nothing to do with the term *old bag*, for an ugly woman (which goes back to the 1920s), or bagman, a term for someone (often a policeman) assigned to collect bribe or extortion money, an expression also dating back to the flapper age. *Bag* has many meanings in American slang, including "to be sacked (bagged) from a job"; "a prostitute" (from douche bags being associated with prostitutes); "a condom"; "to arrest"; "a base in baseball"; and "to be drunk (to have a bag on)." But *bag* here refers to the shopping bags, filled with their possessions, that the unfortunate women we call *bag ladies* carry with them as they wander—from doorway to alley to abandoned car to park bench—through American cities. The *lady* in their name is both ironic and kind.

bagman. In America *bagman* means a racketeer or anyone assigned to collect a bribe, extortion, or kidnapping money. (A bag woman, or bag lady, is a homeless woman characterized by carrying shopping bags containing all her worldy goods.) In England, however, a bagman is simply a traveling salesman, a drummer who carries bags of samples. "In former times," one authority tells us, "these commercial travelers used to ride a horse with saddle bags sometimes so large as almost to conceal the rider."

bah!; bashful; abeyance; etc. *Bah!* is an interjection indicating scorn, contempt, or disgust, but "ba!" is a natural expression of surprise in any language, a sound uttered by both sheep and men when the jaw drops down. It forms the basis for a number of English words. *Bashful* and abash come to us from the French *esbaiss*, which derives from the Latin *ex + ba! Abeyance*, a state of temporary suspension or inactivity, derives from the Latin *badare*, which developed from the elementary sound "ba!" and meant to hold the mouth wide open, to gape—someone "held in abeyance" would stand, jaw dropped, waiting for a decision. The "baying" of hounds, from the old French *beer* (later *bayer*), to gape, is also related to "ba!", the exclamation of surprise becoming the sound of impatience here.

Bahaism. *Bahaism* is an Iranian religion with an Oriental mystical quality that specifically reflects the attitudes of the Islamic Shiah sect, emphasizing religious tolerance. Founded by a Shirez merchant who was executed for heresy in 1850, the religion was named for its founder's leading disciple, known as Baha Allah, who gave it a worldwide following. Baha Allah, in turn, means "splendor of God" in Persian. The Bahais have been persecuted in Iran since the fundamentalists took power in 1979.

Bailey bridge. Portable *Bailey bridges* designed to replace bridges destroyed by retreating forces and to carry much heavier loads than military bridges could previously support, were to a large extent responsible for the Allied victory in World War II, particularly in northwestern Europe. They were invented by Sir Donald Coleman Bailey, an engineer with the British Ministry of Supply, who was knighted in 1945 for his contribution to the war effort. The versatile truss bridges were first used in 1941 and are still employed throughout the world in flood and disaster areas. They consist of some twenty-nine different parts, but are made principally of ten-foot-long, five-foot-wide prefabricated lattice-steel panels weighing six hun-

dred pounds each that are held together by steel pins. Bailey first sketched his bridge on the back of an envelope and he always claimed that his invention was "just part of the job." Field Marshal Montgomery, on the other hand, said, "Without the Bailey bridge we should not have won the war." Bailey died in 1985, at age 83.

bailiwick. Someone in his own *bailiwick* is at home, in a place he knows well. Literally, a *bailiwick* is the county in which an English sheriff (a bailiff of the king) exercises jurisdiction. The term dates back to the 15th century.

Bakelite. Employed chiefly as an electric insulator, *Bakelite* has numerous industrial uses, including the manufacture of phonograph records, machinery, and even buttons, pipe stems, and billiard balls. A heat resistant, synthetic resin or plastic, valuable as a nonconductor of electricity, it is prepared by the chemical interaction of phenolic substances and aldehydes. Bakelite was invented by Leo Hendrik Baekeland (1863-1944), a Flemish chemistry teacher who migrated to the United States from Ghent, Belgium in 1889. Seven years later he announced the invention of Bakelite, a registered name used by the company.

baker's dozen. Bakers in ancient times were subject to severe penalties for shortweighting their customers; in ancient Egypt, for example, they were sometimes nailed by the ear to the doors of their shops when caught selling light loaves. Thus when the English Parliament passed a law in 1266 subjecting the Company of White Bakers and the Company of Brown Bakers to strict regulations regarding bread weight, the bakers made sure that they complied. Since it was difficult to make loaves of a uniform weight at the time, bakers customarily added a thirteenth loaf, the "in-bread" or "vantage loaf," to each shipment of twelve they sent to a shopkeeper or retailer, thus guaranteeing that there would be no shortchanging or ear-nailing. Most authorities believe this led to the expression *baker's dozen* for thirteen.

baksheesh. *Baksheesh* is Persian for a tip or present. But the insolent persistent demands of beggars, servants, and officials in the Near East over the years have made baksheesh seem more a claim or demand upon a traveler than a gratuity in many cases, giving the word an unsavory connotation.

balbriggans. Men's white cotton socks are called *balbriggans*, after Balbriggan, Ireland, a Dublin suburb, where the fabric they are made of was first manufactured in the 19th century.

bald as a coot. The common coot has, in contrast to its black plumage, a white bill extending to form a conspicuous plate on its head, this startling whiteness giving the water bird the name *bald coot*, even though it isn't actually bald. In the 15th century the expression *bald as a coot* was first used to describe a strikingly bald person. (*See* **crazy as a coot**.)

balderdash. Nonsense, a senseless jumble of words or ideas. *Balderdash* is still another word for which no one knows the origin. First recorded in the late 16th century, it meant a light frothy liquid, then came to mean incongruous liquids, such as beer and milk mixed together, and finally took its modern meaning. The Danish *balder*, "noise, clatter," has been suggested as its parent, but this derivation is doubtful at best.

baleboss. This Yiddish expression has no etymological connection with the English word *boss*. To be called a *baleboss* (pronounced bahl-eh-BOHSS) is indeed a compliment, but the term has several meanings. A baleboss, the word deriving from the Hebrew *baal*, "master," and *bayis* "house," can be the head of the household, the owner of a business establishment of any kind, or anyone who assumes authority. A female baleboss is a *baleboosteh*, and she can be the same things as a baleboss, or be the wife of a baleboss, or be an excellent homemaker.

balk. A *balk*, deriving from the Old English *balca*, was a ridge between two furrows made in ploughing. Since the *balk* was an obstacle, the word *balk* came to be applied figuratively to any obstacle, and *to balk* came to mean "to place obstacles in the way of." The baseball term *balk*, an illegal movement by a pitcher when runners are on base, comes from an obsolete meaning of *balk*: "to miss, slip, or fail."

ballast. *Ballast*, loaded in the belly of a ship to help keep her right side up, probably has its ancestor in a Teutonic word meaning "belly load," but no one is sure, though the word has been used for centuries. Everything from rocks to gold bars has been used for ballast.

balled up; balls. Dashing through the snow on a horse-drawn sled could be hazardous in days past. One difficulty was the balls of snow or ice that formed in the curve of a horse's shoe and often made a horse slip and fall. When horses did fall, especially a team of them, the resulting confusion and entanglement gave rise to the expression *all balled up*. That is *almost* everybody traces this term for helpless confusion to floundering horses. Mencken suggests a connection with the ejaculation *balls!* (1890), one for which little proof can be found. A second alternative linking the expression to balls of knitting yarn that the cat got at is a possibility, too. *Balls* has been American slang for testicles since the early 1880s, and slang for guts or courage since about 1935.

ballot. In days past, people voted by dropping little balls, or *ballots*, (from the Italian *ballotta*) into a box or other receptacle. In this ancient method of voting, still used in some clubs today, a white ball signified an affirmative vote and a black ball a negative one. By the 19th century paper was being widely used in place of these balls, but the new form retained the old name.

ballyhoo. The little village of Ballyhooly in County Cork, Ireland once had a reputation for loudmouthed, violent street debates. "The residents engage in most strenuous debate," the *Congressional Record* of March 1934 advises, "a debate that is without equal in the annals of parliamentary, or ordinary discussion, and from the violence of these debates has sprung forth a word known in the English language as *ballyhoo*." However, this is but part of the possible truth. Ballyhooly did have a reputation for violent arguments that drew crowds, but today *ballyhoo* denotes something far from violent, being glib advertising or the spiel of a carnival barker. Possibly the residents of Ballyhooly, noted for their blarney as well as their violent arguments, lent their village's name to a popular British music-hall song of 1885 that used the refrain *bloody hooly truth* as a phrase for "the whole bloody truth." *Bloodyhooly*, in turn, was later applied to the spiels of carnival barkers and acquired its present meaning.

balm. (*See* **no balm in Gilead**.)

balmy. *Balmy*, in its sense of silly, foolish, eccentric, is the Americanized version of the British *barmy*, and may derive from the name of St. Bartholomew, patron saint of the feebleminded. Most etymologists, however, trace the word to the old English *barm*, the froth on fermenting beer, which could indeed make one act *balmy*. Still another theory is that the word derives from the Barming lunatic asylum at Kent in England, meaning that a *barmy* or *balmy* person is "one fit only for Barming." This overlooks the fact that the *Oxford English Dictionary* gives the first use of *barmy* as 1535, whereas Barming was established in the early 19th century, but it may be that the popularity of the word was enhanced by the asylum.

baloney. (*See* **boloney**.)

balsa rafts. Spanish sailors off South American in the 16th century gave the name *balsa*, meaning "float," to the rafts lashed together with vines that the natives used. They later applied the same name to the tree logs, half the weight of cork, that made the rafts so buoyant. That the rafts make even better boats than the Spaniards expected was demonstrated by Thor Heyerdahl centuries later, when he sailed from South America to Polynesia on a balsa raft.

Baltic Sea.   This body of water is named for either the Lithuanian *baltas*, "white," or from the Scandinavian *balta*, "strait." Thus, no one knows for sure whether the Baltic means "the white sea," or "the sea of straits."

Baltimore; Baltimore oriole; Baltimore clipper.   An early dictionary tells us that the *Baltimore oriole* is "so called from the colors of Or (orange) and Sable in the coat of arms belonging to Lord Baltimore." This oriole is not closely related to the orioles of Europe, belonging to the blackbird and meadowlark rather than the crow family. In fact, many American birds with the same names as European species are in reality birds of a different feather. (The American robin, for instance, is really a thrush, and other Old World avian words given new significances include partridge, blackbird, lark, and swallow.) But whatever its true species, the *Baltimore Oriole*, definitely takes its name from the Baltimore family, founders of Maryland, the bright colors of the male bird indeed corresponding to the orange and black in their heraldic arms. The city of Baltimore, Maryland also honors the barons Baltimore, as do the early 19th-century *Baltimore clippers*, more indirectly, the famous ships having been built in the city. The same can be said of baseball's Baltimore Orioles and football's Baltimore Colts. No particular Lord Baltimore has been singled out for the honor. George Calvert, the first baron Baltimore (c. 1590-1632), prepared the charter for the proposed colony that became Maryland, but died before it could be accepted; the charter was granted to his son Cecilius, but the second baron Baltimore never even visited the province; and the third baron Baltimore, Cecilius's son Charles, governed the province from 1661 to 1684. A Catholic who ruled quite arbitrarily over his predominantly Protestant subjects, Charles returned to England and never came back, leaving little more than the family name behind.

baluster.   (*See* **banister.**)

The Bambino.   Taken from the Italian *bambino*, baby, this is a well-known nickname of American baseball great Babe (George Herman) Ruth (1895-1948), also known as The Sultan of Swat. But *Bambino* has for centuries meant an image of the infant Jesus in swaddling clothes.

bambochades.   Genre paintings of rural life, especially rustic drinking scenes treated in an exaggerated or comic manner, are called *bambochades* or *bambociades*, after the nickname of Dutch landscape painter Pieter van Laar (ca. 1600-ca. 1674). Van Laar, or Laer, worked some fifteen years in Italy, where he was nicknamed *Il Bamboccio*, "the cripple." Famous for his landscapes and etchings depicting rustic life—pictures usually in heavy brown tones showing wakes, weddings, and other country scenes—the artist was also called *Michael Angelo des Bambochades*.

bamboozle, bombazine.   How did a fabric used for women's mourning clothes since the early 19th century give its name to our word for "to cheat or swindle"? Probably an early confidence game had a female swindler posing as a bereft widow wearing black bombazine, her costume lending its name to the swindle or hoax she and others like her practiced. Jonathan Swift included *bamboozle* in a list of new distasteful slang words, but it survived nevertheless. *Bombazine* itself comes from the Greek *bombux*, "silkworm."

banana.   *Banana* derives from the Arabic word *banana*, meaning finger, and even today the individual fruits forming the familiar banana "hand" are called "fingers." The banana tree is really a giant herb with a rhizome instead of roots, and its "trunk" is made up of large leaves, not wood. The fruit was given the scientific name *Musa*, comprising eighteen species, by Linnaeus in honor of Antonio Musa, personal physician to the first emperor of Rome. *Musa sapientum*, the most common banana tree species, takes its second name from the Latin word for "wise man," in reference to the Indian sages of old who reposed in its shade and ate of its fruit. Arabian slang and a score of other languages make the fruit a synonym for the male sexual organ, not surprisingly, and "I had a banana with Lady Diana" was British slang for sexual intercourse up until about 1930. "Where the banana grows man is sensual and cruel," Emerson wrote in his *Society and Solitude*, and the Koran says that the forbidden fruit in Paradise was a banana, not an apple. Banana oil, incidentally, is a synthetic—bananas produce no commercial oil—and the banana, like the pear, is one of the few fruits that ripen better off the vine.

banco; Mark Banco.   *Banco*, meaning bank money of account as distinguished from banknotes or currency, is often used in the international exchange business. *Mark Banco* was the mark of fixed value employed as an invariable standard in the old Bank of Hamburg in Germany and used by the Hanseatic League. Since all gold and silver deposits were credited in *Mark Banco* and all banking transactions carried on in *Mark Banco*, it made no difference how the exchange rate varied from day to day.

Band-Aid.   Invented by Robert W. Johnson and George J. Seabury in 1874, the *Band-Aid* was registered by Johnson as a trademark in 1886 when he left Seabury and formed his own business, Johnson & Johnson. Widely used today, the word is a zealously protected trademark and still must be capitalized.

bandanna.   A Hindu method of dyeing called *bāndhnu* consisted of knotting pieces of silk and dipping them in dyes so that parts of the silk would retain their original color. The Portuguese, who reached India during the 16th century, brought clothes dyed in this manner back to

Europe, where the Hindu *bāndhnu*, corrupted to *ban-danna*, soon came to mean a large silk handkerchief, especially one with a background of red with white spots.

bandersnatch. (*See* **Jabberwocky**.)

bandicoot. A word like this is needed in a time noted for both green thumbs and slick fingers, when thefts of shrubs, flowers, and vegetables right from the ground are occurring more frequently from public places and private residences. *Bandicooting* is an Australian word for the practice of stealing vegetables out of the ground, and a *bandicoot* is a thief who does this. The word could have a wider application, covering all vegetative thefts. Human *bandicoots*, like the Australian marsupial they are named for, usually steal root vegetables, leaving their tops protruding from the ground to avoid suspicion for a longer time.

bandwagon. (*See* **hop on the bandwagon**.)

bandy; bandy-legged. This word for bowlegged (legs shaped something like these parentheses), strangely enough, derives from a comparison of bowlegs with the curved sticks used in the 17th-century Irish game of bandy, the precursor of hockey. No one is sure where the word *bandy* that gave us the game of *bandy*, *bandy-sticks*, and *bandy-legged* comes from, though earlier it was a tennis term. In playing ancient hockey, the ball was bandied from side to side and fought for, which led to metaphors like "I'm not going to bandy words with you"; that is, "I'm not going to argue, wrangle over nothing."

bang. (*See* **onomatopoeia**.)

Bang's disease; Brucellosis. These are names for what is probably the most diversely named disease—it is called, variously, undulant fever, Malta fever, Gibraltar fever, rock fever, Mediterranean fever, and goat fever. Its cause, an infectious bacteria called *Brucella*, was discovered in 1887 when Scottish physician Sir David Bruce (1855-1931) performed an autopsy on a patient who had died of the illness on the island of Malta. Later, Danish veterinarians Bernhard L. F. Bang and V. Stribolt isolated a second strain of *Brucella* and in 1895 found that it caused a disease in cattle, which was called *Bang's disease* in that scientist's honor. *Bang's disease*, the name still used for the infection, is thought to have been responsible for the epizootic disease or storms of abortions that commonly occurred in American and European cattle herds in the early 19th century. Scientifically speaking, all diseases caused by *Brucella* bacteria are termed *brucellosis*. The disease affects not only cattle and goats but swine, chickens, dogs, cats, wild deer, and bison as well. It is usually contracted by humans from contact with infected animals or by ingesting infected milk, and is sometimes fatal. No complete cure is known for infected animals, and the incidence of the disease is said to be on the rise throughout the world.

banister; baluster. *Banister*, a support for a handrail on a staircase, is a mispronunciation of *baluster*, first recorded in English over three centuries ago. *Baluster* comes from "balaustion," the Greek name for a specific flower. Because Greek architects used the outlines of these flowers for the shapes of the short pillars supporting handrails, *baluster* came to mean the supports themselves.

banjo. There are two theories about *banjo*'s origin. One holds that the word derives from a black mispronunciation of *bandore*, an English word of Spanish origin denoting a musical instrument similar to the banjo. The other cites the Angoloa Kimbunde language *mbanza*, which also means a banjo-like instrument. It would be hard to prove or disprove either theory.

bank; bankrupt. In medieval times Italian moneylenders used a small bench in the marketplace to conduct their business. The Latin word for such a bench, *banca*, is in fact the source for the English word *bank*. These moneylenders, the bankers of their day, were required to break up their benches if they failed in business, and the Latin expression for doing so, *banca rupta*, later became the English word *bankrupt*.

bank holiday. *Bank holiday* was one of the first of many words and phrases coined during the New Deal in America's Great Depression. President Franklin Delano Roosevelt used it on March 6, 1933, two days after his inauguration. Providing for the reopening of sound banks in a period when most banks had failed and "runs" had abounded, F.D.R. declared a four-day bank holiday while Congress rushed to pass the Emergency Banking Act.

bankrupt. (*See* **bank**.)

bankrupt worm. A little parasite roundworm of the genus *Trichostrongylus* is called the *bankrupt worm* because it often infects cattle herds, sometimes bankrupting those cattlemen whose stock it attacks.

banned in Boston. In its heyday during the 1920s the phrase *banned in Boston* made a number of books bestsellers throughout the rest of the country. Books were frequently banned in Boston for foolish reasons at the time because the local ultraconservative Watch and Ward Society wielded great power in the city. This is no longer the case, but the expression is still used jokingly.

to bant; banting. William Banting (1797-1878) might have made a fortune had he published his booklet on dieting a century later, in our own weight-conscious era. As it turned out, he merely amused Londoners in the mid-1860s, although his name did become a word. Banting was an enormously overweight cabinetmaker and undertaker who couldn't bend to tie his shoelaces and had to walk downstairs backwards to relieve the pressure on his legs. Convinced by his own discomfort, and perhaps from his undertaking activities, that many deaths resulted from overeating, he went on a strict diet, losing forty-six pounds and taking twelve inches off his waist. As so many dieters do, he then wrote a book about his experience, setting forth his method of reducing. "Bantingism" called for a meat diet and abstention from practically everything else—beer, butter, sugar, farinaceous foods, and even vegetables. Needless to say, it wasn't popular very long, but Londoners humorously took to calling dieting *banting* and to diet *to bant*.

bantam. The dwarf fowl called the *bantam* takes its name from Bantam, Java where it was developed, and gives its name to any little, feisty creature.

bantling. (*See* **bastard.**)

Bantu. (*See* **Eskimo.**)

banyan tree. Here is a tree named for merchants who sold their wares beneath it. The Indian tree, which spreads out by sprouting aerial extensions that grow into the ground to form new trunks, can cover an area large enough to shade thousands of people. Noticing this, Hindu merchants set up naturally shaded marketplaces underneath the trees and the British later named the tree after the merchants, *banions*, who traded there.

banzai. Before World War II, when the Japanese Navy and those of the Western powers were on good terms, *banzai parties*, or shore parties, were held where seamen from Japan and other nations mingled. The expression derives from the general Japanese felicitation, *banzai*, which means "May you live forever." During World War II, the once pleasant *banzai* was shouted by Japanese soldiers making bayonet charges.

baptism of fire. There is a strange, little-known story behind this common expression. The phrase had been used from antiquity as a synonym for martyrdom, in reference to Christian martyrs burned at the cross. It came to mean any severe ordeal or painful experience, but not until the late 19th century were the words used to describe a soldier's first experience in battle. We even have an exact date for the phrase used in this sense. At the battle of Searbuck during the Franco-Prussian War of 1870, Napoleon III (Louis Napoleon Bonaparte) ordered that his fourteen-year-old son and only male heir, Prince Louis Napoleon, be sent into battle and be exposed to

enemy fire for the first time. The French ironically called this event the child's *bapteme de feu*, "baptism of fire." The teenaged Prince, who had agreed with his father's order, if that means anything, survived the battle, but went into exile in England with the enigmatic Napoleon III when France was defeated. Later he joined the British army and did die under fire, while fighting the Zulus in Africa, at the age of 22.

BAR. The *Browning automatic rifle*, or BAR, of World War II fame was invented by John M. Browning (1854-1926) of Ogden, Utah, who designed many famous weapons. The BAR, an air-cooled weapon capable of firing 200-350 rounds per minute, was generally assigned one to a squad. It is said that none of the prolific Browning's designs ever failed. These included the light and heavy Browning machine guns, the caliber .45 pistol, the caliber .50 machine gun, the 37mm. aircraft gun, and a number of shotguns and repeating rifles. Browning took out his first patent in 1879, on a breech-loading, single-shot rifle that the Winchester Arms Company purchased. After his entry into the military field, the U.S. Army relied almost exclusively on Browning's automatic weapons.

bar; before the bar. Shakespeare used the word *bar* for a tavern, this *bar* first recorded in 1572 and taking its name from the *bars* that were pulled over the serving counter in taverns at closing time. Similar *bars* or gratings were used in early courts of law, leading to the expression about lawyers practicing *before the bar*.

Barbados. The Spanish *barbados*, "bearded," is the source for this country's name. What they had in mind were the many vines hanging from all the trees in the area, vines so dense that they looked like beards.

barbarian; barber. *Barba* means "beard" in Latin, and when the Romans called hirsute foreigners *barbarians* they were strictly calling them "bearded men," though the word shortly came to mean, rightly or wrongly, "rude, uncivilized people." A barber was, of course, one who cut beards or hair. The barber pole outside barber shops today has its origins in the ancient barber's duties as a surgeon and dentist as well as a hair cutter. It was first the symbol of these medical professions—a blood-smeared white rag. However, *barbarian* may have Greek origins.

barbecue. Here's an English word that comes from the language of the extinct Haitian Taino tribe. The tribe smoked meat on a framework of sticks called a *barbacoa*—at least the name sounded like that to Spanish pirates who visited Haiti in the mid-17th century. *Barbacoa* came to mean the cooking of the meat itself and passed into English as the American *barbecue*. The Tainos also gave us the word *potato* (*q.v.*), which was first their *batata*.

barber. (*See* **barbarian.**)

Barbie doll. I've heard *Barbie doll* used as American slang for a conformist or a dehumanized person since the late 1960s, though the first recorded use of the term seems to have been in a 1973 issue of *Rolling Stone*. The term derives from the trade name of a very popular blue-eyed blond doll made for little girls.

bardash. A *bardash* is a male prostitute, or "a catamite," in the definition of the *O.E.D.* First recorded in 1548, the word may be an adaption of the Arabic *bardaj*, "slave." In 1760 a magazine spoke of the practice of "Publikely maintaining bardassaes and concubines." *Berdache* is an alternate spelling.

Barebone's Parliament. The historically important *Barebone's Parliament* nominated by Cromwell in 1653 wasn't so called because it was a small body, the skeleton of a real parliament. Rather, the assembly, which first met on July 4th of that year, was derisively nicknamed for one of its members. Praise-God Barebones was his name. Barebones, a famous London preacher as well as a leather merchant and man of property, was vociferously opposed to the restoration of the Stuarts. Controversial for his Baptist religious views, Praise-God Barebones's preaching attracted large crowds, the meetings frequently disturbed by riots, and one time a mob stormed his house, Barebones barely escaping with his life. The *Barebone's Parliament* passed a number of reforms, including civil marriage and public registration of births and burials, but was generally unqualified for its task of governing, "more fools than knaves," as someone wrote. Praise-God Barebones, who seems to have taken little part in the debates, long outlived his namesake, dying in 1680, at about age eighty-four.

barefaced liar. *Barefaced*, "beardless, with no hair upon the face," may have been coined by Shakespeare in *A Midsummer Night's Dream*, where it is first recorded. Within half a century or so it came to mean bold, audacious, impudent, or shameless, like many boys, who were barefaced. By 1825 we find "the barefacedness of the lie" recorded, and Harriet Beecher Stowe writes of a *barefaced lie* in *Uncle Tom's Cabin*.

barge in. Useful but clumsy flat-bottomed barges, probably named from an early Celtic word for boat, have been common in England since medieval times. These shallow-water craft are often pulled through canals by conventional vessels or by animals on the bank. But accidents involving the unwieldy vessels were frequent; they were constantly bumping into other boats. By the late nineteenth century, English schoolboys were using the slang term *barge*, "to hustle a person," *to barge about* someone, bump him or move him heavily about. It is this practice, far removed from the water but related to *barges*, that led to the expression *to barge in*—to clumsily or rudely intercede, to butt in—that originated in the early 1900s.

bark up the wrong tree. Coon dogs, which could be almost any breed of dog or even mongrels in Colonial days, commonly chased raccoons through the underbrush and treed them, barking furiously at the base of the tree until their masters came to shoot the "gone coon." But the crafty nocturnal animal, called a *rahaugum* by John Smith, often escaped through the branches to another tree in the dark, leaving the dogs *barking up the wrong tree*, which is the origin of the American phrase. Skilled hunters who could *bark* a squirrel, that is, strike the bark on the lower side of the branch where it sat, killing it by the concussion, have nothing at all to do with the expression. The *bark* of a tree comes to us from the Anglo Saxon *beore*, while a dog's *bark* is related to the Old English *barki*, "windpipe." It's said that dogs in the wild state howl, whine, and growl, but that their barking is an acquired habit—anyway, debarking operations are available to silence dogs whose barks are worse than their bites and dogs that bark at the moon. *Barkable* is an unusual old word. One would take the adjective to be a modern affectation, but it dates back to at least the 13th century, a treatise of the time on estate management advising lords to have "discreet shepherds . . . with good barkable dogs."

barlow knife. Russel Barlow, who has been called "the patron saint of whittlers," invented the *barlow knife* over two hundred years ago and it has been known to Americans under one name or another ever since. The *barlow*, a single-bladed pocket, pen, or jackknife, was the pride, joy and bartering power of many an American boy, and is mentioned in the works of Mark Twain, Joel Chandler Harris, and many other writers. It has also been called the *Russel Barlow knife*.

Barmecide's feast. A *Barmecide's feast* is an illusion of plenty, figuratively a poor meal leaving much to the imagination. The expression comes from the "Story of the Barber's Sixth Brother" in the *Arabian Nights*. A rich noble named Barmecide (based on one of a real family of Baghdad princes) served the beggar Schacabac course after course of imaginary dishes, pretending that the empty golden plates he set before his guest constituted a sumptuous feast. Schacabac got the better of the prince, pretending to enjoy each course and finally boxing his host's ears while feigning drunkenness from the illusory wine. So amused was Prince Barmecide that he gave the beggar a real banquet, but his name is remembered for the first, imaginary meal.

barn; barnstorming. The Old English *bere*, "barley," combined with *ern*, "storage," gives us the word *barn*, which was originally a place to store grain. Only in early America did the *barn* become a joint grain storage place and animal stable, American barns becoming so big that they spawned sayings like *You couldn't hit the broad side of a barn* and *as big as a barn*. Eventually we had *car barns, furniture barns,* and *antique barns. Barnstorming,* first applied in 1815 to a theatrical troupe's performances in upstate New York barns, has come to mean tours of rural areas by political candidates.

barnacle. The barnacle takes its name from the *barnacle goose,* which is so called because of its "bare neck," *barnakylle* in Middle English, for in ancient times people firmly believed that these geese were born from what we now know as *barnacles.* A barnacle's long stalk and rounded body does resemble the neck and body of a goose, and its tentacles, which wave during the feeding process, suggest the wings of an infant bird being born from a shell and straining out to sea. The ubiquitous crustacean takes its scientific names, *Cirripedes,* from the Greek *cirri,* "feet-like curls of hair," in reference to its tentacles.

barnburner; hunkers. *Barnburners* were members of a faction of the Democratic Party in New York State from about 1830-50, so-called because they were so zealous for reform in the party that they would burn the barn (the Democratic Party) to get rid of the (pro-slavery) rats. The Democratic Party majority at the time was called the *Hunkers,* perhaps from the Low German *hunk,* "home, place of refuge," but possibly because they once packed the state convention and nominated a complete ticket for their faction, "took the whole hunk." *Barnburner* is used by wildcat oil men for a big well, a gusher, a strike that lights up the sky. It is common presently in Michigan, among other states, but probably originated in Pennsylvania toward the end of the last century, though I've never seen it recorded.

barnstorming. (*See* **barn.**)

barnyard epithet. This widely used euphemism for plain old *bullshit* was coined by a *New York Times* editor as recently as 1970 in reporting the reply of David Dellinger, one of the Chicago Seven tried for conspiracy to disrupt the 1968 Democratic National Convention, to a police version of his actions ("Oh, bullshit!").

barrage. A *barrage* of artillery is strictly speaking a "barrier," the word deriving from the French *barre.* One can see the logic of this when considering that strategically an artillery barrage is meant primarily to be not an assault but a barrier to any enemy activity. The word in its military sense is first recorded during "the war to end all wars," in 1917.

barrister. (*See* **lawyer.**)

barter. Few, if any, American sports terms derive from the names of great players, no matter how proficient. In baseball a home run is not called a "Babe Ruth," though we may (rarely) say a "Ruthian blast"; a hitting streak is not a "DiMaggio"; nor is a strikeout a "Sandy Koufax." Across the Atlantic this is not the case. *Barter,* for example, is an English cricket term dating back nearly 150 years. It comes from the name of Robert Barter, warden at Winchester College from 1832 to 1861, famed for his half-volley hits. The word is unrelated to the word "barter" meaning to trade, which is of unknown origin, although it may be related to the Old French *barater,* to cheat, exchange.

Bartholomew pig; Bartholomew fair. Shakespeare called Falstaff *a Bartholomew pig.* This has long been the synonym for a very fat person, after the whole roasted pigs that were traditionally sold at the *Bartholomew Fair* in London. The fair, held on St. Bartholomew's Day (August 24th) from 1133 to 1855, was the center of London life. St. Bartholomew, martyred in Armenia in A.D. 44, has as his symbol a knife, in allusion to the knife with which he was flayed alive.

Bartlett pear; Seckel pear. The yellow *Bartlett* grown commercially mostly in Oregon and Washington, where it is less susceptible to blight than in the East, represents 70 percent of the country's 713,000 ton crop and is certainly America's most commonly grown pear. It is a soft European-type fruit, in season from July to November, as opposed to earlier hard Asian varieties like the *Seckel,* which is named for the Philadelphia farmer who first grew it in America just after the Revolution. The *Bartlett* was not, in fact, developed by Enoch Bartlett (1779-1860), a merchant in Dorchester, Massachusetts, as is generally believed. Bartlett only promoted the fruit after Captain Thomas Brewer imported the trees from England and grew them on his Roxbury farm. The enterprising Yankee eventually purchased Brewer's farm and distributed the pears under his own name in the early 1800s. They had been long known in Europe as Williams or William Bon Chretien pears. *Bartletts,* by any name, are one of the most delicious of the over three thousand pear species, and pears have been one of man's favorite fruits from as early as 1000 B.C.

Bartlett's. For many years John Bartlett owned the University Book Store in Cambridge, Massachusetts, where Harvard teachers and students came for assistance in tracking down the source of a quotation. Bartlett's erudition soon made the saying "Ask John Bartlett" a customary one when anyone sought the origins of a phrase, a faith that was justified when *Bartlett's Familiar*

Quotations, or *Bartlett's*, appeared in 1855. John Bartlett died in 1905 at age 85, and his book remains a standard reference work today, unequaled by any similar English work except *The Oxford Dictionary of Quotations*. The Bartlett pear doesn't bear the scholar's name.

Basedow's disease. (*See* **Bright's disease**.)

bash. Meaning a blow or even a wild party, *bash* seems to have originated in the world of boxing, the first use of the word recorded in the 19th century, when a *basher* was a prizefighter. No one is sure whether the word is a blend of "bang" and "smash," or simply of echoic origin.

bashful. (*See* **bah!**)

basil. *Basil* was once believed to have been used in making royal perfume, and so the aromatic herb takes its name from the Greek *basilikos*, royal. In ancient times it was thought to have great healing properties. Boccaccio's *Decameron* tells the story of Isabella, who put her murdered lover's head in a pot, planted basil on top and watered it with her tears.

basilect. (*See* **acrolect**.)

basilisk. This is another name for the legendary *cockatrice* (*q.v.*). The two names seem to have been interchangeable, and the same myths applied to both beasts. Just to look in the basilisk's eyes was enough to kill a person, and the serpent hatched from a cock's egg had breath so fiery that it killed off all vegetation. The *basilisk* took its name from the Greek *basiliskos*, "little king," in reference to the cock's crest on its head that resembled a crown; the mythical creature had a cock's head, a dragon's tail and bird's wings. The monster's killing glance led to the use of *the basilisk* for the killing glance of a wanton woman, who you never looked at while making love, and the term "cockatrice" for a prostitute or whore. Today *basilisk* is the name of a real South American lizard, a harmless two-foot-long creature that has a crest on its head.

basketane. (*See* **Cubane**.)

Basque. *Basque*, which derives from the Latin *vasco*, for an inhabitant of Vasconia, a country up on the slopes of the Pyrenees, is spoken in northern Spain and southwestern France, and has been called "the most difficult language in the world to learn," being the remains of a prehistoric cave language that is related to no other language save a tongue spoken in a small area of the Caucasus Mountains. A Spanish proverb says that when God wished to punish the devil he made him study Basque for seven years. The Basques have jealously guarded their ancient customs and traditions, which include the strenuous national game of *jai alai*, now widely played throughout the world. There are some 200,000 Basques in Spain and France and another 250,000 in other countries.

Basque words. English words that come to us from Basque include: *bizarre, original* (a word for the American moose), and *jai alai* (*q.v.*).

bass. *Bass*, or *bast*, is the inner bark of the linden or basswood tree. This bark has been used to make everything from cloth to shoes and hats; gardeners use it often for packing and tying up plants.

bastard, bantling. Provencal mule drivers on the road in the Middle Ages used packsaddles called *basts* for beds whenever they checked into an inn or stretched out under a tree. Atop his *bast* (from the Latin *bastum*, "packsaddle") the typical muleteer must have fathered many an illegitimate child, for the expression *fils de bast*, "son of a packsaddle" (a child begotten on a packsaddle bed as opposed to a marriage bed) became an epithet for a natural child and the basis for the Old French word *bastard*. Many other attempts have been made to explain the word—even a happy one tracing it to the old English word *besteaerd*, "the best disposition"—but "packsaddle child" is clearly right. *Bantling* has a similar derivation, coming from the German *bank*, "bench," and conveying the idea of a child begotten on a bench instead of in the marriage bed. "Born on the wrong side of the blanket" is a euphemism for *bastard* and indicates prudery at work—implying that sex in marriage should be performed in the dark, under the covers.

bat. To call a woman an *old bat* is not to call her an *old battle-ax*, as many people believe. *Bat* is not a shortening of *battle-ax* here, but English slang for a prostitute that goes back to at least 1612. A *bat* was a prostitute who walked the streets; like a bat she usually worked at night or, if she worked during the day, she hid out in dark recesses like a bat. To go *on a bat*, "a binge" or "a drinking spree," is similarly connected with the nocturnal bat—the "nightbird," not the prostitute. Someone who goes on a bat usually stays out all night, often stumbling around, as people thought a bat did in the dark. (The first such *bat* recorded in literature, in 1848, describes the spree taking place at night. In days past the winged, rodent-like bat was called by the colorful name "flittermouse.")

bathos; pathos. *Pathos*, which derives directly from the Greek word for "suffering," is the quality or power in any of the arts to evoke feelings of tender pity, compassion, or sadness, and gives us pathetic characters in literature such as Ophelia in *Hamlet* or even Dickens's Little Nell. *Bathos* means something quite different and was coined by Alexander Pope from the Greek word *bathos*, "depth" (not related to our English word *bath*), to indicate a descent from the sublime to the depths of the ridiculous. Pope and other writers of the early 18th century, including Swift, Gay, and Arbuthnot, made a sport of parodying contemporary writers. Out of this game of wits came Pope's satire "Bathos, the art of sinking in Poetry" (1727), in which he invented the word because no similar one existed in English to express the idea. "The taste of the Bathos is implanted by Nature itself in the soul of man," he wrote in his essay, and he proceeded to give an example of bathos at its worst:

> And thou, Dalhousie, the great god of war,
> Lieutenant-general to the earl of Mar.

bathukopian. A rare, rather elegant way to say "big breasted" or "deep bosomed," *bathukopian* is first recorded in 1825. Coined apparently as a euphemism, the word comes from the Greek for "deep" and "breast."

bathysiderodromophobia. There are many people afraid of subways, but few who call themselves *bathysiderodromophobes*, people who fear subways and other things underground. A 20th-century coinage, the word is based upon the Greek *bathys*, "deep."

batiste fabric. One account claims that the popular *batiste fabric* takes its name from the soft linen used in medieval times to wipe holy water off the heads of baptized infants. It is more likely that the word derives from the name of one Jean Baptiste, of Cambrai, a 13th-century French linen weaver about whom little is known beyond his name. Cambric was at the time already a trade name for a linen manufactured at Cambrai, or Kamoric. English merchants needed another word for this new Cambrai product, so they named it after the French weaver but misspelled his name. Today *batiste* is no longer only linen material. Sheer cotton *batiste* is used for lingerie, handkerchiefs, and children's wear, and sheer rayon, silk, and woolen *batistes* are common, too.

a bat out of hell. Since bats are nocturnal creatures that loathe the light, the hellfires of the infernal regions would inspire them to flap like hell to get out of there. That may be the idea behind the expression to move *like a bat out of hell*, extremely fast, which *Partridge* traces to 1908 and probably goes back to the late 19th century. It was also slang used by R.A.F. pilots since World War I for "to fly extremely fast."

bats in your belfry; batty. Blind bats flapping about in the vast emptiness of someone's head, which suggested a church belltower or belfry to somebody, form the basis of this expression meaning a little crazy in the head, poco loco in the coco. Apparently no one told anybody *You've got bats in your belfry* until early in this century, for the first recorded use of the words is 1907. *Bats*, meaning crazy or nuts, seems to derive from the phrase, as does *batty*, meaning the same. The expression holds on mainly because of its alliteration, like the much older "bees in your bonnet" (*q.v.*). But the image of bats flapping their wings and squeaking in the dark is a strong one that does suggest craziness.

batten; batten down the hatches. A *batten* is simply a sawed strip of wood. This word gives us the nautical phrase *batten down the hatches*, for battens were once used to fasten canvas over a ship's hatchways during a storm. The phrase probably originated in the early 18th century.

battering ram. Romans of old called this device for battering down the walls of an enemy city an *aries* ("ram"), alluding to the male sheep and its powerful butting horns, and our term *ram* or *battering ram* is just a translation of the Latin term. The long log, sometimes hung on chains, was used until the invention of the cannon and has been depicted in hundreds of film epics. It has never to my knowledge been shown in the form of a huge ram's head, although some ancient armies actually constructed it that way.

batting eyelids. To bat your eyelids is to flutter them, the expression an American one that goes back to the late 19th century. It has nothing to do with bats flapping in a cave, someone "gone batty," or even baseball bats. *Batting* in this case comes from the lexicon of falconry in Tudor times. According to a falconry book written in 1615: "Batting, or to bat, is when a Hawke fluttereth with his wings either from the perch or the man's fist, striving, as it were, to fly away." The old word had long been used by sportsmen, and some American with a lot of *sprachgefuhl*, "feeling for language," found a fresh use for it in the 1880s.

battle-ax. It took over six hundred years for someone to think of this description of a domineering, sharp-tempered wife. Battle-axes were used at least since the Bronze Age, and were so named in the Middle Ages, most of them fearsome weapons that could fell a man with a single blow. Long after the lethal weapons were made obsolete by firearms, they remained a favorite of collectors and were displayed in museums. But it wasn't until the early years of this century that someone, possibly a vaudeville comedian, compared his warring wife to an *old battle-ax*. The expression is still used, often in a humorous, affectionate way. *Old battle-ax*, as slang for a strong man who is disliked and considered mean, has passed out of use.

battle of the giants.   (*See* **war of the giants.**)

battle royal.   Cockfighting does have a lot to do with this metaphor for a free-for-all, a battle in which more than one contestant is involved, but it probably didn't originate with the now outlawed "sport," as is often stated. The earliest quotations using the phrase support the theory that it derives from medieval jousting tournaments, where it was used to describe two sides fighting, each commanded by a king. Later, the expression became cockpit jargon before passing into standard English. In cockfighting, *battle royal* better describes what we mean by a *battle royal* today. It was an elimination tournament for gamecocks in which only the best fighters survived. A number of cocks, say eight, were thrown in the pit. These eight fought until there were only four left. Then these remaining four were rested and pitted against each other until two survived. The two survivors finally fought for the championship.

battology; battologist.   A stammering man named Battos mentioned in the works of the Greek historian Herodotus, "The Father of History," is responsible for the word *battology*, "needless or excessive repetition in speech or writing," The *Oxford English Dictionary* records *battology*'s first use in 1603. It was formed by combining the name of the man Herodotus described, *Battos*, with the Greek *logia*—from *logos*, "word." *Battologist* is a term sometimes applied to boring speakers.

batty.   (*See* **bats in your belfry.**)

Bavius; Maevius.   Virgil sarcastically criticized the two minor Roman poets *Bavius* and *Maevius* in his Third Eclogue and Maevius was further criticized by Horace in his Tenth Epode, making their names forever synonyms for inferior poets or poetasters. In 1794 William Gifford wrote a fierce satire called *The Baviad* and followed it two years later with the *Maeviad*. The works attacked the Della Cruscan school of poetry, founded by sentimental young English poets living in Florence at the time. Ironically, the school bore the name of Florence's famous Accademia della Crusca (Academy of Chaff) whose object was purifying the Italian language, sifting away its chaff. By the way, Virgil himself was much criticized in his time; one critic published eight volumes consisting of resemblances between lines in Virgil's poems and earlier Roman poems.

bawdy; bawdy houses.   *Bawdy*, "obscene, indecent, or lewd," derives from *bawd*, originally a procurer of either sex, and then either a prostitute or the madam of a brothel. Some scholars link *bawd* with Middle French *baud*, "gay, dissolute," but the *O.E.D.* marks *bawd* "of uncertain origin." *Bawd* also means a hare in English, but

as this use of the word is recorded two centuries after the first, it is hard to show any relationship between the fabled sexual energy of hares and the activities of human *bawds*. In the 17th century it was customary on Shrove Tuesday for apprentices to beat or frighten *bawds* on the street or in their *bawdy houses*.

bawl; bawl out.   Dating back to the 15th century, *bawl* for a loud, rough cry probably derives from the Latin for *baulere*, "to bark like a dog." The word was also applied to the sounds of other animals, especially cows and bulls, which supports the theory that to *bawl out* originated as American ranch slang, suggested by the bawling or bellowing of angry bulls.

baying.   (*See* **bah!**)

bayonet.   Originally a short dagger, the *bayonet* almost certainly takes its name from Bayonne in southwestern France, where it was first made in the early 17th century. The word is first recorded, meaning "dagger," in 1611, and first cited meaning "a dagger attached to a musket" in 1674.

bay window.   The *bay window*, devised as early as the 14th century, is so named because in projecting from the house it made the room inside appear to mariners like a little harbor or bay. *Bay window* has been American slang for a "pot belly" since the 1890s.

bazaar.   Used for a store or marketplace where many kinds of goods are sold, *bazaar* is one of the few English words that come to us from the Middle East, in this case deriving from the Persian *bazar*, "marketplace."

bean; string bean; green bean.   Deriving from the Old English *bean*, and possibly akin to the Latin *faba* by a circuitous route, *bean* was long used for the seeds of many plants. "Common beans" (*string beans*, first recorded in 1759; *Lima beans*; *wax beans*; etc.) are native to the Americas. Napoleon wouldn't eat *string beans*, afraid that he would choke on the strings, but today's varieties are virtually stringless and thus are often called *green beans*. As early as 1830, one observer noted: "We do not call it a string bean, because the pod is entirely stringless." Yet *string bean* is still used for the vegetable and Americanisms like *string bean* for a tall, thin person remain in the language. *Bean pole*, another Americanism for a lanky person, takes its name from the tall poles that support climbing bean plants.

beanfeast.   No one is sure about *beanfeast*'s derivation. The annual dinner that British employers gave their workers in the 1800s may be so named because beans were served at the feast or because a "bean goose," a goose "with a beak like a horse bean," was part of the fare.

On the other hand, *bean* here may come from *bene*, "prayer, solicitation," because charitable collections were made at the feasts.

to bear down upon. The nautical practice of *bearing down* on another ship means to sail toward her rapidly from a position upwind. From this naval strategy comes the phrase *to bear down upon*, to put pressure on someone or something, which probably originated late in the 19th century.

to beard the lion in his den. Sir Walter Scott apparently invented this expression, meaning to boldly encounter someone powerful on his own ground. At least Scott first records the words, in *Marmion*, 1808.

a bear for work. In the early 19th century, as Americans pushed on into the wilderness, a number of native expressions arose comparing man with great strength or strong appetites or emotions to bears. *A bear for work* was born at this time, as was *cross as a bear* (*q.v.*).

beast 666.

> Let he who hath understanding
> Reckon the number of the Beast;
> For it is a human number,
> Its number is Six Hundred and Sixty Six.
>
> —Book of Revelations xiii, 18

No one has been able to identify satisfactorily the Beast alluded to in the Bible. Since each digit in 666 falls short by one of the "sacred number" seven, it has been suggested that 666 therefore symbolizes the Antichrist expected by some Christians to precede the second coming of Christ. Others have tried to prove that 666 is a cryptogram based on the names of various men throughout history. The Hebrew letters of the name Nero Caesar, for example, represent numbers which add up to 666. Nero has always been a favorite candidate for the Beast, but Roman emperor Diocletian, Martin Luther, Muhammad, Napoleon, and many others have been suggested, too. The matter is further complicated by the fact that some ancient authorities say the number given in Revelations is 616.

beast-with-two-backs. Shakespeare used this expression for face-to-face sexual intercourse in *Othello*, having Iago say: "I am one sir, that comes to tell you your daughter and the Moor are now making the beast with two backs." The words are often hyphenated today.

beat a dead horse. (*See* **flog a dead horse.**)

to beat a retreat. In early times drums were played when armies retreated from the field. Over the years the drumming and a bugle call came to be the ceremony of retreat at sunset, when day was done and the flag was lowered. *To beat a retreat* now means to retreat or retire from all activities rather than just battlefield withdrawal.

beat around the bush. It's hard not to *beat around the bush* about the origins of this one. Hunters once hired beaters who "started" birds and other game for them by beating the bush and scaring them out into the open. The simplest explanation for the phrase *to beat around the bush*, to approach a matter very carefully or in a round-about way, is that these beaters had to take great care when approaching the bush or they would "start" the game too soon for the hunter to get a good shot. But etymologist Ernest Weekley and others believe that the expression, which dates back to at least the early 16th century, is a mixed metaphor. Weekley suggests that the old proverb "I will not beat the bush that another may have the bird" joined with "to around the bush," an early expression used for a hound hesitating when circling the bush—and gave us *to beat around the bush*.

to beat black and blue. Originally the colors in this phrase, recorded as early as 1300, were *blak* and *bla*, the *blak* for "black," and the *bla*, for "a dark color between black and blue," a livid blackish-blue. These of course are the colors the human body commonly turns when beaten, bruised, or pinched.

beat it! Although most authorities say *beat it!* is American slang first recorded in 1905 for "get out of here, go away!", the expression is much older. The term was used by both Ben Jonson and Shakespeare for "go" and is said to have been coined by Shakespeare. It may be a shortening of "beat the trail" or some similar expression, but no one is sure. (*See* **scram.**)

to be at loose ends. There are at least two good explanations for this expression meaning "not knowing what to do with oneself," or to be unemployed. The saying dates back to the middle of the last century in England and was originally *to be at loose end*. One theory connects it with a string hanging loose from a garment, the end of it attached to nothing. But Weekley in his *Etymological Dictionary of Modern English* says the phrase suggests "freedom from tether," like a horse out to pasture, out of harness, untied and unemployed.

to be at low tide. *To be at low tide* or *water* or *the low watermark* is to have financial difficulties, or no money at all, as if one were stranded by the ebbing tide. Nautical slang in origin and dating back to the early 17th century, the expression is Standard English today.

to beat the band. Banagher, an Irish town on the Shannon, was in the mid-19th century a notorious "pocket borough" where most residents were employed by the local lord and voted as he directed (were "in his pocket"). It became a standing joke in Parliament at the time to quip "Well, that beats (or bangs) Banagher!" whenever someone mentioned a pocket borough where *every* resident was employed by the local lord. Either via this route, or because of an Irish minstrel named Bannagher who told amazing stories, the saying *that beats Banagher,* for "anything amazing or superior," became an English favorite. It's reasonable to suggest, as *Partridge* does, that the later phrase *that beats the band,* derived from it. The alliterative expressions do sound alike and "*bang*" (from both the alternate version of the English phrase and Banagher) would suggest "band"—that beats something louder, bigger, better than a great brass band. Attempts to connect *that beats the band* with several real bands have all failed.

beats; beat generation; beatnik. Novelist Jack Kerouac claimed he invented the word *beat* for Allen Ginsberg's "angel-headed hipsters" of the fifties, and said it meant "beatific, blissfully happy," that "you got the beat," but it probably owes a lot to the early thirties jargon of jazz musicians in which *beat* meant "exhausted, frustrated, played out" (*q.v.*). In fact, *beat* in this last sense was used generally as far back as 1830. *Beat generation* seems certainly to have been Kerouac's name for the fifties' "Lost Generation," though it was first used in John Clellon Holmes's novel *Go!* (1957). Columnist Herb Caen of the *San Francisco Chronicle* coined *beatnik* in 1958. The pejorative though affectionate Yiddish suffix *nik* (as in "nudnik," "no-good-nik," etc.) was probably added to *beat* to make the word, but remember that the Russian sputnik ("fellow traveler of the earth") with its Polish suffix *nik* was launched at the time.

to be at the end of one's rope. *I'm at the end of my rope* means I've gone as far as I can, I can't do anymore, and suggests the image of an animal tied on a tether. The expression is first recorded, however, in the sense of someone finally checked in wrong-doing, in a 1686 translation of a French work. This suggests that the expression may have been inspired by the sight of a man executed by hanging, dangling at the end of his rope.

to beat the living daylights out of someone. To say "I'll let daylight into you!" to an enemy in days past was to threaten that you'd open him up, make a hole in him with a sword, knife, or gun. The expression, in the form of its variant "I'll make daylight shine through you," is recorded in America as early as 1774 and is probably much older. Sayings like "I'll fill him full of holes" replaced the older expression when modern weapons like machine guns made wholesale ventilation easier, but it lived on in the form of *I'll beat the living daylights out of you*—I'll beat you to a pulp, punish you unmercifully. Unlike the old swordsman's words, this makes no sense literally. It is merely the ghost of an imaginative phrase.

Beau Brummell. *Beau Brummell,* born George Bryan Brummel, was more a dandy than a gentleman; it is said that he even refused to tip his hat to ladies, out of fear that he might mess his wig. Brummell's name has indeed been synonymous for a dandy, fop, or fancy dresser for over a century. From his early years at Eton and Oxford the incomparable Beau paid extravagant attention to his dress. There he met the Prince of Wales, later George IV, who became his patron when he left college, commissioning him in his own regiment in 1794. Brummell retired from the service four years later, when he inherited a large fortune, and set up a bachelor apartment in Mayfair, where he held sway as London's arbiter of fashion for almost twenty years. Though he showed good taste and originality in dress, he is remembered for his excesses. *Beau Brummell* often spent a whole day dressing for a royal ball; his gloves were the work of three glovers—one to fashion the hands, another for the fingers, and a third for the thumb. In 1816 he fled to France to escape his creditors. Here he spent his last twenty-four years in exile while struggling to survive, imprisoned once for debt and suffering several attacks of paralysis. He died in an asylum for the poor in Caen in 1840, aged sixty-two. He had long before lost all interest in elegant fashion and manners, his dress becoming slovenly and dirty. (*See also* **Beau Nash**.)

Beaufort scale. The *Beaufort scale,* a means to measure wind velocity, was devised in 1806 by Sir Francis Beaufort (1774-1857), noted surveyor and hydrologist, who later became a rear admiral and served as hydrographer to the British navy from 1829 to 1855. Beaufort's scale consists of numbers from 0 to 12 that indicate the strength of the wind ranging from "light," force 0, to "hurricane," force 12, or in Beaufort's words, "that which no canvas could withstand."

Beaujolais. Often drunk very young—even as early as mid-November of the year its grapes are harvested—*Beaujolais* is a full-bodied fruity wine that has become very popular in America recently. It takes its name from the Beaujolais region in France, north of Lyon, where it is produced.

Beau Nash. Beau Nash is the only "beautiful person" comparable to *Beau Brummell* (*q.v.*). Master of Ceremonies at Bath, then England's most fashionable gambling and cultural center, Nash spent much of his long life preening and strutting, riding in a chariot drawn by six gray stallions and attended by laced lackeys. The

"King of Bath" died in 1761, aged eighty-seven, and the town ordered a full-size statue of him erected in the Pump Room between the smaller busts of Newton and Pope. That Beau Nash, like Brummel, was remembered for his excesses and not his many good works can be seen in Lord Chesterfield's epigram concerning this statue:

The statue placed these busts between
Gives satire all its strength;
Wisdom and Wit are little seen,
But Folly at full length.

beautiful.   (See **broken-hearted**.)

the beautiful people.   *The beautiful people*, in the rather debased sense that it is used today, isn't a 1960s creation but dates back to the 1880s, when it was coined, most appropriately, by Oscar Wilde.

beauty is only skin-deep.   *Skin-deep*, for "superficial" or "shallow," "penetrating no deeper than the skin," can be traced back to the early 17th century, as can the proverbial *beauty is only skin-deep*, expressing the limitations of beauty. The last expression is first recorded in a poem by Thomas Overbury in about 1613: "All the carnall beauty of my wife,/ Is but skin-deep." *Skin-deep*, literally, can range from 1/100th of an inch on the eyelid to 1/5th of an inch on the back.

bechamel.   The Marquis de Bechamel, it is said, made his money financing various fraudulent deals before turning from crookery to cookery, but the French forgave him everything for the sauce he invented. Louis de Bechamel became steward to Louis XIV, the Sun King, as he liked to call himself, whose motto was, "He who eats well works well." While superintendent of the royal kitchens, Bechamel created many sublime dishes for the dedicated gourmet king, under whom the now proverbial Cordon Bleu school of cookery was established. However, what we call a *bechamel*, a *bechamelle*, or a *Bechamel sauce* today—a cream sauce thickened with flour—bears little resemblance to the original, which was a complicated concoction prepared from egg yolks, cream, and butter blended with an elaborate bouillon made from vegetables, wines, "old hens, and old partridges." This may be for the best, though. "Thank goodness," writes the noted chef Raymond Oliver, "[such recipes] are no longer more than pale ghosts of what they were."

beche-de-mer.   *Beche-de-mer*, a lingua franca known only in the Pacific, is a combination of English and native dialects. The *beche-de-mer* was a staple of trade, the natives prizing it for food, and the language takes its name from this sea slug or sea cucumber.

bedbug letter.   According to an old story, a guest at a famous hotel was bitten by a bedbug one night and on returning home wrote a letter of complaint. He received an apologetic letter claiming that this had never happened before; however, the guest's letter was enclosed, with the notation scrawled across the top: "Send him the bedbug letter." Ever since, the expression *bedbug letter* has meant a form letter apologizing for poor service or a defective product.

bed of ice.   A short story I read recently described as a *bed of ice* the water bed a quarrelling couple shared. The expression has a much crueler connotation in history. It seems that for one capricious reason or another Empress Anne of Russia demoted an old noble at her court to court jester and then ordered him to marry an old crone who served her as a chambermaid. At great expense the sadistic Anne had a house of ice built on the frozen Neva River and furnished it entirely with ice. The newlyweds were, amid great fanfare, transported to their home on the back of an elephant, put into their ice bed naked and the house's ice door was moved in place. They did not last until morning.

bed of Procrustes.   Procrustes, sometimes called Damastes or Polypemon in Greek legend, always obliged weary travelers when they came to his house on the road to Eleusis seeking lodging for the night. But the notorious highwayman of Attica makes modern muggers look *namby-pamby* (*q.v.*) in comparison. He had two sadistic M.O.'s. Once he got a short victim inside, he'd lead him to a long bed, tie him up and stretch him on a rack until he fit it. If the victim was tall, Procrustes would show him to a short bed, restrain him, and lop off his legs so that he fit. Either way his victims died in bed and Procrustes stole their money. From his inhumane hospitality we have the expression to put a person *on the bed of Procrustes*, meaning to force him to one standard of thought or action by arbitrary methods.

bedouin.   A *bedouin* has come to mean any wandering person or vagabond, and derives from the French word (*Bedouin*) for the nomadic Arab tribes of the Arabian, Syrian, and North African deserts. The French adapted the word from the Arabic *bidwan*, "a dweller in the open lands." The Bedouins of the Arabian desert, about one million in number, are nomadic camel breeders who trade their camels with Persian (Iranian) and Syrian traders for food and other goods. Living in groups of up to one hundred, they are strongly united through blood relationships, a woman generally marrying her father's brother's son.

bedswerver.   In days past this delightful word served as a synonym for an unfaithful spouse (one of *its* synonyms being a *spouse-break*). Shakespeare used the term in *The Winter's Tale*.

bee. *Spelling bee* is among the last survivors of a large number of *bees* relating to social gatherings (bees being busy, cooperative, social animals) "for performing some task in common." These are American in origin—the first one recorded is a 1769 *spinning bee* in Taunton, Massachusetts, though the term was in use before that. Later came *bees* prefixed by apple, building, candy, checker, chopping, drawing, housecleaning, husking, knitting, logging, paring, picking, political, quilting, raising, sewing, shingle, shooting, shouting, shucking, spinning, squirrel, stone, tailor, and wood. There were even *rattlesnake bees*, where "the venomous reptiles . . . were summarily excised by fire and lethal weapons"; *kissing bees*, parties for young people; *whipping bees*, where toughs beat someone; and *lynching bees*. The affairs, sometimes called "frolics," were often followed by parties.

Beealzebub. (*See* **Old Nick**.)

Beecher's Bibles. *Beecher's Bibles* were Sharps repeater rifles that the Reverend Henry Ward Beecher (1813-1887), one of America's most famous and controversial preachers, raised money for at his Brooklyn Heights church in New York and shipped to "Bloody Kansas" in crates labeled "Bibles." Beecher encouraged his parishioners to join the "underground railroad" and even held mock slave auctions at Plymouth Congregational Church to illustrate the evils of slavery. The church, still in use, was called "The Church of the Holy Rifles," and is now a national historic shrine. Beecher once wrote that "the Sharp rifle was a truly moral agency . . . [had] more moral power . . . than a hundred Bibles." The great preacher, brother of Harriet Beecher Stowe, was a complex man whose interests ranged from involvement in antislavery movements to involvement with female members of his congregation. (*See* **Sharps rifle**.)

beefcake. (*See* **cheesecake**.)

Beef Stroganoff; Beef Wellington. Nineteenth-century Russian diplomat Count Paul Stroganoff has the honor of having the well-known *Beef Stroganoff* named after him. It is beef sauteed with onions and cooked in a sauce of consomme, sour cream, mushrooms, mustard, and other condiments. *Beef Wellington*, another popular dish, commemorates Arthur Wellesley, first duke of Wellington, for whom a number of words were named, including *Wellington boots* (q.v.). *Beef Wellington* combines a choice cut of beef, liver pate, bacon, brandy, and various condiments, all baked in a golden crust of puffed pastry.

bee in his (her) bonnet.

Ah! woe is mee,
woe, woe is mee
Alack and well-a-day!

For pity, sir, find out the bee,
Which bore my love away.
I'le seek him in your bonnet brave,
I'le seek him in your eyes.

Robert Herrick's little-known poem "Mad Maid's Song," above, written in 1648, is supposed to be the basis for the expression *to have a bee in one's bonnet*, "to be eccentric, have a screw loose, especially to be obsessed with one idea." If the gentleman in the poem is implying in the last two lines that the mad maid is slightly insane, this is the case. Herrick was probably playing with an older expression, "to have bees in the head or brain," which means the same and dates back to the early 16th century. Bees humming in the head obviously suggested an obsessive idea busy at work there. A bonnet at the time was either a man's or woman's hat.

been down so long it looks like up to me. This expression is the title of a book by the late Richard Fariña and still has currency today. It dates back to the 1960s or before and is akin to several ancient phrases. For example, in 1590 one writer noted: "They verife the olde Proverb, Charles, which is, That such as were never but in Hell, doo thinke that there is no other Heaven."

beer. *Beer* possibly derives from the Latin *biber*, for "drink." Roman soldiers most likely demanded *biber* in taverns wherever they went in Germany and the tavern owners assumed that this meant the ale in which they specialized. Gradually, the German word for ale became *biber* and then *Bier*, which came into English as *beer*.

beerplants. (*See* **aspidistra**.)

beet; red as a beet. *Beet* comes to us from the Greek *beta*, for a similar plant. *Red as a beet* has probably been used as long as man has used beets. The French *bettereve*, "beet," has served as slang for the penis, an analogy not unknown in history, despite the unlikely shape of the modern beet for such—Catullus wrote about a Roman matron who left her husband because the object of her desires "dangled like a limp beet."

beetle. Born to bite, beetles take their name from the Old English word *bitula*, meaning "biter." The species of beetles called *dermestes* derive their name from the Greek words for "skin or leather" and "to eat," meaning that an entomologist-etymologist in the early 19th century observed that they ate even the hides of dead animals. *Dermestes* are interesting little beetles that *play possum* (q.v.) when touched. Actually, their larvae do the eating, and they demolish everything on a dead animal. They're so thorough that large museums sometimes keep a colony on hand to clean delicate specimens to the bone instead of risking chemical or mechanical means.

beetle-brained.   We don't call someone *beetle-brained* because he acts as though he has a brain about as big as a beetle. The English term, first recorded in 1604, derives from the Old English *betl*, "a hammer," a *betl* or *beetle-brained* person having a head as hard as a hammer head.

beezer.   Rarely heard anymore, *beezer* was once popular slang for the nose, slang brought back by U.S. Marines serving in China, where Westerners were called the insulting *ta-bee-tsee*, or "big-nosed ones." (*See* **Chinese**.)

before the mast.   Seamen on sailing ships in days past always bunked in the forecastle (fo'c'sle), literally "before the mast," which accounts for the title of Richard Henry Dana's classic *Two Years Before the Mast* (1840). But *before the mast* also means to be hauled before the mast of a ship, where the captain held court, to be tried for some offense.

beggar; to beg.   A *beggar*, as Ernest Weekley pointed out in *The Romance of Words*, is not etymologically one who begs, for in the case of *to beg* the verb evolved from the noun. Many scholars share this opinion. Surprisingly, *beggar* is not of ancient vintage, like "eat" and "drink" and "sleep." The word probably derives from the nickname of the 12th-century Liege priest, Lambert le Begue (Lambert the Stammerer), who founded a Belgian lay order devoted to the religious life and chastity as a reaction against the suffering of the Crusades. Little is known about Lambert le Begue besides the fact that he died in 1177, but his secular order, though it demanded communal living, poverty, and self-denial, was a tolerant and popular one. There were no requirements that his followers take vows or lock themselves in a monastery, and members were allowed to own private property, as well as to leave the order and marry. The nuns of the Beguine order were called *beghinae* in Medieval Latin, and the monks belonging to a male group formed in the Netherlands were similarly called *beghardi*, these Latin formations influenced by the name of their order and by the Old Flemish *beghen*, "to pray." But the brotherhood of *beghardi* or *Beghards*, composed mostly of the tradesmen, was very loosely organized, making it easy for thieves and mendicants to pose as members of the poor and ill-clad group. Imposters traveled the Low Countries claiming to be Beghards and asking for alms, and the group was held in low repute by the end of the 13th century—especially because a large number of the Beghards were militant trade unionists who raised havoc wherever they went, and because many other members had become idle, wandering mendicants like their imitators. The old French word *begard*, meaning mendicant, was soon formed from either the Medieval Latin *beghardi*, for *Beghards*, or from the Middle Dutch *beggaert*, meaning the same thing. *Begard*, in turn,

became the Anglo-French *begger*, which was transformed into the Middle English *beggare*, or mendicant, with its verb *beggen*, meaning to ask for alms. Eventually we had the English word *beggar* that we use today, the verb *to beg* thus growing out of what the *beggar* did. Other scholars trace *beggar* to the obscure Old English word *bedecian*, which is only related to a Gothic word meaning mendicant and is so rare it has been found only once. But even if this is correct, there is no doubt that the Beghards at least reinforced the idea of *beggar* in people's minds. (*See also* **bigot**.)

beggar on horseback.   "Set a beggar on horseback and he will ride a gallop," Robert Burton observed in his *Anatomy of Melancholy*. But the proverb, meaning there is no one so arrogant as a beggar who has suddenly made his fortune, probably dates back much earlier. It possibly derives from the old English proverb, "Set a beggar on horseback and he'll ride to the devil." This proverb is common to many languages, its German equivalent, for instance, being "Set a beggar on horseback and he'll outride the devil."

begonia.   Michel Begon (1638-1710) served as a minor navy official at various French ports until a fortunate marriage led to his appointment by Louis XIII as royal commissioner in Santo Domingo, though he wasn't Santo Domingo's governor, as is often claimed. Begon primarily concerned himself with protecting the natives from unscrupulous merchants and attending to their medical needs, but the amateur horticulturist ordered a detailed study of the island's plant life, collecting hundreds of specimens. Among these he found the begonia, now a common house and garden plant, which he took back to France with him and introduced to European botanists. The begonia however, wasn't named for him until sixty-seven years after his death, when it was first brought to England. Begon is remembered for his patronage of science and his public spirit. On the opening of his large private library to the public, for example, friends advised him that he would surely lose numerous books. "I had much rather lose my books," he replied, "than seem to distrust an honest man." The begonia he discovered is a most valuable garden plant because it prefers the shade, where it flowers freely, is available in a large variety of colors, and can be grown for its foliage as well as its beautiful blooms. The *Begonia* genus contains some one thousand species.

begorrah!   *By God!* is the curse this comic Irish euphemism conceals, though practically no one thinks *begorrah!* means that by now. The corruption dates back to at least the late 19th century.

to beg the question.   *Begging the question* doesn't mean evading the question by giving an indirect answer, as is often assumed. The old phrase, which can be traced back to the 16th century, is the rough equivalent of the logician's *petitio principii* and means "to stack the cards in an argument by assuming something that hasn't been proved before the debate begins." *Beg the question* actually means that someone is acting like a beggar, asking his opponent to give him the argument at the beginning. "O shameless beggar, that craveth no less than the whole controversy to be given him!" an early English author wrote in explaining the term.

beg to advise. The much-used phrase *beg to advise*, so often read in business letters, may be dated but isn't incorrect by any means. Here *advise* doesn't mean "to give advice" but "to give information," information being one of the meanings of *advice*. This is seen in another common business expression: "We would appreciate the benefit of your advice."

behind the eight ball. (*See* **eightball**.)

behind the scenes. Though the origins of this phrase are theatrical, as you would expect, it goes back to the English theater in the time of Charles I, when elaborate paintings were commonly used for the first time to create atmosphere on the stage. Since these paintings were often landscapes, they were called "scenes." Behind them much of the important action of a play went on—birth, murders, intrigues, and the like—action that wasn't represented on the stage. As early as 1658 we find the playwright John Dryden writing on "Things happening in the Action of the Play, and suppos'd to be done behind the Scenes." It wasn't long before the phrase began to be used figuratively to describe any important action hidden from the ordinary spectator, especially in places of power.

bel canto. *Bel canto* is virtuoso singing, a vocal technique emphasizing the quality of sound rather than emotion, a style found in some Italian opera. The words are Italian for "beautiful singing." *Bel canto* writing might be writing with more style than substance, though some would say the only substance *is* style.

Belcher scarf; Belcher ring. Jim or Jem Belcher, England's version of Gentleman Jim Corbett, carried and made popular a large pocket handkerchief, its blue background spotted with large white spots with a small dark blue spot in the center of each. Such handkerchiefs or neckerchiefs, often more descriptively called "bird's eye wipes," were named after the boxer, as was the *Belcher ring*, a huge gold affair set with a large stone that was prominent even on Belcher's massive dukes. Jim Belcher, the most celebrated boxer of his time, lost an eye in 1803, thereafter retiring from the ring and owning or operating a pub. He died in 1811, when only thirty years

old. Belcher's name, oddly enough, means "fine gentleman" in French. He bore a remarkable resemblance to Napoleon and was in fact billed as the "Napoleon of the Ring."

belfry. This word for a church steeple isn't directly named for the bells hung inside it; in fact, it owes its life to the worship of war, not God. In their desire to conquer their neighbors, German strategists of the Middle Ages built moveable wooden towers ironically called *bergfieds* ("peace" shelters) that they used in their advances on walled cities. Soldiers concealed inside these primitive, "vertical" tanks could protect themselves from enemy archers, and the devices proved so effective that many other European armies adopted them. By the time the English imported the siege tower in about 1500 it was called the *berfrey* and the English built it even taller, so that their own archers could climb to the top and fire arrows into a walled city or castle. But with the invention of new weapons using gunpowder, the wooden *berfreys* became outmoded in offensive military operations and were hauled within the walls of cities to serve as watchtowers. Here they were equipped with bells so that watchmen inside could sound the alarm of an enemy attack. Over the years people constantly associated the word *berfrey* with the word bell and because of this "klang association"—the hearing of one word in the sound of another—they began to pronounce it *belfrey*, substituting an *l* from bell for the *r*, this dissimilation being *belfry's* only etymological connection with the word *bell*. Later, churches were built with bell towers and the name *belfry* was used for them, too.

Belisha beacon. (*See* **Hore-Belisha**.)

belladonna lily. Belladonna means "pretty lady" in Italian and this flower may be so named because its smooth petals resemble a pretty girl's skin, or because Italian women once used the red sap of the plant as a cosmetic or to brighten their eyes. A beautiful shepherdess in the poems of Virgil and Theocritus gives the *belladonna lily* its scientific name *Amaryllis*.

bellarmine. *Bellarmine* is a historical term referring to a glazed stone beer jug designed to ridicule Italian Cardinal Roberto Francesco Romolo Bellarmino (1542-1621). Cardinal Bellarmine, as he is better known, distinguished himself as a Jesuit scholar and was a friend of Galileo, but is usually remembered for his persecution of Protestants in Flanders. The Flemish later retaliated by caricaturing him with the large *bellarmine*, which was designed as a burlesque likeness, having a huge belly and a narrow neck. The controversial cardinal was canonized in 1930.

bellibone. In the 16th century a pretty lass was called a *bellibone*, the whimsical word an Anglicization of the French *belle et bonne*, "fair and good."

to bell the cat. *To bell the cat* is to take on a dangerous mission at great personal risk for the benefit of others. Cats, of course, have long been belled to prevent them from killing songbirds. But the expression derives from a wise mouse. It is from an old fable retold in William "Long Will" Langland's alliterative poem "The Vision Concerning Piers Plowman," which was written, as far as is known, between 1360 and 1399. "Piers Plowman" tells of a family of mice who hold a meeting to decide what to do about a cat who has been preventing them from foraging for food. One cunning mouse suggests that a brass bell be hung around the cat's neck so that they could be warned of this approach. Everyone agrees that this ploy is perfect, except for one sage mouse, who steps forward and says, "Excellent idea, but who will bell the cat?"

bellwether. Since Anglo-Saxon times a *bellwether* has been a castrated male sheep that usually has a bell fastened around its neck and leads the flock. Later the word was applied humorously to a ringleader, the leader of any mob, conspiracy, or the like, and then was used to describe any leader who assumes the forefront of a profession or industry, etc., as in "New York is the bellwether of the publishing industry."

to bellyache. *Bellyache* had earlier meant "colic" in England, but in the sense of "to complain" it is an Americanism coined about midway through the 19th century and first recorded in 1881. As with so many coined words, no one knows its clever inventor's name.

belly cheater; belly robber; belly burglar. *Belly cheater* is an old American cowboy term for a cook, which may date back to the 19th century but is first recorded as U.S. Navy slang in the form of *belly robber*, specifically referring to a commissary steward. The term has also been used for an Army mess sergeant. Another (later) variant is *belly burglar*.

belly laugh. (*See* **high hat.**)

belly-timber; belly-cheer; belly-god. A synonym for food provisions—timber for the belly—*belly-timber* is recorded as early as 1607 and as late as the mid-19th century, having been used by a number of great writers, including Butler and Smollett. *Belly-cheer*, another delightful word, is perhaps a century older, and refers to food that cheers the belly. A *belly-god* is usually a person who makes a god of his belly, a glutton, though a *belly-god* can be "a god presiding over the appetites": the three belly-gods being Bacchus, Ceres and Venus.

below the belt; Queensberry rules. Boxing enthusiast John Sholto Douglas, the eighth Marquis of Queensberry, put boxing on a more humane basis in 1867 when he and lightweight boxer John Graham Chambers drew up a code of twelve rules to govern boxing matches that were generally accepted by 1875 and standard throughout England by 1889. The rules instituted many modern features, including the use of gloves, a limited number of three-minute rounds, the ten-second count for a knockout, and the outlawing of wrestling, gouging, and hitting below the belt line on a boxer's trunk. The *Queensberry rules* became the basis for all world boxing regulations. The rule that attracted most attention was the one prohibiting hitting below the belt, a practice that had been widely accepted despite the fact that fighters hit in the testicles suffered excruciating pain. *Queensberry rules* mark the first literal use of the expression, and not long after their formation *below the belt* was being used figuratively to describe any dirty, unfair methods.

Beluga caviar. (*See* **caviar.**)

belvedere. *Belvedere* is Italian for "fine or fair sight." Such summer houses commanding a fine view of the garden began to be built on English estates in the 16th century, when the word came into the language from France or Italy.

Ben Day. A New York printer named Benjamin Day (1831-1916) invented the Ben Day process of quick mechanical production of stippling, shading, or tints on line engravings. *Ben Dayed* means produced by the *Ben Day* photoengraving method. The process, which has been used since about 1879, eliminates the shading of a drawing by hand.

Bendigo, Australia. The only city ever named for a prizefighter is *Bendigo*, Australia, which has a population of some fifty thousand and is the third largest sheep and cattle market in that country. *Bendigo*, the site of a famous gold strike in 1851, honors the ring name of English pugilist William Thompson (1811-1889), as does the *bendigo* fur cap popular in the late 19th century. Thompson was born the same year that Fighting Jim Belcher (*q.v.*) died. He may have been one of triplets nicknamed Shadrach, Meshac, and *Abednego*, or his nickname could have stemmed from his evangelical pursuits, but, in any event, in 1835 he signed his first ring challenge "Abed-Nego of Nottingham," and used the nickname *Bendigo* for the remainder of his career—until he gave up fighting to become a full-time evangelist. *Bendigo*, Australia had some second thoughts about its eponymous name, changing it to Sandhurst in 1871, but reverted back to the old application in 1891, two years after Thompson's death.

beneath; beneath contempt. Deriving from an Old English word, *beneath* is first recorded in 1205. As for its prepositional use, the *O.E.D.* puts it this way: "The prepositional use of *beneath* seems originally to have been introduced to express the notion of 'lower than' . . .

But in process of time *beneath* was so widely used for *under* that *below* was laid hold of to express the more general idea . . ." *Beneath* has thus become "more or less a literary and slightly archaic equivalent" of both *under* and *below*, and is preferred to these words only in a few phrases, such as *beneath contempt*, below the level or dignity even of contempt, which seems to have first been recorded in the late 19th century.

benedick; benedict. A *benedick* is strictly a sworn bachelor entrapped in marriage, while a *benedict* refers to a bachelor of marriageable age. The former term derives from the name of the character Benedick in Shakespeare's *Much Ado About Nothing* and the latter honors St. Benedict (d. 543), founder of the Benedictine order and a great advocate of celibacy. Benedict originally meant a perennial bachelor sworn to celibacy and it is probably for this reason that Shakespeare adopted and adapted the name—for its amusing contrast to his Benedick, the young lord who vows at the beginning of *Much Ado About Nothing* to forever remain a bachelor and is finally talked into marriage. Shakespeare may have borrowed his idea from Thomas Kyd's *The Spanish Tragedy*, and the Latin *Benedictus*, "the blessed," probably also influenced his choice of the name. Although there is a distinction between the two words, they are used interchangeably today, meaning not a bachelor anymore, but a newly married man who had been a bachelor for a long time. *Benedict*, as in "a happy *benedict*," is the usual spelling.

Benedict Arnold. *Quisling* (*q.v.*) and a few others have endured, but most traitors have not been included in the dictionaries. *Benedict Arnold* is an exception. The term has been used for over two hundred years in America, and is still a common one. Every schoolboy knows the story of how General Benedict Arnold plotted to deliver the garrison at West Point to Major John Andre, how the plot failed with Andre's capture and how Arnold fled to the British army. Less familiar are the facts that Arnold was a brilliant soldier and that his treason was provoked by shabby treatment at the hands of superiors several times during the course of the Revolutionary War.

Benedictine; Benedictines. Many famous drinks treated in these pages—*champagne, coffee, chianti, mocha, scotch, seltzer,* and *Vichy water*—are named after places, but the celebrated liqueur *Benedictine* is named for the monastery of a famous religious brotherhood. The particular monk who concocted the drink was one Don Bernardo Vincelli, a man whom the medieval archbishop of Rouen declared as important to humanity as any saint for his inspiration. *Benedictine*, one of the oldest liquors in the world, was first made at the *Benedictine* monastery at Fecamp, France in about 1510. Called *Benedictine* in honor of the order, its makers dedicated it "to the greater glory of God." Though the monastery was destroyed dur-

ing the French Revolution, monks managed to save the secret formula, and fifty years later a Frenchman named Le Grand began manufacturing *Benedictine*, his distillery still standing on the site of the abbey. Le Grand labeled each bottle D.O.M., which are the initials of the order and stand for *Deo optimo maximo*, "for the most good and great God."

benefit of clergy. *Benefit of clergy* was until 1827 a procedure in British law whereby a criminal arrested for a felony was exempt from trial in the secular courts if he could recite a passage from the Bible—the passage becoming known as *neck verse*. After reciting the verse, whether he was accused of murder, rape, or burglary (all capital offenses), he would be turned over to an ecclesiastical court, which could not invoke the death penalty for such crimes, and his neck would be saved from the hangman or axman. Originally, this privilege was granted only to the clergy, but as it was based on the biblical injunction, "Touch not my annointed and do my prophet no harm" (1 Chron. 26:22), it was extended to anyone who could read or write, that is, anyone who could *become* an ordained clergyman. This early-day "diplomatic immunity" of course discriminated against the uneducated poor. The *neck verse* that had to be recited was from the first verse of Psalms 51: "Have mercy upon me, O God, according to Thy loving kindness: According unto the multitude of Thy tender mercies blot out my transgressions. . . ." This verse is commonly called the *Miserere* because its opening words in Latin are *Miserere mei Deus*.

benign neglect. *Benign neglect* was used in reference to a proposed policy of giving fewer welfare benefits to U.S. minorities in the 1970s, but it originated long before this. The term was coined in 1839 by the Earl of Durham and described England's treatment of Canada.

benny, benjamin. Today a *benny* is usually American slang for an amphetamine tablet, especially Benzedrine, a trademarked name, but it also signifies both a pawnbroker and an overcoat. A pawnbroker became a *benny* because he often makes loans on overcoats, which are sometimes called *bennies* or *benjies*, a shortened form of *benjamins*. The benjamin, at first a certain tight-fitting style of overcoat and then any overcoat at all, probably derives from the biblical Benjamin, in humorous reference to this brother Joseph's coat of many colors (Gen. 37:3). But some scholars claim that the *benjamin* was created by a mid-19th-century London tailor of that name, the biblical tale rendering the term popular, and *Mencken* suggests that *benny* for an overcoat may have derived from the Romany *bengru*, "a waistcoat." *Benny* is also slang for a derby.

Ben Trovato. *Ben Trovato* comes from the Italian phrase *Se non e vero, e ben trovato* ("If it is not true, it is well invented"), so it has often been used humorously as the authority for a good story that really isn't true—*ben trovato*, in other words, has over the years become the quoted scholar *Ben Trovato*. Every effort has been made to bar Ben Trovato from these pages, but in a work of this size it is impossible to be sure that he hasn't sneaked in somewhere. What can be promised is that if old Benjamin is anywhere on the premises, he'll certainly be spinning a good yarn.

Bering Sea. (*See* **Seward's folly**.)

Berlin blue. (*See* **Prussian blue**.)

berm. *Berm* is first recorded in 1854, in the sense of "the bank of a canal opposite the towing path." The word derives from the German *Berme*, "a path or strip of ground along a dike," and over the years has come to mean the side or shoulder of a road, especially in the southern U.S.

Bermuda. Juan Bermudez, a Spanish colonist, had been migrating elsewhere late in the 18th century when he was shipwrecked in what is today called the Bermuda Triangle. He and a cargo of pigs wound up on the island that now bears his name.

the berries. *The berries* has been American talk for "the best, the greatest" since 1902, when it seems to have originated as college slang. *Berry* had been recorded a few years earlier as slang for a dollar and perhaps this use suggested the expression.

berserk. Old Berserkr ("Bear Skin"), a famous hero in Norse mythology, was a supernatural warrior who fought with feral fury and feared nothing; he even spurned weapons or armor, rushing into battle protected only by the bearskin thrown over his shoulder and clawing and biting his victims to death. His twelve sons bore the same name, and these mad warriors could also turn themselves into wild beasts that neither fire nor armor could kill. Together they terrorized the land. This is the most widely accepted biography of Old Berserkr. Another account says he was a grandson of the eight-handed Starkader and that he got his name not from his bearskin, but from Norsemen calling him *baer-serce*, bare of mail, because he went into battle without armor. At any rate, the legends surrounding Berserkr and his dozen scions became known to the English, who spelled his name Berserkar. Any fierce fighter was soon called a *berserker*, especially one who fought with a fury that seemed almost insane and terrified even his allies. In time *to go berserk* came to mean the violent, furious rage of a madman.

berth. (*See* **give a wide berth**.)

Bertillon system. The first modern scientific method for identifying criminals was the *Bertillon system*, devised by Alphonse Bertillon (1853-1914), French anthropologist and pioneer criminologist. Bertillon developed *Bertillonage*, as the system is also called, when he headed the criminal identification bureau in the Seine prefecture and described it in his book *La Photographie judiciare*. Adopted by France in 1888, the revolutionary method relied on anthropometry—the classification of skeletal and other body measurements, plus the color of hair, eyes, etc., for purposes of comparison. Fingerprints were a late addition to these *Bertillon measurements* and soon supplanted the system itself. The term is still used, though, to describe fingerprints and all anthropometric measurements.

Bessemer converter, etc. We might almost as fairly call the Bessemer process the Kelly process. This revolutionary method for converting pig or cast iron to steel is named after Englishman Henry Bessemer (1813-1898), but it was discovered almost concurrently by American inventor William Kelly (1811-1888). Bessemer, the son of a French artist, was already a respected metallurgist and the inventor of a machine used to reduce gold and bronze to powder when he began experimenting to produce better and cheaper iron for cannons during the Crimean War. He started his work about the year 1854, being granted his first patent a year later, and in 1856 discovered the basic principle involved in his process, which he described in his paper, "The Manufacture of Iron Without Fuel." Bessemer's secret was the removal of carbon and other impurities from pig iron by melting it in his *Bessemer converter* and forcing a blast of air through the molted metal. The Bessemer process, much improved today, produced far better steel more cheaply and faster than ever before, tripling English steel production within a few years after its introduction.

the best laid schemes (plans) of mice and men. In his poem *To a Mouse* (c. 1786) Scottish poet Robert Burns wrote: "The best laid schemes o'mice an'men / Gang aft a-gley." The words have ever since been a common expression for failed plans in both Great Britain and the U.S., often in its original form, often as *the best laid plans of mice and man often go astray*, and often as the abbreviated *the best laid plans of mice and men*.

best of all possible worlds. (*See* **Dr. Pangloss**.)

best-seller. *Best-seller*, for a book that sells many copies, is an Americanism first recorded in 1905. The Sears Roebuck Catalog is probably the "best-seller" of all time, though it was distributed free for more than three-quarters of a century. Over 2.5 billion copies of the Sears Roebuck mail-order catalog have been distributed in the last ten years alone, and 5 billion may be a conservative estimate for its total distribution since 1896. In second place is the Bible. Only recently has Sears begun to charge customers for its catalog.

bet one's bottom dollar.   When one bets his bottom dollar he is betting everything he has, his last dollar. The expression comes from poker, where the chips, or "dollars," are stacked and one takes chips from the top of the pile in betting, betting one's bottom dollar when he bets the entire stack. The phrase dates back to the late 19th century.

better half.   Originally these words bore no hint of male chauvinism, applying to a husband as well as a wife and meant to be taken seriously. The expression can be traced back to the Roman poet Horace, who called his old friend Maecenas his *better half*. But the term became common in England only about 1570, not long before Sir Philip Sidney began writing his prose romance *Arcadia* (1580). The Puritans had used the phrase to describe the soul, the *better half* of the person, but Sidney popularized its use as a description of either partner in a marriage. For three centuries husbands and wives called their mates *my better half* without any humor intended. It wasn't much more than a century ago that it began to be used jocularly and mainly in reference to a wife.

better mousetrap.   (*See* **build a better mousetrap**.)

between a rock and a hard place.   In days past if one was badly in need of money, almost bankrupt, he or she was said to be *between a rock and a hard place*. This expression was probably born in Arizona during a financial panic early in this century, but over the years its meaning changed. It came to mean being in a very tight spot, on the horns of a dilemma in making a hard decision. The words do lend themselves best to this last definition, for wherever one turns in making the decision there is rock or something as hard as or harder than rock.

between Scylla and Charybdis.   The *Odyssey* vividly describes Odysseus's passage between Scylla and Charybdis. In Greek mythology Scylla (Skulla) was a beautiful maiden loved by Poseidon, the lord of the sea. But her rival, Amphitrite, fed Scylla magic herbs that transformed her into a monster with twelve dangling feet, six long necks with a head on each, and three rows of teeth. She dwelt in a high cave overlooking the sea (situated, according to tradition, in the Strait of Messina) and from every ship that passed by, each of her terrible mouths reached down and devoured a sailor. On the other side of the narrow channel, beneath an immense wild fig tree, lay a dangerous whirlpool called Charybdis (Charubdis) that sucked in and regorged the sea three

times a day. It was Odysseus's fate to sail between Scylla and Charybdis, as it is still the fate of anyone steering a mid-course between equally dangerous perils. Odysseus had mixed luck: he lost his crew and ship, but saved his own life by clinging to the fig tree at the base of Charybdis.

between the cup and the lip there's many a slip.   No one knows where this common phrase originated, though it has been traced back to the 16th century. It means of course that anything can happen between the making of plans and their fulfillment.

between the devil and the deep blue sea.   The Devil didn't inspire this old saying, as many people believe. It is thought to be a nautical expression, as its earliest recorded use in 1621 indicates, the "devil" in it referring not to Satan but to a seam between planks in a wooden ship's deck, specifically the long seam nearest to either side of a ship. This seam was "the devil to get at" and any sailor caulking it in a heavy sea risked falling overboard. The seam that ran around a ship's hull at the waterline, another one difficult and dangerous to get at, was also called "the devil," and these two devils inspired the memorable alliterative phrase *between the devil and the deep blue sea*—someone caught on the horns of a dilemma, caught between difficulties that are equally dangerous. Similarly, "the devil to pay" refers to "paying"—waterproofing with pitch—the devil on a ship. *Pay* here comes from the Latin *picare*, for the process, and the original phrase was "the devil to pay and no hot pitch."

between the lines.   (*See* **read between the lines**.)

between wind and water.   Any ship struck by a shell or torpedo in an area that is *between wind and water*—that is, damaged in a part of the hull that dips into the water and then rises to the wind when plowing through rough seas—is usually seriously damaged. The expression *between wind and water* has thus been used since the 16th century to signify hazardous damage in a ship and is used metaphorically to mean an unexpected attack on someone.

between you, me, and the lamppost.   Dickens used this expression in *Nicholas Nickleby* (1838) and it couldn't be much older, for "lamppost" is first recorded in 1790. But the words probably derive from earlier expressions meaning "in confidence," such as "between you and me" and "between you and me and the gatepost" (or "bedpost").

beware of Greeks bearing gifts.   (*See* **Greek**.)

beyond the pale; put to the pale.   There is no connection between this expression and the word *pale,* "of whitish appearance," which comes from the Latin *pallidus*, "pallid." *Pale* here refers to the Latin *palus*, "a stake or boundary marker driven into the ground with others to fence off a territory under the rule of a certain nation." Pale or picket fences (we call them palings today) were erected all over Europe from Roman times to designate territory belonging to a certain country. Later, the "pale" came to be used figuratively, as in the famous 15th-century "English pale" portion of Ireland that the English dominated before Cromwell conquered the whole island. *Beyond the pale* first meant simply to be outside the boundaries or jurisdiction of a nation, but by extension, and with the aid of Kipling's "Beyond the Pale," it came to describe a dismal place to which we assign social outcasts, those regarded as beyond the bounds of moral or social decency. To *put to the pale* often means to defeat someone so badly that he'll be banished from competition with you forever ("Write more poems like this and you'll put Poe to the pale").

be your age.   (*See* **act your age.**)

bialy.   (*See* **bagel.**)

Bibb lettuce.   An amateur gardener named John B. Bibb developed *Bibb lettuce* in his backyard garden in Frankfort, Kentucky, about 1850, and the variety has been an American favorite ever since. Bibb is the most famous and best of what are called butterhead lettuces, having a tight small head of dark green color and a wonderful flavor. Because the variety is inclined to bolt in hot weather, a summer Bibb is now offered by nurserymen for the home garden. Several kinds of lettuce are named after their developers, including blackseeded Simpson, a loose-leaf variety. The vegetable can be traced back to ancient India and Central Asia, but takes its name from the Latin word *lac*, meaning silk, the Romans favoring lettuce for its milky juice and calling it *lactuce*. Bibb is not often found in the market, the most popular sellers in the United States being iceberg lettuce, a heading variety, and loose-leaf Boston lettuce.

Bible.   (*See* **book.**)

biblia a-biblia.   "I can read anything which I call a *book*," wrote Charles Lamb. "There are things in that shape which I cannot allow for such. In this catalogue of books which are not books—*biblia a-biblia*—I reckon Court Calendars, Directories, Pocket Books, Draught Boards, bound and lettered on the back, Scientific Treatises, Almanacs, Statutes at Large, the works of Hume, Gibbon, Robertson, Beattie, Soame Jenyns, and generally, all those volumes which 'no gentleman's library should be without.'"

bibliopoles and other bibliotypes.   A *bibliopole* is simply a bookdealer, while a *bibliotaph* is one who conceals or hoards books, keeping them under lock and key, and a *biblioclast* is someone who collects and treasures books either for their value or for what's in them, and a *bibliomaniac* is a *bibliophile* gone bonkers, one who loves books to the point of madness. Legend has it that Don Vicente, a Spanish friar and scholar, murdered five or six collectors to steal a rare book, which makes him a *biblioklept* as well as a *bibliomaniac*.

Bic.   The *Bic* disposable razor owes its name not to an advertising copywriter, but to its inventor, Frenchman Marcel Biche, who introduced it in the 1970s. He also invented the Bic disposable pen.

Bickerstaff hoax.   Nearly all of Jonathan Swift's works were published anonymously, and he received payment only for *Gulliver's Travels* (200 pounds). In the case of the *Bickerstaff Hoax* Swift made no profit, using the pen name Isaac Bickerstaff. The Dean grew prudently indignant in 1708 when an ignorant cobbler named John Partridge, claiming to be an astrologer, published an almanac of astrological predictions. So he parodied the book under the title "Prediction for the ensuing year, by Isaac Bickerstaff." In his parody the wasp of Twickenham foretold the death of John Partridge on March 29, 1708, and when that day arrived he published a letter affirming his prediction and giving an account of Partridge's death. Partridge indignantly protested that he was very much alive, but Swift wrote what he called a "Vindication," *proving* that he was dead. Poor Partridge was doomed to a literary death as a result, especially when other writers perpetuated the joke. So famous did the pseudonym Isaac Bickerstaff become that Richard Steele used it as his pen name in the *Tatler*. Benjamin Franklin later emulated Swift's hoax in America.

bidet.   Ben Johnson is the first to record *bidet*, in 1630. A low basinlike bath "used especially in France for bathing one's private parts," the *bidet* is "bestridden, one squatting to wash." Someone with a sense of humor named the bath after the small horse called a *bidet* that people had to ride with their legs drawn up to avoid dragging their feet on the ground.

big.   No one really knows the origin of this important monosyllabic word. *Big* has been traced to the Middle English *bigge*, meaning the same, but no further than that. It may come from the Scandinavian *bugge*, "an important man," but it could also derive from the Latin *bucca*, in the sense of "inflated cheek," among other possibilities.

the Big Apple.   A nickname for New York City since the 1960s, *the Big Apple* was first used in New Orleans. In about 1910 jazz musicians there used it as a loose translation of the Spanish *manzana principal*, the main "apple orchard," the main city block downtown, the place where all the action is.

Big Ben. *Big Ben* is not the huge clock in London's Parliament tower, though it is often given this name. The words really describe the huge, deep-toned bell in St. Stephen's Tower that strikes the hours over the British Houses of Parliament. *Big Ben*, cast from 1856 to 1858, weighs 13 1/2 tons, more than twice the weight of the 6 1/2 tons bell in Philadelphia's Independence Hall. The great bell's first stroke, not the last, marks the hour, four smaller bells in the tower striking the quarter hours on the famed Westminster Chimes. The tower clock, 329 feet high, was designed by lawyer and architect Edmund Grimthorpe (1816-1905), and was named St. Stephen's Tower. This was to be the name of the bell, too, but newspapers took to calling it after Sir Benjamin Hall, Chief Commissioner of Works at the time, and the sobriquet stuck. *Big Ben*, though a notable achievement in bell founding, is far from being the world's largest bell. Moscow's Tsar Kolokol, a broken and unused giant weight about 180 tons, is called the "King of Bells."

Big Bertha. On close examination, *Big Bertha*, the famous cannon that shelled Paris during World War I, is not so complimentary to the woman for whom it was named. *Big Bertha* is a translation of *die dicke Bertha*, "the fat Bertha," a nickname the Germans had for their 42-cm. howitzers. They had in mind portly Frau Bertha Krupp von Bohlen und Halbach, whose husband owned the giant Krupp steel and munitions plant at Essen, it being mistakenly believed that the howitzers were manufactured by Krupp, whereas they were actually made at the Skoda works in Austria-Hungary. The *Big Bertha* aimed at Paris, an even larger gun with a range of 76 miles, began bombarding the city on March 23, 1918, firing every third day for 140 days and killing 256 people in all. On Good Friday of that year alone its shells killed or wounded 156 worshippers in the church of St. Gervais. It was at this time that journalists resurrected the term from the German and began applying it specifically to the Paris gun.

big brass. (*See* **brass.**)

Big Brother is watching you. *Big Brother* has come to mean a dictator or a dictatorship, a person or a political system that controls people's minds and lives so that there is nothing private and personal anymore. The reference is of course to the character *Big Brother* in George Orwell's novel *Nineteen Eighty-Four* (1949).

big butter-and-egg man. Speakeasy owner Texas Guinan may have coined this expression for a wealthy big spender during the Roaring Twenties. According to the story, one of her patrons kept buying rounds for the house all evening and showering $50 bills on the chorus girls. Texas asked him to take a bow but he would only identify himself as being in the the dairy business, so Texas put the spotlight on him, asking for "a hand for my big butter-and-egg man." In any case, George S. Kaufman used the phrase as the title of a play in 1925, giving it greater currency.

big cheese. A *big cheese*, for "a boss or important person," is an Americanism dating back to about 1890. But it derives from the British expression *the cheese*, meaning "the thing or the correct thing, the best." The British expression, in turn, is a corruption of the Persian or Urdu *chiz* (or *cheez*), "thing," that the British brought back from India in about 1840. A *big cheese* thus has nothing to do with cheese and should properly be "a big chiz."

the Big Drink; Big Ditch; Big Water; Big Pond. *The Big Drink*, the first humorous American phrase for the Atlantic, Pacific, or any big body of water, seems to have been coined anonymously in 1844 and was also a name for the Mississippi River, which is more commonly called the *Big Ditch* or *Big Water*. *Big Ditch*, coined in 1825, has also been applied to the Atlantic, but is most commonly associated with the Erie Canal. The *Big Pond*, a humorous term for the Atlantic, stems from about 1840, when it was coined by Canadian humorist Thomas Haliburton.

big galoot. *Galoot* or *galloot* is not an Americanism, for British sailors had used it as a contemptuous term for a stupid, clumsy soldier sixty years or so before it was first recorded here, in 1866. It may be that British sailors picked up the contemptuous Dutch expression *gelubt* for "a eunuch" and changed its meaning, though still using it contemptuously. No better explanation has been made.

big gooseberry season. In Victorian times summer was a dull period for the British newspapers. So much space was left for reports of record-size vegetables and fruits grown by one gardener or another that it was nicknamed *the big gooseberry season*.

bignonia. A widely distributed woody flowering vine, the *bignonia* is sometimes confused with the *begonia* (*q.v.*), and the names of the men that the two plants honor are often confused as well. The species are not related, and Abbé John Paul Bignon, court librarian to Louis XIV, did not discover the beautiful *bignonia* vine bearing his name. The *bignonia* was named by the French botanist Tournefort about 1700 in honor of the abbé, who had never ventured from Europe.

Big Noses. Koreans often called all Occidentals *Big Noses*, a slur just as surely as the terms "gook" (*q.v.*) and "slopehead" or "slope" applied to them by Westerners.

bigot. *"Ne, se, bi got!* ('No, by God!')" the Norman lord Rollo is supposed to have shouted indignantly when he was told to kiss the foot or posterior of Charles the Simple as an act of homage, and legend has it that the word *bigot* arose because this phrase of Rollo's was thereafter applied to any obstinate person. But the amusing old story is probably no more than that. Some scholars do suspect, however, that *bigot* stems from the Teutonic oath *bi got,* suggesting that it may have been bestowed as a derogatory nickname upon the Normans, who were regarded as obstinately and intolerantly devoted to their own religion. Nobody knows, but whatever the case, the formation of *bigot* was certainly influenced by the fanatical, intolerant behavior of the Beguine religious order. (*See also* **beggar**.)

big shot. Garibaldi's forces used a 90-millimeter cannon against the Austrians. The big projectile it fired was translated into English by Garibaldi's American followers as the *big shot,* which came to mean a big, important person. Such, at least, is one version of the origin of *big shot,* an Americanism first recorded in 1910, some thirty years after Garibaldi had breathed his last.

big wheel, etc. *Big wheel,* first recorded in 1941, is the latest in a long line of similar earlier expressions. Of these *bigwig, big shot, big cheese, big gun,* and even *big noise* are still heard infrequently, while *big bug, big fish, big dog,* and *big toad in the puddle* are all but dead. The "wheel" in the term could come from the huge wheels in textile mills, or the phrase may derive from the mid-19th-century expression "to roll a big wheel," used by mechanics as a synonym for "to be important or influential."

bigwig. All of Europe's royalty aped France's Louis XIV when he took to wearing long, flowing wigs in his middle years. In England especially, the more important a man was, or imagined himself to be, the bigger the wig he likely would wear. In fact, custom soon dictated that only the nobility, judges, and bishops were permitted to wear the full-length style wig still retained in British courts of law. By then the word *bigwig,* for "an important person," had passed into the language.

bilge. Now meaning nonsense or filth, *bilge* was originally the dirty water than collected in the bottom of a ship. *Bilge* was first spelled *bulge,* which referred to the fact that the dirty water collected in the bulge, or curve, at the bottom of a straight-sided ship.

bilk. *Bilk* comes from the game of cribbage, where this variant of *balk* means to defraud another player of points by sharp, sly tactics. The term was widely used by the mid 1800s in its current general sense of to cheat or defraud in a clever way.

bill; bill of lading; check. *Lading* in this expression simply means "loading." The *bill* part refers not to the modern meaning of bill as a statement of money owed, but to a written, formal, and sealed document. *Bill,* in fact, derives from the Latin *bulla,* for "seal." Today a bill of lading is simply a written receipt given by a carrier for goods accepted for transportation. None are as poetic as the old bills of lading, which ended with the prayer: "And so God bring the good ship to her desired port in safety." Because *bill* meant an "official paper" it came to be applied to paper currency in late 16th-century England. As for the word *check* for a bank check, it originated from a bank draft with a counterfoil. The counterfoil prevented, or "checked," forgeries and alterations of the drafts.

Billies and Charlies. Collectors will still pay premium prices for genuine *Billies* and *Charlies,* even though they are fake historical objects. They are named for antique dealers William (Billy) Smith and Charles (Charlie) Eaton, who in general manufactured such bogus medieval articles from 1847 to 1858, planting them around London and then "discovering" them in excavations.

billingsgate. Coarse and abusive language, *billingsgate* is language similar to that once used by the fishwives in the Billingsgate fish market along the River Thames in London. The area was named for whoever built the gate below the London Bridge leading to the old walled city. But who built Billing's Gate is a matter of controversy. Some historians credit a Mr. Billings (or Billin, or Belin), a builder or famous burgher who owned property thereabouts; others suggest that Billing's Gate was named for an ancient clan called Billings, or for one Belen (Belinus), a legendary monarch, citing a 1658 map that ascribes it to "Belen, ye 23rd Brittish Kinge."

billionaire. There are no British billionaires, for a billion is a million million there, whereas it is "merely" a thousand million in the U.S. The word *billionaire* is first recorded in 1861. Though stingy with his dimes, John D. Rockefeller was the world's first known billionaire—American style. (*See also* **millionaire, trillionaire**.)

billycan. Even an aboriginal language has made its contributions to English. *Billycan* or *billy* for any can in which water can be carried and boiled over a fire, derives from the Aboriginal Australian *billa,* "water." The word has limited use in England and America as well as in Australia.

billycock. (*See* **bowler**.)

bimbo. (*See* **groupie**.)

Binet-Simon tests. The first intelligence tests were developed by Alfred Binet (1857-1911), a French psychologist who directed the laboratory of psychology and physiology at the Sorbonne, in conjunction with psychologist Theodore Simon. The initial tests, later extended in age, determined the intelligence quotient of children three to twelve, each subject being asked questions adapted to the intelligence of a normal child of his age. The *Binet-Simon tests* have been revised many times since their invention in 1905. Intelligence quotient, or I.Q., on such tests is merely a ratio, expressed as a percentage, of a person's mental age to his actual age, his mental age being the age for which he scores 100 percent on all the questions. The score 150 is generally accepted as genius and below 70 is classified as mental deficiency.

Bing cherry. *Bing cherries* are popular dark red, nearly black fruit of the Bigarreau or firm, crisp-fleshed group. The tree was developed in 1875 by a Chinese farmer named Bing in Oregon, where over a quarter of the United States' sweet cherry crop is grown. Other cherry varieties named after their developers include the Luelling, for the man who founded Oregon's cherry industry in 1847, the Lambert, and the Schmidt. Countless varieties honor famous people, such as the "Napoleon," the "Royal Ann," and the "Governor Wood," though none is named for George Washington. Surprisingly, sour cherries outnumber sweets two to one in the United States because they are easier to grow and are more in demand for cooking and canning. Cherries were probably first cultivated in China over four thousand years ago, so Bing was carrying on a great ethnic tradition.

Bingley terrier. (*See* **Airedale terrier**.)

bingo! Nineteenth-century Christian missionaries introduced the game of *bingo* to inhabitants in various parts of Africa while they were enthusiastically converting people to their religion. The people associated the Christian concept of heaven, a Christian's final reward, with a player's shout of *bingo!* when he wins a game of bingo—making *bingo!* their word for heaven. *Bingo* is a corruption of *beano*, an early name for the game, and *beano* was patterned on *Keno*, another game of chance, which takes its name from the French *quine* for "five winning numbers."

bird; birdie. For well over half a century, beginning in about 1849, *bird* was American slang for a person or thing of excellence ("He's a perfect bird of a man"), the expression coming into use at about the same time as the still heard use of *bird* for "fellow" or "guy" ("He's a strange old bird"). In the early 1920s, possibly at the Atlantic City Country Club in New Jersey, the popular expression attached itself to golf in the form of *birdie*, which means "one stroke under par for a hole," an excellent performance. Since about 1880 *bird* has been British slang for a girl.

a bird in hand. This proverbial expression can be traced back in English to the early 16th century, when it is rendered as "A byrde yn hande ys better than three yn in the wode," and probably much earlier, counting variations such as "Some bete the bush and some the byrdes take" (1440). Later, Cervantes used it in *Don Quixote* in the full form best known today: "A bird in the hand is worth two in the bush." Actually, the proverb, which is found in German, French, Italian, and several other languages, has its direct ancestor in an ancient saying from Plutarch's *Of Garrulity*, written in about A.D. 100: "He is a fool who lets slip a bird in the hand for a bird in the bush." It is what *Weekley* calls one of those proverbial expressions "which contain the wisdom of the ages."

bird of ill omen. Birds that appeared to the right of the augur who stood on Rome's Capitoline Hill were considered good luck, and any bird that appeared on his left was said to indicate bad luck. It is from the ceremony of this Roman religious official and fortune-teller that we get the phrase *bird of ill omen*, which is still applied to a bearer of bad news or an unlucky person. Specific birds that have been considered unlucky over the years include the owl, which is said to screech when bad weather (and hence, sickness) is coming, the raven, and the vulture, held to indicate death, as well as the crow and the albatross under certain circumstances.

birrelism; birreligion. The charm and unobtrusive scholarship displayed by Augustine Birrell (1850-1933) in his *Obiter Dicta* and other works led to the formation of the word *birrellism* for shrewd cursory comments on humankind and life in general. Birrell, a barrister elected to Parliament in 1889, became president of the national board of education and chief secretary for Ireland (1907-16). He is noted for Birrell's Educational Bill of 1906 and the founding of the Roman Catholic National University of Ireland. *Birreligion* indicated the political import of his educational bill.

birthday suit. Anyone parading in his *birthday suit* is stark naked. The phrase, first recorded in 1771 but probably older, simply means that someone is wearing nothing, just what he or she wore at birth.

biscuit. *Biscuits* were cooked a second time to keep them from quickly spoiling at sea. Thus their name derives from the French *biscuit*, "cooked twice."

to bishop. Unlike *burke* (*q.v.*) which it resembles, the expression *to bishop* is used only historically today, although the words arose at about the same time and for essentially the same reason. *To bishop* is to murder by drowning. It is named for a Mr. Bishop, who in 1831 so murdered a little boy in Bethnal Green, England in order to sell the child's body to surgeons for dissection, the murderer probably influenced by the earlier work of Burke and Hare.

bistro. When the Russians invaded Paris after Napoleon I's fall in 1815, restaurant owners or their shills would lure them into their places by shouting the Russian word *vee-stra*, meaning "quick," assuring them that they could eat quickly here at a good price. They used the word so often that it became, altered to *bistro*, the common French word for any small unpretentious restaurant where cheap meals could be had, and from there *bistro* soon entered into English.

bitch. Captain Grose defines a *bitch* as "A she dog, or doggess; the most offensive appellation that can be given to an English woman, even more provoking than that of *whore*, as may be gathered from the regular Billingsgate or St. Giles [woman's] answer [on being called a bitch]: 'I may be a whore but can't be a bitch.'" *Bitch* has meant "a lewd woman" and applied opprobriously to a woman since about 1400. It has been applied to a man, "less opprobriously and somewhat whimsically," for almost as long, Fielding, for example, calling the landlord "a vast comical bitch" in *Tom Jones.* The word *bitch* derives from the Old English *bicchu,* meaning "a female dog."

bite the bullet. The cartridge used in the 1850s' British Enfield rifle had a paper tube, the end of which riflemen had to bite off to expose the powder to the spark. A rifle-man doing this had to remain calm when reloading in the midst of a battle, giving rise to the expression *to bite the bullet,* to stand firm while under attack. Another theory, however, has the expression deriving from the bullet patients bit to alleviate pain when they were operated on without aid of an anesthetic.

bite the dust. Everytime we hear of still another desperado *biting the dust* in western films, we are hearing an almost literal translation of a line found in Homer's *Iliad,* written thousands of years ago. American poet William Cullen Bryant translated the words in 1870: ". . . his fellow warriors, many a one, Fall round him to the earth and bite the dust." Earlier, Alexander Pope had eloquently translated the phrase as "bite the bloody sand" and English poet William Cowper had it, literally, as "bite the ground." The idea remains the same in any case: a man falling dead in combat, *biting the dust* in his last hostile, futile act.

to the bitter end. The first theory here is that death has always been regarded as *the bitter end,* as in the phrase

from Proverbs, "Her end is bitter as wormwood." Poetically, then, any unpleasant final result, utter defeat or death would be *the bitter end.* But the anchor rope on early sailing vessels was attached to a device called the *bitt,* from which the anchor and anchor rope were paid out into the sea. The portion of the anchor rope nearest the bitt was called the "bitter end." There was no more anchor rope to be paid out after you came to the *bitter end,* and so you were at the end of your rope. This nautical expression has become widely known and so has at least helped to perpetuate the expression.

a bitter pill to swallow; pill-pusher. Figurative bitter pills were being swallowed more than two centuries before Horace Walpole used the expression in 1779. The phrase may have been proverbial ever since apothecaries began making the round little pellet that the Romans called a *pila* (ball) and from which our word *pill* derives. Though many pills were coated with honey and spices (and later sugarcoated), some bitter ingredients could not be masked. The intensely bitter chinchona bark, which contains quinine and was used to treat malaria, is one example. (Chinchona, incidentally, was named for the Condesa Ana de Chinchon, wife of the Spanish viceroy of Peru, who was stricken with a tropical fever in 1639 and cured by chinchona bark.) Bitter pills are also responsible for the expression *an old pill* for a grouchy person, first recorded in about 1880, and *pill-pusher,* early 20th-century slang for a doctor, which has a derogatory connotation but has its roots in old, nonobjectionable British military slang for a doctor, a "pill," that goes back to about 1860.

blab. *Blab,* first recorded by Chaucer, is supposed to be a shortening of the earlier *blabber. Blabber* in turn, is said to derive from *blaeberen,* an echoic word that imitates the sound of blabbering. It means, of course, "chatter" (*q.v.*), or loose talk, or to chatter, to spill out information.

black arts. As *Weekley* points out, this name for conjuring or the art of divination is a mistake, no matter how apt it seems. It was translated into English directly from the Old French *nigromancie,* "divination by means of the dead." But the Old French word itself had been formed in error from the Greco-Latin *necromantia* meaning the same, people confusing the sound-alike words *necro,* "dead," and *niger,* "black"—and associating black with the dark, secret ways of conjuring. The Greeks and others after them believed that they could divine or foretell the future, or discover hidden knowledge in many ways besides the study of corpses, these methods ranging from the study of animal entrails to the study of water.

blackball. So infamous was the 19th-century Black Ball Steamer Line between Liverpool and New York (the pilfering of its sailors widely known on both sides of the Atlantic and second only to the cruelty of its officers) that the term *blackball* came to mean stealing or pilfering at sea. In its most common use *blackball* means to vote against, to ostracize. When voting by ballot for a candidate proposed for membership in certain social clubs in 18th-century England, club members who accepted the candidate dropped a white ball into the ballot box and those who voted against the candidate dropped in a black ball. The term *blackball* is first recorded in a 1770 letter referring to a lady shunned by polite society.

blackbirder. A *blackbirder* was a ship engaged in the African or Polynesian slave trade in the mid-19th century. A *blackbird* was a captive aboard these slavers and *blackbirding* was used to describe such kidnapping or slaving.

black book. None of the slang dictionaries seem to record it, but a *little black book* has for at least half a century been the name for any Casanova's address book filled with the names, addresses, and especially phone numbers of desirable or compliant companions. But *black book* has far greater historical importance as the synonym for a book containing the names of people liable to censure or punishment, the term used most frequently in the phrase *I'm in his black book*, meaning "in disfavor with someone." The first such *black books* were compiled by agents of Henry VIII, who listed English monasteries under the pretext that they were sinful but really in order to convince Parliament to dissolve them so that the crown could claim their lands—which Parliament did in 1536. Later, the British universities, the army, and the police began the practice of listing censured people in *black books*, which reinforced the meaning of the term.

Black Death; bubonic plague. The bubonic plague that started in Constantinople (now Istanbul) and devastated Europe from 1347-51, killing from one-quarter to three-quarters of the population, was called the *Black Death* because the bodies of plague victims rapidly turned black after death. Over twenty-five million died of the Black Death, far more than in the 1665 plague of London that Defoe described in his *Journal of the Plague Year* and Samuel Pepys in his *Diary*. *Bubonic plague* is carried by rat fleas that have become infected by biting diseased rats (and certain squirrels on the West Coast of the U.S.). It is so named because the rod-shaped bacterium, *Pasturella pestis*, responsible for it causes swellings (buboes) of the glands in the groin or armpit.

black dog. (*See* **black money**.)

black eye; a black-eyed beauty. A *black eye* has had two meanings for over three centuries. In one sense *black eye* is a mask of beauty, an eye in which the iris is very dark and lustrous—hence our expression *a black-eyed beauty.*

In another sense a *black eye* is of course a discoloration of the flesh around the eye by a blow or contusion. Both expressions were coined toward the beginning of the 17th century.

blackguard. The modern meaning of *blackguard*, a low, contemptible person, may derive from the characteristics of medieval kitchen servants, who were humorously called *blackguards* in allusion to their filthy appearance and the black pots and pans that they guarded when the household retinue moved from place to place. These kitchen workers surely weren't always "rough and worthless knaves," as one source has it, so the theory, accepted by most etymologists, isn't entirely convincing. Perhaps the word really derives from some actual band of soldiers who wore black uniforms and whose vicious crimes are lost to history—unlike those of the contemporary *blackshirts*. (*q.v.*).

black hole. The infamous Black Hole of Calcutta gives its name to any *black hole* or hole in a prison where prisoners are confined as a punishment. The original *black hole* in this sense was the 18- by 14-foot room into which the French-supported Nawab of Bengal, Siraj Uddaula, thrust 146 British prisoners on the terribly hot night of June 20, 1756. The only ventilation in the room was two small air holes, and by the next morning 123 of the men had died. Robert Clive retook Calcutta the following year and avenged the atrocity, but the story of the *Black Hole* was never forgotten. Several Indian writers have claimed it was a British hoax, perpetrated to rouse patriotic sentiments, but three witnesses testified to the story and none of the twenty-three survivors ever denied it.

black is beautiful. It has been suggested that this slogan of pride for black Americans since the late 1960s may derive from the Song of Solomon in the Old Testament: "I am black but beautiful." But the "but" in the song casts doubt upon such a derivation.

blacklist; white list. The blacklist is centuries old, having originated with a list England's Charles II made of fifty-eight judges and court officers who sentenced his father, Charles I, to death in 1649. When Charles II was restored to the throne in 1660, thirteen of these regicides were executed and twenty-five sentenced to life imprisonment, while the others escaped. The *white list* is not quite the opposite of a blacklist, usually being a list, often kept by unions, of people suitable for employment.

black magic; voodoo. *Black magic* doesn't divine the future as the black arts do; it is rather the casting of magic spells for an evil purpose. *Black magic* is a synonym for *voodoo*, which is found in its purest forms today in the villages of Haiti, where it was encouraged and practiced by the former Haitian dictator "Papa Doc" Duvalier. *Voodoo* was brought to the New World by African slaves as early as the 1600s, and some authorities believe the word derives from the West African *vodun*, a form of the Ashanti *obosum*, "a guardian spirit or fetish." Others say that *voodoo* takes its name from the Waldensians, followers of Peter Waldo or Valdo (d. 1217), who were accused of sorcery and given the name "Vaudois" by the French. French missionaries later remembered these "heretics" when they encountered the witch doctors who preached black magic in the West Indies, this story says. They called the native witch doctors "Vaudois" and the name was soon applied to any witchcraft similar to the magic spells they cast, "Vaudois" being eventually corrupted to *voodoo*. Americans further corrupted *voodoo* to "hoodoo," but use the word in a playful sense.

blackmail. Sixteenth-century Scottish farmers paid their rent, or mail, to English absentee landlords in the form of *white mail*, "silver money," or *black mail*, "rent in the form of produce or livestock." The term black mail took on a bad connotation only when greedy landlords forced cashless tenants to pay much more in goods than they would have paid in silver. Later, when freebooters along the border demanded payment for free passage and "protection," the poor farmers called this illegal extortion *blackmail*, too.

Black Maria. Maria Lee, an imposing black woman, became a national heroine in 1798 when she delivered swivel guns to outfit the little cutters Alexander Hamilton had ordered built to protect American merchant ships on the high seas. Maria was just as reliable when she opened her boardinghouse for sailors in the early 1800s; her place was the cleanest and her guests the best mannered on the Boston waterfront because even hardened criminals feared her awesome strength. The giant woman aided the police so often that the saying "send for the Black Maria" became common whenever there was trouble with an offender. Fiery Maria sometimes helped escort prisoners to jail, and when the first British police horse vans or paddy wagons were introduced in 1838 they may have been christened *Black Marias* in her honor. But this tradition has skimpy evidence to support it. Critics point out that the first van was *black* and that *Maria* (which is pronounced *mar-eye-ah*) could have come from numerous sources.

Black Friday, etc. The first *Black Friday* in the British financial world fell on May 10, 1886, when certain brokers suspended payments and a widespread panic ensued. America's first *Black Friday* also came in 1886, when Jay Gould and Jim Fisk tried to bribe public officials in an attempt to corner the gold market; their manipulation failed when the government released gold for sale, but it ruined thousands of investors. With the Panic of 1919, the

beginning of America's Great Depression, came *Black Wednesday* (October 23) when stocks began falling; *Black Thursday* (October 24), the day the bottom dropped out of the market; and *Black Tuesday* (October 29), when over 16 million shares were traded. *Black Monday* was Easter Monday in 1360, a terrible day for the English armies in France, while *Black Saturday* refers to August 4, 1671, when there was a violent storm in Scotland. History seems to record no *Black Sunday*.

black money; black dog. In the early 18th century, counterfeit coins were commonly made of double-washed pewter and looked black or dirty. They were therefore called *black money* or *black dogs*, as readers of historical romances know.

Black Sea. The ancient Greeks never gave a derogatory name to any natural force, good or bad. So they named what we know as the *Black Sea*, the Euxine or "the Hospitable," even though it was noted for its storms and rocky shores. The Turks later named it the *Black Sea* because they were terrified of its dangers and large stretches of open water.

black sheep. Black sheep were once thought to bear the devil's mark in their wool. The superstition arose in days when dyestuffs were so ineffective and expensive that it wasn't practical to dye the wool of black sheep. Since black sheep were biological rarities, there weren't enough of them to market black wool, and the animals were regarded as practically worthless. Generations of farmers cursing their bad luck for having black sheep in their flocks evolved the term *black sheep*, for "any disgrace in a family or community." Wild sheep are usually brownish, and American mountain men called the buff wool of the bighorn (*Ovis canadensis*) its "long underwear."

blackshirts. These were first members of the Italian fascist militia, who wore black shirts and were imitated in England and other countries by fascists who wore similar uniforms. The term became much better known as the popular nickname of the elite military unit of the German Nazi party, officially called the *Schutzstaffel* (protection staff), or SS Corps. As its German name implies, the black-shirted SS served as a special protection unit and Hitler's bodyguard.

Black-shoe navy. This derogatory term for the seafaring navy was coined by members of its air arm. Navy fliers, usually not Annapolis graduates, were allowed to wear brown shoes, while the dress code specified black shoes for all others. Airborne officers felt that promotions came too easily for the Annapolis men and *Black-shoe navy* was the kindest of the epithets they hurled at them.

blacksmith. A *smith* is a craftsman who shapes any metal by hammering, and a *blacksmith* takes his name from the iron or black-colored metal he works with, not from the soot that gets on his clothes and skin while he works over a fire. His opposite is called a whitesmith, or tinsmith, one who works with tin or white metal. The *Harmonious Blacksmith* is the popular name of a musical composition by Handel; it wasn't really suggested to him by a smithy hammering at his forge.

blanket. There may have been a Thomas Blanket of Bristol, England who made *blankets*, setting up "the first loom for their manufacture in 1340." But the word *blanket* comes from the Old French *blankette*, originally a "white wool cloth used for clothing" but meaning the *blanket* we know today by the mid-14th century. This is not to say that a Thomas Blanket couldn't have adopted the name *blanket* for his product and popularized the word.

blarney. Built by Corman McCarthy in 1446 and named for a nearby village only a few miles north of Cork, Ireland, Blarney Castle was put under siege by the British in 1602. The story goes that McCarthy Mor, descendant of its builder, refused to surrender the fortress to Queen Elizabeth's Lord President of Munster, Sir George Carew. All Carew got from McCarthy for months were promises that he would eventually surrender. This smooth talk became a joking matter, making Carew the laughingstock of Elizabeth's ministers and *blarney* a byword for cajolery, flattering or wheedling talk. There is today, about twenty feet from the top of the castle wall, a stone inscribed "Cormac McCarthy *fortis me fieri fecit, A.D. 1446,*" which may have been set there to commemorate the verbal defeat of the English by the Irish. This triangular stone is difficult to reach and the legend grew in the 17th century that if you could scale the wall and kiss the blarney stone you would be blessed with all the eloquent persuasive powers of McCarthy Mor, that is, you'd be able to lie with a straight face. The blarney stone that people kiss today is a bit of *blarney* itself—a substitute provided to make things easier for tourists.

blazer. The jacket called the *blazer* may take its name from the "somewhat striking blue-and-white-striped jerseys" that the captain of Britain's H.M.S. *Blazer* ordered his crew to wear in the 19th century. But others say the jackets were called *blazers* because they were the "brightest possible blazing scarlet." According to this theory the jackets were first worn by the crew of the *Lady Margaret*, St. John's College, Cambridge, Boat Club in 1889.

bleachers. When you sit in the open outfield seats of a baseball stadium on a hot day, the sun seems strong enough to bleach your shirt. That is the humorous idea behind the coining of the word *bleachers* for all such seats in a stadium, the term first recorded in the early 1880s.

bleed white. (*See* **pay through the nose.**)

Blighia Sapida. (*See* **Captain Bligh.**)

blimp. The word wasn't coined, as *Mencken's* story goes, by two Britishers while they were having "blunch" (or brunch, as it is called in America) at an airport. Nor was the nonrigid dirigible airship so named by its manufacturer, the Goodyear Company in the early years of World War I. It is often reported that Goodyear's first model, the "A limp" (nonrigid), hadn't worked and that their second model, the "B limp," succeeded and kept its name, but Goodyear has denied that they or anyone else had airships with "limp" or type "B" designations. This leaves us with the possibility that the word is an onomatopoeic one, possibly coined by a Lt. Cunningham of the British Royal Navy Air Service in 1915. Cunningham, according to this story, flicked his thumb at one of the airships while on an inspection tour and "an odd noise echoed off the taut fabric . . . . [He] orally imitated the sound his thumb had drummed out of the airship bag: 'Blimp!' Those nearby saw and heard this unusual interlude in the inspection, and its account quickly spread."

blindman's buff. This old children's game is sometimes called "blindman's bluff," which makes no sense at all. *Blindman's buff* is actually right, the *buff* coming from the buff, or slap on the backside, other players would give the blindfolded player when he tried to grab them to make somebody else the "blindman."

blind pig; blind tiger. No doubt these names for "speakeasies serving illegal liquor during prohibition" owe much of their popularity to the fact that people believed the rotgut served therein would get you blind drunk. The names, however, may have more interesting origins. *Blind pig* is traditionally said to derive from the nickname of a band of soldiers called the Public Guard serving in Richmond, Virginia, in about 1858. Their militia hats had the initials P.G. on them, the sobriquet arising because "P.G. is a pig without an *i*, and a pig without an *eye* is a blind pig." One would have to assume that the soldiers were much disliked and were drunk a lot of the time—and the saloons they drank in named after them—to accept this theory, which has law officers being called "pigs" long before the sixties, as indeed they were. The theory seems all the more unlikely when it is known that *blind pig* is recorded as early as 1840, eighteen years before the Richmond Public Guard was formed. *Blind tiger* (1857) possibly takes its name from the saloons in faro gambling establishments a century ago, the game of faro commonly known as "tiger." But it is just as good a guess to say that both names were suggested because cheap whiskey got people *blind drunk*.

blizzard. In its meaning of a severe snowstorm *blizzard* seems to be an Americanism dating back to about 1835. Its direct ancestor is probably the English dialect word *blisser*, meaning the same, but could be the German *blitz*, "lightning, flash." Before *blizzard* meant a storm in America it meant a violent blow of the fist or a crushing remark.

blockhead. Since the 14th century, when hats began to replace hoods as the most popular headware, head-shaped blocks of oak have been standard equipment in the shops of hatmakers. By the time of Henry VIII these *blockheads*, used to shape hats and wigs, had already been compared to simpletons, stupid people whose heads contain no more brains than a block of wood. "Your wit will not so soon out as another man's will," Shakespeare wrote in *Coriolanus*, "'tis strongly wedged up in a block-head."

block of stock. People have been buying *blocks* of stock, a large number of shares in a company, on the stock market since the late 19th century. In fact, a humorous anonymous poem about a block of stock appeared in Carolyn Wells's *A Whimsey Anthology* (1906):

> He bought a little block of stock
> The day he went to town;
> And in the nature of such things,
> That
> Stock
> Went
> Right
> Straight
> Down!

bloke. Word origins can be lost very quickly. *Bloke*, for a "man," "chap," or "guy" (in America) entered the language only in 1839 or so, but no one has been able to establish its ancestors. Suggestions are that it came from the Hindustani *loke* for "man," introduced by the Gypsies into England; that it derives from an old Irish tinker's cry; and that it is from the Dutch *blok*, for "fool." The Celtic *ploc*, "a large, bull-headed person," reinforced by *plocach*, "a strong, coarse person," has its supporters, too. However, the evidence doesn't prove any of these theories. *Bloke* has been in fairly common humorous usage in America since late in the last century, as in "he's a nice bloke."

Blondin. *Blondin* was the stage name of one of the greatest tightrope walkers of all time, the Frenchman Jean Francois Gravelet (1824-1897). The Inimitable Blondin, whose name became a synonym for a star acrobat or tightrope walker, began his career at a mere five years of age and performed many great feats thereafter. The first man to cross Niagara Falls on a tightrope, on June 30, 1859, he later made the crossing while pushing a wheelbarrow, twirling an umbrella, and with another man on his back. The rope was 1,100 feet long, only three inches thick, and was suspended 160 feet above the falls. *Blondin* is still used occasionally to describe an accomplished acrobat or nimble person.

blood is thicker than water. Neither *Bartlett's* nor the *Oxford Dictionary of Quotations* list it, but *blood is thicker than water* is an old proverb dating back far beyond 1672, when it was first collected in a book of proverbs. It means that one can expect more kindness from family than from strangers, that family relationship has a claim that is generally acknowledged. As Brewer explains: "Water soon evaporates and bears no mark behind; not so blood. So the interest we take in a stranger is thinner and more evanescent than that which we take in a blood relation." It is interesting to note that blood has a specific gravity of 1.06—only slightly thicker than water, which has a specific gravity of 1.00!

bloody. Partridge's *Words!* has a two-thousand-word essay on *bloody*, which has been an objectionable adjective in Britain since the early 1800s, though it had been respectable enough for a century before. Meaning "very," it may have become objectionable because it suggested menstruation, or suggested the profanity "By'r Lady"—many plausible and implausible suggestions have been made. But *Partridge* believed that "the idea of blood suffices" to explain the squeamishness. *Bloody* is often inserted for emphasis within words, as in *abso-bloody-lutely*.

bloody hand of Ulster. (*See* red hand of Ulster.)

bloomers. *Bloomers* take their name from early feminist Amelia Jenks Bloomer (1818-94), who did not invent them as is often stated. *Bloomers* were originally billowing Turkish pantaloons, bound with elastic around the ankles and covered by a short skirt and loose-fitting tunic, a kind of pants suit of the 19th century. They were designed and first worn in 1850 by Mrs. Elizabeth Smith Miller, daughter of the wealthy abolitionist, Gerrit Smith, but Mrs. Bloomer defended the masculine pantaloons with the same vehemence as their detractors and it is her name that they immortalize. Editor of *The Lily*, the house organ of a temperance society, Mrs. Bloomer was an ardent feminist who demanded that the word "obey" be omitted from the marriage vows when she wed. She wore Mrs. Miller's new costume on lecture platforms across the country, insisting that fashionable hoopskirts were both cumbersome and unsanitary, picking up dust and mud on the then largely unpaved American streets. When preachers banned women wearing *bloomers* from church, threatening excommunication and pointing out that the Bible forbids a woman donning anything that pertains to a man (Deut. 22:5), she reminded her religious critics that Genesis made no distinction between the fig leaves of Adam and Eve. Mrs. Bloomer even inspired a troop of Bloomer Girls to sail to England, where they were generally met with laughter or indignation, and her proselytizing, coupled with the fact that the pantaloons "bloomed out" so, made the appellation *bloomers* stick in the public mind.

blossom; flower. In Anglo-Saxon times the word for flower was *blossom*, this changing after the Normans conquered England in 1066 and their *fleur* became the English *flower*. However, both words have the same common ancestor—the ancient Indo-European *blo*, which eventually yielded both *blossom* and *flower*.

blow a fuse. Meaning to explode in anger, this expression, first recorded in 1945, was probably suggested by *to have a short fuse* (q.v.). The *fuse* here, however, is the one in a house's fuse box controlling the electricity.

blowhard. (*See* **blow your own horn.**)

blow off steam. The diesels that have replaced steam engines have robbed us of the literal basis for this metaphor, but it's still widely used. To *blow off* or *let off steam* is to have an emotional outburst, a psychological safety valve. This is reflected in the origins of the term, which goes back to the 1830s. Early steam locomotives had no safety valves and when steam pressure built too high in an engine, the engineer had to pull a handlever to blow off steam to prevent an explosion. The angry looking engine blowing off steam to save itself quickly suggested the colorful metaphor.

blow one's top. For several centuries *blow* has been used in the sense of a violent explosion of temper, and for just as long *top* has meant the top of the head. Yet somehow the expression to *blow one's top* didn't enter the language until about the time of the Great Depression. There have been attempts to link it with the top of a volcano erupting, but the phrase seems to have come down the road to general speech via the offtrail slang of jazz musicians. *Mencken* alludes to its "blushful" sexual origin, but doesn't explain further, probably meaning ejaculation of the male organ.

to blow someone's mind. This was originally an expression employed by drug users, comparing the effect of a drug on the mind to an explosive that blows something up. From this 1960s usage the words came to mean "to experience, or cause someone to experience, great mental excitement."

blow your own horn. The term *blowhard*, for "a braggart," can be traced back to the American West in about 1855. To *blow your own horn*, or "to promote yourself," derives from a much older expression, *to blow your own trumpet*, which goes as far back as 1576. Such "hornblowing" may have its origins in medieval times, when heralds blew their trumpets to announce the arrival of royalty but commoners such as street vendors had to blow their own horns.

blucher boots. This half boot has evolved into today's basic, low-cut men's shoes. Originally laced low boots or high shoes, *bluchers* were named for Gebhard Leberecht von Blucher (1742-1819), a Prussian field marshal who fought with Wellington against Napoleon at Waterloo. Field Marshal von Blucher did not design but sponsored the boots in 1810, considering them better footwear for his troops. Another word commemorating him was the British slang expression *Blucher*, for a cab allowed to take passengers to London stations only after all others had been hired—in allusion to the fact that the old man had arrived at Waterloo too late to be of much help!

blue; blue movies; blue laws. A series of off-color French books called *La Bibliothèque Bleu* contributed to the coining of the word *blue* for obscene, as in pornographic *blue movies*, as did the customary blue dress of prostitutes in the early 19th century when the books were written. *Blue laws*, which might repress *blue movies*, has an entirely different derivation. The term usually means Never-On-Sunday moral laws and may take its name from a nonexistent Connecticut "blue book" rumored to contain fanatical laws. The vengeful rumor was spread by the Reverend Samuel Peters, an American Tory who returned to England after the Revolution. Peters claimed that the fictitious blue-bound book contained laws prohibiting such activities as kissing one's wife on Sunday.

bluebacks. (*See* **greenbacks.**)

Bluebeard. Many of the most famous fairy tales, including "Sleeping Beauty," "Red Riding Hood," "Puss in Boots" and "Cinderella," were collected by Charles Perrault and published in his *Contes du Temps* (1697). Among them was "Barbe Bleue" ("Blue Beard"), in which a sadistic indigo-bearded wife killer is foiled when his last wife, Fatima, discovers the bodies of her predecessors in a secret, locked room and is saved from death herself by her brothers' arrival in the nick of time. According to local tradition in Brittany, the real *Bluebeard* upon whom the story is based was the monstrous Frenchman General Gilles de Retz, the Marquis de Laval, who murdered six of his seven wives and was burned at the stake for his crimes in 1440. But similar stories are common to many languages and other candidates have been nominated as well. A *Bluebeard* has come to mean a man who murders women he has married, and a number of contemporary wife killers, especially the Frenchman Henri Desire Landru, have been called "The Modern Bluebeard."

blue blood; blue-brick.   The warriors of Islam called the Moors (or, more poetically, by the lyrical name Black-amoors) ruled over most of Spain for five centuries. Toward the end of their rule the Spanish aristocrats of Castile began to distinguish themselves from these darker skinned people by adopting the name *sangre azul*, "blue blood," to describe themselves. The expression simply refers to the fact that these nobles had lighter complexions than the Moors and that the veins in their skin showed up a vivid blue. Pure Castilians became known as *blue bloods* and the term was borrowed to describe European noblemen of other countries. Today, the British make use of the expression in an interesting way. Universities with the highest prestige and pedigrees, like Cambridge and Oxford, are called *blue-brick* universities.

blue-chip stocks.   The most valuable counters in poker are the blue chips. Since the early 1900s Wall Street, borrowing the expression from another world of gambling, has called secure, relatively high-yielding stocks *blue-chip stocks*. Among the earliest terms for worthless or speculative stocks is "cats and dogs," first recorded in 1879.

bluegrass.   The *bluegrass* used so widely for American lawns isn't very blue, having only a slightly blue tinge at most. The green grass takes its name from another grass, a pest grass that settlers on the Atlantic coast so named because its leaves were distinctly bluish in color. When these settlers moved into what is now Kentucky they found another grass of about the same size and shape as the bluegrass previously discovered and gave it the same name. *Bluegrass music* is U.S. country music played on unamplified stringed instruments, with emphasis on the banjo.

blue jeans.   In the late 16th century the cotton cloth used to make jeans was called *Genoa fustian* after Genoa, Italy, where it was first woven. *Genoa* was shortened to *Gene* and then *Jean* by Englishmen, fustian was dropped, and the men's work pants made from the material were called *blue jeans* for their color—all this centuries before they reached their present popularity.

blue laws.   (*See* **blue**.)

blue lights.   *Blue lights* became an Americanism for traitors during the War of 1812 when on December 12, 1813 pro-British Americans flashed *blue lights* to British ships off the coast as a signal that Commodore Stephen Decatur's two frigates would soon be sailing from their New London, Connecticut harbor. Acting on this information, the British blockaded the port.

blue movies.   (*See* **blue**.)

bluenose.   The term *bluenose* to describe a person of rigid puritanical habits was first applied to lumbermen and fishermen of northern New England and referred to the color of their noses, the blue induced by long exposure to cold weather. Only later was the word applied to the aristocratic inhabitants of Boston's Back Bay area in the sense that we know it today, possibly in alluding to their apparently "frigid" manner. *Bluenose* is also used as an opprobrious nickname for Nova Scotians, but there the word probably derives from the name of a popular Nova Scotian potato.

blue-nose certificate.   The *blue-nose certificate* was an illuminated diploma once awarded aboard British vessels to those who had crossed a meridian north of the Arctic Circle, the "blue-nose" referring, of course to the cold. The certificate is no longer awarded.

blue peter.   On ships ready to leave port, a signal flag called the *blue peter* is raised to call all crew members aboard and to notify everyone in port that all money claims must be settled because the ship is departing. The flag is blue with a white square in the center. Why the *peter* in the term? It may be a corruption of the French *partir*, "to depart," while most consider it to be a telescoping of the word *repeater*. The flag may have originally been used as a "repeater flag," a signal hoisted to indicate that a message from another ship hadn't been read and should be repeated.

blue ribbon; cordon bleu.   Britain's highest order of knighthood is the Most Noble Order of the Garter, which has as its badge a dark blue velvet ribbon edged with gold that is worn below the left knee. Inscribed on the ribbon in gold is the motto *Honi soit qui mal y pense* ("*Shame to him who thinks evil of it*"). Popular legend says that these words and the name of the order result from the gallantry of King Edward III—the king was dancing with the Countess of Salisbury at a royal ball and when she lost her garter, he retrieved it and slipped it on his own leg to save her embarrassment, uttering the famous words. In any case, Edward III instituted the award in about 1344 and the blue ribbon awarded with it came to symbolize the highest honor in any field of endeavor. The French *cordon bleu* ("blue ribbon"), a decoration suspended on a blue ribbon, also influenced the term's meaning. Under the Bourbons it was the highest order of knighthood in France and was later used to honor great chefs.

blues; blue devils.   *Blues*, for a state of depression or despair, is probably a shortening of the 18th-century expression *blue devils*, or low spirits. Surprisingly, Washington Irving first used the term in *Salmagundi* as far back as 1807: "[He] concluded his harangue with a sigh, and I saw that he was still under the influence of a whole legion of the blues." Later *blue devils* became the hallucinations associated with the D.T.'s, or delirium tremens, and a *blue devil* is now drug users' slang for sodium amytal, suggested by the color of the capsule and the narcotic's effects. *Blue devils, blue, blue-eyed,* and *blue around the gills* all have meant drunk in one way or another, possibly because blue is the color of approaching death and they are all associated with the last of the *seven stages of drunkenness*: verbose, grandiose, amicose, bellicose, morose, stuporous, and comatose. This would also explain the linking of *blues* with depression. *The blues*, toward the end of the 19th century, gave their name to the melancholy jazz music called *the blues*, deriving in part from sad black prison and funeral songs of slavery and oppression.

blue-sky laws. These are American state laws regulating the sale of securities, especially laws designed to inhibit the promotion of fraudulent stocks. Kansas, in 1912, enacted the first law so described by the press as protection against unscrupulous land promoters. Behind the words is the idea that suckers will buy even the blue sky from con artists or that "blue-sky" land or securities lack substance, like cloudless blue skies.

bluestockings. Only one of the original *bluestockings* wore homely blue stockings, and he was a man, a Mr. Benjamin Stillingfleet. The group was founded by Mrs. Elizabeth Montagu in about 1750 as a kind of literary salon based on Parisian models. Leading intellectuals of the era gave talks at Mrs. Montagu's London home and conventional evenings of card-playing were replaced by intellectual discussions. All of the club members dressed simply as a reaction against the ostentatious evening clothes of the time, but only the one male member wore blue-gray tradesman's hose in place of gentleman's black silk hose. Nevertheless, a contemporary wit twisted the fact and called all these intellectual ladies *bluestockings*, the word coming to mean a dowdy, affected literary lady, even though Mrs. Montagu was a beautiful woman and an author whose work was highly praised by Dr. Johnson. These early feminists were held in contempt by "proper ladies" of the time, but male chauvinists were most vehement about them. "A bluestocking," said Rousseau, "is a woman who will remain a spinster as long as there are sensible men on earth."

blue streak. (*See* **talk a blue streak**.)

blue-water sailor. This is a complimentary term for a sailor who customarily sails in the "deep (blue) sea" as opposed to safer coastal waters; it probably dates back to the mid-18th century.

bluff. Mathew's *Dictionary of Americanisms* records *bluff*, origin unknown, as the term for a riverbank as early as 1687, referring to a "Bluffe" in South Carolina. According to Stuart Berg Flexner, in *I Hear America Talking* (1976), this is a historical curiosity, the very first of what would be a long list of Americanisms that the British termed "barbarous." In poker *to bluff* is to deceive an opponent about the strength of one's hand by betting heavily on it. This *bluff* probably derives from the German *bluffen*, "to frighten by menacing conduct." Early names for poker, recorded in 1838, were *bluff* and *brag*. From poker also comes the expression *to call one's bluff*.

blunderbuss. The Dutch gave the name *dunderbluss* ("thunder tube") to this short musket with a wide bore and expanded muzzle, which they used to scatter shots at close range. But the English, who adopted it in the 17th century, soon learned that it was an erratic weapon, changed its name to *blunderbuss*, and applied the word to "a blundering, stupid person" as well.

blurb. Humorist Gelett Burgess invented *blurb* in 1907 with the publication of his *Are You a Bromide?* Burgess's publisher, B. W. Huebsch, later told the story: "It is the custom of publishers to present copies of a conspicuous current book to booksellers attending the annual dinner of their trade association, and as this little book was in its heyday when the meeting took place I gave it to 500 guests. These copies were differentiated from the regular edition by the addition of a comic bookplate drawn by the author and by a special jacket which he devised. It was the common practice to print the picture of a damsel—languishing, heroic, coquettish . . . on the jacket of every novel, so Burgess lifted from a Lydia Pinkham or tooth-powder advertisement the portrait of a sickly sweet young woman, painted in some gleaming teeth, and otherwise enhanced her pulchritude, and placed her in the center of the jacket. His accompanying text was some nonsense about 'Miss Belinda *Blurb*,' and thus the term supplied a real need and became a fixture in our language."

B.O. Lifebuoy Health Soap, better known as Lifebuoy, ran its first "Lifebuoy stops B———O" advertisements (with a two-note foghorn warning accompanying the B.O.) on the radio in 1933. Since then B.O. has become synonymous with *bad* body odor, though it is of course an abbreviation of *body odor*, which isn't necessarily bad.

bob. It has been suggested that this British slang word for a shilling, familiar to all English-speaking peoples, may come from the name of Sir Robert (Bob) Walpole (1676-1745). The first Earl of Walpole was intimately connected with money in his posts as army paymaster, first commissioner of the treasury, chancellor of the Exchequer, and finally as England's Prime Minister. But the word *bob* isn't recorded until about 1810, some sixty-five years after Walpole's death, and so the derivation remains uncertain.

bobadil.   Ben Jonson's play *Every Man in His Humor* (1598) gave us the character Captain Bobadill, an old soldier who gravely boasts of his conquests and is proved as vain and cowardly as he is boastful. From the old soldier's name we have the word *bobadil,* "a braggart who pretends to great prowess." Johnson patterned his character on Boabdil, a late 15th-century Moorish king of Granada. King Boabdil was noted for the same characteristics as the fictional captain.

bobby; peelers; robert.   *Bobby* is among the most familiar of eponymous words, despite the fact that "copper" or "cop" is more often used today to describe an English policeman. The well-known word honors Sir Robert Peel, British Home Secretary (1828-30) when the Metropolitan Police Act remodeled London's police force. Peel, whose wealthy father bought him his seat in Parliament, as was customary in those days, first won fame as chief secretary for Ireland, where he was nicknamed "Orange Peel" for his support of the Protestant "orangemen." It was at this time that he established the Irish constabulary under The Peace Preservation Act (1814), and his policemen were soon called "Peel's Bloody Gang" and then *peelers. Peelers* remained the name for both Irish and London police for many years, *bobby* and *robert* not being recorded in print until about 1851.

bob ruly.   American pioneers called a burned out area a *bob ruly,* which leads some to think that the term might have been named after a notorious firebug of old. But *bob ruly,* first recorded in 1848, though older, is just how the French words *bois brule,* "burned woods," sounded to American ears.

bock beer; lager beer.   Beer drinkers who favor this strong, dark Bavarian lager beer, which is usually brewed in the autumn and aged through the winter, may be surprised to learn that it takes its name from the German word for buck, or male goat—"because of its great strength making its consumers prance and tumble like these animals." *Bock beer* comes from the German *Eimbockbier,* "buck beer from Eimbeck" in Lower Saxony, Germany. A *lager beer* is a beer that, like *bock beer,* has been "bedded-down" in a storehouse for aging, *lager* simply meaning the German for "bed or resting place."

bodkin.   *Bodkin's* origin is uncertain, but it may derive from an unknown Celtic word, or be the corruption of a Gaelic word for "little dagger." A *bodkin* was once a stiletto worn by ladies in their up-swept hair and this is probably the weapon Shakespeare refers to in the famous passage from *Hamlet*: "When he himself might his quietus make with a bare bodkin." (See **quietus.**)

bodock; Osage orange.   *Bodock* is another name for the Osage orange tree (*Maclura pomifera*). It is so called

because the Indians used its wood for making bows and the French thus called it the *bois d'arc* ("bowwood") tree, which became corrupted in English to *bodock.* It is called the *Osage orange* because it grew in Osage Indian country and has large, rough-skinned greenish fruits somewhat suggestive of an orange, but inedible. The spiny-branched tree is often used for hedges and called the Osage thorn. It is first recorded, in 1804, by the Lewis and Clark expedition, as the Osage Apple.

Boeotians.   This is among the oldest of the many words dishonoring an entire people. Meaning ignorant, dull, and lacking in refinement, *Boeotian* recalls the inhabitants of *Boeotia,* a farming district in ancient Greece, whom the urbane Athenians found thick and stupid, with no understanding of art or literature. In truth, as Homer and other knowledgeable Greeks noted, the region produced Pindar and Plutarch as well as country bumpkins. *Boeotian* is also used in terms like "Boeotian ears," ears unable to appreciate good music or poetry.

bogard.   (*See* **don't bogard that joint, Bogard.**)

bogey.   *Bogey,* a word for "an imaginary or real thing that causes fear or worry," may be just a dialectical form of the old word *bug,* "ghost or specter," and it gives us both the *bogeyman* used to scare children and the golf term *bogey,* one stroke over par, which arose from a popular 1890 song called "Coloney Bogey." This latter term at first meant "par" in England, because Colonel Bogey's name was adopted by golfers to signify a fictitious gentleman who could play a course or hole in the lowest number of strokes that a good golfer could play it in. American golfers, satisfied with "par" to express the British meaning of *bogey,* made Colonel Bogey something of a duffer.

bogus.   Most theories about the word *bogus,* meaning "fake or spurious," relate it to some form of bogey, in its sense of an imaginary or false thing. One version claims the word can be traced to May 1827 when the Painsville, Ohio *Telegraph* ran a story about a gang of counterfeiters whose fake coins were so perfect that they were compared to the work of some supernatural bogeyman. Another says the word comes from the name of a device called a *bogus,* used for counterfeiting coins in the same state in the same year, connecting this machine with "tantra-bogus," an old Vermont term for bogeyman. Complicating matters is the fact that the first use of *bogus* isn't recorded until 1838. Although it is certainly possible that the word was in use ten years or so before it appeared in print, another derivation traces it to a counterfeiter who was operating at exactly the time *bogus* was first recorded. "The word *bogus,*" according to a *Boston Courier* of 1857, "is a corruption of the name Borghese, a man who, twenty years ago, did a tremendous business in supplying the Great West of America with counterfeit bills on fictitious banks. The western people came to shortening the name Borghese to *bogus*, and his bills were universally styled 'bogus currency.'" However, there is still another theory that suggests a direct passage from *boghus*, a gypsy word for counterfeit coin. More than one of these speculations has to be *bogus*.

Bohemian. *Bohemian* was first used as a synonym for a gypsy or vagabond during the Middle Ages, people mistakenly believing that the gypsy tribes entered the West via the ancient kingdom of Bohemia. *Bohemian* became synonymous with a poor writer or artist with French novelist Henri Murder's stories in *Scenes de la Vie de Bohème* (1848), his book providing the basis for Puccini's opera *La Bohème*. The English novelist William Makepeace Thackeray made the word a synonym for a nonconforming artist in *Vanity Fair* (1848) when he wrote of his headstrong heroine Becky Sharp: "She was of a wild, roving nature, inherited from her father and mother, who were both Bohemian by taste and circumstance."

bohunk. (*See* **honkie**.)

Bolivia; Boliviano; Bolivar. Commemorative of Simon Bolivar (1783-1830), the legendary South American revolutionary, soldier, and statesman, are the *bolivar* monetary unit of Venezuela and the *boliviano* of *Bolivia*. Simon Bolivar, the Liberator, led Venezuela's revolution against Spain and founded Greater Colombia (then a union consisting of Venezuela, Ecuador, and New Granada, the present-day Colombia). He is one of the few men in history to have a country named after him in his lifetime and probably the only one to create and give that same country its constitution. *Bolivia*, or Upper Peru as it was then known, was first named *Republica Bolivar* in the great soldier and statesman's honor.

boll weevil. *Weevil* comes from the Old English *wifel*, "beetle," and *boll*, first spelled *bowl*, refers to the pod of the cotton plant, which the beetle attacks. In Enterprise, Alabama there is a monument to a *boll weevil*—erected at the turn of the century after the beetle so devastated the cotton crop in the area that farmers were forced to plant peanuts, and as a result became more prosperous than they ever had been as cotton growers. (*See also* **gull**.)

bolo. Paul Bolo, a French traitor popularly known as Bolo Pasha, faced a firing squad in 1917, having been convicted of treason the previous year. *Bolo*, though now generally a historical term, saw extensive use during World War I in describing a traitor, fifth columnist, or spy, someone working underground for the enemy. Bolo's treason consisted principally of spreading pacifist propaganda financed by the Germans.

boloney. Al Smith, governor of New York and unsuccessful presidential candidate in 1928, helped popularize this expression with his remark "No matter how you slice it, it's still baloney." But *boloney* for "bunk" dates back to at least the early 20th century, bologna sausage having been pronounced *boloney* as early as the 1870s, when there was a popular song "I Ate the Boloney." There are those who say that *boloney* for "bunk" has nothing to do with bologna sausage, however, tracing it to a corruption of the Spanish *pelone*, "testicles," and claiming that this meant "nonsense" or "bunk" just as "balls," "all balls," and "nerts" did. The word is also spelt *baloney*.

Bolshevik; Menshivik. Synonymous today for an agitator or radical reformer, *bolshevik* originally signified the left wing of the Russian Social Democratic Party, the designation evolving from a party conference in 1902 when the majority (*Bolshevik*), accepted the views of Nikolai Lenin. The vote was close (25-23), and behind the tactical issues involved lay great differences—such as the minority belief that revolution in Russia should be gradual in contrast to Lenin's insistence that there be an immediate overthrow of the czarist regime. In 1917, the Bolsheviks again gained a majority in the Socialist party congress, though not in Russia itself, and simultaneously overthrew the existing Russian government. Ironically, it was Lenin's view that the Bolsheviks (the majority party) should be composed of a small select minority rather than the masses. "Bolshie," for an agitator, is simply a corruption of *bolshevik*. The Menshiviks (from the Russian *menshiviki*) were the members of the minority in the Russian Socialist party, who favored a more gradual transition to communism.

bolt from the blue. (*See* **talk a blue streak**.)

bomb. *Bomb*, in reference to theatrical productions, has completely opposite meanings in England and America. When a play *bombs* in America it is a complete flop—a *bomb*. When a play *bombs* in England it is a great success—a *bomb*. The British use seems to be built on the explosive force of a real bomb, while the American usage is based upon the destruction a bomb creates. The word *bomb* derives ultimately from the Latin *bombus*, "a booming sound."

bombast. *Bombast* was cotton used as a padding or stuffing for clothes in days past, the word deriving from the word *bombyx*, for "silkworm or silk," which was applied to cotton as well. Just as stuffing or padding in clothing was called *bombast* so was padded, stuffed, inflated, grandiose speech—this figurative use of *bombast* being first recorded in 1589, not long after the word was first used in its literal sense. Write off as entertaining but untrue the old story that *bombast* for inflated speech on trivial subjects comes from the real name of the egotistical Swiss physician, alchemist, and writer Paracelsus (1493?-1541)—Theophrastus Bombastus von Hohenheim.

bombazine. (*See* **bamboozle**.)

bonanza. *Bonanza*, a rich body of gold or silver ore in a mine, or any rich strike, began life as a Spanish word meaning "fair weather at sea." Miners in California probably learned the word from seamen, who also used it to mean prosperity in general, and applied *bonanza* to any rich vein of ore.

Bonaparte's gull; Zenadia bird. *Bonaparte's gull*, one of only two black-headed species in the United States, was described scientifically for the first time in Prince Charles Lucien Bonaparte's *American Ornithology*. Bonaparte, Napoleon's nephew, resided in this country from 1824 to 1833. The gull bearing the naturalist's name breeds hundreds of miles from the sea, becoming a seabird in winter, and inland bird-watchers consider it a harbinger of spring. *Zenadia*, the scientific designation for several species of wild doves and pigeons, is named for Bonaparte's wife, Princess Zenaide.

bon-bon. *Bon-bon* means "good, good" in French and the name was probably given to candies by children, "originating in the nursery," according to the *O.E.D.* The term is first recorded in Thomas Moore's satirical poem "The Fudge Family in Paris" (1818): "The land of Cocaigne . . ./ Where for hail they have bon-bons, and claret for rain."

bond. (*See* **stocks and bonds**.)

bond paper. In the early 1800s a Boston, Massachusetts paper mill made a desirable all-rag paper that was widely used for printing bonds, bank notes, and legal documents. People began to call it *bond paper* when ordering it, and the expression soon was applied to any high-quality paper.

bone; bone up on. Bones were once used to polish shoes, and some scholars have attempted to link such bones to the expression *to bone up on* a subject, to study it hard and thoroughly, especially for an exam. One would then "polish up" his knowledge, presumably, but bones probably have nothing to do with this term. It was first used in the 1860s by collegians, and they apparently first spelled the *bone* in the phrase *Bohn*, probably referring to the Bohn translations of the classics, or "trots," that they used in studying. British scholar Henry George Bohn (1796-1884) was the author and publisher of many books, including the "Classical Library."

bonehead play; pulling a boner. The original *bonehead play* was made on September 9, 1908 by Fred Merkle,

New York Giants first baseman. It was the last of the ninth, two out, and the Giants had Moose McCormick on third and Merkle on first. The next man up singled to center and McCormick scored the winning run, but Merkle ran into the dugout instead of touching second base. Johnny Evers of the Cubs got the ball and stepped on second, forcing out Merkle. The winning run was nullified and the game not counted in the standings. Merkle's play became all the more important later in the season when the Cubs and Giants finished tied for first place and the Cubs won the pennant in a playoff game. Though *boneheaded* had been used in the sense of "stupid" a few years earlier, it was a sportswriter's use of *bonehead play* in reference to Merkle's blunder that introduced the phrase to the language, along with the related *to pull a boner*.

boner. (*See* **bonehead play**.)

a bone to pick. It has been suggested that this expression arose from "an old Sicilian custom" where the father of the bride gave "the bridegroom a bone to pick clean as a symbol of the difficult task of marriage that he was undertaking." If such a custom exists, it has nothing to do with the phrase, which in modern usage means to have an argument to settle with someone. The expression, though its meaning has varied over the years, is some four centuries old and was probably suggested by two dogs fighting over a single bone tossed between them—"a bone of contention"—or by a dog preoccupied with a bone, which suggested the phrase's original meaning of "to mull over something." The idea is conveyed in several earlier phrases common to English and other languages.

bonfire. A pagan festival held in England during the summer was celebrated by burning in huge heaps the bones of cattle and sheep that had been saved during the year. These "bone fires" continued into the Christian era, when they were celebrated on June 24th, St. John's Day, and were held up until two centuries ago in parts of the British Isles. But by the 16th century a *bonefire*, corrupted to *bonfire*, was being used to mean any large outdoor fire.

boniface. Innkeepers are called *Bonifaces* after Will Boniface, a character in George Farquhar's comedy *The Beaux' Stratagem* (1707). Will Boniface is the landlord of an inn in Lichfield, a pleasant old man of 85 with a comic tongue who loves his ale. (*See* **Lady Bountiful**.)

bonne-bouche. An English term since the 18th century, *bonne-bouche* means "a dainty or tasty mouthful or morsel." It comes from the French *bonne-bouche* (*bonne*, "good" + *bouche*, "mouth"), which means "a pleasing taste in the mouth" in that language. French for a dainty morsel would be *morceau qui fait ou donne bonne bouche*.

bonnet. Back in the 14th century, when the word is first recorded, a *bonnet* wasn't a woman's hat but a brimless man's hat, its name deriving from the Old French *bonnet*. ("Off goes his bonnet to an Oyster-wench," Shakespeare wrote in *Richard III*.) It was over a century before *bonnet* meant a headdress exclusively for women.

bonus. Those who have received a bonus for an outstanding piece of work will understand the derivation of the word, for bonus derives from the Latin *bonum*, "a good thing." According to the best conjecture, the term originated as a pun on the classical Latin word early in the 17th century among London stock market traders.

boo. "Boo is a corruption of *Boh*, the name of a terrible Gothic general whose gross brutalities struck terror among his enemies," swears one old source. "It was early used to conjure fear among stubborn children." I like this story as well as the next person, but there is no proof for it. Unfortunately, the *boo!* used to startle someone, first recorded in about 1430, is probably just a loud startling sound—Latin had a similar exclamation, *bo-are!* The O.E.D. claims that the *boo* used to express disapproval, as in *booing*, is a sound imitating the lowing of oxen. It is first recorded in about 1800.

booby; booby trap; booby hatch. *Booby*, for "a dunce, a nincompoop," is recorded in English as far back as 1599, probably deriving from the Spanish *bobo*, "a fool," which in turn, may come from the Latin *balbus*, "stammering." It explains later expressions such as *booby prize* (ca. 1900), "a prize of little value given to the loser of a game," and *booby-trap* (ca. 1850), "a trap set for fools." The last originally described practical jokes played by English schoolboys (balancing a pail of water atop a door that a *booby* would open, etc.), but in World War I *booby traps* became lethal explosive devices, killing wise men and poets as well as fools. "Booby hatch," for an insane asylum, may have its beginnings in the "booby hatch," a police wagon used to carry criminals to jail. This term can be traced back to 1776 and certainly some of the criminals confined (for a short time, anyway) in booby hatches were deranged. Further, a "booby-hutch" was a police cell in the late 19th century—before some unknown American wit coined *booby hatch*. The term may have been suggested, however, simply from the idea of *boobies* confined and crammed under a hatch in some snake pit of an early insane asylum.

boodle. The Dutch in the New World called a bundle of paper money or a sack of gold a *boedal*, which served as the term for any property, goods, or effects. The word's spelling gradually became *boodle* and it was used as underworld slang for counterfeit money and graft or bribery money, later becoming slang for a large bundle of money or money in general, with no implication of dishonesty.

boohoo. *Boohoo*, first recorded in 1525, originally expressed weeping or laughter. (Thackeray wrote that one of his characters "burst into a boohoo of laughter.") The imitative word is today applied only to crying. American humorist Thomas Haliburton made a verb of the word, *to boohoo*, to weep noisily, in 1837.

book; folio; bible; bibliography; volume; code. Smooth-skinned beech trees have always been the favorite of lovers carving their names or initials inside a heart. The outer bark of the beech and slabs of its thin, inner bark were also the first writing materials used by Anglo-Saxon scribes. Saxons called the beech the *boc* and also applied this name to their bound writings made from slabs of beech, the word becoming *book* after many centuries of spelling changes. Numerous terms for things related to writing come from the names of raw material. *Folio*, now a book of the largest size, is from the Latin word *folium*, "a tree leaf," which also gives us the word *foliage*. *Bible* and related words, such as *bibliography*, derive from the Greek *biblos*, "the inner bark of papyrus." *Volume* is from the Latin *volumen*, which meant "a roll of papyrus manuscript"; and *code*, a system of laws, etc., is from the Latin *codex*, "the trunk of a tree," from which wooden tablets were made to write codes upon.

book burner. The term *book burner*, meaning "self-appointed censor" and worse, didn't arrive until 1933 when thousands of pro-Nazi students ended a torchlight parade at the University of Berlin by burning a pile of 20,000 books while Nazi propaganda minister Joseph Goebbels proclaimed: "The soul of the German people can express itself. These flames . . . illuminate the . . . end of an old era and light up the new." But the first mass *book burners* in American history were, oddly enough, the anti-mail-order small merchants at the turn of the century who burned mail-order catalogs to censor not the free expression of ideas, but free enterprise. Local merchants persuaded or arm-twisted people into tossing their catalogs into a bonfire in the public square every Saturday night. Prizes of up to fifty dollars were offered to those who brought in the greatest number of catalogs to be burned. This practice seemingly descended to its nadir in a small Montana town where a movie theater gave free admission or ten cents to any child who turned over a catalog to town authorities for public burning. Yet the Montana orgy of destruction was repeated in other states, all in the name of insuring a continuance of "freedom of opportunity in America."

bookworm. *Bookworms* are literally the larvae or adults of various insects, moths, and beetles that live in and feed upon the pages and bindings of books. No single species can properly be called the bookworm, but the little beetle *anolium*, silverfishes (order *Thysanura*) and book lice (order *Psocoptera*) are widely known by the name. The human of the bookworm species also lives in and feeds upon the pages of books, but doesn't usually destroy them. Human *bookworms* have been scorned since before Ben Jonson wrote of a "whoreson book-worm." Authors especially are fools to be contemptuous of bookworms, but from Elizabethan times to the present few scriveners have had anything good to say about them.

boomerang. *Boomerang* is another loan word from Australia's Aboriginals (like "kangaroo," "dingo," "koala," and "wombat"). Captain Cook noticed the native weapon on his voyages to Australia but did not record its name, which is first mentioned in 1798 in an account of Aboriginal weapons.

boondocks. *Bundok* is the word for "mountain" in Tagalog, the Indonesian language of the Philippines. But during the U.S. occupation there, American soldiers extended its meaning to include any rough back country with wild terrain difficult for troops to penetrate, corrupting the word to *boondocks* in the process. After World War II, Marines brought *boondocks* home with them and it became the name for difficult terrain on the fringes of training camps, where recruits were often taken on long bivouacs. These remote areas naturally suggested the "sticks," rural areas where there is similarly little to do but work and be bored, and *boondocks* began to be applied to them as well. The word is most frequently heard in the expression *out in the boondocks*, way out in the sticks.

boondoggles. One dictionary defines *boondoggles* as: "Useless, wasteful tasks, 'make-work' projects that are often performed by recipients of a government dole." The word was employed in 1929 by Scoutmaster Robert Link of Rochester, New York, who applied it to the braided leather lanyards made and worn around the neck as a decoration by Boy Scouts. Under the New Deal during the Great Depression, the term was transferred to the relief work for the unemployed that some people, not out of work themselves, thought was as useless as making lanyards, and soon *boondoggling* meant to do any work of no practical value merely to keep or look busy. Before Scoutmaster Link applied *boondoggle* to lanyards it had been a word for a belt, knife sheath, or other product of simple manual skill, and in Scottish dialect it means a marble that you get as a gift, without winning it. The yarn about *boondoggle* being suggested by Daniel Boone idly whittling sticks to throw to his dog does convey the sense of the word, but it is just another spurious tale.

booster. Sinclair Lewis's Babbitt was a *booster* who wore a Booster Club button in his lapel. But Lewis didn't invent the term in his novel. This term for an enthusiastic, often puerile supporter or promoter of a person, team, cause, etc., was born in the American Southwest in about

1890, quickly spreading throughout the country, and has its roots in the verb to boost.

boot camp. U.S. sailors serving during the Spanish-American War wore leggings called *boots*, which came to mean "a navy (or marine) recruit." These recruits trained in what were called *boot camps*.

bootlegger. *Bootleggers* got the name because they smuggled illegal whiskey in the legs of their tall boots. The word originated in about 1850, at least seventy years before Prohibition. Today a *bootleg* is a football ploy in which the quarterback fakes a handoff and hides the ball on his hip, running with it himself.

boots and saddles! Most Americans are familiar with the old western song "Give Me My Boots and My Saddle," but this familiar cavalry call has nothing to do with boots and saddles, as one might suspect. It derives from the old French cavalry command *Boute selle!* ("Put saddle!"), which the British corrupted to *boot and saddle* and which American cavalrymen further corrupted to *boots and saddles!*

booze. Mr. E. G. or E. S. Booze of either Philadelphia or Kentucky, circa 1840, was a distiller who sold his *booze* under his own name, the bottles often made in the shape of log cabins. But *booze* probably has its roots in the Middle English verb *bousen*, "to drink deeply," which comes from an earlier German word. However, the English use *booze* only for beer and ale and there is no doubt that the labels on our Mr. Booze's bottles influenced the American use of the word for hard liquor and strengthened its general use. Today booze most often signifies cheap, even rotgut whiskey.

borax. The real source for the term *borax*, for "cheap furniture, or any cheap and inferior merchandise," is probably not a Yiddish expression used by Jewish immigrants on New York's Lower East Side in the late 19th century, as many sources contend, but the premiums for cheap furniture offered by early manufacturers of borax soap.

Bordeaux. The largest of France's great wine areas, the province of Gironde, surrounds the port city of Bordeaux, after which the elegant red and white wines made there are named.

bored. British actor George Sanders committed suicide, leaving behind a note saying that he had been *bored* by it all. Another worldly Englishman, the poet Lord Byron, used the word *bored* for "wearied, suffering from ennui," in *Don Juan* (1823), in which he wrote:

Society is now one polished horde
Formed of two mighty tribes, the bores and the bored.

Bored is first recorded in 1768, apparently being a figurative use of *to bore*, "to pierce, make a hole through," although the French *bourrer*, "to stuff or pad," has also been suggested.

Borgia; nepotism. Whether any Borgia was ever a poisoner is a matter of dispute, but Lucrezia and Cesare Borgia, children of Pope Alexander VI (1431-1503), were reputed to indulge in such activities. Tradition has it that the Borgias employed some secret deadly poison to eliminate their enemies. Historians have never been able to substantiate this, but "a glass of wine with the Borgias" has long been proverbial for a great but risky honor, and a *Borgia* is still a synonym for a poisoner. There is no doubt that the Borgias were murderers, the family generally a pretty unsavory lot. They are also responsible for the word *nepotism*, this directly from the Latin *nepos*, "a descendant, especially a nephew," coined when Pope Alexander VI filled important church offices with his relations. Among the many family appointments Rodrigo Borgia made were the installing of his son Cesare as an archbishop when the boy was only sixteen, and the bestowing of a cardinal's hat on his young nephew, Giovanni.

born-again Christian. This term for a Christian who has found a renewed commitment to Christ has long been known to evangelists, but came into prominence when U.S. presidential candidate Jimmy Carter described himself as a "born-again Christian." The phrase's source is John 3:3 and 3:7: "Jesus answered and said . . . Except a man be born again, he cannot see the kingdom of God . . . Marvel not that I said unto thee, ye must be born again."

born on the wrong side of the blanket. (*See* **bastard**.)

born on the wrong side of the tracks. This is an American expression, if only because the British designation for a train's roadbed with rails is not the *tracks* but *the line* or *the rails*. It arose in the 19th century when railroad tracks, which sometimes split a town in two, did indeed provide a clear social demarcation—well-to-do people living on the right side of the tracks and the poor living on the wrong side, in the seedy area of town. Today, with the spread of suburbia and exurbia made possible by the automobile, the distance between rich and poor has increased and they tend to live in different towns altogether. But the expression *to be born on the wrong side of the tracks*, to be born poor and disadvantaged, persists despite the anachronism.

born to the purple. From earliest times purple has been the color of kings, especially Tyrian purple, a color yielded by a species of Murex shellfish. But the expression *born to the purple*, or "born of royal parentage," doesn't have its origins in the purple robes of royalty. It really derives from an ancient Byzantine custom that dictated that the empress give birth to her royal child in a lavishly appointed special chamber called the *Porphyra*, whose walls were lined with royal purple, *porphyry*. The Greeks had a word for such a royal birth, *porphyrogenitus* (from *porphyra*, "purple," and *gennetos*, "born"), which translates directly as "born in the purple." Today the expression is *born to the purple*, and it is used to describe anyone of exalted birth, not necessarily royalty, or anyone born rich.

born with the gift of laughter and a sense that the world was mad. These words became famous not because they are from Shakespeare, Milton, or any of the great classical writers of antiquity, but because they were inscribed as a hoax over a door in the Hall of Graduate Studies at Yale University. The line is from contemporary novelist Rafael Sabatini's rousing *Scaramouche*, beloved to generations of romantics, and the full quote, referring to the hero, is "Born with the gift of laughter and the sense that the world was mad, and that was his only patrimony." The words apparently were written on Yale's hallowed walls as the result of a hoax. At least the building's architect, John Donald Tuttle, confessed in a letter to the *New Yorker* (December 8, 1934) that collegiate Gothic repelled him. It is, he wrote, "a type of architecture that had been designed expressly . . . to enable yeomen to pour molten lead through slots on their enemies below. As a propitiatory gift to my gods . . . and to make them forget by appealing to their senses of humor, I carved the inscription over the door." Yale authorities apparently didn't enjoy the joke. After employing medievalists, classical scholars, and Egyptologists to find the source of the quotation, only to learn it was from a mere adventure novelist, they planted the ivy that hides the words today.

borrow. *Borrow* was originally a noun deriving from the Anglo-Saxon *borg* and meaning "a pledge of security." This use of the word became obsolete in England by Spenser's time, but early on *borrow* became a verb meaning "to give security for, to take on pledge." Security is no longer essential in a borrowing transaction, but the idea that what is loaned is the property of the lender and must be returned is still preserved.

bosey; googly. A *bosey* is a cricketing term familiar to Australians but not much used anymore in England, where it originated. The term honors the English bowler, B. J. T. Bosanquet, who popularized the technique known elsewhere as the *googly* when he toured Australia in 1903-04. The *googly* is, according to the *Oxford English Dictionary*, "an off-break ball bowled with leg-break action." There is no popularly known technique in American baseball, basketball, or football named after its player-inventor, so B. J. T. Bosanquet is somewhat unique in the world of sports.

bosh. Meaning "stuff and nonsense," *bosh* came into English from the Turkish word *bosh* for "nothing, empty, worthless." The novelist James Morier introduced the word in a book about Turkish life published in 1834.

bos'n; boatswain. *Bos'n* is a corruption of *boatswain*, the boy ("swain") who took care of the ship's dinghy and summoned its crew. The *boatswain* didn't get his whistle until sometime in the 15th century and wasn't called a *bos'n* for two hundred years more.

boss. Early Americans, independent and democratic, never liked the word "master" with all its aristocratic associations. Late in the 18th century they adopted the Dutch word *baas* meaning the same thing, and were soon spelling it *boss.* By as early as 1838 *boss* had achieved common usage and writers as prominent as James Fenimore Cooper were condemning it as a barbaric vulgarization of the language. Some people think that *boss* as an adjective meaning the best, the greatest, is recent teenage slang, but the word has been used in the same sense since the mid-19th century.

Boston fern. (*See* **Bramley's seedling.**)

bosum bread. These were large, flat loaves of bread that black stevedores working the Mississippi steamboats carried in their shirt fronts (against their chests, or *bosums*) for snacks throughout the day. Such fuel they needed, as these longshoremen expended more energy than almost any other workers at the time. Even today barge workers in the Netherlands consume more calories than any other occupational group, ingesting an average of 5,300 calories a working day.

Boswell; boswellize. "I have a notion," Somerset Maugham once observed, "that it is pleasanter to read Boswell's record of the conversations than it ever was to listen to Dr. Johnson." A *Boswell*, for the ultimate in biographers, honors James Boswell (1740-95), whose *The Life of Samuel Johnson* (1791) is the prototype of biographies. Boswell, born in Scotland, met Dr. Johnson only after numerous rebuffs but became both friend and admirer of the great English man of letters. Over a relatively short period, he recorded in detail Johnson's words and activities. "That Boswell was a vain, intemperate man of dubious morals is of no matter to history," writes one biographer. "He shines in the reflected glory of his great portrait." To *boswellize* means to write biography in the same detailed, intimate and faithful manner as "Bozzy" did.

botanomancy. Botanomancy is divination by leaves. The most popular method was to write sentences on leaves as possible answers to a question. The leaves were then left outside exposed to the wind, and those that weren't blown away were supposed to compose the answer. The practice, and word, dates back to at least the early 17th century.

Botany Bay. Captain James Cook named Botany Bay after the many new botanical specimens he found there on his voyage to Australia in 1770. Later, the inlet's name came to be wrongly applied to a convict settlement at Sydney, and even to the whole of Australia.

both ends against the middle. (*See* **to play both ends against the middle.**)

bottom dollar. (*See* **bet one's bottom dollar.**)

botulism. Why, you ask, does the Latin word for sausage, *botulus*, give us the English word *botulism*, first recorded in 1878, for "a form of food poisoning"? The answer is that the earliest cases of such food poisoning through improperly stored food involved canned sausages.

bougainvillaea. The largest island in the Solomon group, two Pacific straits, and a brilliantly flowering South American vine are all named after the French navigator and adventurer Louis Antoine de Bougainville (1729-1811). Bougainville commanded a French expedition around the world in 1766-69, discovering the Solomon Islands and Tahiti. Naturalists in his party named the woody climbing vine family, of which there are about a dozen known species, *Bougainvillaea* in his honor. Bougainville's descriptions of the natives he encountered on his voyages helped popularize Rousseau's theories on the morality of man in his natural state, especially as concerns sexual freedom. He fought for America during the Revolution, and in his later years Napoleon I made him a senator, count of the empire, and member of the Legion of Honor. The plant named after him is often cultivated in greenhouses, can be raised outside in the southern parts of the United States, and is regarded as the handsomest of tropical vines.

boughten goods. Once common as a participal adjective in the U.S., *boughten* is rarely heard any more, though it is listed in the *O.E.D.* as poetic dialect and an Americanism. *Boughten goods* is sometimes used today as a pseudo-rustic term meaning "manufactured or store bought things that are valued above familiar, homemade ones."

bought the farm. As late as the Vietnam War, soldiers killed in action were said to have *bought the farm.* The expression was inspired by the draftees's dream to go home—in many cases to a peaceful farm, or perhaps to buy a farm—in any case, to settle down somewhere far away from the army and war. "Well, he finally did buy the farm," a friend could say on hearing of the death of such a man, and the expression was used so often that *bought the farm* became an ironic synonym for death. The phrase dates to World War II or earlier.

Boulangism; boulangerite. General Georges Ernest Jean Marie Boulanger (1837-91) won the admiration of all France for his exploits during the Franco-Prussian war. That he was a handsome man who looked impressive astride a horse in parades didn't hurt his image, either. In 1886 Boulanger was made minister of war and insisted that he was the man to retrieve the lost glories of France with doctrines of militarism and reprisal against Germany. For a short time a wave of political frenzy called *Boulangism* swept over France, but the movement came to nothing, the general in reality no Napoleon and his backers largely reactionary elements. Boulanger eventually went into exile, ending his life in Brussels as a suicide.

boulevard. Stroll down a *boulevard* and you are literally strolling down a military rampart or bulwark. The first *boulevard* was a wide promenade made from the old defensive walls encircling Paris. This was called *le boulevard* after the abandoned ramparts it followed, and was soon applied to any similar broad street.

bouncer; checker-out. The American *bouncer*, for "a person who acts as a guard in a disco, nightclub, brothel, or bar, someone who bounces out unruly people," dates back to Civil War days. *Checker-out* is the British term for the same, but it seems to have been coined later, in about 1880.

bourbon. *Bourbon whiskey* takes its name from Bourbon County, Kentucky, named for France's Bourbon kings, and home of the first still that produced it. The word *Bourbon* for a political reactionary also derives from France's Bourbon kings, a dynasty that reigned over two hundred years beginning in 1589, and of whom it was said that they "forgot nothing and learned nothing." *The Dictionary of Americanisms* gives its first use for a political diehard as 1876.

the Bourse. The world's first stock exchange, in Belgium, originated in the 14th century. Few people are aware that it takes its name from the Van der Buerse family in Bruges, at whose house early traders congregated.

Bovarian. (*See* **Madame Bovary**.)

bowdlerize. His inability to stand the sight of human blood and suffering forced Dr. Thomas Bowdler to abandon his medical practice in London, but this weakness apparently did not apply where vendors of words were concerned. Bowdler so thoroughly purged both Shakespeare and Gibbon that they would have screamed in pain from the bloodletting had they been alive—to *bowdlerize* became a synonym for "to radically expurgate or prudishly censor." Thomas Bowdler, the most renowned of self-appointed literary censors, was born at Ashley, near Bath, England on July 11, 1754. After he retired from medicine, a considerable inheritance enabled him to travel about Europe, where he wrote accounts of the Grand Tour that seem to have offended or pleased no one. Though he came from a religious family, Bowdler never earned the "Reverend Doctor" title often applied to him, and his early years are conspicuous for the lack of any real accomplishments, unless one counts membership in organizations like the Society for the Suppression of Vice. Only when he was middle-aged did he retire to the Isle of Wight and begin to sharpen his rusty scalpel on the Bard of Avon's bones. His *Family Shakespeare* was finally published in 1818. In justifying this ten-volume edition, Bowdler explained on the title page that "nothing is added to the text; but those expressions are omitted which cannot without propriety be read aloud in a family," adding later that he had also expunged "Whatever is unfit to be read by a gentleman in a company of ladies." He would probably have turned his scalpel to other great authors if death had not excised him in 1825. About ten years later Bowdler's name was first used as a verb, the official definition then being "to expurgate by omitting or modifying words or passages considered indelicate or offensive." Today the word means "prudish, ridiculous censorship."

bowels of compassion. Though not a common expression anymore, these words are frequently encountered in literature. The phrase itself is given in the King James Bible (I John 3:17), and Shakespeare, Congreve, and other great writers all made use of the ancient idea that the bowels are the seat of misery or compassion in the body—just as the liver was supposed to be the location of courage; the heart of affection and learning (*learn by heart*); the head of understanding; and the spleen of passion. The blunt word *bowel* comes from the Latin *botellus*, little sausage or pudding, a diminutive of the Latin word for sausage, *botulus*. Aside from the expression the *bowels of the earth*, it is heard today mainly in medieval references or in the entreaties of parents toilet-training children. Certainly it isn't associated with compassion anymore, so once-current expressions such as *the bowels of compassion, the bowels of pity, the bowels of Christ,* and *child of my bowels* have all but died.

bowie knife; Arkansas toothpick. One writer defines the *bowie* (pronounced "boo-ie") *knife* as "the principal instrument of nonsurgical phlebotomy in the American Southwest." Sad to say, this lethal instrument was not invented by the legendary Colonel James Bowie (1796-1836), friend of Davy Crockett and hero at the Alamo. According to testimony by a daughter of Rezin Pleasant

Bowie, the colonel's older brother, it was her father who invented the knife in about 1827, though Jim Bowie did make it famous in a duel that year at Natchez, Mississippi, in which six men were killed and fifteen wounded. The common long-bladed hunting knife was originally made at Rezin Bowie's direction by a Louisiana blacksmith, who ground a large file to razor sharpness and attached a guard between the blade and handle to protect the user's hand. After he killed one man with it in the Natchez duel, Colonel Bowie is said to have sent his knife to a Philadelphia blacksmith, who marketed copies of it under his name. Its double-edged blade was ten to fifteen inches long, and curved to a point. Once called an *Arkansas toothpick*, it was even carried by some congressmen.

bowing.   *Bowing*, to salute showing someone respect, derives from an Old English word meaning the same, and the custom is recorded as far back as *Beowulf*. While Westerners commonly bend the neck and uncover the head when bowing, people in several other cultures uncover the feet to show their respect. As *Brewer* explains, this is because "with us the chief act of investiture is crowning or placing a cap on the head; but in the East it is putting on the slippers."

bowler; billycock.   The same hat by different names, each probably named for a different person. Its shape can be traced back to the helmet worn by the ancient Greeks, but the *billycock*, a round, soft felt hat with a wide brim, most likely first graced the head of William Coke, a rich British landowner, in 1850. It is said to have been designed at "Billy" Coke's request by a hatter named Beaulieu because Mr. Coke's tall riding hat was frequently parted from his head by tree branches when he rode to the hounds. There is little doubt about the origin of *billycock* then, and *bowler* may derive from the name of the hatter, M. Beaulieu. The only trouble is that some authorities credit a London hatter named William Bowler, quoting a newspaper item tracing his "invention" to 1868. Still others say *bowler* is simply named for the hat's "bowl shape" or from the fact that it is round, stiff brimmed, and can be bowled along.

bowl game; bowl.   The first football *bowl game* ever recorded was the 1916 *Pasadena Bowl* (which was a year later renamed the *Rose Bowl*). *Bowl*, however, had been a synonym for a football stadium since 1914, when the Yale University stadium was first called the *Yale Bowl*.

Boxer Rebellion.   The Chinese anti-foreigner movement early in the 20th century originated with a Shantung secret society known as the I-Ho-Chuan, which the British thought meant "righteous, uniting fists" (it correctly meant "righteous harmony band"). So the British, or "foreign devils," as they were called, punned upon members of what they thought were the "fists" and called them *Boxers*, dubbing their uprising the *Boxer Rebellion*.

box office.   Most likely *box office* derives from the theater office that sold box seats to customers. But an old story insists that the expression originated in Elizabethan times, when theater admission was collected by passing a box attached to a long stick among the audience.

to box the compass.   Mariners who boxed the compass literally named all thirty-two points of the compass, from north through east and back to north. One describes a complete turn in doing so, however, which is why, in the early 19th century, the expression *to box the compass* began to be used figuratively for a complete or full turn.

boy.   The O.E.D. traces *boy*, which came into the language in the late Middle English period, to the Old French *abuie*, "fettered or chained," which suggests that the word originally meant a slave. Other sources, however, suggest the Frisian *boi*, "young gentleman," the German man's proper name *Boia*, and the Old Norse, *bofi*, "rascal," among other choices. Nobody really knows. Male American Indians, black slaves, and white indentured servants who were little more than slaves, were all called *boy* in America before the Civil War, and black men were commonly called the same for more than a century after. The term is insulting, however, not because *boy* here means a male child. This *boy* is a word dating back to the 13th century that originally meant a low menial servant, deriving from the Latin *boiae*, "fetters."

boycott.   Captain Charles Cunningham Boycott (1823-97) lived to see his name immortalized as a synonym for a refusal to deal with a person or business firm, the word current not only in English but in French, German, Dutch, Russian, and a number of Asiatic languages as well. Boycott, a stubborn British soldier turned farmer, had been hired to manage the Earl of Erne's estates at Lough Mask House in Connaught, County Mayo, Ireland. Absentee landlords like the earl owned most of the land in Ireland at the time and were evicting poverty-stricken tenant farmers who could not pay their rents. The fiery Irish leader Charles Stewart Parnell had already formed his National Land League, agitating for land reform by these "English usurpers." In September 1880, Parnell addressed tenants near Connaught, advocating that anyone working a farm from which a man had been evicted, or any landlord refusing to accept his new, reduced rent scales, should be ostracized "by isolating him . . . as if he were a leper of old . . . by leaving him strictly alone . . . ." When Captain Boycott harshly refused to accept more reasonable lower rents and tried to evict one farmer, Boycott's tenants forced his workers to leave him; organized marauders destroyed his property; his fences were torn down and cattle driven into his fields; he was refused service in all local stores; his mail went undelivered; he was jeered in the streets and hanged in effigy;

and his life was repeatedly threatened. So successful had been the famous "excommunication" against him that it was commonly called a *boycott* in the papers within two months.

the boys. *The boys*, for "political hangers-on," has a long history in America, dating back to at least 1832. It is often spelled *b'hoy*, the Irish pronunciation. (*See* **boy**.)

boysenberry. Americans have always been pie makers without peer, thanks to sugar resources close by, an abundance of native fruit, and a willingness to experiment. The blackberry, long regarded as a nuisance and called a bramble or brambleberry in England, is a case in point. Many varieties of blackberries have been developed here, long before anyone paid attention to the family *Rubus* in Europe. Among them is the *Boysenberry*, a prolific, trailing variety that is a cross between the *blackberry* (*q.v.*), *raspberry* (*q.v.*), and *loganberry* (*q.v.*), another eponymous berry. The *Boysenberry*, a dark wine-red fruit that tastes something like a raspberry, was developed by California botanist Rudolf Boysen in the early 1900s. Single plants commonly produce two quarts of the large 3/4-inch round, 1-1/2-inch-long fruit.

boys of the bulldog breed. Pugnacious Englishmen, often sailors, are called *boys of the bulldog breed*. The words come from the popular 19th-century song "Sons of the Sea, All British Born."

bra. The *brazziere*, which Roman matrons wore in the form of leather straps beneath the breasts and which euphemizers have called "breast shields" and "cup forms," probably takes its name from the French *bras*, "arm," and was first coined in about 1914. However, in a punning hoax, one source claims that its inventor in modern times was Otto Titzling, who designed a bra for a hefty opera singer named Swanhilda Olafsen in 1912. Titzling failed to patent his invention, but Mary Phelps Jacobs (a descendant of Robert Fulton of steamboat fame), who had independently invented a similar device, did so, filing for a patent application for a *brassiere* in February 1914. The same source credits dress designer Phillippe de Brassière, who glamorized the "chest halters" and sold them under his name beginning circa 1929, with popularizing *brassiere* and hence *bra*.

Bradbury. One of the few men to have bank notes named for them, even in slang, was J.S. Bradbury, whose signature as President Secretary to the Treasury from 1914-28 was on the British one-pound note, which was widely called a *Bradbury*.

braggadocio. You will look high and low in Italian dictionaries for this word, to no avail. For it was invented by Edmund Spenser (1552-99) in *The Faerie Queene*.

Spenser gave the name Braggadochio to a loud-mouthed braggart in his poem who was finally revealed as a coward, and may have based his character on the Duke d'Alencon, a suitor of Queen Elizabeth. The word came to mean "any braggart," and finally "empty or loud boasting."

Brahmin; Boston Brahmin. A *Brahmin* is a worshipper of the Hindu God Brahma, the creator of the universe. The Brahmin's status as a member of the highest caste in Hinduism inspired the Americanism *Boston Brahmin* for a member of a Boston family thought to be "aristocratic," and *Brahmin* for a person of great culture and intellect. Oliver Wendell Holmes first wrote of "the Brahmin caste of New England" in 1860.

braille. When only three years old, Louis Braille was blinded by an awl driven into his eye while he was playing in his father's leather-working shop. Total blindness extended to both eyes, but young Louis attended the village school in Coupvray outside of Paris, where he learned his alphabet by feeling twigs in the shape of letters, and then the *Institution Nationale des Jeunes Aveugles*, where he learned to read from three huge 400-pound books engraved with large embossed letters. This last method had been invented by Valentin Hauy, Father and Apostle of the Blind, the Institute's founder, but it could not be easily written by the blind and was thus inadequate. At about the time that Louis Braille was made a junior instructor at the Institute, French army officer Captain Charles Barbier introduced his "night writing," a system of twelve raised dots and dashes that fingers could "read," enabling brief orders like one dot for advance, or two dots for retreat to be written with a simple instrument and understood in total darkness. Barbier demonstrated his invention at the Institute and it fired young Braille's imagination. When only fifteen he began work on the improved system that bears his name. Louis Braille, highly regarded as an organist and composer in his own right, also invented a *braille* musical notation, but *braille* was not officially adopted at the Institute where he taught until 1854, two years after his death. Tradition has it that a blind organist performing at a fashionable salon told her audience that she owed everything to Louis Braille, who had died unheralded of tuberculosis in 1852 when only forty-two years old, and that her touching story finally led to universal recognition of his system.

brains knocked out. *To have one's brains knocked out* is not a modern Americanism for to be badly beaten in a fight. It dates all the way back to the late 16th century and the first British bare-knuckle "fistfights," as boxing matches were called at the time. (*See* **below the belt**.)

brain trust. James M. Kieran of the *New York Times* called the group of experts surrounding presidential candidate Franklin Delano Roosevelt the *brains trust* in his 1932 dispatches, the term having previously been used in sarcastic reference to the first American general staff in 1901, not at all in the same sense. Headline writers quickly chopped off the cumbersome s, and by the time Roosevelt became President his larger group of experts was called the *brain trust*. *Brain trust* now is applied to trusted business as well as government advisers.

brainwashing. *Brainwashing* was coined during the Korean War, when a number of American prisoners of war violated military codes after being captured, imprisoned, interrogated, and tortured by the North Koreans and Chinese. The vivid term is not an Americanism, however, being a direct translation of the Mandarin Chinese *hsi*, "to wash," and *nao*, "brain." (*See* **Chinese.**)

Bramley's seedling. *Bramley's seedling* is a delicious English apple, notable not only because it was discovered by a butcher named Bramley of Southwell, Nottinghamshire in his garden, but because it is a "sport," or mutation. Most mutations, or changes in genes, occur in seedlings, but the *Bramley* was the result of a bud mutation, a variation in which only part of a plant is affected. Thus the first *Bramley* as well as the first Golden Delicious apple, and the first New Dawn Rose, among others, developed on one branch of a plant bearing an entirely different race. The Boston fern, which originated in a shipment of ferns sent from Philadelphia to Boston in 1894, is another well-known mutation, but the most famous bud sport is the nectarine.

brand-new. *Brand-new* has nothing to do with the brand name of a product. It is rather associated with the word *brand* that is cognate with "fire," as in firebrand. The product would thus be fresh from the anvil, or as Shakespeare put it in *Twelfth Night*, "fire-new."

the brand of villain. Up until the early 19th century, when the practice ended, British criminals were branded with large letters indicating their crimes. Murderers or manslayers were branded with an *M* on the thumb or back of the right hand, while thieves got a *T* on the left hand; rogues, usually kidnappers, had an *R* branded on their shoulders; and felons were marked with an *F* on the cheek. In early times the English also branded people convicted for brawling in church (*F* for felon), and blaspheming (*B*). Some of these brands were used in colonial America, too, and we had one of our own, the *A* or Scarlet Letter that was sewn on the dress of an adulteress. English criminals often pleaded *benefit of clergy* (*q.v.*) and were released to a church court, where they automatically received lighter penalties. But even if they did so, they were frequently branded before the secular court let them go. Branded criminals were thus a familiar sight on the streets of London and other large cities, and it was their presence that suggested the old expression *he had the brand of villain in his looks.*

brandy. *Brandy* is a shortening of *brandywine*, which comes from the Dutch *brandewijn*. *Brandewijn*, in turn, derives from the Dutch *branden*, "burn" and *wijn*, "wine," translating as "burned (or distilled) wine." The word is first recorded in the early 17th century.

brass; brazen. As the ancient word for an alloy of copper with tin or zinc, *brass* is of unknown origin; it comes directly from the Anglo-Saxon *braes*, not found in any other language, though it may have some relation to the Danish *brase*, "to fire"—as in the firing and hardening of metal. The metal *brass* does give us several other easily explained words, though. *Brass* meaning "shameless impudence" goes back to Elizabethan times and is explained by the 1642 quotations cited by the *O.E.D.*: "His face is of brasse, which may be said either ever or never to blush." *Brazen*, "shamelessly impudent, as bold as brass," is simply from the English word *braze*, "to make hard like brass." The word *brass*, used to describe anyone in authority, is a shortening of the British *brass hat*, for "a high-ranking military officer," a term used before the turn of the century and referring to the oak leaves, commonly thought to be brass, that adorned the brim of a British officer's cap. This term was adopted by U.S. soldiers in World War I, was streamlined to *brass* (or *top brass*, *big brass*, *heavy brass*, etc.) in World War II and was then applied to high-ranking civilian officials, executives, and influential people in general, none of whom had "scrambled eggs" (gold braid) on their hats.

brass tacks. There are no *brass tacks*, only *brass-headed* ones, used because they rust less easily. The American expression, which has been traced back only to 1903, though it may have been common before then, has several possible origins. Brass-headed tacks were used in upholstering chairs, especially at the foundations of the chairs, and in taking a chair apart to reupholster it from the bottom up, craftsmen might have said they were getting down to business, to the root of the matter, getting down to the *brass tacks*. There is no solid evidence for this theory, however, just as there is none for the country-store hypothesis. Merchants in country stores, it's said, hammered brass-headed tacks at intervals into their fabric department counters to indicate lengths of a yard, a half-yard and a quarter-yard. After a customer selected the cloth she wanted, the merchant would say, "All right, now we'll get down to brass tacks—I'll measure it up for you." This certainly was a practice in country stores and a common one at about the time the expression is first recorded.

brawl. Did the British dance called the *brawl*, a kind of cotillion popular into the 19th century in which many dancers held hands and moved closer together, have anything to do with our slang expression *brawl*, for "a party"? Some etymologists believe that it is the origin of the word, but others believe the clamor or disturbance of *brawl* in the sense of "an argument" is responsible.

brazen. (*See* **brass.**)

Brazil. The country of *Brazil* was named for the wood called *Brazilwood*, not the other way around. Brazilwood is a red-colored wood used as a dye source that takes its name from the Spanish *brasa*, "red coal or ember," and was used in Europe centuries before what is now Brazil was discovered. Because so many similar dye-wood trees were found there, Portuguese explorers named the country *terra de Brasil*, "land of red dye-wood," which later became *Brazil*.

bread and circuses. *Bread and circuses* is a translation of a line by the Roman poet Juvenal that refers to the practice in ancient Rome of government feeding the people and providing them with entertainment to prevent rebellion. The term means the same today.

breadfruit. Breadfruit (*Artocarpus incisa*), which grows wild on trees on South Pacific islands, was so named because English seamen who sampled the fruit in the 17th century believed its soft white pulp resembled fresh baked bread—although it tastes something like sweet potato. (*See* **Captain Bligh.**)

breadline. In *The Dictionary of Americanisms*, *breadline* is said to be first recorded in 1900, but no specific account of its origin offered. However, in his fascinating book *Here at the New Yorker*, Brendan Gill attributes the expression to the Fleischmann family from whose yeast fortune rose the *New Yorker* magazine. The family ran the Vienna Model Bakery in New York City during the late 1870s: "In order to call attention to the freshness of Fleischmann's bread and also, it appears, because of an innate generosity, Lewis [Fleischmann] made a practice of giving away at eleven every evening whatever amount of bread had not been sold during the day. The poor lined up to receive it at the bakery door; hence our word 'breadline.'" The term had its widest use during The Great Depression fifty years later.

breadwinner; bread. *Breadwinner* is one of the few words still retaining the meaning of the Anglo-Saxon word *winnan*, "to toil," that gives us the word "win"—a breadwinner being one who toils to obtain bread. As slang for money, *bread* dates back to about 1935 and may derive from the Cockney rhyming slang "bread and honey," for money.

break. When a criminal went to trial or left prison in the late 19th century his friends often took up collections called *breaks* to raise money for a lawyer or to help give him a fresh start. These *breaks* possibly took their name from collections performers had made since medieval times during pauses, or "breaks," in their acts, but there is no solid proof of this. The collections for criminals may have given rise to the expression "to get a break," meaning "to have some good luck." Perhaps collection *breaks* were held long before the first recorded mention of them. Or "to get a break" might come from a *break* in pool or billiards, where once a player breaks the racked balls he has a chance to make a long, successful run.

break a leg! *Break a leg!* means "good luck" in theatrical circles, probably *not* because the great Sarah Bernhardt "had but one leg and it would be good luck to be like her." No one is sure, but one theory has the expression deriving, possibly through Yiddish, from a German expression meaning "May you break your neck and your leg," for which I can find no satisfactory explanation. It may also have something to do with wishing someone a "big break," that is, good luck leading to success.

brevity is the soul of wit. "Since brevity is the soul of wit, and tediousness the limbs and outward flourishes, I will be brief," Polonius says in *Hamlet*. But Shakespeare did not mean *wit* in the sense of a witty remark when he wrote this. He used *wit* here in its older meaning of "wisdom," and what Polonius is really saying is that wise men know how to put things succinctly—which the Bard knew was a dramatically ironic thing for a windy chap like Polonius to say. The newer meaning of *wit* was known in Shakespeare's time; he himself used it in *Much Ado About Nothing*: "They never meet but there's a skirmish of wit between them." Yet "brevity is the soul of wit" meant "brevity is the soul of wisdom" for many years before it took on its present, universal meaning. Swinburne's "An Epigram" (1802) is both witty and wise:

What is an Epigram? A dwarfish whole,
  Its body brevity, and wit its soul.

Brevoortia Ida-Maia. *The floral firecracker*, as this plant is popularly called, shows how oddly things sometimes get their names. Ida May, the daughter of a 19th-century California stagecoach driver, had noticed the bulbous plant many times in her travels and pointed it out to Alphonso Wood, a naturalist always interested in collecting botanical specimens. Wood named the single plant, a member of the lily family *Brevoortia Ida-Maia*, its prenomen in honor of his fellow American naturalist J. C. Brevoort, and its patronym in gratitude to the observant little girl who had brought the scarlet-flowered perennial to his attention.

breeze. John Hawkins and his men heard the Spanish word *breza*, for the northeast trade winds, on their voyage along the Spanish Main in the mid-16th century. They introduced the word to English, where it became the lovely refreshing *breeze*, which within fifty years was used in the sense that we employ it today.

a Briareus of languages.   Briareus was a mythological giant with fifty heads and one hundred hands, but the phrase *Briareus of languages* first honored Cardinal Giuseppe Caspar Mezzofanti (1774-1849), chief keeper of the Vatican library. The term is used to describe an accomplished linguist, having been invented by the English poet Byron, who called the cardinal "a walking polyglot; a monster of languages; a Briareus of parts of speech." Mezzofanti, we are told, learned Latin and Greek fluently while listening to an old priest giving lessons to students next door to the shop where he had been an apprentice to a carpenter. He eventually mastered thirty-nine languages, from Albanian to Wallachian, speaking these as well as he did his native tongue. All in all, he could speak sixty languages and seventy-two dialects fluently and could translate 114 languages. Among these were such exotics as Bimbarra, Geez, Kurdish, Tonkinese, and Chippewa.

bribe.   A *bribe*, a sinister thing today, was originally, in 14th-century France, alms that one gave a beggar. Because beggars began to *demand* such alms the word came to mean "to extort or steal" when it reached England a century or so later. Within a century or so a *bribe* came to mean, instead of an extortion, "a voluntary inducement to get someone to do something for the giver," an ironic change that has carried over into the word's meaning today.

bridegroom.   The *groom* in *bridegroom* is of no relation to the "groom" who takes care of horses. *Groom* here is a corruption of the Old English *guma*, "man." *Guma* became *grome* in Middle English and this word was associated with *grome*, "a lad," finally becoming part of *bridegroom*, first recorded in the early 16th century.

bride of the sea.   Early in the 11th century, the wedding of the Doge of Venice to the Adriatic symbolized the sea power of Venice. Every year the Doge, in his state barge, the *Bucentaur*, sailed into the Adriatic on Ascension Day and dropped a wedding ring into the sea. This practice, still part of the annual ceremony called the *Sposalizo del Mar*, is responsible for Venice's historical name "The Bride of the Sea."

Brie.   "The Queen of Cheeses," as *Brie* is called, takes its name from the town of Brie, southeast of Paris, where it was first made. It is formed in small wheels with tough crusts and soft centers, its flavor mild and delicate.

brig.   Brig, for "a prison on a ship," is an Americanism first recorded in 1852. One theory has it that pirates called "brigands" sailed on "brigandines" or "brigantines," small, two-masted sailing vessels, the name of which was soon shortened to *brig*. Since the brigands were criminals and were often in jail, the name of the type of ship they sailed supposedly became associated with jail cells.

bright and early.   This common expression, meaning "very early in the morning," isn't as old as one would suspect, being an Americanism that is first recorded by Washington Irving in his *The Adventures of Captain Bonneville, U.S.A.* (1837).

bright-eyed and bushy-tailed.   *Bright-eyed* is obvious, and the *bushy-tailed* here is a reference to "the tail of a cat," which fluffs up when the animal becomes excited. The expression means cheerful and lively, and it dates back to the 19th century.

Bright's disease.   One of the scores of maladies named for medical researchers is *Bright's disease*, named after English Dr. Richard Bright (1780-1858), whose findings determined the nature of the kidney affliction. Other words in the same morbid category include *Basedow's disease*, a swelling of the thyroid gland, for German Dr. Karl von Basedow (1799-1854); *Hodgkin's* a disease of the lymphatic glands, after English Dr. Thomas Hodgkin (1798-1866); *Lindau's*, a brain disease, for Arvid Lindau, a Swedish pathologist; *Paget's*, a disease of the breast, after Sir James Paget (1814-99); *Pott's*, a tuberculosis infection, after English surgeon Percivall Pott (1714-88); *Riggs pyorrhea* for American dentist John M. Riggs (1810-85); *Jacksonian epilepsy*, after English Dr. John Hughlings Jackson (1835-1911); and *Vincent's infection*, trench mouth, for French Dr. Jean Hyacinthe Vincent (1862-1950). All also go by far, far longer medical names.

brightwork.   Metal fixtures of a ship that are kept bright by hand polishing are called *brightwork*. The term is an Americanism, first recorded in 1841, but probably older.

Brillat-Savarin.   "The destiny of nations depends on the manner wherein they take their food." "A dessert course without cheese is like a beautiful woman with one eye." "Animals feed: man eats; only a man of wit knows how to dine." Anthelme Brillat-Savarin, author of these and many other well-known aphorisms on *la cuisine*, was seventy when he published his *Physiologie du Goût* (Physiology of Taste) in 1825, his celebrated book thirty years in the making. He was to die the following year but not before he had given the world the most trenchant discussion of food and its effects on trenchermen ever written. The greatest of French bon vivants had been born, appropriately enough, in the town of Belley—"Belley is its name and Belley is its nature," someone wrote over a century later. He became the town's mayor after the French Revolution but had to emigrate to America during the Reign of Terror, living in Connecticut for a few years. Portly and gregarious, the sage of Belley remained a bachelor all his life—perhaps too devoted to food and women ever to marry, possibly because he loved his cousin, the society beauty Madame Récamier. A lawyer who wrote on political economy and law, and penned a few licentious tales as well, he is remembered above all for his bible of gastronomy. "Tell me what you eat and I will tell you what you are," he once declared. Though he was something of an eccentric—he often carried dead birds around in his pockets until they became "high" enough for cooking—Brillat-Savarin's reputation has not suffered for his eccentricities, his name long synonymous with supreme authority on cooking. The greatest of gourmets also has the *savarin*, a yeast cake soaked in a rum of kirsch-flavored syrup, named for him, and there are countless restaurants and a brand of coffee using the last half of his hyphenated name, as well as two classic garnishes, both made in part with truffles, the most extravagant of gourmet foods. *Brillat* was actually Anthelme's real name—he took on the hypen and *Savarin* when his great aunt left him her entire fortune on the condition that he add her name to his, Mademoiselle Savarin wanting a little immortality and getting more than she bargained for. Love of food, in fact, seemed to run in the Brillat family. Anthelme's youngest sister, Pierrette, for instance, died at the dinner table. She was almost one hundred and her last words are among the most unusual in history: "And now, girl, bring me the dessert." *Physiologie du Goût*, incidentally, had to be printed at the author's expense. And when Brillat-Savarin's brother later sold the rights to a publisher, he got only $120—after throwing in a genuine Stradivarius as well.

brilliant diamond. This isn't a diamond that sparkles brilliantly, but a diamond cut in a specific way, a perfect brilliant diamond having 58 facets. The term has been used since the late 17th century, when the Venetian diamond cutter Vincenzo Peruzzi invented the technique.

Brinell hardness; etc. A Brinell machine or tester determines the hardness of a metal, especially steel, by forcing a hard steel or tungsten carbide ball into it under a fixed hydraulic pressure. By dividing the force applied by the indenter into the surface area of the indentation made, the metal's Brinell number is obtained, this indicating its relative *Brinell hardness* on the Brinell scale. The machine and method were devised by the Swedish engineer, Johann August Brinell (1849-1925), who first demonstrated his famous invention at the Paris International Exposition of 1900.

to bring down the house. A performer who *brings down the house* is so good that the theater seems to vibrate from all the applause he receives and it even seems as if the building will collapse. The common expression is from the British theater and is first recorded in 1754.

bring home the bacon. An English custom initiated in 1111 and lasting until late in the 18th century provided that any married couple who swore that they hadn't quarreled for over a year, or had not at any time wished themselves "single again"—and could prove this to the satisfaction of a mock jury sometimes composed of six bachelors and six maidens—was entitled to the Dunmow Flitch, a side of bacon awarded at the church of Dunmow in Essex County. The expression to *bring home the bacon*, "to win the prize," isn't recorded until 1925, but bacon was used as a word for "prize" centuries before, and most scholars believe that the Dunmow Flitch is responsible for the usage. This custom, along with the popular American one of awarding the pig to the winner of "greased-pig" events at county fairs, gives us the phrase, which now means to support a family by working.

bristlecone pine. Called the "oldest living things on earth" some gnarled, twisted *bristlecone pines (Pinus aristata)* in California's White Mountains are more than 5,000 years old. Named for the bristle-like prickles at the end of its cones, this slow-growing tree also goes by the names *Jack pine, cattail pine*, and *foxtail pine*, the last two names alluding to the tufts at the ends of its twigs.

Bristol, CT. The Connecticut city takes its name from its sister city in England. Bristol, England, in turn, got its name from the peculiar habit its residents had of tacking an "l" onto words ending in a vowel. This local dialectical eccentricity, which persists there to this day, changed the seaport's name from Bristowe to Bristol.

broad. *Broad* has meant both a promiscuous woman and any young woman since the 1920s, though it is generally used today, when it is used, to mean a young woman—not necessarily a promiscuous one, but not someone toward whom much respect is shown. The Americanism may derive from *bawd*, but was more likely suggested by broad breasts and buttocks.

Brobdingnagian. A big word that means "giant" or "huge," and honors a race of fictional giants. The Brobdingnagians were the giants who inhabited the island of Brobdingnag in Jonathan Swift's *Gulliver's Travels* (1726). Men were "odious little vermin" to the Brobdingnagians. (*See* **lilliputian**.)

brocard; Brocard's circle and ellipse. Brocard was the French name for Burchard, an 11th-century bishop of Worms. Bishop Brocard published a collection of canons, *Regulae Ecclesiastecae*, celebrated for its short, sententious sentences, and a *brocard* soon came to mean both a brief maxim or proverb in philosophy or law and a pointed jibe or biting speech. *Brocard's circle* and *Brocard's ellipse* are mathematical terms named for French mathematician Henri Brocard (1845-1922).

broccoli. Roman farmers, who must have been more poetic than their contemporary counterparts, are said to have called *broccoli* "the five green fingers of Jupiter." The word has a more prosaic derivation, however, coming from the Latin *bracchium*, "a strong arm or branch," in reference to its shape. According to Pliny the Elder, Drusus, the eldest son of Emperor Tiberius, ate so much broccoli that his urine turned bright green! (*See* **I say it's spinach and I say the hell with it!**)

broderick. His tactics wouldn't be officially approved today, but Johnny (The Boffer) Broderick is still remembered as a tough New York City cop who relied on his fists as much as his police revolver. Known as the world's toughest cop, Detective Broderick worked "the Broadway beat," dealing out punishment with his fists on the spot so often that *to broderick* became a synonym for "to clobber." Broderick once flattened the hoodlum Jack (Legs) Diamond, and he knocked out and captured Francis (Two-Gun) Crowley before Crowley could find the courage to shoot. Another time he battered two men molesting a woman, threw them through a plate-glass window and then arrested them for malicious destruction of property. In fact, Bellevue Hospital used him as an exhibit to show how much punishment the human hand could take. Broderick, an image of sartorial splendor, was used as a bodyguard by many celebrities, including Franklin Roosevelt and Jack Dempsey. Dempsey confessed that the detective was the only man he wouldn't care to fight outside the ring. This graduate of New York's gashouse district was immortalized by Damon Runyon as Johnny Brannigan and played by Edward G. Robinson in *Bullets or Ballots.* By the time he retired in 1947, after twenty-five years on the force, Broderick had won eight medals for heroism. Broadway gamblers once gave 9-5 odds that he would be killed on any given day, but he died in his bed in 1966, seventy-two years old.

brodie. (*See* **do a brodie.**)

brogue. One theory holds that the *brogue* long associated with the Irish derives from the Gaelic *barrog*, for "a wrestling hold"—Irish tongues were held by tradition and couldn't speak any other way. A rival theory says that *brogue* comes from the heavy brogans (from the Gaelic *brog*, "shoe") worn by Irish peasants, who usually spoke with what we now call a *brogue*.

broken-hearted. *Broken-hearted* lovers weren't the inspiration for this word. It was coined in 1526 by William Tyndale, English translator of the Bible, who was later strangled and burned at the stake for heresy. The word first occurs in Luke *iv* 18: "To heale the broken harted," and was preceded by such formations as "broken-minded," "broken-backed," and "broken-winded." Tyndale is also said to have coined the word *beautiful*, in his translation of the Bible (in Mat. 23:27).

broker. *Brokers* today are associated with stocks or real estate, but all brokers were originally *brokieres*, or men who opened up wine casks (usually to bottle and sell the wine inside). This old French word came to be transferred to wine salesmen, or brokers, and finally to one who sold anything at all. Wall Street brokers who work on the floor (or in the pit) of the exchange are called *floor brokers*; they were once called *$2 brokers* because they received a fee of two dollars per transaction.

the Bronx. The Bronx, one of New York City's five boroughs, takes its name from Jonas Bronck, a Dane who first settled the area for the Dutch West India Company in 1641. Points of interest in the celebrated borough are the Bronx Zoo and Botanic Gardens, the Edgar Allan Poe cottage, and Yankee Stadium, "the house that Ruth built." The Bronx River runs from Westchester County through the Bronx and into the East River. The *Bronx cocktail* was named in honor of the borough, or invented there in about 1919. Long associated with baseball, the razz, or raspberry, called the *Bronx cheer* wasn't born at Yankee Stadium, home of baseball's New York Yankees. It may derive from the Spanish word *branca*, "a rude shout," or have originated at the National Theater in the Bronx. We know for certain only that the term was first recorded in 1929.

bronze. Many scholars trace the word *bronze* to the late Latin *brundisium*, "brass from Brundisium," Brundisium being the modern Adriatic city of Brindisi. But since that city doesn't produce exceptional brass or bronze, the derivation is doubtful. Another possible source is the Persian *birindj*, "alloy." In any case, *bronze* is a fairly modern word, first recorded in 1721.

broom. British housewives in early times used the *besom*, "a handful of twigs with the leaves attached," to sweep their homes. Because these "besoms" were often made of twigs from the broom shrub they came to be called *brooms* by about the year 1000. "Besom," however, remained the name for a sweeping implement well into the 19th century. *Brooms* were often placed across the door of a house to ward off witches, for even though witches were believed to ride on brooms, it was thought that a witch had to count every straw in a broom placed across a door before she could open it.

broomstick marriage. Broomstick marriages were common in remote districts of England, Scotland, and the southern U.S. in the 18th century. In order to avoid paying clerical fees and waiting for the preacher to ride by, rural folk devised a ceremony that was regarded as perfectly legal and binding in many communities—all the prospective bride and groom had to do was jump over a broomstick held by two people who knew them and they were declared man and wife. It has been suggested that the broomstick has something to do with "witches riding on their broomsticks to their unholy pleasures," but no one really knows why the superstition developed. At first a *broomstick marriage* meant only a rural marriage, but its meaning deteriorated over the years as laws grew more uniform and it is now regarded as a mock marriage or a common-law marriage.

brothel. Prostitutes in the 15th century were called *brothels*, from the Old English *breothan*, "to go to ruin." *Brothel houses* soon meant houses of prostitutes, or whorehouses, the word shortened to *brothel* by the late 1700s.

brother, can you spare a dime? A popular song published in 1932 had these words as its title and they quickly became the common plea of panhandlers throughout America during the Great Depression.

Brother Jonathan. *Brother Jonathan* was originally Connecticut governor and minister Jonathan Trumbull (1710-85), one of the few colonial governors to stand up for the rights of the colonists. The redoubtable Trumbull was a trusted friend and adviser of George Washington, and an unsupported story has it that General Washington, when he needed ammunition and none of his officers could solve the problem, declared, "We must consult Brother Jonathan on this." Trumbull came up with a solution and Washington's remark became proverbial in time. Washington did rank Trumbull "the first among patriots," and the term *Brother Jonathan* for an American first appeared in print in 1816. Some debunkers point out, however, that Jonathan was a very common American name at the time and that the British had used *Brother Jonathan* in allusion to the Puritans as early as the 17th century.

brother's keeper. (*See* **mark of Cain.**)

brougham. The *brougham*, a four-wheeled carriage for two or four passengers, honors Henry Peter Brougham, Baron Brougham and Vaux (1778-1868). This name for a one-horse carriage with an open driver's seat and a closed, low-slung passenger cab behind also designated the first tall electric automobiles, as well as an early gasoline-powered limousine with the driver's seat unenclosed. The *brougham* was named after Lord Brougham in about 1850, because of his design for the "garden chair on wheels," similar to the old "growler" horse cab. The amazing Lord Brougham, born in Edinburgh, Scotland

was among the most versatile of men—a noted lawyer, orator, politician, statesman, scientist, writer, publisher, abolitionist, reformer, and one of the great wits of this day. In his later years the many-faceted genius built a cottage in Cannes, and his presence there was directly responsible for the French town's great vogue as an international resort.

to browbeat. A *browbeaten* person is literally "someone who is beaten or put down by the knitted or wrinkled brow and frown of somebody else." *To browbeat*, "to belittle someone with sternness, arrogance, or insolence," is first recorded in 1581.

brown as a berry; it's the berries. The first expression was used by Chaucer in 1386: "His palfrey [small saddle horse] was as broune as is a bery." Though most berries aren't brown, the reference is possibly to brown berries like those of the juniper or cedar. *It's the berries*, meaning "it's the best," is an Americanism dating back to about 1900 when collegians used *the berries* to mean "any remarkable, attractive, or satisfying person or thing."

the Brown Bomber. (*See* **Joe Louis.**)

browsing. We associate *browsing* mainly with bookstores today, but the word, from the French *broust*, "young bud or shoot," originally meant the feeding of animals such as cattle, deer, and goats on the leaves and shoots of trees and bushes; *to browse* was recorded as early as 1542 in this sense. Shakespeare seems to have been the first to use the word figuratively, in *Cymbeline*, but Charles Lamb first used it in its modern sense in his largely autobiographical *Essays of Elia* (1823): "He browsed at will upon that fair and wholesome pasturage [a good library]."

Brucellosis. (*See* **Bang's disease.**)

brucine. Another poison named for a real person, but this time not for someone who used it for nefarious purposes. *Brucine* is a bitter, poisonous vegetable alkaloid found in seeds of various *Strychnos* species, especially *Nux vomica*. It resembles strychnine, though it isn't as powerful and it is rapidly eliminated from the body. *Brucine*, used in the denaturing of alcohol, was named for the apparently innocent Scottish traveler and explorer, James Bruce (1730-94), who merely discovered it. (*See* **aqua tofana.**)

bruin. Bears have been called *bruins* ever since medieval times, when the bear in the folk tale *Reynard the Fox* was named Bruin. The tale is Dutch in origin and *bruin* is the Dutch word for "brown." The Swiss capital, Bern, takes it name from the Swiss word for bear.

brumby. An Australian wild horse is often called a *brumby*, or *brumbie*. The word possibly derives from the name of Major William Brumby, an early 19th-century settler from England whose descendants still live in Australia. Major Brumby was a noted breeder of horses, but much of his stock escaped and ran wild. *Brumby* may come, however, from the Aborigine *booramby*, meaning "wild."

brummagem. Counterfeit or cheap merchandise is called *brummagen*, after the city of Birmingham, England, which was often pronounced *Brummagem* locally in the 17th century. The city had a reputation as a manufacturing center of cheap trinkets and a place where counterfeit coins were made.

brunch. *Brunch* is a dictionary-accepted word for a meal. Brunch came into the language back in 1895, when it was introduced in *Hunter's Weekly*, a British publication, to describe a combined breakfast and luncheon. It had probably been a collegiate coinage a little earlier. *Lupper*, a midafternoon meal eaten instead of lunch and supper, is a new portmanteau word "struggling to be born," according to William Sherk in *500 Years of New Words* (1983). *Dunch* and *blupper* are two possible substitutes for *lupper*, suggested by readers of Marian Burros's "De Gustibus" column in the *New York Times*.

brushfire. Two uses of the word *brush* probably suggested this recent coinage for a relatively small, localized war, an expression first recorded about thirty years ago. *Brushfire*, the term invented by early emigrants on the western frontier, was a fire in the *brush*, or scrubby areas where shrubs and small trees grew, a fire relatively easy to control compared to a forest fire. More than a century later the word *brush* became slang for uncivilized regions of any kind. Since they took place in what many considered "uncivilized" areas and were presumably easy to contain, local wars in far-off places became known as *brushfire wars* in the mid fifties. *Brushfire* has also been used as an adjective for other things limited in scope, area, or importance, as in a *brushfire labor dispute*.

brussels sprout. Unknown in America until about 1800, this relatively "new" vegetable is named for the capital of Belgium, where it was developed or improved upon early in the 16th century.

Brutus; et tu Brute. Marcus Junius Brutus (ca. 85-42 B.C.) was, of course, the principal assassin of Julius Caesar and *a Brutus* is any treacherous person, especially a former friend. *Et tu Brute* ("You too, Brutus?"), Caesar's last words when he glimpsed his friend, is among the most familiar of quotations. History holds two opinions of Brutus. One claims that he conspired with Cassius to save the republic from Caesar's tyranny. The other suggests that his reputation as a moneylender and his friendship with the self-seeking Cassius prove that his motives were far more crass. Two years after he took part in Caesar's assassination, Brutus committed suicide, following a battle at Philippi that the republicans lost to Mark Antony and Octavian (later Augustus Caesar). A *brutus*, without the capital, is both a rough, cropped wig and a bronze variety of chrysanthemum, the origin of these terms unknown.

bubby; bubee. Both *Bartlett* and *Webster's* state that *bubby*, a familiar name for "a little boy," is a corruption of "brother," claiming it as an Americanism first recorded in about 1848. More likely, it is from the German *bube*, "little boy." *Bubee*, a Yiddish term of endearment that can be addressed to a child or any loved one, appears to have a separate etymology. It derives from the Yiddish *bubeleh*, meaning the same, which probably comes from the Russian *baba*, "little grandmother," and the Hebrew *buba*, "little doll."

bubonic plague. (*See* **Black Death**.)

buccaneer. *Buccaneer* was the name applied to themselves by the sea raiders roaming the Caribbean. The word derives from the *boucanes*, or little dome-shaped smokehouses, on Hispaniola Island, where strips of boar meat and beef were smoked dry over a slow fire. The men who smoked *viande boucanee*, or "jerky," and sold it in bundles of a hundred for six pieces of eight were called *boucaniers*, "smokers of meat." Pirates in the area so often bought this dried meat from the *boucaniers*—it was perfect food to carry in the days before refrigeration—that they began to be called *boucaniers* or *buccaneers*, too.

Bucephala. (*See* **Peritas and Bucephala**.)

buck; pass the buck. The American slang word for a dollar may have its origins in animal skins that were classified as "bucks" and "does." The bucks, larger and more valuable (some 500,000 of them were traded every year in 18th-century America), could have become a part of early American business terminology (ca. 1800) and later become slang for a dollar. But *buck*'s origin could just as well be in poker. A marker called a *buck* was placed next to a poker player in the game's heyday, during the late 19th century, to remind him that it was his turn to deal next. When silver dollars were used as the markers, they could have taken the name *buck* for their own. Although markers called *bucks* may or may not have given us the slang term for a dollar, they are almost certainly responsible for the expression *to pass the buck*, "to evade responsibility"—just as poker players passed on the responsibility for the deal when they passed the buck.

buckaroo. *Buckaroo*, for "a cowboy," is a corruption of the Spanish *vaquero*, meaning the same. The first recorded quotation using the word, in a letter from Texas, shows the mispronunciation of *vaquero* by Americans: "These rancheros are surrounded by peons and *bakharas* or herdsmen." The mispronunciation "bakhara" was further corrupted to "buckhara," "buckayro," and finally *buckaroo*. *Buckaroo* has probably lasted because it is a good descriptive word, suggesting a cowboy on a bucking horse. It inspired well over fifty other American slang words ending in "-aroo" or "-eroo." *Stinkaroo*, a bad play or movie, still has wide currency, as does *the old switcheroo*, the act of substituting one thing for another. Others not so familiar anymore are *antsaroo*, ants in his pants; *jugaroo*, a jail; and *ziparoo*, energy.

bucket shop. Before it became the term for "an illegal brokerage house that cheats its customers," *bucket shop* was the designation for "an unsavory bar where patrons could buy beer by the buckets." However, in 1882, the Chicago Board of Trade prohibited grain transactions of less than 5,000 bushels. Illegitimate brokerage houses began trading in smaller lots and whenever larger, legitimate houses dealt illegally in smaller lots they sent down for a "bucketful" to the *bucket shops*.

buckeye. American pioneers in what is now Ohio so named this horse chestnut tree because its dark-brown nut resembles the eye of a buck deer "when the shell first cracks and exposes it to sight." A useful tree whose soft wood, cut into long shavings, even made ladies' hats and whose very roots were made into a soap, the *buckeye* (*Aesculus glabra*) eventually gave its name to all the natives of the *Buckeye State*. The nuts, or *buckeye beans*, of the tree were carried as good-luck charms and thought to ward off piles, rheumatism, and chills, among other maladies.

buckhorse. If you gave him a few shillings, the English fighter John Smith, who went by the ring name of *Buckhorse*, would let you punch him on the side of the head as hard as you could. The well-known boxer saw his nickname become slang for "a punch or a blow" beginning about 1850; that is, if he saw anything but stars after a while.

buckle down to work. To buckle oneself, when English knighthood flowered, meant to fasten one's armor, to buckle the straps securely in their holders, to prepare for battle. Soon the expression was used figuratively, meaning "to apply oneself resolutely to any task": "Everie man . . . must buckle himself to a painful kind of life" (1574). The word *buckle* itself comes from the Latin *buccula*, a diminutive of "cheek," which originally was used to describe the strap holder or clamp on Roman battle helmets that rested near the cheek.

buckwheat. The grain of buckwheat resembles the seed of the beech tree, so the Dutch called it *bockweit*, or "beech wheat." From *bockweit* came the English *buckwheat*, which is used in Europe mainly for animal feed ("A grain which in England is commonly fed to horses," Dr. Johnson notes characteristically in his *Dictionary*, "but in Scotland supports the people."), but is used in America to make *buckwheat pancakes* and was the name of one of the most popular characters in the "Our Gang" film comedies.

Buddhism. Buddha, "the Enlightened One," was the title given to Prince Siddhartha (ca. 563-c. 485), the Hindu prince who founded *Buddhism* in the sixth century B.C. It had been prophesied on his conception that the prince would renounce the world upon seeking a sick man, an old man, and a corpse, which human misery he saw while riding through the royal park one day when he was twenty-nine years old. Prince Siddhartha left his wife and child, and after six years of solitude and contemplation, during which he devoted himself to the severest asceticism, living on seeds, grass, and even dung, he emerged as the Buddha, preaching a religion based on salvation by suffering. Existence, he proclaimed, was evil, and desire was the cause of sorrow. Nirvana the absorption into the supreme spirit, was the reward obtained by the suppression of desire. Gautama Buddha (Gautama is from his clan name, and he is called Sakyammuni Buddha from his tribal name) spent all his life as a wanderer, preaching his doctrine from the time he attained enlightenment under a Bo tree at Buddh Gaya in northern India until his death forty-five years later. Buddha, or the Enlightened, derives from the Sanskrit *Bodhati*, "he awakens." It is estimated that Buddhism has about 140 million followers today.

budget. Originally, a *budget* was a leather bag or wallet, deriving from the French *bougette*, wallet. The word's meaning may have been extended to cover a statement of financial requirements when the British Chancellor of the Exchequer, in appearing before Parliament, began the custom of carrying papers containing his annual statement of estimated revenues and expenses in a leather bag and "opening the budget" for the year. Another theory claims that in 1733 Sir Robert Walpole introduced an unpopular excise duties bill and a political pamphleteer compared him to "a mounte-bank at a fair opening his budget of crank medicines," the word *budget* from then on becoming linked with government financial requirements.

Budweiser. Though one of America's most popular beers, *Budweiser*, or *Bud*, as it is often abbreviated, is German in origin. The brand of beer is not named for an American brewmaster, as many people suppose, but takes its name from the German village of Budweis, where a visiting St. Louis businessman "discovered" it.

buff; in the buff. So many buffalo hides were taken in the 19th century that buff coats made of them became very fashionable, the undyed yellowish coats giving us the word *buff*, and the verb *buff*, "to polish," entering the language from the strips of buffalo hide that were used to bring metals like bronze to a high polish. Even the word *buff* for an avid devotee of some activity or subject owes its life to *buffalo*. Buffalo robes were the winter gear of firemen in the middle of the last century. The amateur firefighters who rushed to blazes emulated the professionals by wearing buffcoats made of buffalo skins and were called *buffs* as a result. The expression *in the buff*, "in the nude," derives from the soft yellow buff skins made from buffalo hides, which looked something like bare human skin tanned by the sun.

buffalo. Most people believe that *buffalo* is a misnomer, a name applied with zoological inexactitude to the American bison. Cortes described the creature as "a rare Mexican bull, with crooked shoulders, a hump on its back like a camel and with hair like a lion," but later explorers thought it was the Asian or African water buffalo and called it after the Spanish *bufalo*, already used in Europe as the name for those animals. Actually the water buffalo and the American buffalo both belong to the bison family, so the real mistake of early explorers was in calling the native American animal simply *buffalo* and not qualifying it with a name such as *prairie buffalo*.

Buffalo Bill. Colonel William Frederick Cody (1846-1917), the peerless horseman and sharpshooter who became the original *Buffalo Bill*, earned his nickname as a market hunter for buffalo (bison) hides and as a contractor supplying buffalo meat to workers building the Union Pacific Railroad in 1867. To his glory then, and shame now, he killed 4,280 buffalo in one year, mostly for their hides and tongues. It is hard to separate truth from fiction in Cody's life, his fame owing much to the dime novels that made him a celebrity in the late 19th century. *Buffalo Bill* was a herder, a Pony Express rider, a scout and cavalryman for the U.S. Army in the Civil War, and an Indian fighter who is said to have killed the Cheyenne chief Yellowhand single-handedly. He was a member of the Nebraska State Legislature. His Wild West Show, which he organized in 1883, toured the United States and Europe, bringing him great personal fame, yet financial problems caused this legendary American hero to die in poverty and relative obscurity. Today his name conjures up visions of "sportsmen" picking off buffalo from the platforms of moving trains, abundant buffalo meat rotting on the plains, and the destruction of the great herds. Thanks to early conservationists, some 20,000 American bison survive today, protected on government ranges.

bug; insect. The word *bug* originally had nothing to do with insects, possibly deriving from the Welsh *bwg*, "a specter or a ghost." How *bug* came to mean *insect* (insect is short for the Latin *animal insectum*, an "animal notched near the middle") no one knows, but perhaps the beetles and other insects first called *bugs* terrified some people, suggesting supernatural creatures. Another possibility is the West African word *baga-baga*, "insect," which the English may have encountered in the slave trade. *Bug* is first recorded in 1642. Some etymologists trace the *bug* in "don't bug me" to the West African *bugu*, "annoy." This may be so, but if the term did come to America with slavery, there should be earlier references to it than we have, *bug* only being recorded in this sense since the early 1950s. *Bug* for "annoy" may also have derived in some roundabout way from one of the many other slang uses of *bug*, including an obsessed person, a trick, or even *bugging* a person's telephone calls surreptitiously. It could also derive from *bugger* (*q.v.*) for sodomy, or from "bogey" (*q.v.*). *Bug* in the sense of a defect ("This new model car has a lot of *bugs* in it") does not derive from the moths that supposedly plagued the first U.S. experimental computers in the 1940s, as the old story goes. Used long before then, *bug* is most likely a form of "bogey" (*q.v.*), in this case, "a real thing that causes worry." The *bug* used to wiretap a telephone or a room may have its origin in "bogey" (*q.v.*), being "a device that causes worry, even terror." But the term has its origins in the underworld and could be a shortened form of *burglar alarm*—back in the twenties commercials used to say that premises protected with burglar alarms were *bugged*. In racing terminology, a *bug* means the weight allowance granted to a horse because the jockey riding him is an apprentice; the apprentice jockey himself is also called a *bug*. This term comes from the asterisk appearing on racing forms next to the weight of a horse granted such an allowance. In printing jargon an asterisk, being small, was called a *bug*, and the term was adopted by horseplayers.

The Bug Bible. Numerous editions of the Bible have been named for their translators or patrons, the most famous being the *King James* or *Authorized Version*, which was prepared by a group of British scholars working at the command of King James I from 1604 to 1611. James commissioned this version mainly because other Bibles of the time had marginal notes questioning the divine right of kings. *Coverdale's Bible, Crammer's Bible, Cromwell's Bible, Matthew's Bible, Matthew Parker's Bible, Taverner's Bible, Tyndale's Bible*, and *Wycliffe's Bible* are all famous in history. *Coverdale's Bible* is sometimes known as *The Bug Bible* because it reads "Thou shalt not need to be afraid for any bugs by night" in a passage from *Psalms*, using "bugs" instead of "terror" in the sentence. Other amusing instances of printer's errors occur in *The Wicked Bible* (1805), where the seventh commandment reads "Thou shalt commit adultery"; the *Unrighteous Bible*, which says that "the unrighteous shall inherit the Kingdom of God"; and *The Sin On Bible*, which in the book of *John* reads "sin on more" instead of "sin no more." There is even a *Vegetarian Bible* and one with no references to sex. (*See also* **Gutenberg Bible**.)

bugger. *Bugger* in British English never means a child, as it does in American expressions like "he's just a little bugger." A *bugger* in England is only a sodomite and *to bugger* is to sodomize—in fact, use of the word in print was actionable in England for many years. *Bugger* in this sense, which is American slang as well, derives, down a torturous path, from the Medieval Latin *Bulgarus*, meaning "both a Bulgarian and a sodomite." The word first referred to a Bulgarian and then to the Bulgarian Albigenses or Bulgarian Heretics, an 11th-century religious sect whose monks and nuns were believed to practice sodomy. Some historians claim that the charge of sodomy against these heretic dissenters was a libel invented with the approval of the Church. They had already been banished from Bulgaria, were living in the south of France, and the trumped-up story caused the French to oust or exterminate them, too.

buggy. The horse carriage *buggy* is thought to derive from the old meaning of *bug*—"a specter or a ghost," often called a "bogie" (*q.v.*). It seems that the light carriages were called "bogies" (which later became *buggie*) because they were so fast that they scared people out of their wits.

bug juice. *Bug juice*, for "cheap liquor," is a century-old term that takes its name from the tobacco-colored secretion of grasshoppers.

bugle. The rude ancestor of this musical instrument was made from the horn of a young bull or bullock, a *buculus*, in early Roman times. *Buculus* passed into French and English as *bugle* and the *bugle horn*, or *bugle*, remained the name for the instrument long after it was no longer made from a bull's horn.

to bug out; swanning. *To bug out*, "to retreat hastily," is an expression that dates back to the time of the Korean War, when it was first used by teenagers and then in the United Nations "police action" to indicate a military retreat. Since retreats are generally the result of fear, the expression is another one that probably derives in a roundabout way from "bugaboo" or "bogey." Incidentally, the migrating habits of the swan inspired the word *swanning*, "going purposefully anywhere without a purpose," which meant the same thing that *bugging out* did during the Korean War.

build a better mousetrap. Ralph Waldo Emerson is often credited with "If you build a better mousetrap the world will beat a path to your door," mainly because a book entitled *Borrowings* by Sarah S.B. Yule and Mary Keene, published in 1889, reported that he had said it in a speech. But many scholars believe that Emerson was too wise to believe that the world would always seek out the best, and nothing concerning a mousetrap can be found in any of Emerson's published writings.

build (or set) a fire under. Ornery mules may be responsible for the expression to set a fire under, or "to stir someone to action or movement": Southern farmers, it is said, sometimes built fires under their mules to get the beasts to move when they were standing with four legs spread and refusing to budge despite every other tactic. Palmer Clark, research librarian at the Van Noy Library in Fort Belvoir, Virginia, advises that relatives of hers in the "chuggy huggy hills of Tennessee" were familiar with the practice. "Aunt Clellie," Mrs. Clark writes, "said when she was a young girl, loads of cedar were transported to Murfreesboro from Hall's Hill Pike. She distinctly remembered that her brother-in-law . . . literally and actually built fires under the mules who hauled the cedar to get them going [this about 1921 or 1922 in middle Tennessee]."

bull; phallus. *Bull*, for "the male of any bovine animal," is first recorded in about 1200 and derives from the Old English *bula*, "bull." The word is akin to the Greek *phallos*, "phallus," which comes from an Indo-European root meaning "to swell up." *Bull* as an opprobrious Americanism for a policeman, or prison guard, came into the language in 1893 from the Spanish Gypsy *bul*, policeman.

bull! *Bull!*, in the sense of "a lie, an exaggeration, an incredible concocted story," was first recorded in 1911 and is not a euphemism for the euphemistic "booshwah" (which derives from the French *bois de vache*, "cow's wood" or "dried dung"). It has nothing to do with a papal bull, either or, for that matter, with Irish bulls (ludicrous incongruities such as "It's grand to be alone, especially if your swatheart is wid you"). No one can say for sure just how the expression originated. *Bull!* may have passed into English via the French *boule*, meaning "fraud." Or it could come from a "cock and bull story," an expression that dates back to at least the early 17th century. Another explanation is that it's simply a shortening of *bullshit*, which was first recorded in 1928, but it was probably around long before that. Still another has it deriving from the American expression "I wouldn't trust him as far as I could throw [fling] a bull," dating back to the 1830s. The papal *bull* comes from the Latin *bulla* for the heavy leaden seal attached to papal edicts, while the term *Irish bull* may derive from either the Middle English *bull*, to cheat, or the Old French *boule*, fraud.

bulldog edition. In the 1890s several New York City newspapers brought out early morning editions that came to be called *bulldog editions*, possibly because the newspapers "fought like bulldogs" among themselves in their circulation wars.

bulldogging.   "One of the men . . . reached well over the animal's back to get a slack of the loose hide next the belly, lifted strongly, and tripped. This is called 'bulldogging.'" So did an early writer describe the way cowboys wrestled steers to the ground in the American West. They often, however, leaped from their horses and twisted the cow's neck, flipping it over. Neither method suggests the way bulldogs fought bulls when such cruel contests were held in England—for the bulldog seized the bull's nose in its mouth. Esse F. O'Brien's *The First Bulldogger* (1961) therefore suggests that a black cowboy named Bill Pickett is responsible for the word—Pickett would sink his teeth into a bull's nose while wrestling it to the ground, his method being responsible for the name of the more conventional method!

bulldozer.   The earth-moving bulldozer takes its name from a band of political terrorists. After the Civil War, a group of Louisiana vigilantes, who brutally prevented freed slaves from voting freely, were termed "bulldozers," the word first printed in an 1876 newspaper account of their activities. It is not certain whether they were whites forcing blacks to vote Democratic, Republican Negroes forcing their brothers *not* to vote Democratic, or groups of both. Neither is the exact origin of their name clear—it probably came from *bulldose*, to mete out a "dose of the bull" with the long heavy bullwhip often made from the animal's penis. *Bulldozer* was soon used for "a revolver" and to describe anyone resembling the original terrorist bullies. Later the huge earth-moving machine, which brutally pushes everything in its path aside, became a natural candidate for the designation. Few people realize that when someone is called a *bulldozer* today he is being named not for the machine, but for the vigilantes so much like him. (*See also* **derrick; monkey wrench**.)

bull in a china shop.   Back in 1936 bandleader Fred Waring lost a bet to actor Paul Douglas and had to lead a bull through Plummer's China Shop in New York City. Waring agreed to make good any damage the bull might do, but Ferdinand walked up and down the aisles with aristocratic grace, whereas his leader knocked over a table of china. Obviously bulls aren't as clumsy and reckless in delicate situations as the old saying holds, but the expression has been common in English since before 1834, when Frederick Marryat used it in his novel *Jacob Faithful.*

bullion.   Meaning gold or silver in the mass, or in bars or ingot form, *bullion* derives from the French *bouillir*, "to boil," referring to the boiling or melting of the metal before it is made into bars or ingots. The word is first recorded in the 14th century.

bull pen.   Early in this century the imposing Bull Durham Tobacco signs behind outfield fences in American baseball parks pictured a big brightly colored bull, proclaiming that any batter whose home run hit the bull would get $50 and two bags of Bull Durham. Pitchers usually warmed up near these Bull Durham signs, which may be why warm-up areas for relief pitchers are called *bull pens* today, although the word could have derived from the word *bull pen* that had meant a stockade for prisoners since 1809. Or perhaps the two meanings reinforced each other.

bull's-eye.   There are many plausible ways to explain this term, all of them based on a bull's eye, which is about the same size as the small black spot at the dead center of a target. *Bull's-eye* targets were not used in ancient archery contests, as is commonly thought, but were introduced to England as targets in rifle and hand-gun competition. Perhaps the bull's eyes in them were simply named for their resemblance to a bull's-eye. But it is possible that *bull's-eyes* take their name from a British coin called the *bull's-eye*, which was worth a crown, or five shillings. This coin was in circulation in the early 1800s, about the time *bull's-eye* targets were introduced, and it would seem more logical to name the flat target centers after flat coins than after the round eye of a bull. As for the coin, it was so named in the late 17th century, possibly because the one-crown piece was often bet on the outcome of a bull-baiting contest; when one put money "on the bull's-eye" one was betting on the bull, just as today we are said to put a bet on a horse's nose.

bullshit.   (*See* **shit**.)

bum; on the bum.   No self respecting hobo, or tramp, would allow himself to be called a *bum*, for the word has degenerated from its original meaning of "a vagabond" over a century ago, and today usually stands for a "moneyless, prideless, filthy, hopeless derelict and habitual drunkard." One working definition to distinguish between the three classes of vagabonds is that "a hobo will work, a tramp won't, a bum can't." *Bum* was first recorded in 1855, and during the Civil War was used to describe a foraging soldier. It appears to derive from two words: the German *bummer*, "a high-spirited, irresponsible person," and the old English word *bum*, which has for over four centuries been slang for both "a drunk" and "the buttocks." By the turn of the century a *bum* was the pitiable creature described above instead of a romantic vagabond singing the song of the open road. The term is also used today to describe any no-good person and has a score more uses, including terms like *tennis bum* and *ski bum. On the bum* is an American expression dating back to San Francisco Gold Rush days, when it simply meant living the life of a hobo. Later humorist George Ade used the slang term to mean someone not feeling well, and from this use derives our expression *on the bum* for something that isn't working well. *Bum* for a drunken loafer or vagrant is first recorded in reference to men who lost their fortunes in the California gold rush. To *bum*, to borrow or panhandle money, comes from the practice of bums begging in the streets. *Bum*, for "the buttocks" is a very old word dating from Middle English; only within the past two centuries has it become a vulgar expression. *Bum* now is apparently not an abbreviation of "bottom" but an echoic word. A long-suppressed nursery rhyme goes:

> Piss a bed
> Piss a bed
> Bailey Butt,
> Your Bum is so heavy
> You can't get up!

bumashka.   *Bumashka*, a pejorative form of *bumage*, "paper," is the Russian term for *gobbledygook* (*q.v.*) or "officialese." As much of this exists in the Soviet Union, as in America, one government directive called for "the mobilization of personnel for the removal of dust."

bumboat.   In the early 17th century, *bumboats* (also called *dirtboats*) were scavengers' boats used to remove filth from ships anchored in the Thames. Their name ultimately derives from the medieval *bum*, for "buttocks," a word of echoic origin imitative of "the sound of breaking wind." The bumboats' crews used to sell fresh vegetables to the ships in the harbor, so these craft came to be known as "any boat employed to carry provisions, vegetables, and small merchandise for sale to ships, either in port or lying at a distance from shore."

bump.   The prevailing theory is that *bump* was first an *onomatopoeic* word meaning "a knock or blow," the swelling or protuberance arising from the knocking or bumping becoming known as a *bump* as well. The trouble is that the *bump* for "a swelling" is the first recorded of the two words, by Shakespeare in *Romeo and Juliet* (1592): "It had upon its brow a bumpe as big as a young Cockrel's stone [testicle] . . ." To *bump off*, to murder someone, is American underworld slang of the 1920s, though it originated among U.S. hoboes some years earlier. Being *bumped* from a list, such as an airline passenger list, is a fairly recent and widespread Americanism.

bump on a log.   "Ye ain't goin to set there like a bump on a log 'thout sayin' a word to pay fer yer vittles, air ye?" This recorded use of the above American expression, from Kate Douglas Wiggins's *The Bird's Christmas Carol* (1899), uses the words as they are still used today and best defines them. The metaphor is a good one, for a log is

stolid and stupid and a bump on a log seems all the more so. Also, sitting next to someone who is *like a bump on a log*, who just sits there silently without being able to make conversation, is as uncomfortable as sitting on a bump on a log.

bundling.   In the late 1700s many tracts pro and con were written about the custom of *bundling*, which was all the rage in America at the time. When *bundling*, courting couples would lie in the same bed partly or fully clothed, sometimes with a special bundling board between them. Often the bundling board was breached or hurdled and the couples groped in the dark for additional ways to keep warm, and that is where the controversy came in. In his *Classical Dictionary of the Vulgar Tongue*, Grose defined *bundling* as "A man and woman lying on the same bed with their clothes on; an expedient practiced in America on a scarcity of beds, where, on such occasions, husbands and parents frequently permitted travelers to 'bundle' with their wives and daughters." But there was more to the practice than the scarcity of beds or the lack of heat, as Washington Irving noted in his *History of New York*. Irving cited those "cunning and ingenious" Yankees who permitted young couples to bundle due to their "strict adherence to the good old pithy maxim about 'buying a pig in a poke.'" On the other hand, one old gentleman, explaining the custom to his grandson late in the last century, emphasized the practicality of *bundling* and denied any wrongdoing on the part of the participants. "What is the use of sitting up all night and burning out fire and lights, when you could just as well get under cover and keep warm?" he said. "Why, damn it, there wasn't half as many bastards then as there are now!" In any event, *bundling* was with us from the beginning in America and came close to being a universal custom from 1700 to 1780.

bunk.   The Missouri Compromise was being hotly debated that morning of February 25, 1820 when long-winded Congressman Felix Walker of Buncombe County, North Carolina rose on the floor of the House of Representatives and insisted that he be heard before a vote was taken. "Old Oil Jug," as his fellow congressmen called him after his well-lubricated vocal cords, did not address himself to the monumental question of the extension of slavery; his interminable oration actually had little to do with anything and important members began interrupting him with cries of "Question, Question!" On being asked what purpose his speech served, Walker calmy remarked, "You're not hurting my feelings, gentlemen. I am not speaking for your ears. I am only talking for Buncombe." Old Oil Jug apparently had written his speech some time before and believed he would ingratiate himself with the voters back home if he delivered it in the midst of a great debate, but the strategy didn't work, judging by the fact that he lost the next election.

Yet his reply, "I am talking for Buncombe," was widely published in newspapers covering the debate and became a synonym for talking nonsense. Eventually, *Buncombe* became *bunkum* and it finally took the shortened form of *bunk* (in the 1850s), meaning not only "bombastic, political talk," but "any empty, inflated speech obviously meant to fool people."

bunny. *Bunny*, as in the *Easter bunny* or a *Playboy bunny*, has its origins in the Scottish dialect word *bun*, which according to some scholars, originally meant just the tail of a rabbit or a squirrel. By 1690 *bun* had been extended to *bunny* and had become the pet name for a rabbit.

Bunsen burner; bunsenite. Robert Wilhelm Bunsen (1811-99) invented the *Bunsen burner* that is standard equipment in every chemistry laboratory. This laboratory burner, which mixes gas with air to produce a hot smokeless flame, wasn't the only scientific contribution the German chemist made. He discovered, with Gustav Kirchhoff, the elements cesium and rubidium, and shared with Henry Roscoe the discovery of the reciprocity law, doing much original work in spectrum analysis. The Heidelberg professor also has *bunsenite*, a nickel monoxide, named in his honor.

bunt. The *bunt* in baseball, used mostly by a batter as a sacrifice play to advance another runner into better scoring position, is probably a corruption of the word *butt*, which sounds like *bunt* when spoken through the nose. Hitters *butt* at the ball with the bat when they bunt. *Bunt* dates back to at least 1872, when the strategy's first use is recorded by a player named Pearce on the Brooklyn Atlantics.

buoy; buoyant. Pronounced "boy" in England and by many sailors and some landlubbers in America (as in Lifebuoy soap), the word *buoy* (also pronounced "boo-i") has no etymological connection with "boy." *Buoy* comes from the Old French *boye* meaning "chained," in reference to the chain that holds a buoy in place. However, the chain is invisible to anyone looking at a *buoy* and *buoys* came, ironically enough, to suggest lightness and freedom (the opposite of being chained) to onlookers, giving us the words *buoyant* and *buoyancy*. This was perhaps because of the floating action of the buoy itself.

Burbank; Burbank plum; Burbank potato. There has been muted controversy over whether the plant breeder Luther Burbank (1849-1926) was a "plant wizard" or something of a failure. Burbank was born in Lancaster, Massachusetts and there developed the *Burbank potato*, his most important achievement, while just a boy experimenting with seeds in his mother's garden. At twenty-six he moved to Santa Rosa, California, using the

$150 he made from the sale of his potato to pay for the journey. It was in Santa Rosa, his "chosen spot of all the earth," that he bred almost all the varieties of fruit, vegetables, and ornamentals for which he became famous. These included at least 66 new tree fruits, 12 new bush fruits, 7 tree nuts, and 9 vegetables, of which a number, notably the *Burbank plum*, bear his name. However, only a few of the several hundred varieties developed by Burbank have stood the test of time. Nor was Burbank the first American plant breeder—Thomas Jefferson, George Washington Carver, and Charles Hovey, originator of the Hovey strawberry, came long before him. Yet he undoubtedly deserves his place in history for the contributions that he did make and the example he set for others. Burbank was strongly influenced by Darwin's *Variations of Animals and Plants Under Domestication*. His credo can be summed up in his statement, "I shall be contented if, because of me, there shall be better fruits and fairer flowers."

burbs; suburb. For better or worse, *burbs* has been American slang for *suburbs* for the last decade or so. I record it here mainly because I haven't seen it any dictionary. *Suburbs* wasn't used much in America until about 1940, though the word dates back to 14th-century England, where it meant residential areas outside a town or city, deriving from the Latin *suburbium*, formed from *sub*, "near," and *urbs*, "city."

burgoo. The rich southern American stew called *burgoo* probably takes its name from a similar stew that American seamen used to make, which, in turn, may derive its name from the Arabic *burghul*, "bruised grain." The word, however, is first recorded out West as *burgou*, in 1837, and may be a corruption of "barbecue." Someone has noted about *burgoo*: "No two people tell the same story about its origin and no two people will give you the same recipe."

burgoynade. "Gentleman Johnny" Burgoyne hardly deserved his fate. General John Burgoyne (1722-92), an accomplished dramatist as well as a soldier, commanded the British forces that came down from Canada to capture New York's Fort Ticonderoga during the Revolutionary War. It was his intention to join with Howe's army farther downstate, but due to a delay on Howe's part, excellent American tactics, and enemy forces three times the strength of his own, he was forced to surrender after the battle of Saratoga. English Tories condemned him for his alleged use of savage Indians, and his name in the form of *burgoynade* came to mean the capture of a notable person, particularly a general or high-ranking officer.

Burgundy. The ancient Duchy of Burgundy southeast of Paris has long produced the rich red and white wines called *Burgundies*, which are often made from a blend of wines.

the burial of an ass. This is a biblical term meaning no burial at all, burial with the body thrown on a refuse heap. The expression is from Jeremiah 22:9: "He shall be buried with the burial of an ass, drawn and cast forth beyond the gates of Jerusalem."

Buridan's ass. Buridan's ass is "a hypothetical beast that stands exactly between two haystacks in every respect equal and starves to death because there is no reason why it should eat from one rather than the other." The argument is a sophism, false because it ignores the fact that random choice remains when choice based on knowledge is impossible. Aristotle knew that the argument was specious when he drew the analogy in his *De Caelo* ("On the Heavens"), where he used it to criticize a theory of an earlier writer. However, the French scholastic philosopher Jean Buridan (ca. 1295-1356) accepted it as a philosophical principle when he wrote a commentary on Aristotle's work. Buridan used a dog dying of hunger between two equally tempting dishes of food to illustrate the will's paralysis when confronted with two equal choices and his philosophical sophism should really be called *Buridan's dog*. How *Buridan's dog* became *Buridan's ass* remains something of a mystery. Aristotle used a *man* standing between food and drink in his analogy, so there is no help there. What probably happened was that Buridan's opponents substituted the ass, long a symbol of stupidity, for the dog in Buridan's analogy in order to deride his doctrine. Other myths about the rector of the University of Paris, as false as *Buridan's ass*, insist that he founded Vienna University and was the lover of Joan of Navarre and/or Margaret of Burgundy, both queens of France.

buried; buried in booze. *Buried*, and sometimes *buried in booze*, was popular slang for "dead drunk" in the 1920s during Prohibition, when the ingredients in *booze* (*q.v.*) could kill more quickly.

burke. The best-known of eponymous murderers and among the most unwise, William Burke (1792-1829) was an Irish laborer who emigrated to Scotland in 1817. There he eventually opened a used-clothing store in Edinburgh and, far more important, rented a room from William Hare, a fellow Irishman and owner of a boardinghouse catering to vagrants and elderly pensioners. It was in 1827 that Burke and his partner embarked upon their career. One of Hare's lodgers—an old man named Donald—had died owing him four pounds, and the landlord convinced Burke that they had stumbled upon an easy source of income. Ripping the cover off the coffin in which parish authorities had sealed Donald, the pair hid his body in a bed and filled the coffin with tanner's bark, resealing it and later selling the cadaver for seven pounds ten shillings to Dr. Robert Knox, who ran an anatomy school in Surgeon's Square. Burke and Hare soon expanded their operation. Another boarder lingered too long at death's door and they helped him through, smothering the man with a pillow and selling his body to Knox for ten pounds. Hare and his wife, and Burke and his mistress, Helen McDougal, proceeded to dispatch from fourteen to twenty-eight more unfortunates in similar fashion, receiving up to fourteen pounds for each body. They were careful to smother their victims, leaving no marks of violence, so that it would appear that they were merely graverobbers. Whenever the boardinghouse supply ran low, they lured victims there, usually choosing old hags, drunks, and prostitutes, whom they often plied with drink. If a candidate offered too much resistance to being smothered by a pillow, Burke would pin him down while Hare smothered him, holding his hands over the victim's nose and mouth. But the murderers eventually got careless. First they killed Mary Peterson, a voluptuous eighteen-year-old, so free with her body that it was quickly recognized by Knox's young medical students, who even preserved it before dissection as a perfect example of female pulchritude. Then they did in "Daft Jamie" Wilson, a familiar, good-natured imbecile who made his living running errands on the streets of Edinburgh. Finally, the suspicions of neighbors aroused, police caught them with the body of a missing woman named Mary Dougherty. Hare turned state's evidence at the ensuing trial, which began on Christmas Eve; he and his wife were freed, and Helen McDougal was discharged for lack of evidence. Burke for some reason foolishly refused to give state's evidence. He was convicted and hanged a month later on January 28, 1829, before a crowd of some thirty thousand. The word the murderer contributed to the language was even heard as he stood on the scaffold in the Grassmarket, spectators exhorting the executioner with cries of "Burke him, Burke him!" (*i.e.*, don't hang him but smother or strangle him to death). The crowd wanted to *burke* Hare, too, despite his immunity, but the real brains behind the operation escaped them and is believed to have died of natural causes many years later in England, where he lived under an assumed name.

Burke's Peerage. Like *Debrett's Peerage* (*q.v.*) before it, *Burke's Peerage* has often been called the "studbook" of the British aristocracy. Originally published in 1826, it was fully titled *A Genealogical and Heraldic History of the Peerage and Baronetage of the United Kingdom*, and has been issued annually since 1847. The famous reference book, the first alphabetical guide to the British aristocracy, was the inspiration of John Burke (1787-1848), an English genealogist whose family hailed from Tipperary. Burke's son Sir John Bernard, a genealogist and barrister, assisted him in the compilation, and began its annual re-editing. John Burke also published *Burke's Landed Gentry* (1833-38), another work well known by those interested in tracing lost ancestors.

burning ears; itching ears.   Pliny writes: "When our ears do glow and tingle, some do talk of us in our absence." This superstition probably goes back before the ancient Romans and is recorded early in English, Shakespeare writing of "fire in mine ears." *To have itching ears,* "to enjoy hearing gossip," is perhaps even older, the words recorded in the Bible (2 Tim. 3:3).

burning the midnight oil; it smells of the lamp.

> Wee spend our mid-day sweat, or mid-night oyle;
> Wee tyre the night in thought; the day in toyle.

I've read that this saying is of American origin, but it obviously isn't, judging by the above poem by Francis Quarles, English author and later "chronologer to the City of London," who first recorded the expression in the mid-17th century. Oils of many types were of course widely used for lamps long before American petroleum made low-priced lamplight available. The words mean "to sit up late at night working," especially in the pursuit of learning. *It smells of the lamp* (Latin, *olet lucernam*) is an equally old saying, referring to literary work that is overworked and tired from too much burning of the midnight oil. Of authors who consistently burned the midnight oil, Honoré de Balzac is the best example. Like Pliny the Elder before him, Balzac liked to begin work at midnight and write for eighteen hours at a stretch. He did this for weeks on end and was so meticulous a craftsman that he often completely rewrote his novels in proof.

to burn one's fingers.   To be harmed by meddling with something. Several sources suggest that the allusion here is to taking chestnuts from the fire. But there is no evidence for this in the first recorded use of the phrase in a 1710 book of English proverbs: "The busiebody burns his own fingers."

to burn or hang in effigy.   I've found *effigies* washed up on New York City beaches several times—once two small plastic dolls bound together face-to-face with the names of lovers taped on their foreheads and hundreds of pins stuck in their bodies; on another occasion, an unhusked coconut that represented the head of a real person and had a message carved on it, urging her death. This handiwork of members of local voodoo cults shows that the practice of executing, burning, or hanging people *in effigy* still exists, as it has since prehistory. It means, of course, "to vent one's wrath on a facsimile or copy of a hated person in the hope of insulting him or actually harming him." Apparently, no one gave a name to the practice until the 17th century, when the phrase *in effigy* is first recorded in a beautiful sermon of John Donne (1617): "In those that are damned before, we are damned in Effigie." *Effigy* itself, for "a likeness or image," is from the Latin *effigies,* meaning the same, and was first written

effigies until this was mistaken for a plural and the *s* that should be in the word was dropped. The practice of hanging people in *effigy* to disgrace them publicly dates back long before the French Revolution, when it was customary for the public executioners to hang an effigy of a criminal if the criminal himself couldn't be found.

Burnside carbine; Burnside hat.   (*See* sideburns.)

burn the candle at both ends.

> My candle burns at both ends;
>   It will not last the night;
> But ah, my foes, and oh, my friends—
>   It gives a lovely light!
>
> —Edna St. Vincent Millay, "First Fig" (1920)

These are the words I remember when I hear the above expression; Millay's bright brief candle shows how even an old hackneyed phrase can be transmuted into poetry. The phrase goes back to the early 17th century in English and is much older, for it was translated then from the French *Bruloient la chandelle par less deux bouts.* Originally the expression meant to waste material wealth; that is, to use the candle wastefully. Then it took on its more common modern meaning of wasting one's strength, as when someone goes from his day job to one he holds at night, or works for a worthy cause every moment of his spare time, or even does too much partying after work.

burn your bridges behind you.   This expression may have originally been "burn your boats behind you," which originated with the Romans. Roman generals, including Caesar, often did burn all their boats after invading an alien land to impress upon their legions the fact that there could be no retreat. Later, bridges were burned for the same reason and the phrase to *burn your bridges behind you* came to mean, figuratively, to take a stand from which no withdrawal is feasible.

bury the hatchet.

> Buried was the bloody hatchet;
> Buried was the dreadful war-club . . .
> There was peace among the nations.

Longfellow wrote this in *Hiawatha* (1855), but the expression *bury the hatchet,* "to settle all differences, to let bygones be bygones," goes back much further. Recorded as early as 1794, it stems from an old Indian custom. Crude stone axes, or hatchets, were long the most important weapon of northeastern American Indians. Such ceremony was attached to these tomahawks that when peace was made between two tribes, it was customary to take the tomahawks of both chiefs and bury them. When hostilities broke out again, the hatchets were dug up again as a declaration of war. The earliest record of this practice is found in the letters of American author Samuel Sewall, dated 1680: "Meeting with the Sachem they came to an agreement and buried two axes in the ground . . . which ceremony to them is more significant and binding than all the Articles of Peace, the hatchet being a principle weapon."

busboy. The waiter's assistant in restaurants, who clears dishes off tables and other tasks, takes his name from the *bus*, a "hand-pushed four-wheeled vehicle used typically for carrying dishes in restaurants." The term dates back to the late 19th century.

busby. A *busby*, once a large 18th-century bushy wig, is now the name for the plumed fur cap comprising part of the full-dress uniform of the British Hussars and Royal Home Artillery. It has long been thought to derive from the name of the noted schoolmaster and disciplinarian, Dr. Richard Busby (1606-95). Dr. Busby, headmaster of Westminster School, had among his pupils such greats as Dryden, Locke, and Prior, and once boasted that he at one time or another birched sixteen of the bishops then in office with his "little rod." As far as is known, however, the good doctor did not wear a frizzled wig. Perhaps his hair naturally stood on end, suggesting the wig when it came into vogue, or possibly there was another Busby thus far unknown to history.

bush league. The Dutch *bosch*, "woods or forest," gave us our word early on for *bush*, "wilderness." By 1909 American baseball fans were calling the minor leagues the *bush leagues*, because they were out in the wilderness, away from the cities where professional teams played. *Bush league* and then *bush* soon came to mean anything amateur.

bushwacker. The first *bushwackers* weren't soldiers who hid in the woods or thickets carrying on guerrilla warfare. These *bushwackers* didn't appear until the Civil War, almost fifty years after the first bushwackers got their name by pulling their boats up parts of the Mississippi, by grasping bushes along the bank. In more recent time *bushwacking* has also come to mean making one's way through unbroken forest, off the trail, by pushing bushes aside or breaking them.

business. *Business* derives from an Anglo-Saxon word, *bisigian*, which means "to worry, to fatigue, to occupy." All the earliest recorded uses of the word *business*, dating back to about 950, are to express anxiety, distress, and uneasiness, the word eventually coming to mean "a pursuit, occupation, or employment," its modern sense, only in about 1400.

business tomorrow. After the Spartans seized Thebes, Archias commanded the garrison in that Greek city. The enemy plotted to kill him, but were discovered, their plot revealed in a letter sent to Archias. Archias, however, was enjoying himself at that moment. He put the letter aside, remarking, *"Business tomorrow."* He was assassinated before the sun rose the next day.

busman's holiday. An old story has a London bus driver spending his days off riding the bus he regularly drives, his peculiarity resulting in the expression *busman's holiday*, for "spending one's spare time doing what one regularly does for a living." But the story cannot be authenticated and the phrase, which is first recorded in 1921 but is probably ten years or so older, must still be marked "origin unknown."

busted, by gosh! (*See* **Pike's Peak or bust.**)

busy as a bee. "For aye as busy as bees been they," Chaucer wrote in *Canterbury Tales* (1387), the first recorded mention of the phrase. But bees must have been noticed busily pollinating plants since prehistoric days and no doubt the expression was used long before Chaucer's time. *Bee*, in fact, is a word found in all languages with Indo-European origins. That bees are busy there is no doubt—one pound of honey results from the visiting of some ten million flowers where bees collect nectar, which they change to honey in their bodies.

busy as a one-armed paperhanger. This phrase is often attributed to cartoonist T(homas) A(loysius) Dorgan (1877-1929), but may have originated with O. Henry, who wrote in a 1908 story: "Busy as a one-armed man with a nettle rash pasting on wall-paper."

Busy Lizzie. (*See* **touch-me-not.**)

butcher. There is a story of a 13th-century queen of France wedding a *butcher*, so esteemed was the trade at the time. Our word *butcher* does come to us from the French *bocher*, which derives from *boc*, "goat," all butchers originally having been slaughterers of goats before bloodying their hands with other animals.

butcher's dog. (*See* **to lie like the butcher's dog.**)

Buttercup. Centuries ago English dairy farmers believed that if their cows ate the little yellow flowers that commonly grew in the meadows, the butter they yielded would be colored the same rich yellow. Experience seemed to prove that this was true and so the flowers were named *buttercups*. Actually, the *field buttercup* (*Ranunculus acris*) did improve the quality of Bossy's output, because the flower grows only on good pasture and thus provides good feed. The flower's scientific genus name, *Ranunculus*, is Latin for "a little frog," in allusion to the meadow habitat of the wildflower.

to butter up someone. In the sense of bestowing fulsome flattery upon someone this phrase dates all the way back to Congreve's *Way of the World* (1700): "The squire that's buttered still is sure to be undone." It probably comes from the French *cirer*, which means the same.

butter wouldn't melt in her mouth. Men have been saying this about demure women since the early 16th century; in fact, Heywood listed it as a proverb in 1536: the lady so prim and proper, so cold, that is, that even a piece of soft butter wouldn't melt in her mouth. In *Pendennis* Thackeray used the expression with reference to a girl who "smiles and languishes," but today it isn't usually employed in the sense of suspiciously amiable. In fact, the phrase once had a longer form: "She looks like butter wouldn't melt in her mouth, but cheese won't choke her," *i.e.*, she's really not fastidious at all, but in fact rather earthy.

buttinsky. Someone who interrupts conversations or intrudes in matters not concerning him is said to *butt in*. Most authorities believe the "-sky" ending a play on Russian and Polish names ending in "-sky," *buttinsky* a punning word formed toward the turn of the century when there were plenty of "greenhorn" immigrants among these ethnic groups who had to ask a lot of questions in order to survive. At any rate, the term was soon used to describe all *buttinskies* and still is.

buttock broker. *Buttock broker* is a humorous term for a matchmaker or marriage broker, first recorded in the late 17th century. Used in slang speech until the early 19th century, it also meant the madame of a brothel, equally adept at getting buttocks together.

to buttonhole. "Barricade your door against the button-holding world!" a British magazine warned its readers over a century ago. *Button-holding*, "grabbing a man by the top button of his coat and holding on with all the strength of the boring until you sell him one thing or another," was so common in the early 19th century that *button-holder* was defined in many dictionaries as "one who takes hold of a man's coat by the button so as to detain him in conversation. People must have been button-holding and wearying people in France, too, at the time, for the French had a similar phrase. In those days men's coats had buttons all the way up to the neck, including one on the lapel that could be buttoned in cold weather. When fashion decreed that upper buttons be eliminated, button-holders didn't suddenly reform. Instead, they began grabbing people by the buttonholes designers (for no good reason) left on the lapels and the phrase became *to buttonhole*.

buzz. (*See* **onomatopoeia**.)

B.V.D.s. There is no doubt about the origin of *B.V.D.*s. The initials do not derive form the words "Boys Ventilated Drawers" or any such humorous phrase. *B.V.D.*s comes from the initials of the three men (Bradley, Voorhies, and Day) who founded, in 1876, the company that makes them. *B.V.D.* is a trademark and cannot be legally used to describe the product of any other company, though it is often used, unlawfully, as a generic term for underwear. *Beeveedees* is a variant spelling that is recorded in print as early as 1915.

bwana. The journalist Henry Morton Stanley of Stanley and Livingstone fame first recorded the Swahili *bwana* in 1878. *Bwana* is a title of respect translating as "father of sons," but meaning "sir, Mr., boss, or master." Often applied exclusively to white men in the past, it is today a common form of address to both Africans and whites in many African countries. (*See* **Dr. Livingstone, I Presume!**)

by a hairbreadth; a hairbreadth escape. Since the early 15th century a *hairbreadth* has meant "an infinitesimally small space or distance, one extremely narrow or close." The breadth or diameter of a hair varies from head to head, but is generally given as 1/48th of an inch. A famous early American cartoon strip featured a character called "Hairbreadth Harry" who was always having close calls and barely avoiding trouble.

by and large. *By and large* originated in the days of sailing ships, roughly meaning "to sail a ship to the wind and off it." These instructions to a helmsman were not precise, and so the 17th-century nautical term came to indicate imprecise generalities in everyday English and to mean "generally speaking," "on the whole"—especially when the speaker or writer is telling the substantial truth, despite minor exceptions. Literal-minded linguists object to the expression because *by and large* really describes a more complex marine operation than is indicated in the above definition.

Byerly Turk; Darley Arabian; Godolphin Barb. These are the three Oriental horses from whom, without exception, all modern thoroughbred racehorses descend through the male line. *Byerly Turk*, first of the founding fathers, was the charger of English Captain Byerly at the Battle of the Boyne (1690). Little is known about him except that he was a Turkish stallion purchased abroad a few years before. *Darley Arabian*, most celebrated of the three sires, was sent from Syria to Richard Darley of Yorkshire by his son Thomas in 1704; he was a certified Arabian stallion. *Godolphin Barb* or *Arabian*, called "the mysterious Frenchman," was brought to England from France in 1730 by Edward Coke and later sold or given to the Earl of Godolphin.

by George. Ben Jonson (and presumably his contemporaries) used the mild oath *by St. George!* as far back as 1598, but it wasn't until the late 19th century that the expression began to be shortened to *by George!* St. George has been the patron saint of England since the institution of the Order of the Garter. A historical character about whom little is really known, the patron saint of soldiers was perhaps a soldier in the Roman army who was martyred for the faith in Asia Minor. In legend he is said to have slain a dragon that fed on villagers at Silene, Libya, rescuing the Princess Sabra from its clutches. This tale of course became a Christian allegory for good triumphing over evil. The name George has its roots in the Greek *Georgos*, "a farmer," literally a worker of the earth. The word comes from the Greek *ge*, "the earth," and *legon*, "a work," which also gives us Virgil's *Georgics*, an "agricultural poem" about the land and the men working it.

by hook or by crook. Used by John Wycliffe in 1380 and now standard English, this expression has a dozen explanations that can't be proved or disproved. The most widely accepted theory traces *by hook or by crook* to the forests of medieval England, which belonged to the King and were off limits to all commoners except those gathering firewood. Ancient law restricted these peasant gatherers to dead wood on the ground or dead branches that they could reach with a shepherd's crook and cut off with a reaper's billhook. The story does explain the phrase meaning "by any means possible," but leaves something to be desired regarding the foul means suggested by *crook*. One widely accepted version traces the expression to 1100, when a charcoal burner named Purkiss found the body of William Rufus, King of England, who had been slain by an archer in Hampshire's New Forest. Purkiss carted the king's body to Winchester and was rewarded with permission to gather all the wood in the forest that he needed for his charcoal burners—provided he took only wood that he could reach *by hook or crook*. Almost nine hundred years have passed and the Purkiss family (now spelled Purkess) still live in the New Forest, which is the largest surviving medieval forest in England thanks to such *hook and crook conservation laws*, if I may coin a phrase.

Byronic. George Gordon, Lord Byron (1788-1824), contributed to the creation of the *Byronic* hero with deeds as much as poems. Byron's slight lameness, his good looks (which were likened to the Apollo Belvedere), his myriad and often sensational romantic entanglements, his wanderings on the Continent and his devotion to the cause of Greek freedom, were among many factors that made the English poet the perfect model for the wildly romantic yet despairing and melancholy heroes of his poems. Byron's poetry was the most popular of his day, at home and especially abroad, despite its criticism on what today might be considered ridiculous moral grounds. No English poet but Shakespeare had greater influence on European literature, and all Byron's major works, such as *Childe Harold's Pilgrimage* and *Don Juan*, have stood the test of time. The poet was haunted in his lifetime by the charge that he committed incest with his half-sister, Mrs. Augusta Leigh. His tempestuous life, the panache and bravura of this poet ("His eyes the open portals of the sun—thing's of light and for light," in Coleridge's words; "The only man to whom I could apply the word beautiful," according to another contemporary) were more romantic than any of his poems. Byron died in Missolonghi, Greece of malarial fever when only thirty-five. His heart is buried there, where he had sought a soldier's grave in the name of Greek freedom. His body lies buried in England in a small village church, the authorities having refused his burial in the Poet's Corner of Westminster Abbey.

by the skin of the teeth. Many phrases from the *Book of Job* in the Old Testament are proverbial in English: "Naked I came from my mother's womb, and naked I shall return"; "The Lord gave, and the Lord hath taken away"; "Man is born unto trouble . . . ." The scholars who prepared the Geneva Bible in 1560 were the first to render Job's reply to Bildad that he had barely escaped with his life as "I have escaped with the skinne of my teethe," and their poetic translation was retained by the editors of the King James version of the Bible (*Job* 19:20). The full King James quotation is: "My bone cleaveth to my skin and to my flesh, and I am escaped with the skin of my teeth." Despite objections that the teeth have no skin, centuries of Bible reading have given the expression a permanent place in the language as the description of a close escape, though it has been altered a hairbreadth to *by the skin of the teeth*.

C

C. The letter *C* is probably the highly modified form of an ancient sign for a camel. One of the strangest stories attached to any letter is told about it. It seems that an Admiral George Cockburn led the incendiaries who demolished the *National Intelligencer* when the British burned Washington during the War of 1812. This gentlemanly incendiary ordered his men to melt down all the *C*s in the newspaper office, "so that later they can't abuse my name."

cabal. This word, for a group of conspirators, has for many years been popularly regarded as the most famous acronym in English. Tradition has it that the word was formed from the initials of certain members of King Charles II's infamous ministry in the years 1667-73. *Clifford, Ashley (Shaftesbury), Buckingham, Arlington,* and *Lauderdale* were only five among a number of Charles's ministers who plotted often diametrically opposed secret intrigues. They rarely met all together, although they did constitute the Privy Council foreign committee. The infamous five did, however, secretly sign the Treaty of Alliance with France in 1672, without Parliament's approval, forcing the nation into war with Holland. After this shameful episode, their enemies were quick to point out that their initials formed the word *cabal,* but this does not say that *cabal* originated with the acrostic ministry. *Cabal,* for a society of intriguers, had previously been introduced into English from the Latin *cabbala,* which derives, in turn, from the Hebrew *qubbalah.* The *qubbalah* were doctrines said to be originally received from Moses, enabling their possessors to unlock secrets of magical power. During the Middle Ages, the secret meetings of *cabbala* groups claiming knowledge of such doctrines gave rise to the English word *cabal. Cabal* did, however, take on a new political significance and popularity in English with the machinations of Clifford and the others. The historian Macaulay writes, for example, that "These ministers were called the Cabal, and they soon made the appellation so infamous that it has never since their time been used except as a term of reproach."

cabbage; cabbage head; cabbages & kings. Ask for a head of *cabbage* and you are repeating yourself, for *cabbage* means "head," the name of the vegetable deriving from the Old French *caboce,* "swollen head," and obviously named for its shape resemblance. *Caboce* itself is made up of the Old French *boce,* "a swelling," the *ca* in the word very likely suggested by the Latin *caput,* meaning "head." *Cabbage,* probably the most ancient of vegetables, has been cultivated for more than 4,000 years. In Greek mythology, it is said to have sprung from sweat on the head of Jupiter, and the Greeks also believed that eating it cured baldness. The saying *cabbage head* for "a fool" dates back to the late 17th century and is best explained by the old music hall lyrics: "I ought to call him a cabbage head,/ He is so very green . . ." *Cabbages and Kings,* an expression O. Henry used as the title for his first book of stories, is from Lewis Carroll's *Through the Looking Glass*:

> "The time has come," the Walrus said,
>   "To talk of many things:
> Of shoes and ships—and sealing wax—
>   Of cabbages and kings—
> And why the sea is boiling hot—
>   And whether pigs have wings."

cablegram; telegram. First used in 1868, the word *cablegram* initially met with some resistance, scholars condemning it as a hybrid derived from Latin ("cable") and Greek ("gram"). Use the all-Greek *calogram* instead of the New York City-born monster, they suggested, but few agreed and the coinage proved durable. Something of the same happened with the earlier coinage *telegram,* which we know was invented by a friend of a man who wrote a letter to the *Albany Evening Journal* on April 6, 1852, asking that it be adopted in place of the clumsy "telegraphic dispatch" used at the time. Grammarians pointed out that *telegram* was not properly formed from its Greek elements and suggested "telegraphemie" instead, but the "barbaric new Yankee word" won out in the test of time. Such improperly formed words are of course common in English and there is a liberal supply of hybrids like *cablegram,* including such common words as *because, dentist, grateful, starvation, talkative,* and *parliament.*

caboose. Before it became "the last car on a train," a *caboose,* from the Dutch *kombius,* was a seaman's term for a ship's galley. The word went West in America to become the name for the cook wagon on the range and then became the car on a train carrying provisions.

caca. Though it appears to be simply the imitation of an infant's sounds, *caca,* for "excrement or a bowel movement," has an aristocratic Roman ancestor. The word derives from the Latin *cacare,* "to defecate."

cackle. (*See* **chuckle; onomatopoeia.**)

caconym. A *caconym*, deriving from the Green *caco*, "bad, evil," and *onyma*, "name," is a bad or undesirable name. Many *caconyms* were given to people in German-speaking countries during the early 19th century, when all citizens were required to take surnames and village clerks often assigned objectionable ones unless bribes were given. An apocryphal story is told of two men who paid such bribes. "You can't imagine how much it cost to have the *m* put in my name," said Herr Schmeiss." (*Schmeiss* means "fling" in German, while *Scheiss* means "shit.") "You can't imagine how much I paid to have the *m* taken out of my name," replied his friend, Herr Schutz. (*Schutz* means "protection" in German, while *Schmutz* is "filth.")

caddy; cadet. According to legend, Mary Queen of Scots was the first woman golfer, so avid a player, in fact, that she continued playing her round when she was informed of her husband's murder one day in 1567. An old story also claims that Mary introduced the word *cadet* (from the Gascon *capdet*, "little chief") into English from French. *Cadet* first meant the youngest son of a noble, and by 1630 meant a young no-good who had taken to the streets—its spelling changed to *caddy*. By the mid-18th century a *caddy* came to mean a young porter on the streets and finally, a century later, a young porter who carried golf clubs. Independently, the word *cadet* for the youngest son of a nobleman came to mean a student at a military academy, because the youngest sons of nobles usually became soldiers.

Cadillac. *Cadillac*, which is of course a trade name, has long been to expensive automobiles what *Ford* (*q.v.*) has been to low-priced cars. Ironically, the Detroit Automobile Company, formed by Henry Ford in 1899, was the forerunner of the Cadillac Company, Cadillac later being absorbed by General Motors. The Cadillac, in the United States and elsewhere, has become a symbol of success to some, vulgar pretension to others, and is a synonym for an expensive car to all. It bears the name of Antoine de la Mothe Cadillac (1658-1730), a minor nobleman and French colonial governor who, in 1701, founded Detroit as an important post for French control of the fur trade. Cadillac also established a trading post in what is now Cadillac, Michigan, on Lake Cadillac. Unlike the car bearing his name, the Frenchman seems to have been popular with no one. Neither Indians nor settlers could get along with him at Fort Pontchartrain (present-day Detroit), and his later governorship of the vast Louisiana Territory (1711-16) met with similar hostility. Cadillac, recalled to France, died in his native Gascony.

Cadmean letters; Cadmean victory. Myth is often a reflection of fact, and the sixteen letters of the old Greek alphabet said to be introduced to the Boeotians by the mythological hero Cadmus from Phoenicia really do derive from Phoenician script. It is uncertain whether there was an actual Cadmus, a prototype for the hero who introduced the *Cadmean letters*. A *Cadmean victory* refers to the same mythological warrior. It derives from the story that Cadmus killed a dragon and sowed the dragon's teeth. Armed warriors sprang up and he set them fighting by throwing a stone among them; only five warriors survived, and these became the ancestors of the noble family of Thebes. A Cadmean victory, in remembrance of these five surviving stalwarts, became proverbial for a victory achieved where the victors can hardly be distinguished from the vanquished.

cadre. *Cadre* are trained or key men, generally in the military, who instruct and supervise untrained troops. Thought to be the "skeleton" or foundation of an outfit, they appropriately take their name from the French *cadre*, "frame." The word didn't come into English until the mid-19th century.

Caesarian section. According to Pliny the Elder, the first of the Caesars was brought into the world by the *Caesarian section* operation named in his honor. However, Julius Caesar probably wasn't extracted from his mother's womb by this incision through the abdominal walls, though the operation was commonly practiced on dead mothers in early times. Caesar, whose mother, Julia, lived many years after his death, probably has his name confused with the operation because it became mandatory under the *lex Cesare* ("law of the Caesars," the codified Roman law of the time), just as it had been under the previous *lex regia* ("royal law"), that every woman dying in advanced pregnancy be so treated in an effort to save the baby. It is also possible that *Caesarian section* simply comes from the Latin *caesus*, past participle of the verb *caedere*, "to cut."

Caesar salad. This popular salad was not named after Julius Caesar nor any of his family. It seems to have been invented in the late 1920s by Caesar Gardini, a restaurant owner in Tijuana, Mexico, but there are several contenders for the honor.

cafeteria. A relatively young Americanism, *cafeteria* was probably introduced in 1893 at the Chicago World's Fair. It derives, however, from the Spanish *cafetería*, meaning the same.

cahoots. To be in partnership, often shady partnership, with. There are two theories about *cahoots*. One, that the word derives from the French *cahute*, "cabin," suggesting that the two in cahoots shared a cabin together. Or, two, more probably, that *cahoots* derives from the French *cahorte*, "a gang."

cakes and ale. Long before it became the title of Somerset Maugham's novel, *Cakes and Ale* meant "fun or pleasant activity," as in "life isn't all cakes and ale." Shakespeare may have invented the expression, for he first recorded it in *Twelfth Night* (1600): "Dost thou think, because thou art virtuous, there shall be no more cakes and ale?"

calabash. Since the mid-19th century a *calabash* has meant an empty-headed person, someone with nobody home upstairs, in U.S. slang. *Calabash* in this sense derives from the gourd of the same name, which comes from the Arabic *qar 'ah yābisah*, "empty gourd." Sherlock Holmes's famous pipe, readers may recall, was made from a hollowed-out calabash gourd.

calculate. The abacus, or counting board, was borrowed by the Romans from the Greeks, who called it an *abax*. Although today it contains wooden beads strung on wire, it was first divided into compartments, with pebbles moved from compartment to compartment as the reckoning progressed. Thus, from the Latin name for these abacus pebbles, *calculus*, comes our word for mathematical reckoning, *calculate*.

Calendar Islands. The Calendar Islands in Maine's Casco Bay are among the most appropriately named of island groups—there are exactly 365 of them.

calepin. I don't know of any synonym for a polyglot dictionary, one in many languages, save the unusual *calepin*. The word comes from the name of Italian Augustine friar Ambrosio Calepino, who in 1502 published a famous Latin dictionary that went through many editions and was *the* Latin dictionary of the day. Apparently this Latin dictionary of Calepino's was published in an "octoglot" edition, which led to the man's name being employed as it mostly is. Anyway, *calepin* was used for "a polyglot dictionary, a dictionary or any book of authority or reference" until well into the 18th century, and has had limited use since.

calico. The cotton cloth is named after the Indian city of Calicut (now Kozhikode), from where it was first exported in 1498, when Vasco da Gama took it back to Portugal.

California. Lexicographers aren't positive about the origin of *California*, but the state may be named after a woman named Calafia in an old Spanish romance, Calafia ruling over an island called California. On the other hand, other etymologists insist that *California* is a Catalan word meaning "hot oven"—a story that's not good for the tourist trade.

call his bluff. This widely used phrase certainly originated in American poker games of the early 19th century, bluffing being an integral part of poker, and *to call* meaning to match a bet. Some etymologists trace *bluff* itself back to the Low German *bluffen*, "to frighten by menacing conduct," which became the Dutch *buffen*, "to make a trick at cards," but *bluff* is first recorded in an 1838 account of an American poker game.

callipygian. According to Sir Thomas Browne, *callipygian* refers to "women largely composed from behind." This is a term of admiration (unlike *steatophygous*, q.v.), deriving from the Greek roots for "beauty" and "buttocks." The *Callipygian Venus* is a famous statue of Venus with substantial, nicely shaped buttocks.

call the turn. Someone who *calls the turn* guesses correctly how an affair or transaction will turn out. The expression doesn't derive from "turn out," however, which comes to us instead from the card game faro (q.v.), a very popular game in 19th-century America. One who *calls the turn* in faro, that is, guesses correctly how the last three cards turned over will appear, wins at high odds from the bank.

calumny; libel; slander. The Romans branded false accusers with a *K* on the forehead, this standing for their word *kalumnia*, which became *calumnia* when they gave the *c* the *k* sound and for the most part stopped using the *k*. Our word *calumny*, a false accusation deliberately intended to hurt another's reputation, comes directly from the Latin *calumnia*, which means the same. Shakespeare and Shelley believed that only the dead knew not calumny, the bard writing in *Hamlet*: "Be thou chaste as ice, as pure as snow, thou shalt not escape calumny." A false accuser, the slanderer who spreads *calumnies*, is called a *calumniator*, and those who are the victims of *calumniatory* charges are the *calumniated*. "Calumny," said Queen Elizabeth I, "will not fasten on me forever." *Libel* is written or printed calumny, and *slander* is legally calumny by oral utterance. For example, Whistler's paintings were slandered by English critic John Ruskin, but Ruskin was only sued for libel when he published such statements as "I . . . never expected to hear a coxcomb ask two hundred guineas for flinging a pot of paint in the public's face." Whistler won his case, but was awarded only a farthing, a coin then worth less than one cent.

Calvinism; Calvinist. The system of theological thought called *Calvinism* was founded by French Protestant reformer John Calvin, or Caucin (1509-64). *Calvinist* beliefs, held in much modified form today in Presbyterian and Reformed churches, were formulated as the Five Points in 1618. These are, briefly: 1) Original Sin, man's natural inability to exercise free will since Adam's fall; 2) Predestination; 3) Irresistible grace; 4) Perseverance of the saints or elect; and 5) Particular redemption. *Calvinism* has overwhelmingly been regarded as a bleak, forbidding theology.

Cambridge flag. This was a popular name for the first flag of the American Continental Army at the start of the Revolutionary War. Its official name was the *Grand Union flag* (because it had been patterned on the British Grand Union flag with its red and white stripes and crosses), but was popularly called the *Cambridge flag* because it was first flown near Boston and Cambridge, Mass.

camellia. One of the most beautiful flowering plants, the evergreen *camellia* is named for George Joseph Kamel (1661-1706), a Moravian Jesuit missionary and amateur botanist who wrote extensive accounts of the shrub, which he found in the Philippine Islands in the late 17th century. Kamel, who called himself Camellus, the Latinized form of his name, operated a pharmacy for the poor in Manila, planting an herb garden to supply it. He published reports of the plants he grew in the Royal Society of London's *Philosophical Transactions*, and some authorities believe that Kamel sent the first specimens of the shiny-leaved *camellia* back to Europe. In any event, he was the first to describe the shrub, a relative of the tea plant, and the great Swedish botanist Linnaeus read his accounts in *Transactions* and named the plant *camellia* after him. *Camellias* are used extensively as garden shrubs in southern areas of the United States and England. Their wax-like, long-lasting flowers are white, red, or pink.

camelopard. (*See* **giraffe**.)

Camelot. The legendary spot where King Arthur held court in British fable, which has come to mean any ideal place. The real Camelot has been located in Somerset near Winchester, in Wales, and in Scotland, among other places.

camel's hair. A German artist named Kemul may have given his name to *camel's hair* artists' brushes because he invented them, but there is no evidence to support the theory that *camel's hair* is a corruption of *Kemul's hair*. In any case, the name *camel's hair* is a misnomer: the artist's brushes are made from long tail hairs taken from squirrel species inhabiting cold areas such as Siberia. Most likely the brushes were erroneously named because people thought they were made from the fine hair of the two-humped Bactrian camel when the brushes were introduced in the 18th century. Camel hair, longer than sheep's wool and as fine as silk, had been used in Europe since the early 14th century for cloth, scarves, and other items.

Cameroon. This African country has an unusual name, one that derives from the Portuguese word for shrimp—*camarão*. Not because it was a small country, but due to the abundance of the crustaceans off its shores.

Camille. In *La Dame aux Camelias* (1848), better known on the stage and screen as *Camille*, Alexandre Dumas *fils* wrote about Marguerite Gautier, one of the world's most endearing fictional creations, a courtesan who wore no flower other than the camellia—a white camellia for twenty-five days of the month and a red camellia the other five days. Marguerite was based on a real-life Parisian courtesan, or prostitute, Marie Duplessis, the mistress of many wealthy aristocrats and Dumas's lover for a time. Marie, who used the camellia as a trademark, died of tuberculosis at the age of twenty-three, and Dumas immortalized her in his book, her name becoming synonymous for anyone like her.

camouflage. In Parisian slang, prior to World War I, *camoufler* meant "to disguise." After 1914 the term was "naturalized with remarkable rapidity" by the English as *camouflage* and applied to anything disguised from the enemy, whether a varicolored battleship or a convoy of trucks.

canard. *Canard* means "duck" in French, and the word *canard*, for "a ridiculously false story," comes from the French expression *vendre un canard à moitié*, literally, "to half-sell a duck." The expression means to make a fool out of a buyer, or anyone else, with a false story. Tellers of "half-ducks," or *canards*, were known in France three centuries ago, and the word probably gained a firmer foothold with a hoax played by a Frenchman named Cornelessin, who, testing the gullibility of the public, published a story that he had thirty ducks, one of which he killed and threw to the other twenty-nine, who ate it. He then cut up a second, then a third, until the twenty-ninth duck was eaten by the survivor—an excellent, bull, duck, or *canard* story.

canary; sing like a canary. How did dogs give their name to canaries? It happened that in about 40 B.C. Juba, the native chief of Mauritania, explored a group of islands far off the coast of his kingdom and named the largest of them Canaria, or "Island of Dogs," because of the wild dogs inhabiting it. Later visitors called the whole island group the Canary Islands, and when the grayish-green songbird of the island was tamed and exported in the 16th century, it became widely known as "the bird from the Canary Islands," which was inevitably shortened to *canary*. Informants, or stool pigeons, are sometimes said by police to *sing like a canary* when they reveal everything they know, the expression dating back to the late 19th century.

cancel. Medieval scribes crossed out errors on parchment by drawing lines obliquely across the words. They called such crisscrosses *cancelli*, "lattices," because they resembled such structures, and the word *cancelli* for such cross-outs eventually gave us the English *cancel*.

candidate.   Romans running for public office wore white clothing (signifying they were pure) during the elections. From the Latin word for white or pure, *candidus*, came their name *candidate*, which became our word meaning the same.

can do.   (*See* **no can do**.)

canicular days.   (*See* **dog days**.)

cannel coal.   This is not "channel coal." Found in Kentucky and Indiana, *cannel coal* is "a brightly burning coal rich in hydrogen that burns well in open fireplaces" and is becoming popular again as fireplaces become more common. Because it gives off a lot of light compared to other coals, it was first called "candle coal," the name eventually corrupted to *cannel*.

cannibal.   When Columbus encountered the Caribs upon landing in the Lesser Antilles on his second voyage in 1493, these natives told him their name was *Canibales*. This word was merely a dialectic form of Caribes and these people were Caribs themselves, but the Spanish thereafter called the whole Carib tribe *Canibales*. Because some of these fierce warriors ate human flesh, within a century their name was used in Europe as a synonym for man-eaters, and *cannibalism* was substituted for the classical "anthropophagy." The word was probably also influenced by the Spanish word *canino*, meaning "canine" or "voracious." Columbus, incidentally, thought he had landed in Asia and that the *Canibales* were subjects of the Great Khan, or Cham, another doubtful but possible influence on the word's formation. (*See* **Caribbean Sea**.)

cannoli.   This is a crisp Italian pastry filled with sweetened ricotta, candied fruits, and chocolate chips. The pastry is named from the Italian word for "tube," the pastry being tubular in shape. But a *cannoli* is never called a *cannolo*—at least I have never heard the singular used in America, although one such pastry is technically a *cannolo*.

canoe; paddle your own canoe.   Abraham Lincoln's frequent use of the phrase *paddle your own canoe* did much to make it popular, but Captain Frederick Marryat, that unflattering critic of American manners, seems to have been the first to have used the expression in its figurative sense, "be independent," in his novel *The Settlers in Canada* (1844). *Canoe* probably derives from the Arawak word *canoa*, for "a small boat carved from a tree trunk," which Columbus recorded in his diary and introduced into Spanish.

canoe birch.   The birchbark canoes of Indian fame were made from this birch species, which is the most wide-spread birch in the world. *Canoe birch* is also called white birch, silver birch, and paper birch.

canopy.   The *canopy* we know as an overhanging protection or shelter takes its name from *konops*, the Greek for "gnat." The first canopy was a "gnat curtain" that fishermen and boatmen on the Nile River fashioned from their fine-meshed nets and slept under to protect themselves from gnats and other insects.

cant.   *Cant*, for "a whining manner of speech or pious hypocritical talk," surely derives from the Latin *cantare*, "to sing or chant." Yet some evidence indicates that the word's meaning may have been influenced by the unpopularity of a Scottish preacher named Andrew Cant (1590-1663). In fact, the *Spectator* tried to trace *cant* to the Reverend Cant in an article written in 1711, observing that he talked "in the pulpit in such a dialect that it's said he was understood by none but his own Congregation, and not by all of them." Most dictionaries do not recognize the connection between the preacher's name and *cant*—the usual explanation being that the word evolved from the Latin *cantare*, in reference to the whining speech of beggars. But there seems to be enough evidence to indicate that Reverend Andrew Cant's unpopularity at least strengthened the word's meaning.

Cantab; Cantabrigian.   *Cantabrigian* has been since about 1645 a synonym for a resident of Cambridge, England, deriving from the Latin *Cantabrigia* for "Cambridge." Hence the word has long meant Cambridge or Harvard (in Cambridge, Massachusetts) students who are more commonly called *Cantabs*, even this shortened form dating back to early 18th-century England.

cantaloupe.   The *cantaloupe* is named for Cantalupo, the Pope's country seat near Rome, where the melon was first grown in Italy.

can't cut the mustard; can't cut (hack) it.   Whatever the origins of *can't cut the mustard*, and they are about as clear as mustard, the expression *too old to cut the mustard* is always applied to men today and conveys the idea of sexual inability. *Can't cut the mustard*, however, means not to be able to handle any job for any reason, not just because of old age. Preceding the derivation of *too old to cut the mustard* by about a half a century, it derives from the expression *to be the mustard*. "Mustard" was slang for the "genuine article" or "main attraction" at the time. Perhaps someone cutting up to show that he was *the mustard*, or the greatest, was said *to cut the mustard* and the phrase later came to mean to be able to fill the bill or do the important or main job. In any case, O. Henry first used the words in this sense in his story "Heart of the West" (1907) when he wrote: "I looked around and found a proposition that exactly cut the mustard." Today *can't cut the mustard* is usually *can't cut it* or *can't hack it*. A recent variant on *too old to cut the mustard* is *if you can't cut the mustard, you can lick the jar.*

cantankerous. Oliver Goldsmith coined this word for "contrary or ill-natured" in *She Stoops to Conquer* (1773). Or rather, he fashioned it from an earlier, now obsolete word, *cantecker*, meaning a quarrelsome, disputatious person.

canter. Originally the *canter*—the gait of a horse between a trot and a gallop—was called a *Canterbury gallop*, because it was thought to be the traditional pace of pilgrims riding to the Canterbury shrine in England.

Canterbury bells. Pilgrims to Canterbury in Chaucer's time thought that the bellflowers (*Campanula medium*) they saw along the road resembled the little bells on their horses and called the flowers *Canterbury bells*. *Campanula* itself is the Latin word for "bell."

can't hold a candle to. It was common in the 16th century and later for servants holding candles to guide their masters along the poorly lighted streets of English cities. Theaters also employed candle-holders called link-boys in the days before gas lighting. These were among the most menial of jobs, but some poor wights failed at them for not knowing the roads or the layout of a theater, and they were said to be *not worthy to hold a candle to anyone*. This expression soon came to be used in the sense of comparing the abilities of two people, *he can't hold a candle to you*, meaning "he's greatly inferior to you."

can't make head nor tail of it. I can't understand this, it's totally confusing. The saying, born in a rural world some three centuries ago, is today applied mainly to stories or explanations, though someone will occasionally say he or she *can't make head nor tail of* an object. It is sometimes heard as I *can't make heads or tails of it*, this variation possibly suggested by coin flipping.

can't see the woods for the trees. John Heywood listed this as an English proverb in 1546, using the singular "wood" in the phrase, but most Americans say it "woods" today. Still very common, after perhaps 500 years, the workhorse expression means to be so involved in a mass of details that you don't have a view of the whole.

Canuck. *Canuck* as a derogatory name for a French Canadian has been around since about 1865, with both Canadians and Americans using it. It may be from *Canada* and *Chinook* (*q.v.*), but it may also be from *Canada* + the Algonquin Indian ending *-uck*.

canvasback duck. Courtiers in the 17th century wore doublets that covered them from shoulders to waist.

These were made of leather or other expensive materials, but some impecunious gallants couldn't afford such fine garments and had to settle for doublets made of leather in the front and cheaper canvas in the back. These "canvas back" garments later inspired the name *canvasback* for the North American duck with whitish back feathers.

Capability Brown. "Your estate holds great capabilities" the great English landscape gardener and architect Lancelot Brown (1715-83) often told prospective employers. His words earned the founder of modern English landscape gardening many commissions and the nickname "Capability."

Cape Cod turkey. New Englanders have called baked codfish *Cape Cod turkey* for many years, at least since the mid-19th century, just as melted cheese has been called *Welsh rabbit* (*q.v.*) the world over.

Cape Horn. (See **around the horn**.)

Cape of Good Hope; Greenland. Early Portuguese explorers named this treacherous area off the southern tip of Africa the "Cape of Storms." But King John II of Portugal changed the name to *Cape of Good Hope* to encourage exploration of the area! Earlier the Vikings had played the same public relations game when naming Greenland, which is hardly green.

capital. Our word *capital*, for "wealth," comes to us from the Latin *caput*, "head," dating to days when a person's wealth was reckoned in the number of head of cattle that he owned.

capital punishment. The word *capital* derives from the Latin *caput*, "head," and *capital crimes* in English law were at first crimes for which the offender literally lost his head, had it chopped off on the block. (The first recorded use of the word *capital* shows this: "To have capytal sentence & be beheaded," 1483). *Capital punishment* was used about a century later, by which time commoners sentenced to death were hanged and only nobles were allowed to have their heads chopped off. "Capital (or deadly) punishment is done sundry wayes," observed the first writer employing the term. The death penalty, of course, goes back to prehistoric times. It was originally used only to appease an offended diety because of a grave religious offense, but also came to be imposed for murder and many other crimes. Among the ancient Hebrews adultery, bestiality, blasphemy, cursing father or mother, idolatry, incest, rape, sabbath-breaking, unchastity, and witchcraft were all punishable by death. The Romans punished by death crimes such as forgery by slaves, corruption, sodomy, and seduction, and in 18th-century England more than 200 crimes, most of them against property, called for capital punishment. Since the 19th century, crimes punished by death have been reduced greatly in number throughout the world and many countries have now abolished *capital punishment*.

cappuccino. This Italian concoction of espresso coffee, steamed milk, and whipped cream seems to have been named after the *Capuchin* (*q.v.*) monks, who may have invented it in medieval times.

capsule wisdom. No one has identified the inspired genius who invented small medicine capsules that dissolve in the stomach so that the terrible-tasting stuff inside never touches the tongue. From their shape these capsules seem to have been patterned on plant seeds, pods, or capsules, which take their name from the Latin *capsula*, a small box or case. The medicines were mass produced by the middle of the 19th century, and the first recorded use of their name is in 1875. The little capsules, a clever idea themselves, became so common that soon after they were compared with anything short and concise, as in *capsule wisdom*, "a wise, pithy saying."

Captain Bligh. A *Captain Bligh*, commemorating the captain of *Mutiny on the Bounty* fame, is still used to describe a cruel, cold-hearted task-master. Captain William Bligh is also remembered by the ackee fruit, which looks and tastes like scrambled eggs when properly prepared, but can be poisonous when over- or under-ripe. The ackee tree's botanical name is *Blighia sapida*, after the man who introduced it, along with breadfruit. Bligh was called "Breadfruit Bligh" for his discovery of that fruit's virtues and was in fact bringing specimens of the breadfruit tree from Tahiti to the West Indies in 1789 when his mutinous crew foiled his plans. The lesson of *Bounty* apparently taught him little or nothing, for his harsh methods and terrible temper aroused a second mutiny, the Rum Rebellion, while he served as governor of New South Wales. Bligh, a brave and able officer, retired from the Navy a vice admiral. He died in 1817, aged sixty-three. (*See also* **breadfruit**.)

captain cook. Captain James Cook and his men introduced the domesticated pig to New Zealand. Many of these animals escaped into the wild and multiplied; there were soon so many that settlers took to calling the wild pigs *captain cooks*, after the great explorer.

captain of the heads. A jocular Navy term for the enlisted man responsible for keeping the lavatories, or *heads*, neat and clean. Wrote one proud mother to a friend: "My son is doing very well in the Navy. In only six months he's been promoted to Captain of the Heads!" *Heads* are so called because they were originally in the bow, or head, of a ship.

Capuchin. The order of Capuchin monks, established in 1520, came into being when Franciscan friar Matteo di

Bascio insisted that the habit worn by the Franciscans wasn't the one that St. Francis had worn. He stubbornly fashioned himself a sharp-pointed pyramidal hood (*capuche*), let his beard grow, and went barefoot; the Pope granted him permission eight years later to wear this costume and form a separate order that would preach to the poor. The new offshoot of Franciscans came to be named for the headdress its monks still wear, and it wasn't long before a woman's combined cloak and hood was dubbed a *capuchin* after the monks' cowl. The tropical *Capuchin monkey* and *Capuchin pigeon* are named for the Capuchin's costume—the monkey's black hair and appearance resembling the monastic cowl, and the pigeon having a hoodlike tuft of black feathers.

caput. In medieval times, during bubonic plague epidemics, German burial squads counted each corpse as a head, from the Latin *caput*, "head," the term used so often that the German *kaputt* came to mean anything "broken, wrecked, unserviceable, finished." This is probably the origin of the English slang term *caput*, used in both England and America for "all gone, no more, done for."

car. The word *car* comes from a Celtic word that sounded like *karra* to Julius Caesar, who gave the name to his chariots. *Karra* later was Latinized to *carra*. Surprisingly the word *car* appears first around 1300; *carriage* evolved from it, then *horseless carriage*, and, finally, back to *car* again as a shortened form.

carbine. The carbine, a short, light rifle, probably takes its name from the Medieval Latin *Calabrinus*, meaning "a Calabrian." Calabria in southern Italy was noted for its light horsemen or skirmishers, and the first such weapons were either used or manufactured there. *Carabins*, as the weapons were called in 16th-century England, were originally "large pistols . . . having barrels 3 ft. long." They were much shorter and less cumbersome than muskets, however, and were employed by light cavalry troops. By the early 17th century *carbine* was being spelled in its present form, although it took many years for the weapon to develop into the short, light rifle that we know today.

cardigan. "It is magnificent but it is not war," was Maréchal Bosquet's memorable remark on the Charge of the Light Brigade, famous in history and in Tennyson's poem of the same name. The charge at Balaclava during the Crimean War was led by James Thomas Brudenell (1797-1868), the seventh earl of Cardigan. Cardigan, a foolish, vain, violent-tempered man, somewhat redeemed himself by his great personal courage. Cardigan's troops were the most precisely drilled and splendidly dressed of British soldiers, their commander invariably surpassing them in the last respect. The knitted woolen vest he wore to protect himself against the

Crimean winter was named in his honor during his fleeting moments of fame, but today the *cardigan* is a collarless, three-button sweater or jacket with a round or V-neck, bearing little resemblance to the original.

cardinal. Roman Catholic bishops were called *cardinals*, from the Latin *cardo* ("hinge"), because the election of the pope "hinged" on them. The handsome red bird we know as the *cardinal* was so called because of the cardinal's bright red hat. This name for the North American grosbeak was first recorded in 1802.

careen. *Careening* a ship means to ground her at high tide, and when the tide has receded to heel her over on her side. This is sometimes done with small vessels so their bottoms can be scraped, caulked, or otherwise repaired. The word is first recorded in the late 16th century and derives from the French *carene*, "keel," which comes from the Latin *carina*, "keel." A ship is also said to *careen* when she inclines to one side or heels over when sailing on a wind. From this nautical expression comes our term for any leaning, swaying, or tipping to one side of something while it is in motion, such as, "The car careened around the corner."

Carême. "The king of cooks and the cook of kings" was born in Paris on June 8, 1784, in his own words one of twenty-five children "of one of the poorest families in France." Marie-Antoine Carême worked from the time he was seven as a kitchen scullion. In his teens he was accepted as an apprentice chef and after much study under many masters went on to found *la grande cuisine française*, classic French cooking, as we still know it today. Carême's creations reflected his considerable artistic abilities, his pastries often looking more like sculpture than food, and his supreme taste and meticulous standards illustrated in his many books, as well as his forty-eight-course dinners, made French cuisine sovereign throughout Europe. Among other notables, Carême cooked for Talleyrand, the future George IV of England, Czar Alexander I, Lord Castlereagh, Baron Rothschild, the world's richest man, and France's Louis XVIII, who granted him the right to call himself "Carême of Paris." But his motto was "One master: Talleyrand. One mistress: Cooking." Monarch of the entire culinary empire, his name is today synonymous for a great chef. He died on January 12, 1833 while sampling a *quenelle* of sole prepared by a student in his cooking school. Someone wrote that he had died "burnt out by the flame of his genius and the heat of his ovens."

Caribbean Sea. The Caribs of the South American coast were far more adventurous and warlike than those of the larger islands such as Cuba, and it is from these expert mariners—they were one of the few New World peoples to use sails—that the *Caribbean Sea* takes its name. In fact, at the time of Columbus, the natives in the Lesser Antilles spoke two separate languages, the men one and the women another. This situation developed when fierce South American Caribs invaded the islands some years before, butchering and eating all the relatively peaceful Arawak male inhabitants and claiming their women. In retaliation, the women devised a separate "female language" based on Arawak, refusing to speak *Carib* and maintaining silence in the presence of all males, a revenge that they practiced for generations afterward. (*See* **cannibal**.)

carnation. *Carnation*, "fleshlike," was first the name of a fleshlike color developed by artists in the 15th century, deriving from the Latin *carnis*, "flesh." Soon a gillyflower of this color was developed and took the same name for its pinkish color. The *carnation* has retained its name even though it is today available in many other shades.

Carnegiea. One of the world's richest men, Andrew Carnegie (1835-1919), gives his name to the largest cactus in the world, *Carnegiea gigantea*, or the saguaro. One *Carnegiea* specimen found near Madrona, New Mexico in 1950 had candelabra-like branches rising to fifty-three feet. *Carnegiea* had been named for Carnegie a half century before in gratitude for his help in financing Tucson's Desert Laboratory. The millionaire, whose family emigrated to America from Scotland when he was a youth, rose from rags to riches, starting as a bobbin boy in a cotton factory at $1.20 a week and becoming a multimillionaire with his Carnegie Steel Company, which was merged with the United States Steel Corporation when he retired in 1901 to live on his estate in Scotland. Carnegie believed that it was a disgrace to die rich. He became one of the greatest individual philanthropists in history, his benefactions totaling about $350 million.

carnival. The word *carnival* is associated with fasting. *Carnival* was first the whole season leading up to Mardi Gras, the word deriving from the Latin *carne vale*, "flesh, farewell," signifying that the revelry will soon be over and the lean days of Lent will be upon us.

carpetbagger. In Victorian times luggage made from red carpets became an institution and was so popular among embezzling bankers as a place to stash their loot that the embezzlers themselves were dubbed *carpetbaggers*. After the American Civil War carpetbags were used by most of the unscrupulous northern political adventurers, often poor whites, who packed their few worldly possessions in them to satisfy state property residence requirements and moved to the South to take advantage of the newly enfranchised blacks and to win power and fortune by controlling elections. These greedy, unprincipled men, carrying their red carpetbags, and the previous association of the bags with men who milked banks as these men were milking the South, gave birth to their name, *carpetbaggers*, as well as to the name for the *Carpetbag Era* of American history.

carpet knight. In days of old, when knighthood was in flower, a *carpet knight* was a contemptuous term for a knight who fought all his battles in a lady's bed or on her carpet, one who stayed home from the wars. The expression, first recorded in 1576, came over the years to mean someone who avoids practical work.

carrot. From the Latin *carota* for the vegetable, *carota* deriving from the Greek *karoton*. When carrots were first brought to England, women liked to use the plant's ferns as hair decorations, but didn't much care for them as food. The ancient Greeks extolled them as "love medicine" and called them *philtron*.

carry coals to Newcastle. England's Newcastle upon Tyne was the first coal port in the world, the initial charter granted to the town for the digging of coal given by Henry III in 1239. The fact that no one in his right mind would import coal into this coal-mining county gave rise in the 19th century to the expression *to carry coals to Newcastle*, "to do something superfluous, to take something where it is already plentiful."

Carry Nation. Any intemperate temperance agitator. Carry Nation (1846–1911), convinced that she was divinely appointed to bring about the downfall of the saloon, embarked upon her career in Kansas in 1899, chopping her way through the United States and Europe with her "hatchetings" or "hatchetations." Her temperance lectures were not as interesting as her spectacular destruction of saloon interiors with her trusty axe, but the title of her autobiography, *The Use and Need of the Life of Carry A. Nation* (1904), is a classic. The much ridiculed schoolteacher seemed to believe that she was made for martyrdom; she even enjoyed her frequent stays in jail.

to carry the ball. The person in charge *carries the ball* and has been doing so since the 1920s, when the football term began to be used figuratively by Americans.

carte blanche. *Cartes blanches* is the plural, if anyone dares use it. The phrase simply means "white paper" in French and originated as a military term referring to unconditional surrender—a defeated government signing a blank sheet of paper on which the victor could write whatever terms he pleased. The phrase has been commonly used in English since the beginning of the 18th century, soon after which the expression took on its fuller meaning, by extension, of unconditional authority, total discretionary power.

Cartesian. *Cartesian* refers to the philosophy of René Descartes (1596–1650) and his followers, deriving from *Cartesius*, the Latinized form of his name. The French philosopher was an eminent mathematician who based the starting point of his philosophy on the famous phrase *Cogito, ergo sum* ("I think, therefore I am"). His influence on science, philosophy, and literature has been immense, for he was among the first to rely on the rule of reason, rejecting all philosophical tradition. *Cartesian* also means "the explanation of philosophical problems by mathematics." Descartes spent much of his life in Holland, dying in Sweden, where he had been invited by Queen Christiana. His major work is *Discours de la Méthode* (1637). I remember reading somewhere that Descartes was fascinated all his life by women with a squint, which means absolutely nothing but might be of encouragement to some readers.

Carthage must be destroyed! When Rome destroyed Carthage she became the great power in the ancient world. That she destroyed Carthage is due in large part to the eloquent orator Cato, who inspired the Romans by using *Carthage must be destroyed!* ("*Cartago delenda est!*") as the final words in every speech he made in the Roman Senate.

a Carthaginian peace. A destructive peace settlement, one like the severe Punic War treaties that the Romans imposed on the Carthaginians.

Carvel's ring. Captain Grose, in his *Dictionary of the Vulgar Tongue* (1785), relates the anecdote explaining why *Carvel's ring* means "a woman's private parts or the *pudendum muliebre*": "Ham Carvel, a jealous old doctor, being in bed with his wife, dreamed that the Devil gave him a ring, which, so long as he had it on his finger, would prevent his being made a cuckould: waking he found he had got his finger the Lord knows where." Rabelais also told this story. (*See* **Charles.**)

caryatid; atlas. Caryatids are draped or partially clad female figures used in place of columns or pillars as supports, especially in classical architecture. They take their name from the maidens of *Caryae* (Latin for Karyai, a town in Laconia, Greece). The Karyatids, or maidens of Karyai, danced in temples at the festival of Artemis and occasionally assumed the poses represented in the statues. Some accounts say that their figures were first used by the Greeks as a reminder of Karyai's disgrace, for the Karyatids had supported the Persians at the battle of Thermopylae (480 B.C.). An *atlas*, the male counterpart of a caryatid, takes its name from the Titan who supported the Earth on his shoulders.

Casanova. Giovanni Jacopo Casanova de Seingalt's famous memoirs run to some 1.5 million words and take us only through his forty-ninth year. It is said that his autobiography should be trusted in the main as a portrait of the 18th century, but not in the details, yet it seems relatively tame today and the details are not as licentious or racy as they once appeared. It is often forgotten that the

Italian adventurer was a man of many talents: in turn, journalist, raconteur, soldier, gambler, gastronome, preacher, abbe, philosopher, violinist, alchemist, businessman, diplomat, spy, and so on. Casanova is of course best remembered as a great lover, his name equaled only by Don Juan (*q.v.*) as a synonym for a promiscuous womanizer.

case. Criminals *case* or survey a place in order to get useful information to enable them to rob it. This underworld expression dates back to early 20th-century America and has been adopted by the British and Australians.

Casey at the bat.

> Oh! somewhere in this favored land the
>   sun is shining bright,
> The band is playing somewhere, and
>   somewhere hearts are light;
> And somewhere men are laughing, and
>   somewhere children shout,
> But there is no joy in Mudville—mighty
>   Casey has struck out.

This mock-heroic poem by Ernest Laurence Thayer (1863-1940) was first published in the *San Francisco Examiner* on June 3, 1888, and *Casey at the Bat* has been popular ever since. Its initial popularity was due as much to the actor De Wolf Hopper, who included the thirteen-stanza poem in his repertoire, as it was to the poet, a former editor of the *Harvard Lampoon*. Everyone knows that there was no joy in Mudville when the mighty Casey struck out, but few are aware that Thayer patterned his fabled slugger on a real player, Daniel Maurice Casey, who was still posing for newspaper photographers fifty years after the poem's initial publication. Dan Casey, a native of Binghamton, New York, holds no records worthy of recording—not even as a strikeout king. He was a pitcher and an outfielder for Detroit and Philadelphia, but his career was overshadowed by the exploits of his elder brother, Dennis, an outfielder for Baltimore and New York. Casey died in 1943, when he was seventy-eight, in Washington, D.C. As for Thayer, he was paid only five dollars for his poem, which De Wolf Hopper recited over 5,000 times.

Casey Jones. Engineer John Luther Jones, who died in a wreck of the Chicago and New Orleans Limited on March 18, 1900, probably inspired the perennially popular folk ballad, "Casey Jones." The song's authorship is unknown and it may have been adapted from a ballad about a black railroad fireman. There are numerous versions of both music and lyrics, the folk song based on the tradition that "there's many a man killed on the railroad and laid in his lonesome grave." Casey Jones's story was dramatized in Robert Ardrey's *Casey Jones* (1938).

cashier. *Cashier* is recorded as far back as 1596, as "a person who handles financial transactions." The term derives from the French *caisse*, meaning "money box."

cash in one's chips. (*See* **chip in.**)

cash on the barrelhead. Though there is no proof of it, the origins of this expression most likely lie in the makeshift saloons on the American frontier over a century ago, which were often no more than a room in a log cabin with a barrel serving as both booze container and counter. No credit was extended, and any customer who wanted a smack of tarantula juice, or any rotgut likely to make him brave enough not to want to pay, was required to put down *cash on the barrelhead*, or counter.

cash register. *Cash register* was invented by the machine's inventor—Dayton, Ohio restaurant owner James J. Ritty—who called it the *Cash Register and Indicator* in his patent filed March 26, 1879. Ritty invented the machine to help prevent his cashiers from stealing and, in fact, called it the *Incorruptible Cashier*. Unfortunately, he sold out his company after two years, discouraged by slow sales, never really cashing in on what would prove to be a billion-dollar invention.

castanet. The first *castanets* were made of ivory or very hard wood, but the Spanish dancers who invented this musical instrument saw their resemblance to two chestnuts and gave them the Spanish name for that nut.

Castilloa elastica. This tree species—commonly called the ule or Mexican rubber tree—is not by any means the most important source of rubber today, but is a historical curiosity, having yielded the heavy black rubber balls Columbus was amazed to see natives playing with on his second voyage to South America—the first recorded observation of rubber by a European. The tree *C. elastica* is a species of the *Castilloa* genus of the mulberry family, and is named for Spanish botanist Juan Castillo y Lopez. Like Columbus, later explorers were astounded by the resilient balls made from the tree's vegetable gum, remarking that they rebounded so much that they "seemed alive," but rubber wasn't brought into commercial use in Europe until three centuries after its discovery. The tree *Hevea brasiliensis*, yielding high-grade Para, is by far the most important rubber source today. *Castilloa elastica*, however, still yields a good quality Caucho rubber, the large tree being particularly valuable when Para rubber is high priced. (*See* **rubber.**)

cast-iron plants. (*See* **aspidistra.**)

castles in the air. Boswell's famous remark that he was the first man to live in a *castle in the air* was charming self-analysis, and Bulwer-Lytton's observation that such castles are cheap to build but expensive to maintain is profound. However, the expression came into English long before both writers from the French *un chateau en Espagne* ("a castle in Spain") in about 1400, which later became *castles in the air*. French dreamers had been building castles in far off Spain or *Albanie* or *Asie* since the 11th century, when a poem called "The Roumant of the Rose" introduced the French phrase into English:

Thou shalt make castels thanne in Spayne,
And dream of Ioye [joy] all but in vayne.

to cast pearls before swine.   This is a familiar biblical injunction, from Matt. 7:6: "Give not that which is holy unto the dogs, neither cast ye your pearls before swine, lest they trample them under their feet, and turn again and rend you." John Wyclif, commenting on the passage in 1380, added that "men should not give holy things to hounds," a phrase that has been used much more sparingly.

catamaran.   Today's *catamaran*, a vessel with two hulls held side by side some distance apart by a frame above them, bears only a slight resemblance to the rafts formed by a number of logs tied side by side at some distance apart that the British first saw in India late in the 17th century. But the Tamil *katta-maran*, "tied wood," for the rafts served well as a name for "two boats tied together at a distance apart" and finally for the vessel now called a *catamaran*. How *catamaran* became a synonym for a quarrelsome woman is anybody's guess. The term seems to have originated in America, *catamaran* possibly having been confused with "catamount," a bad-tempered cat also known as the cougar.

cat and mouse.   Surprisingly enough, suffragettes arrested in England in about 1913 inspired the first popular use of this expression. The suffragettes often went on hunger strikes when imprisoned, and the government retaliated by passing the "Prisoners' Temporary Discharge for Ill-Health Act," which said that prisoners could be set free while fasting but were liable for rearrest when they recovered from their fasts to serve the remainder of their sentences. Critics compared the government's action to a big cat cruelly playing with a little mouse and dubbed the legislation "The Cat and Mouse Act." From the act, which wasn't particularly successful, came the popularization of *to play cat and mouse with*, though the expression may have been used long before this.

Catawba grapes; Concord.   A light reddish variety of grape grown in the eastern United States, the Catawba was developed by John Adlum in his vineyard near Georgetown in 1829, its dominant parent being the Northern fox grape. It was named three years later for the *Catawba Indians* of the Carolinas, or for the *Catawba*

River, which takes its name from the Indian tribe. The *Catawba*, long a traditional favorite, contains some vinifera blood and is one of the best grapes for white domestic wines. By 1860, nine-tenths of all grapes grown east of the Rockies were *Catawbas*, but they were thereafter replaced by the Concord, perfected in 1850, as the leading American variety.

catbird; catbird seat.   The slate-colored North American thrush (*Dumetella Carolinensis*) has been called the *catbird* since the early 18th century because "its ordinary cry of alarm . . . somewhat resembles the mew of a cat." The name is also given to several Australian birds with similar cries. *To be in the catbird seat*, to be sitting pretty, is a Southern Americanism dating back to the 19th century but popularized nationally by Brooklyn Dodger baseball announcer Red Barber, who used it frequently, and James Thurber's story "The Catbird Seat." (*See also* **tearing up the pea patch**.)

catboat.   *Catboat* remains a double etymological mystery. No one knows why the name *cat* was given in the late 17th century to "a large vessel formerly used in the English coal trade and capable of carrying some 600 tons." Neither is it known why this name was later transferred to the small single-masted pleasure sailboat known as a *catboat* today. Perhaps the two boats were named independently, the reason for the former's name anybody's guess, and the *cat* sailboat so named because it is small and moves quickly and quietly, like a cat.

catcalls.   Though this word, first recorded in 1659, is inspired by the nocturnal cry, or "waul," of the cat, *catcalls* are actually "human whistles expressing disapproval." A *catcall* was apparently first "a squeaking instrument, a kind of whistle used especially in British music halls to express impatience or disapprobation." It then came to mean a shrill shrieking whistle people made in imitation of the instrument and used for the same purposes. In America, however, such shrill whistles (though in this case not called *catcalls*) can be expressions of approval of a performance.

catch a crab.   When an oarsman *catches a crab* he of course doesn't literally catch one on his oar. The expression, dating back to the 19th century, means that the oarsman has slowed down the speed of the boat either by missing the water on a stroke, or, more commonly, by making a poor, awkward stroke that doesn't completely clear the water when completed.

catchpenny.   Back in 1824 London printer James Catnach sold at one penny each the "last speech by the condemned murderers" of a merchant named Weare. After the sheet sold out in a day, Catnach realized he had a good thing, and he headlined another penny paper WE

ARE ALIVE AGAIN but ran the first two words together so that the banner read WEARE ALIVE AGAIN. Buyers of the Catnach penny paper punned on his name after discovering the cheap trick, referring to his paper as *catchpenny*, which soon came to mean any low-priced, fraudulent item. This is a good story, one of the best and earliest examples of folk etymology. However, the fault in this ingenious yarn lies in the fact that *catchpenny* was used in the same sense, "any flimflam that might catch a penny," sixty-five years before the very real Catnach ploy.

catch-22. Joseph Heller's novel *Catch-22* gave us this expression for an "insoluble dilemma, a double bind." In the novel, American pilots, forced to fly an excessive number of dangerous missions, could not be relieved of duty unless they were diagnosed insane. On the other hand, the same regulations stipulated that a pilot who refused to fly, so that he wouldn't be killed, could not be insane because he was thinking too clearly. There was no way out. By the way, Heller's *Catch-22* was originally titled *Catch-18*, the title changed at the last minute because Leon Uris's novel *Mila-18* came out just before Heller's book was to be published. Save for this we would be saying *Catch-18*.

catchword. *Catchwords* are expressions caught up and repeated for effect. Because catchwords are often used by political parties, the term has become a contemptuous one, applied to insincere, misleading statements. *Catchword*, however, has an honorable history. Books were once printed with the word that began the first line on the next page directly under the last line of the preceding page. Such words, designed to catch the reader's attention and make him turn to the next page, were called *catchwords*. Then the term began to be applied to the last word, or cue, in an actor's speech and finally to any expression that catches the attention.

caterpillar. A *caterpillar* is a *chatepelos*, a "hairy cat," in French and it is from this word that we originally got our word for the "wyrm among fruite," as the English once called the creature. But the meaning and spelling of *caterpillar* were strengthened and changed by two old English words. "To pill" meant "to strip or plunder," as in "pillage," which came to be associated with the little worm stripping the bark off trees, and a glutton was a "cater," which the creature most certainly is. Thus the *caterpillar* became a "greedy pillager" as well as a "hairy cat," both good descriptions of its mien and manner.

catgut. Stray cats aren't killed to get it, as some people believe. *Catgut* is a misnomer, actually being the intestines of sheep, and sometimes horses and mules, used to make the tough cords that violins and tennis rackets are strung with (when nylon isn't employed). Probably the word *catgut* was originally *kitgut*, the word *kit* meaning a small fiddle as well as a kitten, but the English word *catlings*, "small strings for musical instruments," contributed to the confusion, too. The toughest and best *catgut* comes from the intestines of lean, poorly fed animals. "Roman strings," the best *catgut* strings for musical instruments, are made in Italy. *Catgut* is also used for hanging clock weights and for sutures in surgery.

a cat has nine lives. Recorded in 1546, this old English saying surely goes back well before the 16th century. Cats were regarded as tenacious of life because of their careful, suspicious nature and because they are supple animals that can survive long falls, though not from the top of a skyscraper as some people believe.

Catherine wheel. The Christian martyr St. Catherine of Alexandria is said to have confessed her faith to Roman Emperor Maximinus and rebuked him for the worship of false gods. After she converted his wife and the Roman general who escorted her to prison, Maximinus ordered her broken on the wheel, but the spiked wheel was shattered to pieces by her touch. This virgin of royal descent was then put to death by the axe, and tradition has it that her body was carried by angels to Mount Sinai where Justinian I built a famous monastery in her honor. St. Catherine is known as the patron saint of wheelwrights and mechanics, and her name day is November 25. The *Catherine wheel*, fireworks in the shape of a wheel rotated by the explosions; the circular, spoked *Catherine wheel window*; and *Catherine wheels*, lateral somersaults, all derive from her name.

cathode. (*See* **farad**.)

cathouse; cat wagon. *Cat* was slang for a prostitute as far back as 1401, when a poem of the day warned men to "beware of cats' tails." Though the term associating the cat and commercial sex is obsolete, the connotation hangs on in the word *cathouse*, for "a bordello, crib, fancy house, whorehouse, or sporting house." A *cathouse* is usually a cheap bordello, and even cheaper *cat wagons* pulled by horses brought harlots thataway when the West was being won. It's anybody's guess whether the *cathouses* take their names in some obscure way from the old word for harlot or were named independently after the sexual qualities usually attributed to cats.

Catiline; Catilinarian. Catiline's conspiracy (64 B.C.) gives us the term *Catiline* for a conspirator or plotter against the government. Lucius Sergius Catiline (ca. 108-62 B.C.), already guilty of at least one murder and extortion, had plotted with other nobles to kill the consuls, plunder the treasury, and set Rome on fire, but Cicero's eloquent *Catilinarian oration* alerted the public, foiling the conspirators. Catiline, sentenced to death, attempted to escape but was defeated in battle by Antonius and slain near Pistoria. Catiline represented himself as a democrat who would cancel all debts and outlaw all wealthy citizens. Ironically, Julius Caesar, the victim of assassins himself twenty years later, was probably a party to the planned assassinations.

catlinite. A clay stone of pale grayish-red to dark red, *catlinite* honors American painter and writer George Catlin (1796-1872). Catlin, a self-taught artist, is remembered for his primitive but authentic paintings of Indian life. An impresario, too, he displayed troupes of Indians in the East and Europe long before Buffalo Bill or Barnum. Early used by American Indians for making pipes, *Catlinite* is commonly called pipe rock.

cat on a hot tin roof. Best known today as the title of Tennessee Williams's famous play, the expression has been in wide use in America since the turn of the century. *Like a cat on a hot tin roof* derives from a similar British phrase, *like a cat on hot bricks*, which was first recorded about 1880 and also means someone ill at ease, uncomfortable, not at home in a place or situation.

cat-o-nine tails. Some black humorist probably coined the name for this terrible scourge—because it "scratched" the back like a cat—but the fact that the first Egyptian scourges were made of thongs of cat hide may have had something to do with the word's origin. The nine tails of the scourge, similar to the "nine lives" of a cat, could also have suggested the name. Scourging criminal offenders with a whip is a punishment as old as history. There are cases in medieval England of prisoners receiving sixty thousand stripes from whips with three lashes and twenty knots in each tail. But the *cat-o-nine-tails*, composed of one eighteen-inch handle with nine tails and three or more knots on each tail, only dates back to about 1670. Men were flayed alive with this scourge, which people believed was more holy, and thus effective, because its nine tails were a "trinity of trinities" (3 × 3 = 9).

cats and dogs. (*See* **blue-chip stocks.**)

cat's cradle. Word detectives have given this one up as a bad job. The first mention of the child's game is in a little-known book called *The Light of Nature Pursued* (1768), in which the author attempts to explain it: "An ingenious play they call cat's cradle; one ties the two ends of a packthread together, and then winds it about his fingers, another with both hands takes it off perhaps in the shape of a gridiron, the first takes it again from him in another form, and so on alternately changing the packthread into a multitude of figures whose names I forget, it being so many years since I played it myself." Some say that suggestions that the game's name is a corruption of *cratch-cradle*, the manger cradle in which Christ was

born, are not founded in facts. The story I was told when a boy had it that the first figure in the game resembled a *cratch*, a medieval English word for a hayrack, while the last figure resembled a cradle. Supposedly the game was first called *cratch-cradle* and this was changed to *cat's cradle* in later years when the hay cratch was no longer used or familiar to people—not because cats had anything to do with the game but because the word *cat* sounded something like *cratch*. Moreover, before its meaning as a hayrack, *cratch* was a verb meaning "to seize, snatch, grab"—so maybe the *cratching*, or grabbing, of the string became the cat in the name. Then again perhaps I, too, should give this one up.

cat's-paw. A *cat's-paw* is light air during a calm that moves as silently as a cat and causes ripples on the water, indicating a coming storm. The term is recorded as early as 1769. Captain Frederick Marryat wrote in *Jacob Faithful* (1834): "Cat's paws of wind, as they call them, flew across the water here and there, ruffling its smooth surface." In the old folktale a monkey tricks a cat into using its paw to pull chestnuts from a fire, the monkey getting the nuts and the cat getting a burnt paw. From the tale comes our expression *cat's-paw*, for "a dupe."

catsup. (*See* **ketchup.**)

The Cat's Waltz. This Chopin composition is so named because when Chopin was composing his Waltz No. 3 in F major, his cat scat across the keys of his piano and he tried to reproduce the same sounds in his piece.

cattail pine. (*See* **bristlecone pine.**)

cat the anchor. *Catting the anchor* simply means to keep the anchor clear of the ship by hanging it outside the vessel on a piece of timber called the cathead. The term dates back to at least the early 19th century.

cattle; chattel. Capitalists and cows have much in common, *cattle* being a corruption of the Latin *capitale*, "capital or principal holdings," a word that medieval English peasants found hard to pronounce and altered to *catel* and finally *cattle*. Because the principal holdings of peasants were often livestock, especially cows, cattle came to mean what it does today, while the medieval French *chatel*, another corruption of the Latin *capitale*, entered English as *chattel*, our legal term for all personal property.

Cattleya. This most popular of florist's orchids has nothing to do with cattle, having been named for William Cattley (d. 1832), English amateur botanist and botany patron. The *Cattleya* genus includes some forty species, though over 300 hybridized forms are known. *Cattleya labiata*, with its 200 or so named varieties, is the most commonly cultivated orchid in America—the showy magenta-purple-lipped, yellow-throated "florist's orchid"—although the enormous orchid family contains perhaps 500 genera and 15,000 species. The *Cattleyea fly* and the *Cattley guava*, a subtropical fruit, also commemorate the English plant lover.

Caucasian.   When the German anthropologist Johann Blumenbach divided mankind into the Caucasian, Mongolian, Ethiopian, American, and Malayan races in 1795, he chose a skull from the Caucasus, in what is now the Soviet Union, as the perfect type in his collection. He also claimed that the Caucasus area was the home of the hypothetical race known as "Indo-Europeans," to whom many languages can be traced. Blumenbach's theories proved unscientific and tinged with racism. In *Webster's* the word he coined is now given "in default of a better" and as "one of the main ethnic divisions of the human race: [including] the Mediterranean, Alpine, and Nordic subdivisions, and is loosely called the white race."

caucus.   In American politics party leaders hold *caucuses*, off-the-record meetings, to select leaders and form policy. These leaders are in one sense counselors or advisers, and it is probably the Algonquin Indian word *caucauasu*, meaning "counselor or adviser," that gives us the Americanism *caucus*, first recorded in 1773.

caught flat-flooted.   Americans have only used this expression, meaning "to be caught unprepared," since about 1910. However, it has been traced to the reign of Queen Anne in England, where it was first applied to horses left at the line after the start of a horse race. These horses weren't dancing forward on their toes, but had all four feet flat on the ground. In fact, the term *flat-footed* for someone with little or no hollow in the sole and a low instep, was first used to describe animals afflicted with the condition, especially horses with flat hooves and soles near the ground. Later *caught flat-footed* must have been a good description for a runner not on his toes and left at the mark when a footrace began, and it was eventually generalized to anyone asleep at the switch.

caught red-handed.   *To be taken with red hand* in ancient times was to be caught in the act, like a murderer, his hands red with his victim's blood. The use of *red hand* in this sense goes back to 15th-century Scotland and Scottish law. Scott's *Ivanhoe* has the first recorded use of *taken red-handed* for someone apprehended in the act of committing a crime. Not long after, the expression became more common as *caught red-handed*.

caught with his pants down.   *Partridge* has managed to trace this expression only to 1920, to England, where it was, of course, *caught with one's trousers down*. But possibly the phrase is much older and was kept out of print for prudish reasons until the twenties. Two explanations are given for its origins. One that it refers to a man caught with a lady *in media res* by her husband; the other that it arose when a hostile Indian came upon a frontiersman answering the call of nature in the woods without his rifle at his side.

caustic; cauterize.   (*See* **holocaust**.)

caviar.   *Caviar* derives from the Persian *khavyar*, salted sturgeon eggs. The Russians call the fish eggs *ikra*, not caviar, and it is from a select sturgeon species called the Beluga that the highly regarded Beluga caviar comes. Actually, the most prized caviar of all is that made from selected golden sterlet's eggs of the *Acipenser ruthenus* species, produced by sterlets "with a particularly happy frame of mind." While dispelling myths about caviar, we should mention that *malossol* isn't a quality name like *Beluga*; it is just less salty caviar, and you can buy *Beluga malossol, Sevruga malossol*, et cetera.

caviar to the general.   "I heard thee speak me a speech once," Hamlet says to the players at Elsinore, "but it was never acted . . . ; for the play, I remember, pleased not the million, 'twas caviar to the general." When Shakespeare says "general" here, he means the general public, the generality, the masses as they were later called, not the general of an army. The play he refers to (which was actually pretty bad, judging by the fragments presented) is, like caviar, for the tastes of only the most discriminating people; others would find it repugnant because they haven't acquired fine tastes. The rather snobbish remark is still commonplace in describing something for which one has to acquire a taste.

Cavy.   (*See* **uncle!**)

cayenne pepper.   *Cayenne* is an English word contributed by the Tupi language of Brazil. It derives from the Tupi *quiynha*, meaning "capsicum," *quiynha* deriving from the name of the island (now called Cayenne) where the pepper is ground.

cayuse.   Characters in westerns sometimes use the word *cayuse* to describe a horse of little value, but *cayuse*, strictly, is a name for Indian ponies, a breed that western pioneers knew as *kiyuse* and which were rarely properly tamed by white men. The *cayuse* takes its name from the Cayuse Indians of Oregon and Washington, who bred the small horse. In 1847, blaming whites for a smallpox epidemic, the tribe attacked and killed fourteen missionaries near the present city of Walla Walla, Washington. Subdued and put on a reservation in 1855, their ranks decimated by disease, they died as a people, with no full-blooded Cayuse Indian surviving today.

CCCP. There isn't a "Communist" behind any of these "C's". The common abbreviation stands for *Soiuz Sovetskihh Sotsialisticheskikh Respublik*, the Union of Soviet Socialist Republics, written as CCCP in English because in the Russian alphabet *c* is equivalent to our *s* and *p* to our *r*.

Cecil's fast. In an attempt to improve the fish trade in England, Queen Elizabeth's long-time minister William Cecil, Lord Burghley, had legislation passed requiring Englishmen to eat fish and no meat on certain days of the week. Beef-eating and mutton-eating Britons didn't much like the idea and dubbed all fish dinners *Cecil's fasts*. Possibly the idea remained distasteful to Englishmen for over two centuries, because in the early 1800s, cold hash patties were being called *Cecils*—another substitute for "real" meat.

cellar. *Cellar*, for "the lowest position in league rank for a baseball team" is first recorded in a *New York Times* headline of July 9, 1922: "Red Sox Are Up Again. Leave Cellar to Athletics by Taking Final of Series, 4 to 1." Thus the Philadelphia Athletics were the first baseball team to be in the *cellar*. *Cellar*, for "an underground room or basement," dates back to the 14th century and derives from the Latin *cella*, "cell."

Celsius scale. The centigrade thermometer is often called the *Celsius thermometer* in honor of the eminent Swedish astronomer who invented the *Celsius scale*. Anders Celsius (1701-44) first suggested his improvement of the Fahrenheit (*q.v.*) scale before the Swedish Academy of Sciences in 1742, proposing the more obvious gradation between 0 and 100. Today the mercury thermometer patterned on this thermometer scale is widely used in Europe for meteorological and all other temperatures. Celsius also founded the observatory at Uppsala, where he was a professor, and made and collected many observations of the aurora borealis. Boiling water measures 212 degrees on the Fahrenheit scale and 100 degrees on the *Celsius* or centigrade scale; water freezes at 0 degrees centigrade and 32 degrees Fahrenheit.

Celtic words. English words that come to us from Celtic include: *bin, crag, curse*, the color *dun* and possibly *ass* (perhaps a Celtic contraction of the Latin *asinus*). *Whiskey, clan, glen, heather, shillelagh, claymore, slogan, dirk, brouge, wraith, bog, plaid*, and *bard* are Celtic, too, but are modern borrowings from the Irish and Scots. Celtic words also survive in British place names, such as the *Avon* ("water"), *Dover* ("black") and *York* (*q.v.*). (See **Tor.**)

cemetery. With all the talk about the euphemisms used by today's "morticians" it is often forgotten that *cemetery* is a euphemism coined by early Christian writers from the Greek word for dormitory, a place where one sleeps. *Cemetery* is first recorded in English in 1387, over a century after "burial ground" (ca. 1250). "Graveyard" isn't recorded until the early 19th century.

cent. *Cent* is an Americanism introduced during the Revolution by Gouverneur Morris to replace the British word "penny." Though both words are still used today, *cent*, deriving from the Latin *Centum*, for "one-hundredth (of a dollar)," is more common than penny (*q.v.*).

centurion. The Roman noncommissioned officer was named a *centurion* because he was in charge of a *century*, originally a hundred *legionaries*, or ordinary soldiers, members of the Roman legion (a legion consisting of 3000-6000 soldiers).

century plant. *Agave americana*, common to the American West, is called the *century plant* because it is thought to take a century to bloom, and to die shortly after it does. The name is a misnomer, for *century plants*, depending on the variety, take from one year to fifty years to bloom, and none dies immediately afterward.

cereal. Demeter was the Greek goddess of fruits, crops, and vegetation; her Roman counterpart was the Mother Earth goddess Cerus whose name gives us *cereal*.

cha. (*See* **tea.**)

Chablis. Though its name has been widely appropriated in other wine producing countries, true *Chablis*, a dry white Burgundy, is produced near the town of Chablis, southeast of Paris, and made only of Chardonnay grapes.

cha cha. This dance should properly be called the *cha cha cha*, as it takes its name from the sound of its musical accompaniment. In fact, it is called the *cha cha cha* in Cuba, where it originated, and people dancing it call out *cha cha cha*, not *cha cha*.

chaise lounge. The French called it a *chaise longue*, or "long chair," but Americans, on importing it from France, assumed that the *longue* in the term was French for "lounge." *Chaise lounge* it has remained ever since, despite all the efforts of purists.

Chaos chaos. Linnaeus discovered and christened this microscopic animal in 1775. It has since been identified only fifty times. The Swedish founder of scientific nomenclature gave the one-celled animal its name because of the chaos it creates. The voracious *Chaos chaos* never fails to attack and destroy all smaller protozoa it encounters.

chap. The word *chapman*, for "a wandering peddler," lives in the language long after the last chapman has passed from the scene. For the British term *chap*, "fellow or man," as in "he's a good old chap," is simply an abbreviation of *chapman*—a good chapman, or *chap*, became in time a good fellow. The old English word *chop*, "to barter," gave us both *chapman* and *cheap*.

chapel; chaplain. St. Martin of Tours converted to Christianity as a young pagan soldier in the Roman army under Constantine. According to Butler's *Lives of the Saints*, "In a very hard winter, during a severe frost, he met at the gate of the city a poor man almost naked, begging alms of them that passed by. Martin, seeing those that went before take no notice of this miserable creature . . . had nothing but his clothes. So drawing his sword, he cut his cloak into two pieces, gave one to the beggar and wrapped himself in the other half." That night Martin saw a vision of Christ "dressed in that half of the garment he had given away" and decided to enter into the religious life. He eventually became bishop of Tours and was credited with many cures and miracles. After his death in about 400 A.D., Martin became patron saint of the Frankish kings, who preserved the remaining half of his cloak, or *cappella*, as a relic. It was enshrined in a chest in "a special sanctuary," which also came to be known as a *cappella*, and the soldiers who watched over it, or carried it into battle and from place to place, were called *cappellani*. These two words, in French *chapelle* and *chapelain*, are the source of the English *chapel* and *chaplain*, the former deriving initially from St. Martin's cape and the latter from the soldiers who guarded it in its sanctuary.

chaperone. The *chaperone* was originally a hood or mantle worn by priests and others in medieval France, the word itself meaning "little mantle." It was later adopted as a fashion by English ladies, but it wasn't until the 18th century that a *chaperone* meant a married woman who shelters or protects a young woman, much as the hood protects the face.

chard. (*See* **Swiss chard.**)

Charing Cross. In 1290 Edward I erected a cross to the memory of his beloved Queen Eleanor (*chère reine*) in the center of the ancient village of Charin, midway between London and Westminster. He chose the spot because it was there that her coffin rested for the last time before her burial in Westminster. The Puritans destroyed the original cross in 1647 (it stood on the south side of Trafalgar Square, on the site now occupied by an equestrian statue of Charles I), but a new one was erected in 1865 in the courtyard of what is now called Charing Cross Station.

charity begins at home. An ancient saying, *charity begins at home* was probably old when the Roman author Terence expressed the idea in a comic play: *Proximus sum egomet mihi*. Similar words are first recorded in English late in the 14th century.

charlatan. *Charlatan* can be traced to the Italian *ciarlatano*, for "a quack," but a notorious quack dentist may have helped it along. A.M. Latan, it is said, was a 19th-century Frenchman who dressed in a long-robed exotic costume and often toured Paris in a magnificent dispensary car, a horn player heralding his approach. Spectators would cry out "*Voila le char de Latan*" ("There is Latan's car"), the words *le char de latan* popularizing *charlatan*. Most likely Latan was an assumed name, chosen to accompany his *char*, but the mischievous Frenchman probably strengthened the meaning of a word that had been used in English since the early 17th century.

Charleston. This peppy dance, symbolic of the Roaring Twenties, takes its name from Charleston, South Carolina, where it was probably first introduced as a variation of an earlier dance originated by American blacks. The word is first recorded in 1925.

Charles' Wain. Much legend surrounds Charlemagne, Charles the Great (742-814 A.D.), king of the Franks and founder of the Holy Roman Empire. Charlemagne is said to have been eight feet tall and so strong that he could bend three horseshoes at once. He had four wives and five mistresses who between them presented him with fifty children. Charles the Great was also associated, probably erroneously, with the legendary King Arthur. The constellation now better known as the Big Dipper, the Plough, Ursa Major, or the Great Bear was at one time called *Arthur's Wain* because it resembled a wain, or wagon, of old, the stars in the handle of the Dipper being the wagon's shaft. Since there was a legendary association between Charles the Great and King Arthur, the star cluster called Arthur's Wain eventually became known as *Charles's Wain*, too.

Charley; Charlie; charlies. Long before English policemen were dubbed *bobbies*, London night watchmen were called *Charleys*, or *Charlies*. The obsolete designation is believed to derive from the name of Charles I, who extended and improved the London night watch in order to curb street offenses in 1640, or from his son the lascivious Charles II. Charles I, beheaded by Cromwell in 1649, also wore a short, triangular beard called a *Charlie* that is now known as a Vandyke (*q.v.*). The slang *charlies*, for a woman's breasts, one etymologist suggests, derives from "the opulent charms displayed by the mistresses of Charles II"—*charlies* was probably originally *charlie's* because they were "playthings belonging to the king." (*See also* **bobby; charley horse.**)

charley horse. Back in 1946 the *Journal of the American Medical Association* published an article entitled "Treatment of the Charley Horse," rather than "Treatment of Injury to Quadriceps Famoris." This would indicate that *charley horse* has been a part of formal English for at least forty years. But did this term for "a leg cramp" arise from a lame horse named Charley that pulled a roller across the infield in the Chicago White Sox ball park in the 1890s? That's the old story, and there was such a horse, but the expression may have been printed several years before his baseball days, in 1888, to describe a ballplayer's stiffness or lameness. Another derivation that seems likely but hasn't been proved traces *charley horse* to the constables, or *Charleys*, of 17th-century England. According to this theory, *Charleys*, for "local police," survived in America through the 19th century and because aching legs were an occupational disease among *Charleys*, ballplayers suffering such maladies were compared with the coppers and said to be "weary from riding Charley's horse." (*See* **Charley.**)

Charley More. "Charley More—the fair (or square) thing" was the legend on the huge tavern sign of a Maltese publican about 1840. His name became synonymous with fair or straight dealing, and *Charley More* became a British term for one who is honest and upright.

Charley Noble. Commander, captain, or ship's cook Charles Noble (ca. 1840) demanded that the cowl of the copper funnel of his galley stove always be kept brightly polished. So obsessed was he with the idea that galley funnels were dubbed *Charley Nobles* in his honor.

Charlotte Russe; Apple Charlotte. Marie-Antoine Carême, the greatest chef of his day, created a lavish pastry that he called the *Apple Charlotte*, after England's Princess Charlotte, George IV's only daughter. The master chef apparently could not forget Charlotte, for while serving Czar Alexander in Russia, he created a jellied custard set in a crown of ladyfingers that he named the *Charlotte Russe* in her honor. Carême's creations were so valued that it is said that they were stolen from the table at the court of George IV—not to be relished at home, but to be sold in the market at high prices. (*See* **Carême.**)

Charterhouse. Charterhouse, the venerable London public school and hospital, was, in the 14th century, the site of a religious house of the Carthusian monks. When one Thomas Sutton died in 1611, he endowed a hospital, chapel, and school on this property, which had come into his possession that same year. All three institutions were called Charterhouse as was the Carthusian monastery before them, the word deriving from the early English spelling (Chartrouse) of the French *maison Chartreuse,* "Carthusian house." The school moved to Surrey in 1872, but the hospital, or almshouse, still stands on its old site. Many of the Charterhouse buildings were destroyed in World War II. (*See* **Chartreuse liqueur.**)

Chartreuse liqueur. A cordial that takes its name from a monastery of the Carthusian monks. La Grande Chartreuse, the mother house of the Carthusian order, was founded by St. Bruno of Cologne in 1084 near Grenoble, France, the monastery taking its name from nearby Carthusua, after which the Carthusians had been named. Early in the 17th century the Maréchal d'Estrées gave the monks a recipe for a liqueur made from fragrant herbs and brandy; the Carthusians called the liqueur *Chartreuse*. They began to manufacture and sell it on a large scale only when they returned to La Grande Chartreuse after their expulsion during the French Revolution, using the revenues to rebuild and maintain their devastated monastery. Le Chartreux, as the French call the Carthusians, were again expelled from France in 1903, their distillery and trademark being sold and an imitation *Chartreuse* marketed by a commercial firm. Cognoscenti hold that only the liqueur made by the monks is worthy of the name, claiming that *Chartreuse* owes its distinctive flavor to the still-secret formula that employs angelica root and other herbs of the Grenoble region. The Carthusians were allowed to return to Grenoble in 1938, and now sell their liqueur under the *Les Pères Chartreux* trademark. The best *Chartreuse* is a pale apple-green, hence the color *chartreuse*. (*See* **Charterhouse.**)

chaste tree. (*See* **vitex.**)

chat; chatter; chatterbox. *Chat,* like "blab" (*q.v.*), is a truncated form of an earlier word, *chatter,* which is supposed to be an echoic word imitative of the sound of birds chirping. *Chatter* is first attested in about 1225, *chat,* for "to talk idly," about three centuries later. *Chatterbox* is an Americanism first recorded in 1814.

Chateaubriand. One old story tells us that Brillat-Savarin dined in Paris with the Vicomte François René Chateaubriand on the night that an anonymous restaurant proprietor invented *steak Chateaubriand* in his honor. The occasion, according to this version, was the publication of the French romantic's *La Génie du Christianisme,* and the succulent tenderloin was encased between two flank steaks, symbolizing Christ and the thieves. The outer steaks, seared black, were discarded, leaving the tenderloin rare and juicy. More likely, *steak Chateaubriand* was invented and named by the novelist's chef, Montmirel, and served for the first time at the French embassy in London.

chattel. (*See* **cattle.**)

chatterbox. (*See* **chat.**)

chauffeur. The first *chauffeurs* known to the world were members of a band of brigands led by Jean l'Ecorcheur (Jack the Scorcher), a bandit leader who took advantage of the chaos created by the French Revolution to terrorize the French countryside in the late 18th century. Jack's gang would force their way into homes and demand that all hidden valuables be surrendered, tying up those householders who refused and roasting their bare feet in the fire until they capitulated. They thus came to be known as *chauffeurs*, "firemen," their nickname deriving from the French *chauffer*, "to heat or stoke." Many years after its application to Jack the Scorcher and his *chauffeurs*, the word was logically applied to steamship stokers, locomotive firemen, and, finally, to the stokers required to tend early-powered automobiles. These last stokers often operated someone else's car, and the word was retained when *chauffeurs* no longer needed to be firemen in addition to drivers.

Chautauqua. Chautauqua, New York, which takes its name from a Seneca Indian word possibly meaning "one has taken out fish there," was the home of a Methodist summer colony where various cultural activities were offered beginning in 1874. Lectures there came to be called *Chautauquas* and by the end of the century lecturers giving lectures in towns and cities across the country were calling them *Chautauquas* no matter where they were held.

chauvinism. Nicolas Chauvin of Rochefort was a genuine hero, wounded seventeen times in service of the French Grand Armée and retiring only when so scarred that he could no longer lift a sword. How then did his name become associated with excessive nationalism or superpatriotism? Chauvin actually was left with little after his war service. For his wounds and valor he received a medal, a ceremonial saber, and a pension of about forty dollars a year. Instead of growing bitter, the old soldier turned in the opposite direction, for, after all, his sacrifices had to mean something. Chauvin became an idolator of the Little Corporal; even after Waterloo and Napoleon's exile, he spoke of little but his hero's infallibility and the glory of France. The veteran became a laughingstock in his village, but he would have escaped national attention if dramatists Charles and Jean Cogniard hadn't heard of him and used him as a character in their comedy *La Cocarde tricolore* (1831). The play truthfully represented Chauvin as an almost idolatrous worshipper of Napoleon and was followed by at least four more comedies by other authors caricaturing the old soldier. As a result the French word *chauvinisme*, or *chauvinism*, became synonymous with fanatical, unreasoning patriotism and all that such blind, bellicose worship of national prowess implies. The closest English synonym is *Jingoism* (q.v.), while the Germans use *Hurrapatriotismus*.

chaw stick; chew stick. The ancient *chewstick* or *chawstick* is the branches and twigs of the *Gouauia Domingenia* tree. These were and are still used in the West Indies for cleansing the teeth and sweetening the breath, just as the roots of the cola tree, called *chew stick*, are used in Sierra Leone.

cheap as a Sardinian. Many groups of people have been unfairly characterized as cheap, but the Sardinians do not carry this stigma. The phrase *cheap as a Sardinian* refers not to penny-pinching Sardinians but to the fact that the Romans under Tiberius Gracchus auctioned off great numbers of Sardinian prisoners in Rome for whatever price they could get, no matter how cheap.

cheapskate; a good skate. Revolutionary War soldiers liked to sing the Scottish song "Maggie Lauder," the chorus of which chided a *blatherskate*, a gabby person full of nonsense or hot air. The song is a very old one, dating back to the 17th century, and the word blatherskate is older still, formed from *bladder*, an obsolete English word for an inflated pretentious man, a windbag, and a contemptuous use of the word *skate*, referring to the common food fish. Why the skate was chosen for the humorous word isn't clear perhaps because it was believed to inflate itself like a blowfish, or possibly just because it was common. In any case, "Maggie Lauder" made *blatherskate* popular in America and later, in the 19th century, when Americans invented their native word *cheapskate*, for a tightwad, they borrowed the *skate* from it. This is a more roundabout explanation than the theory that the *skate* in *cheapskate* comes from a British slang word for chap, but it seems more logical, as *skate* in the sense of chap never had much currency in the U.S., except in the term *a good skate*, meaning a good person.

cheat. In feudal times *escheators* were officers of the king's exchequer appointed to receive dues and taxes and handle estates that might possibly revert to the crown because of failure of descendants to qualify as heirs. The escheators did so many people out of money unscrupulously that their name was inherited by future generations in the form of *cheat*.

check. (*See* **bill; checkmark**.)

checkmark. As far back as the 17th century teachers were for some unknown reason using the checkmark, (✔) to mean "correct." The word *check* is much older, deriving ultimately from the Persian *shah*, for "king," which became the *check* in the game of chess, and from its use in the game was widely transferred to other meanings in English. (*See* **checkmate**.)

checkmate; chess. Chess was already an ancient game when the Persians introduced it to the Arabs. The Arabs retained the Persian word *shah* for the king, the most important piece in the game, and when the *shah* (pronounced "shag" by the Arabs) was maneuvered into a helpless position, ending play, they exclaimed *shah mat*, "[your] king is dead." Soon after the Arabs introduced chess into Spain in the eighth century this expression became *xague mate*, from which derived the French *eschec mate* and finally the English *checkmate*. For many years *checkmate* was restricted to chess, but by the 14th century Chaucer and other writers were using it in the figurative sense of "to thwart, defeat, or frustrate." Our word *chess* comes from a shortening of the French *eschis*, the plural of *eschec*, so the game's name really means "kings." By a similar process the king in the game, the *shah* that became the French *eschec*, is also the source of every use of the word *check* in English, from bank checks to security checks. (*See also* **checkmark**.)

cheddar. Originally a cheese made in the village of Cheddar in England's Somerset County, *cheddar* today refers to "a wide variety of hard, crumbly cheeses ranging in flavor from mild to sharp and in color from yellow to orange." The word is first recorded in 1666, but the cheese probably was made long before then.

cheek by cheek; cheek by jowl. *Cheek by cheek*, recorded over six centuries ago, implies closeness, intimacy. *Cheek by jowl* is just a variation invented some two centuries later, substituting the French *jowl*, "cheek," for the second cheek in the phrase.

cheer up; cheer up—the worst is yet to come. The British have been using the expression *cheer up* since at least 1597. It took over three centuries but an Americanism finally managed to cheerfully deflate these encouraging words, with *cheer up—the worst is yet to come*, first recorded in 1920.

cheesecake; beefcake. The old story is that in 1912 *New York Journal* photographer James Kane was developing a picture of an actress that included "more of herself than either he or she expected." As he looked at it, he searched for the greatest superlative he knew of to express his delight and exclaimed, "That's real cheesecake!" The word soon became synonymous for photographs of delectable models. In the 1970s, *beefcake* became the male equivalent.

cheese it, the cops! If you've ever wondered why *cheese it* means "stop it," or "watch it," *Partridge* has an answer for you. He suggests that the term, first recorded in England in 1812, is a mispronunciation of "cease it."

chenangoe. Upstate New York farms in Chenango County supplied many of the longshoremen who worked the New York waterfront in the late 19th century. So many, in fact, that *chenangoe* became a term for any longshoreman who loads cargo from railroad barges to ships. Before this the *chenangoe* had been a popular variety of potato.

cherishing a serpent in your bosom. An ancient Greek legend tells of a man who found a frozen serpent that he put beneath his shirt against his breast, only to have the snake, revived by the warmth of his bosom, bite and kill him. The story, adapted by Shakespeare, became the basis of the saying *to cherish* (or *nurse*) *a serpent in your bosom*, "to show kindness to someone who proves ungrateful."

cherry. *Cherries* in English first meant *one cherry*, the word deriving from the French *cerise* (which came from the Latin *cerasus*) for the fruit. *Cerise* became *cherries*, but the *s* in *cherries* was dropped, because it made the singular word sound like a plural, and the result was *cherrie* or *cherry*.

Cheshire cat. (*See* **grin like a Cheshire cat**.)

chess. (*See* **checkmate**.)

chesterfield. *Chesterfieldian* usually means writings on dress and manners, referring to Philip Dormer Stanhope, the fourth earl of Chesterfield (1694-1773), whose posthumous *Letter to His Son* and *Letter to His Godson* are models of their kind. Lord Chesterfield, whose last words were "Give Dayrolles [a visitor] a chair," did not intend his letters for publication. Dr. Johnson described them as teaching "the morals of a whore and the manners of a dancing master"—but then the Great Cham was hardly an unprejudiced judge, Chesterfield having neglected the plan for his great *English Dictionary*, which resulted in Johnson's famous letter rejecting his support when it was finished. The witty *Letters* of the statesman and diplomat were meant to be filled with worldly knowledge and thus reflected the morality of the age. The large overstuffed *chesterfield couch* and the man's velvet-collared overcoat with concealed buttons called a *chesterfield* were introduced in the 19th century. Both may have been named in honor of Philip Stanhope, but it is more likely that they commemorate a later earl of Chesterfield, who may even have invented them. Just which earl no one seems to know.

chestnut. No one is sure about the antecedents of *chestnuts*. The word may derive from the name of Castana in Asia Minor, a city near which chestnuts grew, or from the Armenian *kaskene*, meaning "chestnut."

chew the fat (rag). One guess is that this expression was originally a nautical one: Sailors working their jaws on the tough salt pork rationed out when supplies ran low constantly grumbled about their poor fare while literally *chewing the fat*. *Chewing the rag* also had a grouchy connotation when first recorded in print at about the same time, in 1885. There are a few stories relating these words to actual rag chewing (men chewing pieces of rags when out of tobacco and grousing about it, etc.), but more than likely the expression has its roots in the English verb *to rag*, "to scold," its origin unknown. Both phrases are probably much older than their first appearance in print, and both are used more often today to mean a talkfest between friends than the act of complaining.

Cheyenne. No one is certain about it, but the name of this North American Indian tribe of the Algonquian linguistic family, now found in Montana and Oklahoma, may derive from the French feminine for dog, *chienne*. French traders in Minnesota may have named them so because the tribe, like many Indian tribes, ate dog meat.

Chianti. The *Chianti mountains* in Tuscany, where this wine is produced, give their name to the best-known of Italian reds, their squat flasks traditionally wrapped in straw.

chichi. Slang for the female breasts as sexual objects, *chichi* or *chi-chi* can also mean anything sexually stimulating. The term arose after World War II during the U.S. occupation of Japan and derives from *chisai chichi*, a corruption of the Japanese words meaning "little breasts." The expression had widespread use in Korea.

Chicago. The Windy City unfortunately derives its name from an Indian word that means "place of the bad smell," "place of skunk smells," or "skunktown." There is only a slight chance that the Indian word means "wild onion place," as has been suggested.

chicanery. *Chicanery*, the use of mean, petty subterfuge, especially legal dodges and quibbles, came into English through a French word meaning the same. It seems originally to have derived from the Persian *chaugan*, "the crooked stick used in polo." The stick's name somehow came to mean a dispute in polo and other games, then took on the meaning of a sharp, crooked practice in the same games and in general.

chicken à la King. *Chicken à la King*, diced pieces of chicken in a sherry cream sauce, is now available canned, frozen, and even in Army mess halls, a long way from the éclat tables where it was served in the late 19th century. The dish was not invented for a king, as is popularly believed, yet it's hard to pinpoint just who *chicken à la King* does honor. Some say that New Yorker Foxhall Keene, self-proclaimed "world's greatest amateur athlete," suggested the concoction to a chef at Delmonico's Of the numerous stories surrounding the dish's creation the most reliable seems to be that of the famous Claridge's Hotel in London. Claridge's claimed that the dish was invented by its chef to honor J.R. Keene, whose horse had won the Grand Prix in 1881. Perhaps J.R. passed on the recipe to his son, the peerless Foxhall. At any rate, the Keenes did not hold public interest long enough, and the *Keene* in *Chicken à la Keene* eventually became *King*.

chicken feed. Chickens were fed grain too poor for any other use by American pioneers, and these pieces of poor-quality grain had to be small so the chickens could swallow them. This obviously suggested the contemptuous term *chicken feed* for small change (pennies, nickels, and dimes) to riverboat gamblers fleecing small-town suckers. The first in-print mention of the expression is in *Colonel [Davy] Crockett's Exploits* (1836): "I stood looking on, seeing him pick up chicken feed from the green horns." By extension, *chicken feed* has come to mean any small or insignificant amount of money, and even (rarely today) misleading information deliberately supplied or leaked by a government to spies employed by another government.

chickenhearted; chicken-livered. Not nearly a new expression, *chickenhearted* is first recorded in a 1681 poem by John Dryden: "Where 'tis agreed by bullies chicken-hearted/ To fight the ladies first, and then be parted." *Chicken-heart*, for a heart, or courage, as weak as a chicken's, is first attested in 1602. *Chicken-livered* is a variant of the term, first recorded in America in 1857.

a chicken in every pot. Often attributed to Herbert Hoover, this synonym for prosperity was, indeed, a Republican campaign slogan during the election of 1932—a ridiculous one that helped the Democrats more than the Republicans, with the Great Depression gripping the land. The words can actually be traced to Henry IV of France and his vow on being crowned king in 1589: "If God grants me the usual length of life, I hope to make France so prosperous that every peasant will have a chicken in his pot on Sunday." Assassinated in 1610 when only fifty-seven, Henry wasn't able to provide such prosperity.

chicken-livered. (*See* **chickenhearted**.)

chicken ranch. Unlike most sexual euphemisms, this synonym for "a brothel" takes its name from a real place. The original Chicken Ranch was a bordello in Gilbert, Texas, early in this century, so named because poor farmer clients often paid for their visits with chickens. It is celebrated in the play *The Best Little Whorehouse in Texas*.

chickens come home to roost. Malcolm X stirred up a hornet's nest when he said this about John F. Kennedy after the President was assassinated, possibly alluding to alleged C.I.A. attempts on Fidel Castro's life. But the saying is an old one, dating back to at least 1810 in the form of "Curses are like young chickens; they always come home to roost," which appears to have been the invention of English poet laureate Robert Southey as the motto to his poem "The Curse of Kehama." The idea, of course, is that every curse or evil act returns to its originator as chickens return to their roost at night.

chicken scratch; crow tracks. These are Americanisms for illegible handwriting. *Chicken scratch* is first recorded in 1956 but is probably much older, while *crow tracks* dates back to at least 1875. Variations are *hen tracks* and *turkey tracks*.

chickenshit. Petty rules, especially in the Army, probably had been called *chicketshit* before the first recorded use of the expression in this sense in the 1930s. The early Canadian term *chickenshit* for "information from a superior officer" may be the source for the term.

chicken Tetrazzini. Luisa Tetrazzini, the Italian-born diva whose role of Lucia di Lammermoor made her famous to opera lovers throughout the world early in this century, counted this dish as her favorite. *Chicken Tetrazzini* is diced chicken in cream sauce flavored with sherry and baked in a casserole with thin spaghetti, cheese, and mushrooms. According to those who saw her, Madame Tetrazzini shared a problem common to most opera stars, looking as if she had dined many times on the highly caloric dish. The coloratura soprano made her debut in Florence in 1895 and ended her concert career in 1931, after starring in Spain, Portugal, Russia, England, America, and many other countries. She died in 1941, aged sixty-nine.

chick pea. *Chick pea* came into English in the 16th century from the French *pois chiche* for the vegetable and was originally called the *chiche pea*, until people began to confuse the word *chiche* with *chick*. *Cicer arietium* is also known as the *chick bean*. The word has nothing to do with the *chick* of *chicken*, as is often claimed.

chickweed. This bane of gardeners has been called by the name *chickweed* since the early 16th century. Before that the weedy plant was known as *chickenweed*, so named because it is eaten by chickens. *Stellaria media* is still called *chickenweed* in Scotland.

chigger. Both mites and fleas are called *chiggers*, the name deriving from the African *jigger*, for "a blood-sucking mite." In fact, even in this country *jigger* is sometimes used. *Chigger* came to mean a flea as well as a mite because it was confused with the West Indian *chigoe*, for "a flea," somewhere along the line.

children and chicken must always be pickin'. Both are always hungry and ready to eat, testing everything for food. The saying, first recorded in 1682 as an old proverb, uses *chicken* as a plural, one of the few cases in English where this still occurs.

childe ballad. American ballads are generally classified in three groups: *Childe ballads*, broadside ballads, and native American ballads. *Childe ballads* are not about children but refer to the 305 early songs collected by Harvard English professor Francis James Childe (1825-96) in the late 19th century. Of Childe's *English and Scottish Popular Ballads*, half the songs were brought to America by English settlers; they are considered the best of American ballads, and are still sung today, although many have undergone great transformations through the years.

chili pepper. (*See* **pepper.**)

chime in. When someone butts into a conversation he can interrupt with words of agreement or disagreement, but a person who intrudes by *chiming in* usually echoes the words of the last speaker. The term is often labeled slang in this sense but is really standard English now, common since Byron used it in the early 19th century. It has its origins in the harmonious chimes or bells in church towers, a music known since before the 14th century wherein a simple melody is struck and the other bells repeat it many times. As a musical term, meaning to join in harmoniously or in unison, the expression has been used since the late 19th century.

chimpanzee. *Chimpanzee*, from the Bantu *chimpanzee*, meaning "mock man," entered the English lexicon in 1738 when British explorers shipped the first of such animals to England from Angola. The highly intelligent ape more closely resembles man than any of the other anthropoids. British zoologist Jane Goodall, who spent years in Africa studying chimps, says they don't "have a language that can be compared with ours, but they do have a tremendous variety of calls, each one induced by a different emotion." Studies of chimps raised in captivity show that they use a vocabulary of about two dozen "words" or utterances. One chimp, Viki, raised from birth by Keith and Cathy Hayes in Florida, after three years learned to speak three human words (*papa*, *mamma* and *cup*), none of them very well—at the same age when a human child knows 200 or more words. (*See* **wraaaah!; dolphin; ow aw . . .; parrot**)

China; sinologist. *China* was not the name of the country that ancient Romans in Persia heard about from Chinese traders. The country is so named by mistake, because when asked where they came from, the Chinese would diplomatically give the name of the ruling dynasty at the time, the *Ch'in*, instead of the name of their country, *Chung-kuo*, "the Middle Kingdom" or "Central Country." *Ch'in* was Latinized by the Romans as *Sina*, which became the English *china*, as well as the basis for words like *sinologist*. The *china* (lower-cased here) refers to the fine porcelain brought to Europe from the Far East as early as the 16th century.

a Chinaman's chance. The Chinese immigrants who built so many miles of American railroads often tried to make their fortune by working old claims and streams abandoned by white prospectors during the California gold rush of 1849. They had an extremely poor chance of finding any gold in such abandoned claims, and thus *a Chinaman's chance* came to mean "no chance at all." The poor lot of Chinese in a segregated society probably reinforced the phrase, for the Chinese had as poor a chance on the railroads and other places as they did in the gold fields.

chin chin. Relatively few Americans have been greeted by anyone using this expression, but it is an oriental English greeting often encountered in literature since the early 19th century. There is no connection here with the lower jaw, the word for which derives from the old English *cin*. *Chin chin* is just a corruption of the Chinese salutation *ts'ing ts'ing*.

Chinese home run. Because Chinese immigrants were forced to work for little pay in a segregated society, their name came to mean "cheap" in American slang and formed the basis of a number of expressions. *Chinese home run* is the only one of these that still has much currency. It describes a cheap home run, one that just makes it over the fence. No one is sure who coined the phrase. It either arose in some ball park on the West Coast at the turn of the century and was brought East by the cartoonist "Tad" Dorgan (who is also responsible for the words "yes-man" and "hot dog"), or it originated in a baseball park with a fence a relatively short distance from home, possibly the old 239-foot right-field fence in Philadelphia's Shibe Park, or the short right-field fence in New York's old Polo Grounds.

Chinese language contributions to English. One out of every four people in the world speaks Chinese, "the world's first language." A good number of English words have Chinese ancestors. Among these are: *beezer* for a nose (from the Chinese *ta-bee-tsu* for Westerners, "the great-nosed ones"); *brainwashing* (originally a Korean War term that is a direct translation of the Chinese *hsi nao*, "to wash the brain"); *chop-chop* ("hurry," from pidgen English); *chop suey*; *chow*; *chow mein*; *fantan*; *gung-ho*; *joss*; *kow-tow*; *long time no see* (*q.v.*); *mah-jong* (although the Cantonese Chinese word really means "house sparrow"); *no can do* (from pidgen English); *tong*;

and *typhoon*. The Chinese have a proverb *cat gone, old rat comes out* that is much older than our centuries-old *when the cat's away the mice will play*. Even the insulting abusive word *chink* for a Chinese person is said to be a mispronunciation of the Chinese word *Chung-kuo* for "China." (*See also* **Chinaman's chance; Mandarin; pidgen English**.)

Chink. (*See* **Chinese**.)

Chinook; Chinook wind. *Chinook*, an important pidgin language, enabled 18th- and 19th-century American farmers and traders, French trappers, and even visiting Russian seal hunters to converse with Indians in the Pacific Northwest. Chinook jargon was used for more than one hundred years. Named for the Chinook Indians, who had large settlements along the Columbia River, this lingua franca combined various Chinook dialects, other Indian languages, English, French, and probably Russian. *Chinook wind*, so called by early settlers because it blew from the direction of the Chinook Indian camps, designates a dry wind blowing from the west or north over the Rocky Mountains—warm in winter and cool in summer—while a *wet Chinook* is a warm, moist wind blowing from sea to land in Washington and Oregon.

chintzy. *Chintzy* is American slang for "cheap," or "poorly made," or even "stingy," dating back to about the 1940s. But it comes from the plural of the Hindu word *chint*, for "a glazed cotton fabric with flowery designs" first made in India. The British mistook the plural of the word, *chints*, for the singular, applying it to the cloth and eventually spelling it *chintz*. Regarded as a cheap material in America, *chintz* finally gave us the word *chintzy*.

chip in; blue-chip, etc. Poker chips are the basis of a number of English expressions. To *chip in*, "to share expenses," derives from the practice of each player putting up his ante of chips at the start of the card game and chipping in with each bet. To *cash in one's chips*, or *hand*, that is, "to die," comes from the end of a poker game, when players turn in their chips to the cashier for money. *In the chips*, "affluent," refers to having a lot of poker chips, and *the chips are down*, signifying a situation of urgency, means literally that all bets are in the pot, the hand is over and the cards now have to be shown to determine the winning hand. All of these expressions date back to the 19th century, when poker became our national card game. So does a *blue-chip stock*, a high-priced common stock that pays high dividends consistently over a long period, which derives from poker's highest-valued blue chips.

chipmunk. This small striped squirrel-like rodent takes its name from the way it descends trees. *Chipmunk* comes from the Chippewa Indian *atchitamon*, meaning "head first."

a chip on one's shoulder.   In 1830 the *Long Island Telegraph* in Hempstead, New York reported that "When two churlish boys were determined to fight, a *chip* would be placed on the shoulder of one, and the other demanded to knock it off at his peril." From this New York State boyhood custom, first recorded above, comes the expression *to have a chip on one's shoulder*, "to be sullen or angry, looking for a fight." The phrase itself isn't recorded until 1934, but is probably much older.

Chippendale.   Thomas Chippendale (ca. 1718-79) worked primarily in the French rococo, Chinese, and Gothic styles, sometimes combining them without incongruous results. Setting up his factory in London in 1749, he later published *The Gentleman and Cabinet Maker's Directory* (1754), in which he illustrated some 160 designs. Chippendale almost invariably managed to combine comfort, grace, and solidity in his wide variety of furniture, which is highly valued today. So many of his designs were slavishly copied during the latter half of the 18th century that it has always been difficult to identify his own work, dealers generally using the term *Chippendale* to designate a large variety of furniture in his style.

chippy.   Most sources say *chippy*, first recorded in the late 1880s, comes from *chip*, "to chirp," as a streetwalker might do when a prospective client walked by. But it's hard to believe that prostitutes commonly chirped at men. More likely, this name for a whore derives from the *chips* prostitutes were paid with by clients in Mexican-American whorehouses (*chippy houses*) in the western United States. The customers purchased chips from the madam, paid the women with them and the women cashed them in for their percentage.

the chips are down.   (*See* **chip in.**)

Chisholm Trail.   In the spring of 1866 Jesse Chisholm (ca. 1806-68), a halfbreed Cherokee Indian trader and government agent, drove his wagon loaded with buffalo hides through the Oklahoma territory to Wichita, Kansas. The wheels cut deep into the prairie, providing rut marks for a route that was to become the most important and famous of all western cattle trails, extending from San Antonio, Texas to Abilene and other Kansas railheads. The trail was used for more than twenty years after the Civil War, and 450,000 Texas longhorns were driven up it in 1872 alone. Remnants of the trail, celebrated in folklore and cowboy ballads such as "The Old Chisholm Trail," still remain along the Santa Fe Railroad line.

chit.   *Chit*, for "an I.O.U." or "a voucher of money owed for food or drink," derives from the Hindustani *citthi*, "a short note." In British colonial India, Hindu civil servants seem to have been in the habit of writing an inordinate amount of *citthis* about every conceivable matter. The British found this practice time-consuming and inefficient, criticizing it so often that the word *citthi* eventually became the easier to pronounce *chitty* and then *chit* in their vocabulary. They used *chit-coolies* as a term for Indian messengers, and soon they used *chit* for the notes they signed for drinks and food at their clubs. The *chit* that means a young, often insignificant person or a child ("a chit of a girl") goes back much further in time. Found in Wycliffe, it refers to the young of an animal and probably derives from *kitten* or *kit*.

Choctaw.   *Choctaw*, a fancy step in ice-skating, and Southern slang for unintelligible speech, is from the Choctaw Indian tribe of southern Mississippi. The Choctaws, named from the Spanish *chato* ("flattened") for their practice of flattening the heads of male infants, fought against the British during the American Revolution and aided the United States in later years against the Creeks. They ceded their lands to the government in 1832, the majority moving to reservations in what is now Oklahoma.

chocolate mousse.   One theory has it that this dessert was invented by French artist Henri de Toulouse-Lautrec a century ago. Lautrec gave it the witty name *chocolate mayonnaise*, but this was changed to chocolate *mousse*, ("foam, lather") over the years.

choke pear; chokecherry.   Because of its rough, astringent taste, which could make a person choke, this fruit was called a *choke pear*. Later the term was applied, figuratively, to anything that stopped someone from speaking, such as biting sarcasm or an unanswerable argument. The wild black cherry is sometimes called the *chokecherry* for similar reasons, and there is a berry called the *chokeberry*.
(*See* **choke-pear; pears of agony.**)

choke-pear; pears of agony.   The *choke-pear*, whose name also became the synonym for "a severe reproof" in the 16th century, has to be among the most perverse instruments of torture man has invented. Named after the indigestible pear called a *choke pear (q.v.)*, it was "of iron, shaped like a pear" and originally "used in Holland" by robbers. According to an early source: "This iron pear they forced into the mouths of persons from whom they intended to extort money; and of turning a key, certain interior springs thrust forth a number of points, in all directions, which so enlarged it, that it could not be taken from the mouth: and the iron, being case-hardened, could not be filed; the only methods of getting rid of it were either by cutting the mouth, or advertising a reward for the key. These pears were also called pears of agony."

chop chop. Noticing how fast the Chinese ate with chopsticks, 19th-century traders in China adopted the "chop" from the word *chopsticks* and invented the pidgin English expression *chop chop*—"quick, fast, or make it snappy." The word *chopsticks* itself is a corruption of the Chinese name for the eating implements, *k'wai-tsze*, which means "the quick or nimble ones." (*See* **long time no see.**)

chopsticks.   (*See* **chop chop.**)

chop suey.   *Chop suey* isn't native to China; in fact, most accounts of its origin say that the dish was invented in America. The widely accepted theory, advanced by Herbert Asbury in his *Gangs of New York* (1928), makes the tasty melange the brainchild of a San Francisco dishwasher, though the Chinese dishwasher is sometimes promoted to a "cook in a California gold mining camp." I've traced the term's invention however, to 1896, when it was concocted in New York by Chinese ambassador Li Hung-Chang's chef, who tried to devise a dish appealing to both American and Chinese tastes. Since the ambassador had three chefs, it's hard to say which one invented *chop suey*. The name has nothing to do with the English word "chop," deriving instead from the Cantonese dialect *shap sui*, which means "bits and pieces of mixed bits," *sui* being the Chinese for "bits." The chef who invented it took leftover pieces of pork and chicken and cooked them together with bean sprouts, green peppers, mushrooms, and seasonings in a gravy, serving it with rice and soy sauce.

chortle.   Author Lewis Carroll coined *chortle*, "to chuckle gleefully," in *Through the Looking Glass* (1871)—the word a blend of "snort" and "chuckle."

chouse.   The word *chouse*, "to cheat or swindle," is thought to derive from the Turkish *chaush*, for "an official messenger." How the messenger became a swindler is an interesting story. It seems that in 1609 the English adventurer Sir Robert Shirley, who had been barred from his homeland, sent a Turkish messenger to England to transact business with Turkish and Persian merchants there. The messenger *choused* the merchants of 4,000 pounds and disappeared, the notoriety of his swindle leading to the coining of the word. However, this derivation is not certain because there are no contemporary records of the swindle.

chow.   *Ch'ao*, the Mandarin Chinese for "to fry or cook," probably gives us the word *chow*, an Americanism first recorded in the 1850s in California, where there were many Chinese laborers and cooks working on the railroads. (*See* **chow chow.**)

chow chow.   *Chow chow*, or *chow*, a medium-sized, generally red, black, or brown nonsporting dog of Chinese breed, may derive its name from *chow*, a pidgin word for food, or from *chow-chow*, the Chinese mixed-fruit preserve. Another theory, which seems more plausible, is that it is simply from the Chinese *Chou*, this being the name of the ancient Chinese race that formed the Chou dynasty, which ruled from about 1122 to 256 B.C., and which brought China's first "golden age." The *chow* is noted for its sturdy build, large head, and deep-set eyes. Probably originally bred in northern China, it can be traced back as early as 150 B.C.

chowderhead.   Neither clam chowder nor any other chowder has anything to do with the expression *chowderhead*, for "a dolt, a stupid clumsy person." *Chowderhead* is a mispronunciation of *cholter-head*, which dates back to the 16th century and derived from the older term *jolthead*. Unfortunately, we're all a bunch of chowderheads when it comes to the origin of *jolthead*.

Christian.   The first known usage of *Christians*, for "followers of Christ," is recorded in the Bible, *Acts* 11:25-26: "So Barnabas went to Tarsus to look for Saul; and when he had found him, he brought him to Antioch. For a whole year they met with the church, and taught a large company of people; and in Antioch the disciples were for the first time called Christians." The word *Christ* is from the Greek *Christos*, "the Anointed one." (*See* **Buddhism; Jew.**)

Christmas.   *Christmas* simply means *Christ's mass*. The Christian holiday celebrates Christ's birth, but there are no trustworthy records of the real date—August 28, May 20, April 19 or 20, November 17, and March 28 having all been suggested by scholars as more accurate than December 25. In northern Europe, *Christmas* was originally a pagan feast celebrating the winter solstice, a time when ancient peoples built great bonfires to give the winter sun god strength and to receive him. The early church fathers wisely chose a day near the winter solstice as the date to celebrate Christ's birth, the return of light becoming associated with the hope of the world in the birth of the savior.

Christmas tree.   The Christmas tree is an ancient German custom, though Germans call the small decorated firs or spruces they use a *Weihnachtsbaum*, or "holy-night tree." German settlers brought the custom to America, where English-speaking settlers dubbed it the *Christmas tree* as early as 1838, the first recorded use of the term. Americans thought the trees idolatrous at first, but soon realized the German immigrants weren't worshipping the tree and adopted the custom themselves.

christy.   Also called a *christiania*, the *christy* is a quick turn in skiing, so named for the capital of Norway, Christiania (now Oslo), where it was invented.

Christy minstrels.   Folk music fans may be surprised to learn that the name of this popular group honors an early American songwriter and that the term *Christy minstrels* is a synonym for Negro minstrel-type groups. Edwin Christy (1815-62) popularized his songs through his black-face troupe, which toured America and England and was widely imitated up until the beginning of this century. Christy wasn't the first to perform in blackface, but his group brought the minstrel show to perfection. His name had such great drawing power that it was assumed by the man who assumed leadership of the troupe when Christy retired.

chrononhotonthologos.   The longest words ever delivered on stage were: "Aldiborontiphoscophornio! Where left you Chrononhotonthologos?" which begins Henry Carey's farce *Chrononhotonthologos, the Most Tragical Tragedy That Ever Was Tragedized by Any Company of Tragedians* (1734). Chrononhotonthologos was the King of Queerummania, and his name is now used (though seldom, if ever, verbally) for any bombastic person delivering an inflated address. Aldiboronti-phoscophornio was a courier in the play. Carey, who wrote the popular song "Sally in My Alley," may have written the words and music to the British anthem, "God Save the King."

chubby.   For nearly 400 years now overweight people have been called *chubby* after the thick, fat, and round-cheeked fish named the *chub*, a type of carp common in England and northern Europe. The American fish called the *chub* is not the same fish at all.

chucker-out.   (*See* **bouncer**.)

chuckle; cackle.   The *O.E.D.* says *chuckle* is an echoic word like *cackle*, both perhaps suggested by sounds chickens make. *Chuckle* provides a problem, however, because it meant "to laugh vehemently or convulsively" when first recorded in 1598, and such laughter, to my ear, hardly sounds anything like a chicken. The soft, suppressed laughter that is *chuckle's* meaning today does fit such origins, though. (*See* **onomatopoeia**.)

chum.   *Chum*, for "close friend or pal," came into the English only in the late 17th century, probably from British university slang. It possibly is a shortening and slight alteration of *chambermate* (roommate), but there are no quotations to prove this. *Chum*, for "fishing bait," possibly comes from a Scottish dialect word meaning "food"; in any case, it derives from a different source from the *chum* meaning "pal."

chump.   (*See* **sap**.)

chunnel.   *Chunnel* is the name for the tunnel under the English channel from England to France, which has long been discussed but has not yet been constructed, mainly because of English fears of invasion from Europe through it.

Churchillian.   Often accompanying elegant oratory or prose, great wit, and statesmanship, and even a large cigar, this familiar adjective commemorates British Prime Minister Sir Winston Leonard Spencer Churchill (1874-1965). "On the 30th of November at Blenheim Palace, the Lady Randolph Churchill, prematurely, of a son," read the one line notice in the *London Times* announcing his birth, but Churchill's life was to fill volumes. Soldier, journalist, writer, and statesman, his brilliant public career included service as home secretary of state for war, and chancellor of the exchequer. Yet all his life, he felt, was merely a preparation for his crucial prime minister-ship during World War II. Some have gone so far as to say that England would not have survived the blitz of 1940-41 without his leadership. Great *Churchillian* words and phrases include the much quoted, "I have nothing to offer but blood, toil, tears and sweat"; "Never in the field of human conflict was so much owed by so many to so few"; "The soft underbelly of the Axis"; the "iron curtain"; and his words on the fall of France: "Let us therefore brace ourselves to our duties, and so bear ourselves that if the British Empire and its Commonwealth last for a thousand years, men will still say: 'This was their finest hour!'" On April 9, 1963, Winston Churchill was paid the unique honor of being proclaimed a citizen of the United States.

churl.   (*See* **earl**.)

churrigueresque.   This man's name itself is elaborate, suggesting the style it represents. Extravagant overornate architecture, especially that of 17th- and 18th-century Spain, is called *churrigueresque*, after Spanish architect and sculptor José Churriguera (1650-1725). Churriguera, a native of Salamanca, was an architect of the baroque school whose important works include the great catafalque for Queen Maria Louisa (1688), the palace of Don Juan de Goyeneche, and a portal of the Church of Santo Gayetano. Spanish baroque, with its free lines and vast profusion of detailed ornament, is named for him because he and his two sons were the most successful practitioners of this Renaissance form. *Churrigueresque* strongly influenced the Spanish colonial style in the southwestern part of Spain and in Mexico.

chutzpa.   *Chutzpa*, or *chutzpah*, derives from a Hebrew word meaning "insolence, audacity." Signifying impudence, gall, brazen nerve, incredible cheek, and unmitigated audacity in Yiddish and in American slang, it more often today indicates an admirable quality in a person—guts bordering on the heroic. Leo Rosten gives the classic definition of *chutzpa* in *The Joys of Yiddish*: "that quality enshrined in a man who, having killed his mother and father, throws himself on the mercy of the court because he is an orphan." (No one knows if this ever happened, but a 19th-century anecdote does mention such a man.)

ciao!   *Ciao!* (pronounced "chow") is an Italian word for "hello" or "good-bye" used frequently in the U.S. over the past twenty years or so. *Ciao!* derives from the Italian *schiavo,* "I am your slave."

Cicero; Cicerone; Ciceronian.   If you travel in Italy, any guide you hire will be called a *cicerone,* these guides often being well versed about the places of interest and objects they point out. The Italians invoke the name of Marcus Tullius Cicero (100-43 B.C.) for this word because the eloquent statesman, orator, and writer epitomized the knowledge and style they expected of their *cicerones.* The story, from Plutarch, is that Cicero got his name from the Latin *cicer* ("a wart"), due to the "flat excrescence on the tip of his nose." Cicero is also honored by *Ciceronian,* pertaining to his clear, forceful, and melodious oratorial or prose style, and *Cicero,* a unit of print similar to a pica. Today, *Cicerone* has come to mean a guide in any country.

cider.   That *cider* was originally hard cider—that is, a fermented alcoholic drink—is witnessed by the derivation of the word, which came into English, via French (*cidre*), from the Latin word *sicera,* which comes from the Hebrew *shekar,* "strong drink." General William Henry Harrison of "Old Tippecanoe and Tyler, too" fame (he was called Tippecanoe because he won a battle against Indians at Tippecanoe River), was also known as the "log cabin and hard cider candidate" when he defeated Martin Van Buren for the presidency in 1840. As a campaign song put it:

Let Van from his cooler of silver wine drink
And lounge on his silken settee.
Our man on a log-cabin bench can recline;
Content with hard cider is he!

cigarette.   (*See* **coffin nails.**)

Cimmerian darkness; Crimea.   The ancient Cimmerians were believed to live in total darkness in a land where the sun never shone—hence the expression *Cimmerian darkness,* often "the darkness of ignorance." Homer used the term *Cimmerian darkness* in the *Odyssey.* These wandering nomads also gave their name to the *Crimea* because they lived on the shores of the Black Sea.

Cinchona; quinine.   About 1639 the Condesa Ana de Chinchón, wife of the Conde de Chinchón (ca. 1590-1647), Spanish viceroy of Peru, was stricken with a persistent tropical fever. After European doctors failed to restore her health, she was cured by the powdered bark of a native evergreen tree that Peruvian Indians brought her. The condesa and her husband collected the dried bark, which contained quinine, and sent it back to Spain. There the miracle bark was at first called "Countess bark" or "Peruvian bark," but when Linnaeus named the genus of trees and shrubs yielding it in the condesa's honor, he misspelled her name. What should have been the "Chichona tree" became known to history as the *Cinchona tree.* Today the native South American *Cinchona* is widely grown throughout the world, notably in Java and India. The *quinine* extracted from its bark derives its name from *quinaquina,* its Peruvian Indian name.

Cincinnati.   Cincinnati, Ohio takes its name from the Society of the *Cincinnati,* honoring the Roman statesman Cincinnatus, which former Revolutionary officers in the area founded in 1783.

cinque ports.   From the 13th to the 17th century and even later the British crown granted special privileges to the ports of Hastings, Sandwich, Dover, Romaney, and Hythe, because they provided men and ships for the defense of the English Channel. The ports of Rye and Winchelsea were later added, but the favored ports were still called *cinque* ports, from the Latin *quinque,* "five."

Circassian.   *Circassian beauty* refers to the legendary charms of the Circassian women, inhabitants of a region in the northeast Caucasus once known as Circassia, where fathers often sold their beautiful daughters to Turkish merchants for the harems of Eastern monarchs. No degradation was implied; the women considered their sale an honor. The Circassians had a number of unusual customs: any young man who purchased a bride was required to come with friends, fully armed, and carry her off from her father's house; a younger brother had to rise from his seat whenever an elder brother entered the room and remain silent whenever he spoke; a murderer could escape punishment by rearing the newborn child of his victim until his or her education was completed; and any man pursued by enemies had sanctuary after he touched the hand of a woman, so long as he remained under her roof. Russia finally subjugated these proud, warlike Muslims in 1864, after which many of them migrated to Turkish territory. Today Circassia forms the state of Kuban in the U.S.S.R.

circus; charity circus.   The expression *charity circus* for a circus that donates part of its proceeds to charity dates back to famous American circus owner and clown Dan Rice, who helped popularize his circus by donating part of the proceeds in the 1850s and gave performances for the

Union cause during the Civil War. Circuses in America go back to at least 1785, however, and circuses were popular in Roman times, the word *circus* itself deriving from the Latin *circus* for ring. A *three ring circus* is thus, strictly speaking, "a three ring ring."

clam up.　*Clam up* is an Americanism for "to become silent, refuse to disclose information," dating back to 1916 and referring to the difficulty of opening the "lips" of the clam. *Clam*, for "mouth," has been common in America since the early 19th century. *Close as a clam*, describing a stingy person, refers to the difficulty in opening a clamshell and is an older expression that probably originated in England. (*See* **happy as a clam at high tide.**)

the clap.　The Old French *clapoire* ("bulge, venereal sore"), which comes from the Old French *clapier* ("brothel"), gives us the word *clap* for gonorrhea. *Partridge* advises that the word was standard English from its introduction in the 16th century until Victorian times, noting, interestingly enough, that "They sing, they dance, clean shoes, or cure a clap" (in the poem "London") is "almost the sole instance in Dr. Johnson's work of a monosyllabic sentence."

claptrap.　*Claptrap*, first recorded in 1727, initially meant a playwright's trick or device to catch applause, "a trap to catch a clap by way of applause from the spectators at a play," as the first person to define the term put it. The word finally came to mean pretentious, insincere, or empty language.

claque.　Playwrights have had an advantage over most authors in the past because they or their backers could hire a *claque*, a body of people to applaud their work. The French, who originated the system in 1820 or so, had it down to a science. *Claqueurs* were divided into:

> *Commissaires*—memorized the play and pointed out
> 　　　its literary merits.
> *Rieurs*—hired to laugh at the jokes.
> *Pleureurs*—women hired to cry when appropriate.
> *Chatouilleurs*—kept the audience in good spirits.
> *Bisseurs*—hired to cry "*bis!*," "encore!"

Clarkia; Lewisia.　Captain William Clark (1770-1838) is best known for his leadership with Meriwether Lewis of the Lewis and Clark Expedition to find an overland route to the Pacific, their party being the first to cross the continent within the limits of the United States. But the Army officer and veteran Indian fighter had an avid interest in natural history, describing many plants in his journals covering the 1803-07 expedition. The showy *Clarkia* genus, native to California, was named in his honor. Clark, the youngest brother of the famous frontier military leader, George Rogers Clark, was appointed

superintendent of Indian affairs when his expedition returned. Clark's partner Captain Meriwether Lewis has *Lewisia*, a genus of twelve species of low-growing perennial flowers widely grown in the rock garden, named in his honor. Lewis, who had been Thomas Jefferson's secretary, was appointed governor of the newly acquired Louisiana Territory after the expedition. He died suddenly in 1808, only thirty-five years old, his death shrouded in mystery. He had been traveling to Washington to prepare the expedition journals when he died alone in an inn near Nashville, Tennessee. Suicide, or more probably murder, has been suggested as the cause of his death.

clatter.　(*See* **onomatopoeia.**)

clavicle.　*Clavicle*, or collarbone, derives from the Latin *clavicula*, meaning "little key." According to Littré's *Dictionnaire de la Langue Française* (1863-77) "because it was compared to the key of a vault, or, as others think, because its form is that of the ancient bolts."

clean as a whistle.　One possibility is that the old simile describes the whistling sound of a sword as it swishes through the air to decapitate someone, and an early 19th century quotation does suggest this connection: "A first rate shot . . . [his] head taken off as clean as a whistle." The expression is proverbial, at least since the 18th century, when Robert Burns used a variation on it. More likely the basic idea suggests the clear, pure sound a whistle makes, or the slippery smooth surface of a willow stick debarked to make a whistle. But there is also a chance that the phrase may have originally been *as clean as a whittle*, referring to a piece of smooth wood after it is whittled.

a clean bill of health.　Used generally today this term has its origin in the document issued to a ship showing that the port it left was suffering from no epidemic or infection at the time of departure. Its antonym is *a foul bill of health*, both expressions dating back to the 18th century.

cleanliness is next to godliness.　Writers have variously assumed that this proverb originated with the American Puritans, that Benjamin Franklin created it in *Poor Richard's Almanac*, or that it is from the Bible. The truth is that it can be traced back to writings of Phinehas ben Yair, an ancient rabbi, and is found in the Talmud in this form: "The doctrines of religion are resolved into carefulness; carefulness into vigorousness; vigorousness into guiltlessness; guiltlessness into abstemiousness; abstemiousness into cleanliness; cleanliness into godliness." In this quotation "cleanliness" is literally next to "godliness." The first written record of the expression in English is by John Wesley, the founder of Methodism, who in a 1778 sermon wrote "Cleanlines is indeed next to godliness" and put the words in quotes as if to indicate that he had borrowed or slightly changed them from another source. Wesley said, "I look upon all the world as my parish." His "Rule of Conduct" was:

Do all the good you can,
By all the means you can,
In all the ways you can,
In all the places you can,
At all the times you can,
To all the people you can,
As long as ever you can.

to cleanse the Augean stables.   This means a formidable if not impossible task. It was one of the twelve tasks of Hercules, hero of Greek mythology, given to him by Eurystheus before he could gain immortality. Hercules managed to clean the stables of King Augeus in one day, even though they contained 3,000 oxen, by turning the course of two rivers through the stalls.

clean up.   In the early 19th century American farmers used the expression *to clean up* as a synonym for gathering the harvest, stripping all the grain from a field. However this doesn't appear to be the source when the expression means "to make an exceptional financial success," a "big haul." In this sense *clean up* came into the language after the gold strikes toward the end of the last century. It apparently derives from the mining term *clean-up*, which describes the process of separating gold from the gravel and rock that collected in the sluices or at the stamping mill.

clear the decks.   Make everything ready, especially before a great activity such as a fight. The expression goes back to the 18th century or earlier, when it was a naval command ordering seamen to prepare the ship for a battle.

Cleopatra.   Cleopatra was only thirty-eight when she died in 30 B.C., but in her short life she became one of the great romantic heroines of all time, her name still synonymous with feminine allurement and charm. At the age of seventeen, the Queen of the Nile married her younger brother, as was the custom, and led a revolt against Ptolemy XIII when he deprived her of her royal authority. Inducing Julius Caesar to fight a war to place her on the throne, she became his mistress, living openly in Rome with him after she poisoned her second, younger sibling-husband. Caesar's assassination marked her return to Egypt with their son, Caesarion. There, in 41 B.C., Mark Antony fell under her spell and gave up his wife for her. Cleopatra hoped that Antony would restore her former powers. However, Octavian (later Emperor Augustus) declared war on them, vowing to destroy the two lovers, and defeated Antony at Actium. Cleopatra coldly accepted Octavian's proposal to assassinate Antony

and persuaded him to commit suicide so that "they might die together." Antony took his life by falling on his sword, believing that Cleopatra had already done so, but "the serpent of the old Nile" was unable to win over Octavian, despite her treachery. She ended her own life by putting an asp to her breast. Her three sons by Antony were allowed to live, but Caesarion was put to death soon after.

Cleopatra's Needles.   *Cleopatra's Needles* is a misnomer. The two originally pink obelisks—one 68 1/2 feet tall standing on the Thames embankment, and the other 69 1/2 feet tall in New York's Central Park—really have nothing at all to do with the Queen of the Nile. Hieroglyphics on the needles show that Pharaoh Thotmes III erected them centuries before Cleopatra. Originally raised at Heliopolis in 1475 B.C., the obelisks were moved to Alexandria under Augustus in about 14 B.C., where they adorned the Caesareum. In 1878 and 1880, respectively, Ismail Pasha made gifts of them to England and the United States, and it is said that they have suffered more from erosion in their present locations over the last ninety-odd years than they did over thousands of years in Egypt. The formerly rose-red syenite granite obelisks were probably named for Cleopatra because they stood outside the Caesareum, honoring her dictator lover.

Cleopatra's nose.   "If the nose of Cleopatra had been shorter the whole face of the earth would have been changed," wrote the French philosopher Blaise Pascal (1623-62) in his famous *Pensées*. His proverbial observation refers to the effects of Cleopatra's charms on Caesar and Mark Antony, but a different nose length, at least a moderately different one, would probably have made little difference to history. For Cleopatra's allure did not depend on her physical beauty; most sources, in fact, indicate that she wasn't a beautiful woman at all. What she was was an accomplished, artful lover, and the "salad days" that Shakespeare has her admit to—when she was young and loved unskillfully, like a salad, green and cold—were distant memories long before she had married at seventeen.

Cleopatra's pearl.   *Cleopatra's pearl* concerns a sumptuous banquet Cleopatra gave for Antony. Her lover, the legend tells us, expressed astonishment at the costly meal, and she promptly removed a pearl earring, dropped it in a cup of vinegar and let it dissolve, saying, "My draft to Antony shall far exceed it." Vinegar cannot dissolve a pearl, however, and anything strong enough to do so wouldn't have conveniently been on Cleopatra's table—unless the wileful woman planted it there, in which case it is just as possible that she used a fake pearl.

clerical collar.   Also called the *Roman collar* and the *reversed collar*, the clerical collar is a stiff narrow white collar fastened at the back and worn by some clerics. The term is first recorded in the mid-19th century. (*See* **clerk.**)

clerihew.

> Sir Humphry Davy
> Abominated gravy
> He lived in the odium
> Of having discovered sodium.

This was the first *clerihew* written by Edmund Clerihew Bentley (1875-1956). The English detective-story writer composed it while only a schoolboy, according to his schoolmate G. K. Chesterton, "when he sat listening to a chemical exposition, with his rather bored air and a blank sheet of blotting paper before him." Bentley, one of the few people to have a word honoring his middle name, could in Chesterton's words "write clear and unadulterated nonsense with . . . serious simplicity."

clerk.   Clerks were originally scholars; the word *clerk* is simply a slurred pronunciation of the word *cleric*, which in medieval times meant a member of a religious order, all of whom were regarded as scholars because they could read and write. When education became more widespread, the term *clerk* gradually lost its scholarly connotation and assumed the meaning it has today, surviving in its old sense in legal circles, where, for example, a clerk to a Supreme Court Justice is still considered a scholar.

Cleveland.   Cleveland, Ohio was laid out in 1796 by General Moses Cleaveland and was later named for him. Still later, a descendant of the general, Grover Cleveland, became president.

clicketing.   In days past, people had more names for natural things than we can imagine today. *Clicketing*—not slang, but Standard English—means "the copulation of foxes" and has been used in this sense since the late 16th century or before. This is perhaps a distinct word from *clicket*, meaning "to chatter," the first recorded use of it explaining: "When a bytche foxe goeth on clycqueting . . . she cryeth with a hollow voyce like unto the howling of a madde dogge . . ." The term is also applied to the wolf.

client.   In ancient Rome a *client* (Latin for "learning") was a plebeian under the patronage of a patrician who was called his patron, the *client* performing certain services for the patron in exchange for the patron's protection of his life and interests. Hundreds of years later, in the 15th century, the word's meaning changed to describe a person who employs the services of a legal adviser or a person who employs the services of any professional businessman.

climb a sour apple tree.   First recorded in the early 1900s but probably older, *go climb a sour apple tree* means "go to blazes, go to hell." It is an Americanism that is still occasionally heard.

clink.   *Clink*, which is still heard humorously as the term for a jail, dates back at least to 1515, when a writer noted, "Then art thou clapped in the . . . Clinke." One theory has the word deriving from "a noted jail in the borough of Southwark." Milton is among the distinguished writers to have used the term. *To kiss the clink* was an expression, now virtually obsolete, meaning to be imprisoned.

clipped ears.   Though the term isn't recorded in the *Dictionary of Americanisms*, Australians who migrated to the California gold fields in 1849 were often called *clipped ears*, because a certain number of them had been criminals who had suffered the punishment of ear clipping in Australia.

clipper ship; Flying Clipper.   The origin of the *clipper* in *clipper ship* is not definitely known, but we may owe the expression to Cleopatra. The first authentic *clipper ship* was the *Ann McKim*, built in Baltimore in 1832, but an early French ship of this type was christened *Cleopatra-cum-Antonio*. The French ship's name, some scholars say, was shortened in usage to *Clipster* and then to *Clipper*, the last becoming the designation for all vessels of this class. Other authorities contend that rude *clippers* were being built before the War of 1812 and were known as *Baltimore clippers* because they clipped the surface of the sea as they sped over the waves. Still another source holds that the expression *going at a clip* resulted in the word; and some investigators even claim that *clipper* is an invention of either Robert Burns or Percy Bysshe Shelley. But the French developed the principle for this type of ship in the 18th century, long before the *Baltimore clippers*, and as the *Cleopatra-cum-Antonio* dates from that period, the Cleopatra theory has much to say for it. *Clipper ship* was later applied to transoceanic flying boats, the famed *Flying Clippers*.

clodhopper; country bumpkin; hick; hayseed; rube.   *Clodhopper*, before it became a word for "shoes," was an old 17th-century English term for a farmer or rural dweller who hopped over clods of dirt in the fields. *Country bumpkin*, from the Dutch *boomkin*, "little tree," became common in England a century later. *Rube* (from "Rustic Rueben"), *hick* (a pet name for "Richard") and *hayseed* are 19th-century Americanisms.

close as a clam.   (See **clam up.**)

clothes make the man.   Apparently *clothes make the man* is an "alteration" of Shakespeare's "The apparel oft proclaims the man," which the Bard puts into the mouth of Polonius in *Hamlet*.

Cloud Cuckoo Land.   Unrelated to life, an imaginary state of affairs. The reference is to the imaginary city built in the air in Aristophanes's comedy *The Birds* (414 B.C.).

clue. Tracing *clue*, or *clew*, back in time we find that it first meant (in about 1393) "a ball of yarn or thread." Two centuries passed and *clues*, balls of thread, began to be used to guide people "threading" their way out of garden labyrinths or mazes. This soon led to the use of the word *clue* for something that "points the way, indicates a solution, or puts one on the track of a discovery or solving a mystery."

coach. The little village of Kocs in northwestern Hungary is responsible for the word *coach* in all its senses of the word "carriage" and for academic and athletic *coaches* as well. In the 15th century an unknown carriage maker in Kocs devised a larger, more comfortable carriage than any known at the time. It was called a *Koczi szeter*, a "wagon of Kocs," which was shortened to *kocsi*. Copied all over Europe in the next century it eventually became a *coche* and then a *coach* in English. From the name of the English horse-drawn *coach* came all *stagecoaches*, *motor coaches*, and finally *air coaches*. *Coach*, for "an instructor," arose as college slang—a *coach* was a figurative carriage whose *coaching* would "carry" you through exams. The same idea was applied to athletic *coaches*, who were, however, known as *coachers* up until the late 1880s, when they became *coaches*.

the coast is clear. Though prominent during Prohibition among liquor smugglers, this is a much older term that passed into general use in the 19th century. It originally meant that no coast guards were in sight and it was safe to sail in those waters.

cobbler should stick to his last; ultracrepederian. Alexander the Great's favorite artist, Apelles, corrected his drawing of a man's sandal latchet in one of his paintings when a cobbler criticized it. But when the shoemaker went on to criticize the way Apelles had drawn the man's legs, the artist admonished him: *Ne sutor ultra crepidam*, "The cobbler should stick to his last [the metal foot-model on which shoes are shaped]." Apelles's words give us not only the familiar expression but the term *ultracrepederian*, meaning "criticism ranging beyond the critic's range of knowledge." Its first recorded use is by Hazlitt in an 1819 letter to critic William Gifford, who had savaged Keat's "Endymion" in the *Quarterly Review*.

cobwebs; spiderweb. Dating back to at least 1300, *cobweb* is older than *spiderweb* by about two hundred years. *Cob* is a form of *cop*, a Middle English word for spider. Strangely enough, although *cobweb* is of older ancestry than *spiderweb*, *cob* or *cop* was only rarely used as a separate word for *spider*. It is a back formation from *cobweb*, which means that we have to look elsewhere for the origin of *cobweb*. Possibly the answer may be found in an earlier use of *cob* or *cop* for "head." *Cobweb* may have been suggested by people walking into spiderwebs and brushing their heads (*cobs*) in the webs.

Coca-Cola. (*See* **Coke**.)

cock. The word *cock*, for "the penis or male sexual organ," is included in the great *O.E.D.*, which traces it to the earlier term *cock*, for "the spout or short pipe serving as a channel for passing liquids through . . ." *Cock* for the penis is, however, recorded earlier than the *O.E.D.'s* date of 1730, being first attested in Beaumont and Fletcher's comedy *The Custom of the Country* (ca. 1619). *Cock* for a rooster is recorded much earlier, in ca. 897, its origin unknown, although it is earlier *cocc* in Old English.

cock-a-doodle-doo. English speakers might think that the use of our centuries-old echoic word for the sound of the crowing of a rooster would be universal, but only the "k" sound in the word is common to most languages, their echoic words for the cock's crowing being quite different. German, for example, uses *kikiriki*; Italian, *chicchirichi*; French, *cocorico*; Spanish, *quiquiriqui*; Russian, *kikareku*; Rumanian, *cucuriqu*; Vietnamese, *cuc-cu*; Japanese, *kokekkoko*; and Arabic, *ko-ko*. The same is true for many echoic words. (*See* **meow**.)

cockamamie. *Cockamamie* means something worthless or trifling, even absurd or strange; a *cockamamie* excuse or story is an implausible, ridiculous one. The word may be a corruption of *decalcomania* ("a cheap picture or design on specially prepared paper that is transferred to china, wood, etc."), a word youngsters on New York's Lower East Side early in the century found tiring to pronounce and impossible to spell.

cock and bull story. This long, rambling, unlikely yarn, like the similar *canard* (*q.v.*), takes its name from the barnyard. The phrase first appeared in about 1600 and has been constantly used ever since; even in classics like Laurence Sterne's *Tristram Shandy* (1767), one of our most imaginative and whimsical novels, where the words end the book: "'L———d' said my mother, 'what is this story all about.' '———A COCK and a BULL,' said Yorick—'and one of the best of its kind, I ever heard.'" The expression *cock and bull story* hasn't been traced to the specific fable where it originated, but it arose in all probability from a fantastic tale about a cock and bull who talked to each other in human language. Since people knew that such a conversation was impossible, they most likely labeled any incredible yarns *cock and bull stories*. The French have used the expression *coq-à-l'âne*—literally "cock to the donkey"—in the same sense as cock and bull for almost four centuries, too. But it is also the term for a satirical verse genre that ridicules the follies and vices of society, deriving in this sense from the old French proverbial expression *c'est bien sauté du coq à l'âne*, which signifies incoherent speech or writing.

cockatrice; ichneumon. Thanks to Pliny and other incredulous observers, people were terrified of this fantastic monster with the wings of a bird, the tail of a dragon, and the crested head of a cock until well into the 17th century. Said to be born of a cock's egg, the monster was, according to one old description, about "a foot long, with black and yellow skin and fiery red eyes," but others described it as much larger. It could be killed only by the crowing of a cock and so travelers often carried roosters with them to Africa or wherever they feared a *cockatrice* might be encountered. Otherwise, just a glance from the fabulous creature's eye could kill them, with only the crafty weasel immune to its "death rays." The cockatrice takes its name from the Greek *ichneumon*, which means "a tracker." This was translated into the Latin *calcatrix*, "a tracker," and *calcatrix* was ultimately corrupted to the English *cockatrice*. The mythical creature was called "a tracker" by the Greeks because they believed that it tracked down and devoured the eggs and young of the crocodile. In this respect it was probably given the characteristics of the real Egyptian *ichneumon*, an animal that does hunt down and devour crocodile eggs.

cocker spaniel.   The dog is not so named because it's "cocky," but because it was bred for hunting and retrieving wood*cock*, among other small game birds or, possibly, from the way the dog *cocks* its long, drooping ears. *Spaniel* simply means "Spanish dog," deriving from the Old French *Chien epagneul*, which was shortened to *espagnol*, "Spanish," and became *spaniel* in English. The spaniel may have been a breed developed in Spain, or perhaps the breed's silky hair and soft, soulful eyes suggested the appearance of the Spaniards, though there is no hard evidence of this. *Spaniel* has served as a verb and adjective, a symbol of affectionate humility, as well as a noun. Shakespeare has Antony speak of the "hearts that spaniel'd me at heels, to whom I gave their wishes."

cockles.   (*See* **to warm the cockles of one's heart**.)

cockney.   *Cockney* literally means a "cock's egg," deriving from the Middle English *cokeney*. The word first meant a foolish child or a foolish person who did not know a good egg from a cock's egg or *cockney* (a small egg with no yolk). Country people next applied the term to city people in general, then to Londoners and finally to London East Enders, people born within sound of the bells of St. Mary-le Bow (Bow Bells) in London who share a characteristic accent called *Cockney*.

cockpit; the cockpit of Europe.   Belgium has long been known as *the cockpit of Europe* because so many important European battles have been fought there, from the battle of Oudenarde in 1708, to Waterloo in 1815, and the many battles fought there during World Wars I and II. *Cockpit* is of course an allusion to the arena where gamecocks are set to fight, which also gave its name to the space in fighter planes where the pilot sits.

cockroach.   Captain John Smith must have had a lot of trouble with cockroaches, judging by his description of the nocturnal household pest in his *The generall historie of Virginia, New England and the Summer Isles* (1624). Smith described the insect as "A certaine India Bug, called by the Spaniards a Cacarootch, the which creeping into Chests they wat and defile with their ill-scented dung." His rendition of the Spanish *cucaracha* as *cacarootch* started the long and involved process whereby the name for the bug became *cockroach* in English. The most famous literary cockroach is undoubtedly American humorist Don Marquis's Archy, who wrote modern free verse because he couldn't work the typewriter shift key—along with his friend Mehitabel the Cat, he is immortalized in *archy and mehitabel* (1927) and a number of sequels. It was once thought that the smell of the *cockroach apple*, a Jamaican plant, would kill cockroaches.

cocksure.   Since the word *cocksure* first meant secure, safe, and certain—not dogmatic and self-confident, as it does today—it probably didn't originally have anything to do with the pompous, strutting rooster usually associated with it. But no one is cocksure about *cocksure's* origins, which go back almost five centuries. In its now obsolete sense of lecherous, *cocksure* is much younger, so that eliminates a likely source and a better story. A real possibility is that the word was just a euphemism for *God sure!*—since *cock* was often a euphemism for God in oaths. Or it may have first meant the security of God, as in the following quote from Foxe's *Book of Martyrs* (1563): "Who so dwelleth under . . . the help of the Lord, shall be cock-sure for evermore." Shakespeare uses the word as if it derives from the sureness of the cock on the firelock of a gun, a cock that keeps the gun from going off, and the *O.E.D.* suggests as a source the cock, or tap, on a barrel of whiskey, which secured the liquor inside, preventing its escape. The Welsh word *coc*, "cog," has also been nominated—*cocksure* would thus mean "as sure as cogs fit into one another." So has the Irish *coc*, "manifest," and the old English *cock*, for "the notch of a bow"—an arrow would have to be set *cocksure* to hit its target. No matter which is correct, it's almost certain that the idea of the strutting aplomb of a barnyard cock and the phallic associations of the word contributed to its later meaning of "pert and cocky."

cocktail.   There are well over fifty theories as to the word *cocktail's* origin, H.L. Mencken alone presenting seven plausible ones in his *American Language*. These include a derivation from the French *coquetier*, "an egg cup," in which the drink was supposedly first served in 1800; from *coquetel*, "a mixed drink of the French Revolution period"; from the English *cock-ale*, "fed to fighting cocks"; from *cocktailings*, "the last of several liquors mixed together"; and from a toast to that cock that after a cockfight had the most feathers left in its tail. Just as reliable as any of these guesses is the old folktale that Aztec King Axolotl VIII's daughter *Octel* or *Xochitl* concocted the first *cocktail*; or, in another version, that an Aztec noble sent his emperor a drink made of cactus juice by his daughter, the emperor enjoying it so much that he married the girl and called the drink by her name—again *Octel* or *Xochitl*. According to this story, General Scott's soldiers are supposed to have brought the drink back to America centuries later. Suffice it to say that the origin of the word, first printed in 1806, is really unknown.

coconut, copra.   Safe in its buoyant, waterproof pod, the coconut sailed the high seas from southern Asia in prehistoric times and was propagated and cultivated throughout tropical regions. But it wasn't given its present name until the late 15th century, when Portuguese explorers came upon it in the Indian Ocean islands and fancied that the little indentations at the base of the nut looked like eyes. Thinking that these three "eyes" gave the nut the look of a grinning face, they named it the *coconut*, *coco* being the Portuguese word for "a grinning face." The nut deserves a better appellation, having been "the fruit of life" for ages, providing people with food, drink, oil, medicines, fuel and even bowls, not to mention the many uses of the 60-100 foot tree it grows on. Copra, important to the plot of many a South Sea tale, is the dried meat of coconuts that oil is pressed from, and *coconut* itself is slang for "a head," which takes the word back to its origins. *Copra* derives from the Hindu *Rhopra* for coconut.

coconut crab; robber crab.   The large *robber crab* or *coconut crab* (*Birgus latro*) of the Pacific islands is closely related to the hermit crabs, but has given up carrying a portable dwelling and developed a permanent hard-plated shell. Called the *coconut crab* because it climbs palm trees to get the fruit, it is named the *robber crab* for an entirely different reason. After chasing another crab, *Cardisoma*, into its hole in the ground, the robber crab threatens to enter. When *Cardisoma* thrusts out its big claw to guard the entrance, the robber crab seizes it, twists it off, and scuttles off to enjoy a gourmet feast.

cod; you can't cod me.   Experts have suggested that *cod* might derive from an old Danish word for "bag" (because it was said to be a "bag fish," in reference to its shape), but its origin must be marked unknown due to lack of evidence, even though the word has been with us at least since the 14th century. The North Atlantic cod (*Gadus morrhua*), reaching a length of up to three feet and a weight of up to fifty pounds, has long been one of the most important fish of commerce (*see* **codfish aristocracy**). It is called the *sacred cod* because it is said to be the fish that Christ multiplied and fed to the multitude. According to one early 19th-century writer: "Even today the marks of

His thumbs and forefingers are plainly visible on the codfish. His Satanic majesty stood by and said he, too, could multiply fish and feed multitudes. Reaching for one of the fish it wriggled and slid down his red-hot fingers, burning two black stripes down its side and thus clearly differentiating the haddock from the sacred cod. These markings, in actual practice, do distinguish one fish from another." *You can't cod me* means "You can't get a rise out of me, you won't make me rise to the bait like a codfish."

code.   (*See* **book**.)

codfish aristocracy.

> Of all the fish that swim or swish
>   In oceans deep autocracy,
> There's none possesses such haughtiness
>   As the codfish aristocracy.
>   —Wallace Irwin

It's hard to think of any group haughtier than the Cabots and Lowells (who spoke only to God, according to another old poem), but the Boston nouveau riche who made their money from the codfishing industry in the late 18th and early 19th century apparently gave a grand imitation of them. At any rate, they were disliked enough to inspire the derogatory expression *codfish aristocracy*, for "any pretentious, newly rich person."

codger.   An *old codger* is generally a nuisance or an eccentric old man, but can also be a term of affection akin to "old chap" or "old fellow." No dictionary honors the derivation, but both definitions may have been strengthened by the existence of a club called The Ancient Society of Cogers former in London in the 1860s. The Cogers came onto the scene half a century after *codger* was first used in its whimsical sense, but they were well known, all prominent writers and artists. The debating club derived its name from the word "cognition" and these thinking men, "ancient" at least by title, met at the Barley Mow Tavern on Fleet Street. (The tavern is now named The Cogers in their honor, though they moved to the Cock Tavern in 1921.) Codger probably comes from the Scottish *cadger*, for "a wandering peddler or beggar," but it is not hard to imagine the Cogers' influence on the word. "Ancient . . . Cogers" could easily have become *old codgers*, meant either affectionately or derisively.

codpiece.   The *cod* in the word originally meant "the bag enveloping the testicles, the scrotum." In the 15th century the *codpiece* was introduced as a simple leather bagged appendage attached to the front of breeches, the word first recorded in 1460. But within a century the appendage became a spectacular ornament, brightly colored and often the size of a small melon. In *The Unfashionable Human Body*, Bernard Rudofsky claims that the codpiece died as a fashion in the 17th century because the male genitals "seem too unsubstantial to warrant display." This may be the case, because men often used the codpiece as a kind of pocket, storing things like money and bonbons in it. Robert Herrick wrote of a thieving dinner guest in *Hesperides* (1648): "If the servants search, they may decry in his wide codpiece, dinner being done, Two napkins cramm'd up, and a silver spoone."

codswallop. I came across *codswallop* in a newspaper account about a scientist's charge that a rare and extremely important bird fossil (the Archaeopteryx (*q.v.*), pronounced "arky-opterix") in the British Museum was a fake. The account quoted several British Museum curators on the charge: "It's rubbish," one official said. "Absolutely ludicrous," added another. "Codswallop," echoed a third. *Codswallop?* Does it mean to flop about like a cod, in reference to the scandalmonger's tongue. *Wallop* does mean in one sense "to flop about." Or does it stand for "cod's beer," meaning the charge is an awful concoction? (*Wallop* is British slang for beer.) To tell the truth I don't know. And neither does the *O.E.D.*, *Mencken*, *Flexner*, *Partridge* and all those other high-flying etymology birds. Hawkeyed William Safire, however, noted in his *New York Times Magazine* column that James McDonald's *Wordly Wise* (1984) mentions a 19th-century "inventor called Hiram Codd [who] patented a new type of bottle with a glass marble in its neck. Mineral waters were sold in such bottles, and, *wallop* being a slang term for fizzy ale, the contents became known as *Codd's Wallop.*" And if this explanation doesn't satisfy you, either, perhaps *codswallop*, as Mr. Safire also points out, derives in some way from the British slang *cod*, meaning "to horse around."

coffee. *Coffee* was introduced to England from Turkey, where it was called *qahwah*, pronounced *kahveh*, a word that apparently first meant some kind of wine and derived from a verb meaning "to have no appetite." The word came to England, perhaps from the Italian *caffé*, in about 1600. At first coffee's reputation wasn't good, one early English traveler warning that it "intoxicated the brain." It has had widely varying reviews since.

coffin nails. *Coffin nails* has been American slang for cigarettes since the 1880s, at least twenty years before cigarettes were called *weeds* and forty years before they were called *butts*. *Another nail in my coffin*, said by a person lighting a cigarette, has been a catch phrase since about 1910, when it was first recorded in Australia. *Cigarette* itself is first attested in England in 1842, though these "little cigars" had been smoked for at least two centuries before then.

cognac. The town of Cognac in southwestern France gives its name to this high-quality brandy, produced by the old pot-still method and aged two to five years or more in oak barrels.

coin. Our *coin* takes its name from the wedge-shaped die once used to make pieces of metal money. The French *coign*, deriving from the Latin *cuneus* and meaning wedge, was given first to the die and then to the money made on the die. *Coign* later passssed into English as *coin*. *Coin* came to be a general word for money in early times because most money was in the form of coins.

Coke; cola. *Coke*, or *Coca-Cola* (both registered trademarks), was invented by Atlanta, Georgia druggist Dr. John S. Pemberton in 1886, and is so named because its original ingredients were derived from coca leaves and cola nuts. *Coke* is also slang for *cocaine* and for this reason the Coca-Cola Company long avoided use of this name—especially because, up until 1909, Coca-Cola did contain minute amounts of cocaine. While the Supreme Court declared *Coca-Cola* and *Coke* exclusive trademarks, *cola* was ruled a generic word that anyone could use. Coca-cola's slogans "The pause that refreshes" and "Coke is it" are also well known. In 1985 a Mr. Frederick Koch (pronounced "Coke") of Guilford, Vermont got tired of people pronouncing his last name "Kotch" and changed it to Coke-Is-It. Coca-Cola objected to the use of its trademark, but finally reached a settlement with Mr. Coke-Is-It, letting him keep his new name.

Coke upon Littleton. This expression suggests the shades or subtleties of law and honors British legal experts Edward Coke (1552-1664) and Thomas Littleton (1407-81).

cola. (*See* **Coke.**)

cold blood. Early physiologists believed that the blood actually boiled within the body when a person grew excited and that it grew cold when someone was calm or detached. While the term *in hot blood* suggested by the belief is no longer heard (hot-blooded is), *in cold blood* remains as common as it was back in the late 16th century. Generally it is used today to describe a deliberate act of murder, as in Truman Capote's "fact-fiction" *In Cold Blood*. Mankind has always regarded calculated killing *in cold blood* as something less than human. Trollope summed up the idea in describing one of his characters: "But then Aylmer was a cold-blooded man—more like a fish than a man."

cold burning. *Cold burning?* Yes. In the late 18th to early 19th century *cold burning* was a British navy and army punishment for minor offenses in which ice-cold water ("so cold that it burns") was poured down a man's upraised arm so that it came out "at his breeches-knees." According to one explanation: "The prisoner is set against the wall, with the arm which is to be burned tied as high above his head as possible. The executioner then ascends a stool, and having a bottle of cold water, pours it slowly down the sleeve of the delinquent, patting him, and leading the water gently down him till it runs out at his breeches-knees."

cold enough to freeze the balls off a brass monkey. Here and in Australia the saying is as above; in Canada it is often the euphemistic *freeze the ears off a brass monkey. Partridge* indicates this is a late-19th-century Australian saying for very, very cold indeed, but I have heard others claim it for America and Ireland. Some say the "monkey" here is not the brass image of a monkey but a rack called the "monkey" used on wooden naval ships in the days of sail to hold cannonballs in place, to keep them from rolling all over the deck. But no one as yet has proved the existence of any rack called a "monkey," one made of brass or anything else. And how cold weather could cause cannonballs to spill from a rack also remains to be explained.

cold feet. The old Italian proverb *avegh minga frecc i pee* literally means "to have cold feet" and the proverb in a figurative sense of "to be without money" was used by Ben Jonson in his play *Volpone.* Professor Kenneth McKenzie pointed this out in an article in *Modern Language Notes* (Vol. XXVII, 1912) and also explained how a phrase meaning "to be without money" could come to mean "to lose one's nerve." In card-playing, he wrote, a player "as a pretext for quitting a game in which he has lost money, [might] say that his feet are cold, [and] the expression might come to mean in general 'to recede from a difficult position,' or more specifically, 'to have cold feet.'" This may be true, but if it is, it didn't happen in Ben Jonson's time, to the best of our knowledge. *Cold feet* in the sense of "fear," originated as an American expression in the early 1890s. It could, however, have journeyed here with Italian immigrants, as the Italian proverb was still used in Lombardy at the time. Otherwise the expression must be marked "of unknown origin" and perhaps refers to the association of fright with cold—chattering teeth, shivers and chills, etc.

cold shoulder. Cold shoulders have been turned up to so many passionate advances that this expression is usually thought to be connected with women spurning unacceptable men. But it seems that the phrase has no romantic origins. In the early 19th century, when the phrase was first recorded by Sir Walter Scott, it was the custom of hostesses to serve hot meat to a welcome visitor and to bring out a *cold shoulder* of mutton to someone who had overstayed his welcome or wasn't particularly welcome in the first place. That this is the source of *cold shoulder* can best be seen in the Victorian slang *to give the cold shoulder of mutton*, meaning the same thing.

cold war. *Cold war*, for a situation where two nations aren't actually at war but are doing everything they can to damage each other short of war, is first recorded in 1947, when Walter Lippmann's *The Cold War*, a study of American-Soviet relations, was published.

coleslaw; hot slaw. The word is *coleslaw*, not *cold slaw*, and isn't so named because the dish is served cold. An Americanism of Dutch origin, *coleslaw* derives from the Dutch *koolsla*, composed of *kool*, "cabbage," + *sla*, "salad." First recorded in 1792, it must be older, as Dutch farmers on Long Island cultivated the first cabbage in America long before this. Though there is no *cold slaw*, there is a *hot slaw*, the word for this dish first recorded in 1870.

collage. The device of using pieces of newspaper in paintings was much used by the Cubists, who called the technique *collage*. but Matisse and many other artists before them built pictures partly or wholly of pieces of paper, cloth, and similar materials. The word *collage* comes from the French *coller*, "to stick."

collective bargaining. Beatrice Webb of the *Fabians* (*q.v.*) first suggested this term in 1891. In America *collective bargaining* came to mean, after the 1935 Wagner Act, "the process by which wages and working conditions are negotiated and agreed upon by a union with an employer for all the employees that the union collectively represents."

collie. Though they are generally white and brown today, *collies* were originally black medium-sized shepherd's dogs when bred in 17th-century Scotland. They may have taken their name from their black color, being first called *coalies*, then *collies*. But the dogs could also have been named after the common Scottish name Colin, which in pastoral verse denotes "a shepherd."

cologne. A scent that almost takes its name from a woman. The Roman emperor Claudius established a colony in what was then Oppidum Ubiorum in 50 A.D., renaming the place *Colonia Agrippina* ("colony of Agrippina") after his wife, Nero's mother, who had been born there. This cumbersome name was later modified by the French to *Cologne*, which grew into the beautiful German cathedral city that we know today. When centuries later a resident Italian chemist, Johann Maria Farina, invented a perfume made with alcohol and aromatic citrus oils, it was named *eau de cologne* or *cologne water*, for the city where he had settled in 1709. "Agrippina" had been lost over the years and only a fragment of her *Colonia* remained, but the perfume was unknowingly and obliquely named for her.

colon. (*See* **comma.**)

colonel.   The confusing pronunciation of this word is due to several errors. *Colonel* comes from the Italian *colonello*, which meant "the officer who led 'a little column' of soldiers at the head of a regiment." This became the French *colonelle*, meaning the same. So far, so good. But the French word became corrupted to *coronel* in Spanish through faulty pronunciation and was introduced into England in this form. Until the 17th century the word was spelled and pronounced *coronel*, and then its spelling was changed to the current *colonel*. Yet despite the efforts of teachers and pronouncing dictionaries, people refused to pronounce the word *colonel*. Early habits were too great to overcome and they continued to pronounce it like *coronel*, the experts finally giving up and accepting this as the standard pronunciation.

colophon.   Originally, this word, derived from the Greek *kolophon*, meaning "summit" or "finish," was the "finishing touch" at the end of a book, a bibliographical note on the last page giving the printer, date, place, and so on. Today the word has two meanings—the original one, which has been expanded to include design and typographic information, and a new one, referring to the publisher's trademark or logo, which often appears on the title page of the book.

Colorado.   *Colorado* was the *Colorado territory* before it was admitted to the Union in 1876 as our 38th state. "The Centennial State" takes its name *Colorado* from the Spanish *colorado*, "red land," or "red earth."

color blind.   (*See* **daltonism**.)

Colosseum.   Its size had nothing to do with the name of the Roman arena called the *Colosseum*, which gives its name to all coliseums. The original *Colosseum* took its name for a colossal statue of Nero that stood near it, the statue placed there after the dissolute emperor's palace had been destroyed, when Rome burned.

colporteur.   Today's book salesmen follow an honorable calling, one that dates back hundreds of years to when their kind carried Bibles and other books in a basket or pack hanging from their necks by a strap. For this reason they were, and sometimes still are, called *colporteurs*, from the French *col*, "neck," and *porters*, "to carry." Typical of these was Old Parson Weems, noted for his charming fabrication of George Washington chopping down the cherry tree, not to mention his bold Homeric yarns about Ben Franklin and General Francis "the Swamp Fox" Marion.

colt.   When Samuel Colt (1814-62) ran away to sea from his home in Hartford, Connecticut at sixteen, he spent his lonely nights on deck whittling a wooden model of the *Colt revolver* that was to make him famous. Young Colt had several metal models made of his gun upon arriving home and patented his invention. He built his armory into the largest in the world, his use of interchangeable parts and the production line making him one of the richest men in America. As for the *Colt*, the first pistol that could be effectively employed by a man on horseback, it played a more important part in the conquest of the West than any other weapon, the famed "six-shooter" becoming so popular that its name became a generic term for revolver. *Colt* for a young horse comes from the Old English *colt* meaning the same.

Columbia; columbium.   *America* (*q.v.*) was named for someone else, but Columbus did win fame on the globe as the name for *Colombia*, South America, the U.S. *District of Columbia*, and a number of towns and cities. *Columbus* itself has for centuries meant an intrepid discoverer or explorer; *Columbus Day* (October 12) commemorates the discovery of America; and *Columbia* is the feminine symbol for America from which the element *columbium* is named. Christopher Columbus—Cristoforo Colombo in his native Italian and Christobal Colon in Spanish—discovered America in 1492, a familiar story that needs no repeating here. He may have come ashore in the Bahamas on an island he named San Salvador and which is now called Cat or Watling Island, but his landing site is disputed by historians. A sailor named Rodrigo de Triana first sighted the New World.

columbine.   In medieval times people thought the inverted white flower on this plant bore a resemblance to five doves or pigeons clustered together and it was given the name *columbine* from the latin *columba*, "dove." There are sixty known species of the genus *Aquilegic* comprising columbines, and the flowers' horned nectaries were once symbols of cuckoldry.

Columbus's egg.   Washington Irving told this proverbial tale in his *History of . . . Christopher Columbus*. It relates a classic squelch supposedly made by Columbus at a banquet given by Cardinal Mendoza shortly after the explorer had returned from his first voyage:

> A shallow courtier present, impatient of the honors paid to Columbus, abruptly asked him whether he thought that in case he had not discovered the Indies, there were not other men in Spain who would have been capable of the enterprise. To this Columbus made no immediate reply, but taking an egg, invited the company to make it stand on end. Every one attempted it, but in vain. Whereupon he struck it upon the table so as to break the end and left it standing on the broken part; illustrating in his simple manner that when he had once shown the way to the New World nothing was easier than to follow it.

Although Irving had the tale on good authority, it may really apply to an earlier historical figure, an Italian architect named Filippo Brunelleschi.

Coma Berenices; varnish; vernis martin. Berenice's hair, or *coma Berenices*, is the lock of a woman's hair that became a constellation. It was made famous by the five surviving lines of the poem *The Lock of Berenice* by the Greek poet Callimachus, which is said to be based on a true story. Berenice was married to Ptolemy III, King of Egypt, and when he invaded Syria in 236 B.C. to avenge the murder of his sister, she dedicated a lock of her hair to the gods as an offering for his safe return. The hair mysteriously disappeared, but the court astronomer, Conon of Samos, perhaps to assuage her, pretended to discover that it had been carried to heaven and transformed into a constellation of the northern hemisphere, which has been known ever since as *Coma Berenices*. (A coma is the hazy envelope around a comet, and the word comet itself derives from the Greek and Latin words for hair, alluding to a fancied resemblance between the tails of comets and hair blowing in the wind.) Ptolemy returned from the wars safely, but soon after his death in 221 B.C. the fabled Berenice was murdered at the instigation of her son. Later the Greeks named the town of *Berenike* in Libya for Berenice. Here a paint industry thrived and one new coating was called *Berenice*, its color said to resemble the amber hair of the queen. This paint was called *bernix* in medieval Latin, but the Italians corrupted its name to *vernice*, which became *vernis* in French and *varnish* in English—the chances being that the floor under your feet has something of the color of Berenice's hair. *Vernis martin*, or *Martin varnish*, a finish for furniture, is twice eponymous, being also named for the brothers Martin, 18th-century French craftsmen who invented it in imitation of Chinese lacquer.

come a cropper. To fall head over heels, to fail, or be struck by some misfortune. This is a British expression that originally meant only to fall head over heels from a horse, to fall to the ground completely, *neck and crop*, but it most likely refers to the *crop* or rump of a horse—when a horse falls neck and crop, he falls completely, all together in one heap.

to come down like a ton of bricks on someone. To be very severe with someone, to come down hard on him. This Americanism dates back to the 19th century and sounds much better than the British *come down like a thousand bricks on him*. But it has been pointed out that the British expression is more technically accurate, in that bricks aren't sold or measured by the ton.

come hell or high water. The ancestor of this common expression is apparently *between the devil and the deep blue sea* (q.v.). Between hell and high water seems to have been a 20th-century variation on (or deviation from) the earlier phrase. Then the variation took on a life of its own in the expression *come hell or high water*, meaning "no matter what," as in "Come hell or high water, I'll finish it!"

to come in with one's five eggs. (*See* **to put in one's two cents' worth**.)

come to a head. When we wait for something to come to a head, wait for it to come to maturity, we are doing what farmers have long done in waiting for cabbage leaves to come together and form a head. The expression is an old one from the farm, probably dating back centuries.

comeuppance. Whether this expression is an Americanism or not is the subject of some dispute; it is first recorded in America in 1859 and in England some twenty years later, if that proves anything. *Comeuppance* means "just desserts" or "merited punishment," and has several dialect versions in different areas, including *comings* and *come-uppings*, the British once using *come-uppings* for a flogging. Possibly the expression *come up*, "to present oneself for judgment before a tribunal," fathered the phrase.

come up to scratch. Deaths and maimings were so frequent in the lawless early days of boxing that one rule had to be established if there were to be enough boxers alive to please the crowd. A line was scratched in the center of the ring (in the ground or on the canvas) and a fighter who couldn't "come up to scratch" when the bell sounded for a new round was considered physically unable to fight any longer. This early version of the technical knockout probably led to use of *to come up to scratch* as a figurative expression for fulfilling or meeting requirements of any nature. *Scratch*, however, was the term for a starting point or boundary in cricket, shooting matches, horse racing, and cockfighting as well as boxing, so the expression could have originated in one of these sports, especially from cockfighting, where a cock that doesn't *come up to scratch* and fight is considered an inferior specimen.

comma; colon; period. Before they became common terms used for punctuation, these words were the names of elements of sentence structure. A *comma* was a short phrase or clause, a *colon* a long phrase, and a *period* two or more colons. *Period*, for example, was recorded as early as 1533 for a sentence of several clauses, almost a century before it meant the point or character that marks the end of such a sentence.

commando. This term was adapted by the British during World War II when they established their specially trained commando units to raid enemy territory. It derives, however, from the Portuguese word for "small commands that raided native villages in South Africa," a word the Boers borrowed when they used similar tactics to wipe out thousands of Bushmen in their villages.

commerce. (*See* **merchant**.)

commute. The verb to *commute* developed as a back formation from the noun *commutation* at about the time of the Civil War—Americans were *commuting* to work on the train even at that early date. *Commute* later became the word for a railroad ticket, a shortening of "commutation ticket." *Commute* has its roots in the Latin *commutare*, to change, thus someone *commuting* is changing from one place to another.

company. A business company, in the strictest sense of the word, is a group of people who sit down and share bread together. For *company* derives from the Latin *con* "together," and *panin*, "bread." The idea is that a *company* consists of friends so close that they sit at the same table sharing any bread they have.

company store. (*See* **tommyrot**.)

comparisons are odious. The correct word in the proverb is *odious*, not *odorous*, and the prolific poet and monk John Lydgate was the first to put the idea on paper, in 1430: "Odyous of olde have been comparisons,/And of comparisons engendyrd is haterede." Cervantes, Donne, Swift, and Hazlitt are other great writers who used the proverb, and Shakespeare had Dogberry give his variation on the expression, *comparisons are odorous*, in *Much Ado About Nothing*. Lydgate's version was printed some forty years before that of John Fortescue, to whom *Bartlett's* credits the phrase.

compass plant; polar plant; pilotweed.

> Look at this vigorous plant that lifts its head
>   from the meadow,
> See how its leaves are turned to the north, as true
>   as the magnet;
> This is the compass flower, that the finger of God
>   has planted
> Here in the houseless wild, to direct the traveler's
>   journey
> Over the sea-like, pathless, limitless waste of
>   the desert.

> —Longfellow, *Evangeline* (1847)

A huge coarse-stemmed plant 6 to 8 feet tall with flowers like the sunflower, the compass plant (*Silphium laciniatum*) was much valued by pioneers on the great western plains because its leaves show polarity, always pointing north and south. For this reason it was called not only the *compass plant*, but *polar plant* and *pilotweed* as well.

compound. English merchants in the Orient during the 18th century often built enclosed trading stations to protect themselves and their goods from thieves. They called these stockaded enclosures *compounds*, from the Malay *kampong*, "enclosure." This *compound* is no relation to the chemist's *compound*, which derives from the Latin *componere*, "put together."

comptonia. Henry Compton, Bishop of London, was a collector of rare and exotic plants. The prelate, an anti-papal leader during the Revolution of 1688, had many admirers in England, even after his death in 1713 at the age of eighty-one. One of these was the great naturalist Sir Joseph Banks, who traveled to Newfoundland and Labrador in 1766 to collect native plants and accompanied Captain Cook on his first voyage two years later for the same purpose. Banks expressed his admiration for the plant-loving divine by naming the *comptonia bush* (*Comptonia peregrina*) after him. The *Comptonia* is a single shrub, sometimes called *sweet bush* or *sweet fern*. Native to eastern North America, it is highly aromatic, with fernlike leaves and green, rather inconspicuous flowers.

comptroller. There is really no good reason for this word. It is pronounced the same as *controller* and means the same, except that it looks a bit more elegant than its counterpart. Probably influenced in spelling by the French *compte*, "account," *comptroller* means the official in a business firm who controls funds, just as *controller* does.

computer. *Compute* and *computation* date back to the 15th century. Though there have been a number of *mechanical computers* over the years, the first *electronic computer*, using 18,000 radio tubes, was built in 1946 by three scientists at the University of Pennsylvania— Dr. John W. Mauchly, J. Presper Eckert, Jr., and J.G. Brainerd. Their ENIAC—*E*lectronic *n*umerical *i*ntegrator *a*nd *c*omputer—cost $400,000 and had to be housed in a 30 foot by 50 foot room.

comrade. Three centuries and more ago Spanish soldiers resided in separate chambers called *camaradas*, two or more to the room, instead of barracks. Soldiers who shared the same chambers came to call themselves *comaradas*, which in time became the English word *comrade*.

comstockery. About 160 tons of books, stereotyped plates, magazines, and pictures were destroyed by Anthony Comstock (1844-1915), founder of the New York Society for the Suppression of Vice, in his long career as a self-appointed crusader against immorality in literature. Comstock, who inspired Boston's Watch and Ward Society, headed a YMCA campaign against obscene literature in 1873, the same year in which he came to national prominence by founding his society and securing federal passage of the so-called *Comstock Laws* to exclude objectionable matter from the mails. Appointed special agent of the Post Office Department and chief special agent for the Society, Comstock had the power of an inquisitor, and *comstockery* became a synonym for narrow-minded, bigoted, and self-righteous moral censorship. The crusader particularly objected to George Bernard Shaw's play, *Mrs. Warren's Profession*, and Shaw coined the word, making good clean fun of the censor's name.

Comstock lode. A Nevada sheepherder and prospector named Henry Tompkins Paige Comstock first laid claim to the *Comstock lode* that bears his name. In 1859, Old Pancake, as he was known, had taken possession of a cabin belonging to other prospectors who had discovered the lode but had died tragically before filing their claim. Comstock filed his claim, but he later sold all his rights for a pittance and the Virginia City mine became the world's richest known silver deposit, producing $20 million to $30 million annually at its peak and making great fortunes for many a "silver king." Virginia City mushroomed to 40,000 inhabitants and anyone associated with the mines, hopeful prospector or millionaire, was called a *comstocker.*

con; con game; con man. Just after the Civil War, one of the most common frauds in America was the sale of fake gold mine stock in the West. Sometimes gold would be salted in played-out "mines" to fool "marks," but the swindlers who worked the scheme usually settled for a small score from a great number of investors and never bothered about tricking up a real mine. Investors were often reluctant to advance funds without examining the property, however, and the swindlers asked their victims to make a small investment in advance "just as a gesture of confidence," deposits that they quickly absconded with. The trick was soon dubbed the *confidence game*, and, in time, its fast-moving practitioners became known as *con men.* Reinforcing the word is the idea that victims of a *con game* are bamboozled into confidence that they're going to make a killing. To con, in this sense, has nothing to do with the older English verb *to con*, to study or commit to memory, which derives from the Middle English *cunnen*, "to try." *Con games* were practiced, of course, long before this word for them was coined. On the American continent, for example, Mayan swindlers painstakingly drilled small holes in cocoa beans, emptied out their precious powder and refilled them with dirt before selling them to Europeans.

concatenation; concatenated sins. *Concatenation* simply means a chain, the word deriving from the Latin *catena*, "chain." One early (1688) felicitous writer described two lovers as "the most affectionate couple since the concatenation of Adam and Eve," while John Donne wrote of "concatenated sins."

Concord grape. (*See* **Catawba grapes**.)

condign punishment. Just a fancy way of saying an appropriate punishment, a punishment that fits the crime. *Condign* (pronounced kun-dine) is from the Latin *con dignus*, "altogether worthy." The phrase *condign punishment* has been commonly used since it originated in the Tudor Acts of Parliament, and the two words have become so inseparably yoked that *condign* is rarely used in any other way. Thomas De Quincey complained about this back in 1859, but it did no good: "Capriciously . . . the word *condign* is only used in connection with the word *punishment*. These and other words, if unlocked from their absurd imprisonment, would become extensively useful. We should say, for example, 'condign honors,' 'condign reward,' 'condign treatment' . . . ."

condom. *Condom* derives from either of two real names. Proksch in his *Prevention of Venereal Diseases* traces *condom* to a London doctor in the court of Charles II named Dr. Conton and insists that the contraceptives should thus be called "contons." Dr. Conton's invention is said to have been made from lamb intestines, dried and well oiled to make them soft and pliable. They immediately became popular, and Casanova is on record as buying a dozen, though he called them "English caps." It was only in 1826, Proksch claims, that a papal bull by Leo XIII damned Conton's discovery, "because it hindered the arrangement of providence." Dr. Conton probably did improve upon the *condom*, but an equally reliable source traces the word derivation to a Colonel Condum of Britain's Royal Guards. This authority notes that the colonel devised the *French letter* early in the mid-17th century to protect his troops from the French. (The French, chauvinistic, too, called *condoms* "English letters.") In 1667 three English courtiers—Rochester, Roscommon, and Dorset—even wrote a pamphlet entitled *A Panegyric Upon Condom*, extolling their countryman's invention. A new and excellent monograph of the origin of *condom* is William E. Kruck's *Looking for Dr. Condom* (University of Alabama Press, 1982).

condominium. *Condominium*, meaning "an apartment owned by tenants rather than rented" (although the owners do pay a monthly maintenance charge), is composed of the Latin *con*, "together," and *dominion*, "property." The word has been used for the joint control of a territory by two states since the early 18th century, but its newer usage dates back only to the late 1950s.

Conestoga wagons; stogy. The heavy, covered, broad-wheeled *Conestoga wagons* that carried American pioneers westward, crossing many a waving "sea of grass" like "prairie schooners," were named for the Conestoga Valley in Pennsylvania, where they were first made in about 1750. But as Mencken points out, *Conestoga Valley* derives in turn from the name of a long-extinct band of Iroquois Indians. So little has been done for the Indian that we should honor him where we can. The wagons, pulled by their six-horse teams, also supplied the West with manufactured goods and brought back raw materials, some carrying up to eight tons of freight. *Stogy*, a cheap cigar today, was coined by the *Conestoga* teamsters—either after the *Conestoga Valley* tobacco that they rolled into thin, unbound cigars for their long trips or after the wagons themselves.

Coney Island; coney.   The *Coney* in *Coney Island* should really be pronounced to rhyme with *honey* or *money*. The word derives from *cony* (or *coney* or *cuny*), meaning the adult long-earred rabbit (*Lepus cunicula*) after which the Brooklyn, New York community was named. However, *cony*, pronounced *cunny*, became a term for the female genitals in British slang, and proper Victorians stopped using the word, substituting *rabbit*, which previously had meant only the young of the cony species. The only trouble remaining was that *cony* (pronounced *cunny*) appeared throughout the King James Bible, which had to be read aloud during church services. Proper Victorians solved this problem by changing the pronunciation of cony (*cunny*) to *coney* (rhymes with *boney*), which it remains to this day in *Coney Island* as well as the Bible.

confession magazines.   Confession magazines, which have been with us now for over sixty-five years, are an American invention that were an outgrowth of long soul-searching letters sent to physical culture crusader Bernard MacFadden's *Physical Culture* magazine in 1919. MacFadden's first confession book was *True Story*, the great-grandmother of the genre, which currently has a circulation of 5 million, but there are scores of other *confessions* on the newsstands today. The first stories dealt with sweet young things who were so wicked that they dared to elope against their parents' wishes, etc., while contemporary tales have virtually no taboo themes, ranging from well-written confessions about incest to stories such as "My Bride Is a Man" (where Julie was Jules before her sex-change operation). The yarns, which earn five to ten cents a word, aren't all written by readers. Professional writers turn out a large number, perhaps the majority of them, though some magazines do require an author to sign a release saying his or her story is based on a true experience.

Confucius say; kung-fu.   Historians tell us that there is little positive evidence of the Chinese philosopher's life, but it is said that the Chinese K'ung clan, descendants of Confucius, numbers over 50,000 today and that Confucius's burial place outside Kufow is still a place of homage. Confucius is the Latinized form of the philosopher's name, K'ung Fu-tzu ("philosopher" or "master K'ung"),

which may be the origin of the oriental martial arts *kung-fu*, though no hard evidence supports this theory. Born around 551 B.C. of a poor but noble family, Confucius taught and held a number of government posts. By his death at about 72, the philosopher had attracted some 3,000 disciples who helped spread his ethical teachings, which were based primarily on his "golden rule": "What you do not like when done to yourself do not do to others."

congressane.   (*See* **cortisone**.)

Congressional Medal of Honor.   (*See* **Medal of Honor**.)

conk out.   *Partridge* suggests that this avaiation term for "the stalling of an engine," which is also applied to "someone who falls asleep, passes out, or dies," stems from the words "to be conquered," an ingenious theory, while the *O.E.D.* says it may come from a Russian word meaning "to stall." The word seems to have been coined by World War I military aviators and may just be imitative of the "conking" sound a motor makes when it stalls. Another theory is that *conk out* derives from the *conk* that means "a blow on the head," which has been common in England and America since about 1870. *Conk* in this sense is a direct ancestor of the British slang word *conk*, for the head itself, known in England since the early 19th century: a blow on the *conk* was probably dubbed a *conk* because the blow was associated with the head (*conk*) and sometimes sounded like a "conk" as well. *Conk* for the head, in turn, is probably a variant spelling of the Latin word *concha*, "the head," the same word that gives us the *conch* (pronounced "conk") *shell*. It is also American slang for the head and it gives its name to a black American hairstyle—straightened, pressed hair—that is no longer popular.

Connecticut.   "The Nutmeg State," the fifth to enter the Union in 1788, takes its name from the Mohican Indian *quinnitukqut*, "at the long tidal river," in reference to the state's location on what is now the Connecticut River.

conniption fit.   The English dialect word *canapshus*, meaning "ill-tempered, captious," is the ancestor of the Americanism *conniption*, for "a fit of rage or anger." A person can go into *conniptions*, have a *conniption fit*, or *go into a fit of conniptions*—all mean the same. The expression is first recorded in 1833: "Ant Keziah fell down in a conniption fit."

consistency is the hobgoblin of little minds.   It is hard to understand how Emerson, as reasonable and consistent as anyone and certainly no little mind, could have written this until you look at what he really wrote in his essay "Self-Reliance" (1841). There is quite a difference in the qualification he makes: A *foolish* consistency is the hobgoblin of little minds, adored by little statesmen and philosophers and divines."

conspiracy of silence.   I can find no earlier use of this term than that of popular Victorian poet Sir Lewis Morris (1833-1907), who complained that no one reviewed his work. Approaching Oscar Wilde, he said, "Oscar, there's a conspiracy of silence against me. What shall I do?" Advised Oscar: "Join it."

constable.   *Constable*, for "a police officer," comes from the late Latin *comes stabuli*—any count, or officer, of the stable, or "master of the horse," under the Theodosian Code in about A.D. 438. In England the word first meant the chief officer of the court or of the nation's military forces.

controller.   (*See* **comptroller**.)

conversation; criminal conversation.   As early as 1511 *conversation* was used as a synonym for sexual intercourse, Shakespeare employing it this way in *Richard III* (1594). *Conversation* derives from the Latin *conversari* "to turn oneself about, to move to and fro, pass one's life, dwell, live somewhere, keep company with." It was used in these senses long before it came to mean "to communicate by speech or writing" in the late 16th century. *Converse* no longer means to have sexual intercourse, but *criminal conversation*, used at least since the late 18th century, and often abbreviated to *crim. con.*, is still a legal term for adultery.

Cook's tour.   *Cook's tours* were invented by English travel agent and former missionary Thomas Cook, who founded the venerable Thomas Cook & Son travel agency in 1841. His first tour was a railroad excursion to a temperance convention, for which he charged a shilling a head. Cook's first grand tour of Europe, which he organized in 1856, was more expensive, and its excellent organization, along with the high quality of tours to follow, made *a Cook's tour* the byword for any complete, well-organized travel tour. So reliable was the agency that the British government hired it to convey General Gordon and his troopers to the Sudan in 1884, making it probably the only travel agency ever to accommodate an army.

cook your goose.   The Mad King of Sweden, Eric XIV, was supposedly so enraged because residents of a medieval town he had attacked hung out a goose, a symbol of stupidity, to "slyghte his forces" that he told the residents "[I will] cook your goose" and proceeded to burn the town to the ground. This story is generally disregarded, because Mad King Eric supposedly avenged his insult in about 1560 and the expression *cook your goose*—"to put an end to, ruin"—isn't recorded until 1851. Attempts have been made to relate the phrase to the old Greek fable of the goose that laid the golden eggs. The peasant couple to whom that goose belonged, you'll remember, killed it (and perhaps cooked it later) because they were eager to get at the golden eggs within its body, which turned out to be undeveloped in any case. The first recorded use of the phrase *cook your goose* is in a London street ballad condemning "Papal Aggression" when Pope Pius IX tried to strengthen the power of the Catholic Church in England with his appointment of Nicholas Wiseman as English Cardinal:

> If they come here we'll cook their goose,
> The Pope and Cardinal Wiseman.

cool as a cucumber.   It took scientists with thermometers until 1970 to find out what has been folk knowledge for centuries—that cucumbers are indeed cool, so much so that the inside of a field cucumber on a warm day registers about 20 degrees cooler than the outside air. The belief is ancient, but was first put on paper by Francis Beaumont and John Fletcher in their play *Cupid's Revenge* (1610), when they referred to certain women "as cold as cucumbers." The metaphor describes anyone self-possessed and unemotional. *Cucumber*, which derives from the latin *cucumir*, was considered "bookish" and commonly pronounced *cowcumber* in England in the early 19th century, the way Sara Gamp said it in Dickens's *Martin Chuzzlewit*. Roman Emperor Tiberius is said to have enjoyed the "fruits" so much that he ordered them served to him every day, even though they had to be grown in greenhouses out of season.

coolie.   Coolies did not originally come from China. The word for an unskilled laborer almost certainly derives from the name of the aboriginal *Kuli* or *Koli* tribe of Gujerat, an Indian province. Ironically, *coolie* labor emigration came about mainly as the result of the outlawing of slavery in British colonies in 1834. Cheap labor was needed, and obtained, primarily from India and China in the form of natives hired under five-year contracts that were enforceable by prison terms. Conditions were often intolerable for these coolies, of whom the *Kulis* were apparently the first, their home on the northern Indian coast making it easy to recruit them. Many thousands of them died on the long voyages aboard *coolie ships*, which were often as inhuman as African slave ships. Another possible source for the word *coolie* is the Urdu or Tamil *kuli*—both words meaning "hireling"—but most writers support the Indian tribe theory.

coon.   This racial slur against a black person has nothing to do with the animal called a raccoon, or coon, which derives from an American Indian word. *Coon* here comes from the last syllable of the Portuguese *barracoos*, which is pronounced *coon* and meant "buildings especially constructed to hold slaves for sale."

a coon's age.   Meaning "a very long time," *a coon's age* is an Americanism recorded in 1843 and probably related to the old English expression "in a crow's age," meaning the same. The American term is an improvement, if only because the raccoon usually lives longer—up to thirteen years in the wild—than the crow.

Cooper's Droop.   *Cooper's Droop* provides another name linked forever with female breasts (*see* **charlies**). Honoring 19th-century British surgeon Sir Pastor Cooper, *Cooper's Droop* contradicts the current case for nonsupport, or wearing no bra. It seems that Cooper discovered that going without a support, or without a firm enough one, can stretch Cooper's ligaments, which attach the breasts to the body, causing the breasts to sag—a condition for which there is no recuperative exercise.

to coot; old coot.   Applied to tortoises, the obsolete verb *coot* meant "to copulate." Recorded in 1667, its origin is unknown, but it is responsible for the name of two amorous American turtles commonly called the *cooter* (*Chrysemys concinna*). The first recorded use of the word: "The Tortoises . . . coot for fourteen daies together." The Americanism *old coot* for a foolish or crotchety old man comes from the name of the *coot*, a North American duck of the genus *Oidemea* noted for its laugh-like cry.

cooties.   Our slang word *cooties*, for "body lice," derives from the Malayan-Polynesian *kutu*, "louse," which British sailors became familiar with (both word and nit) in the early years of this century.

copacetic.   The word is also spelled *copesetic*, leading *Partridge* to suggest that this slang for "excellent, all right," or "all safe or clear," as he defines it, is a combination of *cope* and *antiseptic*. But the expression is American and was largely confined to black speech when first recorded in the 1920s. "Bojangles" Bill Robinson may have invented *copacetic* and the great black tap dancer certainly did popularize it in his routines, giving the word wide currency. Robinson claimed he coined it when he was a shoeshine boy in Richmond. But a number of Southerners have testified that they heard the expression used by parents or grandparents long before this. Another theory holds that *copecetic* is from a Yiddish word meaning the same. It's also spelled *kopasetic* and *kopesetic*.

Copenhagen.   In 1807 the British destroyed the Danish fleet in a surprise attack off Copenhagen. As a result, all surprise attacks came to be called *Copenhagens* after the site of the original battle.

Copernican; Copernican theory.   Early in the 16th century the *Copernican theory* established that all the planets, including the earth, revolve in orbits around the sun, in opposition to the older Ptolemaic theory (See **Ptolemaic system**) that the sun and planets move around the earth. It immortalizes Copernicus (1473-1543), the Latinized form of the surname of Mikolaj Koppernigk, whose work revolutionized astronomy, changing man's entire outlook on the universe and influencing a profound change on the inner man as well. The great astronomer, born in Prussian Poland, made his living as a physician and canon of the cathedral of Frauenburg. He completed his theory as early as 1530, when he circulated in manuscript a brief popular account of it, but *De Revolutionibus Orbium Coelestium* wasn't published until thirteen years later, when he lay on his deathbed. Though the work was dedicated to Pope Paul III, it was placed on the church's index of forbidden books. *Copernican* also means revolutionary, in reference to the new system's impact on the world.

copper.   *Copper*, first attested in English in about 1000, comes from the Low Latin *cuprum*, "metal of Cyprus," the island of Cyprus having an exceptional wealth in copper in ancient times.

copperhead.   Northerners sympathetic to the Southern cause during the Civil War were called *copperheads* after the poisonous "sneak snake" of that name that strikes without warning and is so named for its copper color. The term was coined by a *New York Tribune* editorial writer on July 20, 1861 and is still used today to denote "an enemy sympathizer."

copra.   (*See* **coconut**.)

Coptic words.   The Coptic language, now extinct, was superseded by Arabic, but it was the ancient Egyptian language most spoken in early Christian times. Two English words that come to us from Coptic are *oasis* and *ebony*.

coral.   Its ancestor an old Greek word, *coral* first meant the beautiful red coral of the Red Sea and the Mediterranean. It was then extended to mean coral of all colors. In ancient times red coral was a highly prized precious gem and was believed to be a charm against shipwreck, lightning, whirlwinds, and shipboard fire. The Romans hung it in necklaces around the necks of infants to "preserve and fasten their teeth."

cord of wood.   Stacks of firewood were once measured with cords of rope, this practice giving us the term *cord of wood* for "a pile of split logs stacked eight feet long and four feet high and wide." The expression was used, indicating the same dimensions, as early as 1616.

cordon bleu.   (*See* **blue ribbon**.)

corduroy. Plebeian cotton forms the basis for the ribbed cloth we know as *corduroy* today, but the fabric was once woven from regal silk. The word had generally been thought to derive from the French *corde du Roi* ("cord of the King"), no one venturing to say which Gallic king first wore the material. But no such word has ever been used by the French, *velours à côtes* being their name for corduroy. Thus it has been suggested that the fabric had its origins in England, the *O.E.D.* pointing out that an 1807 French list of cloths used the English words "king's cordes." The surname Corderey or Corderoy is one possibility, from its first manufacturer's name, or it may be that some enterprising merchant, relying on snob appeal in advertising, christened the product "cord of the king," using the French *corde du Roi* for even greater distinction. The word was first used for a cloth in 1787.

core. *Core* for the central part of something—anything from an apple to a doctrine—probably derives from the Latin word *cor*, meaning "heart." Words like the French *coeur* and the Spanish *corazon* for "heart" suggest this, though the English word has not been traced back to the original Latin. Core was first recorded in 1398.

corn; maize; alien corn. When in Keats's "Ode to a Nightingale" a homesick Ruth stands "in tears amid the alien corn" (the phrase is Keats's own and not from the King James Bible), she is standing in a field of wheat or rye, any grain but New World *corn*. The English have always used the word *corn* to describe all grains used for food and never specifically for the grain that built the Mayan and Incan empires. *Corn* derives from the Old Teutonic *kurnom*, which is akin to *granum*, the Latin word for "grain." *Kurnom* eventually became the Old Saxon *korn* and then *corn* in Old English. The semantic confusion arose when English settlers here named corn on the cob *Indian corn* and then dropped the cumbrous qualifying adjective "Indian" over the years. The British call our "corn" *maize*, a word that derives from the Spanish *maiz*, which has its origins in *mahis*, a Caribbean Indian tribe's name for the plant. But while "corn" is the most valuable food plant native to the New World and has a fascinating history and manifold uses (employed in over 600 products, perhaps even used as a binding for this book), it is still little known in Europe—perhaps because most corn loses some 90 percent of its sugar content an hour after harvesting and can't survive a transatlantic voyage without losing practically all its taste.

corned beef. There is of course no corn in *corned beef*. The *corned* here is for the corns, or grains, of salt used in preparing this "salted beef."

corner the market. This term arose in U.S. financial circles toward the middle of the 19th century. Used generally today, it originally meant only to buy "one kind of stock or commodity, thereby driving potential buyers and sellers into a corner because they have no option but to yield to the price demands of those controlling the stock."

corny. *Corny*, for something old-fashioned, unsophisticated, and unsubtle, what is often called "tacky" in today's slang, has its origin in America's Corn Belt. Comedians playing unsophisticated "corn-fed" audiences in the Midwest gave them the *corn-fed* humor they wanted, so much so that corn came to be known as "what farmers feed pigs and comedians feed farmers." Soon *corn-fed humor* became simply *corney jokes*, the phrase possibly helped along by the Italian word *carne* "cheap meat," being applied to the "cheap jokes" the comedians told. *Corny* eventually was used to describe anything old-fashioned, full of clichés, or mawkishly sentimental.

coroner. Shakespeare called a *coroner* a *crowner*, which is nearer to the word's meaning of a "crown officer" (from the Latin *corona*, "crown"). *Coroners*, or *crowners*, collected the Crown revenues in Saxon days, and did not assume their official Crown duties of looking over corpses and holding inquests on suspicious deaths until the 18th century.

Corporal Violet; Little Corporal. Napoleon Bonaparte, the Little Corporal, who stood barely 5'2", was nicknamed *Corporal Violet* by his followers after he was banished to Elba and boasted that he would return with the violets. His followers used the question "Do you like violets?" to identify each other.

corporation. *Corporation* can be either singular or plural, depending on whether the writer regards it as an entity or has in mind the individual stockholders. Corporations generally use the plural in their communications ("Write for our catalogue," etc.), but it is equally correct to say "Sears have issued their catalogue," or "Sears has issued its catalogue." Many great writers have mixed a singular verb and a plural pronoun, as in the second example, including the framers of the Constitution. Tertullian, one of the fathers of the Christian church, coined the word *corporation* in A.D. 190 from the Latin *corporare*, "to make into a body," using it in ecclesiastical law. By the 17th century the word began to take on the meaning that it has today.

corpus delicti. *Corpus delicti*, first recorded in 1832, is *not* the corpse in a murder case, as is commonly thought. The term, translating from the Latin as "the body of the offense," refers to the basic element of a crime, which in a murder would be the death of the murdered person.

corsair. *Corsair*, which came into English in the late 16th century, was a Spanish word for someone between a pirate and a privateer, while "sea robbers" and "sea rovers" were German and Dutch inventions, also carelessly applied. At any rate, very few of these thieves of the sea were not the *hostes humani generi*, "enemies of the human race," that the Roman orator Cicero called all pirates centuries ago—though it is important to note that almost all pirates euphemistically called themselves "privateers" (*q.v.*).

corsned. This unusual word means "an ordeal by bread." In medieval times guilt was sometimes determined by making the accused swallow an ounce of bread or cheese consecrated by a priest—if the accused choked on the bread he was considered guilty. Blackstone explained in his *Commentaries* that people believed that the Almighty would "cause convulsions and paleness and [the bread would] find no passage if the man was really guilty, but might turn to health and nourishment if he was innocent." The practice is recorded as early as the tenth century and the word *corsned* derives from the Old English *cor*, "trial," and *snaed*, "piece."

cortisone. The colorless steroid hormone used in the treatment of rheumatoid arthritis and certain allergic diseases is so named because it comes from the adrenal *cortex* of the human brain. This so-called "trivial name" is much easier to say than its scientific name: *17,21-dihydroxypregn-4-ene-3,11,20-trione*. The trivial names of many chemical compounds are far less obvious. *Cubane*, for example, is so named because a drawing of its molecule looks like a cube. *Congressane* was so named "because a drawing of it was used as a symbol of one of the recent [1960s] international congresses of chemistry."

corvette. Originally *corvettes* were cumbersome, ponderous freighters, "old baskets" that took their name from the Latin *corbis*, "basket." Over the years, as the design changed, they became swift, streamlined armored cruisers.

cosine. (*See* **according to Gunter, etc.**)

cosmonaut. (*See* **cosmopolitan.**)

cosmopolitan; cosmonaut. Socrates, Diogenes, and Alexander the Great all claimed to be "citizens of the world," which in Greek is *kosmopolitis*, the root of our word *cosmopolitan*. Today we apply *cosmopolitan* to a man at home anywhere, the word's latest relative being *cosmonaut*, the Russian space pilot.

Cossack. The Cossacks, quartered in eleven communities throughout the country, were four million strong before the revolution in Russia. In return for certain privileges their men were all required to give military service for twenty years, from age eighteen. These cruel, fearless fighters and expert horsemen, constituting an elite Russian cavalry, were used by the czars to suppress revolution and were much feared by the people. A *Cossack* is still often used to describe a brutal or brave warrior. The Cossacks were descended from serfs who had fled their masters in the 15th to 17th century and settled on the border steppes, their name coming from the Russian *Kayaki*, "wanderers." In World War II they were used as cavalry by the Soviet Union.

cot. *Cot*, for a "little house" (hence *cottage*) and *cot*, for "a little boat" were in the language long before it, but neither word has any connection with our word *cot* for a small, often portable bed. This *cot* derives from the Hindi *khat*, for "bedstead, couch, or hammock," which a British traveler in India recorded as early as 1634.

cotangent. (*See* **according to Gunter.**)

Cotterel's salad. Hanged for rape in the early 18th century, Sir James Cotterel had no chance to see his name immortalized in this historical pun. As the baronet was hanged for rape and rape is also the name of a rather hot salad green, *Cotterel's salad* became the synonym for a hemp rope, like the one that burned his neck.

cotton gin. (*See* **engine.**)

to cotton to. Cotton clings readily to many surfaces, and clung to the machines, clothing, and hair of the English weavers who worked with it in the 16th century. This clinging quality of cotton probably suggested the expression *to cotton to*, "to like or be attracted to a person or thing." Although an earlier phrase used the word in essentially the same sense, its first recorded use by itself is in an old English play (1605): "John a Nokes and John a Style and I cannot cotton." Early technical processes of cloth manufacturing may have been responsible for the idea, as the *O.E.D.* points out, but it all amounts to the same thing—cotton sticking to something. No one has offered any proof that the expression derives from *kowtow*, or the French *côté*, "side," or from the obsolete slang *to cotton*, "to perform coition."

Couéism. "Every day, in every way, I am getting better and better." The bowlegged man who repeated this famous psychotherapeutic formula too often and became merely knock-kneed is a myth, but Emile Coué (1857-1926) is not. The French pharmacist and hypnotist turned psychotherapist established a free clinic in Nancy in 1910. Here he put into practice his system of therapeutics, based primarily on his theory that, by means of autosuggestion, ideas that cause illness may be eliminated from the will. This power of the imagination over the will was best expressed in his formula, and Coué claimed to have effected organic changes. He lectured widely abroad and his healing methods became well known in the United States and England during the 1920s.

cough; whooping cough. *Cough* was defined by Dr. Johnson as "a convulsion of the lungs, vellicated by some sharp serosity"! First recorded in about 1325 it is of echoic origin, "representing various sounds and actions made with the breath," as are many words, including *whoop*. Thus *whooping cough* is an echoic term.

cough up. Four centuries ago *to cough up* meant to disclose. It did not take on its present meaning of "to pay up or hand over" until the end of the 19th century, probably originating in this sense as American criminal slang. One theory is that underworld suspects tried to bribe police officers with money instead of coughing up, i.e., disclosing information about crimes, and that *cough up* then came to mean "pay up."

coulomb. Charles Augustin de Coulomb (1736-1806), a French military engineer who became a physicist when bad health forced his retirement from the army, did much work on electricity and magnetism. He designed his torsion balance for measuring the force of magnetic and electric attraction in 1777, while still an army engineer, but didn't publish his findings until about ten years later, finding that Michel had invented the same system independently. Bearing his name are *Coulomb's law* of magnetism; the *coulomb*, a unit for measuring the quantity of an electrical current; and the *coulometer*, which is more often called a *voltameter*. (See **volt**.)

countdown. Ninety-nine people in a hundred would say that the *countdown*, counting backwards for rocket launches, was invented at Cape Canaveral. But the technique was conceived and the word coined by film director Fritz Lang in his science-fiction classic *The Lady in the Moon*, to give the rocket launching in his realistic movie greater suspense. Persecuted by the Nazis, Lang fled Germany in the 1930s, but his *countdown* invention was used in early German rocket experiments leading to the V-2 and brought to America by German scientists who had worked on the early rockets.

counterpoint. Originally, *counterpoint* was the Latin musical term *punctus contra punctus*, "note against note." This means "melody against melody or simultaneous independent melodic lines," and was shortened to *counterpunctus*, which became the English *counterpoint* with its general as well as musical meaning. The word is first recorded in the early 16th century.

country bumpkin. (See **clodhopper**.)

country pay. Trading in early American country stores was often conducted by barter, or *country pay* as it was called, with customers exchanging corn, wheat, rye, and flax, or articles of household manufacture like blankets and baskets for goods on the merchant's shelves.

Homemade Indian brooms, maple syrup, aphrodisiac ginseng (sold in China), barrel staves, dried fruits, the potash and charcoal left when forests were burned down to clear land, even Indian wampum—all these and a hundred other things were used as *country pay*.

couvade. The custom among some American Indian tribes in which a father-to-be retires to bed and simulates childbirth. He believes that by doing this he prevents his regular daily exertions from harming the child, that he is magically assisting in the birth of the child, and that the act is "a symbolic assertion of identification of father and child." *Couvade* is from the French *couver*, "to hatch," which comes from the Latin *cubare*, "to lie down."

Coventry blue. (See **send to Coventry**.)

coward. *Coward* seems to have its roots in the Latin *cauda*, for "tail." There is no proof to be had, but some etymologists believe that the reference is to a frightened animal "turning tail" in flight, or tucking its tail between its legs. The word is recorded as early as the 13th century.

cowlick. This word for "a tuft of hair that refuses to lie down" is British in origin. It almost certainly comes from a comparison with the projecting ridge of hairs on a cow's hide, licked into that shape by the animal. The word is first recorded in 1598.

cowpoke; cowpuncher. *Cowpokes* and *cowpunchers* were originally cowboys who poked cattle onto railroad cars with long poles. The terms, first attested in 1880, were soon applied to all cowboys.

cowslip. This pretty flower takes its name from the droppings, or slips, of cattle, because it grew best and most numerous in English pastures where cattle grazed. The ancient word dates back to at least A.D. 1000.

Coxey's Army. Over his long life—he died in 1951, aged ninety-seven—Jacob Sechler Coxey lived through everything from the Civil War to the atomic bomb. His *Coxey's Army* was one of the first and best remembered groups to march on Washington, D.C., to demand change of some kind. Coxey's followers were a band of unemployed workers who presented Congress with a "petition in boots" the year following the Panic of 1893. It was their leader's plan to have Congress authorize money for public construction, which would provide employment, an idea that would be implemented during the Great Depression in the 1930s. But his highly publicized march from Massillon, Ohio on Easter Sunday failed to accomplish its purpose. The one hundred men who started never swelled to 100,000 as he had predicted, and only about five hundred reached Washington on May Day to protest their situation. "The Commonweal of Christ" came to an anticlimactic end when its leaders were arrested for walking on the Capitol lawn.

coxswain. Several centuries ago a *coxswainn* was the *swain* ("boy servant") in charge of the small cock, or cockboat, that was kept aboard for the ship's captain and used to row him to and from the ship. But with the passing of time the *coxswain* became the helmsman of any boat, regardless of size.

CQD; Mayday. Another telegraph symbol for requesting aid was CQD (*CQ*, the general call alerting other ships that a message follows, and the *D* standing for "danger"). But these letters, proposed after the *Titanic* sank in 1912, proved unsatisfactory for technical reasons and the easy-to-remember dashes and dots that coincidentally spell out SOS were retained. *Mayday*, not SOS, is the *oral* radio signal for requesting aid and probably derives from the French *M'aidez*, "help me." (*See* SOS.)

crabby. Jacob Grimm contended that the German word *Krabbe*, from which our *crabby* ultimately derives, meaning "a cross, ill-tempered person," owes its origin to the crab, "because these animals are malicious and do not easily let go of what they have." But another authority has it that the primary reference here is "to the crooked or wayward gait of the crustacean, and the contradictory, perverse and fractious disposition which this expresses."

cracked; crack-brained. *Cracked* has meant "crazy" in English since at least the 16th century and was indeed Standard English until about 1830, when it was labeled slang. But the expression is much older than this, for a character in Aristophanes's (ca. 448-ca. 388 B.C.) *The Frogs* is said to be *cracked*. A variant is *crack-brained*, first attested in 1557.

cracker-barrel philosopher. One small-town Missouri storekeeper in 1829 sold a line of books that included Homer, Herodotus, Josephus, Shakespeare, Cervantes, Milton, Defoe, Bunyan, Smollett, Hume, Fielding, and Scott. A town's most educated man aside from the schoolteacher and the preacher, the country storekeeper was usually the local *crackerbox philosopher*, and he and others of his breed often sat around on the large cracker barrels in general stores philosophizing on all the issues of the day. Such wise rustics were probably called *cracker-barrel philosophers* at the time, though the term isn't recorded until 1938 in a *Time* magazine piece.

crackle. (*See* onomatopoeia.)

crag. (*See* hog.)

cranberry. This berry grows wild in the marshlands favored by cranes, which leads some experts to trace it to the Low German word *kraanbere*. However, since the word is recorded in America as early as 1647—a time when it is unlikely that Low German terms would have much currency here—it could be that Americans coined the word independently, noting themselves that the berry grew where cranes lived.

crap; crapper. Poor Thomas Crapper, whose name is about as close as anyone would normally want to get to the fourth most expurgated word in the English language, was an Englishman who developed and manufactured the modern toilet bowl, which U.S. soldiers in World War I saw and used everywhere, bringing the name *crapper* home with them to America. The story of his life, of "the power behind the throne," has recently been published under the title *Flushed with Pride*. It is apparently not a put-on, although it has the ring of a classic hoax. Crapper's name, of course, is only a lucky or unlucky coincidence. It does not give us the word *crap* from the Dutch, *krappe*, "scraps," which through the ages has been applied to offal or excrement. Crap is now most often used metaphorically to mean "nonsense or lying," as in "That's a lot of crap."

craps. Dice have been found in ancient Egyptian tombs and in the ruins of Babylon, but the game of dice as we know it today, dates to the early 19th century and may owe its name, craps, to a Frenchman. Johnny Crapaud was the sobriquet of French gambler Bernard Marigny, who introduced dice to New Orleans in about 1800 (*Crapaud* being slang for any Frenchman, owing to the belief that three *crapauds*, or toads, were the ancient arms of France). High-roller Marigny became associated with the game, which was named *Johnny Crapaud's game* after his nickname, this eventually shortened to *craps*. It is said that Marigny even named the present Burgundy Street "Craps Street" in honor of his favorite pastime.

crash. *Crash* in the sense of to *crash a party* is an Americanism that derives from *gate-crasher*, another American expression that originated in about 1920. The latter term has its roots in a person forcing his way through a gate into a sporting event. *Gate-crashing* is not much heard of anymore, but *crashing* and *party-crashing* are commonly used.

Crassus. A *Crassus* describes "a rich man of unbounded avarice and ambition." Marcus Licinius Crassus (ca. 115-53 B.C.), Roman "real estate dealer," military leader, and statesman, personified these qualities. It is said that crafty Crassus made his fortune by forming his own fire-fighting company and forcing the sale of houses on fire by letting them burn until he could buy cheap—holding off his fire brigade until the sale was consummated. Other ploys of his included buying confiscated property at nominal prices from those outlawed by Sulla, under whom he served, by slave trafficking, and usury. By such means he became the richest man in Rome and a force to be reckoned with in the corrupt politics of the day. Crassus suppressed the slave uprising of Spartacus in 71

B.C. and was elected consul with Pompey the following year, both men joining with Caesar in forming Rome's First Triumvirate ten years later. In this last capacity Crassus encouraged the infamous Cataline conspiracy. Finally, his ambitions outran his ability. Lusting for military glory, he launched a campaign against the Parthians in Syria. However, his army was routed by Parthian archers at Carrhae in one of the most notable examples of military stupidity in history. Crassus was captured by the Parthians and put to death; one story has it that they poured molten silver down his throat.

crate. Americans began using *crate* for a beat up old car, or even boat or plane, in about 1920. However, the term dates back before that to 1917, when *Partridge* says it was first applied in the R.A.F. to old planes. The old biplanes would seem to resemble a wooden crate more than any car would and this is probably the word's source. *Old crate* is more common than *crate* today.

cravat. The modern *cravat*, another word for "necktie," was originally a huge colorful linen or muslin scarf edged with lace and worn knotted loosely around the neck. The scarves were introduced into France by mercenaries enlisted in the royal Croatian regiment during the Thirty Years War (1618-48). French men and women, impressed by such sartorial splendor, adopted the scarves, tying them with long flowing ends and calling them *cravats*, after the French word (*Cravate*), for "a Croatian." Croatia, part of Austria at the time, is now a republic of Yugoslavia.

crayfish. This word is an example of folk etymology, deriving not from any fish but from the French *ecrevisse*, which has its roots in the German *krebiz*, "crab." Which is appropriate, of course, since a *crayfish* isn't a fish but a crustacean that includes among its ranks the spiny lobster. First recorded as *creuesse* in English early in the 15th century, the word was corrupted to *crayfish* by 1597.

crazy as a coot. As far back as the 18th century the coot's stupid facial expressions and clownish behavior inspired the expression *silly as a coot, stupid as a coot,* and *crazy as a coot.* "During the breeding season *Fulica americana* acts especially odd, breaking water, flapping wings, sitting on their tails, slashing at one another with taloned feet and thrusting with their bills," one expert explains.

crazy as a loon; loony. The common loon (*Gavia immer*) is noted for what one expert calls its "mirthless laughter, a high, far-crying, liquid tremolo that sets your spine atingle." This water bird's name may come from the Dutch *loen*. The loon has nothing to do with the word *loony*, for "crazy," which is a shortening of *lunatic*, but it does give us the expression *crazy as a loon.*

crazy bone. (*See* **funny bone.**)

credenza. An Italian nobleman's meals in Borgian days, when poisoning was an art, would be placed on a sideboard and tasted by a servant before being served to the noble. If the servant didn't die or get sick, it was safe for his master to eat. From this practice the sideboard where the food rested came to be called a *credenza*, meaning "belief or confidence," no doubt for the belief and confidence it gave the noble, not the servant. This old story, or some variation on it, may well be true; there is no better explanation of why a sideboard or buffet should take its name from the Latin *credere*, "to believe."

credit. According to J.P. Morgan, loans are made safe by character rather than collateral. This idea is reflected in the word *credit*, which derives from the Latin *credo*, meaning "I believe," which indicates that the person giving credit "believes" in the person to whom he gives it. The word, in its financial sense, was first recorded in 1542.

creepmouse. "Here comes a little mouse/creeping up to baby's house" is the rhyme often used in this familiar game played with infants. Most common in the South under the name *creepmouse*, the game is played everywhere, the idea "to tickle bablies to make them laugh by moving the fingers rapidly on their bodies as if a mouse was running over them." The name *creepmouse* is first recorded in 1899.

creosote. *Creosote* was coined in the early 19th century from Greek words that the word's inventor thought meant "flesh saving"; though the Greek meant something else entirely, *creosote* has never been abandoned. Creosote, an oily liquid with a burning taste and penetrating odor, is obtained by the distillation of wood tar, and it is a "flesh saver" because of its early use as a preservative of meat and fish. (Now, when used at all, it is to preserve wood.) The evergreen *Creosote* bush (*Larrea tridentata*), which has a strong odor of creosote, is now regarded as the world's oldest known living plant; a specimen found in 1985 in the Mojave Desert is believed to be 11,700 years old, making it far older than the previous record-holder, a 5,000-year-old bristlecone pine.

crêpe suzette. When or where crêpes suzette were invented in France remains a mystery, but the dessert pancake must have been named for someone's favorite Susy, *Suzette* being the French diminutive for the proper name Suzanne. The thin, rolled pancakes, or *crêpes*, are generally heated in an orange-flavored liqueur sauce and flambéed at the table, making the blazing dessert one of the more spectacular glories of the French cuisine. One theory has the dish created by San Francisco chef Henri Charpentier, but it was more likely invented by a chef known only as M. Joseph at the Restaurant Marivaux in Paris and named in honor of actress Suzanne Reichenberg.

cress.   (*See* **watercress.**)

cretin.   Our pejorative *cretin*, for "an idiot," began as a kindly word. In the Middle Ages many deformed people with a low mentality lived in the Alpine regions, their condition resulting from a thyroid condition now known as myxedema, which was possibly caused by a deficiency of iodine in their drinking water. These unfortunates were called *Chretiens*, "Christians," by the Swiss because the word distinguished human beings like these people from brutes and they believed these childlike innocents were incapable of actual sin. But the kindly word went into French as *cretin*, meaning "idiot," and retained the same meaning when it passed into English.

crib.   Recent slang use of a *crib* for "an apartment" isn't new at all; *crib* has been used in this sense since the early 19th century and not long after became slang for either a bed or a small room in a brothel big enough to contain just a bed. *Cribbing* from *crib sheets* on an examination, a kind of euphemism among students for cheating, has its origins in the use of *to crib* for "to pilfer or take furtively," common since about 1740. The reasoning behind this last was probably the idea that *cribs* or wicker baskets were used by thieves to hide stolen articles. It is said that thieves in London carried baskets, or cribs, in which to stash stolen goods and that they were hard to spot because most women in the marketplaces carried the same baskets.

cricket; it's not cricket.   In 1622 villagers in Boxgrove, England, near the cathedral city of Chichester, were prosecuted for playing the game of cricket on a Sunday, and replied that "It's not cricket!" This is reportedly the first use of the expression and, clearly, if these villagers did say it, they were just trying to get out of paying a fine. In any case, over the years, perhaps after the villagers paid their fine, the phrase *it's not cricket* came to mean it's unfair, it's "not playing the game." I can find no proof of the story except in the one source that gives it and the earliest I can trace the expression to is 1900, though it is foreshadowed in 1867. *Cricket* itself is of unknown origin, possibly coming from the Old English *cric*, "a staff," for the bat used in the game. John Gunther in *Inside Europe* (1943) writes of the British national game of cricket "and the ritualistic attitude to fair play that it has proclaimed."

Crimea.   (*See* **Cimmerian darkness.**)

criminal conversation.   (*See* **conversation.**)

crimson.   The kermes, or scarlet grain insect, which takes its name, ultimately, from the Sanskrit *krmi*, "worm," gives its name to the red dye called *crimson* that it is used to make, the word a familiar one in England since the 15th century.

Crippen.   *Crippen* is used to describe any man wild and unkempt in appearance, but is more common for a doctor-murderer, of which there have unfortunately been too many. Dr. Hawley Harvey Crippen, English murderer, killed his wife, Cora, and was hanged for his crime on November 23, 1910. Captain Kendall of *The Montrose* transmitted a message on July 22 of that year leading to Crippen's capture, marking the murderer the first to be caught by wireless telegraph. Dr. Crippen, born in Michigan in 1861, received his medical education in London and settled there in 1896 with his shrewish wife, who had previously appeared unsuccessfully in opera and on the music hall stage as Belle Elmore. Crippen fell in love with his secretary and on New Year's Eve, 1909, poisoned his wife, dissected the body and, after destroying what he could by fire, interred the remains in the cellar. He and Ethel le Neve, who disguised herself as a boy, eventually fled England, but on the boat crossing the channel Captain Kendall recognized them from their pictures and wired Scotland Yard to come aboard.

crisis.   *Crisis*, strictly speaking, means "the ability to judge," deriving from the Greek *krinein*, "to decide or determine." In ancient times physicians believed that "the humours of the body ebbed and flowed like the tides of the sea." *Brewer* notes that Hippocrates called these tidal days *critical days* and called the tide itself a *crisis*, "because it was on these days that the physician could determine whether the disorder was taking a good or bad turn." From this original use the word *crisis* took on its present meaning of "a turning point."

Crispin.   A word often found in literature for "a shoemaker," but rarely used in everyday speech, *Crispin* commemorates the legendary brothers Crispin and Crispinian, patron saints of shoemakers and all leather workers, noble Romans who left Rome for Gaul in A.D. 303 to preach Christianity, supporting themselves by their craft. They made many converts and survived several attempts by Emperor Maximian to put them to death, but were finally beheaded. The martyrs also have *St. Crispin's lance*, humorous for "a shoemaker's awl," named after them. *St. Crispin's Day* is October 25.

crisscross.   Crisscross sounds like a mere reduplication of sounds similar to zigzag, or ding-dong, but when we call a series of crossing lines *crisscross* we are really saying *Christ-cross*, "the cross of Christ." In the old 16th-century hornbook primer—originally one vellum sheet slotted into a wainscot board frame and protected by a thin transparent front covering of horn—only the alphabet, a few numbers, a little spelling, and the Lord's

Prayer were taught. Most teachers at the time were trained for the ministry and so there was a close connection between education and religion. Thus the alphabet printed on the sheet's top line was preceded by a small cross that was referred to as the *Christ-cross,* or *Christ's cross.* Soon the alphabet row came to be called *Christ-cross* row, this eventually becoming *crisscross* row due to the reduplicative tendency of tongues, or perhaps because the word was pronounced slurred, like "Christmas" or "Christian." Eventually *crisscross* alone was applied to any pattern of crossing lines similar to the cross at the beginning of *crisscross* row.

critic. *Critic,* referring to someone who passes judgment on something, was first attested by Shakespeare in *Love's Labour's Lost* (1588), but we don't know if the bard coined the word, which is based ultimately on a Greek word meaning the same. Shakespeare is said to have first recorded over 1,700 words.

crocodile tears. Crocodiles can't shed real tears, but the myth arose in early times that the creature moaned and cried to attract the sympathetic and helpful, and then snatched and ate its saviors while "wepynge" ("weeping"), as British adventurer and nature faker Sir John Maundeville, the first to record the legend, put it in about 1400. The story was repeated in *Hakluyt's Voyages* (1600) and by many other writers including Shakespeare, and these hypocritical *crocodile's tears* became a term for any feigned sorrow. The crocodile takes its name from the Greek *kroke,* "gravel," and *crilos,* "worm," the newly hatched animal resembling to early observers an oversized worm emerging from gravel on the banks of the Nile.

Croesus. When we say, as the ancient Greeks did, that a man is *as rich as Croesus,* we are invoking the name of the last King of Lydia (560-546 B.C.). As a result of his conquests and trade, King Croesus was regarded by the Greeks as the wealthiest man on earth, his riches proverbial even at that time. Croesus probably minted the first gold and silver coins. Although he had subjugated the Ionian cities of Asia Minor, he was friendly to the Greeks, making spectacular offerings to their oracles. According to a legendary story told by Herodotus, the Athenian Solon once advised Croesus that no man could be deemed happy, despite his riches, until he finished his life happily. Later, after Croesus had been defeated by Cyrus the Great and condemned to be burned alive, he supposedly cried out Solon's name three times from the pile. Cyrus, moved by his explanation and perhaps reflecting on his own fate, is said to have spared his captive's life and they became great friends. The tale, however, is chronologically impossible and only one of a number of legends concerning this very real Midas.

Cromwell; a Cromwellian. His name was once pronounced "Crumwell," hence the historic Royalist toast, "God send this crumb well down!" Royalists had every reason to wish no good to this brilliant military leader and forceful statesman. A devout Puritan and member of Parliament who vigorously supported the Roundheads, Oliver Cromwell (1599-1658) eventually led his new model army to victory over Charles I's forces in battle, had the king executed in 1649, and abolished the monarchy. In 1653 he became England's Lord Protector, rejecting the offer of the crown but accepting what was an undisguised dictatorship. He who had established the Commonwealth and began his career as an opponent of absolutism had become an abolutist himself. To this day, his name is a synonym for *dictator.* Cromwell died a natural death, naming his ineffectual son, Richard, as Lord Protector on his deathbed. He was buried in Westminster Abbey, but when the Royalists regained power in 1660, his body was exhumed, hanged from a gallows, and beheaded. Such was their revenge on the man who had said of Charles I, "I tell you we will cut off his head with the crown upon it." (*See also* **Oliver's skull.**)

crony. *Crony* began its life as college slang for a long-time "chum." That college wits at Cambridge coined it from the Greek *chronios,* "long standing," is evidenced by its spelling in the first recorded use of the term, which we find in Samuel Pepys's *Diary* in 1665: "Jack Coles, my old schoolfellow . . . who was a great *chrony* of mine."

croon. A popular singer who *croons* doesn't need much vocal equipment; he or she sings softly, sadly, uses the voice as little as possible. So *croon* has come to mean "to sing in a melancholy way," a meaning far removed from its original one. Croon first meant "to utter a continued, loud, deep sound; to bellow as a bull, roar; to boom as a bell." Bulls *crooned* to the hills in old poems, and crooning was associated with hearty, virile singers by Burns and other poets. It was only by misuse through the years that the word changed in meaning from a roar to a lamentation and then to the singing we call *crooning* today, which approaches the bellowing of a bull only when the amplifiers are turned way up.

crops. (*See* **Roundheads.**)

cross as a bear. "Major Smalleye war as made as a beaten b'ar," wrote Robert Bird in *Nick of the Woods* (1837). The still common Americanism for "quite cross or mad" goes back at least a decade earlier and is probably even older. (*See* **a bear for work.**)

crossing the line. Anyone who *crosses the line* has sailed across the international date line, an occasion that in days past was celebrated with an initiation ceremony for those who were crossing for the first time. The custom, still practiced to a limited extent, called for a sailor, dressed as King Neptune, and his court to seize novices and lather and shave them, among other antics.

crossing the Rubicon. The Rubicon, a river in Italy, marked the boundary between Roman Italy and Gaul, which was governed by Julius Caesar. When Caesar crossed the Rubicon in 49 B.C. he had invaded the Roman Republic and there was no going back. Thus the expression *crossing the Rubicon* became synonymous over the years for "taking an irreversible step."

cross of gold. It was the gold standard, "the standard of monetary value solely in terms of gold, the single standard," that William Jennings Bryan, an advocate of the silver standard, referred to when he made his famous *Cross of Gold* speech at the National Democratic Convention in Chicago in 1896: "You [the rich and powerful] shall not crucify mankind upon a cross of gold." On the gold standard since 1834, the U.S. legally adopted it in 1900, then abandoned it in 1933.

crowbar. This prying tool is so named because its forked end resembles a crow's foot. It wasn't called a *crowbar* until the early 19th century, having been termed a *crow* as early as 1573.

crow-herd; crow-keeper; scarecrow. We've heard of sheep-herds (shepherds) and cow-herds, but *crow-herds*? *Crow-herds*, it seems, were boys or old men equipped with makeshift bows and employed to keep crows off planted fields. They were apparently first called *crow-keepers*, this term mentioned in Shakespeare's *King Lear*: "That fellow handles his bow like a crow-keeper . . ." A *crow-keeper* could also be called a *scarecrow*, a word first recorded as applying to humans hired to scare off crows (1553) and applied to "a straw dummy dressed like a man" about a half century later.

crow's feet. Small wrinkles "formed by age or anxiety" around the eyes are called *crows-feet* because they are "thought to resemble the impression of the feet of crows," according to an old dictionary. Chaucer used the expression as far back as 1372 in his poem "Troylus and Cryseyde."

crow's nest. A ship's highest lookout station is called the *crow's nest* because old sailing vessels once carried a coop high up on their masts in which land birds, including crows, were kept. If winds carried a ship out of sight of land, the birds would be released and the ship would follow them inland.

crow tracks. (*See* **chicken scratch**.)

crud. An Americanism dating back to the early 1920s in Army use, *crud* doesn't come directly from the Middle

English *crudd*, for "coagulated solids of milk, or curds," even though Shakespeare used the word *crudy* in this sense. It probably derives from the mispronunciation of the word *curdled* as *cruddled*, anything curdled or cruddled being undesirable *crud*. The word first described semen sticking to the body or clothes after sexual intercourse," and was probably so named for this, but is now used mainly as a synonym for feces, or, even more commonly, for "anything dirty, inferior, worthless, ugly, or disgusting."

crummy. Hoboes begging for food on the road often received bread and other baked goods that were so stale they were literally *crummy*, had begun to turn to crumbs. *Crummy* is recorded in this sense in the early 1900s and within twenty-five years or so meant "anything cheap or inferior."

the crying bird. Limpkins (*Scolopaceous Courlan*) are often called *crying birds* in America because the usual cry of this noisy bird "possesses a quality of unutterable sadness," according to one ornithologist.

crying towel. (*See* **get out the crying towel**.)

cry over spilt milk. Canadian humorist Thomas C. Haliburton, whose Down East humor strongly influenced American literature, had a friend say this to his famous character Sam Slick, a shrewd Yankee peddler, in *The Clockmaker; or the Sayings and Doings of Samuel Slick of Slickville* (1836). "What's done, Sam, can't be helped, there is no use cryin' over spilt milk" were the exact words. This is the first use of the expression in print, though to *cry over spilt milk* seems homely enough to be of much older origin. It expresses, of course, the folly of vain regret, meaning to grieve over something beyond saving, something you can't do anything about. Haliburton, a Canadian jurist, later returned to England and became a member of Parliament.

crystal. *Crystal* derives from the Greek word for ice and, indeed, was an early English synonym for ice. When the first quartz crystals were observed by the ancients, they were thought to be merely ice crystals petrified by some natural process over the ages and were thus given the same name. We still retain the old meaning of crystal as "ice" in the fortune-teller's *crystal ball*, which isn't at all like crystal as we know it but does resemble a ball of ice.

cry uncle. (*See* **uncle**.)

Cuba libre. During the Cuban War of Independence in 1896 rebels drank a refreshing energizing drink of sugar and cold water that they called a *Cuba libre*, or "free Cuba." Later some anonymous bartender added rum to the drink, which is now made of rum, cola, and lime juice.

cubane; basketane; squaric acid. Whimsical scientists named these molecules so because of their shapes. In *cubane* the six carbon atoms are arranged in the form of a cube; *basketane's* molecular shape suggests a basket; and in *squaric acid* the atoms are arranged in a square.

cubbyhole. The *cub* or *cubby* in this term has nothing to do with bear cubs who live in a hole or den. *Cub* is a word still used in rural England for any small shelter, from a rabbit hutch to a chicken coop. Possibly first altered to *cubbyhole* by children in reference to a small hiding place, it came to mean "any small, snug place."

cuckold. Instead of building its own nest, the cuckoo eats other birds' eggs and lays its eggs in their place. The cuckoo eggs are then hatched by the sparrow, wagtail, yellowhammer, or whatever. For this reason the bird's name became the basis for the derisive word *cuckold*, "a husband whose wife has been unfaithful," a term that dates back more than a century before Chaucer's time. How cuckold came to be applied to the husband instead of the adulterer isn't clear, though Dr. Johnson believed that "it was usual to alarm the husband at the approach of an adulteress by calling out 'cuckoo,' which by mistake was applied in time to the person warned."
(*See* **cuckoo.**)

cuckold hazel. (*See* **witch hazel.**)

cuckoo. The cuckoo was so named for the one-note song it repeats over and over. Why it became a symbol for stupidity in the 16th century isn't really known. Perhaps it got this reputation because it lays its eggs in other birds' nests, though many would consider this clever. Or we may owe this meaning of *cuckoo* to the folktale "Wise Men of Gotham," in which the villagers tried to prolong summer by fencing in the cuckoo so that it wouldn't fly off. (*See* **cuckold; onomatopoeia.**)

cucumber. (*See* **cool as a cucumber.**)

cue. In the 16th century the Latin *quando*, "when," was abbreviated as *Q* on actors' copies of play scripts as a direction telling an actor when to begin speaking his part. *Q* was read and pronounced *cue*, the abbreviation becoming a word when it was finally written *cue* as well. No play manuscripts with *Q's* on them survive, but several 16th and 17th century writers tell this story and it seems likely, especially since *cue* is first recorded as *q*, in 1553: ". . . a man's *q* in a play."

cul-de-sac. In French *cul-de-sac* (from *cul*, "bottom or anus," and *sac*, "bag") means the bottom of the bag or sack. First used as an anatomical term, *cul-de-sac* was by the early 19th century a military term for the position of an army hemmed in on all sides with no chance of escape, and then came to mean "a dead-end street," one from which there is no exit save the entrance.

Cullinan diamond. Most famous of the precious stones bearing someone's name is the 3,106 metric carat (over 1 1/4 lbs.) diamond found in South Africa's Premier Mine in 1905. The stone, the largest diamond ever unearthed, was named after the mine's discoverer-director, Sir Thomas Major Cullinan. Presented to England's King Edward VII in 1907, it was cut into a number of specimens worth collectively over a million pounds. The Star of Africa made from it is, at 530.2 metric carats, the largest cut diamond in the world.

cumshaw. *Cumshaw*, for "a tip or gratuity," came into the language early in the 19th century from the Chinese Amoy dialect. The Chinese words it derives from were a traditional beggar's phrase that has a literal meaning of "grateful thanks."

cunt. *Cunt*, for the female sexual organ or vagina, dates back (as *cunte*) to Middle English, deriving from a Teutonic word corresponding to the Latin *cunnus*, which is related to the Latin *cuneus*, "a wedge." While the *O.E.D.* records *cock* (*q.v.*) and *prick*, it doesn't include *cunt*, *Partridge* calling this "an injustice to women." The word has been avoided in public speech since the 15th century and been considered obscene since about the 17th century, though it has recently been included in dictionaries and is commonly printed in other works.

Cupid. cupidity. Over the years *cupidity* has changed from its first meaning of a passionate desire for love to a passionate desire for money, that is, greed or avarice. It derives from Cupid, the Roman god of love, whose name remains a symbol of love. Traditionally *Cupid* is a winged blindfolded ("Love is blind") boy carrying a bow and golden arrows and "he whets with blood the grindstone on which he sharpens his arrows."

cuppa char. (*See* **tea.**)

cur. This word, for a mean mongrel or worthless dog, is associated with the growling of such dogs. Used by Spenser in the *The Faerie Queene* (1589), *cur* is an old word that derives from the Scandinavian *kurra*, "to snarl or grumble."

curare. This well-known deadly poison, with which South American natives sometimes tipped their arrows, takes its name from the *wrari* of the Brazilian Tupi Indians. In Tupi it translates as the poetically apt "he to whom it comes always falls."

curate's egg. (*See* **like the curate's egg.**)

curfew. Domestic fires left unextinguished at night caused many devastating fires in medieval times. Therefore laws made it mandatory to cover fires at night, church bells ringing at the hour (usually 8 or 9 o'clock) that this was to be done. The French for "cover fire," *couvre feu* passed into English as *curfew* and the word later was applied to all regulations banning people from the streets at certain hours.

curie. Several words honor the husband and wife co-discoverers of radium, whose work laid the foundation for much later research in nuclear physics. The *Curie point*—the temperature at which the magnetic properties of a substance change—had been named for Pierre Curie (1859-1906) before he married Marja Sklodowska in 1895. He and Madame Curie, who came from Poland to study at the Sorbonne, worked together to extract from pitchblende the twin radioactive elements polonium and radium in 1898, the former being named for Mme. Curie's native country. Marie Curie's name has become more widely known than her husband's; it was she who first suspected the presence of new elements in pitchblende, and she was a pioneer woman scientist as well. But the *curie* or *curiegram*—a unit of measurement for radioactivity—was named for *both* scientists in 1910, as was the radioactive element *curium* when discovered by Glenn Seaborg and his co-workers at the University of California in 1945. Both Curies shared a *Nobel Prize* (*q.v.*) in 1903 for their discovery of radioactivity; Madame Curie received a second Nobel Prize, in 1911, for the discovery of radium. Their daughter, Irène Curie Joliet, shared a Nobel Prize in chemistry with her husband in 1935.

curlicism. John Arbuthnot remarked that English publisher Edmund Curll's inaccurate biographies were "one of the new terrors of death," but Curll was more notorious for the obscene books he published, these including *The Memories of John Ker of Kersland* (1728), *The Nun in Her Smock*, a book on flagellation, and other inspirational works. Today "the unspeakable Curll" might be a rich man, but in his time he was fined, put in the pillory and imprisoned for his efforts. Among the greats who lampooned him were Jonathan Swift and Alexander Pope, who described him as "a fly in amber." No one has identified the anonymous wit who coined the word *curlicism*, "literary indecency," from his name.

currants. *Currants* may taste nothing like them, but they take their name indirectly from grapes. In the early 14th century the chief place of export for the small seedless raisins made from grapes was Corinth, Greece. As Corinth was pronounced *Corauntz* in Anglo-French at the time, these dried raisins were called *raisins of Corauntz*. Later, the tart berries of the Ribes family were given the same name because their plant clusters looked like the dried grapes, or raisins, of Corauntz. *Corauntz* was eventually corrupted to *currants* and this became the tasty fruit's name.

currency. *Currency*, a synonym for paper money, applied to coins when the term was first used in late 17th-century England, there being no paper money at the time. It was so named because it was the *current* medium of exchange.

curry favor. These words are literally meaningless. What does currying, or brushing, favor have to do with bootlicking, or ingratiating oneself by flattery? The expression shows that a mistake repeated often enough can become standard usage. *Favor* here is a corruption of *Fauvel*. Fauvel was a fallow-colored or chestnut horse in the early-14th-century satirical poem *Roman de Fauvel*. The equine hero of this popular French allegory symbolized cunning duplicity; thus cunning people who resorted to insincere flattery in order to gain someone's favor were said to *curry Fauvel*, to groom or brush the rascally fallow-colored horse so that he would look kindly on them and perhaps impart to them his powers of duplicity. *Fauvel* came to be spelled *favel* in English. But because *favel* sounded like *favor* to Englishmen and because the idea of gaining someone's favor is the essence of the phrase, the proverbial expression became *to curry favor*.

the curse. *The curse* is still used for "menstruation" among a large number of American women. How old the expression is hasn't been established, but it is first recorded in John Dos Passos's *42nd Parallel* (1930): "She was afraid her period was coming on. She'd only had the curse a few times yet." Variations are *Eve's curse* and *the curse of Eve*.

curtain lecture. This is a reproof or lecture given in private or secret. *Curtain lectures* date back to the 18th century, when beds were often curtained and within the privacy of them wives often scolded or lectured their husbands, or vice versa.

Curzon line. The *Curzon line* separating Russia and Poland was suggested in 1919 by the British Conservative politician, statesman, and writer George Nathaniel Curzon, first Marquess of Kedleston (1859-1925). Lord Curzon, secretary of foreign affairs at the time, served in many capacities for the British government. As Viceroy of India from 1899 to 1905 and Chancellor of Oxford University from 1907 to 1915, he became noted for his aloof regal manner, which was the butt of many jokes. Behind the facade was a witty, modest, friendly man whose sheer willpower overcame serious physical weakness (a curvature of the spine). Curzon failed in his ambition to become the British prime minister in 1923, when Stanley Baldwin was chosen over him. It is said that he died of overwork. The Curzon line was adopted as Poland's eastern frontier after World War II, having been confirmed at Yalta in 1945. By the way, the diplomat wasn't at all like the rhyme composed about him at Balliol College in the late 1870s: "My name is George Nathaniel Curzon,/ I am a most superior person."

cushlamachree. *Cushlamachree* is one of the few native locutions that Irish immigrants retained after being in America awhile. The expression is a corruption of the Gaelic *cuisle me chroidhe*, "vein of my heart."

cushion; cushy. Plush cushions seem as though they'd have something to do with the word *cushy*, comfortable, or easy, as in "a cushy job." But the word *cushy* derives from the Hindu-Persian *khush*, "pleasant," which the British assimilated in India, while the unrelated *cushion* derives ultimately from the Latin *coxa*, "hip," because it was often put under the hips.

customer. *Customer* first meant one who acquired ownership of a house after long use or possession, the word deriving from the Latin *custodia*, "guarding or keeping." *Customer* also meant a common prostitute in the early 17th century and was used by Shakespeare twice in this sense. By the end of the 15th century it took on its meaning of "one who frequents any place for the sake of purchasing." In this sense, it probably derived from the long-standing satisfied tenant who became an owner, the first *customers* giving all their business and allegiance to one merchant in early times.

to cut. *To cut* someone, "to refuse to recognize someone socially, to shun him," was originally Cambridge slang, dating back to the 18th century. As one contemporary observer put it: "There are several species of the *cut* . . . The *cut direct* is to start across the street at the approach of the obnoxious person in order to avoid him. The *cut indirect* is to look the other way and pass without appearing to observe him. The *cut sublime* is to admire the top of King's College Chapel, or the beauty of the passing clouds, till he is out of sight. The *cut infernal* is to analyze the arrangement of your shoe-strings, for the same purpose."

cut a Dido. (*See* **cutting up**.)

cut and dried. The allusion is probably not to ready-cut timber, as *Brewer* says, but to the cut-and-dried herbs that were sold in the herbalists' shops of 17th-century England. Used as remedies, herbs were more effective cut and dried than they were fresh picked, and herbalists stocked great quantities of them. The phrase came to mean "far from fresh, hackneyed," its first recorded use in this sense being in a 1710 letter to a preacher whose sermon was described as *cut and dry'd*. The words also came to mean "clear cut." By the time Swift used the phrase for hackneyed literary style in his poem "Betty the Grizette" (1730), it was already fairly hackneyed itself:

Sets of phrases, cut and dry,
Ever more thy tongue supply.

cut a wide (big) swath. This Americanism, meaning "to make a big pompous show, to appear important," dates back to the early 19th century or before. "Gracious me! How he was strutting up the sidewalk—didn't he cut a swath!" exclaimed one writer in 1843. The term is a farming one, a *swath* being "the amount of grass or any crop cut down with one sweep of a scythe."

cut it. (*See* **can't cut the mustard**.)

cut neither nails nor hair at sea. An old superstition, which goes back at least to the ancient Romans, has it that the cuttings of nails and hair were votive offerings to Persephone, Queen of Hades. Therefore, Neptune, ruler of the sea, would be jealous and show his displeasure if sailors cut their nails or hair because he would believe his subjects were making offerings to another god and wreck their ship or drown them.

cut off your nose to spite your face. "Henry IV well knew that to destroy Paris would be, as they say, to cut off his own nose in taking spite on his own face," Gedeon Tallemant des Reaux wrote this in his *Historiettes* (ca. 1658), and the fact that he wrote "as they say" indicates that the expression is even more venerable. There may have been an old story about someone angrily cutting off a portion of the long, unattractive nose nature had cursed him with and succeeding only in spiting his face, but, if so, it is lost in time. The expression has survived so long and is still so frequently used simply because it is the most graphic, homeliest, and most grimly humorous of all sayings describing someone injuring himself through pique or anger.

the cut of his jib. The cut of a jib, or foresail, of a ship indicates her character to a sailor and *jib* means "face" in sailor's slang. Thus *don't like the cut of his jib*, which probably dates to a century ago, translates as "I'm suspicious of him; I don't like the expression on his face."

cut one's eyeteeth; wisdom teeth. The eyeteeth are those directly under the eye, the long, pointed canines that are cut at fourteen to twenty months for the first set and at eleven to twelve years of age for the second set. To *cut one's eyeteeth* means "to acquire wisdom and become worldly," because the permanent set is acquired when a child is passing into young adulthood. It is usually said in the negative, as in *he hasn't cut his eyeteeth yet*. The expression was used by Haliburton's Sam Slick in 1837 and Emerson after him, but is British in origin, dating back to the early 1700s, when it was *to have one's eyeteeth*. *Eyeteeth* commonly referred to the canine teeth of dogs and other animals long before this, so the phrase may have been suggested by the fact that fighting dogs were considered dangerous to handle when they developed their eyeteeth. Actually, the words better describe the emergence from infancy or childhood than they do the acquiring of wisdom. If wisdom does come with age, *to cut one's wisdom teeth* is more appropriate, for these are cut at the ages of 17 to 25 and up to age fifty! These molars have been known as *dentes sapientiae*, "teeth of wisdom," since the time of Hippocrates.

to cut one's foot. *To cut one's foot* means to step in cow dung. The euphemism, traced back to the Appalachians, was first recorded in 1899 and still has some currency in rural areas today. A variation is *to cut one's foot on a Chinese razor*.

cut the Gordian knot. The workman Gordius of old was chosen king of Phrygia when he fulfilled an oracle's prophecy that the first man to approach the temple of Jupiter driving a wagon would rule the land. King Gordius dedicated his wagon to the god and tied it to a temple beam with a knot of cornel bark so baffling that another oracle declared that the man who untied it would become lord of all Asia. Enter Alexander the Great, whose hopes lie in that direction. "Well then it is thus I perform the task," says the Conqueror, drawing his sword, and he simply cuts the knot in two. The whole tale is improbable, scholars say, although Gordium, ancient Phrygia's capital, had been named for Gordius, the father of King Midas. But a *Gordian knot* remains an intricate problem and *to cut the Gordian knot* still means "to solve a baffling problem by a single bold and incisive act."

cut the mustard. (*See* **can't cut the mustard.**)

to cut the painter. A painter is the rope by which a ship's boat can be tied to the vessel, a buoy, or a dock, and the word ultimately derives from the Latin *pendere*, "to hang." Thus *to cut the painter*, a phrase much used in the 19th century, came to mean "to sever all connection with something."

cutting up; cut a Dido. To *cut a Dido*, or play a prank, though an almost obsolete expression, may be the origin of the more common phrase *cutting up*. The original cutup could be Dido, the legendary princess who founded and became Queen of Carthage. The daughter of a Tyrian king, Dido married her uncle and upon his murder by her brother Pygmalion sailed to the African coast with his treasure. There she purchased land from a native chieftain, with the provision that all the ground she could cover with an oxhide would be hers. She then cut the hide into thin strips long enough to enclose a space that became the fort of Carthage. In a later myth, Virgil's *Aeneid*, Dido is the lover of Aeneas and commits suicide upon her own funeral pyre when he abandons her at the

command of Jupiter. It's a shame to spoil a good story, but the legend of Dido probably arose because the fortress protecting Carthage was named *Bozra*. *Bozra* meant "hill city" in Phoenician but "oxhide" in Greek, and most likely the tale was fabricated by some ancient Greek seeking to explain a fort named Oxhide.

cut to the quick. The *quick* (*q.v.*) in this sense is the most sensitive or tender flesh in the body, such as the flesh under the fingernails. The word derives from the Anglo-Saxon *cwicu*, "alive or living," as do the adverb and adjective *quick*. *Cut to the quick* means to cut through the skin to sensitive, tender living tissue and, figuratively, to hurt someone deeply. It has been used both ways (by Shakespeare, Dryden, Swift, De Foe) since the early 16th century, sometimes in the form of *galled, touched,* or *stung to the quick*. Other instances of *quick* used in the sense of "living" are the biblical phrase the *quick and the dead* ("the living and the dead"), the phrase *quick with child* ("pregnant with living child") and *quicksilver* (*q.v.*)

to cut up (or split) the melon. This means to divide the spoils or profits of any kind, each person getting a slice of the tasty melon, or profits. Surprisingly, it is a relatively recent term, dating back only to 1906 or so, when it arose as Wall Street jargon for the distribution of extra, unexpected dividends to stockholders.

cyclamen; sowbread. Here is a plant named for the shape of its bulbous roots, *cyclamen* deriving from the Greek *kyklos*, "circle." *Sowbread*, the plant's common name, referred to the fact that its fleshy roots were once fed to pigs.

cyclone. In December 1789 great storm waves claimed 20,000 lives in Coringa, India. Writing about the disaster 49 years later, British East India company official Henry Piddington coined the word *cyclone* for such a storm. Piddington thought he was using the Greek word for "the coil of a snake" in his coinage, "this expressing sufficiently the tendency to circular motion in these meteors," but he actually used the Greek for "circle," or "moving in a wide, whirling manner."

cynic. Disciples of the Greek philosopher Antisthenes (born ca. 440 B.C.), especially his later followers such as Diogenes, were nicknamed *kunikos* (*cynikos*), "doglike" or "snarlers," for their insolent, currish manners. Antisthenes and his pupils believed that independent virtue formed the sole basis for happiness, scorning freedom, honor, art, learning, health, riches—life itself. Insolently self-righteous, this small but influential band of ascetics derided all social customs, even sleeping in kennel-like quarters. From their churlishness and rude manners we probably have our word *cynic*, meaning "a surly, sarcastic person who believes that only selfishness motivates human behavior." It is possible, however, that this nickname is only a coincidence and that *cynic* derives from *Cynosarges* ("white dog"), the Greek gymnasium outside Athens where Antisthenes taught; or perhaps each word contributed to the other. (The gymnasium was supposedly named for a white dog that carried off part of a victim being offered to the gods.)

Cyprus. *Cyprus* was an important source for copper in ancient times, so much so that the country takes its name from the Greek word for copper.

Cyrano de Bergerac. The most famous proboscis in history. Anyone with a prodigious nose is likely to be called a *Cyrano de Bergerac* after the eponymous hero of Edmond Rostand's play of the same name (1897). Rostand's hero was based on the very real Savinien Cyrano de Bergerac (1619-55), who had a nose as long as his fictional counterpart's and whose exploits were even more remarkable. The historical Cyrano was a brave soldier, great lover, and eloquent, influential writer of comedies and tragedies. This swaggering swordsman fought countless duels with those foolish enough to insult or even mention his nose, and his duel single-handedly against one hundred enemies while serving as an officer in the Guards is a well-documented fact. Cyrano's exploits became legend long before Rostand fictionalized him. Surprisingly, he did not perish on the wrong end of a sword. Cyrano died as a result of a wound caused by a falling beam or stone while staying at the home of a friend.

czar; tsar; tsarina; etc. When Julius Caesar died, his proper name was adopted by the Roman emperors, beginning with Augustus, and retained until the fall of the Holy Roman Empire. The title later came to be adopted by various European countries with minor changes in spelling. *Czar* or *tsar* can be traced to the old Slavic word *cesare*, deriving from "Caesar" and introduced into Russia in the 15th century as a title. The word, first spelled *tsear*, was applied to all Russian rulers after Ivan the Terrible assumed it officially to describe his rule as king of Poland. The Russian *tsar* was considered to be appointed by God as head of church and state, his authority unlimited by laws of any kind; his wife was called the *tsarina*, his son the *tsarevitch*, and his daughter the *tsarevna*. Today *czar* is often used for "any tyrannical despot with absolute power," a *czarist* being anyone who believes in such a system of government. Spelling of the word varies in both British and American dictionaries—neither form is accepted by all authorities in either country.

D

D. The letter *D* can be traced back to the ancient Phoenician and Hebrew alphabets where it also had the shape of a rude archway or door (in Hebrew it is called *daleth*, "a door"). (*See* **delta**.)

d for pence. Why is the British written abbreviation for pence or pennies *d* and for the pound L? The abbreviations actually go back to Roman times in Britain when the Latin *denarius*, "penny," was shortened to *d* and *libra*, "pound," was shortened to *l*.

damn Yankee. (*See* **peddler**.)

dachshund. This low to the ground sausage-shaped dog dates back at least to the early Egyptians, but it took its name from the German *Dachs*, "badger," plus *Hund*, "hound," "badger hound." The breed was originally used in Germany for hunting badgers.

Daedal, Daedalist. (*See* **labyrinth**.)

daffodil. No one knows why people began to call the flower *asphodel*, which carpeted Elysium, an *affodill*, in the 15th century. But the mispronunciation stuck and eventually *affodill* was corrupted further to *daffodil*, which remains the flower's name today. The best explanation, according to the *O.E.D.*, is that the change was "due to childish or playful distortions, as in *Ted* for *Edward* or *tante* for *aunt* . . ." *Daffodil* and *narcissus*, though there are differences between them, are often used interchangeably for *daffodil*. The *narcissus* takes its name from the mythological youth who was so enamored of his own reflection that after long gazing at it he was changed into the flower. The "dainty daffodil," the "lamp of beauty," is perhaps English lyric poetry's favorite flower next to roses and rosebuds, from Herrick's "Fair daffodils, we weep to see/You haste away so soon"; to Wordsworth's host "of golden daffodils;/Beside the lake, beneath the trees,/Fluttering and dancing in the breeze . . ./ Continuous as the stars that shine . . ./ Tossing their heads in sprightly dance . . ." (*See also* **narcissus**.)

dago; wop; guinea. *Dago* is an offensive word that may derive from the name of a saint. *Mencken* traces this disparaging term to 1832, when it was used in Louisiana to describe a Spaniard, not an Italian. But *dago* is a corruption of the very common Spanish name *Diego*, or alludes to St. Diego, Spain's patron saint, or both. *Diego* was used in Elizabethan times for a "swarthy" Spanish or Portuguese seaman. As recently as the beginning of this century the word also meant the Italian language, as well as a professor or student of Italian. The pejorative term is not heard as often today as its derivative, *dago red*, "any cheap wine." *Dago* may also come from "day come, day go," a term reputedly used by early Italian laborers in expressing their patient philosophy. Far more offensive is *wop*, which arose toward the end of the last century. This ugly word comes from a relatively innocuous one, the Neapolitan *guappo*, a term used by immigrant laborers signifying a showy, pretentious person. Similarly, the offensive *guinea* may have originally referred to Italian laborers working for the equivalent of a guinea a day.

daguerreotype. (*See* **diorama**.)

dahlia. Over 14,000 named varieties of *dahlias* have been cultivated and crossed from the single plant that the German naturalist, Baron Alexander von Humboldt, discovered in Mexico in 1789. Sent to Spain in that year, the specimen was named there by the head of Madrid's Botanic Garden, Professor Cavanilles. But Cavanilles named the plant for a fellow professor, ignoring Humboldt. Thus the entire *Dahlia* genus honors Swedish botanist and pupil of Linnaeus Anders Dahl (1751-89), who had died at about the time the flower was discovered. The first single-flowered *dahlia* bore little resemblance to the giant, colorful, double-flowered species so important in gardens today. There was, incidentally, a time in the 19th century when *dahlia* roots were touted as an excellent substitute for potatoes. They were easy to grow and unsusceptible to blight, said their advocates, but unfortunately no one seemed to like the way they tasted.

daily bread. The essentials, the food or money needed in order to live. The common term is from the Lord's Prayer (Matt. 6:9): ". . . Give us this day our daily bread."

daisy; fresh as a daisy. *Daisy* still sounds like the Old English word for the flower, "day's eye" or "eye of the day." *Bellis perennis* was so named in allusion to both its appearance and because it closes its ray in the evening to conceal the flower's yellow disk, opening it again in the morning. *Fresh as a daisy* is first recorded in Captain Frederick Marryat's *Peter Simple* (1833) but there is no telling if he coined the popular phrase.

Dallia blackfish. A tasty fish named in honor of William Healey Dall (1845-1927), an authority on marine life for the Smithsonian Institution. Dall wrote one of the first books on Alaska's immense resources, and the edible blackfish of Alaska called the *Dallia*, a species of the genus *Dalliidae*, does honor to his pioneer work in the territory.

dalmatian. The spotted coach dog and fire dog of the past originated in Dalmatia on what is now Yugoslavia's Adriatic Sea coast.

daltonism. So determined was British scientist John Dalton (1766-1844) to solve the mystery of color blindness that he willed his eyes for study after his death. His pioneering paper, "Extraordinary Facts Relating to the Vision of Colours" (1794), is the earliest account of the problem, based on observations of himself, his brother, and other similarly afflicted persons. As a result of his descriptions, *daltonism* became a synonym for color blindness, especially the inability to distinguish between the colors red and green. One of the great pioneers in science, the industrious Dalton also kept a meteorological diary in which he entered 200,000 observations over fifty-seven years. This diary both resulted in a remarkable book on weather conditions (*Meteorological Observations and Essays*, 1793) and contained the germs of his atomic theory, Dalton's major scientific contribution and the basis of modern chemistry.

dam. *Dam* for the female of a horse, sheep or other animals is simply a shortening of the word *dame*. It is first recorded in 1330.

Dame Partington. English politician and author Sydney Smith alluded to the legendary *Dame Partington* in an 1831 speech condemning the opposition of the House of Lords to reform measures. Dame Partington had tried to mop up the Atlantic Ocean, which was flooding her cottage in Devon. Thanks to Smith, her name became synonymous for "anyone futilely trying to hold back progress or natural forces."

Damien's bed of steel. "Such was the end," wrote an eyewitness, "of that poor unfortunate who it may well be believed—suffered the greatest tortures that a human being has ever been called on to endure." He was referring to the public execution of Robert François Damien (1715-57), the madman who tried to assassinate France's Louis XV and inflicted a slight knife wound on the monarch. Early that morning Damien had been racked and wounded deeply with glowing forceps, his torturers pouring molten lead, boiling oil, pitch, and sulphur into his open wounds. His screams never ceased and the stench pervaded the entire court, but many of the thousands who turned out to witness the "spectacle" applauded the prisoner's agonies. Damien's limbs were finally ripped off one by one in the Place de Greve, the man suffering longer because four wild horses couldn't

pull him apart and two more had to found. Until nine o'clock at night the pathetic creature stayed alive, and it is said that his black hair turned completely white, that his rump still twitched up until the moment what was left of him was burned at the stake. *Damien's bed of steel* has become a symbol for the barbaric, sadistic cruelty he suffered.

damn with faint praise. Alexander Pope invented this phrase when satirizing the scholar and author Joseph Addison as Atticus in 1723. The full paradox is seldom quoted anymore but Pope wrote that "Atticus" would:

Damn with faint praise, assent with civil leer,
And, without sneering, teach the rest to sneer.

Damn Yankee. (*See peddler.*)

Damon and Pythias (Phinotias). Two ancient Greeks of the early fourth century whose names became proverbial for devoted friends. In the Greek version of the legend, Phinotias (Pythias) was condemned to death by the tyrant Dionysus. Damon offered himself as a hostage so that his friend could make a last visit home. True to his word, Phinotias returned, but Damon insisted that his own head be put on the block, so impressing the monarch that he freed both the philosophers and begged to be allowed to join their brotherhood. The phrase should therefore be Phinotias and Damon, but when Richard Edwards wrote his play *Damon and Pythias* in 1564, he turned the tale around, using the corruption *Pythias* instead of *Phinotias*, and it was from this source that the story became popular.

Damson plum. (*See plum.*)

dandelion. *Lion's tooth*—referring to the plant's indented leaf—was the old English name for this flower, but some language snob gave it the French name *dent de lion*, meaning exactly the same, in the 16th century. Since the French *dent de* was pronounced "dan de," the word soon became *dandelion*.

dander. (*See get one's dander up.*)

Daniel Boone. "A good gun, a good horse, and a good wife," in that order, were the ingredients for Daniel Boone's prescription for happiness. The American pioneer's name has long been synonymous with a frontiersman, an intrepid explorer or hunter, and a resourceful backwoodsman. Boone's accomplishments have been exaggerated in popular accounts, but there is no doubt that his explorations opened the way for millions. Born near Reading, Pennsylvania, the great folk hero moved to North Carolina with his Quaker family in his early years. After serving under British General Braddock as a wagoner, he explored Florida, and fought as a lieutenant colonel of militia during the American Revolution, among many other activities. But his major contribution was the blazing of the famous Wilderness Road, which he and a band of thirty men forged in March, 1775, to found Boonesboro on the Kentucky River. Daniel and his wife, Rebecca, figure in more frontier lore than any other pioneers, and he has been commemorated in numerous place names. Boone was eighty-six when he died in 1820, a legend in his own time.

danse macabre.   (*See* **macabre**.)

darbies.   *Darbies* is a British expression for handcuffs, but the word, oddly enough, derives from the name of a usurer. It seems that a shrewd 16th-century lawyer and moneylender named Derby drew up an ironclad bond that left no loopholes for debtors to escape through. This contract, used extensively by usurers, came to be called *father Derbie's bands*. Because they were also impossible to "unlock" it wasn't long before all manacles were known as *derbies*, too, the word often pronounced *darbies*. *Darbies* is first recorded in 1576, and no other plausible explanation has been offered for its derivation.

Darby and Joan.

> Old Darby, with Joan by his side,
>   You're often regarded with wonder:
> He's dropsical, she is sore-eyed,
>   Yet they're never happy asunder.

This verse was printed in the *Gentleman's Magazine* in 1735 under the title of "The Joys of Love Never Forgot: a song." The ballad, whose anonymous author may have been poet Henry Woodfall, praises, in a number of stanzas, *Darby* and *Joan* whose names have come to stand for any mutually affectionate and contented old married couple. The poet, if he did write the verse, probably patterned his pair on John and Joan Darby who lived in Bartholomew Close, London. Woodfall had served an apprenticeship under John Darby, the printer, who, with his wife, was widely known for his good works and faithfulness.

the dark and bloody ground.   (*See* **Kentucky**.)

dark horse.   A wonderful story is told about a swift, coal-black horse named Dusky Pete who belonged to Tennessean Sam Flyn. Sam made an easy living riding his horse from town to town and entering him in local races, which Dusty Pete, who looked like a lame plug, always won handily, Sam collecting his bets and going on to his next conquest. But the story is fable as far as scholars are concerned. *Dark horse* was first recorded in England, not America, in about 1830. Benjamin Disraeli used it in his *The Young Duke* (1831) as a racing term indicating more than the color of the horse: "A dark horse, which had

never been thought of, rushed past the grand stand in sweeping triumph." Given Disraeli's widespread popularity as a novelist and public figure, it wasn't very long before the term was introduced in American politics to describe a candidate about whom little is known or who wins unexpectedly. The Democratic Convention of 1844 produced the first political *dark horse* in James Polk, who went on to become president, and the term was in wide use by 1865.

dark meat; white meat.   These were originally American euphemisms for the leg and the breast, respectively, of turkey and other fowl, *leg* and *breast* being embarrassing words in Victorian times. The words are still frequently used, but descriptively now and not euphemistically.

Darley Arabian.   (*See* **Byerly Turk**.)

Darlingtonia.   When an insect enters the pitcher-shaped leaves of the curious California pitcher plant, *Darlingtonia*, it is trapped by down-pointing hairs, which allow it to crawl in but not out. Then it is drowned in liquid from the leaves, and, according to some scientists, ultimately is eaten or digested by the plant. Not a particularly wholesome thing to have named after one, but the single specie's scientific name honors William Darlington (1782-1863), an American botanist who wrote several biographies of famous botanists and published *American Weeds and Useful Plants* (1859). The naming was done by a fellow botanist, John Torrey, there being no record of bad feelings between the two men. *Darlingtonia* is sometimes sold as *Chrysamphora californica* and is not the only insectivorous plant. These include the famous Venus's flytrap, bladderwort, sundew, butterwort, and pitcher plants belonging to the genus *Sarracenia*, all varying in the ways they capture their prey.

darn.   *Darnation* is recorded as a euphemism for *damnation* as early as 1798, with *darn* recorded not long after. Some early scholars held that *darn* derived from *derne*, the Middle English word for secret, while others claimed it was an aphetic form of *eternal*, with the *er* pronounced as in the British *clerk* (*clark*).

d'Artagnan.   Memoirs attributed to Charles de Batz-Castelmore d'Artagnan (ca. 1623-73) were used by the novelist Alexander Dumas père in his fictional series beginning with *The Three Musketeers*. In real life Gascon d'Artagnan did serve in the king's musketeers, but he wasn't a *comte*, as he called himself, claiming the title without right. About all that can be verified about the man is that he captained the contingent that arrested the powerful French superintendent of finances Nicolas Fouquet in 1661, became a brigadier general nine years later, and was fatally wounded at the siege of Maastricht. Yet d'Artagnan will always be remembered for the heroic adventures Dumas and his collaborator Maquet adapted or created from his story.

darts. *Dart* for a pointed missile or spear is first recorded in 1314, deriving from the French *dart* meaning the same. The indoor game called *darts*, in which small darts are thrown at a target, isn't recorded in England until 1901, though this game, so popular in British pubs, must be much older.

Darwinian. "A hairy quadruped, furnished with a tail and pointed ears, probably arboreal in habits." So Charles Robert Darwin (1809-82) described our common ancestor in *The Descent of Man* (1871), which didn't sound at all like Adam or Eve. The epochal theory of evolution was formulated by Darwin in his *On the Origin of the Species by Means of Natural Selection* (1859), *The Descent of Man*, and other works. Evidence gathered during a five-year cruise to South America and the Galapagos Islands as a naturalist aboard the *Beagle* (1831-36) enabled Darwin to confirm organic evolution, and to propose his theory of natural selection, which he explained twenty years later. Darwin deduced that all species descended from a few primal ancestors and that favorable variations within a species better enabled it to survive—*the survival of the fittest*, as Herbert Spencer called the process. Special development and natural selection, he explained, not special creations, accounted for the diversity of species on earth. The Darwinian theory is widely known and accepted today, but provoked a storm of controversy in the 19th century in both religious and scientific circles.

date. Date palms were introduced from the Mediterranean area to America by Spanish missionaries in the early 1700s. The fruit of this palm takes its name from the Latin *dactylus*, "finger," people in ancient times finding that it resembled the human finger.

davenport. In American a *davenport* generally means a large, often convertible sofa, while in England it is a small desk or escritoire. The British meaning came first and nobody is sure where the word derives from. *Webster's* attributes it to its original 19th-century manufacturer, another source to "a Captain Davenport who first commissioned it," and a third to "some now forgotten craftsman." The word, for a desk, was first recorded in 1853 and most likely honors an English furniture maker of ca. 1820-40. The sofa may have been devised by another manufacturer of the same name.

David and Goliath. *See* **Goliath**.)

Davis Cup. While still an undergraduate at Harvard in 1900, American statesman and sportsman Dwight Filley

Davis (1879-1945) donated a silver cup to be presented as a national trophy to that country winning an international championship contest in lawn tennis. The cup still bears his name.

Davisdom. (*See* **Lincolndom**.)

davit. Since the 14th century *davit* has meant a crane-like device used for supporting, raising, and lowering boats and anchors from a ship. Formerly called a *David*, the device is thought to take its name from the proper name David. Several tools at the time were called *Davids* and they may or may not have been named for a specific person or persons.

Davite. (*See* **Davy lamp**.)

davy; I'll take my davy of it. In England *davy* has been used for *affidavit* since at least 1764, which gives us the common extension *I'll take my davy of it*: I'll vouch that it's true.

Davy Crockett. David (Davy) Crockett, as the song goes, was "a son of the wild frontier" from his earliest years. Born in 1786 in Limestone, Tennessee, Davy was hired out to a passing cattle driver by his Irish immigrant father when only twelve; he wandered the frontier until he turned fifteen, before finally returning home. He became a colonel in the Tennessee militia under Andrew Jackson during the Creek War, and after serving as a justice of the peace and state legislator, acted on a humorous suggestion that he run for Congress in 1827. Much to his surprise, he won the election. Crockett served two terms in Congress, and was noted in Washington for his backwoods dress and shrewd native humor, though many of the comments often attributed to him are largely apocryphal. His motto was "Be sure you are right, then go ahead." When defeated for reelection in 1835—mainly because he opposed Jacksonian banking and Indian policies—he moved to Texas, where he joined the Texas war for independence from Mexico. On March 6, 1836, Colonel Crockett was killed with the defenders of the Alamo. The folk hero's famous autobiography, *A Narrative of the Life of David Crockett of the State of Tennessee* (1834), was probably dictated, but is written in his robust style, complete with many examples of the tall tale.

Davy Jones's locker. Since at least 1750 *gone to Davy Jones's locker* has been used by sailors to indicate death, especially death by drowning, but no one has yet fathomed the origins of the phrase. In *The Adventures of Peregrine Pickle* (1751) Tobias Smollett wrote: ". . . I'll be damned if it was not Davy Jones himself. I know him by his saucer eyes, his three rows of teeth and tail, and the blue smoke that came out of his nostrils . . . This same

Davy Jones, according to mythology of sailors is the fiend that presides over all the evil spirits of the deep, and is often seen in various shapes, perching among the rigging on the eve of hurricanes, ship wrecks, and other disasters to which seafaring life is exposed, warning the devoted wretch of death and woe." The original Davy Jones may have been the 16th century owner of an English pub, commemorated in the ballad "Jones Ale is Newe," who stored his ale in a mysterious locker for some reason much feared by seamen. Or *Jones* could be a corruption of Jonah, the unlucky biblical character swallowed by a whale, and *Davy* the Anglicization of the West Indian word *duppy*, meaning "a malevolent ghost or devil." A third, more plausible explanation proposes the Jonah above for *Jones*, but derives *Davy* from St. David, the partron saint of Wales often invoked by Welsh sailors. Jonah was indeed considered bad luck to the sailors aboard the vessel on which he was attempting to flee God's wrath. And the phrase was first recorded in Captain Francis Grosse's *Classical Dictionary of the Vulgar Tongue* (1785) as *David Jones' Locker*, which lends still more support to the Welsh patron saint theory. And the *locker* in the phrase probably refers to an ordinary seaman's chest, not the old pub owner's mysterious locker.

Davy lamp; Davy Medal; davite. Sir Humphry Davy, who "abominated gravy" (see **clerihew**), invented the *Davy lamp* and has the mineral ore *davite* named in his honor. The great English chemist (1778-1829) invented the safety lamp for miners in 1816; largely outmoded today, it is a flame enclosed in a fine-meshed wire cage that prevents high heat from escaping and has saved thousands of lives that would have been lost due to the igniting of explosive gases. Like Madame Curie, the largely self-educated genius refused to take out a patent for his discovery. Among his myriad scientific achievements were his electrical theory of chemical affinity, said to be one hundred years before its time; the discovery of the anesthetic effect of "laughing gas"; the isolation of the alkali metals potassium and sodium; the isolation of calcium, barium, strontium, magnesium, and boron; and the discovery that chlorine is an element. Davy was presented with an expensive silver dinner service by grateful coal mine owners for his invention of the Davy lamp. In his will he decreed that it be melted down and sold, interest from the proceeds to be used to establish the *Davy Medal* of the Royal Society, "given annually for the most important discovery in chemistry made in Europe or Anglo-America."

daymare. On first coming across the word, you might think it a recent coinage by some whimsical writer tuned into the times. But *daymare*, patterned after *nightmare* (*q.v.*) and referring to a similar condition occurring during wakefulness, goes back to at least the early 18th century. It was probably invented by English author

Matthew Green in his poem "The Spleen" (1737), which praised the contemplative life as a cure for boredom:

The daymare Spleen,
by whose false pleas
Men prove suicides in ease . . .

Coleridge confessed that he had *daymares*, an English medical writer called *daymares* "attacks of imperfect catalepsy," and James Russell Lowell implored:

Help me to tame these wild day-mares
That sudden on me unawares.

day of infamy. "Yesterday, December 7, 1941, a date which will live in world history, the United States was simultaneously and deliberately attacked by naval and air forces of the Empire of Japan." So began the first draft of Franklin Delano Roosevelt's historic Pearl Harbor speech, which he wrote himself. In the second draft FDR substituted the infinitely better "infamy" for "world history," and "suddenly" for "simultaneously," making a sentence that will live in world history.

D-day. Many explanations have been given for the meaning of *D-day*, June 6, 1944, the day the Allies invaded Normandy from England during World War II. The Army has said that it is "simply an alliteration, as in H-hour." Others say the first *D* in the word also stands for "day," the term a code designation. The French maintain the *D* means "disembarkation," still others say "debarkation," and the more poetic insist *D-day* is short for "day of decision." When someone wrote to General Eisenhower in 1964 asking for an explanation, his executive assistant Brigadier General Robert Schultz answered: "General Eisenhower asked me to respond to your letter. Be advised that any amphibious operation has a 'departed date'; therefore, the shortened term 'D-day' is used." I like Ike.

dead as a dodo; dodo. The hapless dodo left behind as its epitaph both its common name, which has become a synonym for stupidity and extinction, and its scientific name *Didus ineptus*, which says about the same for it. Barely a century after it was discovered by man on the islands of Reunion and Mauritius, east of Madagascar, the heavy, flightless bird became extinct. Dodoes were not only big (larger than a swan), but they were barely able to run, and the colonists who settled the islands, along with their pigs, found them delicious. By the early 18th century the short-winged bird that seemed "to have been invented for the sole purpose of becoming extinct" was gone, leaving behind only its sad story and a synonym for something utterly extinct or a hopelessly dumb person. *Dodo* is a corruption of the Portuguese *dondo*, silly.

dead as a doornail. Since ordinary nails aren't used in making doors, perhaps the "nail" in this phrase, which can be traced all the way back to 1350, was a small metal plate nailed on a door that visitors pounded with the knockers attached to it when announcing their arrival. Life would eventually be pounded out of the "nail" in that way. Then again the "nail" could be the heavy-handed decorative nails outer doors were studded with, though why these doornails would be regarded as any "deader" than, say, coffin nails is a mystery. It has even been suggested that since nails weren't ordinarily used for doors, the phrase means "dead as something that never existed." Anyway, people are still getting good mileage out of the expression, as did Langland in *Piers Plowman*, Shakespeare more than once, and Dickens in *À Christmas Carol*. *Dumb as a doornail* and *deaf as a doornail* are variations on the phrase that appeared after its coining.

deadbeat.   Though *deadbeat* meant an exhausted, almost dead person at the beginning of the 19th century, by about 1863 it had become American slang for "a hobo or sponger riding the rails." The idea of hobos not paying their way, riding trains free, inspired the present prevailing use of *deadbeat* for "someone who doesn't pay his debts."

dead cat on the line.   Field workers for the *Dictionary of American Regional English* found twenty-one people who used this expression, meaning "there's something suspicious, something wrong"— but not one of them could explain it. When William Safire asked readers of his nationally syndicated word column for help, an old man in Louisiana scrawled a letter explaining that the expression has its roots in fishing for catfish, when trotlines with many hooks on them are set in the water. The lines are checked every day, so if a fisherman checks a neighbor's line and *there's a dead catfish* (cat) *on the line* he knows there's something wrong, something suspicious or fishy is going on.

deadhead.   A spectator who doesn't pay at the theater or at sports events, or one who rides free in a train or other public conveyance. Formed from the noun *deadhead*, the verb *to deadhead* means to drive an empty train, truck, or the like, one with no passengers or freight, on a return trip to a terminal. First recorded as American slang in 1843, most authorities agree that the term derives from railroad use. Conductors on passenger trains possibly counted heads to be sure every passenger had paid and deducted from their total passengers, or heads, those who had free passes—the first *deadheads*. The gardening term to *deadhead*, to pull off spent blooms, is unrelated to the above; in this case the dead blooms are the dead "heads."

deadlock; wedlock.   Though it wasn't applied to stalemates at political conventions until 1888 in America, *deadlock* was first used as a term for a complete standstill in Richard Sheridan's play *The Critic* (1779), which also gave us the word *puffery* (q.v.). *Deadlock*, for "a springless lock that opens with a key" came later. The *O.E.D.* suggests that the expression simply employs the word *dead* in its sense of obsolete, complete. Others have offered, without proof, the theory that *deadlock* comes from the ancient sport of wrestling, where a *deadlock* hold is one that keeps an opponent immobile indefinitely without forcing him to submit. *Holy deadlock* as a term for marriage comes from the title of A. P. Herbert's novel *Holy Deadlock* (1934), but the idea is anticipated by Byron's "A wedlock and a padlock mean the same." The *lock* in *wedlock*, however, is not a lock, deriving instead from *lac*, "a gift."

The deadly nevergreen.   *The deadly nevergreen* has been a humorous term for the gallows in England since the late 18th century, because the gallows bears no leaves but "bears fruit all the year round."

deadman's hand.   James Butler "Wild Bill" Hickok, only 39, had come to Deadwood, Dakota Territory, in 1876 to make a stake for the bride he had just taken, but lawless elements, fearing his appointment as town marshall, hired gunman Jack McCall to assassinate him, giving McCall three hundred dollars and all the cheap whiskey he needed for courage. Wild Bill was playing cards in the No. 10 saloon (his back to the open door for only the second time in his days of gunfighting) when McCall sneaked in and shot him in the back of the head, the bullet passing through his brain and striking the cardplayer across the table from him in the arm. Hickok's last hand, which he held tight in a death grip, was aces and eights, which has ever since been called the *deadman's hand*. McCall, freed by a packed miner's court, was later convicted by a federal court, his plea of "double jeopardy" disregarded on the ground that the miner's court had no jurisdiction. He was later hanged for his crime.

dead men.   There is nothing new about this term for "empty beer or liquor bottles," which originated well before 1700, not in World War I, as has been suggested. It referred to the empty pots or bottles on the tables of English taverns when drinking bouts were held. Swift used the expression in his *Polite Conversations* (1738) and may give a clue to the word's origin: "Let him carry off the dead Men [the empty bottles], as we say in the army." In the Army, where life is cheap, it would be appropriate to call bottles without any spirits *dead men*, after the spiritless bodies of the battlefield. In fact, the term is sometimes *dead marines* and *dead soldiers* today, these phrases dating back to World War I. *Dead soldiers* and *dead men* are also applied to empty beer cans, canned beer having been introduced by Coors in 1935.

deadpan.   *Pan* has been used since at least the early 19th century to mean "the face," possibly because the face is "broad, shallow and often open," as *Webster's* suggests, but just as likely because *pan* meant "the skull or head" as far back as the early 14th century and was used by Chaucer, among many much-read writers. (The word is still used in *brainpan*.) *Deadpan*, a contemporary expression for an expressionless poker face, especially applied to comedians with a dry delivery, is just a combination of *pan* with *dead*, "unanimated." It has nothing to do with Elizabeth Barrett Browning's poem about the "great dead Pan," the god of Greek mythology who, legend says, died when Christ was crucified.

dead ringer. (*See* **ringer.**)

Dead Sea. The *Dead Sea*, actually a salt lake in Palestine, is 51 miles long and 11 miles wide, falls to a depth of about 1,300 feet and is 26 percent salt, as opposed to about 3 or 4 percent in most oceans. Because its limpid blue-green water supports practically no life, the Romans named it the *Mare Mortum*, or *Dead Sea*.

Dead Sea fruit. In days past the apple of Sodom was thought to grow along the Dead Sea, the mythical fruit beautiful to behold but turning to ashes when touched. From this belief arose the expression *Dead Sea fruit* for something promising that turns out to be worthless, the phrase first recorded in 1868 as the title of a novel but probably older.

Deadwood Dick. *Deadwood Dick* became proverbial through many late 19th-century dime novels, especially those written by Edward L. Wheeler, and long stood for a fearless Indian scout and outlaw fighter. The prototype for Wheeler's westerns was Richard W. Clarke (1845-1930), who had been nicknamed *Deadwood Dick* long before his fictional exploits. Clarke, an Englishman attracted to the Black Hills by the gold diggings, won fame as both an Indian fighter and an express guard for gold shipped from the mines in and around Deadwood, South Dakota. Many of the *Deadwood Dick* myths have been debunked, but he was certainly a real character. Clarke lies in a mountain grave near Deadwood.

deaf as an adder. The ancients believed that a serpent could protect itself against the music of snake charmers by holding one ear against the ground and sticking its tail in the other ear. This belief led to the expression *deaf as an adder*, first recorded in the biblical book of Psalms.

deaf ear. (*See* **to turn a deaf ear.**)

dealing from the bottom of the deck; deal me out. Both of these expressions passed into general use from the American poker tables of the early 19th century. *Dealing from the bottom of the deck*, like a crooked gambler, means to take unfair or illegal advantage of someone, while *deal me out*, meaning "I don't want to play this hand," or "I don't want to participate this time," or, as Sam Goldwyn reputedly said, "Include me out."

dear. In times past a "dear of corn" meant a scarcity of corn, for *dear* is related to the word *dearth* meaning "scarcity" and was once used as its synonym. Over the years *dear* came to mean expensive because something scarce, if needed, is bid for competitively until its price rises.

Dear John letter. No one has identified the original jilted John, if there was one, but this term for a letter to a soldier saying that his wife or sweetheart is leaving him for another dates back to World War II. It is often abbreviated to a *Dear John* and can be used for a similar letter to any man distant from the woman writing it. (*See* **that's all she wrote.**)

dear me! This is among the most interesting of interjections, which usually haven't much of a story behind them. *Dear me!* is thought to derive from the Italian *Dio me salvi!*—"God save, or spare, me!"

death and taxes. (*See* **snug as a bug in a rug.**)

deathwatch beetle. When the little beetle *Anobium tesellatum* clicked or tapped, according to an old superstition, death would come to someone in the house. The beetle was therefore named the *deathwatch*. The sound of the *deathwatch* is really the beetle's mating call, which it makes by raising itself on its hind legs and beating its head rapidly against wood.

debauch. To *debauch* someone was originally to entice him away from duty or the service of his master. According to one theory, corrupt friends persuaded workers in small French shops known as *bauches* to go off on sprees, that is, enticed them from the *bauche*, or *debauched* them. The word passed into English in the early 16th century as *debauch*, coming to mean any excessive indulgence in sensual pleasure.

Debrett's Peerage. Another guide to the British aristocracy, *Debrett's Peerage* was published in 1802 as a peerage of England, Scotland, and Ireland, making it the first compilation of its kind. Its publisher, John Debrett, who died twenty years later, also published a *Baronetage of England* (1808). In England *to be in Debrett* means "to be of noble birth." (*See also* **Burke's Peerage**, a term more familiar to Americans.)

debt. *Debt* actually derives from the French *dette*, meaning the same, and should rightly be spelt without a *b*. However, clerical scholars in medieval times assumed that the word derived from the Latin *debita* and changed the spelling accordingly, saddling future generations with their learned error.

debunk. Meaning to strip of false or exaggerated claims, *debunk* was coined from the word *bunk* (*q.v.*) by American novelist William Woodward (1874-1950), who, indeed, wrote a lot of debunking books and introduced *debunk* in one of them entitled *Bunk*.

debut. *Debut*, from the French *début* and meaning "from the mark," was originally a gaming term in French signifying the opening move in a game, similar to the English "your move" in chess, or "your play" in cards. From the old gambling term came the French verb *debuter*, "to lead off in a game," which in time was extended into "to make one's first appearance," this last being the word's only meaning ever since *debut* was first recorded in one of Lord Chesterfield's letters in 1752.

December. (*See* **September.**)

decibel. "Watson, come here; I want you." These were the undramatic words spoken by inventor Alexander Graham Bell to his lab assistant on March 10, 1876, the first complete sentence conveyed over the telephone. Bell was a Scottish immigrant who in 1871 came to the United States, where he lectured to teachers of the deaf on his father's visible speech method and opened his own school of vocal physiology in Boston. In the course of work on his harmonic telegraph, he invented the first practical telephone, an idea he had conceived as early as 1865. Later inventions included the first practical phonograph record, the audiometer, and a telephonic probe for locating bullets in the human body. The Bell Telephone Company was formed in July, 1877. The inventor died in 1922, aged seventy-five. *Bel*, a unit of measuring the loudness of electrical signals, and *decibel*, one tenth of a *bel*, both honor his name.

deciduous; evergreen. Trees that keep their leaves all year long are called *evergreen*, while those that lose their leaves in fall are called *deciduous*. *Evergreen* is of course self-explanatory, while deciduous derives from the Latin *deciduus*, "falling down."

to decimate. After any mutiny in the Roman army, or any cowardice, the standard punishment was to take one man by lot out of each of the ten-man squads and have his fellow squad members kill him. From this disciplinary measure came the word *decimare* (from the Latin *decem*, ten, meaning "to kill one in ten") that became the English *decimate*. *Decimate* strictly means to reduce a military force by one-tenth, but through careless usage has come to mean to destroy a large part of any population, even to obliterate it.

to deep-six. *Deep-six* is an old nautical term meaning "to drown," the *six* meaning "six fathoms down." It has recently taken on the meaning of "to kill a person or thing," as in "we're going to *deep-six* that project."

defenestration. Here is a nonce word that lasted. On May 21, 1618 three Catholic members of the Bohemian National Council were thrown out of a window of the castle of Prague by Protestant insurgents. Though the Catholic members landed in the moat and weren't badly injured, this incident marked the beginning of the Thirty Years War that spread throughout Europe. The incident became known as the *defenestration of Prague*, the word *defenestration* coined to describe it from the Latin *de*, "from," and *fenestra*, "window." *Defenestration* has since meant "the act of throwing a person out of a window."

deipnosophist. Anyone seeking a big word meaning "a master of the art of dining" need look no further. The word derives from an early work entitled *Deipnosophistai*, which might be best translated as *Gastronomes at Dinner*, written by the Greek writer Athenaios of Naucratis in about A.D. 200. *Deipnosophist*, first recorded in 1656, is formed from the Greek *deipnon*, "dinner," plus *sophistes*, "learned person." The word is first recorded in the late 15th century.

defalcate. *Defalcate* may have originally been a gardening term, deriving as it does from the Latin *de*, "off," and *falx*, "sickle." Translating as "to cut off with a sickle," the word's meaning was extended to "take away," especially in the sense of taking away or embezzling money.

Delaware. *Mencken* points out that the map of this country is "besprinkled with place names from at least half a hundred languages, living and dead." Of the eight classes he lists as their sources, "surnames" comes first. *Delaware* falls into this category, being the first alphabetically of American states that take their names from the names of individuals. The Diamond State commemorates English soldier Thomas West, Baron De la Warr (1577-1618), who in 1609 was appointed the first governor of Virginia by the Virginia company. *Delaware Bay* was named for Lord De La Warr by Sir Samuel Argall, who discovered it when the governor sent him on an expedition to locate supplies for the starving settlers at Jamestown; both *Delaware* and the *Delaware Indians* derive their names from this body of water. De la Warr had been appointed governor of Virginia for life, but died on his second trip from England to the colony and was buried at sea.

Delilah. A *Delilah*, from the name of the biblical courtesan, signifies both a temptress and a seductive wife or mistress who turns to treachery. Delilah in the biblical story (Judges 16:4-20) had been bribed by the Philistines to learn the source of Samson's strength. Samson lied to her three times, but on her fourth attempt she learned that his power lay in his long hair, had his head shaved while he slept upon her knees, and betrayed him to his enemies. Little is told of Delilah except that she was a "woman in the valley of Sorek." After she collects "eleven hundred pieces of silver" for her tonsorial treachery, she is heard from no more.

delirium.   In Latin *lera* means the ridge left by ploughing, so the verb *de-lerare* means to make an irregular ridge when ploughing. A *delirus* was one who couldn't make a straight furrow when ploughing and thus came to mean "a crazy, disoriented person whose mind wandered from the matter at hand." The state of such a person was called *delirium*, which is still our word for the condition today. (*See also* **prevarication**.)

delta.   The Greek letter for *D* (*q.v.*), *delta* was drawn in the form of a triangle: △. *Delta* was thus applied to the area of the mouths of the Nile, which was of a triangular shape. It has since been applied to similar formations of other rivers. The Mississippi Delta, by the way, is not, strictly speaking, a delta. Far from the sea, it is simply a flood plain.

dem bums.   This nickname for the Brooklyn Dodgers, beloved of memory, was given to them by an irate fan seated behind home plate at a home game in Ebbets Field during the Great Depression. Particularly incensed at one error he shouted, "Ya bum, ya, yez bums, yez!" and his words, reported by a baseball writer, stuck as an endearing nickname for the team. It was in 1900 that the team was named the *Dodgers*, after all Brooklynites, who were called *trolley dodgers* by Manhattanites, contemptuous of all the trolleys in the borough. (*See* **the Dodgers**.)

demijohn.   The shape of a portly lady is suggested by the *demijohn*, which is narrow at the neck and round in the body. For this reason some etymologists trace the word, first recorded in 1769, to the French *Dame Jeanne*, "Lady Jane," theorizing that the large glass bottle was named for some forgotten French housewife whose bulging figure it resembled, or for such portly women in general. The theory that *demijohn* is a corruption of *Damaghan*, a Persian town where glassware was manufactured, is not generally accepted. A demijohn generally hold five gallons and is usually encased in wickerwork. (*See also* **bellarmine**.)

democracy.   (*See* **encyclopedia**.)

demoralize.   The great American lexicographer Noah Webster claimed to have coined only one word—*demoralize*, in a pamphlet he wrote in about 1793. But *demoralize* was not pure invention, Webster taking it from a word of the French Revolution, *démoraliser*, a coinage the conservative French Academy condemned but finally admitted to the language in 1798.

Demosthenic.   There are legends that the great Greek orator Demosthenes was a stammerer, that he could not pronounce the letter *p*, that he overcame his impediment by practicing with pebbles in his mouth against the sound of the surf, or by declaiming as he ran uphill. According to still another tradition, Demosthenes also mastered language by copying Thucydides' direct and graphic *History of the Peloponnesian War* eight times. Whatever the truth of these stories—and there is little doubt that Demosthenes did have some speech defect as a boy—the Greek statesman ranks as the greatest orator of all time, surpassing even Cicero, who patterned himself on the Athenian. Demosthenes (ca. 383-322 B.C.) is particularly noted for his denunciations of Philip of Macedonia (See **philippics**), which roused his countrymen to the danger of the subjugation of Greece. The word *Demosthenic* refers to his oratory and also means eloquent, patriotic speech, for his two most constant themes were the greatness of Athens and the need to preserve her traditions.

den of thieves.   *Den* is recorded as "the lair or habitation of a wild beast" at least as far back as *Beowulf*, written sometime in the tenth century. By the 18th century the word began to be used for a secret hiding place of thieves or the like, Daniel Defoe first recording the expression *den of thieves* in *Robinson Crusoe* (1719).

dénouement.   The resolution of a play or any literary work following its climax is called a *dénouement*. The word came into English intact as the French *dénouement*, meaning "untying of the knot," being first recorded by Lord Chesterfield in one of his letters.

deodand.   *Deodand* itself derives from the Latin *Deodandum*, something "given to God." Under the law of *deodand* any automobile that hit and killed a pedestrian would be sold and the proceeds given to the church. This custom was abolished in England in 1846, but previously any personal chattel—such as a bull that killed a man—was forfeited by the owner and sold for some pious purpose. It was reasoned that, as a person meeting such an accidental death had died without extreme unction, the money could be used to pay for masses for him.

department store.   The term *department store* isn't recorded until 1887, when a New York establishment advertised itself as H.H. Heyn's Department Store, though the idea of separate departments in stores can be found in print at least forty years earlier, when an article in *Hunt's Merchandising Magazine* told of "tubes connecting with each department of a store, from the garret to the cellar, so that if a person in a department . . . wishes to communicate with the employer, he can do so without leaving his station."

dephlogisticated air. (*See* **phlogiston**.)

derby. *Derby* is the American name for a version of the dome-shaped, felt hat that the English call a bowler. The man it honors also has the *English Derby* at Epsom Downs and the *Kentucky Derby* at Churchill Downs named for him. The twelfth early of Derby, Edward Stanley (d. 1834), came from a family that traced its origins to William the Conqueror. He had a great interest in horse racing but little in his wife—a mutual feeling—and so devoted most of his time to the improvement of the breed. Races had long been held at Epsom Downs, but in 1780 the earl started a series of annual contests for three-year-olds, the races named in his honor both because he suggested them and was such a convivial host each season at The Oaks, a house near the course that had belonged to this uncle General "Johnny" Burgoyne. The *Derby* became so popular that almost a century later, in 1875, the *Kentucky Derby* adopted part of its name. After the Civil War, American spectators at the "blue Ribbon of the Turf" noticed that English sportsmen often wore odd-shaped bowler hats. A few were brought back home, where it is said that a Connecticut manufacturer made a stiff felt, narrow-brimmed version that an unknown New York store clerk sold as "hats like the English wear at the Derby." In any event, the *derby* became not only the American term for bowler, but the most popular headwear for men up until the 1920s.

derelict. Deriving from the Latin *derilictus*, "to forsake wholly, abandon," *derelict* at first meant any piece of property abandoned by its owner, being first recorded in 1649. Within ten years, however, the word was applied to abandoned ships and it came to be used mainly in this sense over the years.

der Führer. (*See* **Führer**.)

derrick. The large crane for lifting heavy objects that we call the *derrick* takes its name from English executioner Godfrey Derrick. Derrick was responsible for some 3,000 hangings and beheadings in his long career as public executioner, which extended into the reign of James I. His name was most likely applied to the gallows itself and then to the crane which resembled the gallows, though the comparison might have been made between his and the crane's great strength or huge stature. Ironically, Derrick, a convicted rapist, had been pardoned by Robert Devereux, Earl of Essex, his commander in a military expedition, when he agreed to become executioner at the infamous Tyburn Prison just outside London. The young

and handsome Essex, long a favorite of Queen Elizabeth, was later condemned for treason and sentenced to be executed at Tyburn in 1601. By an odd twist of fate, Derrick became his executioner, though as a headsman, for even then nobles were exempt from hanging. (*See* **dick; dirk**.)

derringer. This is the small but deadly large-bored gun that in real life has been the choice of a large variety of villains, including assassin John Wilkes Booth. The pistol is named for Philadelphia gunsmith Henry Deringer, who invented it in 1835. Posterity cheated Deringer a bit, though, for the stubby gun came to be spelled with a double *r*.

despot. The original Greek *despotes*, the source of *despot*, simply means "master," not a tyrannical master or ruler. But over the centuries the title was bestowed upon many kings, emperors, and bishops who were tyrannical, and by the time of the French Revolution the word came to mean an absolute, tyrannical ruler.

despotism by dynamite. (*See* **absolutism tempered by assassination**.)

dessert. The French word *servir* means to serve a meal, while *desservir* means to clear away or remove the dishes from the table. Because *dessert* is served after the table is cleared, it takes its name from the French *desservir*. The word is first recorded in English in 1600.

desultory. Circus riders in ancient Rome jumped from one horse to another during their acts, which led to their being called *desultors*, or leapers, from the Latin *salire*, "to leap." They were soon compared to people who fitfully jump from one idea to another in conversation, which resulted in the word *desultorious*, "to be inconsistent, aside from the point," the ancestor of our English word *desultory*.

deuce. *Deuce* for "the devil" may have its origin in the hairy demon of Celtic mythology called the Dus. Other suggestions are the Old German *deurse*, "a giant," the Latin expletive *Deus!*, "My god!," or the two, or deuce, which is an unlucky throw (snake eyes) in a dice game. Congreve first recorded the expression *the deuce take me!*, in 1694. *Deuce* for the number "two" comes from the Latin *duos*, two.

deus ex machina. Some unlikely event that extricates one from a difficult situation, usually in a play or other work of fiction, is called a *deus ex machina*, which literally means "a god (let down upon the stage) from a machine." In ancient Greek drama a god was often lowered onto the stage by a pulley system to help the hero out of trouble, this practice giving rise to the expression. Euripides used the device widely, while Sophocles and Aeschylus avoided it—as almost all writers avoid it today. Much later Bertolt Brecht parodied the practice at the end of *The Threepenny Opera* when Mack the Knife is saved from hanging by Queen Victoria's proclamation.

devil.   *Devil* has a more complicated history than the old story that it is a contraction of "do-evil." It is a translation of the Hebrew "Satan" in the Old Testament, where it meant "adversary." When the Old Testament was translated into Greek, its translators chose the word *diabolos* to convey the meaning of "adversary," *diabalos* coming from the Greek verb *diaballian* "to slander or accuse." *Diabolos* thus meant "accuser," and the devil, whose name derives from *diabolos* via the Old English *deofol* is "the slanderer or accuser of the soul."

the devil dances in his pocket.   Someone who is broke, penniless. This early 15th to 19th century expression derives from an old belief that the cross on ancient coins prevented the devil from entering one's pockets.

devil dogs.   The Germans in Word War I called the U.S. Marines of the 4th Brigade *Teufelhunden*, or *devil dogs*, because they were such fierce fighters. The name stuck as a nickname for marines. So did the marine slogan *Retreat, hell!*, a shortening of the reply Marine Captain Lloyd Williams gave a Frenchman when asked to fall back at the Battle of Belleau Wood: *Retreat, hell! We just got here!*

devil's advocate.   Deriving from the Latin *Advocatus Diaboli*, the *devil's advocate* was first an official appointed by the Roman Catholic Church, his job to argue the case against a person's canonization, or recognition as a holy person. From this the term came to mean anyone who argues against an idea to test it.

devil's darning needle.   Thoreau and other New Englanders called the dragonfly the *devil's darning needle* and *devil's needle* because of its big eerie eyes, which are far out of proportion to its long, needlelike body. But the two colorful expressions yielded to the shorter *darning needle* over the years. Another colorful Americanism was *devil's riding horse* for the praying mantis. It was also called the *devil's horse, cheval du diable, devil's mare, devil's rear horse,* and *devil's war-horse*.

Devil's Island.   *Devil's Island*, the former French penal colony off the coast of French Guiana, isn't so named because it was like hell for prisoners sent there, or because the climate was as hot as hell. The island, one of the three Safety Islands, takes its name from the dangerous turbulent waters surrounding it, the major reason why escape from it was so difficult.

the devil's picture book.   A colorful, little-known term for "playing cards" that was used by the Puritans, who

considered it sinful to play cards or even have a deck of cards in the house. In fact, it wasn't until the mid-19th century that playing cards were deemed permissible in devout New England homes. Long before this, however, 16th-century clergymen issued playing cards bearing scriptural passages and Cardinal Mazarin taught France's Sun King history, geography, and other subjects by printing instructive text on "educational" playing cards. We take our 52-card deck from the French, but there is a 56-card deck (Italian), a 32-card deck (German) and many others around the world. Playing cards are called *pasteboards* because they were made of pasteboard for centuries, the paste making them opaque so that they couldn't be seen through. It was only after 1850 that designs on the backs of cards were used, for early gamblers had felt that plain white backs couldn't be so easily marked as decorative ones.

devil to pay.   (*See* **between the devil and the deep blue sea.**)

Dewar flask.   The *Dewar flask*, the original thermos bottle, is named for its inventor, Sir James Dewar (1842-1923), a Scottish chemist and physicist who devised the vacuum-jacketed vessel in 1892 for the storage of liquid gases at low temperatures. The *thermos* takes its name from the company that adapted Dewar's invention commercially. Originally a trademark, the word is now spelled without a capital in most dictionaries.

dewberry.   *Dewberries*, which are trailing blackberries similar to boysenberries, are a native American fruit, although they are cultivated today by gardeners in other parts of the world. Not that there aren't native European varieties of dewberries as well. In Europe the dewberry can be traced back to the 16th century, when Shakespeare praised it. Its name, in fact, may be a corruption of "dove berry," which it has been called for centuries in Germany, but it has long been associated with "dew" in English usage.

Dewey Decimal system.   The father of American library science, Melvil Dewey (1851-1931), first proposed his famous *Dewey Decimal system* in 1876 while serving as acting librarian at Amherst College. It is now used by some 85 percent of all libraries. The classification scheme, invented when he was in his early twenties, divides the entire field of knowledge into nine main classes (from 000 to 999), a second set of numbers following a decimal point indicating the special subject of a book within its main class. A man of fantastic energy and originality, Dewey later became chief librarian at Columbia College (1883-88), where he founded, in 1887, the first American school of library science. As director of the New York State Library (1889-1906), he reorganized the state library, making it one of the most efficient in the nation, and originated the system of traveling libraries. Dewey also helped found the American Library Association, the New York State Association, and the *Library Journal*. He crusaded for simplified spelling and use of the metric system, among many other causes.

dewitt. To *dewitt*, or brutally lynch, is chiefly a historical expression today. The brothers DeWitt—Jan (b. 1625) and Cornelius (b. 1623)—were Dutch statesmen opposed to the war policies of their monarch when the French invaded the Netherlands in 1672. Jan DeWitt, King William III's major opponent and a wise, eloquent statesman, was arrested that same year and tortured in the Gevangenpoort at The Hague. When his brother Cornelius came to visit him in jail, an incensed chauvinistic (*q.v.*) mob gathered and broke into the prison, hacking the two men to pieces and hanging their limbs and parts on lampposts. For many years after, *to dewitt* meant to perform such grisly lynchings or mob murders, one of the few such verbs in English deriving from someone's name.

dewlap. The lap, or fold, of skin hanging loosely from the throat of certain dogs, cattle, and other animals, including humans, may be so named because someone humorously observed that such folds "brushed the dew of the grass." However, no one is sure about the origins of this old word, which is first recorded early in the 14th century.

dextrous. (*See* **right**.)

D4D. (*See* **K-9 Corps**.)

dharna. This Indian word means "persistence." Those practicing *dharna* in India have in fact been known to seek justice by sitting at the door of someone who owes them money, and fasting to death.

dialect. *Dialect* is first recorded in 1577, deriving from the Latin *dialectus*, "way of speaking," and is defined as "one of the varieties of a language arising from local peculiarities of vocabulary, pronunciation and idiom." It is often forgotten that dialects sometimes become languages. Italian, Spanish, Portuguese, French, and Rumanian, for example, began life as regional dialects of Latin.

Diana's tree. This is not a plant but an amalgam of crystallized silver obtained from mercury in a solution of silver. It is so called because to alchemists silver was represented by Diana, the Roman nature goddess. The substance is also known as *philosopher's tree*.

diaper. Baby's *diaper* has no relation to the town of Ypres in France, as has been suggested. The word probably comes from the French *diapre*, "a white cloth vari-

egated with flowers," which, in turn, derives from the Greek *dia*, "through," and *aspros*, "white" or "white in places." First used to mean such a cloth in 1350, *diaper* wasn't used for a baby's "clout" or napkin until the 19th century. In fact, in Britain the term has never been applied in this way.

dick; dirk. *Partridge* suggests that *dick*, as a common slang synonym for penis, comes indirectly from the English hangman Godfrey Derrick's (see *derrick*) name. It seems that among the dreaded hangman's victims were many sneak thieves and picklocks, who often carried short daggers. These came to be called *dirks* after Derrick (which is a Dutch name identified with Dirk). The dagger called the *dirk* then gave its name, in the form of *dick*, to the penis.

dickens. The expression *what the dickens* has nothing to do with author Charles Dickens's name, as is often believed, the *dickens* in this case probably being an old euphemism for *devil*.

dicker. Deriving from *decem*, "ten," *decuria* was the Latin word for the bundle of ten animal hides that Caesar's legions made a unit of trade in Britain and elsewhere, this word eventually corrupted to *dicker*. On the frontier in America the haggling and petty bargaining over *dickers* of pelts became the meaning of the word itself.

Dick test. Like the more famous Curies (*q.v.*), Drs. George Frederick and Gladys H. Dick form a famous husband and wife scientific team. In 1923 they isolated the streptococcus that causes scarlet fever. The following year the Dicks devised the test used to determine an individual's susceptibility to the disease and developed a serum providing immunity. In the *Dick test* scarlet fever toxins are injected into the arm; if the individual is not immune, the skin reddens around the injection. George Frederick Dick (b. 1881) was professor of clinical medicine at Rush Memorial College when he and his wife made their discoveries. He served as chairman of the department of medicine at the University of Chicago Medical School from 1933 to 1945.

to die for the want of lobster sauce. Vatel, the chef of the French Prince de Condé, is said to have killed himself because the lobsters (or fish) he needed for a sauce he was preparing for Louis XIV didn't arrive on time. Thus, *to die for the want of lobster sauce* is said of someone who suffers greatly because of some small disappointment.

diehard. The British won the battle of Albuera on May 16, 1811, and although the battle is generally considered a strategic mistake it provided the éspirit de corps that aided Wellington in future battles against Napoleon's superior forces. The victory was due in large part to the heroic action of the famous British 57th Foot commanded by Colonel William Inglis. His regiment, part of a thin line of 1,800 redcoats, occupied an important strategic position in the small Spanish village and had been pinned down by deadly French fire. "Die hard, fifty-seventh, die hard!" Inglis cried out from where he lay wounded. His men responded. Of 579 troops, 438 were killed or wounded and the regiment passed into legend as the *Die Hards*. Later their nickname was used to describe ultraconservative political groups or individuals refusing to change with the times, many of them far less honorable than the 57th.

to die like a dog.   (*See* **dog's life.**)

Diervilla.   (*See* **Weigela.**)

diesel.   German mechanical engineer Dr. Rudolph Diesel developed the heavy-duty internal combustion engine bearing his name from 1892-97 at the Krupp factory in Essen and spent the rest of his life perfecting it and manufacturing *diesel engines* at a factory he founded in Augsburg. Today it is employed in locomotives, ships, generators, cars, trucks, submarines, and much heavy equipment. Diesel became rich and famous as a result of his invention, yet he may have ended a suicide in 1913, when he was only fifty-five. It is possible that he fell overboard while crossing the English Channel on a mail steamer on the night of September 30, but his hat and overcoat were found by the rail, suggesting tht he had jumped.

dig.   *Dig*, for "to understand," is first recorded in about 1935, which is not to say that it couldn't have been in use much earlier. No one knows how the Americanism came to be, but there are two contending theories: (1) the Celtic *twig*, "to understand," is the word's ancestor, and (2) the West African *degu* yielded *dig*. *Dig* for an insulting remark, a *dirty dig*, goes back to the turn of the century and may derive from the *dig* meaning a poke or jab.

digger.   (*See* **Aussie.**)

digging one's grave with a knife and fork.   This humorous expression for gluttony was first recorded in England during the late 19th century and is still occasionally heard there and in America these weight-conscious days.

digit.   Roman numerals first represented human fingers, so the numbers one to nine were called *digitis* after the Latin *digitus*, "finger."

digitalis.   The flower *digitalis*, long known as a heart stimulant, is so named because a human finger, or *digit*, fits snugly into one of its deep-throated bells.

dildo.   Several derivations have been suggested for this instrument of sexual pleasure, which the French call a *consolateur*: 1) a corruption of the Italian *deletto*, "delight"; 2) a corruption of the English *diddle*; 3) the cylindrical *dildo* tree or bush, which grows ten feet or so straight up. The *O.E.D.* says only that the word is of obscure origin and offers an earlier date (1610) for its use for a phallus than its use for a plant.

dilly.   In its meaning of "some outstanding thing or person," *dilly* is first recorded in the early 1930s. But it was used as an adjective in America before then and probably has a long history, deriving either from the 17th-century English *dilling*, "darling," or from the first four letters of *delightful*.

dime.   *Dymes*—the word's origin from the Latin *decema*, "a tenth part"—were originally the tithe, or tenth, of one's income paid as a tax to the church by temporal rulers. Chaucer so used the word in 1362 and it was not employed in its present sense—for a U.S. coin representing one-tenth of a dollar—until 1786.

dimity.   This durable cotton cloth woven with raised patterns isn't so named after Damietta, Egypt, as is often claimed. It takes its name from the Greek *di-mitos*, "double-thread."

dine.   Meaning to eat, possibly to eat well or to eat "seriously" (not to eat a sandwich, for example), *to dine* originally meant "to eat dinner, the principal meal of the day." In this respect the word is a contradiction, deriving as it does from the Latin *disjunare*, "to breakfast, to eat the *first* meal of the day."

dine with Duke Humphrey.   It was popularly believed in days of yore that Humphrey, Duke of Gloucester (1391-1447), a man noted for his hospitality, was buried in London's old St. Paul's Cathedral. For many years after his death those poor who remained in the cathedral during dinner hours, or those debtors afraid to leave the sanctuary for fear of imprisonment, were said to be *dining with Duke Humphrey*. Although the good duke had actually been buried at St. Albans, the expression *to dine with Duke Humphrey* remained linked with St. Paul's and came to mean to go without any dinner at all. It is now solely a literary expression, often found in the novels of Dickens and other great English authors.

dingbat; dingus, etc.   *Dingbat*, a favorite expression of Archie Bunker's, is American in origin, going back to at least 1861, when it meant "anything that can be thrown with force or dashed violently at another object," according to Farmer's *Americanisms* (1899). The word possibly derives from *bat*, "a piece of wood or metal," and *ding*, "to throw." But *dingbat* came to be used in describing anything of which the proper name is unknown to or forgotten by a speaker, much as we more frequently use such meaningless words as *thingamabob* (an extension of the word *thing* that goes back to the late 17th century), *thingamajig, dingus, doohickey, whatsit,* and other infixes. A father describing how to assemble a complicated piece of equipment, such as a child's toy, might say: "You put this *thingamajig* into this *doohickey* and tighten this *doodad* and this *thingamabob*; then you take this *dingus* over here near this *gismo* and attach it to this *hickeymadoodle* so that it barely touches the *thingamadoodle* there near the *whatchamacallit*—then you have to grease it up with this *jeesalamsylborax* or the damn *dingbat* won't work!" *Dingbat* has also served over the years as a slang term for "a gadget, money, buns or biscuits, a woman, and a hobo or bum." But Archie Bunker's contemptuous use of the word for a "nut," an ineffectual, bumbling fool (that is, anyone he doesn't agree with), may come directly from the Australian *dingbats,* meaning "eccentric or mad."

dinghy. Small boats carried on larger vessels take the name *dinghy* from the Hindi *dingi,* "little boat." In the late 18th century British mariners noticed small native rowboats called *dingis* in Indian waters and brought the word for the boat home with them, changing its spelling a bit.

dinosaur. In 1841 zoologist Sir Richard Owen gave the name *dinosaur* to these huge creatures reconstructed from fossilized bones, fashioning the word from the Greek *dinosauria,* "terrible or fearful lizard." The creatures would have more appropriately been named *dino-crocodilia,* as they are more closely related to crocodiles than to lizards.

Diogenes; Diogenes crab; Diogenes cup; Diogenic. He is said to have walked the streets of Athens with a lantern in broad daylight searching for an honest man, thus expressing his contempt for his generation. His home was a narrow, open earthenware tub or barrel that he trundled about with him. On seeing a child drinking from cupped hands, he threw away his only worldly possession, a wooden bowl. On being asked by Alexander the Great if the emperor could oblige him in any way, he replied, "Yes, by standing out of my sunshine." More lore surrounds Diogenes of Sinope (c. 412-322 B.C.), a relatively minor philosopher, than many a more deserving thinker. Diogenes the Cynic held that the virtuous life was the simple life and advocated a return to such ways; self-control, the lack of all pleasure, and even pain and hunger, he considered essential to achieving goodness. The Greeks nicknamed him "dog" for what they considered his shameful ways (*see* **cynic**), but Diogenes considered himself a governor of men; in fact, he once told pirates who had captured him that he would like to be sold to a

man who needed a master. Diogenes died on the same day as Alexander the Great, who had said, admiringly, "If I were not Alexander, I would be Diogenes." Today a *Diogenes* or a *diogenic* person is a cynical, churlish, but independent one, while a West Indian hermit crab bears the philosopher's name because it lives in empty shells reminiscent of his tub.

diorama; photography. Invented in 1822 by Louis Daguerre (1787-1851), who later invented the *daguerreotype,* the first permanent photographic process that really worked, the *diorama* is a scene, often in miniature, reproduced in three dimensions. The French inventor probably patterned the word on *panorama,* which comes from the Greek *(h)orama,* view. The word *photography* was coined from Daguerre's *photo*genic drawing process plus his helio*graphic* system.

Dioscorea. While many genera and species of flowers and fruits are named for people, the yam is the only major vegetable, excluding vegetable varieties, to take even its scientific name from a real person. The yam's botanical name is *Dioscorea Batatas*; the genus, containing many species, was named by Linnaeus for Pedanius Dioscorides, or, more correctly, Dioscurides, a 1st-century physician and an early father of botany. A surgeon in Nero's Roman army, Dioscorides gathered information about 600 medicinal plants and other remedies of the period, which he recorded in his *De Materia Medica,* translated in 1934 as the *Greek Herbal of Dioscorides.* Dioscorides' work remained standard for centuries and he is considered to be the first man to establish medical botany as an applied science. *Dioscorea Batatas,* the yam, is often incorrectly called a sweet potato, to which it is no relation, despite the similarity in appearance and taste.

diploma; diplomat; diplomacy. *Diplomas* were originally official documents that were folded in two and sealed, taking their name from the Greek *diploma,* "a letter folded double." Though mainly a document given to graduates today, they were at first government documents and the government officials who carried these *diplomas* were called *diplomats.* English statesman Edmund Burke apparently coined *diplomacy* from *diplomat* in 1796 while writing about international relations: "The only excuse for all our mendicant diplomacy is . . . that it has been founded on absolute necessity."

dirge. In medieval times the memorial song at funeral services for the dead was based upon the eighth verse of the fifth Psalm, which in English is "Guide, O Lord, my God, my way in Thy sight." The song was sung in Latin, however, where the line is *"Dirige, Domine, Deus meus, in conspectu tuo viam meam."* The first word of the song in Latin was heard so often through the years that it became, slightly altered, *dirge,* the name of such a funeral song.

dirty dig. (See **dig**.)

dirty dog. (See **to go to the dogs**.)

dirty dozens. (See **the dozens**.)

discount. The French practiced discounting as early as 1500, calling the practice *déscompte* because it first involved "selling by the count" rather than knocking down prices. For example, a buyer was charged for only nine items when buying ten, the tenth item set aside from the count and given to him free—a practice that would better be called the premium technique. By the time *déscompte* spread to England in the early 17th century, however, its name transformed to *discounting*, it meant the reduction in price that discounting is today.

discretion is the better part of valor. Shakespeare probably coined this old saw, in *Henry IV, Part I*. But what he wrote exactly was "The better part of valor is discretion."

dish. The round flat quoit that the Romans called the *discus* probably gives us the word *dish* for "a plate." Apparently, German soldiers jokingly called their mess tins *diskaz*, after the *discus* and *diskaz* passed into English as *dish*. *Dish* is not an Americanism for "a pretty or sexy girl," as many slang dictionaries claim. Shakespeare called Cleopatra Antony's *dish* in *Antony and Cleopatra* (1606), when Enobarbus remarked of Antony: "He will to his Egyptian dish again."

distance lends enhancement to the view. (See **few and far between**.)

divan. *Divan* has an involved but logical history. Originating as a Persian word meaning "a brochure," it came to mean, in order: "a collection of poems"; "a register"; "a military pay book"; "an account book"; "a room in which an account book was kept"; "an acccount office or custom house"; "a court"; "a great hall"; and, finally, by 1597, "the chief piece of furniture in a great hall"!

a Dives. Dives is not named in current versions of the Bible, but he is the rich man mentioned in the parable told by Jesus in Luke 16:19-31 and his name has become proverbial for a wealthy, often insensitive person.

÷ (division sign). British mathematician John Pell (1611-85), who taught mathematics at Cambridge and Amsterdam, invented the division sign ÷ that we still use today. (See also **ampersand**.)

Dixie; Dixieland. It sounds incredible, but the first *Dixieland* or *Dixie* may have been in New York City. Some etymologists lean to the following derivation of the word given by the *Charlestown Courier* of June 11, 1885:

"When slavery existed in New York, one Dixie owned a large tract of land on Manhattan Island, and a large number of slaves. The increase of the slaves and of the abolition sentiment caused an emigration of the slaves to more thorough and secure slave sections, and the Negroes who were thus sent off (many being born there) naturally looked back to their old houses, where they had lived in clover, with feelings of regret, as they could not imagine any place like Dixie's. Hence it became synonymous with an ideal location combining ease, comfort, and material happiness of every description." Although no slave "lived in clover," the explanation seems somewhat less doubtful than other theories about Dixie—that it derives from the 18th-century Mason Dixon line, or that the word comes from the French-Creole word *dix*, meaning "ten," which was prominently printed on the back of ten-dollar notes issued by a New Orleans bank before the Civil War.

Dixie cup. The American Water Supply Company's vending machines sold a drink of water in a disposable paper cup for one cent beginning in 1906, the cup possibly called a *Dixie cup* because it was so reliable—like the old ten-dollar bills issued in Louisiana prior to the Civil War (see **Dixie**). In years to come the Dixie cup was frequently applied to ice-cream sold in a small cup as opposed to Popsicles, or ice-cream pops, and cones.

do a Brodie. As a result of his famous leap off the Brooklyn Bridge, Steve Brodie's name became a byword—in the form of to *do (or pull) a Brodie*—for "taking a great chance, even taking a suicidal leap." Brodie made his jump from the Manhattan side of the Brooklyn Bridge on July 23, 1886, to win a $200 barroom bet. Eluding guards on the bridge, the twenty-three-year-old daredevil climbed to the lowest cord and plummeted 135 feet into the water below, where friends were waiting to retrieve him in a rowboat. He was arrested for endangering his life and reprimanded by a judge, but that didn't stop him from making future leaps off other bridges. Some say that Brodie never jumped at all, an unproved theory, and many at the time belittled his claim. It is said that Brodie once angered boxer Jim Corbett's father by predicting that John L. Sullivan would knock his son out. "So you're the fellow who jumped over the Brooklyn Bridge," the elder Corbett said when the two met for the first time. "No, I jumped *off* of it," Brodie corrected him. "Oh," replied Corbett, "I thought you jumped *over* it. Any damn fool can jump off it."

to do a number on. When this voguish slang expression first appeared in the late 1960s, it simply meant "to deceive." It derives, in this sense, from the old vaudeville days, when acts were called *numbers* because they were numbered on theater programs. The meaning evolved from an act to a pretense and then to an outright deception. Recently, however, the meaning has been softened and extended and *to do a number on* often means only "to affect," though still usually in a devious way.

Doberman pinscher. Louis Dobermann, a German breeder of Apolda in Thuringia probably helped develop the ferocious, medium-sized guard dog we know as the *Doberman pinscher*. The *Dobermans* were originally bred from *pinscher* hunting dogs to be used as herders for livestock. About all that is known about the breed is that it was developed by Dobermann in about 1890, its origins before that being a mystery. The short-haired, fearless dog is generally black or rust in color, proud of bearing, and the male stands twenty-four to twenty-seven inches, weighing sixty to seventy-five pounds. *Dobermans* are used extensively by the military and as guards for department stores and other commercial establishments. Their ferocity is fabled, and there are tales of them holding onto a gunman's arm after being shot to death.

Dr. Fell; Fell types.

I do not love thee, Dr. Fell,
The reason why I cannot tell;
But this alone I know full well,
I do not love thee Dr. Fell.

Dr. John Fell's classes at Oxford must have been something to see. The English divine (1625-1686) was quite a permissive teacher for his day, initiating many educational reforms and even allowing classroom debates, which often ended in fistfights. Fell, a dean of Christ Church, Oxford, and bishop of Oxford, is also noted for the *Fell* (printing) *types* he collected for the university press and for the extensive building program he began at the university. Yet his name is used to describe someone disliked for no apparent reason. He owes his unjust fate to Thomas Brown (1663-1704), once his student at Christ Church and later an author and translator. Dean Fell had threatened to expel Brown for some offense if he could not translate a Martial couplet. The resulting jingle above bore little resemblance to the thirty-third epigram, but Dr. Fell, to his credit, good-naturedly accepted the paraphrase. As for Tom Brown, he never wrote anything else that was remembered.

Dr. Jekyll and Mr. Hyde. In Robert Louis Stevenson's novel *The Strange Case of Dr. Jekyll and Mr. Hyde* (1886), Dr. Jekyll, a physician, discovers a drug that creates in him a personality that absorbs all his evil instincts. This personality, which he calls Mr. Hyde, is repulsive in appearance and gradually gains control of him until he finally commits a horrible murder. *Jekyll* can rid himself of *Hyde* only by committing suicide. Stevenson, who wrote the novel in three days locked in his study after he had had a dream about the story, based the main character on an Edinburgh cabinetmaker and deacon named William Brodie (1741-1788), who was a "double being," by day a respected businessman and by night the leader of a gang of burglars. Brodie was finally hanged for his crimes, but Stevenson, who was raised in Edinburgh, knew his story well and in fact wrote a play entitled *Deacon Brodie, or The Double Life* when he was only fifteen. This was the germ of the idea for the later work.

Dr. Livingstone, I Presume! The phrase is still used in a humorous sense, as it was several generations ago. It recalls, of course, the very British greeting of journalist Sir Henry Morton Stanley when after a long, arduous journey—only 700 miles in 236 days—he found the ailing Scottish missionary-explorer David Livingstone on the Island of Ujiji in the heart of Africa. The star reporter had completed one of the greatest manhunts of all time. Deserted by his bearers, plagued by disease and warring tribes, he was probably too tired and overwhelmed to think of anything else to say. Stanley (1841-1904) had been sent to Africa by the *New York Herald* to locate the famous explorer, Livingstone, feared dead or swallowed up by the Dark Continent. Born John Rowlands in Denbigh, Wales, Stanley assumed the name of his adoptive father when he emigrated to America as a youth. He later became a noted explorer in his own right. Dr. Livingstone died, aged sixty, a year after the reporter left him in 1873. His body was shipped back to England and buried in Westminster Abbey.

Dr. My-book. British surgeon Dr. John Abernethy (1764-1831) wrote a number of books on medicine, the best-known of which was *Surgical observations on the constitutional Origin and Treatment of Local Diseases* (1809). Very popular with his patients, he got the name Dr. My-book because like many an author he invariably told his patients, "Read my book," whenever a medical question came up.

Dr. Pangloss. Any incurable optimist is called a *Dr. Pangloss* after the pedantic old tutor of the same name in Voltaire's *Candide, or the Optimist* (1759), which was an attack against Rousseau's philosophy. Dr. Pangloss remained optimistic to the end, despite all his misfortunes, believing "all is for the best in this best of all possible worlds."

doctrinaire. This word for a pedantic theorist is taken from the nickname of Pierre Paul Royer-Collard (1763-1845), whose political party, in turn named the "Doctrinaires" in his honor, made it their business "to preach a doctrine and an orthodoxy." Royer-Collard's party arose in France in 1815 after the second restoration of Louis XVIII. Moderate royalists, he and his colleagues desired a king who would govern liberally, accepting the results of the French Revolution, and were noted for the rigidity of their arguments. Unattuned to political realities, the "Doctrinaires" were destroyed by a reactionary Charles X in 1830. Before being applied as a nickname to Royer-Collard the word had been the popular name for a religious order founded in 1592. Today *doctrinaire* is used contemptuously to describe an inflexible theorist, as distinguished from one who tries to accomplish something within the existing political system.

the Dodgers. The incomparable Brooklyn Dodgers, who became comparable after their move to Los Angeles, were called *the Dodgers* because Manhattanites contemptuously referred to all Brooklynites as "trolly dodgers" at the turn of the century, the bustling borough being famed for its numerous trolleys, especially in the central Borough Hall area. Attempts were made to change the name to the Superbas, the Kings, and the Robins, all to no avail. Some baseball team names just seem to catch on while others don't. The Boston Bees, for example, were named by a distinguished committee of baseball writers from a choice of 1,300 names, but people stubbornly called them the Braves, a name they retained after they moved to Milwaukee. The Cincinnati Reds tried to become known as the Redlegs to avoid identification with communism, but their name remains the Reds. (*See also* **dem bums.**)

dodo. (*See* **dead as a dodo.**)

(he) doesn't know beans. Boston, home of the "bean eaters," "home of the bean and the cod," may be behind the phrase. Walsh, in his *Handbook of Literary Curiousities* (1892), says that the American expression originated as a sly dig at Boston's pretensions to culture, a hint that Bostonians knew that Boston baked beans were good to eat, that they were made from small white "pea beans"—even if Bostonians knew nothing else. It may also be that the American phrase is a negative rendering of the British saying "he knows how many beans make five"—that is, he is no fool, he's well informed—an expression that probably originated in the days when children learned to count by using beans. But *he doesn't know beans*, "he don't know from nothing," possibly has a much simpler origin that either of these theories. It probably refers to the fact that beans are little things of no great worth, as in the expression "not worth a row (or hill) of beans."

dog. First recorded in 1050 but probably born before then, *dog* is an early example of a "native" invented English word not borrowed from any other tongue. Before its introduction, the Teutonic *hund* had been the Old English word for the canine. Then *dog* (*docga*) first appeared in English as the name for a now unknown breed of powerful *hunds*, the word *dog* eventually passing into other Continental languages.

dog days. Mad dogs don't give us this name for the hot, close days of July and August, though perhaps the prevalence of mad dogs at that time of year has kept the phrase *dog days* alive. The expression originated in Roman times as *canicularis dies*, "days of the dog," and was an astronomical expression referring to the dog star Sirius, or possibly Procyon. The Romans linked the rising of the Dog Star, the most brilliant star in the constellation, *Canis Major*, with the sultry summer heat, believing that the star added to the extreme heat of the sun. "Canicular days," of course, have nothing to do with heat from the Dog Star, but the ancient expression remains popular after more than twenty centuries.

doggerel. (*See* **pig latin.**)

dogie. The American cowboy has been shouting "git along little dogie" for more than a century, but no one knows where the word *dogie*, for "a motherless calf," comes from. Maybe it derives from "dough-guts," referring to the bloated bellies of such calves, perhaps dogie is a clipped form of the Spanish *adobe*, ("mud"), possibly the cows were so small that they were playfully called "doggies" and the pronunciation changed. Since some American cowboys were black there is also the possibility that the Bambara *dogo*, "small, short," is the source, or the Afro-Creole *dogi*, meaning the same. Your guess is as good as any etymologist's.

dog latin. (*See* **pig latin.**)

dogmerd. British novelist Anthony Burgess apparently invented this new word a few years ago, employing the English *dog* and the French *merde* (for "excrement"). It is a word more adult than all other euphemisms we have for good old Anglo-Saxon expressions, and yet it conveys the nose-squinching reaction one has to stepping in the stuff. The word *merd* for excrement has of course been used in English for centuries, first recorded in 1477 and employed by Ben Jonson and Richard Burton, among other great writers.

dog rose. The wild, hardy dog rose (*Rosa canina*, called *cynorrodon* by Pliny) is said to have been so named because the Romans thought that eating the flower cured the rabid bites of wild dogs. But then the Romans also believed that shortening a dog's tail was a preventative for rabies, and the Greeks thought that dogs could cure many diseases by licking patients. Today the *dog rose* is more realistically valued for the high vitamin-C content of its "hips."

dog's letter. (*See* **R.**)

dog's life; to go to the dogs; die like a dog; dirty dog. Dogs aren't the prized, often pampered pets in other countries that they are in America. In the East they are often considered pariahs, scavengers of the streets, and the Chinese, Koreans, and Japanese, among other Asians, commonly eat them. Englishmen of earlier times used dogs primarily for hunting and kept them outside or in a rude shelter, not generally as house pets. The dogs were fed table scraps there wasn't any further use for, and these they had to fight over. It didn't seemideal, a dog's life, and Englishmen of the 16th century began to compare anyone who had become impoverished, who was going to utter ruin naturally or morally, to their maltreated canines. *To lead a dog's life* was to be bothered every moment, never to be left in peace; *to go to the dogs* was to become just like the helpless animals; and *to die like a dog* was to come to a miserable, shameful end. There were many other similar phrases that arose before the dogs had their day in England and America, including *throw it to the dogs*, "to throw something away that's worthless"; and of course *a dirty dog*, "a morally reprehensible or filthy person."

dog tags. The metal identification tags worn by soldiers were not dubbed *dog tags* until World War I, when they were so called because they resembled a license tag on a dog's collar. Identification tags became required in the Army in 1906, but men had worn them on their own initiative since the Civil War. Two are worn so that, in the event of death, one can be buried with the body and the other kept as a record. The Army is now experimenting with an embedded microchip dog tag that can hold up to 12,000 characters—an individual's vital medical data and personnel file as well as his service number, blood type, and religion.

dogwatch. The *dogwatch* at sea is the period between 4:00 and 6:00 P.M. (the first dogwatch) or the period between 6:00 and 8:00 P.M. (the second dogwatch). The other watches aboard ship are:

12:00 to 4:00 P.M.—afternoon watch
8:00 to 12:00 P.M.—first night watch
12:00 to 4:00 A.M.—middle watch
4:00 to 8:00 A.M.—morning watch
8:00 to 12:00 A.M.—forenoon watch

The dogwatches are only two hours each, so that the same men aren't always on duty at the same time each afternoon. Some experts say *dogwatch* is a corruption of *dodge watch*, and others associate *dogwatch* with the fitful sleep of sailors called *dog sleep*, because it is a stressful watch. But no one really knows the origin of this term, which was first recorded in 1700.

dogwood tree. John C. Loudon wrote in *The Hardy Trees and Shrubs of Britain* (1838) that the tree "is called Dogwood because a decoction of its leaves was used to wash dogs, to free them from vermin." This may be true,

but no evidence has yet been found to support the theory. The beautiful ornamental (*Cornus florida*) was in early times called the *dogger tree*, the *dogge berie tree*, the *hounder tree* and the *hounde berie tree* as well as the *dogwood*. Another possibility is that it was named the *dogberry tree* because its dark purple berries resembled the berries of another, now unknown tree that was used as a medicine for dogs, and that *dogberry* became *dogwood* in time. No link between the tree's wood and dogs has been found, but the *dog* in *dogwood* may be a corruption of the Old English *dogge*, "skewer," for wood of the European variety was often used for skewering meat. In short, no one really knows why *Cornus florida* is so named.

doily. It is probable that a London linen draper named Doily, Doiley, Doylet, or Doyly sold and perhaps invented the first *doily* napkins. Eustace Budgell, a cousin of British essayist Joseph Addison, uses the first spelling in the January 24, 1712, number of *The Spectator*, noting, "The famous Doily is still fresh in everyone's memory, who raised a Fortune by finding out Materials for such Stuffs as might at once be cheap and genteel . . . [a] frugal method of gratifying our pride . . ."

doing a land-office business. Before the Civil War, the U.S. government established land offices for the allotment of government-owned land in western territories just opened to settlers. These agencies registered applicants, and the rush of citizens lining up on mornings long before the office opened made the expression *doing a land-office business*, "a tremendous amount of business," part of the language by at least 1853. Adding to the queues were prospectors filing mining claims, which were also handled by land offices. After several decades the phrase was applied figuratively to a great business in something other than land, even, in one case I remember, to a land-office business in fish.

doldrums. The *doldrums* has come to mean any area where a ship is likely to be becalmed, especially that area near the equator between the northeast and southeast trade winds. *Doldrums*, first recorded in 1811, probably derives from the words *dull* and *tantrum*, as if the dullness of such an area could drive one to tantrums. The phrase *in the doldrums* means "down in the dumps," much like mariners felt when they weren't moving anywhere.

dollar. The word *dollar* can be traced to the name of a saint. The most likely candidate is St. Joachim, father of the Blessed Virgin, for whom the small mining town Sankt ("Saint") Joachimsthal in Bohemia had been named. It happened that the town and valley, or *thal*, belonged to a vast estate containing a rich silver mine from which one-ounce coins were minted. These silver coins, with a picture of St. Joachim on the face, were at first called *Joachimsthalers* ("of the valley of Joachim"). But the cumbersome name was soon shortened to *thalers*, pronounced *dahlers* in northern German dialect. The name eventually got to England as *daller* and by the end of the 17th century *dollar* was the accepted term applied to any foreign coin, especially Spanish pieces of eight. When the newly formed United States adopted its monetary system in 1785, it completely broke with England and "resolved that the money unit of the U.S.A. be one dollar (Spanish)." The first silver dollars were coined here in 1792, and greenback dollars as we known them were first printed during the Civil War.

dollar-a-year man. Someone who serves the federal government for patriotic rather than financial reasons is called a *dollar-a-year man*. The term came into use during World War I when such volunteers were paid a dollar a year because one dollar was the "valuable consideration" needed to make their contracts binding.

dollar sign—$. $—the dollar sign—probably doesn't derive from the figure "8" on Spanish "pieces of eight," the usual explanation. The dollar sign was most likely modified from the twisted Pillars of Hercules stamped with a scroll around them on the pieces of eight. It may, however, result from a combination of the two symbols, or a corruption of the Spanish *Ps*, the contraction for "peso." Anyway, if George Washington threw a silver dollar across the Potomac or Delaware, it must have been a foreign coin—for, as noted, American silver dollars weren't minted at the time.

dolphin. The *dolphin*, its name derived from the Latin *delphin*, for "the cetaceous mammal," has long been regarded as "man's best finned friend." *Dolphinet* is an old word for a female dolphin. Wrote Spenser: "The Lyon chose his mate, the Turtle Dove Her deare, the Dolphin his own Dolphinet." In recent experiments dolphins have been taught to understand twenty-five words arranged in sentences. (*See* **dorado; parrot; ow ah . . .; chimpanzee.**)

Dom Pérignon. Dom Pierre Pérignon (1638-1715), the man who put the bubbles into champagne and after whom Moet et Chandon named its most famous vintage some years ago, was a blind man who renounced the world when only fifteen and joined the Benedictine order. Cellarmaster of the monastery near Epernay, France, Dom Pérignon eventually found that corks tightly drawn in his bottles would not be forced out, as would rags, and yet would retain naturally expanding gases, allowing for the so-called second fermentation in the bottle that is essential for any true sparkling champagne. Although unproved, the old story certainly rates a toast, if only as an excuse for another glass.

donate. The verb *donate* is a back formation from the noun *donation*. An Americanism recorded as early as

1795, it is firmly established today, but at first met with vociferous opposition, having been placed on William Cullen Bryant's *Index Expurgatorius* and denounced as "a pretentious and magniloquent vulgarism" by a British writer as late as 1935.

Don Juan. Of the names most frequently applied to libertines and lovers—*Casanova, Don Juan, Cyrano, Valentino, Romeo,* and *Lothario*—only the last is completely fictional. *Don Juan,* though immortalized in Byron's incomplete cantos, Mozart's *Don Giovanni,* and the myths and literature of many countries, is supposedly based on the 14th-century Spanish nobleman Don Juan Tenorio. That this original Don Juan had 2,594 mistresses, according to the valet's figures in Mozart's opera, is doubtful if not impossible, but the aristocratic libertine's conquests were legion. His last was the daughter of Seville's commandant. While attempting to ravish young Dona Anna, the legendary lover was surprised by her father, whom he dispatched in a duel. But local Franciscan monks decided that this was one debauchery too many and lured Don Juan to their monastery, where he was killed with his boots on. The monks, to conceal their crime, claimed that he had been carried off to hell by a statue of the commandant on the grounds, and thus the legend of *Don Juan* had its basis in fact.

donkey's years. *Donkey's years* means a very long time. The usual explanation for this expression, which is first recorded in 1916, is that *donkey's years* is a play on donkey's *ears,* which are very long indeed.

Donner Pass; Donner Lake. The scene of one of the most gruesome tragedies in western history is named for the two Donner families who were part of a California-bound wagon train of emigrants that set out across the plains from Illinois in 1846. The Donner party, beset by great hardships, paused to recoup their strength at what is now *Donner Lake* in eastern California's Sierra Nevada mountains, only to be trapped by early snows that October. All passes were blocked deep with snow and every attempt to get out failed. Forty of the eighty-seven members of the party, which included thirty-nine children, starved to death during the winter, and the survivors, driven mad by hunger, resorted to cannibalism before expeditions from the Sacramento Valley rescued them in April. The Donner party's gruesome yet heroic adventures have figured in much native literature. California's Donner State Historic Monument commemorates the event; the *Donner Pass* is traversed by U.S. Highway 40 today.

Do-nothing Congress. (*See* **The Useless Parliament.**)

Donnybrook. Too much flowing *usquebaugh* and too many flailing shillelaghs made the Donnybrook Fair a dangerous place to visit in old Ireland. The two-week-long fair, held in August every year since King John licensed it in 1204, was the scene of so many wild free-for-alls that the town's name became a synonym for any knock-'em-down-drag-'em-out brawl involving a group of people. By 1885 things had gotten so bad that they were too much for even those legendary Irishmen who love a good fight and the fair was finally closed. Donnybrook is now a relatively peaceful suburb about a mile and a half from Dublin.

don't bogart that joint; Bogard. In his films Humphrey Bogart often left cigarettes dangling from his mouth without smoking them. This led to the counterculture expression *Don't bogart that joint*; that is, "don't take so long with, don't hog that stick of, marijuana; smoke and pass it on to the next person." The term became widely used after appearing in a song in the film *Easy Rider*. Among those who practice the long-standing, widespread habit of communally smoking marijuana cigarettes, *bogarting* is considered both selfish and a waste of the expensive weed. Bogart's name, in the form of *Bogard*, also became inner-city slang for "to act tough or in a forceful manner" in the 1950s, deriving from the tough-guy heroes Bogart portrayed.

don't change horses in midstream. The phrase, possibly suggested to Abraham Lincoln by an old Dutch farmer he knew, is recorded almost a quarter of a century before Lincoln said it. But Lincoln immortalized the expression when he accepted his nomination for the presidency in 1864. Waving aside any suggestions that the honor was a personal one, he told the Republicans that he was sure they hadn't decided he was "the greatest or the best man in America, but rather, . . . have concluded it is not best to swap horses while crossing the river, and have further concluded that I am not so poor a horse that they might not make a botch of it in trying to swap." Over the years "the river," which was of course the Civil War, was abbreviated to "midstream" and the saying *don't change horses in midstream* came to mean "don't change leaders in a crisis."

don't count your chickens before they're hatched. Don't count on profits before you have them in hand. "I woulde not have him to counte his chickens so soone before they be hatcht," is the first recorded use of this expression, in 1579. Perhaps the idea behind the words goes all the way back to Aesop's fable of the woman who brings eggs to market, announcing that she will buy a goose with the money she gets for her eggs, that with her profits from the goose she will buy a cow, and so on—but in the excitement of all her anticipations kicks over her basket and breaks her eggs. *Don't count your chickens before they're hatched* is also used as the moral of Aesop's tale "The Milkmaid and Her Pail."

don't give a rap. Counterfeiters took advantage of the scarcity of copper coins in the early 18th century and

began flooding Ireland with bogus halfpence. These worthless coins became known as *raps* and inspired the expression *not worth a rap*, "of no value at all," and *I don't give a rap*, "don't care in the slightest."

don't give holy things to hounds. (*See* **to cast pearls before swine**.)

don't give up the ship. We have all been taught that Captain James Lawrence shouted these immortal words while mortally wounded when the U.S. frigate *Chesapeake* was lowering its flag in surrender to the British off Boston during the War of 1812. Lawrence actually said: "Tell the men to fire faster and not give up the ship; fight her till she sinks." Despite his order, the Americans were defeated.

don't go to the bad for the shadow of an ass. Though little heard today, this expression, meaning "don't fight over foolish things," has a long history. Demosthenes told the story of a young Athenian traveler who rented an ass or donkey. When he took shelter from the sun at midday under the shadow of the beast its owner appeared and claimed the shadow for his own, saying he had rented the ass to the traveler but not its shadow. The two fought and fought over the shadow, then took the matter to the law courts, where both men were ruined because the suit lasted so long.

don't hurrry, Hopkins. A Mr. Hopkins, late of Kentucky, once returned a promissory note to a creditor along with instructions that "The said Hopkins is not to be hurried in paying the above." Since that day in the middle of the last century, it is claimed, said Hopkins has been remembered by the admonition *Don't hurry, Hopkins*, an ironic reproof to deadbeats late in paying their bills or persons slow in anything else. But the phrase was used in England almost a century before with just the opposite humorous meaning, implying "don't be too hasty." In this sense it derived from a Mr. Hopkins, or Hopkin, "that came to jail over night, and was hanged the next morning."

don't know him from Adam. Many have observed that only a fool wouldn't know someone from Adam, since Adam had no navel and wore only a fig leaf. But the old proverb persists. *I wouldn't know him from Adam's off ox* is possibly an attempted improvement on the original expression, *off ox* referring to the yoked ox farthest away from the driver—the one even less familiar than the near ox, and surely less distinguishable than old Adam.

don't look a gift horse in the mouth. The age of a horse can be roughly determined by examining its teeth. That people knew this long before A.D. 400 is witnessed by the appearance of the above expression in the writings of St. Jerome, who called it a familiar proverb at the time. *Don't* *look a gift horse in the mouth*, an injunction to accept presents gracefully without trying to find something wrong with them or determine how much they're worth, is literally reproduced in German, French, and other languages, though its first English use is *don't look a given horse in the mouth*.

don't look back, something might be gaining on you.   Sage advice from baseball great Leroy "Satchel" Paige, who would have been one of the greatest pitchers in the major leagues if the color barrier had been broken earlier. Paige's five additional rules were: 1) avoid fried meats which angry up the blood; 2) if your stomach disputes you, lie down and pacify it with cool thoughts; 3) keep your juices flowing by jangling around gently as you move; 4) go very gently on the vices, such as carrying on in society—the social ramble ain't restful; and 5) avoid running at all times.

don't make two bites of a cherry.   The expression is an old one warning against dividing things too small to be divided, against prolonging for two days jobs that should take only one. It may have some connection with those polite European courtiers three centuries ago who acted so dainty in public that they always took two bites to eat a cherry.

don't stick your neck out.   Chickens, for some reason still known only to chickens, usually stretch out their necks when put on the chopping block, making it all the easier for the butcher to chop their heads off. Probably our expression, a warning to someone not to expose himself to danger or criticism when this can be avoided, which is American slang from the late 19th century, originating from the bloody barnyard image. Lynchings have also been suggested, but lynched men rarely stick their necks out for the noose.

don't take any wooden nickels.   First recorded in about 1915, this expression was originally a warning from friends and relatives to rubes leaving the sticks in the great migration from rural areas to the big cities at the turn of the century. It was a humorous adjuration meaning beware of those city slickers, for no real wooden nickels were ever counterfeited—they would have cost more to make than they'd be worth. Ironically, country boys were the ones who possibly *did* succeed in passing off wooden objects as the real thing. Yankee peddlers as early as 1825 allegedly sold wooden nutmegs, which cost manufacturers a quarter of a cent apiece, mixed in with lots of real nutmegs worth four cents each.

don't wash your dirty linen in public.   Anthony Trollope didn't coin this phrase in *The Last Chronicle of Barset* (1867). What the hardworking novelist did was turn around the old French proverb *Il faut laver son linge sale*

en famille, "One should wash one's dirty linen in private." Both sayings mean the same: don't expose family quarrels or skeletons in public, keep discreditable things within the house where they in all decency belong. The *dirty linen* is considered discreditable to the person who washes it as well as his family and is usually exposed out of anger at a relative.

Doolittle do'd it!   In World War II days Red Skelton's "mean widdle kid" used to say "I do'd it!" on the comic's radio show. A news story borrowed Skelton's words on April 18, 1942, when Lt. Colonel James "Jimmy" Doolittle and his men took off from the carrier *Hornet* and made the first air attack on the Japanese mainland, greatly uplifting American morale in those dark days. *"Doolittle do'd it!"* became a popular catchphrase throughout America.

doornail.   (*See* **dead as a doornail.**)

dope; dopey.   *Dope* for drugs is an Americanism of Dutch origin, deriving from the Dutch *doop*, "sauce or gravy." It is only since the late 1890s that stupid people have been called *dopes*, or *dopey* (like Dopey of *Snow White and the Seven Dwarfs*), as if they were under the influence of dope. The word was first recorded as *doop*, or "gravy," in 1807 by Washington Irving. It then came to mean any preparation containing unknown substances (1872), and then drugs (1895), possibly because these were mysterious unknown substances to most people. How *dope* came to mean information, or knowledge, a usage first recorded in 1901, is anybody's guess. Maybe knowing the *dope*, or "inside information," first alluded to knowing what was inside preparations whose constituents were unknown to most people. Try to dope it out for yourself.

dorado.   The *dorado* (*Coryphaena hippuras*) is for reasons unknown sometimes called the *dolphin* (*q.v.*), but this game fish is no relation to the friendly mammal. The fabled "dolphin" of sports fishermen has been clocked at 40 miles an hour while chasing flying fishes. Among the most majestic of fish, old male dorados have a high narrow crest which gives the forehead a vertical profile. All dorados are beautifully colored—marked with blues, purples, golds, and bright yellows. When taken from the water, pink and green flushes run over their sides. Byron and many another poet has celebrated the beauty of the dorado's colors when it is dying. The splendid creature's name appropriately comes from the Latin *deaurare*, to gild.

do, re, mi, fa, so, la, ti, do.   The work of Italian musician and singing teacher Guido d'Arizzo, born toward the end of the tenth century, forms the basis of the modern system of musical notation. In about 1040 this inspired genius devised the *Guido scale*, or *Artinian syllables*, that still sing his praises. The names he gave to the musical notes of the scale are still used today in modified form (*do, re, mi, fa, sol, la*). The Benedictine monk based them on six lines of a Latin hymn to St. John the Baptist, which happened to form the scale. Over the years the final syllable *ti* was added to the scale and two centuries ago the syllable *do* joined it in English. *Solfeggio* is the English word, taken from the Italian, to describe the musical exercise sung with *Guido's scale*.

dormouse. A member of the rodent family that the Romans raised for food, the little six-inch-long *dormouse* (*Glis glis*) resembles a small squirrel in looks and habits. Its name—about five centuries old—is something of a mystery, but many etymologists believe the creature is named for its appearance of sleepiness, that dormouse derives from the Swedish *dorsk*, "sleepy," or the Latin *dormire*, "to sleep." In fact, the dormouse, which Alice had such a hard time keeping awake at the Mad Hatter's tea party, is one of the legendary "seven sleepers" of the animal world, along with the ground squirrel, marmot, hedgehog, badger, bat, and bear. A hibernating dormouse—coiled up with its forefeet tucked under its chin, its hind feet clenched in front of its face, and its tail curled over its face—can be rolled across a table like a wheel and won't come awake. The savage garden dormouse will immediately devour any dormouse that begins its winter sleep before the others, even its own mother.

Dorothy Perkins's rose. Ranking with Peace and Crimson Glory as the best known of American roses, the *Dorothy Perkins* is a pink rambler introduced by the famous Jackson & Perkins Nursery of Newark, New York, in 1901. It is a small, cluster-flowering type and though ramblers have bowed in popularity to larger-flowered varieties, remains a sentimental favorite much mentioned in literature. The rose was named for the wife of the firm's co-owner.

d'Orsay pump; dossy; Quai d'Orsay. The last of the dandies, Count d'Orsay, Alfred Guillaume Gabriel (1801-52), designed the innovative *d'Orsay pump* that became the model for women's footwear. Like his contemporary Beau Brummel, d'Orsay, the son of a distinguished French general, was an *arbiter elegantarium* of English society, and the slang term *dossy*, for "elegant or smart," may also derive from his name. The man's shoe he devised in 1838 fit more snugly than any pump before it, due to its low-cut sides and V-shaped top, and was soon adopted by women. D'Orsay, an ex-soldier who came to London from France in 1821, won fame as a painter, sculptor, diarist, and wit, being "the most perfect gentleman of his day." Named for d'Orsay's famous father is the *Quai d'Orsay*—that quay along the south bank of the Seine in Paris that has become synonymous for the French Foreign Office, Department of Foreign Affairs, and other government offices located there.

do-si-do. The square dance call, sometimes *dozy dozy*, instructs partners to circle back to back and, appropriately, comes from the French *dos-à-dos*, "back to back."

doublecross. *Doublecross* came into use only in about 1870, apparently as an English racing term describing the common practice of winning a race after promising to arrange a *cross*, to lose it. *Cross*, for "a prearranged swindle or fix," dates back to the early 19th century and was used by Thackeray in *Vanity Fair* to describe a fixed horse race. The adjective *double* here is meant in its sense of "duplicity," so *doublecross* really means "dishonesty about dishonesty"; in fact, the earlier expression "to put on the double double" meant the same as *doublecross*.

double entendre. *Double entendre*, "double meaning" (one often of doubtful propriety), is a French term that came into English in the 17th century. While the French expression for the same is *double entente* today, it was *double entendre* when the term was adopted.

double in brass. To be versatile, to be able to do more than one thing well, or to hold two jobs in order to make more money. In its earliest recorded use, the American expression meant to play in a circus act and perform in a circus band as well. It was very common for a circus performer in the 1880s to play in the brass band when not performing as a clown, acrobat, or equestrian, and it is still sometimes the practice in small one-ring circuses. So *to double in brass* became circus talk of the day, was adopted by actors to describe an actor playing two parts in the same play, and then passed into general use.

doubting Thomas. History's first *doubting Thomas* was St. Thomas, one of the twelve apostles. Because he doubted the resurrection of Christ (John 20:24-29) and questioned Christ in an earlier passage in the Bible (John 14:5) early readers of the Scriptures gave his name to any faithless doubter. Thomas, however, reformed when the resurrected Christ let him touch the wounds He suffered on the cross and admonished him, "Blessed are those who have not seen and yet believe." Tradition has it that later, when no longer a doubter, Thomas went on a mission to India where a king gave him a large sum to build a magnificent palace. He spent the money on food for the poor instead, "erecting a superb palace in Heaven," and so became the patron saint of masons and architects.

doughnuts. American *doughnuts* go back to the time of the Pilgrims, who learned to make these "nuts" of fried sweet dough in Holland before coming to the New World. It is to the Pennsylvania Dutch that we owe the hole in the middle of the *doughnut*, or *sinker*, as the doughnut is sometimes called.

Douglas fir. Only the giant sequoias and redwoods of California among North American trees exceed the *Douglas fir* in height and massiveness. The coniferous evergreens grow to heights of three hundred feet and reach twelve feet in diameter, yielding more lumber than any other American species. The *Douglas fir*, or *Douglas spruce*, as it is sometimes called, was named for its discoverer, David Douglas (1798-1834), who came here from Scotland in 1823 to study American plants and to collect specimens for the Royal Horticultural Society. The former gardener at Glasgow's botanical gardens collected more than two hundred plants and seeds then unknown in Europe. His eleven-year journal became historically valuable because he was one of the first travelers in the Pacific northwest. The *Douglas fir*, which he first observed in 1825, is botanically of the pine family, and yields a hard, strong wood of great commercial importance. Douglas died one of the strangest of deaths; in 1834 he extended his travels to the Hawaiian Islands, where he was killed by a wild bull.

dove's dung. During a famine in Samaria, the Bible tells us (2 Kings 6:25) "an ass's head" was sold for fourscore pieces of silver and a quantity of "dove's dung" for five pieces of silver. This implies that dove's dung was eaten by the Samarians, surely one of the most disgusting substances ever used as food. It is said that the Hebrew for "lentils" and "locust pods" might easily be mistaken for "ass's head" and "dove's dung," but many modern versions of the Bible still translate the words as the latter. The expression might have been used for dramatic impact, but people have eaten some strange foods throughout history, including rats, cats, dogs, all manner of insects, and other people.

Dow Jones. Short for the *Dow Jones Industrial Average*, the *Dow Jones* is the average daily price of selected industrial stocks. It was first published in 1884, five years before its founders, Charles Henry Dow and Edward D. Jones, began to publish the *Wall Street Journal*. In 1909 their company was acquired by Walker Barron, of *Barron's Financial Weekly*.

down. A completed play has been called a *down* in football since the late 19th century, *Walter Camp's Book of College Sports* (1893) explaining that it was so-named because a tackled ball carrier cried "down" when he was stopped by the opposite side and could go no farther. This got the other side off his back.

down at the heels. (See **well-heeled**.)

Downing Street; Downing College; a George Downing. Like its French counterpart, the Quai d'Orsay, England's *No. 10 Downing Street* is another famous diplomatic address deriving from a family name. *Downing Street* is used figuratively to mean the British foreign office or government in power, No. 10 Downing Street having been the official residence of almost all British prime ministers since George II gave the house to Sir Robert Walpole for that purpose in 1735. The street in London, which also contains the British foreign and colonial offices, is named for soldier and diplomat Sir George Downing (ca. 1624-84). Downing, a nephew of Massachusetts' governor John Winthrop, was graduated in the first class at Harvard, but returned to England, where he performed the difficult trick of serving under both Cromwell and then Charles II. A talented but selfish man, his character is said to have been "marked by treachery, servitude, and ingratitude." In his own time *a George Downing* was proverbial for "a false man who betrayed his trust." *Downing College*, Cambridge, derived its name later from his generous grandson, but *Downing Street* was on the king's property and named for the statesman during Charles II's reign. The facade of No. 10 Downing is the same as it was in 1735. Who's at No. 11? The Chancellor of the Exchequer. The government whip's office is No. 12. (See **d'Orsay pump**.)

down in the dumps; dump. Someone *down in the dumps* may momentarily feel ready to be hauled off to the *garbage dump*, but the *dumps* in the expression derives from the Dutch *domp*, "mental haze or dullness," or from the German *dumpf*, "close, heavy, oppressive, gloomy." The *dump* in *garbage dump* has an entirely different origin and is an old echoic word like *bump* and *thump*, common to many languages—from garbage being thrown down heavily and making this sound. *Garbage dump* gets its name from this, as does *dumping stock* on the market, or *dumping* ("accepting a bribe to lose") a basketball game.

down the hatch! This toast originated in the 18th-century British navy, the mouth compared to the *hatches*, or openings, leading to various parts of a ship. *Hatch* comes from the Old English *haecc*, grating or hatch. It is unrelated to the verb *hatch*, to incubate, which derives from the Greek *hecken*, meaning the same.

Down Under. (See **Aussie**.)

the dozens. The art of hurling invective at one's enemies is an ancient one (see **logomachy**) and American slaves probably brought the verbal exchange called *the dozens* or *dirty dozens* with them from Africa, basing it on the Tuareg and Galla game of two opponents cursing one another until one man lost his temper and began fighting with his hands instead of his mouth; he was considered the loser. Alive and thriving today among blacks, the game takes its name not from dozen, "twelve," but probably from the Americanism *bulldoze*, which meant "to bullwhip someone," especially a slave, the insults likened to whip lashes. (*see* **bulldozer; logomachy**.)

Dr. Everybody knows that *Dr.* is an abbreviation for "doctor"—and it has been for about four centuries. Few are aware, though, that *Dr.* is also an abbreviation for "debtor"—in bookkeeping jargon.

Draconian. "The Draconian Code is written in blood," one Greek orator declared, and Plutarch observed that under Draco's code "for nearly all crimes there is the penalty of death." They referred to the severe laws—now largely lost—codified and promulgated by the Athenian legislator Draco about 621 B.C. Draco was the first to collect Athens' unwritten laws, but his assignment wasn't to modify them and he is therefore not really responsible for their proverbial harshness. The written *Draconian Code* proved valuable because it substituted public justice for vendettas and made it impossible for magistrates to side openly with the nobility. Its severity may have been exaggerated by future generations. Draco's laws, except for those dealing with homicide, were abolished or ameliorated by the wise Solon thirty years later, but they were so harsh, or thought to be so harsh, that the word *Draconian* remains a synonym for "severe" and *Draconian laws* still means any code of laws or set of rules calling for ironhanded punishment of their violators.

draftee. First recorded in an 1866 Civil War memoir, *draftee* was surely used before this during the war, probably as soon as the Confederate Conscription Act of 1862 and the Union Draft Law of 1863 were passed. In the North single men 20 to 45 and married men 20 to 35 were drafted, while the South conscripted all men 18 to 35. Most men volunteered, however; only about 2 percent of the Union Army consisting of *draftees*. During World War II *draftee* and other *ee*-ending words (such as *trainee, enlistee, escapee,* and *amputee*) were widely used. *Draft* in the sense of conscription comes from the "to draw or pull" meaning of the verb *to draft*.

drat it! Charles Dickens, among other great writers, used the word *drat* as a mild expletive. *Drat* was first recorded in the early 19th century as a contraction of "God rot"; thus *drat it!* means "God rot it!"

to draw a blank. To search hard but fail to find out about something. The reference is to the losing ticket in a lottery in which people buy numbered tickets to win prizes; a blank ticket wins nothing. The expression dates back to the late 19th century.

drawers. *Drawers*, "women's or men's underwear," were originally made something like women's pantyhose, their name bestowed upon them back in the 16th century when they were drawn on over the feet and legs.

drawn and quartered. (*See* **hanged, drawn, and quartered**.)

to draw in one's horns. *Horns* here refers to the horns of the land snail, which draws in its horns and remains in its shell when threatened with danger, or when weather conditions aren't favorable. The snail's actions do suggest someone who *draws in his horns*, that is, draws away from a situation and takes no action while reconsidering the matter. The expression is first recorded in the early 1300s and clearly indicates that the land snail is its source.

draw the line. When we say "This is where I draw the line," we are of course laying down a definite limit beyond which we refuse to go. Several attempts have been made to trace actual sources of the figurative "line" in the phrase. One says that it referred to tennis, a sport almost as popular as cricket in England by the 18th century. When tennis was introduced from France four centuries before, according to this story, there were no exact dimensions for the court and players drew lines that they agreed the ball couldn't be hit beyond. Another explanation says that the line was cut by a plowhorse across a field to indicate the boundary of a farmer's holding in 16th-century England. No examples of the figurative expression *to draw the line* have been found recorded before 1793, but either theory could be right. The phrase could also derive from early prizefights, where a line was drawn in the ring that neither fighter could cross. For a famous American use of *drawing the line, see* **teddy bear**.

dreadnought. With her ten 12-inch guns, 11-inch armor belt, and 21.6-knot speed, the 17,940-ton British battleship *Dreadnought* out-classed any battleship on the seas and made all others virtually obsolete. Before *Dreadnought's* 1906 debut, battleships commonly had four 12-inch guns and a number of smaller ones. The British built the *Dreadnought* in just four months, but it was three years before Germany could produce a comparable ship. The *Dreadnought* marked a turning point in naval military history, and her name became synonymous for any big ship of comparable size. By 1916 Britain had twenty-nine dreadnoughts, enabling her to defeat Germany in the Battle of Jutland. Indeed, by that time Britain had super-dreadnoughts like the 27,000-ton *Warspite* with her eight 15-inch guns and 13-inch armor belt, and the original *Dreadnought* did not even see service at Jutland.

drink like a fish. Fish don't intentionally drink water, getting whatever water they need from their food. Most of the water they appear to be drinking while swimming along is actually passing through their gills to supply them with oxygen. But they certainly do *seem* to be drinking continually, many swimming with their mouths open. That is why what has been called an "idiotism" (like "cold as hell") has been a common synonym for drinking excessively, especially alcohol, since at least the early 17th century.

droit du seigneur. *Droit du seigneur*, French for "the lord's right," is also called "the right of the first night" in English. It is said to have been a custom in medieval Europe, permitting the lord of a manor to have sexual relations with all brides of his vassals on their wedding nights. The story is part of folklore and literature in many countries and often finds its way into history books, but there is little evidence that such a custom really existed. A suspect 1392 French document mentions such a law and that is the only "proof" we have of it in history.

a drop in the bucket. This venerable metaphor first appears in the Bible (Isa. 9:15), the King James Version reading: "Behold, the nations are a drop of a bucket and are counted as the small dust of the balance." Since then *a drop in the bucket* has meant anything much too small.

drop of a hat. No one has offered a convincing explanation for this very common American expression, and both *Webster's* and the *O.E.D.* ignore it entirely. It has been suggested that it is Irish in origin and that since the words are most often heard in the form of "he's ready to fight at the drop of a hat" the phrase parallels challenges like "roll up your sleeves," "take off your coat," and other expressions used at the start of a fistfight. Another possible explanation lies in the duels with guns, knives, whips, or fists so common in the 19th century. The referee who judged these duels usually dropped a handkerchief or hat as a signal for the fight to begin. The expression seems to have originated in the West and was first recorded in 1887.

drown the shamrock. (*See* **shamrock.**)

a drug on the market. We use this expression for "something not in demand, something unsaleable because the market is glutted with the same or the woods are full of them." But since the phrase's first appearance in 1661 no one has figured out just what it means. What drug is referred to? Is it possibly items of trade like the tea and spices that were sometimes called drugs in the past, and, if so, when in early times were markets ever glutted with such rare commodities? Or is *drug* here just a pronunciation of *dreg* in certain English dialects? Take your choice, but the theory that apparently has the most supporters claims that the drug here is from the French word *drogue*, meaning "rubbish." The word *drug* has been used in this sense, as when Robinson Crusoe, discovering the coins in the wreck, cried out: "O Drug! what art thou good for?"

drugstore. *Drugstore* is an Americanism for the appellations "chemist's shop," "apothecary," and "pharmacy," used in England. But before they were called *drugstores* here, pharmacies were called *druggist shops* (1786) and *druggist stores* (1817). *Drugstore* is first recorded in 1818 and *drugstore cowboy* in 1925, the latter being a man who lounges around public places trying to impress young women by showing off.

drumhead court-martial. In days past, battlefield courts-martial trying soldiers for desertion, cowardice, and similar offenses, were held around a large drumhead (animal skin stretched upon a drum) that served as a table. The brief courts-martial, which usually resulted in immediate death sentences, were thus called *drumhead courts-martial*, this term first recorded in 1835.

Drummond light; in the limelight. Anyone in the limelight is—or was—in the *Drummond light*. Thomas Drummond (1797-1840) invented this first limelight, utilizing calcium oxide, or lime, which had been isolated by Sir Humphry Davy in 1808 and gives off an intense white light when heated. Royal Engineer Drummond, a Scottish inventor, devised his light as an aid in murky weather while assisting in a land survey of Great Britain, and later adopted it for use in lighthouses. He became secretary of state for Ireland in 1835, noted as an able administrator who told absentee Irish landlords that "property has its duties as well as its rights." The incandescent *Drummond light* wasn't perfected as a spotlight for the stage until after his death. It has long been replaced by arc and klieg lights, but the phrase *in the limelight* still survives. (*See also* **klieg light.**)

drumstick. The *drumstick* of a turkey or other fowl is so called because it resembles a drumstick in shape. But the word is a euphemism of British origin, invented as a substitute for "leg," which the Victorians found offensive enough to call a "limb."

drunk as a lord. Both *drunk as a lord* and *drunk as a beggar* were coined in the mid-17th century, but only the former expression survives today—perhaps because most drunks like to consider themselves lords rather than beggars. Three hundred years ago there were no class restrictions on drinking in England and anyone could buy enough gin to get drunk on for a penny.

as drunk as David's sow. Very drunk, "beastly drunk." The wife of David Lloyd, "a Welchman who kept an alehouse at Hereford" became known to history as *David's sow* early in the 17th century. "David," according to one old story, "had a living sow, which was greatly resorted to by the curious; he had also a wife much addicted to drink. . . One day David's wife having taken a cup too much, and being fearful of the consequences [David's wrath], turned out the six-legged sow and lay down to sleep herself sober in the stye. A company coming to see the sow, David ushered them into the stye, exclaiming, 'There is a sow for you! Did any of you ever see such another?,' all the while supposing that the sow had really been there. To which some of the company, seeing the state the woman was in, replied, it was the drunkenest sow they had ever beheld; whence the woman was ever after called *David's sow.*"

Drury Lane Theatre. This long-famous street and theatre in London get their name from the Drury House, which once stood just south of the present lane. The house was built by English statesman and soldier Sir William Drury (1527-1579) during the reign of Henry VIII. There have been four Drury Lane theatres, including the present one; the first was originally a cockpit that was converted into a theatre under James I. All the great English actors, from Booth and Garrick on, have performed at one or another Drury Lane.

druthers. *If I had my druthers* means "if I were free to choose." It is based whimsically on *I'd ruther*, an American dialect form of *I'd rather*, which dates back to the 19th century.

dry goods. *Dry goods stores* ("drapist's shops" in England) may take their name from stores run by New England merchants, many of whom were shipowners and direct importers in Colonial times. Two chief imports were rum and bolts of calico, which were traditionally carried on opposite sides of the store—a wet-goods side containing the rum and a dry-goods side holding the calico. "Wet goods" disappeared from the language, but all stores that sell goods are still called *dry goods stores.*

Dubuque, Iowa. (*See* **the old lady in Dubuque.**)

dubok. This Russian word reportedly became part of the CIA's vocabulary in the 1960s. *Dubok* is Russian for "oak tree" and the CIA supposedly adopted it to mean a secret "drop" where papers or money can be hidden.

duffel bag. A coarse woolen called *duffel* was named for the town of Duffel in Belgium near Antwerp. The word came to be applied to military clothing and finally to the large round canvas *duffel bag* that holds them.

duffer. A *duffer*, for "a bad golf player" is a British expression that dates back to the early 1840s. It probably comes from the Scottish *duffar*, for "a dull or stupid person."

dukes. (*See* **put up your dukes.**)

dull as ditchwater. Uninteresting people and tedious undertakings have been called *dull as ditchwater* for over two centuries. The allusion is to the dull muddy color of water in ditches, which were much commoner in days past. *Dull as dishwater* is a later variant.

Dumb Dora. U.S. cartoonist T.A. ("TAD") Dorgan contributed this term for "a scatterbrained young woman" to the language. *Dumb Dora* was originally the name of a dizzy cartoon character he invented.

dumb ox. When he was a young monk in Germany (ca. 1250) other members of his Dominican order thought St. Thomas Aquinas was stupid—perhaps because they weren't intelligent enough to understand what he said. They dubbed him the *Dumb Ox*, which has become synonymous for "a stupid person." *Lummox*, an Americanism first recorded in 1825, apparently derives from *dumb ox*, perhaps combined with *lumbering* or another word suggesting clumsiness. (*See* **dunce.**)

dumdum bullet. This particularly hideous bullet—it expands on impact, creating an ugly wound—is named for the Dum-Dum arsenal in Bengal, India, where the British made it to stop the charges of "fanatical tribesmen." *Dumdum*, or softnose, bullets were outlawed by many world powers under an international declaration made in 1899, but that has not entirely stopped them from being used since.

dump. (*See* **down in the dumps.**)

dumpy. *Dumpy*, for "a short fat person," is thought to be related to *dump* in its sense of melancholy (*see* **down in the dumps**), but no one knows exactly how. Perhaps because such people appeared melancholy, perhaps from the German adjective *dumpf*, which means "heavy" in another sense.

dun. "Send Dun after him," creditors would say when a person was slow to pay his debts. According to the old story, they referred to Joe Dun, a London bailiff during the reign of Henry VIII who had proved himself particularly efficient in collecting from defrauding debtors. But most authorities trace *dun* to various words meaning din or thundering noise, sometimes connecting this with the drum that town criers pounded when they shouted out the names of debtors. Only a few Celtic words survive in English, and most of these must be marked "doubtful." Philologists do think that a word similar to *dun*, for the dull brown color, was spoken by the Celts 2,000 years ago.

Duncan Phyfe. Duncan Phyfe's furniture workshop stood on the site of the present Hudson Terminal Building in New York City. The Scottish-born master craftsman had arrived in New York in 1783 at the age of fifteen and later opened his own shop, changing his name from Fife to Phyfe. Duncan Phyfe and Sons employed more than one hundred artisans at its height of popularity, but the master craftsman's best work was done in the early period up until 1820, when he evolved his own style, using the creations of Sheraton, Hepplewhite, and the Adam brothers as models. This work has become known as the *Duncan Phyfe style*, characterized by excellent proportions, graceful, curving lines, and beautifully carved ornamentation.

dunce. Ironically, one of the most brilliant scholars and philosophers of the Middle Ages is the source for the word *dunce*. Little is known about John Duns Scotus outside of his new theology. He was probably born in 1265 in Scotland, most likely died while still a young man, aged forty-three or so, and his middle name is presumably a place name, either from the village of Duns, Scotland, Dunse in Berwickshire, or Dunston in Northumberland. The "Subtle Doctor," as he was called, apparently taught at Oxford and the University of Paris, but again there is no hard evidence available. Duns Scotus did found a school of philosophy that attracted numerous followers. A Franciscan, he successfully opposed the teachings of St. Thomas Aquinas and the Dominicans, challenging the harmony of faith and reason, and insisted on the doctrine of the Immaculate Conception, for which he was known as the Marian Doctor. After his death—tradition has it that he died in Cologne, buried alive—Duns Scotus remained a great influence on scholastic thought. His works were studied in all the great universities throughout Europe and his followers, called Scotists, reigned supreme. However, these same Dunsmen sabotaged his reputation some two hundred years later. During the Renaissance, blindly resistant to change, "the old barking curs" raged from the pulpit against the new learning, being scorned and ridiculed as hairsplitters and stupid obstructionists. *Dunsmen* became *dunses* and finally *dunces*, "blockheads incapable of learning or scholarship." Exactly the opposite of the precise, learned mind of the man who started it all. (*See* **dumb ox.**)

dunderhead. *Dunderhead* for a dunce or blockhead, may come from the Dutch *donderbol*, cannonball, the head of a dunce thus compared to a thick iron ball. However, the origin of the word, first recorded in 1625, is obscure.

dundrearies. Long silky whiskers drooping in strands from both cheeks were high fashion during the 1860s and after. They are named for Lord Dundreary, the witless indolent chief character who sported such whiskers in English dramatist Tom Taylor's play *Our American Cousin* (1858). Abraham Lincoln was watching the play at Ford's Theatre on the night he was assassinated.

dungarees. *Dungarees* isn't used as much as *jeans* or *levis* for these coarse blue cloth pants today, but the word

is still frequently heard. The name derives from what *Partridge* calls the "disreputable Bombay suburb" where the cloth used for the pants was first made and exported to England early in the 1830s.

duodenum. This word for the first part of the small intestine is the Latin for "twelve fingerbreadths [inches] long," the measurement early physicians and anatomists gave the organ. The term is recorded as early as 1398.

duotrigintillion. (*See* **googol.**)

dupe. Because its cry sounds like "up up," the south European bird *Upupa epops* was called the *upup* or *upupa* by the Romans. The bird, about the size of a large thrush and noted for its long, curved beak, variegated plumage, and beautiful orange erectile crest in the male, became known in French as the *huppe* and in English as the *hoopoe*, or *hoop*. The French considered it to be an especially stupid bird because it laid its eggs most anywhere without a nest (in a hole in a wall, tree, or bank, etc.). They commonly said that any fool had the head of a *huppe*, *tete d'huppe*. *D'uppe* in the expression eventually became *duppe* and passed into English in the late 17th century as *dupe*, a person who is easily fooled or deceived.

the duration. *For the duration* means without a fixed time limit for as long as is necessary or may be. The phrase originally referred to the duration of World War II.

dust bowl. Severe dust storms beginning in 1934 destroyed crops and dried the soil in the southern High Plains of the United States, largely because this land in Kansas, Colorado, Oklahoma, New Mexico, and Texas had been poorly farmed for years. The Great Depression, drought, and the dust forced large numbers of people to migrate from the area, which was first called the *dust bowl* in a story written by Associated Press reporter Robert Geiger in April 1935. The dust storms lasted almost a decade and dust from them blew as far as 300 miles out into the Atlantic, where it coated ships. (*See also* **okies.**)

Dutch. The Dutch people have been so offended by the English language over the past three centuries that in 1934 their government ordered its officials to drop the word *Dutch* and use "Netherlands" instead whenever possible. But the strategem didn't succeed in stopping the dike. *Dutch* remains what one dictionary calls "an epithet of inferiority." Three examples of a few score such expressions, are *Dutch courage*, courage inspired by booze; *in Dutch*, in trouble; and *Dutch treat*, a meal or entertainment where each pays his own way. To complicate matters, the name *Dutchman* from the German *Deutsch*, has been applied to German people, such connections and the world wars adding still more derogatory expressions to the list such as the *Dutch Act*, suicide.

Dutch words in English. Dutch and other Low German languages (Frisian, Flemish, and Plattdeutsch) have contributed a great many words to English. These include: *date, dotard, bowsprit, golf, gin, uproar, wagon, bounce, snatch, huckster, tackle* (fishing), *boy, booze, wainscot, hobble, splint, kit, mart, hop* (plant), *spool, rack, sled, excise, buoy, hoist, hose* (stockings), *bulwark, boor, loiter, snap, groove, luck, placard, brandy, stoker, smuggle, sloop, cruise, walrus, jib, yawl, knapsack, furlough, blunderbuss, sketch, stipple, decoy, slur, hanger, snort, snuff, hustle, snow* and *mangle.* Many Dutch words became part of American English. These include: *bush, hook* (of land), *boss, patroon, Yankee, sawbuck, stoop* (porch), *hay, barrack, boodle, dingus, dope, dumb, logy, poppycock, Santa Claus, snoop, spook, skate, coleslaw, cruller, cookie, pit* (of fruit), *pot cheese, waffle span* (of horses), *sleigh, caboose, scow, bedspan, bedspread, cuspidor, keelboat, landscape* and *a good scout.*

duxelles sauce. A *duxelles* today is a purée of mushrooms and onions, the tasty sauce once made from a much more elaborate recipe. It was named for the Marquis d'Uxelles, employer of the too often ignored chef François Pierre de la Varenne. Varenne's *Le Cuisinier François* (1651) is a landmark of French cuisine, and his rare pastry book *Le Patissier François* has been called the most expensive cookbook in the world. The chef is said to have been trained by those Florentine cooks brought to France by Marie de' Medici, second wife of Henry IV. It is often claimed that these Italians taught the French the art of cooking, but Varenne's cuisine was much more delicate and imaginative than that of his masters; and if anyone can be called the founder of classical French cuisine he deserves the honor. Varenne did not name the *duxelles* after his employer; this was done at a later date when it became customary to honor a man's name in a recipe.

D.V. When someone writes or says, "I'll be home next week, D.V.," he is saying "I'll be home next week, God willing," *D.V.* being an abbreviation of the Latin *deo volente.* First recorded in 1873, the term appeared on church posters, etc., before that, and is still heard occasionally.

dyvour. This synonym for "a bankrupt" is an old Scottish term. Dyvours were once compelled by law to wear a half-yellow, half-brown shirt along with a particolored cap and hose.

dyed in the wool. (*See* **spoils system**.)

E

E. *E* is the most commonly used letter in English. It is followed in order of use by: *t, a, i, s, o, n, h, r, d, l, u, c, m, f, w, y, p, g, b, v, k, j, q, x,* and *z*. The most common vowel in English is obviously *e* and the most common initial letter is *t*. Called *he* in Hebrew, the letter *E* was representative of the Phoenician and Hebrew sign for "a window."

eager beaver. Referring, of course, to the industrious beaver, this near-rhyming expression is a Canadian Army one that isn't recorded before 1940, although it obviously derives from such phrases as "as busy as a beaver," which dates back to the early 18th century. Unlike the early expression, however, *eager beaver* is usually applied derisively to someone who is overly industrious, zealous, gung ho in his work, one who tries to impress his superiors by his diligence and becomes obnoxious to his associates as a result.

the eagle shits on Friday. At least since the years of the Great Depression, U.S. workingmen have used this phrase meaning "payday is Friday," and the term may date back to the Spanish-American War. The eagle, of course, is the one on the U.S. dollar. A euphemism for the expression is *the eagle screams on Friday.*

eaglestones. These lumps of ironstone, often the size of small eggs, are so called because the ancient Greeks believed that an eagle's eggs wouldn't hatch unless the bird deposited one in her nest. Nobody knows how the myth originated, but the Greeks called the ironstones *aetites*, which translates into the English *eaglestone.*

earl. Any *Earl*, third in rank among the British peerage, below a Duke and a Marquess, takes his name from the Old English *eorl*, "a man of position," as opposed to a *ceorl*, or *churl*, "a freeman of the lowest rank." A *churl* is today a peasant, a rude surly person, and a miser.

early to bed, early to rise . . . . (*See* **snug as a bug in a rug.**)

earmark. Back in the 16th century English farmers began to notch their own identifying marks in the ears of their sheep and cattle to prevent them from being stolen. This practice didn't always work, for many thieves were adept at altering earmarks, but the animal earmark was so common that it soon gave its name to any kind of identifying mark and, figuratively, to something, such as money, marked or set aside for some special purpose. Incidentally, thieves who altered an *earmark* ran the risk of being sent to prison where *they* would be earmarked—slitting the ears of pilloried criminals, earmarking them, was as common as nose-slitting or earmarking animals in those days.

earthlight. *Earthlight* is not light on the earth; it is light reflected from the earth to the moon and back that is visible on the dark side of the moon. British astronomer John Herschel seems to have coined the word in 1833. (*See* **asteroid**, for a word his father coined.)

ear to the ground. Ramon Adams wrote in *Western Words* (1944) that old plainsmen often placed a silk neckerchief on the ground and thus could hear the sounds of men and horses miles away. Even if plainsmen and American Indians didn't hear distant footfalls by putting their ears to the ground, so many writers of Westerns have attributed this skill to them that the practice has become well known. The phrase is first recorded in 1900 in the *Congressional Record*, meaning to use caution, to go slowly and listen frequently. Since then someone with *an ear to the ground* has become someone trying to determine signs of the future, trying to find out what's coming.

earwig. The nocturnal earwig (*Forficula auricularia*) is a common garden pest, but it won't wiggle or wriggle into people's ears and then drill its way into the brain with the aid of its large pincers. Yet it was exactly this popular superstition that gave the *earwig*, or *ear-wiggle*, its name over a thousand years ago. One English writer even instructed: "If an earwig begotten into your eare . . . spit into the same, and it will come forth anon . . . ." Good trick if you can do it. To *earwig* someone is to fill his mind with prejudices by insinuations, by whispering into his ear and wriggling into his confidence.

easel. The three-legged frame used to hold a painting while the artist works on it suggested a donkey to 17th-century Dutch painters because it somewhat resembled one and because it carried a burden. So they named this piece of equipment an *ezel*, Dutch for "donkey," the word becoming *easel* in English, as use of the device increased. The idea seems to be a widespread one, however, as the French call an *easel* a *chevalet*, a wooden "horse."

Easter. The pagan festival held at the vernal equinox to honor Eastre, the goddess of dawn, was called *Eastre* in Old English. Since the Christian festival celebrating Christ's resurrection fell at about the same time, the pagan name was borrowed for it when Christianity was introduced to England, the name later being changed slightly to *Easter*.

Easter Island. Over 2,300 miles west of Chile and some 1,200 miles east of its closest inhabited neighbor, lonely Easter Island is so named because it was discovered by Europeans on Easter Sunday in 1722.

easy as rolling off a log; logrolling. No one seems to know the origin of the first expression, which dates back to Colonial times. One ingenious theory suggests that colonists searching for home sites in the wilderness would leave their toddlers seated on dry logs temporarily while they explored the area and that the round-bottomed children often rolled off the logs, not knowing how to keep their balance. The metaphor could just as likely have derived from colonists rolling logs off toward a building site, across a meadow or down a hill. Logs can be quite heavy, though, and difficult to move, which explains the origins of *logrolling*. When an early settler in the West was building a log cabin, his neighbors helped him roll the heavy logs to the home site, or helped him clear the land of felled trees, with the understanding that he would do the same for them if need be. Eventually the frontier expression *logrolling* came to describe this mutual "back-scratching," passing into politics by 1838 as the practice of one lawmaker voting for a bill sponsored by another if his colleague reciprocates and votes for a bill sponsored by him—the political deal, "help me roll this one, I'll help you roll that one past the opposition."

easy does it. (*See* **take it easy**.)

Easy Street. The earliest known reference to this expression, for "living in comfortable, prosperous circumstances," is in 1901. It appears to have been coined by American author George V. Hobart in his novel *It's Up to You*, where he describes a prosperous young man who had it made and "could walk up and down Easy Street." *On Easy Street* could, however, have some relation to the old English expression *an easy road*, "a road that can be traveled without discomfort or difficulty," an expression that was used figuratively by Shakespeare.

eat crow. During an armistice toward the end of the War of 1812, an American soldier out hunting crossed the Niagara River past British lines. Finding no better game, he shot a crow, but a British officer heard the shot and surprised him. The Britisher tricked the Yankee out of the rifle with which he shot so well. He then turned the gun on the American, demanding that he take a bite out of the

crow he had shot as a punishment for violating British territory. The American complied, but when the officer returned his weapon and told him to leave, he covered the Englishman and forced him to eat the rest of the crow. That is the origin of the expression *to eat crow*, "to be forced to do something extremely disagreeable," as related in an 1888 issue of the *Atlanta Constitution*. Although *to eat crow* is possibly a much older expression, the saying first appeared in print in 1877 and the story may well be true—nothing better has been suggested. The concept behind *to eat crow* is that crows are not good eating, but the flesh of young ones was once esteemed and I have it on the authority of the Remington Arms Co. that even old crows aren't so bad if you simply "skin the bird, salt and cut it into pieces, parboil till tender and then fry with butter and onions." I'll eat crow if someone conclusively proves that the recipe isn't authentic.

to eat dog for another. Various American Indian tribes ate dog meat and at least one was called *the Dogeaters* by their enemies. When white men sat at Indian councils where dog meat was served, those who didn't relish the comestible could, without offending their host, put a silver dollar on the dish and pass it along, the next man taking the dollar and eating the dog. From this practice arose the American political expression *to eat dog for another*.

eat drink and be merry. "A man hath no better thing under the sun than to eat, and to drink, and to be merry," says the Bible, in Eccles. 8:15, this the source of the well-known expression.

to eat humble pie. Here is an expression probably born as a pun. The *humble* in this pie has nothing to do etymologically with the word *humble*, "lowly," which is from the Latin *humilis*, "low or slight." Umbles or numbles (from the Latin *lumbulus*, "little loin") were the innards—the heart, liver, and entrails—of deer and were often made into a pie. Sir Walter Scott called this dish "the best," and an old recipe for it (1475) instructed "For to serve a Lord"—but some thought it fit only for servants. When the lord of a manor and his guests dined on venison, the menials ate umble pie made from the innards of the deer. Anyone who ate umble pie was therefore in a position of inferiority—he or she was humbled—and some anonymous punster in the time of William the Conqueror, realizing this, changed *umble pie* to *humble pie*, the pun all the more effective because in several British dialects, especially the Cockney, the *h* is silent and *humble* is pronounced *umble* anyway. So the play upon words gave us the common expression *to eat humble pie*, meaning to suffer humiliation, to apologize, or to abase oneself.

eatin' a green 'simmon. The *'simmon* in the 19th-century Southern Americanism is a *persimmon*, which takes its name from the Cree *pasiminan* meaning "dried fruit." While the fruit is delicious when dead ripe, a green unripe persimmon is so sour it could make you whistle, which led to the expression he (or she) *looks like he's been eatin' a green 'simmon. Ripe* persimmons suggested *walking off with the persimmons*, "walking off with the prize," which also dates back to the 1850s.

eat one's hat.   This is an asseveration, as the *O.E.D.* so neatly puts it, "stating one's readiness to do this if an event of which one is certain should not occur." A woman named Miss E.E. Money first recorded the phrase, in 1887, and it is sometimes given as *I'll eat Rowley's hat*. One persistent folk etymology has the *hat* here being "a food made of eggs, veal, dates, saffron, salt, and spices" that no one else seems to have heard of.

to eat one's words.   "God eateth not his word when he hath once spoken" is the first recorded use of this expression meaning "to retreat in a humiliating way"—in a 1571 religious work. There are several instances of people literally eating their words, the earliest occurring in 1370 when the pope sent two delegates to Bernabo Visconti bearing a rolled parchment, informing him that he had been excommunicated. Infuriated, Visconti arrested the delegates and made them eat the parchment, words, leaden seal, and all. I doubt that this suggested *to eat one's own's words*, but it is a good story.

eavesdropper.   The eaves of a house is simply the edge of the roof that overhangs the side. (*Eaves* is the singular, there being no word *eave*.) In ancient times, English law forbade the building of a house less than two feet from another person's property, because rainwater dropping off the eaves might injure a neighbor's land. So the space beneath the eaves of a house and about two feet out came to be called the *eavesdrip* or *eavesdrop*. Later, in the 15th century, persons standing in this space near a window trying to overhear conversations inside a house were called *eavesdroppers*, and it was from their name that the verb *to eavesdrop* was formed. One 16th-century English writer warned of "eavesdroppers with pen and ink outside the walls," and the great jurist Sir William Blackstone called "eavesdroppers" a "common nuisance."

eccentric.   *Eccentric* derives from the Latin *ex centrum*, "out of center, deviating from the center," the word originally an astronomical term and used this way early in the 16th century. Not for almost another two hundred years was *eccentric* applied to odd, whimsical people who deviated from the center. (The *eccentricity* of the earth's orbit is 0.017, should anyone have need to know.)

ecdysiast; stripteaser.   Stripteaser Georgia Sothern, or her press agent, wrote H. L. Mencken in 1940 asking him to coin a "more palatable word" to describe her profession. The Sage of Baltimore, who had hatched other neologisms (*i.e.*, "bootician" for a bootlegger), gallantly responded, suggesting that "strip-teasing be related in some way or other to the zoological phenomenon of molting." Among his specific recommendations were lizards, called the Geckonidae (not very appetizing, either), and *ecdysiast*, which comes from *ecdysis*, the scientific term for "molting." Miss Sothern adopted the last and it was publicized universally; born to the world was a new word and a new union called the Society of Ecdysiasts, Parade, and Specialty Dancers. But not every artfully unclad body was happy with Mencken's invention. Said the Queen of Strippers, Gypsy Rose Lee: "'Ecdysiast,' he calls me! Why the man is an intellectual slob. He has been reading *books. Dictionaries.* We don't wear feathers and molt them off . . . What does he know about stripping?" Most would agree that *stripteaser* is far more revealing. *Striptease*, first recorded in 1938, and *stripping* seem to have been coined within the last 65 years or so, but the word *stripping* for a woman removing her clothes to sexually stimulate men goes back at least 400 years. "Be sure that they be lewd, drunken, stripping whores," says a character in Thomas Otway's comedy, *The Soldier's Fortune* (1581). Joseph Addison wrote in *The Guardian* (1713): "At a late meeting of the stripping ladies. . . it was resolved for the future to lay the modesty price aside." Synonymous for *stripteaser* are: *peeler* and *shucker*. (*See* **G-string.**)

echo.   The Greek nymph Echo talked so much that Zeus and his wife Hera couldn't hear what any of the other nymphs were saying. Hera punished this *yenta* (*q.v.*) by depriving her of all speech save the ability to repeat the words of others, giving her heartaches—she lost her love, Narcissus—but giving us the word *echo*.

economist.   *Economist* is a lofty occupational title but has its roots in a very common calling —housekeeping—deriving from the Greek *oikonomia*, meaning "house management." An *economist* was a household manager in England at least after 1580, when we find the first known use of the word; the term did not acquire its present meaning until the 18th century. The old meaning of the word is retained in the home economics courses still taught in schools.

Ecuador.   The Spanish named this South American country after the equator, which passes through it.

Eddyism.   *Eddyism*, a synonym for Christian Science, honors its founder, Mary Baker Eddy (1821-1910). Though she lived until nearly ninety, Mrs. Eddy was plagued all her life by illness and unhappiness. Married three times, her first marriage was ended by her husband's death and the second by divorce. A serious accident in 1866 turned her to the Bible. The story in

Matthew of Jesus healing the paralyzed man brought her the spiritual enlightenment she attributed to her discovery of Christian Science. "The Bible was my textbook," she once wrote. "It answered my questions as to how I was healed, but the Scriptures had to me a new meaning . . . I apprehended for the first time . . . Jesus' teaching and demonstration, and the Principle and rule of spiritual Science and metaphysical healing—in a word, Christian Science." Before this, however, Mrs. Eddy had been treated by Phineas P. Quimby, a faith healer of Portland, Maine, and his influence may be reflected in her work. An indefatigable worker, she remained the leader of the movement until her death. In 1908 she established the famous international newspaper, *The Christian Science Monitor*.

edelweiss.   The *edelweiss*, well-known in song and picture (the little Alpine flower is featured in many Swiss designs) takes its name from the German *edel*, "noble," and *weiss*, "white" or "pure."

Eden.   (*See* **abyss**.)

Edgar.   The *Edgar* is a small bust of Edgar Allan Poe presented annually to the best writers of detective stories by the Mystery Writers of America. *Edgars* are awarded in several categories, such as best novel and best short story. Poe himself once won a prize for his "Gold Bug" (1843), the code in the story developing from his interest in cryptography. Though he did invent the detective story in his "Murders in the Rue Morgue," "The Purloined Letter," and "The Mystery of Marie Roget," the writer is best remembered for his poetry and horror tales. Among his greatest stories are "The Fall of the House of Usher," "The Black Cat," "The Pit and the Pendulum," and "The Tell-Tale Heart." He died at forty, perhaps addicted to drugs, having spent his last days stumbling into Baltimore polling places and casting ballots for drinks. "Three-fifths genius and two-fifths sheer fudge," was James Russell Lowell's facile opinion of Poe, but Yeats declared him "always and for all lands a great lyric poet."

edgy.   *Edgy* for nervous or irritable is an Americanism first recorded as late as 1931. However, it derives from the expression *on edge*, which has been common since the beginning of the century. No doubt the latter is patterned on someone on the edge of a precipice, close to falling. The *mulligrubs, jimjams, shakes, fantods,* and *willies* are all earlier synonyms.

Edison effect.   On Thomas Alva Edison's death in 1931, aged eighty-four, the *New York Times* devoted four-and-a-half pages to his obituary, calling him the greatest benefactor of humanity in modern times. His name is a synonym for inventor, and his more than 1,300 United States and foreign patents establish him as probably the world's greatest genius in the practical application of scientific principles. Many of his inventions spawned giant modern industries—the electric light, his telephone transmitter, the phonograph, and the motion-picture camera being only four such discoveries. Ironically, the *Edison effect*, one of the few discoveries named for him, was not exploited by the inventor. It is the principle of the radio vacuum tube that made radio and television possible.

editorial.   *Editorial* is an Americanism for what the British call a *leader* or *lead article*, that is, an article expressing the views of the editor or publisher of a periodical. The word is first recorded in 1830 and still hasn't caught on in England.

Edsel.   Named in 1957 for Edsel Ford, founder Henry's grandson, the Ford Motor Company's *Edsel* was, and is still, so ridiculed for its defects that its name became almost a synonym for a car that doesn't work. Edsel Ford, to his greater and probably longer lasting fame, also has the Edsel Ford Range in Antarctica named for him.

education.   (*See* **encyclopedia**.)

eena, meena, mina, mo; eeny, meeny, miny, mo.   Look in the *O.E.D.*, *Webster's Second*, Mathews's *Dictionary of Americanisms*, Partridge's *Dictionary of Slang*, Brewer's *Dictionary of Phrase and Fable*—look anywhere, in any etymological reference work—and still you will not find the "counting out" expression *eena, meena, mina, mo*, or *eeny, meeny, miny, mo*, as it is perhaps more often said. Yet this is a very familiar phrase in both the United States and Britain, used at one time or another by almost all children and frequently employed by adults. It is, of course, part of a counting out expression used in children's games to determine who will be "it" among a group of players. The full rhyme, probably dating back to the 19th century, was originally the insensitive (at best): "Eena, meena, mina, mo,/ Catch a nigger by the toe,/ If he hollers, let him go,/ Eena meena, mina, mo." Sometimes the fourth line is "My mother says I should pick this here one," and, happily, the second line is much more frequently today "Catch a tiger by the toe." The rhyme is said, of course, with the counter pointing at each player in rotation with each word, the player who is last pointed at being "it." One tradition has it that counting-out rhymes are relics of formulas Druid priests used to choose human sacrifices.

effigy.   (*See* **to burn** or **hang in effigy**.)

effing.   *Effing* or *effen* has been a euphemism for *fucking* in America since at least the early 1960s, though it is first recorded in a *New York Times Magazine* article by

Anthony Burgess in 1972: "I have already had several abusive phone calls, telling me to eff-off back to effing Russian, you effing, corksacking limey effer."

eggnog. *Eggnog* is an American invention, the word first recorded at the time of the Revolutionary War. Made of eggs, milk, sugar, spices, and rum or other spirits, it takes its name from the eggs in it and *nog* for "strong ale."

egg on. The expression *to egg on* has nothing to do with hen's eggs or any kind of eggs. Neither does it derive from Norman invaders pricking Anglo-Saxon prisoners in the buttocks with their *ecgs* ("the points of their spears") when urging them to move faster, as one old story claims. *To egg on* is just a form of the obsolete English verb "to edge": to incite, provoke, encourage, urge on, push someone nearer to the edge. To *egg* someone meant the same as *to edge* someone and was used that way until about 1566, when the expression was first lengthened and became *to egg on*.

egg phrases   (a dozen more, ungraded).

• *To teach one's grandmother to suck eggs*—to lecture one's elders or betters—dates from about 1700 and was originally *to teach one's dame to grope* (handle) *ducks* (1590).
• *To turn up the eggs of the eyes*—the whites of the eyes—"the eggs of their eyes were at their highest elevation" (1635).
• *To walk on eggs*—to walk warily, 1734.
• *To put all your eggs in one basket*—to risk all on a single venture—"'Tis the part of a wise man to keep himself today for tomorrow, and not venture all his eggs in one basket," Cervantes, *Don Quixote*, 1605. "Put all your eggs in one basket and WATCH THAT BASKET," Mark Twain, *Pudd'nhead Wilson*, 1894.
• *To take eggs for money*—to be fooled with something worthless, 1611.
• *To break an egg in someone's pocket*—to spoil someone's plan, 1734.
• *As alike as eggs*—"We are almost as like as eggs"—Shakespeare, *The Winter's Tale*, 1611.
• *To have eggs on the spit*—to have business in hand, 1598.
• *In egg and bird*—in youth and maturity, 1711.
• *To crush in the egg*—to crush at the very beginning, as in crushing rebellion, 1689.
• *Egg-shell blonde*—a bald man—Australian slang, 1945.
• *To find a hair upon an egg*—to make a picky criticism—"Critics that spend their eyes to find a hair upon an egg" (1606).

eggplant. Variously called the "mad apple" and "apple of love" in Europe, *eggplant* takes its common American name from its supposed shape resemblance to a large egg. The vegetable is known as the *aubergine* to the English.

Eggs Benedict. Oscar of the Waldorf once confirmed the story that *Eggs Benedict* was invented by a man suffering from a hangover. It seems that early one morning in 1894, Samuel Benedict, a prominent New York socialite, tread softly into the old Waldorf-Astoria Hotel after a night of partying—his head hurt that much. But he had what he thought was the perfect cure for his splitting headache—a breakfast of poached eggs served on buttered toast and topped with bacon and hollandaise sauce. Oscar, the maitre d'hotel, thought this combination excellent, but substituted an English muffin for the toast and ham for the bacon, naming the dish in Benedict's honor. Whether the cure worked or not isn't recorded, and another version of the tale claims that the dish was created between Oscar and New Yorker Mrs. Le Grand Benedict.

egri bikaver. This distinctive red wine of Hungary takes its first name from Eger, a leading Hungarian wine center. Its second name, *bikaver*, means "bull's blood," so it is literally the "bull's blood of Eger."

Eiffel Tower. At the time it was erected in the Champ-de-Mars for the Paris Universal Exposition of 1889, the *Eiffel Tower*, standing 984.25 feet high, ranked as the world's tallest structure. The structural iron tower had been designed by French engineer Alexandre Gustave Eiffel (1832-1923), the earliest and foremost builder of iron structures in France and a pioneer in the science of aerodynamics with his *Resistance of Air* (1913). The tower, with three platforms at different heights, reached by stairs and elevators, has since become as much a symbol of France as the fleur-de-lis. The interior structure of the Statue of Liberty, presented to the United States by France in 1884 and a symbol of America, was also designed by Eiffel, although the statue itself was created by F.A. Bartholdi.

eightball. In a version of rotation sometimes called Kelly pool, players must sink all fifteen balls in numerical order, except for the black eight ball, which must be pocketed last. Furthermore, if a player hits the eight ball with the cue ball prematurely, he loses points. Thus anyone who makes a shot and finds the cue ball behind or very close to the eight ball is in a difficult position, for unless he makes a difficult cushion shot, he'll probably hit the eight ball when he shoots and be penalized. From this hazardous position in Kelly pool came the expression meaning to be "in an unfortunate position with little or no hope of winning, to be up the creek, out of luck." It seems to be black poolroom slang from about 1920. The later *eightball* for a maladjusted or inefficient person derives from the phrase (such a person is always *behind the eight-ball*), with some help from the armed services "Section 8" discharge for mental instability in World War II.

eight-hour day; five-day week. Henry Ford brought attention to the *eight-hour day* and *five-day week* for workers in 1926 when he instituted them at the Ford Motor Company plant in Detroit. However, a small number of workers had worked such hours before this, and the former term is recorded a quarter-century earlier.

Einstein; einsteinium. Albert Einstein (1879-1955) was unquestionably one of the greatest thinkers of all time, and *an Einstein* is still widely used as a synonym for a genius. *Einsteinium*, a man-made radioactive element, was named for the physicist in 1953 by its American discoverer, Albert Ghiorso, who formed it in the laboratory after it had been detected among the debris of the first H-bomb explosion the year before. Einstein's genius wasn't apparent in his early years. Born in Ulm, Germany, he had been regarded as a dullard and even "slow, perhaps retarded" in his first years at school there. The same opinion may have been shared by his parents, for he did not learn to walk until a relatively late age, nor begin to talk until he was past three. Einstein was graduated from the Polytechnic Institute of Zurich and took employment with the Swiss Patent Office, devoting all his spare time to pure science. In 1905, at twenty-six, his genius suddenly, inexplicably, burst into full bloom with three discoveries in theoretical physics that included his revolutionary theory of relativity, which reshaped the modern world. He was awarded the Nobel Prize in 1921—but not specifically for his theory, which few understood at the time.

Eisenhower jacket; I like Ike. One of the most popular presidents in American history, Dwight David Eisenhower (1890-1969) was elected to a second term of office in 1956 by a landslide. Graduated from West Point in 1915, the Texas-born soldier later became General Douglas MacArthur's aide in the Philippines. "General Ike," or "Ike," as he was known to G.I.'s, was appointed commander of the Allied armies in World War II, and was noted for his success as both a strategist and a diplomat who fashioned his command into a smoothly functioning machine. At this time the *Eisenhower jacket*, a waist-length woolen jacket once worn as part of the service uniform, was named in his honor. He is also remembered by his presidential campaign slogan *I like Ike*.

Elberta peach. (*See* peach.)

elbow; elbow bender; elbow grease; etc. *Elbow grease* has been a term of "hard manual labor" since before 1639, B.E.'s *Dictionary of the Canting Crew* (ca. 1698) calling it "A derisory term for Sweat." The old joke that *elbow grease* is the best brand of furniture polish was probably common centuries ago, too, in some form. The phrase was known in France from early times as well (*huile de bras*). *Elbow-bender*, for "a habitual drinker," someone who

does little more than bend the elbow to lift a glass to his mouth, is also of ancient vintage in both languages. *Out at the elbows*, shabby, "down at the heels," has aged equally well, Shakespeare using it in *Measure For Measure*: "He cannot (speak), Sir; he's out at Elbows." *Elbowing*, "jostling," is another elbow term going back to Shakespeare's time, and the Elizabethans used the term *elbonic* for "a rude, awkward verse or sentence that seemed to be pushing with the elbow." *Elbow* is from the Anglo-Saxon *el*, "length of arm," plus *bow*, "bend."

El Dorado. A mythical land filled with gold, jewels, and other great riches. El Dorado, "the gilded one," was in the original 16th-century story an Indian chieftain in what is now Colombia, who was coated with gold dust during festivals and thought so little of it that he washed it off in a lake. Explorers from many European countries tried to find him, to no avail, and the yarn grew more fantastic with each telling, *El Dorado* becoming a country filled with riches, often spelled as one word—*Eldorado*.

Eleanor blue. Like *Alice blue* (*q.v.*), this color is named for a Roosevelt, in this case, Anna Eleanor Roosevelt (1884-1962), whose dresses popularized the dark blue shade while she was "first lady of the world." Eleanor Roosevelt married her distant cousin Franklin Delano Roosevelt in 1905, two weeks after her uncle, Theodore Roosevelt, had been inaugurated as president. When F.D.R. was stricken with polio, she encouraged him to overcome his handicap and return to politics. He became the only man ever to be elected to the presidency four times, breaking the two-term tradition, and from 1933 to 1945, when he died, Eleanor was by far the most active first lady in American history. Among many activities, she wrote the syndicated newspaper column "My Day" and traveled extensively abroad on good-will missions. Outspoken on all important issues, she remained active even after her husband's death, serving as a delegate to the U.S. general assembly and chairman of the U.S. Commission on Human Rights. Orphaned at ten and starved for love and affection in her childhood, Mrs. Roosevelt nevertheless became one of the most compassionate human beings of modern times, always an enemy of prejudice and poverty despite her aristocratic origins.

electricity. English scientist William Gilbert published his researches on magnetism in 1600, writing in Latin and using the Latinized word for amber, *electricus*, because he had rubbed amber in his experiments to attract light substances. Gilbert himself later translated *electricus* into English as *electric* and gave the name *electricity* to the agency through which he had effected magnetism.

electrocute. There was no need for a word "to put to death by electricity" before Thomas Edison began using electricity to light cities beginning in about 1875. Many workers lost their lives in this great endeavor and such a word was clearly necessary. From many new coinages Americans came to prefer *electrocute*, a hybrid word formed from the Greek *electro* and the Latin *cute*, even though scholars thought *electricute*, a pure-bred word formed from *two* Greek words, was a better choice. In the final analysis people just decided *electrocute* sounded better. (*See* **electricity**.)

elementary, my dear Watson. (*See* **Sherlock Holmes**.)

eleven; at the eleventh hour. This expression, meaning "the latest possible time, with not a moment to spare," comes from the Bible, where Jesus used it in the parable of the laborers (Matt. 20:1-16). *The eleventh hour*, as the parable shows, referred not to the hour before midnight but to the last hour of sunlight, for in Jesus' day hours were counted from dawn to dusk, with the twelfth hour bringing darkness. The parable says that it is never too late to earn the right to enter the kingdom of heaven: "For the kingdom of heaven is like unto a householder, which went out early in the morning to hire laborers into his vineyard. And when he had agreed with the laborers for a penny a day, he sent them into his vineyard . . . And about the eleventh hour he went out and found others standing idle, and saith unto them, Why stand ye here all the day idle. They say unto him, Because no man hath hired us. He saith unto them, Go ye also into the vineyard; and whatsoever is right, that shall ye receive." And when evening came, all the laborers, those who arrived both early and *at the eleventh hour*, received the same penny for their wages.

elfin. The English poet Edmund Spenser invented *elfin*, "of an elfish nature, like an elf," in *The Faerie Queene* (1589), where he writes about an "elfin knight." Some say the word was suggested to Spenser by the phrase *elvene land*, "land of elves," or the proper name Elphin in the Arthurian romances.

elk. (*See* **lamb**.)

Elmer. Many given names derive from the last names of famous persons. *Elmer*, which has come upon bad times recently, is the most surprising of them. *Elmer* was even more popular than Washington as a given name during the Revolution. Its origins have long been forgotten by most, but *Elmer* may have originally honored the brothers Ebenezer and Jonathan Elmer, Revolutionary War patriots from New Jersey—"pamphleteers, organizers of Revolutionary militia, surgeons and officers in command of troops throughout the Revolution, members of Congress and fierce debators of a hundred stirring issues of their times." Some experts disagree with the derivation, but no better explanation has been given.

Said a *New York Herald Tribune* editorial on January 18, 1935: "The name Elmer . . . has such an honorable genealogy that it is time for America's countless Elmers to stand up for it."

Elmira, New York. A local legend tells us that Elmira, New York, was named for a little girl whose mother called her home so frequently and stridently ("Elmira! Elmira!") that people in the neighborhood named the town after the child.

an embarrassment of riches. A great amount of wealth, or anything, almost too much to have and certainly too much to conveniently use. The expresssion apparently came into English from the French *embarras de richesse*, meaning the same, which seems to have originated as the title of a 1753 play by the Abbe d'Allainvail. *Embarras de richesse* is also much used in English.

embezzler. *Embezzle* derives from the French word *embeseiller*, meaning "to make away with, cause to disappear, fraudulently destroy." One theory has it that this word was formed from the French *bezel*, "a chisel," and referred to the practice of con men shaving small bits off gold and silver coins, passing off the shaved coins at face value, and melting down the shavings into bullion. *Bezelers*, who used the *bezel*, were these first *embezzlers*, according to this theory.

emcee. (*See* **M.C.**)

Emerald Isle. Doctor William Drennan claimed that in 1795 he invented the term *Emerald Isle* for Ireland, obviously because the island is so brilliantly green. In any case, the expression is first recorded in Drennan's poem *Erin*, which contains the lines:

Arm of Erin! Prove strong, but be gentle as brave,
And, uplifted to strike, still be ready to save,
Nor one feeling of vengeance presume to defile
The cause or the men of the Emerald Isle.

Emmenthaler. The classic "Swiss" cheese laced with holes, *Emmenthal*, or *Emmenthaler*, is formed in huge wheels weighing up to 145 pounds. It is named for Switzerland's Emma Valley, where it is made.

emporium. Since the 16th century, *emporium* has been used to describe principal centers of trade, the word deriving from the Greek *emporion*, a place where merchants come together, the Greek for merchant being *emporos*, which was formed from the prefix *em*, "in," and *porous*, "travel"—the first merchants being traveling salesmen. Early on we had the words *emporial*, pertaining to an emporium, and *emporentic*, of or pertaining to trade, both now obsolete, but *emporium* wasn't applied to a single store until well into the 19th century. Today the latter meaning has almost entirely replaced the former, and though it is considered grandiloquent by some, *emporium* is frequently used for a large store selling a great variety of articles and having a luxurious air.

Empress Eugénie hat. A number of fashions that held sway in the 19th century commemorate the French Empress Eugénie, wife of Napoleon III. This beautiful, elegant, and charming woman, the undisputed leader of French fashion, which led the world then as now, was especially celebrated for her smart hats. She sometimes wore five different specimens in a day, one of her favorites being a small model with the brim turned up on the side and often decorated with ostrich plumes, named the *Empress Eugénie* in her honor. Born Eugenía Maria de Montijo de Guzmán, the empress was the daughter of a Spanish grandee and a Scottish noblewoman. Prince Louis Napoleon at first offered to make her his mistress, but she intrigued to become his wife and prevailed. Their marriage was celebrated in 1853 at Notre Dame. "The Spanish Woman" seemed too conservative in politics to be popular with the French at the time, but strongly influenced Napoleon, often efficiently governing the Empire as regent in his absence. When the Second Empire fell in 1871, she fled to England with her husband, where she died almost half a century later in 1920, ninety-four years old and a legend in her time.

Emu War. (*See* **war of the stray dog**.)

encomium. High praise or a eulogy is called an *encomium*, from the Greek *enkomion*, meaning a eulogy or a panegyric honoring a victor in the Bacchic games, which was sung in a procession moving from *kome* to *kome* ("village to village").

encore. *Encore* is not what the French call out in the concert hall for "repeat it, do it again," as many people believe; the French use *bis bis* for this. But since the early 18th century the word has been used in this sense in English, possibly because *encore* does mean "another" (*encore une tasse*, "another cup") and "once again" (*encore une fois*) in some French phrases.

encyclopedia. Statesman-scholar Sir Thomas Elyot (1499?-1546), whose translations helped popularize the Greek classics in England, coined the word *encyclopedia* from the Greek *en kyklos*, "in a circle," and *paedia*, "teaching of children," the two words possibly suggesting to him "some kind of universal classroom or round table," as someone has suggested. Elyot also naturalized the Greek *democratia* into *democracy* and was the first to use *education* (Latin *educare*, "to raise a child") in its modern sense.

end of his rope. An executed murderer dangling at the end of a rope didn't inspire this old saying for someone

who has outrun fortune, exhausted all his resources. It derives from an earlier phrase *at the end of his tether*, which refers to an animal who has come to the end of the rope he is tied to and can graze no more. The exact words aren't recorded in English until 1809, but similar expressions are recorded as early as the 16th century, and Locke used something like it in *Human Understanding*. The expression *give him enough rope and he'll hang himself* (*q.v.*) probably did reinforce the stronger meaning of the phrase.

engine, engineer. The *gin* in Eli Whitney's *cotton gin* is no more than another word for "engine," an old word that dates back to the 13th century as the synonym for a mechanical contrivance or device. *Engine* itself has a more interesting history. The word is from the Latin *ingenium*, "the powers inborn," the same word that gives us *ingenious*. In English it first meant "native talent, mother wit, genius," Chaucer noting three qualities of the mind: "Memorie, engin and intellect." By extension *engine* came to mean "trickery or device," and Shakespeare used it this way when he wrote in *Othello* that men's lures and promises are "engines of lust." But as more complicated machines were developed the word came to mean the "products of engine or wit," the name for the power transferred to its product, and it is only in this sense that it is used today. An *engineer* was first a wit, one who might have invented a phrase, or even a tricky political plot. Only later was the name applied to constructors of military engines (Shakespeare writing in *Hamlet*, "For 'tis sport to have the enginer hoist with his own petard") and in this sense applied to anyone who *operated* an engine, like a railroad engineer. The only *engineers* to whom the title applied in early times, however, were military engineers, who constructed military engines and works intended to serve military purposes. It wasn't until the mid-18th century that the title was used for those who designed and constructed public works such as roads, bridges, and tunnels—these men called *civil engineers* to distinguish them from their military counterparts.

England. The four tribes that invaded Britain from western Germany and the Jutland (Danish) peninsula after the Romans left in 410 A.D. were called the Saxons, the Frisians, the Jutes, and the Angles. The Angles, last to arrive, in A.D. 547, eventually acquired dominance and by the year 1000 the country as a whole became known as *Englaland*, land of the *Angles* (the shift of the A in *Angle* to the E in *England* known technically as a front mutation). The land's language, however, was known as *Englisc* three-hundred years earlier. (*See* **English**.)

England expects every man will do his duty. These were Lord Nelson's famous words to his men at Trafalgar on October 21, 1805. A British member of Parliament has written that the officialese or gobbledygook so common in government services everywhere today would express the same sentiment this way: "England anticipates that, as regards the current emergency, personnel will face up to the issues and exercise appropriately, the functions allocated to their respective occupational groups." It should be noted that Nelson's famous sentence was first reported as "Say to the fleet, England expects that every man will do his duty." Nelson's flag lieutenant, Captain Pasco, suggested that it be changed to the above.

English.   As the designation for a language *English* is first recorded in about 1000 A.D. At the time English contained perhaps 30,000 words. Today the most complete dictionary (*Webster's Second International*) contains some 650,000 words, but there are probably 5 to 10 million English words if all scientific and technical terms were included. (We should also remember that there are a vast number of personal names in English. In *The Mountain of Names*, 1985, Alex Shoumatoff reports that an estimated 69-110 billion names have been bestowed since humans first made their appearance in the world and that 6-7 billion names of the dead are believed to be extinct!). In any case, the average English-speaking person has a vocabulary of about 3,000 words, while a very well-educated or well-read person might have a vocabulary of 60,000 words. Shakespeare used 19,000 to 25,000 different words to write his plays.

English letters.   (*See* **condom.**)

English sparrow.   People have compared the destructive *English sparrow* to the rat because of the damage it does in eating tree buds and grain. The bird is so named because eight pairs of them were brought from England to Brooklyn in 1850 and freed in an attempt to rid the area of a caterpillar pest called the inchworm. The birds thrived, ultimately proved more of a liability than an asset and are now ubiquitous pests throughout the country.

Enoch Arden.   Enoch Arden, Philip Ray, and Annie Lee grow up together in a little seaport town. Though both boys love Annie, Enoch wins her hand and they live together happily until Enoch sails aboard the merchantman *Good Fortune* to make his fortune. Shipwrecked for ten years on a deserted island, Enoch is finally rescued. Annie, meanwhile has been reduced to poverty and Philip asks her to marry him, certain that Enoch is dead. Enoch is brokenhearted when he returns after the ten years and witnesses, unknown to them, Annie and Philip's happiness, but he vows never to let them know of his return until after his death, sacrificing his happiness for theirs. Such is the plot of Alfred Lord Tennyson's long poem "Enoch Arden," which he based on the true story of a sailor thought drowned at sea who returned home after several years to find that his wife had remarried. A similar case was reported after the *Arctic* went down in 1854; a

New Orleans merchant named Fleury was believed drowned and his young widow remarried. The "widow" had three children by her new marriage and lived happily until a letter arrived from Fleury six years later. A whaler just setting out on a long voyage had rescued him and when the whaler was also wrecked, Fleury was rescued by still another whaler starting out on a long voyage, thus accounting for the many years he had spent at sea. An *Enoch Arden* has come to mean that rare creature who truly loves someone better than himself.

enough to make the angels weep.   Something so foolish that it causes one to lose all hope. Shakespeare appears to have invented the expression in *Measure for Measure* (1604): ". . . man,/ Drest in a little brief authority,/ . . . Plays such fantastic tricks before high heaven/ As make the angels weep."

ensign.   No *ensigns* served in the early American navy, for ensign only became the lowest commissioned rank in 1862. *Ensign* simply means "banner," and the first ensigns were British Army officers who led a group of men under a flag.

to enter the lists.   To compete, to join in the game. *Lists* in this old expression is no listing of names but the borders of a field in medieval times when armed horsemen fought each other for the sport of it.

entire horse.   *Entire* is used to indicate any ungelded animal, including uncastrated stallions. The expression seems to be a Victorian one first recorded in 1881, when a sportsman wrote. "He bought two young bay entires . . ."

environment.   Thomas Carlyle invented the word *environment* (from the English *environ*) in its modern meaning of "the aggregate of external circumstances, conditions, and things that affect the existence and development of an individual, organism, or group." The word, first recorded in 1827, is his rendering of the German *Umgebung*, meaning the same, which had apparently been coined by Goethe.

epicure.   "The fountain and root of every good is the pleasure of the stomach," is a quotation attributed to Epicurus by the Greek writer Athenaeus five centuries after the philosopher's death. Nothing could be further from the spirit of Epicurus. The Greek philosopher (341-270 B.C.) did not teach that mere sensual pleasure is man's reason for being. He argued, rather, that while pleasure constitutes the happiness of life, pleasure means peace of mind and freedom from want and pain, which can be achieved only through noble thoughts, self-control, and moderation. Though this generous, brave man regarded virtue as having no value in itself, the real harm in his philosophy lay in the fact that it was an escapist one—permitting, for example, no marriage, children, or participation in public life. Later students of his garden school in Athens—which lasted over two hundred years—distorted his teachings completely, using them as an excuse for selfish hedonism and heedless indulgence. Seizing upon his idea of pleasure, they magnified it so that an *epicure* became one entirely devoted to gluttony, debauchery, and every wanton sensual pleasure imaginable. It took centuries before the word acquired its present meaning of "gourmet or connoisseur," one with refined tastes and knowledge of food and drink, and even today's *epicure* is still far removed from the simple serene philosophy of Epicurus.

epiphany. *Epiphany* is the Christian "Little Christmas," January 6th, commemorating the manifestation or appearance of Christ to the gentiles, as represented by the Magi. The word, first recorded as far back as 1310, comes to us from a Greek word meaning "to manifest or appear" and originally referred to the gods of the Greeks making sudden appearances. Today an *epiphany* can be a sudden insight into the reality or meaning of something as well as an appearance.

epizootic. Deriving from the Greek *epi*, "upon or among," and *zoo*, "animal," epizootic diseases include rabies and hoof-and-mouth disease. The Great Epizootic (the word can be either a noun or adjective) of 1872 claimed almost a quarter of America's horses (some four million) and left the nation's business without the power it needed to function for three months—most power at the time being horsepower. Scientists never isolated the virus that caused the epizootic, and it ended its ravages only when cold weather killed the mosquitoes that transmitted the deadly virus. By that time the financial losses suffered had helped bring on the Panic of 1873. To a nation wholly dependent on horsepower, the epizootic was indeed a tragedy. In cities across the country homes went without heat, fires blazed unfought, garbage wasn't collected, deliveries halted, public transportation ceased, stores closed, and unemployment soared. Racetracks closed their gates, and at least one great American thoroughbred, Pocohontas, fell to the disease. In several cities unemployed men were even harnessed to carts and trolleys in place of horses.

E Pluribus Unum. The motto on the obverse side of the Great Seal of the United States may come from an expression found on the title page of the British *Gentlemen's Magazine*, widely circulated in America for several decades after 1731. The title page of the magazine's first volume shows a hand holding a bouquet over the epigraph, *E. Pluribus Unum*. The Latin words mean, in this case, "From many, one," and are as fitting for a bouquet of flowers as they are for a nation composed of many former colonies. Other possibilities, however, include a line in Virgil's poem "Moretum," which deals with the making of a salad and reads *color est e pluribus unus*, probably the first use of the phrase in any form, and an essay by Richard Steele in *The Spectator* (August 20, 1711), which opens with the Latin phrase *Exempta juvat spiris e pluribus unus* ("Better one thorn plucked than all remain"). The Continental Congress ordered the President of Congress to have a seal in 1776 and *E Pluribus Unum* appeared on the first seal, as well as on many early coins. Congress adopted the motto in 1781 and it still appears on U.S. coins as well as on the Great Seal.

Epsom salts. *Epsom salts*, whose composition is essentially the same as that of seawater, derive their name from the mineral springs in Epsom, England, where the natural hydrated magnesium sulphate baths attracted many people searching for good health.

equalizer. Inventors Daniel B. Wesson and Horace Smith founded the Smith & Wesson Arms Company at Springfield, Massachusetts, three years after they published the first firearms magazine in 1854. Their Smith & Wesson pistols replaced the Colt to a large extent and have been famous ever since. In fact, the term *equalizer*, for "a gun," may come indirectly from their names. It is said that the term derives from a remark made by Chicago gangster Tim Smith, who died in a gangland killing on June 26, 1928. "Smith and Wesson made all men equal," this non-related Smith is supposed to have said.

Erlenmeyer flask. Emil Erlenmeyer put his name in mothballs for posterity when he devised the first formula for naphthalene, used in making them. The German organic chemist also invented the cone-shaped, flat-bottomed *Erlenmeyer flask* made from thin glass and commonly used in chemistry laboratories. Erlenmeyer, who taught at Heidelberg, conducted many important experiments in his long, fruitful career. He died in 1909, aged eighty-four.

ermine. The lovely fur takes its name from a rat, *ermine* deriving from the Latin for the Old World weasel, *Armenius mus*, "the Armenian rat"—so called because it was thought to come from Armenia.

erosion. *Rodere*, the Latin for "to gnaw," gives us both the *rodent* and the word *erosion*, which is common to most languages today. *Erosion* was first used in medieval times to describe acid eating through metals, and in the 19th century was applied to the gnawing action of water upon land.

ersatz. Not recorded in English until 1919, *ersatz* came into English from German, where it meant "substitute," deriving from *ersetzen*, "to replace." The meaning of "substitute" changed in English to "an inferior or artificial substitute," something not as good as the real thing.

Esau's mess of pottage. There are two versions of the proverbial story in the Bible. In one (Genesis 25:27-34) Esau sells his birthright to his twin brother Jacob for a mess of red pottage, while in the other (Genesis 27) Jacob conspires with his mother Rebekah to cheat his older twin out of his paternal blessing. Historians believe that the stories symbolize conflicts between the Edomites, led by the eponymous Edom or *Esau*, and the Israel tribe headed by Jacob. The Edomites were probably wandering hunters, as represented by *Esau* in both stories, and the Israelites more civilized pastoral nomads. The phrase is generally used today without Esau's name (*mess of pottage*). Incidentally, the "mess" was most likely tempting. Arabians still prepare lentils in what is thought to be a similar way, blending onions and rice with them and simmering the concoction in sesame seed oil—a delectable dish, it is said.

escape. The Latin word *excappare* (from *ex*, "out of," and *cappa*, "cloak"), "to slip out of one's cloak," is the ancestor of our word *escape*, though the Greeks had a similar word meaning literally "to get out of one's clothes." The idea behind these words is probably someone slipping out of a cloak or coat held by a robber or jailer—and escaping, leaving the villain or keeper with the cloak in his hands.

Escoffier sauce; Escoffier garnish. If one man had to be chosen to epitomize modern gastronomy it would have to be Auguste Escoffier (1847-1935). Escoffier, made a member of the French Legion of Honor in 1920, was renowned as a chef and restaurateur, operating, with César Ritz, the Ritz in Paris, London's Savoy, and the Grand Hotel in Monte Carlo. Author of a number of books on the art of cooking, Escoffier invented both the basic sauce and the chopped, carmelized almond topping for peach melba that bear his name.

Eskimo. *Eskimo* is an Algonquin word meaning "eaters of raw flesh." The Eskimos do not recognize it. They proudly call themselves *Innuit*, "the People," or "the human beings." "Bantu," "Navaho" and "Ainu" also translate as "the People" or "all the People," as do the names of many primitive tribes.

Eskimo pie. Invented in 1919 and originally called an "I Scream Bar," this still-popular chocolate-covered ice-cream bar was manufactured in 1921 by Russell Stover (for whom the well-known chocolate-covered candies are named) and given the trade name *Eskimo Pie*.

Esperanto. Over the past seven centuries scores of artificial universal languages have been invented. The French philosopher Descartes devised one in 1629; there is another called Sobresol, based on the notes of the musical scale; and a third, Timerio, is written solely in numerals (*i.e.*, 1-80-17—"I love you"). *Esperanto* is far better known than any other such invention. It takes its name from the pseudonym chosen by its inventor, Lazarus Zamenhof, when he wrote his first book on the subject, *Linguo Internacia de la Doktoro Esperanto*. Dr. Lazarus Ludwig Zamenhof (1859-1917), the "Doctor Hopeful" of the title, was a Warsaw oculist who believed that a world language would promote peace and understanding. He launched his system in 1887 and today the movement has some eight million supporters, with from half a million to a million people capable of speaking *Esperanto* fluently. Advocates claim that the language—based primarily on words common to the major tongues, with a Latin-type grammar—is much easier to learn than any other and can be mastered in a relatively short time. Esperanto is now taught in over 750 schools in 40 countries around the world, has textbooks for study in 54 languages, has been used in more than 8,600 books, and is the subject of some 145 periodicals.

-ess (Feminine termination). Unlike most feminists today Mrs. Sara Josepha Hale thought that the *-ess* or feminine termination in words, declining steadily since Chaucer's day, should be revived in many cases or carried much further. So in 1867 the editor of *Godey's Lady's Book* recommended the following words: *actress, adventuress, arbitress, authoress, citizeness, doctress, governess, huntress, instructress, monitress, murderess, negress, paintress, poetress, postmistress, preceptress, professoress, sculptress, shepherdess, songstress, sorceress, stewardess, tailoress, teacheress, tormentress, traitress, victress, waitress.* Of these only *actress, waitress* and *governess* are commonly used today. *Songstress, sorceress* (historical) and *stewardess* (despite *flight attendant*) still have some currency, but the rest are rarely, if ever, heard. I have never heard anyone called a *teacheress* or a *victress*, a female victim—and many feminists today would feel that a woman called any of these terms would qualify as a *victress*.

essay. Montaigne's *Essais*, published in France in 1580, were the first in history to bear the name *essay* for a literary composition, while Bacon's *Essays Dedicated to Prince Henry* (1597) were the first in English to use the name. "To write treatises," Bacon explained, "requireth leisure in the writer and leisure in the reader . . . which is the cause which hath made me choose to write certain brief notes . . . which I have called essays. The word is late, but the thing is ancient." There are three words for short essays, none of which is used very much, if at all, anymore: "essaykin," "essaylet," and "essayette."

essence. *Essence* derives from a Latin word that is thought to be a corruption of the Greek phrase for "What is it?" It means what a thing basically is, its primary kind of being, the word first recorded in 1576.

Essenes; Essenian; Essenic. According to unsubstantiated traditions, both Jesus and John the Baptist were originally Essenes, a sect of pre-Christian Jews that emphasized ascetic self-discipline, communal property, ceremonial purity, and baptism. The Essenes dressed in white, strictly obeyed the Sabbath, ate no meat, and drank only water. They led a monastic life, shunning marriage and wealth, and similarly ascetic persons are sometimes called *Essenes* or *Essenic* today. Little accurate historical information is available about the Essenes, but since the discovery of the Dead Sea Scrolls in Qumràn, thought to be the *Essenian* homeland, there has been renewed interest in the group.

E.T.; extraterrestrial. H. G. Wells first recorded, and perhaps invented, *extraterrestrial* as an adjective at the turn of the century. Meaning "ouside the limits of the earth," the word was first used as a noun by American author L. Sprague de Camp in the May 1939 issue of *Astounding Science Fiction,* the author inventing the abbreviation *e.t.* in the same article. *E.T.* has since become the name of the extraterrestrial being in the popular film *E.T.* Wells, or someone before him, may have patterned *extraterrestrial* on *extraterritorial,* which dates back to at least 1665.

ethnophaulism. A term for ethnic slurs, *ethnophaulism* was coined (from the Greek *phaulos,* "ugly") by A.A. Rodack in the subtitle of his authoritative *Dictionary of International Slurs* (1944). Such insults—usually cheap humor—have been known since the earliest times and still prevail. The Irish call the English names, the English insult the French, the French defame the Germans, and so on ad infinitum, or ad nauseam.

et tu Brute. (*See* **Brutus.**)

Euclidian. The Greek mathematician Euclid's *Elements,* written in the third century B.C., was a collection of theorems and problems that formed the basis for geometry. So famous were Euclid's mathematical works—the *Elements* alone consisted of thirteen "books"—that they completely overshadowed his life; almost nothing known about the man himself. The mathematician probably received his training from pupils of Plato in Athens, and it is certain that he founded a school in Alexandria about 306 B.C. Euclid is said to have told Ptolemy that "there is no royal road to geometry" when the ruler asked if there wasn't an easier way to learn it. Much of his *Elements* owes a great debt to the work of earlier mathematicians.

eudaemonia. The *Eudaemonic Pie,* a recent book by Thomas A. Bass, brings this rare but useful word to mind.

It means, according to one dictionary definition, "a state of felicity or bliss obtained by a life lived in accordance with reason," and was apparently coined by Aristotle in that sense, deriving from the Greek word for happiness. *Eudaemonia* also means, quite simply, plain old uncomplicated "happiness."

euhemeristic. *Euhemeristic* is an adjective applied to attempts to interpret myths, especially primitive religious myths, on a historical basis. The Greek writer Euhemerus is responsible for the word, it being this mythmaker's theory that the gods popularly worshipped in the 4th century B.C. had all originally been kings and heroes. In his philosophical romance *Sacred History* Euhemerus depicted the gods thus, insisting that they had merely been deified by their subjects or admirers. The writer claimed that he had discovered an inscribed gold pillar confirming his theory in a temple on an island in the Indian Ocean.

eunuch. A little consciousness-raising for *eunuchs!* At one time *eunuchs* were "keepers or guardians of the bed," hence their name, which derives from the Greek *eune,* "bed," and *echo,* "keep." Today the term refers to any castrated human male and is used figuratively to describe a man with no courage, strength, or backbone, a weak, powerless, spineless person. Strictly speaking, however, all of our uses of *eunuch* are wrong, for *eunuchs* were never what most people still think them to be. Eunuchs were *not* deficient in courage and intellect. From earliest times throughout the world they took charge of harems or were the chamberlains of royal households and their confidential position often enabled them to rise to stations of great power. Neither were eunuchs always castrated. And even when they were castrated, in certain cases—if the castration took place after puberty and only the testicles were removed—they were still capable of sexual intercourse, some ladies of ancient Rome preferring them as both natural birth control devices and lovers best at prolonging the sex act. Among famous eunuchs in history were the Italian *castrati,* young boys who were castrated so that they could be trained as adult soprano singers, and the *Skopski,* a Russian religious sect whose members castrated themselves as an act of salvation and numbered over 5,000 before the Russian government prosecuted them in 1874.

euphuism. (*See* **Guevarism.**)

eureka. When Archimedes discovered the principle of buoyancy in his bathtub while determining by specific gravity the proportion of base metal in Hiero's golden crown, he supposedly ran naked through the streets of Syracuse shouting *"Eureka, Eureka!"* ("I have found it! I have found it!") Since the 16th century the term has been used allusively as an exulting cry of discovery. Plutarch tells the story about Archimedes, and it could well be true, for the Greeks commonly exercised in the nude and a naked man running through the streets wouldn't have been at all unusual.

even keel. The expression *to get things on an even keel*, "to make things move smoothly," dates back to at least the early 19th century. It, of course, derives from the nautical term *an even keel*, which one early writer defined this way: "A ship is said to swim on an even keel when she draws the same quantity of water abaft as forward."

even steven. Contrary to some accounts, there was never a gentleman named Steven who matched his wife blow for blow. The term apparently stems from a far less equitable character in Jonathan Swift's *Journal to Stella* (1713): "'Now we are even,' quoth Steven, when he gave his wife six blows to one." Stella was Swift's name for Esther Johnson, and his *Journal* letters to her described his daily life in London. Their relationship was a complicated one. Swift, fourteen years Stella's senior, taught her to read and write, loved her all his life and when he died was buried beside her, but the two lovers probably never married.

evergreen. (*See* **deciduous.**)

every dog has his day. Cervantes apparently deserves credit for this proverb, which is given in *Don Quixote* (1605-1615). Two centuries later, English author George Borrow wrote: "Youth will be served, every dog has his day, and mine has been a fine one." No one has been able to trace the proverb to the Himalayan valleys north of India, where all dogs literally do have a day. *Dog's Day* in the region is called *Khich Mavas* by the Kashmiris and *Swana Boli* by the Nepalese. It is a day when humans pay reverence to dogs as their brothers and sisters among living things. Choice food is set out for the dogs; even the mangiest strays get flower garlands hung around their necks and the Nepalese dogs wear the red spot of Hindu holiness imprinted on their foreheads. The following day things get back to normal until the next Dog's Day and the dogs lead a dog's life, 364 days of curses, kicks, and stonings from humans who consider them unclean and contemptible.

every inch a man, etc. In every way. *Every inch* phrases are nothing new, having been popular ever since Shakespeare used one in *King Lear* (1606): *Gloucester*: Is't not the king. *Lear*: Ay, every inch a king.

Everyman. The term *Everyman* means "every man and woman." It derives from the central character of the 15th-century morality play *Everyman*, of unknown origin, which is still read and performed today.

every man has his price. Some cynic other than Sir Robert Walpole coined this phrase. The British prime minister said something entirely different and referred only to corrupt members of Parliament, according to William Coxe in his *Memoirs of Sir Robert Walpole* (1798). Wrote Coxe of Sir Robert: "Flowery oratory he despised. He ascribed to the interested view of themselves or their relatives the declarations of pretended patriots, of whom he said, 'All those men have their price.'"

every man jack. Everybody without exception, even the most insignificant. This apparently isn't a nautical phrase; at least it is first recorded by Dickens in *Barnaby Rudge* (1840). Dickens may have coined the precise phrase, but Shakespeare used a similar term in the same sense in *Cymbeline*: "Every Jack-slave hath his belly full of fighting."

everything's all tiggerty-boo. The American *O.K.* is generally replacing *right-o* in England, but *right-o* is still heard, as is its synonym *tiggerty-boo*, especially in the above expression. The *tiggerty* here (sometimes pronounced *tickerty*) is from the Hindustani *teega* and is said to have been introduced to Britain by Lord Mountbatten.

every which way. In every way, in all directions. The first recorded use of this Americanism, in 1824, says it was originally an "odd phrase" taught by slaves to the children of Virginia gentry.

Eve's curse. (*See* **the curse.**)

evil-starred. (*See* **moonlit.**)

Excalibur. King Arthur's famous sword, which Arthur pulled from a stone in which it had been fixed by magic, proving him "the right born king of all England." *Excalibur* is so called from the name of a sword famous in Irish legend: *Caledvelch* or *Caladbolg*, meaning "hardbelly," that is, voracious, capable of consuming anything.

excelsior. *Excelsior*, or "wood shavings," takes its name from New York State's Latin motto *Excelsior*, "Yet higher, ever higher." The word was originally a trademark of the New York-based Excelsior Mattress Company, which borrowed *Excelsior* for its name from the State's Great Seal in 1868 and also applied it to the wood shavings used to stuff its mattresses.

exclamation mark (!). Like *&* (*q.v.*) *!* goes by a number of names. In America it's usually called an *exclamation mark* or *point*, but the British call it, more simply, an *exclamation*, and sometimes a *note* or *point of exclamation*. Anyone using the older rhetorical terms *ecphonesis* ("the outcry") or *epiphonema* for the grammatical interjection rates an *!* of surprise, which is called *a note of admiration*, or, depending on your taste, "a note of detestation." Shakespeare used the phrase *note of admiration* (!) effectively in *The Winter's Tale*: "The changes I perceived in the King and Camillo were very Notes of admiration." But sometimes writers slashed pages with scores of them following words and phrases intended to be uttered with an intonation of exclamation or surprise, leading Swift to write that a reader should skip over sentences with *notes of admiration* at the end. For that matter the exclamation has had few friends throughout history. Dr. Johnson defined it as "a note by which a pathetical sentence is marked thus!" while Spenser said, "The lowest form of language is the exclamation, by which an entire idea is vaguely conveyed through a single sound." But the powerful points do have their uses in small doses—showing strong emotions or emphasizing commands or warnings. They seem to have been invented by the Italians and came into English use about four centuries ago. Tradition says that the mark derives from the Latin *io* (exclamation of joy), written vertically as ϕ, which became ! in time.

excruciating. This interesting word should not be used lightly when describing pain. It comes from the Latin *crucifigere*, "to crucify," and reflects the fact that the Romans thought that crucifixion was the most painful of all ways of execution.

Exeter's daughter. (*See* **rack one's brains.**)

expedite. An old story that no one has been able to prove or disprove holds that the Latin word *expedire*, the ancestor of *expedite*, derives from the name of St. Expeditus, a soldier in the Roman Army before being martyred at Melitene, Armenia, in the fourth century. St. Expeditus, it seems, was the advocate of *urgent* causes. The *O.E.D.* merely says that the Latin word *expedire* means "to free a person's feet (ped) from fetters, to help forward, to dispatch, send off."

expletive deleted. *Expletive deleted* has quickly become a euphemism to use in place of a curse, especially for four-letter words. The phrase originated in the 1970s after Watergate, deriving of course from the transcripts of President Nixon's White House tapes in which many curses are rendered as "expletive deleted."

extraterrestrial. (*See* **E.T.**)

extrovert. (*See* **Jungian.**)

eyeballs in, eyeballs out. Test pilots in the 1960s coined this term to describe the physical effect of acceleration on the person being accelerated. For example, the acceleration experienced by an astronaut at lift-off is *eyeballs in*, while the expression of an astronaut when the retrorockets fire is *eyeballs out*.

eyeless in Gaza. (*See* **gauze; Samson.**)

eyeteeth. (*See* **cut one's eyeteeth.**)

F

F. *F* was the sixth letter in the Phoenician and Latin alphabets, as it is in ours. In both Phoenician and Hebrew its character was a peg. An *F* branded on a person's left cheek in medieval times signified that he was a felon.

F. *F.*, following temperatures, has become the shortest and one of the most widely used eponymous words. In 1714 Gabriel Daniel Fahrenheit perfected and manufactured the first practical mercury-in-glass thermometer, and invented the scale for measuring temperature that is named after him. Galileo had developed a faulty air-thermoscope long before this, and there were numerous contact thermometers employing alcohol in 1654, but Fahrenheit's was the first fairly precise instrument of its kind. Even at that, his thermometric scale has had to be revised since he invented it—his thermometer being inaccurate enough for him to regard 96 degrees as the temperature of a healthy man. Today only two of his fixed reference points—32 degrees and 212 degrees, the freezing and boiling points of water under standard atmospheric pressure—are still used on the *Fahrenheit scale*. The inventor, a German born in Danzig, Poland, lived most of his life in Holland and England after being orphaned at fifteen. He was elected to Britain's Royal Society before his death in 1736 when only fifty years old.

Fabian tactics. Such delaying tactics are named after Quintus Fabius Maximus, the Roman dictator who over a ten-year period defeated Hannibal's superior Carthaginian army. His strategy was to avoid open engagements and employ his troops only in harassing raids and skirmishes in the hills, where Hannibal's cavalry was ineffective. Marches, countermarches, and other hit-and-run tactics were among the "masterly inactivities" devised by this cool, unemotional man to gradually erode Hannibal's forces, despite the objections of the subjects who had elected him dictator. After his victory in the Second Punic War, in 209 B.C., he earned the agnomen, or official nickname, of "Cunctator," the "slow-goer" or "delayer," for his wariness. England's socialist *Fabian Society*, founded in 1884, adopted Fabius Cunctator's name upon rejecting Marxist revolutionary theory and decided to accomplish "the reorganization of society" without violence, "by stealing inches, not by grasping leagues," this giving the word a new, political significance. *Fabian policy* is thus patient, long-range planning.

face the music. Though not listed by *Mathews*, this appears to be an Americanism first recorded in 1850. Meaning "to face up to the consequences of one's actions" it may have originally been Army slang, alluding to the "Rogue's March" being played when an offender was drummed out of the service.

fad. A persistent old story holds that *fad*, a temporary fashion, derives from the initials of *for a day*, but there is no proof of this. Most authorities believe that the word, first recorded in 1834, comes from the English dialect *fad*, "to busy oneself with trifles," which may be a contraction of the *faddle* in *fiddle faddle*, "trifling talk or trivial matters"—but there is no real proof of this theory either.

Fahrenheit scale. (*See* **F.**)

fail-safe. The *fail-safe system*, intended to help prevent nuclear war, was developed by the Strategic Air Command of the U.S. Air Force in the 1950s. Under the fail-safe procedure a bomber had to return home without dropping its bombs if specific orders to drop the bombs weren't received. Thus a failure to receive such a radio message would be a failure on the safe side that wouldn't accidentally trigger a nuclear war. The term *fail-safe* is now used to describe any precautionary system.

fairy rings. Fairies dancing on the spot were once thought to cause the dead or withered circles of grass often found on lawns. The *fairy rings* are, sad to say, caused by more prosaic fungi below the surface that envelop the grass roots and prevent them from obtaining water. The term is first recorded in 1598 when Ben Jonson used it in his satirical play *Every Man in his Humour*, in which Shakespeare acted at its first performance at the Globe Theatre. (*See also* **fascinate**.)

falderol. First used as a meaningless refrain in Scottish songs (as in Browning's line *Fol-di-rol-di-rido-liddle-iddle-o!*) *falderol* or *folderol*, attested early in the 18th century, came within a century or so to mean "nonsense, empty talk or ideas."

fall. (*See* **autumn**.)

to fall in love. "So fare I—falling into love's dance;" wrote a man smitten back in 1423, the first recorded use of the expression. It took over a century more for *falling in love* to detach itself from *falling into love's dance*, but since then the phrase has been indispensable, suggesting so simply and well the dizzy loss of control of the love struck.

false front. Gay Nineties merchants often built the facades of their stores in such a way as to give the appearance of greater size, which they thought appropriate in an era of great prosperity. But in time these *false fronts* became the symbol of pretense or sham that the expression means today.

fanfare; fanfaron. *Fanfare,* an "ostentatious display or flourish," was originally a flourish or short air played by trumpets when important people, or self-important people, arrived. In this sense it derived from the Spanish *fanfarria,* meaning "bluster, haughtiness," haughty people often demanding that heralding trumpets be played when they came upon the scene. Another word deriving from the Spanish *fanfarria* is *fanfaron,* for a braggart.

Fannie Mae. (*See* **Ginnie Mae.**)

fanny. This euphemism may be an unknown personification, the diminutive of the feminine name Frances, or it may have a more objectionable history than the word it replaces. For *Partridge* suggests that the euphemism for "backside" comes from the eponymous heroine of John Cleland's hardly euphemistic novel *Fanny Hill* (1749). The term in this sense is originally an American one, however, probably deriving from the English slang use of Cleland's *Fanny* for "the female pudenda." Or else Americans were reading *Fanny Hill* long before it was legally permissible to do so. Cleland's classic of brothel life, which he wrote to escape debtor's prison, has already been made into a movie, had had vast sales in paperback and, judging by recent examples, may indeed finally prove euphemistic for its genre. Another etymologist feels that *fanny* may come from the obsolete expression "fancy vulva"; still another source traces the word to a pun on "fundament" (which became "fun," then "fan," then *fanny*), and *Webster's* derives it from "the fanciful euphemism 'Aunt Fanny' for the buttocks."

Fanny Heath raspberry; Lloyd George raspberry. Raspberries have not been cultivated for nearly as long as apples, peaches, and pears. Called a brambleberry and considered a nuisance in England, it was not until about 1830 that the delicate, delicious fruit began to be developed in America. The *Fanny Heath* variety is a tribute to a determined pioneer woman who immigrated to North Dakota in 1881. This young bride had been told that she could never grow anything on the barren alkaline soil surrounding her house, but forty years later her homestead was an Eden of flowers, fruits, and vegetables. After her death in 1931, the black raspberry she developed was named in her honor. A red raspberry variety honoring a famous person is the *Lloyd George,* named after British Prime Minister David Lloyd George (1863-1945), who led Britain to victory in World War I and dominated British politics in the first quarter of this century.

fans. *Fans* for enthusiasts or devotees, is a shortening of *fanatics,* the Americanism first recorded in 1889. *Fans* were originally sports enthusiasts, but soon the word was applied to the devoted followers of thespians as well.

farad; faraday. Born into extreme poverty, he had virtually no formal education and is said to have possessed a very poor memory, yet Michael Faraday (1791-1867) became probably the world's greatest experimental genius in the physical sciences. As both a physicist and chemist Faraday became one of the immortals of science—discovering the principle of the electric motor, developing the first dynamo, formulating the laws of electrolysis, producing the first stainless steel, and discovering benzene and butylene, among many other brilliant accomplishments. His discovery of electromagnetic induction alone provided the basis for our modern electrified world and produced his "field concept," which in turn was the basis a century later of Einstein's revolutionary theory of relativity. The *farad* named for the scientist is an electromagnetic unit, while a *faraday* is a unit of electricity used in electrolysis. Faraday invented the electrical terms "anode" and "cathode."

farce. French theatrical programs used to be stuffed, or completed, with brief broad comedies based on swift action and surprising situations—which gave us the word for such broad comedies, *farce,* from the French *farcier,* "to stuff." The word is first recorded sometime in the 15th century in connection with religious dramas.

farm. A French *farmer* was originally a tax collector, for the word *farm* came into English from the French *ferme,* which in turn derives from the Latin *firmus,* "fixed or settled," and meant the fixed annual rent paid for a tract of land. The French *fermes générales* were tax collectors who made a handsome living up until the French Revolution. In England, *farm,* a corruption of *ferme,* long meant "the fixed rent on agricultural land," but over the years came to be applied to that land itself.

faro. *Faro,* which is now a card game principally played in gambling houses, derives its name from an Egyptian pharaoh, but so far as we know, from no particular king except the king of spades. The game came to England from France or Italy and little more is known about it than that. The French version was named *pharaon* (pharaoh), but this was altered to *faro* as it grew popular among the English. It is assumed that at a certain stage in the game's history, a likeness of an Egyptian pharaoh appeared either on all the cards, or, more likely, on the king of spades.

a farrago of nonsense. *Farrago*, from the Latin *farrago*, is "a mixed fodder for cattle," and figuratively means "a confused mixture, a hodgepodge." Since the 17th century the word has been used in expressions such as a *farrago of doubts, cant, fears, nonsense*, etc.

fascinate. Ben Jonson first recorded the word *fascinate* in his play *Every Man in his Humour* (1598), which had in the cast Shakespeare, who would fascinate the world forever. The word derives from the Latin *fascinum*, "a spell," and meant in Jonson's time "to literally case a spell by means of the evil eye," not taking on its present meaning, "to be irresistibly attractive," for another half century. (*See also* **fairy rings.**)

fast one. (*See* **to pull a fast one.**)

Fata Morgana. Mirages of houses, ships, and mirror images, often seen in the water as well as in the air, and often doubled—inverted above each other—have frequently been reported in the Strait of Messina and other places. They are named *Fata Morgana* after Morgan le Fay, a sorceress in Arthurian legend, the words *Fata Morgana* being an Italian translation of Morgan le Fay.

Father Damien. *Father Damien*, the religious name of Joseph De Veuster (1840-1889), is often used to describe "a selfless, heroic man of God." Damien de Veuster, a Belgian Catholic missionary of the Society of the Sacred Heart of Jesus and Mary, was sent to the Hawaiian Islands in 1863 to replace his ailing brother, and was ordained as a priest the following year. He volunteered to be the first resident chaplain for the leper colony on Molokai ten years later. For many years the courageous priest labored almost single-handedly to improve the condition of the seven hundred lepers there, contracting leprosy himself but remaining in the colony among his people until he died.

Father Mathew. A Capuchin priest and Irish social worker, Father Mathew took a pledge of total abstinence in 1838 and through his campaigning in Ireland, England, and America, gained a tremendous following, coming to be known as "the Apostle of Temperance." His name became proverbial for a temperance reformer, his good work rewarded by a pension Queen Victoria bestowed upon him. Father Mathew was sixty-six when he died in 1856.

fathom. A fathom is now a nautical measure of six feet, but it was once defined by an act of Parliament as "the length of a man's arms around the object of his affections." The word derives from the Old English *faethm*, meaning "the embracing arms."

fatted calf. (*See* **kill the fatted calf.**)

fatten the kitty. (*See* **sweeten the kitty.**)

fauna. Linnaeus first used *fauna* as a term for "animals" in his 1746 book *Fauna Suica*, a companion volume to his *Flora Suica* (1745). The great naturalist took *fauna* from the name of a Roman rural goddess.

fava bean. The *Fava bean* takes its name from *faba*, the Latin word for "bean." It is often called the broad bean, horse bean, or Windsor bean. Since antiquity this widely grown legume has been known to cause *favism* in people of African and Mediterranean origin with a certain enzyme deficiency, fava-bean poisoning sometimes proving fatal.

feague. In times long past, fortunately, horse trainers would insert ginger or even a live eel, it is said, into a horse's anus to liven him up and make him "carry his tail well" when he was to be shown to prospective buyers. This was called *feaguing* a horse. The expression, coming to mean "encouraging or spiriting him up," was used well into the 19th century. The origin of *feague* is unknown though it may derive from the German *fegen*, to polish.

fearnought. Heavy woolen clothing worn by sailors was called *fearnought* in the 19th century. Men wearing clothing made of *fearnought* needed to "fear nought" from the weather.

featherbedding. "What do you want, feather beds?" management supposedly snapped when Rock Island Railroad freight crews complained that their caboose bunks were too hard. This has been cited as the origin of the term *featherbedding*, for "unions forcing employers to hire more men than necessary for a job." It is certain, however, only that the expression was first recorded during a labor dispute in 1943.

a feather in his cap. American Indians of various tribes often wore feathers to show their past bravery in wars. This custom led to the Americanism *a feather in his cap*, "an honor or an accomplishment of which a person can be proud."

feather one's nest. Birds commonly use their breast down to make a soft, comfortable lining for their nests when they will be hatching eggs for a long period. This practice gave rise, in the early 16th century, to the expression *to feather one's nest*, "to accumulate wealth for one's comfort in the future."

February. February is named for *Februaria*, the name Juno was given as goddess of fertility. February had been the month when the festival of Lupercalia was held and youths roamed the streets supposedly making barren women fruitful by striking them with magic thongs called *februa*, fashioned from the hides of goats sacrificed to *Februaria*. By the way, February originally had 29 days, but the Romans took one from it to give to July, so that July, named after Julius Caesar, wouldn't be inferior to August, named after Augustus Caesar.

fecalemia. Medical school students in relatively recent times invented this term for "cowardice." The mocking word was made from *fecal*, "feces," and *emia*, "of the blood," literally meaning "shit in the blood."

fee. The Anglo-Saxons used cattle for trading, these cattle called *feoh*, like all farm animals. Eventually *feoh* came to mean "payments of any kind." Altered to *fee*, the term finally was used for any public or private charges as well.

feel one's oats. Someone *feeling his oats* or *full of oats* is in high spirits, full of pep, so full of himself that he may even be showing off a bit. The allusion is to lively horses fed on oats and the expression is American, first recorded in 1843 by Canadian Thomas Haliburton, the humorist whose Sam Slick gave us "cry over spilt milk" and other expressions. Men, women, and children can *feel their oats*, but only young men are said to *sow their wild oats*.

feet of clay. The phrase comes from the Old Testament (Dan. 2:31-32). There the Hebrew captain Daniel interprets a dream for Nebuchadnezzar, founder of the new Babylonian Empire. Nebuchadnezzar had dreamed of a giant idol with golden head, silver arms and chest, brass thighs and body, and iron legs. Only the feet of this image, compounded of iron and potter's clay, weren't made wholly of metal. Daniel told Nebuchadnezzar that the clay feet of the figure made it vulnerable, that it prophesied the breaking apart of his empire. Over the years readers of the Bible were struck with the phrase *feet of clay* in the story and it was used centuries ago to describe an unexpected flaw or vulnerable point in the character of a hero or any admired person.

feisty. A *feist*, first spelled *foist*, *fice*, or *fise*, was in George Washington's time a little, ill-natured cur full of fight. An Americanism, the term probably has its roots in the British *fysting curre* and *fisting hound*, which date back to the 16th century and have their origins in the word *fist*. By the early 20th century *feist* had evolved into the adjective *feisty*, "belligerent, high-spirited, and fidgety."

fellowfeel. As a synonym for empathy, the ability to get inside the other fellow's skin and feel like him, *fellowfeel* was commonly used from the 17th through the 19th century. The word is a back-formation from *fellowfeeling*, a rendering of the Latin *compassio*.

Fell types. (*See* **I do not love thee, Dr. Fell.**)

♀ **(female) and** ♂ **(male).** Perhaps you've wondered about the derivation of these standard scientific symbols for female and male. The female symbol is the representation of a hand mirror and is associated with Aphrodite, the Greek goddess of beauty; it also serves as the symbol of the planet Venus (the Roman equivalent of Aphrodite). The male symbol represents the shield and spear of Mars, the Roman god of war; it serves also as the symbol of the planet Mars.

fence-mending. Secretary of the Treasury John Sherman, later to author the Sherman Anti-Trust Act, decided to run for the Senate in 1879, knowing that he would shortly lose his Cabinet post because President Rutherford B. Hayes wouldn't be running for reelection. When he visited his Ohio farm, he told reporters "I have come back to mend my fences" and reporters assumed he meant political fences, not the ones around the farm. Soon after, *fence-mending* came to mean "trying to gather political support at home by making personal contacts," and "patching up disagreements," the last its most common use today.

fennel; finochio. *Finochio* or *fennel* can be traced to a Latin word, *feniculum*, meaning "product of the meadow." *Florence fennel*, a sweet variety, is often called *finochio*.

fermium. *Fermium*, like *einsteinium* (*q.v.*), is an artificially produced radioactive element first detected by American physicist Albert Ghiorso in the debris of the first H-bomb explosion. Element 100 was named for Enrico Fermi (1901-54), "the father of the atomic bomb," the year after his death. Professor Fermi, Italian born, left Italy in 1936 to receive the Nobel Prize for his theory of radioactive substances known as *Fermi statistics*. Opposed to Mussolini's anti-Semitic policies, he did not return, immigrating to America and becoming a citizen of the United States. Fermi directed the scientific team that produced the historic self-sustained nuclear chain reaction at the University of Chicago in 1942, and worked on the development of the atomic bomb at Los Alamos, New Mexico.

ferret. This domesticated polecat has been much used over the centuries to drive rats and rabbits from their burrows, thus giving us expressions like *to ferret out the facts*, etc. The animal, however, takes its name from the Latin *fur*, "thief," probably because it had a bad reputation for killing and stealing domestic fowl.

Ferris wheel. Not even Little Egypt, the first belly dancer to perform in America, outdrew the *Ferris wheel* at the World's Columbian Exposition held in Chicago in 1893. The ride was the work of George Washington Gale Ferris (1859-96), a Galesburg, Illinois railroad and bridge engineer. A giant steel structure weighing over 1,200 tons, the first *Ferris wheel* stood 140 feet high and measured 250 feet in diameter, with 36 cars at its rims capable of carrying 1,440 riders. The chief wonder of the "World's Fair" had been built on the tension spoke principle, the large power-driven vertical wheel revolving on a stationary axis and rotating between two pyramids. So great was the wheel's success that imitations soon became standard at all amusement parks worthy of the name.

fertilizer. The first recorded mention of the word *fertilizer* came in 1661 when an English writer noted that "Saint-foime [Saint-foin] or Holy-hay [*Onobrychis sativa*, a member of the pea family, also called Holy Clover] . . . [is] a great Fertilizer of Barren-ground." Fertilizers, however, have been known since time immemorial. The word *fertile*, from which *fertilizer* derives, comes from the Latin *ferre*, "to bear." While animal and plant fertilizers date far back in history, chemical fertilizers weren't developed until the first half of the 19th century.

ferule. *Ferula communis*, or the giant fennel, is a plant that became famous as a switch or stick used in classrooms on disobedient students. This member of the fennel family, which takes its name from the Latin for "stick," grows up to 8 to 12 feet high and was grown by the Romans both for its handsome yellow flowers and for the dried pith of its stems, which provided excellent tinder for starting fires. But by the 16th century the pliable stalks of the plant were being used as schoolroom switches, their name slightly changed to *ferule*. Eventually *ferule* was applied to "a sort of flat ruler, widened at the inflicting end into a shape resembling a pear . . . with a . . . hole in the middle, to raise blisters."

fetus. *Fetus* is the etymologically correct spelling of this word for "the young of viviparous animals," not *foetus*, as the word derives from the Latin *fetus*, "offspring." The word is first attested in English as *fetus*, in 1398.

few and far between. Scottish poet Thomas Campbell's poem "The Pleasures of Hope" (1799) contains this line, as well as "distance lends enhancement to the view." *Few and far between* is "Like angel-visits, few and far between" in the poem and is adapted from Robert Blair's "Like angels' visits, short and far between." (*See also* **Iberia's pilot.**)

fey. *Fey* usually means "being in unnaturally high spirits, or unreal, enchanted," as in "elves and other fey creatures." In times past someone who suddenly acted so lighthearted was thought to be on the point of death, *fey* deriving from the Anglo-Saxon *faege*, "on the verge of death."

fez. This well-known traditional Arab red hat with a flat top and black tassel was first made in Fes, Morocco (spelled Fez by the Europeans), where the berries yielding the red dye for it grew abundantly. The hat is brimless, so that Moslems wearing it can touch their heads to the ground when praying.

Ff. Personal names beginning with a double *f* in English, such as Ffoulkes or Ffrench, originated as mistakes when the medieval or Old English capital *F*, which in script appears to be two small entwined *f*s, was transferred to print as two lowercase *f*s. No word in English should really begin with two *f*s.

fiacre. *Fiacres* are small horsedrawn cabs that take their name from an old town house called the Hôtel de St. Fiacre in Paris, where they were first rented out from a stand in 1648. The hotel, in turn, took its name from an image of St. Fiacre that hung outside it. St. Fiacre, who can be invoked as the patron saint of both gardeners and cab drivers, was an Irish priest who founded a monastery with a hospital and extensive gardens near Paris in about A.D. 615. Legend has it that his Bishop granted him as much land as he could turn over in a night and that the ground miraculously opened at the touch of his spade. It is also St. Fiacre's fate to be invoked for perhaps the most unpleasant assortment of diseases that any saint is responsible for—including diarrhea, venereal diseases, and even warts on the knees of horses. But this saint was the first man to restore people to mental health by hard work in the garden, by what psychiatrists now call *hortotherapy*, and he is thus best remembered as the patron saint of gardeners. His monastery eventually grew into the village of St. Fiacre, and his day is August 30, appropriate for the harvest. French gardeners have observed his anniversary for generations, attending services in the flower-decked chapels dedicated to him.

fiasco. Our word for "a total, foolish failure" derives from the Italian *fiasco*, "bottle," but no one seems to know why. First recorded in England as a theatrical term in the late 19th century, the word may have something to do with a bottle breaking—either accidentally or as part of the plot—in some forgotten Italian play. Perhaps also a brand of wine in some bottles was flat or sour—a complete failure or fiasco—or imperfect bottles made by glassblowers were called *fiascos*. There is no proof for any theory.

fiat money. *Fiat money* is currency that is convertible into coin or specie. *Fiat* derives from the Latin for "let it be done."

fiddle. The word fiddle comes from the Anglo-Saxon *fithele*, which may have derived from the Latin *vitula* that gives us violin. In any event, no musical instrument is involved in as many common English expressions as the fiddle, which is usually called the violin today but, surprisingly, still retains its homely name among a

FIG 195

number of prominent musicians. With the exception of *fit as a fiddle*, a metaphor that goes back at least to the early 17th century and shows the great pride with which the English regarded their well-made fiddles, these expressions generally reflect a Puritanical scorn of fun and gaiety, the notion that hard work is the only important thing in life. They include "fiddlesticks," "fiddling around," "to play second fiddle," "drunk as a fiddle," "to play the fiddler," "fiddle-faddle," and many others.

fiddler crab. Any tiny crab of the genus *Uca*, the crab so named because it moves its big claw rapidly, the way a fiddler moves his arm.

Fiddler's Green. Since the 19th century, British sailors have called the traditional heaven of mariners *Fiddler's Green*, "a place of unlimited rum and tobacco."

to fiddle while Rome burns. The origin of this old expression is an incident described by the Roman historian Suetonius, who said that Nero set fire to Rome in 64 A.D. because he wanted to see what Troy had looked like when it burned centuries before. Suetonius added that Nero regarded the blaze with cynical detachment, singing his own composition "The Sack of Ilium" and playing the harp while flames consumed the city. Tacitus, a more reliable historian and one who, unlike Suetonius, lived in Nero's time, says that the last of the Caesars was at his villa at Antium fifty miles away when Rome burned. However, it could be that Nero climbed the tower of Maecenus on the third day of the fire and recited Priam's lament over the burning of Troy to musical accompaniment, as other accounts say. The tyrant did rebuild Rome in a much improved way, but he blamed the fire on the Christians to save his own skin and persecuted them with such fury that these first martyrs regarded him as an Antichrist (he is possibly the fantastic beast referred to as 666 in Rev. 13:11-18).

field. The Anglo-Saxons called any place that had been cleared of trees a *feld*, which by the 15th century or so became *field* and meant "open land" as opposed to woodland. *Feld* is probably related to the Old English word *felde*, "earth."

a field day. The expression *to have a field day* means "to enjoy oneself as if the time were a special festive occasion, a holiday." *Field day* in the phrase refers to "a special day on which soldiers parade or practice maneuvers before high-ranking officers."

Fielding guide. (*See* **Baedeker**.)

fifth column. During the Spanish Civil War (1936-39), a group of sympathizers within Madrid worked secretly to help Franco's Falangist rebels overthrow the Loyalist Republic and establish his dictatorship. These sympathizers were first called the *fifth column* in 1936 by Lt. General Queipo de Llano, a Falangist propagandist who broadcasted the following in an attempt to demoralize Loyalist forces in Madrid: "We have four columns on the battlefield against you and a fifth column inside your ranks." When a little later that year the Falangist commander General Emilio Mola was leading four columns of Fascist troops on Loyalist Madrid from various directions, he said essentially the same thing, and so the term has often been credited to him. *Fifth Column* is a direct translation of the Spanish *quinta columba* and has come to mean "any group of secret agents or traitors at work within a country." The expression gained wide currency because Ernest Hemingway used it as the title of a 1940 play about espionage in the Spanish Civil War.

fifth wheel. Looking at the fifth wheel of wagons and carriages many people thought it had no function, but this wheel, or circular plate, which was attached to the upper side of the front axle and never touched the ground, supported the vehicle's body when it made a turn. Ignorance prevailed, however, and the expression *fifth wheel* came to mean "a useless or needless person or thing in any enterprise."

fifty-fifty. *Fifty-fifty*—50 percent for one party, 50 percent for the other—is still a common Americanism for "equally divided." An expression that one would guess is much older, it is first recorded in a 1913 *Saturday Evening Post* article, though it may date back to the late 19th century or earlier.

fifty-four forty or fight. James Polk won election to the American presidency in 1844 with this slogan, which referred to the ousting of the British from the whole of the Columbia River country up to latitude 54 degrees 40 minutes N. After his election Polk discarded the slogan and settled the Oregon question without going to war. The sarcastic Whig slogan "Who is James K. Polk?" inspired the myth that Polk was a political nonentity and weak president. In truth, he was one of the hardest-working of all presidents, attained almost all his stated aims, and added more territory to the U.S. than any president except Jefferson.

fifty-seven varieties. (*See* **Heinz's 57 varieties**.)

fig. When someone says "I don't care a fig," he isn't referring to the delicious fruit (whether he knows it or not), but to the ancient *Spanish fig*, a contemptuous gesture made by thrusting the thumb forth from between the first two fingers. The insult is said to be an invitation to "kiss my ass" and to have its origin in a classic piece of revenge Frederick I took on two Italians who insulted his wife: he forced them, under threat of death, to extract a fig with their teeth from deep within the anus of an ass. *Figs* themselves are mentioned in the biblical story of the Garden of Eden, and it was under a Nepal species of fig tree called Bo that the Buddha's revelations came to him. The fruit takes its English name from the Latin *ficus* ("fig"), which became the Provençal *figa*. It figures in a number of phrases of its own. English, for example features it in various expressions from the euphemistic *fig you* to far worse, and in French *faire la figue* means "to give the obscene finger gesture." The euphemistic *frig you* has nothing to do with the *fig you* etymology, deriving from the Old English *frigan*, "to love," which in the 15th or 16th century took on its present meaning.

to fight fire with fire. An Americanism, possibly deriving from the use of backfires to help extinguish great prairie and forest fires in the early West. Settlers would set fire to a circle or strip of land in the path of a blaze but at a good distance from it, then extinguish it and leave a barren patch so that the advancing fire would have nothing to feed on and so would burn itself out. Fighting fire with fire could be a dangerous practice, for the backfire might get out of control itself, so the expression came to mean "any desperate measure involving great risk."

to fight like Kilkenny cats. During the Irish rebellion or revolution of 1798, Hessian mercenaries stationed in Kilkenny amused themselves by tying two cats by their tails and throwing them over a clothesline to fight to the death. Just before an officer interrupted their banned "sport" unexpectedly one day, a quick-thinking trooper reportedly cut off the two tails and let the cats escape, telling the colonel that the soldiers had nothing to do with the fight—the two cats had just devoured each other except for the tails. The above tale may have inspired the expression *to fight like Kilkenny cats*, to fight bitterly until the end. But another story has it that two Kilkenny cats fought so ferociously in a sandpit that they devoured each other except for their tails. And still another yarn has a thousand fabled Kilkenny cats fighting an all-night battle with a thousand cats selected by "sportsmen" from all over Ireland, the tough Kilkenny cats killing them all. Most authorities go along with Jonathan Swift, who, more conservatively, prefers the explanation that *cats* in the phrase refers to men. It seems that in the 17th century residents of Englishtown and Irishtown in Kilkenny—which was bisected by a stream—were constantly fighting over boundary lines and were compared to battling cats. But nobody has offered convincing proof for any of these stories.

fight the good fight. (*See* **keep the faith, baby!**)

fig leaves. In prudish Victorian times *fig leaves* were used to cover the genitals on statuary in many museums. But the practice began thousands of years before, dating to the story in Gen. 3:7, that Adam and Eve covered their nakedness with fig leaves after the Fall.

figurehead. Ship figureheads are carved figures or busts attached below the bowsprit directly over the cutwater. They have great ornamental value, but no function whatsoever and the ships would sail just as well without them. The carvings do inspire pride and confidence among seamen, however, and lend prestige to ships. Thus, *figurehead* has been used for at least a century to describe "a person who normally heads an organization, who lends his good name to it, but has no real duties in it."

filbert. About the only connection between St. Filbert and filbert nuts is that the saint's feast day falls on August 22, the height of the nut-harvesting season. This was enough reason, however, for Norman gatherers to name the nuts *philberts* in his honor. St. Philibert, his name *Filuberht* in Old High German, was a Benedictine who founded the Abbey of Jumieges in 684. What Americans call *filberts* after him are actually hazelnuts. *Filberts* are confined botanically to two European nut varities—about 250 million pounds of them bearing the saint's name each year. A *Gilbert Filbert* was British slang for a very fashionable man about town early in this century, deriving from the popular song "Gilbert the Filbert, Colonel of the Nuts." *Cracked in the filbert* meant "eccentric or crazy."

filibuster. Deriving from the Dutch *vribuiter*, "freebooter or pirate," *filibuster* was originally used in American English to describe gun-runners in Central America, men who engaged in war with a country with whom their own country was at peace. Over the years the word came to mean "obstruction of legislation in the U.S. Senate by prolonged speechmaking," after a congressman described one such obstruction as "filibustering against the U.S."

fill the bill. Theatrical companies in the 19th century advertised mainly on posters and handbills that were distributed in towns by advance men several weeks before a show came to town. The name of the troupe's star performer was featured on these bills in large letters, to the exclusion of the rest of the company—he or she *filled the bill*, was the show's star. Soon the vivid image behind this theatrical expression meaning "to star" came to encompass a more complex, broader thought, and by 1860 *to fill the bill* meant "to be very competent, effective, to do all that is desired, expected, or required."

filthy lucre. *Lucre*, in the form of *lucrum*, is a Latin word that means "profit or wager." The term *filthy lucre* comes to us from the letters of St. Paul to his followers, Timothy and Titus. In these letters the Apostle denounced religious leaders who were greedy lovers of money and taught Christianity for dishonorable gain. But when William Tyndale translated the New Testament from Greek to English in 1525, he mistranslated Paul's figurative expression "dishonorable gain" as "filthy lucre." Paul's words didn't mean "dirty money," or *filthy lucre*, but the phrase was retained by the authors of the great King James Version of the Bible in 1611 and soon entered English as a term for money in general, no matter how honorably earned.

fin. The Yiddish word *finnif* is probably the ancestor of our slang for a $5 bill. *Finnif* meant a five-pound note in mid-19th century England. Shortened to *fin* in England, it became American underworld slang by the 1920s. The Yiddish word, in turn, derives from the German *funf*, or "five." The *fin* of a fish comes from the Old English *finn* meaning the same.

finagle. Unlikely as it seems, a Mr. Feinagel, a German mesmerist and whist expert of the Regency (1812-20), is most likely the person who gave us this word for "to manage by trickery or sharp practice." Since an early definition of *finagle* meant "to cheat at cards," Mr. Feinagel's name, slightly altered, almost certainly is responsible for the word's coining.

finalize. *Finalize*, despite the objections of many critics, is recognized by most dictionaries and has been current in both American and British English for about half a century in both formal and casual writing. Such formations as *neutralize*, *minimize*, and *generalize* don't seem to bother people, but *finalize* rankles many, perhaps because most critics believe it is a pretentious bureaucratic synonym for "to complete." But it has a meaning different from "complete." It means "to put into a final form a set of conclusions that has been agreed upon roughly through a preceding series of discussions or actions."

fine as silk.   (*See* **quicker than hell can scorch a feather**.)

fine fettle. The expression *in fine fettle*, "in excellent condition," isn't recorded until 1890, but expressions like *in poor fettle*, *in good fettle*, etc., were common long before this. *Fettle* here probably comes from the belts or girdles, called *fettles*, that ancient warriors bound themselves with before going into battle; when their fettles were on they were "in good condition, ready for battle."

a fine kettle of fish. A *kiddle* or *kiddle net* is a basket set in the sluice ways of dams to catch fish, a device well known from the time of the Plantagenets. Royal officials had the perquisite to trap fish in kiddles, but poachers often raided the traps of fish, frequently destroying the kiddles in the process. Possibly an official came upon a destroyed trap and exclaimed, "That's a pretty kiddle of fish!" or something similar, meaning "a pretty sorry state of affairs!" and the phrase was born. Repeated over the

years, *kiddle* was corrupted in everyday speech to *kettle*, giving us the expression as we know it today.

F'ing.   (*See* **effing**.)

a finger in the pie. This expression, recorded in 1659, has nothing to do with being meddlesome, as has been suggested. It means simply "to have something to do with, to have a part in something." "Lusatia . . . must needs, forsooth, have her Finger in the Pye" is the first attested use of the words.

finger man.   (*See* **to point the finger**.)

fingers were made before forks. An old expression dating back several centuries, *fingers were made before forks* is still used as an excuse when someone is chastised for eating with his fingers. Forks are a relatively new culinary innovation, dating back to 14th-century Italy.

fink. The original *fink* may have been either a Pinkerton man or a cop named Albert Fink, who worked for railroads in the American South. *Mencken* prefers the former explanation, tracing the term to the 1892 Homestead steel strike when Pinkerton men were hired as strikebreakers, these brutal "Pinks" becoming *finks* in time, the word synonymous with the earlier "scab" or the British "blackleg." Finks were anathema to the early labor movement, but the word is now used to describe not only "a strikebreaker but any treacherous, contemptible person or a police informer." Mr. Albert Fink could just as well have inspired the term in similar fashion. The German-born Fink, according to a reliable source, long headed a staff of detectives with the Louisville and Nashville Railroad and then switched to the New York Trunk Line Association in about 1875. He was not involved in railroad labor disputes, but his operatives probably policed rates charged on the lines and some of them were likely planted spies who came to be known as *finks*. This gives the word more a management than a labor flavor, but is is possible that *fink* gained currency in this way before being adopted by union men. It is at least as plausible as the transformation of "Pinks" to finks. *Ratfink* is a stronger variant of *fink* that originated in the U.S. within the last thirty years or so. (*See* **Pinkerton**.)

Finnan haddie. *Haddock* gives us the *haddie* for this fish dish, while the *Finnan* comes from either the River Findhorn or the village of Findon, both, of course, in Scotland.

Finnish words in English. This remarkably constant language, which has changed little over the centuries and in which letters of the alphabet can be pronounced only one way, has only contributed a few words to English, the best known of these being *sauna*.

fire. First recorded in 1871, *to fire out* meant "to throw out or eject a person from a place." Thirteen years later the term, shortened to *to fire*, was first recorded as a synonym for "dismissing an employee." Both terms have their origins in the firing, or discharging, of a gun.

firebug. *Firebug* derives from those *bugs* who have enthusiasms often amounting to manias. That this is an old American expression is evidenced by the fact that Oliver Wendell Holmes used it figuratively, writing of "political firebugs" in his *The Poet at the Breakfast Table* (1872). That is the first recorded use of the term, which generally means "a pyromaniac, someone mentally unbalanced who lights fires for his pleasure." But people with a mania for anything have been called "bugs" in America since at least the early 19th century; we have had our *slavery bugs*, those who wished to see slavery extended into the West, and we still have our *money bugs*, whose sole interest is money.

firecracker. *Firecrackers* were called *crackers* in England, because of the sound they make when ignited, long before they became known as *firecrackers* here because a distinction had to be made between them and the "crackers" Americans eat, which are called "biscuits" in England.

firewater. A traveler in North America in 1817 reported that "[the Indian chiefs] called the whiskey fire water." An accurate description of whiskey's taste going down, especially the whiskey Indians were traded, *firewater* is probably a translation of the Algonquin Indian *scoutiouabou*, meaning the same.

first catch your hare. Writers still attribute these humorous directions to a recipe in Mrs. Hannah Glasse's *Art of Cooking Made Plain and Easy* (1747). What the lady really wrote was "Take your hare when it is cased and make a pudding . . ." To "case" a hare is to skin it. The joke, which is all the phrase was, is first recorded in Thackeray's *Rose and Ring* (1855), and he used the words as if his readers would be familiar with them.

the first fruits. John Wycliffe mentions *first fruits* in the first translation into English of the whole Bible (1382), specifically in Num. 18:12 with reference to the custom of making offerings to the Lord of the first fruits gathered in a season. Over two centuries passed before the expression was used figuratively to mean "the first products of one's efforts," as in *the first fruits of our labor.*

first rate, etc. From Elizabethan times up until the 19th century, British warships were rated by the number of guns they carried and the weight of those guns, rather than by the weight of the ships themselves. Six rates, or categories, were applied, a mighty first-rate ship being the highest. Before long these technical navy terms were being used to describe degrees of excellence generally.

first string; second string. Archers in medieval times are responsible for these terms, so common on athletic fields today in describing first and second teams. An archer was only as good as the bowstring on the stout, five-foot English longbow, and in competitions a marksman always carried two—a *fyrst-string* to be used as his best and a second to be held in reserve lest the other should break. This led to the popular Elizabethan saying *two strings to his bow*, meaning to carry something in reserve in case of accident, which fathered our *first string* and *second string*.

first water. Arab diamond traders graded gems as first water, second water, and third water—diamonds of the first water being perfect, flawless ones. ("Water" here signified the transparency of a diamond and may be the translation of an Arabic word for luster.) Europeans used the Arab grading system for more than 300 years, and even when it was discarded in the mid-19th century the expression *of the first water* remained in English as a synonym for unsurpassed perfection in anything.

fiscal. In ancient Rome merchants used a small basket called a *fiscus*, so named because it was made of rush or reeds (fiscus), to carry money from one place to another. From these little baskets, so common in Rome, the public treasury was named the *fisc*, and over the centuries anything to do with money matters came to be called *fiscal*.

fisherman's joke. *Scherzo del pescatore* means *a fisherman's joke*. It is a fried Italian dish of small squid, or calamaries, which are usually eaten by popping them in the mouth. One of the squid, however, has a sac filled with hot red pepper.

fishfall; frogfall. *Fishfalls*, or a rain of fish falling from the sky, have occurred fairly often throughout the world, probably due to waterspouts that suck up fish and water and release them miles away. Similarly, *frogfalls* are surprisingly common phenomena, too. The term seems to have been first recorded in the late 19th century.

to fish in troubled waters. *To fish in troubled waters*, meaning "to take advantage of another's marital troubles and gain something for yourself," refers to the fact that fish bite best in rough waters, as all good fishermen know. The expression probably dates back to the 19th century, its origin unknown.

fish or cut bait. These words, associated with politics since the late 19th century, demand that someone "take a definite stand, take action instead of procrastinating, or else stop trying and give somebody else a chance to act."

Someone in a choice fishing spot on land or aboard a ship was possibly told to stop fooling around, to either drop his line in the water and fish, or cut the bait from his line and let another fisherman take his place.

a fish out of water. Older by at least several hundred years than the dates cited in the *O.E.D.* and the *Oxford Dictionary of Quotations*, this expression may even have originated with the fourth-century Greek patriarch St. Athanasius. Its earliest recorded use, however, is by English theologian and religious reformer John Wycliffe in his *English Works* (ca. 1380): "And how thei weren out of ther cloistre as fish is withouten water." The metaphor, as widely used as ever today, describes "anyone floundering in an element or environment to which he is unaccustomed and in which he is practically helpless."

five-day week. (*See* **eight-hour day.**)

fjord; fjeld. *Fjord* and the seldom encountered *fjeld* are the only two words in English beginning with *fj*. Both are Norwegian in origin. The latter, pronounced *fyeld*, means an elevated rocky plateau virtually without vegetation, and the former, pronounced (and sometimes spelled) *fiord*, is a long narrow arm of the sea running up between high banks or cliffs, as on Norway's coast.

flabbergasted. Astounded or utterly confused. A relatively new word, *flabbergast* is first recorded in a British magazine article called "On New Words" in 1772. It is possibly a combination of *flabby* and *aghast*, but neither the source of the word nor its inventor is known.

flack. This term has been used since the mid-1940s for "advertising copy," ever since the similarity between rapid gunfire and exaggerated advertising copy or publicity writing was first noticed. *Flack* probably derives from the World War II acronym *flak* (from the German *Flieger abwehr Kanone*, "aircraft defense gun"). A *flack* can also mean a public relations person today.

flamingo. This long-legged pink wading bird is named for the people of Flanders, the *Flemings*, as they were called. Flemings were widely known for their lively personalities, their flushed complexions, and their love of bright, gay clothing. Spaniard explorers in the New World thought it was a great joke naming the bird the *flamingo*, which means "a Fleming" in Spanish and became the English *flamingo* in time.

Flanders poppies. In England the artificial red flowers sold on Remembrance Day for the benefit of war veterans are called *Flanders poppies*. A 1915 poem by John McCrae called "In Flanders Fields" seems to have been the first to connect this flower with the dead of World War I:

If ye break faith with us who die
We shall not sleep, though poppies grow
    In Flanders fields.

flash in the pan. Old flintlock muskets had a pan, or depression, that held the priming powder. The guns fired after the trigger was pulled and sparks produced by the steel hammer striking a flint ignited the powder, which exploded the main charge. That is, the guns *sometimes* fired. Flintlocks, used since the 17th century, were unreliable weapons and frequently didn't work. Often the powder just flared or flashed up in the pan, failing to explode the main charge because the charge was wet or because the touchhole linking the two was clogged. Flintlocks "hanging fire" like this were common enough to make the term a *flash in the pan* a natural figure of speech for "any short-lived brilliance yielding no results in the long run" and, long after the old flintlocks were relegated to museums, it is still used to describe a person who fails to live up to his early promise.

flashy. Nineteenth century *Flash men* from outside the village of Flash in England's Derbyshire were squatters, who, like some gypsies, traveled from county fair to county fair in the district doing no good. Their slang dialect, called *Flash talk*, and their distinctive clothing, often bright and showy, made them quite conspicuous. The word *flashy*, used to describe conspicuous dressers, among many showy, ostentatious things, could well have been applied to anyone like them, for the word came into use at a time when they were the cause of much trouble. On the other hand, some investigators say the word simply derives from "a sudden flame" or "a lightning flash."

flattop. Though the *Langley*, a converted coal ship, commissioned in 1922, was America's first aircraft carrier, no one thought of calling any aircraft carrier a *flattop* until World War II, when the United States built 150 carriers.

flaybottomist; bum brusher. Here is a jocular synonym for a schoolteacher in the days of "spare the rod and spoil the child." The term for a schoolmaster originated in the mid-18th century and lasted for some two hundred years. *Bum brusher* was a synonym.

fleabitten. *Fleabitten* has since the late 16th century been a *color* as well as a condition. It describes a dog, horse, or other animal with a light coat flecked with red, the reddish flecks reminiscent of the bites of fleas on human skin.

flea market. These bargain markets have nothing to do with fleas. *Flea market* has been an American expression as far back as Dutch colonial days when there was a very real Vallie (Valley) Market at the valley, or foot, of Maiden Lane in downtown Manhattan. The Vallie Market came to be abbreviated to *Vlie Market* and this was soon being pronounced *Flea Market*.

fledgling nation.   A *fledgling nation* usually means a newly formed, poor nation that the United States has taken under its wing. The euphemism was probably coined by Eleanor Roosevelt after World War II.

Fleet Street.   Fleet Street in London has been synonymous with journalism since the end of the 18th century, when the first newspaper was published there. The street takes its name not from fleet reporters writing stories while type is being set, but for the Fleet River that ran alongside it.

Flemish.   When rope is flemished it is coiled down concentrically in the direction of the sun, or like the coil of a watch spring, beginning in the center. *Flemish* also once meant "to force or score the planks." The terms seem to have arisen in the early 19th century and take their name from Flemish sailors, considered to be neat seamen and who may have coiled their rope like this.

flesh-spades; flesh-tailer.   In *Tom Jones* (1749) Fielding writes about "The injury done to the beauty of her husband by the 'flesh-spades' of Mrs. Honour." The humorous term *flesh-spade* for fingernails, those digging tools protruding from our fingers, may have been invented by the British novelist, but there is no proof of this. *Flesh-tailor* was a 17th-century term for a surgeon, used by John Ford in his play *'Tis Pity She's a Whore* (1633).

fletcherize.   The author of *Glutton or Epicure* (1899) advocated cutting out regular meals and eating only when really hungry, consuming very small amounts of food at one time, and chewing each tiny mouthful vigorously and thoroughly before swallowing. Horace Fletcher (1849-1919), a Lawrence, Massachusetts businessman turned nutritionist, believed that this regimen—which he had followed from the time he went on a diet and lost sixty-five pounds at age forty—would promote better digestion and health as excellent as his own. *Fletcherism*, described more fully in a later book of that name, swept the country; thousands attended Fletcher's lectures and followed his instructions to the letter. As a result of the health fad, the word *fletcherize*, "to masticate food thoroughly," became a common expression that still remains in the dictionaries. Fletcher had really borrowed his idea of thirty-two chews to the bite from British Prime Minister Gladstone, who "made it a rule, to give every tooth of mine a chance," and who claimed he owed much of his success in life to this rule. Slogans like "Nature will castigate those who don't masticate" won Fletcher many famous converts, including John D. Rockefeller, Thomas Edison, William James, and the cadets at West Point.

fleur-de-lis; iris.   The *fleur-de-lis*, or lily flower, is the French name for the *iris*, which is so named because its striking colors reminded the Greeks of Iris, goddess of the rainbow. The French symbol of empire since the 12th century, the *fleur-de-lis* was chosen by the 14th-century Italian navigator Flavio Gioja to mark the north point of the compass in honor of the King of Naples, who was of French descent.

flibbertigibbety.   Silly restless actions are called *flibbertigibbety* after Flibbertigibbet, one of the five fiends who possessed "poor Tom" in Shakespeare's *King Lear*. Shakespeare borrowed the character and his name from an earlier work.

flog (or beat) a dead horse.   Though he supported the measure, British politician and orator John Bright thought the Reform Bill of 1867, which called for more democratic representation, would never be passed by Parliament. Trying to rouse Parliament from its apathy on the issue, he said in a speech, would be like trying to *flog a dead horse* to make it pull a load. This is the first recorded use of the expression, which is still common for "trying to revive interest in an apparently hopeless issue." Bright's silver tongue is also responsible for "England is the mother of Parliament," and "Force is not a remedy," among other memorable quotations. He was wrong about the Reform Bill of 1867, however. Parliament "carried" it, as the British say.

floozie.   "The Flat-Foot Floogy with the Floy Floy," a popular song in 1945, spelled *floosie* differently, but it meant the same. A *floosie, floogy, flugie*, or even *faloosie* is a gaudily dressed, dumb, disrespectable, frequently high-spirited woman, often a prostitute. If the word derives from *Flossie*, a nickname for Florence, no one has proved it, and the word was first recorded in the form of *flugie* at the turn of the century. Hollywood's Hays Office banned *floozie*, along with *red-hot mamma* and other words, but the term got a breath of new life with the song mentioned above, which describes a *floozie* with what it seems is a kind of venereal disease, the *floy floy*. This American slang, as a British writer observes, is "picturesque" and should be retained for its "blousy flowery atmosphere" suggesting "good spirits, gaudy flowered dresses, and bad but delightful perfume."

Florida.   "The Sunshine State" was the *Florida Territory* before being admitted to the Union as the 27th state in 1845. *Florida* means "land of flowers" in Spanish, Ponce de Leon naming it in 1513 with "flowery Easter" in mind.

flotsam and jetsam.   *Flotsam*, from the Old French *floter* (Latin *fluere*), "to float," means the contents or parts of a wreck found floating on the sea, and belonged to the

Crown. *Jetsam*, which could be claimed by the lord of the manor, derives from the French *jeter* (Latin *jacere*), "to throw out," and means cargo or equipment purposely thrown overboard, or jettisoned, in order to lighten a ship in an emergency. Jetsam was considered flotsam only if it were found between the high and low waterlines, because no one could tell whether it had been jettisoned there or had floated there.

flower. (*See* **blossom**.)

floy floy. (*See* **floozie**.)

fly a kite; kiting. *Go fly a kite!* means "get lost, don't bother me, go do something somewhere else." To *fly a kite* is another story. This is Irish, not American, slang dating back to the early 19th century and means "to raise money on a fraudulent note or to cash a check without having the funds in the bank to cover it." The expression possibly derives from an older Irish phrase *to raise the wind*, "to borrow money," but in any event it suggests an action far removed from down-to-earth reality and honesty. *To fly a kite* isn't heard much anymore, the expression *kiting* being used in its place. Someone *kites* a check when he overdraws his account and quickly cashes another check somewhere else, depositing this cash in the bank to cover the original shortage. The *kiting* can go on for sometime, with new obligations incurred again and again to discharge old ones—a kite soaring farther and farther away from firm ground.

a fly-by-night. A *fly-by-night* was originally an ancient term of reproach to an old woman, signifying she is a witch, according to Grose's *Dictionary of the Vulgar Tongue*. From a witch flying about at night on a broom, the term was applied, at the beginning of the 19th century, to anyone who flies hurriedly from a recent activity, usually a business activity and usually at night—someone who is a swindler and whose activities are fraudulent. The first fly-by-night operator recorded in English makes his appearance in Thomas Love Peacock's novel *Maid Marian* (1822), a parody of the Robin Hood legend in which a character refers to Maid Marian and the outlaw: "Would you have her married to an old fly-by-night that accident made an earl and nature a deer-stealer?" *Fly-by-night* has also been, in British slang, a prostitute and a prostitute's vagina.

flying clippers. (*See* **clipper ship**.)

Flying Dutchman. The legend of the *Flying Dutchman* trying to round the Cape of Good Hope against strong winds and never succeeding, then trying to make Cape Horn and failing there too, has been the most famous of maritime ghost stories for over three hundred years. The cursed spectral ship sailing back and forth on its endless voyage, its ancient white-haired crew crying for help while hauling at her sails, inspired Samuel Taylor Coleridge to write his classic "The Rime of the Ancient Mariner." The real *Flying Dutchman* is supposed to have set sail in 1660.

fly in the ointment. "Dead flies cause the ointment of the apothecary to send forth a stinking savour; so doth a little folly him that is in reputation for wisdom and honour." The unknown author of the biblical book of Ecclesiastes (a Greek rendering of the Hebrew word *Koheleth*, "preacher") wrote this sometime in the third century B.C. Like many other vivid figures of speech in the twenty-first book of the Old Testament ("Vanity of vanities, saith the preacher; all is vanity . . ." "For everything there is a season . . ." "He who digs a pit will fall into it . . ." etc.), these words from the first verse of the tenth chapter became proverbial when translated into English. For five centuries now *a fly in the ointment* has meant a small defect that spoils something valuable or is a source of annoyance.

fly off the handle. Axes in American pioneer days were frequently handmade, frontiersmen whittling their own handles and attaching axe-heads shipped from back East. Because they were often crudely fitted to the helve, these axe-heads often flew off the handle while woodsmen were chopping down trees or preparing firewood, sometimes injuring the axeman or people nearby. The sudden flying of the head off the axe, and the trouble this caused, naturally suggested a sudden wild outburst of anger, the loss of self-control, or the losing of one's head that the expression *to fly off the handle* describes. The expression is first recorded in John Neal's novel *Brother Jonathan; or the New Englanders* (1825) as *off the handle*, but isn't known in its full form until 1844, when it was used in still another of Thomas Haliburton's "Sam Slick" tales. (*See* **feel one's oats**.)

flyting. (*See* **logomachy**.)

fly-up-the-creek. We don't hear this expression today, but it is recorded as early as 1845 as the nickname for a resident of Florida. Floridians were so called because *fly-up-the-creek* is a popular name of the small green heron common in the state. Walt Whitman used the expression in this sense and it later meant "a giddy capricious person."

F.M.C.; F.W.C. There were a good number of freed and escaped slaves in America long before the Civil War. By 1840 the terms *F.M.C.*, for "free man of color," and *F.W.C.*, for "free woman of color," are recorded, and blacks for many years proudly affixed the terms after their names.

fo'c'sle. (*See* **forecastle**.)

focus. In Latin the word *focus* means fireplace or hearth. The word was probably first employed outside of its Latin literal use as "the burning point of a lens or mirror," in optics, and then came to mean any central point. The German astronomer Johannes Kepler first recorded the word in this sense in 1604.

fofarraw; fanfaron. Meaning haughty or proud, *fofarraw*, first recorded in 1840, is a corruption of the Spanish *fanfarron*, "a braggart." *Foo-foo-rah* and *froofraw* are other pronunciations. *Fanfaron*, recorded some eight years later, means the same and comes from the same source.

Foggy Bottom. The U.S. State Department has been humorously called *Foggy Bottom* at least since the early 1960s, due to its location near the Potomac River on a piece of land long called "Foggy Bottom." The designation caught on because of the "foggy" gobbledygook (*q.v.*) emanating from the Department.

folio. (*See* **book.**)

fontange. Through the ages women's hair has been tortured into shapes of full sails, bird nests with fledglings in them, and even windmills, but no style has ever topped the *fontange* created by Louis XIV's beautiful red-haired mistress. In the brief time that they were lovers "The Sun King" made Marie Angelique de Scorraille de Roussilles *duchesse de Fontanges*, a territory in France. She died all too soon in 1681, when only twenty, but a year before her death the lovely young woman introduced what was probably the most extravagant, expensive hairdo in the history of coiffures. Called a *fontange* after her, this pile of style rose to heights of two feet and more above the wearer's head, including feathers, bows, and a large assortment of jeweled ornaments in the gummed-linen circular bands that held them in place. So great a nuisance did *fontanges* become that Louis XIV had to issue a royal decree abolishing them in 1699. To the duchess's further shame, the hairdo was dubbed a "commode" in England, and *fontange* itself was adopted as a polite word for a commode, the piece of furniture having come into use in the late 17th century and serving as a toilet among other uses.

fool. The Latin word *follis*, which literally meant "bellows" but came to mean a "windbag," gives us our word *fool*—foolishness and tongue-wagging being equated early on.

foolscap. A size of drawing or printing paper measuring 13 1/2 x 17 inches that is so named because the watermark of a fool's or jester's cap was formerly used on such paper. One old story holds that in 1653 Cromwell invented the design to replace the royal crown used on the paper, but the fool's cap design dates back to at least 1540.

for crying out loud. An Americanism first recorded in 1924, but probably dating back earlier, *for crying out loud* is what is called a "minced oath," a euphemism that may have originated when someone started to say "For Christ's sake!" but got only as far as the first syllable of the second word, realized the curse was inappropriate in the circumstances, and changed the offensive word to "crying." It's hard to believe that this common expression was consciously invented by someone. But it has been traced to American cartoonist and prolific word coiner Thomas Aloysius (TAD) Dorgan (1877-1929).

Ford. John Dillinger, the first "public enemy number one," once wrote Henry Ford extolling the performance of his car as a getaway vehicle. That curious incident shows just how widespread was the Ford's really incalculable influence on society, both good and bad. Henry Ford's motor cars, though not the first invented, put America and the world on wheels, his assembly-line and mass-production methods marking the beginning of modern industry, and his "Five Dollar Day" heralding a new era for labor. Ford (1863-1947), born on a farm near Detroit, Michigan, founded the Ford Motor Company in 1903. First came his two-cylinder Model A and then in 1909 the immortal Model T, the Tin Lizzie, the flivver, America's monument to love, available in any color so long as it was black. Fifteen million of these cars were built over almost twenty years—a record that lasted until the Volkswagen broke it in 1972—and any cheap, dependable car became known as a *ford*. The word is usually capitalized now, but *Ford* still remains a symbol of American mechanical ingenuity. Though he was often controversial and foolish in his public life, no one has ever doubted the inventor's genius. He is honored today by both the motor company bearing his name and the philanthropic Ford Foundation. (*See also* **Cadillac.**)

fore! This golfing term meaning "watch out" hasn't been with us for much more than a century, being first recorded in 1878, though the game of golf is much older. Deriving from the word *before!*, "in front of," it probably was coined when the harder golf ball came into use at that time.

forecastle (fo'c'sle). By the 14th century the forward part of many large ships had an area that was raised and protected like a castle, from which the captain could overlook the decks of an enemy ship. Today the forecastle is simply "that part of the upper deck forward of the foremast or, in merchant ships, the forward part of the vessel under the deck, where the sailors live." *Forecastle* is almost always spelled and pronounced *fo'c'sle* (fo'ksl).

forget it! As an expression of annoyance or anger meaning "never mind," *forget it!* has been popular since before 1912, when the Americanism, in the form of *aw, forget it,* was discussed in a scholarly work on slang. The term enjoyed a resurgence of popularity in the hippie 1960s.

fork. The dinnertable *fork* takes its name from the farmer's pitchfork. The first such eating instrument was brought to England in the mid-15th century and named for the big fork it resembled in miniature. The pitchfork called a *fork* is recorded in England more than four hundred years earlier.

forlorn hope. This expression is one of the best, or worst, examples of folk etymology recorded anywhere. The Dutch called a small squad of volunteer soldiers assigned to an extremely perilous mission a *verloren hoop*, "a lost troop." Such a squad of doomed death-defiers was called *enfants perdus* ("lost children") by the French, *verloren kinder* by the Germans and in modern times might be described as *shock troops* or *point men* in the U.S. Army, or *kamikaze*, "suicide pilots," by the Japanese. Though *verloren* does not mean "forlorn" and *hoop* does not mean "hope," the Dutch words sound like these English words, and *verloren hoop* was spelled *forlorn hope* by the Englishmen. The expression was first applied to similar bands of English soldiers picked to lead attacks, but by 1641 *forlorn hope's* common meaning of any undertaking almost surely doomed to failure, any vain expectation, was established. The poor chances of success and high casualties suffered by *forlorn hope* squads are mainly responsible for the expression's staying power, but the pathos and word music of "forlorn"—alliterative and suggesting "forgotten," "forsaken"— were helpful, too.

fornication. *Fornication* was one of the words Noah Webster tried to *bowdlerize* (q.v.) from the Bible in 1833. He substituted *lewdness* for it, but *fornication* remained popular in love and language. The word comes from the Latin *fornix*, for "an arch or vault." Since brothels in ancient Rome were often in caves or under arches (not always: they were sometimes even located in baker's ovens), *fornix* became the Latin for a brothel, which eventually gave us the English word *fornicate*. *Fornicate* strictly means "voluntary sexual intercourse between unmarried men and women," but it more generally means the four-letter word nobody wants to print.

for openers. (*See* **just for openers.**)

forsythia. These handsome yellow-flowered shrubs, their bloom the first obvious sign of spring in many places, were named for William Forsyth (1737-1804), a Scottish gardener and horticulturist who became superintendent of the royal gardens at St. James and Kensington in London. Forsyth introduced many unusual ornamental plants to England and may have personally brought the *forsythia* from China. Also the inventor of a plaster that

stimulates new growth in dying diseased trees, he received formal thanks from Parliament for this contribution. The *Forsythia* genus is especially valuable to gardeners because it is easy to propagate, is virtually care-free, and does well in partial shade. Incidentally, most people in the U.S. pronounce the plant's name *for-sith-ia*, though it should strictly be pronounced *for-sigh-thia* since Forsyth pronounced his name *For-sigh-th*.

fortnight. (*See* **se'nnight.**)

fortune cookies. The cookie with a fortune inside was invented in 1918 by David Jung, a contemporary Chinese immigrant who had established Los Angeles's Hong Kong Noodle Company. Jung got the idea after noting how bored customers got while waiting for their orders in Chinese restaurants. He employed a Presbyterian minister (the first fortune cookie author!) to write condensations of biblical messages and later hired Marie Raine, the wife of one of his salesmen, who became the Shakespeare of fortune cookies, writing thousands of classic fortunes such as "Your feet shall walk upon a plush carpet of contentment." The Hong Kong Noodle Company is still in business, as are hundreds of other fortune cookie "publishers." Notable ones include Misfortune Cookies of Los Angeles: "Look forward to love and marriage, but not with the same person." Today fortune cookies are of course served at the end of a meal.

fortunella. *Fortunella*, or the kumquat, is the only genus of well-known fruit trees to be named for a living person, and no more deserving eponym could be found than Robert Fortune (1813-1880), Scottish botanist and traveler. Few men have equaled Fortune as a plant hunter. The author of *Three Years' Wanderings in the Northern Provinces of China* (1847) and other botanical books began traveling in the Orient for the Royal Horticultural Society in 1842. A former employee in the Society's English gardens, his express orders were to collect flora and he brought many beautiful plants back to Europe, including the kumquat, tree peonies, the Japanese anemone, and a number of chrysanthemums. Fortune also introduced the tea plant into India for the East India Company, founding its cultivation there. The tallest species of *Fortunella* is only ten feet high, the smallest a bush of about three feet, and the kumquat fruit is orange-like but smaller, having three to seven cells, or sections, as opposed to eight to fifteen in the orange. The kumquat, which is eaten fresh or preserved, has been crossed with other citrus fruits into a number of strange hybrids, such as the citrangequat and limequat.

forty rod lightning. Whiskey in the early West could literally kill a man and was thus given colorful names, none more vivid than *forty rod lightning*—which likened it to a rifle or shot that could kill a man at forty yards.

forty winks.   Why *forty* winks for a short nap? One story suggests that the Thirty-Nine Articles, the articles of faith that Church of England clergy have been required to accept since 1571, are responsible for the phrase. It seems that a writer in *Punch* (November 16, 1872) quipped: "If a . . . man, after reading through the Thirty-Nine Articles were to take forty winks . . . " and that his joke about the long and often tedious Articles led to the expression for a short nap. But this isn't possible unless the writer was repeating a very old joke indeed, for *forty winks* is recorded in print as early as the middle 1820s, George Eliot using it in 1866. More likely the *forty* follows the old tradition of using forty to designate an indefinite number, as in Shakespeare's "I could beat forty of them," Ali Baba and the Forty Thieves, and many other instances.

foul play.   Shakespeare may have invented the term *foul play.* At least he used it first in print, in *King John,* where Salisbury says "It is apparent foul play," when suspecting (wrongly) that Hubert has killed the young Prince Arthur. *Play* is a strange word to associate with murder, rape, and other crimes, even if the term originated in some gambling den, as has been suggested.

founder.   When a ship *founders* it fills with water and goes to the bottom. And *bottom* is the key to the ancestry of the word *founder,* which comes from the Latin *fundus,* meaning "bottom."

fountain pen.   The first fountain pens weren't made in late 19th-century America, as many people believe. There is an account of one dating back to 1657 and in 1712 the term *fountain pen* is first recorded in an advertisement in a Welsh almanac.

fourdrinier.   The brothers Fourdrinier, Henry and Sealy, invented the *fourdrinier* machine that makes most of the paper we use. In 1807 they patented the first practical machine for converting woodpulp into paper, but labored thirty years in perfecting it, aided only by a partial grant from Parliament. The English papermakers revolutionized the industry with their *fourdrinier,* which is today a huge automatic machine working on the same basic principle but bearing little resemblance to the original.

fourflusher.   A *flush* in poker is five cards all of the same suit, the hand taking its name either from a flush, or flight, of birds, or more likely, from the Latin *flux,* "a copious flow." A four-card *flush* is worthless, but in open-handed poker, if four cards of the same suit are face up on the table a player is in an excellent position to bluff, nobody knowing whether he has a fifth card of the same suit as his concealed "hole" card. Gamblers in the American West at the turn of the century bluffed so often with such *four-card* or *bobtail flushes* that the term *fourflusher* spread from the gambling tables into politer society, where it came to signify anyone who bluffs or pretends, especially someone who pretends to be more than he is while living on money borrowed from others.

the Four Horsemen.   This expression is a shortening of *The Four Horsemen of the Apocalypse,* who are mentioned in the biblical book of Revelation, the four horsemen being Conquest, Slaughter, Famine, and Death. *The Four Horsemen* in modern times also means the Notre Dame University football team's backfield during the 1922-24 seasons, the four backs being James Crowley, Don Miller, Elmer Layden, and Harry Stuhldreher.

the Four Hundred.   Society columnist Ward McAllister coined this term in 1889, when he claimed only 400 people formed New York City's high society. The old story says "400" was chosen because Mrs. Astor's ballroom held only that number, but the truth is that she often invited twice that many people to parties held there.

Fourierism.   *Fourierism,* or utopian socialism, has inspired at least forty-one experimental communities around the world at one time or another, all of them failures. Developed and introduced by François Marie Charles Fourier (1772-1837), a French merchant reacting against his commercial background, the system advocates dividing the world into phalanxes of 1,620 people. Each phalanx would live in a common building, or phalanstery, with separate apartments. One common language, a federal world government, and the encouragement of talent and industry were among other features of this very elaborate scheme, its ultimate goal being a systematic agricultural society. Fourier made a number of converts in France and wasn't dismayed when the only community established in his lifetime failed. His disciples later brought his doctrine to America, where several *Fourier communities* were established, none of them remaining today.

the four-letter word.   *The* four-letter word, as it is called, is YHVH, the Hebrew word for God, which many pious Jews will neither speak nor write. It is the oldest four-letter word under taboo in history. In Greek it is rendered as *Tetragrammaton.*

fourteen hundred!   This obsolete phrase is a good example of secret language used in a profession. For many years, starting in about 1870, the London Stock Exchange had only 1,399 members. To ensure secrecy in the Exchange, the catchphrase *fourteen hundred!* was cried as a warning whenever a stranger came onto the floor.

fox grape.   *The Theatre of Plants* (1640) by John Parkinson informs us that "The Foxe Grape . . . is white, but smelleth and tasteth like unto a Foxe," which is presumably why the American grape is so named. There are two species of wild fox grapes, the northern (*Vitis labrusca*, which is the source of the cultivated Concord grape and other varieties) and the southern (*Vitis rotundifolia*, which is the source of the scuppernong). The wine term *foxy* refers to the pungent fruity flavor of Concord wine and other wines made from native American grapes, these wines reminiscent of jelly or jam to many people.

foxtail pine. (*See* **bristlecone pine.**)

fox-trot. One story has it that actor Harry Fox's original trotting type of dance was a show-stopper in a 1913 Broadway hit musical. The show's producers realized the dance had promotional value and hired the noted social dancing teacher Oscar Duryea to modify it and introduce it as the *Fox Trot* to the public. This he did and the *fox-trot* has been America's most popular slow dance ever since. The story does jibe with the fact that the term is first recorded as *Fox* (with a capital *F*) *trot* in an RCA Victor Catalog in 1915.

fragging. *Fragging* came into the language during the Vietnam War. Meaning the intentional wounding of an officer by his own troops, it takes its name from the fragmentation grenades sometimes used to accomplish this.

franc. This French unit of currency honors "John the Good" (1319-64), King John II of France. Captured by the British after the battle of Poitiers, John was freed in 1360 so that he could return to France and raise a ransom of three million gold crowns. He failed to do this, but in trying he ordered a new gold coin struck that was equivalent in value to the livre. John was pictured on horseback upon the coin's face, the Latin legend beneath his effigy reading, *Johannes Dei gracia Francorum rex*, "John, by the grace of God King of the Franks." It is from this coin, and a similar one honoring his successor Charles V, that the word *franc* derived. John, though he debased the currency, proved to be a man of honor. He returned to England when one of the hostages held for him escaped.

France; frank; etc. Late in the sixth century the warlike Francs conquered Gaul, giving their name to *France* and the *French*. The Gauls had named these Germanic tribes after the Latin *Franci*, the name the Romans bestowed upon the fearless warriors for the javelins they carried. Soon *Franc* itself, *Frank* in English, came to mean "free"—for the barbaric tribes reduced the Gauls to virtual slavery and were the only truly free nobles in the land. This meaning eventually led to such English words as *franking privilege*, free use of the public mails, but the Frank influence does not end there. Similarly, our *frank*, for "straightforward, or candid," derives from the Franks'

blunt integrity in dealing with others—they were so powerful that there was no need for subterfuge; and *frankincense*, an incense of "pure or high quality," refers to what they at least considered their racially pure origins. (*See* **frankfurter.**)

frangible booster. This space-age term describes a booster rocket with a casing of material that fragments easily so that there will be no large pieces to create a hazard if the rocket is destroyed in flight. *Frangible*, meaning breakable, comes from the Latin *frangere*, to break.

frangipane. The Marquis Muzio Frangipani, a general under Louis XIV, is said to have invented the pastry cake filled with cream, sugar, and almonds called *frangipane* or *frangipani*. The name is also applied to the fragrant but ugly *Plumeria rubra* tree or shrub, and to a perfume either originally prepared from or imitating the odor of its flowers. The perfume is usually associated with the name of its otherwise unknown inventor—possibly a Frangipani relative or the marquis himself. An alternate suggestion is that both pastry and perfume may have been introduced by an earlier member of the Italian Frangipani family, a relative who came to France with Catherine de' Medici a century before the marquis. Considering Catherine's many contributions to French cooking, this is not unlikely.

Frankenstein. *Frankenstein* is the name of the young scientist who created a soulless monster out of graveyard corpses in Mary Wollstonecraft Shelley's novel by that title published in 1818. *Frankenstein's monster* is the proper name of the creature, not *Frankenstein*.

frankfurter; frank. The *frankfurter* is named after Frankfurt, Germany, where it was first made centuries ago. Frankfurt itself was so named because it was the "ford of the Franks," the place from which the Franks set out on their raids. The *frankfurter* seems to have been introduced to the U.S. in St. Louis in about 1880 by Antoine Feuchtwanger, an immigrant from Frankfurt. *Frank* for *frankfurter* isn't recorded until the 1920s. *Franks* are also called *hot dogs* (*q.v.*) and *New York tube steaks*. (See **France; hamburger**)

Franklin conductor; Franklin stove; etc. Benjamin Franklin (1706-1790), one of the broadest and most creative minds of his time—statesman, scientist, writer, printer, and inventor—devised the *Franklin stove*, a great improvement over its predecessors, in 1743. This portable, coal-burning iron fireplace had a pipe connecting it to the chimney, producing heat cheaply and relatively efficiently. Franklin's other inventions include *Franklin's bifocals*, and his famous experiment with a kite during a thunderstorm in 1762 led to his development of the *Franklin lightning rod*. Every branch of science held his interest, but Franklin's contributions to mankind did not end here. Among many civic achievements, he founded America's first circulating library, set up Philadelphia's first fire company, established what is now the University of Pennsylvania, organized the American Philosophical Society, wrote and published *Poor Richard's Almanack*—which sold ten thousand copies a year—and published the *Pennsylvania Gazette*, the most widely circulated newspaper in Colonial America. The *Franklin tree*, or *Franklinia*, is also named after Benjamin Franklin. This species has an unusual history—introduced into cultivation from the wild in 1770 by American's first botanist, John Bartram, no one has been able to find it in its wild state since.

Franklin's gull. *Franklin's gull*, the only bird ever to have a monument erected to it, is intimately connected with English and American history. The black-headed gull was named in honor of Sir John Franklin (1786-1847), the English explorer who died in discovering the Northwest Passage that so many other mariners had striven to find. The story of his expedition and his wife's later attempts to find him is one of the most interesting in maritime history. *Franklin's gull (Laridae pipixcan)* has the same upland-breeding and seashore-wintering habits as the *Bonaparte's gull* (q.v.). (*See also* **gull.**)

frankly my dear, I don't give a damn. (*See* **give a damn.**)

free lance. A *free lance*, for a self-employed writer, is a term with an unsavory history. The original *free lances* were medieval Italian (*condottiere*) and French (*compagnies grandes*) knights, free men who would sell their skills with the lance to any master, whether his cause was good or bad. However, the name *free lance* for these knights was invented by Sir Walter Scott in *Ivanhoe* (1820). *Free lance* doesn't seem to have been applied to writers until about sixty years later.

freesia. There is some question about the naming of this fragrant and beautiful genus of South African herbs. Comprising three species but scores of horticultural forms, *freesias* grow from a bulblike corm, belonging to the iris family and bearing typically white or yellow flowers at the end of their stems. They are generally raised in greenhouses and are a popular florist's flower. Some authorities, including *Webster's Biographical Dictionary*, say the genus was named for E.M. Fries (1794-1878), a Swedish botanist; others cite F.H.T. Freese, a pupil of Professor Klatt, the christener of the genus.

free soil, free speech, free labor, free men. This was the slogan of the American *Free-soil Party* during the election of 1848. The slogan referred to the party's opposition to the extension of slavery into any of the territories newly acquired from Mexico. With former President Martin Van Buren as its candidate, the Free-soilers polled nearly 300,000 votes and were a decisive factor in the victory of the Whigs over the Democrats. In 1854 the Free-soil Party was absorbed into the new Republican Party.

freewheeling. A *freewheeling* person is one who moves about freely, independently, one who might even be irresponsible, or someone who isn't governed by rules and regulations. The term comes from bicycling in the old days before the coaster brake was invented, when cyclists coasted, *freewheeling* down the hills. The term *freewheeler* for a bicycle is first recorded in 1889.

the French disease. *Syphilis* (q.v.) has been blamed on nearly every country and continent, always by residents of other countries and continents. For Poles, it was *the German sickness*; the Russians blamed it on the Poles; to the Dutch it was the *Spanish Pox*; and carried to India, China, and Japan it was there branded *the Portuguese disease*. But the French have been blamed far more than most nations, mainly because they have long been widely associated with anything sexual. When in 1496 an Italian wrote that "the French disease is a new plague . . . contracted by lying together," the phrase was quickly adopted throughout Europe. In later years *syphilis* became *French pox*, *French marbles*, *the French goods*, *the French gout*, *the French sickness*, and *a Frenchman*. Furthermore, *French crown* long meant baldness produced by syphilis, *to be Frenchified* meant to be venereally infected, and *a French pig* was a venereal sore. As for the French, they steadfastly refused to call the disease anything but the *Italian* or *the Naples disease*.

French fried potatoes. Many youngsters think McDonald's invented them, but they were conceived in Belgium toward the middle of the 19th century. From there the Belgian fries spread in popularity to France, and the method of deep frying them soon imported to America, where they are still known under the misnomer *French fries*.

Frenchified. Since the late 16th century *Frenchified* has been a contemptuous term for having French manners or qualities. Ben Jonson, the first to record the word, wrote of "Monsieur Fastidious Brisk, otherwise called the fresh Frenchified courtier." The phrase once also meant "to be infected with the venereal disease," this usage recorded as early as 1655.

French letter. (*See* **condom.**)

French words in English. French words came into English by the thousands after the Norman Conquest in 1066 and many had entered the language long before then. It would take a volume to list these basic contributions, but here is a brief sample of just those words that have come into American English: *crappie* (fish), *gopher, pumpkin, cache, carry-all, pirogue, portage, voyageur, brioche, chowder, jambalaya,* [pie] *à la mode, praline, cent, dime, mill, bayou, butte, chute, crevasse, flume, levee, prairie, rapids,* [Indian] *brave, Cajun, calumet, Canuck, lacrosse, lagniappe, parlay, picayune, rotisserie, sashay, bureau, depot, shanty.*

fresh as a daisy. (*See* **daisy.**)

fret. Tracing *fret* back to Middle English we find that the word, related to the German *fressaen,* primarily meant "voracious eating by animals." Today *fret* means only to worry, its new sense probably arising from the idea that worry eats into one, as in the expression "What's eating you?"

Freudian. No other contemporary thinker has influenced 20th-century intellectual thought more profoundly than Dr. Sigmund Freud (1856-1939), the founder of psychoanalysis. His *Freudian theories,* though often modified and even discarded over the years, emphasize the importance of the unconscious, infantile sexuality, and the role of sexuality in the development of neuroses, while *Freudian methods,* such as free association, are methods for treating mental disorders. A *Freudian slip* is popularly a slip of the tongue revealing a repressed subconscious thought or desire. The Austrian physician and psychoanalyst met with extreme hostility when he published *The Interpretation of Dreams* in 1900, but his views became increasingly accepted.

Friday. The Scandinavian goddess of love Freya was deserted by her husband Odin, or Wotan, god of war, wisdom, agriculture, and poetry, because she paid too much attention to a life of luxury and not enough to him. Odin may have forgotten her, but history didn't, the Old English for her name, Freya, becoming the basis for our *Friday: Fria daeg,* or *Freya's day. Wednesday* (q.v.) is named for Wotan.

fried chicken. (*See* **Southern fried chicken.**)

frig. (*See* **fig.**)

frogfall. (*See* **fishfall.**)

from A to izzard. Chiefly British in usage and rare today, *from A to izzard* means *from A to Z,* from alpha to omega (q.v.), from beginning to end. *Izzard* here may be a 1597 dialect variation of *zed* (z) according to the *O.E.D.*

from China to Peru. Throughout the world, this literary phrase still has currency, though seldom in speech. It is from these lines in Samuel Johnson's *On the Vanity of Human Wishes* (1749): "Let observation with extended view/ Survey mankind from China to Peru."

from hell, Hull, and Halifax, Good Lord deliver us. British vagabonds and beggars often recited this famous prayer in the early 17th century and after. *Hell* was to be avoided for obvious reasons, the town of *Hull* demanded hard labor for any "charity" given, and *Halifax* had a celebrated Gibbet Law that provided for the execution of prisoners *and then* a trial to determine whether they were guilty or not!

from scratch. (*See* **start from scratch.**)

from soup to nuts. One would think that this expression for a full-course meal that came to mean "everything" was an ancient one, but the expression is an Americanism that hasn't been tracked beyond 1938, many years after huge multicourse meals were common.

frozen words. An old story from the Texas Panhandle tells of a winter so cold that spoken words froze in the air, fell entangled on the ground and had to be fried up in a skillet before the letters would reform and any sense could be made of them. The idea is an ancient one, used by Rabelais and familiar to the Greek dramatist Antiphanes, who is said to have used it in praising the work of Plato: "As the cold of certain cities is so intense that it freezes the very words we utter, which remain congealed till the heat of summer thaws them, so the mind of youth is so thoughtless that the wisdom of Plato lies there frozen, as it were, till it is thawed by the refined judgement of mature age."

fuchsia; Fuchsian group; fuchsin. *Fuchsia,* a vivid bluish or purplish red, takes its name from the ornamental fuchsia shrubs that honor German physician and botanist Leonhard Fuchs (1501-66). These principally Mexican and South American shrubs, which are of the evening primrose family and can have purple, red, yellow, or white flowers, were named for Fuchs in 1703 by the French botanist Charles Plumier. Dr. Fuchs was noted for his treatment of the "English sweating sickness," a plague that had spread to Europe. He became professor of medicine at the University of Tubingen in 1535, remaining there until his death over three decades later. His herbal *De historia stirpium* (1530) was widely known, this compendium of medicinal and edible plants probably the main reason why the genus *Fuchsia* was named in his honor. The genus contains some one hundred species, with *fuchsia* shrubs being only one of its many widely cultivated plants. *Fuchsin,* or *fuchsine,* is a purplish red aniline dye, and *Fuchsian group* is a mathematical term that derives from the name of I.L. Fuchs (1833-1902), an eminent German mathematician.

fuck. Originally a quite acceptable word, *fuck* was recorded in an English dictionary as early as John Florio's *A World of Words* (1598). The word doesn't derive from the police blotter entry "[booked] *for unlawful carnal knowledge*," as some people still believe. Our word for the act of sexual connection may remotely come from the Latin for the same, *futuere*, but most probably is from the Old German *ficken/fucken*, "to strike or penetrate," which had the slang meaning "to copulate." As *Partridge* points out, the German word is almost certainly related to the Latin words for *pugilist*, *puncture*, and *prick*, through the root *pug*, which goes back to prehistoric times. Before *fuck* came into English in the late 15th century—its first recorded use is in 1503—*swyve* was the verb most commonly used for *fucking*. *Fuck* began to become more rare in print in the 18th century when human experience began to be disguised behind a "veil of decency," and the last dictionary it was recorded in up until recent times is Francis Grose's *Dictionary of the Vulgar Tongue* (1785), in the form of *f**k*. The great *O.E.D.* banned it, just as it banned *cunt* (but not *prick*, for some reason), and this made the word's acceptance all the harder. Though great writers like D.H. Lawrence, James Joyce, and Henry Miller tried to restore *fuck* to its proper place in print, it wasn't until 1960 that Grove Press in America won a court case that permitted publishers to print *fuck* legally for the first time in centuries. The book containing the word was D.H. Lawrence's *Lady Chatterley's Lover*, written in 1928.

fudge. Isaac D'Israeli, father of the British prime minister, had an interesting story about the word *fudge*, for "lies or nonsense," in his *Curiosities of Literature* (1791): "There was sir, in our time one Captain Fudge, commander of a merchantman, who upon his return from a voyage, how illfrought soever his ship was, always brought home a good cargo of lies, so much that now aboard ship the sailors, when they hear a great lie told, cry out "You fudge it!" A notorious liar named Captain Fudge, called "Lying Fudge," did live in 17th century England. His name, possibly in combination with the German word *futch*, "no good," may well be the source of the word *fudge*. Where the word *fudge* for candy comes from no one seems to know, though it probably dates back to the 19th century.

Fugger. (*See* **rich as a Fugger**.)

führer; Hitler; Schicklgruber. Before Adolf Hitler preached his doctrines of the "master race" and The Thousand Year Reich, *führer* was simply a German word for "leader." But Nazi blood purges, millions dead in gas chambers and concentration camps, towns like Lidice wiped off the map, broken treaties, and planned world conquest made both his name and title symbols for terror, horror, and evil, synonyms for a mad tyrant or mega-lomaniac. *Der Fuhrer* was the title Hitler chose when he combined the offices of president and chancellor in 1934. Hitler is said to have committed suicide in his Berlin bunker in 1945, aged fifty-six, but legends persist that he still lives, which indeed he does, if only symbolically. *Schicklgruber* is another word often used to describe someone like him, but contrary to widespread belief, it was not his legal name—Hitler's father, Alois, an illegitimate child, bore his mother's name, Schicklgruber, for a time, but changed it to Hitler, his father's name, before Adolf was born. A *Hitler* or a *Mr.* or *Mrs. Hitler* is a blustering, domineering person.

Fulbright scholarship. A *Fulbright* is a scholarship grant provided under the U.S. Congress Fulbright Act (1946), which was introduced by Senator James William Fulbright (b. 1905) and has been awarded to a large number of now prominent Americans.

full nelson. The name for this wrestling hold didn't come into use until the 19th century, when it was named either for some celebrated grappler who excelled at the pressure hold, or for Nelson, a town in Lancashire, England, once famous for its wrestling matches. The town of Nelson changed its name from Marston in the 19th century, calling itself after the popular Lord Nelson Inn there, which in turn honored England's great naval hero.

full of beans; etc. The phrase is used like *full of baloney*, *full of soup*, and worse, but it usually means someone who is full of energy, high-spirited, lively—sometimes in a foolish or silly way. Some say it is a horsey expression, like *full of oats*, going back to the days when horses were fed "horse beans" raised for fodder. The saying, however, is a British one from about 1870 and may derive from an earlier phrase, *full of bread*. Beans, a high-protein food, certainly should make one lively; in fact, they have long been regarded as an aphrodisiac. As an old English ballad, "The Love Bean," put it:

My love hung limp beneath the leaf
  (O bitter, bitter shame!)
My heavy heart was full of grief
  Until my lady came.
She brought a tasty dish to me,
  (O swollen pod and springing seed!)
My love sprang out right eagerly
  To serve me in my need.

The gas that beans inspire also has something to do with the expression; as the word *prunes*, substituted in the phrase for *beans* some seventy years later, would indicate, both beans and prunes have a laxative effect. In fact, beans were primarily regarded as an aphrodisiac by the ancients because the eructations they caused were thought to produce prodigious erections. But the U.S. Department of Agriculture has recently developed a "gas-less variety," "a clean bean" seed guaranteed not to cause social distress at the dinner table or elsewhere. So bean eaters can now be as *full of beans* as ever and much less obnoxious, though maybe not as sexy.

full of oats.   (*See* **feel one's oats.**)

funk; funky.   *Funk*, for "fear of panic," still has its best explanation in the Flemish phrase *in de fonck siin*, "in a state of panic." Yet this literally means "to be in the smoke" and no one has been able to explain the connection between smoke and panic. Possibly smoke was associated with a panic-stricken person trying to find a way out through the smoke of a fire, or with the smoke of hell fire. The word owes part of its long popularity to its similarity to the most famous of four-letter words beginning with *f*. Since its introduction to England in the early 18th century it has also come to mean a dejected mood, especially in the phrase *in a blue funk*, "blue" intensifying the phrase by suggesting "the blues." If there is an eponymous Funk somewhere, he or she would be glad to know that *funky* which derives from *funk*, means good jazz with an earthy blues-based character. This *funky* is popular recent slang for anything very good or beautiful (clothes, hairstyle, etc.), but it can also mean something cheap or no good, depending on the context.

funny bone.

They have pull'd you down flat on your back,
And they smack, and they thwack,
Till your "funny bones" crack,
As if you were stretched on the rack,
   At each thwack!
Good lack! what a savage attack!

Reverend Richard Harris Barham, well known for his punning, wrote the above in *The Ingoldsby Legends* (1840) and it is the first mention of the expression *funny bone* in literature. The *funny bone*—Americans called it the *crazy bone* in the past—is technically the medial condyle of the humerus, that is, the enlarged knob on the end of the bone of the upper arm, which lies below the ulnar nerve. The unpadded nerve hits the humerus as if against an anvil when we strike it on something, causing sharp, tingling pain. Nothing is very funny about this—it inspires cursing rather than laughter. But Barham or some punster before him probably saw the pun *humorous* in the *humerus* bone and dubbed it the funny bone, adding one of the few puns that have become words to the language.

furlong.   In medieval times a *furlong*—from the Old English *furh*, "furrow," and *lang*, "long"—was the length of an ideal furrow in a plowed field, which was one-eighth of a Roman mile. Though the length of furrows and other land measurements changed over the centuries, a *furlang*, changed slightly to *furlong*, remained the same eighth of a mile, or 220 yards, and became a measurement used primarily in horse racing.

furphy.   Any baseless report, a latrine rumor, is in Australian military slang called a *furphy* and honors, or dishonors, one of two possible candidates: either the firm of Furphy & Co., whose name appeared on World War I latrine buckets supplied to the Australian forces; or a contractor named Furphy who supplied rubbish carts to Melbourne army camps about 1915.

F.W.C.   (*See* **F.M.C.**)

G

G. According to the old Phoenician alphabet, *G* represented the outline of a camel's head and neck.

gabfest. *Gabfest* is an Americanism, which like all *fest* words (*e.g.*, talkfest, funfest) half derives from the annual family *fest* (from the German *fest*, "festival") held by the German-American Turner family beginning in the mid-19th century. The *Turner fest* was the model for *gabfest*, first recorded in 1897, but *gab* had been used in England for "to talk fluently, very well, or too much." *Gab* may be an old Norse word, or may be onomatopoeic like *gabble*, and has been used since at least 1670. *Gift of gab* ("He's got a gift of gab"), the ability to talk well or convincingly, dates back to 1681 in England, while *gabby*, too, is British, first recorded in 1719.

Gabriel's hounds. *Gabriel's hounds* are wild geese, so called centuries ago because their sound in flight is like a pack of hounds in full cry. Legend has it that they are the souls of unbaptized children wandering in space until the Judgment Day. *Gabriel* here refers to one of the biblical archangels.

gadget. *Gadget*, as it is usually employed, is a relatively new word, dating only to 1886 and possibly deriving from the French *gachette* for "a little mechanical thing." Its latest and most ironic use (ca. 1970) is a widely used synonym for an atomic bomb, especially among scientists who make the monsters.

gadolinite; gadolinium. In 1794 Finnish chemist Johann Gadolin analyzed a black mineral found in rare-earth elements at Ytterly, near Stockholm, Sweden. The mineral, from which he extracted the oxide yttria, was named *gadolinite* in his honor eight years later. Gadolin (1760-1852) also has the metallic chemical element *gadolinium* to commemorate him. It was discovered in 1880 by the Swiss chemist J.C.G. de Marignac, being one of several elements extracted from *gadolinite*. Marignac did not name the new element for Gadolin until six years after his discovery.

Gaelic words in English. Gaelic, still spoken by about 600,000 people in Ireland and Scotland, has contributed a number of words to English, including: *bard, bog, glen, slogan, blarney, shillelagh, shamrock, colleen, brogue, galore* (all Irish Gaelic); and *clan, loch,* and *ptarmigan* (Scots Gaelic).

gaff; to stand the gaff. To *stand the gaff* means to endure goading or kidding by someone, but its roots extend to the Provençal word *gaf*, for "a boathook." *Gaff*, for "a hoax or trick" possibly derives from the idea of "hooking some poor fish," from the time when a large fishhook was referred to as a gaff.

gaffer. *Gaffer* means an old man, so *an old gaffer* is somewhat redundant, but that is how the expression is mostly used. *Gaffer* is thought to be a contraction of either *grandfather* or *godfather*, and is believed to be much older than its first recorded use at the end of the 16th century. *An old gammer*, for "an old woman," derives from either *grandmother* or *godmother* and is rarely heard outside rural England.

gaga. Someone cuckoo, off his rocker, mentally unbalanced. It has been suggested that *gaga* is of French origin, the word deriving from the name of the French artist Paul Gauguin, who gave up banking to become a painter at the age of thirty-five, having experienced considerable mental anguish toward the end of his life. The word seems inappropriate, however, to express Gauguin's tortured genius and would be a cruel and stupid coining if true. Alternatives are the theories that *gaga* derives from the French *gateux*, "an old man feeble-minded and no longer able to control his body," or that it is in imitation of an idiot's laugh. The phrase has been artist's slang, which would support the Gauguin theory, but according to the *gateux* theory, *gaga* originated in the theatrical world about 1875, eight years before Gauguin (1848-1903) became a painter.

gag rules. *Gag rules* restrict or prevent discussion on a particular subject by a legislative body. The term is an Americanism first recorded in 1810, though *gag tactics* were used as early as 1798 in Congress to try to restrict freedom of the press.

Gainsborough hat. Paintings have inspired a number of fashions, but no artist has been more influential than English portrait painter and landscapist Thomas Gainsborough in this regard. The *Gainsborough* is a wide-brimmed, large hat, turned up at the side, similar to those included in many of his portraits. Gainsborough (1727-88) did not invent the plumed velvet or taffeta hat, but painted it so well that it has been revived several times by designers, as have a number of the gracious fashions he depicted.

Galahad. The term is not much used anymore, except in jest, but a true gentleman is still sometimes called *a Galahad*, after the noble knight Sir Galahad of Arthurian legend. The noblest knight of all, Galahad was the son of Lancelot.

Galatea. Here is a cotton fabric named for a ship. *Galatea*, often used to make children's sailor suits in the past, honors H.M.S. *Galatea*, a mighty British warship of the 1860s. The *Galatea*, in turn, took her name from the sea nymph Galatea of Greek mythology.

galaxy. The Greek *galaxis*, "circle of milk," a reference to the Milky Way, gives us our word *galaxy*, first recorded in about 1398.

gallium. French chemist Paul Emil Lecoq de Boisbaudran named this element after *Gallia*, the Latin name for present-day France, on discovering *gallium*, in 1874. Some etymologists suspect that the scientist may have been crowing a bit, however, as *le coq* means "rooster" in French and "rooster" is *gallus* in Latin.

Gallup Poll. The Gallup Poll is the best-known, though not the first public-opinion poll. It was originated by Dr. George Horace Gallup (b. 1901), a professor of journalism at Northwestern University. Gallup developed his technique about 1933, basing it on carefully phrased questions and scientifically selected samples. He became prominent nationally by predicting the outcome of the 1936 American presidential election, when many other pollsters failed. His poll, operating both at home and abroad, has proved remarkably accurate but is far from infallible. In the 1948 national elections, for example, Gallup chose the late Governor Thomas E. Dewey over incumbent President Truman.

galoot. (*See* **big galoot**.)

galumph. (*See* **jabberwocky**.)

galvanic; galvanism; etc. These words enshrine Luigi Galvani (1737-98), a brilliant physiologist at Italy's University of Bologna—although *galvanism* originally proved something less than brilliant. Galvani's experiments began in about 1771. No one knows if his observant wife Lucia pointed out the first *galvanic* reaction, or if the professor had been preparing frog legs for her dinner—the tale has numerous versions—but one evening Galvani did notice that the skinned leg of a frog he was dissecting twitched when he touched it with a scalpel. After experimenting for about twenty years, Galvani wrote a paper concluding that the reaction had been produced by "animal electricity." Actually, the original frog's leg had twitched because his scalpel had touched the brass conductor of a nearby electrical machine, the charged knife shocking its muscles involuntarily "into life" with a current of electricity. Alessandro Volta quickly pointed out that the contact of two different metals really produced the electricity, but controversy raged between his and Galvani's supporters for years. Despite his monumental mistake, Galvani's name was lionized in numerous scientific terms indicating the use of direct current. Technically, we speak of *galvanizing* by shocking with an electric current, or *galvanizing* metal by giving it a protective zinc coating, while *galvanic* refers to electricity produced by chemical action. Yet the words have much broader nontechnical meanings when they imply arousal or stimulation. As when we say someone is *galvanized* into action by a *galvanic* happening—shocked into an excited response like Galvani's frog. (*See* **volt**.)

gamble away the sun before sunrise. This saying about gold and riches might be considered the first American proverb, though it isn't recorded in *Bartlett's* or any other book of quotations. The expression surely is old enough, dating back to 1533, when Pizarro conquered Cuzco, the capital of the Inca empire, and stripped the Peruvian metropolis of gold and silver. One cavalryman got as his share of the booty a splendid golden image of the sun "which raised on a plate of burnished gold spread over the walls in a recess of the great temple" and which was so beautifully crafted that he did not have it melted down into coins, as was the usual practice. But the horseman came to symbolize the vice of gambling. That same night, before the sun had set on another day, he lost the fabulous golden image of the sun at cards or dice, and his comrades coined the saying *Juega el Sol antes que amanezca*: "He gambles (or plays) away the sun before sunrise," which crossed the ocean from America on Pizarro's gold-laden galleons and became proverbial in Spain.

game as Ned Kelly. It cost nearly half a million dollars to finally capture Australia's Kelly gang, even though the band was only four in number. Ned Kelly (1854-80), the son of a transported Belfast convict and a convicted horse thief himself, took to the hills with his brother Daniel when the latter was charged with horse stealing. Joined by two other desperados, the brothers held up towns and robbed banks for two years until the police finally caught up with them. Ned Kelly became something of a folk hero, and the great deprivations he suffered led to the phrase *as game as Ned Kelly*. When the gang was traced at last to a wooden shanty hideout, police riddled it with bullets, burned the shack down and found Ned Kelly alive and dressed in a suit of armor. He was tried, convicted, and hanged for his crimes, without the iron suit.

game leg. A *game leg* is a bad leg, the *game* here probably from the English dialect *gam* or *gammy*, both meaning crooked. The expression isn't recorded until late in the 18th century.

the game of the arrow. American artist George Catlin recorded this favorite (though little known) amusement of the plains Indians: "The young men . . . assemble on the prairie [and] . . . step forward in turn, shooting their arrows into the air, endeavoring to see who can get the greatest number flying in the air at one time, thrown from the same bow."

gamesmanship. British author Stephen Potter coined this word in his 1947 book *The Theory and Practice of Gamesmanship, or The Art of Winning Games Without Actually Cheating. Gamesmanship* means "the use of dubious or seemingly improper methods that are not strictly illegal" and is almost an antonym of *sportsmanship,* upon which Potter probably based it.

gammer. (*See* **gaffer.**)

gammon and spinach. The expression *gammon and spinach* for "nonsense, humbug" is not as familiar today as it was in Dickens's time, when he used it in *David Copperfield*: "What a world of gammon and spinnage it is, though, ain't it!" The phrase, most likely an elaboration of the slang word *gammon,* which meant nonsense or a ridiculous story, is probably patterned on the older phrase *gammon and patter,* the language of London underworld thieves. The nonsense part of it was possibly reinforced by the old nursery rhyme "A Frog He Would A-wooing Go" (1600) heard by millions: "With a rowley powley gammon and spinach/Heigh ho! says Anthony Rowley."

gamp; brolly. *Gamp* is a term for an umbrella, especially an untidy one, in England, but is rarely, if ever, used in the U.S. The word comes to us from Charles Dickens's *The Life and Adventures of Martin Chuzzlewit* (1843-44), in which the garrulous and disreputable nurse Sarah Gamp always carries a bulky cotton umbrella. Her name is sometimes used for a midwife as well. *Brolly,* first recorded in 1873, is more commonly British slang for an umbrella today.

gams. In the U.S., since about 1900, *gams* has referred only to women's legs. But before then, in England, *gamb* meant any leg, especially a bare leg, and long prior to that *gamb* meant the leg of an animal, deriving from the Latin *gamba,* "leg," from the Greek *kampi,* "bend, curve."

gandy dancer. There are several theories about this term for a railroad construction worker, which is immortalized in the song "The Gandy Dancer's Ball." One says *gandy dancer* is an American hobo term for fellow tramps who helped build the transcontinental railroad. Another claims the expression comes from the gander-like movements of these men as they worked, while a third and most probable theory opts for Chicago's Gandy

Manufacturing Co., which made prominently marked track-laying tools used by the workers.

gangplank; gangboard; gangway. Whether it's called a *gangplank* or *gangboard,* the plank connecting a ship to land takes its name from the Old English *gang,* a way of passage, because it was a way of going on or off a ship. In time, *gangway* became a synonym.

Garand rifle. In the early 1930s, Canadian-born John Cantius Garand invented the semiautomatic *Garand,* which works on the principle of expanding gas, while employed as a civilian ordnance engineer at the U.S. Armory in Springfield, Massachusetts. The famous M-1 was adopted in 1936 as the official U.S. Army rifle. The .30-calibre, 8-shot, clip-loading weapon proved to be a great improvement on the old standard Springfield, firing up to four times as many shots, or 100 rounds per minute, and contributed greatly to the Allied victory in World War II. Garand was never paid a cent in royalties for his invention, and never earned more than $12,000 a year in his 34-year service with the U.S. Ordnance Corps.

garbage. There are several possibilities here. Folk etymology has it that *garbage* derives from the Latin *gerbe,* "green stuff," from the nobility's scorn for vegetables in centuries past. Another possibility is the French *garbe,* "wheat, hay and other vegetative matter chopped up together for horse fodder." But *garbage* most likely derives from the Italian *garbuglio,* for "confused intrigue," hence confusion, a mess—the intrigue part appropriate for our modern-day *garbologists,* people who apparently first appeared in the 1970s to make their living by poking through the garbage of celebrities and others at the top of the heap and learning their deep, dark, dirty secrets.

garden. In Latin a formal garden was called a *hortus* (cultivated land") *gardinus* ("guarded"), that is, cultivated land guarded or enclosed by a wall. This ultimately came into English, early in the 14th century, as the shortened *garden,* which actually refers to the wall rather than the cultivated land.

gardenia. "Mr. Miller has called it Basteria. But if you will please to follow my advice, I would call it Gardenia, from our worthy friend Dr. Alexander Garden of S. Carolina."

"If Dr. Garden will send me a new genus, I shall be truly happy to name it after him, Gardenia."

These quotations from an exchange of letters between a friend of Linnaeus and the great botanist himself, 1757-58, reveal the politicking that is sometimes involved even in naming something. Linnaeus did honor his promise to their mutual friend and two years later dedicated a newly discovered tropical shrub to Garden, even though the amateur botanist did not discover the beautiful, sweet-smelling *gardenia*. Dr. Alexander Garden (ca. 1730-91), a Scottish-American physician, resided in Charleston, South Carolina, where he practiced medicine and also devoted much of his time to collecting plant and animal specimens, discovering the Congo eel and a number of snakes and herbs. Garden carried on an extensive correspondence with Linnaeus and many other European naturalists, probably as much out of loneliness as for intellectual stimulation. An ardent Tory, he returned to England during the Revolutionary War, resuming his practice in London and becoming vice-president of the Royal Society. Dr. Garden was by all accounts a difficult, headstrong man. When his granddaughter was named Gardenia Garden in his honor, he still refused to see her. After all, her father had fought against the British!

Gargantua. Broad, coarse exuberant humor and sharp satire mark the *Rabelaisian* spirit or style. The word honors the prodigious French humanist and humorist François Rabelais (ca. 1490-1553), who "drank deep as any man," of life as well as wine. Rabelais, whose voracious appetites would have sufficed for any two ordinary men, started out as a Benedictine monk, later turning physician, but his reputation rests on his ribald writing, a paean to the good life—love, drink, food—a satire on the bigotry and blindness of Church, state, and pedant. Gross and noble at the same time, marked by vast scholarship, his masterpieces are *Pantagruel* (1533) and *Gargantua* (1535). The last book, though Gargantua had been a figure in French folklore, gives us the word *gargantuan*—"enormous, gigantic"—from the giant prince of prodigious appetite, who was eleven months in the womb, as an infant needed the milk of 17,913 cows, combed his hair with a 900-foot-long comb, once ate six pilgrims in a salad, and lived for several centuries. Pantagruel, Gargantua's son, is just as famous and classic a character.

Garibaldi shirt; Garibaldi fish. In the crowning achievement of his eventful life, Giuseppe Garibaldi, commanding his one thousand Redshirt volunteers, conquered Sicily, crossed back to the Italian mainland and expelled King Francis II from Naples. One year later in 1861, Italy was united under King Victor Emmanuel II and Garibaldi became an international hero. Both a woman's loose, high-necked blouse with full sleeves—similar to those worn by his followers—and a currant biscuit were named for him, as well as an edible, brilliant orange fish (*Hypsypopa rubicundus*) discovered off the southern California coast by Italian-American fishermen.

garlic. Owing to its resemblance to the leek, the herb that "makes men drink and wink and stink" takes its name from the Old English *garleac*: *gar*, "spear," and *leac*,

"leek." The Romans believed garlic contained magical powers and hung it over their doors to ward off witches, just as some people wear cloves around their necks to protect themselves against colds and diseases.

Garret election. Presumably, there are no more bawdy garret elections *anywhere*, but such popular ceremonies were held near Wandsworth, London in the 18th century. There in the borough of Garret, a small hamlet consisting of "a few struggling cottages," the ludicrous "election" was held with the opening of every new parliament, the only voting qualification being "open-air coition in or near Garret." According to an account of the time: "The ceremony consists of a mock election of two members to represent the borough of Garret. The qualification of a voter is having enjoyed a woman in the open air within that district. The candidates are commonly fellows of low humour who dress themselves up in a ridiculous manner. As this brings a prodigious concourse of people to Wandsworth, the publicans of that place jointly contribute to the expenses, which is sometimes considerable." Similar elections might prove the answer to voter apathy in the U.S.

Garrison finish. Holding Montana back from the pack until they came into the homestretch, "Snapper" Garrison suddenly stood high in the stirrups, bending low over the horse's mane in his famous "Yankee seat" and whipped the mount toward the finish line, moving up with a rush and winning the 1882 Suburban Handicap by a nose. This race made jockey Edward H. Garrison an American turf hero. Garrison, who died in 1931, aged 70, used his new technique many times over his long career, winning many of his races in the last furlong, and the *Garrison finish* became so well-known that it was applied to any close horse race, finally becoming synonymous with all last minute efforts—in sports, politics, or any other field.

garryowen. In rugby a *garryowen* is a high punt the offensive team uses to gain ground when the forwards are rushing downfield. It takes its name from the Irish rugby club Garryowen, well-known for using the tactic.

gas; gasoline. Though it is also the abbreviation of *gasoline*, *gas* is the older of the two words. *Gasoline* made its debut in the late 19th century when scientists coined it (from *gas* plus the Latin *oleum*, "oil," and *ine*) to describe the colorless liquid obtained by the fractional distillation of petroleum. *Gas* itself was coined nearly three centuries earlier by Dutch physician and chemist Jean Baptiste van Helmont (1577-1644). Van Helmont thought that he had discovered an occult principle contained in all bodies and named his discovery *gas* from the German *chaos*, "chaos." He had little understanding of the nature of gases, and no one knows exactly what sense of the word *chaos* he had in mind when he coined *gas* from it. But despite all this chaos, he was *cooking with gas*, for his invention has become part of almost every language.

gasconade. The Gascon inhabitants of Gascony, France, a region and former province near the Spanish border, have traditionally been regarded by other Frenchmen as flamboyantly boastful, a poor people except in bravery and bragging. This tradition can be seen in Dumas's *The Three Musketeers*, where brave, boastful D'Artagnan is the model of a Gascon. Many old French *contes* illustrated Gascon braggadocio. One tells of a Gascon being asked how he liked the great Louvre in Paris. "Pretty well," the braggart replies, "It reminds me of the back part of my father's stables." Such stories and the sentiments that inspire them led to the coining of *gasconade*, "extravagant boasting or swashbuckling braggadocio," a word that became universal because it described so many people other than Gascons.

gat. (*See* **Gatling gun.**)

gate crashing. (*See* **crash.**)

gathering nuts in May. Since there are no nuts to be gathered in May, the old children's song that goes, "Here we go gathering nuts in May" seems to make no sense—and indeed, it may have been intended as a nonsense song. But the *nuts* in the phrase has been explained as being *knots* of May, that is, bunches of flowers. In Elizabethan England Elizabeth herself gathered *knots of May* in the meadows, one author tells us, and this is a plausible explanation, even though there are no recorded quotations supporting the use of *knots* for flowers, except possibly the English knot gardens of shrubs.

Gatling gun. The *Gatling gun* won fame as the best of the eleven mostly eponymous Civil War machine guns (including the Ripley; the Ager "Coffee Mill"; the Claxon; the Gorgas; and the Williams, which, when used by the Confederates on May 3, 1862, became the first machine gun to be fired in warfare). Designed by Doctor Richard Jordan Gatling (1818-1903), a North Carolina physician and inventor, the *Gatling* was perfected by 1862 but adopted by Union forces too late to be used in more than a few battles. Mounted on wheels, it had a cluster of 5 to 10 barrels that revolved around a central shaft. The gunner, by turning a hand crank, controlled the rate of fire, up to 350 rounds per minute. Despite the weapon's late introduction, the Gatling's effective range of two thousand yards had a strong psychological effect on the Confederacy; adopted by many nations after the Civil War, it remained in use until about 1900. Although the weapon is of only historical importance today, as the precursor of the modern machine gun, another word deriving from it has wide currency. *Gat*, a slang term for a small gun, appar-

ently arose as a humorous exaggeration. By 1880, however, fictional characters were talking of having *gatlins* under their coats and it wasn't long before *gatlin*, or *gatling*, was shortened to *gat*.

gauntlet. (*See* **throw down the gauntlet.**)

gauss. Known as "the prince of mathematicians," and possibly the greatest mathematical genius of all time, Karl Friedrich Gauss (1777-1855) was a German prodigy who when only ten discovered independently how to sum up complex arithmetic series. He did much important work in his field before turning twenty-one, including a proof of the fundamental theorem of algebra, but did not confine himself to mathematics. Of his many important contributions in topology, physics, and astronomy—he headed the Gottingen Observatory—one of the most valuable is his founding of the mathematical theory of electricity. Thus the *gauss*, a unit of intensity of the magnetic field, pays honor to his name.

gauze. *Eyeless in Gaza* and the *Gaza strip* are phrases well known to readers of the Bible and history, but few people know that the city of Gaza on the Mediterranean Sea gives its name to the light filmy fabric called *gauze*, which was first manufactured there.

gay. Some commentators have argued that *gay*, used to describe a homosexual, makes obsolete older, more traditional uses of the word, and that, besides, homosexuals are as morose as anybody else. But no one can legislate word usage, and what the language at the time needs, it takes. *Gay* came into use in the 1950s, possibly originating from the older (ca. 1935) term *gaycat*, for "a homosexual boy." In addition to suggesting gaiety, *gay* has also had strong links with "affectation, dissipation, and immoral life" for over three centuries.

gay Lothario. Lothario's boastful speech from Nicholas Rowe's tragedy in blank verse *The Fair Penitent* (1703) explains why his name became a synonym for a libertine or seducer. Lothario isn't by any means a model lover, for Calista, the fair penitent, stabs herself after being seduced by him. Wounded in a duel, he dies claiming: "In Love I Triumphed: Those joys are lodg'd beyond the reach of Fate . . ." Rowe apparently stole the plot for his play from Massinger and Field's *Fatal Dowery* (1632), shortening it and modifying the ending, and borrowed Lothario's name and character from William D'Avenant's tragedy *The Cruel Brothers* (1630), though Lothario is also the name of characters in Cervantes's *Don Quixote* and Goethe's *Wilhelm Meister*. Rowe's play, a favorite of Dr. Johnson's, was extremely popular for over a century, the legendary David Garrick playing the lead for a time, and made "the haughty, gallant, gay Lothario" proverbial. Lothario's philosophy might be summed up in his lines: "The driving storm of Passion will have way, and I must yield before it."

gazebo. The German *Gasse-bau*, "bow window" has been suggested as the source for *gazebo*, but this word for a summer garden house, or lookout, or belvedere, is probably a humorous play on the verb *to gaze*. First recorded in 1752, it could also be a corruption of some unknown Chinese word, for it was called a *Chinese tower* at the time.

gazette. Newspapers were first called *gazettas* in 16th-century Venice, where they were so named because one could be bought with a Venetian coin of small value called a *gazeta*. By 1605 we find Ben Jonson using the word in English, though it wasn't spelled in its present form for another 75 years or so.

gear. 1980s slang for clothes, replacing "threads," "vines," etc., in the inner city, the word *gear* derives from the common term for military or outdoor equipment, including clothing, and was either introduced by Vietnam veterans or associated with the Army-Navy "surplus stores" where the young often buy clothing that sets styles. French designer Jean Charles de Castelbajac had even introduced the *Gear Look* for the not so young with money, "rough-hewn outdoorsy materials translated into high fashion." *Gear* was standard English for the female and male sexual organs from the 16th to the 19th century.

gee! An American euphemism for "Jesus!", *gee!* dates back to only 1895. Its antecedents are *jewillikin* (1851); *gee whillikins!* (1857); *gee whiz!* (1895); *gee whitaker!* (1895); and *holy gee!* Since then we have had *jeez!* (1900); *jeepers!* (1920s); and *jeepers creepers!* (1934). (*See also* **Jiminy Cricket.**)

gefilte fish. Hot or cold it is delicious, but the Jewish delicacy, made with many ingredients and traditionally served on Friday nights, is *not* a separate species of fish. Gefilte fish is a kind of fish loaf made of various ground fish, eggs, onions, pepper, salt, and sometimes sugar—every good cook having her or his secret recipe. The Yiddish word derives from the German for "stuffed fish."

Geiger counter. The *Geiger counter* is sometimes called the *Geiger-Muller counter*, for both German physicist Hans Geiger (1882-1945) and the scientist who helped him improve upon it in 1927. Actually it might better be named the *Geiger-Rutherford-Muller counter*, because the British physicist Ernest Rutherford had invented the device, with Geiger, fifteen years earlier. The clicking electronic counter, which measures nuclear radiation, is owned by many hopeful prospectors today and

widely used as a safety device; it is also employed in medicine to locate malignancies. Geiger designed other types of counters as well.

gelati. Italian *gelati* has become more popular in America over the past ten years. *Gelato* is the Italian for ice cream, and the delicacy, which is folded rather than churned when made, has a much higher butter-fat content than any other kind of ice cream.

gelt; mazuma; shekels. This slang term for money owes its currency to Yiddish. *Gelt* derives from the German *geld*, "money," and has been common here since the mid-19th century, in England since 1698. *Mazuma*, usually a more humorous term, possibly derives from the Chaldean *m'zumon*, "the ready necessary," or money. For some strange reason *mazuma* was first recorded (1907) in a book about Kansas, of all places. The *shekel*, the first money mentioned in the Bible (Gen. 33:12-16), was a silver coin weighing about two-thirds of an ounce, common in ancient times. In the plural it has come to mean money in general, since at least the mid-19th century.

genocide. Acts intended to destroy national, ethnic, racial, or religious groups are called *genocide*, the word based on the Greek *genos*, "race," and the Latin *cadere*, "to kill." The word was invented by Professor Raphael Lemkin of Duke University and used in the official indictment of Nazi criminals in 1945; three years later the United Nations made genocide a crime against international law.

gentian. Among the loveliest wild flowers, the *fringed gentian* has been immortalized by Bryant and other poets, and the large *Gentiana* genus to which it belongs, containing some 400 species, provides us with many valued alpine plants for the rock garden. *Gentians* take their name from the powerful monarch Gentius, who reigned as king of Illyria about 180-167 B.C. and who was first to experience the medicinal value of *gentians*, according to Pliny and Dioscorides. Since early times the roots and rhizome of the European *yellow gentian* (*Gentiana lutea*) have been used to dilate wounds, as a bitter tonic and counterpoison, and in curing diseases. Certain alcoholic beverages are made from the plant, too. The beautiful flowers, predominantly blue, despite *Gentians lutea*, are generally found at high altitudes. Difficult to cultivate, they are nevertheless extensively grown in the home garden. *Gentianaceae*, the *Gentian* family, consisting of 800 species and 30 genera, also bears the Illyrian king's name.

Gentoo. *Gentoo*, for prostitute, is a South African word that may come from a disparaging Hindi term for a Hindu who speaks Teluga rather than Hindi. But it possibly derives from the name of the *Gentoo*, a ship transporting female servants to Africa that was wrecked on the South African coast. The women were saved but lost all their belongings and were forced to work as prostitutes in *Gentoo houses* to support themselves. *Gentoo*, first recorded in 1638, also means a heathen.

georgette. Whether she invented it or not isn't known, but the finespun fabric *georgette* honors Madame Georgette de la Plante, a celebrated Parisian dressmaker and modiste of the late 19th century. The formerly trademarked sheer silk crepe is used primarily for blouses and gowns. It is sometimes called *georgette crepe.*

Georgia. Georgia is named for George II of England (1683-1760). Discovered by Hernando de Soto in 1540, it became the last of the thirteen original colonies in 1732 when a British charter was granted for the establishment of "the Colony of Georgia in America." George II, a methodical man who "took the greatest pleasure in counting his money piece by piece, and . . . never forgot a date," wasn't a particularly popular monarch. Historians straining for something interesting to say about him seem only to be able to tell us that he was the last British sovereign to command an army in the field—at the battle of Dettingen (June 27, 1743) in the War of the Austrian Succession.

geranium. The beaked seed pods of these flowers resembled the head and beak of a crane, the Greeks thought, and so they named the plant for their word for crane, *geranos.* This family of flowers, containing about 250 species, does not include the very popular common garden geranium (*Pelargonium*) so widely grown today, which were mistaken for it over the years and so share its name. *Pelargonium*, however, is from the Greek for "stork," an allusion to the shape of its fruit.

germ. The Latin word *germen*, "sprout," is the ultimate root of *germ.* Long before it meant the seed of a disease, a usage first recorded in 1803, *germ* meant "any portion of a living thing, animal or vegetable, that is capable of development into a likeness of that from which it sprang." Hence the name *wheat germ* for the tiny living protoplasm in the wheat kernel.

German measles; German shepherd; etc. During both World Wars anything *German* was anathema to her enemies. As *Mencken* points out, Bismarck herring became *Eisenhower herring*, sauerkraut, *liberty cabbage*, and German measles even became *liberty measles*. *German measles*, or rubella, is a milder virus disease than measles, though particularly dangerous to the offspring of pregnant women who are exposed to it; the *German* may be spurious in that sense, but the disease could be so named because it was first identified by Dr. Friedrich Hoffmann, a German physician, in 1740. Similarly,

German silver was initially made at Hildburghausen, Germany, although the fact that it is a silvery alloy, a *fake* silver compound of copper, nickel, and zinc, may have influenced its name. Typical of words using the national adjective is the now ubiquitous *German shepherd* guard dog, which is properly an Alsatian. (*See* **measly.**)

German words in English. English is of course structurally Germanic and is considered a Germanic language because of its Anglo-Saxon roots, but many words from Germanic languages have come into English at a later time in history, from the Middle Ages up until the present. A brief sample of these include: *junker, lobby, carouse, plunder, saber, zinc, hamster, cobalt, shale, quartz, feldspar, gneiss, nickel, meerschaum, waltz, zigzag, iceberg, poodle, spitz, dachshund, zither, leitmotiv, yodel, protein, paraffin, ohm, poltergeist, rucksack, semester, kindergarten, seminar, poker,* and *bum.* Words in American English of German origin include the following: *fresh* (impudent), *bub, hex, hausfrau, loafer, nix, ouch, phooey, wunderkind, spiel, Kris Kringle, Christmas tree, semester, seminar, noodle, sauerkraut, pretzel, lager beer, bock beer, frankfurter, hamburger, liverwurst, sauerbrauten, pumpernickel, schnitzel, delicatessen, snits, wienerwurst, zweiback, stollen, dunk, bake oven, and how!, cookbook, ecology, gabfest, check* (restaurant tab), *hold on, hoodlum, klutz, loafer, rifle, scram, slim chance, shyster, gesundheit, schnapps, standpoint, wisenheimer, wanderlust.*

Geronimo! Chiricahua Apache leader Geronimo is said to have made a daring leap on horseback to escape U.S. cavalry pursuers at Medicine Bluffs, Oklahoma. As he leaped to freedom down a steep cliff and into a river below he supposedly cried out his name in defiance of the troopers. There is no mention of this incident in the great warrior and prophet's autobiography, which he dictated to a white writer before his death under military confinement at Fort Sill, Oklahoma, in 1909. But by that time Geronimo was an old man, well over seventy, and had converted to the Dutch Reformed Church; little remained of the brave leader who in protecting his people's land against white settlers had terrorized the American Southwest and northern Mexico with cunning, brutal raids and whose actions became western legend. The cry *Geronimo!* is part of that legend and was adopted as the battle cry of American paratroopers leaping from their planes in World War II. The 82nd Airborne at Fort Bragg, North Carolina first used it, taking it either from the oral legend about Geronimo or from the popular movie featuring the Indian warrior, showing near the paratrooper training center at the time.

gerrymander. Above editor Benjamin Russell's desk in the offices of the *Centinel*, a Massachusetts Federalist newspaper, hung the serpentine-shaped map of a new

Essex County senatorial district that began at Salisbury and included Amesbury, Haverhill, Methuen, Andover, Middleton, Danvers, Lynnfield, Salem, Marblehead, Lynn, and Chelsea. This political monster was part of a general reshaping of voting districts that the Democratic-Republican-controlled state legislature had enacted with the approval of incumbent Governor Elbridge Gerry. The arbitrary redistricting would have happily enabled the Jeffersonians to concentrate Federalist power in a few districts and remain in the majority after the then yearly gubernatorial elections of 1812, and was of course opposed by the Federalists. So when the celebrated painter Gilbert Stuart visited the *Centinel* offices one day before the elections, editor Russel indignantly pointed to the monstrous map on the wall, inspiring Stuart to take a crayon and add head, wings, and claws to the already lizard-shaped district. "That will do for a salamander," the artist said when he had finished. "A *Gerry*-mander, you mean," Russell replied, and a name for the political creature was born, *gerrymander* coming into use as a verb within a year.

Gestapo. *Gestapo* is a contraction formed from *Geheime Staats Polizei*, the Nazi secret state police agency that was formally declared a criminal organization at the Nuremberg trials. Founded in 1933 by Hermann Goering, it came under Heinrich Himmler's control as part of the S.S. the following year. The group's ruthless methods of capture, torture, and extermination, the fact that it was responsible for all concentration camps, and its exemption from any control by the courts made it the symbol for brutal, sadistic repression that it is today.

to get a rise out of someone. These words first applied to fish rising to the bait. Writers on the art of angling popularized the word *rise* in this sense three hundred years ago, and the metaphor from fly-fishing became standard English. Just as the fish rises to the bait and is caught, the person who *rises* to the lure of a practical joke becomes the butt of it. From its original meaning of raising a laugh at someone's expense, the expression has been extended to include the idea of attracting attention in general—getting a rise out of a sales prospect, etc.

to get by the short hairs. It is widely assumed that the *short hairs* here are the pubic hairs, and *short hairs* is, in fact, slang for the hair around the genitals. George P. Burnham first used the expression in the form "get where the hair is short" in his *Memoirs of the United States Secret Service* (1872), and some department of dirty tricks no doubt invented it. But to get complete mastery over a person by grabbing his or her pubic hair would be difficult, to say the least, even if he were naked. So would holding someone by the short hairs at the nape of the neck, another explanation. Maybe the relatively short hairs of the beard provide a logical answer, and there is a

much earlier expression *to take by the beard* that means about the same thing.

to get in one's hair. Shakespeare wrote "Thou art ever in my beard," but it took almost another three centuries before someone invented "You get in my hair." That someone is anonymous, but the expression describing somebody or something persistently annoying a person is of American origin. The phrase is first recorded in an Oregon newspaper in 1851 and no explanation is given for it. The obvious explanation is that the original comparison was to lice, or "cooties," getting in the hair and irritating the scalp, but the possibilities are limitless.

to get one's back up. Once upon a Tom someone noticed the hair standing up on a cat's humped back and coined this expression. No one knows exactly when the aggressive arching of an angry cat's back suggested this phrase for humans aroused into anger, but it's surprising that the phrase seems no more than two centuries old, for an angry cat with its back arched high is an impressive sight, and a common one wherever there are felines wild or domestic. Cats were introduced to Europe long before the Crusades and became valued pets, despite their aloofness, when they demonstrated a proficiency at rat killing at least equal to the ferret's, and they proved far more prolific and easier to keep.

to get one's dander up. Many of the early Yankee humorists—Seba Smith, Charles Davis, Thomas Haliburton—used this Americanism for "to get angry," and it is found in the *Life of Davy Crockett*. It is one of those expressions with a handful of plausible explanations. The most amusing is that the *dander* in the phrase is an English dialect form of *dandruff* that was used in the Victorian era; someone with his dander up, according to this theory, would be wrathfully tearing up his hair by the fistful, dandruff flying in the process. Another likely source is the West Indian *dander*, a ferment used in the preparation of molasses, which would suggest a rising ferment of anger. The Dutch *donder*, "thunder," has also been nominated, for it is used in the Dutch phrase *op donderon*, "to burst into a sudden rage." And then there is the farfetched theory that *dander* is a telescoped form of "damned anger." And if these aren't enough, we have the possibilities that *dander* comes from an English dialect word for "anger"; from the Scots *danders*, for "hot embers"; and from the Romany *dander*, "to bite."

to get one's Ebenezer up. (*See* **that gets me.**)

to get one's goat. High-strung racehorses often have goats as stablemates, on the theory that the goats have a calming effect on the thoroughbreds. But the horses grow attached to their companions and become upset if they are removed, throwing off their performance on the track.

It is said that 19th-century gamblers capitalized on that fact by stealing on the preceding day the goat of a horse they wanted to lose a race and that this practice gave us the phrase *to get one's goat*—they got the horse's goat and he became upset or angry. It's as good an explanation as any, but isn't supported by much evidence. Jack London was the first to record the expression, in his novel *Smoke Bellew* (1912), though its usage there has nothing to do with racing. Attempts have also been made to connect the goat in the phrase with the *scapegoat* of Hebrew tradition; with the word *goad*, "to anger, irritate"; and to an old French phrase *prendre la chevre*, literally meaning "to take the goat," which dates back to the 16th century and certainly took a long time making the journey to America if it is the source of our expression.

to get one's Indian up.　(*See* **that gets me.**)

to get one's Irish up.　(*See* **that gets me.**)

to get one's monkey up.　Monkeys have quick tempers, though they calm down sooner than humans, which suggested the phrase *to get one's monkey up*, "to become angry," an expression that is British in origin, and is first recorded in a popular 1853 song.

to get out the crying towel.　Originally a military expression, probably dating back to about the beginning of World War II, *get out the crying towel* is a sarcastic reply to a chronic complainer who consistently bemoans his often minor misfortunes, meaning that he is complaining too much and should desist.

get thee to a nunnery.　Shakespeare gives these words to Hamlet, when he spurns Ophelia's advances. The prince is telling her to go to a whorehouse, for which *nunnery* was Elizabethan slang.

to get up on the wrong side of the bed.　The wrong side of the bed is the left side, according to a superstition that goes back to the time of the Romans. People have been saying other people *got up on the wrong side of the bed*, "awoke surly or grouchy," for well over three centuries now, usually not knowing the real meaning of what they are saying, but the equally old expression *got up left foot forward* tells the story. The supposedly sinister nature of the left is reflected in many English superstitions and expressions, such as the belief that it is unlucky to put on your left shoe first, or to walk into a house left foot first. The Romans, especially Augustus Caesar, were very careful that they got up on the *right* side of the bed, but there is no evidence that they were less grouchy than anyone else.

geyser.　All spouting hot springs called *geysers* take their name from the Geysir, a particular hot spring in Ice-

land that the English learned about in the mid-18th century. *Geysir* itself derives from the Old Norse *geysa*, "to gush."

ghetto.　*Ghettos* are now generally areas in which racial minorities are forced to live through economic necessity, though the word has been applied loosely to areas where higher-income groups live as well, even in such terms as *middle-class ghetto*. But originally a ghetto was an area where Jews in western Europe were cruelly forced to live by law. The practice dates much earlier, but the word derives from the Venetian Jewish quarter in Italy, where the island of Ghetto was used to confine Jews. The island's name itself, Ghetto, meant "iron foundry."

ghoti.　When George Bernard Shaw and others proposed "simplified" phonetic spelling systems early in this century, the word *ghoti* was created as a ridiculous example of such systems. *Ghoti* spells "fish" phonetically. The *GH* as in tou*GH*, the *O* as in w*O*men and the *TI* as in mo*TI*on.

giants in the earth.　(*See* **there were giants in the earth in those days.**)

gibberish.　Geber, or, more properly, Jabir ibn Hazyan (*Jabir* is the Arabic for *Geber*) was an eighth-century Arabian alchemist who wrote his formula in seemingly unintelligible jargon and anagrams in order to avoid the death penalty for sorcery. For this reason Dr. Johnson, Grose, and other prominent word detectives believed that *gibberish*, "nonsense or words without meaning," derives from his name. Geber could not have written all the 2,000 books attributed to him, but he was a prolific writer, respected enough for many medieval scientists to cite him as an authority, and for one 14th-century Spanish alchemist to go so far as to adopt his name. Today many authorities speculate that *gibberish* is imitative of the sound of nonsense, an echoic word like "jabber," "gabble," "giggle," and "gurgle," and at most was only influenced by Geber's name. *Gibberish* does not derive from the verb *gibber*, which it preceded in use, and has no roots in "gypsy jabber," as has been claimed.

gibbon.　Is this long-armed ape really named after a man? Possibly, if it's true that the naming was the practical joke of an eminent naturalist. Several respected etymologists believe that this is the case. Apparently the French naturalist Buffon first named the Indian ape in his *Natural History* (1749-1804). The witty Buffon may have been aware that the tombs of the English Gybbon family in Kent, "dating from about 1700, are surmounted by an ape's head, the family crest." A less inspired derivation suggests that *gibbon* comes from an Indian dialect, but there is no abundant evidence for either theory.

Gibraltar. Rock of Gibraltar signifies any impregnable stronghold. Gibraltar was called Calpe in ancient times, and forms the renowned Pillars of Hercules with Abyla on the opposite coast; but when the Saracen conqueror Tarik captured it from the Visigoths and built a castle there in A.D. 710, it was named Jebel el Tarik, "the mountain of Tarik," in his honor. *Gibraltar* is simply an English corruption of the longer name. The island, a rocky promontory on Spain's southern coast, acquired a further reputation for impregnability when the British captured it in 1704, made the island a fort and naval base, and successfully repelled several attempted invasions in future years. *Gibraltar* remains in British hands today, despite recent demonstrations for its return to Spain. Strategically important because it commands the only entrance to the Mediterranean from the west, the island is honeycombed with natural and man-made caves used by the military. It is also an important tourist center, a major attraction being the Barbary apes that live there.

gibson cocktail; Gibson girl. A bartender at the New York Players Club is supposed to have run out of olives and garnished artist Charles Dana Gibson's martini with a pearl onion instead, giving us the *gibson cocktail*. Gibson was no stranger to such honors. The popular American artist's *Gibson girls* appeared on the covers of national magazines in the period 1896 to about 1920 as frequently as Norman Rockwell's work has in more recent times. His pen-and-ink drawings typically depicted slender, wasp-waisted beauties clad in sweeping skirts, shirtwaists, and large hats. The well-bred *Gibson girls*, widely imitated, were the ideals of young men and women alike up until about the end of World War I, when their vogue ended, but their creator remained active until his death in 1944.

gibus. A gibus is the folding opera hat invented by Paris hatmaker Antoine Gibus in 1837. This cloth top hat with collapsible crown proved ideal for gentlemen attending the opera, who could fold it flat and put it out of the way, the patented gimmick making a considerable fortune for its inventor and his heirs. By now almost a relic of the past, the gibus is rarely used today.

giddy. The Greek word that gives us *giddy*, first recorded in about 1000, translates as "possessed by a god." *Giddy*, however, started off meaning mad, insane and foolish, in English, and today generally means frivolous and lighthearted, flighty, though it sometimes means to be dizzy or affected with vertigo.

Gideon Bible. In 1910 one very proper Bostonian sought an injunction to prevent the Gideon Society from distributing the Bible—"on the ground that it is an obscene and immoral publication." But not even crackpots have deterred the organization of traveling salesmen from their goal of placing a Gideon Bible in every hotel room and Pullman car in America. The Gideon Society, formally the Christian Commercial Young Men's Association of America, was founded in Boscobel, Wisconsin in 1899 and is now based in Chicago. Its name derives from that of the biblical Gideon, a judge of Israel who became a warrior and ingeniously delivered Israel from the Midianites, giving his country forty years of peace (Judg. 6:11-7:25).

gigaton. A word born with the hydrogen bomb, a *gigaton* is a measure of energy equal to one billion tons of T.N.T. *Giga* means "one billion times," deriving from the Greek *gigas*, "giant." A *kiloton*, from the Greek for "one thousand," is a measure of energy equal to 1,000 tons of T.N.T.

GIGO: garbage in—garbage out. This U.S. catchphrase was coined back in the 1960s when computers were first widely used for data processing. The phrase is now common among computer people wherever English is spoken and is, in fact, so well known that it is abbreviated as *GIGO* (with a long *i*).

gilbert. Physician to Queen Elizabeth I, and author of the first scientific book published in England, William Gilbert, or Gylberde, (ca. 1544-1603) was the most distinguished scientist of his day. His work on magnetism—he was the first European to accurately describe the behavior of magnets and the earth's magnetism—led to the *gilbert*, a unit of magnetic force, being named in his honor. Gilbert first used the terms *electricity, electrical force*, and *magnetic pole* in English, and introduced the Copernican theory to his countrymen.

Gilbert filbert. (*See* **filbert.**)

Gilderoy's kite. (*See* **hung higher than Gilderoy's kite.**)

to gild the lily. Everybody knows that this expression is wrong and hackneyed as well, but it is still used to describe something superfluous, and I'd bet that it comes to mind first as *gild the lily* even to most of those fastidious few who correctly say *paint the lily*. The fault lies, of course, in confusing what Shakespeare really wrote in *King John*, when the Earl of Salisbury makes his protest against the king's second coronation.

> Therefore, to be possessed with double pomp,
> To guard a title that was rich before,
> To gild refined gold, to paint the lily,
> To throw a perfume on the violet,
> To smooth the ice, or add another hue
> Unto the rainbow, or with taper-light
> To seek the beauteous eye of heaven to garnish
> Is wasteful, and ridiculous excess.

Since *to gild* comes first in the pertinent line and it is just as ridiculous to gild a lily as to paint one, the phrase was often remembered as *to gild the lily*. Perhaps the old phrase to *gild the pill* also helped create the confusion. It meant to coat a bitter pill with sugar and gave *gild* wide currency as a word meaning "to cover over, to paint" (*not* to paint with gold necessarily). As for King John, he was far from "ridiculous." The unscrupulous king, who had unjustly seized the throne after the death of his brother Richard in 1199, wanted a second coronation because like any shrewd politician he knew that the awe-inspiring spectacle would win him more support among his subjects.

gimlet. A "healthy" cocktail invented by a naval officer. Anyway, it was a lot healthier than drinking gin neat, which is exactly why Sir. T.O. Gimlette devised the *gimlet* that commemorates him. Gimlette, a British naval surgeon from 1879 to 1917, believed that drinking straight gin harmed the health and impaired the efficiency of naval officers, so he introduced a cocktail that diluted the gin with lime juice. Today the gimlet is made with gin or vodka, sweetened lime juice, and sometimes soda water.

gimme a dope. *Gimme a dope* still means "give me a Coca-Cola" in the southern U.S., especially among teenagers. This isn't recent slang, but dates back to the late 19th century, when the fabled soft drink was touted as a tonic and contained a minute amount of cocaine. Coca-Cola's inventor, druggist John S. Pemberton, brewed the stuff in his backyard and knew it was done when he smelled the cooked cocaine—no reactions among the man or his neighbors are reported. (*See* **Coke**.)

gin and it. A term more familiar with the British than Americans, the *gin and it* is a type of martini, a drink made of gin and vermouth. The *it* is short for *It*alian vermouth. The drink seems to have been invented in the last 25 years.

gin and tonic. *Tonic*, deriving from the Latin *tonicus*, had only the meaning of "pertaining to tension" when first used in the 17th century. But the word took on the meaning of a medicine that restored the tension or tone of the body, and the first *tonic* drinks weren't far behind. When people began adding alcohol to such drinks in the 19th century or thereabouts, *tonics* became the mixers that are today used in concoctions like *gin and tonic*, enough of which can destroy the tone of the body.

gingham. Originally all *gingham* cloth may have been striped, for the origin of this word, which came into English from French in the 18th century, is probably the Malay *gingam*, "striped."

Ginnie Mae. Despite talk of an eponym behind this term, this is really simply a nickname for the Government National Mortgage Association, fashioned from its initials, GNMA. There are a number of similar nicknames, such as the *Fannie Mae*, for the Federal National Mortgage Association, and *Sally Mae*, for the Savings Loan Mortgage Association.

gin rickey. *Rickeys* can be made of any liquor, carbonated water, and lime juice, but the most famous drink in the family is the *gin rickey*, invented in about 1895 and named after "a distinguished Washington guzzler of the period," according to H. L. Mencken. Just which Washington Colonel Rickey was so honored is a matter of dispute, however. Several theories have been recorded by Mencken in his *American Language, Supplement I*, and other sources, but none is generally accepted.

Giotto's O. Tradition holds that the great Italian artist Giotto di Bondone was a shepherd boy when discovered by the Florentine painter Giovanni Cimabue. While serving his apprenticeship to Cimabue, he was approached by a messenger of the Pope, who had been sent all over Italy to find artists to work on a new church. Giotto was asked to submit a drawing that could be shown to the Pope as evidence of his talent and with a single flourish of his brush he drew a perfect circle on a panel, *Giotto's O* being proof enough for the Pope.

giraffe. The *camelopard* is not a mythical monster, but a very real animal, though you might not have believed it existed if you hadn't seen it in a jungle or zoo. The ancient Greeks came across the beast on the African plain and called it *kamelopardalis*, believing it to be a cross between the camel—because of its height—and the leopard—because of its spots. It was called the *camelopard* in English for many years, beginning in at least 1398, until its present designation began to be used in the late 16th century: *giraffe* (from the Arabic word for the animal). The giraffe, the world's tallest quadruped, at up to twenty feet (so tall that newborn calves come to life with a jolt, falling six feet to the ground), also has the highest blood pressure of any animal (an average 260/160, as opposed to 120/80 in humans) to compensate for the pull of gravity while it is supplying blood to a brain ten feet above the heart.

gird one's loins. A good wife, says the Bible (Prov. 31:17), "girds her loins with strength and makes her arms strong." That is, she prepares for action, usually hard physical work. The expression *gird one's loins* came into the language directly from this biblical phrase, though today it can refer to mental as well as physical labor. Workers preparing for strenuous jobs used to tuck or gird the skirts of their long garments into the girdles or belts about their loins so that they could move more freely and not worry about soiling their clothes—much as men roll up their sleeves today. *Gird*, incidentally, is either *girded* or *girt* in the past or past participle, so "He girt up his loins" is correct. Today the expression is usually the shorter *gird one's loins*.

girl. The origin of *girl*, first attested in 1290, is obscure. Among many suggestions as to its ancestor are the Anglo-Saxon *gyrlgyden*, "virgin goddess"; the Anglo-Irish *girlun*; and the Irish *cailin* or *colleen*. It may also come from the Low German *göre*, "a young person" and, indeed, in some Scottish dialects *girl* means either a young male or female. A synonym probably just as old as girl is *gay girl* (*gaye girle*) for a young woman. (*See* **boy**.)

girl Friday. (*See* **man Friday**.)

gismo. Did this word come from the Arabic *shu ismo*, meaning a gadget, as at least one philologist suggests? The theory is that American soldiers were introduced to the expression in Morocco during World War II, and the theory has not been proved or disproved. A *gismo*, or *gizmo*, of course, is a thingamajig.

give a damn. The above was originally "I don't give a *dam*," the expression probably brought back to England from India by military men in the mid-18th century. A *dam* was an Indian coin of little value. *I don't give a damn* is first recorded in America in the 1890s. Its most famous use was in *Gone with the Wind* (1939), when Rhett Butler tells Scarlett O'Hara: "Frankly, my dear, I don't give a damn."

give a deaf ear. (*See* **to turn a deaf ear**.)

give and take. The expression *give and take* is first recorded (1769) in British horse racing as "a prize for a race in which the horses which exceed a standard height carry more, and those which fall short of it less, than the standard weight." By 1816 we find the phrase being used on and off the track for making allowances or concessions, the practice of compromise. In an interesting study of the words *give* and *take*, researchers found that over a given period among an observed group *give* was used 2,184 times, while *take* was used 7,008 times.

give a whaling to. Many etymologists believe this phrase should be *give a waling to*, as a *wale* is a mark raised on the flesh by the blow of a stick or whip. But the key word in the phrase has been spelled with an *h* ever since it first appeared, two centuries ago. This suggests that a *whaling*, "a terrible beating," was one given with a whalebone whip, though the wales it raised may have contributed to the phrase, making it more vivid. Riding whips were commonly made of whalebone in the 18th and 19th centuries and were used to beat more than horses. Whalebone, incidentally, is a misnomer: It's not made from the bones of a whale but from a substance found in the whale's upper jaw.

give a wide berth to. Berth, its origin unknown, has since the 17th century meant working or operating room for a ship. *Giving good berth* to a ship, the earliest version of this nautical expression, meant to avoid or keep far away from her, which is what *give a wide berth to* means today, in reference to ships or anything else.

give 'em hell! Harry S Truman and his supporters didn't originate this Americanism during the Presidential election of 1948. The expression has been traced back to the early 19th century and has military origins. In 1851 it was recorded in *Harper's Magazine*: "At daybreak old Rily shouted, 'Forward and give them h-ll!'" Four years earlier, during the Battle of Buena Vista in the Mexican War, General Zachary Taylor had exhorted his men to "Give 'em hell!" after the enemy launched a fierce attack.

give her the gun; jump the gun. *Give her the gun* means to accelerate a car, plane, boat, or any machine. Originally it was an RAF term for "open the throttle wide," dating to about 1920 and referring to the noise generated by a wide-open airplane motor. *Jump the gun*, on the other hand, is an expression about fifty years old that derives from both foot racing and hunting. An anxious runner often *jumps the gun*, that is, starts before the starter fires his pistol in a track event, and a startled pheasant will frequently take flight before a hunter can fire his gun, both situations responsible for our figurative use of the phrase—to begin something before preparations for it are complete.

give him an inch and he'll take a mile. The expression may someday become "give him a millimeter and he'll take a meter," or something similar. It has already been put this way humorously and might someday be standard English. Which shouldn't be surprising. In fact, the above expression was originally *give him an inch and he'll take an ell*, a very old proverb that goes back before the 16th century. An *ell*, the word deriving from the Anglo-Saxon *eln*, "the forearm to the tip of the middle finger," varied in length from 27 to 48 inches, depending on in which country you were measuring forearms (the English had it at 45 inches). No matter what the measurement, past or present, the expression means the same—give him a small concession and he'll take great liberties.

give him enough rope to hang himself. Originally *give him enough rope to hang himself* took the form of *give him enough of rope*, recorded in about 1659 and meaning to allow someone free scope or action enough to embarrass himself. The image behind this is an animal tied up on a long rope, but within another thirty years we have the crude beginnings of *give him enough rope to hang himself*, a critic of poet John Dryden saying "Give our Commentator but Rope and he hangs himself." Executions by hanging no doubt suggested the stronger version.

give him Jesse. Still heard infrequently, *give him Jesse* means "give him hell." A 19th-century expression of obscure origins, it has been credited to the 1856 presidential campaign slogan of General John C. Fremont, "Give them Jessie!", which referred to his wife Jessie. But *Jesse* was used earlier than this and probably stems from the biblical "rod out of the stem of Jesse" mentioned in *Isaiah.*

to give short shrift to someone. To treat someone curtly, swiftly, and unsympathetically. *Short shrift* was originally, in the 16th century, the few minutes given a condemned man to make his confession to a priest before he was executed, *shrift* meaning "a confession."

to give someone the gate. *Giving someone the gate,* "firing him, showing him the door," has been American slang since at least 1921, when it first appeared in print. There is some precedent for it, however, in the old English phrase *to give* or *grant the gate to,* that is, to let someone pass through the castle gate and out to the road, which the *O.E.D.* traces back to 1440. The American term is of course negative, but ironic use of the earlier *give the gate to* could have inspired it.

to give the hook. Amateurs competing in early vaudeville talent nights were sometimes difficult to coax off the stage no matter how unfavorably the audience reacted to their performances. In order to prevent egg and tomato damage to the theater, all obstinate hams were yanked offstage and into the wings before the audience got violent. The instrument used was a long pole with a hook on the end, which inspired the expression *to give the hook.* Today the phrase is used to describe anyone fired for incompetence.

give up the ghost. The belief that the ghost, or soul, is an alter ego independent of the body, a spirit that departs the body when we die, is behind this phrase. The words are recorded in the Bible (Job 14:10): "Man dieth, and wasteth away; yea, man giveth up the ghost, and where is he?" That is the majestic King James Version speaking. The Revised Standard Version of the Bible cuts out the words as if they had no history, substituting: "But man dies, and is laid low; man breathes his last, and where is he?" *Ghost* comes from the Old Teutonic root *gaistjam,* "to terrify," and so was always associated with something frightening. English printer William Caxton was the first to add the *h* to *ghost,* in error, and this spelling didn't become standard English until about 1600.

gladhander. Indiana humorist George Ade is supposed to have invented *gladhander,* for a demonstrative, even overfriendly person in his *Artie* (1896): "She meets me at the door, puts out the glad hand and . . ." (*See* **panhandler; tightwad.**)

gladiolus. *Gladiolus* used to be called *sword lilies.* Long before this the Romans named the flower *gladiolus,* "little sword," from the Latin *gladius,* "sword," because their long brilliant spikes of flowers, or the shapes of their leaves, resembled the swords Roman gladiators used in the arena.

Gladstone bag; etc. At least one writer claims that English statesman and orator William Ewart Gladstone (1809-98) never carried the *Gladstone bag* named after him. Neither did the four-time prime minister *invent* the light, hinged leather bag, but he did do much traveling in his long public career and the flexible bag was made with the convenience of travelers in mind. Gladstone's name was given to certain cheap clarets—*Gladstone wines*—because he lowered the customs duty on French wines while Chancellor of the Exchequer in 1860, and a two-seated, four-wheeled carriage also paid him honor. Gladstone has been rated as the most inspiring and among the five greatest British prime ministers, but his private life sometimes provoked comment. Until he was well past seventy-five, for example, he made it his habit to walk the streets of London at night trying to persuade prostitutes to convert to a different way of life. When the prime minister left office for the last time, he was eighty-five years old.

a glass of wine with the Borgias. It was rumored that Lucretia and Cesare Borgia, the children of Pope Alexander VI, used some secret deadly poison to eliminate their enemies. One never knew whether he was an enemy of the Borgias, so *to have a glass of wine with the Borgias,* or *to dine with the Borgias* has been proverbial for a great but risky honor since the 16th century. Historians haven't been able to substantiate whether any Borgia was a poisoner, but there is no doubt that some of the Borgias were murderers, the family being a pretty unsavory lot. Sir Max Beerbohm gave the proverb his attention in his *Hosts and Guests:* "I maintain that though you would often in the fifteenth century have heard the snobbish Roman say, in a would-be off-hand tone, 'I am dining with the Borgias tonight,' no Roman was ever able to say, 'I dined last night with the Borgias.'"

glass slippers. Cinderella's glass slippers in the old fairy tale should almost certainly be made of fur, not glass. It is widely believed that when French author Charles Perrault took the story from the Old French in 1697, he mistook *voir,* "ermine or fur," for *verre,* meaning "glass." In no other of the scores of versions of the Cinderella tale in other languages are the slippers glass.

glitch. This scientific word, meaning a sudden change in the rotation period of a neutron star, has its roots in the Yiddish *glitch,* "a slip," which, in turn, comes from the German *glitschen,* "slip." Apparently a scientist familiar with Yiddish is responsible for the coining, but he remains nameless. Today the term is most used in computerese for a mechanical malfunction, or for any problem or emergency due to a defective or broken machine.

glossary; to gloss over. The two words *gloss* constitute one of the 700 or so sets of homonyms in English, words that are spelled the same but have different meanings. The earlier *gloss*, from the Greek *glossa* which meant "tongue," then "word," and finally "explanation of the word," came to be used in the sense of language and gave us both the term *to gloss*, "to explain, or translate a text," and *glossary*, alphabetical wordbook or "collection of explanations" (*glosses*) sometimes printed in the backs of books to explain difficult words or passages. The Middle High German *glos*, "shun," had nothing to do with language, but yielded our word *gloss*, for "superficial luster." However, the words were often confused by early writers and influenced each other, *to gloss over* coming to mean "to excuse or explain something away, to provide a false or superficial appearance or explanation." Possibly, too, the idea of careless or lazy scholars changing the meaning of difficult passages in classical works by making incorrect, superficial *glosses* or marginal comments reinforced the meaning of *to gloss over*.

gnu. There are hundreds of thousands of these large antelopes in Africa, where they are also called "horned horses," but elsewhere they are mainly encountered in crossword puzzles. Their unusual name is a corruption of the even more unusual and difficult to pronounce *ngu* that Bushmen call the animal.

goatee. The style of chin whiskers cut in the form of a tuft like that of a he-goat apparently became popular in mid-19th-century America, when the word *goatee* is first recorded. *Goatee* simply means "little goat" and the Americanism is first recorded in 1842 as *goaty*. *Billygoat beard* or *billygoat whiskers* means the same and is first recorded in the mid-1880s.

goatsucker. This nocturnal bird (*Caprimulgus europaeus*), also known as the nightjar because its calls "jar the night," is called the *goatsucker* in Greek, Latin, French, German, Spanish, and several other languages besides English, its name reflecting the widespread belief that it attacks and sucks the udders of goats for food. Aristotle was among the first to note the legends, writing that "flying to the udders of she goats, it sucked them and so it gets its name. They say that the udder withers when it has sucked it and that the goat goes blind." Even this bird's scientific name, *Caprimulgus*, honors the story, deriving from the Latin *caper*, "goat," and *mulgere*, "to milk." The short-billed, wide-mouthed bird actually feeds on insects it captures in the air.

gob. The U.S. Navy banned the use of *gob* for a sailor in the early 1920s, claiming it was undignified. Like most such comstockery (*q.v.*), the ban on *gob* failed, but the Navy might have been right about its lack of dignity, considering the word's possible origins. *Gob*, first recorded in 1909, probably comes either from *gobble*, an allusion to the way many sailors reputedly ate, or from the word *gob*, for "spit," in reference to English coast guardsmen who were called *gobbies* in the past because they were in the habit of expectorating so much. Little better is the suggestion that the word is from the Irish *gob*, "mouth," as in the expression *shut your gob*. Sailors might then have been compared to "big mouths" or something similar.

gobbledygook. *Gobbledygook* means obscure, verbose, bureaucratic language characterized by circumlocution and jargon, and usually refers to the meaningless officialese turned out by government agencies. The late Representative Maury Maverick coined the word in 1944 when he was chairman of the Smaller War Plant Committee in Congress. Maverick had just attended a meeting of the committee, at which phrases such as "cause an investigation to be made with a view to ascertaining" were rife. He wrote a memo condemning such officialese and labeled it *gobbledygook*, later explaining that he was thinking of the gobbling of turkeys while they strutted pompously. *Bafflegab, jargantuan, pudder*, and *pentagonese* are all synonyms. George Orwell's "translation" of Lord Nelson's immortal phrase "England expects every man to do his duty" is a good example of gobbledygook: "England anticipates that, as regards the current emergency, personnel will face up to the issues, and exercise appropriately the functions allocated to their respective occupational groups." (*See* **maverick**.)

to go by the board. This expression, originating in England, literally means to go overboard, to fall down past the *board*, or side of a ship, into the sea. Since the mid-18th century it has also figuratively meant to be utterly lost, as in the first recorded use of the expression: "Every instinct and feeling of humanity goes by the board."

go-by-the-ground; go-by-the-wall. A little person, man or woman, has been jocularly called a *go-by-the-ground* in England since the 18th century, though today the term is heard only in English dialect. A *go-by-the-wall* meant a creeping, helpless person, or a coward.

God bless you. The custom of saying *God bless you* after someone sneezes supposedly arose with St. Gregory the Great, who said it to people during a plague in which sneezing was often a symptom. The custom has been widespread throughout the world since ancient times, though notably among the Greeks and the Romans, who exclaimed *Absit omen*!

goddam. English-speaking people have been quick on the draw with curses since earliest times. So often did the English in medieval times take the Lord's name in vain, for example, that the French called them *goddams*. Later, in the American Southeast, Indians gave the Anglos the same name for the same reason.

Godolphin Barb. (*See* **Byerly Turk.**)

God speed the plough; Plough Monday. *God speed the plough*, "a wish for success or prosperity," was originally a phrase in a 15th-century song sung by ploughmen on *Plough Monday*, the first Monday after Twelfth Day, which is the end of the Christmas holidays, when farm laborers returned to the plough. On this day ploughmen customarily went from door to door dressed in white and drawing a plough, soliciting "plough money" to spend in celebration.

God tempers the wind to the shorn lamb. Since lambs are never shorn, Laurence Sterne's phrase, from his *Sentimental Journey* (1782), seems to make little sense. Sterne coined it from an earlier, less poetic expression—invented some 140 years before—that said *To a close-shorn sheep, God gives wind by measure*. But George Herbert, its author, got it in turn from a French saying in Henri Estienne's *Premices* (1594), which said *God regulates the cold to the shorn lamb*. Poetry usually triumphs.

God wills it! No ancient phrase spilled more blood than *God wills it!* (*Dieu le veult!*), words uttered by Peter the Hermit that launched the Christian Crusades to deliver the Holy Land from the Muslims. The Holy Land, once conquered at great cost in human lives, could not be held.

go-go funds. In the late 1960s go-go dancers inspired the name for these "exciting" mutual investment funds, which were "very attractive" to investors. Mutual funds themselves date back to early 19th-century Belgium.

going by shank's mare. This means to go somewhere by walking, to use "Walker's bus," and as far as is known no horseless Mr. Shank is responsible for the two-hundred year old phrase, which is probably Scottish in origin. Neither is there any proof that the expression refers to King Edward I, nicknamed "Long Shanks" because whenever he rode a pony his long legs reached to the ground. The *shank* is the leg, or that part of the leg below the knee, and a mare is usually slower than a stallion. Going by *marrow-bone stage*, a play on the once real Marylebone (pronounced "Marrybun") stage in London, means the same.

going like sixty. In 1860 a terrible drought in the Missouri and Arkansas valleys devastated that part of the country, lasting for over a year. Some tracers of lost word origins believe that the memory of the drought was so vivid that people began linking the year 1860 with extremes of any kind. But the drought could only have reinforced and possibly accelerated the meaning of the popular expression *going like sixty*, for it was used by James Russell Lowell in his *Biglow Papers* in 1848 ("Though like sixty all along I fumed an' fussed") and was recorded in an early 1860 slang dictionary as "[to go] at a good rate, briskly." Perhaps *sixty* is used simply to express a large number, as an abbreviation of "like sixty miles an hour," or something similar. "Forty" was used in this way at least since Shakespeare's *Coriolanus* (1607), and in *Uncle Tom's Cabin* (1852) a character says: "I has principles and I stick to them like forty."

to go into extra innings; good innings. A baseball game that goes into extra innings goes beyond the normal time played (nine innings). *To go into extra innings*, a phrase I've heard recently but which is recorded nowhere, means to live a long life, as when someone says, "He's over eighty, he's already gone into extra innings." A similar British phrase *to have a good innings* means the same, but comes from the game of cricket, where an *innings* (the singular would be *inning* in baseball) is the time during which a team or player is batting.

golconda. Any source of great wealth is *a golconda*. The term owes its life to the town of Golconda in India, which the British in the 16th century thought was the site of extensive diamond mines. Though the area actually was a diamond-cutting center without mines, the term lasted in the language.

gold. Gold is one of the four oldest words in English, deriving from the Indo-European substrate word *gol* (the other three are *apple*, from *apal*; *bad*, bad; and *tin*, tin). Hundreds of expressions, some of them covered in these pages, are based on gold, from *all that glitters is not gold* and *good as gold* to *heart of gold* and *gold digger*. (*See* **bad; apple.**)

goldbacks. (*See* **greenbacks.**)

goldbrick. Con men working Western mining properties toward the end of the 19th century sometimes sold gullible investors lead or iron bricks coated with gold paint, representing them as the real thing. One Patrick Burke of St. Louis is recorded as having paid $3,700 for such a "gold" brick in 1887. This all-too-common confidence scheme gave the name *goldbrick* to any swindle or fakery. Later, soldiers picked up the expression and used the phrase *to goldbrick* in its present meaning of avoiding work or shirking duty. The phrase is first recorded in 1914 in this sense, applied to army lieutenants appointed from civilian life.

gold digger. Long before *gold digger* meant a mercenary woman, a use first recorded in 1915, it signified a miner in California gold fields such as Jackass Gulf, Puke Ravine, Greenhorn Canyon, and Rattlesnake Bar. In fact, the term *gold digger*, for a miner, is recorded in 1830 during America's first gold rush, which took place in northern Georgia. It was gold diggers of the most mercenary kind that a humorous Western song referred to in one of its verses:

> The miners came in '49
> The whores in '51
> And when they got together
> They produced the native son.

golden calf. (*See* **to worship the golden calf.**)

the golden horde. This was the name given to the Mongolian Tartars who invaded Russia in the 13th century and established an empire there under Bator, a grandson of Genghis Khan, that lasted two centuries. They were so called because the color of their skin appeared golden to their adversaries. *Hordes* has always been a favorite word of Europeans for Asian armies. (*See* **Asiatic hordes**.)

the gold of Tolosa. Ill-gotten gains that will never leave one prosperous. The Roman consul Caepio looted the temple of Apollo at Tolosa of all the gold and treasure belonging to the Cimbrians. Not only were the gold and treasure stolen from him shortly after, but he was defeated on the battlefield by the Cimbrians, who killed 112,000 of his men.

Goldwynism. "Include me out," "In two words: impossible," and "We have passed a lot of water since this" (for "a lot of water has passed under the bridge") are but three legendary *Goldwynisms.* An American film pioneer, Samuel Goldwyn has long been considered a modern "Mr. Malaprop," unrivaled for his fractured English. Goldwyn, born in Warsaw, Poland on August 27, 1882, founded Goldwyn Pictures Corporation, which became part of Metro-Goldwyn-Mayer in 1924, and later turned independent producer. (*See* **malapropism**)

golf links. All golf courses were originally built on ridges of virtually flat land along the seashore. They were called *links* from the Old English *hlinc,* for "ridge of land."

Goliath. The original Goliath stood between 9 feet 9 inches and 11 feet 3 inches tall, depending on how you value the "6 cubits and a span" given as his height in the Bible. Nevertheless, the stripling David slew him with a stone from his sling (I Sam. 17:49-51) and defeated the Philistines. A *David and Goliath* contest is one between a great and a small man. Not to take anything away from David, Goliath was a stripling compared to the giant Og

(16 feet 2 1/2 inches) and other biblical big men. All such claims, however, are most likely based on our ignorance of ancient measurement units.

gondolas. The little American *gondolas* of the Revolutionary War take their name from the Italian double-ended boats used on the Grand Canal in Venice, but there the resemblance ends. The Continental gondolas were rigged with sails and fitted with guns.

a gone goose. No connection has been made between this American expression and the much older phrase *cook your goose* (*q.v.*). Apparently, the Americanism dates only from about 1830, and there is no story about a goose in a helpless, hopeless state to explain it. Probably *a gone goose, a gone beaver, a gone chick,* and similar expressions all derive from the earlier *a gone coon,* which, according to one of several legends, goes back to the Revolutionary War. It seems that an American had disguised himself in raccoon skins and climbed a tree to spy on the British. But an enemy soldier discovered him that night while coon hunting and took aim, ready to shoot the biggest coon he had ever seen, when the spy cried out, "Don't shoot—I'll come down! I know I'm a gone coon!" According to the legend, the British soldier was so terrified to hear an "animal" talk that he dropped his gun and ran. The tale need not be true for it to have popularized the expression *a gone coon,* and other animals could have been substituted for the coon by storytellers in different areas of the country.

gone to pot. Marijuana isn't even a contender here. Neither is there reason to believe that *gone to pot* has its origins in cremation; that is, in the placing of human ashes in an urn or pot. Neither has it any connection with drunkards dissipating in wine pots. Most authorities agree that this expression for being ruined, disintegrated, which dates back before Elizabethan times, was inspired by pieces of meat being chopped up and going into the pot for a stew. They were usually inferior cuts of meat, this stew meat, the kind rich men trimmed off a joint in old England and gave to the servants for their stew pot. "Going to the pot" suggested going down in the world, because a mere stew didn't compare to more savory ways of preparing meat. When you went to the stew pot, like a piece of meat, your identity was destroyed, you literally disintegrated, all but vanished. Nevertheless, the old story persists that a tailor who lived near a cemetery in a small European town dropped a stone in a pot for every funeral that passed by. When he himself died, a wag quipped that he too had *gone to pot.*

gone where the woodbine twineth. Woodbine is a honeysuckle (*Lonicera periclymenum*) that was often planted on graves in years past. An 1870 song written as a tribute to those who died in the bloody Civil War went:

"Then go where the woodbine twineth,/ When spring is bright and fair,/ And to the soldier's resting place/ Some little tribute bear." From this song by Septimus Winner the expression *gone where the woodbine twineth* came to mean someone who had died, or even someone who had gone someplace from which he would never return.

Gongorism. It is only fair to say that the arrows that were transferred into "flying asps" and the birds that became "feathered zithers" were part of a larger plan. Luis de Gongora y Argote (1561-1627) wrote in a twisted, torturous style in his later years, his syntax deliberately distorted in order to highlight words and create an unreal world. But he inspired many imitators, who inspired many critics and, unfortunately, his name is now a synonym for a deliberately obscure, meaningless, and affected ornamental style. The Spanish poet after whom *Gongorism* is named was essentially a lyric poet in his early years; his work was much admired by Cervantes, though no poem of his was published in his lifetime. Readers have discovered that his baroque *Gongorisms*, a great influence on modern poetry, are far from meaningless, as difficult as the long poems like *Soledades* are to read. Gongora, who adopted his mother's name, was a priest as well as a poet and dramatist. Toward the end of his life he turned back from cultivated obscurity to a simple, unaffected style.

goober. *Goober*, for "peanut," was not coined in the southern U.S. It originated in Africa as the Bantu *nguba*, for "peanut," and was brought to the America South by African slaves in about 1834. A dialect term for many years, it has achieved wider currency over the past fifty years. *Pindal*, another word for peanut, comes from the Kongo *npinda*.

good. *Good*, first recorded circa A.D. 800, derives from the Old English *god*, which is akin to earlier words basically meaning "suitable," so that, according to the *O.E.D.* "the original sense of *good* would be 'fitting' . . ." Thus, unlike *bad* (q.v.), *good* has its roots in "the suitable, the fitting, the natural."

good egg. (See **bad egg**.)

good field, no hit. This baseball catchphrase is sometimes applied jokingly to other things, to anyone who does one thing better than another, who is good in one field and not another. The expression dates back to 1924 when coach Miguel "Mike" Gonzales scouted Dodger player Moe Berg for the St. Louis Cardinals. Observing Berg at Brooklyn's Clearwater, Florida training camp that spring, Gonzales wired his boss the four-word evaluation: "Good field, no hit." The Cardinals didn't offer a contract, but the scholarly Berg, who spoke seven languages, including Chinese and Japanese, became an American spy during World War II, spying on German atomic scientists.

goodnighting. Students of the old West may be aware that bulls on long cattle drives often suffered from chaffing of the testicles, which frequently swelled so large that the animal sickened and died. The remedy was to cut off the testicle bag, push the testicles up into the body and sew the cut—a process that enabled the bulls to travel well and did not impair their breeding. This remedy was called *goodnighting*, after cattleman Charles Goodnight, who invented it, and is surely among the most unusual of words named after people.

good Samaritan. The *good Samaritan* is nameless in the biblical story (Luke 10:30-85) told by Christ; he is only referred to as "a Samaritan" and Christ tells how he helped a man who had been assaulted and left half dead by robbers, how he cared for the stranger and paid for his room in an inn after two holy men passed him without helping. This anonymous man of Samaria, a district of ancient Palestine, the northern kingdom of the Hebrews, became over the centuries the *good Samaritan*, lending his name to the countless kind, helpful, philanthropic people who do good for others with no thought of worldly gain. The *Samaritans* are also a religious community who claim that they are descendants of the ten tribes of Israel and that their religion contains the true undiluted teachings of Moses. These Samaritans, who broke with the Jews in about 458 B.C. but are said to observe the Torah even more scrupulously than orthodox Jews, are now represented by a few families living in Jordan.

a good scout. A *good scout*, "a regular person, a good fellow," is probably much older than its first recorded date of 1912. The *scout* here most likely comes from the Dutch *schout*, "a sort of combination town mayor-sheriff"—not the English word *scout*, which derives ultimately from a Latin word for "to listen," *ascultare*.

a good skate. (See **cheapskate**.)

good times. (See **playing the market**.)

good to the last drop. This slogan for Maxwell House coffee, coined in 1960, is a good example of advertising slogans that have come into general use, and means "thoroughly or completely good or enjoyable." Another example is Ivory soap's *99 and 44/100ths % pure*, which, though coined in 1925 and no longer used in the company's ads, still persists in the language. Similar slogans have enjoyed popular use, even if only comic, for over a century, like the old patent medicine *Pink pills for pale people*, coined in the mid-19th century and still used, though rarely, today. Another example is Alka-Seltzer's more recent *I can't believe I ate the whole thing . . .*

a good wine needs no bush.   Dating back some 2,000 years to ancient Rome, this expression refers to the vine leaves or ivy (honoring Bacchus) frequently depicted on signs outside Roman wine shops or taverns. The Romans continued this custom when they occupied England, where the saying arose that *a good wine needs no bush*, that is, it isn't necessary to advertise a good wine with a bush outside the tavern—its good quality will soon make it known to everyone anyway. Today the words mean generally that "excellent things speak for themselves."

goof off; goofy.   *Goofing off*, "wasting time," originated in the U.S. armed forces during World War II. It implies shirking like a silly or goofy person, a *goof*, which word derives from the English dialect word *goff*, "a simpleton," first recorded in 1570.

googly.   (*See* **bosey.**)

googol; googolplex.   A nine-year-old child invented *googol*—a word for the number one followed by a hundred zeroes, or ten to the hundredth power (10^{100}), which is frequently used in mathematics. Distinguished American mathematician Dr. Edward Kasner asked his nephew to make up a name for the big number and the boy replied *googol*. Possibly the word was suggested by childish sounds like *goo, coo*, etc., or possibly the comic strip *Barney Google* had something to do with it. A *googol* can also be called 10 *duotrigintillion*, if you want to go to the trouble. Dr. Kasner, who died in 1955, is also, along with his nephew, responsible for the term *googolplex*. This is ten raised to the power of a *googol*, or one followed by a *googol* zeroes. Using *googolplex* as shorthand for this finite number certainly saves a lot of time, for as Kasner wrote, "there would not be enough room to write it, if you went to the farthest star, touring all the nebulae, and putting down zeroes every inch of the way."

gook.   *Gook* is among the most universal of derogatory words, in that it has been applied by Americans, Englishmen, Canadians, and Australians to practically every nationality group but Americans, Englishmen, Canadians, and Australians. Most commonly it is used as a nickname for Filipinos, Pacific islanders, Japanese, Chinese, Vietnamese, and Koreans. The word probably derives from *goo-goo* and *gu-gu*, military names for a Filipino during the Spanish-American War. The Korean *kuk* (pronounced *kook*), used to convey the idea of nationality (as in *Chungkuk*: "China"), probably reinforced the word during the Korean War. So did the later slang use of *gook* (pronounced like "book"), which means "slime or dirt" and is a blend word formed from *goo* and *muck*.

goon.   Alice the Goon, a big stupid creature who appeared in E.C. Segar's comic strip "Popeye, the Thimble Theatre" in the late 1930s, gave her name to both stupid people called *goons* and the big stupid thugs called *goons*. Segar (1894-1938) may have fashioned the name from the 1895 slang term *goony*, for "a simpleton," but he could also have blended *gorilla* and *baboon* or even *goof* and *baboon*.

gooney bird.   (*See* **albatross.**)

to goose.   *Mencken* characterized *to goose* as "one of the most mysterious of American verbs . . ." No other language employs this term for "to jab sharply with the thumb in the anus, with the intention of startling or stimulating," which is only about sixty years old and has taken on the additional meaning of goading someone into action. There are many theories about the word's etymology. Most experts lean to the explanation that pugnacious geese "sometimes attack human beings, and especially children, by biting their fundaments." Since they are also said "to attack women by striking at the pudenda," the sexual associations are obvious. Others say that goose breeders examine their birds' rear parts for eggs before turning them out from the pens each day, and that thrusts of a similar nature are the only way to distinguish between male and female geese in certain varieties—either practice could have inspsired the expression. *To goose* could also be a euphemism for *to roger*, 18th century British slang for to have sexual intercourse, since Roger, like Dobbin for a horse, was a conventional English folk name for a goose. Finally, there is the suggestion that *to goose* is named from a poolroom receptacle called "the goose" that jokers frequently jabbed into the fundament of a pool player just as he was about to make a shot.

gooseberry.   How the *gooseberry* got its name is a puzzle to historians and etymologists. One theory claims that "gooseberry" is a mispronunciation of "gorge berry," an early name for the fruit; a nice theory, except that *gooseberry* was used before *gorgeberry*, according to what records there are. For similar reasons, most word detectives do not believe that gooseberry is a corruption of *groseille*, the French name for the fruit, or the Dutch *kruishes*, which means "cross berry." Perhaps a better explanation is that *gooseberry* is a corruption of the German *Jansbeeren* (*John's berry*, so named because it ripens during the feast of St. John), which corrupted into the German *Gansberren* and was translated into English as *gooseberry* because *gans* means "goose" in German. That, in fact, is the only thing linking geese with the berry or plant—the goose doesn't like berries, isn't even averse to them, just ignores them entirely. Neither were gooseberries customarily served with roast goose, as is sometimes stated. The consensus is that *gooseberry* does come from some unknown association with the goose, plant names associated with animals often being inexplainable. There is even a theory that holds, simply put, that the goose gave its name to a fool or simpleton (as in *a silly goose*) and that the green berry (suggesting a "green-horn" or fool) became known as a *goose* (or fool) *berry*.

gooseberry fool. Probably the most famous dish made from gooseberries is *gooseberry fool*, a dessert made of the fruit stewed or scalded, crushed, and mixed with milk, cream, or custard. Some say the *fool* in the dish is a corruption of the French verb *fouler*, "to crush," but this derivation seems to be inconsistent with the use of the word. More probably the dish is simply named after other, older fruit trifles, the use of *fool* in its name in the sense of "foolish or silly" being suggested by "trifle." In any case, gooseberry fool has been an English favorite since at least 1700. So widely known is the dish that a *plant* is named after it, the English calling the willow herb *Epilobium hirsutum* gooseberry fool because its leaves smell like the dessert!

goose egg. (*See* **lay an egg**.)

goose pimples; horripilation. When geese are plucked, the thousands of tiny muscles that pull their feathers erect to form a natural insulation system continue to contract in the cold. The contracted muscles look like bumpy, pimply skin on a bare bird and as far back as the 17th century suggested the bumps on human skin caused by cold or fear. At first this condition was called *gooseflesh* or *goose skin*, or "creeping of the flesh." A fancier name is *horripilation*, "erection of the hair on the skin by contraction of the cutaneous muscles caused by cold, fear, or other emotion." This word effectively suggests fear and derives from the Latin *horrere*, "to bristle or shudder," which gives us the word *horror*. It is first recorded in 1623.

goosestep. The military *goosestep* is in modern times most associated with German troops during World War II and has unpleasant connotations, to say the least. However, the "elementary drill in which the recruit is taught to balance his body on either leg alternately, and swing the other backwards and forwards" dates back to the end of the 18th century. Apparently there were many who didn't much like it then, hence the contemptuous name *goosestep*. Wrote an observer in 1806: "The balance or goose-step introduced for this practice excites a fever of disgust." By 1900 *goosestep* came to mean the slow, stiff-legged march step now associated with the Nazis.

G.O.P.; G.O.M. These initials stand for *Grand Old Party*, the official nickname of the U.S. Republican party. First used in 1887, when it also meant "get out and push" (your own horse or car), it was probably suggested by *G.O.M.*, which the English called their *Grand Old Man*, Prime Minister Gladstone.

gopher. *Gopher* is probably theatrical in origin, dating back to the 1940s. The word is a corruption of words *go for* and describes an errand runner, hired to do menial chores—to go for coffee and doughnuts or whatever else the boss and other higher-ups can't acquire from a sedentary position. A *gopher* can also be a zealous salesman, from "go for broke." The burrowing animal called the gopher has nothing to do with the expression.

Gordian knot. (*See* **cut the Gordian knot**.)

Gordon setter. In contrast to the red-coated Irish setter, bred at about the same time, the *Gordon setter* is a brilliant black and tan. The breed originated in Scotland, partially developed by Alexander, the second duke of Gordon (1743-1847), a Scottish breeder and sportsman who also served in the House of Lords and wrote a number of folk ballads. The long-haired Irish and *Gordon setters*, extensively used by sportsmen for game pointing, both descend from the English setter, developed some three centuries before them.

Gorgon. A terribly ugly person, especially a woman. The three snaky-headed Gorgons of classical Greek mythology, the best known of whom is Medusa, were so hideous that they turned to stone all humans who met their gaze.

Gorgonzola. Similar to Roquefort (*q.v.*), veined *Gorgonzola* cheese is an Italian product named for the village of Gorgonzola, not far from Milan, where it was first made.

gorilla. Tough, hairy men aren't named after the *gorilla*, as most people believe. Such men actually gave their name to the ape. Originally, *Gorillai* seems to have been the name of a hairy African tribe known to the Greeks in about 500 B.C. This word came into English as *gorilla*, which first meant a hairy aboriginal person. Then in 1847 the American missionary and naturalist Dr. Thomas S. Savage observed the largest of the anthropoid apes in West Africa, naming them *gorillas* in an article published in the Boston *Journal of Natural History*. For other instances of animals named after men *see* **gibbon, shark, shrimp, guppy, molly, petrels, lynx, flamingo, halcyon, Capuchin, booby, husky, chow, cayuse, brumby,** and **maverick.**

to go someone one better. A common American expression today, *to go someone one better* means to excel the performance of someone else. It began life as a poker term (which it still is) in the early 19th century, meaning to raise the bet one more chip over someone who has bet before you.

gossamer. (*See* **St. Martin's Day**.)

gossip. A *gossip*, the word a corruption of *god-sib*, "related to God," was originally a sponsor of a child at a baptism; Shakespeare used the term in this sense in *Two Gentlemen of Verona*. There was so much chatter at christenings, as at funerals, that the word came to mean "a tattler or newsmonger."

Gotham. Washington Irving first called New York *Gotham* in his *Salmagundi Papers* (1807), because its residents reminded him of the legendary inhabitants of the English town of Gotham. An old tale has it that these villagers had discouraged King John from building a castle in their town, and taxing them for it, by feigning madness—trying to drown fish, sweep the moon's reflection off the waters, etc. This legend led to more stories about the villagers, collected in a book called *Merrie Tales of the Mad Men of Gotham*, and Irving, reading of these alternately wise and foolish people, thought that they resembled New Yorkers.

Gothic. After overthrowing Rome in the fifth century, the Gothic tribesmen, an east German people, dominated much of Europe for the next three hundred years. Not much is known of them, and their architecture was certainly not *Gothic*, but Renaissance architects nevertheless bestowed their names on all buildings characteristic of the Middle Ages, considering such structures crude and barbaric, suitable for the Goths. The 12th-to-16th-century building style, characterized by the pointed arch, as well as *Gothic art*, *Gothic type*, and myriad other things, was thereby named for a people who had nothing to do with it.

go to the devil. The Devil Tavern was one of the most famous taverns in London, standing in Fleet Street and taking its name from its sign, which showed the devil tweaking St. Dunstan's nose. The tavern was a favorite hangout for lawyers, and 17th-century wits spread the story that whenever a lawyer was wanted and couldn't be found in his offices, his clerk would tell the client to "go to the Devil." This has been suggested as the source of the above phrase, but is not to be believed. To *go to the devil*, "to go to ruin or hell," dates back to at least 1384, and there are many examples of its use through the centuries. William Caxton, for example, wrote: "Let them go to a hundred thousand devils!"

to go to the dogs. Dogs aren't the prized, often pampered, pets in other countries that they are in America. In the East they are often considered pariahs and scavengers of the streets, and the Chinese, Koreans, and Japanese, among other Asians, commonly eat them. Englishmen of earlier times used dogs primarily for hunting and kept them outside or in a rude shelter, not generally as house pets. The dogs were thrown table scraps, which they had to fight over. It didn't seem very pleasant, a dog's life, and

Englishmen of the 16th century began to compare anyone who had become impoverished, who was going to ruin, with their maltreated canines. *To lead a dog's life* was to be bothered every moment, never to be left in peace; *to go to the dogs* was to become just like the helpless animals; and *to die like a dog* was to come to a miserable, shameful end. There were many other similar phrases that arose before the dogs had their day in England and America; *throw it to the dogs*, to throw something away that's worthless; and, of course, *a dirty dog*, a morally reprehensible or filthy person.

to go to the wall. A traveler set upon by robbers in medieval times tried to protect his back against the wall of a street or country lane so that he didn't have to worry about anyone running him through from the rear while he defended himself with his sword. But *to go to the wall* nevertheless suggested serious difficulties, for someone in such a position still had to fight off attackers from three sides. So the phrase came to describe anyone in serious straits, anyone up against it, down to his last resources, physical or financial. The expression *driven to the wall* and *up against the wall* derive, just as early, from the same situation.

gourmet. The first gourmet was a *groumet*, "a horse groom." The word changed to *gourmet* in French and was applied to grooms and any minor servants in a household. Among these servants were boys who tasted wine, and such wine tasters, or *gourmets*, were given the same name when they worked as assistants in wine shops. Eventually the wine-shop *gourmets* became connoisseurs of fine wines and food in general, giving us the *gourmet* we know today. The word is not recorded in English until 1820.

gout. Regarded today as a form of arthritis, *gout* derives from the Latin *gutta*, "drop," because it was once believed that drops of bad blood or acrid matter dropped from the bloodstream into the joints and caused the painful swellings associated with the disease. The word came into English via the French *goutte* in about 1290.

to go west; occident. An unknown poet may have independently coined the phrase *to go west*, "to die," in the trenches of World War I. The expression was common then, possibly suggested by the setting of the sun in the west. But the phrase is much older. In America, Indian legend had it that a dying man had gone to meet the setting sun, and, later, when explorers and prospectors didn't return from dangerous country west of the Mississippi, they were said to have *gone west*. In 16th-century England the phrase was used of criminals going to be hung at Tyburn, which is west of London, and an early 14th-century English poem with the refrain "his world is but a vanity" had the lines: "Women and many a willful man,/ As wind and water are gone west." The idea behind the expression is even older. The Egyptians spoke of the west as the home of departed spirits, and among the Greeks the association of death with the west was proverbial, as in *Ulysses*:

My purpose holds
To sail beyond the sunset, and the paths
Of all the western stars, until I die.

Even our word *Occident*, for "the west," is associated with death. It comes from the Latin *occidens*, "the place where the sun died at the end of each day," which is from the verb *occidere*, "to die."

go west, young man, go west.   In America *go west* came to stand for new life and hope instead of death (*see* **to go west**) with the expansion of the frontier. There is some controversy about who said *go west, young man* first, however. Horace Greeley used the expression in an editorial in his *New York Tribune*: "Go west, young man, and grow with the country." Later, as the phrase grew in popularity, Greeley said that his inspiration was John Babsone Lane Soule, who wrote "Go West, young man" in an 1851 article in the *Terre Haute Express*. Greeley even reprinted Soule's article from the Indiana newspaper to give credit where it was due, but several writers insisted that Greeley had given them identical advice before Soule had written the piece. William S. Verity said that the great editor had coined the expression a full year before Soule.

go whistle for it.   One story claims that this saying arose as a perversion of the old nautical superstition that one could raise the wind for a becalmed ship by whistling (the basis of the "magic" was that air would come from the sky just as air came from your mouth). But another tale, also unproved, attributes the words to the whistle tankards once used in British pubs, drinkers blowing a whistle on the side of each when they wanted a refill. Thus both possible sources imply the opposite of the phrase's meaning: "You'll never get it from me, you won't get it at all."

to go whole hog.   Probably the expression *to go the whole hog*, or *to go whole hog*, "to go the limit, all the way," has its origins in William Cowper's poem "The Love of the World Reproved; or Hypocrisy Detected" (1779). Cowper told a story about pious but hungry Muhammadans who were ordered by Muhammad not to eat a certain unspecified part of the pig. Unable to determine what part, they began to experiment:

But for one piece they thought it hard
From the whole hog to be debar'd;
And set their wit at work to find
What joint the prophet had in mind . . .
Thus, conscience freed from every clog,

Mohometans eat up the hog . . .
With sophistry their sauce they sweeten,
Til quite from tail to snout 'tis eaten.

goy.   *Goy* is a Yiddish word for a gentile, and can be completely innocent or disparaging, depending on who is using it and how it is used—just as *Jew* can be either, depending on the circumstance. Leo Rosten notes that the word itself is not derogatory and discusses it at length in his *The Joys of Yiddish*, one of the best and brightest word books of this or any other time. *Goy* derives from the Hebrew *goy*, nation, and dates back at least to the 19th century.

Grable-bodied seamen.   Movie actress Betty Grable, her "million dollar legs" insured by Lloyds of London, was the pin-up girl par excellence during World War II. British sailors used the term *Grable-bodied seamen* to describe long-stemmed lovelies in the Wrens (Women's Royal Naval Service) who fit the description.

graft.   This American term for dishonest earnings, usually of politicians, isn't recorded until 1859. Its origins are unclear, but the word may derive from the British slang *graft*, for "any kind of work, especially illicit work," which, in turn, may come from the British *graer*, "to dig," influenced, *Partridge* says, by the gardening *graft*. The gardening *graft* derives, ultimately, from the Greek word *grapheion*, "a bone or wood pencil-like instrument used for writing on wax tablets." Someone in early times possibly thought that a *grapheion* resembled a twig for grafting.

Graham crackers, etc.   Young Presbyterian minister Sylvester Graham (1794-1851) became so ardent a temperance advocate that he not only traveled far and wide to lecture on the demon rum, but invented a vegetable diet that he was sure would cure those suffering from the evils of drink. Graham soon extended his mission to include changing America's sinful eating habits. Meats and fats, he said, led to sexual excesses and mustard and catsup could cause insanity, but Graham mainly urged the substitution of homemade unsifted whole wheat flour for white bread. Modern science has affirmed his belief that refining flour robs it of vitamins and minerals, and most of his regimen, including vegetables and fruits in the diet, fresh air while sleeping, moderate eating, and abundant exercise, is now widely accepted. His memorials are the *Graham flour*, *Graham bread* and *Graham crackers* that his followers ate and dedicated to him.

grain of salt.   (*See* **take with a grain of salt**.)

Gramont's memory.   The name is often spelled *Grammont* due to its misspelling in the *Mémoires du comte de Grammont*. A *Gramont's memory*, a convenient one, derives from a tale told about the count and Lady Elizabeth Hamilton. While visiting England in 1663, the sharp-tongued Gramont is said to have grossly insulted and refused to apologize to La Belle Hamilton, whose brothers followed him as he prepared to leave the country, drew their swords, and asked if he hadn't forgotten something. "True, true," he replied, unruffled. "I promised to marry your sister." This he did. Only the year before his marriage, Philibert, comte de Gramont, had been exiled from Paris for attempting to rival King Louis XIV in a love affair. The French diplomat's memoirs, a masterpiece of their kind, vividly describe the licentious court of England's Charles II. They were written by Gramont's brother-in-law, Anthony Hamilton, from materials supplied by the count. So sharp-tongued was Philibert that one writer describes the immense feeling of relief expressed by the French court when, in 1707, it was announced that he had died. Even at eighty-seven he was still a threat to anyone who crossed him.

grand climacteric. As far back as 1653, people have been writing about the *grand* or *great climacteric*. This is a superstition involving the age 63 (a number that is the product of the "magic numbers" 7 and 9) and holding that if you survived that dangerous year you would live to a ripe old age. The word *climacteric* itself, which also refers to the female menopause, derives from a Greek word meaning "a critical period."

Grand Guignol. Violent, sensational plays were the staple of the Théâtre du Grand Guignol in Paris up until recent times, these short plays giving us the name *Grand Guignol* for such works, or the staging of them. The theater took its name, ultimately, from the French *guignol*, "puppet or marionette", in relation to the violence and brutality of Punch and Judy shows.

grand old flag. The original title of "You're a Grand Old Flag" (1906) was "You're a Grand Old Rag." George M. Cohan changed it when critics protested that he was profaning the Stars and Stripes. Cohan (he pronounced his name Cohen) wrote his famous song "Harrigan" in honor of his friend, vaudeville performer, Ed Harrigan, of Harrigan and Hart fame.

Grand Panjandrum. (*See* **no soap!**)

grandstanding. (*See* **playing to the grandstand.**)

Grand Tetons. French voyageurs early named these mountains in northwestern Wyoming the *Grand Tetons*, the "big breasts," because of their resemblance to a woman's breasts. For the same reason the rounded hillocks or mounds west of the Mississippi are called *mamelle*, from the French *mamelle*, for "a woman's breast."

grangerize. Reverend James Granger (1723-76) himself clipped some 14,000 engraved portraits from other books to use as possible illustrations for his *Biographical History of England*. Some of the books he pillaged were rare ones, and to make matters worse, he suggested in his preface that private collections like his might prove valuable someday. This resulted in a fad called *Grangerizing*, or extra-illustration, with thousands of people mutilating fine books and stuffing pictures and other material into Granger's. Editions following the 1769 *Biographical History . . . adapted to a Methodical Catalogue of Engraved British Heads* provided blank pages for the insertion of these extra illustrations; the book eventually increased to six volumes from its original two. Sets of Granger illustrated with up to 3,000 engravings were compiled, and so many early English books were ravaged that *to grangerize* came to mean the mutilation that remains the bane of librarians today.

to grant (give) no quarter. *To grant (give) no quarter* originally meant to spare no life of an enemy in your power, but it has come to mean "to be unmerciful." The expression has its origin in its opposite, *to grant quarter*, which may derive from an ancient agreement between the warring Spaniards and Dutch that the ransom of a soldier be a quarter of his pay. More likely the words have their origin in the old custom of a victor providing his captives temporary housing. *Quarters* (from the Latin *quadrus*, "square"), for "a residence or a place where an army lodges," is recorded as early as 1591.

grape; grapefruit; wineberry. *Grapefruit* (*Citrus paradisi*) resemble grapes only in that they grow in clusters on their trees, but that was sufficient reason to bestow the name upon them, early explorers in Barbados thought. *Grapes* themselves look nothing like their namesakes. Grapes were named for the *grape*, or grapple, the small hook that the French used to harvest them. The English called grapes *wineberries* until they imported the French word toward the end of the 11th century.

the grapevine. Some fifteen years after Samuel Morse transmitted his famous "what hath God wrought" message, a long telegraph line was strung from Virginia City to Placerville, California, so crudely strung, it's said, that people jokingly compared the line with a sagging grapevine. I can find no record of this, but, in any case, grapevines were associated with telegraph lines somewhere along the line, for by the time of the Civil War a report *by grapevine telegraph* was common slang for a rumor. The idea behind the expression is probably not rumors sent over real telegraph lines, but the telegraphic speed with which rumormongers can transmit canards with their own rude mouth-to-mouth telegraph system.

grass roots. "A little classic of the poetic imagination," the *New York Times* once called this phrase, but whose "poetic imagination" we don't know. In 1935, when the Republican Party was seeking a broader base of support among the voters, John Hamilton of Topeka, Kansas used the words in describing the "new" G.O.P. No one has traced the phrase back further in print, but one respected etymologist has testified that he heard the expression back in rural Ohio in about 1885. A term dear to politicians, it simply means to get down to basic facts or underlying principles, its appeal becoming more nostalgic as more concrete replaces grass. *Grass roots* itself, for "basics, fundamentals," has been traced to 1932 when used, appropriately enough, to describe the candidacy of Oklahoma Governor William H. ("Alfalfa Bill") Murray for the Democratic presidential nomination. It, too, probably stems from the prairie farms of the West.

grass widow. The old story that this synonym for a divorcée derives from *veuve de grace*, "a divorcée or widow by courtesy or grace of the Pope," has no basis in fact—for one thing, *grace widow* is nowhere recorded in English. Just as unlikely is the theory that the phrase originated with the custom of British officers in India sending their wives on vacation to the cool grassy hills during intensely hot summers, where, separated from their husbands, they were humorously referred to as *grass widows*. There is also a yarn that "forty-niners" in America "put their wives out to grass," boarding them with neighbors until they returned from prospecting. The most plausible explanation of this old English expression, which dates back to at least the early 16th century, is that it formerly meant an unmarried mother and just changed in meaning over the years. "Grass" probably referred to the grass in which the grass widow's child might have been begotten, outside of the proper marriage bed, and "widow" to the woman's unmarried state. We find the same parallel in many languages, including our current slang *a roll in the hay*; the German *Strohwiteve*, "straw widow"; and the Middle Low German *graswedeue*, an obsolete word for a woman with an illegitimate child. One joke has it that a *grass widow* is a forlorn middle-class matron whose husband spends all his spare time playing golf.

graveyard. (*See* **cemetery.**)

graveyard stew. During the Great Depression we ate toasted bread and milk, sweetened with a lot of sugar when no one was looking, for too many meals. There were complaints about this *graveyard stew* or *soup*—so named because it was often fed to old people with no teeth or because a steady diet of it might send you to the grave—but it doesn't seem that bad anymore.

gravy train. In the 1920s, railroad men invented the expression to *ride the gravy train* to describe a run on which there was good pay and little work. The words were quickly adopted into general speech, meaning to have an easy job that pays well, or, more commonly, to be prosperous. *Gravy*, however, had been slang for easy money since the early 1900s.

graybacks. (*See* **greenbacks.**)

greased lightning. Lightning is fast enough, striking before it can be heard, but *greased lightning*! Why, this is the kind of American exaggeration for emphasis that British grammarians sneered about all through the 19th century. Americans surely are a hyperbolic people, but the trouble here is that *like greased lightning*, "faster than anything," is a British expression, despite some disclaimers. At least it first appeared in the *Boston, Lincoln, and Louth Herald* of January 15, 1833. The hyperbole is of course not meant to be taken seriously. No more than the everyday expressions *as old as the hills, a million thanks, I haven't seen you for ages*, or even Shakespeare's famous poetic device in *Macbeth*:

> No; this my hand will rather
> The multitudinous seas incarnadine,
> Making the green one red.

grease one's palm. *To grease one's palm* was originally *to grease one's hand*, an expression first recorded by the poet John Skelton in 1526. From such early times, *to grease one's hand, palm*, or *fist*, or simply *to grease*, has meant to bribe or tip. There is an identical old expression in French, *graisser la patte*, and the idea behind the expression is the same as that behind greasing the wheels, making things run smoothly—greasing the hand or palm of a person will make his hand work more smoothly for you.

Great American Desert. The idea of a Great American Desert in the West discouraged many people from settling in the region, which they thought was uninhabitable. The term *Great American Desert* was used in newspapers and geographies as early as 1834. Before this, the area, which is part of the Great Plains, was called the *Great Desert*, this term recorded fifty years earlier.

The Great American Novel. This term sprang up toward the end of the 19th century. Frank Norris wrote: "The Great American Novel is not extinct like the Dodo, but mythical like the Hippogriff . . . the thing to be looked for is not the Great American Novelist, but the Great Novelist who shall also be American." Observed Jack London a little later: "I'd rather win a water-fight in a swimming pool, or remain astride a horse that is trying to get out from under me, than write the great American novel."

the great commoner. This nickname was applied to a number of American political leaders with a populist bent after it was first given to Henry Clay in the early 1840s—among them: Thaddeus Stevens, William Jennings Bryan, and Thomas Jefferson.

greatest show on earth. (*See* **there's a sucker born every minute.**)

great fleas have lesser fleas. All of us, no matter how great, have our troubles, our enemies who prey on us. The expression has its roots in Jonathan Swift's volume of satirical advice to a poet, *On Poetry, a Rhapsody* (1733), with its lines: "Hobbes clearly proves that every creature/ Lives in a state of war by nature;/ So naturalists observe a flea/ Has smaller fleas that on him prey,/ And these have smaller still to bite 'em/ And so proceed *ad infinitum*."

great hulking man. *Hulk* has its origins in the ancient Greek *holkas*, "a trading vessel," originally a towed ship, the word akin to the Greek *helkein*, "to drag," because such ships were towed or dragged behind. The English word first meant a large sailing ship, then became the hull of a ship, and today means the body of an abandoned ship. Shakespeare was the first to record *hulk* as the synonym for a big unwieldy person and this comparison to a large unwieldy ship remains in the language today, both in the names of wrestlers ("The Hulk") and other big people called *hulks* and the expression *a great hulking man*.

Great Scott! Old Fuss-and-Feathers, General Winfield Scott, a brigadier general at only twenty-eight, was well known for his arrogant swagger, and his opponents may have jeeringly dubbed him "Great Scott" with this in mind. On the other hand, the hero of the Mexican War and the Whig candidate for president in 1852 wasn't the only Scottophile in the country—his many supporters may have named him "Great Scott" in admiration of his great dignity. At any rate, the exclamation *Great Scott!* hasn't been traced back before Old Fuss-and-Feathers' day and he could certainly have been responsible for the expression in one way or another. That the term is just a euphemism for "Great God!," a play on the German *Gott*, is a simpler but not necessarily truer explanation.

the great unwashed. In 1901 the *Congressional Record* noted that "the Democratic Party has long been known as the 'great unwashed.'" By then the epithet was at least fifty years old. *The great unwashed* is still heard today occasionally in reference to what the speaker believes are "the lower classes," but is not applied to the Democrats. In the late 18th century the British had called the rabble of the French Revolution *the great unwashed*.

Great White Fleet. The United States decided to show the world its naval power in 1907 and sent sixteen battle-ships and four destroyers on a world cruise. Because all these ships were painted white, they were popularly called the *White Fleet* or *Great White Fleet*.

Great White Hope. (*See* **Jack Johnson**.)

the Great White Way. This nickname for the Manhattan theatrical or entertainment district, a reference to all the lights there, was coined by Albert Bigelow Paine, best known today as Mark Twain's first biographer, and used as the title of his novel *The Great White Way* (1901), which is about the Anarctic not Broadway.

Greek. The Greeks are the subject of many proverbs still heard. *Beware of Greeks bearing gifts* dates to a line in Virgil, "I fear the Greeks especially when they bring gifts," and refers to the fabled wooden horse containing soldiers that the Greeks gave to the Trojans. *Greek trust* was to the Romans no trust at all; and *when Greek meets Greek then comes the tug of war* commemorates the resistance of the ancient Greek cities to the Macedonian Kings Philip and Alexander the Great. Putting something off *until the Greek calends* is to never do it, for the Greeks, unlike the Romans, had no term like "calends" for the first days of their months. To *play the Greek* is to live a luxurious life, while the modern expression *when Greek meets Greek, they open a restaurant* at least admits that Greeks are enterprising. Then there's *it's all Greek to me*; and the slang term *Grecian bend*, a posture bent forward from the waist much affected in the late 19th century, and the straight-lined *Grecian profile*, among other expressions. To many, Grecian itself is the term "for all civilized and subtle thoughts and feelings," the Grecians "swelling o'er with arts," as Shakespeare wrote. Lastly, there's *Greek fire*, the mysterious ancient naval weapon that burned when wet and was so effective against wooden ships from A.D. 700 to 900, which is said to have been invented by the Greek Callimachus. No one knows its constituents, but it is thought to have been composed of sulphur, naphtha, and pitch. Water helped *Greek fire* spread and it could be extinguished only with wine.

Greek words in English. Classical Greek and Latin borrowings possibly account for a majority of English words. Many Greek words have come into English, often through Latin and other languages. These include: *anthology, barometer, Bible, catastrophe, cheer, cyclone, elastic, idiot, magic, tactics, tantalize*, and *hoi polloi* (*qq.v.*).

Greenacre!. *Greenacre!*, a word popular in the 19th century, is a good example of true gallows humor. The rope broke when they hanged James Greenacre at Newgate Prison in 1837 and he had to be strung up again. However, little sympathy was shown for the murderer, who had hacked up his victim and buried sections of the body under various London landmarks. Stevedores, in fact, promptly adopted the killer's name to indicate the falling of cargo. Whenever rope slings broke while goods were being loaded or unloaded, the cry *Greenacre!* went up along the docks.

greenbacks.   Union troops in the Civil War named U.S. Treasury legal-tender banknotes *greenbacks* for the obvious reason that the backs of the bills were green. Over a half-billion dollars' worth of them were issued. The Confederacy issued more than a billion dollars' worth of "bluebacks" and "graybacks," which were worthless because they had no gold or silver behind them. "Gold-backs" (1873) and "Yellowbacks" (1902) were other colorful U.S. banknotes.

green bean.   (*See* **bean**.)

the Green Book.   The *Green Book*, with its 6,000 entries, is "The Social List of Washington, D.C.," encompassing "socially acceptable" Washington and official Washington, there being quite a distinction between the two. It was begun by Helen Ray Hagner in 1930 and is run by her granddaughter today. To get in it one has to be recommended by two people already there and approved by an anonymous board of governors. The book also serves as an arbiter of protocol.

green-eyed monster.   Why since the 16th century has the color green been associated with jealousy? It has been suggested that oriental jade ground into powder and used as a love potion by jealous suitors to win their loved ones has something to do with it, but that seems a farfetched explanation. Shakespeare was the first to use the expression *green-eyed monster*, in *Othello*, where Iago says: "O, beware, my lord, of jealousy;/ It is the green-eyed monster which doth mock/ The meat it feeds on." Clearly the reference here is to cats toying with their victims before killing and eating them, so the first green-eyed monster is a cat. However, before this, in *The Merchant of Venice*, Shakespeare wrote of *green-eyed jealousy* without any reference to a feline. We must mark the ultimate origin "unknown."

Greengage plum.   *Greengage plums* are actually yellow with a tinge of green. The renowned plum, which has two eponymous names, was brought from Italy to France about 1500, where it was named and is still called the *Reine-Claude*, after Claudia, *la bonne reine*, queen to Francis I from their marriage in 1514 until his death. In about 1725 Sir William Gage, an amateur botanist, imported a number of plum trees from a monastery in France, all of which were labeled except the Reine-Claude. A gardener at Hengrave Hall in Suffolk named the unknown variety *Green Gage* in honor of his employer and the Reine-Claude has been the *greengage* in

England ever since. The blue and purple gage were developed from their illustrious ancestor on the fertile grounds of Gage's estate, probably much to the delight of his eight children.

greenhorn.   Authorities reason, without any proof, that *greenhorn* was first the name for a young ox, one with young, or "green," horns. Because young oxen were inexperienced and untrained as farm work animals, they were undesirable, and their name became attached to raw Army recruits by the 16th century and finally to any raw, inexperienced person. *Greenhorn* is also remembered as a derogatory term for newly arrived immigrants in turn-of-the-century America.

Greenland.   (*See* **Cape of Good Hope**.)

greenmail.   Patterned on *blackmail* (*q.v.*), *greenmail* became popular during the 1980s. It describes, in the takeovers of companies, "the payment of a premium by a company that is a takeover target for the shares held by an unwanted suitor."

greenroom.   This lounge in the theater where performers rest when they aren't on stage, or where people who are to appear on television wait before they go on, probably takes its name from such a room in London's Drury Lane Theatre, which just happened to be painted green sometime in the late 17th century. Most authorities reject the old story that the room was painted green to soothe the actors' eyes.

green thumb.   No one, it seemed, knew why the Italian monk Fra Antonio could make plants grow so well in the cloister garden. But one day an elderly monk watching Fra Antonio observed that he had a green thumb on his right hand, which made him an excellent gardener—the green thumb, no doubt, colored by the plants he had been handling. This is a nice little story, but so far as we know the term *green thumb* doesn't go back to medieval times. In fact, it is first recorded in 1925 by Dean Middleton, a BBC broadcaster and garden-book author. It is probable that Middleton merely popularized the phrase, which many people remembered hearing around 1910 and is probably a generation older.

Greenwich time.   A borough of London, at latitude 51 degrees 28' 38" No., and longitude 0 degrees 0' 0", Greenwich was long the place where the world's time was officially measured, specifically at the Royal Observatory there. At a meeting in Washington, D.C. in 1884 most nations agreed to the place. In 1985, however, a decision was made to dismantle the historic Greenwich clock.

Gregg system.   *Gregg*, the most widely used shorthand writing in the world and by far the most popular in the

United States, was invented by John Robert Gregg (1864-1948), an Irishman who explained Gregg in *The Phonetic Handwriting* (1888) and emigrated to introduce it in America. Once called "Light-Line Phonography," it is an improvement on the earlier phonetic *Pitman* (*q.v.*) and is much easier to write.

Gregorian calendar. While an improvement on its predecessors, the inaccurate *Julian calendar* resulted in the calendar year gradually losing on the actual solar year, or the time it takes the earth to travel around the sun. By the 16th century, for example, the first day of spring came on March 11, instead of March 21. As this interfered with seasonal church celebrations, Pope Gregory XIII introduced a modified calendar in 1582. He decreed that the day after October 4 in that year would be October 15, making up for the lost days in this way and ensuring that they would not be lost again by ruling that century years would no longer be leap years unless divisable by 400. Pope Gregory himself probably did not devise the "new style" calendar, but it was named in his honor. Immediately accepted in Catholic countries, the *Gregorian calendar* wasn't adopted in England or America until 1752—when the calendar gained twelve days overnight. Imperfect itself, it is nevertheless used today throughout most of the world.

Gregorian tree. The English so valued one hangman, Gregory Brandon, that they granted him a coat of arms for his gruesomely efficient work on the scaffold. Gregory, whose son succeeded him as public executioner and beheaded Charles I in 1649, lived to see his name become a synonym for the gallows in the form of *Gregorian Tree*.

grenade; pomegranate. The grenade was developed as an antipersonnel weapon in the late 16th century and so named because it resembled the pome*granate* in shape and size and exploded like a ripe pomegranate when thrown against anything—jagged chunks of metal spewing out instead of pulp and seed. *Pomegranate* itself derives from the Latin *pomum granatum*, "grainy apple," which refers to the fruit's hundreds of seeds.

Gresham's Law. Though the tendency of bad money to drive good money out of circulation is known as *Gresham's Law*, it was formulated as an economic principle long before Sir Thomas Gresham (ca. 1519-1579). Gresham, a London merchant and founder of what is now the Royal Exchange, noted that the more valuable of two similar coins would be hoarded, but Copernicus and others had already made similar observations. Unaware that he had not formulated the principle, the economist H. D. MacLeod named the law for Gresham in 1857.

griffin. The *griffin*, half lion and half eagle, was an enormous aerial monster of antiquity that fed living humans to its young. It took its name from the Greek *grypos*, "hooked," because of its large hooked beak. The griffin was known to the Sumerians, under the name *chumbaba*, as early as 3000 B.C.

gringo. Many scholars trace this disparaging term for an American to the Spanish *gringo*, "gibberish," which is a corruption of the Spanish word *Griego*, "a Greek." *Gringo*, by this theory, would be related to the old saying "It's all Greek to me," indicating that the Yankees were strange and unfamiliar in their ways to the Mexicans who so named them. But we haven't exhausted all the conjectures by any means. Another etymologist boldly claims "green coat" as the base for *gringo*, and a second theory says that the first two words of the Robert Burns lyric "Green grow the rashes O," a song sung by American soldiers in the Mexican war, is the origin of the contemptuous word—somehow one can't imagine battle-hardened veterans riding along singing: "Green grow the rashes O/ The happiest hours that ere I spent/ Were spent among the lasses O!" If the "gibberish" theory is to be challenged, the most likely contender is Major Samuel Ringgold, a brilliant strategist dreaded by the Mexicans during the Mexican War until he was killed at the Battle of Palo Alto in 1846. Ringgold's name, pronounced with a trilled *r* and without the last two letters as it normally would be by a Mexican, might yet prove the correct source for the word.

to grin like a Cheshire cat. The pseudonymous British satirist Peter Pindar (John Wolcot) first used this expression for a broad smile in the late 18th century, but Lewis Carroll popularized it in *Alice's Adventures in Wonderland* (1865)—the Cheshire cat in the story gradually faded from Alice's view, its grin the last part of it to vanish. No satisfactory explanation of the allusion has been made. *To grin like a Cheshire cat* probably goes back much further than Pindar, and the source could be Cheshire cheeses that were at one time molded in the form of a cat—supposedly, the cat was grinning because the former palatine of Cheshire once had regal privileges in England, paying no taxes to the crown, etc. Another story relates the expression to the attempts of an ignorant sign painter to represent a lion rampant on the signs of many Cheshire inns—his lions supposedly looked more like grinning cats. The most unlikely yarn credits an eponymous forest warden of Cheshire named Caterling. In the reign of Richard III, it's said, this Cheshire Caterling stamped out poaching, was responsible for over one hundred poachers being hanged, and was present "grinning from ear to ear" at each of these executions. *To grin like a Cheshire Catling* became proverbial and was later shortened *to grin like a Cheshire cat*. Another fanciful story makes the same Catling the "cat" of the nursery rhyme "Hi Diddle Diddle, the Cat and the Fiddle."

grocer. *Grocers* in medieval times were so named from the Latin *grossus*, "large," because they sold only in large quantities. England's Company of Grocers, an association incorporated in 1344, were wholesale dealers in spice and foreign produce.

grog. Mount Vernon was named after Vice Admiral Sir Edward Vernon by George Washington's half-brother Laurence, who served under "Old Grog" when he led six little ships to the West Indies and captured heavily fortified Portobello during the War of Jenkins' Ear (1739). This action made Vernon England's hero of the hour, Parliament voting him formal thanks and street pageants being held on his birthday to celebrate his humbling of the Spaniards. But the arrogant former war hawk MP never won popularity with his men. Old Grog had been nicknamed for the impressive grogram cloak he wore on deck in all kinds of weather, the coarse taffeta material symbolizing his tough and irascible nature. Then, in August 1740, the stern disciplinarian issued an order that made his name a malediction. In order to curb drunken brawling aboard ships in his command, and to save money, he declared that all rum rations would henceforth be diluted with water. Incensed old sea dogs cursed Vernon roundly, for half a pint of rum mixed with a quart of water seemed weak stuff indeed to anyone on a raw rum liquid diet. Furthermore, the rationed bilge was divided into two issues, served six hours apart. His men soon defiantly dubbed the adulterated rum *Grog*, using the nickname they had bestowed upon the admiral. Vernon's order served its purpose and "three water rum" became the official ration for all enlisted personnel in the Royal Navy, but *grog* quickly took on the wider meaning of any cheap, diluted drink. (*See* **booze**.)

Grolier binding. Rich, ornate book bindings are called *Grolier bindings*, after Jean Grolier, Vicomte D'Auigsy (1479-1565), who was not a bookbinder or printer but a prominent French bibliophile. Grolier collected books and had them bound by the best artisans of his day, each book bearing the inscription *Groliere et Amicorum*. All the books in his library, sold in 1675, are world-famous collector's items. The Grolier Club, which has published many books and catalogs of its exhibitions, was founded in New York City (1884) "for the study and promotion of the arts pertaining to the production of books."

groovy; in the groove. *In the groove* has lasted longer than most slang expressions, possibly because of a popular song of the same name. The phrase, meaning "exciting, satisfying, or functioning smoothly," isn't heard much anymore, nor is its offspring, *groovy*. But from the thirties to the fifties it was all the rage, was even translated into Latin: *in canaliculo*. The allusion is to the quality of music reproduced when a good phonograph needle traverses the grooves of a record without jumping out. Oddly enough, an older English expression *groovy*, dating back to the late 19th century, means just about the opposite—to be in a rut, like a cart stuck in the grooves of a muddy road.

grotesque. In the 16th century, excavated chambers, or *grotte*, in ancient Roman buildings revealed murals on the walls depicting figures that were unnaturally distorted or comically exaggerated. These figures were called *grotesca*, after the *grotte* they were found in, *grotesca* eventually becoming the English *grotesque*, for any similar figure.

groundhog; woodchuck. American settlers named the marmot, or woodchuck (*Arctomys monax*), the *groundhog*, perhaps because this member of the squirrel family seems hoggish in the way he burrows through the ground. Or, possibly groundhog is a translation of the Dutch *aardvark* made by Dutch settlers in America, even though the South African aardvark, or earth hog, is a larger burrowing animal than the groundhog. The groundhog isn't a hog then, but his other American name, woodchuck, is no more accurate, for he doesn't chuck wood, either, a fact even the old tongue twister implies: "How much wood would a woodchuck chuck if a woodchuck could chuck wood?" "Woodchuck" has no connection with wood at all, simply deriving from the Cree Indian word *wuchuk* or *otchock* for another animal, the fisher, or pekan, which early settlers corrupted finally to "woodchuck" and applied through mistaken identity to the groundhog. *Groundhog day*, February 2, is the day when the groundhog is supposed to emerge from his hibernation, look outside, and go back to bed again if he sees his shadow, in anticipation of more severe weather unfit for man or groundhog.

groupie. Originally describing a very young girl who followed rock 'n' roll groups on concert tours, worshiping them in an idolatrous fashion, this word has since the early 1960s come to mean a young woman who makes herself available for sexual intercourse with a member of a rock group or other celebrity without charge. A *groupie* can also be a young girl constantly on the make. The groupie's counterpart in sports is sometimes called a *bimbo*, this word common for a promiscuous woman since about 1930 and probably deriving from *bambino*, "baby."

groves of academe. According to legend, the Athenian hero Academus helped Castor and Pollux rescue their little sister Helen when she was kidnapped by the Athenian Prince Theseus. Academus revealed Helen's hiding place, and she was spared marriage with Theseus, growing up to become the famous "face that launched a thousand ships," in reference to her later abduction by Paris, which caused the Trojan War. As a reward for his help the Spartans gave an olive grove on the outskirts of

Athens to Academus, the place later becoming a public park called the Grove of Academus in his honor. Much later, around 387 B.C., the philosopher Plato had a house and garden adjoining this park and opened a school of philosophy there. He walked and talked with his students in the peaceful olive grove for the rest of his life, was buried near the grove, and his peripatetic successors taught there as well, so his school of philosophy became known as the *Academia*, after the olive grove honoring the eponymous hero Academus. Renaissance scholars later adopted the name *académe*, or "academy," for an institution devoted to learning, from the learning of philosophy to the learning of war, and it is from the word *academy* that our word *academic* derives. Possibly the most famous of academies is the French Académie Française founded in 1635, but this literary school has its detractors, too, having been called the "*hôtel des invalides de la littérature.*"

to grow like Topsy. "Never was born, never had no father, nor mother, not nothin' . . . I 'spect I growed," the slave child Topsy replies when Aunt Ophelia, a white woman from the North, questions her about her family. The scene in Harriet Beecher Stowe's antislavery novel *Uncle Tom's Cabin, or Life Among the Lowly* (1852), the most popular book of its day, had great impact, especially in dramatic versions of the novel, and inspired the saying *to grow like Topsy*, describing any unplanned, often sudden growth. Little Eva's companion, like Uncle Tom and the brutal, drunken planter Simon Legree, has become part of the language, and Mrs. Stowe's book, despite its faults, has spawned more new words than any other American novel.

Grub Street hack.

> Here lies poor Ned Purdom, from misery freed,
> Who long was a bookseller's hack;
> He led such a damnable life in this world,
> I don't think he'd wish to come back.
>
> —Oliver Goldsmith

Grub Street in London was known a century before Dr. Johnson's lifetime as the stamping ground of (depending on your perspective) needy writers or literary *hacks* (from *hackney*, "a horse or carriage anyone could hire"). When compiling his famous *Dictionary of the English Language* (1755) the Great Cham defined Grub Street as "much inhabited by writers of small histories, dictionaries and temporary poems, whence any mean production is called grubstreet." The term lasted even after the street name disappeared, probably because it suggests writers *grubbing* (from the Middle English *grobben*, "to dig") for money for *grub* (as Johnson himself was forced to do) and often producing cheap works in the process. Grub Street has been called Milton Street since 1830—not in honor of the great poet John Milton, but after a landlord who owned most of the houses on the street at the time.

grue.   Grues are grisly little comic poems with sadistic content and trick last lines. They are sometimes called *Little Willies* in honor of the "hero" of so many, but the name *grue*, coined by Robert Louis Stevenson from "gruesome," is more appropriate. Though their content is never worse than the daily news, most *grues* are anonymous:

> Willie poisoned father's tea;
> Father died in agony.
> Mother looked extremely vexed;
> "Really, Will," she said, "what next?"

grueling.   No matter how you cook it, *grueling*, meaning exhausting or punishing, has something to do with *gruel*, a light, cooked, thin cereal usually made of oatmeal. There's no doubt that the word derives from the expression *to get*, or *take*, *one's gruel*, first recorded in the late 18th century. Why eating oatmeal came to be associated with a punishment is open to question. The traditional story is that *to get one's gruel* is an allusion to Medici poisonings. The Medici family, which directed the destiny of Florence from the 15th century to 1737 and produced two queens of France, did much good and evil, ranging from patronage of the arts to political tortures and poisonings. In fact, they were so prone to dispose of each other by assassination that their genealogy is highly complicated. Catherine de' Medici (1519-89), Queen of France, was particularly infamous for political assassinations, especially for her part in the attempted assassination of Admiral Coligny and the St. Bartholomew's Day Massacre (1572) in which 30,000 Protestants were killed. She was also rumored to give poisoned drink to her enemies under the guise of friendship, usually serving it in a thin drink of gruel. It wouldn't be unreasonable to assume that Catherine's alleged poisonings inspired the expression *to get one's gruel*, except that the words aren't recorded until some two hundred years after her death. The Medici family is a more likely candidate, but most word sleuths now believe the poisonings have nothing to do with the phrase. *Partridge* suggests that it comes from an earlier nautical expression, *to serve out the grog*, "to mete out punishment," making it comparable to humorous expressions such as *settle one's hash* and *cook one's goose*.

G-string.   Stripteasers, who sometimes call this a "gadget," aren't responsible for the word. *G-string* is an Americanism first used to describe an Indian's loincloth or breechclout in the 19th century. It could be that some fiddler in the West compared the heaviest of violin strings, the G string, to the length of sinew or gut that Indians tied around their waists to hold up their breechclouts. But even the heaviest of violin strings wouldn't really do the job. Perhaps the g is just a euphemistic shortening of "groin," an indecent word at the time. The burlesque G-string is of course far smaller than the Indian variety and must have seemed even skimpier a century ago, considering the Brunhildian builds of yesterday's ecdysiasts. One burlesque company of the day proudly advertised "two tons of women" and had only twenty strippers. (*See* **ecdysiast**.)

the Guard dies but never surrenders.   History courses teach us that General Pierre Cambronne, the commander of Napoleon's Imperial Guard at Waterloo, made the above reply to a British surrender demand. What Cambronne really said was "Shit! The Guard never surrenders!" The polite French call this episode *le mot de Cambronne*, "the word of Cambronne."

guerilla.   *Guerilla* means a "little war" in Spanish, the word first becoming popular when Napoleon Bonaparte invaded Spain in 1808. The Spanish peasants took up arms and Napoleon, used to fighting trained armies, couldn't cope with these small units of men that seemed to be everywhere and yet could rarely be found. The Spanish peasants, with English help, eventually expelled Napoleon, and ever since then *guerilla army* has meant small bands of men fighting in unconventional ways.

Guevarism; euphuism.   Spanish writer and moralist Antonio de Guevara (ca. 1480-1545) has been regarded as the father of *euphuism*, for which his name is equivalent. But *euphuism*, an ornate, artificial writing or speaking style characterized by alliteration, eloquence, and high-flown phrases, was coined more than a century after his death. *Euphuism* takes its name from *Euphues: the Anatomy of Wit* (1579) by John Lyly, who displayed such a style in his book in an attempt to "soften" the English language, Euphues being the name of the main character in his romance. Guevara may have been among Lyly's inspirations, for the Spanish author's *The Golden Book of Marcus Aurelius* (1535) and other works were translated early into English.

guillotine.   Dr. Joseph Ignace Guillotin (1738-1814) did not invent the *guillotine*, did not die by the *guillotine*, and all his life futilely tried to detach his name from the height reducer. The confusion began on October 10, 1789, when the eminent Parisian physician, a member of the National Assembly during the French Revolution, suggested that a "merciful" beheading device replace the clumsy sword and degrading rope then used by French executioners. Dr. Guillotin remained in the public's mind for his eloquent speech and one of many popular songs about the new machine claimed that he had invented it. Not much time passed before "La Louisette" (this name honoring its real inventor, Dr. Antoine Louis) lost out to *La machine Guillotine*, *Madame Guillotine*, and then *guillotine* itself.

After his death, Guillotin's children petitioned the French government to change the name of the *guillotine*, but won only permission to change their own names.

Guinea.   The area on the African west coast and the countries there called *Guinea* may take their name from a misunderstanding. One story claims that the first Portuguese seafarers to land in the area asked local tribesmen the name of the coast. The residents thought they were pointing at a group of women nearby and answered *guiné*, their word for women, which became the name of the area. In any case, the name of the country first appears in Portuguese as *Guine*. (*See also* **dago; indri; kangaroo; llama; Luzon; Nome; Pago Pago; Sierra Leone; wop; Yucatan**.)

guinea hen.   The ancestor of today's tasty *guinea hen* hailed from Guinea in western Africa, unlike the *guinea pig* (*q.v.*).

guinea pig.   The South American rodent isn't a pig and doesn't hail from Guinea in West Africa. Native to Brazil, the guinea pig takes its first name from the fact that it was first brought to Europe on the *Guinea-men* slave ships that sailed from Guinea to South America to deliver their human cargo and to fill their holds with whatever cargo was available for the return trip to Europe. How the creature came to be called a pig is anybody's guess.

gull.   The *gull*, the only bird ever to have a monument erected to it, is intimately connected with American agricultural history. All gulls take their name from the Breton *guylan*, for the bird, which derives from the Breton *gwela*, "to weep," in reference to the bird's cry. In 1848 an invasion of grasshoppers threatened starvation for the Mormon settlers near the Great Salt Lake and it was checked only by the appearance of flocks of gulls, which devoured the crickets and saved the crops after all other means had failed. The Sea Gull Monument on Temple Square in Salt Lake City is dedicated to the species, "in grateful remembrance of the mercy of God to the Mormon pioneers." In a similar 1947 incident, gulls destroyed a plague of caterpillars in Scotland. (*See also* **boll weevil**.)

Gullah.   The American dialect called *Gullah*, with some five thousand African terms in it, takes its name either from *Ngola* ("Angola") or from the West African Gola tribe. It is spoken on the Sea Islands and along the South Carolina-Georgia coast.

the Gum Nebula.   The name of this star, which may have shone as bright as the full moon 11,000 years ago, has nothing whatever to do with chewing gum. It is named for Australian astronomer Colin Gum, its discoverer in 1950.

gumption. Born as a Scottish word, first recorded in 1719 and meaning "common sense, mother wit, shrewdness," *gumption* changed in meaning after emigrating to America, coming to mean determination, spirit, courage. Perhaps the hard cider called *gumption* known here during the early 19th century, and possibly before, gave the word this sense because of the spirit and courage it gave to those who drank it.

gum up the works. The expression *gum up the works* possibly derives from our national gum-chewing habit. The phrase became popular at the turn of the century and may refer to youngsters who went into the woods on gumming expeditions and got covered hair to foot with tree resin, which their parents had to work for hours to remove. But clogged machines in factories were referred to as *gummed up* as early as 1889, in reference to gummy substances such as inspissated oil clogging or stiffening them. It seems more likely that our expression for throwing a project into confusion derives from clogged machines (or works) than from youngsters daubed with gum.

gun. *Gun* doesn't derive from the echo of its sound, as has been suggested. *Gunnr* and *hildr* meant "war" and "battle" in Icelandic, so the Scandinavian female name Gunhildr was a favorite among missile-throwers in the Middle Ages as a pet name for their ballistic devices. It is also possible that some anonymous soldier named a specific ballista *Gunhildr* for his sweetheart, the name gaining currency in this way. Whatever the case, we find *Gunhildr* recorded before 1309 in England, where it was shortened to *gunne*, and then *gun*, the last designation transferred to firearms after the cannon was invented. A "large ballista called Lady *Gunhilda*," a mechanized catapult used to hurl huge stones and balls of fire at troops, is listed in a weapons inventory made at Windsor Castle in 1330. This particular ballista, its name derived from the Scandinavian, must have been around for a number of years and may even have been the particular Gunhilda abbreviated to *gunne* some years before.

gunboat diplomacy. Not until 1927 is there a printed reference to *gunboat diplomacy*, which might translate as "getting one's way by force," but the expression may date back to 1841, when American ships exacted trade concessions from the Chinese by sending gunboats to Canton, after the British had done the same in the First Opium War. *Gunboat* itself dates back to 1793. The expression has, however, long been associated with President Theodore Roosevelt's Latin American policy.

gung ho. *Gung ho* means "work together" in Chinese, but after Carlson's Raiders, the 2nd Marine Raider Division commanded by Lt. Colonel Evans F. Carlson, a veteran of the China campaign, adopted the expression as their slogan in World War II, it took on a different meaning. Carlson's Raiders were a remarkably brave, loyal, and enthusiastic band, so *gung ho* came to describe these qualities. Yet when noncombat marines and soldiers displayed the same enthusiasm in picayune matters such as white-glove inspections, *gung ho* was disparagingly applied to them, resulting in its present meaning of overzealousness.

gun moll. This term arose from the mistaken belief that the female accomplices of criminals carried their guns for them. The *gun* in the term does not refer to a firearm but derives from the Yiddish *goniff*, "a thief," and *moll* is 18th-century slang for a woman. A *gun moll* in the 1920s was originally a female pickpocket, before newspaper reporters mistakenly took to calling any racketeer's girl a *gun moll*.

gunnysack. Still another word that was brought back from India by the British, *gunnysack* derives from the Hindi *goni*, for the coarse hemp fabric from which the sacks are fashioned.

gunsel. *Gunsel*, for "a cheap thief or criminal," is another word reinforced by "gun" in the mind but which really has nothing to do with any weapon. *Gunsel* derives from either the German *ganzel* or the Yiddish *gantzel*, both meaning a gosling. At the beginning or this century prisoners and hoboes called young, inexperienced boys, especially homosexuals, *gunsels*. From constant underworld use, where it later meant a sly, sneaky person, it was adopted generally as a term for a "run-of-the-mob," usually second-rate criminal. *Cannon*, for a male pickpocket, has a similar roundabout derivation. As far back as 1840 a pickpocket was called a *gun*, from the Yiddish *ganov*, "thief"; *cannon* was simply an elegant variation on this word adopted by criminals in about 1910. Thus the popular belief that a male pickpocket is so named because he carries a gun or cannon is all wrong—in fact, pickpockets don't usually carry guns.

guppy. The *guppy*, or "rainbow fish" (*Lebistes reticulatus*), is also called *the millions fish*. It takes its name from R. J. Lechmere Guppy, once president of the Scientific Association of Trinidad, who presented the British Museum with specimens of the species in the late 19th century. A namesake of the guppy is the little *guppy submarine*, developed toward the end of World War II, but the sub's name is also an acronym, the first four letters standing for "greater underwater propulsion power."

gusset. (*See* **all gussied up**.)

Gutenberg Bible. The first printed Bible, long erroneously thought to be the first book to be printed from movable type in the Western world, is named for

Johannes Gutenberg (ca. 1398-1468), the German printer generally believed to be the inventor of movable type. Few great men of relatively modern times have left such meager records of their lives as Gutenberg. No likeness exists of him, and his life is veiled in obscurity. Gutenberg may have adopted his mother's maiden name, for his father's surname appears to have been Gensfleisch. It is known that the goldsmith Johann Fust loaned the printer money to establish his press in Mainz, which Gutenberg lost to him in 1455 when he failed to repay the loan. But no book extant bears Gutenberg's name as its printer and though he is still regarded as a likely candidate, he may not have invented printing in the West or even printed the *Gutenberg Bible* (1450).

guts. *Guts* has been an Americanism for courage since about 1880 and is still much heard, though *balls* is used more among men. *Grit, spunk,* and *gumption* are early synonyms rarely heard today.

guy. American expressions often vary greatly in meaning from their identical British cousins. *A regular guy* to many Englishmen means "a thoroughly grotesque person," not "a decent chap" at all. The difference is not as pronounced as in the past, but the American meaning still has a strange ring to British ears. For the English, *guy* owes its origin to the grotesque effigies of Guy Fawkes, a leader of the infamous Gunpowder Plot, which are carried through the streets of England and burnt in bonfires on November 5, *Guy Fawkes Day.* All of the festivities through the years probably mellowed the meaning of the word to include both good and bad *guys.* But only in America, far removed from the Gunpowder Plot in distance as well as time, is *guy* widely used for any "chap" or "fellow," no ridicule intended. In England to this day a *guy* remains a ridiculous-looking person. Since the 1970s *guys* in America has been used in referring to women as well as men, especially in mixed groups of men and women (i.e., "Do you guys want to come over?").

guyot. A *guyot* is a flat-topped submarine mountain or seamount rising above the deep-sea floor. It is named after American geologist Arnold Guyot (1807-84).

gymnast; gymnasium; gymnite. Greek atheletes were required to train in the nude to allow their bodies maximum freedom of movement. The famous Olympic track meets were run in the nude, wrestlers competed naked, and all exercises were performed without clothes. Thus the Greek word *gymnazo,* "to train naked," gives us the words *gymnast* (literally someone in the nude exercising), and *gymnasium,* a place where naked exercises are done! The ancient Greeks considered the physical training of boys and young men as essential as mental training, and one of the best gymnasiums in Athens was in Plato's Academy. An amusing sidelight on all this nudity is the mineral *gymnite,* a hydrated silicate of magnesium, so named because it is found at Bare Hills, Maryland.

gyp. According to the popular etymology, *to gyp,* "to cheat," derives from the name of the much maligned gypsies, who got *their* name because 16th-century Englishmen erroneously assumed that they hailed from Egypt. The *O.E.D.,* however, doesn't dishonor the Romany people, deriving gyp from *gee-up,* which meant "to treat roughly" in some localities of England. The *gippo* theory also saves face for the gypsies. A *gippo,* later shortened to *gyp,* was a short jacket worn by the valets of Oxford undergraduates in the 17th century. The word *gyp* this theory holds, was eventually applied to the servants themselves, who were often cheats and thieves.

H

H. *H* can be traced back, through the Roman and Greek alphabets, to the Phoenician alphabet, where the letter was called *Heth* and represented a fence, having two crossbars instead of one: �. The reason Dr. Johnson made his famous remark "I'd rather dine with Jack Ketch [the public hangman] than Jack Wilkes" is seldom told. John Wilkes had written a comic review of Johnson's *Dictionary* in which he addressed the great man's pronouncement that "The letter 'h' seldom, perhaps never, begins any but the first syllable." Wilkes wrote: "The author of this observation must be a man of quick apprehension and of a most comprehensive genius," going on in the same fashion for several paragraphs. Johnson never forgave him.

haberdasher. A 17th-century source derives *haberdasher*, a dealer in men's furnishings such as shirts and ties, from the German *Hab' Ihr das?*, "Have you that?", which such shopkeepers asked when waiting on a customer. Another possibility is the Old French *hapirtus*, "a fur dealer," for haberdashers did originally carry fur hats along with other small wares and notions. We only know surely that *haberdasher* has been part of the language for almost seven centuries.

hack. (*See* **grubstreet hack.**)

hack it. (*See* **can't cut the mustard.**)

Hadassah. The benevolent Jewish women's organization takes its name from the Hebrew name of Queen Esther, mentioned in the Old Testament, Esther 2:7.

ha-ha. Here is an exclamation that became a word, one of the most peculiar of derivations. A *ha-ha* is "an obstacle interrupting one's way sharply and disagreeably, a ditch behind an opening in a wall at the bottom of an alley or walk." It is used in English gardens as a boundary that doesn't interrupt the view from inside, and can't be seen from the outside until you come very close to it; it is in effect a sunken fence, the inner side of the ditch perpendicular and faced with stone, while the outer side is turfed and sloping. When these ditches, or fosses, were first used extensively in the 17th century, etymologists tell us, people out for a stroll in the country were frequently surprised to find a sudden check to their walk. Their exclamations of "ha-ha!," "ah-hah!," or "hah-hah!" in expressing their surprise became the name of the ditch or sunken fence.

hail fellow well met. The exclamation of welcome or greeting, *hail*, goes back over a thousand years, as in the Anglo-Saxon expression *wes hal*, "may you be in good health." *Hail fellow well met*, for "a jovial, convivial person, a good mixer," is one of the longest phrases treated as a descriptive word in English and is recorded in print as early as 1550. No doubt it is older still and it possibly originated as a greeting: "Hail, fellow! Well met!" Today the exclamation *Well met!* is sometimes, though rarely, used to mean "Glad I met you!"

hairbreadth escape. A very narrow escape; just how narrow is shown by the old English formal unit of measurement called the hairbreadth, the forty-eighth part of an inch, or twelfth part of a line. The measurement is said to have been used by the Jews in ancient times. *Hairbreadth*, the breadth or diameter of a hair, is recorded as early as the 15th century, but Shakespeare appears to have coined the phrase *hairbreadth escape* in *Othello*, where his leading character speaks of the "hair-breadth 'scapes" he has experienced throughout his life. *Hairbreadth* is often corrupted to *hair's breadth* in everyday speech and has indeed been said this way since the 16th century. Every *hair's breadth Harry*, anyone who is always having narrow escapes, honors an old comic strip hero of that name.

hair of the dog that bit you. Like cures like, *similia similibus curantur*, the Romans believed, like many ancient peoples before them, and they commonly bound hairs of a dog that had bitten someone to that person's wound in order to make it heal better—even if the dog was rabid. The treatment was recommended for centuries by serious medical books, about the only change until medieval times being that *burnt* hair of the dog that bit you was prescribed. By then it was also believed that the best cure for a hangover was a drink of the same poison that "stifflicated" you the night before, and the old proverb *a hair of the dog that bit you* applied to this practice. The first mention of the phrase in reference to hangovers is in John Heywood's *Proverbs* (1546): "I pray thee leat me and my felow have a heare of the dog that bote us last night—and bitten were we both to the braine aright."

hair-raising. This Americanism came into the language too late, about 1910, for it to be associated with Indians or Indian hunters taking scalps. There is no evidence that horrible accounts of Indians or whites "lifting or raising hair" inspired the synonym for "frightening." Most likely the term is a streamlining of the old expression *to make one's hair stand on end*.

hairy. *Hairy*, as slang for unpleasant or rough, seems to be of Army origin, from about 1935, when a *hairy patrol* was an unpleasant one that met with resistance. Its origin is unknown, but the word may have something to do with *to make one's hair stand on end* and "scary." Another possibility, a longshot, is the English expression *hairy at the heel*, common in the late 19th century. A horse with hair about the heels or fetlocks was an underbred one, so the expression was used figuratively for an ill-bred, bad-mannered, thoroughly unpleasant person, as was *hairy*.

hairy quadruped. There have been many variations on Charles Darwin's description of humankind's common ancestor in *The Descent of Man* (1871), but his words were: "A hairy quadruped, furnished with a tail and pointed ears, probably arboreal in habits."

halcyon days. A storm killed her mortal husband and the heartbroken goddess Alcyone, daughter of Aeolus, the wind god of Greek legend, drowned herself in the sea. Punishing the suicide, the angry gods turned both Alcyone and her husband Ceyx into birds later known as *halcyons*, or kingfishers as we call them today. Yet the goddess' father took pity on the couple and decreed that during the halcyon's breeding season, the seven days before and the seven days after the shortest day of the year, the sea would always be perfectly calm and unruffled. Thus, during the fourteen days, at about the time of the winter solstice, the halcyons could sit on their nests, which floated securely on the tranquil water, borne by currents across the world, hatching their eggs. This legend was widely believed through Roman times, when Alcyone's name became Halcyone, and well into the 15th century. The halcyon days had an actual place on ancient calendars, and the legend inspired much poetry. Eventually, the legend turned the phrase *halcyon days* into not only windless days of peace and calm but any time of peace, serenity, and rejoicing.

haler. This small Czechoslovakian coin was first minted in the German town of Hall, Swabia, West Germany, from which it takes its name.

half-baked. Anything or anyone raw, incomplete, or not thoroughgoing has been called *half-baked* since at least the early 17th century, the allusion being to under-cooked baked goods. Some say, however, that the expression *half-baked* as applied to half-witted, uncultured persons is of American origin. This seems unlikely, for although the term is first recorded here in the mid-19th century, an old Cornish proverb cited in 1868 defines a fool as "only half-baked; put in with the bread and taken out with the cakes."

half-seas over. Half-seas over indicates a person quite drunk but not yet under the table. British in origin and dating back to the late 17th century, the phrase probably originated in the resemblance of a drunk's stagger to that of a man walking on the deck of a storm-battered ship, one side heeled over in the sea. Or perhaps the expression is a corruption of *op-zee-zober* ("oversea beer"), a strong, heady beer imported from Holland in the 17th century. The earlier phrase *halfway across the sea* for a drunk suggests the former theory, however.

half-wit. Humorists take note that *half-wit* was first used in English to mean an ineffectual writer of humor, "a dealer in poor witicisms," someone who wasn't funny half of the time. Wrote John Dryden in *All For Love* (1678), the first recorded use of the term: "Halfwits are fleas;/ so little and so light,/ We scarce could know they live,/ but that they bite." It wasn't until nearly a century had passed (1755) that *half-wit* was applied to anyone who hasn't all his wits.

halibut. Five hundred years ago every flatfish from the flounder to the skate was called a *butt*, even the largest of the flounders, *Hippoglossus hippoglossus*. The most esteemed was *Hippoglossus*, which was only eaten on Church holy days and became known as the *holy butt*. This fish is no longer reserved for holy days, of course, but it is still known as the *halibut*, or "holy flounder."

hallelujah. According to an Italian folktale the word *hallelujah* was born when three Roman legionnaires—a Roman, a Piedmontese from northern Italy, and a German—were guarding Christ's body in the sepulchre after His crucifixion. When Christ rose from the dead the Roman exclaimed *Ha!*, the Piedmont man cried *L'e lii!* ("It's him!"), and the German shouted *Ja!*—which gave us *Hallelujah*. But, as good as the story is, *hallelujah* derives from the Hebrew *hallelu-yah*, "praise ye Jahveh."

Halley's comet. *Halley's comet*, the first comet whose return was accurately predicted, was observed by English astronomer Edmund Halley in 1692, when he correctly estimated its reappearance in 1758, sixteen years after his death, as it turned out. Halley based his calculations on Newton's theory; a long-time friend of the great scientist, he had paid for the initial printing of Newton's *Principia*, collaborating on the section dealing with comets. Over his eighty-six-year lifetime Halley made a number of important discoveries, which resulted in his appointment as astronomer royal in 1720. The comet that blazons his name across the sky last appeared in 1986.

hallmark. *Hallmarks*, "marks of excellence on products," owe their origin to the official stamp of the Goldsmiths' Company of London, which in 1300 was ordered by Edward I to stamp all gold and silver with such a mark to indicate its purity. They were called *hallmarks* because the stamping was done at Goldsmiths's Hall in London.

ham. Actors prefer to think that this word derives from the old theatrical use of ham fat to remove blackface makeup—actors were thus called *hamfatters*, or *hams*. Many scholars lean to this theory, but *ham* in the sense of an amateur actor or a tenth-rate actor who outrageously overplays his scenes has enough folk etymologies to make a one-act play. Since none really seems capable of absolute proof, I'll simply list three: 1) Ham derives from the Cockney slang *hamateur*, for "amateur actor." (Unlikely, as the term *ham* in this sense is American from about 1880.) 2) The word structure of *amateur* itself suggested *ham*. (A good possibility, but why did it wait so long to suggest itself?) 3) It comes from the role of *Hamlet*, which actors frequently misperformed. (Another good possibility, but, if so, *ham* should have been with us since Shakespeare's time.) *Ham* for one of the rear quarters of a hog, or its meat, derives from Old English *hamm* for the bend of the knee.

Hamal. The name of the star *Hamal* in the constellation *Aries* (the ram) is an example of a word that comes to us from ancient Sumerian, which flourished over five thousand years ago and dates back even further than that. *Hamal* derives from the Arabic *al-Hamal*, "the full-grown lamb," which is a modified form of the Sumerian *mul LU-LIM*, which means "the constellation of the lamb." Thus fragments of the Sumerian survive, as they do in the names of a few other stars.

hamburger. Most authorities say that the hamburger first appeared in the U.S. in 1884 under the name of *Hamburg steak*, after the place of its origin, Hamburg, Germany. But the town of Hamburg, New York persistently claims that America's favorite quick food was invented there in the summer of 1885 and named for the burger's birthplace. According to this tale, its inventors were Charles and Frank Menches from Ohio, vendors who ran out of pork at their concession at the Erie County Fair. Since the first recorded use of *hamburger* seems to have been in 1902, according to the *O.E.D.*, Hamburg, New York could be the source. *White Castles, McDonalds* and *Wimpeyburgers* (for the Popeye comic-strip character who ate prodigious amounts of them) are synonyms for hamburgers. (*See* **frankfurter.**)

Hamiltonianism. U.S. founding father and statesman Alexander Hamilton (1757-1804), in his essentially conservative political philosophy, advocated a strong central government and protective tariffs. A *Hamiltonian* is one who supports this doctrine of *Hamiltonianism*, the word loosely describing a levelheaded political conservative.

hamlet. The English term *ham*, for "a small village," survives in place names like *Shoreham, Oakham,* and *Hamton. Hamlet*, for a small village, is simply a diminutive of *ham*, and has been part of the language since medieval times.

Hamlet-like. Someone who cannot make up his mind is often called *Hamlet-like*, after Shakespeare's tragic character. The expression is used too loosely, however, and should be reserved for those indecisive because—like Hamlet—they are faced with impossibly difficult choices.

hammer and tongs. "To go at it *hammer and tongs*" means to literally or figuratively fight with all one's resources with no hold barred, with might and main. The blacksmith has become a rarity and a curiosity, but this 17th-century expression alluding to his art lives on. It refers of course to the brawny smitty taking red-hot metal from the forge with his long-handled pincers, or tongs, and vigorously beating it into shape on the anvil with his hammer.

to hamstring someone. The part of the leg behind the knee was once called the *ham* in English and the tendons there were given the name *ham string*, a designation still used today. To cut the hamstrings was to cripple or disable someone, which gives us the expression *to hamstring* "to cripple, or destroy the activity or efficiency of," an expression first recorded by John Milton in 1641.

handbook. Dr. Richard French, the philologist who first suggested the great *Oxford English Dictionary* in 1857, called *handbook* "an ugly unnecessary word . . . scarcely . . . ten or fifteen years old," a very poor substitute for the Latin "manual." Actually, the handy *handbook* had reentered the language after a long absence. It dated back to the Anglo-Saxon *handboc*, used before Alfred the Great.

hand of glory. This is an example of a new custom or superstition created by an etymological error. *A hand of glory* was originally a charm made of a mandrake root, which was believed, among other things, to double one's money when put beside it overnight. *Hand of glory* was a translation of the French *main de gloire*, meaning exactly the same, but the French expression was a corruption "by popular etymology" of what had originally been the Old French for *mandragore*, "mandrake." Thus, when the term came into English early in the 18th century, people couldn't help but think that the charm consisted of a human hand. This led to a completely new superstition due to the deformation of the word. By 1816 we find a writer explaining that *the hand of glory* "is a hand cut off from a dead man, as has been hanged for murther, and dried very nice in the smoke of juniper wood." Such charms made from the hands of executed criminals were said to help one sleep, that is, lull one into a dead sleep, among other things.

hand over fist. Seamen reached the rigging on old sailing ships by climbing hand over hand up a thick rope—a skill sailors prided themselves on—and when sails were hoisted, the same *hand over hand* technique prevailed, just as it did when ropes or even fish were hauled in. American seamen in the 19th century changed this expression to the more descriptive *hand over fist*, which shows one fist clenching a rope and a loose hand passing over it to make another fist on the rope, etc. The rapid ascent on the ropes and the act of hauling in nets soon suggested someone rising rapidly in the business world and hauling in money, which is what we still mean when we say someone is making money *hand over fist*.

hand to mouth. One of the earliest uses of this phrase best explains it: "Hungry folkes that are fed from hand to mouth." The expression arose in the 16th century, when famines in which thousands of people starved to death were frequent for the first time in England, usually occurring with the failure of grain crops. People living under such conditions had no choice but to cram a piece of bread into their mouths as soon as they got it in their hands, so great was their hunger; there was no thought or possibility of saving for the future. Later, a *hand to mouth existence* came to describe a life of poverty in general, and even, especially among those who had never lived *hand to mouth*, a thriftless, improvident life.

handyman. *Handy*, "ready or clever with the hands, dextrous," dates back to the early 17th century, but the term *handyman*, for a person useful for all kinds of odd jobs, doesn't appear in print for almost two hundred years more. *Handywright* is an older synonym rarely, if ever, used today.

to hang by a thin thread. The flatterer Damocles annoyed Dionysus the Elder of Syracuse with his constant references to the ruler's great power and consequent happiness. Deciding to teach the sycophant the real perils of power, he invited Damocles to a magnificent banquet, surrounding him with luxuries only a king could afford. Damocles enjoyed the feast until he happened to glance up and see a sharp sword suspended by a single thin thread pointing directly at his head, after which he lay there afraid to eat, speak, or move. The moral was "Uneasy lies the head that wears a crown"—that there are always threats of danger, fears, and worries that prevent the powerful from fully enjoying their power, the sword of Damocles symbolizing these fears. From this fifth-century story, recounted by both Cicero and Horace, comes our expression *to hang by a thin thread*, to be subject to imminent danger.

hangdog look. It's said that hunting dogs living in the great English country houses of the past, eating scraps tossed from the table and sleeping as close to the fire as they could get, were kept orderly by special handlers who broke up dogfights, whipped their charges, and even hanged incorrigible dogs. Shakespeare, no dog lover, does refer to the hanging of dogs five times in his plays, but I've been unable to find any reliable record of actual cases of a dog hanging, though there are other cases of animals tried and executed by law (*see* E.P. Evans, *The Criminal Prosecution and Capital Punishment of Animals*, 1906). Nevertheless, since the late 17th century anyone with a cringing, abject appearance, or a base, sneaky demeanor has been said to have a *hangdog look*. Whether real or the product of someone's imagination, the allusion was originally to a despicable, degraded person fit only to hang a dog, or to be hanged like a dog. Nowadays a *hangdog look* has almost entirely lost its meaning of contemptible and sneaky and generally describes someone browbeaten, defeated, intimidated, or abject—someone who looks a little like a bloodhound.

hanged, drawn, and quartered. At first this punishment for high treason and other crimes in England was called *drawn, hanged, and quartered*—that is, the criminal sentenced to death was drawn (dragged) through the streets behind a horse to the gallows, hanged, and then his head was cut off and his body torn into four pieces, often by horses. In the 15th century a further barbaric penalty was added and *drawn, hanged, and quartered* became *hanged, drawn, and quartered*. In this case the victim was hanged and drawn (eviscerated) before he was torn to pieces. Often he was only partially hanged, his body cut down, and his "bowels burnt before his face." There was even a legal term in Latin for the perversion: *detrahatur* ("drawn, dragged"), *suspendatur* ("hanged"), *devaletur* ("disemboweled"), *decolleter et decapitetur* ("beheaded and quartered").

hanged high as Haman. The biblical Haman, King Ahasuerus's counselor, built a "fifty cubits high" gallows on which he planned to hang Mordecai and other Jews. But Esther turned the king against him and he was hanged on his own gallows, giving Ahasuerus pleasure, Mordecai great relief, and posterity the expression *hanged high as Haman*, "destroyed by one's own machinations."

hanging out. Present-day slang for a group of people congregating at a place, usually on a regular basis, *hanging out*, dates back to the early 19th century, when it was first used in the British underworld. *Partridge* says the expression derives from "the ancient custom of hanging out signs" indicating that one resided at a certain place. *Hangout*, a place where people congregate, derives from the verb.

hangman's wages.

For half of thirteen-pence ha'penny wages
I would have cleared all the town cages . . .
　　　　—The Hangman's Last Will and Testament

This term is referred to occasionally in English literature from the late 17th to early 19th century. It means thirteen pence and a halfpenny, which was the execution fee (a Scottish mark) set by James I—one shilling for the work and three halfpence for the rope. The nobility were expected to give the executioner up to 10 pounds for beheading them. As time went on, of course, hangmen and headsmen raised their prices like everyone else.

hangnail. The Anglo-Saxon word *angnaegl* meant "a painful corn on the foot," deriving from *ang*, "pain," and *naegel*, "nail," a hard corn resembling the head of a nail. Later, its meaning was extended to include a painful corn on the finger as well, or anywhere on the skin for that matter. This word, eventually pronounced *angnail*, appropriately defined a painful corn, but through mispronunciation an "h" was added to it. *Hangnail* served only as the term for a painful corn or swelling until someone in the early 17th century realized that it perfectly described the small strip of skin that sometimes tears away and hangs down from the fingernail, causing considerable pain. The mispronunciation that was superfluous in the old meaning of the word has become essential to the new meaning.

hang on by the eyelashes. As late as this expression came into the language—it is traced by *Partridge* to 1860—we still don't know who or what is responsible for it. Two centuries earlier something *hung by the eyelids* was something in a state of suspense, but the other phrase, used literally or figuratively, means to hang on precariously, to be barely able to hang on to the most meager of holds. As with the much older expression *hang on by the skin of one's teeth*, no real situation inspired the imaginative description.

hang out your shingle. To become a doctor or lawyer, among other professions. The Americanism comes from pioneer days, when doctors did use shingles for their signs.

hanky-panky. A synonym for trickery, *hanky-panky* may have been coined, with the help of reduplication, from the magician's handkerchief, or *hanky*, under which so many things have mysteriously appeared and disappeared through clever sleight of hand. Probably related to *hocus pocus*, it is first recorded in *Punch* (1841).

Hansard. What the *Congressional Record* is to the United States Congress, the *Hansard* is to the British Houses of Parliament. A *Hansard* is the official printed report of proceedings in Parliament, the name in honor of Luke Hansard (1752-1828) and his family after him, private printers who published the reports from 1774 until 1889. Today the proceedings are recorded by the government, but the reports still bear the printing firm's name.

hansom. If Joseph Aloysius Hansom invented the hansom cab, once the most popular of horse-drawn carriages—"the gondolas of London," as Disraeli called them—he certainly gained nothing from his invention. Most word authorities vouch for Hansom, but one source claims that Edward Bird invented the vehicle, presenting the idea gratis to his brother-in-law, Edward Welch, a partner in Hansom's Birmingham architectural firm. Hansom (1803-82) was an English architect specializing in churches and public buildings. He did patent the cab—possibly as Bird's Patent Safety Cab—but the financial arrangement he made upon selling his patent rights proved disastrous. Promised ten thousand pounds, Hansom received, according to conflicting accounts, either nothing or a mere three hundred pounds for his patent. *Hansom cabs*, however, made millions for their manufacturers. The low, two-wheeled covered carriage, with the driver's seat above it in the back, was noted for its maneuverability and safety features as well as its privacy and unobstructed view for passengers. Soon after its appearance in 1834, it became the most popular cab in London and around the world. The last hansom disappeared from London in 1944, but a few are still available for hire in New York's Central Park.

happy as a clam at high tide. Clams are usually dug at low tide, so a clam might be happy indeed at high tide. This expression is an Americanism, first noted in 1834.

happy hunting grounds. Perhaps American Indians invented this synonym for heaven, but it seems more like the work of an author like Washington Irving, who first recorded it in one of his books (1837).

happy landin' with Landon. The Republicans coined this campaign slogan for Alfred M. Landon in 1936, when he ran against Franklin D. Roosevelt for president. It was more like a crash landing than a "happy landin," Landon suffering one of the most devastating defeats in American political history.

hara-kiri. The word isn't spelled *harikiri* or *hari kari* and doesn't mean "happy dispatch," as many people believe. Formed from the Japanese *hara*, "belly," and *kiri*, "to cut," *hara-kiri* literally means "belly cutting." It is, of course, the Japanese method of suicide by disemboweling, practiced especially when honor is lost, and is said to have been first turned to by Tametomo, brother of ex-Emperor Sutoku, in the 12th century, after he suffered a devastating military defeat. *Hara kiri*, which *Mencken* also gives as the name of a cocktail, was one of the first Japanese words to come into English, introduced shortly after "tycoon" in 1856. *Jujitsu, geisha, rickshaw, kimono, soybean, banzai, kamikaze*, and other words were to follow. *Hara-kiri* is seldom used by the Japanese, who find it vulgar and offensive.

harass. Though it means inflicting any kind of unpleasantness today, to *harass* originally had a much stronger meaning, as its derivation shows. *Harass* derives from the Old French verb *harer*, meaning "to set a dog on," and came into English early in the 17th century.

harbinger of spring. The robins flying north or the swallows returning to Capistrano are *harbingers*: messengers who announce that spring is coming. It's hard to imagine this expression having its roots in war, but it does. *Harbinger* derives from the Old High German *hari*, "an army," and *bergan*, "to lodge." In English it was first spelt *herbergeour* and meant one who provides or obtains lodgings for the military. Later the word changed in meaning, describing someone sent ahead to obtain lodging for a party of travelers, and finally it came to mean someone who goes forth in advance to announce the coming of travelers or things—like the swallow, robin, and other *harbingers of spring*.

hard-boiled. A *boiled* or *boiled shirt* was, on the American frontier, a shirt boiled in water, in contrast to one newly washed in cold water. Later the term came to mean a stiff or hard-starched white shirt. By 1886 we find Mark Twain using the term *hard boiled*, probably suggested by a hard-boiled shirt, for "a rigid narrow person," and by 1898 *hard-boiled* was being used to mean hard-headed and heartless. Later, in 1919, New York City saloon keeper Jack Doyle coined the similar expression a *hard-boiled egg*, for "a heartless person."

hard hat. *Hard hat* used to be a designation for a man who wore a derby hat, especially Eastern bankers and businessmen during the 1880s. A century later, in the late 1960s, it came to mean a construction worker, because of the metal or plastic safety helmets such workers wear. Because these *hard hats* often clashed with antiwar demonstrators during the early 1970s and supported the war in Vietnam, the term *hard hat* also came to mean a political conservative.

hard-on; heart-on; horny. The taboo slang term for an erection is often slurred in speech out of embarrassment, so that it is difficult to tell if the first word is pronounced *hard* or *heart*. Both words are actually used interchangeably in the expression, *hard* obviously referring to the erect penis and *heart* perhaps referring to the shape of the glans of the *membrum virile*. The term goes back only to about 1860 and was preceded in use by the expression *to have the horn*, which gives us the slang *horny*: lustful, sexually aroused.

hardtack. A century ago, *tack* meant food of any kind. Sailors took to calling hard biscuit—biscuit that was hard and lasted through long voyages in rough weather—*hard tack*, or what we'd more often call *dog biscuits* today.

hard up. When the weather was bad at sea *Hard up the helm!* was the order given and the tiller had to be put up as far as possible to the windward in order to turn the ship's head away from the wind. These words came to mean "to weather the storm as best you can" and then took on the meaning of being short of money or some other necessity—that is, the condition of someone weathering a "storm."

harem. Used by the Greeks before any Arabian, and called a *gynaeceum* by them, the *harem* does take its name from the Arabian *harim*, "sacred or forbidden place." *Harem* first meant the section of a house in which the wives and concubines of a Muslim lived and then was applied to the women themselves.

harlot. William the Conqueror, known in history as the Bastard, *was* the result of a union between Arlette or Herleva, the attractive daughter of the tanner Falbert of Falaise, and Robert le Diable, duke of Normandy—perhaps even, as the old tale says, when Robert the Devil came cantering by, saw Arlette kneeling naked washing her clothes and dismounted from his horse. But Arlette's name doesn't give us the word *harlot*, which was born long before her illegitimate son and most probably derives from the old German *hari*, "army," and *lot*, "loiterer," meaning "an army camp follower." *Harlot* first signified a person of low birth and applied to both men and women before taking on its present meaning of a female prostitute.

harmonica. (*See* **stormonter**.)

harp. Long synonymous for an Irishman, this derogatory expression stems from the use of the harp as the national symbol of Ireland. One of many legends about the word's origin says that an early King David of Ireland took the harp of the psalmist as his badge. Another story says the Irish were so called because in days past they were often gamblers who flipped coins, calling "harp!" for tails because the shilling had a harp engraved on one side. The musical instrument called a *harp* takes its name from the Old English *hearpe* meaning the same. (*See* **dago; kike; wasp; welch**.)

Harpers Ferry, West Virginia. This beautiful little town in easternmost West Virginia on the bluffs at the confluence of the Potomac and Shenandoah rivers is famous in American history because the old fanatic abolitionist John Brown was captured and hanged there just before the Civil War. The town takes its name from one Robert Harper, who established a ferry at the site in 1747.

harridan. The French *haridelle* means a worn-out wreck of a horse. From this word comes the English *harridan,* "a haggard, disreputable old woman, a vicious or violent old hag."

Harriet Lane. *Harriet Lane* is a merchant-marine term for Australian canned meat, because it supposedly resembled the chopped-up body of this girl, murdered by a man named Wainwright in about 1875.

Harvard beets. *Harvard beets,* often called pickled beets, are made from sliced beets cooked in sugar, cornstarch, vinegar, and water. There is no record that the dish was invented at Harvard University, but it is said that the unknown chef who did noticed the resemblance in color of the deep red beets to the crimson jersies of the then vaunted Harvard football team. Harvard, the first institution of higher learning in North America, bears the name of John Harvard (1607-38), an English minister who lived for a time in Charlestown, Massachusetts, and later willed the fledgling university half his estate and his library of over four hundred books. Cambridge, Massachusetts, where Harvard is located, was named for England's Cambridge University.

harvest. The harvest was so important in ancient times that the word *haerfest,* "or harvest," became the Old English term for autumn as well as for the gathering in of crops. This usage prevailed well into the tenth century, when harvest began to be used exclusively to mean the gathering in of wheat (called "corn" in England) and finally crops in general.

a Harvey Smith. Here is a man whose name means "the finger," or, anyway, two fingers, meaning the same. Harvey Smith, a well-known British show-jumper, saw his name become better known after he "was alleged to have raised two fingers" at the judge of a 1971 competition. *A Harvey Smith* came to mean "the obscene gesture" in English, and still does, though, of course, the gesture dates back much further than Mr. Smith, and will almost certainly last longer than this probably ephemeral, eponymous word.

hash. Horne Tooke's *Diversions of Purley* (1786) derived *hash* from the Persian *ash,* or stew. An ingenious derivation, but completely wrong, as *hash* comes from the French *hacher,* "to cut up," which also gives us the word *hatchet.* As a noun meaning the common meat dish, *hash* is first recorded in Samuel Pepys' *Diary* (13 Jan. 1663): "I had . . . at first course a hash of rabbits, a lamb."

haul over the coals. Heresy in medieval times was determined not by a jury trial but by ordeal by fire. Accused persons were hauled or dragged over the coals of a slow fire and those who burned to death were considered guilty of departing from the teachings of the church; those who survived were pronounced innocent. From

this and similar barbarous practices in 15th- and 16th-century England, comes the expression *to haul over the coals,* for "a severe reprimand or censure."

Haussmannization. *Haussmannization* is frequently heard today in connection with the blight and plight of cities around the world. To *Haussmannize* means to remodel a city along beautiful lines and celebrates Baron Georges Eugène Haussmann (1809-91), who administered a face-lifting to Paris, starting in the middle of the 19th century. While Prefect of Paris, Haussmann completely remodeled the city. He laid out the Bois de Boulogne and other parks; constructed new streets and widened old ones; instituted a new water supply and sewer system; created wide, open spaces and vistas; and built new bridges, railroad stations, and numerous public buildings. These and many other improvements required expenses and loans that resulted in a public debt of hundreds of millions and eventually led to Haussmann's dismissal in 1870, seventeen years after he had begun his plan. Interestingly, Haussmann was trained not as an architect but as a financier. The *Boulevard Haussmann* also bears his name.

to have a bear by the tail. This is another of those colorful expressions (*see* **a bear for work**) that arose in America during the first half of the 19th century. *To have a bear by the tail* is to be in a bad situation—you're in trouble whether you hold on or let go!

have an oar in another's boat. (*See* **all in the same boat.**)

to have at one's fingertips. To have thorough familiarity or knowledge of a subject. The phrase isn't recorded until 1870 in America, but it is obviously an elaboration of the much earlier *to have at one's fingers' ends,* which is recorded in England in 1553 as a familiar saying.

havelock. Sir Henry Havelock (1795-1857) was rarely in fashion—it took him twenty-three years to be promoted to captain, for example—but this most British of British soldiers did eventually do well. Havelock, an evangelist as well as a soldier, served over thirty-four years with the British Army in India, taking only one leave home in all that time. Known as "the Saint" to his men for his habit of trying to convert everyone under his command to temperance and moderate ways, he was indeed among the fussiest and most tiresome of men. But as to his military ability and bravery there is no doubt. Havelock led his troops to many victories during the Sepoy Rebellion (1857) and is remembered for his recapture of Cawnpore and his stand at Lucknow until reinforcements arrived. The general died of dysentery brought on by the arduous Lucknow defense. The *havelock,* or covering, that he had devised for his "Ironsides" brigade wasn't his invention; similar helmet coverings had been used since the Crusades. This trademark of the French Foreign Legion in films was fashioned of white linen, hanging halfway down the back and protecting the neck from the sun.

to have (or put) one's nose out of joint.   Sometimes this expression is used wrongly to describe a conceited person. The only connection here is that it really means to humiliate a conceited person, as well as to supplant a person in another's affections and to upset someone's plans. Recorded as early as the 16th century, the phrase suggests the altering of a nose that is always confidently stuck up in the air, the down-fall of vanity. Samuel Pepys wrote that the marriage of Charles II to Catherine of Braganza, "a very fine and handsome lady" would put his mistress's (Madame Castlemaine) "nose out of joynt."

to have something up one's sleeve.   Fifteenth-century garments had few if any pockets, so men often carried whatever things couldn't be hung from their belts in their full sleeves. It is probably from this source, rather than magicians with rabbits up their sleeves, that we derive our expression for having something in reserve or an alternative plan, although the phrase in its sense of a scheme or trick was most likely influenced by magicians concealing their professional paraphernalia. Another expression deriving from the same source is *to laugh up* (or *in) one's sleeve*, "to ridicule a person secretly." A man wearing a garment with capacious sleeves was quite literally able to conceal a laugh by hiding his face in his sleeve.

have the goods on.   The *goods* here are stolen goods, those found by the police on a criminal and almost assuring his conviction. The phrase dates back only to the early 1900s, and "goods" may have referred specifically to bogus money made by counterfeiters before it was applied to stolen goods in general. Soon after its introduction, the expression was being used generally for "to have knowledge giving one a hold over another."

to have words with someone.   These words, denoting a verbal altercation, go back at least five centuries, though in a slightly different form. We find the expression was first *at words* (1462). After that, various phrases such as *to fall at words with, to have hard words with, high words with,* and *sharp words with* have all served to express the same idea.

Hawaii.   Hawaii is from *Owykee* or *Hawaeki*, which means "homeland" in the native language. Our 50th state, admitted to the Union in 1959, was previously known as the *Sandwich Islands* (see **sandwich**) and is nicknamed "the Aloha State" (see **aloha**).

Hawaiian words in English.   Hawaiian and South Sea Island languages such as Tongan and Tahitian have contributed a number of words to English, including *tattoo, taboo, lei, atoll, muumuu, poi, ukelele* and *sarong.*

hay is for horses.   One of the earliest and most enduring of catch phrases, *hay is for horses* is a retort to someone who cries out *hey!* It is first recorded in Jonathan Swift's *Polite Conversations* (1738):

Neverout: Hay, Madam did you call me?
Miss: Hay! Why; hay is for horses.

Hayism.   "Acidosis," Dr. William Howard Hay advised in his book *Health Via Food* (1933), causes almost all bodily ills. Therefore, since proteins need acid for their digesting and carbohydrates require alkaline conditions, such foods should not be eaten in combination—no milk with your potatoes or vice versa—for "no human stomach can be expected to be acid and alkaline at the same time." Hays ignored the fact that most foods contain mixtures of proteins and carbohydrates. Like most food fads his regimen had its loyal, even fanatical followers. *Hayism*, incidentally, recommended frequent fasting—which is said to cause acidity or acidosis.

haymaker.   "Gentleman Jim" Corbett used this colorful expression for a heavy, swinging blow, usually a knockout, in his autobiography *The Roar of the Crowd* (1925). It originated a decade or so earlier, in about 1910, and was popularized by radio boxing announcers. The term probably derives from the slang expression *to make hay,* "to take full advantage of one's opportunities," and *the hay,* "sleep or unconsciousness." The idea of a worker swinging a scythe while haymaking is also suggested.

Hays Code.   Long the moral code of the American film industry, the *Hays Code* commemorates Will Harrison Hays (1879-1954). "Czar" of the movies, Hays served as first president of the Motion Picture Producers and Distributors of America from 1922 to 1945. A former chairman of the Republican National Committee and postmaster general under Harding, he helped formulate the so-called *Hays Code* in 1934 and zealously administered it from what was dubbed the Hays Office.

hayseed.   (See **clodhopper**.)

haywire.   A recent autobiography entitled *Haywire* shows that this Americanism still has a long life ahead of it, even though its rural origins are remote from most Americans now. Someone or something gone haywire is confused, out of order, deranged, crazy. The expression is first recorded toward the beginning of the century and was suggested by the baling wire, or haywire, that farmers and ranchers used to tie bales of hay. When a bale of hay was opened with a hatchet to feed livestock this thin sharpened wire would spring out and whirl about a farmer, the sharp ends frequently cutting him or snagging in his clothing. Old haywire lying around—and there was of course much of it—also wound about the legs of horses and other livestock, hopelessly tangling them up. Finally, farmers used old haywire to make temporary repairs on everything from machinery to fences and houses —temporary repairs that were often never made permanent and gave their places a disorderly look. All of these associations, from the crazy leaping of the wire to the tangling up of livestock and the disorder created by haywire, contributed to the coining of the colorful expression, which probably dates back to the 19th century, though first recorded in 1910.

head. *Heads*, "latrines," are so called because they were originally in the bow, or head, of a ship. Our word *head* for the upper part of the body joined to the trunk by the neck comes from the Old English heāfod for the same.

head over heels. As you might suspect, *head over heels*, for "a state of helplessness" ("He's head over heels in love with her") was originally *heels over head*. For nearly five hundred years it was used that way, until in the late 18th century it was popularly corrupted to its present topsy-turvy form. The allusion is probably to a somersault. There is no proof that the phrase is a translation of Catullus's *per caputque pedesque*, "over head and heels," or that it alludes to the practice of hanging criminals by the heels as a warning in medieval times—though anyone so hanged would certainly have been helpless.

hear, hear. As a murmur of approval, the exclamation is more common in England than America, but it is sometimes heard in the U.S. Originally the expression was *Hear him! Hear him!*, a ploy used by Whigs in the Parliament of 1689 to drown out Tory hecklers and call attention to the opinions a speaker from their own party expressed. Calling attention to a speaker's opinions became equivalent to agreeing with the speaker and the phrase took on its present significance, the "him" eventually dropped for the sake of brevity.

Heaving Day. (*See* **Lifting Monday**.)

Heaviside layer. Increasing deafness forced Oliver Heaviside (1850-1925) to retire from his post with the British Great Northern Telegraph Company when he was only twenty-four. The mathematical physicist and electrician devoted the remainder of his long life to theoretical investigations into electricity. In 1902 he suggested that a conducting layer of ionized gas exists in the upper atmosphere that conducts, reflects, and refracts radio waves. This Heaviside layer, about sixty miles above us, reflects radio waves back to earth, and enables reception around the globe. Because Edison's former assistant

Arthur Edwin Kennelly (1861-1939) postulated the same theory shortly before the British scientist, the stratum is also called the *Kennelly-Heaviside layer*. Today it is more generally known as the ionosphere.

heavy brass. (*See* **brass**.)

heck. Contrary to popular legend, Mark Twain didn't invent *heck* as a euphemism for "hell" to please his prudish wife. The word goes back to Lancashire dialect several centuries ago, deriving from *(h)eck!*, an expression of surprise, or possibly from the Lancashire oath *go to ecky* meaning "go to hell."

Hebrew words in English. Among the many Hebrew words that came into English, sometimes through other languages, are: *amen, hosanna, manna, rabbi, Sabbath, Satan, seraphim, cherubim, sapphire, babble, behemoth, leviathan, cabal, shibboleth, jubilee, kosher, shekel, Torah, kibbutz,* and *hallelujah.* (*See also* **Yiddish**.)

to hector. Why did Hector, Troy's mightiest, bravest defender in Homer's *Iliad*, become a blustering, domineering bully? His name, symbolic for a gallant warrior in early English literature, today means not only a bully, but to bully, torment, or treat insolently. The change seems to have taken place toward the end of the 17th century when a gang of young bullies, who considered themselves paragons of valiant courage, adopted the honorable name "Hectors." This ruffian band insulted passers-by, broke windows and became notorious for their bullying, terrorizing the streets of London. It is probably from their name that *hector* and *to hector* derive, rather than from that of the exalted magnanimous Hector, noble in victory and in defeat. Some scholars point out, however, that Hector was represented in medieval drama as boastful and domineering, possibly from the notion that any hero is swashbuckling and blustering. There also might be some connection with "heckle."

to hedge. *Hedge*, in the form of *hegge*, is recorded in English as early as 785, referring to rows of bushes or trees, such as privet or hawthorn, planted in a line to form a boundary. In time the word *hedge* came to mean a safeguard and by the 16th century writers were using the word as a verb, meaning to protect oneself with qualifications, to avoid committing oneself. Shakespeare was the first to record the expression, in *The Merry Wives of Windsor*.

the heebie jeebies. Cartoonist Billie DeBeck (1890-1942), who invented "hotsy totsy," "hot mama" and other slang expressions, is credited by *Mencken* with this coinage, for "a feeling of nervousness, fright, or worry"—the willies or jitters. What he based the rhyming compound on, outside of a sheer joy of sound, is hard to say. One guess is that it is a "reduplicated perversion" of "creepy" or "the creeps." More likely DeBeck took the expression from the name of a dance called the Heebie-Jeebies popular in the 1920s, a dance that inspired a popular song titled "Heebie Jeebies" (1926). The dance, bearing an American Indian name, is said "to represent the incantations made by Red Indian witch doctors before a sacrifice."

heeler.   In the early days of Texas dogs were trained to catch and herd cattle. Often of the bulldog breed, they were called *heelers* because they typically caught the heel of the cow in their jaws.

hegira.   Any flight, often a political one, to a more desirable place than where one is, is called a *hegira*. It is so called from the flight of Muhammad from Mecca to Medina in A.D. 622 to escape persecution by wealthy traders, a date regarded as the beginning of the religion of Islam.

he hath slept in a bed of saffron.   This old Latin expression refers to the supposed exhilarating effects of saffron, meaning "he has a very light heart." As an old poem puts it:

> With genial joy to warm his soul,
> Helen mixed saffron in the bowl.

One of the most expensive spices, saffron is made from the dried stigmas of crocuses.

Heinz's 57 varieties.   The original Mr. Heinz, forebear of the millionaire senator, adapted his company's famous slogan from a New York City billboard ad he saw featuring "21 Styles of Shoes." Heinz actually had 60 varieties at the time he coined the slogan in 1892, but he thought an odd number sounded better. The company used its "57" slogan until 1969.

Heisman Trophy.   The *Heisman Memorial Trophy* has been called the ultima Thule for undergraduate football players, being awarded annually since 1935 to the best of their breed in the country. It is named for John W. Heisman, former Georgia Tech coach. Called "Shut the Gates of Mercy" Heisman, the coach was a great mentor, though not noted for being a gentleman on the playing field. On one occasion he allowed his team to rack up an incredible 222 points against an opponent. Notable *Heisman Trophy* winners include Tom Harmon of Michigan (1940), Paul Hornung of Notre Dame (1956), and O. J. Simpson of Southern California (1968). Jay Berwanger of the University of Chicago won the initial award in 1935.

he is not being executed, he is being shot.   The death penalty had been abolished in Soviet Russia when Admiral Aleksie Shchastny was sentenced to be shot. Spectators in the court that day in 1918 began to stir when the state prosecutor explained: "What are you worrying about? Executions have been abolished. But he is not being executed; he is being shot." This most extreme of euphemisms is recorded in Aleksandr I. Solzhenitsyn's *Gulag Archipelago* (1974).

he kept us out of war.   The political slogan *He kept us out of war* has been used in *two* American presidential campaigns. The Democrats used it in 1916 to help return Woodrow Wilson to the White House, only to have Wilson ask Congress to declare war on Germany a year later, "to make the world safe for democracy." In 1956 the Republicans used it to sell Dwight D. Eisenhower as a peacemaker in Korea, though it took a backseat to the very popular "I like Ike." (*See* **Eisenhower jacket**.)

heliotrope.   Many plant leaves and flowers turn toward the sun. The ancient Greeks noticed that this fragrant vanilla-scented perennial flower (*Heliotropium arborescems*), often called "cherry pie," did so and called it the *heliotrope*, from the Greek *heleos*, "sun," and *trepos*, "turning to go into it." Another fragrant flower sometimes called *heliotrope*, and also called "cherry pie" for its blossoms, is common *valerious* (*Valeriana officinalis*), probably named for the Roman Emperor Valerianus. A Greek legend says the god Apollo loved the ocean nymph Clytie but abandoned her for her sister, whereafter she died of sorrow. A remorseful Apollo changed the dead Clytie into a living flower that always turns toward the sun.

hell afloat.   Usually old hulks no good for sailing anymore, British prison ships were the concentration camps of the Revolutionary War. It has been estimated that they took the lives of more American fighting men (11,000 to 15,000) during the Revolution than enemy rifles did. Such ships were often dubbed *hell afloat* by the prisoners, whatever the ship's real name.

hello.   *Hello*, one of the most frequently used words in everyday speech, isn't recorded until 1883 or thereabouts. But in the form of *hallow*, its earliest ancestor, the word dates back to at least 1340 and was used by Chaucer. *Hallow* probably derives from the Old French *hallo-er* "to pursue crying or shouting." *Hello* came into fashion with the invention of the telephone late in the 19th century, replacing the earlier variant *hullo*. *Hello girl*, once used for a telephone operator, is an Americanism first recorded by Mark Twain in *A Connecticut Yankee in King Arthur's Court*.

hell on wheels.   Union Pacific Railroad construction gangs in the 1860s lived in boxcars that were pulled along as the line progressed. Traveling and living with these hard-drinking, often violent men were gamblers, prostitutes, and other unsavory characters. The wild congregation assembled in the boxcars suggested the population of hell to settlers, and the transient town was called *hell-on-wheels*, a colorful term soon applied to any violent, vicious person or lawless place.

to hell or Connaught. During the Commonwealth, under Oliver Cromwell, the native Irish were dispossessed of their land in the other provinces and ordered to settle in Connaught or be put to death. This led to the phrase common throughout Ireland, or wherever Irishmen emigrated, of *to hell or Connaught*.

hell or high water. (*See* **come hell or high water.**)

Hell's Angels. The best-known, if not the first, of the motorcycle gangs came into prominence in the 1950s in the San Francisco Bay area. *Hell's Angels* founders were descendants of the *Okies* (*q.v.*) of the Great Depression.

hell's bells! The more colorful curse *hell's bells and buckets of blood*! was the original of the imprecation, which probably originated at sea during the late 19th century, under what circumstances no one knows.

helot. The original *helots*, slaves or serfs, were inhabitants of the town of Helos in Laconia, enslaved by the Spartans in ancient times. The Spartans actually ranked their *helots* midway between citizens and slaves, but certainly treated them like flunkeys. As an object lesson to Spartan youth that drunkenness is evil, *helots* were often forced to drink more than they could handle and then exhibited in the public square.

helpmeet. *Helpmeet*, "a companion or helper, a wife or husband," is the source of the more familiar *helpmate*, meaning the same. *Helpmeet* is a misreading of the biblical Gen. 2:18, which refers to "a help meet for him," *meet* in this sense actually meaning "suitable" (a "suitable help").

hem and haw. As an expression for hesitancy, to *hem and haw* isn't recorded until 1786. But it is found centuries earlier in similar expressions such as *to hem and hawk, hem and ha*, and *hum and ha*, which Shakespeare used. These are all sounds made in clearing the throat when we are about to speak. When a speaker constantly makes them without speaking he is usually hesitating out of uncertainty, which suggested the phrase. Said the first writer to record the idea in 1469: "He wold have gotyn it aweye by humys and by hays but I would not so be answered."

henpecked. The *pecking order* among hens, according to the famous study made by biologist W. C. Allee, has a definite prestige pattern: Hens, like many humans, male and female, freely peck at other hens below their rank and submit to pecking from those above them. Although hens rarely peck at roosters in the barnyard, where the rooster is the cock of the walk, it was widely believed in the 17th century that they often pulled feathers from young roosters below them in the pecking order. This led to the comparison of domineering wives to aggressive hens. Samuel Butler defined the term first, Dryden complained that he was *henpecked*, and Steele called Socrates "the undoubted head of the Sect of the Hen-pecked." There was even a noun *henpeck*, for a wife who domineered over her husband, and Byron, in *Don Juan*, wrote his celebrated couplet: "But—oh! ye lords of ladies intellectual,/ Inform us truly, have they not hen-peck'd you all."

henry. Scientist Joseph Henry's career constitutes a series of famous firsts and foremosts. The U.S. Weather Bureau was created as a result of his meteorological work while first director of the Smithsonian Institution, and Henry was the first "weatherman" to make forecasts from collected scientific data. Not only a brilliant administrator who initially planned the Smithsonian's scope and activities, Henry has been acknowledged as the leading physicist of his day. His researches on sound gave America the best fog signaling service among maritime nations, he stimulated geologic and geographical exploration, and his influence on the character of science, especially concerning the free publication of scientific results, was exceeded by no contemporary. Before becoming secretary of the Smithsonian in 1846, Henry taught physics at Princeton, where he built the first electromagnetic motor (1829) and devised the first practical telegraph (1830-31). It is *not* for the theory of electromagnetic induction that the *henry*, the measurement unit of induction, is named in his honor. This theory is credited to the English scientist Faraday, although Henry's experiments may have preceded his, and it is for his theory of producing induced current (1832) that the International Congress of Electricians gave the celebrated American's name to the standard electrical unit in 1893. He died in 1876 at the age of eighty-one.

Henry rifle. The *Henry rifle* has been called the grandfather of repeating arms. Invented by Benjamin Tyler Henry (1821-98), one of the Henry family of gunsmiths, the weapon was tested under fire by Union forces in the Civil War. The breech-loading, lever-action rifle never became popular as a military weapon but saw some use on the frontier and is featured in many a western. Henry may also have worked on the Martini-Henry rifle adopted by the British army in 1889. This was basically an improvement on the Martini, invented by Swiss mechanical engineer Frederic de Martini (1832-97), but another Henry, a Scottish gunsmith, possibly deserves the credit for it.

hepatica. These charming little wildflowers have three-lobed leaves that resemble the human liver. Noticing this, someone in medieval times named them from the Greek *hepatikos*, "of the liver."

Hepplewhite style. Nothing is known about the British furniture designer George Hepplewhite except that he operated a fashionable cabinetmaking shop in the parish of St. Gile's, Cripplegate, London, died in 1786, and willed his business to his wife, Alice. But his furniture was widely imitated in England and the United States, resulting in a style often eloquent and graceful. It has been assumed that the original *Hepplewhite styles* were delicate and soundly constructed. The cabinetmaker invented or popularized the shield-back chair and the "spider leg" for chairs, tables, and sideboards, and was among the first to inlay much of his furniture with exotic woods. Hepplewhite's small pieces, such as inlaid knife boxes, fire screens, and tea caddies, are highly valued by collectors. His *The Cabinet-Maker and Upholsterer's Guide*, published by his wife in 1788, inspired a host of imitators at home and abroad.

herba sacra. Vervain (*Verbena officinalis*), the *herba sacra* or "divine weed" of the Romans, who believed that, among other things, it cured the bites of rabid animals, arrested the progress of snakebite, cured the plague and scrofula, reconciled enemies, and warded off witches. The Romans so esteemed vervain that they held annual feasts called *Verbenalia* in its honor. Ambassadors in ancient times wore vervain as a badge of good faith.

herb of grace. Rue is called the *herb of grace* because it is the symbol of repentance, owing to its extreme bitterness. Shakespeare used the expression in *Richard II*, and there are many old records telling of the use of rue in ceremonies of exorcism.

herculean task. A *herculean task* may not require great strength, even though the expression derives from the name of the mythical Greek superman, Hercules. Such a task is a difficult or dangerous one and refers to the fabled twelve labors of Hercules that he performed while overcoming great difficulties.

herd's grass. (*See* **timothy grass.**)

here's mud in your eye. This toast was originally made in the muddy trenches of World War I, or in the cafes where English and American soldiers spent their leaves trying to forget them.

Hermannia. (*See* **Mahernia.**)

hermaphrodite. Hermaphroditus, the son of Hermes and Aphrodite in Greek mythology, gives his/her name to any human or animal combining characteristics of both sexes. The handsome Hermaphroditus was loved by the beautiful nymph Salmacis, but didn't love her in return. She persisted in pursuing him, however, and throwing her arms around him begged the gods to fuse their bodies together—which they did.

hermetically sealed. Mystic philosophers in the third century claimed that their magical secrets had been dictated to them by Hermes Trismegistus, his name meaning "Hermes thrice greatest [three times as great as the original Greek god Hermes]," and that this Hermes was really the Egyptian god of wisdom, Thoth. The wisdom of Hermes Trismegistus became the basis for the 42 *Hermetic Books* containing secrets for alchemists, and one formula in these books told how to seal a container so that no air could get in. Today we don't claim to seal bottles, cans, and jars by any "magical" method, but all such airtight containers are called *hermetic* or *hermetically sealed* in Hermes' honor.

heroin. Formerly a trade name, *heroin* was discovered around 1897 by Professor Paul Dresser, chief of the research department of Germany's Elberfeld Farben Fabriken. It was named from the Greek *heros*, "hero," apparently "because of the inflation of the personality consequent on taking the drug," because it made a user feel like a hero, for a short while.

hero sandwich, etc. New York's *Italian hero sandwiches*, the term first recorded in the 1920s, are named for their heroic size, not for Charles Lindbergh or any other hero. *Poor boys*, similar huge sandwiches on split loaves of French (not Italian) bread, are said to be so named because they were given to New Orleans beggars in the late 19th century. Heros are called *hoagies* in Philadelphia and thereabouts, *submarines* or *subs* in Pittsburgh, *torpedos* in Los Angeles, *wedgies* in Rhode Island, *Garabaldis* (after the Italian liberator) in Wisconsin and *rockets* and *bombers* in various other places. *Hero* for a man of great courage or brave deeds comes from the Greek *heros* meaning the same.

he's (I'm) a poet but don't know it. The rhyme in this expression has kept it alive for nearly three centuries. The catchphrase dates back to at least 1700, when it was first directed at people who rhyme words accidentally in conversation.

Hessian. As an American epithet *Hessian* can be traced back to the Revolutionary War, when the British employed thirty thousand Hessian mercenaries and their name, justly or not, came to mean any boorish, uncouth person of low moral character. The Hessians came from the former Grand Duchy of Hesse in Germany. Their name is also found in the high-tasseled *Hessian boots* fashionable in early 19th-century England; *Hessian cloth*, a strong, coarse jute or hemp cloth originally made in Hesse; *Hessian*, for any mercenary; and the *Hessian fly* so destructive to wheat, which was erroneously believed to have been brought to America by the Hessian soldiers.

heterosexual.   (*See* **homosexual**.)

hewers of wood and drawers of water.   *Hewers of wood . . .* describes people who aren't particularly clever, those who depend more on physical labor for their livelihood. The old expression is from the Bible (Josh. 9:21).

hey!   The exclamation *hey!*, to attract attention, first attested in about 1225, but probably as old as English, has its counterparts in all languages. In ancient times the Romans used *eho!*, and the Greeks before them cried out *eia!*

hiccup.   No matter how it is spelled, the word is pronounced *hiccup*. Why is hard to say. Only in the 17th century did people begin to use *hiccup*, closely allied to the Danish *hicke* and the Dutch *hikke*. The *hic* in this echoic word is fine, but any connoisseur of *hiccups* would agree that a *cup* is rarely if ever heard in a *hiccough*.

hick.   (*See* **clodhopper**.)

hickery dickery dock.   Some authorities call this familiar phrase an "onomatoplasm," an attempt to capture a sound (in this case that of a ticking clock) in words. However, it has been argued in the *Oxford Dictionary of Nursery Rhymes* that "the shepherds of Westmorland once used *Hevera* for 'eight,' *Devera* for 'nine' and *Dick* for 'ten.'"

hickory.   *Pawcohiccora* was the name American Indians near Jamestown, Virginia gave to the milky liquor they obtained from nuts from a tree that abounded in the area. Colonists called the milky liquor and nuts *hiccora*, or *hickory*, abandoning the first part of the Indian word, and eventually applied the word *hickory* to the useful tree the nuts came from, which supplied them with a stony, tough wood good for many purposes.

hidebound.   Cramped, constricted people, those who are rigidly opinionated, have been called *hidebound* since the 16th century. The word derives from a term applied to emaciated cattle in days before veterinary science had made many advances. Feeding and care of cattle was so poor in England at the time that by winter the animals were often thin and diseased and had lost the fatty tissue under the skin. As a result their skin clung tightly to their bones, they moved stiffly, and their hides couldn't be removed from their backbone or ribs when they died. Their physical condition naturally suggested the inelastic, constipated minds of some people.

to hide your light under a bushel.   Early translations of the Bible introduced the above phrase from Matt. 5:14-15 into English. Jesus, after urging his disciples to be "the light of the world," added that "A city that is set on a hill cannot be hid. Neither do men light a candle and put it under a bushel, but on a candlestick." The *bushel* in the phrase is a bushelbasket, not today's loosely made type, which lets some light through, but a sturdy earthenware or wood container. Thus *to hide your light under a bushel* was to unduly conceal your abilities so no one could see them, to be excessively modest.

Hi Diddle Diddle.   (*See* **to grin like a Cheshire cat**.)

highball.   Long drinks were first called *highballs* in the 1890s, and were so named because they came in tall glasses and all glasses were called "balls" in bartender's slang. There is some reason to believe that the common, much older, railroad term *to highball* helped keep the drink *highball* in the public mind. *To highball* means to travel at top speed. In the early days of railroading a large metal ball hanging from two crossarms at the approach to railroad stations signaled locomotive engineers as to how they should proceed. A lowered ball meant come to a full stop and a ball raised to the top of the mast, a high ball, meant to proceed full speed ahead.

highbinder.   A *highbinder* can be a swindler and cheat, especially a confidence man, or a gangster or rowdy. The word, first used in its latter meaning, derives from a gang of ruffians called the *Highbinders* that plagued New York City about 1806. Later their name was applied (in the lower case) to members of American-Chinese secret societies believed to be employed in blackmail and assassination.

highbrow.   Dr. Franz Joseph Gall (1758-1828), founder of the "science" of phrenology, gave support to the old folk notion that people with big foreheads have more brains. Gall's lifelong studies purportedly showed that the bigger a person's forehead was, the higher his brow, the smarter he would be. This theory was widely accepted through the 19th century, until phrenology was discredited by scientists, and the belief led to the expression *highbrow* for an intellectual, which is first recorded in 1875. The term is often used disparagingly and is the source of the similar terms *lowbrow* and *middlebrow*. *Highbrowed* people can be supercilious, meaning disdainful, and this word has a connection with the brow, too. *Supercilious* is from the Latin *supercilium*, "eyebrow," and the Latin suffix *-osus*, "full of." Thus a supercilious person is literally one "full of eyebrow," an etymology that goes well with the image of someone lifting the eyebrow slightly in disdain. *New York Sun* reporter Will Irvin popularized *highbrow*, and its opposite *lowbrow*, in 1902, basing his creation on the wrongful notion that people with long foreheads have bigger brains and are more intelligent and intellectual than those with short foreheads. At first the term was complimentary, but *highbrow* came to be at best a neutral word used to describe such things as *highbrow books*, and at worst sank as low as *lowbrow*, being used by lowbrows and other anti-intellectuals to describe supercilious intellectuals or psuedo-intellectuals. *Life* magazine coined the term *middlebrow* in the mid-1940s.

high dudgeon. *Dudgeon* is a feeling of anger, resentment, or offense, so *high dudgeon*, which dates back over a century, means great anger or resentment. S. J. Perelman's *in a low dudgeon* is a decided improvement on the timeworn phrase. No one seems to know where *dudgeon* itself comes from. An Italian word meaning "to overshadow" has been suggested, implying that someone who cuts off another's sunlight provokes anger. This is an idea that at least goes back to Diogenes the Cynic, who on being asked by Alexander the Great if the emperor could oblige him in any way, replied: "Yes, by standing out of my sunlight." But *dudgeon* has also been linked to a much earlier word for "the handle of a dagger." By this theory, which isn't documented or widely accepted, an insulted man reached for his dagger handle, or *dudgeon*, in anger. By extension the dagger handle became the dagger, and the dagger, or *dudgeon*, was used to describe the anger that led to its use.

highfalutin. The Americanism *highfalutin* means "high-flown," bombastic, and is first recorded in 1839. Its origins are obscure and *high-flown*, *high-flying*, the Yiddish *hifelufelem* and the Dutch *verbooten* are among the many words suggested as its source.

high-handed. In the Bible (Num. 23:3) the direct ancestor of this phrase means "triumphantly." It is used in describing the departure of the Israelites from Egyptian bondage: ". . . on the morrow after the passover the children of Israel went out *with a high hand* in the sight of all the Egyptians." The description does suggest a certain amount of arrogance, however, and it is probably from this passage that *high-handed* came, with the passage of time, to mean arrogant or overbearing.

high hat. Jack Conway, a former baseball player and vaudevillian who became editor of the show business newspaper *Variety*, coined the expression *high hat*, for "a snob," in 1924. It suggests an affected rich or nouveau riche man in a high silk hat and tails strolling about town with his nose almost as high as his hat, and it gave birth to the expression *to high hat*, to snub or act patronizingly. The prolific Conway—Walter Winchell called him "my tutor of slanguage"—died in 1928. *Belly laugh, pushover, to click* (succeed), *baloney* (bunk), *S.A.* (sex appeal), *payoff*, and *palooka* are among his other memorable coinages.

high horse. In the royal pageants of medieval England nobles and others of high rank customarily rode "high horses," great chargers a hand or so taller than the average mount. Riding such a high horse naturally came to be equated with superiority and the arrogance superiority often breeds. *To ride the high horse* came to mean to affect arrogance or superiority, and this phrase gave us the still common *to get up on one's high horse*, to scorn what we consider "beneath us."

high jinks. *High jinks*, a somewhat dated expression for fun and pranks, was originally the name of an ancient drinking game played with dice, and the antics of the players gave birth to the phrase. Sir Walter Scott describes the game in his novel *Guy Mannering* (1815): "Most frequently the dice were thrown by the company, and those upon whom the lot fell were obliged to assume and maintain for a time a certain fictitious character or to repeat a certain number of fescennine [obscene] verses in a particular order. If they departed from the character assigned . . . they incurred forfeits, which were compounded for by swallowing an additional bumper, or by paying a small sum toward the reckoning."

highlight; high spot. The *high light* or *high lights* of a painting, the brightest parts of a subject, which are focal points in the composition, was a technical term, well-known to artists in the early 17th century. These focal points of highest light intensity became familiar in photography, too, and by the beginning of this century the expression *high light* began to be used frequently for any bright, prominent, or outstanding feature of any occasion, subject, or situation. The much newer American expression *high spot* (1928), meaning the same and deriving from *spotlight*, doesn't seem to be used as often.

high muckey-muck; mogul. A *high muckey-muck*, or *muck-a-muck*, is someone in a position of authority, especially an overbearing person in such a position. *Muckey-muck* may be a childish play on the word *muckle*, "great," or is possibly a corruption of *Great Mogul*. The Great Mogul (mogul itself being a corruption of *mogol*) was originally the Emperor of Delhi, and eventually his title was used to describe any big shot.

high on (off) the hog. Well aware that the best cuts of meat on a hog—the hams, pork chops, bacon, tenderloin, and spare ribs—are high up on a hog's sides, American Southerners used the expression *eating high on the hog*, "good eating," as opposed to *eating low on the hog*—eating the pig's feet, knuckles, jowls, and sow belly, well known today as "soul food." By extension, *living high on* (or *off*) *the hog* came to mean living prosperously.

high seas. *High* in the term *high seas* means "chief" or "principal." The high seas, or the "main," are the open seas—those waters beyond any territorial limit that belong to no one nation.

High Street. (*See* **Main Street**.)

hightail it. Mustangs, rabbits, and other animals raise their tails high and flee quickly when they sense danger. Trappers in the American West noticed this, over a century ago, probably while hunting wild horses, and invented the expression *to high-tail it*, to make a fast getaway.

hijack. Back in Prohibition days, the story goes, criminals who robbed trucks of their loads of whiskey commanded their drivers to "Stick 'em up high, Jack!" or "Up high, Jack!" From their command they were called *highjackers*, then *hijackers*, and the word *hijack* became part of the language. Another explanation is that the crooks pretended to be friends of the drivers, calling out "Hi, Jack!"

the hills are closing in on him. He's going mad. This expression, heard in America, England, New Zealand, Australia, and Canada, originated with United Nations troops during the Korean War, or Conflict. Korea of course has many forbidding hills and mountains.

hip. There was supposedly a cool cat named Joe Hep who tended bar in Chicago during the 1890s and it was from this aware, all-knowing, disaffiliated man that we get the word *hep*, of which *hip* is a variant. Most scholars don't go along with this theory, dividing their loyalties between the opium smoker's term for smoking opium, *on the hip* (opium smokers often reclined on one side while smoking), or the West African *hipi*, "to be aware," or the African Walof *hipicat* (hence *hepcat*, too) meaning "one who has his eyes wide open." All we really know is that *hep* was recorded first in 1903 and has by now been almost totally replaced by its variant *hip*, which gave us the word *hippy* in the 1960s.

hip! hip! hurrah! The old story here can be taken for what it's worth, which isn't much. *Hip*, we're told, derives from the initials of the Latin words *Hierosolyms est perdita*, "Jerusalem is destroyed." German knights, not a very bright bunch, were supposed to have known this and shouted *hip*, *hip!* when they hunted Jews in the persecutions of the Middle Ages. *Hurrah!* by the same strained imagining, is said to be a corruption of the Slavonic word for Paradise (*hu-raj*). Therefore, if you ever shout *hip! hip! hurrah!* you are supposedly shouting: "Jerusalem is destroyed [the infidels are destroyed] and we are on the road to Paradise!" There is not the slightest proof for any of this, and the phrase, which doesn't date back earlier than the late 18th century, almost certainly comes to us from the exclamation *hip, hip, hip!* earlier

used in toasts and cheers, and *huzza*, an imitative sound expressing joy and enthusiasm.

Hippocratic Oath. The original version of the *Hippocratic Oath*, which in altered form is still administered to medical school students upon graduation, begins with an invocation to the gods: "I swear by Apollo the physician . . ." All forms of the oath memorialize Hippocrates (ca. 460-377 B.C.), "The Father of Medicine," but not a line of it was written by the Greek physician and surgeon, it being rather the body of Greek medical thought and practice of his day. The words do, however, embody Hippocrates's ideals. Believed to have been born on the island of Cos off the coast of Asia Minor, the son of a physician who claimed descent from the Greek god of medicine, Hippocrates apparently studied medicine with his father and philosophy under the famed Democritus. He separated medicine from superstition, and his acute observations have been used in medical teaching for centuries. Hippocrates was at least 85 when he died, and some estimates put his age at 110.

hippopotamus. The ancient Greeks thought the *hippopotamus* looked like a horse and, since it spent so much time in the water, called it "river horse," from the Greek *hippos*, "horse," and *potamos*, "river." British historian Thomas Macaulay wrote: "I have seen the Hippo both asleep and awake, and I can assure you that, asleep or awake, he is the ugliest of the Works of God."

hippopotomontrosesquipedalianism. This word (I won't repeat it out of pity for the typesetter) is the term for "the practice of using long words." Composed of 32 letters itself, it is far longer than its synonym *sesquipedalian words*, from Horace's *sesquipedalia verbs*, words a foot and a half long. The Greeks, too, had a word for mile-long words: *amaxiaia remata*, "words large enough for a wagon." (*See also* **bovine**.)

hirquitalliency. James Crichton, the Admirable Crichton, took a prince's lady to bed, according to Sir Thomas Urquhart in his *The Discovery of a Most Exquisite Jewel* (1652), the love scene described by Urquhart with majestic euphemisms:

> . . . the visuriency of either, by ushering the tacturiency of both, made the attraction of both consequent to the inspection of either: here it was that Passion was active, and Action passive: they both being overcome by each other, and each the conqueror. To speak of her *hirquitalliency* at the *elevation* of the *pole* of his Microcosm, or of his luxuriousness to erect a *gnomon* on her *horizontal* dial, will perhaps be held by some to be expressions full of obsceneness, and offensive to the purity of chaste ears.

Not today, Sir Thomas. The italics and spellings are Urquhart's as is the opinion that the Admirable Crichton was killed in medias res by the jealous prince. So is the word *hirquitalliency*, which the author apparently coined for the occasion from the Latin *hirquitallire*. The nonce word, meaning to acquire a strong voice (like an infant's), is apparently found nowhere else in literature. *Visuriency*, another nonce word, means "the desire of seeing."

hisn.

> Him as prigs what isn't hisn
> When he's cotch'd he goes to prison.

The old proverbial adage is proof that *hisn* isn't a backwoods Americanism. *Hisn* has a long and respectable lineage, dating back to the early 15th century and used by Richardson in *hisn* novel *Clarissa*. Nowhere, however, is the word properly used in place of *his* today.

hiss.   (*See* **onomatopoeia.**)

Hitchcock chairs.   *Hitchcock chairs* were so well made that they have become collector's items even though they were originally mass produced in 1818. Lambert H. Hitchcock (1795-1852) established a factory in Barkhamsted, Connecticut, where some one hundred employees turned out his product. *Hitchcock chairs* came in a variety of designs and sizes, but were characterized by strong legs, curved-top backs, and seats (initially rush-bottomed) that were wider in front than in the back. The chair maker won such renown that Barkhamsted renamed itself Hitchcocksville in his honor, although the town changed its name again to Riverton in 1866. The sturdy chairs, all identified by Hitchcock's signature stenciled on the back edge of the seat, include the first rocking chair designed and made as such—i.e., not made by just adding rockers to a regular chair.

Hitchcock ending.   An often ironic, surprise ending characteristic of the fifty-three films, numerous television plays, short-story anthologies, and magazine stories directed, sponsored, collected, and published by Alfred Joseph Hitchcock. Hitchcock's films have received high critical praise as well as a great popular following. The English director, born in London in 1899, began his career as a scenario writer, becoming an art director and production manager before starting to direct films in 1925. His many suspenseful thrillers, object of a cult for their brilliant camera technique, include *The Lodger, Blackmail, The 39 Steps, The Lady Vanishes, Rebecca, Suspicion, Foreign Correspondent, Shadow of a Doubt, Lifeboat, Spellbound, Rope, Strangers on a Train, North by Northwest, Psycho,* and *The Birds.*

hit on all six.   In the early days of motor cars this phrase was *hitting on all fours*, referring of course to the four cylinders of automobiles and meaning that all the pistons in the cylinders we hitting, or firing, perfectly. With bigger cars came the expression *hitting on all six*, and though engines got even bigger, the expression never exceeded this number. Most sources have the expression as *hitting on all six* today, but mostly I've heard it as *hitting on all sixes* to describe any good performance.

to hit the jackpot.   The "progressive jack pot" in draw poker has been explained as follows: "If a pot is not opened on the first deal, the opening hand for the next deal increases from jacks or better [to open], to queens or better . . . on the second deal . . . from queens, or better, to kings, or better . . ." Since the players bet on each hand until someone can open, the pot can grow larger than usual, which led to large pots in poker being called *jackpots*. From poker the word passed into general usage, first recorded in a nonpoker use in 1884 and subsequently employed in phrases like *to hit the jackpot*, "to have great luck," first attested in 1944, but probably older.

hit the nail on the head.   Although the allusion is obvious here, no one knows who invented the expression. John Stanbridge's *Vulgaria* (1520) has "Thou hyttest the nayle on the head" and English poet John Skelton used it a little later, but the phrase was probably proverbial before then. One suggestion is that it derives from the Roman saying *acu rem tangere*, "you have touched the thing with a needle," which refers to the custom of probing sores. To be *off the nail* was slang over a century ago for being slightly drunk.

hobby; hobbyhorse.   *Hobby* first meant only a small Irish horse, or pony, in English, the word first recorded in 1375. By the late 16th century the toy *hobbyhorse*, also called a *hobby*, had been invented and within another century people were comparing their favorite occupations for amusement to the riding of such toy horses, which they had found so pleasurable in their youth. These favorite pastimes we first called *hobbyhorses*, the word not shortened to *hobby* until the early 19th century. *Hobbyhorse* is sometimes used as a synonym for a rocking horse today.

hobnob.   To *hobnob* with someone is to be very close friends with him. The word is formed from *hob*, "give," and *nob*, "take," which derive from the Anglo-Saxon *hab* and *nab*, meaning the same. To *hobnob* involves giving and taking, as has always been the way with true friends.

hobo.   True *hoboes* claim that they will work whereas tramps and bums will not, and, indeed, the first *hoboes*, in the 1890s and early 1900s were often migrating workers who carried their IWW union cards. The word *hobo* is of uncertain origin. Perhaps it derives from a once common greeting of vagabonds to each other: "Ho! Beau" (*Ho!* a form of "Hi!" and *Bo* meaning "guy or brother"). This seems to be the most popular explanation, but wandering *homeward bound* Civil War veterans have also been suggested, as have *hoe boys* who left the farm and were on the road. The word is first recorded in the American Pacific Northwest, about 1889.

hobsonize. Lieutenant Richmond Pearson Hobson (1870-1937) won fame during the Spanish-American War, stepping into the national limelight when he tried to sink the collier *Merrimac* and block Santiago harbor. The young naval engineer was honored with parades and dinners wherever he went when he returned to the United States in August 1898. His good looks and popularity led to his name becoming a verb meaning *to kiss*: women often flung their arms around him and showered him with kisses when he appeared in public. Though *hobsonize* is an obsolete expression today, it remains in historical dictionaries as one of the most curious of linguistic curiosities.

Hobson-Jobson. The substitution of native English words, unrelated in meaning, for foreign ones, especially oriental expressions, is called *Hobson-Jobsonism*. Hobson and Jobson were applied to the Muslim processional chant "Ya Hassan! Ya Hussein!" by British soldiers in 19th-century India because these traditional English surnames sounded something like the repeated exclamations of the parading Muhammadans (*Hodge* was the first of the English names, but it became *Hobson* by reduplication). The Hassan and Hussein of the chant are the grandsons of Muhammad, their names still honored at the festival of Murarram. The term *Hobson-Jobson*, for "a kind of pidgin language," was popularized with the publication of a book of the same name by the English Sanskrit scholar Arthur Coke Burnell in 1886.

Hobson's choice. This expression has lasted for over three centuries, even though it derived from the name of an obscure English carrier and innkeeper, Tobias or Thomas Hobson, who for some fifty years drove his stage from Cambridge to London, sixty miles away, often at breakneck speeds, and kept some forty horses on the side to rent to students at Cambridge University. Hobson, a humane man who realized that "the scholars rid hard," put his mounts on a strict rotation basis so that the best and most often chosen horses would not be ruined. When you rented a horse from Hobson, you rented the horse nearest the livery stable door, the one best rested, no matter what your preference or how many horses were available. Hence, *Hobson's choice* is no choice at all.

hock. *Hock*, for any white Rhine wine, is simply an abbreviation of *Hockamore*, which is what the English called *Hochheimer*, a fine white wine made in Hochheim on the River Main in Germany. In commerce the name *hock* became extended to all white Rhine wines, fine or not. (*See also* **be in hock.**)

hocus-pocus; hoax. "I will speake of one man . . ." wrote Thomas Ady in *A Candle in the Dark* (1656), "that went about in King James his time . . . who called himself, The Kings Majesties most excellent Hocus Pocus, and so was called because that at the playing of every trick, he used to say, *Hocus Pocus, tontus talontus, vade celeriter jubio*, a dark composure of words, to blinde the eyes of the beholders, to master his trick pass the more currantly without discovery." Whether this juggler's assumed name became the basis for our *hocus-pocus*, "deception or trickery," no one really knows. Ochus Bochus, "a wizard and demon of Northern Mythology," or "a 17th-century magician," whose identity has been established in neither case, has also been nominated. Neither is there proof positive that *hocus-pocus* is a blasphemous Scandinavian corruption of the first words of the consecration in the Catholic Mass, *Hoc est corpus (filii)*, "This is the body [of the Son of God]." Many scholars lean to this last theory, pointing out that *hokus-pokus-fileokus* is still unwittingly used in Norway and Sweden, just as *hocus-pocus-dominocus* (for *hoc est corpus Domini*, "this is the body of the Lord"), is an expression common in children's play in America. (I remember the possibly euphemistic *hocus-pocus-minniocus*.) Perhaps the word does originally come from the perversion of the sacramental blessing, reinforced by the nickname that the ancient juggler assumed from his diverting pseudo-Latin patter, and further strengthened by the names of other successful jugglers and magicians named after him. We do know that many Tudor conjurors famous for their legerdemain were called Hocus Pocus or Hokas Pocas after their predecessor and that Master Hocus Pocus became a symbol of illusion and deceit. From *hocus-pocus* came, in all probability, the words *hoax*, "a trick"—*hoax* is merely *hocus* said quickly—and *hokum*, which is a blend of *hocus-pocus* and "bunkum" or "bunk."

Hodgkin's disease. (*See* **Bright's disease.**)

hoecake. It seems unlikely that the cakes of coarse cornmeal called *hoecakes* are so named because they were baked on hoes, for the hoe was a valuable tool on the frontier and baking bread on one would damage and eventually destroy it. More likely the cake takes its name from the Indian *nokehick*, for "coarse cornmeal," which the earliest settlers pronounced *nocake*. These settlers called the cake baked from this meal *nocake*, too, but the name changed to *hoecake* over the years, perhaps because this was close in sound to *nocake* and people thought that *nocake* couldn't possibly be the name for a cake that did exist!

to hoe your own row. Unlike *a long row to hoe* (*q.v.*) this expression means to be independent, to paddle one's own canoe. It is also an agricultural phrase, dating back to the 18th-century, when farm workers, unaided by machinery, did hoe their own rows. The saying first appeared in print after John Tyler became president on William Henry Harrison's death in 1841, when it became apparent that Tyler wouldn't follow Harrison's policies, but would "hoe his own row."

hog. Few English words that were used by the Britons remain. *Hog* is such a native word, deriving from the British *hukk*, probably first referring to a certain aged pig, such as a yearling, and then coming to mean pigs in general. "Crag" and "tor" are other words the Britons used.

hogan; Hogan's goat; etc. Goats don't eat tin cans (they eat the paper labels off them), but they do stink. For this reason, and no other, anything said to be like *Hogan's goat* (a play, a book, or whatever) is something that is very bad, that really stinks. *Hogan* is just a common name affixed to this Americanism that dates back to the turn of the century—no real Hogan has anything to do with it. "Hogan's brickyard," for a rough-hewn baseball diamond—one usually in a vacant lot—is a similar expression, but *Hogan*, a variety of cotton, is named for its 19th-century developer, William Hogan. The Navaho Indian *hogan*, from the Navaho word for the same, is a dwelling constructed of earth and branches and covered with mud or sod.

Hogarthian. His paintings uncompromisingly realistic in style, his name came to indicate the same, but English painter William Hogarth (1697-1764) wasn't above fantastic flights of the imagination. Once when an ugly client refused to pay for a realistically ugly portrait, Hogarth threatened to add a tail and other appendages to his likeness and dedicate it to "Mr. Hare, the famous wild-beast man." His client paid on condition that the portrait be destroyed. Hogarth's great ability as a painter was overshadowed by his consummate skill as a caricaturist, which he used in his engravings to expose the hypocrisy and degeneration of English society. Among his numerous satiric works the most celebrated are *The Rake's Progress*, the *Marriage à la Mode* series, *Gin Lane*, and *Four Stages of Cruelty*, all noted for their frank humor and realistic attention to detail. It has been said that Hogarth, despite his great skills, was less a painter than an author, "a humorist and satirist upon canvas." Yet he was capable of painting such masterpieces as the *Shrimp Girl* and *Captain Coram*.

hog latin. (*See* **pig latin**.)

hogwash. "They in the kitchen, for jest, poured hogwash on her head," says the first mention of *hogwash* in English. This wasn't much of a joke, even in 1440, for hogwash was then the common term for the garbage or slops fed to pigs. *Hogwash* is thus not slang but colloquial En-

glish; even in its figurative sense of insincere talk, "garbage," or misleading propaganda, the term dates back nearly 300 years.

hog wild. To become wildly excited or irrational due to excitement, anger, or even happiness. The Americanism probably originated in the mid-19th century, though it isn't recorded until about fifty years later. It obviously refers to the way hogs become wildly excited when aroused and is just as obviously another phrase from the farm, still hanging in there long after most Americans began buying their bacon wrapped in cellophane.

hoi polloi. *Hoi polloi* means the masses, the crowd, deriving from the Greek *hoi pol'oi* "the many." It shouldn't really be written as *the hoi polloi*, which is equivalent to saying "the the many," though great writers like Dryden have made this usage acceptable. *Hoi polloi* is often erroneously associated with snobs because of its resemblance to *hoity-toity*, (*q.v.*), "haughty or snobbish," another English word that dates back more than three centuries.

hoist with his own petard. The petard of medieval times wasn't a derrick, but a kind of rude hand grenade or mine that invaders would fasten to castle walls or gates. It took its name, oddly enough, from the French *peter*, "to break wind." Metal and bell-shaped, it contained an explosive charge that was fired by a slow-burning fuse, but it was often poorly constructed and went off prematurely, blowing up the man who lit it as well as the castle wall. Such a man was said to be *hoist* (lifted or heaved) *by his own petard*. (See **derrick**.)

hoity-toity. A pretentious upper-class Frenchman a few centuries ago often took the opportunity to literally look down from his *haut toit*, or "high roof" on the lower classes, his *haut toit* becoming through mispronunciation the English *hoity-toity*, "haughty, pretentious." Or so goes one theory on *hoity-toity's* origins. The *O.E.D.* claims the word is a rhyming compound based on *hoit*, "to romp," now obsolete. By this theory *hoity-toity*, first recorded as meaning giddy behavior (1668), came to mean haughty by 1830—possibly because the same socialites who were *hoity-toity*, "silly," were haughty as well.

hold at bay. Surprisingly, scholars haven't been able to connect this expression with hunting dogs that ran down big game like stags and held them at bay by barking, or baying, until the hunters arrived. Perhaps the baying of big-throated hounds bred for this purpose in medieval times did reinforce the expression; but *hold at bay*, to hold at a standstill, to keep someone on the defensive, derives from the French phrase *tener a bay*, which means "to hold in a state of suspense, to hold in abeyance." The

French expression, in turn, comes from the Italian *tenere a bada*, meaning the same. *Bada* in the latter phrase indicates the state of suspense or expectation, deriving from the Latin *badare*, "to open the mouth." So although the idea of dogs baying at a trapped stag conveys the idea behind the expression perfectly, it literally means to hold agape, or to hold with mouth open.

hold your horses.   Harness racing at American country fairs about a century and a half ago probably inspired the expression *hold your horses*. The amateur drivers, frequently young and inexperienced, often started their charges before a race had begun, leading the starter and the spectators to shout "Hold your horses!" By the 1840s the expression was being used to urge human patience in general.

holistic.   Though the word hardly fits in with that country's policy of apartheid, South African prime minister General Jan C. Smuts coined this term from the Greek for "whole" in his book *Holism and Evolution* (1926). Smuts wrote that "The whole-making, holistic tendency . . . operating in and through particular wholes, is seen at all stages of existence . . . There is a synthesis which makes the elements or parts act as one, or holistically." Thus *holism* is defined as "the theory that whole entities, as fundamental components of reality, have an existence other than as the mere sum of their parts."

holly.   The Romans used *holly* as a decoration in their wild festival of Saturnalia before the early Christians in Rome adopted it for Christmas. Related to the word *holy*, *holly* derives ultimately from the Anglo-Saxon *holen*, for the holly tree.

hollyhock.   The old favorite garden flower wasn't introduced to England by the Crusaders and named after the Holy Land as legend has it. *Holly hock* is a corruption of *holy hock*, which the plant was first called. *Hock* is an old name for "mallow," and the plant probably became *holy* because it had been known as *St. Cuthbert's cole* at one time. St. Cuthbert, who lived in the seventh century and also has an eider duck named for him, was of course holy and had his retreat on Holy Island (the Isle of Farne) off the English coast as well. He lived in a hermit's cell on the island, where the mallow grew in marshes, and pilgrimages were made there as early as the ninth century.

Hollywood.   The film capital of the world, laid out in 1887, is probably named for the California holly or toyon (*Heteromeles arbutifolia*), a large shrub that isn't a tree holly but whose scarlet berries, borne from Christmas to Easter, suggest the holly and are much used for Christmas ornaments. *Hollywood* may, however, be the transferred place-name of another Hollywood named for a true holly someplace where hollies are a native tree.

There is no proof for the tale that the town was first called Holywood by its pious founders, this corrupted to Hollywood as the town corrupted.

holocaust.   *The Holocaust* refers to the slaughter of over twelve million people, including six million Jews, in Nazi concentration camps, many murdered in cyanide gas showers, their bodies desecrated and burned in bake ovens. The word has been used in the sense of a great slaughter or massacre, usually by fire, for over three centuries, one writer noting that France's Louis XII "made a *holocaust* of 1,300 people in a church." *Holocaust* is also used today to describe a great fire, such as the firebomb raids of World War II, or Hiroshima and Nagasaki. A *holocaust* was originally a sacrifice completely consumed by fire, a burnt offering to the pagan gods, the word deriving from the Greek *holokaustos*, "burnt whole." *Kaustos*, "burnt," is also the basis of the English words *cauterize* and *caustic* (used literally of *caustic lime*, which burns, and figuratively of *caustic words* that "burn" their recipients).

holy deadlock.   (*See* **deadpan**.)

holystone.   Soft sandstone, often used to scrub the decks of ships, is called *holystone* because it is full of holes. First it was spelled *holeystone*, losing the "*e*," it's said, because sailors who used it knew no ease ("*e*'s") and had to kneel as if in prayer (a holy attitude) when scrubbing the decks.

homage.   When we pay homage to someone we are acknowledging our respect for him. This is what peasants were required by law to do in a medieval ceremony called *homage* (from the French *homme*, "man"), which demanded that a vassal kneel before his lord on the feudal estate and swear allegiance that he would ever be his man. From the ceremony comes our word *homage*, first recorded in 1390 in anything like its modern sense.

homburg.   The *homburg* hat, a soft felt *trilby* (*q.v.*), was first made at Homburg in Prussia. It was introduced to England by King Edward VII, who often enjoyed the hot springs in Homburg.

home, James, and don't spare the horses.   Passengers in autos still use this phrase humorously to friends when given lifts home by them. *Horses* here has nothing to do with engine horsepower, however. The old expression, dating back perhaps to the 17th century, was once a common command of English nobility to their private coachmen.

home, sweet home.   "Home, Sweet Home," its words written by John Howard Payne in 1823, may have used the melody of an old Italian folk song that Englishman Henry Bishop adapted when he wrote the music. Payne received 250 pounds from an English producer for the words and other material, the song first sung in a popular British opera of the time. Legend says that the author wrote the song while homesick in Paris. The Payne family cottage in East Hampton, Long Island, New York is a national landmark today.

Homeric laughter; Homer sometimes nods.   *Homeric laughter* is hearty, lusty laughter like that of the Gods in the greatest of epic poems. No one really knows who wrote the *Iliad* and *Odyssey*. Some authorities doubt that there was even a poet Homer, pointing out that the name means "one who puts together"; instead, they ascribe his work to a number of authors. But modern scholars tend to support the traditional story that the author was the blind Greek Homer, who lived in the ninth century B.C., wandered from city to city writing his poems, and whose life remains a blank historically. *Homer sometimes nods* is another expression associated with the author, meaning that the best of authors can make mistakes. This phrase comes from Horace's "Ars Poetica": "Sometimes even good old Homer nods."

hominy.   Hominy isn't a vegetable, as so many believe, but the inner part of corn (maize) that has been soaked to remove the hull. The word derives from the Algonquin Indian *rockhominy* for the dish.

homo sapiens.   Carolus Linnaeus (1707-78), the great Swedish botanist and methodical classifier of things animal, vegetable, and mineral, gave the name *homo sapiens*, "thinking man," to the human species. Before this the Latin *homo*, "man," had been similarly used, Shakespeare writing in *Henry IV, ii*: "Homo is a common name to all men." Linnaeus also first used the Mars (♂) and Venus (♀) symbols as symbols for male and female.

homosexual; heterosexual.   *Homosexual* does not derive from the Latin word *homo*, for "man," as *homo sapiens* does. It comes from the Greek *homos*, meaning "the same," like many other English words, including *homogenized* and *homonym*. Therefore, contrary to popular belief, it can be applied to females as well as males. Its antonym, *heterosexual*, comes from the Greek *heteros*, "other."

honey.   Several dictionaries of slang call *honey*, as a personal term of endearment for a lover, an Americanism originating in the 1880s. But among the Greek betrothal rings in the British Museum's collection is a gold ring from the fourth century B.C. engraved inside with the Greek word *meli*, "honey."

honkie; bohunk.   *Bohunk*, a low expression for a Polish- or Hungarian-American, arose at the turn of the century, and is probably a blend of *Bohemian* and *Hungarian* (both

Poles and Hungarians were called Bohemians). *Bohunks* were also called *hunkies*, and black workers in the Chicago meat-packing plants probably pronounced this as *honkie*, soon applying it as a derisive term not just for their Polish and Hungarian co-workers but for all whites.

honky-tonk.   The first printed use of this word for a cheap dance hall featuring gambling or burlesque shows, in a February 1894 Oklahoma newspaper, described a *honk-a-tonk* "well attended by ball-heads, bachelors and leading citizens." No one is sure how the word originated. The British attribute it to America, calling *honky-tonk* "Negro slang," while one American authority claims it is from the English dialect word *bonk*, "to idle about." Either way *honky-tonk* is a reduplication, with tonk repeating the sound of *honk*. ". . . It was nothing for a man to be drug out of them dead," testified a jazz musician of an early *honky-tonk*.

honorificabilitudinitatibus.   The making of long words was a popular game in Elizabethan England and *honorificabilitudinity*, meaning "honorableness," was one of the most absurd ones made. Shakespeare made fun of this word by stretching it out still longer in *Love's Labour's Lost*, using its original Latin ablative plural when he has Costard the clown say to the servant Moth: "I marvel thy master hath not eaten thee for a word, for thou art not so long by the head as *honorificabilitudinitatibus*" This is the word, incidentally, that to some "prove" Bacon was the author of all plays attributed to Shakespeare. For its rearranged letters form the Latin sentence *Hi ludi F. Baconis nati tuiti orbi*, which says, translated: "These plays born of F. Bacon, are preserved for the world."

hooch.   The American soldiers who first occupied Alaska in 1867 were forbidden any liquor, but the long Alaskan nights were cold. They apparently made do with crude firewater, a brew made in their own rude stills from yeast, flour, and sugar or molasses. This *booze* (*q.v.*) has been blamed on a local Indian tribe called the *Hoochen* by slightly *chauvinistic* or *groggy* (*q.v.*) etymologists, but these Alaskan natives only happened to live nearby—they were in reality the Hutsnuwu, Tlingit Indians, a name easy to mispronounce, and probably had no part in brewing the potent *hoochino* that the soldiers named after them. The brew's name remained *hoochino* or *hoochinoo* until the Klondike gold rush in 1897, when more of it was needed more often, in a hurry, and it was shortened to *hooch*. Being firewater, *hooch* was splendidly accurate to describe the bathtub concoctions, made during Prohibition, which wasn't called the Grand Experiment, however, for this reason. The name caught on and is still with us, though more in a comic sense for all liquor. *Hootch* is a variant spelling. A *hooch* to those among U.N. troops in Korea, 1951-54, was a temporary shelter, but there the word derives from the Japanese *uchi*, "house."

hood. Robin Hood, a good guy really, has nothing to do with the *hood* or *hoodlum*. But take your choice again; it's another word that stumps the experts. *Hoodlum* is first recorded in 1871. *Bartlett* tells us on hearsay evidence that a San Francisco reporter exposed a street gang at that time and changed its leader's name from Muldoon to Noodlum because he feared reprisals. The Irishman's name became *Hoodlum*, and soon a synonym for a cheap gangster, when the paper's compositor mistook the reporter's handwritten *N* for an *H*. The second variation on this tale has the Irish leader's name spelled backward, but associated with Hooligan and receiving the *H* that way. Variation number three suggests that this scourge of the Barbary Coast was so feared by the crusading newsman that he spelt the name *Hoodlum* all the way. But there are multifarious versions, aside from the variations. One, unlikely, is that *hoodlum* comes from the gang cry *Huddle 'em*. Another, very unlikely, has the word deriving from the pidgin English *hood lahnt*, "very lazy mandarin," in some vague reference to the many Chinese in San Francisco. In addition to the Chinese, the Spanish and Germans have also been called upon to take the Hibernians off the hook. Some authorities claim that the derogatory word is of Spanish origin, explaining no further, and the latest theory, which *Mencken* supports, suggests that *hoodlum* comes from the Bavarian dialect term *hodalump*, meaning "a small-time gangster." There were numerous German-Americans in the San Francisco area at the time and for this reason a mispronunciation of *hodalump* for *hoodlum* has its loyal supporters. However, the *hoodlums* I know pronounce the word like *mood*, not *hood*.

hooiaioia. *Hooiaioia* is the Hawaiian word for "certified." It has the distinction of having the most consecutive vowels, eight, of all the words in the world. The English leader is *queueing*, with five.

hook, line and sinker. Any extremely gullible person who swallows a fantastic yarn *hook, line, and sinker* is like a hungry fish who gulps down not only the fisherman's baited hook but the entire tackle. This Americanism has been traced back to the age of Davy Crockett, when tall tales hooked many a fish hungry for belief. But a 16th-century British expression, to *swallow a gudgeon* (a small bait fish), conveyed the same idea.

hooker. *Hooker*, for "a prostitute," may derive from the name of the small vessels called hookers that traded between British ports and the Hook of Holland in the 19th century. Prostitutes, it was said, would wait at the Hook for sailors from the hookers and lure them to their rooms. Another theory is that U.S. Civil War General Joseph Hooker, a fiery, opinionated man, didn't believe that his men should dissipate their energies in the Washington, D.C., red-light district, putting the area off-limits. His

troops, it seemed, counterattacked by dubbing all prostitutes, *hookers*. Still another theory traces hooker to the way a prostitute "hooked" prospective customers by linking arms with them.

Hookey Walker! Dickens used the variation *Walker!* in *A Christmas Carol*, but most Victorian writers wrote *Hookey Walker!* as a synonym for *incredible!* or *Nonsense!* on hearing a tall story. Several writers have suggested a hawk-nosed liar named John Walker as the source, but the origin of the expression is really unknown.

hooligan. A proper name is the origin for this word for a violent roughneck, a fact conclusively established when British etymologist Eric Partridge brought to light Clarence Rook's *Hooligan Nights* (1899) in his *Dictionary of Slang*. Excerpts from Rook's sociologically valuable work follow: "There was, but a few years ago a man called Patrick Hooligan, who walked to and fro among his fellow men, robbing them and occasionally bashing them . . . It is . . . certain that he lived in Irish Court, that he was employed as a chucker-out [bouncer] at various resorts in the neighborhood. Moreover, he could do more than his share of tea-leafing [stealing] . . . being handy with his fingers . . . Finally, one day he had a difference with a constable, put his light out . . . He was . . . given a lifer. But he had not been in gaol long before he had to go into hospital, where he died . . . The man must have had a forceful personality . . . a fascination, which elevated him into a type. It was doubtless the combination of skill and strength, a certain exuberance of lawlessness, an utter absence of scruple in his dealings, which marked him out as a leader among men . . . He left a great tradition . . . He established a cult." This man called Hooligan made the Lamb and Flag pub in the Southwark section of London his headquarters, attracting a gang of followers around him. The entire rowdy Hooligan family, the nucleus of his gang—their real name was probably Houlihan—"enlivened the drab monotony of Southwark," as another observer put it. The entry "Hooligan gang" is found on many police blotters in the late 1890s. *Hooligan* has also been used as a synonym for a prison guard, screw, or hack.

hoosegow. *Hoosegow* is a western word of the 1860s that derives from Spanish *juzgado*, "a court or tribunal," which to Mexicans means a jail and was borrowed in this sense by American cowboys. Our slang word *jug* for a jail probably also comes from *juzgado* and was recorded a half century or so earlier.

hootchie-kootchie. The Turkish belly dance that many of us "have no stomach for," as Beatrice Lillie once said. This name for the "mildly lascivious" dance—"not as sensuous as actual bumps and grinds since the hips are swayed rather than the pelvis rotated," we're told—has no source in an oriental name unless it possibly comes from the Bengal state of Coach Behar. The best guess is that *hootchie-kootchie* derives from the English dialect words *hotch*, "to shake," and *couch* (pronounced cooch), "to protrude." But this fails to explain why the dance was first recorded as the *cootchie-coot* in the 1890s. Dancer Little Egypt (Catherine Deviene) made a fortune and got herself arrested several times by dancing the hootchie-kootchie in the nude at the 1893 Chicago World's Fair and a number of private parties. A lowdown *hootchie-kootcher*, like Danny Kaye's Minnie the Moocher, is a *hootchie-kootchie* dancer.

Hoover hog.   (*See* **armadillo**.)

Hooverize, etc.   Before becoming the thirty-first President of the United States Herbert Clark Hoover (1874-1964) had a distinguished career as an engineer and administrator, popularizing scientific management among businessmen and inspiring the building on the Colorado River of Boulder (now *Hoover*) Dam, for example. Hoover first came to national attention as the head of various European relief agencies and as U.S. Food Administrator during World War I. In the latter capacity he met the food crisis by ending farm hoarding of crops, curbing speculation, and urging Americans to live by "the gospel of the clean plate" and to institute "wheatless and meatless" days. It was only a few days after these suggestions that the term *to Hooverize* began to appear in newspapers around the country, and housewives soon adopted the phrase when discussing ways to stretch food. Later, when Hoover was president during the Great Depression, more than a few derogatory terms bearing his name were invented. Shoes with hobs in them were *Hoover shoes*, and Hoover blankets were newspapers bums slept under. The *Hoover cart* was a southern mule-drawn wagon made from the rear axle and chassis of a discarded automobile, and a *Hooverville* was a collection of shacks housing the unemployed at the edges of cities throughout the country. Later *Hoover Commissions* under both Truman and Eisenhower studied the reorganization of the executive branch of government and suggested many improvements that were adopted. The *Hoover vacuum cleaner*—a *hoover* long a synonym for a vacuum cleaner—is named for the man who founded the Hoover company in the 1920s. (*See also* **armadillo**.)

hop on the bandwagon.   Barnum and earlier showmen perfected the American bandwagon—a brass band perched atop a brightly decked dray pulled by a team of horses—but politicians quickly adopted it for national and local election campaigns. It wasn't, however, until the handsome silver-throated champion of silver, William Jennings Bryan, ran for president for a second time in 1901 that the expression to *hop on the bandwagon*, "to rush to join a popular movement," entered the language.

The phrase remembers local politicians and ward heelers hopping up on Bryan's bandwagons as they banged and rolled through town, to show the support for their candidate and help create enthusiasm for him.

hopscotch.   The Scottish didn't invent the ancient children's game, and the *scotch* in its name had nothing to do with them, either, deriving from the lines that are hopped in the game, these being *scotched*, or scored, in the ground. In fact, the game was once called hop-score.

Horatio Alger story.   Ironically, none of the heroes Horatio Alger, Jr. (1834-99) created in his novels ever became rich. His poor but honest characters struggled to get ahead against overwhelming odds and always succeeded in improving their lot, even found fame and glory (at least one became a senator), but great monetary rewards never came to Ragged Dick and company. Nevertheless a *Horatio Alger story* became synonymous with a rags-to-riches story. Alger's books, of little interest to anyone but historians and nostalgia buffs today, served a real need in his time. Dull and unimaginative, as filled with preachments as his pages might be, his philosophy of hard work and clean living influenced three generations of Americans. In recent time historians have claimed that this author of moralistic books for children was a pederast obsessed with young boys.

horde.   (*See* **Asiatic hordes**.)

Hore-Belisha.   These black-and-white striped posts topped with yellow globes honor Lord Leslie Hore-Belisha, British Minister of Transport, 1934-37, who introduced them to indicate pedestrian crossings. A colorful, controversial figure, Hore-Belisha instituted a campaign to halt "mass murder" on the highways, and the beacons were a warning to drivers that pedestrians had the right-of-way at approaching intersections. Not overly modest, Lord Leslie seems to have named the lights after himself. The British statesman, born in 1895, fought in World War I as a major, was a member of Parliament, and served as head of the British War Office at the beginning of World War II. The beacons are often called *Hore-Belishas*.

hormone.   British scientist Dr. E. H. Sterling coined the word *hormone* from a Greek root meaning "to set in motion," in a 1905 article he wrote for the *Lancet* about such "chemical messengers." A hormone can be defined as "a substance formed in one organ and carried by the blood-stream to another organ, which it stimulates [sets in motion]."

horns of a dilemma.   *Lemma*, in Greek, means a thing taken for granted, deriving from *lampanien*, "to take." Affixing the Greek *di*, "two," we have *dilemma*, two things taken for granted. Therefore, in logic, a dilemma is an argument that forces a person to choose one of two things taken for granted, both of which may be untrue and unacceptable (*e.g.*, "Do you still beat your wife?"). Philosophers in the Middle Ages also called each *lemma* of a *double lemma* a horn, because it was so easy to get caught on the sharp point of each, even coining the Latin expression *argumentum cornutum*, "a horned argument." Since both terms meant the same, they were eventually wedded in the phrase *to be caught on the horns of a dilemma*, to be unable to make up one's mind about which course of action to choose.

hornswoggle. *Hornswoggle*, "to bamboozle or cheat," is one of the few extravagant American phrases of the early 19th century surviving today. It is described as "a fanciful formation" by *Mathews* and first attested in 1829 in Kentucky, but no one knows who coined it. It may be related to the English dialect word *connyfogle*, "to deceive in order to win a woman's sexual favors," which is rooted in the English slang *cunny* for vagina.

horsefeathers! As a euphemism for "horseshit!" this word has been around at least since 1925. It may or may not be related to the term *horsefeathers* once used in carpentry, these horsefeathers being the feathering strips used in roofing and siding houses. Because they are *big* feathering strips, they may have been called *horse feathers* (like *horseradish* (*q.v.*), etc.), but how these *horse feathers* came to be a euphemism for "horseshit!" is not clear—unless it came easily to some roofer's tongue when he had half-said "horseshit" and a lady abruptly appeared upon the scene. On the other hand, *horsefeathers* may have first been a synonym for "nonsense," originating with a saying such as, "That's nonsense, that's like saying horses have feathers!"

horse latitudes. The *horse latitudes*, region of calms found at 30 degrees north and south latitudes, may be so named because sailing ships carrying horses to America became becalmed and had to throw horses overboard in order to lighten the vessels and to take advantage of any slight breeze that did blow up. However, the name may simply be a translation of *golfo de las yeguas*, "gulf of the mares," which was the Spanish name for the ocean between Spain and the Canary Islands and compares the supposed fickleness of mares with the fickle winds in these latitudes.

horselaugh. A *horselaugh* is a loud, coarse, vulgar laugh, a guffaw. The word probably alludes to the loud neigh of a lusty horse, but an obscure pun on the word *horse* has also been suggested as a source. The expression has been common since Pope used it in 1710.

a horse of a different color. Cut into the chalk downs of Berkshire, England is the enormous crude outline of a galloping white horse covering some two acres. The figure possibly dates back to Saxon times, when a white horse was the emblem of Saxons invading Britain, and over the ages local residents have kept it clear of overgrowth. It is thought that this might be the source of the expression *a horse of a different color*, something of a different nature from what is under consideration, for the White Horse of Berkshire changes from green to white periodically when the locals clear grass and weeds from its outline. The expression may, however, come from races in medieval tournaments, where armored knights were distinguished by the color of their horses. A favored knight might have lost a race, leading one of his supporters to say "That's a horse of a different color" as the winner crossed the finish line. But both explanations are conjectures. The phrase is first recorded in Shakespeare's *Twelfth Night*, Shakespeare using the expression as if it were quite familiar to his audience.

horsepower. A car's *horsepower* is actually about one and a half times the power of a horse. Seeking a way to indicate the power exerted by his steam engine, inventor James Watt calculated that a strong dray horse averaged 2,200 foot-pounds per minute working at a gin on an eight-hour-a-day basis. Increasing this by 50 percent, Watt got 33,000 foot-pounds, which has ever since been one horsepower: "The standard theoretical unit of rate of work, equal to the raising of 33,000 pounds one foot high in one minute."

horseradish; etc. There is apparently no truth to old tales that the fiery horseradish (*Cochlearia armoricia*) is so named because it was once used to cure horses of colds, or because it made a good seasoning for horse meat. *Horse* is used as an adjective before a number of plants to indicate a large, strong, or coarse kind. Others include the horse-cucumber, horsemint, and horseplum. The *horseradish* is of course hotter, and has a much larger root and leaves than the ordinary radish. However, many plants *are* named after the horse because they were used to feed or train horses or because they resemble the animal. The horsebean is used as horse feed; horse-bane was supposed to cause palsy in horses; the horse-eye bean was thought to resemble a horse's eye; and the pods of horse-vetch are shaped like horseshoes. The horse chestnut, Gerade says in his famous *Herbal* (1597), bears its name because "people of the East countries do with the fruit thereof cure their horses of the cough . . . and such like diseases." But the horse chestnut is big, too, and when a slip is cut off the tree "obliquely close to the joint, it presents a miniature of a horse's hock and foot, shoe and nails." Incidentally, Samuel Pepys in his *Diary* mentions a *horseradish ale*, ale flavored with horseradish, which must have been hot indeed.

horse sense. *Horse sense* for good plain common sense comes from the American West, about 1850, inspired by the cowboys' trusty intelligent little cow ponies, trained even to do a good deal of cattle-herding work without directions from their riders (as noted in *The Nation*, August 18, 1870).

horses for courses. A mostly British expression urging someone to stick to the thing he knows best, *horses for courses* comes from the horse racing world, where it is widely assumed that some horses race better on certain courses than on others. In 1898 a British writer noted, in the first recorded use of the expression: "A familiar phrase on the turf is 'horses for courses.'"

horsmandering. This old word would serve well today in describing the efforts of the many public officials, even corrupt ones, who write books about their experiences. Meaning just that, *horsmandering* comes from the name of an 18th-century American judge who was "one of the first public servants to use his records of a public experience as the basis of a full-length book."

Hosackia. Few people know that New York City's Rockefeller Center was once the site of the famous Elgin Gardens, one of the first botanic gardens in America. The Elgin Gardens were established by Dr. David Hosack (1769-1835) who subsequently deeded them to Columbia University, long the landlord of Radio City. Hosack, a professor at Columbia, is remembered as the physician who attended Alexander Hamilton after his fatal duel with Aaron Burr. He served on the first faculty of Columbia's College of Physicians and Surgeons, and helped found Bellevue Hospital as well as founding and serving as first president of the now defunct Rutgers Medical College. Hosack wrote a number of medical and botanical books, including a biography of Casper Wistar (*see* **wisteria**). *Hosackia*, a genus of over fifty species of perennial herbs of the pea family, is named for him. Its most cultivated species is *H. gracilis*, "witch's teeth," a rock-garden plant about twelve inches high with pretty rose-pink flowers borne in small umbels.

hot as hell. The expression is heard so frequently that it's surprising that a compressed word such as *hotshell* hasn't evolved; it is certainly not slang anymore and is surely colloquial if not standard English by now. *Hot as hell* and *hot as hades* have been traced back only to the 18th century, but the idea is doubtlessly much, much older in one form or another. *Hell* is mentioned twenty-one times in the New Testament alone under various names (Hades, Gehenna, Hell, and Tartarus), and it was always thought to be hot in the nether regions. Internal heat in the form of hot springs and volcanoes and the fact that the temperature of the earth goes up as one digs deeper, no doubt gave early man the idea of a fiery underground hell. (*See* **drink like a fish**.)

hot-blooded; cold-blooded. One would guess such a basic term as hot-blooded, for "passionate or excitable," would go back to early English. But the term appears to have been coined by Shakespeare. Wrote the Swan of Avon, in *The Merry Wives of Windsor* (1598): "Now the hot-blooded gods assist me." Shakespeare had earlier coined, or at least first recorded, the antonym *cold-blooded*, in *King John* (1595): "Thou cold-blooded slave, hast thou not spoken like thunder on my side?"

hotcha. The Spanish word *muchacha*, for "a girl," may be the source of this expression of delight, pleasure, or approval over seeing someone sexually attractive. *Hotcha*, a favorite of Jimmy Durante, isn't used much anymore and could simply be an elaboration of *Ah-hah!* rather than a corruption of the Spanish exclamation for "What a girl!" It doesn't have anything to do with *cha*, the Cantonese word for tea that the British occasionally use.

hot dog. According to concessionaire Harry Stevens, who first served grilled franks on a split roll in about 1900, the franks were dubbed *hot dogs* by that prolific word inventor sports cartoonist T. A. Dorgan after he sampled them. "TAD" possibly had in mind the fact that many people believed frankfurters were made from dog meat at the time, and no doubt heard Stevens's vendors crying out "Get your red hots!" on cold days. Dorgan even drew the *hot dog* as a dachshund on a roll, leading the indignant Coney Island Chamber of Commerce to ban the use of the term *hot dog* by concessionaires there (they could be called only *Coney Islands*, *red hots* and *frankfurters*). *Hot dog!* became an ejaculation of approval by 1906, one that is still heard occasionally; *hot diggity dog!* was invented during the Roaring Twenties. Dorgan at least popularized the term *hot dog*, which may have been around since the late 1880s. (*See* **frankfurter**.)

hot pillow joint. (*See* **No-tel Motel**.)

hot slaw. (*See* **coleslaw**.)

Hottentot. The *Khoi-Khoin* were a proud tribe, and their native name meant "men among men," but they had the misfortune to be the first Africans to come in contact with the Dutch settlers of the Cape of Good Hope, eventually losing most of their land and now numbering less than twenty thousand. Even their name was taken from them and they became the *Hottentot* tribe, a word that means gibberish in English, describes a stupid, depraved person as well, and is sometimes used as an ugly slang word for a black person. *Hottentot* is the name that Boers gave to this South African tribe closely allied to the Bushmen. The Dutch and other Europeans, imposing their own values on another civilization, had long thought the pastoral people small and stupid; hence Hottentot's second meaning. As for *Hottentot* meaning "gibberish," the Khoi-Khoin dialect is full of harsh, staccato clicks and clacks and kissing sounds, unique in that it is spoken by breathing in rather than out. These noises made by the tongue (similar to the way we say "tsk tsk") sounded like so much stammering or clucking to Dutch ears. The Boers therefore named the people after what the language sounded like to them, calling them *Hottentots* from the Dutch *hateren en tateren*, to "stammer and stutter," and it wasn't long before *hottentot* was applied to any gibberish at all.

a hot time in the old town tonight.   "A Hot Time in the Old Town Tonight," by Theodore Metz, was the rallying song of Teddy Roosevelt's Rough Riders during the Spanish-American War and was so popular with all the troops that the enemy thought it was our national anthem!

hot toddy.   Today this drink, often used as a folk remedy to ward off colds, is made of brandy mixed with hot water, sugar, and spices. Originally, however, it was a drink called *tari*, made from the fermented sap of the palmyra tree, which the British encountered in India and brought home, changed in name and content, and called the *toddy*.

Houdini.   Someone who *pulls a Houdini* performs an amazing disappearing act or escape, and *a Houdini* is anyone with seemingly magical powers in any field. The expressions lionize Eric or Ehrich Weiss (1875-1926), an American magician who adopted the stage name Harry Houdini. Houdini named himself after Jean Eugene Robert Houdin (1805-71), a celebrated French magician noted for the fact that he did not attribute his feats to supernatural powers. Harry Houdini became world famous for his escapes from "impossible traps" such as locks, handcuffs, and straitjackets while suspended high in the air, or chained in chests submerged under water—all tricks, it is said, that can be explained today. A magician's magician who invented many magic tricks, he exposed numerous spiritualists and other fraudulent performers. Houdini also wrote a number of books and left his extensive magic library to the Library of Congress, where there is now a Houdini Room. The supreme magician has become the object of almost cult-like worship among fellow necromancers. Once he claimed that if anyone could break the shackles of death and contact the living from the grave, he could. Since his death—"He was fifty-two when he died, his life like a deck of cards"—followers have periodically held seances where he is buried in Glendale, New York in Machpelah Cemetery, a granite bust of the magician staring down at them. He has inspired a Houdini Hall of Fame at Niagara Falls, New York, and a worldwide research committee has been formed to determine whether the "Handcuff King" was really born in Budapest, Hungary on March 24, 1874, or in Appleton, Wisconsin on April 6, 1874.

to hound someone.   *Hound* derives from the common Teutonic *hund*, related to "hunt," and may be related to the Teutonic verb *hinpan*, "to seize," in reference to big hunting dogs that actually seized their prey. Eventually, however, the designation *hound* was reserved for hunting dogs that followed their quarry by scent. There were many breeds of these from early times, but all were noted for their tenacity as well as for their keen sense of smell. Hounds would follow a trail for hours, doubling back to find a scent if they lost it. By the late 16th century their grim persistence had suggested the expression *to hound someone*, to relentlessly pursue someone with the determination of a hound.

household words.   Shakespeare may have invented this workhorse phrase, for it is first recorded in his *Henry V*: ". . . then shall our name,/ Familier in their mouths as household words . . ." More likely, the Bard was repeating an already common expression.

houyhnhnms.   These are the intelligent breed of horses that Jonathan Swift created in *Gulliver's Travels* (1726). Swift said he coined their name from the characteristic whinny of a horse as it sounded to him. The talking horses, endowed with reason, ruled over the brutish Yahoos, another word coined by Swift in the book. *Gulliver's Travels* also gives us *brobdingnagian*, for any immense thing, after the giants Gulliver encounters in the county of Brobdingnag, and *lilliputian*, after Lilliput, a country of tiny people. *Houyhnhnms* is pronounced "whinims."

how!   Some etymologists believe the *how!* used by western Indians as a salutation is an abbreviation of "How do you do?" It could just as well derive from the Sioux *hao* or the Omaha *haw*, these ejaculations used in a variety of ways, signifying "come on" and "let us begin" as well as "hello."

Howard Libbey Tree.   The redwood, native to the coast of California and a few miles into Oregon, is probably the tallest tree in the world, and towering above all other redwoods is the specimen called the *Howard Libbey* or *Tall Tree* growing along Redwood Creek in California's Redwood National Park. Standing 367.8 feet tall, the Tall Tree may be the tallest tree of all time, although there are unconfirmed reports that an Australian eucalyptus felled in 1868 reached 464 feet. It was first named the *Howard Libbey* after the president of the Arcata Redwood Company, on whose land it was located until Congress established the park.

how come?   *Bartlett's* (1848) says *how come?* is "Doubtless an English phrase, brought over by the original settlers . . . the meaning . . . [being] How did what you tell me happen? How came it?" Others opt for the Dutch *hockum*, "why?," which the "original settlers" heard in New Amsterdam.

how do I love thee? let me count the ways.   The famous line above, from Elizabeth Barrett Browning's *Sonnets from the Portuguese*, is one of the best known in English poetry, but up until recently no one thought to actually count the ways Miss Barrett loved Mr. Browning in Sonnet XLIII. Author Randy Cohen did so and published the results in *New York* magazine, finding that she loved him "nine ways—unless 'with the breath,/ Smiles, tears, of all my life' is considered to be three separate ways, in which case she loved him a total of eleven ways." *Sonnets from the Portuguese* was written for Robert Browning and published, reportedly, only because Browning felt: "I dared not keep to myself the finest Sonnets written in any language since Shakespeare's." There is, of course, no Portuguese model for the sonnets and they were probably called *Sonnets from the Portuguese* because Browning's pet name for his wife was "my little Portuguese."

howdy.   Generally regarded as an expression born in the American West, *howdy*, a contraction of "how do you do?," began life as a Southern expression and was taken West by Confederate Civil War veterans. It is first recorded in 1840.

how the other half lives.   This expression for "how people belonging to another class live" usually refers to the rich today, but it originally referred to the poor. The words derive from the title of social reformer Jacob Riis's book *How the Other Half Lives* (1890), describing the lives of New York City poor people.

hubba-hubba.   "A delirious delight in language making," *Mencken* calls the coining of *hubba-hubba*. The expression was ubiquitous during World War II, made famous by a leering Bob Hope, the linguistic equivalent of a wolf whistle that was uttered lasciviously when an attractive woman walked past a group of men. Sexual but highly complimentary, it was often *hubba hubba hubba*, the third awesome *hubba* thrown in for added emphasis if body language warranted it. Anyway, we're told that the term originated with "flyboys," U.S. airmen who got it from Chinese airmen being trained at a Florida air base early in World War II. Supposedly it is a corruption of the familiar Chinese greeting *how-pu-how*. A second theory, wholly unpalatable, traces the expression to *Hubba*, "a cry given to warn fishermen of the approach of pilchards."

hubbub.   An ancient Irish war cry may be responsible for this word, meaning an uproar of confused sound from a crowd of voices. The O.E.D. suggested as a source the cry of *abu! abu!* repeated again and again by hordes of warriors running into battle. The word has been spelled

many ways. In its first recorded use (1555) it was an "yrishe (Irish) whobub." *In The Present State of Ireland* (1596) Edmund Spenser wrote: "They come running with a terrible yell and *hubbabowe*, as if heaven and earth would have gone together, which is the very image of the Irish *hubbabowe*, which theyr kerne [soldiers] used at theyr first encounter." Shakespeare called a *hubbub* a *Whoo-bub* in his *The Winter's Tale*.

huckleberry.   The first American settlers noticed the wild huckleberry, comparing it with the English bilberry, and first calling it a *hurtleberry or hirtleberry*, from which its present name derives. Huckleberries were so little, plentiful, and common a fruit that *a huckleberry* became early 19th-century slang for a small amount or a person of no consequence, both of these expressions probably inspiring Mark Twain to name his hero Huckleberry Finn. The berry was also used in the colloquial phrase *as thick as huckleberries*, very thick, and *to get the huckleberry*, to be laughed at or ridiculed, a predecessor of sorts of the raspberry (razz), or Bronx Cheer. *To be a huckleberry to someone's persimmon* meant, in 19th-century frontier vernacular, to be nothing in comparison with someone else. Huckleberries, which are not a true berry but a drupe fruit, belong to the *Gaylussacia* genus, which was so named in honor of French chemist Joseph Louis Gay-Lussac (1778-1850).

hue and cry.   For at least 600 years, up until the 19th century, *hue and cry* was the legal name in England for the outcry of someone who had been robbed, someone calling "with horn and with voice" for others to join in the chase after the thief. *Hue* is from the Old French *huer*, "to shout," and may have meant in ancient times the sound of a horn as well, while the cry was probably "Stop thief!" or something similar. In any case, the clamor that attended such chases (any man who refused to join in could be punished under the law) led to *hue and cry* becoming a synonym for any public clamor, protest, or alarm.

hulk.   (*See* **great hulking man**.)

hullabaloo.   (*See* **hurly-burly**.)

hull down over the horizon.   Sailors have long—no one knows how long—used this phrase to describe the phenomenon of the masts of an approaching ship appearing before her hull does. The phenomenon itself is one way observant people proved to themselves that the world was round and not flat long before Magellan's men circumnavigated the globe in 1522.

human.   (*See* **Adam**.)

humbug.   *Humbug*, a fraud or hoax, has long outlived those purists who so vehemently attacked the word when it entered the language from underworld slang in the 1750s. No one is sure just where *humbug* came from. Several authorities suggest the Irish *uim bog*, "soft copper," referring to the debased money with which James II flooded England from the Dublin mint. But *bug* in its slang sense had meant to cheat or "sting" before *humbug* was coined, and in former times people expressed approbation, perhaps even false encouragement, by humming. Then again, since the original meaning of bug is "bogey," a humbug may first have been a really harmless bug that hums and frightens us. Dickens's Scrooge with his "Bah, humbug!" gave the word great popularity worldwide, as did P. T. Barnum, "the Prince of Humbug."

humdrum. Maybe the *drum* got in the word just because it rhymed with the monotonous *hum*, but *humdrum* does suggest both the monotony of a humming bee or other insect and a monotonous drumbeat. Anyway, *humdrum* sounds like the boredom it imitates, meaning routine, monotonous, and dull. The term has been around since the early 16th century. Addison in *The Spectator* (1711) told his readers about "The *Hum-Drum Club* . . . made up of very honest Gentlemen of peaceful Despositions, that used to sit together, smoke their pipes and say nothing till Mid-night." A later writer, fed up with the *humdrumishness* of the world, said it was made up of "hum-drums and jog-trots." *Humdudgeon* means an imaginary illness, "nothing . . . but low spirits."

humility. (*See* **to eat humble pie**.)

hummums. *Hummums* is standard English for a Turkish bath, a corruption of the Arabic *hammam*, meaning the same. The word came into the language in the late 17th century and soon became, in the form of *hummum*, British slang for a brothel, because so many Turkish baths were corrupted into brothels.

humongous. *Humongous* has gotten a lot of play in the mid-1980s as a term for a huge, monstrous person, often wrestlers standing 6'8" or so and weighing about 300 pounds. The word is often used humorously and though its origin is obscure it seems to be based, consciously or subconsciously, on words like *huge, monstrous,* and *mountainous.*

Hun. After the Great Wall of China was built to contain them, the warlike nomadic tribe called the Huns thrust westward to Europe, where under Attila the Hun European Russia, Hungary, Poland, and Germany were tributary to them. The Hun's ethnic origins are unknown and there were at least four peoples bearing the name, but Attila, "the scourge of God," and his tribe destroyed the Burgundian German kingdom in A.D. 437 and occupied a large part of Germany. However, the use of *Hun*

for a German did not occur until 1900, when the Kaiser himself lovingly applied it to German soldiers leaving to fight in China. The name stuck because their behavior in the Orient proved *hunnish* and headline writers gladly adopted the nickname during World War I. In World War II *heinie, kraut,* and *gerry* were substituted by the British for Hun, but none of these terms was much used in America, *Nazi* taking their place.

a hundred of these days. *A hundred of these days* is a birthday wish commonly expressed by Italians and sometimes by Italian-Americans. Italians, however, attach less attention to birthdays than to a person's *name day,* the feast day of the patron saint after whom a person is named.

hundreds and thousands. *Hundreds and thousands* is an old name used mainly in England for the multicolored little sugar "sprinkles" used to decorate cakes and cookies. Their French name is *nonpareilles,* meaning "peerless."

Hungarian. (*See* **ogre**.)

Hungarian words in English. Hungarian is not an Indo-European language like most European tongues, but it has contributed a few words to the English lexicon, including *paprika, goulash,* and *coach.*

hunger. An ancient word deriving from the Old English *hungor.* There are few synonyms for hunger in English. By way of contrast, Otto Jesperson tells us in *The Growth and Structure of the English Language* that the Araucanian Indians speak a tongue "that distinguishes nicely between a great many shades of hunger."

hung higher than Gilderoy's kite. Patrick Mac Gregor, a handsome highwayman regarded as something of a Robin Hood in folklore, was nicknamed "Gilderoy" for his red hair (from the Scottish dialect words *Gillie roy,* "a red-headed lad"). The daring Gilderoy, who boasted that he had robbed old Cardinal Richelieu in the presence of the king and picked Cromwell's pocket, made the mistake of hanging a much-hated judge. A bad tactical error, for the judge who sentenced the outlaw after his capture in 1636 was a hanging judge who didn't want to encourage the hanging of hanging judges. He sentenced Gilderoy to be hanged far higher than his four confederates, "high aboon the rest" as the old ballad goes. Gilderoy's gallows stretched thirty feet into the Edinburgh sky, and he was left hanging there for weeks as a warning. No *kite,* or "body," had ever been hung higher than Gilderoy's, it was said by the thousands who saw him, and since that sad June day to be *hung higher than Gilderoy's kite* has signified the most severe punishment possible.

hunk.   (*See* **piece.**)

hunky-dory.   No one is certain about it, but a product called Hunkidori, a breath freshener introduced in 1868, may have given us the American expression *everything is hunky-dory*, or O.K. We do know for sure that *hunky-dory* is first recorded the same year that Hunkidori was introduced. The old tale that the word comes from the name of a pleasure street in Yokohama much frequented by American sailors seems to be spurious.

hunting pink.   The famous English *hunting pink* jacket is scarlet, not pink. Moreover, it never was pink, taking its name instead from the London tailor named Pink who designed it for fox hunting in the 18th century.

hurly-burly; hullabaloo.   The famous "When the Hurley-burley's done, When the Battaile's lost, and wonne," of *Macbeth's* witches seems to support the old story that *hurly-burly*, an uproar or noisy disturbance, derives from the excitement of burly men hurling spears in battle. But no proof of this exists. Neither does *hurly-burly* appear to have derived from *hullabaloo*, the Irish word for wailing at funerals, which now means any loud noise or uproar. The word may just be imitative of the howling of the wind—*burly* chosen to reduplicate *hurly* simply for the rhyme.

hurrah!   (*See* **hip! hip! hurrah!**)

hurricane.   A *hurricane*, the word deriving from the Spanish *huracan*, was first a violent tropical cyclonic storm of the western North Atlantic, but it eventually came to mean a violent storm in general. A hurricane is called a *hurricane* in the Caribbean Sea, but a *cyclone* in the Indian Ocean, and a *typhoon* in the China Sea.

hush puppy.   These cakes of deep-fried cornmeal batter, very popular in the South, have been traced back only to the time of World War I; at least the name isn't recorded before then. The most common explanation for the odd name is that hunters tossed bits of the cakes to their dogs, telling them to "*hush, puppy.*" A perhaps more authentic version notes that the cakes were first made in Florida, where people often fried fish outdoors in large pans, attracting dogs who would whine and bark. To quiet the dogs, the cook would fry up some cornmeal cakes and throw them to the dogs, shouting, "Hush, puppies!" *Hush puppies* for soft shoes or slippers seem to have been so named by the first company to manufacture them, in the 1960s.

husk.   Corn husks, the outer coverings of the corn, probably take their name from the German for "little house," *huske*. This name was first applied to the shells of various nuts and finally to corn when it was discovered in America.

husky.   Any man called *husky*, "stocky and muscular," is actually being compared to a sled dog—specifically, to a *husky*, or Eskimo dog, a strong breed capable of pulling great loads and covering sixty miles a day. Husky is used loosely for any arctic dog, but the breed is a recognized one. An unusual animal that yelps or howls like a wolf, although not closely related to the wolf, the husky normally feeds on fish and sleeps without shelter in the snow. Its name is a corruption of either the Tinneh Indian *uskimi*, "an Eskimo"; *Esky*, English slang for Eskimo; or the word *Eskimo* itself. Early explorers in the far north named the dog after the natives who bred it, and the dog's name was later applied to trappers who exhibited the breed's vigor, endurance, and stocky build.

hussy.   *Hussy*, a bold or lewd woman, was originally no more than another word for housewife, simply a phonetic reduction of the earlier term, which was first pronounced *hussif*. Justly or not, housewives were associated so often with impudence, boldness, or lewdness that the word *hussy* began to be used as early as the 17th century to describe bold and lewd women, possibly to provide a distinction in the language between most housewives and such women. Over the years *hussy* became more degraded, until we find Henry Fielding writing in *Tom Jones* (1749): "Hussy . . . I will make such a saucy trollop as yourself know that I am not a proper subject of your discourse."

hustings.   (*See* **take to the hustings.**)

hyacinth.   According to Greek legend, Hyacinthus was a handsome Spartan youth beloved by both the gods Apollo and Zephyrus, the West Wind. Jealous Zephyrus caused Apollo to kill Hyacinthus by making a heavy disc he had thrown while playing quoits go astray and strike the boy on the head. Although grief-stricken Apollo could not restore the youth's life, he made a beautiful new flower spring from the red earth and named it the *hyacinth*.

hybrid.   The offspring of a tame sow and a wild boar was called a *hybrida* by the Romans, and this Latin word came into English in the early 17th century to describe such animal offspring. *Hybrid* wasn't applied to plants until almost two hundred years later. A hybrid is, strictly speaking, the offspring of a cross-fertilization between parents differing in one or more genes, and a great many, possibly the majority, of cultivated plants have resulted from either natural or artificial hybridization, according to several experts.

hydroplane.   Almost as soon as the airplane became a reality in the early 20th century, inventors began experimenting with seaplanes with floats that were able to take off from and land on the sea. These were called *hydroplanes*, and some of the first examples were built in France. But the name created some confusion, and still does, for it had, since 1870, also been used for a light, high-powered boat designed to plane over the water at high speeds. Invented by English pastor Charles Meade Ramus in the mid-19th century, the hydroplane boat did not become a reality until about the same time as the seaplane. It is often called the *sea sled* or *hydrofoil* today.

hygiene. *Hygiene* derives from the name of *Hygeia*, the Greek goddess of health, who was daughter of Aesculapius, the god of medicine. Legend has it that Aesculapius once appeared in Rome during a plague in the form of a serpent; thus Hygeia's symbol is a serpent drinking from a cup in her hand.

hymen; hymn. *Hymen*, for the vaginal membrane, may derive either from the Greek *humen*, "membrane," or from the name of the Greek *Hyman* (Latin *Hymen*), "the god of marriage." The god could have taken his name from the membrane or the membrane may have been named for him. Our word *hymn* is related to *hymen*, coming from the related *hymnos*, "wedding song."

hype; hyperbole. Although there lived in the fourth century B.C. an Athenian demagogue named Hyperbolus given to exaggerated statements, his name does not give us the word *hyperbole*, or *hype*, as it is abbreviated today. *Hyperbole* derives from the Greek *hyper*, "over," plus *bole*, "throw," which conveys the idea of excess or exaggeration. Hyperbolus was just appropriately named.

hypochondriac. *Hypochondriac*, for a person morbidly anxious about his health, comes from the Greek *hypo*, "below, under," and *chondros*, "rib cartilages." This is puzzling until one learns that "under" the "rib cartilages" lies the upper abdomen, once thought to be the seat of melancholy. *Hypochondriac* is first recorded in its modern sense midway through the 17th century.

hypocrite. The Greek *Hypokrites* originally described an actor on the stage, but came to mean any pretender or liar. It is recorded in English late in the 13th century, for a person pretending to beliefs or feelings he doesn't really have.

hysteria. Early physicians decided 1) that women are more liable to emotional disturbances than men, and 2) that this was because of the malfunctioning of an organ men didn't have, the womb. This mistaken notion gave us the word *hysteria*, from the Greek *hysterikós* "of the womb."

I

I. The letter *I* comes from the stylized drawing of the Phoenician alphabet and is thought to have been based on a picture of the human finger. People at first did not have to remember to dot their *i*'s. The dot on the *i* wasn't added to the letter until the 11th century, when scribes introduced it to distinguish two *i*'s coming together (as in *filii*) from the letter *u*. Up until the 19th century the written and printed *i* and *j* were interchangeable and dictionaries didn't treat them as separate letters. Our word *I* is a shortening of the much older *ik*. The vowel in this word was originally pronounced like the *i* in *his*. (See **iota; tittle**.)

I am going to telephone Hitler (je vais téléphoner à Hitler). A euphemism members of the French Resistance used during World War II when they excused themselves to go to the toilet.

Iberia's pilot. Since 500 years will soon have passed since Columbus sailed the ocean blue in fourteen hundred and ninety-two we should record this little-known name for the great navigator, first recorded in the poem "Pleasures of Hope" (1799), by Scottish poet Thomas Campell. (*See also* **few and far between**.)

I cannot tell a lie (Pa). The folktale of George Washington cutting down the cherry tree and admitting it to his father ("I cannot tell a lie, Pa") is one of the most persistent in American history. It is first recorded in the Reverend Mason L. Weems's *Life of Washington* (1800), told to him by an old lady who had spent much time with the family. No one has ever *disproved* this story, though there is some evidence that it was current as a country tale before Parson Weems printed it. Weems's book went through over forty editions, and millions of Americans were raised on the story, including Abraham Lincoln, who borrowed a copy of the book, and when it was damaged by a sudden rain had to work three days to pay its owner for it. All we can say with certainty is that like most folklore the tale was exaggerated over the years: a tree stripped of bark becoming the chopped-down tree, "I can't tell a lie, Pa," becoming "Father, I cannot tell a lie."

I can't believe I ate the whole thing. (*See* **good to the last drop**.)

Icebergia. (*See* **Alaska**.)

iceblink. Seamen gave the name *iceblink* to a luminous sky caused by light reflected from ice. The term is first recorded late in the 18th century and was shortly applied as well to the huge ice cliffs of Greenland.

ichor. *Ichor* (rhyming with "liquor") is in classical mythology "the ethereal fluid that flows in the veins of the gods" in place of blood. From such lofty heights *ichor* fell to become the English name for the blood of animals, little used today, and, finally, the water discharged from a wound or ulcer!

iconoclast. A debunker, one who attacks cherished beliefs, is called an *iconoclast*. The word dates from the time of Byzantine emperor Leo III, who in 726 began a program of destroying icons, or images, in churches because he believed his people actually worshipped the icons, not the religious figures they represented. The monks fanatically opposed Leo and called him, among other things, an *iconoclast*, "image breaker," the first recorded use of the word.

Idaho. *Idaho* may be the only state name that is a complete fraud—at any rate, its name may mean nothing at all. Many sources derive the word *Idaho* from a Shoshonean Indian word meaning "gem of the mountain," but the Idaho State Historical Society claims that there never was any such Indian word and that *Idaho* and its translation was the phony creation of a mining lobbyist who suggested it to Congress as the name for the territory we now know as Colorado. Congress rejected the name, but it caught on among gold prospectors along the Columbia River and when it was proposed in 1863 as the name for what we know today as Idaho, Congress approved it and the *Idaho Territory* was born. The origin of the word may be Shoshonean, however, though it does not mean "gem of the mountain" or "Behold! The sun is coming down the mountain," as another writer suggested. Idaho residents, in fact, ought to forget about the real Shoshone word that *Idaho* may have derived from, for that word would be *Idahi*, a Kiowa curse for the Comanches that translates roughly as "eaters of feces," "performers of unnatural acts," "sources of foul odors," etc.

idiolect. (*See* **acrolect**.)

idiot. When Horace Walpole dubbed Oliver Goldsmith "The Inspired Idiot," he wasn't aware that the ancient Greeks had often termed prose writers idiots. The word *idiot* first meant an uneducated, ignorant person, which the Greeks considered prose writers (but not poets) to be. This can be seen in the Greek expression "A poet or an idiot" (prose writer). In more recent times Georges Simenon said that Count Keyserling once called him an "imbecile de genie." Today *idiot* usually means a foolish person or, scientifically, someone with a mental age no higher than that of a child of 3 or 4 years of age.

I disapprove of what you say, but I will defend to the death your right to say it. Voltaire didn't say it. In her book *The Friends of Voltaire* (1906), E. Beatrice Hall, using the pen name S.G. Tallentyre, proposed this well-known quotation on freedom of speech as a paraphrase on a thought in Voltaire's *Essay on Tolerance*: "Think for yourself and let others enjoy the privilege to do so too."

I do not love thee, Dr. Fell.

I do not love thee, Dr. Fell,
The reason why I cannot tell;
But this alone I know full well,
I do not love thee, Dr. Fell.

Dr. John Fell (1625-86), dean of Christ Church, Oxford, and bishop of Oxford, was quite a permissive teacher for his day, even allowing classroom debates, which often ended in free-for-alls. Yet, well liked as he was, his name is still used to describe someone disliked for no apparent reason. He owes his unjust fate to Thomas Brown, once his student at Christ Church and later an author. Dean Fell had threatened to expel Brown for some classroom offense if he could not translate a couplet of Martial. The resulting jingle above bore little resemblance to the Thirty-third epigram, but Dr. Fell good-naturedly accepted the paraphrase. Dr. Fell is also remembered for the *Fell types* he collected for the university press. Thomas Brown never wrote anything else that was remembered.

I'd rather dine with Jack Ketch. (*See* **H.**)

if I can't dance, it's not my revolution. A favorite among women (especially on T-shirts) in the ferment of the 1960s, this expression actually originated with anarchist Emma Goldman half a century earlier. She supposedly said this when her lover and fellow anarchist Alexander Berkman berated her one night for dancing wildly in a radical hangout.

if the mountain will not come to Muhammad, Muhammad must go to the mountain. The saying arises from the time when Muhammad, founder of the Moslem religion and prophet of its God Allah, brought his message to the Arabs, and they demanded miraculous proof of his claims. He ordered Mount Safa to move, and when it failed to do so, explained that God had been merciful—for if the mountain had moved it would have fallen on and

destroyed them all. Muhammad then went to the mountain and gave thanks to God. The proverb is used to indicate that it is wise to bow before the inevitable after failing to get one's way. (*See* **Muhammadanism.**)

if you can't lick 'em, join 'em. This Americanism probably dates back to the late 19th or early 20th century. Cynical and pragmatic, it comes from the political precincts, as one would expect.

if you've got the money, honey, I've got the time. There is a popular song of this title, but the expression has its roots in the *any day you 'ave the money, I 'ave the time*, an approach said to have been much used by prostitutes and "enthusiastic near-amateurs" in London toward the beginning of the century.

if you want peace, prepare for war. Whether this advice remains good in our nuclear age is debatable, but there is no denying that this is an ancient phrase. It is a translation of the Latin proverb of the Romans: *Si vis pacem, para bellum.*

ignoramus. Up until the 17th century *ignoramus* was just the Latin plural for "We don't know" and was written by grand juries across the backs of indictments if they thought there wasn't enough evidence in a case for the accused to be prosecuted. *Ignoramus* took on its present meaning in 1615, when George Ruggle wrote a play entitled *Ignoramus*, after the name of its main character, a lawyer who didn't know anything about the law. Soon this ignorant fictional lawyer's name was being applied to any ignorant person, lawyer or not. (*See* **ignore.**)

ignorance is bliss.

Yet ah! why should they know their fate?
Since sorrow never comes too late,
And happiness too swiftly flies
Thought would destroy their paradise.
No more; where ignorance is bliss,
Tis folly to be wise.

English poet Thomas Gray wrote the above in his *Ode on a Distant Prospect of Eton College* (1742), and unintentionally added a proverb to the language. It has been observed that Gray didn't mean it is better to be ignorant than wise at all times, the popular usage given to his words, for he makes an important qualification by using the word *where*. But a reading of the whole poem shows that he did mean it is better for man to be blissfully ignorant of his fate.

ignore. *Ignore*, in the sense of "pay no attention," was a word scorned by pedants well into the 19th century. It apparently derives from the old law term *ignoramus*. Indictments not to be sent to court were marked *ignoramus,* "not found," on the back by the grand jury. They were thus given no attention by the court, or *ignored*. (*See* **ignoramus**.)

I have not yet begun to fight.   (*See* **sir, I have not yet begun to fight**.)

IHS.   This well-known abbreviation, used as a symbol or monogram, is simply the first two letters and last letter of the Greek word for Jesus, capitalized and Romanized. It does not stand for *in hoc signo* ("in this sign") or any other phrase.

an Iliad of woes.   This old expression was used in a similar form by the ancient Greeks. It refers, of course, to the myriad human woes mentioned in Homer's *Iliad*, which ignores virtually no calamity that can befall humankind.

I like Ike.   (*See* **Eisenhower jacket; he kept us out of war**.)

ilk.   *Of that ilk* means of the same class or kind, *ilk* coming from the Old English *ilca*, meaning "same." The expression has been traced back to about 800 A.D.

I'll be there with bells on.   Early 18th-century Conestoga wagons usually arrived at their destination with bronze bells ringing, giving rise to this Americanism. These same Conestogas are responsible for traffic moving on the right side of the road in the U.S. rather than on the left as in Britain. According to one authority, the Conestogas were "best guided from the left and so afforded a clear view ahead only when driven from the right side of the road. Drivers of other vehicles found it not only wise not to argue but convenient to follow in the ruts made by the heavy wagons and habit soon became law." (*See* **stogy**.)

illeist.   The word for the habit of referring to oneself excessively in the third person singular is *illeism*. A nonce word modeled on the Latin *ille* ("he") and *egoism*, it was apparently invented by Coleridge, or at least he is the first author recorded to have used this coining for "a consummate egoist" (in about 1809). Using *he* does sound better than employing the royal *we*, and even a little better than constantly using *I*, for which Victor Hugo was called "a walking personal pronoun."

Illinois.   This central "Prairie State" is named for the Illinois Indians, as the French called the confederation of six Indian tribes in the area. Frenchmen were the first Europeans to enter Illinois territory, in 1673. They changed the Indian name *Hileni* or *Ileni*, meaning "man," to *Illin*, adding their *ois* plural. Since the Indian plural is *uk*, *Illinois* might be *Illinuk* today if they hadn't done so.

The Illinois group is almost extinct today, numbering between two and three hundred, compared to an estimated eight thousand in the 17th century.

I love everything that's old.   The expression refers to the preference of Squire Hardcastle in Oliver Goldsmith's *She Stoops to Conquer* (1773), who "loves everything that's old: old friends, old times, old manners, old books, old wine."

Ima Hogg.   Perhaps this is the *best known* of humorous American names, for *Ima Hogg's* father was the governor of Texas and she was a prominent socialite (her sister's name was Ura Hogg). It is not necessarily the *best* humorous real American name, for we have hundreds of gems like the following to choose from: Virgin Muse, Fairy Guy, Lance Amorous, Etta Turnipseed, Fannie Bottom, Arsie Phalla, and Dill L. Pickle (who was a pickle salesman). There was even someone named La Void.

I'm all right, Jack.   First recorded in the late 19th century, *I'm all right, Jack* was originally British naval slang employing the *Jack* of *Jack Tar* (*q.v.*) and a shortening of the lustier "Fuck you, I'm all right, Jack," common in the military at the time.

I'm from Missouri.   During the Civil War, "an officer of the Northern army fell upon a body of Confederate troops commanded by a Missourian. The Northerner demanded a surrender, saying he had so many thousand men in his unit. The Confederate commander, game to the core, said he didn't believe the Northerner's boast of numerical superiority and appended the now famous expression, "I'm from Missouri; you'll have to show me." Dr. Walter B. Stevens recorded this proud derivation of the phrase in *A Colonial History of Missouri* (1921), but other authorities support the following derogatory origin: Miners from the lead district of southwest Missouri had been imported to work the mines in Leadville, Colorado, sometime after the Civil War. They were unfamiliar with the mining procedures in Leadville and fellow workers regarded them as slow to learn, their pit bosses constantly using the expression, "He's from Missouri; you'll have to show him." Residents of the "Show Me" state obviously favor the former theory, and "I'm from Mizorra," as they said, is a badge of distinction, signifying native skepticism and shrewdness.

immelmann maneuver.   A word still familiar to flyers and aviation buffs, *immelmann* honors a World War I ace. German pilot Max Immelmann devised this aerial maneuver in which a pursued flyer pulls up and comes over in a sharp turn that puts him on the offensive at his pursuer's tail. Immelmann was only twenty-six when he was shot down and killed in combat in 1916.

immolate.   *Immolate* means to sacrifice by fire or other means, but it derives from the Latin *immolare,* "to sprinkle with meal." This is because the ancient Romans sprinkled wine and pieces of the sacred cake, made from meal, on the heads of humans to be sacrificed to the gods.

imp.   A graft or shoot was called an *impian* by the Anglo-Saxons and this word, shortened to *imp,* later came to mean an offspring or a child. At first *imp* meant any child, but the word is now almost always applied to a mischievous child.

impatiens.   (*See* **noli me tangere.**)

imperial beard.   Louis Napoleon (1808-73), nephew of Napoleon Bonaparte, staged a coup d'état in 1851 that made him emperor the following year. As Napoleon III, the despot reigned until his empire was overthrown twenty years later and he retired to England. While emperor, Napoleon sported a small, pointed tuft of hair under the lower lip that was named an *imperial beard* in his honor.

impressionism.   A painting by Claude Monet entitled *Impression-Sunset* is responsible for the name of the school of art called *impressionism.* French critic Louis Leroy coined the term in a review he wrote on April 25, 1874, ridiculing Monet's painting and others of an experimental nature that he had seen exhibited at a photographer's studio in Paris. Meaning to be sarcastic, he entitled his review *L'Exposition des Impressionists.* Soon the term caught on, losing its pejorative sense.

in a hole.   The expression *in a hole,* "in debt or some other kind of trouble," can be traced to gambling houses of the mid-19th century where the proprietors took a certain percentage of each hand for the house. This money, according to a gambling book of the time, was put in the "hole," which was "a slot cut in the middle of the poker table, leading to a locked drawer underneath, and all checks deposited therein are the property of the keeper of the place." When one had put more money into the poker table hole than was in his pocket, he was *in a hole.*

in a pretty pickle.   *In de pikel zitten,* a Dutch phrase going back at least four centuries, literally means to sit in the salt solution used for preserving pickles. This saying apparently suggested the expression to be *in a pretty pickle,* an uncomfortable or sorry plight—like someone sitting in such a bath. Our word *pickle* comes from the Dutch. A sour pickle is perhaps the last thing anyone would expect to be named after a man, but at least one source claims that the word *pickle* derives from the name of William Beukel or Bukelz, a 14th-century Dutchman who supposedly first pickled fish, inventing the process

by which we shrink and sour cucumbers. This pickled-herring theory may be a *red herring* (*q.v.*), however. All the big dictionaries follow the *O.E.D.'s* lead in tracing pickle to the medieval Dutch word *pekel,* whose origin is ultimately unknown.

inaugurate.   (*See* **auspicious.**)

inauspicious.   It has been remarked that "no other word ever had such a premiere as *inauspicious,* which made its debut in Shakespeare's *Romeo and Juliet,* Romeo crying:

> Here, here, will I remain . . .
> And shake the yoke of inauspicious stars
> From this world-wearied flesh.

Shakespeare probably invented *inauspicious,* as he did *auspicious* (in *The Tempest*), meaning favorable, conducive to success. Its roots are in the Latin *auspex,* a corruption of *avispex,* for the Roman birdwatcher who deduced omens from the flight of birds.

in a word.   Briefly, shortly. Shakespeare may have coined this phrase, for he is the first to record it, in *Two Gentlemen of Verona* (1591): "And in a word . . . he is compleat in feature and in mind."

Incas.   The Peruvian Indians of South America did not call themselves the Incas, as the Spanish did. Inca in their language meant lord, king, or ruler, a "man of the royal blood" or a king's relative, not any one of their people. The king himself was sometimes called the *Capa Inca,* or "sole lord."

incorporated; Inc.   No one seems to know what corporation first abbreviated *incorporated* to *Inc.* after its name. *Incorporated* means to be united in one body, *incorporate* and *incorporated* having been used in the sense of legal or formal business corporations since the 15th century.

incubate; incubus.   (*See* **nightmare.**)

incunabula.   The word *incunabula* (the singular form is *incunabulum*) is used to signify books produced in the infancy of printing from movable type, usually those printed before 1500. Caxton's edition of *The Canterbury Tales,* printed in 1478, is a famous incunabulum. The Germans coined the name *incunabula* for these early books in the 19th century, using the Latin word for swaddling clothes and cradle.

indenture.   *Indenture* strictly means "a document with serrated edges," deriving from the Latin *dens,* "tooth," and referring to the once common practice of cutting a document into halves with serrated edges—one half to each party of agreement—so that the document could be authenticated by fitting the edges together. The word's legal meaning today is "a contract in which two parties bind themselves to an exchange of services and observances." *Indentured servitude*, sometimes called "white slavery" and banned under the U.S. Constitution, bound a person to service to another for a period of time, usually seven years, and could amount to virtual slavery. A number of noted early Americans were once indentured servants.

India ink. In France *India ink* is called *China ink* as it rightly should be, for it was invented in China and first traded there. *India ink* it is in America and England, as it has been since 1665, when the dark black ink is mentioned in Samuel Pepys's famous *Diary*.

Indian. At least one writer has speculated that *Indian* may have been suggested to Columbus as a name for the Taino people he encountered because they were so friendly, peaceful, and gentle, *una gente in Dios*, a people of God. But there is no proof of this, most etymologists believing these people were mistakenly named by Columbus because he thought he had reached the Indies of Asia, the first but not the worst mistake immigrants made regarding the native Americans.

Indiana. Indiana's name denotes that it was the domain of Indians. Before it became our 21st state in 1816 the *Hoosier State* had been called the *Indian Territory*.

Indian bread. Pioneers called the strip of fatty meat extending from the shoulder along the backbone of the buffalo *Indian bread* because the Indians favored it. As one writer put it: "When scalded in hot grease to seal it, then smoked, it became a 'tit-bit' the buffalo hunter used as bread. When eaten with lean or dried meat it made an excellent sandwich."

Indian giver. Tradition holds that American Indians took back their gifts when they didn't get equally valuable ones in return. Some Indians were no doubt *Indian givers*; others, however, got insulted if they received *more* than they gave. Instances of Indians *Indian-giving* are hard to come by, and even the *Handbook of American Indians* (1901), published by the Smithsonian Institution, defines the practice as an "alleged custom." Perhaps the expression is explained by the fact that *Indian* was once widely used as a synonym for bogus or false. Many of the nearly five hundred terms prefixed with *Indian* unfairly impugn the Indian's honesty or intelligence—even *honest Injun* was originally meant sarcastically, and *Indian summer* means a false summer.

Indian post office. Indians in the American West often piled sticks and stones in a mound to indicate that they had been at a certain point and would return there in a certain number of days, depending on the number of rocks and sticks piled there. Cowboys called such a mound an *Indian post office* because messages could be left there.

Indian words in English. It is estimated that nearly a thousand basic English words derive from words in Hindu, Sanskrit and Romany, all Indian languages. Some of these are: *panther, ginger, pepper, sandal, guru, pundit, nabob, punch* (drink), *chintz, mongoose, dungaree, cot, bungalow, juggernaut, tomtom, mugger, bandana, jute, sari, chit, myna, jingle, shampoo, puttee, cashmere, thus, pajamas, gazelle, dumdum, loot, dinghy, polo, chutney, zen* (through Japan), and *loot*.

indri. The little short-tailed lemur of Madagascar was so named a century ago when a French naturalist and his Madagascan guide were identifying animals in the jungle. The guide saw a lemur and cried "Indry! Indry!" This actually meant "Look! Look!," but the naturalist recorded it as the animal's native name and the lemur has been called the *indri* (*Indri indri*) ever since. (*See* **kangaroo** for a similar story.)

infant; infantry. First recorded by John Wycliffe in 1382 *infant* comes from the Latin *infans*, "unable to speak." It once meant a "childe" or "a young knight, a youth of gentle birth" as well as a baby. Thus we have the word *infantry* for foot soldiers, "soldiers too young and inexperienced to serve in the cavalry."

inferiority complex. Carl Jung established the psychoanalytical term *complex* in a 1907 work, but it had been coined by his colleague A.L.S. Neisser a year before. *Complex* means in this sense "a system of interrelated, emotion-charged ideas, feelings, memories, and impulses that is usually repressed and that gives rise to abnormal or pathological behavior." *Inferiority complex* became a psychiatric term at about the same time and came generally to mean "lack of self esteem, lack of confidence."

infernal machine. President John Tyler once had White House ushers defuse a package that he thought to be *an infernal machine*, or bomb, but that turned out to conceal a mere cake. *Infernal machine* has been synonymous for a bomb concealed as some harmless object since at least 1810, and in the form of *infernal apparatus* is recorded in 1769. The *infernal* in the phrase derives from the Latin *infernalis*, "of the realms below, or hell."

inflation. The word *inflation*, used in relation to inflated prices and money, is first recorded in 1838, during the Panic of 1837, which actually lasted three years. President Martin Van Buren did nothing to alleviate the

Panic or the bread riots that it brought, enabling William Henry Harrison to defeat him in his 1840 bid for reelection.

influenza. *Influenza* first entered the language about 1743, when an outbreak of "a contagious distemper" was reported in Rome. This was called "the Influenza" because it was believed to have been evilly "influenced" by the stars, and such occult *influenzas* were said to cause plagues and pestilences as well. The Italian word for influence, anglicized in pronunciation, became the English specific name.

infra dig. This is short for the Latin *infra dignitatem*, "beneath one's dignity," and means something not befitting one's position, station, character, or talent.

in German a young lady has no sex, but a turnip has. Mark Twain said this and he was referring to the fact that while vegetable names are given a gender in the German language, the words *Madchen*, for "girl," and *Weib*, for "wife," "female," and "woman," are not feminine but, curiously, neuter.

in God we trust. *Mind Your Business* was the first motto used on a U.S. coin. *In God We Trust*, the motto now found on all American coins large enough to hold it, was authorized by two Congressional acts of 1865. It was used on the eagle (the $10 gold piece), the double eagle (the $20 gold piece), the half eagle (the $5 gold piece), the silver dollar, the half dollar, and the quarter—and still appears on those latter three coins. This motto inspired the humorous slogan *In God We Trusted, In Kansas We Busted* that settlers in Kansas, bankrupt by the severe droughts from 1887 to 1891, painted on their old covered wagons when they returned East.

in hock. In the game of faro, much played in 19th-century America, the last card in the box was called the *hocketty card* (from a word of unknown origin), this card later said *to be in hock*, as was any player who bet on the last card. This was a bad bet, most often a losing one, so that *to be in hock* soon meant "to owe money." Pawnshops were a convenient place to get money to pay debts, so they became known as *hock shops*, and *to be in hock* soon meant to have some or all one's valuable possessions in a hock shop or, generally, to be in very bad financial shape.

in Hoover we trusted, now we are busted. Herbert Hoover won the U.S. Presidency in 1928 with his party's slogans "A chicken in every pot" (*q.v.*), and "Rum, Romanism and rebellion" (*q.v.*), the latter a reference to his opponent Al Smith's Catholicism. He lost the presidency in 1932, in the midst of the Great Depression, Franklin D. Roosevelt's supporters calling for "New Deal" and chanting *in Hoover we trusted, now we are busted*. (*See* **Hooverize.**)

in like Flynn. Chicago's "Boss" Flynn's machine never lost an election and was always "in office," inspiring the expression *in like Flynn*, meaning "to have it made." The popularity of movie actor Errol Flynn and his amorous activities helped popularize the phrase in the early 1940s.

innocuous desuetude. President Grover Cleveland coined this phrase and first used it in a message to Congress on March 1, 1886. It means "harmless disuse" and describes a law, custom, or anything else long disregarded, something on the junk pile. Said President Cleveland: "After an existence of nearly twenty years of almost *innocuous desuetude*, these laws are brought forth." Later, Cleveland explained that he thought such sesquipedalian words (*i.e.*, words a foot-and-a-half long) "would please the Western taxpayer," give them something for their money.

Inuit. (*See* **Eskimo.**)

in one ear and out the other. Only slightly changed over the past four centuries, this expression, said of things that make no impression on the mind, dates back to at least 1583, when an annoyed preacher said that his sermon "goes in one ear and out the other." Almost two centuries earlier, in about 1400, the expression is used in the poem "Romaunt of the Rose" in the form of "out at oon er/ That in at that other."

insane root. Banquo says to the witches in *Macbeth*:

> Were such things here as we do speak about?
> Or have we eaten the insane root
> That takes the reason prisoner?

Either henbane (*Hyoscymus niger*) or poison hemlock (*Conium maculatum*), the hemlock that killed Socrates, is the *insane root* of the ancients that was supposed to deprive anyone who ingested it of his senses.

insect. (*See* **bug.**)

intelligentsia. Another Russian borrowing. The Latin *intelligere* (*inter*, "between" + *legere*, "to choose"), "to perceive or understand," is the ultimate basis of our word *intelligentsia* for the "intellectual elite," but the word comes to us through the Russian *intelligentsiya*, taken from the Latin. It came into English in the 1920s.

interloper. The Russia Company, operated by Englishmen, had a virtual monopoly on Russian trade in the late 16th century, but Spanish traders bribed czarist officials in trying to break the monopoly, and the English in propagandizing against them coined the word *interloper* to describe the trespassers, building it from the Latin *inter*, "between," and the English *lope*, "to run."

international. Eccentric English philosopher Jeremy Bentham coined the much used word *international* in 1780. He is also responsible for *maximize* and *minimize*, and thus the ancestor of a lot of less desirable advertising words ending in "ize."

the Internationale. The song of revolutionaries the world over today, the *Internationale* was first sung in France, in 1871. It was not the anthem of the French Revolution, as many people believe. (*See* **Marseillaise**.)

intestinal fortitude. The head coach of Ohio State University's football team, Dr. John W. Wilce, is said to have invented this word for "guts" in 1915 as "a protest against the lurid language of the gridiron and locker room," *guts* then being considered "improper for drawing-room conversation." They don't make coaches like Dr. Wilce anymore, nor locker rooms so mild.

in the bag. It's usually assumed that this metaphor derives from hunting, where it refers to birds and other small game already safely in the game bag. *Bag* has been used as an abbreviation for *game bag* since at least the 15th century, but the expression *in the bag* is first recorded in 1925. William Bancroft Miller, writing in *Verbatim* (February 1977), offers another explanation, attributing the phrase to cockfighting: "Until comparatively recent years, it was common to transport game chickens to the scene of battle in cloth bags rather than in the comfortable and elaborate carrying cases now in vogue, and the roosters were not removed until the fight was about to begin. A cocker, confident of the prowess of his feathered warrior, would say that victory was *in the bag* for him." Neither theory is supported by quotations and neither explains the sinister implication these words often have, for the expression frequently means "rigged" or "fixed."

in the chips. (*See* **chip in**.)

in the doghouse. The expression *in the doghouse*, "out of favor or undergoing punishment," isn't of ancient origin but is an Americanism first recorded toward the end of the 19th century. Possibly the term originated during the African slave trade, when sailors locked the hatches at night, to prevent slaves from escaping, and slept on deck in tiny sleeping cubicles called "doghouses." There is no evidence, however, to support this theory, or any other for that matter.

intoxicated. There are more synonyms for *intoxicated* in *Webster's Collegiate Thesaurus* than for any other entry in the book, 46 of them in all. *Intoxicate*, ironically enough, comes from a Greek word meaning poison—*toxikon*, the poison into which war arrows were dipped. Then in the Middle Ages, the Latin *toxicum* became a general term for any poison. This resulted in the English *toxic*, "poisonous," our *intoxicate*, meaning "to poison," becoming limited to the temporarily "poisonous" effects of too much liquor. Which is something to remember the next time someone quips, "Name your own poison."

intransigent. *Los Intransigentes* was the nickname of a Spanish political party that tried to introduce a form of communism into Spain in 1873, five years after Queen Isabella II had been deposed and the country was without a sovereign. This splinter group, the left wing of a party favoring a republic, called themselves "the volunteers of liberty," but they were dubbed *Intransigentes* (*in*, the Latin for "not," and *transigo*, Latin for "to come to an agreement") because they stubbornly refused to compromise in any way with other political viewpoints. A dictator outlawed the party the following year, and in 1875 Isabella's son Alfonso restored the monarchy, but *Los Intransigentes* lived on. Their name quickly came into English as *Intransigeant*, and then *intransigent*, meaning "any unyielding, inflexible person or doctrine."

introvert. (*See* **Jungian**.)

in two shakes of a lamb's tail. A lamb can shake its tail twice quite rapidly, apparently more quickly than many animals can shake their tails once, which explains this Americanism, meaning "in hardly any time at all." The expression dates back to the early 1800s and no one knows who coined it. Possibly it is a humorous extension of the older British phrase *in two shakes*, meaning the same, and probably alluding to the quick shaking of a dice box.

Inuit words in English. There are only about eighty thousand speakers of Inuit, but even this little-spoken language has contributed words to the English lexicon, including *kayak*, *igloo*, and *makluk* (a large bearded seal).

Inverness. Sherlock Holmes wore one of these warm overcoat-cape combinations, which were named for the Highlands town of Inverness, Scotland, where they were apparently invented one bone-chilling winter in the 1850s. The cape is removable from the coat or cloak.

Io; Europa; Ganymede; Callisto. These four objects or satellites that endlessly circle the planet Jupiter (the Roman *Jove*) weren't named by Galileo, who discovered them, but by a rival astronomer, Simon Marius, who falsely claimed the discovery. Marius named them after the four objects of the god Jove's sexual desire, even writing a poem to make it easy for all to remember the names: "Io, Europa, the boy Ganymede, and likewise Callisto,/ Aroused to excess the lust of Jove."

ionosphere. (*See* **Heaviside layer.**)

iota. The *i* or *iota* is the smallest letter in the Greek alphabet, so when we say *not one iota* we are saying "not the smallest amount." The expression is found in Matt. 5:18, with *j*ot, a synonym for *iota*, being used. (*See* **tittle.**)

IOU. The term *IOU*, for a signed document acknowledging a debt, is an old expression dating back to at least the early 17th century. In 1618 a writer described "fellows" who: "play tricks with their Creditors, who in stead of payments, write I O U, and so scoffe many an honest man out of his goods." *IOU*, of course, stands for "I Owe You."

Iowa. Nicknamed the *Hawkeye State* (after a resident sharp-eyed Indian chief) our 29th state, which entered the Union in 1846, is so called from the name of the Sioux *Ioways* or *Aiouez*, meaning "sleepy ones." The tribe, however, didn't consider themselves lazy, calling themselves the *Pahoja*, "gray snow." A rival tribe had named them "the sleepy ones."

Iran. (*See* **Ireland.**)

Ireland. The English, no slouches at national slurs, dubbed the urinary organs *Ireland* as far back as the 16th century, the term recorded in Shakespeare's *Comedy of Errors*. A writer on British slavery later explained that the denigration was deserved because Ireland's wet climate made her "The Urinal of the Planets." (For a similar Irish slur on an Englishman, *see* **Twiss.**) *Ireland* is perhaps the only word left in English that derives from the language of the Iberians, the first inhabitants of the British Isles—so the name of the country might well be the earliest surviving word spoken on British shores. The Iberians probably gave their tribal name to the island of *Iveriu*, which over the years was shortened to *Eiri*, this finally anglicized to *Ireland*. The Iberians, however, may also have named Britain itself. One cannot call either of these words "native" words, though, for the Iberians came to the British Isles from somewhere else in Europe. One scholar, taking *Ireland* or *Erin* back to its ultimate ancestor, says the name comes from the Indo-European *ariyan*, "noble." *Iran* derives from the same source. (*See* **dog.**)

iris. Iris, the Greek goddess of the rainbow, gives her name to the colored portion of the eye called the *iris* and the *iris* flower, which has varieties in all the colors of the rainbow. Orrisroot is a powder used in perfumes and other products that is made from the roots of certain irises.

Irish. No one would think that those with "the gift of tongues" could be bested when it came to the English language. But the Irish have been done more harm than ever they inflicted. In fact, many expressions bearing their name seem too good to have been coined by anyone but an Irishman himself, as indeed some undoubtably were. The English began this verbal war on the Hibernians with expressions like *Irish mail*, a sack of potatoes; *Irish draperies*, cobwebs; *Irish lantern*, the moon; *Irish wedding*, the emptying of a cesspool; *Irish hurricane*, a flat sea; *Irish battleship*, a barge; *Irish bull*, any obvious contradiction in terms; and *Irish blunder*, which Swift defined as "to take the noise of brass for thunder." But when the Irish emigrated to America, the other immigrants, old and new, did worse by them, appropriating some ancient expressions and adding some new ones. *Irish evidence* here was perjury; an *Irish beauty*, a girl with two black eyes; an *Irish diamond*, a rock; an *Irish spoon*, a spade; an *Irish apple*, a potato; an *Irish bouquet*, a brickbat; an *Irish promotion*, a demotion; an *Irish dividend*, an assessment; *Irish confetti*, bricks; and an *Irishman's dinner*, a fast. It all was enough for them to *get their Irish up*, which they occasionally did, though it didn't hurt as much as the common *No Irish Need Apply* signs. Somehow all the favorable coinings didn't help matters much. These include *Irish daisy, Irish potato, Irish moss, Irish setter, Irish stew, Irish terrier, Irish wolfhound* and, of course, *Irish whiskey* and *Irish coffee*. (*See* **Gaelic.**)

Irish pennants. Nautical slang often reflects hostility toward particular groups of people. This is the case with *Irish pennants*, which originated as British naval slang for untidy ropes hanging from the rigging aloft. In another age, when the Dutch were England's major foes on the high seas, *Dutch pennants* meant the same thing.

iron curtain. Winston Churchill did not invent this expression, as is commonly believed. Many pages have been devoted to tracking down its originator, but the first person known to use the phrase in a political sense was Queen Elizabeth of Belgium, who said in 1914: "Between [Germany] and me there is now a bloody iron curtain which has descended forever." Before this, H. G. Wells referred to a man held incommunicado by the police as "held behind an iron curtain" in his story "The Food of the Gods" (1904). After Belgium's Queen Elizabeth, several military writers used *iron curtain* with reference to a curtain of artillery fire. Then, in 1945, Nazi propaganda minister Joseph Goebbels employed the phrase in the exact same sense as Churchill would use it eight months later, with reference to Russia, and so did German statesman Count Schwerin von Krosigk. The expression refers of course to the impenetrable secrecy with which happenings in the Soviet Union and countries occupied by it are concealed from the world, the image that inspired the saying probably being the iron fireproof curtains long used in European theaters. Five months before Churchill made his famous Iron Curtain speech on March 5, 1946, at Westminster College in Fulton, Missouri ("From Stettin in the Baltic to Trieste in the Adriatic, an iron curtain has descended across the continent . . ."), his countryman Sir St. Vincent Troubridge, a former British staff officer of SHAEF, had written an article in the *Sunday Empire News* headed "An Iron Curtain Across Europe."

Iroquois. These Indians often ended their speeches with "Hiroquoue!"—meaning "I have spoken with strong emotion!" To the ears of French explorers in North America this sounded like *Iroquois*, the name they gave to the Indian tribe.

isabel; isabelline. Traditionally, this lady's soiled underwear gives her name to the brownish-yellow or grayish color *isabel*. The full story is rarely told. Archduchess Isabella of Austria was the daughter of Spain's Philip II and his fourth wife, Anne of Austria, daughter of Austrian ruler Maximilian II. In 1598 King Philip married Isabella to Austrian Archduke Albert, and as part of a plan to reconquer the United Provinces, handed over the whole of the Netherlands to the newly married couple as a sovereign state. Philip died that same year, but his war continued, which is where Isabella's underwear makes its contribution to history. Supposedly, Isabella vowed never to remove her underwear, even for washing, until husband Albert took the city of Ostend by siege. But Ostend's Flemish defenders had little sympathy for either Isabella or Albert. They held out for *three years*, playing a glorious role in the Dutch struggle for independence. Ostend was in ruins and forty thousand Spanish lives had been lost before the Belgian port city surrendered in 1604. After three years Isabella's underwear certainly must have been *isabelline*, and she might have worn it even longer, for we are told that Albert did not win Ostend at all. General Ambrogio Spinola captured the city. Perhaps this led to jokes about why Albert and Isabella had no children, but, at any rate, the couple ruled wisely after a twelve-year truce was effected in 1609, the war resuming again at the truce's expiration. Albert died in 1621 and Isabella thirteen years later. Some authorities, such as the *Oxford English Dictionary*, flatly reject the dirty-underwear hypothesis, while others, like *Webster's*, admit it with a cautious "It is said," and with still others it washes well.

I say! This British exclamation of surprise or astonishment is thought to be typical of Englishmen by most Americans but is considered rather old-fashioned in England, though it is still heard there. The expression probably dates back before the late 18th century.

I say it's spinach and I say the hell with it. E. B. White wrote the caption that became this catchphrase, for a 1928 Carl Rose cartoon in the *New Yorker* showing a spoiled little girl who rejects her mother's offer of broccoli with these words—which have come to mean, "When I'm indulging my prejudices I don't want to be confused with facts." The phrase's abbreviated form, *spinach*, however, means the same as boloney, malarkey, bull, etc.

Ishmael. An *Ishmael* is an outcast, which is one reason why Herman Melville gave the name to his narrator in *Moby Dick*. Ishmael was the son of Abraham and Hagar; he and his mother were banished to the wilderness by Sarah, where an angel predicted that he would forever be at odds with society (Gen. 21:9-21). The Muslims, however, do not share this biblical tradition, considering Ishmael their progenitor.

I should of stayed in bed. (*See* we wuz robbed.)

isinglass. *Isinglass*, derived from the Dutch *huizenblas*, "sturgeon's bladder," is a semitransparent substance made from that fish's bladder. Isinglass is still employed in cooking as a form of gelatin used as a thickening agent, though it was once much more popular.

I smell a rat. No one can say with irrefragable certainty how this expression originated, but the allusion may be to a cat smelling a rat while being unable to see it. Terriers and other rat-hunting dogs could also be the inspiration. The expression dates back to about 1780, but long before that *to smell* was used figuratively for "to suspect or discern intuitively," as when Shakespeare writes "Do you smell a fault?" in *King Lear*. St. Hilarion, the Syrian hermit who died about 371, could allegedly tell a person's vices or virtues simply by smelling his person or clothing.

I swan. People who say *I swan!* in historical novels are merely saying "I swear!" The old expression derives from British dialect and is a corruption of either "I'se warrant!" or "I'se warn you!"

it. The little workhorse pronoun *it* derives from the Anglo-Saxon *hit*, neuter gender of "he." Though *it* is used to describe anything sexless, among other things, *it* also means sex appeal in slang usage. Clara Bow was Hollywood's *It girl*, but the first use of *it* to represent sex appeal was in Rudyard Kipling's *Mrs. Bathurst* (1904) when he writes: "'Tisn't beauty, so to speak, nor good talk necessarily. It's just It. Some women'll stay in a man's memory if they once walked down a street." The expression became very popular in the late 1920s when Clara Bow starred in the 1926 movie version of Elinor Glyn's novel *It*. As the *It girl* Miss Bow was one of a long line of types loved by American men, including the *Gibson girl*, the *Ziegfeld girl*, the *Vamp* (Theda Bara), the *flapper*, the *oomph girl*, the *sweater girl*, the *pinup girl*, the *Playmate*, and the *Bunny*. *It* may be somewhat euphemistic as well, as it is in the slang synonyms for a chamber pot and the male and female sexual organs. Calling the unlucky player who does all the work *you're it* in a game of tag or hide-and-go-seek dates back to about 1888. In modern slang this *it* has also become someone who is appointed to do a certain job, usually an undesirable one, in an office or elsewhere.

Italian. There has been much controversy recently about the use of the word *Mafia*, which recalls prohibition days in Chicago, when *Italian* was used so frequently in describing gunmen that newspapers bowed to Italian objections and, ironically, began to use *Sicilian* instead. In reality, Italians have been abused as much as any group in the country, but the adjective *Italian* is attached to few derogatory expressions. Aside from the *Italian malady* (*see* **French disease**), an ancient synonym for syphilis used no more, it is hard to think of even one popular expression defaming the name. *Italian aster, Italian clover, Italian honeysuckle*—all innocent terms describing innocuous things. Compared with groups like the Dutch and Irish, the Italians have indeed fared well, linguistically. Sometimes home gardeners curse *Italian ryegrass*, not realizing that it is an annual grass that won't come up the next year, but that's about the extent of *Italian's* infamy.

Italian words in English. The contributions of Italian to English are vast, including three-quarters of our musical terms. Examples are: *alarm, million, ducat, florin, brigand, bark* (ship), *tunny* (fish), *race, nuncio, artisan, doge, magnifico, mountebank, umbrella, gondola, carnival, mustachio, attack, cavalier, musket, squadron, battalion, citadel, bankrupt, contraband, carat, cornice, pedestal, piazza, stucco, portico, grotto, balcony, corridor, sentinel, catacomb, dado, concert, madrigal, viol da gamba, fugue, pastel, fresco, volcano, sonnet, stanza, canto, caprice, regatta, lagoon, balloon, muslin, mercantile, risk, opera, serenade, sonata, spinet, largo, piano, intaglio, profile, vista, miniature, cartoon, chiaroscuro, burlesque, ghetto, incognito, broccoli, sketch, casino, mafia, vendetta, malaria, influenza, bronze, area, lava, braccia, travertine, mezzanine, figurine, soprano, trombone, viola, cantata, trio, concerto, aria, violin, quartet, finale, andante, adagio, crescendo, tempo, bravo, piccolo, prima donna, sextet, scherzo, contrapuntal, fiasco, imbroglio, tirade.* Italian words that have entered American English include: *spaghetti, pasta, lasagne, tortoni, spumoni, antipasto, minestrone, Chianti, provolone,* and many other food and drink terms. *America* (*q.v.*) itself, named after Amerigo Vespucci, could also be said to be an Italian word, as could Washington D.C., the District of Columbia, from Columbus's name. (*See also* **spic; wop.**)

italic type. *Italic type,* in which the first two words of this sentence are printed, was invented about 1500 by the noted Italian printer Aldus Manutius, the Latin name of Teobaldo Mannucci. There is a tradition that the printer modeled his invention on the fine Italian hand of the poet Petrarch, but the Italian hand, a beautiful cursive style, had been widely used for copying manuscripts since its development by scholars in the 12th century. In fact, it was so well known that *a fine Italian hand* had already become an ironic synonym for the scheming Machiavellian politics of assassination by stiletto for which Italian nobles were notorious. Manutius, also a classical scholar, had his type cast by Francesco Griffi of Bologna and in 1501 first used it to publish an edition of Virgil, dedicating the book to his native Italy. Because of that Aldine Press dedication, the new slanting style—the first type that wasn't upright—came to be known as *Italicus,* which means "Italian" or "italic." Today words are *italicized* in print mainly to give them emphasis, and to indicate titles and foreign-language words. This is not the case in the King James or Authorized Version of the Bible, however, a fact that creates confusion for many people. Words italicized in the Bible should not be emphasized in reading, for they merely indicate that the original translators, who considered the text sacred, arbitrarily supplied a word not existing in the text in order to make its meaning clearer—similar to the way bracketed words are used within quotes today.

itch. Itching of various bodily parts has been thought to indicate different cravings for centuries. An itching foot, for example, purportedly means a craving for travel, and itching lips mean a craving for a kiss, or that you're about to be kissed. Shakespeare put these beliefs to use in *Julius Caesar,* where he used an itching palm as a synonym for the readiness to take a bribe, making Brutus say to Cassius ". . . you yourself/ Are much condemned to have an itching palm." Shakespeare was the first to record the words, but long before him an itching palm probably signified a craving for money or was taken as an omen that a person was about to receive money from an unexpected source. An *itch,* as in the seven-year itch, has been synonymous for sexual desire since 1660. *Seven-year itch* had no sexual connotation when first recorded in 1899, simply meaning "a type of itch allegedly requiring seven years of healing." Influenced by the sense of *itch* as sexual desire, it came to mean a married man's urge to roam after seven years of marriage, a meaning widely popularized by the Marilyn Monroe movie *The Seven Year Itch* (1955).

itching ears. (*See* **burning ears.**)

it doesn't go on all fours. Unlike similar Madison Avenue expressions, this saying, meaning "something isn't quite right," goes back to the ancient Latin proverb *Omnis comparatio claudicat,* which literally means "every simile limps," but which British historian Thomas Babington Macaulay translated as "No simile can go on all fours."

it is harder for a rich man to enter the kingdom of heaven than for a camel to go through the eye of a needle. There may be some sense in this last part of this ancient proverb. In ancient Middle Eastern walled towns the rear gate was called the Needle's Eye, after its narrow rise and pointed top. A camel could pass through this Needle's Eye, though with extreme difficulty, by kneeling down. It has been suggested that this is the source of the expression, an equivalent of which is found in the Koran ("The impious shall find the ages of heaven shut; nor shall he enter till a camel shall pass through the eye of a needle").

it rains on the just and unjust alike; scholium. The phrase above can be traced to the biblical (Matt. 5:45): "He . . . sendeth rain on the just and on the unjust . . ." A *scholium* on the verse by Charles, Baron Bowen (1835-94) has it a little differently:

> The rain it raineth on the just
>   And also on the unjust fella:
> But chiefly on the just, because
>   The unjust steals the just's umbrella!

Scholium means "an explanatory note or comment," deriving from the Greek for "school" and first recorded in the early 16th century.

its. There is a tale of literary ratiocination involving this little word. Before the 17th century *its* wasn't used to indicate the possessive case, *it* and *his* serving this purpose (e.g., "For love and devocion toward God also hath *it* infancie . . ."; "Learning hath his infancy . . ."). When he was only sixteen, English poet Thomas Chatterton (1752-70) wrote a number of poems purporting to be the work of an imaginary 15th-century monk, Thomas Rowley. These poems were published after the destitute, despairing Chatterton committed suicide by drinking arsenic, and they were hailed as works of poetic genius. But critic Thomas Tyrwbitt later revealed that the poems were forgeries, finding, among other errors, that one of Chatterton's lines read: "Life and its goods I scorn."

it's all over but the shouting. Victory is certain. The expression seems to have appeared in print for the first time in 1842, when a Welsh sportswriter used it, but it may have its roots in local elections settled by voice vote in rural England. These elections, associated with great noise, came to be called "shoutings." There is no proof of this, but perhaps some candidate or observer of the day was so sure of the outcome of a "shouting," so certain of victory, that he remarked "It's all over but the shouting" and the phrase passed into popular usage.

it's a naive domestic burgundy without any breeding but I think you'll be amused by its presumptions. This originated as the caption under a James Thurber drawing of a pretentious oenologist offering a glass to a friend. It is an expression that has been used jokingly by many a host pretending to be a "wine expert" while dispensing a $3.99 special.

it's a new ball game. Since about 1940 Americans have been using this catchphrase to mean "What's past is past, we start over from here." Though it could have come from several sports, the saying almost certainly has its origins in baseball and sounds like something a baseball announcer may have spontaneously invented. The expression is often "It's a whole new ball game."

it's how you played the game. Sportswriter Grantland Rice, who coined the term the "Four Horsemen" to describe Notre Dame's famous backfield in an account of a Notre Dame-Army game ("Outlined against a blue-gray October sky, the Four Horsemen rode again . . .") is also responsible for *it's how you played the game*. The much loved writer, who died in 1954 at the age of 73, first used the expression in a poem he published in one of his "The Sportlight" columns:

> When the One Great Scorer comes
> To mark against your name,
> He writes—not that you won or lost—
> But how you played the game.

it smells of the lamp. (*See* **burning the midnight oil.**)

it's not cricket. (*See* **cricket.**)

it's not what it's cracked up to be. *To crack* was standard English for "to boast or brag" until about 1700. Today this sense of the word is only found in the expression above, which can refer to a person as well as a thing. Davy Crockett was the first to use the phrase when he wrote in 1835 that "Martin Van Buren is not the man he's cracked up to be," an opinion of the president that history has affirmed.

it's the pits. Grape pits, orange pits, etc. contributed nothing to this relatively recent derogatory slang expression, which describes something of the worst order, though you might suspect that the bitter, unpalatable pits of a fruit would logically have something to do with the term. *It's the pits* was originally junkie talk from "Needle Parks" across the country, the armpits being among the last and most painful places a drug addict can shoot dope when the rest of his body is pocked and diseased, the blood vessels collapsed.

it suits you to a "T." Most dictionaries attribute the expression to the accuracy of the draftsman's T-square, but this is impossible, according to the *O.E.D.*—for the phrase was around many years before the T-square got its name. The expression has been used to indicate exactness or perfection since at least the early 17th century and is probably an abbreviation of the older expression *to a tittle*. *Tittle* or *titil* was the English name for small strokes or points made in writing the letters of the alphabet, a corruption of the word seen today in the Spanish *tilde*. Thus *to a tittle* meant to a dot, precisely, and was used this way more than a century before someone shortened it to *to a T*.

I vant to be alone. Aside from some *Goldwynisms*, (*q.v.*) this may be the single most famous quotation to come out of Hollywood, partly because it is a sentiment uncharacteristic of most film stars. Too bad that Greta Garbo didn't say it. The legendary actress, who still savors her solitude, has made it clear for history that what she really said was: "I want to be *let* alone."

Ivory soap. Procter and Gamble's *Ivory soap* started life in 1870 as The White Soap, Harley T. Procter renaming it *Ivory soap* nine years later, from, of all things, the biblical 45th Psalm: "out of ivory palaces they have made thee glad." The soap had to compete with the more expensive, completely pure Castile soap, and that same year the company introduced the famous Ivory slogan, "It floats—*99 and 44/100 %* pure," the last part of which has come to have some general usage to describe anything or anyone pure.

ivory tower. In the *Song of Solomon* the poet sings that his beloved's neck is "as a tower of ivory," but the phrase in its modern sense has nothing else to do with biblical poetry. French literary critic Charles Augustin Saint-Beuve used *un tour d'ivoire* in 1837 to charge that romantic poet Alfred de Vigny evaded the responsibilities of life by retiring to an *ivory tower*. Whether the charge was justified or not, the image did evoke someone sitting cool and elegantly detached, above it all and looking down on life. The phrase has become a cliché, especially when applied to scholars or intellectuals. It is seldom used anymore in a kind sense, that is, to indicate a place of refuge from the world's strivings and posturings.

Ivy League. The colleges referred to as the *Ivy League* are Harvard, Yale, Princeton, Dartmouth, Cornell, Brown, Columbia, and the University of Pennsylvania. They are all "old-line institutions," with thick-vined, aged ivy covering their walls, and the designation at first applied specifically to their football teams. Sportswriter Caswell Adams coined the term in the mid-thirties. At the time Fordham University's football team was among the best in the East. A fellow journalist compared Columbia and Princeton to Fordham, and Adams replied, "Oh they're just Ivy League," recalling later that he said this "with complete humorous disparagement in mind."

I wouldn't know him from Adam's off ox. (*See* **Adam.**)

IWW. The initials of the "Wobblies," a labor organization important in the early years of this century, do not stand for International Workers of the World, as many people think. The organization was the *Industrial Workers of the World*.

ixnay. (*See* **pig latin.**)

Izvestia. (*See* **Pravda.**)

J

J. The letter *j*, along with *v*, came into the language in post-Shakespearean times, about 1630, making it one of the two youngest letters in the English alphabet. Before this it had shared its form with *i*.

jabberwocky. In its twenty-eight lines Lewis Carroll's immortal nonsense poem "Jabberwocky" has contributed at least four new words of common usage to the English language, more than any other poem by far. *Jabberwocky* itself means "nonsense or gibberish"; a "bandersnatch" is an imaginary wild fierce animal or a person who is a menace or a nuisance; "galumph" (from *gallop* + *triumphant*) means to move heavily or clumsily; and "chortle" (from *chuckle* + *snort*) means to chuckle or utter with glee. Cases could also be made for *frabjous*, *frumious*, *slithy*, and other words in the poem, though these haven't yet been admitted to most dictionaries.

jack. *Jack*, for money in general, is an Americanism first recorded in 1859, but the expression is probably older, possibly deriving from the expression *to make one's jack*, "to succeed in one's endeavors," first attested in 1778. This expression, in turn, may come from the British slang *jack*, for "a farthing and a counter used at gaming tables," which dates back to about 1700.

jackanapes. Applied to any pretentious upstart who apes his betters, the word *jackanapes* probably comes from the nickname of William de la Pole, Duke of Suffolk. Jack was a common name for a tame male ape in England at the time (attached to the word, as it was to jackrabbit, jackass, and others), and Suffolk's coat of arms bore the clog and chain of a trained monkey. When, in 1450, the duke was arrested and beheaded at sea off Dover for alleged treason against Henry VI, he was derisively styled "the Ape-clogge" and later won the nickname Jack Napes, or Jacknapes. The ending might mean "of Naples," the source of apes brought to England in the early 15th century, but there is little doubt that the word earned its popularity and present meaning through Suffolk's nickname, which was even recorded in a satirical song of the day.

Jack Armstrong, the all-American boy. Jack Armstrong, and Frank Meriwell before him, seem to have no counterpart today on the airwaves, unless television's Hardy Boys qualify. "Jack Armstrong, the All-American Boy" was presented afternoons, right after school, by "Wheaties—Breakfast of Champions," during the thirties and early forties. No more than an animated ideal, he often inspired cynical jokes, but the name of this Wheaties-eating hero certainly became part of the language, frequently as a kind of sarcastic description for someone too square or goody-goody, in the language of the time. I had thought Jack's name might have been suggested by the real-life bully Jack Armstrong, who lost that legendary wrestling match with young Abe Lincoln and later became his friend. But it appears that General Mills (Wheaties) executive Sammy Gale had roomed with a real Jack Armstrong in college and decided to use his name for the program's hero because it seemed to convey "all-American virtues of courage, a sense of humor, and the championing of ideals." Jack Lawrence Armstrong, the real Jack Armstrong, the son of a retired British Army officer, moved to the U.S. from Canada at the age of four and later received a civil engineering degree from the University of Minnesota. He was a much-decorated Army Air Force officer during World War II and later served on the Atomic Energy Commission and worked for the Apollo and Gemini space programs. He died in 1985, aged 74.

the jackass express; jackass mail. Any stagecoach pulled by mules in the early American West was called *the jackass express*. *Jackass mail* was the name used for the mail that was carried on the jackass express.

Jack Dempsey. The Amazonian fish named after the former world heavyweight champion is described as a "very aggressive species," although "the fighting between males . . . is ritualized."

Jack Frost. *Jack Frost* has been the personification of frost or cold weather since at least 1826, when the term is first recorded in a British sporting magazine.

Jack Horner. "He put in his thumb and pulled out a plum/ And said, 'What a good boy am I!'" The Jack Horner of the nursery rhyme is supposed to have been, in reality, steward to the abbot of Glastonbury at the time that the monasteries were being dissolved in England. Jack somehow obtained deeds to the Manor of Mells in the area, either by subterfuge or, as the popular story states, when he found the papers hidden in a pie he was delivering from the abbot to Henry VIII. By this account, he lifted the crust, put in his thumb, and pulled out the "plum," becoming owner of the property himself. This may be the only nursery rhyme based on fact. In any event, the real Jack Horner's descendants have owned the manor for generations.

Jack Johnson. John Arthur (Jack) Johnson, his memory recently revived by the play *The Great White Hope*, loudly proclaimed that he reigned as the first black world heavyweight champion in 1908 when he KO'd Englishman Tommy Burns—though his title claim was disputed and not settled until he demolished Jim Jeffries, the original *great white hope*, in 1910. Johnson held the title until 1915, when giant Jess Willard knocked him out in twenty-six rounds in Havana, Cuba. The American fighter had often been called the "Big Smoke" in the United States, "smoke" being common slang at the time for Negro. For this reason, and because he was so powerful a man, the German 5.9 howitzer, its shell, and its shell burst were named after Johnson. A formidable weapon, whose shells emitted thick black smoke upon exploding, the *Jack Johnson* saw action against the Allies during World War I, when Johnson's name was prominent in the news for his fights and love affairs. Johnson, in fact, had fled to Europe in 1913 after being convicted of violating the Mann Act, unjustly or not. The great boxer died in 1946, aged sixty-eight.

Jack Ketch. Jack Ketch, appointed public executioner in 1663, was generally regarded as a clumsy, barbaric bungler who had taken several strokes to sever William, Lord Russell's head after he moved slightly when the axe was falling. He later apologized for his clumsiness, explaining that Russell did not "dispose himself as was most suitable" and that he had been disturbed while taking aim. No one believed him though, and his name became a mark of execration long before he died in 1683—"There stands Jack Kitch, the son of a bitch" went one contemporary rhyme. Of all the public executioners who hung commoners and beheaded nobles his name would be remembered longest, given, as Macaulay wrote, "to all who have succeeded him in his odious office." (*See* **H**.)

jackknife. The ubiquitous American *jackknife* may take its name from the earlier Scottish *jocktilig*, a clasp knife named for its original manufacturer, Frenchman Jacques de Liege. A respected Scottish historian traced the word to this source in 1776, but modern scholars have been unable to confirm his derivation.

Jack of all trades and master of none. The eloquent term for *a Jack of all trades and master of none* is a *sciolist*, which is Latin for "smatterer," and means someone having a smattering of knowledge, a little learning. *Jack of all trades and master of none* extends the little learning to a lot of things, meaning someone who can turn his hand to anything but isn't expert at any work. The expression is first recorded in 1618 as *Jack of all trades* and seems to have been a complimentary term for someone who could

do any kind of work. But within a century the work of *Jacks of all trades* was being disparaged as not expert enough (specialization becoming more important every year) and by at least 1878 the derogatory expression *Jack of all trades and master of none* was being used.

jackpot. (*See* **to hit the jackpot**.)

jackrabbit. *Jackrabbit* is an abbreviation of *jackass-rabbit*, the large hare of North America so named because of its long jackass-like ears and legs. *Jackass-rabbit* is first recorded in 1847 by a traveler in the West: "[We] started a number of hares [called Jackass rabbits] and had no little amusement in witnessing some animated runs." Within fifteen years the same hares were being called *jackrabbits*. They were also called *mule rabbits*.

Jack Robinson. *As quick as you can say Jack Robinson* has no connection with Jackie Robinson, the first black major league baseball player, though he was quick enough to beat out many a bunt and steal many a base. Notable attempts have been made to trace this 18th-century British phrase, all unsuccessful. One popular explanation, first advanced by *Grose*, is that the saying has its origin in the habit a certain Jack Robinson had of paying extraordinarily quick visits to his friends, the gentleman leaving even before his name could be announced. But *Jack Robinson* was probably used in the phrase simply because it is a very common name in England and is easy to pronounce.

Jackson Haines. The well-known sitting-spin of figure skating is called the *Jackson Haines*, after American skater Jackson Haines (1840-79), a former dancer, who is largely responsible for creating modern figure skating by applying dance techniques to the sport.

Jackson Hole, Wyoming. The *hole* in this place name isn't a hole in the ground, as many people believe. *Hole* here means a piece of meadow, or a grassy valley surrounded by mountains (which might resemble a hole in the ground).

Jacksonian democracy, etc. Jacksonism is the term for the political principles and policies advocated by Andrew Jackson, seventh president of the United States, and his followers. Old Hickory, so called because he was as tough as hickory wood, commanded troops in the War of 1812. Elected to the presidency in 1829, General Jackson served two terms, espousing a widespread *Jacksonian democracy* while vigorously opposing nullification and the national Bank of the United States. His famous "kitchen Cabinet," the first of its kind, was simply a group of intimate advisers, and by adopting the "spoils system," the granting of political jobs and favors to loyal supporters, he established a well-knit Democratic Party but intensified evils that were not removed until the Civil Service came into being half a century later. *Jackson boots, hats, jackets,* and *trousers* were all named after the hero, who died in 1845, aged seventy-eight. Today almost one hundred places in the nation bear his name. *Jackson Day,* January 8, is a legal holiday in Louisiana, celebrating his victory at the Battle of New Orleans in 1815.

Jacksonian epilepsy.   (*See* **Bright's disease.**)

jackstraw. A worthless person, a man of straw. Jack Straw was the name or nickname of a leader of the Peasants Revolt, Wat Tyler's rebellion of 1381. This revolt against English king Richard II mainly protested restrictions on pay increases to laborers and repudiated higher poll taxes. Richard agreed to the peasants' demands, but the revolt was suppressed and his promises unfulfilled when Tyler was slain by the mayor of London at a meeting held between the two men. In the original march on London to petition the king Tyler and his followers burned and wrecked much property, incurring the wrath of many. The protestor called Jack Straw must have been particularly hated, for his name soon took its present meaning.

Jack Tar. One story has it that the name Jack Tar, for "a sailor," arose in the 17th century, when sailors wore canvas breeches often spotted with tar from work done on ships. According to another tale, sailors in Lord Nelson's navy wore overalls and broad-brimmed hats made of the tar-impregnated tarpaulin cloth commonly used aboard ship. The hats, and the sailors who wore them, were called *tarpaulins,* which was finally shortened to *tar.*

Jack the Ripper. After eighty-two years, *Jack the Ripper's* name remains the most familiar of all murderers; no other single criminal has been so exhaustively examined in literature and on stage and screen. The Ripper murdered and disemboweled at least five and possibly nine or more prostitutes and gin-soaked whores in London's East End in 1888, in one of the most gruesome, gory serial killings in British or any other history. "Saucy Jack" was never captured in the foggy night streets of Whitechapel or Spitalfields, and his pseudonym was derived from his signatures on the bizarre, mocking notes he reputedly sent to the police. (Sept. 30th: "Double event this time. Number one squeeled a bit—could not finish straight off—had no time to get the ears for police.") "Bloody Jack" was described as a man of medium height who wore a deerstalker cap, sported a small mustache and "talked like a gentleman." For almost a century writers have speculated on the Ripper's real identity, naming literally hundreds of "suspects," including even Prime Minister Gladstone and Albert Victor Christian Edward, Duke of Clarence and Avondale, Queen Victoria's grandson and heir to the throne of England.

Jacobin. During the French Revolution the Société des Jacobins, a radical club or society active beginning in 1789, was responsible for many extreme measures, including the bloody Reign of Terror in which thousands were killed. Though it began as a liberal organization, its name in the form of *Jacobin* came to mean any extreme political radical, as it does today. The Jacobins, only 3,000 strong, managed to control the French Revolution until their leader Robespierre's death in 1794, when they went underground. Five years later the group was finally suppressed.

Jacob's ladder. A *Jacob's ladder* is a ship's wood-runged rope or chain ladder primarily used to let people ascend from or descend to smaller boats alongside. The name is also given to a steep flight of steps up a cliff, an herb or flower in the shape of a ladder, and a burglar's ladder. All take their name from the ladder seen by the biblical patriarch Jacob in a vision (Gen. 28:12-13), the ladder in the dream symbolizing the hopes of Jacob for his descendants.

Jacob's rod.   (*See* **asphodel.**)

Jacquard loom. This early automated machine (controlled by punched cards) could weave patterns in many fabrics. Napoleon quickly purchased the loom for the state and declared it public property, rewarding Joseph Marie Jacquard (1752-1834), a former Lyons weaver, with a 3,000-franc yearly pension and a royalty on each machine sold. Jacquard improved on his creation in 1806, adapting several features of a similar invention. Though he hadn't foreseen the widespread unemployment caused by the loom, his belief that it would greatly increase output was more than justified; the *Jacquard loom* revolutionized the textile industry, and created a new era in manufacturing.

jade. Spaniards in medieval times believed that this gem helped cure kidney ailments. They called it *piedra de ifada,* "stone of the side," which became shortened and corrupted in English to *jade.* The *jade* for an old horse or a worthless woman, and the adjective *jaded* derive from another unknown word, of Middle English origin.

jaegers. Though *jaegers* can be any of several rapacious seabirds, in England they are also woolen underwear. The underwear is named for Dr. Gustav Jaeger, whose Dr. Jaeger's Sanitary Woolen System Co. Ltd. manufactured and marketed the various undergarments he designed, beginning about 1890. Americans are familiar with the term through *The Bishop's Jaegers* (1932), a novel by Thorne Smith, creator of the inhibited banker Cosmo Topper, and his ectoplasmic friends.

jai alai. The name for this court game is Basque in origin, formed from the Basque *jai,* "festival," and *alai,* "joyous," indicating that people have always had a good time playing *jai alai*. Other English words that come from the Basque include *bizarre* and *orignal*, a mostly Canadian word for the American moose.

jalousie. First called *jealousies* in 16th-century England, *jalousies*, their name taken from the French for jealousy, were originally blinds or shutters with wooden horizontal slats that admitted air and light but "jealously guarded" one's privacy. Today they are also made of glass.

Jamie Duff. A professional mourner. There is a story that this Scottish nickname for a mourner at a funeral comes from the name of one James Duff, an odd character who attended many funerals in the mid-19th century because "he enjoyed the ride in the mourning coach." More likely the term is from the name of an old firm that supplied mourners for a price.

Jane or Jane's. Often referred to as an authority in arguments about warships, *Jane* or *Jane's* generally refers to the prime reference on the world's navies, *Jane's Fighting Ships*, an illustrated book published periodically in England for almost a century and founded by Fred T. Jane. A volume on airplanes is also published by Jane's.

janissary. A collective bodyguard or household guard is called a *janissary* after the sultan of Turkey's *yeni-tshari*, or "new army," originally recruited by the Sultan Orchan in his reign from 1329-59. To strengthen the then feeble military, Orchan at first ordered every fifth Christian youth to be surrendered by his parents to the service of the sultan, given instruction in Muhammadanism, and specially trained in the arts of warfare. The *yenitshari*, the word corrupted into the English *janissary* in the process of passing through several languages, became the flower of the newly independent kingdom's standing army. Its reputation for courage and discipline was highly respected and the fur-capped corps received many privileges, soon making compulsory recruitment no longer necessary. But by the 19th century the "new army" numbered some 135,000 and had begun actively defying the government. In 1826 specially trained Muslim troops were employed to abolish them, and a brutal massacre that year resulted in the death of almost every *janissary*.

January. Because it was the gateway of the new year, January was named for the Roman god Janus, keeper of the gates of heaven, who had two faces, one at the back to look at the old year and one at the front to view the new year. The Roman *Januarius* became *Januarie* in English and then *January*. Janus is also remembered in the word "Janus-faced," for "a two-faced person," a deceiver or double-dealer.

Janus-faced. (*See* **January**.)

Japanese words in English. Among Japanese words that have enriched English over the centuries are: *kimono, karate, judo, tycoon, kamikaze, sukiyaki, samurai, hara-kiri, haiku, kabuki, geisha, sake, tsunami,* and *Nisei*.

jape. *Jape*, possibly from the French *japer*, "to bark like a dog," combined in English with the French *gaber*, "to mock or deride," meant to trick or deceive, or to joke, when first recorded in the 14th century. Then, strangely enough, it lost this sense and came to mean "to seduce a woman" or "to have carnal intercourse with a woman." Labeled an obscene word by the 16th century, *jape* was rarely used in print. Only three hundred years later, in the 19th century, did it resurface with its original meaning, a *jape* becoming a joke or trick again.

jargantuan. (*See* **gobbledygook**.)

jargon. *Jargon*, or *jargoun*, meant "a twittering sound" or "meaningless chatter" in medieval French. It later came to mean the argot or special vocabulary of a trade or profession, because such vocabularies were unintelligible to the outsider. Many trades have their own jargon, which facilitates things for the initiated.

jaunty. Every *jaunty* person, "one who swaggers about cocksurely," takes the adjective describing him from the *jaunty*, or master-at-arms, aboard British naval ships who supervised floggings. This jaunty in turn took his name from a mispronunciation of the French *gendarme*, or "policeman."

java. *Java*, for "coffee," originated as slang among American tramps in the late 19th century. It is obviously an allusion to the coffee-producing island.

the jaws of death. Shakespeare is often credited with the coining of this phrase, in *Twelfth Night* ("Out of the jaws of death"), but it appears earlier in *Divine Weekes and Workes* (1578) by Guillaume de Salluste du Bartas. Shakespeare must have read the man for he precedes the Bard with a number of "Shakespearean" phrases, including *The world's a stage*, *Night's black mantle*, and *the four corners of the world*.

jay. While some writers suggest that the name of this common bird is of origins unknown, it probably derives, via Old French, from the Latin *gaius*, for the bird, and *gaius* probably comes from the Latin proper name Gaius. A number of birds are named after very common proper names, including "jackdaw" and "robin." *Jay* is recorded in English as early as 1310.

Jay Hawk. This word for a Kansan may come from the nickname of a "Doc" Jennison, who led a regiment of

Kansas Free State men in the years preceding the Civil War. It is said that abolitionist Jennison, "a frolicsome immigrant from New York State," was called *Gay Yorker*, and that the name was naturally applied to his band as well. Even the pro-slavers, at least Quantrill's raiders, were eventually called *Jayhawkers* in Kansas, as were all residents of the *Jayhawk State* in time. The transformation from *Gay Yorker* to *Jayhawker* does seem unlikely, though, and can at best be regarded as doubtful. Since *Jayhawker* was also 19th-century slang for a bandit, I would hazard that the word has something to do with the quarrelsome, thieving blue jay and the warlike hawk. Or perhaps there really was a rapacious jay hawk bird, as someone has suggested but nobody has ever confirmed.

jaywalker. *Jaywalker*, which is far more succinct than "a pedestrian who crosses the streets in disregard of traffic signals," was one of the abundant expressions (*backseat driver*, *joyride*, *step on the gas*, etc.) made necessary by the automobile. First recorded in 1917, the word incorporates the then-current slang term *jay*, for a stupid, inexperienced "hick." *Jay* itself probably either derives from the "*j*" in the slang term *jughead*, or is a reference to the blue jay, a bird once commonly identified with rural areas.

jazz. Enough men to form a good *jazz* group are credited with lending their names to the word. One popular choice is a dancing slave on a plantation near New Orleans, in about 1825—*Jasper* reputedly was often stirred into a fast step by cries of "Come on, Jazz!" Another is Mr. *Razz*, a band conductor in New Orleans in 1904. Charles, or *Chaz*, Washington, "an eminent ragtime drummer of Vicksburg, Mississippi circa 1895," is a third candidate. A variation on the first and last choices seems to be Charles Alexander, who, according to an early source, "down in Vicksburg around 1910, became world famous through the song asking everyone to 'come on and hear Alexander's Ragtime Band.' Alexander's first name was Charles, always abbreviated Chas. and pronounced Chazz; at the hot moments they called, 'Come on, Jazz!', whence the *jazz* music." Few scholars accept any of these etymologies, but no better theory has been offered. Attempts to trace the word *jazz* to an African word meaning hurry have failed, and it is doubtful that it derives from either the *chasse* dance step; the Arab *Jazib*, "one who allures"; the African *jaiza*, "the sound of distant drums"; or the Hindu *jazba*, "ardent desire." To complicate matters further, *jazz* was first a verb for sexual intercourse, as it still is today in slang.

jeans. (*See* **blue jeans**.)

jeep. Eugene the Jeep, a character in Elzie Crisler (E.C.) Segar's widely syndicated comic-strip "Popeye," had supernatural powers and could do just about any-

thing. Introduced in 1936, the mythical little animal was well known by World War II when Willis-Overland began manufacturing their versatile, open, 1 1/4-ton, four-wheel-drive vehicles for the armed forces. No one knows for certain, but the vehicle was probably named a *jeep* by U.S. servicemen from the sound of the Army term GP (general purpose), this reinforced by the popularity of Eugene the Jeep and the "jeep" noise that he constantly made. In any event, *jeep* was "in the air at the time," as *Mencken* says, used as the name for many contrivances, and the official army name for the vehicle—"half-ton-four-by-four command-reconnaissance car"—was definitely in need of improvement. A *peep* was the term invented to distinguish the new half-ton truck from the *jeep*, but it never really caught on.

jeez, jeepers. (*See* **gee!**)

Jeffdom. (*See* **Lincolndom**.)

Jefferson Bible; Jeffersonian. The *Jefferson Bible*, or *Jefferson's Bible*, is a collection of Jesus's teaching compiled from the New Testament by Thomas Jefferson and published at various times under his name. The author of the Declaration of Independence, founding father, and third president of the United States led an almost incredibly active life, but history best remembers Jefferson for his idealistic championship of democracy and *Jeffersonian* has become synonymous with democratic. Jefferson was eighty-three when he died on July 4, 1826—the fiftieth anniversary of the Declaration of Independence and the same day on which his friend and fellow patriot John Adams died. Some forty-four towns and counties bear his name.

Jehovah. The ancient Hebrews considered JHVH (the sacred tetragrammaton, meaning "I exist") so holy that they never pronounced it and disguised it in the form of *Jehovah*, adding the vowels of *Adonai*, another word for God, to suggest that anyone reading it should say *Adonai* instead of JHVH. During the Renaissance the vowels and consonants added to JHVH were mistaken for part of the name itself and *Jehovah* was pronounced *Jehovah* or *Yahwe* (*See* **Seven Names of God**).

Jehu. (*See* **Jezebel**.)

jell; it didn't jell. *Jell* is an Americanism meaning "to congeal or jelly" and may have been invented by Louisa May Alcott in her book *Little Women* (1869), where it is first recorded. The expression *it didn't jell*, "it didn't work, it failed," is first recorded in 1949.

jelly. Jellies were originally frozen desserts, this reflected by the Latin word *gelata*, meaning "frozen," that is the ancestor of our *jelly*, which is first recorded in 1393. The

Romans made their jellies by boiling animal bones. After cooking they set the liquid in a cool place where it solidified, the process suggesting freezing to them.

Jenny Haniver. Seamen once fashioned strange figures from dried skates, rays, or mantas they had caught, and gullible landlubbers often bought these "mermaids" and "dragons," believing them to be real. Beginning in the 13th century, sailors turned out such *Jenny Hanivers*, many specimens lasting for six hundred years or more, but their name remains a mystery. The surname may be a corruption of Antwerp, a bustling seaport of the time, but it is just as possible that some anonymous sailor bestowed the name of his sweetheart or another real woman on the lifelike mummies.

Jenny kissed me. Poet Leigh Hunt had been ill for several weeks during an influenza epidemic that had taken many lives, when he suddenly recovered and unexpectedly visited his friend Jane ("Jenny") Welsh Carlyle. Mrs. Carlyle impulsively jumped up and kissed him as he came in the door. This inspired Hunt's famous verse:

> Jenny kissed me when we met,
>   Jumping from the chair she sat in;
> Time, you thief, who love to get
>   Sweets into your list, put that in:
> Say I'm weary, say I'm sad.
>   Say that health and wealth have missed me,
> Say I'm growing old, but add,
>   Jenny kissed me.

Jenny Lind. One of the less sensational P. T. Barnum attractions was Jenny Lind. The incomparable showman brought his *Swedish Nightingale* to America in 1850 for a concert tour, the golden-voiced operatic soprano giving ninety-five concerts in nineteen cities and grossing some $712,000—with over half a million being Barnum's share. Jenny Lind, at the height of her powers, became the most famous singer of her time, due in large part to Barnum's hoopla. Her name and nickname are only rarely heard today, but were once commonly used to describe a gifted singer, and many fashions of the day, including a carriage, were named after her. There were rumors that Barnum and the singer were romantically involved, but she married composer Otto Goldschmidt in 1852, the couple later living in England. She died in 1887, aged sixty-seven.

jeopardy. *Jeu parti* was originally a French chess term meaning "a divided play or game." It thus came to mean "an uncertain chance, uncertainty" and entered English in this sense, spelled *jeuparti*, early in the 13th century. By the end of that century it had attained its present meaning of "risk of loss; peril, danger," but its spelling is not recorded as *jeopardy* until 1597.

jeremiad. A lengthy tale of woe or complaint that takes its name from Jeremiah, the major Hebrew prophet of the Old Testament—Lamentations and Jeremiah. Jeremiah's long and sorrowful complaints were a protest against the sins of his countrymen and their captivity, his tirades and dire prophecies rarely equaled in history. Strangely enough, Jeremiah, who lived in the sixth century B.C., is also thought to be the author of several of the *Psalms*. (*See* **no balm in Gilead**.)

jerk. Though *jerk* has been since the 1940s harmless, everyday slang for a fool, the word originally meant "a masturbator," in the form of *a jerk off*, this expression having meant to masturbate since at least 1590.

jerky. *Jerky*, first recorded in 1850, is dried and smoked strips of dried beef. Much used by travelers in the West, *jerky* is simply the Anglicization of the Spanish *charqui* for dried meat, and the Spanish word was often used instead of *jerky*. *Charqui*, in turn, comes from the Incan *echarqui* for dried meat.

jerkwater town. If you've ever traveled on a railroad line where trains are all steam-powered—and some still exist around the world—you'll know that this expression, first recorded in 1896, has nothing to do with "jerks" who live in small, or *jerkwater*, *towns*. Steam engines often make stops in small stations for no other reason but to obtain water, the fireman jerking a cord attached to a long spigot extending from the water tower to fill the engine's water tender. Similar practices, universal in the early days of railroading, gave rise to the Americanism *jerkwater town*, for any small, out-of-the-way place where no train stopped except to "jerk water."

jeroboam; rehoboam. Jeroboam reigned as the first of the kings of Israel, "a mighty man of valor," who "did sin and make Israel to sin" (I Kings 14:16). Which may be why the oversized wine bottle, holding from eight to twelve quarts, was named after him by some scholarly wit at the beginning of the 19th century. The bottle is certainly "mighty" enough, anyway, and its contents can surely cause "sin." The *rehoboam*, two *jeroboams*, is named after Solomon's son, who was at least wise enough to carry on his father's marital policies: Rehoboam had eighteen wives, plus sixty concubines. *Jeroboam* also describes the large bowl or goblet better known as the "jorum," the latter name in allusion to another biblical king who brought King David "vessels of silver, and vessels of gold, and vessels of brass" (II Sam. 8:10).

jerrican. The Germans developed this four-and-a-half-gallon gas container for the Afrika Korps during World War II. But the British stole the idea, naming the can the *jerrican*, after the jerries, or Germans.

jerries. During World War I *jerry* was perhaps the most offensive of the derogatory names given the Germans by Allied soldiers, these names including *Boche* (from the French for "blockhead"); *kraut* (from sauerkraut); *Heinie* (from the German name Heinrich); and *Hun* (after the ancient barbarous warriors). But over the years *jerry* came to be the mildest of such words, once its origins were forgotten: German soldiers were called *jerries* by the British because their helmets resembled the chamber pots the British called *jerries*, which took their name from the slang *jeroboam*, for a chamber pot. (*See* **jeroboam**.)

jerry-built. The cheap, flimsy constructs of a Mr. Jerry of the Jerry Bros. of Liverpool may have inspired the word *jerry-built*. *Jerry-built* could also be connected with the trembling, crumbling walls of Jericho; the prophet Jeremiah, because he foretold decay; the word *jelly*, symbolizing the instability of such structures; or the Gypsy word *gerry*, for "excrement." Still another theory suggests a corruption of *jerry-mast*, a name sailors and shipbuilders gave to makeshift wooden masts midway through the last century. Jerry-masts or rigs derive their name from the French *jour*, "a day," indicating their temporary nature.

Jersey. Jersey, the largest of England's Channel Islands, was named for the Caesars, having been called *Caesarea* when the Romans ruled over it, *Jersey* being simply a corruption of *Caesarea*. In the eighth century B.C., *ey*, the suffix of the word *Jersey*, meant "an island," so therefore *Jersey* is "the island of Caesar," or "Caesar's island." Little evidence of the Roman occupation remains in Jersey or any of the islands in the English Channel. The Romans added the island to their empire after the Gauls had ruled there and, more than 1,500 years later the only evidence of their occupation is traces of Roman buildings found in Alderney. *Jersey* also refers to a breed of cattle, raised on Jersey and noted for yielding milk with high butterfat content. Close-fitting knitted sweaters and skirts, or similar women's garments, are called *jerseys* because they were first made from *jersey cloth*, machine-woven fabrics of wool, etc., manufactured on the island of Jersey. (*See* **caesarian section**.)

Jerusalem artichoke. (*See* **artichoke**.)

Jesse James. Jesse Woodson James became a kind of American Robin Hood in his own brief lifetime. A member of the Confederate Quantrill gang in his youth, he and his brother Frank later led the most notorious band of robbers in the country's history. The gang's daring bank and train robberies caused many deaths, but James was regarded as a hero by a public that hated foreclosing banks and greedy railroads. In 1882, changing his name to Thomas Howard, Jesse went into hiding at St. Joseph, Missouri. There, six months later, Robert Ford, "the dirty little coward that shot Mr. Howard," killed him for a reward. Jesse James was only thirty-five when he died. He is still a folk hero, commemorated in a popular ballad, folktales, movies, novels, and at least one play. Besides being slang for a criminal, a *Jesse James* is a truckman's name for a police magistrate and has been applied by baseball players to umpires.

Jesse tree. There is no such tree growing in nature. The *Jesse tree* is a vine with many branches, tracing the ancestry of Christ that is called "rod out of the stem of Jesse" in the Bible and is represented in church stained-glass *Jesse windows*, Jesse often represented in reclining position with the vine rising out of his loins.

Jesus bug. *Jesus bug* is the popular name for the water strider, several insects of the family *Gerridae*, whose long slender legs fringed with hair enable them to walk on the surface of water—as Jesus was said to do in Matt. 14:25.

jet black. *Jet black*, the blackest black, takes its name from *jet*, the black mineral, which is named for the river and town of Gagas in Asia Minor where it was first mined. The Greeks called this town *Gagates*, the French later changing this to *Jayet*, which became the Modern French *Jaiet* and then the English *Jet* in the late 14th century.

jetsam. (*See* **flotsam and jetsam**.)

Jew. *Jew* comes from the German *Jude*, which is a shortened form of *Yehuda*, the name of the Jewish Commonwealth in the period of the Second Temple. Since the Commonwealth's name derived from the name of Jacob's son Yehuda (Judah), both *Jew* and *Jewish* ultimately derive from this proper name. *Jew* is first recorded in English in 1275, in the form of Gyu. (*See* **Buddhism; Christian; mosaic**.)

Jezebel. Jezebel "painted her eyes, and adorned her head, and looked out the window" when Jehu entered Jezreel. But Jehu, not to be tempted, promptly cried out, "Throw her down," and appropriately enough, three eunuchs responded. Jezebel's defenestration was complemented with her body being trampled by horses and eaten by dogs in one of the bloodiest of vengeful Old Testament passages (2 Kings 9:30-37). What had she done? The wicked ways of this worshipper of Baal were said to have brought evil upon the kingdom of Israel. So much so that *Jezebel* is still used figuratively for "a woman who flaunts loose morals," "a harridan," "a shameless bitch," or "a bold-faced prostitute." Jezebel was the wanton wife of the wicked King Ahab and daughter of the King of Tyre. *Jehu* is an old expression for "an intrepid coachman." The son of Jehoshaphat (of *Jumping Jehoshaphat!* fame) "rode in a chariot" when he went to war, the Bible tells us, a hot rodder that "driveth furiously."

jigger. Our word for the small 1 1/2 ounce shot glass used to measure whiskey probably derives from *chigger* (*q.v.*), for "tiny mites and fleas."

the jig is up. The expression suggests that the dance is over, and that the time has come to pay the fiddler. However, its derivation is more complicated. *Jig* is a very old term for a lively dance, but in Elizabethan times the word became slang for a practical joke or a trick. *The jig is up*—meaning your trick or game is finished, has been exposed, we're onto you now—derives from this obsolete slang word, not the *jig* that is still a gay and lively dance.

Jim Crow. Blackface minstrel Thomas D. Rice, "the father of American minstrelsy," introduced the song "Jim Crow" in 1828, claiming to have patterned it on the song and dance of an old field hand named Jim Crow he had observed in Kentucky. Rice's routine, part of a skit called "The Rifle," became so familiar here and on tour in England that a few years later a British antislavery book was titled *The History of Jim Crow.* It is from this book and similar uses of *Jim Crow* to signify a black that the discriminatory laws and practices take their name, though the first Jim Crow laws weren't enacted until 1875 in Tennessee.

Jiminy Cricket. Pinocchio's friend, whether Walt Disney knew it or not, bears a name that is a euphemism for *Jesus Christ.* An old one, too, the *Jiminy* portion dating back to 1664, when it was recorded as *Gemini*, probably deriving from the Latin *Jesu domini.* The mild exclamation of surprise *Jimmy!*, still heard occasionally, has the same origin, of course. (*See also* **gee.**)

Jimmy Valentine. O. Henry's story, "A Retrieved Reformation," turned into the play *Alias Jimmy Valentine* (1909), popularizing the term *Jimmy Valentine*, for a safecracker. Jimmy Valentine, the story's main character, a master yegg, or safe-breaker, was said to be based on a character O. Henry met while serving time for embezzlement.

jimsonweed. *Jamestown-weed* was the original name of *jimsonweed*, or the thorn apple, a plant that can be deadly poisonous when its foliage is wilted. *Datura stramonium* was named *Jamestown-weed* because it was first noticed growing in America near Jamestown, Virginia, where the Indians smoked it like tobacco; in fact, soldiers among the insurgents in Bacon's Rebellion of 1675 are said to have eaten this weed when defeated and driven into the wilderness, many almost dying of it. Over the years *Jamestown-weed* was slurred to *jimsonweed* in pronunciation and by the 19th century was the common name for the plant.

jinete; jennet. The Zenetes, a North African Berber tribe, were such skilled horsemen and horse trainers that anyone who trains colts to the saddle is called a *jinete* in their honor. They also give their name to the *jennet*, a small Spanish horse and a female ass or donkey.

jingoism.

> We don't want to fight, yet by Jingo
>   if we do
> We've got the ships, we've got the men,
>   and the money, too . . .

This refrain from the British music hall song "The Great MacDermott" (1878), urging Great Britain to fight the Russians and prevent them from taking Constantinople, gives us the expression *jingoism*, for "bellicose chauvinism or excessive patriotism." *Jingo* is a euphemism for "by Jesus" that dates back to the late 17th century. The British fleet did scare off the Russians from Constantinople.

jinx. Baseball Hall of Famer Christy Mathewson was among the first to use the word in print when he wrote in his *Pitching in a Pinch* (1912): "A jinx is something which brings bad luck to a ballplayer." Bix Six didn't know that the word may owe its life to a bird called the jynx, which was used to cast charms and spells. The *jynx*, known in America as the wrynecked woodpecker or wryneck, takes its name from the Greek *iynx* for the bird. In the Middle Ages this rara avis, with its grotesque, twisted neck, its odd breeding and feeding habits, its harsh, strident cries during migration and its near silence the rest of the time, was thought to have occult powers. Jynx feathers were used to make love philters and black-magic charms, the bird's name itself coming to mean a charm or spell, especially a black-magic spell, on a selected victim. It's easy to see how the slang term *jinx* arose from *jynx*, but the long flight of the jynx from medieval times to the printed page circa 1912 is not easily explained. That's why the *O.E.D.* and *Mencken* don't attempt to give the origin of *jinx.* *Webster's* admits the *jynx* version, however, as does the *Random House Dictionary* and other sources. *Partridge* traces *jinx* to the old Scottish word *jink*, "to make a sudden turn," "the implication being [that jinxes] are all *twisters.*"

jix. Among the most interesting of acronyms is the eponymous *jix*, a word coined from the letters of a person's name. *Jix* was a synonym for "prudish interference" popular in England during the late twenties and early thirties. Journalists nicknamed British Home Secretary Sir William Joynson-Hicks "Jix" and the word only passed out of use with his death in 1932.

jo. *Jo*, as in "John Anderson, my jo," means beloved one, darling, or sweetheart in Scotland. The word is simply a variant of the word "joy" and dates to the 16th century or farther back.

job.   First attested in about 1627, but probably used long before this colloquially, *job*, for "a piece of work," may derive from the earlier word *job*, meaning "a small piece, a lump." The earlier *job*, in turn, may derive from *gob*, for "a lump," which has its roots in the Old French *gober*.

Job's comforter; patience of Job.   A *Job's comforter* is someone who in meaning to comfort you adds to your sorrows, especially by advising that you brought your troubles upon yourself. "Miserable comforters are ye all," Job told the three friends who came to console him in his misery, the scolding lectures they delivered to him now known as *Jobations*. The Book of Job in the Old Testament is one of the world's greatest writings, questioning the existence of justice and moral order in the universe, its magnificent poetry more appropriate with each passing year. Job's myriad misfortunes—his stock stolen, his sons, daughter, and servants slain, his body afflicted with "loathsome sores"—and his patience with these afflictions by which Satan is said to have tested him, led to the expression *the patience of Job*, great patience, indeed.

jock; jockstrap.   Beginning in the late 1960s *jock* meant a big brainless college football player, but within a decade it covered any athlete at all, although the athlete does not necessarily have to be big or dumb—*jock* is a kinder word today. No one knows if the term is directly related to the racing *jockey* or to the *jockstraps* most athletes wear, though the latter derivation seems more plausible. *Jockstrap* takes its name from the centuries-old English slang *jock*, for "penis," which derived from the common nickname *Jock* for John.

jodhpurs.   The horseback-riding pants were brought back to England in the 19th century from the district of Jodhpur in northwest India, where riders had been wearing them for many years.

Joe Echoes.   People who were called *Echoes* in late 19th-century and early 20th-century America (Joe Echoes, Johnny Echoes, Eddie Echoes, etc.) weren't called that because they echoed other people's words. Those bearing this common nickname, usually the offspring of poor, recent immigrants, often echoed *themselves*, in sentences like "I betcha ya can't do it, I betcha," or "I tell ya it's mine, I tell ya!"

Joe Louis.   Joe Louis, perhaps the greatest of all heavyweight fighters, came to be nicknamed the *Brown Bomber* for his blockbusting right and the color of his skin. Joe Louis Barrow, born on May 13, 1914, in Lafayette, Alabama, was the son of a sharecropper who died when Joe was four. The family moved to Detroit where Joe helped support them when he was only sixteen by taking odd jobs that included work as a sparring partner in a local gym. This led to a boxing career that finally saw him take the heavyweight title from Jim Braddock in 1937. He defended his title more often than any other champion in ring history, and only Jack Dempsey outpolled him in the Associated Press survey of 1950 in which sportswriters picked the best boxers of the century. Louis lost three times in a career interrupted by service in World War II, once (before he became champion) to Max Schmeling, whom he knocked out in a rematch, and then to Rocky Marciano and Ezzard Charles, after he had retired as undefeated heavyweight champion but was attempting a comeback. His ring record included sixty-four K.O.s, eight decisions, and one win by default. A *Joe Louis* is synonymous for the utmost in a fighter, a heavyweight without peer.

a Joe Miller.   The English comic actor and barfly Joseph or Josias Miller (1684-1738), a favorite at the Drury Lane Theatre in parts such as Hamlet's first gravedigger, was an illiterate; he reportedly married his wife, in fact, only to have someone to read his parts to him. When Miller died leaving his family in poverty, his friend playwright John Mottley gathered a collection of jokes attributed to Miller—and there were many, either because he was famed for his wit, or because it was something of a joke to credit this "grave and taciturn" actor with any joke making its rounds of the pubs. The proceeds of the 72-page book went to Miller's family, and being the only joke book extant for many years it went into numerous editions over the next two centuries. Because the jokes were widely quoted and imitated on the stage so long, any stale joke came to be called *a Joe Miller*.

Joe-Pye weed.   A weed, according to the old saying, is only an uncultivated flower. Sometimes even more. The *Joe-Pye weed*, for instance, may have been named for an Indian medicine man of that name because he "cured typhus fever with it, by copious perspiration." This tall, common plant, with clusters of pinkish flowers, might well be the only weed ever dedicated to a real person. Records from 1787 reveal the existence of a Josephy Pye, or Shawquaathquat, who was possibly a descendant of the original Salem, Massachusetts healer, but the colonial Joe Pye has not yet been unequivocally identified.

Joey.   A coin named after a real person is the *Joey*, a four-pence piece honoring Joseph Hume, M.P. from Kilkenny, who in 1835 recommended that groats be coined for the sake of paying short cab fares and other small transactions. American circus performers coined the word *Joey* for a circus performer in honor of English actor Joseph Grimaldi (1779-1837). An infant of one year when he made his London debut at the Drury Lane Theatre, Grimaldi performed for almost half a century in England. Starting his career as a dancer, he later became internationally famous as the first of modern clowns, one of the best known and beloved performers of his time. Grimaldi, the London-born son of an Italian actor, had no equal in pantomime and his much-acclaimed portrayal of a clown in *Mother Goose* has been revived many times over the years.

John; John Thomas. The common first name John derives from the Hebrew *Yohanan*, "God is gracious." It is the most popular of all U.S. and European first names, appearing in various languages as John, Jean, Juan, Johann, Joao, Johannus, Hans, Giovanni, Yan, Yannis, and Yahya—not to mention feminine versions such as Jean and Joan. The origins of "John Thomas," long a slang expression for the penis, and "john," a modern synonym for a toilet and a prostitute's client, will probably never be established beyond a doubt. But a British tradition, running counter to all known facts, derives the expression from the name of a real man of prodigious dimensions. According to this story, the expression "John Thomas" dates to the Middle Ages, about 1400. At the time there lived in a Wiltshire village a farmer named John Thomas, whose outlandishly large member constantly attracted the attention of people even when safely concealed beneath his codpiece. But John Thomas succumbed to the sin of pride. Confusing astonishment with praise, he took to exhibiting himself to anyone who happened by. Young John was finally tried, hanged, drawn and quartered—except for the real offender, that is. Puritans being then as they are still, John Thomas's enormous penis was preserved in an economy-size pickle jar and Barnums of the time toured the countryside exhibiting dead what he had been executed for exhibiting alive. And so, according to the tale, the expression *John Thomas* became part of the language. The trouble is that no etymologist has traced the expression back further than 1840. All we have is the legend and the expression *John Thomas*, which, interestingly enough, D.H. Lawrence first used as the title for *Lady Chatterley's Lover.* In about 1650 the expression, broken down to *john*, became the common name for a toilet. Then again it may all be a phallic fallacy.

John B. (*See* **Stetson.**)

John Dory. The *John Dory*, or St. Peter's cock (*Zeus faber*), a flat, highly valued European food fish, had its religious name long before its humorous one. *John Dory* is most likely a humorous designation for some real or imaginary person, perhaps the notorious privateer of that name active in the 16th century, and the subject of a popular song of the time. Like the haddock, which also has a dark black spot on each side, the golden-yellow *John Dory* has the reputation of being the fish from which the apostle Peter extracted money. In France, it still bears the name St. Peter's cock; its oval spots are said to be the finger marks left when Peter held the fish to take the coin from its mouth.

John Hancock. If John Hancock had done nothing else, he would be remembered for his big, bold, belligerent signature, the first on the Declaration of Independence, writ "so big no Britisher would have to use his spectacles to read it." "King John" Hancock (1737-93), also known as the King of Smugglers, was a Revolutionary patriot who led local merchants in protesting the Stamp Act, heading as he did the largest mercantile firm in Boston. Immensely popular in his own lifetime, he became a major general of militia, a member and president of the Continental Congress, and, except for one term, was elected annually as governor of Massachusetts from 1780 until his death. His name, as everyone knows, is commonly used to mean a signature or as a synonym for *name* itself. (*See* **John Henry.**)

John Henry. Like *John Hancock* above, this is a synonym for a signature or name, but we don't know how the term arose. There is probably no connection here with the black folk hero John Henry, who outdrove a steam drill with his hammer. *John Henry* originated in the American West as cowboy slang and that's all anyone has been able to establish about it.

johnnycake. "New England corn pone" someone has dubbed this flat corn bread once cooked on a board over an open fire. Most scholars agree that no cook named Johnny had a hand in inventing the bread. *Johnnycake* is usually traced to *Shawnee cakes* made by the Shawnee Indians, who by Colonial times were long familiar with corn and its many uses in cooking. Not everyone agrees, though, and one popular theory holds that *johnnycake* is a corruption of *journey-cake*, which is what early travelers called the long-lasting corn breads that they carried in their saddlebags. However, *johnnycake* is recorded before *journeycake* in the form of *jonikin*, "thin, wafer-like sheets, toasted on a board . . . eaten at breakfast with butter"; *jonikin* is still used for griddle cakes on the eastern shore of Maryland. The word apparently progressed from *Shawnee cake* to *jonnikin* and *johnnycake*, and then to *journeycake*. Probably when people no longer needed to carry the cakes on journeys, *johnnycake* became popular again.

Johnny-come-lately. Back in the early 1800s, British sailors called any new or inexperienced hand *Johnny Newcomer*. American sailors apparently adopted the expression, changing it to *Johnny Comelately*. The first recorded mention of the term—in an 1839 novel set on the high seas—uses it in this form in referring to a young recruit. The expression soon came to describe newcomers in all walks of life, changing a little more to the familiar *Johnny-come-lately.*

John O'Groat's house. *From John O'Groat's [house] to the Land's End* is a colloquial expression for from one end of Britain to the other. The house in question once stood on the northeastern coast of Scotland, having been built by John de Groat, who settled there with his two brothers from Holland in about 1500. The brothers' descendants eventually grew to eight families and quarrels began over the matter of precedency when they met each year at John O'Groat's. Old John solved this problem neatly by building an eight-sided room with a door to each side and an eight-sided table, so that each family would be at the "head of the table." A small green knoll in the vicinity of Duncansby Head is said to be the site of the house. It is not the northernmost point of Scotland, as is often claimed.

a John Roberts. This is an amusing historical expression for a huge tankard of ale. In 1886 John Roberts, a Member of Parliament, sponsored the Sunday Closing Act for Wales, the law closing all pubs on Sundays. Confirmed drinkers took revenge by giving the name *John Roberts* to a large tankard that they filled on Saturday night with enough beer to last them through Sunday.

Johnsonese; Johnsonian. Dr. Johnson, as the great English man of letters Samuel Johnson is usually called, remains most famous for his monumental *Dictionary* published in 1755 and the immortal *Life of Samuel Johnson* written by James Boswell, generally considered the greatest English biography. A man of enormous energies who would have done even more were it not for the debilitating scrofula and often dire poverty that plagued him all his days, Johnson was revered as a moralist and a brilliant conversationalist. His *Dictionary* was the first to introduce examples of word usages by prominent authors, and along with his *Lives of the English Poets* (brilliant but essentially one-sided appraisals), it is still read today. Anecdotes about Johnson abound, but appropriate here is his reply to the lady who asked him why in his dictionary he defined *pastern* (part of a horse's foot) as the *knee* of a horse. "Sheer ignorance, Madam!" he explained. The two words that do Johnson honor reveal opposite sides of the Great Cham. *Johnsonian* refers to the good common sense reflected in his writings and conversation, while *Johnsonese* remembers the rambling polysyllabic style into which he would often slip—the very opposite of pithy *Johnsonian* phraseology. Partridge notes a third term honoring Johnson in his *Dictionary of Slang*: "*Doctor Johnson, the membrum virile*: literary: ca 1790-1880. Perhaps because there was no one that Dr. Johnson was not prepared to stand up to." Dr. Johnson died in 1784, aged seventy-three. (*See also* **Boswell**.)

joint. "I have smoked opium . . . in every *joint* in America" (1883), is the first recorded use of the word *joint* for "a place." Joints are possibly so named because people join together in them. Marijuana cigarette *joints* are, similarly, often smoked jointly by two or more people. Another interesting theory holds that *joint* was first applied to Chinese opium dens, and took their name from the bamboo walls in such places, bamboo having prominent joints!

jolly boat. There is nothing particularly jolly about the *jolly boat*, a small craft usually hoisted at a ship's stern. The name of this little workboat, used mostly in harbors, is simply a misspelling of the Dutch *jolle*, meaning a small yawl.

Jolly Roger. French buccaneers may have flown a flag called the *joli rouge* ("pretty red") and this term may have been corrupted to "Jolly Roger" by English pirates when they transferred it to their black flag. *Jolly Roger* could, however, derive from the 17th-century English word "roger," meaning "rogue or devil." Or it may come from the widely used Tamil title Ali Raja, meaning "king of the sea"—English pirates at first pronouncing "Ali Raja" as "Ally Roger," then "Olly Roger" and, finally, "Jolly Roger."

a Jonah. A *Jonah* means a bringer of bad luck who spoils the plans of others. The phrase is so popular that it has even become a verb, as in "Don't *jonah* me!" The biblical Jonah sailed to Tarshish instead of preaching against the evils of Nineveh as the Lord bade him. But the Lord sent a mighty storm to punish him for fleeing, so "that the ship was like to be broken," the frightened sailors aboard deciding that he was an evil influence, a loser, bad luck. "And they said . . . Come, and let us cast lots, that we may know for whose cause this evil is upon us. So they cast lots, and the lot fell upon Jonah" (Jon. 1:7). After they jettisoned Jonah, calm returned to the seas, but Jonah, of course, was swallowed by a giant fish (possibly a whale) and after three days and nights was "vomited out upon dry land," whereupon he did what he was supposed to have done in the first place.

Jonathan apple. The *Jonathan apple*, named after Jonathan Hasbrouck, an American judge who died in 1846, is fifth in order of commercial importance in America. It is a late fall-ripening apple, bright red and often yellow-striped, its round fruit mildly acid and the trees bearing it very prolific. The *Jonathan*, grown mainly in the northwest, is but one of numerous apple varieties commending their growers or other notables. The *Gravenstein, Grimes Golden, McCoom,* and *Stayman* are only a few others that come to mind. (*See also* **Micah Rood's apple**.)

jonquil. It is good that we no longer pronounce the name of this pretty flower the way it should be pronounced. "Junkwill" is the proper pronunciation if we consider the word's Latin ancestor *juncus*, meaning "rush" (from its long, rush-like leaves). But in the 19th century the *jonquil* (*Narcissus Jonquilla*) began to be pronounced "John-quill," which sounds much better.

Jordan almond. *Jordan almonds* come from Spain, having no connection at all with the country named Jordan, as many people think. *Jordan almond* is simply a corruption of the French *jardin almande*, which translates as "garden almond."

jorum. (*See* **jeroboam**.)

Joseph coat. "Now Joseph was handsome and good looking. And after a time his master's wife cast her eyes upon Joseph, and said, 'Lie with me.'" Joseph refused but Potiphar's wife persisted. ". . . One day, when he went into the house to do his work and none of the men of the house was there in the house, she caught him by his garment, saying 'Lie with me.'" Again Joseph abstained, this time fleeing from her and leaving his upper coat limp in her hand. Mrs. Potiphar proceeded to frame Joseph for attempted rape and her husband, captain of the Pharaoh's guard, had him flung into prison, though all went well with our hero "because the Lord was with him." It is from this story, recorded in Genesis 30, and the "coat of many colors" that Joseph's father made him, that the name of the woman's long riding coat, the *joseph*, derives. The name was probably applied by the 18th-century tailor who designed the short riding coat, later being given to the women's long coat and a cloaklike one worn by men.

josh. The best guess is that the Americanism *josh*, for "to kid" or "fool around," is a merging of *joke* and *bosh*. The pseudonym of an American writer may have something to do with the word, though. Henry Wheeler Shaw (1818-85) wrote his deliberately misspelled crackerbox philosophy under the pen name Josh Billings. Employing dialect, ridiculous spellings, deformed grammar, monstrous logic, puns, malapropisms, and anticlimax, he became one of the most popular literary comedians of his time. The expression *to josh* was used about eighteen years before Josh Billings began writing in 1863, but his salty aphorisms probably strengthened its meaning and gave the term wider currency.

jot. (*See* **iota**.)

joule. Though he made his living as the owner of a large brewery, James Prescott Joule (1818-89) had devoted himself to scientific research since inventing an electromagnetic engine as a youth. In 1840, the English physicist formulated *Joule's Law* of conservation of energy, the first law of thermodynamics. That same year he was the first to determine the mechanical equivalent of heat and the heat equivalents of electrical energy, the unit of work or energy called the *joule* later named in honor of the measurements he made. Only twenty-two when he had these valuable discoveries to his credit, Joule went on to perform other important research, becoming one of the first to broach the kinetic theory of gases.

journal. Deriving from the Latin *dies*, "day," the English *journal* doesn't contain a single letter belonging to its ultimate ancestor. The Latin *dies* was the basis for the Latin *diurnus*, which became the Italian *giorne*, "journal," and the French *jour*, meaning the same, and then passed into English as *journal* in about 1590.

journalism and strong drink. (*See* **take to journalism and strong drink**.)

jovial. *Jovial* derives from the Latin *jovialis*, of or pertaining to Jupiter or Jove, the Romans' highest deity. In its sense of a hearty, merry person, qualities the planet Jupiter was said to impart, *jovial* is said to have been coined or first used by British author Gabriel Harvey in about 1590. At least Thomas Nash claimed that Harvey invented the word, along with *conscious, extensively, idiom, notoriety,* and *rascality*—all of which Nash abhorred and said would not last. There are, in fact, no earlier citations for any of these words than the year Nash cites.

Judas; Judas goat; etc. On Holy Saturday in Corfu the people still throw crockery into the streets, enacting their traditional stoning of Judas Iscariot. Thousands of years have passed, but Christ's betrayer remains the most infamous traitor of all time, his name recorded in many expressions, including *Judas* or *Judas Iscariot*, any treacherous person who turns against a friend for some reward, as Judas did for thirty pieces of silver; *Judas kiss*, outward courtesy clothing deceit, alluding to the way Judas identified Jesus to the high priests in the Garden of Gethsemane; *Judas tree*, any of the several *circis* species, whose purple flowers suggest dark blood and upon which, tradition says, the traitor hanged himself after his act of betrayal; and *Judas goat*, the stockyard goat that leads unsuspecting animals to slaughter.

jug; jughead. Ernest Benzon, a wealthy playboy, was dubbed "Jubilee Juggins" because he foolishly squandered his entire fortune—a quarter of a million pounds—within two years after beginning to bet at the track during Queen Victoria's Jubilee in 1887. One source claims that the nickname "Silly Juggins" also attached itself to him, and perhaps we do refer to young Jubilee when we use that term. *Juggins*, however, was synonymous with simpleton long before Jubilee Juggins. Possibly it is a rhyming variation of *muggins*, which derives from an unknown personal name and means the same. Or *juggins* may be a diminutive of *Jug*, a 16th-century pet name for Judith, Jane, or Joan. Jugs, Judiths, Janes, or Joans were often maidservants or barmaids at the time, and most servants of the day were considered dull and stupid, at least by their masters. The word *jug*, for "a pitcher," could also come from these maidservant Jugs, who often handled them, but the Greek word *keramos*, "potter's earth," is another possibility. Most authorities regard these etymologies as incapable of proof, yet it is likely that all these words—and thus *jughead*—make fun of a personal name. *Jug*, in fact, may have arisen from some squat Joan or Jug's resemblance to a drinking vessel of similar shape. (*See also* **hoosegow**.)

jukebox. A *juke house* or *juke* is a house of ill repute, a whorehouse, taking its name from the black dialect called Gullah spoken on the islands off the coast of South Carolina, Georgia, and Florida. The Gullah word *juke*, or *jook*, in turn, apparently derives from the Wolof West African word *dzug* or *dzog*, meaning "to misconduct oneself, to lead a disorderly life." *Juke* naturally came to be associated with anything connected with a *juke house*, even the early *jook* or *juke organs*, coin-operated music boxes that sounded like *hurdy-gurdies* and were often found in *juke houses*. When coin-operated phonographs became very popular in the early 1940s they were called *jukeboxes* after their early counterparts, so the name of this ubiquitous electrically operated machine can be ascribed to a West African tribe.

Jukes and Kallikaks. Their names happen to be fictitious, but the Jukes and the Kallikaks are real families whose histories showed early 20th-century sociologists that heredity, rather than environment, was the cause of feeblemindedness as well as the poverty and crime often resulting from it. The Jukes were a New York family given their pseudonym by Richard L. Dugsdale, a prison sociologist who traced the clan back several generations after finding its members in various state prisons. Tracing the family to a backwoodsman named Max, who had married two of his own sisters, Dugsdale uncovered a fantastic record of criminal activity, disease, and poverty. Of the 709 descendants on whom he obtained precise information, he established that 140 Jukes had been in prison, 280 had been paupers, and that the Jukes family in seventy-five years had cost New York State $1,308,000. The Kallikaks, another real though pseudonymous family, were studied in New Jersey and revealed the same pattern of a high incidence of crime, disease, and delinquency, the two names soon linked together by writers on the subject. *Kallikak* combines the Greek *kallos*, "beauty," and *kakos*, "ugly, bad."

Julian calendar; etc. You can clip precious time from your age if you immigrate to Addis Ababa, the capital of Ethiopia, where the *Julian calendar* is still used locally. The "slow" Julian calendar, instituted by Gaius Julius Caesar, was corrected and replaced by the *Gregorian calendar* in 1582, although it continued to be used in England until the middle 18th century, when it was proclaimed in 1752, that Wednesday, September 2, would be followed by Thursday, September 14. Inaccurate, but a great reform at the time, the *Julian calendar* had been introduced in 46 B.C. It established the year as 365 1/4 days, with a leap year of 366 days every fourth year. Caesar's calendar divided the months into the number of days they presently contain, except for *August*, which Augustus Caesar insisted have thirty-one days when it was later named in his honor, not wanting Julius's *July* to contain more days than his month. The *Julian day* also pertains to Julius Caesar. It is a chronological reckoning used by astronomers enabling every day since the beginning of the *Julian era* (fixed at January 1, 4713 B.C.) to be numbered consecutively, thus avoiding complications due to months and years of unequal length. The Julian day was devised by Joseph Scaliger in the same year as the Gregorian calendar (*q.v.*).

julienne. One celebrated word sleuth seems to feel sure that *julienne*, when applied to a clear soup garnished with vegetables cut into thin strips, comes from the French *potage à la julienne*, the name bestowed by the chef of the Comte de Julienne. The *Oxford English Dictionary* is not so sure, citing "the French Jules or Julien, personal name," and another big dictionary, sweeping any male chauvinism aside, gives us "French, special use of Julienne woman's name." *Webster's* brings our French male chef to America, without a master, and has *julienne* named "after Julien, a French caterer of Boston," as do several American writers on food. While the controversy simmers, people will go on enjoying the soup, and all kinds of other foods cut into *julienne strips*.

Juliet. (*See* **Romeo and Juliet**.)

Juliet cap. Actresses playing Juliet in Shakespeare's *Romeo and Juliet* were the first to wear the little mesh cap decorated with pearls that women in later times adopted for dressy occasions and called the *Juliet cap*.

July. Mark Antony named the seventh month of the year in honor of Julius Caesar because it was the month he was born in. Up until about 1800, *July* was pronounced like the girl's name Julie in English, rhyming with "newly." In the southern United States, the word is still generally accented on the first syllable.

jumbo. P.T. Barnum purchased the fabled elephant *Jumbo* from the London Zoological Society in 1881 for "The Barnum and Bailey Greatest Show on Earth." Jumbo, captured by a hunting party in 1869, was one of the largest elephants ever seen in West Africa; the natives called the six-and-a-half-ton beast by the Swahili word *jumbo*, meaning "chief." He became a great favorite in the London Zoo, giving rides to thousands of children, and his sale to the American showman caused quite an uproar. Within six weeks the incomparable P.T. had reaped $336,000 from the $30,000 investment, and he made Jumbo's name a synonym for "huge" throughout America and the world.

jumper. Only in recent times has the *jumper* become a woman's garment. Originally it was a coarse canvas shirt reaching to the hips that was worn by sailors. The word derives from the *jump*, a short coat men wore in the 18th century.

jumping Jehoshaphat! (*See* **Jezebel.**)

jump the gun. (*See* **give her the gun.**)

June. One of ancient Rome's leading class, the Junius family, had *June* named in its honor, the naming probably influenced by the fact that the festival of Juno, goddess of the moon, fell on the first of that month.

Jungian. *Jungian psychology* differs from *Freudian* (*q.v.*) essentially in that it believes that the libido, or energy, derives not from sexual instinct but from the will to live. Carl Gustav Jung (1875-1961), an early disciple of Freud, broke with the master over what he considered an excessive emphasis on sex as a cause of neurotic disorders and a regulator of human conduct. He became a world-renowned figure, postulating the existence of two unconscious influences on the mind—the personal unconscious, containing an individual's own experience, and the collective or racial unconscious, holding the accumulated memories of generations past. The Swiss psychiatrist divided mankind into *introverts* and *extroverts*, using those or similar terms for the first time. Among many other innovations, he invented the *word-association test*.

jungle. Another word that the British brought back from India, *jungle* began life as the Hindi *jangal*. In Hindi it first meant "a desert"; then it took on the meaning of "uncultivated land"; and finally, it came to mean "land wild with trees and other uncultivated growth."

junk. "Junk" was the best pronunciation 18th-century British mariners could make of the rude little Javanese sailing boat called a *djong*. Junk, therefore, became the name for the small boat and possibly the word for the things scattered about any ship that seemed as untidy as the *djongs* appeared, though the origin of *junk* in this last respect isn't certain.

junket. "The term *junket* in America is generally applied to a trip taken by an American official at the expense of the government he serves so nobly and unselfishly," noted a *Detroit Free Press* writer in 1886. The Americanism had been used similarly by Washington Irving in 1809. Our *junket* comes from the British *junket*, for "a banquet," which may derive from the old Norman word *jonquette*, meaning a reed basket in which fish and other things were carried, or "in which sweet cream cheese was brought into town for sale." *Jonquette*, in turn, comes from the Latin *juncus*, "a reed."

just as leave. When someone says "I'd just as leave stay home as go to that party," he or she should properly use *lief*, meaning "gladly or willingly," not *leave*, in the phrase. However, people have used *leave* incorrectly for so long that *lief* is slowly but surely becoming obsolete in the expression. Nevertheless, *just as lief*, or *had as lief* can be traced back almost a thousand years.

just deserts. *Deserts* is the right word here, not *desserts*. The expression, meaning the proper punishment for an offense, *he got his just deserts*, dates back to at least 1599, and is recorded in similar forms two centuries earlier. *Deserts* is from the French *deservir*, to deserve, as is the word *desserts*.

just for openers. Originally a poker term dating back to the early 19th century and strictly meaning someone's first bet in a game, *just for openers* quickly extended to many other realms, especially the world of business, where it is still frequently used to mean someone's first action or first offer.

just in the nick of time. Up until the 18th century, both time and transactions were commonly recorded by scoring notches, or nicks, on a stick called a *tally* (*q.v.*). These nicks account for the *nick* in the common expression *just in the nick of time*, "not a second too soon."

K

K. Representing the Greek *kappa* and the Hebrew *kaph* before it, the letter *K* was used by the Romans in place of the *C*, which they abandoned, assigning the *K* sound to it. Roman libelers, for example, were branded on the forehead with a *K*, for *kalumnia*, "calumny."

"K" for a strikeout. The practice of using the letter *K* for a strikeout dates as far back as 1861, according to Joseph L. Reichler of the baseball commissioner's office. In those days, when a hitter struck out, it was said that "he struck." Letters were used for scoring, as they are today: *E* for an error, *S* for a sacrifice, etc. Since the letter *S* could not also be used for "struck," the last letter, *K*, of the word "struck" was used, and it has remained the symbol for a strikeout. Henry Chadwick, the newspaperman credited with inventing the box score, invented these symbols, the term *K* used at the time "for a player who missed the ball in three swings." It is first recorded in about 1880.

kaffeeklatsch. This expression is used, mainly among housewives, as a synonym for the more popular "coffee break." *Klatsch* is German for "a good gossip or gabfest," one held over *kaffee*, or "coffee."

kaffir. Long a derogatory term used by whites to describe blacks in Africa, *kaffir* derives from the time when Arab slavers first came to the east coast of Africa. The slavers called the people there *qafirs*, "unbelievers," because they had not yet accepted Islam, and *qafir* became the pejorative *kaffir*.

kaiser. Like *czar* (*q.v.*), *kaiser* too derives from the surname of Gaius Julius Caesar, being merely the German word for caesar. *Kaiser* was the title of the emperor of the Holy Roman Empire and the emperors of Germany and Austria. The word has less of a stigma attached to it than czar. Another title for a ruler often attributed to Caesar is *shah*. *Shah*, however, actually derives from a Russian word, meaning "dominion."

kale. *Kale* is 20th-century American slang for money, as well as a vegetable. The word derives from the Middle English *cale*, a variant of *cole*, for "cabbage." American settlers called this primitive member of the cabbage family *colewarts*.

Kamerad, Kamerad! *Kamerad* doesn't mean "I surrender" in German, as many people believe. It is German for "comrade," German soldiers who used *Kamerad, Kame-*rad! in surrendering during World Wars I and II appealing to the mercy of "comrade" human beings. The expression, however, has taken on the meaning of "I surrender" in English.

kamikaze. Toward the end of World War II improved defenses and better U.S. aircraft made it difficult for Japanese planes to get close to U.S. ships and bomb or strafe them. *Kamikaze* planes on suicidal missions were employed as a last resort. The planes, heavily loaded with explosives, were flown in mass formations and crashed into enemy ships. Scores of ships were sunk or disabled by this suicidal tactic. The planes and their pilots took their names from the *kamikaze*, or "wind of the gods" of 1281 that had wrecked a Mongol fleet invading Japan.

kangaroo. The great English explorer Captain James Cook asked a native of the Australian Endeavor River tribe for the name of a strange marsupial Cook had spotted. The native answered, "kangaroo," or "I don't know." Cook assumed that this was what the native called the animal, which is how *kangaroo* (or "I don't know") got in the dictionaries. At least that is the derivation several etymologists suggest, there being no better theory, though the story isn't mentioned in any official account of Cook's voyages. The *O.E.D.* says the story "lacks confirmation" but can find no similar word in any Australian language. (*See also* **indri; Luzon; llama; Nome; Yucatan.**)

kangaroo court. While this expression may have originated in Australia, it was first recorded in America during the California gold rush. Perhaps Australian "forty-niners" did bring it with them to the gold fields. According to this story, the source for the term are kangaroos in Australia's back country, who when out of spear range sat staring dumbly at men for long periods of time before leaping off for the horizon; their staring was thought to be similar to the dumb stares of jurors sitting on a mock jury, and their leaping away suggesting the quick decisions of such an extralegal court. But there are no quotations supporting the use of *kangaroo court* in Australia at any time. The expression could have been coined in America, in fact, based on the several uses of the word *kangaroo* in England for anything unusual or eccentric. Another guess is that Americans familiar with the kangaroo's jumping habits, or Australians here with gold fever, invented *kangaroo court* as a humorous term for courts that tried "claim-jumpers," miners who seized the mining claims of others.

kan pei! Thousands of war veterans, among others, know *kan pei* as a Japanese, Korean, and Chinese drinking toast. It translates as "dry cup," and a person making the toast often downs his drink to the last drop and holds his empty glass upside down over his head to show that the glass is drained dry.

Kansas. The Sunflower State, admitted to the Union in 1861 as our 34th state, takes its name from the name of a Sioux tribe meaning "people of the south wind." It had previously been called *the Kansas Territory*.

katydid. John Bartram, America's first great botanist, first recorded *katydid* (or a word similar to it) in 1751 as the name of the large, green arboreal insect of the locust family known scientifically as *Microcentrum rhombifolium*. The word is of imitative origin, the chattering noise the insect makes sounding like "Katy did! Katy did!"

keelboat. "These boats were long and narrow, sharp at the bow and stern, and of light draft. They were provided with running boards, extending from bow to stern, on each side of the boat," a writer noted in the *American Pioneer* (1843). *Keelboats*, also called *keels* at the time, were first recorded in the language in 1785 and the word derives from the *kiel boot* (meaning the same thing) of early Dutch settlers. *Keelboatmen* were among the roughest of men on the frontier.

keelhauling; keelraking. *Keelhauling* today means merely a tongue-lashing from a superior, hardly a punishment compared to the original *keelhauling* used as a discipline for Dutch sailors in the 16th century. Erring Dutch sailors, and later seamen in many other navies, were *keelhauled* by being tied to the yardarm, weighted down and then hauled by a rope under the vessel from side to side. Sometimes they suffered an even more dreaded punishment, being *keelraked*, or hauled under the ship from stem to stern.

keel over. To *keel* a boat is to roll her over on her keel; that is, to turn up the keel—the bottom of the boat—or to turn her upside down, wrong side uppermost. This nautical practice and term led to the Americanism *to keel over*, first recorded in 1832, which means "to turn a man or beast over on his back, to upset or capsize."

keep a stiff upper lip. (*See* **stiff upper lip**.)

keep a straight face. To refrain from laughing. One story has this expression deriving from Irish peat diggers, who have to make their spade thrusts perfectly vertical when digging out peat (thus keeping a straight spade face—"face" here the working side of the implement). I can find no proof of this and the words more likely were suggested by someone trying to keep his face from squinching up in laughter. The phrase is first recorded in an 1897 issue of the *Spectator*: "The story is one which few people, to use an expressive vulgarism, will be able to read 'with a straight face.'"

keeping up with the Joneses. According to his own account, cartoonist Arthur R. ("Pop") Momand lived in a community where many people tried to *keep up with the Joneses*. Momand and his wife resided in Cedarhurst, New York, one of Long Island's Five Towns, where the average income is still among America's highest. Living "far beyond our means in our endeavor to keep up with the well-to-doclass," the Momands were wise enough to quit the scene and move to Manhattan, where they rented a cheap apartment and "Pop" Momand used his Cedarhurst experience to create his once immensely popular *Keeping Up with the Joneses* comic strip, launched in 1913. Momand first thought of calling the strip "Keeping Up with the Smiths," but "finally decided on *Keeping Up with the Joneses* as being more euphonious." His creation ran in American newspapers for over twenty-eight years and appeared in book, movie, and musical-comedy form, giving the expression *keeping up with the Joneses* the wide currency that made it a part of everyday language.

keep it under your hat. Keep something under your hat and it is kept to yourself, it remains a secret to anyone but you. Unlike "blockhead," which goes back to the first hats, the expression is of surprisingly recent origin, having been first recorded in a similar form in 1909 and recorded in its present form in P. G. Wodehouse's *The Inimitable Jeeves* (1923).

keep the ball rolling. The election of 1840, which pitted President Martin Van Buren running for reelection against "Tippecanoe and Tyler, too"—General William Henry Harrison, legendary hero who fought against the Indians at Tippecanoe, and Virginian John Tyler—brought with it the first modern political campaign. Some historians believe that the election gave us the expression *keep the ball rolling* as well as the word *O.K.* One popular advertising stunt that helped Harrison win was "to keep the ball rolling" for the "log cabin and hard cider candidate." Ten-foot "victory-balls," made of tin and leather and imprinted with the candidate's name, were rolled from city to city for as far as three hundred miles. These victory balls did popularize the expression *keep the ball rolling*, keep interest from flagging, but the saying undoubtedly dates back to the late 18th century. Of British origin, it alludes either to the game of bandy, a form of hockey where the puck is a small ball, or the game of rugby. In either sport there is no interest in the game if the ball is not rolling. The first form of the expression was *keep the ball up*. (*See* **bandy; O.K.**.)

keep the faith, baby! This expression was common among Civil Rights workers in the 1960s and became a popular slang expression meaning "don't give up." It is much older than this, however, and has its origins in the Bible (2 Tim. 4:7): "I have fought the good fight. I have finished my course. I have kept the faith." *Fight the good fight* has also been a popular expression through the ages.

keep your eye on the ball. Many sports could have spawned the American expression meaning "be closely attentive." Baseball, tennis, golf, and basketball are all candidates, but the saying seems to have derived from the exhortations of college football coaches to their charges at the turn of the century. *To be on the ball*, to be vitally alert or in the know, is apparently an offshoot of this phrase, even though in baseball it has been said of a pitcher who has a wide variety of effective pitches.

keep your eyes peeled. To *keep your eyes peeled* for something is to keep them wide open, to keep a sharp lookout. The earliest known form of the frontier expression, recorded in 1833, was to *keep your eyes skinned* (presumably meaning with the lids drawn back): "I wish I may be shot if I don't think you had better keep your eyes skinned so that you can look powerful sharp . . . "

keep your fingers crossed. Making the sign of the cross has long been thought to be effective in averting evil, but the use of crossed fingers as a symbol of the cross is American in origin, probably originating as a superstition among blacks in the 17th century. The practice was also thought to bring good luck and resulted in the expression to *keep your fingers crossed*, as well as the belief among schoolchildren and others that a lie told with the fingers (or toes, or legs, etc.) crossed "doesn't count."

keep your pecker up. These words shouldn't be X-rated; *pecker* here refers not to the penis, as many people believe, but to the lip. *Pecker* has been slang for lip, corresponding as it does to the beak, or pecker, of a bird, since the middle of the 19th century, when we first find this expression meaning "screw up your courage, keep a stiff upper lip." (*Pecker*, for the male organ, has been slang only since the late 19th century.) The first recorded use of the phrase is impeccably British: "Keep up your pecker, old fellow," (1853). A more specific explanation is that it refers to a gamecock's bill, the bird's bill or pecker sinking lower toward the ground as he grows more tired and near defeat.

keep your shirt on. The stiff, starched shirts worn by American men back in the mid-19th century when this expression originated weren't made for a man to fight in. Therefore, men often removed their shirts when enraged and ready to fight, a practice that is reflected in the older British expression *to get one's shirt out*, "to lose one's temper." *Keep your shirt on* was a natural admonition from someone who didn't want to fight and realized that an argument could be settled if both parties kept calm and collected. "Keep your hair on" and "keep your back hair up" are earlier related expressions for "don't get excited."

kelpie. Wives of Scottish fishermen believed that a black horse with red eyes called the *kelpie* rose from the sea to warn them of forthcoming maritime disasters. Kelpie would then descend into the deep until it could be of help again. Yet another Scottish legend has it that an equine water spirit called the *kelpie* delighted in drowning travelers.

Kelvinator; Kelvin scale. Barely ten years old when he entered Glasgow University, William Thompson was appointed a full professor of natural philosophy there when only twenty-two. The Scottish mathematician and physicist early became one of the greatest scientists of his or any other era and toward the end of his career was created first Baron Kelvin of Larga. In his long lifetime Lord Kelvin made fundamental theoretical contributions in numerous scientific fields including thermodynamics, electricity, solar radiation, and cosmology. He also personally supervised the laying of the transatlantic cable in 1866, initiated the determination of electrical standards, and invented many useful instruments —among them the modern compass, a deep-sea sounding apparatus, an electric bridge, a standard balance, the mirror galvanometer, the siphon recorder, and a variety of instruments for electrical engineers. This great, good, and kind man invented the absolute or *Kelvin temperature scale*, which has the advantage of expressing any temperature in a positive number, and the British *Kelvinator*, or refrigerator, was named in his honor in 1914 when theories he had advanced made the appliance possible. Lord Kelvin retired from Glasgow University after teaching there half a century, but three years later finally matriculated as a student in order to maintain his connection with the university—thus making him, at seventy-five, the oldest genius ever to go back to school. He died in 1907, aged 83.

kenning. A *kenning* is a poetic phrase used in place of or in addition to the usual name of a person or thing. It is used to introduce color or suggest associations without distracting from the essential statement made. The word for these compound metaphors comes from the *Old Norse* phrase *kenna eitt vio*, "to express or describe one thing in terms of another." For example, the sea in Old English was called "swan's road" (*swansrad*), or "whale's path"; a boat was a "wave traveler" or "foamy necked"; darkness was "the helmet of night"; the queen was "peace weaver"; and a sword was "hammer leaving."

Kentucky. The Blue Grass State was admitted to the Union in 1792 as our 15th state, formerly having been

Kentucky County, Virginia. It takes its name from the Iroquois *Kentake*, "meadowland." Historically Kentucky was called *the dark and bloody ground* because it was an Indian no-man's-land used by several tribes as a burial and hunting ground.

Kentucky rifle. Famous in American history as the rifle of the pioneers, the long, extremely accurate *Kentucky rifle* is recorded by this name as early as 1838. The flintlock muzzleloader should, however, be called the *Pennsylvania rifle*, for it was first made in that state by Swiss gunsmiths in the 1730s and perfected there. "The British bayonet was no match for the Kentucky rifle," wrote one early chronicler.

ketchup. Is it *ketchup*, *catsup*, *catchup*, or *kitchup*? Since the word derives from the Chinese Amoy dialect *ke-tsiap*, "pickled fish-brine or sauce," which became the Malay *kechap*, the first spelling is perhaps the best. The original condiment that Dutch traders imported from the Orient appears to have been either a fish sauce similar to the Roman *garum* or a sauce made from special mushrooms salted for preservation. Englishmen added a "t" to the Malay word, changed the "a" to "u" and began making *ketchup* themselves, using ingredients like mushrooms, walnuts, cucumbers, and oysters. It wasn't until American seamen added tomatoes from Mexico or the Spanish West Indies to the condiment that tomato *ketchup* was born. But the spelling and pronunciation "catsup" have strong literary precedents, as witness Dean Swift's: "And for our home-bred British cheer,/ Botargo [fish roe relish], catsup and cabiar [caviar]." (1730). "Catchup" has an earlier citation (1690) than either of the other spellings, predating *ketchup* by some twenty years. *Ketjap*, the Dutch word for the sauce, and *kitchup* have also been used in English. Anyway, a red tide of half a billion bottles of ketchup, catsup, catchup, or kitchup is slopped on everything from Big Macs to vanilla ice cream(!) in America each year.

khaki. The *khaki* cloth used for soldiers' warm-weather uniforms, which are called *khakis*, owes its name to its color. *Khaki*, twilled cloth originally made in India, means "dust-colored or dusty," deriving from the Persian *khak*, "earth."

kibitzer. It seems that German card players of the 16th century found meddlesome onlookers just as annoying as card players do today. The constant gratuitous "advice" of these chatterers reminded them of the kiebitz (the lapwing, or plover) whose shrill cries frightened game away from approaching hunters. Thus all *kibitzers* are named for this troublesome bird, our peewit, which inspired the German word *kiebitzen*, "to look on at cards."

kibosh. The Gaelic *cie bas*, pronounced "kibosh," means "cap of death" and seems to offer the most logical explanation for the expression *to put the kibosh on* something, "to put an end to it, to dispose of it." But another theory has the expression as Yiddish in origin, deriving either from the German *keibe*, "carrion," or from the Yiddish word *kibosh*, meaning eighteen pence. Regarding the latter, it's said that bidders at small auctions *put the kibosh on* other bidders, forced them out, by jumping their bids to eighteen pence. Dickens first recorded the phrase in his *Sketches by Boz* (1836). Two women are fighting in the East End of London and a young playboy shouts to one of them, "Hooroar, put the kye-bosh on her, Mary!"

to kick against the pricks. This expression is from the Bible (Acts 9:5). Meaning "to show opposition to those in power," it refers to cattle kicking because they are being driven by someone pricking them with a sharp stick.

Kickapoo joy juice. A humorous term for any cheap liquor, *Kickapoo joy juice* remembers the Algonquin Kickapoo Indian tribe formerly resident in Pennsylvania, Ohio, and Wisconsin, but now living in Oklahoma and numbering about 800. The Kickapoos weren't notorious drinkers; their name just seemed right for the alliterative phrase. Before the Civil War a *Kickapoo ranger* meant a violent pro-slaver in Kansas. American cartoonist Al Capp gave the expression *Kickapoo joy juice* wide currency in his comic strip "Li'l Abner."

kicks; to get a kick out of. Cole Porter's "I Get a Kick Out of You" isn't the source of this expression, though nowhere are the words put to better use. The phrase goes back to the turn of the century and was first used to describe the effects of liquor or drugs, not love. The case for drugs is strong, for the related expression *to get a charge out* of something derives from addicts' use of *charge* for the injection of a narcotic. *Kicks*, anything that gives one a thrill or satisfaction, comes from the same source as the phrase.

kickshaws. Tidbits of food, trifles of small value. The word, spelled *kickshaws*, was used by Shakespeare in *Henry IV, Part 2*, but had formerly been spelled *kickhose*. The confusion is understandable when we realize that the word is merely a corruption of the French *quelque chose*, "something," which comes from the Latin *qualis causa*, "of what kind."

kick the bucket. A suicide who stands on a pail, slips a noose around his neck and kicks the pail, or bucket, out from under him would be the logical choice for the origin of this old slang term meaning to die. However, some etymologists say the phrase comes from an entirely different source. Slaughtered hogs, their throats slit, used to be hung by their heels, which were tied to a wooden block and the rope then thrown over a pulley that hoisted the animals up. Because hoisting the block was similar to raising a bucket from a well, the wooden block came to be called a "bucket," and the dying struggles of the hogs kicking against this "bucket" supposedly gave birth to the phrase. There are other theories, however, and this old expression—it may date back to the 16th century—must be marked "of uncertain origin."

kid.   *Kid* is an adaptation of the Old Norse *kio*, also meaning the young of a goat, and seems to have come into the language in about 1200. The word was applied to the young of certain other animals not long after, but isn't recorded for a young child until 1599, as low slang, though it is now standard English. Since *kid* can mean a child or a young goat *to kid* came to mean to hoax in early 19th-century England, to make a child or goat of someone.

kidney bean.   The *haricot bean* takes its name from the French *haricot*, which derived from the Nahuatl Indian *ayacotl* for the bean; it is better known as the *kidney bean* for its shape resemblance to a kidney.

kike.   One respected authority offers the surprising theory that this vulgar, offensive term of hostility and contempt, often used by anti-Semites, offends not only persons of Jewish descent but the Italians and Irish as well. The *Random House Dictionary of the English Language* suggests that it is "apparently modeled on *hike*, Italian, itself modeled on *Mike*, Irishman, short for Michael." In other words, the deliberately disparaging term painfully illustrates the transfer of prejudice from one newly arrived immigrant group to the next. This view runs counter to the prevailing theory, however. *Mencken* and others, including *Webster's*, believe that the word "derived from the 'ki' or 'ky' endings of the surnames of many Slavic Jews." Neither theory offers absolute proof. (*See* **dago; harp; wasp; welsh.**)

Kilkenny cats.   (*See* **to fight like Kilkenny cats.**)

killed with (by) kindness.   Shakespeare recorded this expression first in *The Taming of the Shrew* (1596) and Thomas Heywood later wrote a play *A Woman Killed with Kindness* (1603). The words, meaning to destroy or harm by excessive kindness, may be much older. There is a story that the Athenian lawmaker Draco, a popular man despite the stern *Draconian laws* (*q.v.*) he imposed, was literally killed with kindness. While he was sitting in the theater at Aegina in about 590 B.C., other spectators hailed him by throwing their cloaks and caps in tribute. So many landed on Draco that he smothered to death.

killer instinct.   It is said that when former heavyweight champion Jack Dempsey fought all he thought of was killing his opponent. In any case, the expression *killer instinct* seems to have been coined in the 1920s after

Dempsey's beatings of Jess Willard, Georges Carpentier, and Luis Firpo. From boxing the term became extended to all areas of life, though no major dictionary records this very common expression.

killer ship.   A *killer ship* is a ship of any size on which "death has been caused by her sea behavior"; for example, if someone falls overboard or to the deck from aloft; if there is a fatal accident aboard of any kind; or if she rams another ship and causes death. The expression dates back to at least the 19th century.

killie.   The *killie*, often caught by children in shallow water, is a minnow-like fish of several species often used as hook bait for bigger fish. The word is short for *killfish*, which comes from the Dutch *kille*, "channel or stream," plus *visch* or fish, and is first recorded in 1814.

to kill the fatted calf.   When the Prodigal Son returns home in the biblical story (Luke 15:23) his father prepares a great feast for him saying: "Bring hither the fatted calf and kill it." The story gives us the old expression *to kill the fatted calf*, to make a sumptuous feast to welcome someone.

kill the ump.   Umpires were often the targets of rocks, pop bottles, and tomatoes in the early days of baseball, and were frequently assaulted on and off the field by players and fans, as the following little ditty written in 1886 illustrates. Things got so bad that it was suggested that umpires be put in protective cages suspended over the field. Fans of the day much as now claimed that umpires couldn't see a foot in front of them: "Breathes there a fan with soul so dead,/ Who never to the ump hath said:/ Yer blind, you bum!" This charge so infuriated National League president Thomas Lynch, a former umpire, that in 1911 he had a committee of oculists test the vision of all the umpires in the league. The committee reported that every umpire had 20-20 vision or better. Was *kill the ump* ever more than an idle threat? Several minor league umpires did indeed lose their lives on the diamond over close calls. And in 1911 one Patrick Casey, a convicted murderer at Nevada State Penitentiary, was granted the customary last request. Casey wanted to umpire a baseball game before he died and so a game was arranged on the prison grounds and he was named umpire. When the game ended, he was executed.

Kilroy was here.   No catchphrase has ever rivaled Kilroy since it appeared on walls and every other available surface during World War II. It was first presumed that Kilroy was fictional; one graffiti expert even insisted that *Kilroy* represented an Oedipal fantasy, combining "kill" with "roi" (the French word for "king"). But word sleuths found that James J. Kilroy, a politician and an inspector in a Quincy, Massachusetts shipyard, coined the slogan.

Kilroy chalked the words on ships and crates of equipment to indicate that he had inspected them. From Quincy the phrase traveled on ships and crates all over the world, copied by GI's wherever it went, and Kilroy, who died in Boston in 1962 at the age of sixty, became the most widely "published" man since Shakespeare.

kindergarten. That young children should be taught according to their natural instincts, by stimulating and creating interest, is an accepted view today in educational circles. But when Friedrich Wilhelm August Froebel (1782-1852) put such ideas into practice in the world's first kindergarten ("children's garden"), which he founded in Blankenburg, Germany in 1837, his "Froebel teaching methods" met with wide disapproval. The German schoolmaster and former forester nevertheless remained convinced that preschool education was essential, devoting his life to establishing kindergartens and training teachers for them. Pleasant surroundings, self-activity, the use of play, the study of nature, and the importance of the family were stressed in these schools. Froebel's *The Education of Man* (1826) set forth his views, which were strongly influenced by an unhappy childhood both at home and in school.

Kinderhook. Old Kinderhook, the nickname of President Martin Van Buren, is the basis for the universal expression *O.K.* (*q.v.*) Old Kinderhook's birthplace, Kinderhook, New York, in turn, takes its name from children. When Henry Hudson anchored the *Half Moon* near this hook of land, he was greeted by Indian children, *kinder* in German and Dutch.

kind-hearted. Miles Coverdale, who translated the Bible from German and Latin versions in 1535, coined the term *kind-hearted*: "O give thanks therefore unto the Lord; for he is kind harted." Coverdale in the same year also invented *noonday*, for the middle of the day. He had as a precedent the earlier "noontime."

kinesics (body language). This modern branch of linguistic science studies body motion as related to speech, taking its name from the Greek *kinein*, "to move." There are said to be over 700,000 distinct movements of the arms, hands, fingers, and face "by which information can be transferred without speech," and an *O.E.D.* of *body language* (a term introduced in the 1970s) can be spoken by other parts of the body as well.

King Bomba. *King Bomba* is an expression very rarely used today, but might well be revived. The original King Bomba was Ferdinand II (1810-1859) of Naples, who reigned from 1830-1859. At one point in his reactionary reign the treacherous monarch held 40,000 political prisoners. He was called *King Bomba* for his ruthless bombardment of Sicilian cities in 1848, in which much damage was done, many atrocities committed, and many innocent people hurt. Since then *King Bombas*, whatever their motives, have been all too common.

King Cole. The "merry old soul" of nursery rhyme fame is in British tradition a king of the third century. The monarch is mentioned in *Historia Regum Britannica* (1508) by Geoffrey of Monmouth, who says nothing about him calling for his pipe, bowl, or fiddlers three, and whose veracity, in fact, has been questioned. Old King Cole may also have been the grandfather of the Emperor Constantine. The city of Colchester doesn't derive from his name, as is often stated, but is probably named from the Latin *colonia*.

Kings County; Queens County; Richmond. Since we have covered New York and the Bronx, it's only fair that the origins of New York City's remaining three counties, or boroughs, be touched upon here. *Kings County*, better known as *Brooklyn*, is named for England's King Charles II; *Queens County* honors Catherine of Braganza, Charles's Queen; and *Richmond*, better known as *Staten Island* (*q.v.*), is named for King Charles's son, the Duke of Richmond. Since New York County, or Manhattan, was named for King Charles's brother James, Duke of York, that leaves only the *Bronx* (*q.v.*) of New York City's four boroughs that isn't named for Charles II's royal family.

the King's English. Several English kings didn't speak English, but this term has nevertheless meant "proper English, English as it should be spoken," since the mid-16th century. It was used by Shakespeare in *The Merry Wives of Windsor* (1600) and three centuries earlier Chaucer wrote "God save the king, that is lord of this language."

the king's evil. *The king's evil* is an old name, sometimes encountered in literature, for scrofula. Scrofula, a constitutional disorder of a tubercular nature, characterized by swelling of the lymphatic glands in the neck, was believed to be susceptible to cure by the royal touch. France's Louis IX is thought to be the first king to employ the practice, which soon spread to England, where Macaulay records that Charles II touched 92,107 persons during his reign. The practice ended with Queen Anne, Dr. Johnson being one of the last persons to be "touched" by royal hands in 1712.

King's peace. (*See* **Queen's (or King's) peace.**)

a king's ransom. Just how much is a king's ransom? When Richard the Lion-Hearted was kidnapped by Duke Leopold of Austria while returning from the Third Crusade, he was ransomed for nearly $5 million in today's dollars, a sum that almost bankrupted England when added to the cost of the Crusade. How far back this expression for "a large sum" goes is anybody's guess. We only know that the first recorded mention of it dates from about 1470. Marlowe used the term in his masterpiece *Faust* (ca. 1590).

King Tut. Egyptian King Tutankhamen's tomb was discovered in 1922 by George E.S.M. Herbert, earl of Carnarvon, and Howard Carter in the valley of the tombs of the kings at Karnak. Tutankhamen, heretic king of the XVIII dynasty in the 14th century B.C., lay swathed in a gold sarcophagus surrounded by a fortune in jewels, furniture, and other relics that threw much light on Egyptian history. His difficult name was condensed to *King Tut* and his immense wealth caught the public's imagination. *Don't act like King Tut* or *he think's he's King Tut* became expressions applicable to any person pretending to be much more than he was, acting as if the world should pay him homage as it did King Tutankhamen.

Kinkaider. American Congressman Moses Kinkaid (1854-1922) saw his Kinkaid Act granting homesteads to Nebraska settlers passed into law in 1904. The homesteaders who settled these 640 acre grants under the provisions of the act were called *Kinkaiders* by the newspapers of the day and his name passed from the pages of the *Congressional Record* to the dictionaries.

kinnikinnik. Deriving from a similar but unrecorded word "in the Cree or Chipewa dialects of Algonquian" that means literally "what is mixed," *kinnikinnik* was first a nontobacco mix of dried sumac leaves, ground dogwood bark, and other ingredients that the Indians and early American settlers used. Later tobacco was often added to the mixture. *Kinnikinnik* is also the longest palindromic word in English and can have twelve letters when spelled *kinnik-kinnik*, as it sometimes is.

a kiss-cow. This unusual term, probably obsolete, can be traced back to early 19th-century England, where a *kiss-cow* was someone who would suffer any indignity for a consideration, a sycophant who would "kiss the cow for the milk."

kissing bug. There are several species of venomous bloodsucking Hemiptera of the family Reduviidae called kissing bugs, these assassin bugs inflicting sharp bites on the lips that cause painful sores. There was, in fact, a great kissing-bug scare for two or three months in the U.S. in 1899, with many people bitten by such bugs while they slept. The insect called the *kissing bug* seems to have inspired the punning *kissing bug* for a person who kisses a lot. This is an American expression, not Canadian as *Partridge* claims, first recorded in the late 1890s, and perhaps first applied to naval hero Richmond "Kissing Bug" Hobson, who was showered with kisses by so many women that his name, in the form of *hobsonize* (q.v.), took

on the meaning "to kiss." Hobson, however, was always the *kissee* (first recorded in England in 1827), not the *kisser*.

kissing cousin. *Kissing cousins* is a Southern Americanism that dates back before the Civil War. The term first implied a distant blood relationship, but today more often means a very close friend who is considered family. It still is used in its original sense, however, in the sense of a relative far removed enough to permit marriage, "an eighth cousin" in the North.

a kiss-me. In New England and the southeastern part of the U.S. a *kiss-me* or a *kiss-me-quick* was a ridge or depression in a roadway, one that caused a carriage to jolt and possibly throw a girl into her young man's arms. The usage is recorded as late as 1945 in the Southeast and many still be used there to a limited extent. (*See* **wham, bam, thank ye, m'am.**)

kiss-me-quick-before-mother-sees-me. The *kiss-me-quick-before-mother-sees-me* was a bonnet young women wore in the mid-18th century, a small hat set far back on the head that was considered daring for the day. It was also called a *kiss-me-quick*.

the kiss-my-arse latitudes. The *kiss-my-arse latitudes* is used mostly in the British merchant marine for the "home stretch," when a ship is close to port and the crew cares about nothing but getting ashore and tends to ignore orders—especially if the crew has been paid.

kit and caboodle. (*See* **whole kit and caboodle.**)

kit-cat. Though pastry cook Christopher (Kit) Catt—or Cat or Catling—created little mutton pies, he nevertheless travels in the company of Titians of the art world. Kit Catt's mutton delights were called *kit-cats* and some leading Whigs of the early 18th century enjoyed them so much that they formed a club on his pastry shop premises in London. However, when Sir Godfrey Kneller was commissioned to paint forty-two portraits of the *Kit-Cat Club's* prominent members, who included Steele, Addison, Congreve, and Walpole, a problem soon presented itself. The rooms were so low in height that Kneller had to restrict his portraits to three-quarter size, each canvas measuring exactly 28 by 36 inches. Such canvases were called *kit-cats*, after the club in which they hung and the term is still used for any portrait of these dimensions representing less than half the length of the sitter but including the hands.

kiting. (*See* **fly a kite.**)

kitsch. *Kitsch* derives from the German *kitschen*, "to throw together a work of art," which dates back to the

19th century. The Viennese novelist Hermann Broch has been credited with adding the noun *kitsch* to the vocabulary of literature, in its sense of "art or literature judged to have little or no aesthetic value, especially when produced to satisfy popular taste." The Czech novelist Milan Kundera adds that "Kitsch translates the stupidity of conventional ideas into the language of beauty and feeling."

Kiwanis. Upper Michigan Indians used the term *keewanis* to mean "make one's self known" or "to express one's self." When a Detroit club promoting good fellowship and civic interests was founded in 1915, a local historian suggested that this Indian word be used for the club name. Feeling that "self-expression" suited the purpose of the club, which of course later became a national organization, members adopted the name with its spelling slightly changed to *Kiwanis*.

kiwi. *Kiwi*, like *mako* (q.v.), is an English word that comes to us from the Maori language used by the Polynesian natives of New Zealand. *Kiwi-kiwi* is the Maori word for the flightless bird called a *kiwi* (*Apteryx australis*), which is often termed an *apteryx* in crossword puzzles. *Kiwi* is also slang for a non-flying member of the Royal Air Force and Australian slang for a New Zealander. *Kiwi* fruit (*Actinidae sinensis*), also known as the Chinese gooseberry and *Yangtao*, is native to China but called *kiwi* because most of the fruit sold in American and British markets is grown in New Zealand.

klaxon. *Klaxon* was coined in 1908 from the Greek *klazein*, "to make a noise," by the inventor who patented the first electrically operated horn on an automobile. When the patent expired, this trademark passed into the dictionaries without a capital as a word for any horn.

klieg eyes; klieg light. Hollywood movie stars adopted the dark glasses that became their trademark because of the intense *klieg light* introduced to stage and studio early in this century. These bright incandescent lights, rich in ultraviolet rays, caused a form of conjunctivitis marked by burning of the eyeballs, redness, tearing, and photophobia that was common to all who worked under the arcs. In order to protect their *klieg eyes* the stars, as well as lesser lights, took to wearing "shades," and have traditionally done so ever since. The *klieg light* was the invention of the German-born brothers Kliegl, John H. (1869-1959) and Anton T. (1872-1927), who immigrated to the United States and in 1897 established the firm of Kliegl Brothers, pioneering in the development of lighting equipment and scenic effects for the stage and early motion pictures. The light they invented was first called the *Kliegl light*, which proved too difficult to pronounce, their real name modified like those of many of the actors who worked with them.

kmit. When foreign reporters questioned him about the name of a new ministry the Bolsheviks formed after the Russian revolution Leon Trotsky told them it was named KMIT. Newspapers all over the world called the agency by these initials until someone found out what they stood for. Trotsky had been playing a contemptuous joke on the reporters and their capitalist employers. KMIT stood for the Yiddish *kuss mir im tuches*, "kiss my ass."

knapsack. *Knapsacks* were originally small sacks that German soldiers carried containing their rations, the word deriving from the German *knappen*, "to eat."

knee-high to a grasshopper. *Knee-high to a toad*, first recorded in 1814, was the original of this Americanism, and *knee-high to a mosquito* as well as *knee-high to a frog* appeared before *knee-high to a grasshopper* came on the scene some thirty-seven years later. But *knee-high to a grasshopper* has outlasted all the others, including the later *knee-high to a duck*. It is generally used in comparisons, emphasizing youth, smallness, or remoteness in time. There are some 120,000 varieties of grasshoppers, and to be literally knee-high, or tibia-high, to a grasshopper a person would have to range from one millimeter tall to a little more than an inch tall.

knee jerk. Used to indicate an automatic, unthinking response to anything, *knee jerk* (as in *knee-jerk liberal*) is one of those relatively few terms that can be traced back to its exact origins. In 1948, the distinguished etymologist Sir Ernest Gowers proudly gave us the expression's medical roots: "Some 70 years ago a promising young neurologist made a discovery that necessitated the addition of a new word to the English vocabulary. He insisted that this should be 'knee jerk,' and 'knee jerk' it has remained, in spite of the effort of 'patellar reflex' to dislodge it. He was my father; so perhaps I have inherited a prejudice in favor of homemade words." Sir Ernest's contention seems to be borne out by the *O.E.D.*, which gives as 1878 the first recorded use of the term, in Sir Michael Foster's *Text-book of Physiology*: "Striking the tendon below the patella gives rise to a sudden extension of the leg known as the 'knee-jerk.'" The first figurative use of the term isn't known, but it seems to have been soon after the phrase's coining.

knickers. In England women's *panties* are called *knickers*, which take their name from a man. When in 1809 Washington Irving burlesqued a pompous guidebook of his day with his two-volume history of New York, he decided to capitalize on the name of Harmon Knickerbocker, head of Albany's old, prominent Knickerbocker family, and chose the pseudonym Diedrich Knickerbocker. Soon Irving's humorous work became known as *Knickerbocker's History of New York*, but it wasn't until English caricaturist George Cruikshank illustrated a later edition in the 1850s that the Knickerbocker family name was bestowed on the loose-fitting, blousy knee breeches still worn today. In that English edition Cruikshank depicted the alleged author and his fellow Dutch burghers wearing voluminous breeches buckled just below the knee. His drawings of this style that the early Dutch had worn were widely copied for boys' knee pants, baggy golf trousers four inches longer, and even women's silk bloomers—all dubbed *knickerbockers*, after the family Irving had immortalized.

knight errant. (*See* **arrant thief.**)

K-9 Corps. The army's *K-9 Corps*, organized during World War II, was originally called D4D, an acronym for "Dogs for Defense." But the much cleverer and more memorable *K-9 Corps*, a pun on "canine," quickly replaced the former term.

Knock! Knock! First recorded in about 1936, this appears to have originally been an American catchphrase used by someone about to tell a dirty story. Then it came into use by someone entering a room without knocking. Perhaps it is from the old schoolboy joke "Knock! Knock! Who's there? Grandpa. Whaddya want . . ." But one writer claims it may come from the Porter's scene in *Macbeth* (Act II. Scene iii): "Knock, knock, knock! Who's there . . . Knock, knock! Who's there, in the other devil's name . . . Knock, knock, knock! Who's there? . . . Knock, knock! Never at quiet! . . ."

knocked into a cocked hat. To *knock someone into a cocked hat* is to beat him badly in a game of skill. The expression derives from the old game of ninepins, where three pins were arranged in the form of a triangle (like a three-pointed cocked hat). When all pins but these three were knocked down, the set was said to be *knocked into a cocked hat.*

to knock galley west. No one has been able to explain why a ship's galley or the compass point west have anything to do with this expression meaning "to knock into smithereens." They may not. The words may be a corruption of the English dialect term *collyweston*, which in turn derived from the town of Colly Weston in Northamptonshire, a town reportedly given to excessive violence. Colly Weston itself may have been named for a local, violent troublemaker named Colly Weston. All speculative maybes once again.

knock-kneed. *Knock-kneed*, having knees that knock together in walking, the opposite of "bandy-legged" (*q.v.*), is, surprisingly, not an ancient term. At least it isn't attested until 1807, when recorded in the statement that "children . . . from bad nursing become knock-kneed."

knock on wood. Why do we say *knock on wood* and tap wood or our heads after declaring that some calamity has never happened to us? The superstition is an old one and has many possible explanations, none sure. It may be of pagan origin, deriving from the practice of rapping on trees to ask protection from friendly spirits who were believed to reside inside. Or it could be a Christian superstition similar to touching wooden crucifixes or rosary beads. One theory even holds that the practice comes from games like hide-and-seek in which players who succeed in touching wood are safe from capture. A last, farfetched possibility is that the superstition is linked to a verse in the sixth chapter of Galatians: "God forbid that I should glory save in the cross of our Lord Jesus Christ." You will be forgiven any vainglorious boast, according to this story, if you quickly recall the wooden cross Christ carried.

knock them in the aisles. (*See* **lay them in the aisles.**)

to knock up. In England *to knock up* has been standard English for "to arouse by knocking at the door" or "to visit" since at least 1663, when Samuel Pepys, in his *Diary*, recorded constables knocking him up. In American slang, however, *to knock up* has since about 1920 meant to make a woman pregnant, usually outside of marriage.

knots. Knots measure the speed of a ship at sea, each knot equaling a nautical mile (6,076 feet), which is slightly longer than a land-measured mile (5,280 feet). Since six nautical (geographical) miles are about equal to seven statute (land) English miles, a ship making 12 knots an hour is actually traveling 14 land miles. A ship's speed came to be measured in *knots* because the log line thrown overboard to record distance was marked off by knots and had been used to measure a ship's speed since early times. In its nautical sense *knot* is first recorded in 1633.

to know a hawk from a handsaw. Shakespeare made this phrase immortal in *Hamlet*, but its origins may never be established. The expression means "to be smart, to know one thing from another" and is usually employed negatively today: *he doesn't know a hawk from a handsaw. Handsaw* in the phrase is said to be a corruption of *hernshaw*, a heron (thus it is literally "I know a hawk from a heron"), but there is no proof of this. The expression is quoted nowhere before Shakespeare and he could have been referring to the handsaw carpenters use, as he did in another play. Similarly, *hawk* here could refer to the tool called a hawk, which has long been used by plasterers.

know beans. (*See* **he doesn't know beans.**)

to know him when. American poet and journalist Arthur Guiterman (1871-1943) popularized this expression, meaning "I knew him before he became rich or prominent," in a parody he wrote of Whittier's lines (in *Maud Muller*) "of all sad words of tongue or pen,/ The saddest are these: 'It might have been.'" Wrote Guiterman, in *A Poet's Proverbs* (1924): "Of all cold words of tongue or pen,/ The worst are these, 'I knew him when.'"

to know like a book. "Complete understanding" is the meaning of *to know like a book*, and the Americanism obviously dates from times when there were few books in most homes. Those that were present, like the Bible, were often committed to memory, hence the familiar expression. *To know one's book*, a British saying, means something different—"to know one's best interest, to have made up one's mind." *To speak by the book*, is to speak meticulously, and *to speak* or *talk like a book* is to speak with great precision, usually pedantically.

know-nothing. Pledged to complete silence about their organization, members of New York's Order of the Star-Spangled Banner told anyone who inquired about their secret society: "I know nothing about it." Thus as early as 1850 they were called *know-nothings*. Later, when they merged with other groups into the national American Party in 1856, this stock reply became "I know nothing in our principles contrary to the Constitution." A strange statement for a party that was anti-Catholic, whose members vowed to vote only for native Americans, and which supported a twenty-five-year residence requirement for citizenship, among other reactionary principles. The *Know-Nothings* achieved considerable success in local contests, but fared badly in the 1856 national elections, even with ex-President Millard Fillmore as their candidate and they ceased to be a political power after 1860. However, their name lives on as a synonym for any reactionary political group or individual that appeals to base emotions. Other political parties have fared just as badly over the years and one wonders which modern party will go the way of the Doctrinaires, the Intransigents, and the *Know-Nothings. (See* **doctrinaire; intransigent.**)

to know one's cans. Cowboys on the range in the 19th century were usually starved for reading matter and often read the labels on the cook's tin cans, learning them by heart. A tenderfoot could always be distinguished because he didn't *know his cans*. The expression isn't recorded in the *Dictionary of Americanisms* but is given in Ray Allen Billington's *America's Frontier Culture* (1977). One wonders how the cowboy would have handled modern ingredients like "monosodium glutamate," etc., included among contemporary label ingredients.

know the ropes. Though common in horse-racing circles, these words are almost surely of nautical birth, referring to the complex system of lines on full-rigged sailing ships that bewildered recruits had to master before they became seasoned seamen. Dana used the term in *Two Years Before the Mast* (1840), indicating that it was an old expression he'd heard.

to know what's what. Wrote Samuel Butler in *Hudibras* (1663): "He knew what's what, and that's as high/ As metaphysic wit can fly." *To know what is what* is still to be a shrewd person, to know what is going on. The phrase is thought to derive from the old question in logic *Quid est quid?*, "what is what," one which someone would have to be very shrewd to answer.

knuckle down. Marble players may have been responsible for this expression, which dates back to 17th-century England. One rule in the game provides that a player must shoot directly from the spot where his marble lands, which requires that he put his knuckles on the ground, or "knuckle down." Since marbles was a popular pastime with adults as well as children at the time, *knuckle down* possibly came to express earnest application to any job. However, the bones of the spinal column were also known as "knuckles" in the 17th century, and the expression may therefore derive from the act of "putting one's back into a task."

knuckle under.

> He that flinches his Glass, and to Drink is not able,
> Let him quarrel no more, but knock under the table.

This anonymous verse, from the late 17th century, suggests that our expression to *knuckle under*, or "to admit defeat," derives from an earlier British phrase, *to knock under.* People in taverns apparently rapped on the under side of the table when beaten in an argument. But another equally reasonable theory connects the term with an ancient form of submission to one's conqueror. As a token of submission a person fell to his knees. Since *knuckles* in Anglo-Saxon and medieval English meant the knee joints as well as the joints of the fingers, this would account for the phrase.

Kodak. After inventing this camera in 1888, George Eastman claimed that he intentionally set out to coin a short, easy-to-remember name for it that could not be stolen. He chose *k* as the first and last letters in the word because *k* was the first letter in his mother's family name. The rest of the word came by experimenting with other letters in combination with the two ks, though some have suggested that he might have had Alaska's Kodiak Island in mind.

Korean Conflict; Korean Emergency. (*See* **police action**.)

kowtow. The Chinese *k'o-t'ou*, which we spell *kowtow* (rhymes with "know how"), means "knock your head"—that is, to kneel and bow before a superior by touching the floor with your forehead. The Mandarins required the *k'o-t'ou* of their "inferiors," and adventurers in China at the turn of the century brought back the word if not the practice. To *kowtow* to someone has come to mean to show obsequious behavior, everything but banging one's head on the floor.

K.P. *K.P.* became the abbreviation for *kitchen police*, those soldiers selected to peel potatoes, wash pots and pans, clean grease traps etc., in World War I, not World War II, as is commonly believed. The verb *police*, meaning "to clean up an area," is first recorded in 1893, and may be a corruption of *polish*.

K-rations. You may have wondered what the "K" stands for in this well-known term for emergency Army field rations containing a nutritional meal. The "K" isn't some mystery nutrient. It honors the American physiologist, Ancel Keys (b. 1904), who invented *K-rations*.

Kreutzer Sonata. Beethoven dedicated his famous violin sonata (op. 47) to violinist and fellow-composer Rodolphe Kreutzer in 1803 and it has since been universally known as the *Kreutzer Sonata*. The musician, a Frenchman of German extraction, was professor of violin at the Paris Conservatoire and conductor at Vienna's Imperial Theater. A prolific composer with some forty operas, numerous concertos and sonatas, and forty unsurpassed études for the violin to his credit, Kreutzer died in 1831, aged sixty-five. Tolstoy's novella, *The Kreutzer Sonata* (1890), takes its title from the Beethoven work.

Kris Kringle. After nearly a century and a half this synonym for Santa Claus is still heard, even though the words have nothing at all to do with Santa. The term originated in America in about 1830 and was spelled *Krisskring'l* before taking its present form. *Krisskring'l* stemmed from a misunderstanding of the word *Christkindlein* used by German immigrants, its meaning not "Santa Claus" but "the Child in the Manger," or "the little Christ child."

kulak. Millions of kulaks were exterminated by the Communists in the years following the 1917 Russian Revolution because these small farmers refused to collectivize their farms. These farmers had been named *kulaks* before the Revolution from the Russian for "fist," because they were said to be "tightfisted," cheap employers who took advantage of farm workers.

Kung-fu. (*See* **Confucius say**.)

L

L. Our twelfth letter has been traced to the early Phoenician and Hebrew alphabets, where it was drawn as an oxgoad or *lamed*.

£. The symbol for the British pound comes from the Latin word *libra*, just as our *lb.* for pound does. *Libra* in this case is part of the Latin phrase *libra pondo*, which means a pound by weight.

labanotation. This little-known word describes an important notation system that amounts to a graphic shorthand for dance, enabling a choreographer to delineate every possible movement of the human body individually or in ensemble. Introduced by its creator Rudolph Laban in his book *Kinetographie Laban* (1928), *labanotation* was the first practical method capable of scoring the various complex movements and positions of an entire ballet or musical comedy. Unlike the old numbered-footprint plans familiar to us all, the Laban system amounts to a complete break with tradition. It dispenses entirely with the musical five-line horizontal staff, using a three-line vertical staff that is divided in the center. Code symbols on each side of the line indicate foot and leg movements, while symbols in parallel columns outside the lines pertain to all other body gestures. Every slight movement from toe to head can be noted, as well as their direction, timing, and force, and by grouping together the staffs for individual dancers an entire work can be "orchestrated." Laban did for the dance what Guido d'Arezzo did for musical notation almost a thousand years before him (*See* **Guido scale**). Prior to his system dancers had to rely on their memories of performers who had appeared in classical ballets, but now almost exact revivals can be given and ballet composers can finally adequately copyright their creations. Born in Pressburg (Bratislava) on December 15, 1879, the German dance teacher and choreographer died in London on July 1, 1958.

labor. Adam Smith in *The Wealth of Nations* (1776) was the first person to use the word *labor* in its modern sense of work done to supply material wants. Before that, the word had the same meaning as its parent, the Latin *labor*, which means toil, distress, and trouble.

a labor of love. A *labor of love*, a work undertaken for the love or liking of it more than for any compensation, has been a common English expression since the 17th century, and it is much older, deriving from the biblical "Your worke of faith and labour of love" (1 Thess. i,3).

labyrinth. Though there were mazes before his, the Labyrinth, "double-headed axe," of Greek legend built by the artificer Daedalus to confine the man-bull Minotaur may give us our word *labyrinth*. The only way out of this maze was through the help of a skein of thread. Later, the King of Crete imprisoned Daedalus and his son Icarus in the Labyrinth. Daedalus made wings for them and they escaped, but Icarus flew too close to the sun, melting the wax binding the feathers to his wings, and fell to his death. The story also gives us the words *daedal*, anything cleverly made, and *daedalist*, for an air pioneer.

Lachryma Christi. *Lachryma Christi* is an Italian wine, its Latin name meaning "tears of Christ." (*See* **Liebfraumilch**.)

lackadaisical. A *lackadaisical* person, a lethargic, listless lazy person, was originally someone given to sighing "lackaday, lackaday," a shortening of *alack-a-day* ("woe is the day"). Laurence Sterne may have coined *lackadaisical* from the earlier *lackaday*; anyway, he first recorded the word in his *Sentimental Journey* (1768).

lackey. Military commanders of the Moors were called *al-kaid*, "chief," but when the Spanish captured these commanders and their men in regaining control of Spain during the Middle Ages, they enslaved them and made them servants. From their once proud name, corrupted to *alcayo* in Spanish, came our English word for the lowest of servants.

lackluster. *Lackluster* originally referred only to a lack of luster or brightness in the eyes; in fact, we don't find it to describe anything else lackluster until Dickens's time. The word was invented or first recorded by Shakespeare in 1600: ". . . looking on it with lack-lustre eye, he says . . ."

laconic. "If we enter Laconia, we will raze it to the ground," an Athenian herald (or Philip of Macedon) is said to have announced to the Laconians. "If," was the reply he received from the sententious Spartan magistrates. The Lacadaemonians were all supposed to be so parsimonious with words, and were noted in the ancient world not only for their stoic Spartan life-style but also for their short, brusque, and pithy way of speaking and writing, which was appropriate for their outward lack of emotion. Not only in Sparta, the capital, but throughout the country youths were taught modesty and conciseness of speech, taught so well that the word *laconic* comes to us by way of Latin from the Greek *Lakonikos*, meaning "like a Laconian." A *laconic* person is generally one who expresses much without wasting words, who is terse, to the point, and usually undemonstrative.

lacrosse. *Lacrosse* is probably the only sport whose name has religious significance. When French priest Pierre de Charlevoix saw Algonquin Indians playing their game of *baggataway* in 1705, he thought that the webbed sticks they used resembled a bishop's cross and called the game *lacrosse*, which eventually supplanted the Indian name. While playing lacrosse "to celebrate George III's birthday" on June 4, 1763, Obijway and Sac Indians propelled the ball over the walls of Fort Michillimackinac and rushed in on the pretext of retrieving it, seizing weapons hidden by their squaws and massacring the garrison.

lad; lass. Many authorities cite the Middle English *ladde*, "serving man," as the source for *lad*, "boy or young man." Others, however, suggest the Anglo-Saxon proper man's name *Ladda* as the word's ancestor. *Lass* may be a truncated form of *laddesse*, the feminine of *ladde*, but it could derive from the Swedish *losk kona*, "an unmarried woman."

la-di-da. *La-di-da*, or *la-ti-da*, is still used to put affected people in place. Probably imitative of the accents of such people, the expression became very popular in the 1880s, twenty years after its origin, due to the British music hall song "He Wears a Penny Flower in His Coat, *La-di-da!*"

Ladies and gentlemen. *Ladies and gentlemen*, as a form of address to a mixed audience, used to be the reverse: it was traditional to say "gentlemen and ladies." The change, putting ladies first, came in early America and first took place in the North, not in the chivalrous South.

ladies of the line. We have all heard of the self-explanatory *ladies of the night*, for prostitutes, but why *ladies of the line*? The expression comes to us from the American West, where prostitutes did business in tents and jerry-built shacks stretched out in lines at the outskirts of towns, mining camps, or railroad yards.

ladies of the night. This American euphemism for prostitutes was popular in the 1870s and is still used today. Interesting collective nouns for such ladies include: *a horde of hookers, a jam of tarts, a wiggle of whores, a flourish of strumpets, an essay of Trollope's, an anthology of pros.*

Ladik; Ladikiyeh; Latakia. Every mother should have a boy like Seleucus, founder of the Syrian dynasty. The emperor is said to have named *five* cities after his mother Laodice in the middle of the 3rd century B.C. This able Macedonian general of Alexander the Great tried hard to build his kingdom in the way that Alexander built his, founding Greek colonies governed along Persian lines wherever he could. Three of the at least five cities Seleucus Nicator named for his mother remain standing today, their names now pronounced *Ladik, Ladikiyeh,* and *Latakia*. Latakia, a seaport of Syria opposite the island of Cyprus, is the most prominent of these and is noted for its Latakia tobacco. (For the story of a city Seleucus Nicator's *grandson* named after *his* Laodice, his wife in this case, *see* **Laodician**.)

lady. (*See* **lord**.)

ladybird. (*See* **ladybug**.)

Lady Bountiful. British playwright George Farquhar (1678-1707) wrote his last and best play, *The Beaux' Stratagem*, on his deathbed with the help of a small gift of twenty guineas from an actor friend. A former actor himself who quit the stage after accidentally wounding an opponent in a dueling scene, Farquhar maintained his cheerful disposition to the end and left behind a genial realistic comedy when he died in poverty at the age of 29. Lady Bountiful, a wealthy character in his play, has come to represent any benevolent lady who contributes much of her wealth to a community. (*See* **Boniface**.) The expression is today used mostly satirically, as in "She's always playing Lady Bountiful."

ladybug; ladybird. In *ladybug*, *lady* refers to "Our Lady," the Virgin Mary, in whose honor the beneficial insect was named—not to the erroneous belief that all ladybugs are female. These brightly colored beetles of the family *Coccinellidae*, which feed on aphids and other destructive garden pests, are known in England as *ladybirds*, due to a British aversion to the word *bug*, which is strongly associated there with buggery, or sodomy. Some American Southerners favor the British word, which is why Claudia Taylor Johnson, our former first lady, bears this familiar Southern nickname.

Lady chapel. (*See* **Lady's-mantle**.)

Lady fern. (*See* **Lady's-mantle**.)

Lady Godiva. Strategically arranging her long golden tresses, Lady Godiva rode through Coventry, relieving herself of her clothes and inhibitions in order to relieve her people of oppressive taxation. According to the traditional story, Lady Godiva (ca. 1040-ca. 1080) had jokingly agreed to ride naked through the crowded streets at high noon if her husband, Leofric, earl of Mercia and lord of Coventry, and one of the most powerful nobles in England, would lift burdensome taxes he had imposed on the townspeople. At least Leofric *thought* she was joking. To the delight of his twice-blessed tenants, the earl had to keep his promise when his wife took him at his word. He removed the levy almost as soon as she had removed her clothes and displayed herself in the marketplace. *Lady Godiva*, a title more humorously applied to any undraped woman, was apparently the benefactress of several religious houses in the reign of Edward the Confessor, and founded the Benedictine monastery at Coventry. Her real name was Godgifu, and her legendary ride, as famous and more interesting than that of Paul Revere, was first recorded in *Flores historiarum* by Roger of Wendover (d. 1237), who quoted from an earlier writer. (*See also* **Peeping Tom.**)

lady-killer. People have been humorously calling men "credited with a dangerous power over women" *lady-killers* since the early 19th century, though such *lady-killing* has been with us much longer.

lady of pleasure. James Shirley's play *The Lady of Pleasure* (1635) may have suggested this term for a prostitute, but the lady in the play was not a shady lady. Shirley's play was about "the cure of a wife's desire for a life of fashionable folly by her husband's feigning to engage in gambling and intrigue." Nevertheless, *lady of pleasure* took its present meaning not long after the play was produced.

Lady's-mantle; Lady chapel; Lady fern. A *Lady's-mantle* (*Alchemilla*) is a flowering plant whose large, serrated, and many-lobed leaves resemble "the mantle of Our Lady," and a *Lady chapel* is a chapel attached to a large church and dedicated to the Blessed Virgin. The delicate *Lady fern* (*Athyrium filix-femina*) does not refer to the Virgin Mary, as is commonly believed, taking its name from the legend that possession of its seeds could render a woman invisible.

Lady with the Lamp. Florence Nightingale, the greatest of war nurses, is generally considered to be the founder of modern nursing. Born in the Italian city for which she was named, "the Lady with the Lamp" spent her childhood in England. At seventeen, she is said to have heard the voice of God calling her to service, and several years afterward she decided that she was meant to be a nurse. Despite the objections of her wealthy parents, she embarked upon a career in public health, in spite of the fact that nursing at the time was a disreputable profession filled with prostitutes and worse. World fame came to her when she and thirty-eight other nurses offered their services to the British army in the Crimean War (1854). Overcoming the initial suspicion of the troops, sometimes working as long as twenty hours a day, she became venerated as the *Lady with the Lamp* because she unfailingly made rounds of the wards each night to check

on her patients. When the Lady with the Lamp died on August 13, 1910, aged ninety, she was buried in the family plot in a small country churchyard in Hampshire, in a private service in which six British soldiers carried her coffin to the grave.

Laelia. These tropical American orchids, comprising about thirty-five species and prized for their showy flowers, may be named for Gaius Laelius, a Roman statesman and general who died about 165 B.C., or for his son Gaius Laelius, a Roman consul nicknamed Sapiens, the wise. Both father and son were soldiers and excellent orators, the father the best friend of Scipio Africanus Major, and the son famous for his friendship with Scipio Africanus Minor. The younger Laelius was also a close friend of Cicero, who wrote that he and Scipio used to like to go on holidays to the seaside, "where they became incredibly childish and used to collect shells and pebbles on the beach." Sapiens probably had a hand in writing the plays of Terence; his wide learning was admired throughout Rome. Another candidate English botanist John Lindley may have had in mind when he named *Laelia*, was a vestal virgin of that name, in allusion to the delicacy of the flowers. The vestal virgins, six in number, were daughters of the best Roman families, trained in youth to serve the goddess of hearth and home in her temple in Rome, where they prepared sacrifices and tended a perpetual sacred fire. Their vows included obedience and chastity, and after serving Vesta for thirty years they were allowed to leave the temple and marry, which they seldom did in practice. The virgins were influential, even having the power to pardon criminals, but if they broke the vows of chastity the penalty was a public funeral followed by burial while they were still alive. Needless to say, most remained vestal virgins.

lager beer. (*See* **bock beer**.)

lagniappe. *Lagniappe*, a "bonus gift" often given by merchants to customers, derives from the American Indian *yapa*, "a present to a customer," which came into Spanish first as *la napa*, "the gift." Pronounced *lanyap*, the word has also been used in Louisiana to mean small-scale bribery.

laissez faire. The 18th-century Physiocratic school of French economists were free-traders who wanted all custom duties abolished. Their motto "*laissez faire, laissez passer*" ("Let us alone, let us have free circulation for our goods") later became the term for the principle of noninterference by government in commercial affairs, for allowing things to look after themselves.

Lake Hubbs. Marine scientist Dr. Carl L. Hubbs has more marine namesakes than anyone in history. Besides the lake above, twenty-two species of fish, one genus and one species of lichen, one bird, one whale, one crab, two insects, two mollusks, three species of algae, and a research institute are named after this scientist. In addition, a minnow and a lantern fish are named *Lauri*, for his wife.

Lake Itasca. *Lake Itasca*, the source of the Mississippi River, was originally named *Lake Veritas Caput*, "the true source," by one of the explorers who found it. But his companion thought this Latin name too long and cut it in half, to *Lake Itasca*.

Lake Webster. The longest named body of water is located near Webster, Massachusetts, and is called Lake Webster by almost everyone. However, its official, Indian-derived name is composed of forty-three letters and fourteen syllables, translating into English as "You fish on your side; we fish on our side; nobody fish in the middle." Should anyone want to try pronouncing it, the lake is called Chargoggagoggmanchaugagoggchaubunagungamaug.

lallapalooza. According to one story, when the French landed at Killala in 1798 the Irish heard them cry *"Allez-fusil!,"* "forward the muskets!," and somehow transformed this into their County Mayo provincialism *lallapalooza*, for "a sturdy fellow." Later, when *lallapalooza* came to America, it took on the meaning of any extraordinary or exceptional person, thing, or event. The word is also spelled *lollapaloosa*, *lollapalooza*, and *lalapalooza*.

lamb. Somehow the Greek *elaphos*, for "deer," is the basis for our words *elk* and *lamb*, two animals with little else in common. No one has satisfactorily explained this linguistic curiosity, but apparently the Greek word for deer, or one of its derivatives, was mistakenly thought to mean lamb somewhere long the way.

lambert. The son of a poor tailor and largely self-educated, Johann Heinrich Lambert nevertheless managed to win fame as a physicist, philosopher, mathematician, and astronomer. The German scientist, though he died of comsumption in 1777 when only forty-nine, made important discoveries in many fields. In mathematics Lambert proved the irrationality of pi and developed several trigonometry concepts, while in philosophy his *Neues Organon* (1764) pointed out the importance of beginning with experience and using analytical methods to prove or disprove theories. Lambert also made valuable contributions in electrical magnetism, mapmaking, and meteorology; several theorems in astronomy bear his name. It is for his work in physics on the measurement of light intensity and absorption that his name is honored in the dictionaries, the *lambert* being the unit of brightness in the metric system.

lame duck. Before the adoption of the Twentieth Amendment to the Constitution in 1930, any president or congressman who was defeated for election in November elections still held office until the following March 4th. These elected officials were called *lame ducks* because they were mostly ineffectual, although they could help pass legislation embarrassing to an incoming administration. The "Lame Duck Amendment" eliminated them, but lame-duck appointments to diplomatic posts, etc., can still be made by a defeated, outgoing president. No one is sure where the term *lame duck* comes from. It originated about 125 years ago and may have been suggested by the British *lame duck*, "a person who has lost all his money, who has been financially crippled on the stock exchange." On the other hand it could be native born, a qualification of the American phrase *a dead duck*, an outgoing congressman being not quite dead yet, merely "lamed" until March 4th of the following year.

lampoon. The French *lampons*, "let us drink," is said to be the source of our *lampoon*, for a sharp or scurrilous satire ridiculing someone or something. The source suggests the coarseness and crudity of the form, which dates only from the 17th century and is used more in graphic caricature than in prose or verse—although there are notable examples in literature, including Pope's attack on Hervey in *Epistle to Arbuthnot*. Libel laws today make it much more difficult for a writer to really lampoon someone.

landlubber. Six centuries ago *lubber* meant "a clumsy lout," a word sailors originally applied to green seamen who didn't know a sail from a rudder. Eventually the term was lengthened to *landlubber* and applied to all nonsailors.

land-office business. Prior to the Civil War, the U.S. government established "land offices" for the allotment of government-owned land in Western territories just opened to settlers. These offices registered applicants, and the rush of citizens lining up mornings long before the office opened made the expression *doing a land-office business*, "a tremendous amount of business," part of the language by at least 1853. Adding to the queues were prospectors filing mining claims, which were also handled by land offices. After several decades the phrase was applied figuratively to a great business in something other than land, even, in one case I remember, to a land-office business in fish.

land of Nod. Jonathan Swift, as fond of puns as the next man and better at them than most, is responsible for this expression meaning "the land of sleep." In his *Polite Conversation* (1738) Swift wrote that he was "going into the land of Nod," that is, going to sleep. The *land of Nod*, which suggests the nodding of a sleepy head, was a pun on the "land of Nod" or "land of wandering," the place where Cain was exiled after he slew Abel (Gen. 4:16).

land of the midnight sun. Norway is generally called *the land of the midnight sun*, but strictly speaking many areas in high latitudes above the Arctic Circle deserve the name. During the summer in these places the sun never descends below the horizon within the day and does indeed shine at midnight.

the land up over. (*See* **Aussie.**)

langley. In 1896 Samuel Pierpont Langley, already a celebrated physician and astronomer, constructed and flew the first heavier-than-air model plane. This pilotless steamdriven model traveled a distance of 4,200 feet over the Potomac River and though it included no provision for takeoff or landing, convinced many aviation pioneers that powered mechanical flight was possible. The government appropriated $50,000 for the inventor to build a full-size craft, powered by a 50 horsepower gasoline engine, which failed in two 1903 test flights. This subjected Langley to great ridicule, but the fault was in the launching apparatus, and the plane was reconstructed and flown successfully in 1914, seven years after Langley's death. Samuel Pierpont Langley (1834-1906) had a rich and varied career in science. *Langley Field* in Virginia pays tribute to his pioneering aviation work, and his accomplishments in physics are honored by the word *langley*, a measurement unit of solar radiation.

language. The word *language*, first recorded in about 1290, has its roots in the Latin *lingua*, "tongue." At least 2,796 different languages are spoken on earth, these divided into about sixty families, with Chinese having the most speakers (one billion) and English the second most (300 million, with an additional 200 million speaking it as a second language). Besides our 2,796 languages on this planet there are some 8,000 dialects or language variants.

language barrier. "He [his language] erects a barrier between himself and his reader," a literary critic wrote in the late 18th century. But Oscar Wilde's quip about British and American English is the earliest mention I can find of the common phrase above. "We and the Americans have much in common," he observed, "but there is always the language barrier."

Laodician. The word *Laodician*—usually meaning someone lukewarm or indifferent in religion or politics—derives from the name of a Syrian city. Its ruins can be seen today close to the Gonjele station on the Anatolian railway. Little is known of *Laodicea's* history, but it was one of the earliest homes of Christianity. Yet the Church of Laodicea grew lazy and indifferent, leading to its chastisement in the Bible. This biblical rebuke led to

the word *Laodicean* being applied to all people indifferent to religion, with a Laodicean attitude remaining a major problem to churches today. Ultimately the word came to mean a person unconcerned about politics or even life itself. The city of Laodicea seems to have been named by Antiochus I after his wife Laodice.

Lapageria. French Empress Josephine, Napoleon Bonaparte's first wife, was born Marie Josephe Rose Tascher de la Pagerie. A Creole of French extraction, she had been married to Viscount Alexandre de Beauharnais, who was guillotined after the French Revolution, Josephine escaping the blade herself only because of powerful friendships. The empress brought Napoleon much happiness, including two children from her first marriage—Eugène, later viceroy of Italy, and Hortense, who became queen of Holland—but her numerous love affairs caused him to consider divorce several times. On one occasion, it is said, the glass cracked over the picture of Josephine that Napoleon always carried. The emperor turned pale and declared, "My wife is either sick or unfaithful";—his latter premonition proved true. In any case, Napoleon finally did have his marriage with Josephine annulled in 1809 on the alleged grounds of sterility, and the emperor married Marie Louise of Austria. Josephine lived out her life in retirement at her private retreat, La Malmaison, near Paris, and the emperor continued to consult her on important matters, always having valued her keen mind. She died in 1814, aged fifty-one. An avid botanist as well as an ardent lover (her garden at Malmaison contained the greatest collection of roses in the world), the beautiful Josephine has the monotypic genus *Lapageria*, containing only one species, named for her. This showy Chilean vine of the lily family is among the most attractive climbing vines, its flowers rose-colored, trumpet-shaped, and, unlike Josephine, usually solitary.

Lapp words in English. Even a little-known language like the Lappish spoken by Laplanders has contributed a few words to our English vocabulary, these including *lemming* and *tundra*.

larboard. (*See* **starboard.**)

large as life. We owe this popular phrase to one of Thomas C. Haliburton's Sam Slick tales, *The Clockmaker* (1837), in which Sam Slick of Slicksville says of another character: "He marched up and down afore the street door like a peacock, as large as life and twice as natural." Sam's words became a popular catchphrase in America and still survive in both the original and abbreviated versions.

lark. *Lark*, for "a spree or good time," only came into the language in the late 17th century. It is probably an adaptation of the British dialect term *lake*, "sport," which comes from Middle English *laik*, "play," and has nothing to do with the bird called a *lark* (despite the later term *skylarking*, meaning the same).

Larousse. The famous series of *Dictionnaires Larousse* commemorates the French grammarian and lexicographer Pierre Athanase Larousse (1817-75). In 1852 Larousse helped found the publishing house that bears his name. He later compiled the fifteen-volume dictionary and encyclopedia *Grand dictionnaire universal du XIX siecle* (1866-76).

larva. One meaning of *larva* in Latin is "a mask." Linnaeus first used the term as the scientific (yet poetic) term for a caterpillar because, as one writer puts it, "such a creature wears a disguise, the future insect is not recognizable in the present grub, its form a 'mask' which will one day be cast off." (*See* **pupa.**)

laser. (*See* **radar.**)

lass. (*See* **lad.**)

Lasthenia. Among the students who attended the philosopher Plato's lectures at the Academy in Athens was a woman named Lasthenia, who stole in by disguising herself as a man. Little more is known of her, but centuries later her story inspired the naturalist Cassini to name the plant genus *Lasthenia*, for Plato's woman pupil. The small genus contains but three species, two native to California and the other to Chile. All are tender annual herbs, and their showy flowers are yellow on long, often nodding, peduncles.

last infirmity of noble mind. That infirmity is the desire for fame, according to the proverb, being the last vice an otherwise noble person retains as he grows old. Though Milton said this in his elegy *Lycidas* (1637) on the death of his old friend Edward King, the poem *Sir John van Olden Barnevalt* called glory "that last infirmity of noble minds" sixteen years before. An amazed Swinburne was sure that this was "the most inexplicable coincidence in the whole range of literature," but the idea was simply in the air at the time and can be traced back even earlier. Incidentally, both *Bartlett* and the *Oxford Dictionary of Quotations* still credit the words to Milton.

the last of the Mohicans. The Mohicans live—contrary to James Fenimore Cooper's famous story, we have not seen the last of them. Cooper adopted the name of the Algonquian-speaking confederacy of tribes for the second of his "Leatherstocking Tales," and the title *The Last of the Mohicans* became an expression still used to indicate the last of any group with a certain identity. But the Mohicans—at least mixed-blood remnants of the con-federacy—still survive near Norwich, Connecticut and in Stockbridge, Indiana. The Mohicans, or Mahicans, were a powerful group in the past, occupying both banks of the upper Hudson in New York, while another branch, the Mohigans, lived in eastern Connecticut. While settlement and war with the Mohawks pushed them out of these areas—Dutch guns supplied to their enemies hastening their dispersal—and they almost entirely lost their identity. Probably some eight hundred survive today.

last straw. (*See* **the straw that broke the camel's back.**)

the last word. Since the end of the 19th century *the last word* has meant the ultimate in fashions. The expression, however, had been used in its literal sense three centuries before this.

last words. The first record we have of *last words*, for the final utterances of a dying man, is the title of a book, *The Last Words of a Dying Penitent*, published in 1672, but the expression is probably much older.

lather. (*See* **work into a lather.**)

Latin. We find the word *Latin*, for the language of the Romans, first recorded in about 950. Latin was a second language to cultivated Englishmen for over four centuries, from about 1400-1800, and it was then a supreme insult to call someone a "Latinless dolt." According to Trevelyan, grammar school boys were permitted to speak nothing but Latin even out of school and "a spy aptly named *lupus* was sometimes paid to report whether they used English words while at play—if they did, they were flogged."

Latin words in English. Though many Latin words and phrases are the basis for words in the English lexicon, very few can be traced directly back to the Roman occupation of Britain, which lasted almost four hundred years, A.D. 43-410. Strangely enough, there are more ruins than there are words attesting to the Roman stay, the latter including *port, portal, mountain*, and the *cester* (from the Latin *castra*, camp) that forms part of place names such as *Winchester* and *Manchester*. Latin words form about half of the English vocabulary, but the great majority came into the language during and after the Renaissance.

laugh and the world laughs with you. After Ella Wheeler Wilcox (1850-1919) published her poem "Solitude" in 1883, John A. Joyce claimed that he had written it twenty years earlier. Mrs. Wilcox offered $5,000 for any printed version of the poem dated earlier than her own and none was ever produced. Joyce, however, had the last word when he died in 1915, aged seventy-two. The most famous lines from the poem are attributed to him on his gravestone in Oak Hill Cemetery, Washington, D.C.; they have become proverbial:

Laugh and the world laughs with you
Weep and you weep alone.

the Laughing Philosopher. (*See* **the Weeping Philosopher.**)

to laugh up one's sleeve. (*See* **to have something up one's sleeve.**)

to launch. Deriving from French, with its first recorded nautical use in about 1400, *to launch* did not first mean to break a bottle of champagne against a vessel and slide it into the water. Animal blood was used long before champagne as a sacrifice to the sea gods, red wine later substituted for the blood, and finally more precious champagne substituted for the red wine.

Laura.

It was the day when the sun's heavy rays
  Grew pale in the pity of his suffering Lord
When I fell captive, lady, to the gaze
  Of your fair eyes, fast bound in love's strong cord.

The Laura of Petrarch's immortal love poems was no figment of the poet's imagination. According to tradition, the poet laureate of Rome wrote his poems for Laura, the daughter of Audibert de Noves and the wife of Count Hugues de Sade, an ancestor of the French nobleman who gave us *sadism* (*q.v.*). Petrarch never revealed the real Laura's identity, guarding his secret jealously, but he wrote that he saw her for the first time in the church of St. Clara at Avignon on April 6, 1327, and that his first sight of her inspired him to become a poet. In the 18th century the Abbé de Sade identified her as the wife of Hugues de Sade, who bore the old man eleven children before dying of the plague in 1348 when she was only forty. But this identification is not certain. It is known only that Laura was a married woman who accepted Petrarch's devotion but refused all intimate relations. Their platonic love inspired the long series of poems that are among the most beautiful amorous verse in literature, the most famous being the sonnet in praise of their first meeting quoted above. The Italians call this collection of lyrics the *Canzoniere* and it is titled *Rime in Vita e Morte di Madonna Laura*. Petrarch died long after his Laura (whoever she was), in 1374 in his seventieth year.

lava. *Lava* is not a Samoan word, as I read in one place. The word derives from the Latin *labes*, "a sliding down," in reference to the molten rock that flows from a volcano down a mountain. It is first recorded in 1750.

Laval. After the liberation of France, Pierre Laval was tried for treason, sentenced to death, and executed on October 15, 1945. The French politician, born in 1883, held many national offices before becoming premier of the collaborationist Vichy government in 1942. Believing that Germany would win World War II, he was instrumental in organizing a policy of collaboration with the Nazis within occupied France. Under Nazi pressure Laval instituted a rule of terror, authorizing a French fascist militia and agreeing to send forced labor to Germany. His name became a hated one, synonymous with traitor, though he claimed at his trial that his motives were patriotic. Laval fled to Spain when France fell to the Allies, was expelled, and finally surrendered himself. After his conviction, he tried to commit suicide, but was saved for the firing squad.

lava-lava. Unlike *lava* (*q.v.*) *lava-lava* is a Samoan word, meaning clothing. A piece of printed cloth worn as a skirt or loincloth, it is the principal garment of both sexes in Polynesia.

lavaliere. Louis XIV, the Sun King, had a voracious appetite for women as well as food. Louise Françoise de La Baume Le Blanc, whom he later made Madame la Duchesse de La Vallière, was only his first *maîtresse en titre*, or official mistress to the king. Louise, an innocent girl, never asked for anything, and it was only toward the end of their affair in 1667 that Louis made her a duchess, granting her the estate of Vaujours. Long before that she had become famous throughout Europe for her great beauty and the glamorous fashions she introduced. One of these, called the *lavalliere* in her honor, was transferred to the ornamental jeweled pendant, usually worn on a chain around the neck, that we know as the *lavaliere*. Today the small television microphone that hangs on a cord from the neck is also called a *lavaliere*, taking its name from the pendant necklace that honors the famous beauty.

law and order. This very common expression isn't an Americanism as one would expect. It is first recorded in 1881, in reference to England's troubles with Ireland.

law of the jungle. Some people, by words and actions, insist that we still live by the *law of the jungle*, that is, like animals not governed by the rules of civilization. The term probably dates back to the late 19th century. *Law of the prairie*, a similar U.S. term, is first recorded in 1823.

lawrencium. While a physics professor at the University of California in 1930, Ernest Orlando Lawrence invented and built the first atom-smashing cyclotron, for which he was awarded the Nobel Prize nine years later. The physicist also played a prominent role in the development of the atomic bomb while director of the radiation laboratory at Berkeley, California, conducting research into the separation of U-235. Lawrence died in 1958, aged fifty-seven. In 1961 Albert Ghiorso, Almon Lash, and Robert Latimer created a new synthetic radioactive element at the laboratory dedicated to its former director. *Lawrencium*, its atomic number 103, is believed to be a "dinosaur element" that first formed when the world was born and decayed out of existence within a few weeks.

Lawsonia. Linnaeus probably named *Lawsonia inermis*, the mignonette tree and the source of the dye henna, for John Lawson, a traveler in North Carolina said to be burned alive by Indians. Lawson came to America from England in 1700 and traveled about a thousand miles through unexplored territory, recording his observations of native flora and fauna in his *A New Voyage to Carolina* (1709). A founder of Bath and New Bern, North Carolina, he was appointed the state's surveyor general in 1708, but was captured and put to death in the Tuscarora uprising three years later. Whether Linnaeus related red men and death by fire to the red dyestuff taken from the eastern tree's leaves is unknown, though not impossible. At least one authority, however, claims that the Swedish botanist named the plant for a Dr. Isaac Lawson, a Scottish botanical traveler who published an account of a voyage to Carolina in 1709.

lawyer; attorney; barrister; solicitor. In America, *lawyer* or *attorney* describes anyone who does any kind of legal work, whereas in England a *barrister* is an attorney who does trial work and a *solicitor* one who does general legal work. Attorney in its legal sense dates back to about 1330, lawyer to 1377, solicitor to 1527, and barrister to 1545. *Advocate* and *counsellor* are also words used for a lawyer. All of these terms have finer distinctions in England than in the U.S. There are probably as many derogatory expressions for lawyer as there are honored ones, ranging from *ambulance chaser* to *mob mouthpiece*.

lay an egg. Comedians and other entertainers complain that they *laid an egg*, that their act "bombed," utterly failed, but the phrase originated in the sports world, not in show business. Stranger still, the expression comes from the sport of cricket, England's national game. *Duck's egg* was British slang for "no score" in cricket for many years, and in about 1860 the expression *achieved a duck's egg* was used to describe a team that hadn't scored and had only large oval zeroes shaped like duck's eggs on the scoreboard. Ten years later the phrase became the more expressive *laid a duck's egg* and this came into American baseball slang as *laid a goose egg*. In baseball the expression for "zero" soon became just *goose eggs*, and it still is, but early vaudevillians adopted the expression "they killed the goose that laid the rotten eggs" and changed it to *laid an egg*.

lay them in the aisles. Theatrical slang for "to have a sensational success," to *lay* (or *knock*) *them in the aisles* may derive partly from the expression *to knock 'em cold*, which has its origins in boxing. Both expressions date from only about the 1920s. British listeners would have trouble making sense of the phrase, because until fairly recently they have used *aisle* for a section of a theater, not a passageway. Since the word is from the Latin *ala*, "a wing"—this corrupted to *aisle* over the years possibly because of some confusion with *isle*—their use of the word is more proper.

lazar. *Lazar* has almost dropped out of use as a word for a diseased beggar or leper, but *lazarone* still describes a beggar of Naples. Both words are named for Lazarus, the only character in all His parables to whom Christ gave a proper name. During the Middle Ages *lazar* was the name given to those suffering from leprosy and other diseases, outcasts who were allowed to do nothing but beg. A *lazaretto*, or *lazar-house*, is a hospital for such persons, taking its name from *lazar* plus (N)*azaretto*, the popular name of a hospital in Venice managed by the Church of Santa Maria di Nazaret. The name Lazarus comes from the Hebrew *Eleazar*, meaning "God-aided," or "God will help." (*See* **Lazarus**.)

Lazarus. Strictly speaking a *Lazarus* is someone risen from the dead, but the word is used allusively in many ways. It recalls the brother of Mary and Martha of Bethany, whom Jesus raised from the dead after he had been in his tomb four days (John 11:38-44). One authority notes that "in the fourth century the house and tomb of Lazarus were shown to pilgrims, and the gospel narrative . . . may be based on the story told to first-century visitors to Palestine." (*See* **lazar**.)

lazy as Lawrence. What does a Roman judge do with a saint of a man who when told to bring forth the treasures of his church comes forward with all its poor people? The Romans under Emperor Valerian did not appreciate St. Lawrence's philosophy, and this deacon to Pope Sixtus II (later St. Sixtus) soon followed his bishop to a martyr's death in 258. The Romans burnt him alive on a gridiron over a slow fire, and legend has it that he addressed his torturers ironically with the words "I am roasted enough on this side, turn me round, and eat." Over the years the legend has become more British and St. Lawrence's words are now "Turn me around, for this side is quite done," which is supposed to signify that the martyr was too lazy to move in the flames. More probably the expression *lazy as Lawrence* refers to the heat of St. Lawrence Day, August 10th. In fact, the speech over the fire probably comes from a much older story told by Socrates and others about the Phrygian martyrs.

lazy as Ludlam's dog. Tradition tells us that old Mrs. Ludlam, an English sorceress, had a dog who lived with her for many years in her cottage in Surrey near Farnham. So lazy was her dog that when strangers approached he always lay down or leaned up against a wall to bark, or didn't bother to bark at all. There are several versions of the tale, all of them responsible for the proverbial as *lazy as Ludlam's dog.*

lazybird. The cowbird (*Molathrus ater ater*) is called the *lazybird* in America because the female of the species lays her eggs in the nests of other birds instead of building her own. The term is probably an old one, though first recorded in 1917.

Lazy Susan. The British call our *Lazy Susan* a dumbwaiter, which the revolving servitor was called in America until relatively recently. It is said that the first use of the term dates back to about seventy-five years ago when the device was named after some servant it replaced, Susan being a common name for servants at the time. But the earliest quotation that has been found for Lazy Susan is in 1934, and it could be the creation of some unheralded advertising copywriter. Therefore, *lazy* may not mean a lazy servant at all, referring instead to a hostess too lazy to pass the snacks around, or to the ease with which guests can rotate the device on the spindle and bring the sections containing different foods directly in front of them.

lb. *Lb*, as an abbreviation for *pound* comes from the Latin word *libra*, just as the symbol for the British pound Sterling does. *Libra* in this case is part of the Latin phrase *libra pondo*, a pound by weight.

l'chayim. *L'chayim* is the Yiddish drinking toast equivalent to the English "To your health," the words translating as "to life." It derives from similar Hebrew words meaning the same, and is pronounced *l-khy-im.*

LCI. (*See* **LSD.**)

LCT. (*See* **LSD.**)

to lead a dog's life. (*See* **to go to the dogs.**)

lead by the nose. The allusion here is to animals like oxen, horses, and asses who from early times were led around by bit and bridle or by a rope attached to a ring hanging from the septum of the nose. Even wild animals like bears and lions were led around Roman arenas by a rope attached to a ring in the nose. Therefore, someone who leads another by the nose dominates him or holds him under submission. The idea is found in the Bible (Isa. 37:29): "Because thy rage against me, and thy tumult is come up into mine ears, therefore will I put my hook in thy nose, and thy bridle in thy lips, and I will turn thee back by the way which thou camest."

to lead down the garden path. The origin of this common expression remains a mystery. Not recorded in print until 1926 it may be the creation of the novelist Ethel Mannin, in whose book, *Sounding Brass*, it first appeared. But this seems unlikely. In the book *to lead down the garden* (path) means "to seduce," but the expression's common meaning is "to deceive in any way." The *garden path* suggests that the deception is done in a pleasant way, so that the victim suspects nothing.

lead-pipe cinch. A cinch, borrowed from the Spanish *cincha*, is a saddle-girth used on horses or a girth used on pack mules. Because a well-fastened cinch holds the saddle securely to the horse so that a saddle won't slip off, about a century ago the word *cinch* became a natural synonym for something sure and easy, a surefire certainty; that is, by extension it indicated "a grasp of anything so firm that it cannot get away." *Cinches*, however, are usually made out of leather, canvas, or braided horsehair, not lead pipe. So the expression *a lead-pipe cinch* is something of a mystery. One guess is that the phrase is from the underworld. Criminals using lead-pipe blackjacks, according to this theory, found it a cinch to dispatch their victims and a cinch to dispose of the "blackjack" should police near the scene of the crime stop them and frisk them for weapons.

lead with your chin. The allusion here is to boxing, where if he doesn't protect himself with a right- or left-handed lead, but sticks his chin out, leads with his chin, a fighter is exposing himself to a knockout blow. *Leading with your chin* or "sticking your chin out" has been slang for taking a big chance since the 1920s, while "taking it on the chin" has meant to suffer severe failure since about the same time. The expression *take it* as in "He can really take it," that is, "he can deal with adversity well," is probably a descendant of *take it on the chin.*

lean over backwards. Judicial reforms in 18th-century England brought the appointment of many judges sensitive to the civil rights of accused persons, in marked contrast to older judges notorious for favoring or "leaning" toward the crown. The new justices were said to *lean over backwards* toward the accused and away from the crown or prosecution, in judging cases. In order to prove how honest, fair, and disinterested they were, despite their connections with the government, they went beyond the normal and expected. "Fall over backwards" means the same and "two inches beyond upright" is a synonym for "excessive rectitude" that should be heard more than it is.

learn by heart. The ancient Greeks believed that the heart, the most noticeable internal organ, was the seat of intelligence and memory as well as emotion. This belief was passed on down the ages and became the basis for the

English expression *to learn by heart*, which is used by Chaucer (1374) and must have been proverbial long before that. "To record" reminds us again of this ancient belief in the heart as the seat of the mind. When writing wasn't a simple act, things had to be memorized; thus we have the word *record*, formed from the Latin *re*, "again," and *cor*, "heart," which means exactly the same as *to learn by heart*. (*See* **bowels of compassion; lily-livered**.)

least said, soonest mended. (*See* **little said is soon amended**.)

leave in the lurch. *Lourche*, or "lurch," was an old French dicing game resembling backgammon, popular in the 16th century. Any player who incurred a lurch in the game was left helplessly behind the goal, so far behind his opponent that he couldn't possibly win, which led to the figurative meaning of leaving someone in a helpless plight. The expression persists in English despite the fact that no one plays the old dicing game anymore, possibly because *lurch* describes a similar losing position in the game of cribbage.

to leave in the soup. To leave someone in the lurch or in trouble. The expression is an Americanism first recorded in 1889 in connection with some South Dakota con man who skipped town with a lot of money, leaving many investors in trouble.

to leave no stone unturned. So familiar is this saying that no one has trouble understanding Ogden Nash's pun, "When I throw rocks at seabirds, I leave no tern unstoned." It was advice that the Delphic oracle gave when the Theban general Polycrates asked how he could find treasure that the defeated Persians had hidden somewhere on the field after the battle of Plataea in 479 B.C. "Move all things," the Delphic oracle said, and Polycrates did so, finally locating the horde. The expression has meant "to show great industry" in English since the mid-16th century, probably first as a variation of the earlier *leave no straw unturned*, in reference to the straw-covered floors typical of the time.

ledger. In medieval times ledgers were large breviaries (books of daily prayers, readings, etc.) used in English churches, their name deriving from the Old English dialect *liggen*, "to lie," because they were books that lay in one place at all times, being too heavy to carry like other books. By the mid-16th century the same name was given to large record books used by businessmen that were also too heavy to move from place to place, and soon *ledger* was applied to any business record book.

leech; leechcraft. *Leechcraft* was the Anglo-Saxon word for the practice of medicine. Only a relatively few doctors are leeches today, but in Anglo-Saxon times doctors were

called *leeches*, the term probably deriving from an Old English word meaning "to heal." One theory holds that the bloodthirsty worms called *leeches* were named after the doctors called leeches, because the doctors so often employed the worms in trying to cure people. A second theory has it that the bloodsucking worm's name derives from another similar Old English word that was confused with the Old English word for doctor and was eventually pronounced and spelled the same. *To leech* began to be used figuratively in the late 18th century, meaning "to cling to and feed upon and drain" (the way the worm does), a *leech* becoming a person who does this. In the last century *to stick to someone* (or something) *like a leech* became proverbial and Tennyson wrote of a world swarming with *literary leeches*.

leek. The national emblem of Wales takes its name from the Old English *leac*, for this member of the onion family; but the plant is native to central Asia and many peoples have had different names for it—Nero was nicknamed "Porrophagus" because he ate so many leeks, believing that they improved his singing voice. The leek has only recently been identified as the fabled store-henge that the Greeks considered a love potion.

Leeuwenhoek's little animals. Anton von Leeuwenhoek (1632-1723), a former Dutch linen maker who designed a very powerful single-lens microscope, changed the course of science with his observations of the "animalcules" in a drop of pond water and his observations helped disprove the doctrine of spontaneous generation (that eels are generated from sand, grubs from wheat, and so on), making *Leeuwenhoek's little animals* a phrase that has lived for centuries.

left-handed compliment. The expression *left-handed compliment*, "a thinly disguised insult that poses as praise," apparently has its origins in the practice of morganatic marriage widely prevalent among German royalty in the Middle Ages and even practiced in modern times—Archduke Ferdinand and his wife, who were both killed in the assassination that set off World War I, were married *morganatically*. These were usually marriages between royalty and commoners, the commoner agreeing that she would have no claim to her royal husband's title or property, nor would any children of the marriage—all she received was a *morning gift* (from the Latin *morganaticum*) on the morning after the marriage was consummated. In the special wedding ceremony held for these marriages, common up to the 17th century, the groom gave the bride his left hand instead of his right and thus morganatic marriages came to be known as *left-handed marriages*. Since they were a thinly disguised insult, it is possible that they later lent their name to the deceptive *left-handed compliment*. (*See* **right**.)

leghorns. These prolific egg layers are a breed of chickens originally bred in Livorno, Italy, which the English, never good at pronouncing foreign words, called *Leghorn*. Highly regarded straw hats called *leghorns* are also made in Livorno.

lemon sole. Sour lemons have nothing to do with *lemon sole*, except that lemon juice might be squeezed on the fish before eating. The term is an established redundancy; when we say *lemon sole* we are saying "sole sole," for the *lemon* part is a corruption of the French *limande*, for "sole." The *sole* was so named because its shape was thought to resemble the sole of the foot.

le mot Cambronne. (*See* **the Guard dies but never surrenders!**)

Leningrad; Leninism. N. Lenin was the pseudonym Vladimir Ilyich Ulyanov adopted toward the end of 1901, variants such as V.I. Lenin coming into use a little later as his revolutionary activities in Russia became more prominent. He is thus known in history as Nikolai Lenin or Vladimir Ilyich Lenin, his real name rarely used. Only fifty-four when he died in 1924, he must still be regarded as one of the most effective political leaders of all time, though not "mankind's greatest genius," as *The Great Soviet Encyclopedia* calls him. But Lenin's name is legendary in the communist world, his body embalmed in a tomb in Moscow's Red Square that has become a shrine to Soviet citizens. The former capital city of *Leningrad*, previously St. Petersburg and Petrograd, was named for him in 1924. *Leninism* refers to the particular communistic principles based upon Marxism propounded by the founder of the modern Soviet state, which are collected in his twenty-two volume life and works. *Leninism's* central point is the creation of the dictatorship of the proletariat, or working class.

lentil; lens. Lentils are the beans that made the mess of pottage that the Bible implies Esau traded his brother for (though Scripture nowhere mentions the phrase "a mess of pottage"); they take their name from the Latin word for the bean, which also gives us the word *lens*, a double convex lens resembling a lentil bean in shape.

leonine contract. Aesop's fable about the lion who hunted with several other animals has the lion claiming all the spoils of the hunt. One-quarter of the spoils he claimed as king of beasts; a second quarter because he was braver than any other animal; a third for his mate and cubs; "and as for the fourth, let him who will dispute it with me." Another version of the tale has the lion saying the last share belongs to everyone, "But touch it if you dare!" In any event, from "The Lion and His Fellow-Hunters" derives our term a *leonine contract*, "a completely one-sided agreement," and *a lion's share*, "the largest portion of anything."

a leopard doesn't change its spots. Leopards are so named because they were once thought not to be a separate species but a cross between the lion (*leo*) and the *pard*, a Tibetan wildcat or panther. Like the creature's name, the saying *a leopard doesn't change his spots* also goes back to ancient times. It is an allusion to the pessimistic rhetorical question found in Jer. 13:23: "Can the Ethiopian change his skin or the leopard his spots? Then also you can do good who are accustomed to evil." (*See* **giraffe**.)

leotards. We owe this word to 19th-century French aerialist Jules Leotard, who claimed in his *Memoirs* to have invented the outfit still worn by circus performers. Originally the costume was a one-piece elastic garment, snug-fitting and low at the neck and sleeveless. Leotard, born to the circus—when he was a baby, his aerialist parents would hang him upside-down from a trapeze bar to stop his crying—intended his costume for men, not women. "Do you want to be adored by the ladies?" he exhorts his male readers in his *Memoirs*. "[Then] put on a more natural garb, which does not hide your best features!"

lesbian. Lesbos, a Greek island in the Aegean Sea off the west coast of Turkey, was a center of civilization in the seventh and sixth centuries B.C. There Sappho, the most famous poetess of her time, taught the arts of poetry to a select group of young women. The legend has never been proved but the romantic ardor of some of Sappho's lyrical poems probably accounts for the tradition that she and her followers engaged in homosexual love, female homosexuality being named for the *Lesbians*, or residents of Lesbos. The word *Lesbian* (with a capital) designates any inhabitant of the island, which is noted for its rich soil as well as its sardine and sponge fisheries. Here Epicurus and Aristotle once lived and the philosopher Theophrastus was born. Sapphism, from Sappho's name, is a synonym for lesbianism. The poetess, according to legend, threw herself into the sea when spurned by the handsome youth Phaon, but the story is generally regarded as pure invention. Sappho may have married and had a son. Her simple, passionate verse, characterized by matchless lyricism and vivid use of words, originally formed nine books, but only fragments of these are extant today. The "Tenth Muse," as she was known, used the four-lined verse form now called sapphics in her honor, and is in fact noted for her careful control over meter.

lese majesty. An offense against the sovereign power in a state, especially a ruler, or even an attack against any belief or institution revered by large numbers of people is called *lese majesty*, which comes from the Latin for "imperial greatness." The term is first recorded in 1430.

lespedeza. Japan or bush clover, sometimes called the hoop-coop plant but widely known as *lespedeza*, is believed to have been brought to America in the early 19th century with a cargo of tea unloaded at Charleston or Savannah. The plant became an escape that was first identified at Monticello, Georgia in 1846, and this initial collected specimen is now preserved at Harvard's Gray Herbarium. A member of the pea family, *lespedeza* has become a very important crop not only for hay and forage but for improving poor soils—it has been shown that corn and cotton crops can be increased 10 to 30 percent by turning under a crop of *lespedeza* previous to their planting. The slender plant grows to a height of about eighteen inches, its leaves divided into three leaflets on many branched stems. The genus *lespedeza*, however, contains 125 species, of which Japanese clover (*Lespedeza striata*) is only one. Many of these species are native to America and it was to them that the botanist Michaux referred when he named the genus in 1803. *Lespedeza* was named in honor of V. M. de Zespedz, Spanish governor of Florida in 1795, whose name Michaux misread as Lespedez.

les sommobiches.   Just as they dubbed the English *goddams* (*q.v.*) in earlier times, the French during World War I called the Americans *les sommobiches*—because the Yanks used the epithet *son of a bitch* so often.

let George do it.   We say this satirically today when there is work to be avoided, but France's Louis XII was serious when he said, "Let George do it." He referred to his brilliant advisor Cardinal Georges d'Amboise (1460-1510) and entrusted important affairs of state to him so often that the phrase "let Georges do it; he's the man of the age" became proverbial, eventually losing its *s* and becoming "let George do it" and bestowing more glory on the cardinal than his magnificent tomb in the Rouen Cathedral. Louis's minister of state, a prodigy who became a bishop when only fourteen, was truly "the man of the age," a Renaissance man who excelled in everything he did, from literature to science.

lethal; lethargy.   The waters of Lethe refers to the River Lethe, one of the rivers of Hades in Greek mythology. The dead were required to taste these waters in order to forget the past and find oblivion. From the myth derive our words *lethal* and *lethargy*.

let her rip.   Letting things go at full speed was called *let-her-rip-itiveness* in mid-19th century America. The Americanism derives from another American expression, *let her rip*, which apparently first referred to railroad locomotives. Americans were always obsessed with speed. Wrote one early train traveler out West: "Git up more steam—this ain't a funeral! Let her rip!"

let sleeping dogs lie.   Chaucer seems to have expressed this idea first in *Troilus and Criseyde* (1374), though he put it in the reverse form: "It is nought good a slepyng hound to wake." For at least four hundred years the saying remained basically the same, until in the 19th century it became the familiar *let sleeping dogs lie*, "leave well enough alone."

let's see the color of your money.   When this saying originated in the early 18th century paper money wasn't in general use, so it couldn't allude to the inferior color of counterfeit money, as has been suggested. So-called *red money* (gold) and *white money* (silver) was in existence, however. Probably the expression was born when someone selling something refused to discuss the matter until the prospective buyer proved that the more valuable red money, not white, was jingling in his purse or pocket.

letter.   The first private letter written in English dates from about 1392 (before then letters had been written in French), and manuals for letter writers abound from about that date on. *Letter*, for "a missive," is first attested in about 1225. The word derives from the Latin *littera*, "a letter of the alphabet."

letter (sports).   The practice of awarding college varsity athletes *letters*, or monograms of the first letter of the college's name, began with the great University of Chicago football coach Amos Alonzo Stagg, in the early 1900s.

let the cat out of the bag.   *Let the cat out of the bag* may have originally referred to the master-at-arms aboard a British naval ship taking the cat-o'-nine tails from its blood-red carrying bag before a seaman was flogged. The connection between this and an untimely revelation is a tenuous one, but no better explanation has been offered so far.

let the dead bury their dead.   Don't worry about things over and done with, forget what happened in the past. The expression comes from the Bible (Matt. 8:22): "But Jesus said, Follow me, and let the dead bury their dead."

let them eat cake.   Marie Antoinette may have said this in referring to the Paris proletariat after they pleaded for bread in 1770, but she did not invent the famous retort. Rousseau's *Confessions*, written two or three years before the remark is attributed to her, told of a "great princess" who said the same thing to her peasants at least fifteen years before Marie Antoinette was born. Some claim that the thoughtless remark was circulated to discredit Marie, while others say she repeated it herself, and she was certainly capable of such a "little joke." The French phrase is *Qu'ils mangent de la brioche* and may mean "they" should eat the outer crust (*brioche*) of the bread, the "stale" part as opposed to the soft inside part.

lettuce. *Lettuce* probably takes its name from a form of the Latin *lactuca*, "milky juice." The Roman gourmet Apicius watered the lettuce in his garden with mead every evening so that it would taste like "green cheese cakes" when he picked it mornings.

let your hair down. I can't find an old quotation to support the theory, but this expression may have originated in the days of Louis XIV, when elaborate hairstyles such as the *fontange* (*q.v.*), a pile of style that rose two feet and more above the wearer's head, were popular among Frenchwomen. These styles were such a nuisance that several were actually banned by the Sun King. Certainly none permitted informality or intimacy and only when a woman let down her hair at night in privacy did she relax any and shed at least one inhibition.

Levi's. The word *Levi's* has become more popular in the eastern United States recently as a synonym for jeans, denims, or *dungarees* (*q.v.*)—probably due to the bright-colored styles that Levi Strauss and Company are manufacturing today. The trademarked name has been around since the gold rush days, though, when a pioneer San Francisco overall manufacturer began making them. Levi Strauss reinforced his heavy blue denims with copper rivets at strain points such as the corners of pockets, this innovation making his product especially valuable to miners, who often loaded their pockets with ore samples. Within a few years the pants were widely known throughout the West, where the name *Levi's* has always been more common than any other for tight-fitting, heavy blue denims.

lewd. Beginning with its original meaning of lay (as in *layman*), *lewd* has had seven different meanings through the years: unlettered, low, bungling, vile, lawless, and licentious. Today only the last meaning is much used and it is first recorded in 1712, for the biblical "lewd fellows of the baser sort" (Acts 17:5) refers to lawless fellows, not lascivious ones. No one knows why, although the word is in good company with those many words in English that begin with an "l" and have something to do with sexual debauchery. They have a rather revolting, loathsome pronunciation; you sort of squinch up your nose and sneer when saying them: leer, lecherous, loose, libidinous, lustful, even luxury. Probably the pronunciation does not have a lot to do with the prevailing meaning. But like many words associated with sex, *lewd* is undergoing a change today. It is being used more playfully, with less high-mindedness, and may have an eighth meaning in another century or so. We already have the precedent of Shakespeare calling Falstaff an old lewdster, and Falstaff, after all, was eminently likeable, no one you would squinch up your nose at.

Lewisia. (*See* **Clarkia.**)

lexicographer. Dr. Johnson, working on his great dictionary, invented a definition almost as well-known as the word itself—"Lexicographer: A writer of dictionaries, a harmless drudge." The word, from the Greek meaning the same, is first recorded a century earlier.

Lhasa apso terrier. The "forbidden city" of Lhasa in Tibet gave its name to this long-haired terrier bred as far back as the 12th century.

libertine. Early in the 16th century a group of European freethinkers dubbed themselves the *Libertines*, a word that had previously meant "a freed slave." Because they believed that there was no sin, and acted accordingly, these Libertines saw their name become a synonym for any morally or sexually unrestrained person, a rake, or a profligate.

liberty, equality, fraternity! The motto of the French Fifth Republic today, these words were originally the motto of Revolutionary France. Napoleon, an imperialist, employed them most effectively.

lickety split. Bartlett's *Dictionary of Americanisms* (1859) defines *lickety split* as "very fast, headlong; synonymous with the equally elegant phrase 'full chisel.'" Today *lickety split* is only heard infrequently and it is folksy rather than "elegant." The *lick* in the phrase is probably associated with speed because of the rapidity with which the tongue moves in the mouth, and *split* is perhaps associated with "split second." The Puritans used the phrase, but it wasn't very popular until the mid-19th century. *Lickety cut, lickety switch, lickety click, lickety liver,* and *lickety brindle* were variations on the expression.

lick into shape.

> Beres ben brought forth al fowle and transformyd and after that by lyckynge of the fader and moder they ben brought in to theyr kyndely shap.
> —The pylgremage of the sowle, 1400

For at least ten centuries people believed that bear cubs were born just formless masses of grotesque flesh and that both Mama and Poppa Bear took turns literally licking them into shape. No one debunked this legend for so long because bears usually keep their cubs hidden for a month or so after their birth, and any debunker who ventured into a bear den in search of evidence probably didn't come out to do his debunking. So the story was widely believed—by Pliny, Montaigne, Shakespeare—up until and even after the discovery of America. By the time the marvelous tale was disproved the expression *lick into shape*, "make ready, make presentable," had gained a permanent place in the language.

lido. The many places throughout the world called Lido Beach literally mean "Beach Beach." *Lido*, meaning "beach" in Italian, was originally the famous resort near Venice, but came to be used generically for any spit of land enclosing a lagoon.

Liebfraumilch. The German white wine's name translates as "milk of the Blessed Mother," referring to the Virgin Mary. The name originally applied only to wines made near the Liebfraukirch in Worms. (*See* **Lachryma Christi**.)

Liechtenstein. Liechtenstein is one of the few countries named after a family. It is a principality created in 1719 by uniting the barony of Schellenburg and the country of Vaduy, both of which had been purchased by the Austrian family of Liechtenstein.

lief. (*See* **just as leave**.)

to lie like a butcher's dog. Grose, in the 1788 edition of his *Classical Dictionary of the Vulgar Tongue*, tells us this was "a simile often applied to married men," who, "like the butcher's dog" would often "lie by the beef without touching it." The humorous expression for involuntary sexual abstinence didn't last until Victorian times, when it might have achieved wider currency.

life is just a bowl of cherries. Attempts have been made to link this expression with a much older one, *life is but a cherry-fair*. However, the older phrase, from the early 17th century, means life is all too short and fleeting, as short as the annual English fairs held in orchards where cherries were sold each spring. Evanescence is not the spirit of *life is just a bowl of cherries*—which means life is joyous, wonderful and seems to have originally been the title of a popular song of the late 19th century.

the life of Riley. In a comic song written by Pat Rooney of the "Dancing Rooneys" in the 1880s and performed by him on the vaudeville circuit, the song's hero, Riley, tells of what he'd do if he "struck it rich." He promises New York will "swim in wine when the White House and Capitol are mine." Many word ferrets believe that the phrase *the life of Riley* derives from the Rooney song, though *Mencken* champions the tune "The Best in the House Is None Too Good for Reilly," written by Lawlor and Blake toward the turn of the century. Yet the Hoosier poet James Whitcomb Riley (1849-1916) may just lend his name in some way to the saying. Riley's simple, sentimental poems depicting the lives of barefoot boys loafing and living a life of ease in the summer were immensely popular at the time the phrase came into use.

Lifting Monday; Lifting Tuesday. Easter Monday was called *Lifting Monday*, or *Heaving Day*, in the English counties of Shropshire, Cheshire, and Lancashire because of an ancient custom that allowed men to lift up and kiss any woman met in the street that day. On *Lifting Tuesday* women could do the same to men. "Lifting or heaving differs a little in different places," one writer explained. "In some parts the person is laid horizontally, in others placed in a sitting position on the bearers' hands. Usually, when the lifting or heaving is within doors, a chair is produced." According to another observer, "the woman's heaving-day was the most amusing," with the women trying to lift and heave the men, but the custom, recorded as late as the 1870s, caused too many disturbances and was abandoned before the end of the 19th century.

lift yourself up by the bootstraps. Riding boots and many other long boots have inside, near the top, loops or straps that make it easier to pull on a tight-fitting boot. When yanking on these straps it feels as if you are laboriously lifting yourself upward instead of putting on a boot, and no doubt such struggles inspired the saying to *lift yourself up by the bootstraps*, to raise yourself in the world exclusively through your own efforts. Such bootstraps, and even specialized boot hooks to pull them with, date back to Cromwellian times, but when the expression was invented is a mystery. It hasn't been traced back before 1944, although it is almost certainly much older.

light a fire under. (*See* **build or set a fire under**.)

light colonel. Army slang going back sixty years or more, a *light colonel* is a pun on Lt. (Lieutenant) Colonel and indicates that Lt. Colonel is a lower and less weighty rank than full colonel.

lightning never strikes twice. Not only does lightning strike twice in the same place, it is *more likely* to strike in the same place than not, simply because the tree or whatever else serves as the conductor for the first strike is the highest, most attractive point in the area. Nevertheless, the old superstition has been around for centuries and is often used in the expression *lightning never strikes twice*, meaning that anything, either bad or good, that happened once won't happen again. The ancients held that persons struck dead by lightning were incorruptible and they honored them, but many used various charms to protect themselves against lightning, which kills about 150 people a year in the U.S.

lightning pilot. A pilot on the Mississippi River in the 19th century who was lightning quick, who got all the speed possible from his ship, was called a lightning pilot. The term was used by Mark Twain and many other contemporary writers.

light on a bush.   Folk poetry for the berries of the bayberry bush (*Myieca pennsylvanica*), the phrase *light on a bush* originated among American pioneers in the 17th century. The waxy berries were of course used to make candles; in fact, in Colonial times September 15th was known as Bayberry Day, "a time when old and young sallied forth with pail and basket, each eager to secure his share in the gift of nature."

like a house on fire.   Although log cabins weren't the homes of the earliest American settlers—Swedes settling in Delaware introduced them in 1638—they became a common sight on the Western frontier in the 18th and 19th centuries. As practical as they were, these rude wooden structures were tinderboxes once they caught fire. So fast did they burn to the ground that pioneers began to compare the speed of a fast horse to a log cabin burning to the ground, saying he could go *like a house on fire*. By 1809 Washington Irving, under the pseudonym Diedrich Knickerbocker, had given the expression wide currency in his *History of New York from the Beginning of the World to the End of the Dutch Dynasty*, the first great book of comic literature by an American. The phrase soon came to mean "very quickly or energetically."

like the curate's egg.   Something satisfactory in some ways but not in others: "The play was rather like the curate's egg." The expression originated with a story in the British magazine *Punch* (November 9, 1895) in which a timid curate had been served a bad egg while dining at the home of an important parishioner. He is asked how the egg tastes and, not wishing to offend his host, says that parts of it are excellent.

like trying to nail jello to a tree.   Teddy Roosevelt seems to have invented the idea behind this metaphor, if not the exact words, in a July 2, 1915 letter to William Roscoe Thayer, in which he described the difficulty of negotiating with Colombia regarding the Panama Canal. His exact words were: "You could no more make an agreement with them than you could nail currant jelly to a wall—and the failure to nail currant jelly to a wall is not due to the nail; it is due to the currant jelly."

likker'll make you not know your mama.   "Liquor will make you not know your mother" is the translation of this Gullah proverb, which dates back at least to the 18th century and probably before this, possibly being adapted from an African proverb brought to America by South Carolina slaves. Little-known and recorded in no word book, it is as colorful as *knee-walkin' drunk*, a 19th-century Americanism of southern U.S. origin.

lilacs.   There are lilacs white, blue, pink, red, and purple, in many variations, but the word *lilac* means "blue." *Lilac* began as the Persian word *nilak*, "bluish," for the flower, passed into Arabic as *laylak*, and became *lilac* in Spanish, whence it came into English in the same form.

Lillian Russell.   Beautiful and flamboyant Lillian Russell was the toast of the town almost from the night she made her debut at New York's Tony Pastor's Opera House in burlesques of Gilbert & Sullivan comic operas. Only eighteen at the time, the singer and actress was fresh from Clinton, Iowa, where she had been born Helen Louise Leonard in 1861. For the next thirty years Lillian Russell's beauty and talent for light opera brought her fame and fortune unsurpassed by any contemporary performer. Success included her own company, a collection of male admirers that has probably never been matched since, and a number of sumptuous apartments and houses, such as her summer home in then fashionable Far Rockaway, New York, where she entertained lavishly. Among several things named for her were the *Lillian Russell* dessert, half a cantaloupe filled with a scoop of ice cream, and the town of *Lillian Russell* in central Kansas, which today has a population of about 6,200.

lilliputian.   The Lilliputians of the island of Lilliput in Jonathan Swift's satiric novel *Gulliver's Travels* (1726) are little people averaging six inches tall. Thus *lilliputian*, which suggests "little" in sound as well, has come to mean tiny or diminutive. (*See* **Brobdingnagian**.)

lily-livered.   The liver, the largest gland in our bodies, was once believed to be the seat of passion. It was also believed that the liver of a coward contained no blood, not as much "as you find in the foot of a flea," since a coward wasn't capable of passionate violence. Hence the expression *white-livered* and *lily-livered* for cowardly. Shakespeare wrote of cowards with "livers white as milk" and later came lusty expressions such as "a lily-livered, action-taking knave." (*See* **learn by heart; bowels of compassion**.)

lima beans.   Named for Lima, Peru by early European explorers who found them there, tender *lima beans* are often called "butter beans" in the U.S. The *succotash* made from them (and corn) derives from the Narragansett Indian *msiquatash*, literally "fragments."

limbs.   In the early 19th century "leg" was considered an indelicate word in America and *limb* (from the Anglo-Saxon *lim*, meaning the same) served as a euphemism for it. English novelist Captain Frederick Marryat described a visit to a young ladies' seminary in 1837: "On being ushered into the reception room, conceive my astonishment at beholding a square *pianoforte* with four *limbs*. However, that the ladies who visited their daughters might feel in its full force the extreme delicacy of the mistress of the establishment, and her care to preserve in their utmost purity the ideas of the young ladies under her charge, she had dressed all these four limbs in modest little trousers with frills at the bottom of them!"

Limburger cheese. *Limburger cheese* was introduced to America by German immigrants in the 19th century and was soon well known for its pungent smell. The soft cheese takes its name from the Limburg province of Belgium (not Holland) where it is made.

limelight. Royal Engineer Thomas Drummond, a Scottish inventor, devised the *Drummond light* as an aid in murky weather while assisting in a land survey of Great Britain, and soon after adapted it for use in lighthouses. Drummond, who later became secretary of state for Ireland, utilized calcium oxide, or lime, which had been isolated by Sir Humphry Davy and gives off an intense white light when heated. The *Drummond light* wasn't used on the stage as a spotlight or called *limelight* until after the inventor's death in 1840, when the expression *in the limelight*, "in the full glare of public attention," naturally arose from it. Limelights have long been replaced by arc and *klieg lights* (*q.v.*), but the phrase *in the limelight* still survives.

limericks. Poet Edward Lear's (1812-88) nonsense verses were labeled *learics* by M. Russell, a Jesuit wit of the day, the new word a play on the poet's name, on the fact that what he wrote weren't dignified *lyrics*, and on the *leering* grins some such verses even then produced. It wasn't until fifty-two years after Lear's book was published that the one-stanza poems, by now immensely popular, were dubbed *limericks*. One theory has it that the name arose then because a popular contemporary song had a chorus that went, "We'll all come up, come up to Limerick." It seems that there was also a party game played at the time in which each guest would invent and recite a *learic*, the whole group singing the chorus about "coming up to Limerick" between recitations. This may be true, but it is just as likely that the *learic* became the *limerick* because people believed that the verses were invented in Ireland, the land of poetry.

limey. As far back as 1795, lime juice was issued in the British navy as an antiscorbutic, or protection against scurvy. After about fifty years, Americans and Australians began calling English ships and sailors *lime-juicers*, and later *limeys*. The term *limey* was eventually applied to all Englishmen, and today the designation and the story behind it are widely known. Originally a contemptuous term, an international slur, *limey* is now considered rather an affectionate designation.

limousine. Originally any closed car, the limousine takes its name from a hood of that name worn by Limousens, inhabitants of the French province of Limousin. In recent times *limo* is increasingly being used in place of limousine, and very long custom-made limos are called *stretch limos*.

Lincolndom; Davisdom; Jeffdom. Southerners used *Lincolndom* as a humorous designation for the North during the Civil War, the term first recorded in 1861 and referring, of course, to President Abraham Lincoln. On the other side of the lines, the South was called *Davisdom*, (and, more rarely, *Jeffdom*), after Jefferson Davis, president of the Confederacy, these words being coined a few months before *Lincolndom*. (*See also* **Franklin conductor, Jacksonian democracy**.)

Lincolnian; etc. It is surprising that only some twenty-five place names in the United States honor our sixteenth president, little more than half those commemorating Jefferson and less than one third named for Andrew Jackson. But this can be explained by early bitterness toward Lincoln in the South. For none of his countrymen, not even Washington, has become a folk hero and giant in American tradition equal to Lincoln, and he is certainly more loved and respected the world over than any other American. His story, from his birth in an Illinois log cabin to the Emancipation Proclamation, the immortal Gettysburg Address, and the assassination by John Wilkes Booth, is so widely known in its smallest details that it is, rather than history or myth, a living part of the American legend from generation to generation, making Lincoln a father image to us all. A *Lincolnite* was a supporter of President Lincoln during the Civil War. *Lincolniana* is any material, such as writing, anecdotes, or objects, pertaining to Honest Abe, the Rail Splitter, or The Great Emancipator, while *Lincolnian* pertains to his character or political principles. Lincoln's Birthday, February 12, is a legal holiday in many states.

Lincoln shingles. Hardbread, also dubbed *sheet-iron crackers*, was called *Lincoln shingles* by U.S. troops on the frontier. The term is first recorded in Captain Eugene F. Ware's *The Indian War of 1874*, but must date back to Civil War times, given the use of Abraham Lincoln's name. A synonym was *teeth dullers*.

Lindau's disease. (*See* **Bright's disease**.)

Lindy. Even today's astronauts returning from the moon did not receive the hero worship heaped upon Charles Augustus Lindbergh when he made the first solo flight across the Atlantic on May 20-21, 1927, in his *Spirit of St. Louis*. Lindbergh was awarded the Congressional Medal of Honor for his 33 1/2-hour nonstop flight from New York to Paris, promoted to colonel in the Air Force, and received the French Cross of the Legion of Honor, the English Royal Air Force Cross, and the American Distinguished Flying Cross among hundreds of national and international honors. There had never been such adulation and perhaps there never will be again—in June 1927 alone, it is reported, Lindbergh received 3,500,000 letters, 14,000 parcels, and 100,000 telegrams. The Hero, the Lone Eagle, Lucky Lindy, the Flying Fool symbolized the beginning of a new technical age that in itself made great personal heroism less likely. Lindbergh's unprecedented fame even resulted in the *lindy* or *lindy hop*, a jitterbug dance very popular up until the mid-1950s, being named in his honor. His name made headlines again in 1932 with the tragic kidnaping and killing of his infant son, for which Bruno Richard Hauptmann was found guilty and which led to the Lindbergh Law passed by Congress in 1934. The law made all kidnapings across state lines and the use of the mails for ransom communications federal offenses.

a line-of-battle ship. In the days of sail, a line-of-battle ship, as opposed to other vessels such as frigates, was a capital ship fit to take part in a major battle. "Line of battle" simply referred to the formation of ships in a naval engagement.

lingua franca. A *lingua franca* is any hybrid language, a combination of various tongues. Pidgin English and *beche-de-mer*, or *beach-la-mar*, are two such trade languages in the Pacific, but the earliest one recorded is *lingua franca* itself, meaning "the Frankish tongue" in Italian. Lingua franca arose along the Mediterranean, a medley, or babble, of Italian, French, Spanish, Greek, Turkish, and Arabic common to many seamen in the ninth century or earlier. A Frank was any West European at the time, for the tribe ruled over most of Europe. The language enabled Muslims to conduct business dealings with Europeans, and Mediterranean traders still find it very useful in the Levant.

linguine. Linguine is thin, flat pasta, so thin that it reminded some poetic person centuries ago of "little tongues," which is what *linguine* means in Italian. (*See also* macaroni; vermicelli.)

lining one's pockets. Despite all the other foppish British Beaus before and after Beau Brummell, only Brummell's name lives on as a synonym for a dandy or fancy dresser. Beau Brummell, aided by the patronage of the Prince of Wales, later George IV, was the *arbiter eleganitarum* of London fashion for almost twenty years, a man noted for his excesses as well as his good taste; he often spent an entire day dressing for an affair, had all his gloves made by three glovers—one to fashion the hands, another for the fingers, and a third for the thumb, etc. So valued was his patronage that one tailor presented him with a coat whose pockets were lined with money, which gave rise to the expression *lining one's pockets*, for "bribery or graft."

links. The old English *hlinc*, "rising ground," is the ancestor of our *links* for a golf course; the first course called a *links* was located at Leith, Scotland in the late 16th century. The most famous poem about *golf links* is American poet Sarah N. Cleghorn's quatrain:

> The golf links lie so near the mill
> That almost every day
> The laboring children can look out
> And see the men at play.

lionize. To *lionize* a person can be to show him sights worthy of him, the term taking its name from the old practice of showing visiting dignitaries the lions that used to be kept at the Tower of London menagerie, a major tourist attraction until it was abolished at the beginning of the 19th century. An earlier use of the word, however, is to *lionize* a person by making a fuss over him, by making him feel like a lion. Both expressions date back to the early 1800s.

lion's share. (*See* leonine contract.)

liquor will make you not know your mother. (*See* likker'll make you not know your mama.)

Listerine. A trademark that is practically synonymous today for a mouthwash, *Listerine* takes its name from Joseph Lister, first Baron Lister (1827-1912), famous for founding antiseptic surgery. Basing his methods on Pasteur's theory that bacteria cause infection, Lister in 1865 used a mixture containing carbolic acid as a germicide and invented methods of applying it to wounds and incisions, such procedures greatly reducing postoperative fatalities from infection. Lord Lister, who became president of the Royal Society, tried unsuccessfully to disassociate his name from *Listerine* when the product was first marketed, much preferring to see himself commemorated by the Lister Institute of Preventive Medicine in London, of which he was a founder.

lists. (*See* to enter the lists.)

Literary Emporium. Boston used to be known as America's *Literary Emporium*, due to the comparatively large number of literati and publishing houses there in the early 19th century. British actor Edmund Kean coined the term in one of his speeches from the stage when on a tour of America.

litterbug. *Litterbug*, meaning someone who habitually litters, is an anonymous coinage, probably based on *firebug* (*q.v.*), dating back to the end of World War II. It owes its popularity to the Lakes and Hills Garden Club of Mount Dora, Florida, which used the slogan "Don't be a litterbug!" in a 1950 roadside cleanup campaign.

a little bird told me. One scholar suggests that this familiar saying may have originated with the similar-sounding Dutch expression *Er lift'el baerd*, which means "I should betray another." More likely the idea behind the phrase is in the noiseless flight of a bird, reinforced by a biblical passage from Eccles. 10:20: "Curse not the kind, no not in thy thought, . . . for a bird of the air shall carry the voice, and that which hath wings shall tell the matter." Used by Shakespeare and Swift, the expression dates back to at least the 16th century.

Little Jack Horner. (*See* **Jack Horner.**)

Little Lord Fauntleroy. The hero of the novel of the same name written by Frances Hodgson Burnett in 1886 gives us the expression *a little Lord Fauntleroy*, for a sissyish boy or man. *Fauntleroy* clothes are frilly velvety ones like those worn by the little Lord.

littleneck clams. Littleneck clams don't have little necks, but hailed originally from either Little Neck Bay, Long Island, New York, or Little Neck Bay, Ipswich, Massachusetts. No one knows which for sure.

little said is soon amended. This proverbial phrase, also *least said, soonest mended*, possibly derives from a rhyme Oliver Goldsmith may have written for John Newberry's edition of *Mother Goose's Melody . . .* in 1760:

> There was a little man,
> Who wooed a little maid,
> And he said, little Maid, will you wed, wed, wed?
> I have little more to say,
> So will you aye or nay,
> For the least said is soonest men-ded, ded, ded.

Little Willies. (*See* **grue.**)

llama. "*¿Como se llama?*" ("What is it called?") Spanish invaders asked South American Indians when they first encountered this unfamiliar animal. Not knowing what the Spanish were saying, the Indians repeated the Spanish word *llama*. The Spanish thought this was the name of the animal and dubbed it the *llama*, whose name therefore means "name." So goes the old story about the origin of *llama*. The *O.E.D.* and others claim that it probably comes from "a Peruvian word." (*See* **indri; kangaroo; Luzon; Nome; Yucatan.**)

Lloyd's of London. (*See* **A-1.**)

lo.

> Hope springs eternal in the human breast;
> Man never is, but always to be blessed.
> The soul, uneasy, and confined from home,
> Rests and expatiates in a life to come.

> Lo, the poor Indian! whose untutored mind
> Sees God in clouds, or hears him in the wind;
> His soul proud sciences never taught to stray.
> For as the solar walk, or milky way;
> Yet simple nature to his hope has giv'n,
> Behind the cloud-topped hill, an humbler heav'n.

Alexander Pope's well-known words *Lo, the poor Indian* in the above lines from his *Essay on Criticism* (1711) inspired the term *Lo*, for an American Indian. The word isn't recorded in this sense until 1871, but must be considerably older. "Is it longer a matter of astonishment," someone wrote in 1873, "that the Lo's are passing so rapidly from the face of the earth?"

loaded for bear. Any pioneer who went out into the woods made sure that his gun carried a charge powerful enough to bring down a bear, for the most dangerous of American animals ranged everywhere. "*Loaded for b'ar*" eventually came to mean not only to be prepared for bear but to be well prepared for any contingency, and toward the end of the 19th century became a common American term meaning "drunk."

loaded to the gills; loaded to the guards. Anyone *loaded to the gills drinks like a fish* (*q.v.*) or has drunk alcohol "like a fish drinks water" and is obviously drunk. Sailors use a younger version of the old expression when they say *loaded to the guards*. The "guards" here are part of the *Plimsoll marks* (*q.v.*) on vessels, lines beyond which it is dangerous to load a ship.

loafer. Loafer, for "a lazy do-nothing, an idler, or lounger," is apparently an Americanism, first recorded in 1830, deriving from the German *Landlaufer*, "vagabond." Other possible ancestors are the English dialect word *louper*, "vagabond," the expression *to loup the tether*, "to wander," and the Dutch *loof*, "weary." The verb *to loaf* is apparently a back-formation from the noun. *Loafer* has been the name for a slip-on shoe without laces in the U.S. since the 1940s.

lobbying. Although it is an Americanism that isn't recorded until 1808, a *lobby*, a group trying to influence the government to promote its own special interests, seems to derive ultimately from the large entrance hall to the British House of Commons that was called the Lobby as early as the 17th century. In the Lobby people could talk to members of Parliament and many tried to influence MPs there.

Lobelia. Linnaeus named over a thousand plants, including hundreds that have come to be household words. Many of the botanist's namings honored people. Indeed, by labeling species as well as genera, the Swedish botanist sometimes commended two people with the same plant. This is the case with *Lobelia dormanna*, the water lobelia.

Linnaeus named the plant's family *Lobeliaceae* and its genus *Lobelia* after Matthias de l'Obel, or Lobel (1538-1616), a distinguished Flemish botanist and physician who lived a century before Linnaeus. But he called *L. dortmanna*, one of its three hundred species, after an obscure druggest named Dortmann whom he met while studying in Holland. Nothing is known about Dortmann, but Lobel had been both physician and botanist to England's learned King James I. A native of Lille, Lobel tried to classify plants according to their leaf formations long before Linnaeus and wrote several of the earliest botanical books. The *Lobeliaceae* family commemorating him contains twenty-four genera and over seven hundred species, some of which are trees and shrubs, but its *Lobelia* genus consists of about 300 species of annual or perennial herbs widely grown for their mainly blue, red, yellow, or white flowers. The species *Lobelia inflata* was used by American Indians like tobacco, has a tobacco-like odor, and was also employed as the base for a popular home remedy, though it is considered poisonous in quantity. Another species, *Lobelia syphilitica*, the blue syphilis, was used by the Indians to treat syphilis; it was even introduced into Europe centuries ago for this purpose.

loblolly pine. *Loblolly* is first recorded in 1597 in Gerarde's *Herbal* as a thick gruel or stew. It is probably an onomatopoeic word, one writer noting that "it describes a semi-liquid state" and "itself shakes in pronunciation like jelly, which is most nearly what it describes." In America settlers began to apply *loblolly* to miry muddy places and called *Pinus taeda*, a long-leaved Southern pine, the *loblolly pine* because it commonly grew in such swampy places. The name is first attested in about 1730. There is also a *loblolly bay* (*Gorclonia lasianthus*) and in 19th-century America a mudhole was humorously called a *loblolly.*

lobster. Lobsters are, in fact, a kind of bug. The word *lobster* itself is a melding of two foreign words: the Latin *locasta*, meaning "locust," and the Anglo-Saxon *lappe*, which means "spider." "Real" lobster is not the freshwater lobster that the French call *ecrevisse*, or crawfish, the small European crustacean with no claws; or even the warm-water spiny lobster from which *lobster tails* are obtained and labeled *langosta* or *langouste* in some restaurants. The true lobsters number among their ranks only *Homarus americanus*, often called Maine, or North Atlantic lobsters; the smaller blue lobster of Europe, *H. vulgaris*; *Nephrops norvegicus*, the orange Norwegian lobster, variously called lady lobster, scampi, or prawn and *H. capensis*.

Lobster Newburg. The most famous of lobster dishes, *Lobster Newburg*, should have blazoned the name of Benjamin J. Wenberg (1835-1885), a late 19th-century shipping magnate, across the pages of menus everywhere, but gastronomical lore has it that he was foolish enough to displease the great restaurateur Lorenzo Delmonico. It's said that Wenberg discovered the dish in South America and described it glowingly to Delmonico's owner. Lorenzo, instructing his chef to prepare the shelled lobster in its rich sauce of sherry, thick cream, and egg yolks, served the dish to his wealthy patron and named it *Lobster Wenberg* in his honor. It remained thus on Delmonico's menu for almost a month, until one evening when Wenberg got drunk, started a fight in the posh restaurant's dining room and was evicted. Soon after, the dish appeared on an enraged Lorenzo's menu as *Lobster Newburg*, probably in honor of the city on the Hudson.

lobster shift. *Lobster shift*, for the newspaper shift commencing at four in the morning, is said to have originated at the defunct *New York Journal-American* early in this century. The newspaper's plant was near the East Side docks and workers on this shift came to work at about the same time lobstermen were putting out to sea in their boats.

locate. Probably the earliest of all American back formations, the verb to *locate* derives from the noun *location*. It is recorded by a traveler in 1652 and counted among its early users Ben Franklin and George Washington, who apparently didn't care that some considered it a "vulgarism."

lock, stock, and barrel. The firing mechanism, or lock (by which the charge is exploded); the stock (to which the lock and barrel are attached); and the barrel (the tube through which bullets are discharged) are the three components of a firearm that make up the whole gun. Thus the expression *lock, stock, and barrel* means the whole works, the whole of anything. The saying is an Americanism first recorded in Thomas Haliburton's Sam Slick stories (1843), but likely goes back to the muskets of the American Revolution. However, the expression might also be rooted in the *lock* on a country store's door, the *stock*, or goods, inside, and even the *barrel* on which business was often transacted.

to lock horns. Possibly New Englanders who witnessed moose fiercely battling over a female, their massive horns locked together, invented this expression for "a violent clash." There is no evidence of this in the first American literary use of the phrase in 1839, however. When Swinburne used the phrase in 1865, he spoke of a heifer and her mate locking horns, which could also be the source of the expression.

to lock the barn door after the horse is stolen. The venerable rustic aphorism for "taking a precaution too late" hangs in there; it is still heard in cities that haven't seen a barn for half a century. Back in England in the 1300s we would have recognized the expression, its first literary use being in John Gower's *Confessio amantis* (1390): "For whan the grete Stiede Is stole, thanne he taketh hiede, and maketh the stable dore fast."

loganberry. California Judge James Harvey Logan (1841-1921), who had been a Missouri schoolteacher before working his way west as the driver of an ox team, developed the *loganberry* in his experimental home orchard at Santa Cruz. Logan, formerly Santa Cruz district attorney, was serving on the superior court bench in 1880 when he raised the new berry from seed, breeding several generations of plants to do so. Though a respected amateur horticulturist, he never adequately explained how the berry was developed. One account claims that the *loganberry* originated "from self-grown seeds of the Aughinbaugh [a wild blackberry], the other parent supposed to be a raspberry of the Red Antwerp type." Several experts believe that it is a variety of the western dewberry, or a hybrid of that species, crossed with the red raspberry. The dispute may never be resolved, but experiments in England have produced a plant similar to the loganberry by crossing certain blackberries and red raspberries. In any case, there is no doubt that the purplish-red *loganberry* is shaped like a blackberry, colored like a raspberry, and combines the flavor of both—or that it was first grown by Judge Logan and named for him. Its scientific name is *Rubus loganbuccus* and the trailing blackberry-like plant is grown commercially in large quantities, especially in California, Oregon, Washington, and other places having fairly mild winters.

at loggerheads. *At loggerheads*—"engaged in a violent quarrel, or a dispute"—seems to refer to medieval naval battles during which sailors bashed each other with murderous instruments called loggerheads. These loggerheads were long-handled devices with a solid ball of iron on the end that was heated and used to melt pitch or tar, which could be flung at the enemy. The loggerheads themselves apparently made for handy lethal weapons *after* the boiling pitch was used up, and mariners from opposing ships probably engaged each other with them, being *at loggerheads*. *Loggerhead* also has an earlier meaning of "an ignorant blockhead, a knucklehead," and this idea of stupidity most likely contributed to the popularity of a phrase that suggests that the people *at loggerheads* in the dispute are headstrong and unwilling to compromise. The expression is first recorded in 1685.

logomachy. *Logomachy*, from a Greek word meaning "word contest," is "fighting about words," often about verbal subtleties. However, it can be loosely used to mean fighting with words, actual "combats of curses," the most colorful example of these being the poets who led pre-Islamic Arabs into combat, hurling curses at the

enemy (warfare and the arts were specialized even then). But a better word for word fighting is *flyting*. Flytings (from the Old English *flyte*, "to contend or jeer") were contests held principally by 16th-century Scottish poets in which two persons "assailed each other alternately with tirades of abusive verse." Following is one of thirty-two stanzas directed at Scotland's James V by his former tutor, Sir David Lindsay. Bear in mind that this vitriolic diatribe *lost* the *flyting*.

Purse-peeler, hen-stealer, cat-killer, no I qyell thee;
Rubiator, fornicator by nature, foul befal thee.
Tyke-sticker, poisoner Vicar, Pot-licker, I mon paz thee.
Jock blunt, dead Runt, I shall punt when I slay thee.

(*See* **the dozens.**)

logorrhea. *Logorrhea*, apparently patterned on *diarrhea*, comes from the Greek *logos*, "word," plus *rhein*, "flow, stream." It is first recorded as a psychological term in 1904: "Logorrhea refers to the excessive flow of words, a common symptom in cases of mania." As with many similar terms the word came to be loosely used and can now describe any big mouth who talks too much.

logrolling. "You scratch my back and I'll scratch yourn" was the idea behind this term, which was invented by American pioneers on the Western frontier. Settlers clearing land and building their log cabins could always count on neighbors for help in rolling down logs, with the tacit understanding they'd do the same for their neighbors whenever asked. The good neighborly expression, with its associations of rum, food, and fiddling, became tainted when politicians in many fields adopted it. Legislators are still well-known for *logrolling* with representatives from other states; that is, one congressman will support the pet project of another if he assists in passing a bill furthering the interests of the first. *Literary logrollers* form mutual admiration societies, favorably reviewing each other's books in order to promote sales and reputations. Commenting on one instance of such a practice, A. E. Housman said there had been nothing like it since the passage in Milton where Sin gave birth to death.

Lolita. A Lolita has in the last twenty-five years become the word for a nymphet or adolescent nymphomaniac. Capitalized still, the term derives from the name of the main character in Vladimir Nabokov's novel *Lolita* (1955).

lollapalooza. An extraordinary person or thing; an exceptional example of something. The French expression *allez-fusil*, "Forward the musket!," became common in Ireland after French troops landed at Killala in 1798. County Mayo residents pronounced it "ally foozee" and coined a new word from it meaning "sturdy fellow."

Mencken, among others, believes that our *lollapaloosa*, which is also spelled *lallapalooza*, comes from this word. Surprisingly few words came to American English from the eloquent Irish, the list almost limited to *lollapaloosa*, *paddy wagon*, *shanty*, *shebang*, *shenanigans*, *shillelagh*, *smithareens*, and possibly *speakeasy*. Phrases, as these pages show, are another story.

lollipop. Is the *lollipop* named after a racehorse? The story goes that in the early 1900s one George Smith, a Connecticut candy manufacturer, "put together the candy and the stick" and named it in honor of Lolly Pop, the era's most famous racehorse, the name "lollipop" then becoming an exclusive trade name used by the Bradley-Smith company of New Haven. It is true that candy on a stick wasn't known in America before about 1908 and neither was the word *lollipop*. Smith may have invented the confection (there are no other claimants) and he may even have named his candy on a stick after the horse in question. But the word *lollipop*, for a piece of sucking candy that dissolves easily in the mouth (*not* one, however, that is attached to a stick) was widely used in England as early as the late 18th century. It apparently derives from the English dialect word *lolly*, used in northern England to mean "tongue," plus the word *pop*, in reference to the sound children made when sucking the candy. Somehow the lollipop remained unknown to Americans until the candy on a stick was invented in the early 20th century, but this is not to say that the racehorse Lolly Pop couldn't have been named for the earlier British term.

lollygagging. *The Dictionary of Americanisms* quotes an indignant citizen in the year of our Lord 1868 on "the lascivious lolly-gagging lumps of licenteousness who disgrace the common decencies of life by their love-sick fawnings at our public dances." This is the first recorded use of *lollygagging*, which means "to fool around, dawdle, waste time" and can mean "lovemaking," though this last is no waste of time and my dear old grandmother never used the word in such a way to me.

London. *London*, loosely translated, meant "the wild place," being so named by Celts who found a harbor in the Thames there near two desolate gravel hills, calling the area *lond*, "wild."

lonely. Shakespeare coined *lonely*, or first recorded it, from *lone* + *ly*, in *Coriolanus* (1608): "I go alone Like to a lonely Dragon . . ." The word *loneliness* had been invented before this and may also have suggested *lonely* to him.

longboat. In the days of sail *longboats* were so named because they were the largest boats carried by ships. Up to forty feet long, they were up to eight feet abeam and were built to hold great weights.

long green. The first U.S. greenback dollars were printed in 1863 and this term came into use soon after. *Long green* means "a lot of money," suggesting green bills laid in a long line, end to end.

long in the tooth. That horses' gums recede and their teeth appear longer as they grow older, owing to their constant grinding of their food, is the idea behind this ancient folk phrase, which means one is getting on in years.

a long row to hoe. Rows in American home gardens today, usually a dozen feet or so in length, can't compare to the long rows of corn, beans, and other crops on early American farms. These rows, which often stretched out of sight, had to be weeded by hand at the time and approaching one with hoe in hand was dispiriting, to say the least. The expression *a long row to hoe* was probably well established for any time-consuming, tedious task many years before Davy Crockett first recorded it in 1835. It is still heard in a day when mechanized equipment has replaced hoes on farms, perhaps because, according to a recent poll, some 100 million Americans consider themselves vegetable gardeners.

longshoreman. The *longshoreman*, who helps load and unload ships, takes his name from a contraction of "along-shore-man," while the synonym *stevedore* is from the Spanish *estibodor*, "one who packs things." A *shenango* is a specialized longshoreman, one who handles cargo on railroad barges. His name derives from the county of Chanango in upstate New York, from which many such workers were once recruited.

long time no see. One of the most widely used of all catch phrases, *long time no see* came into the language from *pidgen English* (*q.v.*), brought home from the Far East by U.S. and British sailors in the early 1900s along with other expressions such as *chop chop* for "hurry" and *no can do* (*qq.v.*). *Long time no see* is said to be a direct translation into pidgen of the Chinese expression *ch'ang chih mei*, meaning the same. (*See also* **Chinese**.)

loo. *Loo*, a slang word for "toilet" and British in origin, may be a mispronunciation of *le lieu*, French for "the place." But no one is sure. It could also be a shortening of *gardy loo*! a warning cry housewives made when they emptied chamber pails out the windows into the street, *gardy loo* being a corruption of the French *gardez l'eau*, "watch out for the water." A man traditionally walks on the outside of a woman in the street because chamber pots were emptied out the window in Elizabethan times; in those days a man was expected to take the greater risk of walking near the curb and protecting his lady by shielding her with his body as well. Among men walking together without women brutal fights were fought over who would *take the wall*. (*See* **John Thomes; Twiss**.)

look one way and row another. This phrase means to be aimed at one thing, but in reality to be seeking something quite different, like an oarsman rowing a boat. The expression is an old one that John Bunyan used in *Pilgrim's Progress*.

looney tunes. Looney Tunes was originally the name of a Warner Brothers cartoon series that first appeared in 1930, taking its name of course from *looney*, which comes from lunatic. In recent times, *looney tunes* has been used by law enforcement authorities to mean a crazed subject and has had increased general usage in the same sense. President Reagan referred to terrorists and their supporters as *looney tunes*. It was street slang long before this, however.

loony. (*See* **crazy as a loon.**)

loophole. Medieval castles and other fortifications were often built with narrow windows that widened inward but were no more than vertical slits on the outside. Enemy archers found these defensive positions difficult targets, but archers behind the windows had ample room to fire on attackers. Called *loopholes* from the old word *loop* for "a narrow window," these windows became obsolete when the invention of gunpowder made castles and city walls unimportant in warfare, but the word came to represent an outlet or way to escape, a purpose loopholes had never really served. By the 17th century, writers were using *loophole* to signify a narrow way out and today we associate the word with a clever, tricky way out of a situation, especially in regard to evading a law.

loose lips sink ships. World War II posters urged sailors and others not to talk about war-related matters, for "The slip of a lip may sink a ship," "Slipped lips sink ships," and "Idle gossip sinks ships." The most memorable of such slogans was *Loose lips sink ships*. Another was *Don't talk chum/chew Topp's gum.*

loosestrife. One credulous author wrote that the Romans put *loosestrife* flowers under the yokes of oxen to keep the animals from fighting with each other. Many people believed similar myths about loosestrife (Lysimachia) in ancient times, this belief stemming from the fact that the plant's name was derived from the Greek *lusi*, from *luein*, "to loose," and *mache*, "strife." Actually, loosestrife was named *lusimachon* by the Greeks from the name of one of Alexander the Great's generals, Lysimachus, who supposedly discovered it.

loot. *Loot*, wrote Rudyard Kipling, is really "the thing that makes the boys get up and shoot." The word derives from the Hindi *lut*, meaning the same, which the British found plenty of in India.

lord; lady. Each of these dignified words (though today we have terms like *baglady*) has its roots in a loaf of bread. The lord, or head of a household, was the *loaf-protector*, the Old English for this term, *hlaford*, eventually yielding the word *lord*. Similarly, the lord's wife, or mistress of the house, eventually took the name *lady* from the Old English *hlafdige*, "loaf-kneader," or maker of the loaf of bread.

Lord Hawhaw. A *Lord Hawhaw* is especially one who makes propaganda for the enemy. William Joyce (1906-46) earned the sobriquet for his mocking broadcasts from Berlin during World War II. The American-born British fascist is examined at some length in Rebecca West's brilliant *The Meaning of Treason* (1947). Joyce was captured after the war, adjudged a British subject because he held a passport, and hanged for his crimes.

Lorelei. The *Lorelei*, rising 433 feet high on the right bank of the Rhine River near St. Goar, is a rock cliff noted for its strange echo. Centuries ago the legend grew that the steep cliff was the home of a young maiden who had leaped into the Rhine and drowned in despair over a faithless lover. She was transformed into a siren whose song lured sailors to death in the dangerous Rhine narrows. Those who saw her lost their sight or reason, and those who heard her were condemned to wander with her forever.

Los Angeles. *Los Angeles* is a shortening of the California city's original name: *El Pueblo de Nuestra Senora la Reina de los Angeles de Porcinúncula* ("The town of Our Lady Queen of the Angels of Porcinúncula"). It is more often called *L.A.* Call it "L.A." and it loses 54 letters.

losing face. The Chinese, as would be expected, have a phrase for losing one's dignity before others, and *tiu lien* was simply translated into *to lose face* by English traders there in the late 19th century. These same English, however, invented the phrase *to save face*, "to maintain one's dignity," using the Chinese model.

lose one's shirt. *Lose one's shirt* used to mean to be very angry, giving us the present-day *keep your shirt on*, "keep cool, be calm." Only in this century did the expression come to mean to lose everything. It has many antecedents that convey the same idea, including *He'd give you the shirt off his back*, his last possession, and *not a shirt to his back*, meaning someone penniless and propertyless, with nothing at all. Chaucer, in "The Whf of Bathes Tale," wrote of someone he admired though "had he nought a schert."

the lost generation. *"Une génération perdue,"* remarked Monsieur Pernollet, owner of the Hôtel de

Pernollet in Belley. He was speaking to Gertrude Stein and pointing at a young mechanic repairing her car. Young men like the mechanic, Monsieur Pernollet said, had gone to war, had not been educated properly in their formative years, and were thus "a lost generation." Stein remembered Pernollet's phrase and applied it to Ernest Hemingway and his friends. Hemingway quoted her in *The Sun Also Rises* (1926) and the words became the label for an entire literary generation.

lotus-eater. A daydreamer, someone who leads an indolent, dreamy life of ease indifferent to the busy world, is sometimes called a *lotus-eater*. In the *Odyssey* Homer writes that the Lotus-eaters, or Lotophagi, were a people who lived on the northeast African coast and ate what later Greek writers identified as the fruit of the shrub *Zixxphus Lotus*, which made them dream all day, forget friends and family, and lose all desire of ever returning to their homes. Any traveler who ate the sweet fruit or drank a wine made from it wanted only to live in Lotus-Land. Lotus, however, is a name given to many plants. The Chinese make a lotus seed dessert called *pinh tan lian tye*, reputed to be an aphrodisiac, and the delicious sugarberry or hackberry (*Celtus australis*), grown in the northern U.S., has been called the fabled food of the Lotus-eaters. Even jujubes, long a favorite candy, were once thought to be flavored with lotus fruit.

Louisette. (*See* **guillotine**.)

Louis heel. There is no doubt that France's Louis XIV, called *le Roi Soleil*, the Sun King, because he adopted the rising sun as his personal emblem, was a vain and haughty man who surrounded himself with pomp and ceremony. *Le Grand Monarque* is characterized by the apocryphal remark attributed to him, *L'état, c'est moi*, "the state is I." He is therefore a likely candidate for the inventor of the high *Louis heel*. Because Louis was a short man, the story goes, he ordered his shoemaker to add cork to his shoe heels to make him taller and kept having more and more cork added to them, his loyal court aping the style. The tale is a good one, but probably isn't true. Most likely Louis's grandson, Louis XV, is responsible for the *Louis heel*, which became the imposing carved French heel on men's shoes that was ultimately copied by women. The heel, which is only medium today, once reached such ridiculous heights that court ladies had to use balancing sticks to navigate.

Louisiana. The Creole or Pelican State was named Louisiana in 1682 by the French explorer Robert de La Salle as a homage to the Sun King, France's Louis XIV, applying the designation to the entire Mississippi Valley. The Louisiana Purchase, engineered by President Jefferson because he believed Napoleon might close the Mississippi to United States commerce, brought the one-million-square-mile area under American ownership in 1803 for a mere $15 million. In the history of this country only *Seward's Folly* and possibly *Manhattan* Island (*q.v.*) were shrewder real estate deals. The purchase included part or all of eleven states—Arkansas, Colorado, Iowa, Kansas, Louisiana, Missouri, Montana, Nevada, North Dakota, South Dakota, and Wyoming. *Mencken* notes there was a child named Louisiana Purchase to commemorate the event—but then the boy's sister bore the name Missouri Compromise.

Louisville; Louisville Slugger. *Louisville*, the largest city in Kentucky, was named for France's Louis XVI in 1780 in recognition of the assistance he had given America during the Revolutionary War. Home of Fort Knox, the Kentucky Derby, the mint julep, many bourbon distilleries, and the only inland United States Coast Guard station, *Louisville* also houses the famous Hillerich & Bradsby's baseball bat factory, where the renowned *Louisville Slugger* has been made since 1884. The bat is of course named after the city named after a king. *Louisville Sluggers* are made from prime white ash, one mature tree is needed to make sixty bats, and more than six million are turned out each year. Some 2 percent of the annual production goes to professional ballplayers, these fashioned from specifications noted in a fifty-thousand-card file covering the bat preferences of ballplayers past and present.

lounge. Longinus, according to the apocryphal gospel of Nicodemus (7:8), was the Roman soldier who pierced the crucified Christ's side with a spear. Later, tradition tells us, the soldier converted to Christianity and in medieval times was honored as a saint. Contemporary mystery plays may have depicted Longinus, or Longis, as he was also called, as a tall, lazy lout leaning on his spear—at least in the centurion phase of his life. It has been suggested that *to lounge* could have derived from the posture of Longis, *lounges* and *lounge lizards* following after the verb. The theory isn't likely to be confirmed, but *Webster's* and other authorities do give *longis*, the Old French for "an awkward, drowsy person," as the source for the word.

love. A person who fails to score in tennis might be said to be playing for the love of the game. According to this theory, which is widely supported, *love*, for "zero in tennis," comes from the expression "play for the money or play for love [nothing]." The idea here is similar to that behind the word *amateur*, which comes from the Latin *amare*, "to love," and strictly speaking means a person who loves a game or subject. But there is another explanation for the term *love* in tennis, an expression used since at least 1742. *Love* for *goose egg*, or "nothing," may have been born when the English imported the game of tennis from France. Because a zero resembles an egg, the

French used the expression *l'oeuf*, "egg," for "no score." English players, in mispronouncing the French expression, may have gradually changed it to *love*.

love affair.   Shakespeare may have invented the term *love affair*. We find no use of the words earlier than in *Two Gentlemen of Verona* (1591), where the Bard writes: "I'll . . . confer at large all that may concern thy love affairs."

love apples.   Why tomatoes were dubbed "love apples" is a matter of some dispute. First cultivated by the Mayans and called the *xtomatl*, the tomato was named the *pomi del peru* and *mala peruviane* when Cortez brought it to Europe from America. That tomatoes hailed from exotic climes and were a scarlet shapely fruit undoubtedly helped, but the designation *love apple* owes just as much to semantics as sexuality. All Spaniards at the time were called Moors, and one story has it that an Italian gentleman told a visiting Frenchman that the tomatoes he had been served were *Pomi dei Moro* ("Moor's apples"), which to his guest sounded like *pommes d'amour*, or *apples of love*. However, another version claims that "apples of love" derives in a similar roundabout way from the Italian *pomo d'oro*, "golden apple," and a third tale confides that courtly Sir Walter Raleigh presented a tomato to Queen Elizabeth, coyly advising her that it was "an apple of love." In any case, the tomato quickly gained a reputation as a wicked aphrodisiac, and justly or not, it has held this distinction ever since. "These Apples of Love . . . yield very little nourishment to the body and the same naught and corrupt," the English traveler John Girard wrote in his 16th-century gardening guide. In Germany the tomato's common name is still *Liebesapfel*, or "love's apple," and the expression *hot tomato*, for "a sexy woman," is common to many languages.

lovebird.   The West African parrot *Agapornis pullarius* was apparently the first bird to be called the *love bird*, because of the remarkable affection it shows for its mate. This usage is recorded in the late 1500s, over three centuries passing before *lovebirds* is recorded as applying to humans (as an Americanism in the 1930s). But the phrase *like a pair of lovebirds* was common before this and one doubts that human *lovebirds* weren't so called much earlier.

love child; love brat.   *Love child*, for "a child born out of wedlock," isn't a euphemism from Victorian times, as is often said. The kind words date back at least to 1805, when recorded by a writer referring to *love-child's* use in another locality. Before this Pope used the similar *babe of love* in the *Dunciad* (1728): "Two babes of love close clinging to her waist." *Love brat*, a nastier variant, is recorded earlier than either expression, sometime in the 17th century.

love day.   The ancient custom of settling disputes on legally appointed special days called *love days* is one that might well be revived. The custom is so old that the words are a translation of the medieval Latin *dies amoris*. Shakespeare mentioned such *love-days* in *Titus Andronicus* and the words also came to mean "a day devoted to love-making" in the 16th century, "when bonny maides doe meete with Swaines in the valley . . ."

lovee.   We tend to associate nonce words like *lovee* with modern comics. "Amos and Andy," for instance, were consistently coining things like the *hitter* and the *hittee*, the *kisser* and the *kissee*, etc. But *lovee*, in the sense of the one loved by a lover, a recipient of love, dates back at least to the mid-18th century when Samuel Richardson used it in his novel *Sir Charles Grandison* (1735): "The Lover and the Lovee make generally the happiest couple."

love is blind.   Shakespeare possibly coined this now proverbial phrase. At least it is first recorded in *The Merchant of Venice* (1596):

> But love is blind, and lovers cannot see
> The pretty follies that themselves commit.

love lay.   A *love lay* is a love song, the term dating back to the 14th century. A *lay*, from the Old French *lai*, "song," was originally a short narrative or lyrical poem intended to be sung, but has come to include historical narrative poems (ballads) such as Scott's *The Lay of the Last Minstrel*.

lovelihead.   A rare word, meaning "loveliness," *lovelihead* has its origins in a line by Ben Jonson: "Those Sweet and Sacred fires Of Love betweene you and your Lovelyhead"—in his poem "Underwoods" (1633).

lovelock.   Courtiers in the time of Queen Elizabeth I wore *lovelocks*, which were long locks of hair hanging in front of the shoulders that were curled and decorated with ribbons. Later, *lovelocks* came to mean a small curl plastered to the temples. The man's version was called a *bell-rope*.

lovelorn.   No Mr. Lonelyhearts invented the word *lovelorn*, for "someone forlorn or pining for love." John Milton coined the word in *Comus, A Masque* (1634), a pastoral entertainment in which a character says to another: "Where the love-lorn Nightingale Nightly to thee her sad Song mourneth well." Milton also coined *all-conquering*, *earth-shaking*, and *smooth-shaven* (q.v.).

love me, love my dog.   What the phrase means is "if you want to love me, you'll have to take me faults and all." Almost nine hundred years ago St. Bernard (1091-1153), famous abbot of the monastery of Clairvaux, said this in

Latin: "*Qui me amat, amat et canem meum.*" Despite the canine association, he is not St. Bernard de Menthon (923-1008), who founded the Alpine shelter now called the Hospice of the Great St. Bernard and after whom the *St. Bernard dog* (*q.v.*) is named.

love money. Romantic couples used to break coins in two, each lover keeping a half as a remembrance or pledge of fidelity. The broken coins were called *love money* and the custom is recorded in Roman times.

love nest. Considering that *lovebirds* (*q.v.*) goes back several centuries, it is hard to believe that *love nest*, for "an apartment where two lovers meet, usually clandestinely," dates only to the beginning of this century. But it is, so far as is known, an Americanism first recorded in 1900.

love tap; love pat. People were probably calling gentle taps indicating love *love taps* long before Mark Twain used the expression in *A Connecticut Yankee in King Arthur's Court* (1889). But Twain's is the first recorded use of the expression, which may have been suggested by the earlier *love pat*, recorded in 1876.

love tooth. *Love tooth*, similar to *sweet tooth*, once meant an inclination for love, a liking of love. "I am nowe old," wrote John Lyly in *Euphues* (1580), "yet still have I in my head a 'love tooth.'"

lovey-dovey. *Lovey-dovey* is often cited as an Americanism, but it is recorded first in England in 1769 as a term of affection: "The domestic Lovies and Dovies." By 1819 we find recorded: "My dearest love—lovey, dovey!" *Dovey*, of course, stands for "little dove."

lowbrow. A word invented in 1902 by a *New York Sun* reporter to describe anti-intellectuals. (*See* **highbrow**.)

lower the boom. *Lower the boom* can mean to hit someone hard, as in "Clancy lowered the boom," or to ask someone for a loan. The idea behind the American expression, which probably dates back to the late 19th century, is a cargo-loading boom hitting someone.

lox; gox. There is, in addition to the illustrious *lox* (from the Scandinavian *lax*, salmon) of *bagel and lox* fame, a word *lox* used in space research terminology. *Lox* here means liquid oxygen, the term used in *lox tank*, *lox unit*, etc., and as a verb meaning to load the tanks of a rocket vehicle with liquid oxygen. This *lox* came into use in the 1960s and is the antonym of *gox*, gaseous oxygen.

LSD; LCI; LCT. Many people are confused by these acronyms for World War II landing ships. The *LSD* (*Landing Ship Deck*) was a large ship that carried the smaller landing craft that took men and equipment to the beach during amphibious landings. The smaller troop carriers stored in the LSD's large inner compartment, which was flooded to launch them, were called LCIs (*Landing Craft Infantry*), and LCTs (*Landing Craft Tank*) and were used for landing tanks.

L7. One rarely hears or sees this late-fifties Hollywood slang for "a square" anymore, perhaps because while it is clever visually, it has no ear appeal. *L7* means square, "not with it" according to Artie Shaw, because "if you form an L and a 7 with your finger, that's what you get."

lucifer. Like *Vesuvius* and *Promethean*, *lucifer* was a colorful name for "matches" in the 19th century. Their origins are obvious except in the case of *lucifer*, which doesn't derive from the name of the devil, as one would suspect, but from the morning star, the "Light-Bringer," *lucem ferre*. *Lucifer* is also the only one of the three to still have some currency, in the song "Pack Up Your Troubles In Your Old Kit Bag": "strike up a lucifer to light your fag . . ."

a lucky fluke. A *fluke*, in the sense of lucky things that happen to someone, is possibly from the dialect word *flack*, "a blow." The word *fluke* here seems to come from billiards, where a fluke means aiming at one thing and hitting another, a lucky blow that is to your benefit. *Lucky* is redundant here, but is usually yoked to *fluke* in the phrase. The expression dates back to the 19th century.

Lucullus will sup with Lucullus. Lucius Licinius Lucullus (ca. 119-57 B.C.), a celebrated Roman general and consul who drove Mithridates's fleet from the Mediterranean, among other military successes, had been relieved of his office by Pompey in 67 B.C. But he had amassed a fortune and retired into the elegant leisure for which he has become famous, spending huge sums on public displays and on his estates. Horace tells us he lavishly entertained the artists, poets, and philosophers with whom he surrounded himself, and that his feasts were famous throughout Rome. The gourmand even had files of menus listed according to cost, serving the most expensive ones to his most important guests, and it is said that on one occasion an unparalleled dinner cost him the equivalent of more than eight thousand dollars. Another time, Plutarch says, he ordered his cook to prepare a particularly magnificent meal and was reminded that he was dining alone that night. "Lucullus will sup tonight with Lucullus," he replied, or "Today Lucullus is host to Lucullus." These sayings are now used to indicate a luxurious meal enjoyed by a gourmet who dines alone. The Roman general's military prowess is almost forgotten, but the adjective from his name lives on as a synonym for "gastronomically splendid" and a sumptuous and extravagant meal is still called a *Lucullan feast* or *banquet*.

lucus a non lucendo. An etymological contradiction, an absurd conclusion or explanation. The Latin words literally mean "grove from not giving light," that is, a grove (*lucus*) is so called because it doesn't shine (*lucere*). The Roman grammarian Honoratus Maurus Servius invented the term to illustrate how words are falsely derived from those having a contrary sense (for example, deriving *ludus*, Latin for "school," from *ludere*, Latin for "to play." Addison gave another example in the *Spectator*: "One Tryphiodorus . . . composed an Epick Poem . . . of four and twenty books, having entirely banished the letter A [Alpha] from his first book, which was called *Alpha* [as *Lucus a non Lucendo*] because there was not an *Alpha* in it."

Lucy Stoner. Use of the "Ms." form of address for a woman today recalls the all but forgotten *Lucy Stoners* active earlier in this century. A woman who refused to change her maiden name upon marriage was often called a *Lucy Stoner*. The term recalls American feminist Lucy Stone (1818-93), who deserves far greater recognition than she has received. On graduation from Oberlin, the only college accepting women at the time, Lucy Stone was 29, and she plunged headlong into the woman suffrage and antislavery causes. Her important work included helping to form the National Woman's Association, of which she was president for three years, and the founding of the *Women's Journal*, the association's official publication for nearly fifty years. An eloquent speaker for women's rights, Lucy Stone became well-known throughout the U.S. In 1855 she married Dr. Henry Brown Blackwell, an antislavery worker, but as a matter of principle she refused to take his name, and she and her husband issued a joint protest against the inequalities in the marriage law. Lucy Stone would never answer to any but her maiden name all her married life, and the Lucy Stone League later emulated her, defending the right of all married women to do so.

Luddite. The masked bands of workers who made night raids on English factories from 1811 to 1816 were protesting layoffs, low wages, and poor-quality goods, all caused by the large-scale introduction of textile machines to replace handicraft. The riots began in Nottingham and spread throughout England, the raiders directing their rage against the machines and systematically destroying them. Led by a "General" or "King Ludd"—named for a probably mythical Ned Ludd, said to have destroyed stocking frames in a Leicestershire factory thirty years earlier—the rioters soon became known as *Luddites*. Increasing prosperity in the country, combined with even more repressive measures, finally put them down. But not the memory of them. Today a Luddite is anyone who fears and would eliminate automation—not only for the unemployment it creates, but for its effect on the quality of life and for the human destruction that the machinery of war might cause. In our rebellion against an impersonal society, the word is used much more sympathetically than before. Indeed, some serious observers believe that the Luddites were right.

luff. (*See* **aloof.**)

lulus. The *lulus* we hear most about today are those taken by state legislators, who have been known to abuse them. A *lulu*, in this respect, is any tax-free item in an official expense account that is regarded as "in lieu of" part of a salary. The term is a recent one, dating back only twenty years or so, and apparently derives from the word "lieu." If it does, *lulu* is one of the simplest of reduplications, that is, new words formed from the repetition of elements in an older word. Like *mama* and *papa*, it contains one basic sound that is repeated. But some authorities think that *lulu* is just a special use of the earlier term *lulu*, for "any remarkable or outstanding person or thing." The earlier word has been traced back to 1886, and since it as often used to describe an attractive woman ("She's a real lulu") is thought to derive from the common girl's name Lulu, often a nickname for Louise. The *lulu*, or *loo* (*q.v.*), is a British euphemism for toilet.

lumber. Our story begins with the *Longobardi*, or long beards, a Germanic tribe that in about 568 invaded Italy, where their name became *Lombardi* in Italian, and settled the region now called Lombardy after them. The merchants of Lombardy, who gradually migrated to the area from all parts of Italy, eventually won fame or infamy as bankers, moneylenders, and pawnbrokers. In time, the moneymen and their *Lombards*, or pawnshops, radiated out from Milan and other parts of Lombardy to greener pastures. But *Lombard* came to be pronounced *Lumbard*, or *Lumber* in English. London's Lombard Street had its *Lombard shops*, pawnshops, and these had their *Lombard rooms*, storage rooms—all pronounced "lumber," too. Over the years the *Lumber* rooms on the street grew filled with unredeemed pledges on loans—large crates, cumbersome furniture, and other odds and ends that are still called *lumber* today. At this point, however, the word *lumber* was put to a new use. There are several explanations for the change, which is recorded as early as 1662. One is that American homesteaders in clearing their land for farming, left many discarded trees lying around, this clutter, or *lumber*, later cut or split into the wooden planks we know as lumber today. The word *lumber* for "to walk clumsily or heavily" does not derive from the Longbeards, coming directly from the Middle English verb *lomeren* meaning the same thing.

lummox. (*See* **dumb ox.**)

lunatic. *Lunatics* are literally "moon struck persons," the word deriving from the Latin *luna*, "moon." At least since Roman times it has been popularly believed that the mind is affected by the moon and that "lunatics grow more and more frenzied as the moon increases to full." Recorded in English as early as 1290, *lunatic* is no longer used medically. "The lunatic, the lover and the poet," wrote Shakespeare in *A Midsummer Night's Dream*, "are of imagination all compact." (*See* **looney tunes**.)

lurch. (*See* **leave in the lurch**.)

lush. Near Drury Lane Theatre in London was the Harp Tavern, where a club of hard drinkers called The City of Lushington had been founded in 1750. Lushington's had a chairman, the "Lord Mayor," and four "aldermen," who presided over the wards of Poverty, Lunacy, Suicide, and Jupiter (the supreme Roman god who presided over all human affairs). The club members, we are told, "were want to turn night into day," and by example their convivial fraternity may have given us another word for a sot, or habitual drunk. *Lush*, at least as a generic term for beer or drink, first appeared in about 1790, long after The City of Lushington's formation, and it could very well be a contraction of the club's name. For in years to come a number of phrases employed the name Lushington. *Alderman Lushington is concerned*, 1810, meant "somebody drunk;" *to deal with Lushington*, 1820, meant "to drink too much," as did *Lushington is his master*, 1825; and by 1840 *a Lushington* meant "a drunkard." Even before this a *lush cove* had become a slang term for a drunkard, and *lush* itself both a verb for "to drink" and an adjective meaning tipsy. By the end of the 19th century we finally find *lush* alone being applied to any habitual drunk, as it is to this day.

Lusitania. This famous British liner was named for the Roman province of Spain. One of the most famous ships in history because her sinking by a German submarine set America on the path into World War I; many Americans were among the 1,195 people on the *Lusitania* when she went down off Old Head of Kinsale in 1915. Most historians believe the tragedy was the fault of both a brutal submarine commander and the pigheaded skipper of the *Lusitania*, who refused to stay away from dangerous waters or even to speed through them. Some historians have also maintained that the *Lusitania* was surreptitiously carrying munitions.

Lutetia; Lutece. (*See* **Paris**.)

Luzon. When anchored in the Philippines, Magellan's men supposedly asked an old fisherman the name of the place nearest them. "*Luzon?*" the fisherman replied in Tagalog, meaning "What did you say?" But the sailors thought he meant the place was called *Luzon*, which remains the Philippine island's name to this day. Though quite possibly folk etymology, the story bears repeating, both for its entertainment value and for want of a better derivation. (*See also* **indir; llama; kangaroo; Nome; Yucatan**.)

Lycoris. Mark Antony is mainly remembered for his fatal romantic entanglement with Cleopatra, and it is often forgotten that he led a riotous life while a youth, having had four wives—Fadia, Antonia, Fulvia, and Octavia—before he committed suicide for his Egyptian queen. One of his outside interests was Lycoris, a Roman actress who became his mistress. Centuries later the English botanist Herbert named the six lovely fragrant flowers of the *Lycoris* genus after this beautiful woman. The amaryllis-like *Lycoris* grow from a bulb and are lilac-pink or pink, the flower cluster a loose umbel. Native to China, Japan, and central Asia, they are generally grown in greenhouses in the United States and England.

lyddite. (*See* **shimlose**.)

lynch. Our word for extralegal hanging definitely comes from the name of a man, but just who was the real Judge Lynch? At least a dozen men have been suggested as candidates for the dubious distinction. Scholarly opinion leans toward Virginia's Captain William Lynch (1742-1820), who was brought to light by Edgar Allan Poe in an editorial on "lynching" that he wrote in 1836 when he edited the *Southern Literary Messenger*. Poe claimed that the *lynch law* originated in 1780 when Captain Lynch and his followers organized to rid Pittsylvania County of a band of ruffians threatening the neighborhood. Poe even affixed a compact drawn up by Lynch and his men to the editorial. William Lynch's identity was further verified by Richard Venables, an old resident of the county, in the May 1859 issue of *Harper's Magazine*. But without evidence of any actual hanging there was still room for doubt. Finally, additional proof was found in the diary of the famous surveyor Andrew Ellicott, who visited Captain Lynch in 1811 and gained his friendship. William Lynch related how his *lynch-men*, as they were called, were sworn to secrecy and loyalty to the band. On receiving information accusing someone of a crime, the accused was seized and questioned before a court of sorts. If he did not confess immediately, he was horsewhipped until he did, and sometimes hanged whether he confessed or not.

M

M. *M* in the Phoenician alphabet represented the wavy appearance of water and was, in fact, called *mem*, "water," in Hebrew. In medieval times an *M* was branded on the brawn (fleshy part) of the left thumb of a person convicted of manslaughter. *M* is always pronounced in English, except in Greek words such as "mnemonics." In Roman numerals the capital letter *M* stands for 1,000 (Latin, *mille*).

macabre; danse macabre. *Macabre*, "gruesome, ghastly, or grim," comes directly from the *danse macabre*, or dance of death, which probably originated with a 14th-century German morality play eventually known throughout Europe. Death debates all his victims in this drama, winning his arguments with young and old, rich and poor, wise and foolish—and a weird dance ends the play as he leads his victims offstage. The dance of death survived in many allegorical paintings, sculptures, and tapestries, notably the engravings by Hans Holbein (1538), its popularity due to the overpowering awareness of death during the Hundred Years War and the Black Death, a plague that wiped out two-thirds of Europe's population. *La danse macabre* is believed by most scholars to have been suggested by and received its name from the dance of the seven martyred Maccabee brothers recounted in 2 Maccabees, an apocryphal book of the Old Testament. The Medieval Latin *chorea Machabaeorum* became corrupted to *danse macabre* in French, the adjective *macabre* not appearing in English until the end of the 19th century.

macadam; tarmac. Perhaps the smooth, perfectly drained miniature stone roads that John Loudon McAdam (1756-1836) built in his father's garden as a child inspired the first *macadam* roads, but his system seems to have been the improved version of an older French model. McAdam, a Scotsman whose name is also spelt Macadam and MacAdam, began experimenting in road-building at his own expense at Ayrshire and then at Falmouth, where he had moved in 1798, and his persistent efforts finally got him appointed as surveyor for all Bristol roads in 1815. McAdam had discovered that an expensive French roadbuilding method invented 20 years before his first experiments offered the best solution to the problem of drainage. The roads he began to build were layers of small, sharp-angled, broken stones placed over a drained, gently sloping roadbed, each layer compacted by the traffic that passed over it, and with water running off into ditches on each side. McAdam's roads revolutionized transportation, gradually replacing the common dirt road, and in 1827 he was made general surveyor for all highways in England. But his method was improved just as surely as he had improved on the French method. Subsequently his stone layers were crushed into the earth with heavy rollers and their surface coated with a bituminous covering, and these blacktop roads came to be called *macadam* or *tarmac* (a shortening of "tar" and "macadam") roads.

macadamia. *Macadamia*, a genus of Australian trees often called the Queensland nut and valued for its edible seeds, is not named for the roadbuilder John McAdam. It honors a Doctor John Macadam, secretary of the Victoria Philosophical Institute.

macaronic verse. This is verse where the poet mixes words of his own language with those of another language, forcing his native words to fit the grammar of the foreign tongue, his intention almost always comic or nonsensical. The form seems to have been popularized in 1517 by Italian poet Teofilo Folengo, who called it the literary equivalent of macaroni (which is of course commonplace and a mixture of a number of ingredients). The Germans call it *Nudelverse* (noodle verse). (*See* **spaghetti**.)

Machiavellian. A politician whose last name is a synonym for political immorality, Niccolò Machiavelli first conceived the idea of military conscription, and his first name was once thought to be the model for "Old Nick," or the devil. Not a man to be much loved in an age where honor is given great lip service, Machiavelli still wasn't all that bad. Through his famous book *The Prince*, Niccolò di Bernardo Machiavelli (1469-1527) has become known as the father of political science. But this remarkable work is remembered mainly for its insistence that while his subjects are bound by conventional moral obligations, a ruler may use any means necessary to maintain power, no matter how unscrupulous. Thus *Machiavellian* has come to mean cynical political scheming, generally brilliant and always characterized by deceit and bad faith. The legend of this thin-lipped, sarcastic, hyperactive man gave rise in later years to the theory that his first name was the basis for *Old Nick*, a synonym for the devil. No one really knows how *Old Nick* originated, but the Niccolò origin is wrong. The rumor stems from Samuel Butler's humorous identification in *Hudibras*: "Nick Machiavel had ne'er a trick/(Though he gives name to our Old Nick)."

machine politics. Volunteer firemen in the early 19th century learned to work smoothly as a team on the levers of water-pumping machines, and perhaps, as one investigator suggests, their well-organized political associations suggested the term *machine politics* for this reason. Aaron Burr, who converted New York's patriotic Tammany Society into the political Tammany Hall we know today, is often credited with inventing the phrase, but then so are Nathaniel Hawthorne and even the Duke of Wellington. The use of *machine* in a political sense, however, doesn't seem to have been recorded until 1865.

Mach number; Mach angle. *Mach number* is the ratio of the speed of a body to the speed of sound in air. Almost exclusively used to measure flight speed, it has only become common in the last few decades, as increased aircraft speeds have made old MPH measurements too cumbersome. *Mach 1*, for instance, is the speed of sound, 762 miles per hour at sea level, while *Mach 2* is twice the speed of sound. The word derives from the name of German scientist Ernst Mach (1838-1916), who died thirty-one years before Captain Charles Yeager first broke the sound barrier over Edwards Air Force Base in Muroc, California. (On October 14, 1947 Chuck Yeager flew his Bell X-I rocket plane at Mach 1.015.) Because of Mach's investigations into the supersonic speed of projectiles and the shock waves produced at these speeds both the measurement unit and the *Mach angle*, the angle a shock wave makes with the direction of flight, were named in his honor.

mackerel. *Mackerel* derives from the French *maquereau*, which is of unknown origin. One unproved story has the French word for the fish deriving from the French for "panderer" or "pimp," which is the same *maquereau*. According to this theory, the fish is so-named because it is popularly believed to lead female shads to their mates every spring!

Mackinaw blanket; Mackinaw coat. John S. Farmer, in *Americanisms Old and New* (1889) first gave the origins of this term common in America since about 1830: "A superior kind of blanket which derived its distinctive name from the island of Mackinaw, formerly one of the chief posts at which Indian tribes received their grants from the government. A provision of one of the Indian treaties was that part of the payment made to the redskins should be in these superior blankets, and from that fact the name *Mackinaw Blankets* or *Mackinaws* simply was derived." A *Mackinaw coat* is a coat made from a Mackinaw blanket, or from any blanket.

mackintosh. (*See* **rubber.**)

Madame Bovary. Gustave Flaubert and his publisher were charged with "immorality" when his great novel

Madame Bovary appeared in magazine form in 1856, but both were acquitted and the book was published a year later. The fictional Madame Bovary is based in part on Louise Colet (1810-76), a French poet and novelist with whom Flaubert carried on an affair for some nine years, beginning in 1846. The real Madame Bovary lived in Paris with her husband, Hippolyte Colet, and her affair with Flaubert was the author's only serious liaison. It is hard to see where Flaubert could have gained his amazing insights into feminine psychology except by his intimate observations of this woman. Louise Colet's story is told in her novel *Lui: roman contemporain* (1859). A *Madame Bovary* has come to mean a woman with an inflated, glamorized opinion of herself. Bovarism, a rare word which should have greater currency, means, to quote Aldous Huxley, "the power granted to man to conceive himself as other than he is," *bovaric* and *bovarize* deriving from it. Whether Louise Colet shared these qualities with Madame Bovary is debatable, but her name is linked with the words.

mad as a hatter. Lewis Carroll's Mad Hatter in *Alice in Wonderland* (1865) isn't responsible for this phrase. *Mad as a hatter*, "crazy, completely demented," was used by Thackeray in *Pendennis* (1849) and by that prolific American phrasemaker Thomas Haliburton in *The Clockmaker* (1837), almost thirty years before Carroll. Several explanations for the expression have been advanced. One holds that the term was originally *mad as an adder* (an adder being a venomous viper whose bite was once thought to cause insanity) and that British mispronunciation corrupted *adder* to *atter* and then *hatter*. The curious metaphor is best explained by hatmaking itself, though. The mercuric nitrate long used in making felt hats often poisoned hatters, the effects of this mercurial compound causing men who worked with it for years to be afflicted with uncontrollable twitching muscles, a lurching gait, incoherent speech, and confused minds.

mad as a march hare. Erasmus used the expression *mad as a marsh hare*, claiming that "hares are wilder in the marshes from the absence of hedges and cover." But Chaucer had the phrase *mad as a hare* before him, and *march hare* seems to have preceded *marsh hare* in use. Buck hares are wild frolickers in March, their breeding season, which has made them a synonym for lunacy for centuries. Lewis Carroll gave the expression new life with his creation of the March Hare in *Alice in Wonderland*.

mad as a wet hen. Hens don't become very upset from getting wet, so this old expression isn't a particularly apt one. An Americanism that dates back to the early 19th century, it was apparently based on the false assumption that a hen, being exclusively a land animal, unlike, say, the duck, would go beserk if caught in the rain or doused with water. Better was the old expression *wet hen*, for "a prostitute."

madcap scheme. Today a *madcap scheme* is a rash, reckless, wildly impulsive scheme, while a *madcap* is a person with the same characteristics. But in times past a madcap was simply a crazy person, the word deriving from *mad* for "crazy" and *cap* as a synonym for "head." This term, used by Shakespeare, is first recorded by his detractor Robert Greene, in 1589.

Madeira. The Portugese islands of Madeira off the west coast of North Africa give this fortified wine its name. *Madeira* is said to have originally had its unique taste because of the rolling motions of the ships that carried it on the long sea voyages to Europe.

madeleine. These small, rich, shell-shaped cakes are doubtless the most famous pastry in all literature. They are said to be named for their inventor, Madeleine Paulmier, a 19th-century pastry cook of Commeray, France, though André Simon and other gastronomes credit their invention to "one Avice, chief pastry cook to the Prince de Talleyrand." At any rate, Madeleine Paulmier and the anonymous Madeleine, for whom Avice may have named the cakes, both take their given names from Mary Magdalene. It was on a visit to his mother that Marcel Proust was served the scalloped *petite madeleine*, "so richly sensuous under its severe religious folds," whose taste brought back the flood of memories resulting in his 16-volume masterpiece *A la Recherche du Temps Perdu*. One cynic has called Proust's work "the tale of a man who fell in love with a cookie." Proust's fragile *madeleine*, made with flour, butter, sugar, and eggs, "the same weight of each," flavored with lemon rind and baked in a small but deep scallop-shaped mold, has no relation to the English sponge bun bearing the same name.

madstone. Any hard substance extracted from the digestive system of an animal (such as a hair ball in a deer's stomach) and used to treat the bites of mad dogs was called a *madstone* by Americans in the 19th century. Thousands of people believed that they were cured of snakebites, bee stings, spider stings, and other bites by madstones. Abraham Lincoln, in fact, had his son treated for dog bite with a madstone applied to his wound.

madwort. (*See* **alyssum**.)

maelstrom. Undoubtedly the best-known whirlpool in the world, the Maelstrom is found in the waters of the Lofoten Islands off Norway's west coast. *Maelstrom* is a Norwegian word deriving from the Dutch *malen* ("to grind or whirl"), and *strom* ("stream")—hence "grinding stream." A legend surrounding the Maelstrom has it that two magic millstones aboard a vessel sailing this passage

ground out so much salt that the ship foundered, but the millstones still continued to grind away underwater, making the surrounding waters "forever turbulent and salty." First used to describe this Norwegian phenomenon alone, the word since has come to mean all large whirlpools the world over and widespread turmoil in general.

Maevius. (*See* **Bavius**.)

Mae West. This inflatable life jacket was introduced at the beginning of World War II and named for one of the world's most famous sex symbols because it "bulged in the right places." Mae West (1893-1980) starred on Broadway until two of her plays, *Sex* and *Pleasure Man* were closed by the police in 1928. Migrating to Hollywood, she won fame as "Diamond Lil," the "Screen's Bad Girl," and the "Siren of the Screen." Her name, *Webster's* advises, is also given to a twin-turreted tank, a malfunctioning parachute with a two-lobed appearance, and a bulging sail.

magazine. "This Consideration has induced several Gentlemen to promote a Monthly collection to treasure up, as in a Magazine, the most remarkable Pieces on the Subjects abovemention'd," explained the editor of *Gentleman's Magazine* (1731), the first publication to be called a *magazine*. The word *magazine* itself, however, is from the Arabic *makhzan*, "storehouse," and has been used in that sense in English since the 16th century.

magenta. This red-purple dye was synthesized by French chemists in 1859, just after Napoleon had defeated the Austrians at Magenta in Italy. The reddish dye and its color were named in honor of the battle, because there was so much blood spilled there. Magenta, the place, had been named for a would-be Emperor of Rome, General Maxentius, who in 306 had established a camp there called Castra Maxentia, "Maxentius's camp," which came to be called simply Magenta.

magic lantern. The first magic lanterns were rude optical instruments employing a lens to cast a magnified image of a transparent picture drawn on glass onto a wall in a dark room. Such devices were known in Europe by the mid-17th century, but the first one called a *magic lantern* was the brainchild of a Danish inventor who exhibited it in France in 1665, the French dubbing the machine a *lanterne magique*.

Maginot line. André Maginot (1877-1932) barely escaped with his life in World War I when he was severely wounded during the defense of Verdun, but it was contaminated oysters that finally caused his death from typhoid. Decorated with the Cross of the Legion of Honor and the Médaille Militaire, the former sergeant, who had enlisted as a private despite the fact that he was French Undersecretary of War in 1913, returned to government service and eventually became Minister of Defense. Determined that France would never be invaded again, he and his generals proceeded to plan and have built a fortified wall along the eastern border from Switzerland to Belgium, a wall that extended 314 kilometers at $2 million per mile. The *Maginot line*, complete with self-sufficient forts dug seven floors deep into the earth, was meant to warn against surprise attacks from Germany in Alsace and Lorraine, but only engendered a false sense of security in France (which became known as the *Maginot mentality*), even though the wall was never extended to the coast. Maginot's death spared him from seeing his defenses easily bypassed by the Germans in World War II when they entered France through Belgium. The line's impregnability was never tested, but it could easily have been blasted by bombs, battered by tanks, or circumvented by paratroopers if it had been finished. The fault lay not so much with Maginot as with a war-weary country almost wanting to be lulled into a sense of false security.

Magna Charta. The *Magna Charta* is the "great charter" of English liberty that the nobles extorted from King John in 1215. It was intended to guard against abuses of power by the Crown, including the guarantee that no subject be kept in prison without trial and judgment by his peers.

magnolia. Like Matthias de L'Obel, for whom Linnaeus named the *lobelia*, Pierre Magnol (1638-1715) was a French physician and botanist who published a book classifying plants. Professor of botany at Montpelier University, Magnol had somehow obtained an education despite the fact that he had been denied entrance to French colleges because he was a Protestant. Through his courses in botany his name became celebrated, and Linnaeus honored him further by applying it to the beautiful magnolia tree upon devising his own monumental system of classification. The magnolia had been introduced into Europe from Japan in about 1709, but wasn't named for the professor until after his death. Linnaeus owed much to Magnol, who originated the system of family classificaton of plants, and picked a large plant family to honor him—*Magnoliacea*, including ten genera and over one hundred species. The magnolia family, native to Southeast Asia and the southeastern United States, contains some of the most beautiful garden shrubs and trees. Its lemon-scented fragrance was once used by the Chinese to season rice. The tree's huge, showy flowers, sometimes ten inches across, are commonly white, yellow, rose, or purple, appearing with or before the first leaves of spring, and the magnolia grows to heights of up to one hundred feet. Leaves of one species, the southern umbrella tree, are often two feet long, and the attractive

leaves of *Magnolia grandiflora* are used to fashion funeral wreaths. Mississippi calls itself *The Magnolia State*.

Magyar. *Magyar*, the language of the Hungarians, is unrelated to English, not stemming from the Indo-European languages like most European languages and belonging to a group that includes Finnish, Estonian, and Samoyed. Aside from meaning the Hungarian language, *Magyar* means "an individual of the Mongoloid race, now forming, numerically and politically, the predominant section of the inhabitants of Hungary." Magyar words that have come into English include *hussar, vampire, goulash, paprika,* and *coach*—from the Hungarian town of Kocs, where horse carriages were made.

Mahabharata; Ramayana. The longest poem in the world is the *Mahabharata*, which tells the story of the descendants of the Hindu King Bharata. *Mahabharata* means "the great Bharata," and the poem's 110,000 couplets, or 220,000 lines, make it four times longer than the Bible and eight times longer than Homer's *Iliad* and *Odyssey* combined. The Indian poem is really the combined work of many generations of writers, written between the years 400 B.C. and 150 B.C. Though its main theme is the war between descendants of Kuru and Pandu, it is a vast repository of philosophy and legend. The *Ramayana*, named after the god Rama, is another great Indian epic poem, containing 24,000 stanzas in seven books as we know it today.

Mahernia; Hermannia. One of the most unusual words, the plant genus *Mahernia* is an anagram of *Hermannia*, another genus to which it is closely allied. Linnaeus must have been in a playful mood when he coined the word from *Hermannia*, which he had also named. Linnaeus named *Hermannia* for Paul Hermann (1646-95), a professor of botany at the University of Leyden, who is surely the only man to be honored by two genera in this odd way. *Hermannia* is a large genus, including some 80 species of ornamental, greenhouse evergreen shrubs, their flowers usually yellow. The closely related anagram genus, *Mahernia*, includes about 30 species, which are pretty greenhouse herbs or small undershrubs of which the yellow, fragrant honeybell (M. *verticillata*) is most notable. Both genera are native to South Africa. (*See also* **mho; Quisqualis.**)

mah-jongg. (*See* **Chinese language.**)

Maidenhead. Legend has it that the English town of *Maidenhead* is so named because the severed head of one of 11,000 virgins martyred in Cologne, Germany is buried there. Actually, only one virgin, named Undecemilla, was beheaded in Cologne centuries ago and later elevated to sainthood. But in transcribing her saint's day to the Roman Catholic Church calendar a scribe erred, indicating in shorthand Latin that on her day, *Undecem militia Virg. Mart.*, "eleven thousands of virgins were martyred," And not even Undecemilla is buried in Maidenhead. She has nothing to do with the town's name, which is a corruption of the town's older name, Maydenhythe, a "dock midway" between two other towns.

mailed fist.   The term *mailed fist* means "aggressive military might" and though it refers to the mail armor of the medieval knight, who even wore steel gloves, it came into use only in relatively recent times. The phrase derives from an order Kaiser Wilhelm II of Germany gave to his brother, Prince Henry of Prussia, when he sent him to China in 1897 at the head of forces that were to restore order after two German missionaries had been killed. "If any man dares impugn our right," the Kaiser declared, "smite him with your mailed fist!"

Maine.   The Pine Tree State, admitted to the Union in 1820 as our 23rd state, had previously been called the Province of Maine, taking this name from a province in France.

main liner.   The main line of the Pennsylvania Railroad borders an exclusive suburban area just northwest of Philadelphia. Hence the expression *main liner*, for "a wealthy, socially prominent person, a member of the upper crust." The expression isn't heard as much anymore as the other *mainliner*, "a drug addict who takes his narcotics by intravenous injection."

Main Street.   *Main Street* is the typically American designation for the principal thoroughfare in a town, while the British synonym is High Street (the *high* denoting importance, not elevation). In early Colonial days, along the East Coast, there were High Streets, some surviving today, but *high* came to suggest elevation in America as the pioneers moved inland toward the mountains.

Maintenon.   Born in 1635 in a French prison where her father was being held as a counterfeiter, Françoise D'Aubigné's life seemed to grow no better as she grew to young womanhood. She married the famous comic poet Paul Scarron while still a girl of sixteen, serving mainly as his nurse until his death in 1660. Several years later she finally got a break of sorts when the King's mistress, Madame Montespan, interceded with Louis XIV to put her in charge of their illegitimate children. Gradually she supplanted Montespan in the Sun King's esteem, and in time he made her the Marquise de Maintenon. Madame de Maintenon became Louis's *maitresse en titre* when Montespan left the court and was even a great favorite of Queen Marie Thérèse, who died in her arms in 1683. Two years later Louis married his older, official mistress in a secret ceremony. Maintenon's influence on court life was considerable, though it has probably been exaggerated as concerns matters of state. Madame de Maintenon was no slouch as a cook, and her name is remembered in *lamb chops à la Maintenon* and other creations, in addition to being a synonym for "a mistress." She died in 1719, four years after Louis. (*See* **lavaliere; Montespan; Pompadour.**)

maize.   (*See* **corn.**)

makari.   *Makari* are poets, from the rare word *makar* (a variant of "maker") an archaic Scottish term for poet.

make a clean breast of it.   "That man of peace . . . hath been entrusted with King's breasts," someone wrote of an early diplomat. *Breast* has been a synonym for the heart since ancient times and, like the organ it houses, was long thought to be the seat of consciousness, the repository of all private thoughts, emotions, and secrets. To memorize something was to *know it on breast* as well as *learn it by heart* and a person burdened by guilt had a *stained breast*. These expressions are obsolete now, but the phrase *to make a clean breast*, "to make a full confession or disclosure," has remained part of the language since the early 18th century. One suspects that it is much older, going back to days "when men had breasts like lions" and ceremonial heart burials like Robert Bruce's were common in England.

make a mountain out of a molehill.   In his "Ode to a Fly" the ancient Greek satirist Lucian conveyed this same idea, "to give something much greater importance than it deserves." His "to make an elephant out of a fly" remains a French and German proverb to this day, but for some unknown reason the expression never passed directly into English. Instead, the elephant became a "mountain" and the fly a "molehill." Foxe's *Book of Martyrs* (1570) first recorded "makeying mountaines of Molehils."

to make a scene.   The display involved in *making a scene*, "making a disturbance, usually in public," suggests that the expression is theatrical in origin. Strong emotions often portrayed in short scenes of stage plays probably are responsible for the phrase. In fact, the first literary use of the idea is in Samuel Foote's farce *The Liar* (1762), where one of the characters says, "We parted this moment. Such a scene!"

make both ends meet.   This phrase seems to be merely a shortening of *to make both ends of the year meet*, meaning the same—"to live within one's income." Smollett first recorded the saying in his picaresque novel *The Adventures of Roderick Random* (1748).

make bricks without straw.   Trying to do anything without the proper tools or materials is said to be *making* *bricks without straw.* The expression goes back to biblical times and is found in Exodus, it being necessary to make bricks with chopped straw to prevent them from shrinking and cracking as they dry.

to make fur fly. The cruel "sport" of trapping raccoons and setting dogs on them to see how long the coons could last may have suggested this expression to American pioneers. Certainly the air was filled with fur during such fights. By at least 1825 the saying meant "to attack violently." In the autobiographical *A Narrative of the Life of David Crockett, of the State of Tennessee* (1834) we read: "I knew very well that I was in the devil of a hobble, for my father had been taking a few horns, and was in a good condition to make the fur fly."

make hay while the sun shines. Sun is the best and cheapest way to dry grass for fodder, and this proverb thus reminds us to take full advantage of any opportunity before it passes. "When the sunne shinth make hay," John Heywood wrote in his *All the Proverbes in the English Tongue* (1546), and the saying has been a common one ever since.

make my day. This expression is first attested in Florence Barclay's 1909 novel *The Rosary*, where a character says: "I knew I wanted her; knew her presence made my day and her absence meant chill night . . ." *Make*, however, had been used as a verb meaning "to secure the success of" (as in *Clothes make the man*), since the 16th century. Today *go ahead and make my day* has come to mean "give me the chance to do what I'd like to do—to hurt you badly!" The expression was popularized by the Clint Eastwood character Dirty Harry (a tough police detective) in the recent movie *Sudden Impact.*

make no bones about it. Someone who talks frankly or straight from the shoulder about a subject *makes no bones about it.* Possibly the phrase refers to "not making much" of the dice or bones when rolling them in a dice game, but the theory seems farfetched. The allusion is probably to a person making no fuss or objection about eating soup or stew if there are bones in it. (*I can't swallow that, I can't stomach that,* and *That sticks in my craw* are other expressions in which acceptability is related to terms of eating.) *Make no bones about it* is an ancient saying; Nicholas Udall's translation of Erasmus's *Paraphrase of Luke* in 1548 relates that Abraham, when commanded to sacrifice Isaac, "made no bones about it . . . but went to offer up his son."

make one's gorge rise. Hunting falcons are fierce, gluttonous creatures that store the food they eat in a pouch called the crop, or gorge. Their trainers in medieval times noticed that they frequently overate and vomited part of their food, which came to be called *gorge,* after the pouch it came from. To *make one's gorge rise* therefore became a synonym for "to make someone sick." The saying at first indicated extreme disgust and later expressed strong resentment, so that today the phrase means to make a person violently angry.

to make one's hair stand on end. Surprisingly, this metaphor isn't recorded before 1530, in a French phrase, but the idea behind it is found in the Bible (Job 4: 14-15): "Fear came upon me and trembling . . . the hair of my flesh stood up." The hair on cats, humans, and other animals can stand on end and become rigid with fear; the tiny muscles controlling this reaction are so effective that even baldheaded men feel a prickling of the scalp from sudden terror. An English clergyman at an execution in the early 19th century observed the following: "When the executioner put the cords on the criminal's wrists, his hair, though long and lanky . . . rose gradually and stood perfectly upright, and so remained for sometime, and then fell gradually down again."

to make one's mouth water. In his *The Decades of the Newe Worlde or West India* (1555) historian Richard Eden wrote: "These Craftie foxes . . . espying their enemies afarre of, beganne to swalowe theyr spittle as their moths watered for greediness of theyr pray." No one knows who invented the phrase *to make one's mouth water,* "to salivate in anticipation, to look forward to something eagerly," yet it is interesting that this first known use of the expression had reference not to any gourmet food as we know it today but to human meat that West Indian cannibals spotted in the distance.

to make the grade. A train that makes the grade is one that manages to surmount a steep grade, or slope. Probably someone coined the expression which means "to win despite great obstacles," after a long, heavy effort laboring up a steep hill. But the phrase, which has been traced to only about 1930, may derive from milk making the grade, "reaching a proper standard" and being good enough to be labeled Grade A.

make the horn. The Greek hunter Actaeon came upon Artemis bathing and, either because he saw her naked or because he had boasted that he was a better hunter than she, the goddess of wildlife (she is called Diana in Roman mythology) changed him into a stag and he was torn to pieces by his own hounds. Because he had had horns—at least for a short time—Actaeon's name became a synonym for a man with an unfaithful wife. In fact, *to actaeon,* now obsolete, was once a verb meaning "to cuckold." No one really knows why horns are a symbol of cuckoldry, but one guess is that stags, which are of course horned, have their harems taken from them in the rutting season by stronger males. At any rate, *making the horn*—thrusting out a fist with the first and last fingers extended—has been a gesture of contempt, implying a person is a cuckold, since Roman times.

to make things hum.   Since at least the early 18th century, humming, suggesting the blending of many human voices or the activity of busy bees, has been used to express a condition of busy activity. Two hundred years later the expression *to make things hum* was invented in America. Possibly the hum of machines in New England textile factories was the inspiration for the phrase, in reference to the fabled Yankee mechanics who made things hum again when the machines broke down.

make whoopee.   *Whoopee* has been an American exclamation of joy or approval since about 1860. However, it was apparently newspaper columnist Walter Winchell who coined the expression *making whoopee*, for "wild merrymaking," the expression then made very familiar by the popular song "Making Whoopee" (1930).

mako shark.   A New Zealand Indian fisherman named Mooris is said to have hunted this shark for its long center tooth, hunted it so well in his canoe that the shark was named for him. It may, however, be named for the Maori of New Zealand, who also hunted it in canoes. The *mako shark (Isurus oxyrinchus)*, also called the mackerel shark, is found in both the Pacific and the Atlantic—not to mention seafood restaurants. (*See* **kiwi**.)

Malagasy words in English.   Malagasy, the Malayo-Polynesian language of Madagascar, has contributed several words to English, including *bantam* and *kapok*.

malakoff.   Malakoff, or Malakhov, a fortified hill overlooking Sevastopol from the east, was the scene of one of the most publicized battles of the Crimean War. After a long siege, the French finally stormed Malakoff and took it on September 8, 1855. The historic hill is supposed to be named for a drunken Russian sailor who set up a liquor shop on the heights after being fired from his job in the Sevastopol shipyards. Houses and finally fortifications were built around him and he ultimately won more fame than most of his more sober contemporaries. At one time a crinoline also honored the man's name and today the reformed drunkard is remembered by *malakoff*, a form of four-handed dominoes, and for *malakoff*, a small French cream cheese, both of which commemorate the battle fought on his famous hill.

malamute.   This blue-eyed Arctic dog, descended from the wolf, is named for the Eskimo tribe called the Malemuit, who originally bred the breed of sled dogs.

malapropism.   "Then, sir, she should have a supercillious knowledge in accounts;—and as she grew up, I would have her instructed in geometry, that she might know something of the contagious countries . . . and likewise that she might repreheand the true meaning of what she is saying." The preceding is a speech of Mrs. Malaprop in the first act of Richard Brinsley Sheridan's *The Rivals*. Mrs. Malaprop is the name of an affected talkative woman in the play, the aunt of the heroine, Lydia Languish. Sheridan coined her name from the French *mal à propos*, "unsuitable, out of place," for he had her ludicrously misuse many "high sounding" words out of her ignorance and vanity, just as Shakespeare had Dogberry do in *Much Ado About Nothing* and had Mistress Quickly do in *Henry IV, Parts I & II*. Sheridan's *The Rivals* was produced in London in 1775, when he was only twenty-four. Mrs. Malaprop's name soon became a synonym for the misuse of words, especially by those who are trying to sound important. (*See* **Goldwynism; slipslop**.)

Malay, Tamil, and Telegue words in English.   These Dravidian languages give us a number of English words, including *calico, mango, copra, curry, coolie, pariah, junk, atoll, teak, ketchup, bamboo, gong, orangutang, fetish, caste, anaconda, catamaran,* and *mulligatawny*.

male.   (*See* **female**.)

mall.   (*See* **shopping mall**.)

Malpighian.   His name is not well known outside scientific textbooks, but the Italian physiologist Marcello Malpighi (1628-1694) deserves recognition as the founder of microscopic anatomy, the discoverer of the movement of blood through the capillaries, which completed the theory of circulation formulated by William Harvey, and for his pioneer work in the study of plant and animal tissues. Malpighi, a professor of medicine at Messina University, later served as private physician to Pope Innocent XII. He was one of the first men to use the microscope to study animal and vegetable tissue and the first to attempt an anatomical description of the brain with this instrument. He is commemorated by several words, including the *Malpighiaceae* family of ornamental tropical plants. The technical terms *Malpighian corpuscle, Malpighian layer, Malpighian tube,* and *Malpighian tuft* recall his important work in anatomy.

malted milk.   *Malted milk*, used today for the popular soda fountain drink made of malt, milk, ice cream, and syrup, was once a trademark for a baby food. In 1881 James and William Horlick patented a dried extract of wheat, malted barley, and whole milk "For infants, Invalids, the Aged, and Travelers." The inventors coined the trademark *Malted Milk*, which they enjoyed for many years until it was infringed upon and was eventually applied to the ubiquitous fountain drink.

Malthusian.   Thomas Robert Malthus (1766-1834), an English curate, published his *An Essay on the Principle of*

Population As It Affects the Future Improvement of Society in 1798, and his name almost immediately aroused a storm of controversy throughout the world. His essay contained what came to be called the *Malthusian theory*: that population increases faster, geometrically, than the means of subsistence, which increases arithmetically. According to this theory, population would always outstrip food supply unless checked by natural controls such as war, disease, or famine. Malthus later revised and refined his pessimistic outlook, including a control that he called "moral restraint"—late marriage and sexual abstinence. Most of the economist's predictions haven't been borne out, but his analysis remains correct in many respects and the Malthusian principle still operates in parts of the world where the birthrate has not dropped through birth-control practices. A *Malthusian* is one who accepts the pioneer demographer's theory, or, more generally, an advocate of birth control. It is interesting to note that Charles Darwin was struck by the phrase "struggle for existence" when reading Malthus's *Essay*, the words stimulating him "to find the key to biological change in the process of natural selection."

mama; mammal. (*See* **babe**.)

mamelle. (*See* **Grand Tetons**.)

mammon; the mammon of unrighteousness. *Mammon* became the personification of greed or a passion for money, the god of this world, only in medieval times. In the Bible the word (from the Syriac *mamuna*) means riches or gain, as in "Ye cannot serve God and mammon" (Matt. 6:24) or "The mammon of unrighteousness" (Luke 16:9). In Ben Jonson's *The Alchemist* (1610), Sir Epicure Mammon is a wordly sensualist, a greedy, voluptuous knight who is conned by the alchemist.

mammoth. Some scholars believe that a Tatar word, *mamont*, "earth," gives us the word *mammoth*, first recorded in 1698. According to this theory, when huge bones of a prehistoric creature were dug up in southern Russia, the Tatars believed the animal had been a huge mole that lived underground and gave it their name for earth. Over the years *Mamont* changed in spelling to *mammoth* and in meaning to *any* huge thing.

mamser; momser. Some Hebrew words have been standard in English for centuries. *Mamser*, for example, first recorded in 1562, was frequently used to mean "bastard" during the Middle Ages, and people were familiar with the word from its use in Deut. 23:3. *Mamser* became obsolete by the late 19th century, but is still heard in the Yiddish *momser*, meaning the same and a half-dozen other things, including: an untrustworthy man, a difficult man, and impudent man, a detestable man, a scalawag, and even a clever, quick fellow.

man. (*See* **woman**.)

man about town. This expression has been popular since the mid-17th century, for "a fashionable person who is often seen at public and private functions." *Girl about town*, invented at about the same time, is rarely, if ever, used anymore.

manager. *Managers* were originally horse trainers, the word *manage* deriving from the Italian *maneggiare*, meaning "to train horses." But not long after *manage* was introduced in England the word came to be applied to the military, meaning to handle weapons as well as horses and then to conduct a war. By the late 16th century it had assumed its current meaning.

man bites dog. "If a dog bites a man," editors used to instruct cub reporters, "that's an ordinary occurrence. But when a man bites a dog, that's *news*." The inspiration for both the advice and the saying *man bites dog* can be traced back to Oliver Goldsmith's poem "Elegy on the Death of a Mad Dog" (1757), about a dog that "went mad and bit a man," which concludes with the lines:

> The man recover'd of the bite,
> The dog it was that died.

According to *Partridge*, this touching poem passed into folklore in a number of versions, possibly including a funny one where a man *did* bite a dog, and finally became the journalistic advice.

mandarin orange. This fruit either takes its name from the orange, flowing robes of Chinese mandarin officials or from the superiority implied in the title "mandarin." The word is first recorded in an 1816 botanical treatise.

a man doesn't get his hands out of the tar by becoming second mate. During the age of sail only the *first* mate was exempted from the dirty work of sticking his hands into the tar bucket for tarring the rigging. Hence this British expression, which probably originated in the 18th century, is used colloquially to indicate that responsibilities don't end with promotion.

mandrake. The "magical" mandrake was at first called the *mandragora* in Latin, because its root uncannily resembles a miniature man and it was as magical or awe-inspiring as a dragon. But in medieval times the word for dragon was *drake*, so the plant became known as a *mandrake*. Like ginseng roots, and even peony roots to some extent, the roots of mandrake were associated with many fantastic beliefs. One theory claimed they were an aphrodisiac (especially if shaped like a woman); another held that they caused barrenness in women; still another claimed they could cure any illness. Many people believed that mandrake would shriek like a human when uprooted and that one should not touch the roots when pulling them up. To avoid the last, a dog was actually tied to the plant to tug it out of the ground after the soil around it had been loosened!

man for breakfast.   Lawlessness often went unpunished in the American West and people reading their morning newspapers had their *man for breakfast*, or murder, every day. The expression persisted from the late 19th century well into the 20th century.

man Friday; girl Friday.   The cheerful, hardworking companion of Robinson Crusoe in the 1719 novel of that title by Daniel Defoe gives his name to both *man Friday*, "a male general helper," and his modern-day female counterpart. *Girl Friday* is more often *gal Friday* today.

Manhattan; Manhattanization.   According to one statistician, the Algonquin Manhattan Indians who sold Manhattan Island to the Dutch for $24 in trinkets probably got the better of the deal. He figures that if the Indians had invested their $24 at the prevailing interest rate, they would now have some $13 billion—$4 billion more than the value of all the real estate in Manhattan. Since 1898 *Manhattan* has been the name of New York's central borough, and has always been a synonym for New York City itself. From the Manhattan Indians, indirectly, we also have the *Manhattan cocktail*, made with whiskey, sweet vermouth, and bitters, first mixed about 1890; *Manhattan clam chowder*, made with tomatoes, unlike the traditional New England milk clam chowder; and *Manhattan District*, the code name for the project that developed the first atomic bomb. *Manhattanization* is a word that seems to have originated only recently. In the 1971 fall elections, San Francisco residents were urged to vote for an amendment halting the construction of tall buildings to avoid the Manhattanization, or gentrification, of San Francisco.

the man in the gray flannel suit.   *The man in the gray flannel suit* remains a synonym for a conformist corporation man, although dress styles have changed considerably in the business world since Sloan Wilson coined the phrase in his novel *The Man in the Gray Flannel Suit* (1957).

the man in the street; man of the cars.   The "ordinary" or "average" person. The first term is recorded in 1831, when British statesman Charles Greville refers to it as a racing term in his diary. A similar 19th-century American phrase was *man of the cars*, referring to the streetcars of the time.

man is a wolf to man.   Both *Bartlett's* and *The Oxford Dictionary of Quotations* attribute this expression, in a slightly different form, to Bartolomeo Vanzetti in his eloquent last speech to the Massachusetts court trying him and Nicola Sacco on charges of robbery and murder in 1927. But the expression is much, much older. In 1577 a British author wrote: "Lyons doo not one encounter another, the Serpent stingeth no Serpent: but Man is a Woolfe to Man." The expression was afterward used by many writers, including Cowper.

Manitoba.   The Canadian province *Manitoba* is named for God, or Manitou, the Great Spirit of the Algonquins.

a man of few words.   Shakespeare wrote that "men of few words are the best men." This expression for a laconic, taciturn person who is often "a man of action" was born several centuries before the Bard, however, being first recorded in about 1450.

man of letters.   First attested in English in 1645, *man of letters* may come from the French *homme de lettres*. Originally the term meant "a scholar, a man of learning," but today it is mostly applied to authors, critics, or literary scholars.

a man of men.   *A man of men* or *a man among men* means an excellent man, the kind one encounters once or twice in a lifetime, if at all. Christopher Marlowe first recorded the term in 1594, and Shakespeare, the writer of writers, used it not long after.

a man of straw; straw man.   A man made of straw would certainly be one without a heart or conscience, so that this expression is apt for "an unscrupulous person who will do anything for gain." However, the words may refer to real "straw men," who in the past loitered near English courts with a straw in one of their shoes—this indicating that they would be willing to give false testimony or swear to anything in court for enough money.

the man of Sumter.   General P.G.T. Beauregard (1818-93) is known as *the man of Sumter* in American history because he headed the forces that bombarded Fort Sumter, South Carolina on April 12, 1861 to begin the Civil War. His troops called him "Old Borey" or "Peter."

man of the cloth.   It wasn't until the 17th century that *man of the cloth* was applied to a clergyman of any faith. Until then the term had meant anyone wearing any uniform in his work.

the man of the Revolution.   The patriot called *the man of the Revolution* in American history isn't George Washington, as one might suspect. Samuel Adams has the honor "because of the leading part he played in bringing about the War of Independence."

the man on the horse. We know that this expression meaning "the person in authority or in charge" is an Americanism, but it is first recorded in England. In 1887 a British newspaper writer noted: "The man on the horse . . .to use the picturesque American phrase, is not now Lord Salisbury." No doubt the expression dates back at least twenty years earlier, perhaps to Civil War days.

man proposes, God disposes. These words were probably proverbial long before they appeared in William Langland's *The Vision Concerning Piers the Plowman* (1362). The form is often *man proposes, but God disposes.*

mansard. This type of roof, unlike the conventional peaked shape, has a double, almost vertical, slope on each side, with the upper part almost flat. *Mansard* refers to the roof and the high room under it, both designed by Nicolas François Mansart (1598-1666), a French architect of the Renaissance who is generally known as François Mansard. The roof he devised allows for high-ceilinged attics and was widely adopted by Victorian architects. Mansard's great Church of Val-de-Grace, Paris, is said to have influenced Christopher Wren's plan for London's St. Paul's Cathedral. One of the most influential architects of his time, his pure classical designs have been an inspiration to others for centuries. Mansard, the son of a carpenter to the king, was chosen to design the Louvre, but refused to allow his design to be altered during construction, and so the Italian Bertini replaced him. His nephew Jules Hardouin-Mansart designed the magnificent Hall of Mirrors at the Palace of Versailles, the Hôtel des Invalides (which houses Napoleon's tomb), and the Place Vendôme, among other architectural masterpieces.

manticore The *manticore*, a vampiric man-eating monster of ancient times, takes its name from the Persian *martya*, "man," and *xvar*, "to eat." The mythical monster is first mentioned by the Greek physician Ktesias in the 5th century B.C. It was usually represented as a monster the size of a horse with the body and claws of a lion, but it was depicted in many ways, sometimes with the head of a man and the breasts of a woman.

Mantuan Swan. (*See* **swan song.**)

manufacture. Mass-produced products that are *manufactured* on assembly lines in the world's factories would be made by hand if we took the word's meaning literally. For *manufacture* derives from the Latin *manu*, "by hand," and *factura*, "a making," from which our word *factory* also derives.

manure. *Manure* originally meant "to work by hand," to do manual labor, especially to work the soil by manual labor, deriving from the Old French verb *manouvrer*, meaning the same. The English verb yielded the noun *manuere*, which at first meant "the action of cultivating the soil" and was extended to include the dung put into the soil when a euphemism was wanted for "dung."

the man without a country. Contrary to what many people have believed since grade school, Edward Everett Hale's famous story "The Man Without a Country" is fictional. Only the name of the main character is real. In the story Lt. Philip Nolan cries out, "Damn the United States! I wish I may never hear of the United States again!" and is of course sentenced to sail the seas all his life on a Navy ship without ever hearing his country's name again. Nothing like this ever happened to the real Philip Nolan, an adventurer whose career Hale used as background. Hale later regretted using the man's name and wrote a book called *Philip Nolan's Friends* (1876), "to repair my fault, and to recall to memory a brave man," as he put it.

many happy returns. Up until the 19th century this was a New Year's Day and even April Fool's Day greeting as well as the birthday greeting that it exclusively is today. What the words wish, of course, is that the happy day returns again many times, not the hope that one will get many "returns," or birthday presents, as some children think.

many small potatoes and few to a hill. New Englanders, especially Mainers, use this expression for something or somebody of small consequence. It dates back about a century.

Maori words in English. Maori has contributed several words to the English language, including *kiwi* and *mako*.

maple syrup; maple sugar. "There can't be a remedy better for fortifying the stomach" than maple sugar, a pioneer wrote in 1705. *Maple sugar*, boiled from *maple syrup* and the only sugar the first settlers had, has a long history that dates from the time American pioneers learned how to make it from the Indians. The same, of course, applies to *maple syrup*, another maple-tree product Americans are still familiar with, but there were also maple-derived products like *maple water, maple vinegar, maple molasses, maple wax, maple beer*, and even *maple wine*.

Marcel wave, marcelling. Every hairdresser might wish to have the success Marcel Grateau had with his curling iron. In 1875, when only 23, this Frenchman invented *marcelling*, a process that makes soft, continuous waves in the hair. The *Marcel wave* became so popular with Parisian women, and women everywhere, that Marcel Grateau made a fortune and was able to retire before turning 30. He lived a long life of luxury in an elegant chateau, and just before his death in 1936, aged 84,

France's hairdressers held a week-long celebration honoring him and his contribution to their craft.

March. When spring came in days of old the Romans apparently thought it was a better time to make war than love. Anyway, they named the month, then the first month of the new year, for Mars, the god of war, perhaps in the hope that he would help them in their spring campaigns.

Mardi Gras. *Mardi Gras*, literally "fat Tuesday" in French, takes its name from the fat ox (*boeuf gras*) paraded through Parisian streets in ancient times by mock priests at the head of the carnival procession on the day before the beginning of Lent. The fat ox was a reminder of the abstinence from meat during the coming Lenten season of fasting and prayer. Called Shrove Tuesday in England, and previously Pancake Tuesday because pancakes were traditionally served on the day before Ash Wednesday, the festival of Mardi Gras may have its origins in the old Roman fertility festival of Lupercalia once held at the same time of the year.

Marenisco, Michigan. Another unusual place name, *Marenisco*, Michigan, was coined from the first syllables of the *four* names of its first woman settler: *Mary Relief Niles Scott*.

margarine. The Latin *margarita*, "pearl," is the ancestor of *margarine*, which, before dyes were commonly added, was a white, pearl-like substance extracted from hog's lard. *Oleomargarine* (from the Latin *oleum*, "oil," + *margarine*) was coined first, in 1854, by the French chemist Berthelot, and shortened to *margarine* in the U.S. by 1873.

marigold. There are several genera whose flowers are called *marigold*, the chief ones being *Tagetes*, which includes the misnamed French and African *marigolds* among about thirty other species, and *Calendula*, a genus that counts the popular *pot marigold* among its twenty species. The flower was found by the early Crusaders and brought back to Europe, where it was probably named after the Virgin Mary and its golden color, being called "Mary's gold" or "Marygold" before it became the *marigold*. Linnaeus gave the pot marigold its scientific designation, *Calendula officinalis*, but he merely used a name that had been given to the plant centuries before. For the herbalist Gerad remarks that the name *Calendula* was bestowed upon the plant because it supposedly bloomed regularly "in the calends" or first days of almost every month, *calends* meaning the first of the Roman month. The *pot marigold* was once used as a poultice for wounds and is still grown as a flavoring for soups and other dishes. *Calendula officinalis* differs from the so-called French and African species mainly in that its leaves are not strong smelling. But the flowers of the *Tagetes* genus, also herbs, do resemble the *pot marigold*, and early American settlers gave them the same name. *Tagetes* possibly honors the Etruscan god Tages, but this is not certain. All flowers of the genus are native from North Mexico to the Argentine, which does make the marigold an ideal candidate for our national flower, although Congress recently voted the rose this honor.

marijuana. *Cannabis sativa* goes by some 200 names in practically every language throughout the world, including *pot, grass, seed, weed, tea, dope, reefers, joints*, and *Texas tea*. But the hemp plant's crushed leaves, flowers, and, sometimes, twigs, are best known as *marijuana*. The word comes from the Spanish prenomens *Maria* and *Juana*, translating as *Maryjane*, and no one knows why. The Chinese used *Cannabis* at least five thousand years ago, and George Washington is said to have grown it at Mount Vernon—for the rope produced from the hemp. One hundred years ago, according to the National Institute of Mental Health, "extracts of *Cannabis* were as commonly used for medicinal purposes in the United States as aspirin today."

marine. The term *marine* for a type of soldier didn't originate with the U.S. Marines but dates back to the early 17th century when the word (from the Latin *marinus*, "of the sea") was used in England to describe specially trained soldiers serving on British warships.

Marinism. II Cavalier Marino, as the pompous Neapolitan poet Giambattista Marino (1569-1625) was called, headed the *seicento* school of Italian literature, which became noted for its flamboyance and bad taste. Poems like his 45,000-line *Adone* show brilliant mastery of technique but were intended to dazzle the reader at any cost, their extravagance leading to his name standing for any florid, bombastic style, pages full of sound but signifying nothing. Marino, or Marini, had his trouble with censors, too. His satirical works were not appreciated by his satirized patrons and he was forced to leave Italy, taking refuge in Paris for eight years before he could return home safely.

marivaudage. Important advances in the development of the novel were made by French writer Pierre Carlet de Chamblain de Marivaux (1688-1763), who is undeserving of his fate at the hands of the dictionaries. *Marivaudage*, however, means an affected, overstrained style, as exemplified by the witty bantering of lovers in his two unfinished novels and thirty plays. Marivaux's subtle, graceful works are mostly excellent psychological studies of middle-class psychology and led a contemporary to remark that his characters not only tell each other and the reader everything they have thought, but everything that they would like to persuade themselves that they have thought. *Marivaudage* has also been described as "the metaphysics of love making." The author was much admired in his own time, though not by Voltaire, whose work he criticized, and it is said that Madame de Pompadour secretly provided him with a large pension.

marjoram. *Marjoram* is any of several mints, including *sweet marjoram* and *pet marjoram*. The old saying *as a pig loves marjoram* (that is, not at all) is still heard occasionally. *Marjoram* is an alteration of the Latin *amaracus* for the herb.

Mark Antony's wig. Cleopatra reputedly gave the virile but balking Mark Antony a wig made of her pubic hairs, and *Mark Antony's wig* was later brought back to Rome. According to the old story, this wig was worn by many Roman emperors on "revel evenings" and finally presented to the Pope by Constantine in 328. The papal treasures supposedly included a sporran of pubic hair that the Queen of Sheba had lost to Solomon in a riddling contest, and this was allegedly added to the wig and presented to England's licentious Charles II by Pope Clement X as part of an attempt to convert his kingdom to Catholicism. Charles, it is said, added pubic hairs plucked from his mistresses before he tired of plucking and gave the wig to the Earl of Moray, who donated it to his club of ribald rakehells called the Ancient and Most Puisant Order of the Beggar's Benison and Merryland. There the head of the Order wore the wig at all ceremonies, and initiates were required to augment it with pubic hairs of their wives or mistresses. *Mark Antony's wig* was last heard of when some members of the Order reportedly absconded with it in 1775 and formed a new group called The Wig Club. (*See* **Cleopatra's pearl**.)

market. The Latin word *mercari*, "to trade," altered to *markatte* and finally *market*, came to be applied, by the 12th century, to the place where the trading took place. The word may possibly have been used three to four hundred years before that.

mark of Cain. The *mark of Cain* is not described in the Bible, which simply says in Gen. 4:15: "And the Lord put a mark on Cain . . ." The mark was not made to identify Cain as a murderer, but to warn the world that Cain was condemned to be forever "a fugitive and a vagabond . . . in the earth," i.e., that it was forbidden to kill him. Cain, the first born of Adam and Eve, and the first biblical murderer, through jealousy slew his brother Abel, and lied to the Lord that he did not know his whereabouts ("I know not: Am I my brother's keeper?"). The curse of Cain refers to the legend that he was never to die or reach home again. Why Cain's hair (or Judas Iscariot's) is traditionally represented as reddish-yellow, or *Cain-colored*, remains a mystery. Cain and Judas were usually depicted with such hair and beards in ancient tapestries, but not

necessarily because their acts suggested murder or the shedding of blood. The term probably has as much to do with yellow being the traditional color used to depict jealousy and betrayal.

to mark time. First mention of the military parade ground term *to mark time* is in a British Army manual *Regulations for the Instruction of the Cavalry* (1833). "On the word 'mark time,'" the manual says, "marching is continued without gaining any ground." Naturally the process of marking time suggested any action that fills time but doesn't lead to progress, and not long after its first military use the phrase was used as a metaphor for just that.

mark twain. *Mark twain!* is a slurred mispronunciation of "Mark on the twine, six fathoms!," called out when riverboat leadsmen sounded the river with weighted twine. It is well known that former riverboat pilot Samuel Langhorne Clemens took his pen name Mark Twain from the leadsman's call *mark twain!*

marmalade. Though made today of oranges and lemons, the conserve called *marmalade* takes its name from the Latin *milimelum*, or "honey apple," which was some variety of apple grafted on quince stock. The Latin for "honey apple" became the Portuguese word for "quince" and the first marmalades recorded, in the early 16th century, were made of quinces and brought to England from Portugal. But over the centuries there have been plum, cherry, apple, and even date marmalades as well. Natural marmalade is the name of the fruit of the marmalade tree (*Lucuma mammosa*). In the 18th century a *Marmalade Madam* was a tart or strumpet.

Marrowsky. Spoonerisms (*q.v.*), the unintentional shifting of sounds at the beginnings of words (for example, "It is customary to kiss the bride" becomes "It is kisstomary to cuss the bride"), were first called *Marrowskis*, a name said to derive from the name of Polish Count Joseph Boruwlaski, who suffered the same affliction as Reverend Spooner. The word is first recorded in 1863 and soon after intentional *marrowskis* became the basis for a kind of slang called *marrowsky language*. Metathesis, the process of shifting letters or sounds, is responsible for a number of English words, including *dirt*, which was earlier *drit*.

marsala. Italy's best-known fortified wine, with its molasses-like flavor, takes its name from Marsala, the town where it is made on Sicily's west coast.

Marseillaise. First entitled "War Song for the Rhine Army," the French national anthem is called "the Marseillaise" because it was sung with great spirit by soldiers from Marseilles while advancing on the Tuileries on August 10, 1792. The song was actually written by a royalist army officer, not a revolutionary—Captain Claude Joseph Rouget de Lisle—who wrote it as a marching song. (*See* **the Internationale**.)

marshal; Marshall Plan. The German *marahscalh*, meaning "servant in charge of the mares," became *maréchal* in French and *marshal* in English, having been adopted by the French as the title for a high-ranking general of armies when cavalry became important in warfare as early as the fifth century. Though never used in the American military, it is said that *marshal* was being considered for the one rank above four-star general during World War II. It didn't sound right with the name of the man selected for the job, however, and instead of being made Marshal Marshall, George Catlett Marshall was named General of the Armies Marshall. As Secretary of State, General Marshall later proposed the broad European Recovery Plan aiding Europe after the war, the plan popularly named the *Marshall Plan* in his honor.

Martha. St. Martha is the patron saint of housewives, and a *Martha* is a woman somewhat too devoted to her domestic duties. Both references are to the New Testament Martha, the sister of Mary and Lazarus, who unlike Mary, was preoccupied with her household duties. Though Martha, encumbered with her duties and mildly rebuked by Jesus, represents the active as opposed to the contemplative life, she is later said to have become a missionary in Gaul. St. Martha (her feast day is July 29) is traditionally represented in a plain housedress, a bunch of keys hanging from her belt, and a ladle in her hand. The dragon pictured with her is the fearsome Tarasque, which legend tells us she slew at Aix-la-Chapelle while it ravaged Marseilles. Active she certainly was.

Martha's Vineyard. Possibly discovered by Leif Eriksson in the 11th century, *Martha's Vineyard*, an island about five miles off Massachusetts's southeast coast, was once an important center for whaling and fishing. The Indians called the island *Noe-pe*, "Amid the Waters," while the Norsemen named it *Staumey*, "Isle of Currents." It was christened *Martin's Vineyard* by English navigator Bartholomew Gosnold in 1602, apparently for no reason in particular. After a century it took the name *Martha's Vineyard*, probably because its name was confused with that of a little neighboring island to the southeast called Martha's Vineyard that had also been named by Gosnold. That little island is now called *No Man's Land*, after an Indian named Teque*noman*.

Martian canals. The myth of man-made canals on Mars is no longer believed by many people, after recent space explorations. In any case, the search by astronomers for life on Mars in years past was probably inspired by a linguistic accident. When in 1877 the astronomer

Giovanni Virginio Schiaparelli observed faint lines on Mars through the telescope he called them *canali*, Italian for "channels." *Canali* was erroneously translated into English as *canals*, "carrying with it a strong connotation of being man-made, which *canali* does not."

Martin drunk. (*See* **St. Martin's Day**.)

martinet. Colonel Martinet, the strict disciplinarian from whose name *martinet* originated, was "accidentally" killed by his own troops while leading an assault at the siege of Duisberg in 1672. Jean Martinet, sometimes called the Marquis de Martinet, had been a lieutenant colonel of the king's regiment of foot and inspector general of infantry in the army of France's Louis XIV. The Grand Monarch, then only twenty-two, and his brilliant nineteen-year-old war minister the Marquis de Louvois had formed a model standing army in 1660, replacing the old system where the state hired entire units for its army—a regiment, for example, being in the employ of its colonel and a company in the pay of its captain. But these old units had to be molded together into an efficient, homogeneous group and Colonel Martinet's exacting work with the Sun King's own Royal Regiment made him just the man for the job. As inspector general, Martinet was assigned the task of designing all drill systems for the new army and training its infantrymen to fight as a unit in battle. His methods, several of them named for him, were later copied by many European countries. In the process, however, his strict and tedious drills made Martinet's name synonymous with not only sharp military efficiency but stern spit-and-polish discipline inflicted by a goose-stepping stickler for details, who insists that his men carry out his rigid orders as if they were puppets. Today his name is applied to excessively severe soldiers and civilians alike. (*See* **martins**.)

martingale. Residents of the town of Martigues in Provence, France once wore economical breeches with a strap belt. Some authorities think that these *chausses à la martingale* give us the word for the part of a harness used to keep down a horse's head, as well as part of the rigging of a ship. Other etymologists discount *Martingalo*, "an inhabitant of Martigues," and trace the word to the Spanish *almartaga*, "a rein or harness." How the reckless *martingale*—a betting system in which the stakes are doubled or raised even higher after each loss—derived from either the stingy *Martingalos* or a harness is anybody's guess.

martini. H. L. Mencken traced the *martini* to 1899 and derives the cocktail's name from the Martini and Rossi firm, maker of a popular vermouth. Others say the drink originated with a now forgotten Italian or Spanish bartender named Martini. The dry martini is made, according to the classic recipe, by drinking a little vermouth, exhaling into the interior of a cocktail glass and filling it with gin—after you drink it, you'll forget that you forgot the olive. Mencken also mentions the *martini sandwich*, a dry martini between two glasses of beer, which he says "is favored by many American linguists."

martins.   St. Martin gives his name to the small bluish-black swallows called *martins* that begin to migrate southward from France and England at about the time of *St. Martin's Day* and return again in March, the Martian month. The martin was first called the *martinet* in France. Numerous martins occur all over the world, including the American purple martin, a bird valued by farmers because it eats harmful insects and drives away hawks and crows.

Martin varnish.   (*See* **Coma Berenices**.)

martyr.   *Martyr* ultimately derives from the Greek word for "witness" and was applied as a designation of honor by early Christians to those who accepted the penalty of death rather than renounce their faith. But by the 14th century the word was being generally and even sarcastically used. The expression *a martyr to science*, one who loses his life through his devotion to science, seems to have been first applied to Claude Louis, Count Berthollet (1748-1822), who died trying to determine the effects of carbolic acid on the human body.

Marxian.   After the German economist and revolutionary socialist Karl Marx (1818-83). Marx was a founder of the First International Workingmen's Association, but his most important contributions to history by far were the *Communist Manifesto* (1848), which he wrote with Friedrich Engels, and the enormously influential *Das Kapital* (1867). The dialectical materialism set forth in this last work has come to be known as *Marxism*, and a *Marxist*, depending on one's political inclinations, is either one favoring *Marxian* economic teachings or one who is economically doctrinaire and extremist.

Mary had a little lamb.

> Mary had a little lamb,
>   Its fleece was white as snow
> And everywhere that Mary went
>   The lamb was sure to go;
> He followed her to school one day,
>   That was against the rule;
> It made the children laugh and play
>   To see a lamb in school . . .

There seems to be no doubt that the Mary and little lamb in the well-known nursery rhyme were real, but there is some uncertainty about who wrote the poem. Sara Josepha Hale first published the 24-line verse over her initials in the September 1830 issue of *Juvenile Mis-*

cellany. Over the years it became known that it was based on the true experiences of eleven-year-old Mary Sawyer, who had a pet lamb that followed her to the schoolhouse at Redstone Hill in Boston one day in 1817. In fact, Mary Sawyer a half century later confirmed the story during a campaign to save the famous Old South Church of Boston from being torn down.

Maryland.   A popular but incorrect belief has it that *Maryland* was named for the Virgin Mary because it was originally settled by Catholics. The *Old Line State* actually bears the name of Henrietta Maria (1609-69), wife of England's King Charles I and daughter of France's Henry IV. When Maryland was settled under Lord Calvert in 1632 as a haven for persecuted Catholics, Henrietta Maria was a natural selection for its name, and in the original Latin charter the area is called *Terra Mariae*. It seems that Maryland was to be named for King Charles at first, but he already had the Carolinas named after him and suggested "Mariana," as a name honoring his queen. This was rejected by Lord Baltimore because it was the name of a Jesuit who had written against the monarchy and *Terra Mariae* was adopted instead. Maryland, one of the thirteen original colonies, bears the name "Old Line State" because of the bravery of her soldiers—men of the line—during the Revolutionary War.

masher.   The first *mashers* may have been not men but Gypsy women who flirted with men. This may be the case if the word for a man who makes passes at women in public places comes from the Gypsy expression *masher-ava*, "to allure, entice with the eye." *Masher* could, however, derive from the Standard English sense of *mash*, "to crush, pound, smash." *Mash* in the lewd sense is first recorded in America in 1860, *masher* in 1875.

mashie.   Golf's number 5 iron may take its (now rarely heard) name from the way unskilled golfers "mashed" a ball with it, or it may have resembled some Scottish kitchen utensil used to mash potatoes when the club was introduced in 1888. But more likely it derives from the French word for club, *massue*.

masochism.   A masochist derives sexual pleasure from having pain inflicted on himself, but, as with *sadism* (*q.v.*), the use of the term has broadened to now include pleasure derived from self-denial and from suffering in general. The word is taken from the name of Leopold von Sacher-Masoch (1835-95), an Austrian novelist whose characters dwelt lovingly on the sexual pleasure of pain, just as he did. A prolific, talented novelist who had published several scholarly histories and had once been a professional actor, Sacher-Masoch became a leading literary figure of his time. But he finally suffered a complete breakdown before turning fifty, and his second wife committed him to an asylum after he tried to kill her on several occasions. In a fitting ending to his bizarre life, his wife officially announced that he had died, even mourning him, ten years before his actual death in confinement. The pre-Freudian psychiatrist Richard Krafft-Ebing probably first used Sacher-Masoch's name to describe his ailment, recording *masochism* in 1893.

Mason-Dixon line. Although *Dixie* wasn't named for the *Mason-Dixon line*, the latter term has come to be used as a figure of speech for an imaginary dividing line between North and South. The *Mason-Dixon* line has an interesting history. Originally the 244-mile boundary set between Pennsylvania and Maryland in 1763-67 by English surveyors Charles Mason and Jeremiah Dixon, it was extended six years later to include the southern boundary of Pennsylvania and Virginia. The line had been established by English courts to settle a territorial dispute between the Penns of Pennsylvania and the Calverts of Maryland, but the use of *Mason-Dixon line* in Congressional debates during the Missouri Compromise (1819-20) gave the expression wide currency as a dividing line between free and slave states. After the Civil War the term was retained as the boundary between North and South, especially as a demarcation line of customs and philosophy. Its existence probably did influence the popularity of the word *Dixie* (*q.v.*).

mason jar. With the renewed interest in vegetable gardening and fresh, healthy foods that are raised for taste and not ease of shipping, the *mason jar*, used for home canning, is coming into prominence again. The wide-mouthed glass jars with either glass or metal screw tops were named for their inventor, New Yorker John Mason, who patented them in 1857.

massa. This American term for "master," long used by slaves, could derive from the English "master," or from the West African *masam*, "chief," or it could be a blend of both. No one knows for sure.

Massachusetts. "Place of the big hill" is the English translation of the Algonquian *Massachusetts*. The Bay State was admitted to the Union in 1788 as our sixth state and had been called the Massachusetts Bay Colony before then. It is now officially called the Commonwealth of Massachusetts.

massage. (*See* **matzo.**)

massive retaliation. (*See* **agonizing reappraisal.**)

masterpiece. Long before *masterpiece* became associated with the fine arts during the Renaissance, it meant the perfect piece of work that an apprentice under the English guild system had to make before he was recognized as a master. After he had served his apprenticeship and was able to make a piece worthy of a master, a *masterpiece*, he became a master himself and was no longer required to work under supervision.

mastic; masticate. Mastic, the chewing gum discovered by Columbus in Santo Domingo, is an exudation obtained from the lentisk, or mastic shrub (*Pistacia lenticus*), cultivated mainly on the Mediterranean island of Chios. The resin, found in the lentisk's bark, speedily exudes when the bark is cut, hardening into oval tears the size of peas that are transparent and of a pale yellow or faint greenish tinge that darkens slowly with age. Mastic's primary use since ancient times has been as a masticatory to sweeten the breath and preserve the teeth and gums. People throughout southeastern Europe and the Near East have used it for this purpose, and Dioscorides, the great Greek physician and botanist of the first century, refers to mastic's curative powers in his *De Materia Medica*. In fact, mastic goes so far back in history that it may have constituted the Greek word *mastichon*, "to chew," which is the root of the English word *masticate*. Today a chewing gum made with mastic and beeswax is still enjoyed by many Greeks and Middle Easterners.

Mata Hari. Behind the patina of the pseudonym *Mata Hari* ("Eye of the Dawn") is a rather prosaic Dutch name. Margaretha Geertruida Zelle (1876-1917) used *Mata Hari* as both her stage name and *nom de guerre* when she chose to become a spy for the Germans before World War I. Acclaimed throughout Europe for her interpretations of naked Indonesian dances, she met many men in high places, including German officials in Berlin who recruited her as a spy in 1907. During World War I, her dancing was the rage of Paris and she became intimate with top Allied officers, who confided military secrets to her. Mata Hari, who slept with literally hundreds, thrived on the deceit of espionage, but she was eventually betrayed to the French secret service by another German agent, Captain Walther Wilhelm Canaris, later to become head of the German secret service in World War II. Her trial was the most publicized of the many espionage trials held during the war, and her name become synonymous for a glamorous female spy and femme fatale. She was convicted by a French court-martial and executed by a firing squad.

matzo. This unleavened bread in the form of large, square corrugated crackers takes its name from the Hebrew-Arabic *massah*, "to touch, handle, squeeze," in reference to making the bread. *Matzo* thus has the same root as "massage."

maudlin. Christ exorcized Mary Magdalene of evil spirits, and *Magdalene* has become a synonym for a reformed prostitute. However, in classical paintings and old folk plays, based on the Bible stories relating to her, Mary was often shown with eyes red and swollen, disheveled and weeping endlessly for her sins. Her name—pronounced *maudlin*, just as Oxford's Magdalene College is pronounced today—was applied by the British, with their mistrust of easy emotion, to the excessive, tearful sentimentality that is often associated with drunkenness. In fact, the fifth stage of drunkenness in Thomas Nashe's analysis of intoxication presents us with the "maudlin drunk," and *maudle*, "to talk in a drunken way," comes from this use of the word. But it should be added that biblical scholars cannot agree on the identity of Mary Magdalene. The Mary of Magdala who was the first witness to the Resurrection may not have been the Mary who washed Christ's feet with her tears, wiped them with "the hairs of her head," and whom Christ forgave because "she loved much." Legend, however, combines the three Marys figuring in Christ's ministry into one.

Maundy Thursday. The day before Good Friday. *Maundy Thursday* takes its name from Christ's "new commandment" beginning *Mandatum novum do vobis*, "I give unto you" (John 13:34), with which the ceremony of the washing of the feet is initiated. The ceremony commemorates Christ washing the feet of his disciples on Holy Thursday.

Mauser. The original *Mauser*, and subsequent improved models, were used by the German army for many years following the rifle's introduction in 1871. Its inventors were Peter Paul Mauser (1838-1914) and his older brother Wilhelm (1834-82), the younger Mauser also inventing the Mauser magazine rifle in 1897.

mausoleum. Queen Artemisia of Caria was so grief-stricken when her husband, King Mausolus, died in 353 B.C. that she collected his ashes and mixed a portion of them with her daily drink until she died of inconsolable sorrow three years later. But she had ordered a sepulchral monument erected to her husband's memory in the Carian capital of Halicarnassus that became one of the Seven Wonders of the World. Built on a base of about 230 x 250 feet and towering over 100 feet high, the tomb of Mausolus (or more correctly Maussollus) wasn't completed until after Artemisia's own death, in 350 B.C. Caria, located in what is now southwest Turkey, attracted the greatest Greek architects to work on the vast white marble edifice, which was richly decorated with the sculpture of Scopas and Praxiteles and included statues of Mausolus and his queen. Nothing quite like this ornate super tomb had ever been seen before, and the Greeks called it a *Mausoleion* after the dead king, *Mausoleum*, the Latin form of this word, becoming our *mausoleum*. The imposing structure stood for almost 1,800 years before it crumbled in an earthquake in 1375. The Crusaders who occupied Halicarnassus in the 15th century used much of its marble to build a castle, but in 1859 Sir Charles Newton brought some of the structure's remains, including the statue of Mausolus, to the British Museum.

maverick. Texas lawyer Samuel Augustus Maverick (1803-70) reluctantly became a rancher in 1845 when he acquired a herd of cattle in payment for a debt. Maverick, a hero who was imprisoned twice in the war for independence from Mexico, eventually moved his cattle to the Conquistar Ranch on the Matagorda Peninsula, fifty miles from San Antonio. But he was too involved in other activities to prove much of a rancher. When in 1855 he sold out to A. Toutant de Beauregard, their contract included all the unbranded cattle on the ranch. Since careless hired hands had failed to brand any of Maverick's calves, Beauregard's cowboys claimed every unbranded animal they came upon as a *Maverick*. So, apparently, did some of Maverick's neighbors. Though Sam Maverick never owned another cow, his name soon meant any unbranded stock, and later any person who holds himself apart from the herd, a nonconformist. (*See* **gobbledygook**.)

mawkish. *Mawkish* originally meant having a sickly, nauseating or insipid flavor, but also means "characterized by sickly sentimentality, feebly emotional." Whatever the meaning, anything mawkish is being compared to a maggot, the word deriving from the obsolete English *mawk*, maggot, which comes from a Scandinavian word meaning the same.

Maxim gun; Maxim silencer. Sir Hiram Stevens Maxim, inventor of the first automatic machine gun, also invented a better mousetrap, an automatic fire sprinkler, a gas meter, a delayed-action fuse, a smokeless powder, a heavier-than-air flying machine, an inhalator for bronchitis, and sundry other items. The world did beat a path to his door, for his arms company merged with the Vickers firm in 1896 to become the giant Vickers Armstrong Ltd. and he was knighted for his accomplishments. Sir Hiram (1840-1916) was born in Maine, but became a naturalized British subject in 1881, after serving as chief engineer for America's first electric power company. The *Maxim machine gun*, invented in 1883, is a single-barreled, recoil-operated weapon that fires some ten rounds a second, the first modern machine gun in that the recoil from one cartridge was used to both expel the empty shells and reload the weapon. But what has turned out to be the greatest of the Maxim inventions is the *Maxim silencer* devised by Hiram's son Hiram Percy Maxim (1869-1936), who remained an American and who invented the Maxim automobile as well. *Maxim silencers* were weapon attachments originally developed only to make the explosion of firearms practically noiseless. But they were soon perfected to eliminate noise from many modern machines. Thanks to the silencer, noise pollution is much less than it would be, the invention prolonging lives rather than making it easier to take them.

maximize. (*See* **international**.)

May. The merry month of May may have been named for Maia, the goddess of spring, or to honor the Maiores, the Roman senate in early times. No one is sure, but the Latin *Maius* for the month became our *May*. The Romans, incidentally, thought May was an unlucky month for marriages, for their feast in honor of Bona Dea, the goddess of chastity, was held in the month of May.

Mayday. (*See* **CQD**.)

the Mayflower Compact. The former wine ship that transported the early settlers to America took its name from the mayflower, another name for the blossom of the hawthorn tree. In the *Mayflower Compact*, signed by the fifty-one adult passengers aboard ship, all agreed to stay together where they landed, choose their own leader, and abide by majority rule, this being the rude beginning of American democracy.

mayonnaise. Port Mahon gave its name to *mayonnaise*. The story is that the Duc de Richelieu attacked the Spanish island of Minorca and drove out the British for a while in 1756. But Richelieu was ravenously hungry after the battle. The Frenchman stormed the nearest kitchen ashore, tossed all the food he could find into one pot and blended it all together. This apocryphal tale got back to Paris, where chefs concocted a dressing of blended-together ingredients that they named *Mahonnaise* in honor of Richelieu's victory at Port Mahon.

may your shadow never grow less. An expression of Eastern origin, dating back in English at least to the 19th century and meaning "may your health and prosperity always continue." According to *Brewer*: "Fable has it that when those studying the Black Arts had made certain progress they were chased through a subterranean hell by the devil. If he caught only their shadow, or part of it, they became first-rate magicians, but lost either all or part of their shadow. This would make the expression mean, May you escape wholly and entirely from the clutches of the foul fiend." More likely the expression is just a colorful way of saying "May you never waste away."

Mazda. Ahura Mazda, the Persian god of light, has lent his name to the lamps and light bulbs of the General Electric Company since 1910, when G.E. borrowed it and registered it as a trademark. According to Persian belief, Ahura Mazda created all the 486,000 good stars—the lucky stars that people are born under as opposed to the like number of evil stars. Today *Mazda* is also the name of a Japanese auto.

mazel tov. One of the better-known Yiddish expressions, *mazel tov* literally means "good luck." However, Leo Rosten, in *The Joys of Yiddish*, says it has come to mean "Congratulations" or "Thank God!" rather than its literal meaning. Advising us that "the distinction is as important as it is subtle," Rosten offers an example: "Say *mazel tov*! to an Israeli ship captain when he first takes command: this congratulates him on his promotion; don't say *mazel tov*! when the ship reaches port: this suggests you're surprised he got you there." Though Rosten and most others say *mazel tov* "literally" means "good luck" (from *mazel*, "luck," *tov*, "good"), *mazel* is actually the Hebrew for "star," so the expression literally means "Good star," or "May a good star shine upon your days."

mazuma. (*See* **gelt**.)

M.C., emcee. In this case the initials became the word. *M.C.*, an abbreviation of *Master of Ceremonies*, came first. This began to be used as a verb in the early 1940s and was spelled *emcee*. The term *femcee*, for a female *emcee*, never caught on.

McCarthyism. Here is one word whose exact origins are recorded. *McCarthyism* was coined by author Max Lerner and introduced for the first time in his newspaper column on April 5, 1959. The word notes the witch-hunting practices and disregard of civil liberties that his critics accused Senator Joseph McCarthy (1905-57) of using and inspiring during the "Red" scare in the early 1950s. The Wisconsin senator, a great patriot to his supporters, first charged the Democratic administration with allowing Communist infiltration of the State Department. After taking on other government departments, he finally met his match when he attacked the Army for alleged security lapses. The Army, in turn, accused him of seeking special privileges, and while McCarthy was acquitted by the Senate of this charge, he was censured by a vote of 67-22 for his insolent behavior toward Senate committees. Earlier, the McCarthy hearings were televised and his countenance and repeated "Point of order, Mr. Chairman, point of order" became familiar throughout America. His low tactics ruined the lives of many innocent people.

McGuffey's reader. More than 123 million copies of *McGuffey's readers* have been sold since they were first published in 1836, and as many as 30,000 copies were sold as recently as 1960. The school readers, noted for their moral lessons and selections from great English writers, have had a profound effect on the shaping of the American mind. They were the work of educator and linguist William Holmes McGuffey (1800-1873). McGuffey, reared on the Ohio frontier, was possessed of a phenomenal memory that enabled him to become a teacher at the age of thirteen. After graduating from

Washington and Jefferson College in 1826, he became in turn a professor of languages at Miami University in Ohio and president of both Cincinnati College and Ohio University. He later served as a professor at Woodward College, Cincinnati, and the University of Virginia, and was a founder of the Ohio public school system. The educator's initial book was published under the title *McGuffey's First Eclectic Reader*. Five more were to follow, the last being issued in 1857.

McIntosh. Like many fruit varieties, the *McIntosh* apple was discovered accidentally. It is named after John McIntosh, an Ontario farmer, who found the late red apple in 1796 while clearing woodland in Dunclas County and was so impressed by it that he began to cultivate the variety. Today the Early McIntosh, one of the best early red apples, bears the same name, as does the Sweet McIntosh, regarded by many as the sweetest of all red varieties. The original *McIntosh* is still grown, however, a self-sterile type with whitish-yellow flesh and a superb though slightly acid taste. *McIntosh* apples account for some 10 percent of apples grown in this country, but they constitute about 75 percent of the New England harvest and 50 percent of the New York State crop. Most connoisseurs rate them superior in taste to the Red and Golden Delicious apples that have become the dominant American varieties. (*See* **Micah Rood's apple**.)

mealy-mouthed. A person called mealy-mouthed in ancient times was being complimented, for the expression is from the Greek *meli-muthos*, "honey-speech," and meant honey-mouthed or velvet-tongued. However, the insincerity of too many sweet talkers over the ages led to *mealy-mouthed* becoming synonymous for someone soft-spoken to the point of insincerity, someone so afraid to give offense that he became smarmy and hypocritical.

meander. *Meander*, "to wind in and out, to wander aimlessly," comes from the ancient name of the crooked Menderes River in Phrygia, now in western Turkey. The river, noted for its wandering course, is still called the Menderes, which became *Maiandros* in Greek, the Greek word eventually yielding *meander*, which came into English late in the 16th century via French.

measly. Measles has generally been considered an insignificant disease, despite the fact that a form of the measles used to kill many and can lead to serious birth defects if contracted by a pregnant woman. Hence our word *measly*, "insignificant or worthless," coined sometime in the middle of the 19th century.

meat. *Meat* in Middle English meant food in general. The word became confined to the flesh of animals only when there was a large increase in flesh eating and *meat* by the 17th century lost its meaning of food in general.

Medal of Honor. The United States' highest military decoration, awarded to a serviceman who distinguishes himself beyond the call of duty, this blue-ribboned gold star was established by Congress in 1862 as an award for Union heroes in the Civil War.

meddlesome Matty. A *meddlesome Matty* is a woman who is always poking her nose in others' business, or anyone who constantly fidgets with someone else's belongings. The expression derives from the character in the eponymous poem "Meddlesome Matty" (1804) written by Ann Taylor of "Twinkle, twinkle, little star" fame.

Medicean. Immensely wealthy Florentine banker Giovanni Medici (1360-1429) founded Italy's powerful Medici family. The Medicis ruled in Florence from the 15th to the 18th century, their influence felt throughout Italy, especially since the family produced three Popes—Leo X, Leo XI, and Clement VII. Catherine de Medici, Lorenzo's daughter, became queen of France, as did Marie de Medici. A genealogical table of the Medici would yield a score of figures who greatly influenced their times, but this family did so much, both good and evil—ranging from patronage of the arts to political poisonings and tortures—that their name came to mean a variety of things. *Medicean*, then, is simply "pertaining to the Medici," its meaning depending on the way it is used, or to which Medici it refers.

Mediterranean Sea. Formed from the Latin *medi*, "middle," and *terraneus*, "earth," the *Mediterranean* means "the sea in the middle of the earth," which, indeed, the ancients believed it to be.

meeting a deadline. *Deadline*, in the sense of a final demarcation of time, a time line beyond which one is not permitted to go, isn't recorded until the 1920s. This Americanism may derive, however, from another uniquely American term *deadline*. This earlier word was used in prison camps during the Civil War. According to Benton Lossing's *History of the Civil War* (1868) the original *deadline* was a line 17 feet from the inner stockade in prison camps over which no prisoner was permitted to go—any prisoner crossing it would be shot. Today's deadlines are not so final as that, but they do bother people, I reflect, as I consider how much more work I have on this book before my deadline for finishing it.

megabucks. This synonym for "big money" is first recorded in 1946, deriving from the Greek *megas*, "large, powerful," and probably reinforced by the constant use of *mega* in *megabombs*, etc.

melba toast; peach melba. *Melba toast*, according to the traditional story, originated as several pieces of burnt toast served to the Australian opera star Dame Nellie Melba at the Savoy in London. The prima donna had been on a diet, ordered toast, and enjoyed the crisp, crunchy, overtoasted slices that were served to her by mistake. The maitre d' named them in her honor and put *melba toast* on the menu. Whether the story is true or not, thin crispy melba toast honors Dame Nellie, as does the *peach melba*, which the French chef Escoffier concocted for her. Nellie Melba was the stage name adapted from the city of Melbourne by Helen Porter Mitchell (1861-1931), who became a Dame of the British Empire in 1918. The world-famous soprano made her debut in *Rigoletto* in Brussels (1887) and went on to star at London's Covent Garden, the Paris Opera, La Scala, and New York's Metropolitan among numerous opera houses. Unlike many opera stars, Nellie Melba did not study singing until she was over twenty-one years old, although she had previously been trained as a pianist.

meltdown.   No more serious accident can happen in a nuclear power plant than a *meltdown*. The term, first recorded in the 1960s, signifies a condition where the reactor core (the assembly of the fuel elements) burns through or melts into the ground below the nuclear power station, releasing highly dangerous radiation.

melting pot.   In his play about immigration entitled *The Melting Pot* (1908) English author Israel Zangwill wrote: "America is God's Crucible, the great Melting Pot where all the races of Europe are melting and re-forming!" Though Zangwill didn't stew blacks and Asians in his pot, the phrase quickly came to include everybody in America, "a homogeneous melting pot of heterogeneous individuals," as someone said. The term, by the way, doesn't refer to the loss of ethnic identity but to the breaking down of racial and national prejudices.

memsahib; sahib.   Indians used to address British women as *memsahib* in the days when the sun never set on the Empire. The word is simply a feminine form of the Urdu *sahib*, "sir or master," *mem* representing the English "ma'am." The respectful title is first recorded in 1857, *sahib* attested to as far back as 1696. The terms are still used in India, but aren't exclusively applied to the British anymore.

mendelevium.   All attempts to classify the elements had failed before Dmitri Ivanovich Mendeleyev (1834-1907) invented his own system in 1869-71. The Russian chemist's *Periodic Law of the Chemical Elements* arranged the elements in order of increasing atomic weight, which made it easy to check the now commonplace tables of the vertical columns, and left spaces into which undiscovered elements would probably fit. Mendeleyev taught organic chemistry at the University of St. Petersburg. Known as one of the greatest teachers of his time, his

Principles of Chemistry (1869) was a standard textbook. The artificially produced radioactive element *mendelevium* was named in Mendeleyev's honor in 1955 when four American scientists—Glenn Seaborg, Bernard Harvey, Gregory Choppin, and S.G. Thompson—formed it in the laboratory by bombarding the element *einsteinium* (*q.v.*) with alpha particles.

Mendel's law.   Mendel's law is the theory of heredity formulated by the Austrian Augustinian abbot and botanist Gregor Johann Mendel (1822-84). Mendel's painstakingly careful experiments, crossing different strains of peas in his monastery garden at Brunn, led to Mendel's law, reported in 1865, stating that characteristics of the parents of crossbred offspring reappear in successive generations in certain proportions and according to fixed laws. His *Mendelian* laws were neglected until long after his death, when Hugo de Vries and others independently rediscovered his findings in about 1900. They soon became the foundation for the modern study of heredity. Mendel was not uneducated as is sometimes inferred, having studied natural science at the University of Vienna 1851-53.

menhaden.   This abundant oily fish has a name related to its use. Caught in great numbers by American Indians and buried in their corn fields, it bears an Algonquian name meaning "fertilizer." It is also called the *mosbunker*, the *bunker*, the *marshbunker*, and by some thirty more popular names (see the *American Naturalist* XII, 1878, pp. 735-39 for a listing). In 1949 *Brevoortia tyrannus* was called "America's No. 1 fish . . . yielding some $10 million worth of oil, meal, and dry scrap last year."

Mennonites.   (*See* **Amish.**)

mentor.   Mentor, in Greek mythology, was the friend of Odysseus and took charge of his household when the hero of Homer's *Odyssey* went off to war. When problems arose Pallas Athene descended from heaven to inhabit Mentor's body and, through him, to give good advice to Odysseus's son Telemachus. *Mentor* has since meant an advisor, teacher, or coach.

meow.   *Meow* has been the English echoic word for the sound of a cat for centuries. The word is similar to those in many languages (German *miaw*, Italian *miao*, French *miaou*); but the Japanese hear the sound slightly differently as *nya nya*, and in Arabic our *meow* is *nau-nau*. (*See* **Cock-a-doodle-do.**)

Mercator's projection.   Gerardus Mercator, his name being the Latinized form of Gerhard Kremer, devised *Mercator's projection* in 1568. His famous cylindrical chart gave all meridians as straight lines at right angles to the parallels of latitude, and is the basis of mapmaking today. Mercator, born in 1512, was a Flemish geographer and mathematician whose accurate maps and globes revolutionized mapmaking and freed geographers from "the tyranny of Ptolemy," the earlier astronomer and geographer, who had underestimated the earth's size.

Mercedes-Benz. The Mercedes-Benz auto isn't named after two men who designed it, as most people believe. Emil Jellinik, an Austrian, manufactured the car in 1886, and he named it for his daughter, Mercedes. When the Daimler company later merged with Jellinik's Benz automotive works, the name assumed its present form.

mercerize. A mercer is a dealer in textiles, but the old word has nothing to do with the method for treating cotton textiles called *mercerization*. The process was invented by John Mercer (1791-1866), an English calico printer who discovered it in 1850. *Mercerizing* involves treating material under tension with a caustic soda solution and then acid to neutralize the alkali used. This shrinks, strengthens, and gives a permanent silky lustre to the yarn or fabric, also making it easier to dye. Mercer's method wasn't widely successful until long after he died, the breakthrough coming in 1895 when the 25 percent shrinkage was virtually eliminated by treating the material under tension, the one factor he had overlooked. The inventor had named his process "sodaizing," but the hundreds of millions of yards of material and thread annually produced by the method are called *mercerized* in tribute to his pioneering work.

merchant. The swift Roman god Mercury, for whom *mercury* (*q.v.*) is named, was the god of business. Thus from his name come the words *merchant, merchandise, mercer, commerce,* and *commercial,* among others.

merchants of death. *Merchants of death* is applied to any group of manufacturers or businessmen who make money from war and even promote wars in various ways so that they can make money. This is another term from the title of a book—*The Merchants of Death* (1920) by H.C. Engelbrecht and F.D. Hanighan, which argues that munition makers were among the major causes of World War I.

mercury; mercurial. Mercury, with his winged hat and sandals, was the fastest and busiest of the Roman gods, as our old saying *quick as Mercury* reflects. For the same reason the liquid metal *mercury* was named for him, because it flowed quickly from place to place. The planet *Mercury*, also named for the god, gives us the word *mercurial*, "rapid, unpredictable changes in mood," astrologers in ancient times believing that because Mercury was the planet closest to the sun those born under its influence were most subject to such shifting moods. (*See* **merchant**.)

meretricious. The Latin root of *meretricious*, meaning "tawdry, gaudy, deceitful," is *meretrix*, "whore." The English word first meant "pertaining to a prostitute," taking on its later meanings because prostitutes often dressed gaudily and were deceitful.

mermaid. *Mermaids*, whose name derived from the Latin *mer* ("sea"), date back long before history was written. In Greek mythology the fifty daughters of Nereus, the god of the sea, were beautiful mermaids who rode the waves on the backs of dolphins, and any sailor lucky enough to catch one could demand that the mermaid predict the future as a price for letting her go.

mermaid's purses; mermaid's glove. The horny skate, ray, and shark egg cases often washed up on the beach by wave action are popularly called *mermaid's purses. A mermaid's glove* is a British sponge (*Halichondria palmata*) whose branches resemble human fingers.

Merry Andrew. Henry VIII's personal physician, Dr. Andrew Borde or Boorde (ca. 1490-1549), has been regarded by some as the original *Merry Andrew*, at least since Thomas Hearne designated him so in the preface to his *Benedictine Abbas Petroburgensis* in 1735. Borde did have a reputation for a salacious wit and a bedside manner that mixed facetiousness with healing, but to call the eccentric doctor a buffoon or clown would be stretching the evidence too far. He did not author a contemporary joke book, as is sometimes alleged, but he was a man known for his vast learning as well as his reputation for enjoying a good joke. The *Oxford English Dictionary* notes Hearne's statement, and like most authorities dismisses it, claiming that the author based his identification on little evidence or even intrinsic probability. The expression did arise in Borde's time, but probably from the generic name for men servants or serving men, "Andrew" being commonly bestowed on servants in those days. The first *Merry Andrew* was most likely such a servant, the cognomen later being applied to any conjurer's assistant who engaged in buffoonery to help make the magician's hands quicker than the eye.

merrythought. *Merrythought*, first attested in 1607, is a charming synonym for the wishbone in the breast of a fowl, taking its name from the tradition of two persons pulling on the bone until it breaks, the one who holds the longer piece getting any wish he has made.

merry widow. Late in the 19th century Merry Widow was a U.S. trade name for a brand of condoms. Within thirty years or so, however, *merry widow* had become a synonym for any kind of condom and remained so until the firm making Merry Widows went out of business in the 1940s. The product preceded Franz Lehar's operetta of that title, which was first produced in 1905. *Merry* does figure in several British slang expressions, all obsolete, including *merry-legs*, a harlot; *merry-maker*, the penis; *merry bout*, sexual intercourse, *merry bit*, a willing wench; and, merriest of all, a *merry-arsed Christian*, a whore.

mervousness. A short-lived political word and only an amusing historical footnote today, *mervousness* is a blend of *Merv* and *nervousness*. The Duke of Argyll coined it in the early 1880s when the British government worried nervously about Russia having designs upon the area of Merv in Turkestan. In fact, the British *mervousness* was warranted, for the Russians grabbed Merv in late 1883.

mesmerize. Franz Anton Mesmer doesn't entirely deserve his centuries-old reputation as a charlatan. Though he wasn't aware of the fact, Dr. Mesmer was one of the first to treat patients by hypnosis, and his motives generally seem to have been beyond reproach. The Austrian physician, garbed in the flowing, brightly colored robes of an astrologer and waving a magic wand, would arrange his patients in a circle, have them join hands in the dimly lit room and then pass from one to another, fixing his eyes upon, touching, and speaking to each in turn while soft music played in the background. Apparently he never did understand that the supernatural had nothing to do with his success, that his hypnotic powers accomplished this. Many physicians supported his claims but when Louis XVI appointed a scientific commission—which included Benjamin Franklin—to investigate his practice, they labeled him an impostor. A man born before his time, the hypnotist died in obscurity in Switzerland in 1815, aged eighty-two. Freud and others would profit from his work, but he would mainly be remembered as a quack occult healer. *Mesmerism* was used for hypnotism before the latter word was coined, but today is employed mostly in the sense of to spellbind, to enthrall by some mysterious power, in fact, to sway a group or an individual by some strange personal magnetism.

Mesmerizer Creek, Texas. Over a century ago a settler on the banks of this Texas town actually tried to domesticate American bison by hypnosis, his colorful ways inspiring the colorful placename *Mesmerizer Creek*.

message to Garcia. In his inspirational *A Message to Garcia* (1899), Elbert Hubbard dramatized the true adventure of Lt. Andrew Summers Rowan, U.S. Bureau of Naval Intelligence, who during the Spanish-American War was sent by the U.S. Chief of Staff to communicate with General Calixto Garcia, leader of the Cuban insurgent forces. No one knew just where the elusive Garcia might be, but Rowan made his way through the Spanish blockade in a small boat, landing near Turquino Peak on April 24, 1898, where he contacted local patriots, who directed him to Garcia far inland, and returned to Washington with information regarding the insurgent forces. The brave and resourceful Rowan became a hero, but Hubbard transformed him into an almost Arthurian figure and it was his essay that made *carry a message to Garcia* a byword.

Messalina; messaline. The notoriously cruel, greedy, and venal Valeria Messalina managed to cuckold her weak-minded husband Emperor Claudius I so many times that even in corrupt Rome her name became proverbial for a lascivious, unfaithful woman. One of the profligate empress's favorite tricks was to make love to men and learn about their real estate holdings, later condemn them to death for treason, and then confiscate their property. But she went too far when she eliminated the freedman Polybius. Shortly afterward, in her husband's absence, the empress forced her current lover, a handsome youth named Gaius Silius, to divorce his wife and marry her in a public ceremony. The freedman Narcissus, alarmed at Polybius's fate, took this opportunity to inform Claudius of her treachery and he ordered his third wife put to death. She was either killed in the gardens of Lucullus, which she had obtained by confiscation, or forced to commit suicide there with her paramour. She was only twenty-six when she died in A.D. 48. No one knows why, but the fabric *messaline*, a thin, soft silk with a tweed or satin weave, also pays the empress homage.

Messerschmitt. This was the most famous German fighter of World War II and the main support of the Luftwaffe. The aircraft, technically the ME-109 and ME-110 pursuit planes, were designed by German aircraft engineer and manufacturer Wilhelm or Willy Messerschmitt (b. 1898). Messerschmitt built his first plane when he was eighteen and owned his own factory by 1923, his early experience in gliding leading to his interest in power-driven aircraft. Besides the renowned fighter he built a remarkable twin jet, the ME-262. The inventor had been awarded the Lilienthal prize for aviation research in 1937, but was declared a minor offender in the postwar trials of Nazis.

Mexico. *Mexico* derives from the Aztec name of the great war god Mextli.

mho. It is safe to make the earthshaking claim that this is the only word deriving from a man's name spelled backwards. This unusual crossword puzzle and Scrabble word means just the opposite of the *ohm* (q.v.), being the electrical unit of conduction, while the ohm is the electrical unit of resistance. The inverted word, whose plural is *mhos*, was coined by Lord Kelvin and of course honors physicist Georg Simon Ohm, just as the ohm does. In fact, the *mho* is often called a reciprocal ohm. (*See* **Mahernia; Quisqualis.**)

MIA. This abbreviation for "missing in action" didn't originate during the Vietnam War, as many believe. The initials were used in military parlance at least during the Korean Conflict and probably further back, though they did pass into general use in the Vietnam era.

Micah Rood's apple. An apple with streaks of red running through the white flesh. The tale is that on a spring day in 1693 a jewelry peddler visited old Micah Rood's farm at Franklin, Pennsylvania. Shortly afterward the peddler was found murdered under an apple tree in Rood's orchard, but his jewelry was never recovered and the farmer never was convicted of the crime. According to legend, though, all the apples harvested from the tree that autumn had streaks of blood inside. Rood died of fright after seeing them, the "damned" spot or streaks called "Micah Rood's curse" from that day on. When recounting this one, don't ruin a good story by quibbling that apples with red running through the flesh were common before Rood's time, that they are simply a "sport," like the famous golden delicious variety and many others. There seems to be no record of a farmer named Micah Rood, but two other peddlers were involved in sensational murders at the time he was allegedly murdered; perhaps these cases inspired the story. (See **McIntosh**.)

Michigan. Our 26th state, admitted to the Union in 1837, takes its name from *Michigaman*, both the name of an Indian tribe and a place, translating as "great water." The Wolverine State had first been the Michigan Territory.

Mickey Finn. This term, for "a powdered knockout drug or purgative slipped into a drink to render its drinker unconscious or otherwise helpless," seems to have originated in Chicago in the late 19th century and has been attributed to a gangland figure named Mickey Finn, remembered for his sleight of hand but nothing else. The original *Mickey Finn* is said to have been a laxative commonly used for horses. Possibly some unknown bartender named Mickey actually administered it, but one guess is as good as another here.

Mickey Mouse. Mickey Mouse only began to lose popularity when he was streamlined for later films, his tail cut off and his bare chest covered, among other "modernizations." He looked like he had come off an assembly line of drawing boards, and this commercial slickness was reflected in phrases like *Mickey Mouse music*. In the armed forces during World War II and the Korean War *Mickey Mouse* meant anything childish or silly, such as white-glove inspections. "Mickey Mouse movie" was a humorous term G.I.'s gave the frightening films servicemen were shown that gruesomely detailed the effects of gonorrhea and syphilis and that caused many men to swear off sex—for a few days. Mickey Mouse was of course invented by the late Walt Disney (1901-66) in 1923. Disney called his creation Mortimer Mouse at first, but changed the name when his wife suggested Mickey Mouse instead. The cartoonist was Mickey's voice in the early Mickey Mouse cartoons. In Disney's words, "He was my firstborn and the means by which I ultimately achieved all the other things I ever did—from Snow White to Disneyland."

Mickey Mouse rules. One theory holds that World War II U.S. Navy Military Indoctrination Centers, or M.I.C.'s, where undisciplined sailors were restrained, gave their initials to this expression for petty rules. The term has been around since early in World War II and probably can be explained by the fact that such rules seem silly and childish, like Mickey Mouse cartoons. Mickey Mouse was better honored when his name became the password chosen by intelligence officers in planning the greatest invasion in the history of warfare—Normandy, 1944. *Mickey Mouse diagrams* were maps made for plotting positions of convoys and bombarding forces at Normandy.

microcosm. *Microcosm* derives from the Greek for "little world," the Greeks applying the word to man, whom they considered as the world in miniature. The term is now used for anything regarded as a world in miniature. Its opposite is *macrocosm*.

Midas; Midas touch. Just as the title Pharaoh was bestowed upon all Egyptian rulers, Midas was the title of the kings of Phrygia, an ancient kingdom in what is now central Turkey, but the Midas who became the basis for the Midas legends has never been positively identified. In legend King Midas is the father of Gordius. Several tales are told of him in Greek mythology, the most famous of these making his name proverbial. This story had King Midas befriending Silenus, the Greek god of wine and fertility, a jolly old man, often drunk but gifted with great powers of song and prophecy. Midas led Silenus to Dionysus, his pupil and boon companion, and this grateful god of fertility and wine rewarded him by promising to fulfill any wish he might make. King Midas told Dionysus that he wished everything he touched would turn to gold, and his wish was granted. But Midas got much more than he bargained for—even his food and drink turned to gold, and he nearly starved to death before the greedy king's appetite for gold decreased and he asked the god to lift the spell. Dionysus commanded him to bath in the Pactolus River, which washed him clean of his cursed power and has ever since had gold-bearing sands. From this original morality tale, on which there have been many embellishments, we have the *Midas touch*, referring to anyone who effortlessly makes money from every project he undertakes.

Middle America. Capital columnist Joseph Kraft (1925-1986) coined *Middle America* in the mid-1960s as a term for "the middle-class America whose views were often overlooked by the opinion-molders on the two coasts," according to one of his editors.

middle of the road. Toward the end of the 19th century this term came into use to describe political parties or factions of political parties that took a cautious, moderate position between extremes supported by their opponents. Highways at the time were often unpaved, with untended roads whose left and right sides were well below the grade of the middle. After a heavy rain cautious travelers stayed in the middle of the road, which may have suggested the political phrase.

the middle passage. In the so-called triangular trade, ships carried New England rum to the African Gold Coast on the first passage, traded the rum for slaves and transported the shackled slaves to the West Indies on the *middle passage*, where the slaves were sold for molasses and sugar, which were brought back to New England to make more rum on the final passage. The middle passage was, of course, the worst and most inhuman of the three legs of the journey.

midshipman fish. Native to mainland America, the midshipman fish (*Porichthys notatus*) has golden spots on each side like the brass buttons on a midshipman's coat. Familiar along the Pacific coast, the luminescent midshipman is also called the *talking fish*, the *grunter*, the *grunt*, and the *singing fish*. The sound it makes when disturbed—made by vibrating its air bladder—is actually similar to the croak of a tree frog.

midsummer madness. Something completely mad, unreasonable, or foolish. Shakespeare is the first to record this expression, in *Twelfth Night* (1600). In the Bard's day midsummer was believed to be a time when madness was common.

midsummer men. The *Orpine* (*Sedum telephium*), also known as live-forever, is called *midsummer men* because it used to be potted and hung in the house to tell young women if their sweethearts were true—the plant's leaves supposedly bending to the right if they were faithful, to the left if they were false.

MIG. All Russian fighter planes called by the acronym *MIG* honor the original aircraft's inventors, designers *Mi*(koyan) and *G*(urevitch). It is sometimes written *MiG* and *Mig*.

might as well be hung (hanged) for a sheep as a lamb. In former times thieves were sentenced to death when caught stealing either a sheep or a lamb, which led to this originally British expression that dates back to at least the early 19th century and means if the punishment is the same for either action one might as well commit the worse (and more profitable) one.

migraine headache. Migraine comes from the Greek *hemikrania*, "half the skull," this extremely severe type of headache usually confined to one side of the head. The word seems to have been a fashionable one when Horace Walpole first recorded it in a 1777 letter to a friend.

a Mike Fink. In days past, *a Mike Fink* was used to mean "a rough and ready hero given to exaggeration about his exploits." Mike Fink was a real American frontier hero (ca. 1770-1822), a river boatman and Indian fighter whose tall tales contributed greatly to the American folklore of exaggeration, a fact witnessed by the twelve or more different accounts of his death.

mile. The Latin *mille*, "one thousand," is the ancestor of our word *mile*, which is 5,280 feet, because it once referred to a thousand paces of the Roman legion's formal parade step, left foot and then right foot, each pace equalling 5.2 feet.

to mill. *To mill about* is to move aimlessly in a circle. First recorded by Kipling in 1874, the expression is related to the circular motion of mill wheels. (*See* **to be put through the mill**.)

milliard. *Milliard* is the British word for the American English "billion" (*q.v.*), or one thousand million. This term is also used in the Soviet Union and Germany. The American English *trillion* is equivalent to the British English *billion*. *Milliard*, from the French *milliard*, which comes from the French *mille*, "thousand," is first recorded in 1793. Wrote Byron in *Don Juan*: "I'll bet you millions, milliards."

milliner. One of the great fashion centers of the world in the early 16th century, Milan, Italy set styles for all Europe. *Milan gloves*, *Milan hats*, *Milan point lace*, *Milan ribbons*, *Milan needles*, and even *Milan jewelry* were among the many items imported to England from the Paris of its day. Shopkeepers who sold these imported articles, only some of them merchants from Milan, were naturally named *Milaners*, but the English pronounced and spelled the word *Milliners*, which eventually lost its capital. The small shops, run primarily by men at first, did often specialize in making and selling ladies' hats, but the use of *milliner* exclusively for a designer or a seller of women's headgear is fairly recent.

millionaire. Fur and real estate tycoon John Jacob Astor (1763-1848) was probably the first American to be called a *millionaire*, for the word entered English from the

French *millionnaire* in about 1820, but there were Americans who accumulated millions before him, the first probably being the Virginia planter and banker Robert "King" Carter, who owned more than 300,000 acres in the late 17th century. (*See also* **billionaire; milliard; multimillionaire; myriad; trillionaire**.)

millions for defense, not one cent for tribute. (*See* **XYZ Affair**.)

Milquetoast. Timorous men are still called *Caspar Milquetoasts*, or *Milquetoasts*, even though the cartoon character of that name, created by H. T. Webster as "The Timid Soul" in the 1930s, has long ceased to appear in the Sunday comics.

mimosa. *Mimosa* is from the Greek "to mimic," in allusion to the sensitive collapse of the leaves in some species of this tree, which were thought to be mimicking the motions of animals at one time. The mimosa's reaction to shock or cloudy weather is one of the strangest cases of physiological response among plants, its leaflets folding up face to face at the slightest irritation and its leaves collapsing entirely if the shock is sufficient.

Mimulus. These showy flowers were once thought to resemble a monkey's face and were thus named from the Greek *mimo*, "face." Other names for them are the *monkey flowers* and the *cardinal monkey flower*. One species, *Mimulus moschatus*, is called *monkey musk*, but actually has no smell at all. Experts are at a loss to explain why the flower mysteriously lost its perfume at the end of the 19th century.

mind your p's and q's. Be very careful, precise. We have been using this expression since at least the late 18th century without any definite proof of where it comes from, and we still don't know. Not that there is any want of theories. Of the top ten contenders, three are listed here:

- The obvious explanation is that English children learning to write the alphabet were told to mind their *p*'s and *q*'s, to be careful not to reverse the knobs on the letters and make *p*'s look like *q*'s and vice versa. Why wasn't the admonition mind your *b*'s and *d*'s, though?
- A similar theory holds that apprentice printers were told to mind their *p*'s and *q*'s, to be very careful in picking out type, especially since a typesetter has to read letters upside down. The trouble with this theory is that the reverse of a *p* isn't a *q* but a *d*.
- Word delvers always come up with a good barroom story whenever it's possible to work one in, and a third explanation has British tavernkeepers minding their *p*'s and *q*'s when figuring up the monthly beer bill—being careful, that is, not to confuse pints and quarts.

miniature. *Miniature* doesn't derive from the Latin *minor* or *minimus*, "small," as seems the case. It comes from *minium*, a Latin borrowing from Basque. *Minium* (from the Basque *arminea*) means "red lead, vermilion," Basque Spain being a major source of red lead in ancient times. Miniature first meant "a manuscript containing letters illuminated with red vermilion." The word was then erroneously applied to small portraits, because it was confused with the Latin *minimus*, and later came to describe anything small.

minimize. (*See* **international**.)

minister. The first meaning of *minister* in English was "a servant or attendant," the word deriving ultimately from the Latin *minister* meaning the same. *Ministers* waited on table or worked in the kitchen. *Minister*, for "a clergyman," possibly owes its life to the fact that such men were "servants of God."

Minnesota. No one is sure exactly what *Minnesota* means, for the Sioux word translates as either "sky-blue water" or "cloudy water." The Gopher State had been called the Minnesota Territory before being admitted to the Union in 1858 as our 32nd state.

minnie ball. French Army Capt. Claude Étienne Minié (1814-79) invented the *minnie* or *minié ball* bullet that became famous around the world and was extensively used in the American Civil War. Minie's invention came in 1849, designed for the *Minié rifle*, but more important something of a final answer in the search for an ideal bullet. The elongated bullet, one of the first of its shape, was more accurate and could be loaded faster than any shell before it. Experts thought it to be the ultimate in ballistic ingenuity and it was certainly the first step in the development of the modern bullet. With it a soldier could fire *two* aimed shots a minute!

mint. *Mint* derives from the name of the Greek nymph Minthe, who was transformed into the herb by Proserpine, the jealous wife of Pluto, god of the underworld. Wild mint (*Mentha sativa*) has been chewed since earliest times and is often regarded as an aphrodisiac. Aristotle forbade the chewing of mint by Alexander the Great's soldiers because he felt it aroused them erotically and sapped their desire to fight. (For a *mint* where money is made, *see* **money**.)

Miranda. (*See* **Uranus**.)

miserere. (*See* **benefit of clergy**.)

mishmash. *Mishmash* isn't a Yiddish expression but Standard English dating back to the 15th century. Meaning a hodgepodge or conglomeration, the term has been influenced by Yiddish in recent times and is often pronounced *mishmosh*.

a miss is as good as a mile.   Charlemagne's faithful warriors Amis and Amile shared many things in common, even their martyrdom—but they aren't the inspiration for this old saying. The expression is really meaningless until you study its original form: "An inch in a miss is as good as an ell." In the 19th century the phrase was shortened by Sir Walter Scott, who also substituted the alliterative *mile* for "ell."

Mississippi.   The Chippewas named the river for which the state is named the *mice sipi*, the "big river," which white men spelled *Mississippi*. The Magnolia State was admitted to the Union in 1817 as our 20th state.

Missouri.   *Missouri* is either from the name of a Sioux tribe, "people of the big canoes," living in the region, or from an Algonquian word adapted by the French meaning "muddy water," in reference to the Missouri River. The Show Me State was admitted to the Union in 1821 as our 24th state, having previously been the Missouri Territory.

Mr. Micawber.   A *Mr. Micawber* is an incurable optimist and to be *micawberish* is to be incurably cheerful and optimistic. The words honor Mr. Wilkins Micawber of Dickens's *David Copperfield*, one of the immortal author's immortal characters. Mr. Micawber fails at every scheme he tries, but remains certain that "something will turn up," and is always optimistic and cheerful. No fool, he is an honest, able man and his optimism does prevail, for he finally emigrates to Australia and becomes a magistrate.

Mr. Watson, come here: I want you.   This was the first complete sentence transmitted over the telephone, by American inventor Alexander Graham Bell to his assistant Thomas A. Watson on March 10, 1876. (*See* **telephone; telegraph**.)

mistletoe.   The traditional Christmas decoration *mistletoe* derives from the Old English *mistel*, "misteltoe." The word might be translated as "the plant propagated by dung," for Old English *mistel* comes from the Old High German *mist*, "dung," reflecting the fact that birds eat the mistletoe's berries, the berries in their excrement propagating the plant.

mithridatize.   Mithridates VI trusted no one. Coming to the throne when only eleven, this king of Pontus, an area in Asia Minor along the Black Sea, eventually murdered his mother, his sons, and the sister he had married in order to retain power, and once killed all his concubines to prevent his harem from falling into enemy hands. All his days he had guarded himself against poisoning by accustoming his body to small amounts of poison, rendering himself immune by gradually increasing these daily doses. Then, weary of his son's treachery, he decided to commit suicide and found that he had *mithridatized* himself far too well. No poison in any amount worked, for he had total immunity. Instead, he had to have a mercenary or slave stab him to death. Such is the story, anyway, that the credulous Pliny the Elder tells us about Mithridates, King of Pontus (120-63 B.C.), betrayed by the very poisons he himself had so often used to kill. A *mithridate* is the antidote to all poisons that Pliny claims Mithridates had developed. It contained seventy-two ingredients, none of them given by the historian. (*See* **take with a grain of salt**.)

mob.   Englishmen often criticize Americans for their laziness in shortening words like *fanatic* to *fan*, but they were doing the same thing long before. Early in the 17th century some British Latin scholars introduced the phrase *mobile vulgus*, "movable (or fickle) crowd," for an excited or fickle crowd. People shortened this to one word, *mobile*, which they pronounced "mobilly," and then further abbreviated it to *mob*. Language purists were quite indignant. "This Humour of speaking not more than we need . . . has so miserably curtailed some of our words," Addison complained, citing *mob* as a new vulgarism. "I have done my utmost for some years past to stop the progress of 'mob' . . ." Steele wrote in the *Tatler*, "but have been plainly borne down by numbers, and betrayed by those who promised to assist me." *Mob*, of course, survived all its critics. Said Swift of the word in *Polite Conversation*, "Abbreviations exquisitely refined: as *Pozz* for 'positively,' *Mobb* for 'Mobile.'"

Moby Dick.   Mocha Dick, the stout gentleman of the latitudes, the prodigious terror whale of the Pacific, the redoubtable white sperm whale that fought and won over a hundred sea battles against overwhelming odds—such was the reputation in the extravagant language of the time of the whale Herman Melville immortalized as *Moby Dick*. Melville probably first read about Mocha Dick in a piece by Jeremiah N. Reynolds in the May 1839 *Knickerbocker Magazine*; undoubtedly, though, he heard of him long before in the forecastles of ships he sailed on. The last mention in history of Mocha Dick is dated August 1859, when off the Brazilian banks he is said to have been taken by a Swedish whaler. He had already become legend when Herman Melville wrote *Moby Dick* in 1850—Melville changing his prenomen to *Moby* probably to suggest his amazing mobility and to avoid association with the color mocha for his white whale.

mogul.   (*See* **high muckey-muck**.)

Mohammedanism.   (*See* **Muhammadanism**.)

Mohawks.   The Mohawk Indians were one of the smallest tribes of the Iroquois League of Five Nations, but were probably the most fierce and aggressive. In fact, *Mohawk* comes from *Mohawauuk*, "man-eaters," a name given the tribe by their enemies, the Narragansett. Living along the Mohawk River in New York State from Schenectady to Utica, the Mohawks sided with the British during the Revolution, but the British did not honor their name in English, *Mohawk* or *Mohock* being used as early as 1711 to indicate one of a class of aristocratic ruffians who infested the streets of London. These *Mohocks* were said to have mauled passers-by "in the same cruel manner which the Mohawks . . . were supposed to do," being in Swift's words: "a race of rakes . . . that play the devil about the town every night, slit people's noses, and beat them."

mohole.   One of the few people to have a hole in the ground named for him is Yugoslav geologist A. Mohorovicic. The first two letters of his name, *Mo*, plus *hole*, give us the world *mohole*, for a hole bored through the earth's crust for geological study.

mole.   John le Carré did not originate the term *mole*, for "an undercover agent in the enemy camp," we are told by retired intelligence officer Walter L. Pforzheimer. According to a news feature in the *New York Times* (Feb. 7, 1984), Mr. Pforzheimer's extensive library of spy literature contains a rare Elizabethan manuscript that proves the term was coined by Francis Bacon. The sense behind the term, of course, is that a mole burrows underground and sleeps there for long periods.

moll.   (*See* **gun moll**.)

molly.   Of the many tropical fish kept in millions of home aquariums only guppies are more popular than *mollies*, but few enthusiasts know that the fish takes its feminine name from a man. Count Nicolas Grancois Mollien (1758-1850) wasn't a tropical fish collector—the hobby dates back only to about 1860—but a French financial genius who served several governments. Mollien was often consulted by Napoleon, who unfortunately refused to accept his advice against instituting his ill-fated "continental system." The tropical freshwater fish genus *Mollienesia* was irregularly named in Mollien's honor and since then all *mollies* with their female nickname bear this man's abbreviated surname.

mollymawk.   (*See* **albatross**.)

Molotov cocktail.   This "cocktail for Molotov" was so named by the Finns while fighting the Russians in 1940. The Russians were dropping bombs on Helsinki at the time, but Russian statesman Vyacheslav Mikhailovich Molotov (1890-1986) claimed that they were only drop-

ping food and drink to their comrades. This equation of food and drink with bombs quickly resulted in the black-humorous term *Molotov breadbasket* for an incendiary bomb and then *Molotov cocktail* for a gasoline-filled bottle with a slow burning wick that is ignited before the crude incendiary is thrown; when the bottle hits the ground it bursts and the ignited gasoline spreads over its target. The weapon had first been used by the Chinese against Japanese tanks in 1937. Molotov was Soviet premier at the time the Finns derisively named the "cocktail" after him. He had only the year before negotiated the infamous Russo-German nonaggression pact, which is sometimes called the Molotov-Ribbentrop pact but is best known as the Pact of Steel. Molotov, a communist from his early youth, changed his name from Skriabin to escape the Czarist police. (*Molotov* comes from *molot*, Russian for "hammer.") He rose quickly in the party hierarchy, serving in many capacities. In 1940 the city of Perm was renamed Molotov in his honor, but the wily diplomat later fell into disfavor, being sharply attacked by Khrushchev at the 22nd Party Congress in 1961, and was expelled from the Communist Party, to which he was readmitted in 1984.

moment.   *Moment* has always been used to mean a portion of time too brief to be taken into account, an instant. But as the name of a definite measure of time it has varied throughout the years. Today a *moment* specifically means a minute, sixty seconds, while, according to one old English time unit, a *moment* took 1 1/2 minutes and in medieval times a *moment* was either 1/40th or 1/50th of a minute. Rabbinical reckoning makes a *moment* precisely 1/1.080 hour. In 1767 a writer described a clock with three hands, "one for the hours, one for the minutes, and a third for the moments."

momser.   (*See* **mamser**.)

Momus.   Momus, the Greek god of ridicule, was banished from heaven for his censures upon the gods—he once blamed Zeus for not having put a window in the breast of a man that Zeus had made. His name has been used in English for a faultfinder or captious critic since at least the 16th century.

Mona Lisa smile; Gioconda smile.   The *Mona* of *Mona Lisa* is short for Madonna or Milady. Leonardo da Vinci worked over a period of four years on his celebrated portrait of Madonna Lisa, who may have been the wife of the Florentine gentleman Francesco Giocondo. Little is really known about the portrait, among the most beautiful in the world, which was completed in 1506 and is still famous for the enigmatic smile that the sitter wears, which has generally been regarded as subtly sensual, a smile of feminine mystery expressing some secret pleasure or emotion. Leonardo is said to have had music played during Madonna Lisa's sitting so that the strange rapt expression wouldn't fade from her face, but this is only one of the many legends attached to the painting, as is the story that Leonardo was in love with the lady. The painting was sold to Francis I for 4,000 gold florins and has remained a treasure of the Louvre ever since, except for a brief period when it was stolen and returned to Italy. The *Mona Lisa smile* is sometimes called the *Gioconda smile*, and the enigmatic Madonna's husband is sometimes identified as Zanobi del Giocondo of Naples rather than Florence.

Monday.   Monday was called *Monandaeg*, "the day of the moon," by the ancient Anglo-Saxons.

money.   In Roman mythology Juno was the wife of Jupiter and queen of the heavens, the goddess whose prime responsibility, among many, was to warn people of dangers. The Romans were so grateful that she had warned them of the Gallic invasion in 344 B.C. that Lucius Furius built a temple to Juno Moneta, as she was called (her last name deriving from the Latin word *moneo*, "warn"), on the Capitoline Hill. Later, the first Roman mint was attached to the temple and Juno Moneta became the goddess and guardian of finance. The coins coined there were called *moneta*, after the goddess, and the word became *moneai* in French, which later became our *money*. The word *mint*, a place where money is made, also derives from *moneta* via the old English *mynot*. (*See also* **mint**.)

money bags.   (*See* **playing the market**.)

money doesn't stink.   Roman Emperor Vespasian (A.D. 9-79) supposedly quipped *pecunia non olet*, "money doesn't stink," when criticized for taxing the public urinals in Rome, these later dubbed *Vespasiennes* (*q.v.*), after this frugal successor to Nero.

money is the root of all evil.   According to the biblical passage from which the expression derives, Paul wrote to Timothy in 1 Tim. 6:10: "For the *love* of money is the root of all evil." Not the same thing at all.

money talks.   Now a folk saying rather than slang, *money talks* means that wealth is power, or money buys anything. Though it is probably older, no one has been able to trace the phrase back before 1910. J.D. Salinger used it in *Catcher in the Rye* (1950): "In New York, boy, money really talks—I'm not kidding."

monger.   (*See* **warmonger**.)

mongoose.   The Marathi name *mangus* for this Indian animal is the basis of our word *mongoose*. The *gus* in *mangus* sounded like *goose* to British ears, even though the mongoose is not even remotely related to the goose.

moniker.   *Moniker*, for "a name," is apparently of hobo origin, dating back to the late 19th century. The word may be a corruption of *monogram*, which is recorded for "a signature" as early as 1859, but there are several other possibilities, including a Shelta word meaning "sign"; and the Latin *monitor*, "an advisor."

monkey.   *Monkey* may derive from a proper name. In one Low German version of the *Reynard the Fox* fable, published in about 1580, *Moneke* is the son of Martin the Ape. *Moneke* either took his name from the German surname *Moneke*, which has many variants, or from the Italian *monna*, "a female ape." However, it is certain that the name for *monkey* persisted due to the popularity of *Reynard the Fox* and the little *moneke* that the tale included.

monkey's fist.   *Monkey* is generally nautical talk for anything small. A *monkey's fist*, dating back at least to the 19th century, is thus the nautical term for the knot or weight at the end of a heaving line that makes it easier to throw.

monkeyshines; monkey business.   "You may have barefooted boys cutting up 'monkeyshines' on trees with entire safety to themselves," observes one of the earliest writers to use *monkeyshines*, monkey-like antics, which is first recorded in 1828. *Monkey business* was recorded a little earlier, at the beginning of the century, both words suggested by the increasing number of monkeys imported by America's growing circuses and zoos.

monkey suit.   Organ grinders used to dress their simian employees in bright-colored little coats and pants that looked ridiculous on them. Feeling that a tuxedo made him look much the same, some anonymous wit dubbed his tux a *monkey suit*, back a century or so ago.

monkey wrench.   One would think that the *monkey wrench* was so named because the wrench's sliding jaws reminded someone of a monkey's chewing apparatus. This may be the case, but there is some reason to believe that the tool was named after its inventor. One source suggests that this mechanical wizard was London blacksmith Charles Moncke, but the British do not commonly call the tool a *monkey wrench*, using instead the term *adjustable spanner wrench*, or just *spanner*, so this theory is suspect. A more likely explanation turned up some years ago in a collection of clippings on word origins collected by a Boston doctor. One article from the *Boston Transcript*, appearing in the winter of 1932-33, attributed the wrench's invention to a Yankee mechanic by the name of Monk employed by Bemis & Call of Springfield, Massachusetts. Monk supposedly invented the movable jaw for a wrench in 1856 and although it was given another name at first, workers in his shop were soon calling it *monkey wrench.* The tale has not been confirmed, but the 1856 date coincides with the first use of the word in the *Oxford English Dictionary* (1858). None of the standard dictionaries make an attempt to trace the word's origin, not even to say that the wrench resembles a monkey's jaw, just as a crane resembles a crane's neck.

monkshood.　(*See* **aconite.**)

the monosyllable.　(*See* **The venerable monosyllable.**)

Monrovia.　Monrovia, the seaport capital of Liberia, was named for U.S. President James Monroe in 1822 when the American Colonization Society founded it as a haven for ex-slaves from the United States. *Mencken* quotes a Liberian diplomat who says that the descendants of these American slaves, now Liberia's ruling class, "prefer to be called . . . Monrovian Liberians to distinguish themselves from the natives of the hinterland, who are generally called by their tribal names."

Monsieur and Madame Veto.　(*See* **veto.**)

Montana.　*Montana*, previously the *Montana Territory*, takes its name from the Spanish word for "mountainous." The Treasure State was admitted to the Union in 1889 as our 41st state.

Montespan.　Another of Louis XIV's favorites whose name became synonymous with "mistress." Françoise Athénaïs de Pardaillan, the Marquise de Montespan, was the daughter of a nobleman, Gabriel de Rochechouart, duc de Montmart. While serving as maid of honor to Louis's Queen Marie-Thérèse in 1663 she married the Marquis de Montespan. The Sun King's first mistress, La Vallière, introduced Madame de Montespan to him, which she eventually regretted, as the beautiful and brilliant woman replaced her in the king's affections. La Vallière was cruelly discarded and Montespan became Louis's mistress, bearing him seven children, all of whom were later legitimized by the crown, in addition to the two she bore her husband. In the end, however, Montespan lost out to Madame de Maintenon, her companion and the governess of her children, suffering the same fate as her predecessor. But Montespan did not give up so easily. When Louis's affections showed signs of ebbing and he turned to Madame de Maintenon in about 1673, Montespan tried resorting to magic, consulting the infamous sorceress La Voison. She even tried to poison the Sun King's food, but Louis had such fond memories of her that the assassination attempt was hushed up. In 1691, she retired to a convent with a large pension from the king, and she died sixteen years later, aged sixty-six. (*See* **lavaliere; Maintenon; pompadour.**)

Montezuma's revenge.　(*See* **Aztec two-step.**)

Moog synthesizer.　This computer-like musical instrument, able to duplicate the sounds of twelve instruments simultaneously, was named in the 1960s for its American inventor, Robert Moog.

mooncussers.　*Mooncussers* were so called because they cussed the moon and the light that it brought, which robbed them of their livelihood. During the early 19th century, these lowlifes lured merchant ships to shore on dark nights by waving lanterns that were mistaken for the lights of other vessels. When ships were destroyed on the rocks, their cargo was collected as salvage.

moon hoax.　Quite a few Americans have walked on the moon by now and none has seen evidence of life there, but in 1835, according to *New York Sun* reporter Richard Adams Locke, the eminent British astronomer Sir John Herschel trained a new, powerful telescope on the moon and observed some fifteen species of animals, including what seemed to be a race of winged men. Locke's article, supposedly reprinted from the actually defunct Edinburgh *Journal of Science*, raised the circulation of Locke's newspaper from 2,500 to 20,000, and inspired one ladies' club to raise money to send missionaries to the moon. The book that the *Sun* reporter wrote based on the article sold over 60,000 copies, and was studied assiduously by a scientific delegation from Yale. Locke finally admitted his hoax the following year, calling it a satire on absurd scientific speculations that had gotten out of hand. His friend Poe, who never believed a word of the story, nevertheless admitted that it had anticipated most of his own "Hans Pfall," which was the reason he left that story unfinished.

the moon is made of green cheese.　Often credited to Sir Thomas More and Rabelais, this proverb actually dates back to at least the early 15th century. Even then it was assumed that anyone who believed the moon was made of green cheese, or "cream cheese", as one writer put it, was a complete fool. Originally the expression was *The moone is made of a green cheese.* Green cheese wasn't a cheese green in color, but a new cheese that hadn't aged properly yet and resembled the full moon in shape.

moonlighting.　*Moonlighting* has taken on the meaning of working at a second job after one's regular job, especially by public servants such as policemen, who are sometimes prohibited from doing so. But the word dates back to at least the late 19th century when, in England and Ireland, it meant "the performance at night of an illicit action," especially an expedition to steal or harm another's property.

moonlit.　*Moonlit* is an adjective one might have guessed had been invented by a young romantic poet, and so it was. Tennyson coined the word in his *Arabian Nights*

(1830), when he was only 21: "The sloping of the moon-lit sward. . ." The British poet laureate, successor to Wordsworth, also invented *evil-starred*, in "Locksley Hall," 1842.

moose. Early American Indians noticed that the creature we call a *moose* ate tender bark that it ripped off trees. They named the herbivore *mus*, meaning "to tear away," this Algonquian word becoming the English word *moose*.

moot point. A moot point is either a question that is debatable or a point that is purely hypothetical. The Anglo-Saxon words *mot*, "to meet," and *gemot*, "a meeting," are the parents of the term. In ancient times a moot was an assembly of the people, usually a court where important questions were settled by means of the public assembly. Debates on important issues were common in such courts, giving the word *moot* its present meanings. Moot courts, where hypothetical cases are discussed by law students for practice, originated at the London law colleges called the Inns of Court in the 16th century, and these moot courts reinforced the current meaning of *moot point*.

mop-up operation. Along with *concentration camp*, another horror of modern warfare, this military term traces back to the Boer War, when the British cleared the last traces of the enemy from territory they had just won—the way a housewife mops up something spilled on the floor. The word *mop* probably comes from the Latin *mappa*, "cloth," which also gives us the word *map*. *Mop fairs*, or hiring fairs, were held in England over two centuries ago, with domestics gathering on the fair grounds ready to be inspected by potential employers.

mora. Deriving from the Italian *mora*, of unknown origin, *mora* or *morra* is a game in which one player guesses the number of fingers held up simultaneously by another player. The ancient Romans called the game *micare digitis* and a Chinese version is called *chai mei*. The game, explains one writer, "consists in showing the fingers to the other across the table, and mentioning a number at the same moment; as if one opens out two fingers, and mentions the number four, the other instantly shows six fingers, and mentions that number—if he errs in giving the complement of ten, he pays a forfeit by drinking a cup." A similar game called "love" was recorded in England about a century earlier (1585), a player in this version holding up a certain number of fingers and the other player, eyes closed, trying to guess that number. The old game was played by Rabelais and, no doubt, Shakespeare.

more than one way to skin a cat. *There are more ways of killing a cat than choking it with cream*, was the older form of this British expression. This implied that the method under discussion was rather foolish, since cats like cream and wouldn't likely choke to death on it. But the saying evolved until it took on its present meaning—that there are more ways than one of accomplishing an undertaking. The expression shouldn't be confused with the American saying *skinning the cat*, which describes the maneuver where a child, hanging from a tree branch, draws up his legs up through his arms and over the branch and pulls himself into a sitting position atop the branch.

morganatic marriage. (*See* **left-handed compliment**.)

Morgan horse. Justin Morgan is the only American horse ever to sire a distinctive breed. A bay stallion foaled in about 1793, he belonged to Justin Morgan (1747-98), a Vermont schoolteacher. The horse bearing Morgan's name was probably a blend of thoroughbred and Arabian with other elements, fairly small at fourteen hands high and 800 pounds. Morgan, an aspiring musician, bought his colt in Massachusetts, naming him Figure and training him so well that he won trotting races against much larger thoroughbreds. Eventually, Figure came to be called after his master. After his owner died, Justin Morgan was bought and sold many times in the twenty-eight years of his life. One of those unusual horses whose dominant traits persist despite centuries of inbreeding, his individual characteristics remain essentially unchanged in the *Morgan* breed of horses he sired. *Morgans* are still compact, virile horses noted for their intelligence, docility, and longevity, many of them active when thirty years of age or more. Heavy-shouldered, with a short neck but delicate head, they are noted for their airy carriage and naturally pure gait and speed. Morgans were long the favorite breed for American trotters until the Hambletonian strain replaced them.

Mornay sauce. French Protestant leader Philippe de Mornay (1549-1623) invented *sauce Mornay* for King Henry IV. Made with fish broth, the white sauce is enriched with Parmesan and Gruyere cheese and butter. Popularly known as the Protestant Pope, Mornay was Henry's right-hand man until the king converted to Catholicism and the Seigneur Duplessis-Mornay fell out of favor. After Henry's assassination, Louis XIII finally retired Mornay as governor of Saumur because of his opposition to the government's rapprochement with Catholic Spain. Mornay's spiritual writings and organizing abilities strongly influenced the development of a Protestant party in France.

moron; amp. It is often noted that *moron*, as a scientific designation for a feebleminded person, was the only word ever voted into the language. It was adopted in 1910 by the American Association for the Study of the Feeble

Minded from the name of a foolish character in Molière's play *La Princess d'Elide*. This claim overlooks the fact that the unit of electric current called an *ampere*, or *amp*, was adopted at the International Electrical Congress held in Paris twenty-nine years earlier. The ampere, the unit by which the strength and rate of flow of an electric current can be measured, was named for the brilliant French scientist André Marie Ampère (1775-1836). His name also gives us such technical terms as *amperehour*, *Ampère's law*, *ampereturn*, and *amperometric titration*.

morpheme. A *morpheme*, from the Greek *morphema*, "unit of form," is the smallest part of speech that conveys a meaning. In the word *dogs*, for instance, *dog* is one morpheme, while *-s*, indicating plurality, is another.

Morris chair. Something of a complete Renaissance man was English poet, artist, and pamphleteer William Morris (1834-96). His collected works fill twenty-four volumes, and it would take a good many volumes to do justice to his full life. In addition to his poetry and art, Morris found time to help establish England's Socialist Party and can be counted an architect, interior decorator, master craftsman, novelist, translator, editor, publisher, and printer as well. In 1861 he founded a company to reform Victorian tastes by producing wallpaper, furniture, stained glass, metalware, and other decorations. Thus began the arts and crafts movement in England, which emphasized naturalness and purity of color in objects produced by hand. Among the furniture made by the company was the *Morris chair*, a large easy chair with an adjustable back and removable cushions.

Morris dance. The *Morris dance*, originally a "Moorish dance," derived from the ancient military dances of the Moors. Introduced into England from Spain by John of Gaunt in about 1350, its name in French was *danse mauresque* and in Flemish *mooriske dans*. But the dance, which used the tabor as an accompaniment, eventually assumed a very British flavor. It was usually performed by groups of five men and a boy—the five miming Robin Hood, Little John, Friar Tuck, Allan-a-Dale, and other characters from the Robin Hood stories, while the boy played Maid Marian. Generally danced on May Day and in various processions and pageants, the fantastic spectacular was banned by the Puritans but was later revived. It has been revived recently with the renewed interest in folk dancing.

Morse Code. "What hath God wrought?" were the famous words sent in *Morse Code* by its inventor on May 24, 1844. Samuel Finley Breese Morse (1791-1872) had begun experimenting with his electric telegraph twelve years earlier, and Congress later granted the penniless inventor $30,000 to build the experimental line from Washington to Baltimore over which he sent his historic message. The *Morse Code* he invented in conjunction with his telegraph was first called the *Morse alphabet* and is of course a system of dots and dashes representing letters, figures, and punctuation, the dash in the system equaling three times the length of the dot in time. Morse didn't start out as a scientist. After graduation from Yale, he studied in England and began a career in art, earning a reputation as a portrait painter. Though his interest in electricity began during his college days, he was unaware that a number of telegraphs had been independently invented before 1830. Morse was forced to defend his invention in various patent suits, but emerged a victorious and very wealthy man.

mortal coil. Shakespeare of course made this term famous in *Hamlet*, but many who use the phrase have some vague idea that the *coil* in it is a synonym for the globe or sphere. This is not so, the *coil* here deriving from Elizabethan slang for turmoil or bustle.

mortarboard. The caps worn with their gowns by high school and college graduates in America were apparently named by some anonymous mid-19th century wit who thought they resembled the square boards masons still use for holding mortar. The cap began life as ecclesiastical headgear in the 17th century and wasn't worn by university students until the early 1800s or thereabouts.

mortgage. English jurist Sir Edward Coke explained in the early 17th century why the Old French expression *mortgage* meant "dead pledge," taking its name from *mort*, "dead," and *gage*, "pledge": "It seemeth that the cause why it is called mortgage is, for that it is doubtful whether the Feoffer will pay at the day limited such summe or not & if he doth not pay, then the land which is put in pledge upon condition for the payment of the money, is taken from him for ever, and so dead to him upon condition, & c. And if he doth pay the money, then the pledge is dead as to the Tenant . . ."

mosaic. The two words *mosaic*, "a design or picture made from small pieces of stone or other material," and *Mosaic*, referring to the prophet Moses, are unrelated. In fact, the strict Jewish and Muhammadan interpretations of the Ten Commandments Moses brought down from Mount Sinai hold that the second Commandment forbids the making of any likeness of anything, so the capital letter in *Mosaic* is an important distinguisher. The word for the design *mosaic* comes to us via French and Latin from the Greek *Mousa* ("a Muse"), *mosaic* work being associated with the Muses in ancient Greece. (*See* **Moses' cradle**.)

Moses' cradle; Mosaic code. A *Moses' cradle* is a shallow wicker bassinet, its name deriving from the basket made of bullrushes that Moses' mother hid him in when oppressed Israelites were ordered to kill all their male children (Exod. 2:1-5). Pharaoh's daughter found the child, named him Moses, "Because I drew him out of the water," and let his mother nurse him. As a young man, Moses, who grew up in the splendor of the court, killed an Egyptian oppressing a Jew and fled into the wilderness, but at an age of eighty he was called by God, through a voice from a burning bush, to return to Egypt and free the Hebrews. Pharaoh refused God's demand until ten plagues were sent and Moses then led his people to Mount Sinai. For forty years after he led them through the wilderness, drawing up religious and ethical rules known as the *Mosaic code* during this time. The first five books of the Bible, the Hebrew Torah or the Pentateuch, are regarded as Moses' work. After viewing Canaan from Mount Nebo, he died alone at 120, his people compelled to wander in the wilderness until one generation had passed away because they had rebelled against crossing into the Promised Land. (*See* **mosaic.**)

mosey. According to *Webster's* and most authorities the Spanish *vamos*, "let's go," became *vamoose* in American English, which begot the slang word *mosey*, "to stroll or saunter about leisurely." But it is possible, one theory holds, that the word instead takes its name "from the slouching manner of wandering Jewish peddlers in the West, many of whom were called Moses, Mose, or Mosey." Neither explanation seems ideal, but nothing better has been offered.

the most unkindest cut of all. "This was the most unkindest cut of all," Shakespeare had Antony say in *Julius Caesar*. This most famous of literary double superlatives wasn't the only such "grammatical crudity" he used. The double superlative and double comparative ("more larger") were considered excellent devices for emphasis by Elizabethan writers. So were multiple negatives like the Bard's "Thou hast spoken no word all this while—nor understood none either."

motel. Most sources credit West Coast motor lodge owner Oscar T. Tomerlin with coining the word *motel* in 1930, Tomerlin welding it together from *motor hotel*, which he had previously called his place. But in her book *Palaces of the Public, A History of American Hotels* (1983) Doris E. King says that the word originated in 1925 with a San Luis Obispo, California establishment that offered a garage with its roadside cottages and called itself a *Mot-el Inn.* (*See* **No-tel Motel.**)

moth-eaten. People have been using this expression for at least 600 years to describe something eaten by moths or old. However, it isn't adult moths, but moth larvae that destroy clothing that isn't stored properly. The moths we see fluttering around in the closet don't eat clothing, and some species eat nothing at all during their brief adult lives.

Mother Carey's chickens. *Mother Carey's chickens* is a mystery because no real Mother Carey has ever been found. But many etymologists uphold *Brewer's* theory that the phrase is a corruption of the Latin *Mater Cara* ("Dear Mother"), another name for the Virgin Mary. However, in the absence of evidence, Ernest Weekley's conclusion in *The Romance of Words* still seems best: "Mother Carey's chickens, probably a nautical corruption of some old Spanish or Italian name; but, in spite of ingenious guesses, this lady's genealogy remains as obscure as that of Davey Jones or the Jolly Roger." The sea birds are also called *petrels* (*q.v*).

Mother Goose. The famous book of nursery rhymes often called *Mother Goose's Melodies* is said to have been printed in Boston in 1719 by Thomas Fleet, from verses his mother-in-law, Mrs. Elizabeth Goose, created or remembered and repeated. There is no doubt that Mrs. Goose (1665-1757) existed. She was born Elizabeth Foster in Charlestown, Massachusetts, and at the age of twenty-seven married Isaac Goose (formerly Vergoose) of Boston, inheriting ten stepchildren and bearing six children of her own. One of her daughters married the printer Fleet, who had a shop on Pudding Lane in Boston. At this point the facts become unclear, yielding, at any rate, many a good story.

Mother Shipton. A female *Nostradamus* (*q.v.*), *Mother Shipton* is a legendary figure in English literature who is supposed to have foretold the death of Cromwell and the great London fire of 1666, among other accurate predictions. According to the *Life of Mother Shipton*, written by Richard Head in 1667, more than a century after her death, her real name was Ursula Shipton and she lived in Knaresborough, Yorkshire, from 1488-1561. Born Ursula Southill or Southiel, her peasant mother was regarded as a witch by villagers, and Ursula appears to have been so ugly that she was called the "Devil's child", though not so ugly as to prevent a builder named Tobias Shipton from marrying her. Virtually nothing is known about her life, all the "facts" at best traditions, but Mother Shipton's prophecies, like Mother Nixon's, had a phenomenal hold on the minds of rural folk until as late as 1881. In that year the rumor that she had predicted the end of the world caused people to flee their homes and pray in the fields and churches all night. It developed that this prediction, along with others foretelling the coming of the steam engine, telegraph, telephone, and other modern inventions arose out of a forgery of the early *Life* by Charles Hindley, in which he added many "predictions" that had already come to pass.

Motown. Southern American blacks originated this term for Detroit early in the 1940s, after emmigrating there to work in defense plants. *Motown* is of course short for *Motortown*.

mountain oysters. (*See* **prairie oysters.**)

Mount Vernon. (*See* **grog.**)

mountebank. Quacks often sold their nostrums at medieval fairs by mounting a bench and giving their pitch—so often that they were given the name *mountebanks*, from the Italian *montambanco*, "mount on bench."

mourning tree. Once cut, the *cypress* never grows again, which probably led to its being dedicated to Pluto, the king of the infernal regions in Roman mythology. For this reason the beautiful *Cypressus funebris* was often planted in cemeteries along the Mediterranean and its wood was used to make coffins, the tree often referred to as the *mourning tree*.

mousse. (*See* **chocolate mousse.**)

moxie. The rather tart flavor of Moxie, a popular New England soft drink, or tonic, as soda pop is often called in the area, may be the reason it yielded the slang word *moxie*, for "courage, nerve, or guts." Or maybe Moxie braced up a lot of people, giving them courage. These are only guesses, but the tonic, a favorite since at least 1927, is definitely responsible for *a lot of moxie* and other phrases, which, however, aren't recorded until about 1939. I've read that Moxie was originally a nerve tonic, dating back to the 1880s. This would go far in explaining *moxie*, "nerve or courage," if earlier uses for the term could be found.

Mr.; Mrs. Because it was originally an abbreviation of *mistress* (wife), a word that has completely changed its meaning since then, *Mrs.* can no longer be spelled out in full form and is considered a word in itself—unlike *Mr.* which can be written out as *Mister*.

Mrs. Grundy.

> They eat, and drink, and scheme, and plod,
>   And go to sleep on Sunday—
> And many are afraid of God—
>   And more of Mrs. Grundy.

These lines from Frederick Locker-Lampson's poem "The Jester" (1857) were inspired by a character in British playwright Thomas Morton's comedy *Speed the Plough*, first staged at London's Covent Garden in 1800. Actually Mrs. Grundy is something less than a character, for she never appears on stage and is never described physically. She is the epitome of propriety, the narrow-minded, straitlaced neighbor of Farmer Ashfield and Dame Ashfield, his wife, who is obsessed with Mrs. Grundy's opinion of things. "What will Mrs. Grundy say? What will

Mrs. Grundy think?" is on Dame Ashfield's lips so often that the words became proverbial for "What will that straitlaced neighbor say? What will the neighbors think?" and Mrs. Grundy herself became a symbol of prudish propriety or social convention. Dickens's Mrs. Harris, the mythical friend of Sara Gamp in *Martin Chuzzlewit* (1843) is a similar character.

Ms. Though it became popular only in the 1960s, this useful title for either a married or unmarried woman (taking the place of both Mrs. and Miss and pronounced "Miz") was coined by Kansas newspaperman Roy F. Bailey in 1950.

mucilage. (*See* **nose.**)

muckraker. Teddy Roosevelt used the expression *man with the muckrake*, taken from *Pilgrims Progress*, as a derogatory term for those who indiscriminately and irresponsibly charged others with corruption. Lincoln Steffens and other reformers, however, gladly wore the epithet *muckraker* as a badge of honor.

mucus. (*See* **nose.**)

mug; mugging; mugger. Mugging seems first to have been New York City slang for what was called "yoking" in other parts of the country, that is, robbery committed by two holdup men, one clasping the victim around the neck from behind while the other ransacks his pockets. The term either derives from the *mugs* who commit such crimes or from the expression on the victim's face as he is brutally yoked, which can appear as if he is mugging, grimacing, or making a funny face. The term is now well-known throughout the country. As often as not the *mugger* acts alone today, and *mugging* has become a synonym for holding someone up. The spelling "mugg" seems to be yielding to *mug*. The word *mug*, for "a grimace" was introduced to England by the Gypsies and may derive from the Sanskrit word *mukka*, "face." *Mug*, was used as slang for "face" in England as early as 1840. *Mug* for a heavy cup may come from the Swedish *mugg* meaning the same.

mugwump. The term for great chief in Algonquin Indian dialect sounded like "mugquomp" to settlers in what is now the northeastern U.S. and soon came to mean any pompous "big shot," its spelling altered to a simpler *mugwump*. A century later *mugwump* took on another meaning in politics when regular Republicans attached it to those Republicans who bolted the party to support Democrat Grover Cleveland, instead of the corrupt James Blaine. Since then any party member who doesn't accept the party leadership and supports the opposition is called a *mugwump*.

Muhammadanism. Muhammad (or Mohammed, or Mahomet) "the praiseworthy," was the title given to the founder of the Muslim religion, his original name having been Kotham or Halabi. The prophet of the Arabs was born after his father's death in about 570 A.D., grew up as an orphan in Mecca, and died in Medina in 632. A camel driver at twenty-five, he married his employer, a rich widow fifteen years his senior, who became the first of his ten wives. Muhammad was forty when he felt he had been called to be a prophet and began receiving messages he believed were from God, who commanded him to relay them to his countrymen. He called the monotheistic religion he preached Islam, not *Muhammadanism*, *(q.v.)* its keystone being that "There is no God but Allah and Muhammad is his prophet." (*See* **If the mountain will not come to Muhammad**.)

mulberry. An Asiatic legend recounted in Ovid's *Metamorphoses* tells how mulberries became red. Pyramus, a Babylonian youth, loved Thisbe, the girl next door, and when their parents forbade them to marry, they exchanged their vows through an opening in the wall between their two houses. Thisbe agreed to meet her lover at the foot of a white mulberry tree near the tomb of Ninus outside the city walls, but on reaching their trysting place she was frightened by a lion, and, dropping her veil, fled deep into a cave. The lion, its mouth red from another kill, ripped up the veil, covering it with blood, and when Pyramus arrived and found the bloody veil, he thought Thisbe had been killed and devoured by the beast. Throwing himself on his sword, he committed suicide just as Thisbe emerged from the cave. Distraught at the sight of her dying lover, Thisbe, too, fell upon his sword, the blood of young love mingling and flowing to the roots of the white mulberry, which thereafter bore only red fruit. Legend also has it that the mulberry takes its botanical name, *Morus*, from the Greek *morus*, meaning "a fool." This has no connection with the Pyramus myth, according to the *Hortus Anglicus*, but is related to the fact that it "can't be fooled," that the tree "is reputed to be the wisest of all flowers as it never buds till the cold weather is past and gone." As for the word *mulberry* itself, which should properly be *morberry*, it more prosaically derives from the Latin *morus*, which became *mure* in French. The English called the berry the *mureberry* at first, but this was difficult to pronounce (too many *r*'s) and was eventually corrupted to *mulberry* in everyday speech.

mulberry mania. Much has been written about *international tulipomania* (*q.v.*), but virtually none of our history books even mentions our *American mulberry mania* of the 1830s. This was a craze for planting the Philippine white mulberry variety *Morus multicaulis* ("many stemmed") in expectation of making great profits in the silk industry. The leaves of these trees were said to be superior to all others for silkworm feeding and millions of them were planted in the *multicaulis fever* that ensued.

The fever began in Connecticut, where the seven Cheney brothers founded America's first silk mill at South Manchester in 1838, after having experimented with silk culture for five years. One year, from 300 mulberry trees laid horizontally in the ground, there sprang 3,700 shoots, enough to feed 6,000 silkworms. This meant bushels of cocoons and yards of much wanted silk. Many farmers followed the Cheney's example, and across America books and articles were published about raising mulberry trees. Silk societies were formed and bounties offered. Prices spiraled crazily. In 1838, 2 1/2-foot cuttings skyrocketed from $25 to $500 per hundred. In Pennsylvania alone, as much as $300,000 changed hands for mulberry trees in a week, and trees were frequently resold by speculators at great profits within a few days. But by 1840 mulberry trees glutted the market at 5 cents each. When speculation collapsed and the so-called "golden-rooted trees" were uprooted from plantations in 1839, disgruntled investors coined a new word from the mulberry's scientific name that served as slang of the time: *multicaulished*, meaning "run out, good for nothing, disliked." After the *mulberry blight* struck in 1844, killing whole groves of trees, the mulberry mania faded completely.

mule rabbit. (*See* **jackrabbit**.)

muller. Our murderer wore a low-crowned felt hat pulled down over his face in an attempt to disguise himself. But his scheme didn't work. Mr. Muller was arrested and convicted of murder, the publicity attending his hat making it more famous than the killer himself. Not only was Muller the prototype for countless real and fictional villains with large-brimmed hats pulled down over their eyes, but his name came to mean "a deerstalker hat" in England from about 1855 to 1885, a *muller* probably being the only hat in history that was named for a murderer.

mulligan. When you're allowed to take a *mulligan* in golf—a free shot not counted against the score after your first one goes bad—you may not be emulating some duffer of days gone by. *Mulligan* probably comes from the brand name of a once popular sauce that was standard in barrooms. This potent seasoning of water and hot pepper seeds was sometimes mixed with beer and jokers swore that it ate out your liver, stomach, and finally your *heart*—just what happens when you accept too many *mulligans* on the golf course. On the other hand, there are those who say that *mulligan* derives from the name of Canadian David Mulligan, who in the late 1920s was allowed an extra shot by his friends in appreciation for driving his friends over rough roads every week for their foursome at the St. Lambert Country Club near Montreal.

mulligan stew. *Mulligan stew* is made of meat and vegetables—whatever is available or can be begged or stolen. It is an American term, honoring an Irishman whose first name has been lost but who may have made a tasty Irish stew. *Mulligan*, popular among American tramps, is also called *slumgullion*, or slum, the term coming into use during the American gold rush when slumgullion was originally the muddy residue remaining after sluicing gravel.

mulligrubs. The *O.E.D.* calls *mulligrubs*, "a state of depression," a "gross arbitrary formation," and lets it go at that. The word is from British dialect, first recorded in 1599, and is possibly a corruption of "moldy grubs." Besides meaning *the blue devils* it can mean a stomachache. A variant is the obsolete *mubblefubbles*.

mullion. There are indeed "millions of mullions" in modern skyscrapers, for a *mullion* is the slender vertical member separating windows. The word is an alteration of the synonymous *monial*, and is first recorded in 1567.

multimillionaire. *Multimillionaire* was first applied to John Jacob Astor, soon after his death in 1848, aged 85. Astor had made his money in fur and New York City real estate, "the richest man in America" amassing a fortune of well over $75 million—which made a person a lot richer back then than it does today. (*See also* **billionaire; millionaire; milliard; myriad; trillionaire.**)

multiplication, division, and silence. A historical expression no longer much used that gives the qualities most needed by a machine politician, who had to *multiply* the sources of graft, *divide* it among his flunkies, and *keep quiet* about it all. New York's "Boss" Tweed (1823-76) may have invented the phrase when asked what qualities he looked for when selecting his henchmen.

mumbo jumbo. *Mama Dyumbo* was really more a male chauvinist god than anything else. The English explorer Mungo Park writes in his *Travels in the Interior of Africa* that *Mama Dyumbo* was the spirit protecting the villages of the Khassonke, a Mandingo African tribe on the Senegal. His name literally means "ancestor with a pompon," or wearing a tuft on his hat. *Mama Dyumbo* was mostly a ploy used by crafty husbands to silence their noisy wives. He was called upon when a man thought one of his wives talked too much, causing dissension in his house. The husband or a confederate disguised himself as *Mama Dyumbo* and seized the troublemaker, frightening her with his mask, tufted headdress, and the hideous noises he made. He'd then tie the offender to a tree and "whip her silent" amid the jeers of onlookers. (The custom recalls the ducking stool procedure employed in America.) Mungo Park dubbed the bogey employed in this ritual "Mandingo," but he became known as *Mumbo Jumbo*, a corruption of *Mama Dyumbo*. Because the god bewildered offending women, *mumbo jumbo* came to mean confusing talk, nonsense, and meaningless ceremony, or even technical jargon that could just as well be put into plain English.

mummy. The Egyptians preserved the corpses of their dead in elaborate ways, concluding the process by wrapping a corpse in bandages and waterproofing the bandages with a waxy pitch that their Persian conquerors called *mum*. This word became *mummia* in Arabic and, over a thousand years later, changed to *mummy* in English, coming to mean not only the waxy pitch covering the bandages but the preserved body itself.

mum's the word. *Mum's the word* didn't enter into the language through that punning advertising slogan of an underarm deodorant manufacturer so familiar to millions. For about four centuries *mum* has meant "quiet" or "hush" in English, deriving from the Middle English *momme*, meaning the same, which is imitative in origin. *Mum's the word* is an Americanism dating back to at least 1856.

Munchausen. Baron Munchausen once shot a stag with a cherry stone and afterwards found the stag with a cherry tree growing out of its head. At least so Rudolph Erich Raspe wrote in his *Baron Munchausen's Narrative of his Marvellous Travels and Campaigns in Russia* (1785). Raspe was a German librarian who fled to England to escape the consequences of a jewel theft he had committed and wrote the very successful book to restore his resources. But he did base his character and many of his adventures on an actual Karl Friedrich Hieronymus, Freiherr von Munchausen (1720-97), a German officer who served in the Russian cavalry against the Turks and was known to grossly exaggerate his experiences. Thanks to Raspe's further exaggerations of his escapades in his one-shilling book, and many additions afterward in editions fathered by other authors, the real baron's name soon meant both a fantastic liar and a marvelous, classic lie.

mung bean; bean sprouts. The Asian mung bean takes its name from the Tamil *mungu* meaning the same. These are the beans that are easiest to sprout, taking barely three days, and are used for Chinese *bean sprouts*.

Murcott Honey orange. (*See* **orange.**)

murder will out. "Mordre wol out, that see we day by day," Chaucer wrote in "The Nun's Priest's Tale." Before this we find a similar phrase, *Murder cannot be hid*, used with the same meaning: Your sins will find you out, your sinful secret will be revealed.

a Murmansk run.   During World War II *a Murmansk run* became a synonym for a dangerous sea voyage because hundreds of cargo ships were sunk by Nazi subs and planes while crossing the North Atlantic to the ice-free Russian port of Murmansk.

murmur.   (*See* **onomotopoeia**.)

murphy.   A *murphy* is a confidence game, originating in America, in which the victim is let in on "a good thing" and asked to put up evidence of his good faith in the form of cash. When he supplies the required amount, the con man pleads that he must leave somewhere quickly on business, but will return shortly, depositing the envelope containing the cash with his victim. Only when the mark opens the envelope later does he realize that paper cut to size has been substituted for his money. There are endless variations on the game, including the trick where a prostitute collects from a customer first and then goes out the back door. No one has identified the Murphy who first used this ruse to *murphy* someone. The same holds true for the *murphy* that is an Irish or white potato, named so because Murphy is a very common Irish name and potatoes, the English believed, were the staple food of the Irish diet. *Donovan*, another common Irish name, is also used by the English as slang for a white potato.

Murphy bed.   A *Murphy bed* is a space-saving bed that can be folded or swung into a closet or cabinet; it is named after American inventor William Lawrence Murphy (1876-1950).

Murphy's Law.   Who the illustrious Mr. Murphy was remains anybody's guess, but some swear that he formulated two other laws besides the immortal "If anything can go wrong it will." The other two are "Everything will take longer than you think it will" and "Nothing is as easy as it looks." It is said that Murphy was killed by a car driven by an Englishman just arrived in the U.S. while taking a stroll down a country road and carefully walking on the left-hand side of the road to face the approaching traffic. *O'Toole's Commentary on Murphy's Law*, a law in itself, says basically that "Murphy was an optimist."

Musa.   The banana tree, really a giant herb whose collection of fruits, or "fingers," forms the familiar banana "hand," was given the scientific name *Musa* by Linnaeus in honor of Antonio Musa, personal physician to Augustus, the first emperor of Rome. *Musa sapientum*, the most common banana tree species, takes its second name from the Latin word for "wise men," in reference to the sages of old who reposed in its shade and ate its fruit. The banana is one of the oldest fruits known to man and among the first to be cultivated, our word *banana* (*q.v.*) being of later African origin. As previously mentioned, the Koran says that the forbidden fruit was a banana, not an apple. Together with the plantain, a *Musa* species commonly called the *cooking banana*, the fruit is a staple foodstuff throughout the world. The most common eating variety today is the Cavendish (*Musa cavendishi*), a dwarf plant less resistant to disease and wind damage that was discovered in southern China in 1829 and named either for its discoverer or developer. (*See* **Adam's apple tree**.)

muscular Christianity.   This expression has nothing to do with the spread of Christianity by force, as some people think. An anonymous admirer so named Charles Kingsley's brand of religion in the middle of the last century; the reverend taught that Christianity should be hearty and strong-minded in order to help one "fight the battle of life bravely and manfully." Reverend Kingsley himself found the term "painful if not offensive," but it didn't need his approval. Dickens's amiable canon Mr. Crisparkle in the unfinished *The Mystery of Edwin Drood* is a good example of the type in literature. Kingsley, an advocate of social reform, is famous for his novels *Westward Ho!* and *Water Babies*.

mush!   French trappers in the Northwest used to urge on the dogs pulling their sleds across the snow with *Marchons*!: "let's go!, hurry up!" This was corrupted to *mush on!* in English and by 1862 had become *mush!* "Dog French," one writer called it.

mushroom.   When Englishmen in the 15th century tried to pronounce the French word for this succulent fungus, *moisseron*, it came out *Muscheron*, which over the years became *mushroom*, this pronunciation probably to some extent influenced by the common English words *mush* and *room*. All in all, they may have been better off with their native name for the edible fungus: *toad's hat*. "Toad's hat" is no longer heard, but *toadstool* is of course still the name for inedible, poisonous mushrooms. The French word *moisseron*, from which mushroom sprang up, is generally accepted as a derivative of *mousse*, "moss," upon which mushrooms grow. Cities that sprang up rapidly, that seemed to spring up like mushrooms overnight, were called *mushrooms* in England as early as 1787. Within another century the name became a verb meaning to spread out, being first applied to bullets that expand and flatten, then to fires, and then to anything that grows rapidly. The fungus called a *mushroom* takes its name from the Latin *mussirio* meaning the same.

music of the spheres.

> Forward and backward rapt and whirled are
> According to the music of the spheres.
> —Sir John Davies, *Orchestra* (1596)

Pythagoras taught that the spheres, or planets, made

harmonious sounds as they moved through space and Plato said that on each planet there sat a siren singing a sweet song that harmonized with the songs of all the other planets. Even further back, in biblical times, the Book of Job relates that "the morning stars sang together." The reasoning behind the belief is that "planets move at different rates of motion . . . and must make sounds in their motion acccording to their different rates," but "as all things in nature are harmoniously made, the different sounds must harmonize." At any rate, Chaucer, Milton, and Shakespeare all believed this theory and gave expression to it in poetry, although the phrase *music of the spheres* didn't find its way into the spoken language until the end of the 18th century.

mussel. Both the muscles in our bodies and the mussels in the sea take their name from the common house mouse. The early Romans rather whimsically thought that body muscles, appearing and disappearing as men competed in athletic games and then rested, resembled tiny mice appearing and disappearing at play. Similarly, little dark-colored mice were also thought to resemble the dark-colored marine bivalves the Romans liked to serve at their banquets. Thus, both the muscle and the mussel were named *musculus*, or "little mouse." The marine mussel's name is spelled differently today only because this makes it easier to distinguish it from *muscle*.

mustard gas. Poisonous *mustard gas*, dichlordiethyl sulfide, invented by the Germans during World War I, in about 1917, and one of the most terrible weapons of that wretched war, is really an atomized liquid rather than a gas. It produces burns, blindness, and death, often blistering the face and mouth. The so-called gas takes its name from its color, smell, and its mustard-like effects on eyes and lungs—though there is no mustard in it.

mutt. *Mutt*, for a "mongrel," has a long pedigree and was first a contemptuous term for a common, stupid man. As early as 1508 *mutton* was a Scottish word for a dumb man; by the 18th century *muttonheaded* was being used in England; and by the early 1900s Americans were calling commonplace stupid men *mutts* before applying the word to commonplace mongrel dogs. Every dog is of course a mutt, if you go back far enough in its ancestry.

Mutt and Jeff. We use this expression frequently to compare two friends or a loving couple, one short and one tall. The term is from the comic strip "Mutt and Jeff" created by Henry Conway (Bud) Fisher in 1907, but the little guy is named after former heavyweight champion James J. Jeffries. It happened when artist Fisher had Augustus

Mutt, the tall, chinless member of the duo, visit a sanitarium in an early strip; there Mutt met a pleasant little inmate who fancied himself the boxing great Jim Jeffries. Mutt dubbed him Jeff for this reason. Jeffries (1875-1953) was one of the few heavyweight champions to retire undeafeated, but just as Joe Louis was KO'd when he made a comeback so was Jeffries—by Jack Johnson in 1910. (*See* **mutt**.)

mutual admiration society. Two or more people form a *mutual admiration society* when they continually praise each other. Oliver Wendell Holmes coined the expresion in his *Autocrat of the Breakfast Table*, published in book form in 1858.

my back teeth are floating. "I have to urinate—badly." This U.S. expression, still heard, originated in the early 1900s and is used in England as well.

my lips are sealed. I'll keep it a secret, I won't tell a soul. This has been traced to British Prime Minister Stanley Baldwin in 1936-37. Baldwin vowed confidentiality several times when asked about the abdication of King Edward VIII. "My lips are sealed," he said on one occasion, "I am bound to keep silence." Whether or not he invented the expression is unknown, but this is the first record of it. (*See* **loose lips sink ships**.)

myna bird. (*See* **parrot**.)

myriad. Before *million* (*q.v.*) was introduced in about the 12th century the largest number word was *myriad*, which derives from a Greek word meaning countless, infinite, and was then Greek for 10,000. One ancient eclessiastical historian wrote of "a hundred and ten myriads" (1,100,000) slain and starved to death over a certain period, and Archimedes wrote of *the myriads of myriads of myriads* of poppy seeds in the world. Today *myriad* is used chiefly to mean countless or innumerable.

myrmidons of the law. When the inhabitants of the island of Aegina were wiped out by a plague, the Greek god Zeus rewarded his son Aeacus, the island's leader, by creating new human beings from ants to repeople the place. According to Greek legend, these people were called Myrmidons, after the tribe of ants (*Myrmax*). The Myrmidons later followed Achilles to the Trojan War, in which they were noted for their faithful obedience and brutality. Their name is applied to officers of the law—policemen, sheriffs, etc.—who carry out any order unthinkingly and without scruples.

N

N. The letter *N* was originally a wavy line ($\curlywedge$) in Egyptian hieroglyphs and meant "the sea" or "a fish." In Phoenician the letter was called *nun*, "fish."

nabob. The *nawabs* who governed provinces in India from the early 16th century through the Raj were Moguls who owed allegiance to the Mogul emperors of India but grew so wealthy and powerful that they kept all tributes from the people and made their offices hereditary. Europeans, noting the immense wealth and power of these men, took to calling any wealthy, powerful man a *nabob*, which is merely a corruption of nawab.

Nabokov's Pug. Just to indicate the thousands of specialized eponymous words that can't be included here, we might mention the butterfly *Nabokov's Pug*. It is named for the Russian-born author and lepidopterist Vladimir Nabokov (b. 1899), who, most specifically, discovered *Eupithecia nabokovi McDonough* "on a picture window of (publisher) James Laughlin's Alta Lodge in Utah" in 1943. The prose stylist, author of *Mary, Invitation to a Beheading, Lolita, Pale Fire*, and other novels, emigrated from Russia shortly after the Revolution, residing in the United States and Europe. Once a Harvard research fellow in lepidopterology, a number of his discoveries are named for him. *Butterfly* itself, incidentally, may be a *Spoonerism* (*q.v.*) for "flutter-by."

the naked bear. *Hush or the naked bear will get you!* was an expression mothers stilled their crying children with a century ago. First recorded in 1818 the words refer to a tradition American Indians had of "a very ferocious kind of bear, which they say once existed, but was totally destroyed by their ancestors." Longfellow mentions the naked bear in one of his poems.

naked truth. According to an old Roman fable, when Truth went swimming in the river, Falsehood stole Truth's clothes. Truth went naked rather than put on the clothes Falsehood had left behind. Such is the origin of *nuda veritas* or the *naked truth*, which can be traced back as far as the writings of Horace.

nail a lie to the counter. Early country store proprietors often protected themselves against the many types of bogus money in circulation by keeping a copy of *Day's New York Bank Note List and Counterfeit Detector* (1826) on the shelf by the cashbox. They have also been said to nail all counterfeit coins one had been cheated with to the counter as an aide against clerks being cheated in the future and a warning to would-be sharpies trying to pass bad money in the store. Some say that this practice was the inspiration for the Americanism *to nail a lie to the counter*, "to expose anything false."

to nail one's colors to the mast. Crews on warships in the days of sail often nailed their ship's flag or colors to the mast to signify that they would never surrender and would fight to the last man. From this practice came the expression *to nail one's colors to the mast*, to make one's principles or position clear and stick to them no matter what.

namby-pamby. Poor Ambrose Philips (ca. 1675-1749) had the bad luck to accidentally tread on Alexander Pope, easily the most venomous and malicious of the great English poets. Politics and envy had more to do with Philips's misfortune than insipid versifying, for he was a Whig and Pope a Tory, and in 1713 the Whig *Guardian* praised the Whig pastoral poet as the only worthy successor of Spenser. This inane criticism enraged "the Wasp of Twickenham" and initiated a quarrel between the two poets that Samuel Johnson described as a "perpetual reciprocation of malevolence." Pope's friend, poet and composer Henry Carey soon joined in the fray. Carey, rumored author of the words and music of the British anthem "God Save the King," satirized Ambrose in the same book that included his popular song, "Sally in Our Alley," parodying Philips's juvenile poems and writing: "So the nurses get by heart Namby-pamby's little verses." The author of *Chrononhotonthologos*, a burlesque that he characterized as "the Most Tragical Tragedy that was ever Tragedized by any Company of Tragedians," even entitled his parody of Philips's *Namby-Pamby*—taking the *amby* in each word from the diminutive of Ambrose and the alliterative *P* in the last word from *Philips*. Pope, ready for the kill, seized upon the contemptuous nickname and included it in the edition of his enormously popular poem "The Dunciad," which appeared in 1733. The phrase immediately caught the public fancy and much to his distress, Ambrose Philips saw his name come to stand for not only feeble, insipidly sentimental writing, but a wishy-washy, weakly indecisive person as well. Philips, incidentally, is the author of the well-known palindrome "Lewd did I live, evil I did dwel." (*See* **palindrome**.)

Napoleon.   Emperor Napoleon exacted heavy tolls on those he defeated, which is why this 19th century card game is named for him. In five-card *Napoleon* the winner collects chips from each of the other players.

napoleon pastries.   These were not named for Napoleon. A traditional story says the emperor carried *napoleons* in his breast pocket when retreating from Moscow, a tale that persists despite the fact that *napoleon* in this case is simply a corruption of *napolitain*, the pastries were first made in Naples, Italy.

narcissus; narcotic.   Like Hyacinthus (*see* **hyacinth**), Narcissus was a handsome youth of Greek mythology. The nymph *Echo* (*q.v.*) wished that he would fall in love with himself after he spurned her love. When Narcissus chanced to see his own reflection in a still pool, that is just what he did, and he drowned while gazing at his own image. After his death, the gods changed his body into the beautiful flower that has been called a *narcissus* ever since. Narcissus's name is also remembered in *narcissism* and in *narcotic*, named after the narcissus because some narcissus varieties contain substances that induce sleep. (*See also* **daffodil**.)

narwhal.   The arctic narwhal, a whale that grows up to twenty feet long and has an eight-foot-long tusk, takes its name from the Scandinavian *nar*, "ghost" or "corpse" (for its white color) and *whal*, the Scandinavian word for whale. The narwhal is probably responsible for the legend of the unicorn so widely believed in medieval times. This "unicorn of the sea" uses its long tusk, or left incisor tooth, which grows outward in a counterclockwise spiral, to battle other narwhals. Only the male of the species has the tusk, employing it during the mating season when fighting over females.

nasturtium.   "Nosetwister" is the translation of the two Latin words, *nasus* and *torqueo*, that make up this word. The name *nasturtium* was given by the Romans to watercress (*Nasturtium offinale*) because of its pungency; "it received its name from tormenting the nose," Pliny said, and the English called it *nosesmart*. In the 16th century *nasturtium* was applied to the showy orange-colored flowers we call by that name today, which were also known as Indian cress. The flower is today considered part of the genus *Tropaeolum*, its scientific name no longer *Nasturtium Indicum*, but it is still popularly called *nasturtium*, while watercress never is.

nasty.   A word used at least since the early 15th century, *nasty's* history is obscure, but it possibly comes from the Aryan *niz'd* for "bird's nest," from which our word *nest* may also derive. According to this theory early Teutons noticed that birds fouled their nests and called anything fowl and stinking *nesty* or *nasty*. The *O.E.D.* notes that "the original force of the word has been greatly . . . toned down."

a nation of shopkeepers.   Napoleon applied this term contemptuously to the English, but he didn't invent it. Apparently he read it in Adam Smith's *Wealth of Nations* (1776) or quoted the phrase of a contemporary. Smith wrote in full: "To found a great empire for the sole purpose of raising up a people of customers, may at first sight appear a project altogether unfit for a nation of shopkeepers; but extremely fit for a nation that is governed by shopkeepers." Thirteen years before him Josiah Tucker, Dean of Gloucester, had written in his *Tract Against Going to War for the Sake of Trade*: "A Shop-keeper will never get the more Custom by beating his Customers; and what is true of a Shop-keeper, is true of a Shop-keeping nation."

Naumachia.   Roman emperors held "sea battles" on land in the *Naumachia* (from the Greek for "sea battle"), a flooded amphitheater Augustus built on the right bank of the Tiber River. The combatants in the two opposing fleets, who were usually prisoners or criminals, fought to the death unless spared by the emperor. As many as twenty-four triremes fought in these bloody contests.

Navaho.   White settlers bestowed the name *Navaho* upon this Indian tribe, which called itself the *Diné*, or "people." *Navaho* comes from *tewa navaho*, "great planted fields," a term other Indians used in referring enviously to the great land holdings of the wealthy, powerful *Diné* tribe.

navel orange.   The first navel orange was a "bud-sport" that originated for reasons unknown from the bud of an otherwise normal orange tree in a monastery garden in Bahia, Brazil, from where it was imported into the U.S. in 1870. This sweet, usually seedless orange takes its name from the depression in its rind resembling a human navel, which contains an aborted ovary that appears as a small secondary fruit within the fruit. Many other varieties, however, exhibit this characteristic at times.

navvy.   (*See* **work like a navvy**.)

navy.   The color *navy blue* made its debut in the Royal Navy in 1857, when for the first time an act of Parliament required English sailors to wear identical uniforms. This outfit included a blue jacket, which inspired the name of the color *navy blue* or just *navy* shortly after it became standard issue. Today any navy blue or navy clothing takes its name from the color of that first *navy blue* jacket.

Nazi.   A *Nazi* has come to mean any brutal dictatorial person, the word deriving, of course, from Adolf Hilter's National Socialist party, which came to power in 1933 and ruled Germany through World War II. The German *National Sozialist* yields *Nazi*.

Neanderthal. This is among the most ironic of etymologies. It is seldom noted (no English dictionary records the derivation) that *Neanderthal*, for "a primitive backward person," is named after a gentle poet—and a learned, pious churchman to boot! The early forms of *Homo sapiens* called *Neanderthals* were so named because the first skeletons of them recognized as a distinct group of archaic humans was found in the Neander Valley (the Neander Thal) near Dusseldorf, Germany in 1856. But the Neander Valley had been named for the German poet and hymn writer Joachim C. Neander (1650-80), a schoolmaster who wrote the beautiful hymn on the glory of God in creation, "Lo Heaven and Earth and Sea and Air!" There is further irony in the fact that the poet's great-grandfather's name had been *Neuman*, the great-grandfather changing this to *Neander* in the 16th century at a time when Germany was undergoing a rebirth of learning and many were translating their names into Greek. Thus, traced to its ultimate source, *Neanderthal*, which today means a primitive and brutal man, translates as "the man from the valley of the new man [the man of the future]"!

Nebraska. Nebraska, previously the Territory of Nebraska, takes its name from the Omaha Indian *ni-bthaska*, "river in the flatness," for the Platte River. The Cornhusker State was admitted to the Union in 1867 as our 37th state.

neck verse. (*See* **benefit of clergy**.)

negotiate. Those who *negotiate* are often worried and under a strain. This is reflected in the origin of the word *negotiate*, which derives from the Latin *negotium*, composed of *neg*, "not," and *otium*, "ease," or "not at ease." The word is first recorded in the 16th century.

negus. History tells us little about Col. Francis Negus except that he lived in Queen Anne's reign and concocted the first *negus* known to be devised by man. A *negus* is brewed by mixing wine, usually port or sherry, with hot water, sugar, lemon juice, and spices such as nutmeg. Walpole and other writers have praised the hot drink, which warms a body up but can be perilously potent. Colonel Negus died in 1732 and ten years later people were commonly calling his bequest by his name.

neither hide nor hair. In *hide and hair*, meaning "completely, wholly, every part," goes back to Chaucerian times, but its opposite, *neither hide nor hair*, is a 19th-century Americanism, probably arising on the frontier. A hungry predator devouring his prey "hide and hair" has been suggested as the source of the first

metaphor, but that is hard to swallow for man or beast. Anyway, the reverse phrase means "nothing whatsoever" and its earliest record is in an 1858 book by Timothy Titcomb, the pseudonym of the American writer Josiah G. Holland, who founded *Scribners' Magazine*: "I haven't seen hide nor hair of the piece ever since."

Nelly Bly. American journalist Elizabeth Cochrane Seaman (1867-1922) adopted the pen name Nelly Bly from a song by Stephen Foster. She is said to have taken it when an editor insisted that she use a pseudonym and an office boy happened to walk by whistling the tune. One of the first female reporters, Nelly Bly began her career when only eighteen. Her forte became exposés, such as her account in *Ten Days in a Madhouse* (1887) of the horrible conditions on New York's Blackwell's Island, where she was an inmate for ten days after feigning insanity. In 1889 the *New York World* sponsored her famous trip around the globe, which she completed in the record time of seventy-two days, six hours, and eleven minutes and which brought her international fame far exceeding that of any woman of her day. Flowers, trains, and racehorses were named for Nelly Bly and songs were written in her honor.

nelson. (*See* **full nelson**.)

Nelson's blood. After Lord Horatio Nelson, Britain's greatest naval hero, was killed at the battle of Trafalgar in 1805 by a sniper firing from the top of the French ship *Redoubtable*, his body was brought back to England to be buried in St. Paul's Cathedral. The fabled hero became the subject of many legends, including one that his body was brought home pickled in rum. Needless to say, it wasn't long before British sailors were calling rum *Nelson's blood*.

nematode. Beginning gardeners might be puzzled by the term *nematode-resistant* affixed to many plants, especially tomatoes. A *nematode* is simply a small, microscopic worm that attacks the roots of plants and often causes great damage. The word is a learned borrowing from the Greek word for "thread" applied to threadlike things such as these unsegmented worms. Some plants have a better ability to repel these worms than others and are called nematode-resistant.

nemesis. Nemesis was the Greek goddess of justice or revenge, her name deriving from the Greek for vengeance; thus a *nemesis* became anyone who avenges or punishes. Shakespeare used the term in *I Henry VI*, but it is first recorded a few years earlier in 1576.

nepotism. Deriving directly from the Latin *nepos*, "a descendant, especially a nephew," *nepotism* was coined when Pope Alexander VI (1431-1501), the most notorious of political popes, filled important church offices with his relations. Among the many family appointments the Spaniard Rodrigo Borgia made to consolidate his political power were the installing of his son Cesare as an archbishop when the boy was only sixteen and the bestowing of a cardinal's hat on his young nephew Giovanni. Alexander's detractors were so many and so widespead that the new term soon entered all the languages of Europe, referring not only to politics but to business and any other place where such favoritism was practiced.

Neptune. *Neptune*, the Roman god of water, is usually represented as a stately old man carrying a trident and sitting astride a dolphin or huge sea horse called a hippocampus. The ruler or king of the sea, his name is used for the sea itself. Poseidon was the god of the sea in Greek mythology, his wife Amphitrite, the goddess of the sea. Other sea gods include Triton, their son; Nereus, his hair seaweed green, who lives with his wife Doris at the bottom of the Mediterranean; Portunus, the protector of harbors; and Oceanus, god of the ocean. There were also fifty nereids, daughters of Nereus, and the oceanids, daughters of Oceanus.

Nero. Cruel, vindictive, dissolute, profligate, treacherous, tyrannical, murderous—it would take a far longer string of adjectives to describe Nero, the last of the Caesars. A *Nero* is a bloody-minded tyrant for reasons apparent to any high school history student and it is enough to say here that the memory of Nero Claudius Caesar Drusus Germanicus, born Lucius Domitius Ahenobarbus, was publicly execrated when he died. Nero is also remembered by *nero antico*, a black marble found in the Roman ruins and later used for ornamental purposes; in *Neroinize*, "to rule, oppress, or make depraved in the manner of Nero"; and by *Nero's crown*, the grape jasmine. The word *coliseum* also owes something to him. An eleven-foot-high statue, or colossus, of him by Zenodorus stood near where the emperor Vesparian built the huge amphitheater called the Colosseum, the amphitheater taking its name from Nero's colossus and giving its name to *coliseum*. (See **Adam's apple tree**.)

nescience. Though *nescience* (from the Latin *nesciens*, "ignorant") can be a synonym for ignorance, some writers make an important and useful distinction between the words. While ignorance is "not knowing something one should reasonably be expected to know," *nescience* means "not knowing something one cannot be reasonably expected to know."

nesselrode. A mixture of preserved fruits and nuts used over desserts, *nesselrode* is believed to have been invented by the chef of the Russian court, Karl Nesselrode (1780-1867).

Nessiteras rhombopteryx. *Nessiteras rhombopteryx* was suggested by British naturalist Sir Peter Scott as the scientific name for the fabled Loch Ness Monster, which many have claimed, without much proof, to have seen rising from the depths of Loch Ness in Scotland. Believers rejoiced that a noted scientist was on their side, until it was found that *Nessiteras rhombopteryx* is an anagram of "Monster hoax by Sir Peter S."

nest egg. People saved *nest eggs* as early as the 17th century. The expression relates to the pottery eggs once put in hens' nests to induce the hens to lay their own eggs. Persons who start saving a *nest egg* put a little money (like a porcelain egg) aside, which encourages them to save more.

Nestor. There may have been a real King Nestor behind the character the poet Homer describes both in the *Iliad* and the *Odyssey*. Nestor, in Homeric legend, was the youngest of Neleus's twelve sons and the King of Pylos in Greece. At about seventy, he was the oldest and most experienced of the Greek chieftains besieging Troy, being represented as a wise and indulgent prince who lived so long that he ruled over three generations of subjects. Nestor counseled moderation among the quarreling Greek leaders. Full of wise advice and stories of his exploits in days gone by, his wisdom was revered and much sought after despite his prolixness. But the fact that Nestor talked too much was redeemed by the fact that he had a lot to talk about. He had been, for example, the only person spared when Hercules took Pylos. His name is frequently used today to describe a wise old man, and *Nestor* does not imply that said sage is garrulous.

neurobat. (*See* **acrobat**.)

Nevada. The Spanish for "snowed upon" or "snowy" is the basis for *Nevada*. The Silver State, which had first been part of the Washoe Territory, was admitted to the Union in 1864 as our 36th state.

never give a sucker an even break. (*See* **there's a sucker born every minute**.)

never-never land. Today *never-never land* usually signifies an unreal, imaginary, or ideal condition or place, as in "the never-never land of the movies." Originally, however, it was Australian slang for an isolated, sparsely settled region and was first applied to all of Australia and then to the remote Australian outback of Western Queensland and central Australia. This region was probably called *never-never land*, or *country*, because those who visited there vowed "never, never" to return. Sir James Barrie first gave the meaning of an imaginary place to *never land* in his play *Peter Pan*, having Peter teach the Darling children to fly away to the wonderful realm of a child's imagination. Today the British sometimes call installment plans "never-never plans," because one's ownership of the goods bought on such plans lies far in the distance in *never-never land*.

never up, never in. Its sexual implications have helped this golfing expression last since the early 1920s as a catchphrase of pessimism. It means, literally, never up near the hole with the first putt, never in the hole with the second putt.

New Deal. The Agricultural Adjustment Administration, or A.A.A., was among the first of the "alphabet agencies" (government agencies, administrations, authorities, offices, etc.) created for relief and recovery in the early days of the New Deal during America's Great Depression. *New Deal* comes from Franklin Delano Roosevelt's acceptance speech at the Democratic National Convention on July 2, 1932: "I pledge you, I pledge myself, to a new deal for the American people." Coined by Roosevelt's speechwriters, Raymond Moley and Judge Samuel Rosenman, the phrase incorporated elements of Woodrow Wilson's *New Freedom* and Teddy Roosevelt's *Square Deal*.

New England. Captain John Smith thought that the area called New England in North America greatly resembled England. He was the first to record the name, on a map he made in 1616: "That part we call New England . . . betwixt the degree 41. and 45."

Newgate Calendar. Often used today as a synonym for a who's who of crime and notorious criminals everywhere, the *Newgate Calendar* was begun in 1773 as a biographical record of the most notorious criminals confined at England's famed Newgate Prison. Newgate Calendar is also today the pseudonym for the reviewer or reviewers of crime books for the *New York Times Book Review*.

New Hampshire. When Captain John Mason was granted the land including this state in 1622 he named it after his homeland—England's Hampshire County. The Granite State was admitted to the Union in 1788 as our ninth state.

New Jersey. Though it doesn't look like it at first glance, the state's name is another that has to be credited to the Caesars. *New Jersey* was named after *Jersey*, the largest of England's Channel Islands, in honor of Sir George Carteret, who had been governor of the Isle of Jersey and successfully defended it against Cromwell's forces. In 1664 Charles II had granted all lands between the Delaware River and Connecticut to his brother, the Duke of York, who in turn granted the New Jersey portion to Carteret and Lord Berkeley. England's Isle of *Jersey* (a corruption of *Caesaria*) had been named for the Caesars

when the Romans added it to their possessions, and so *New Jersey* also bears the immortal name. The relationship can be best seen in New Jersey's official Latin name, *Nova Caesaria*.

New Mexico. Spanish explorers from Mexico named this area Nuevo Mexico, "New Mexico," in 1562. The Land of Enchantment became our 47th state in 1912, previously having been called the New Mexico Territory. (*See* **Caesar**.)

news.

> News is conveyed by letter, word or mouth
> And comes to us from North, East, West and South.

Contrary to the old rhyme above, which helped popularize the myth, the word *news* wasn't coined from the first letters of the major points of the compass. The word was originally spelled *newes* and derives from the Old English word *niwes*, meaning "new." The legend possibly originated with old newspapers printing a replica of the globe with compass points on their masthead. But the word is much older than the earliest newspapers.

Newton's apple. Everyone knows the story about Sir Isaac Newton sitting under an apple tree pondering the question of gravitation when an apple fell on his head and inspired the train of though that led to his law of universal gravitation. But the particulars are usually omitted in this tale. According to Voltaire, who first told the story, and got it from Newton's niece, Mrs. Conduit, the apple fell in his mother's garden at Woolsthorpe, where he was visiting her in 1666. Even the name of the apple is known—it was a red cooking variety called the Flower of Kent. (If you want to sample it, plant the same tree Newton sat under—grafted scions of the tree have been taken over the years since 1666 and are available from English nurseries.) The apple that bopped Newton must have inspired a long train of thought, for the law of universal gravitation didn't come to fruition for nearly twenty years. Such charming stories have become part of the Newton legend, whether reliable or not. Perhaps the greatest figure in the history of science, Newton could still say of himself: "I do not know what I may appear to the world, but to myself I seem to have been only a boy playing on the sea-shore, and diverting myself in now and then finding a smoother pebble or a prettier shell than ordinary, whilst the great ocean of truth lay all undiscovered before me."

New York. *New York* is named for James, Duke of York and Albany, who in 1664 was granted the patent to all lands between the Delaware River and Connecticut by his older brother, King Charles II. The Duke gave away the Jersey portion, but held on to what was then the Dutch colony of New Netherlands. York became the patron of Col. Richard Nicholls, who that same year set sail for the New World, captured New Amsterdam from the Dutch and named both the city of New Amsterdam (New York City) and the colony of New Netherlands (New York State) after the Duke. New York State's capital, Albany, is also named for the Duke of York and Albany. (*See* **York; put up your dukes.**)

Next year in Jerusalem.   Jerusalem belongs to the Jews again, so these words are no longer a wish or a promise. But the ritual declaration *Next year in Jerusalem!* had been made by Jews at Passover for over 2,000 years, ever since Jerusalem was lost to the Romans.

n.g.; n.n.   The expression *n.g.* has been an abbreviation for "no good" since at least 1839 in America, and it meant "no go," "completely unacceptable," some five years before this. The term *n.n.* is a British one dating back to the beginning of this century and means "a necessary nuisance," especially a husband.

Nicaragua.   The Indian chief Nicaro, who reigned in the country before the Spanish conquered it, gives his name to *Nicaragua.*

nice guy.   *Nice* has undergone a complete change in meaning since it came into English late in the 13th century. Deriving from the Latin *necius,* "ignorant," *nice* originally meant foolish, or simpleminded, and came to mean "wanton or ill-mannered" before another century had passed. By the early 1400s *nice* was being used for "extravagant dress," but before the century was out "extravagant dress" (as is so often the case in the world of fashion) had changed to "fashionable dress" and by Shakespeare's time *nice* meant "fastidious or refined." It took another one hundred years or so before "refined" yielded to "agreeably delightful," this definition first recorded in 1769.

nice guys finish last.   This cynical proverb has been attributed by *Bartlett's* to former Brooklyn Dodger manager Leo Durocher, who has written a book using it as the title. Back in the 1940s Leo was sitting on the bench before a game with the New York Giants and saw opposing manager Mel Ott across the field. "Look at Ott," he said to a group of sportswriters. "He's such a nice guy and they'll finish last for him." One of the writers probably coined the phrase *nice guys finish last* from this remark, but the credit still goes to The Lip. This is one of several baseball expressions that have become proverbial outside the sport.

nice work if you can get it.   Common in the U.S. since at least the late 1930s, this phrase—which means "a favorable or agreeable arrangement"—is in Noel Coward's *Peace in Our Time* (1947). A musical comedy song of the same title popularized the expression in America (in *A Damsel in Distress,* 1937).

nickel.   *Nickel* has stood for a U.S. five-cent piece since 1881, but has never been the official designation for the coin. The coin is so called because it is made partly of nickel. Before *nickel* was applied to the five-cent piece it was the name for a U.S. nickel penny authorized in 1857 and a nickel three-cent piece.

nickel curve.   In baseball a *nickel curve* is a curve that doesn't break much. The term has been traced to William Arthur (Candy) Cummings (1848-1924), a Hall of Famer who is credited with inventing the curveball over 120 years ago. Cummings's curve was inspired by the half clam shells that he skimmed across a Brooklyn beach as a youngster, but he perfected it by experimenting with a baseball that cost a nickel.

nickname.   *Nickname,* first recorded in 1440, derives from an earlier Old English *ekename,* meaning "an extra name." Sloppy pronunciation of the words eventually turned an *ekename* into a *nekename* and finally a *nickname.*

nick of time.   (*See* **just in the nick of time.**)

nicotine. $C_5H_4NC_4H_7NCH_3$, as the nicotine staining my fingers is scientifically described, is named for Jean Nicot, Lord of Villemain (ca. 1530-1600), French ambassador to Lisbon in 1560 when Portuguese explorers were first bringing back tobacco seeds from the new continent of America. Nicot was given a tobacco plant from Florida, cultivated what is said to be the first tobacco raised in Europe, and sent the fruits of his harvest to France's Queen Mother Catherine de Medici and other notables. After introducing what Catherine called *the ambassador's powder* (snuff) into France, the enterprising Nicot proceeded to grow a tobacco crop that he brought back to Paris and built a tidy fortune on. The *American powder* became so popular that the tobacco plant itself was called *nicotina,* after Nicot, and Linnaeus later officially named the whole *Nicotiana* genus of the nightshade family in his honor, this group including the tobacco plant most commonly cultivated today, the species *Nicotiana rustica. Nicotine,* the oily liquid found in tobacco leaves, wasn't so named until 1818, when it was first isolated. It is one of the most physiologically active drugs known, producing most of the observed effects of smoking. The alkaloid is poisonous to bugs as well as humans, and is used as an insecticide in agriculture.

Nietzschean.   The philosophy of Friedrich Wilhelm Nietzsche, much distorted by the Nazis and other "supermen," did however champion the "morals of master men," especially in the philosopher's famous four-part work *Thus Spake Zarathustra* (1883-91). The son of a German pastor, Nietzsche was acidly antagonistic to humble and compassionate Christianity—a slave morality born of resentment, he thought. The philosopher denied the values of beauty, truth, and goodness and asserted that man is perfectible through the will to power. Nietzsche did not claim that the Germans were a master race, as Nazi propagandists insisted; his Nietzschean doctrine of the *Ubermensch*, or dominant men, above good or evil, applied to no particular nationality. *Ubermensch*, incidentally, means "overman" or "beyondman" in German, not "superman." George Bernard Shaw coined the latter word from Nietzsche's term when he wrote *Man and Superman* in 1903. Nietzsche, rejected and reviled by his contemporaries, died insane at the age of 56 in 1891, eleven years after suffering a physical and mental collapse that prevented him from doing more work. It is interesting to note that the philosopher criticized anti-Semitism and many other tendencies that led to Nazism. Few other men have had so strong an influence on 20th-century thought. (*See* **superman**.)

nifty. *Nifty* for "smart, stylish, fine, or clever" may have originated as American theatrical slang. It is first recorded in an 1865 poem by Bret Harte, the author claiming that the word derived from *magnificent*. Another possible source is the older *snifty*, "having a pleasant smell."

nightmare. Bad dreams in Roman times were attributed to demons called the *incubus* and *succubus*. The incubus (from the Latin *incubare*, "to lie on," which also gives us the word *incubate*) was said to consort with women in their sleep. This explained the heaviness or suffocation a woman might feel during a bad dream. The superstition was so widely believed in the Middle Ages that any woman who gave birth to a "witch" was supposed to have been visited by a male demon. The female counterpart of the incubus was the succubus (from the Latin *suc* or *sub*, "under," and *cubare* "to lie"), who slid beneath a male sleeper. In the Dark Ages, there were laws against these demons whose existence was recognized by both Church and state. Soon they became known as the "night hag," "the riding of the witches," and the *nightmare* as well. The *nightmare*, however, had nothing to do with a female horse, taking its name from *night*, plus the Anglo-Saxon *mare*, meaning "incubus." *Nightmare* eventually replaced the older Latin word *incubus*, which is now used to describe an opressive load. Although the word wasn't born from a horse, it caught the popular imagination because of the graphic picture it suggested of a terrible horse bearing sleepers off on a frightening ride.

night of the long knives. On the night of June 29, 1934 Hitler and his allies killed or had imprisoned a number of

Nazi party members he wanted out of the way. Since then a *night of the long knives* has meant "a time when an act of great disloyalty is done," especially when several people form a conspiracy to do it.

night soil. Because cesspools used to be cleaned during the night in the 18th century, their contents were called *night soil* and the cleaners "night men." That the contents were sometimes added as fertilizer to soil at night could account for the *soil* in the expression.

nihilism. Meaning total rejection of established laws and institutions, and denial of all real existence, *nihilism* was coined from the Latin *nihil*, "nothing," by Russian novelist Ivan Turgenev to name and describe the principles of a Russian revolutionary group in the late 19th century.

Nimrod. In the Bible Nimrod is the son of Cush and the founder of Babel. He may have been an Assyrian king who built the city of Nineveh, the capital of the Assyrian empire. According to Scripture, Nimrod was "a mighty hunter before the Lord" (Gen. 10:8-10), and historians tell us that the Assyrian kings were noted for their prowess in hunting. Aramaic translations of the Old Testament say "that mighty hunter before the Lord" means "sinful hunter of the sons of men," which accounts for Pope's and Milton's description of Nimrod as "a mighty hunter, and his prey was man." But a *Nimrod* is more generally the nickname for a great, daring, and skillful hunter, or even sportsman.

nincompoop. Dr. Johnson suggested that *nincompoop*, "a fool or blockhead," came from the Latin *non compos mentis*, "of unsound mind," but the earliest forms of the word, first recorded in about 1676, are *nicimpoop* and *nickumpoo*, making this unlikely. The word is probably "a fanciful formation," as the *O.E.D.* puts it, of obscure origin.

nine days' wonder; ninety-day wonders. Minor marvels, things that cause great sensations for a short time and then pass into limbo, have probably been called *nine days' wonder*, or something very similar, since Roman times. Kittens, puppies, and other young animals have their eyes closed for a number of days after birth and then open them and see the light—just as astonished people eventually "open their eyes" and see astonishing things in their true perspective. This is probably the reasoning behind the expression, *nine* being used because it has always been regarded as a mystical number and might have been thought to be the number of days young animals keep their eyes closed. Robert Burton gave us a proverb that seems to confirm this theory: "A wonder lasts but nine days, and then the puppy's eyes are open." In both World Wars and the Korean conflict, the nickname *ninety-day wonders*, an offshoot of the earlier phrase, was given to young, sometimes zealous second lieutenants who were trained for only three months in Officer Candidate School (OCS).

nineteenth hole. *Mencken calls the nineteenth hole* "the one American contribution to the argot of golf." While this isn't quite true (*par, birdie, eagle, chip,* and *sudden death* are among U.S.-invented golf terms) the expression has been with us at least since the early 1920s and means "a convivial gathering place," such as a locker room or bar, after a game of golf.

the 98-cent man. For many years it was estimated that the value of a human life, in chemical terms, was 98 cents, leading to the expression *the 98 cent man*. Inflation has changed this figure in recent times. Today the chemical elements in the body—5 pounds of calcium, 1 1/2 pounds of phosphorus, 9 ounces of potassium, 6 ounces of sulfur, about 1 ounce of magnesium, and less than an ounce each of iron, copper, and iodine—are worth about $8.37.

99 and 44/100% pure. (*See* **Ivory soap**.)

ninny. *Ninny*, for "a fool or simpleton," is probably an abbreviation or pet form of *innocent*, it being only a short step from "adorably innocent" to "foolishly simple." The word is first recorded in 1592 and an early synonym, used by Rabelais, was *ninny-whoop*. Thus it predates *nincompoop* (*q.v.*).

ninth wave. A nautical superstition of old holds that waves become progressively higher until the ninth wave (some say the tenth) and that then the progression begins all over again. While waves sometimes form larger ones when they meet, there is no fixed interval when a large one can be predicted.

Niobe of nations. Byron called Rome or Italy the *Niobe of nations* because of her lost empire. Niobe in Greek mythology lost all her twelve children when she taunted Latona because she had only two offspring. Latona commanded her two children—Apollo and Diana—to avenge the insult and cause the death of all Niobe's sons and daughters. Inconsolable, Niobe "wept herself to death and was changed into a stone from which ran water."

nip and tuck. *Nip and tuck* pretty much means "neck and neck," but the latter phrase suggests, say, two runners racing at the same speed with neither one ahead of the other, while *nip and tuck* describes a close race where the lead alternates. The earliest recorded form of the expression is found in James K. Paulding's *Westward Ho!* (1832): "There we were at rip and tuck, up one tree and down another." Maybe the *rip* originally came from

"let 'er rip" and later became *nip* because of the expression "to nip someone out," to barely beat him, while the *tuck* was simply an old slang word for "vim and vigor." Other guesses at the phrase's origins are even wilder.

nip in the bud. To obtain larger peonies or tomatoes, to get larger flowers or fruit of any kind, gardeners have long pinched off excessive blossoms on plants, nipped them early in the bud to channel all a plant's strength into a few remaining buds, which will then yield large flowers or fruit. No fruit comes from a nipped-off bud, of course, and so the gardening term *to nip in the bud* became proverbial in Elizabethan times for calling a halt to something before it has a chance to develop, especially in regard to bad habits or plans with little chance of success.

a nip of whiskey. A *nipperkin* (possibly from the Dutch *nypelkin*) was a small container holding a half pint or less of liquor, usually wine or ale, the term being first recorded in 1694. *Nipperkin* was shortened to *nip* within a century or so and came to mean even less, no more than a shot glass full of spirits.

Nissen hut. (*See* **quonset hut**.)

nitpicker. "She can wel pyke out lyce and nitis," William Caxton, the first English printer, wrote in a book of fables he translated from the French and published in 1484. But it took centuries before a *nit picker*, "one who picks lice eggs [nits] from one's body or clothes," changed in meaning to one who looks for and finds small errors (as small as nits), a pedant. I'd guess that the expression is a Americanism dating to the late 19th century.

nitwit. This Americanism, first recorded in 1926, may be a combination of the German *nicht*, "not," and the English *wit*—*nichtwit*, "not with wits, without wits"—corrupted in speech to *nitwit*. Another theory has *nitwit* deriving from "a scornful English imitation" of Dutchmen who answered questions asked in English with the Dutch expression *Ik niet wiet*, "I don't know." This, however, would date *nitwit* to Dutch days in New York and there are thus far no examples of the word's use that far back.

nix. *Nix* is probably a British borrowing from the German *nichts*, "nothing." Meaning "nothing" or "no," it dates back to the late 18th century, when it is recorded as *nichts* in British slang, the word being spelt *nix* by 1812 at the latest. The expression *nix on that*, "nothing doing," is an Americanism first attested in 1902. The famous *Variety* headline STIX NIX HIX PIX widely popularized *nix* in America.

Nixon's the one! This political slogan was turned against Richard Nixon in 1968 when he ran for the presidency—the button with the slogan was sometimes worn by pregnant women (Democrats, of course). In any case, Nixon won, perhaps more because of his slogan "Let's Get America Going Again."

n.n. (*See* **n.g.**)

a no-account.   Our first record of *no-account*, applied to a worthless person, is in 1922, when a popular novelist had one of his characters say: "Yer fired, yer a loafin', windy, clumsy, bunglin' no-account." But the expression is recorded almost a century earlier in reference to worthless things. In 1845 another writer confided: "I'll jist tell you that the land I'm after is a damn little, no-account quarter acre that nobody would want but me."

Noah's brig.   *Noah's Brig*, a tiny rockbound island in the Hudson River, is named for one Captain Noah, an 18th-century captain of a fleet of rafts who had the misfortune of encountering the island under adverse conditions one night. Noah sighted "a dark object floating the waters," which looked like a brig under sail. "Brig ahoy!" he cried, but no answer came. "Brig ahoy!" he shouted. "Answer or I'll run you down!" There was still no reply and Captain Noah stubbornly held his course. Then a crash—wood crunched on rock: Noah had mistaken two trees on the island for masts with sails set.

no balm in Gilead.   "Is there no balm in Gilead; is there no physician there?" Jeremiah laments in the King James Version of the Bible. His words, from Jer. 8:22, give us the common expression meaning there is no consolation, no remedy. *Balm* is simply a shortening of *balsam*, a resinous gum long noted for its healing and soothing properties. But the Hebrew word *tsori*, rendered as *balm* in the King James Version, really means resin, probably the resin yielded by the mastic tree, another ingredient in many ancient remedies. So Jeremiah should literally be saying "Is there no resin in Gilead?" or "Is there no mastic in Gilead?" Not knowing exactly what substance Jeremiah referred to caused early translators of the Bible a lot of trouble. John Wycliffe and others used the word *gumme* or *resin* in the phrase, and in the so-called Bishops' Bible (1568) the translators had Jeremiah say "Is there no treacle in Gilead?" The bishops who did this translation were using treacle in its early sense of a salve, but later generations knew the substance as molasses or any sickeningly sweet substance and humorously referred to the Bishops' Bible as the Treacle Bible. (*See* **jeremiad**.)

Nobel Prize.   "The day when two army corps will be able to destroy each other in one second," Alfred Nobel predicted, "all civilized nations will recoil away from war in horror and disband their armies." The Swedish inventor of dynamite proved to be wrong in his prophecy, which may have been a rationalization for his invention, but the $9 million he left in his will to set up the Nobel Prize Foundation has greatly aided the cause of peace. *Nobel Prizes* are awarded to persons, irrespective of nationality, who have done outstanding work in the five fields Nobel considered most important to the benefit of mankind: physics, chemistry, medicine and physiology, literature, and peace. The prizes, given in Stockholm and Oslo on December 10th of each year in which awards are made, consist of varying amounts of money, a diploma, and a gold medal. The first ceremony was held in 1901.

no better than she should be.   An early 18th century translation by Peter Motteux of *Don Quixote* is the first to record this classic understatement, meaning "an immoral woman." Whether it was coined at this time no one knows.

noblesse oblige.   *Noblesse* has been used as a synonym for nobility in English since it was borrowed from the French in the early 14th century. However, *noblesse oblige*, the French for "nobility obliges," seems to be a recent coinage of the last fifty years or so. It generally means the obligation of the nobility, or the rich, to help others worse off than they.

nobody home!   Knocking themselves on the head, people sometimes say *Nobody home!* or *Nobody's home upstairs!* after forgetting something or after making a foolish statement. This is not contemporary slang, but dates back to the 1700s and an epigram of Alexander Pope's called "The Empty House":

> You beat your pate, and fancy wit will come:
> Knock as you please, there's nobody at home.

A more modern equivalent is "The lights are on, but nobody's home."

no can do; can do.   The negative phrase, and its opposite, are not contemporary expressions, as many people believe. They date back about a century and a half to England, where they probably originated in the Royal Navy.

no great shakes.   That monument of noncomputerized scholarship, the great *Oxford English Dictionary*, suggests that this expression alludes to the shaking of dice. Someone who is *no great shakes* is nothing extraordinary, like a gambler who shakes the dice and throws a low point—no sevens or elevens. Considering its first recorded use, the expression must have been known as early as the 17th century. Lord Broughton, recalling an 1816 art show in his *Recollections of a Long Life* (1865), wrote: "W. said that a piece of sculpture there was '*nullae magnae quassationes*,' and the others laughed heartily." The others, proficient linguists, got the joke immediately when they translated the Latin for *no great shakes*. Another suggestion is that the expression derives from the provincial word *shake*, "to brag"—according to this highly improbable theory someone who is *no great shakes* would be nothing to brag about.

no hits, no runs, no errors.   Dating back to at least the 1930s and deriving from literal use in reports of baseball games, *no hits, no runs, no errors* has come to mean either complete failure (like the team shut out with no hits, no runs, no errors), perfection (like the pitcher who pitches a perfect game with no hits, no runs, no errors), and even something uneventful or without hitches (as in a game where there were no hits, no runs, no errors).

no ifs, ans or buts about it.   In British usage *ifs and ans* describe wishful thinking, as in the old jingle:

> If ifs and ans
> Were pots and pans
> Where would be the tinker?

Ans in this case is the plural of the old *an*, meaning "if." But the American expression *there'll be no ifs, ans, or buts about it* means something entirely different. *An* here is an old form of *and*. The saying is a strong negative meaning there will be absolutely no argument about something. A child might say, as children do, "I'll mow the lawn if there's no game this afternoon and Johnny can't come over, but not if it's too hot, Dad," and his Dad might reply, as fathers do, "You'll mow the lawn, period. There'll be no ifs, ans, or buts about it!"

noisette.   The hardy, widely grown garden rose named the *noisette*, a cross of the moss rose and the China rose, originated in America in about 1816. It was named after an early cultivator (not the originator) of the hybrid, Philippe Noisette of Charleston, South Carolina. It is less often called the Champney rose, for its discoverer, John Champney of Charleston.

noli me tangere.   *Noli me tangere*, "touch me not," are the words Christ spoke to Mary Magdalene after His resurrection. The impatiens (*Impatiens holotii* and other species) are called *noli me tangere* and *touch me not* because their seed pods burst and scatter their seeds when touched. They are also called snapweed and Busy Lizzie, in reference to their frequent blooming. *Impatiens* is from the Latin for impatience, in allusion to the bursting of the seed pods.

no love lost.   This has been called "an ambiguous phrase" that meant both "they have no love for each other" and "their affection for each other was mutual" when it was first recorded in the late 17th century. Today, however, these words always mean "they dislike each other, have no love for each other."

no-man's land.   World War I created many a *no-man's-land*, but isn't responsible for the phrase. *No-man's-land* was first used in the early 14th century for the unowned wasteland outside the north wall of London that was used as an execution site for criminals. For many years no one wanted to own this land where criminals were beheaded, hanged, or impaled, their rotting bodies left on display as a warning to lawbreakers. The place became known as *no-man's-land* because no one claimed it, and the expression was soon applied figuratively to other places. About four hundred years later *no-man's-land* was applied to the little-used place on a ship's forecastle where blocks, ropes, and tackle were stored. The term was first used in its military sense of the area between hostile entrenched lines in about 1900 and became famous in this sense during World War I. The dead could be seen in these *no-man's-lands* just as they had been seen in the original six centuries before. "A wilderness of dead bodies," the writer who first used the military term called it. In a letter to his mother British poet Wilfred Owen, killed in the war, wrote: "No Man's land is pockmarked like the body of foulest disease and its odour is the breath of cancer . . . No Man's Land under snow is like the face of the moon, chaotic, crater-ridden, uninhabitable, awful, the abode of madness." In another letter he spoke of "Hideous landscapes, vile noises . . . everything unnatural, broken, blasted; the distortion of the dead, whose unburiable bodies sit outside the dug-outs all day, all night, the most execrable sights on earth."

Nome.   The Alaskan seaport, according to one persistent story, was dubbed *Nome* after a British naval cartographer aboard the *Herald* working on a map of Alaska noted a cape without a name and wrote "Name?" above it. In London the printer misread "Name?" as *Nome* and so the cape was named. Later, Cape Nome's monniker was transferred to the port near it, which had been called Anvil City. No other plausible explanation has been given for Nome's name. (*See also* **indri; kangaroo; llama; Luzon; Yucatan.**)

nonpareilles.   (*See* **hundreds and thousands.**)

noon.   Why does *noon*, or 12 P.M., derive from the Latin *nono*, meaning "nine"? *Noon* actually first meant the ninth hour of the day—counted from sunrise, which comes at 6 A.M. on the average. *Noon* was thus at 3 P.M., halfway between midday and sunset, or the middle of the afternoon. Early in the 13th century the meaning of noon began to change from 3 P.M., or the middle of the afternoon, to 12 P.M., or the middle of the day itself, possibly because it was a handy word to apply to the time when the midday meal was eaten.

noonday.   (*See* **kind-hearted.**)

Norfolk Howard. There are many notable name changes in history. One of the most famous among them would have to be the change made by Italian Cardinal Grugno in 1009, which began the custom of Popes taking a new name on accession. The cardinal had an excellent reason for adopting the name Sergius IV; Grugno means "swine snout" in Italian. Usually people do have good reasons for legally changing their names—like C.J. Crook who changed his name to C.J. Noble. This type far outnumbers the logically unaccountable changes like W. Jones to W. Smith (1798). Sometimes even the most logical name changes backfire, though. On June 26, 1862, Joshua Bug of Norfolk tired of his "base" name, took an ad in the *London Times* announcing that he would henceforth be known as Norfolk Howard, this being one of England's most aristocratic names. His countrymen soon foiled the poor man's grandiose plans for metamorphosis, however, displaying the British sense of humor so many say doesn't exist and adopting *Norfolk Howard* as a slang synonym for "bedbug."

no room to swing a cat. This phrase probably has something to do with the old "sport" of swinging cats by the tails as targets for archers. The expression goes back at least to the mid-1600s, and *cat-o'-nine-tails* (*q.v.*) isn't recorded until about 1670, which makes it unlikely that the phrase originated with some sea captain having no room to punish a rebellious sailor with a "cat." The only other plausible explanation is that *cat* in this case refers to a sailor's hammock or *cot*, there being little room on olden ships to swing one, but there are no quotations to support this theory.

North Carolina; South Carolina. Both states really honor three kings—deriving from the Latin *Carolus*, meaning "Charles." Originally dedicated to France's Charles XI in the 16th century, the territory now comprising *North* and *South Carolina* was next named for England's Charles I. Charles I granted the patent for the *Carolinas* to Sir Robert Heath in 1629, Heath calling the territory *Carolana* (the Latin form of "Charles") in his honor. This it remained until 1663, when Charles II granted a new patent and the colony was called *Carolina* in *his* honor.

North Dakota; South Dakota. These states are named for the Dakota tribes in the area, *Dakota* meaning roughly, "allies" from *da*, "to think of as," and *koda*, "friend." (For other friendly Indians, *see* **Texas**.)

nose; mucus. Our word *nose* derives directly from the Anglo-Saxon *nosu*, but can be traced back to the Anglo-Saxon *nasa*, which meant "dual or double" and is the tap root for *nosu*, the nose having two nostrils. The nose's mucus, from the Latin *mucus*, "slime from the nose," gives us the word *mucilage* for glue, which someone thought resembled it.

no-see-um. Northwestern loggers and others use this term, which comes from Chinook jargon or a Pidgin English once spoken between loggers and Indians. The *no-see-um*, also called the *punkie*, is a minute, almost invisible fly or midge of the family Chironomedae that has a terrific bite.

nosegay. A bunch of sweet-smelling flowers has been called a *nosegay* since at least the early 15th century. *Nosegay* has survived because it reminds us of how the nose delights in or is made gay by the smell of flowers, but the charming, playful *tussie-mussie*, or *tuzzy-muzzy*, for the same (as well as a gold or silver representation of a bunch of flowers) is extinct now. *Posy*, for a bunch of flowers or flower-like words, is little heard, but lives on in the language forever thanks to Marlowe's "Passionate Shepherd," who rhymed: "I will make the beds of roses/ And a thousand fragrant posies."

nose writing. Aldous Huxley often wrote with his nose, though he produced none of his masterpieces this way. "A little *nose writing*," he notes in *The Art of Seeing*, "will result in a perceptible temporary improvement of defective vision." Huxley's eyesight was so bad that he learned Braille to relieve his eyes; he often read at night in bed, hands and book under the covers. A follower of Dr. William Bates, the author practiced the ophthamologist's exercises for improving eyesight. Any myopic writer or reader who wants to try need not dip his nose in ink. Simply fix your eyes on the end of your nose and move your head as if you were writing a word, sentence, or anecdote.

Nosey Parker. Matthew Parker, who became Archbishop of Canterbury in 1559, acquired a reputation for poking his nose into other people's business. Actually, he was an intelligent, if somewhat overzealous, churchman of marked Protestant persuasion who introduced many administrative and ceremonial reforms into the Anglican Church. His reputation is largely undeserved, but Catholics and Puritans alike resented his good works, taking advantage of his rather long nose and dubbing him *Nosey Parker*, which has meant an unduly inquisitive person ever since. Parker had been chaplain to Anne Boleyn and Henry VIII before becoming archbishop. A scholar of some note, he died in 1575 aged seventy-one. The above, at least, is the most popular folk etymology for *Nosey Parker*. But other candidates have been proposed. Richard Parker, leader of the Sheerness Mutiny in 1797, is one strong contender. This Parker poked his nose so deeply into what the military thought their exclusive bailiwick that he wound up hanged from the yardarm of H.M.S. *Sandwich* on July 30th of that year.

no skin off my back. Originally *no skin off my nose* was the form of this Americanism, which dates back seventy-five years or so. It means "it is no concern to me, not my business, doesn't hurt me one bit." Perhaps *nose* better fits the phrase than *back*—if you don't stick your nose into someone else's business, you won't get it punched.

no soap! In 1775 young actor and author Samuel Foote (1720-1777) composed the following speech when pompous fellow actor Charles Macklin boasted that he could repeat anything after hearing it once: "So she went into the garden to cut a cabbage leaf to make an apple pie; and at the same time, a great she-bear coming up the street pops its head into the shop—What! no soap! So he died; and she very impudently married the barber; and there were present the picaninnies and the Jobilies, and the Garyuloes, and the grand Panjandrum himself, with the little round button at top." "Old Macklin" (he lived to be a hundred) gave up in disgust, unable to memorize this nonsense, but the mnemonic exercise gave the language both the phrase *no soap!*, for the failure of some mission or plea, and *grand Panjandrum*, which was first used as a derogatory term by Edward Fitzgerald in his translation of the *Rubaiyat*, when he applied it to a self-important local official. Foote, disliked by Dr. Johnson, once announced that he was going to do an imitation of the Great Cham on the stage. Johnson sent word that he had ordered a new oak cudgel and would be present that evening to correct any faults in the impersonation with it. Foote canceled the show.

Nostradamus. *The Centuries* of Nostradamus, a book of rhymed prophecies, was published in 1555. The French doctor and astrologer gained a reputation as a seer when some of his predictions came true and as a result he won an appointment as personal physician to Charles IX. His real name was Michel de Nostredame, and his book, divided into centuries, was drawn from the whole body of medieval prophetic literature. Nostradamus was sixty-three when he died in 1566. The papal court condemned his prophecies in 1781, but they have enjoyed wide attention since on a number of occasions, one generation or another applying them to contemporary situations. Detractors claim that the prophecies are so ambiguously worded that they could mean anything, and when *Nostradamus* is used for a seer or prophet it is generally employed in a contemptuous sense. (*See* **Mother Shipton**.)

not a dry seat in the house. The drama critic's cliché *there wasn't a dry eye in the house*, to describe a moving play, suggested this humorous expression, which has been fairly common in England since about 1930 for a play or movie so funny that the audience was helpless with laughter—in fact, wet their pants laughing.

not all there. (*See* **playing without a full deck**.)

not by a long shot. Whether it was suggested by a difficult long shot attempted in archery or shooting isn't known, but the expression *a long shot* first arose in British racing circles some 128 years ago as a bet laid at large odds, a bold wager. *Not by a long shot* therefore means hopelessly out of reckoning. Attempts have been made to derive the saying from the slightly earlier *not by a long chalk*, which comes from the use of chalk for reckoning points in tavern games. But *not by a long chalk* means "not by much," so it seems that the phrase derives from either archery or shooting.

not by bread alone. This ancient expression, meaning that a person's spirit must be cared for as well as his body, comes from the Bible (Deut. 8:3): "Man doth not live by bread alone, but by every word that proceedeth out of the mouth of the Lord doth man live."

No-tel Motel. Over the last decade or so *hot pillow joints* (the pillows are still warm from the last occupants when you get the room, so rapid is the turnover) have sprung up all over America. These swingers' motels usually offer rooms with porno films on closed-circuit TV, water beds, mirrored ceilings, etc. They often advertise on billboards ("Special Two-Hour Rates $11.95 Only") and are of course usually places of sexual assignation for businessmen and housewives, which is why they have been humorously dubbed *No-tel Motels*. (*See* **motel**.)

not for love or money. Not at any price or by any means. The phrase is recorded as early as A.D. 971 and has been commonly used ever since, almost always in this negative form. Swift used it in his *Journal to Stella* (1712).

nothing to fear but fear itself. Franklin D. Roosevelt is often cited as the originator of "The only thing we have to fear is fear itself" in his first inaugural address, when the country was at the bottom of the Great Depression. F.D.R., however, had many ghostwriters past to help him:

• "The only thing I am afraid of is fear."—Duke of Wellington

• "Nothing is so much to be feared as fear."—Thoreau

• "Nothing is terrible except fear itself."—Francis Bacon

• "The thing of which I have most fear is fear."—Montaigne

• "Be not afraid of sudden fear."—Proverbs 3:25

no tickee, no washee. People have always had a hard time getting their wash back from the laundry without having the receipt for it. This expression was common among Chinese laundrymen starting in the late 19th century or earlier and is still occasionally heard. The words have taken on the new, wider meaning of "no credit without collateral."

not so hot. *Not so hot* is often denoted as an American slang expression dating back to the Roaring Twenties, but Shakespeare used and possibly invented this expression meaning "not very good."

not the only pebble on the beach. (*See* **you're not the only pebble on the beach.**)

not to be sneezed at. At the beginning of the 19th century the expression *to sneeze at* meant to consider something unimportant or boring. "It's the sort of thing a young fellow of my expectations ought to sneeze at," said the first writer who used the saying in print. This is guesswork, but the expression may have been suggested by the habit of snuff-taking common among the upper classes at the time. Snuff, also called "sneeze," was a mixture of tobacco, a little pepper, and other ingredients, snuffed into the nostrils to induce a hearty sneeze, which was considered exhilarating. Since a gentleman bored with a conversation might resort to snuff-taking and sneezing, perhaps the phrase *to sneeze at* and its opposite *not to be sneezed at* arose from the practice.

not to turn a hair. Not to show any signs of distress, to be unruffled, unaffected by exertion or any agitation. This is a "horsey" term from the stables, where the first sign of distress in a horse is sweating, which roughens the animal's coat, his hair remaining smooth and glossy as long as he keeps cool. Jane Austen first recorded the expression in *Northanger Abbey* (1797), writing of a horse: ". . . he had not turned a hair till we came to Walcot church."

not to worry. *Not to worry,* "don't worry, there isn't anything to worry about," became very popular in the late 1950s, but probably dates back earlier as British army slang. Some scholars trace it to the Italian *non tormentarsi* and others suggest a Maltese connection, but *not to worry* is more likely simply a shortening of the British "You are not to worry."

not what it's cracked up to be. Martin Van Buren, not a very popular president, though he gave us the expression *O.K.* (*q.v.*), was once disparaged by Davy Crockett, who said he "is not the man he is cracked up to be." The expression, meaning "not what he is generally believed to be," is apparently an Americanism dating back to the 1830s, but it may have British roots that go back much further, for *cracked* here has the old meaning of to boast or brag, a usage that dates back to at least the 16th century.

not worth a continental. Before the U.S. Constitution was adopted, the Continental Congress had no power of taxation to raise revenue. The Congress issued bills of credit called Continentals, the dollar bills of the time, printing bills with a face value of more than $250 million though there was virtually no bullion or specie in the treasury with which to redeem them. To make matters worse, the British and Tories circulated immense amounts of counterfeit Continentals, selling them for the price of the paper they were printed on and sending the fake currency out of New York City by the cartload with persons going into other colonies. By 1790 Continental dollars were worth so little that it took forty paper dollars to buy a dollar in silver and the expression *not worth a continental*—worthless—had become part of the language.

not worth a rap. This *rap* isn't a knock, as many people believe. The rap in the phrase was a half-penny circulated in Ireland in 1721; worth very little, it gave rise to our expression *not worth a rap,* "worth nothing at all."

not worth a red cent. American pennies—once made with more copper, and thus redder—were formerly called *reds,* which is what a Californian describing a card game in 1849 meant when he observed, "Silver is not plenty . . . on the tables and anybody can . . . bet a red on any card he chuses." This accounts for the expression *not worth a red cent,* which has roots in the British "not worth a brass farthing" and which remains a good descriptive phrase because the penny still has enough copper in it to appear reddish.

not worth a row (hill) of beans. The meaning behind this phrase is that beans have little value compared to other crops because they are so easy to grow and prolific. *Not worth a bean* is one of the oldest expressions in English, recorded as early as the 13th century and colloquial since at least 1400. The *hill* in *not worth a hill of beans,* in the American version of the English expression, was a common term a century ago when the saying was born. It means not an actual hill, but a group of bean plants planted close together in a circle. Because most people now plant beans in straight rows and the meaning of hills is unclear to many, the phrase is usually *not worth a row of beans* today.

not worth a tinker's damn (dam). There are numerous old expressions, some dating back over four hundred years, indicating the profanity of tinkers in general. The tinker, who takes his name from "tink," the sound of a hammer on metal, is remembered by *to swear like a tinker* and *not worth a tinker's curse,* among other sayings. Obviously he threw "damns" around so casually that they became meaningless, worthless, giving us the expression *not worth a tinker's damn.* There have been attempts, however, to link the phrase to the little temporary "dams" tinkers fashioned to hold solder in place when they repaired pots and pans.

not worth his salt. (*See* **salt.**)

November. (*See* **September.**)

now Barabbas was a publisher. These lines are often attributed to Lord Byron. Byron supposedly received a lavish copy of the Bible from publisher John Murray in gratitude for a favor, only to return it with *thief* changed to *publisher* in John 18:40. English poet Thomas Campbell (1777-1844) had earlier made a similar quip after Napoleon had had German publisher Johann Pal put to death for printing subversive pamphlets. At an authors' dinner, Campbell proposed this toast: "To Napoleon. [Voices of protest] I agree with you that Napoleon is a tyrant, a monster, the sworn foe of our nation. But, gentlemen—he once shot a publisher!"

nudnik; Phudnick. A *nudnik* is a man "whose purpose in life is to bore the rest of humanity," according to poet Morris Rosenfeld's essay on the subject. *Nudnik*, indeed, derives from the Russian *nudna*, for "a bore." Leo Rosten's *The Joy's of Yiddish* says the recently coined *Phudnik* is "a nudnik with a Ph.D."

nuke. *Nuke* is relatively new American slang for a nuclear weapon, being first recorded in 1964 in a *Time* magazine article, which discussed the possibility of using nuclear bombs to dig a new canal in Panama. *Nuke* as a verb, "to attack with nuclear weapons," is first attested in a July 4, 1970 *New Yorker* interview with Eugene V. Rostow.

number, please. Telephone operators had been advised by Thomas Edison to greet callers with *ahoy* (*q.v.*) instead of *hello*, but operators fell into the habit of opening with a curt "What number?" However, according to Stuart Berg Flexner's *Listening to America* (1982) by 1895 the city manager of the Chicago Telephone Company, one J. W. Thompson, issued the following instructions to the company's chief operator in a memorandum: "In answering calls the query 'Number Please?' spoken in a pleasant tone of voice and with rising inflection must be invariably employed." Within ten years all of the Bell System followed suit.

nuts! When Brigadier General Anthony McAuliffe, known as Old Crock to his troops, was asked to surrender Bastogne during the Battle of the Bulge in World War II, his 101st Airborne outnumbered four to one, he reportedly replied "Nuts!" to the German officer who awaited a reply. There are those who believe that McAuliffe, a tough airborne officer, after all, said something much stronger—Shit!, to be exact—but no proof has been offered. In any case, he meant "Go to hell!" and *Nuts!* has become immortal. (*See also* **the Guard dies but never surrenders!**)

nylon. Though it was first mass produced during World War II and hurt our enemy Japan's silk industry, *nylon* is not an acronym of "*Now You Lousy Nips*," as the old story goes. Formerly a trademark, *nylon* is an arbitrary name with no meaning, though the symbols NY in its chemical formula may have suggested the word.

O

O. Of all twenty-six letters in the alphabet *O* has, perhaps, the most interesting and best documented story. The oldest of letters began as a pictograph common to many languages describing the human eyeball within its protected socket; some drawings of it in ancient alphabets even give it a dot in the center for a pupil. In time the socket and pupil were eliminated from the pictograph and we find it in North Semitic as a plain, full circle that was called "the eye." From there it passed into the Greek alphabet. Unlike any other letter, it has undergone no other major structural change in over 2,700 years. In Anglo-Saxon O's name was *oedel*, "home." It later became probably the only English letter to have a poem written about it by a philosopher (Dr. William Whewell). *O* is also the commonest single-letter surname, there being thirteen in the Brussels telephone directory alone. But there is no evidence of an O being in the Japanese town of O. (*See also* **Giotto's O.**)

O'. The *O'* common in Irish names such as O'Connor, O'Reilly, etc., derives from the Gaelic *ogha* or the Irish *oa*, both meaning "a descendant." Denis O'Connor strictly means "Denis, a descendant of Connor."

oaf. *Oaf* is a corruption of the Old Norse *alfr*, which became *aulf* and *ouph* in Old English and was recorded as *oaf* by 1625. An *alfr* was a child supposedly left by fairies in exchange for a child they had stolen, the changeling held to be an idiot, an abnormal child worse than the stolen one. *Oaf* softened in meaning over the years until it came to refer to a clumsy, foolish, or stupid person, the word most commonly used in the expression *a big oaf.*

oak. *Oaks* were said to be sacred to the god of thunder in ancient times because the trees were believed to be more likely to be struck by lightning than any other tree. Though it was venerated by the Druids, the origins of the oak's name are lost in history, the word first recorded in the sixth century but much older. One oak still standing in England is said to be 1,600 years old.

Oberon. (*See* **Uranus.**)

obese. *Obese* means very fat indeed, but the word comes from the Latin *obesus*, which is, ironically, the past participle of *obdere*, "to gnaw, to eat away, to thin." It is first recorded in the early 17th century.

obscene. According to one theory, *obscene* originally meant "off the stage" in ancient Greek drama, deriving from the Greek *ob*, "against," and *scaena*, "stage." What was kept off the stage in Greek drama was violence (always reported by messenger), not sex, of which there was plenty in comedies and satyr plays complete with actors fitted with huge artificial phalluses. Obscenity wasn't associated with sex until the word made its appearance in England toward the end of the 17th century. However, *obscene* is of obscure origin, and another theory, less likely, derives the word from the Latin *caenum*, "mud." Shakespeare was the first to use *obscene* in the sense of offensive to the senses, that is, disgusting, filthy, foul, etc., in *Richard II*: ". . . so heinous, black obscene a deed." The Bard probably based the word on the French *obscene*, meaning the same, which came from the Latin *obscenus*. Within five years or so, *obscene* was being used to mean "indecent and lewd" as well.

obsidian. Obsidian is a glasslike rock of volcanic origin formed by the rapid cooling of lava on the earth's surface. Usually it is a bright, glossy black, but some examples are gray, green, brown, or red, ranging from opaque to translucent. Usually sharp-edged, the rock was often used for arrows and other weapons by the ancients. Pliny the Elder tells us in his *Natural History* that obsidian was named for its discoverer Obsius, who first found it in Ethiopia. In early editions of his work Pliny's *obsianus*, for the mineral, was misprinted as *obsidianus*, this explaining the mysterious "d" in the word.

Occam's razor. *Occam's razor*, the philosophic principle of economy or parsimony, holds that universal essences should not be unnecessarily multiplied, which means simply that a scientific explanation should contain only those elements absolutely necessary. The axiom is named for William of Occam (ca. 1280-1349), an English philosopher and Franciscan who was a pupil of Duns Scotus and who dissected every question as with a razor. Occam became general of the Franciscan order and his philosophy helped pave the way for pragmatic Renaissance science. He and his followers held that the existence of God and immortality are not capable of philosophical proof and must be accepted on faith alone. His name comes from the town of Ockham in Surrey, where he was probably born. "The Invinceable Doctor," as he was called, so formidable was he in debate, opposed

Pope John XXII over a question of monastic poverty, which led to his imprisonment and excommunication.

Occident. (*See* **to go west.**)

occupy.

> All you that in your beds do lie
> Turn to your wives and occupy,
> And when that you have done your best
> Turn arse to arse, and take your rest.

The old song, quoted in John S. Farmer's *Vocabula Amatoria* (1890), shows that *to occupy* was once a synonym for cohabitation. In fact, as Joseph Shipley points out in an article in *Maledicta* (to which I owe most of the information in this entry) the word *occupy* in all its senses became increasingly rare throughout the 17th and 18th centuries, when the verb took on this meaning. People ceased to use it, even Shakespeare commenting on this in *2 Henry IV, II*: "A Captaine? Gods light, those villains will rake the word as advises as the word occupy, which was an excellent good word before it was ill sorted." Luckily, *occupy* survived the puritanical onslaught. Other words haven't. The "cock", for example, is now almost always the "rooster," the "ass" is the "donkey," "haycocks" are "haystacks," "weathercocks" are "weather vanes" and "apricocks" are "apricots." Old Bronson Allcox even changed his name to Alcott, so that the author of *Little Women* isn't known as Louisa May Allcox.

ocean. *Ocean* came into English later than sea (*q.v.*), being first recorded in about 1290. The word ultimately comes from a Greek expression meaning "the great stream or river," which became the Latin *oceanus*. The Greeks personified this water encompassing the disk of the earth as Oceanus, "the god of the great primeval water." In early times, when only the eastern hemisphere was known, the ocean was "the Great Outer Sea of boundless extent everywhere surrounding the land, as opposed to inland sea."

oceanaut. (*See* **aquanaut.**)

October. (*See* **September.**)

octopus. The name for this creature may have been coined by a scientist in the late 18th century. *Octopus* was not used by the Romans, though the Greeks had the word *oktopous*, "eight-footed." Since the animal we know as the *octopus* has eight *arms*, not feet, whoever named it should have called it the *octobrach*.

od; odic force. Though only an odd term today, *od* was once supposed to stream from female fingertips, "burning blue." It was a natural force said to pervade all nature, especially manifesting itself in persons of sensitive temperament, and the *odic force* was a basic force underlying many natural activities—including magnetism and chemical reactions. The word was an arbitrary coinage of German scientist Baron von Reichenbach, who proposed the *odic theory* in 1850.

oddwoman; oddsman. The Scottish *oddwoman*, common during the 16th century, was a female arbiter or umpire who helped settle disputes and was chosen by both parties to the conflict. Her male counterpart was called the *oddsman*. Both took their names from the term *odd man*, the third or fifth man on a committee of arbitrators, the one who in the event of a tie vote cast the deciding ballot.

ode on a Grecian urn.

> Thou still unravished bride of quietness,
> Thou foster-child of Silence and slow Time . . .

No one would argue that Keats's poem isn't among the most beautiful and best known of all time, but the vase that he wrote about might be called kitsch today. The story begins with the great English potter Josiah Wedgewood (1730-95), who achieved his fame despite the fact that a childhood illness had caused the amputation of his right leg, barring him from using the potter's wheel. Wedgewood, the grandfather of Charles Dickens, was already renowned as a potter when he began to make the ubiquitous blue and white vases that still bear his name. These he copied from the famous "Grecian" *Portland* vase that Sir William Hamilton, husband of Lord Nelson's great love, Emma, purchased when he served as ambassador to Naples, and sold to the Duchess of Portland, for whom it is named, before she donated it to the British Museum in 1784. The Portland vase, however, wasn't a Greek vase as everybody thought, but a heavy-handed Roman imitation from the time of Augustus. The vase that John Keats saw and that inspired him to write his poem was a Wedgewood copy of a Roman copy of a Greek vase—a doubly fake Grecian urn:

> Beauty is truth, truth beauty - that is all
> Ye know on earth and all ye need to know.

O'Donohue's white horses. Every seventh May Day, the Irish chieftain O'Donohue returns to the Lakes of Killarney riding his great white steed, gliding over the waters to sweet unearthly music, a host of fairies preceding him and strewing his path with spring flowers. Foaming waves on a windy day are thus known as *O'Donohue's white horses*. Legend has it that more than one beautiful young girl believed so strongly in O'Donohue that she threw herself into the water so that he would carry her off to be his bride.

odor of sanctity; odor of iniquity. In medieval times people believed that the bodies of saints or holy people gave off a sweet fragrance after death, an *odor of sanctity*; and that the bodies of evil people smelled to high heaven, *an odor of iniquity*. The followers of Emanuel Swedenborg, called the *Swedenborgians*, later attributed the delightful fragrance to the angels present at a saintly person's deathbed. At any rate, the *odor of iniquity* never took on a figurative meaning, but an *odor of sanctity* came to mean "a reputation for holiness."

oersted. The Danish physicist and chemist Hans Christian Oersted (1777-1851) founded the science of electromagnetism when he discovered that direct electric current causes a magnetic needle to take a position at right angles to the wire carrying it. This basic fact of electromagnetic induction was the starting point for all future work in the field. Unlike many scientific discoveries, the Copenhagen professor's attracted immediate and widespread attention when he published a Latin monograph describing it in July 1820, about a year later. The scientist's name in Danish is actually Orsted, but has become anglicized to Oersted. The *oersted* honoring him is a unit of magnetic field intensity.

oesophagus. When Mark Twain wrote his satire on Sherlock Holmes stories called "A Double-Barrelled Detective Story," he began the tale as follows:

> It was a crisp and spicy morning in early October. The lilacs and laburnums, lit with the glory-fires of autumn, hung burning and flashing in the upper air, a fairy bridge provided by kind Nature for the wingless wild things that have their homes in the tree-tops and would visit together; the larch and the pomegranate flung their purple and yellow flames in brilliant broad splashes along the slanting sweep of the woodland; the sensuous fragrance of innumerable deciduous flowers rose upon the swooning atmosphere; far in the empty sky a solitary oesophagus slept upon motionless wing; everywhere brooded stillness, serenity, and the peace of God.

The "solitary oesophagus" in the passage was solitary all right, for it never existed outside of Twain's teeming imagination. He had of course invented the bird—which know-it-alls were quick to describe to friends—and later remarked that few readers ever questioned him about it.

ofay. (*See* **pig latin**.)

off the cuff. (*See* **on the cuff**.)

of the same kidney. Of the same sort, or disposition. This expression was British slang in the early 18th century, its use deplored by Jonathan Swift along with words like *banter* and "bamboozle." All have since become Standard English. The expression has its origins in the ancient belief that the kidneys were "the seat of the affections" and thus largely determined one's personality or temperament.

o-grab-me acts. The Embargo Act of 1807, and acts of following years, restricted American ship departures to prevent hostilities on the seas. But since it hurt our British and French enemies less than American shipowners (the policy having the reverse effect then the one intended), shipowners began spelling *embargo* backward and called the acts the *o-grab-me acts*.

ogre. The Magyars were a fearsome Asian people who invaded Europe in about A.D. 900 and eventually settled in what is now Hungary. In fact, another name for them was Uigurs or Ugrians, which, with the addition over the years of an initial *H*, an *n*, and an *a* became *Hungarians*. But because these savage invaders were so feared, Uigur also became *ogre*, which is still the word for "a terrible man-eating monster" in many languages. At least so goes the apocryphal story most often told about *ogre's* origin, which, unfortunately, is historically unfounded. *Ogre* was in fact coined by French author Charles Perrault in his *Contes* (1697) as the name for a race of hideous man-eating giants, Perrault possibly constructing the word from the name of *Orcus*, the god of Hades. *Ogre* has come to mean a man likened to such a monster in appearance or character.

O. Henry ending. An immensely prolific author, O. Henry wrote tales characterized by ironic, surprise endings, "twists," "stingers," or "snappers" which while they aren't supposed to be fashionable anymore are still widely used by authors and known as *O. Henry endings*. O. Henry was the pen name of American writer William Sydney Porter. While working as a bank teller in Austin, Texas, Porter was indicted for the embezzlement (really mismanagement) of a small amount of money and fled the country to South America. On returning to his dying wife, he was imprisoned for three years and adopted the pseudonym O. Henry to conceal his real identity when he began writing and selling the stories that would make him famous. Released from prison he pursued his literary career in New York, where he published at least fifteen books of short stories, including such perennial favorites as the "Gift of the Magi," before he died when only forty-eight. O. Henry suffered from hypoglycemia, the opposite of diabetes, his classic summary of the condition being "I was born eight drinks below par." His famous last words, quoting a popular song, could have ended one of his stories: "Turn up the lights, I don't want to go home in the dark."

Ohio. In Iroquois *Oheo* means "beautiful water," referring to the Ohio River for which this state is named. The *Buckeye State* (so called from its buckeye or horse chestnut trees) was admitted to the Union in 1803 as our 17th state.

the oil of angels.   A British expression that has some American currency, *the oil of angels* means money or gold, particularly money used as a bribe. The *angel* here refers to a 15th-century coin bearing the visage of Michael the Archangel. As Robert Greene wrote in 1592: "The palms of their hands so hot that they cannot be cooled unless they be rubbed with the oil of angels."

O.K.   Most word authorities believe that *O.K.* comes from the nickname of Martin Van Buren (1782-1862), who rose from potboy in a tavern to president of the United States. Van Buren was elected in 1836. He became an eponym during the campaign of 1840, when he ran for reelection in a tight race against "Tippecanoe and Tyler, too," General William Henry Harrison, legendary hero who fought against the Indians at Tippecanoe, and Virginian John Tyler. The election of 1840 had brought with it the first modern political campaign—mostly to President Van Buren's disadvantage. Harrison's followers, trying to identify Van Buren with the aristocracy, christened the general the "log cabin and hard cider candidate," and tagged Van Buren "Little Van the Used Up Man," "King Martin the First," "The Enchanter," "The Red Fox," "The Kinderhook Fox," the "Little Magician," and several other of the derogatory nicknames he had earned over the years. But "Old Kinderhook," a title bestowed upon the president from the name of his birthplace in Kinderhook, New York, sounded better to his supporters, better even than "the Sage, Magician, or Wizard of Kinderhook." In order to stem the tide somewhat, a group in New York formed the Democratic O.K. Club, taking their initials from "Old Kinderhook." These mystifying initials, appealing to man's love of being on the inside of events, became a sort of rallying cry for the Democrats. The mysterious battle-cry spread rapidly and soon acquired the meaning "all right, correct," probably because "Old Kinderhook," or *O.K.*, was all right, correct to his supporters. The new word did Van Buren no good, for voters remembered the Panic of 1837 and he was defeated in his bid for reelection, but the word honoring his name is undoubtedly the best known of American expressions, international in use, and what *H.L. Mencken* calls "the most shining and successful Americanism ever invented." It is increasingly being pronounced *K* today, making it even shorter and more useful. (*See* **A-O.K.; spoils system.**)

O.K. by me.   In use for at least half a century or so this expression is a Yiddish one given wider currency by the media. The *by me* in the phrase comes from the Yiddish *bei mir*.

Okies.   The migrant farm workers of the Great Depression called the *Okies* took their name from Oklahoma, where many of them originally lived before they left the Dust Bowl and began their journey west searching in vain for a golden land. They were of course immortalized in John Steinbeck's *The Grapes of Wrath*.

Oklahoma.   *Oklahoma* takes its name from a Choctaw word meaning "red people," for the Indians who lived in the region. The Sooner State (so called after those "sooners" who "jumped the gun sooner" and grabbed choice land there before they legally should have) was admitted to the Union in 1907 as our 46th state.

okra.   Okra was so valuable in ancient Angola that tribes made "sharp knife" raids into neighbors' fields to steal the vegetable, killing anyone who stood in their way. *Okra* derives ultimately from the Tshi *nkruman*. The Arabs held it to be a rare delicacy fit for weddings and other special occasions, naming it *uehka*, which means "a gift." *Okra* is sometimes called *ladyfingers* in England, this name being suggested by the shape of the pods.

old as Methuselah.   As *old as Methuselah*, "incredibly old," refers to the grandfather of Noah, who the Bible tells us lived until 969 before he perished in the year of the Deluge. The patriarch is the oldest person mentioned in the Scriptures and is the son of Enoch, descended from Seth, son of Adam. This primeval ancestor of mankind is mentioned in Luke 3:37 as well as Genesis. To recap Methuselah's longevity: "Thus all the days of Methuselah were nine hundred and sixty-nine years; and he died" (Gen. 5:21-28).

old as the hills.   This old phrase for someone very old may have its origins in a similar biblical expression (Job 15:7): "Art thou the first man that was born?, or wast thou made before the hills?"

Old Blighty.   Old Blighty became popular as an endearing name for England during World War I, but it can be traced to Englishmen in India some years before this, *blighty* itself deriving from the Hindustani *bilati*, "a distant country."

Old Brains.   Only one person in American history has the honor of being called *Old Brains* and he probably didn't deserve it. Union General Henry Wager Halleck (1815-72) was a fortifications expert and able organizer, but the prestige he enjoyed for the victories of U.S. Grant and others under his command were unwarranted—he wasn't the "old brains" behind them, as many believed, contributing little to Union strategy.

old chestnut.   English playwright William Dimond's melodrama *The Broken Sword* (1816) is all but forgotten, along with its characters, plot, and dialogue, and the author himself isn't remembered in most guides to literature. Yet Dimond had found immortality of sorts in the expression *an old chestnut*, "a stale joke or story," which probably derives from an incident in his play. *The Broken Sword's* principal character is crusty old Captain Xavier, who is forever spinning the same yarns about his highly unlikely experiences. He begins to tell the following one to Pablo, another comic character:

> *Captain Xavier:* I entered the woods of Golloway, when
>   suddenly from the thick boughs of a cork tree—
> *Pablo:* A chestnut, Captain, a chestnut!
> *Captain Xavier:* Bah, I tell you it was a cork tree.
> *Pablo:* A chestnut; I guess I ought to know, for haven't I
>   heard you tell this story twenty-seven times?

Fame didn't come immediately. The lines lay at rest in Dimond's play for almost seventy years before American actor William Warren, Jr. repeated them at a stage testimonial dinner in Boston, after hearing another speaker tell a stale joke. Other actors present adopted Warren's *chestnut*, elaborated on it, and it became the timeworn *old chestnut*.

old coot. (*See* **to coot.**)

old crate. (*See* **crate.**)

old fogey. Originally a Scottish term, dating back at least to the late 18th century, *old fogey* means an old person far behind the times. Its derivation is unclear, but the *fogey* here may come from an old use of the word *fog*, for "moss-grown."

Old Glory. The many paintings that show the Stars and Stripes flying at Valley Forge and in major battles of the Revolution are all in error, for no official stars-and-stripes flags were used by the Army until 1783. *Old Glory* was named by Captain William Driver of the brig *Charles Doggett* on August 10, 1831. Captain Driver had brought back the British mutineers of the H.M.S. *Bounty* from Tahiti to their home on Pitcairn Island, and some say that in recognition of this humane service a band of women presented him with a large American flag. Others claim that friends gave him the flag as a present. In any case, as he hoisted the flag to the masthead, he proclaimed, "I name thee Old Glory." His ship's flag became famous and by 1850 its name became common for the flag in general.

old guard. This term for the conservative wing of a political party, or anyone who opposes change, dates back to Napoleon's Imperial Guard, troops chosen in 1804 to be the elite of the French military. Devoted to Napoleon, they were treated better than the rest of the army and opposed any change in the status quo, the French calling them the *Vieille Garde*, or "old guard." In their bearskin hats and colorful uniforms they made the last charge at Waterloo.

old hat. Today *old hat* means out of date or not new, and it has meant this for at least a century. But back as early as 1754 it was "used by the vulgar in no very honorable sense," as Fielding put it. It then meant, in Grose's punning definition from his 1785 *Classical Dictionary of the Vulgar Tongue*: "a woman's privities: because frequently felt."

Old Ironsides. Built six months after the *Constellation*, the *Constitution* is America's oldest warship still afloat and in commission. A national historic monument today, she is moored in Boston Harbor flying the flag of the commandant of the First Naval District. The high point of her illustrious career came on August 19, 1812, when she engaged and defeated the British frigate *Guerriere* off Nova Scotia. During the battle an American sailor, watching British shots fall into the sea, cried: "Huzza! Her sides are made of iron!" and *Old Ironsides* she has been since that day. In 1830 Oliver Wendell Holmes, hearing that she was to be sold by the Navy, wrote his famous poem "Old Ironsides" in protest and she was saved.

the old lady in Dubuque. Dubuque, Iowa is named for its first settler, a French Canadian lead miner named Julien Dubuque. But what about that famous symbol of prudery, *the little old lady in Dubuque*? The phrase seems to have originated in this sense with Harold Ross, when he promised in a prospectus of the *New Yorker* that his magazine would *not* be edited for "the old lady in Dubuque." According to Brendan Gill, in his fascinating *Here at the New Yorker*, (1975) Ross may have been inspired by "Boots" Mulgrew, a former Broadway musical comedy skit writer forced by drinking and financial problems to retreat from New York to his birthplace. Mulgrew soon after began contributing squibs to a widely read *Chicago Tribune* column called "A Line o' Type or Two." These pieces, describing "the provincial absurdities of Dubuque" were signed with the pseudonym "Old Lady in Dubuque" and Gill suggests that "Ross read them, admired them, and, whether consciously or not, got the old lady in Dubuque fixed in his mind as a natural antagonist."

the Old Lady of Threadneedle Street. The Bank of England, located on Threadneedle Street in London, is called *the Old Lady* because the institution has traditionally been fiscally conservative or overly cautious. The bank was first called *the Old Lady of Threadneedle Street* in the late 18th century. The street was originally known as "Three Needle Street," this name recorded in 1598.

Old Ned. The Americanism *to raise Old Ned* means "to raise hell or start a row," *Old Ned* being recorded as a name for the devil, along with *Old Splitfoot* and *Old Scratch* as early as 1859. (*See* **Old Nick; Old Scratch.**)

Old Nick. The legend of the thin-lipped, sarcastic, hyperactive Florentine politician Niccolo Machiavelli gave rise to the theory that his first name was the basis for *Old Nick*, a synonym for the devil. The author of *The Prince*, who founded modern political science, did give us the word "Machiavellian," for brilliant, cynical political scheming characterized by deceit and bad faith, but no one really knows how *Old Nick* originated. One theory says that it derives from the German *nickel*, "a mischievious elf," and *nixie*, "a water sprite." The Niccolo origin is clearly wrong, anyway, stemming from Samuel Butler's humorous identification in *Hudibras*:

Nick Machiavel had ne'er a trick
(Though he gives name to our Old Nick)
But was below the least of these.

Satan, another sobriquet for the devil, means "the adversary" in Hebrew, while "Beelzebub" was the god of flies worshipped in Ekron. "Auld Hornie" (Old Horney), "Clootie," and the little used "Demogorgon" are other devil names. (*See* **Old Ned; Old Scratch**.)

Old Probabilities. Americans have been having fun with the weatherman for several centuries now. Knowing that weather forecasters always hedge their bets with a "probability" ("There is a probability of rain tomorrow"), they dubbed such prognosticators *Old Probabilities* in the late 19th century. The term is first recorded in 1873 for the superintendent of the weather bureau in Washington, D.C. *Old Probs* was the nickname of Cleveland Abbe (b. 1838), the first American to make daily weather predictions. Today, weather forecasters are even vaguer, generally saying "there is a possibility."

Old Scratch. This term for the devil may come from the old Scandinavian word *skratta*, meaning a monster or goblin, but the Teutonic wood demon called the *Scrat* is a better possibility. *Scrat*, for "the devil," is recorded early in the 11th century, but *Old Scratch* didn't evolve from it for another seven hundred years. (*See* **Old Ned; Old Nick**.)

Old Splitfoot. (*See* **Old Ned**.)

old stamping grounds. An interesting theory connects this Americanism, used before the Revolution, with the mating of male prairie chickens, who congregated in spring on hills and performed elaborate courtship dances, stamping the hills bare. Another guess is that the stamping of stallions while they covered mares suggested the phrase. All that's known is that *stamping grounds* were first referred to as places where horses or other animals customarily gathered. It wasn't too long (1836) before the term became a place where people customarily gathered. The British definition of a *stamping ground* as "a place for amorous dalliance," like a lover's lane, gives some support to the prairie chicken or stallion theories. The expression is generally used by or about males.

old tar. (*See* **Jack Tar**.)

oliver; Oliver's skull. Oliver Cromwell's name "fairly stank" to the Royalists, which is why they dubbed their chamber pots *Oliver's skulls*. The term was popular slang in England from 1690 to 1820 and puts Cromwell in the select company of the relatively small handful of people who have been discommoded by commodes. On the other hand, Cromwell's supporters so admired the way he hammered at the Royalists that the *oliver*, a small smith's hammer, was probably named after him. Whether the British underworld term *oliver*, for "the full moon," is a compliment or an insult is uncertain, but it definitely arises from the fact that Oliver Cromwell led the Roundheads. (*See* **crapper; Furphy; sacheverell; Twiss; vespasienne**.)

olla podrida; potpourri. *Olla podrida* is Spanish for "a putrid or rotten pot" and literally refers to a stew made of many kinds of meat, fowl, vegetables, and spices boiled in a large pot. Like the French *pot-au-feu*, it is made of many scraps, the "rotten" in the term referring not to its smell or taste, which is delicious, but to the way everything is cooked "leisurely, til it be rotten (as we say) and ready to fall in pieces." Since the 16th century *olla podrida* and *olio*, another word for the stew, have also meant an incongruous mixture, a hodgepodge, a farrago. *Olla podrida* isn't always used disparagingly when applied to miscellaneous collections of any kind, such as literary pieces, drawings, and musical medley. Often it just means a medley or *potpourri*, which, in fact, is the French translation of *olla podrida*. Some samples of the expression's use: "His work is an *olla podrida* of error, confusion's masterpiece;" "This *olla podrida* of a brain of mine." The nonce word *ollapodridical* means heterogeneous.

omelets can't be made without breaking eggs. A common expression that for some reason isn't in *Bartlett's* and *The Oxford Dictionary of Quotations*, this saying isn't recorded in English until 1859. Meaning that some things can't be accomplished without sacrificing others, the phrase is a translation of the French proverb *On ne saurait faire une omelette sans casser des oeufs*.

onanism. "Then Judah said to Onan, 'Go in to your brother's wife, and perform the duty of a brother-in-law to her, and raise up offspring for your brother.' But Onan knew that the offspring would not be his; so when he went in to his brother's wife he spilled the semen on the ground, lest he should give offspring to his brother. And what he did was displeasing in the sight of the Lord, and he slew him also." This passage from the Revised Standard Version of the Bible (Gen. 38:8-11) shows what scholars have long told us, that Onan was not a habitual masturbator as the word *onanism* suggests. It is not even clear from the biblical passage whether Onan's one such mentioned act was masturbation or coitus interruptus, and many biblical scholars tell us that his real sin was not *onanism* but his refusal to take the childless Tamar to bed, get her with child and rear their offspring as the son of his dead brother in accordance with the law of the levirate marriage.

on a shoestring.   This expression may come from faro, but it isn't recorded until 1904, although *shoestring gambler*, for a "petty tinhorn gambler," is attested to ten years or so earlier. Meaning to start a business with a small amount of money or capital, *on a shoestring* suggests that one's resources are limited to the shoestrings on one's shoes.

once in a blue moon.   To say that the moon is blue, to believe an absurdity, is an old proverb first recorded as far back as 1528:

> Yf they saye the mone is beleue
> We must believe that it is true.

At first, then, it was ridiculous to think of the moon as blue and when the expression *till a blue moon* came on the scene in the mid-19th century, it usually meant "never" rather than "extremely seldom" as it does now in the phrase *once in a blue moon*. Perhaps the slight but important change in meaning to "hardly ever" was influenced by the observation that the moon does seem to have a blue tinge on rare, unusually clear nights. This must have been noticed centuries before, but doesn't seem to have been recorded before the last century. Since then songs like "Blue Moon" (Rodgers and Hart) have made us more aware that there are blue moons, real and imaginary.

on cloud nine; seventh heaven.   *On cloud nine*, meaning "blissfully happy," was originally *on cloud seven*, perhaps deriving from *seventh heaven*, the highest of heavens in Jewish literature, the heaven in which God lives. "Nine" may have been substituted for "seven" because it is an even luckier, more sacred number. The expression dates back to the late 19th century.

on deck; in the hole.   A baseball player batting next in an inning is said to be *on deck*, this obviously an old nautical term put to use on land. So is *in the hole* for the man scheduled to bat third, this a corruption of *in the hold*—the reasoning being that the third batter is *in the hold*, or *hole*, since the second is *on deck*. No one knows just how these nautical words were transferred to baseball early in this century.

one degree under.   *One degree under* is a relatively recent expression, dating back fifty years or so, which means "feeling a bit poorly, slightly unwell." The phrase may be modeled on *under the weather* (q.v.), but the reference is to body temperature, not the thermometer. Someone one degree under the normal 98.6 body temperature would indeed be "feeling a bit poorly."

one foot in the grave.   The expression did not originate with the famous Grecian statue of an old man standing at the bottom of a long flight of stairs with one foot in the grave, as Roman tourist guides frequently claim. Fifteen centuries before the statue was carved, Roman emperor Julian said, "I will learn this even if I have one foot in the grave," which is probably the origin of this phrase meaning at the brink of death. Julian may have gotten the idea from the ancient Greeks, who had a similar expression, "With one foot in Charon's ferryboat"—that is, the legendary ferryboat that transported the dead across the river Styx to the Elysian fields.

one for Ripley.   Cartoonist Robert Leroy Ripley traveled widely from his California home to gather bits of odd information for his "Believe It or Not" newspaper series, books, and radio program, though much of the material he used was library researched. His name became as well known as "Believe It or Not" itself, the phrase *one for Ripley* used to describe any strange, almost unbelievable happening. Though he died in 1949, aged 56, Ripley's series still runs in newspapers throughout the world today, along with a host of imitators. There was a Ripley "Odditorium" at the Chicago World's Fair of 1933-34 and today seven "Believe It or Not" Wax museums are doing a thriving business in the United States and England.

one hundred percent American.   (*See* **Ananias**.)

one over the eight.   Heard more in England than in the U.S., this expression means to be drunk. It derives from the old superstition that one always becomes drunk after the eighth drink and not before!

one people, one country, one leader!   How many remember that this was the slogan and rallying cry of the Nazis (German National Socialists) under Hitler? *Ein Volk, ein Reich, ein Führer!* were the German words that led to so many horrors.

one picture is worth a thousand words.   The Chinese proverb that inspired this cliché goes to greater extremes: *One picture is worth more than ten thousand words*. Pictures certainly aren't always, or mostly, ten thousand or a thousand times more versatile than words. "If you're not convinced," author William Childress writes, "fall in a lake and start gulping water—and then, instead of screaming the word HELP, hold up a picture of yourself drowning. If someone pulls you out, I lose my argument."

one's own man. Today this expression (*he's his own man; I'm my own man,* etc.) generally means to be one's own master, beholden to no one, but in the past it also meant to be fully in control of all one's faculties and powers. The expression dates back to the early 16th century.

one swallow does not a summer make. The proverb was first recorded in English as *It is not one swallow that bryngeth in somer. It is not one good qualitie that maketh a man good* (1539). However, Aristotle recorded the Greek proverb *One swallow does not make a spring* long before this. The migratory swallow is still regarded as a harbinger of summer. The nests of some species, formed from the spawn of fish and seaweed bound together by the bird's solidified saliva, are used for *bird's nest soup,* among the most recherché of exotic gourmet foods. They are the subject of many legends—e.g., that they mate while in flight and that they bring good luck to any house they build a nest upon. Scandinavian tradition says that swallows hovered over the cross of Christ crying *Svala! svala!* ("Console! console!"), hence their name *svalow,* "the bird of consolation." *One swallow does not a summer make* means that all of one's troubles aren't over just because one difficulty is surmounted.

one to show, one to blow. Handkerchiefs became uniform in length after Marie Antoinette issued a royal decree declaring that they should be. They then became quite fashionable and men began to wear one in the breast pocket for show, while carrying another in the rear pocket to blow their noses with. This led to the now rare expression *one to show, one to blow,* implying that "all isn't what it seems, someone has something hidden in reserve."

one touch of nature . . . The complete phrase is *one touch of nature makes the whole world kin* and it has come to mean that any appeal to the basic emotions of people will reveal, by their sympathetic response, the common humanity, the basic kinship of all people. Shakespeare, however, meant something quite different when he invented the line for the cynical Ulysses in *Troilus and Cressida.* There are no eternal verities of the heart, Ulysses says to Achilles; the one natural trait we all share is our preference for what's *au courant,* or "in," latest, no matter how superficial it may be:

One touch of nature makes the whole world kin,
That all with one consent praise new-born gauds [gaudy novelties]
Then marvel not, thou great and complete man,
That all the Greeks begin to worship Ajax;
Since things in motion sooner catch the eye
Than what not stirs . . .

In a world where there is perpetual chasing of things in motion, Shakespeare's meaning is far from obsolete.

onion. *Onion* comes from the Latin word *unio,* "oneness" or "union," in reference to the many united layers in an onion; the Romans used the same word for the multilayered pearl; thus our pearl onion would have been a Roman *uniō uniō.* Onions were fed to the Egyptian laborers who built the great Cheops pyramid, dispensed by Alexander the Great to his troops to promote valor, and praised by General Grant, who once wired the War Department that he would not move his army farther without onions. The onion is believed by some to be an aphrodisiac as well as strength-giving, though as Shakespeare wrote, "Eat no onions or garlic, for we are to utter sweet breath."

the only good Indian is a dead Indian. General Phil Sheridan is credited by *Bartlett's Familiar Quotations* with this prejudicial remark so often quoted in old Western movies. But Sheridan said, "The only good Indians I ever saw were dead," which is a condensation of the words of the originator of the slander, Montana Congressman James Cavanaugh, who earlier said: "I have never in my life seen a good Indian . . . except when I have seen a dead Indian." Which kind of ruins the old story about Sheridan making the remark at Fort Cobb, Indian Territory, in 1869 after the Comanche Chief Toch-a-way ("Turtle Dove") was presented to him. Chief Toch-a-way reportedly said: "Me Toch-a-way, me good Indian." Sheridan reportedly replied: "The only good Indians I ever saw were dead."

onomatopoeia. The Greek for "making of words" is the ancestor of *onomatopoeia,* which is the term for forming a word by imitating the sound associated with the object designated. Examples of such words are *bang, buzz, cackle, clatter, crackle, cuckoo, hiss, murmur, pop, sizzle, tingle, twitter, whiz, whoosh,* and *zoom.*

on the ball. Depending on how it is used, the expression has two different origins. *To be on the ball,* "to be alert, knowledgeable, on top of things," probably refers to close and clever following of the ball by players in British soccer or American basketball. The phrase may have arisen independently in each sport, or it may have originated in the 1940s with the "bop and cool" jazz musicians and fans as the *American Dictionary of Slang* suggests. There is no hard evidence for any theory, but the sports analogy seems more logical. To *have something on the ball,* "to be talented or effective in some way," is surely of American origin, a baseball term referring to the various "stuff"—curves, spin, etc.—a good pitcher can put on the ball to frustrate a batter. (*See* **keep your eye on the ball.**)

on the beam.   At first glance *to be right on the beam*, "to be on the right course, accurate, functioning well," might be mistaken for an old expression connected with carpentry. The familiar phrase, however, is modern and has nothing to do with beams of wood. It probably originated in the RAF around 1938 and refers to the directional radio beams that guided planes to airfields. When a pilot is on course, the continuous beam is loudest; when he strays off course, the signal from the beacons along the route grows weaker.

on the carpet.   When carpets first were used as floor coverings they were walked on only by the master or mistress of the house, and servants usually stood on them only when they were called before the gentry to be reprimanded for some misdeed. From this practice, dating to the early 1800s, came the meaning of *on the carpet*.

on the cuff.   *On the cuff* apparently arose at the turn of the century. Since bartenders commonly wore starched white cuffs at the time, the theory that our term for "on credit" derives from bartenders jotting down the debts of patrons on their cuffs during the rush of business is an appealing one. *On the arm* probably derives from *on the cuff*, while *off the cuff*, unrehearsed or extemporaneous, may come from impromptu notes early Hollywood directors jotted down on their cuffs while shooting a difficult scene in a movie. These ideas, not in the script, were conveyed to the actors when the scene was reshot.

on the fritz.   No one seems to have discovered where the *fritz* comes from in *on the fritz*, which means out of working order, in disrepair, worthless, or ruined. Since *on the fritz* isn't recorded before the 1920s, it may have something to do with the derogatory term "Fritz," for a German soldier in World War I. Fritz is the nickname for the common German name Friederich, and was popularized in the nickname of Frederick the Great of Prussia—Old Fritz—long before World War I. Someone out of working order or ruined, could have been compared to the defeated Germans. Another wild guess is that *fritz* is a corruption of "frittered," in its old sense of broken or torn into pieces—as in "the sail frittered in a thousand pieces." Maybe the phrase even refers to little Fritz of the early comic strip "The Katzenjammer Kids," who along with his twin brother Hans put a lot of things *on the fritz*.

on the house.   This phrase originated in English public houses, "tippling houses" as they were called in Elizabethan times. It used to be common for tavern keepers to dispense a free drink with every three or so bought, one that was *on the house*. Bartenders still give drinks on the house, where the law doesn't prohibit this practice, but normally after a lot more than three are paid for. The expression is now common for anything given away free.

on the level.   The phrases *upon* or *on the level* and *by* or *on the square* probably originated with the Freemasons in the 14th century. Freemasons, before they accepted honorary members several centuries later, were exclusively a class of skilled workers in stone who traveled from place to place wherever buildings were being erected. From their use of the square, which drew a straight line and made you go straight, and their use of the level, which made sure a surface was true or even, came these expressions meaning honestly, truthfully, and on the up-and-up.

on the make.   In mid-19th century America, *on the make* meant only to be out for money, to be ruthlessly ambitious. During the Great Depression, interests shifted outwardly from money to sex, there being more of the latter around then than the former, and the expression acquired its second meaning of to be "out for love." The words probably are the source of to *make it with* someone, "succeed in having sexual intercourse"; *make time*, "have relations," *make out* and *make-out artist*. The earlier meaning remains primarily in *to make it*, "to succeed in any endeavor, to rise to the top."

on the nail.   (*See* **pay on the nail**.)

on the nose.   To *win by a nose* is an old horse racing expression, but *on the nose*, "exactly on time, perfectly correct, right on the button," originated in the early days of radio. Directors in their soundproof control rooms signaled their assistants on stage that the various segments of a program were running exactly on time by touching their forefingers alongside their noses. If portions of the program were running behind schedule, the director would relay other signs, and whole pages of a script might have to be cut out. The signal to cut something entirely, for example, was to saw violently at the throat with one hand. When everything was really copacetic, the director held up his thumb and forefinger pressed tightly together.

on the pad.   Since the late 19th century this Americanism has referred to policemen who accept bribes, the *pad* meaning the account book in which the bagman recorded the bribes paid and the officers sharing in the split.

on the qui vive.   French sentries once shouted "*Qui vive?*," literally "who lives?" as a challenge to discover to which party the person challenged belonged —appropriate answers being [*vive*] *le roi* [*king*], "*la France*", etc. Thus to be on the *qui vive* is to be watchful (like a sentry), to be on the alert for something. The expression is first recorded in English by Jonathan Swift in 1726.

on the rocks. The allusion here is to a ship grounded off a rocky coast, battered by waves and ready to sink, and the expression arose among seamen, as would be expected. The figurative use of rocks for a symbol of destruction or ruin dates back to at least the early 16th century, but it wasn't until three hundred years later (1889) that the phrase *on the rocks* appeared or is first recorded. When we use the expression today we always refer to ruin or impending disaster. Someone *on the rocks* can be stone broke, or bereft of sanity. A marriage *on the rocks* is wrecked and about to be sunk unless it is saved at the last minute. *On the rocks* is also a drinking term, meaning a drink served with ice in the glass, the expression dating back to the 1920s.

on the shady side of forty. As the sun sets, shadows lengthen. Thus the allusion in this 19th century expression is to late life, when one has become part of the shadows.

on the side of the angels. The phrase has long been used for someone who takes a spiritual view of things, or for someone who is on "our" side. Benjamin Disraeli coined it in 1864, before he became Britain's prime minister, in a speech he made at the Oxford Diocesan Conference opposing the Darwinian theory of organic evolution proposed in *The Origin of the Species.* "The question is this," he asserted. "Is man an ape or an angel? I, my lord, am *on the side of the angels.*" Two years later Disraeli gave us another famous quotation. "Ignorance," he told the House of Commons, "never settles a question."

on the spot. (*See* **put on the spot.**)

on the square. (*See* **on the level.**)

on the town. "On the Town" has been the title of several society columns over the years, the expression meaning "in the swing of fashionable life, pleasure." Steele first recorded the phrase, in *The Spectator* in 1712.

on the wagon. The original version of this expression, *on the water wagon* or *water cart*, which isn't heard anymore, best explains the phrase. During the late 19th century, water carts drawn by horses wet down dusty roads in the summer. At the height of the Prohibition crusade in the 1890s men who vowed to stop drinking would say that they were thirsty indeed but would rather climb aboard the water cart to get a drink than break their pledges. From this sentiment came the expression *I'm on the water cart*, I'm trying to stop drinking, which is first recorded in, of all places, Alice Caldwell Rice's *Mrs. Wiggs of the Cabbage Patch* (1901), where the consumptive Mr. Dick says it to old Mrs. Wiggs. The more alliterative *wagon* soon replaced cart in the expression and it was eventually shortened to *on the wagon. Fall off the (water)*

wagon made its entry into the language almost immediately after its abstinent sister.

on tick. *Tick* here is just an abbreviation of *ticket.* First recorded as early as 1648, *on tick* originally meant a written I.O.U. or "ticket," then came to mean "on credit."

on velvet. In the game of faro, money won from the house was called *velvet* and any player who won a lot of money was said to be *on velvet.* From these early 19th-century beginnings *on velvet* passed into general use as a synonym for "an unusual unexpected profit or gain."

on your own hook. In the 19th century fishermen on boats fishing the Grand Banks were paid according to what they caught individually on their own hooks and lines. To this practice we owe the expression *to be on your own hook*, "to be on your own."

oo. Sometimes called *Bishop's oo (Moho bishopi)* this most unusually named bird is a member of the honey eater family, birds that can eat nectar and flowers as a part of their diet. The *Bishop* of the bird's name honors no churchman, but American Charles Reed Bishop (1822-1915), who married a Hawaiian princess and became powerful in the islands' business and political affairs. *Oo* is simply the Hawaiian word for unknown, perhaps because so little was known about the bird before it was named.

open and shut. First recorded in 1848, *open and shut* probably didn't originate in a lawyer's office. A good bet is that it had its origins in some card game, probably either poker or faro. Simpler versions of these games didn't allow complicated betting but shut the pot after it was opened, after the ante was put in it. The term could have passed into general use from the card tables to take on the meaning of "easily decided or immediately obvious," as in an open-and-shut case of murder.

open sesame! Ali Baba, of course, overheard the robbers use these magic words to open the door of their cave of riches in the tale of "The Forty Thieves" from the *Arabian Nights.* Sesame is a common herb producing an oily seed long important in cooking and soapmaking in the lands of the *Arabian Nights*, so its use by the robbers is logical. If sesame is also a laxative, as several reference books say, then the thieves were also remarkable punsters.

opsimath; opsigamy. A rare word that should make a comeback with recent interest in the aged and the problems of growing old. An *opsimath* is a person who begins to learn or study late in life, the word deriving from the Greek for "late in learning." Formerly, the word was often used in a derogatory sense, to suggest a laggard, but there is no reason why it shouldn't be applied to old people learning new thing in new fields. *Opsigamy*, a rare related word, is marriage late in life, an act that the Spartans punished with flogging but which is common today judging by all the *opsigamists* around.

orange. Thousands of varieties of fruits are named after their developers and the orange is no exception. The best-known eponymous orange variety is the *Temple*, named after its early propagator, Floridian William Chase Temple. Others include the Murcott Honey orange, named for Florida grower Charles Murcott Smith, and the Parson Brown, which honors Nathan L. Brown, a Florida clergyman. Oranges are one of the oldest known fruits, the word deriving from the Arabian *naranj*, and today the United States is by far their largest producer, growing some 25 billion a year. An orange's color, incidentally, has nothing to do with its ripeness. Oranges turn orange only as a result of cold weather, which breaks down a membrane protecting their green chlorophyll. This is why summer oranges are often dyed and stamped with those familiar words, "color added."

orchard. *Hortyard*, one of the old spellings of *orchard*, best explains its origins. The word originally meant "a garden yard," deriving from the Old English *geard*, "yard," and the Latin *hortus*, "garden."

orchid. *Orchids* were once called *ballocks stones*, dog-stones, and similar names—all because their tubers resemble human testicles. Indeed, the name *orchid* derives from *orchis*, the Greek for "testicle." An *orchotomy* is, in fact, medical castration.

ordeal of battle; ordeal of fire; etc. *Ordeal* here comes from the Anglo-Saxon *ordel*, "to judge." In these ancient practices, outlawed since the 13th century, guilt or innocence was supposed to be left to supernatural decision: God would defend the just, even by miracle if necessary. In *ordeal of battle* the accused (if a noble) was allowed to fight his accuser, with the winner presumed right. *Ordeal of the bier* consisted of the accused touching a corpse, whose blood would start to flow if he was guilty. In the *ordeal of the eucharist* the eucharist would choke a guilty person trying to swallow it. *Ordeal of fire* had the accused holding his hand over red-hot irons or walking barefooted and blindfolded among nine red-hot ploughshares, his innocence established if he emerged unharmed. *Ordeal of water* consisted of ordeal by hot water and ordeal by cold water. In the former the accused plunged his arms to the elbow in boiling water—if his skin wasn't injured, he was innocent. In the latter the accused was bound and thrown into a river—if he floated he was a witch; if he sank he was innocent and lived, that is if he survived the sinking. Nobles, incidentally, could use stand-ins for their ordeals!

Order of the Garter. (*See* **blue ribbon**.)

Oregon. *Oregon* may come from the Spanish *oregones*, meaning "big-eared men" and referring to Indians who lived there. Other possibilities are the Algonquian *Wauregan*, "beautiful water," for the Colorado River, and an unclear Indian name possibly meaning "place of the beaver" that was misspelled on an early French map. The Beaver State was admitted to the Union in 1850 as our 33rd state.

organdy. The silk dress fabric called *organdy*, first recorded in 1835, takes its name directly from the French *organdi*, meaning the same. But its roots are ultimately in the ancient town of *Urgendi* in Turkestan, a place renowned for its weaving.

organoleptic analysis. Decomposition of shellfish is detected by *organoleptic analysis*, the federal Food and Drug Administration reported recently. Pressed for a definition the *FDA Consumer* explained that this meant "by smelling the product with the nose." (*See* **gobbledygook**.)

orgy. Every *orgy*, or drunken, licentious feast, takes its name from the secret nocturnal festivals the ancient Greeks and Romans held in honor of Dionysus or Bacchus, the god of wine. These ceremonies, called the *orgia*, featured wild drinking, dancing, and sexual license.

oriflamme. The early kings of France carried the red banner of the abbey of St. Denis, near Paris, as a military ensign. The flag, called the *oriflamme*, was crimson, cut into three pennants to represent tongues of fire, and carried on a gilded staff. Legend had it that men were blinded by merely looking on the *oriflamme*, but it was replaced by the *fleurs-de-lis* in the 15th century. It took its beautiful name from the Latin for "golden flame."

Orlando, Florida. The site of Disneyworld in Florida has an interesting etymology. It was originally named for its first settler, Aaron Jernigan, but rechristened *Orlando* in 1857 in memory of Orlando Reeves, who had been killed in a skirmish with Indians.

orrery. All planetariums can trace their ancestry to the first *orrery* invented in about 1700 by George Graham. This complicated mechanical device showed the movements of the planets and satellites around the sun by means of rotating and revolving balls. Graham sent his model to instrument maker John Rowley, who made a copy that he presented to his patron Charles Boyle (1676-1731), fourth earl of Orrery, the apparatus being named in the earl's honor. Orrery, who used the device to help educate his children, was a noted patron of science and a descendant of the physicist Robert Boyle.

Osage orange. (*See* **bodock**.)

Oscar. Hollywood's gold-plated Oscars remained nameless for years after the Academy of Motion Picture Arts and Sciences first awarded them in 1927. Called simply the Statuette, the ten-inch high trophy was designed by Cedric Gibbons, weighed about seven pounds, was bronze on the inside, and originally cost about one hundred dollars. The statuette quickly became a symbol of film fame, but not until 1931 did it get a name. At that time Mrs. Margaret Herrick, librarian of the Academy, was shown one of the trophies and observed, "He reminds me of my uncle Oscar." As fate would have it, a newspaper columnist happened to be in the room and soon reported to his readers that "Employees of the Academy have affectionately dubbed their famous statuette 'Oscar.'" The name stuck. Mrs. Herrick's uncle Oscar was in reality Oscar Pierce, a wealthy Texan from a pioneer family who had made his fortune in wheat and fruit and migrated to California, where he could now bask in glory as well as the sunshine.

Oscar Asche. Another famous *Oscar* (*q.v.*) is the Australian Oscar Asche (1872-1936), a musical comedy star who made a tidy fortune on the stage and whose full name became Australian rhyming slang for cash. "*Oscar Asche* for cash" was eventually shortened to *Oscar*, making him the only man whose prenomen means money in a generic sense.

oslerize. In a widely reported speech, Canadian-born physician Sir William Osler (1849-1919) opined that all business and professional men should retire at sixty. He mentioned Anthony Trollope's novel *The Fixed Period*, the plot of which "hinges upon the admirable scheme . . . into which at sixty men retired for a year of contemplation before a peaceful departure by chloroform." Generally misinterpreted in the press, Osler's plan enraged more than half of the population when his plan was interpreted as meaning that all men over forty should be put to death as useless. His scheme actually provided for retirement at sixty on a generous pension, but the misconception prevailed and from 1905 on *to oslerize* implied just the opposite of "life begins at forty." It is interesting to note that Dr. Osler made some of his most valuable scientific contributions *after* he turned sixty, his proposed date for compulsory retirement.

os sacrum. The *os sacrum*, "the triangular bone situated at the lower part of the vertebral column," is said to be so named because it was the sacred part used in ancient sacrifices. In rabbinical lore (where it is also known as the *luz*) the *os sacrum* is said to be called sacred because it resists decay and "will be the germ of the 'new body' at the resurrection."

ostracism. *Ostracism*, "to banish socially," derives from *ostrakon*, the Greek word for oyster shell. It seems that a vote of banishment in ancient Athens had to be a written one, for it was, of course, a serious matter to send a person into exile for crimes against the state. Because paper was scarce, the banishment ballot was written on pieces of tile called *ostrakon*, this name having first been applied to the shell of the oyster, which the tile resembled. It followed that the name *ostrakismos* was bestowed upon the act of banishment itself, which gives us our word for "to banish socially"—to *ostracize* or "oyster shell."

ostrich stomach. *Ostrich stomach* was the name for vitriol in medieval alchemy, because people believed at the time that the ostrich had vitriolic stomach juices that digested all the many things it was thought to swallow. The ostrich was considered a monstrous bird that could eat anything, often so insatiable that it plucked the iron shoes off horses. In heraldry it was represented chewing a horseshoe.

ottoman. Osman I (1259-1326) would not appreciate the fact that many readers are resting their feet on him, or his namesake, while reading this. But the *ottoman*, a stuffed footstool more often called a hassock, its Old English designation, is definitely named for him. Osman, sometimes called Othman, led his Muslim followers farther west from Asia Minor in the late 13th century to found the Ottoman Empire, principally what we know as Turkey today. Tales of this great empire, which lasted until its dissolution in 1918, excited the imagination of Europeans and toward the end of the 18th century merchants saw that there was a ready market in Europe for items of Eastern luxury, for the carpets, pillows, and divans that people imagined sultans lounged upon in their luxurious harems. These included a small, backless couch for two that the French called the *ottoman* because they imported it from the Ottoman Empire, ignoring its Turkish name. The couch or divan eventually became both the overstuffed English *ottoman sofa*, acquiring a back in the process, and, in a much smaller form, the *ottoman footstool*.

ouija board. The *ouija board* pronounced ("wee-jee board") was apparently intended to answer most questions put to it in the affirmative. Its name is simply a combination of the French *oui*, "yes," and the German *ja*, "yes." Obviously its inventor intended to stress the positive, to stress hope, whether the player be of French or Teutonic background.

an ounce of prevention is worth a pound of cure. (*See* **snug as a bug in a rug**.)

our cake is dough. This expression, for "miscarried plans and disappointments," goes back before Shakespeare, who used it in *The Taming of the Shrew*. It is first recorded in Thomas Beacon's *Prayers* (1559): "Or else your cake is dough, and all your fat lie in the fire."

our Perry and our Porter were too much for John Bull to swallow! A popular Yankee slogan after the War of 1812, this punning expression refers to American naval heroes Oliver Perry, whose last name means a hard cider made of pears, and David Porter, whose last name means a strong, dark beer. John Bull, of course, is the national nickname for England.

out at the elbows. (*See* **elbow**.)

to out-Herod Herod. Shakespeare used this in *Hamlet*: "It out-Herods Herod: pray you avoid it," Hamlet says to the actors. The reference is to a king infamous for his barbaric cruelty. *Herodes* or *Herod*, King of Judea in 4 B.C., ordered all Bethlehem's infants to be killed (Matt. 2:16). The expression means, of course, to outdo the worst tyrant in wickedness and violence.

out of kilter. Many have tried to explain the origins of *kilter* in this expression meaning to be out of order, out of whack, but no one has succeeded. The best suggestions, I think, are the *kilter*, meaning a "useless hand in cards," the dialect *kilt*, "to make neat," and the Dutch *keelter*, "stomach," because stomachs are often "out of order" with digestion problems. We only know that the expression is first recorded in 1643, as *kelter*.

out of sight, out of mind. (*See* **absence makes the heart grow fonder**.)

out of touch. Military drills of the late 18th century employed tight formations where every soldier in the ranks had to be close enough to the man on the left and right of him so that his swinging elbows brushed against his companions. A soldier who failed to do this and caused a gap in the line was said to be *out of touch* and the military use of this expression yielded the civilian saying, meaning "to lose contact with a situation."

outta sight! Often regarded as original college slang of the 1960s, *outta sight*, for "something remarkable or wonderful," has been part of the language since the 1840s, in the Bowery expression *out of sight*. Stephen Crane used it in his final novel *Maggie: A Girl of the Streets* (1896): "I'm stuck on her shape. It's outa sight . . ."

ovarimony. (*See* **testify**.)

over a barrel. Here the person over the barrel is in the other person's power or at his mercy. In the days before mouth-to-mouth resuscitation and other modern methods of lifesaving, lifeguards placed drowning victims over a barrel, which was rolled back and forth while the lifeguard tried to revive them. Victims were certainly in the lifeguard's power, and the process is probably the origin of the Americanism *to have someone over a barrel*.

over-the-counter stocks. In the days before stock exchanges, banks used to sell securities over the counter. It is from this practice that we derive the term *over-the-counter* stocks. Today over-the-counter stocks are those not sold on the New York and other major stock exchanges, usually being those of smaller companies.

overwhelm. Overwhelm means essentially the same thing as *whelm*, "to be completely overcome by something," but *overwhelm* is a more emphatic term. *Whelm* has its roots in the Middle English *whelven*, meaning to capsize or turn a vessel upside down. The English *whelm* was first recorded in the 13th century and soon took on the sense of turning a vessel upside down "so as to cover it" with water, which led to its modern meaning.

oxymoron. Deriving from the Greek for "pointedly foolish" an *oxymoron* is a figure of speech in which incongruous and apparently contradictory words are combined for a special rhetorical effect by paradoxical means. A well-known example is Tennyson's "Lancelot and Elaine":

The shackles of an old love straitend' him
His honour rooted in dishonour stood,
and faith unfaithful kept him falsely true.

Many famous English writers have used this device. Other *oxymora* include the phrase *an eloquent silence* and the word *sophomore*, which derives from two Greek words meaning "wise" and "foolish."

oyez! oyez! oyez! This call made by a court officer is the French second-person plural imperative of *oyer*, "to hear," meaning "hear ye! hear ye! hear ye!" and was introduced to England by the Normans. It was formerly used by town criers, and Shakespeare rendered it as *O yes!*

oysters Kirkpatrick. Oysters Kirkpatrick was named in honor of James C. Kirkpatrick, manager of San Francisco's Palace Hotel in the late 19th century. The Palace Hotel, born during the gold rush of 1849, destroyed in the earthquake of 1906 and rebuilt to become one of America's greatest eating places, offers the following simple original recipe for the delectable dish: "Open oysters on deep shell, put in oven for about 3 or 4 minutes until oysters shrink. Pour off the liquor, then add small strip of bacon and cover with catsup and place in very hot oven for about 5 to 6 minutes until glazed to a nice golden brown."

Ozarks. The *Ozark Mountains* in Missouri, Arkansas, and Oklahoma, ranging up to 2,300 feet high, cover an area of 50,000 square miles, and are noted more for their beautiful scenery and mineral springs, which make them a resort area, than their rich deposits of lead and zinc. The *Ozarks* are named for a local band of Quapaw Indians who lived in the Missouri and Arkansas region of the mountains. "The French were in the habit of shortening the long Indian names by using only their first syllables," an article in the *St. Louis Globe-Democrat* explains. "There are frequent references in their records to hunting or trading expeditions 'aux Kans,' or 'aux Os,' or 'aux

Arcs,' meaning 'up into' the territory of the Kansas, Osage, or Arkansas tribes." This *aux Arcs* seems to be the more likely explanation for *Ozarks*, although the local Arkansas band may have been named from the French *aux Arcs*, meaning "with bows," which could also have been corrupted to *Ozarks* and later applied to the mountains where the Indians lived.

ozone. Although *ozone* means "fresh, pure air" in everyday speech (the reason for place names like *Ozone Park*, New York), it translates as "stinking air," deriving from the Greek *ozein*, "to stink." German chemist Christian Friedrich Schonbein coined the name of this stable, pale bluish gas in 1840. Schonbein wrote that he named this most reactive form of oxygen (O_3) "*ozone* because of its strong smell," which he thought was similar to chlorine.

P

P. The ancient Phoenicians and Hebrews called our sixteenth letter *pe*, "mouth." *P.* in music means "piano," while *the five P's* is Englishman William Oxberry (1784-1824) who was for his all too brief forty years a Printer, Poet, Publisher, Publican, and Player (actor). The 16th-century Dominican monk Placentius wrote a poem of 253 verses called *Pugna Porcorum* in which every word begins with a *p*, the first line translating as "Praise Paul's prize pig's prolific progeny."

pablum. *Pablum* was a trademark name for a specific infant's cereal, although the word has become generic and is used to mean childish or insipid ideas. The trademark was coined from the Latin *pabulum*, food or fodder, early in this century.

Pacific Ocean. Portuguese explorer Ferdinand Magellan gave this great ocean its name in 1520, because of the calm, peaceful weather he enjoyed on it after a stormy passage in adjoining straits.

package-goods store. Liquor stores are so named not because liquor is sold in packages in such stores, but because of the quest for euphemisms after Prohibition was repealed. State legislatures did not want to offend "drys" at the time, or wanted to offend them as little as possible, and, in making liquor stores and saloons legal again, referred to them by such names as *package-goods stores* and *taverns*.

paddle your own canoe. (*See* **canoe.**)

paeans; peony. The gods wounded in the Trojan War were cured by the physician Paeon, according to Greek mythology. Thus many plants once prized for their curative powers were named for Paeon, including the flower called the *peony*. Because they believed their god Apollo often disguised himself as Paeon, the Greeks sang hymns of thanks and tribute to him that came to be called *paeans*, these the source for our expression *paeans of praise*.

Paget's disease. (*See* **Bright's disease.**)

Pago Pago. *Pango Pango* should be the name of this Pacific island, the chief harbor of American Samoa, and that, in fact, is the way the locals pronounce the name. An old story, which may be true, explains that the island is called *Pago Pago* because missionaries transliterating the local speech into the Latin alphabet found that there were many sounds that had to be "represented by *n* in combination with a following consonant." So many, in fact, that there weren't enough *n*'s in their type fonts to enable them to set all such words in type. So they quite arbitrarily eliminated the *n* from some words—leaving us with *Pago Pago* instead of *Pango Pango*.

pain in the . . . The *you give me a pain in the . . .* expressions all originated in the early 20th century. Of the various parts of the anatomy included, the *rear end* was first—*neck, back* and *arm* being euphemisms for *ass* in the expression. *Neck* is now as frequently heard as the latter, as is *balls*, while *arm* and *back* are rarely heard. The British have, or had, the expression *you give me the ball's ache*. All of these aches are mental, not physical, and the person who causes one is intensely irritating, at least at the moment of anger in which the words are said.

to paint the town red. If Indians burning down a town suggested this phrase meaning to go on wild sprees, to make "whoopee," no one has been able to find the actual culprits. More than one scholar does nominate the flames Indians on the warpath often left behind for the "red" in the phrase, and the expression did originate in the American West, where it was first applied to the wild partying of cowboys in about 1880. Another good guess suggests a link with the older expression *to paint*, meaning "to drink," which, coupled with the way a drunk's nose lights up red, may have resulted in the phrase. Or *red*, a color commonly associated with violence, could have derived from the way the "painters" did violence to the town or to themselves.

Pakistan. Pakistan is probably the only country whose name was constructed as an acronym, its letters standing for the the regions that make up the nation: *P* for Punjab; *A* for Afghani border tribes; *K* for Kashmir; *S* for Sind; and *tan* for Baluchi*stan*. A number of other place names are acronyms. Pawn, Oregon, for example, is composed of the first letters of the names of the men who founded it—Poole, Aberley, Worthington, and Nolen.

pal. Recorded in late 18th-century England for an "accomplice," *pal* came within fifty years or so to mean a chum or friend. Originally a Gypsy word, it derives from the Romany *pal*, "brother, or mate," which comes from the Turkish Gypsy *pral*, meaning the same.

398

palace. Augustus Caesar, the first Roman emperor, built his home on the most imposing of the seven hills of Rome, the Mons Palatinus, so named for the fence of stakes (Latin, *palus*) around it. His royal mansion was called a *palatium*, which became the French *palaise* and finally the English *palace*, for the same.

palaver. The Portuguese *palavra* journeyed to Africa before it came to England in the form of *palaver*. Meaning "word," *palavra* was used to mean "talk" by Portuguese traders in East Africa when they bargained with natives in the area. By the early 18th century English sailors had adopted the word and brought it back home in the form of *palaver*.

paleface. It is almost certain that no Indian coined this word meaning "white man." Most likely, it was invented by American novelist James Fenimore Cooper (1789-1851).

palindrome. So scurrilous in his satires was Sotades, a Greek poet of the third century B.C., that Ptolemy II had him sewn up in a sack and thrown into the sea. But his coarse, vile verses must have been clever, for Sotades is reputed to have invented palindromes, which are sometimes called *Sotadics* in his honor. Palindromes take their more common name from the Greek *palin dromo*, "running back again," and they are simply anagrams that read the same backward as forward. Making palindromes has been a favorite word game at least since early Grecian times, but English, with the largest and most varied vocabulary of all languages, offers the most fertile ground for the creator of palindromes. It's said that Sir Thomas Urquhart even invented a universal language based entirely on palindromes. Probably the longest common English palindromic word is *redivider*. The longest half-way sensible palindrome is one coined by an anonymous 19th century English poet: *Dog as a devil deified/Deified lived as a god*. Another famous palindrome is the one English author Leigh Mercer wrote for Ferdinand de Lesseps, the man who began the Panama Canal: *A man, a plan, a canal: Panama!* (See **namby-pamby**.)

palma Christi. The castor-oil plant (*Ricinus communis*) is called *palma Christi* because its leaf shape resembles the palm of the hand and in early times it brought to mind an image of Christ's hand nailed to the cross. The name is first recorded in a herbal published in 1548, but is certainly older.

palooka. (See **high hat**.)

pamphlet. *Pamphilus, seu de Amore* was the title of an erotic love poem of the 12th century; nothing is known about its author Pamphilus except his name in the title. No more than a few pages in length, the Latin verses became very popular during the Middle Ages, the best-known love poem of their time. Just as the small book containing *Aesop's Fables* came to be familiarly called *Esopet* in French, the little poem became known as *Pamphilet*, the English spelling this *Pamflet*, and eventually *Pamphlet*. By the 14th century any small booklet was called a *pamphlet* and within another three hundred years the word had acquired its sense of "a small polemical brochure," the transition completed from sensuous love poem to political tract. Generally, a *pamphlet* is defined as a paperbound or unbound booklet of less than one hundred pages.

to pan. Apparently the parent of this is the expression *it didn't pan out*. American prospectors long before the California gold rush were expert at using metal mining pans to separate gold from the sand and gravel they scooped from a stream bed. When gold wasn't found after the pan was shaken, miners would say that it hadn't *panned out*. Similarly, when any effort, say a stage play, didn't pan out, it didn't succeed. After enough literary critics had said plays or books didn't pan out, to criticize a production severely came to be known as *panning it*. Another suggestion is that *to pan* derives from the head, or "pan," of a tamping bar, which receives the blows of a sledgehammer, but the first recorded use of the word in this sense contains several allusions to mining processes, including panning.

Panacea. A daughter of Aesculapius, the Greek god of medicine, Panacea (her name formed from the Greek *pan*, "all," and *akeisthal*, "to heal") could cure any ailment. Over the years her name came to mean a cure-all, a *panacea* now being a remedy that will cure any problem, medical or otherwise.

Panama hat. Made from the plaited leaves of a palmlike plant (*Carludovica palmata*) of South America, the *Panama hat*, or *Panama*, is something of a misnomer. The hats originated in Ecuador, but have been called Panama hats since they were first recorded in English in 1833—probably because Panama was the major distribution center for them.

panda. (See **polo**.)

pandemonium. English poet John Milton gave us this word for wild lawlessness, tumult, or chaos when he dubbed the capital of hell *Pandaemonium* in *Paradise Lost*. He coined the word from the Greek for "all demons."

panhandler. *Panhandler* is said to derive from the Spanish *pan*, meaning both bread and money (just as the American slang *bread* does today). But though it is supposed to have been first recorded in 1890, the earliest quotation I am able to find for it is in humorist George Ade's *Doc Horne* (1899): "He had 'sized' the hustler for a 'panhandler' from the very start." However, the fact that Ade put the word in quotation marks probably indicates that he did not invent it, as has often been claimed. (*See* **tightwad; gladhander**.)

panic. All panics can be linked with the great god Pan of the dark forests and fields—etymologically at least. The word *panic* derives from the name of Pan and the Greek term *panikon deima*, "the panic fear," a fear of the woods on a dark evening when eerie frightening sounds are heard.

panic button. (*See* **push (hit) the panic button**.)

pansy. The french *pensée*, "thoughtful," is the source of this flower's name, some poet in ancient times believing that the flower had a thoughtful, pensive face. The flower was called *pensee* in English during the early 16th century, but changed gradually in pronunciation and spelling to *pansy*. Other fanciful names for the *pansy* (*Viola tricolor hortensis*) have included *heartsease, call-me-to-you, three-faces-under-a-hood, love-in-idleness,* and *kiss-me-at-the-garden-gate. Pansy* has been a derogatory term for homosexuals since about 1930, this expression originating in England.

pants; panties. *Panties* has become acceptable only in relatively recent years, despite the fact that the word has its roots in the name of a saint. St. Pantaleone, a Christian doctor who treated the poor without charge, was condemned to death by the Romans in A.D. 305, and miraculously survived six execution attempts before his persecutors finally beheaded him. The courageous saint (*Pantaleone* means "all lion") became patron saint of doctors and a martyr revered by the Venetians, his name all the more popular because so many boys were baptized in his honor. Probably for this reason, and because it was considered comical to call a foolish character "all lion," the saint's name attached itself to the buffoon in the 15th-century *commedia dell'arte*, in which an emaciated, bespectacled old man called Pantaloon wore slippers and one-piece, skintight breeches that bloused out above the knees and came to be known as *pantaloons*. Pantaloons later came to be a designation for trousers in general, the word introduced to America in the early 18th century and soon shortened to *pants. Pants* quickly replaced *trousers* in American speech and its diminutive form, *panties*, was used to describe women's underwear. In Britain, however, *pants* refers to men's underwear and is not a synonym for *trousers*.

paparazzi. Free-lance photographers called *paparazzi* have been in the news for twenty years or so, usually for their altercations with the celebrities they relentlessly pursue and try to photograph. They are so named from the Italian *paparazzi*, "buzzing insects," which they resemble as they swarm about a celebrity victim.

papaya. The versatile *papaya*, or tree melon, is a staple food in many parts of the world, and its enzyme *papain* aids in the digestion of food, one reason why its leaves are used as a meat tenderizer in some countries and the fruit is the basis for commercial tenderizers. Indians of Central America gorge themselves with *paw paw* so that they can eat large quantities of food at their feasts without becoming ill. The word *papaya* is a corruption of the Carib Indian *ababai*. In Cuba and some other Spanish-speaking countries the large fruit (it sometimes weighs up to twenty pounds) is called *fruita bomba*, or "bomb fruit." *Papaya* itself has come to be slang for "the female fruit," or breasts, in Cuba, but isn't used in polite conversation.

paper. In ancient times paper was made from the pith and stem of the Egyptian papyrus plant soaked in water and pressed into sheets. The Latin *papyrus*, for the plant, came to mean paper and passed into French as *papier*, which gave us the English word *paper*.

paper chase. Thanks to a film and television series about the trials of Harvard Law School, *the paper chase* has since the late 1970s had currency as a synonym for the hectic, often self-defeating chase after good grades in school as a means for advancement in life. The phrase apparently derives from the ancient game of hares and hounds, also called *the paper chase*, in which some players (hares) start off in advance on a long run scattering pieces of paper called "the scent" behind them, with the other players (hounds) following the trail and trying to catch the hares before they reach a designated place.

papist. Usually a hostile or opprobrious term, *papist* means an adherent of the Pope, one who advocates papal supremacy; or, simply, a member of the Roman Catholic Church. Appropriately enough, Martin Luther coined the word from the Latin *papa*, "pope," also coining the obsolete variants *papastres, papanos*, and *papenses*. Luther also invented the term *Romanist*, for a Roman Catholic. The words came from German into English, unchanged, in the early 16th century.

Pap test. This simple, painless test can detect cancer of the womb in its early stages, enabling it to be treated before it is too late. Best known as the *Pap test*, although the more accurate *Papanicolaou's stain* and *Pap smear* are also used, the procedure involves no more than the insertion of a small wooden spatula into the vagina to remove fluid mixed with uterine cells. This fluid is then dyed, spread on a glass slide and examined under the microscope. Few people know that Greek-born American physician George Nicholas Papanicolaou (1883-1962) invented the Pap test, his rather difficult name corrupted to the shortened form and obscuring the fame he so richly deserves. Pap smears can be taken of respiratory, digestive and genitourinary secretions, too.

par. (*See* **up to par.**)

paradise. Paradise often means the Garden of Eden, and the word *paradise* itself derives from the Old Persian word for an enclosed garden surrounded by walls, *pairidaeza*. Such gardens, and the word for them, were known over 3,000 years ago in the Near East, where they were such prized retreats that they took on religious significance.

paradise shoots. Legend has it that paradise shoots (genus *Burera*) is the only plant left from the Garden of Eden. When Adam left Paradise he took a shoot of this tree with him and it has since been prized for the pleasant aroma of its wood. It is also called the East Indian aloe tree and the legin aloes.

parchment. *Parchment*, "animal skins prepared for writing," is said to have been developed at the great ancient library in Pergamum, Asia Minor, when Ptolemy, a rival book collector, refused to export Egyptian papyrus to Pergamum. The Romans called the writing material *pergamena charta*, "paper of Pergamum," which became the French *parchemin*, this yielding the English *parchment* in the early 14th century.

parentheses. First recorded in 1568, *parenthesis* comes from a similar Latin word meaning the same. A *parenthesis* is a word, phrase, or clause inserted in a sentence that is grammatically complete without the insertion. The device goes back to at least the 16th century, when the *parentheses*, or "upright curves" themselves (the marks enclosing these words), were sometimes called "halfe circles" and "round brackets." Parenthetical remarks, however, can be made between dashes and commas as well as within parentheses. Mark Twain had the last word on parentheses. "Parentheses in literature and dentistry are in bad taste," he wrote, comparing *parenthetical expressions* "to dentists who grab a tooth and launch into a tedious anecdote before giving the painful jerk."

par for the course. *Par* is an American golfing term dating back to 1898 and deriving from the Latin *par*, "equal." It means the score an expert is expected to make on a hole or course, playing in ordinary weather without errors. The expression *par for the course*, meaning just about normal or what one might have expected, owes its life to the golfing term and dates back to about 1920.

pariah. The Indian class called the *Paraiyar* in Tamil are not outcasts at all. The *Paraiyar* were forced into

menial positions with the Aryan invasion some two thousand years before Christ and now form one of the lower castes in southern India, but, although they are regarded as "untouchables" by the Brahmins, they are not the lowest Hindu caste. Their name derives from *parai*, "a large drum," for their duty was to beat the drum at certain religious festivals. Eventually the *Paraiyars* became field workers in the Tamil country of Madras; however, when the British came to India they employed most of their household servants from that class, whose name they corrupted to *Pariah*. Believing that they were the lowest caste or had no caste at all, many British and other Europeans began to use *pariah* for the lowest of the low, an utter social outcast among his own kind—unjustly degrading the *Paraiyars* in language just as their countrymen degraded them in life.

Paris. The French still use the names *Lutetia* and *Lutece* for Paris, and though the words are considered poetic today, they actually serve to remind us that the beautiful city was once little more than a swamp. For *Paris* is simply a shortening of the Latin *Lutetia Parisianorum*, meaning "mud flats of the Parisi tribe," the longer name not dropped until after the Roman occupation.

parking meter. This expression became common only after July 16, 1935, when the world's first parking meter was installed in Oklahoma City, Oklahoma. However, two Oklahoma State University professors developed the first *Park-O-Meter* in 1933 and it had been suggested by journalist Carl C. Magee a year or so before that. Park-O-Meter No. 1 is now on display in the Oklahoma Historical Society. It originally cost five cents for one hour's use and the first person to be arrested for a meter violation was a minister.

Parkinson's Law. *Parkinson's Law* (1957), formulated by and named after C. Northcote Parkinson, distinguished British author and scholar, puts down succinctly what employers have known for generations: "Work expands to fill the time allotted to it, or, conversely, the amount of work completed is in inverse proportion to the number of people employed."

Parliament. The British Parliament, where so many debates are heard, takes its name from the Old French *paler*, "to talk." In fact, the word came into Middle English as *parlement*. A *Parlement* under the old régime in France was the sovereign court of justice, a kind of Supreme Court that had some administrative powers.

parliamentary language. Language that is not restrained, unlike the language generally heard in the British Parliament; an uncivil and discourteous way of speaking or arguing. *Parliamentary language* is first recorded in 1818 and *unparliamentary language* probably made its appearance shortly afterward.

parlor.   From the French *parler*, "to talk, to converse." The *parlor* was traditionally the room in which general conversation took place. Such reception rooms were originally found in monasteries, where talking might be forbidden elsewhere on the premises.

Parmesan cheese.   *Parmesan cheese*, a hard cheese that is often grated and used on pasta, and possibly the most famous of classic Italian cheeses, was first made near and named for the city of Parma, Italy.

Parnassus; to climb Parnassus.   The 8,000-foot-high Greek mountain Parnassos, called Parnassus by the Romans, had one of its summits consecrated to Apollo, the god of music, and thus the mountain near Delphi became associated with poetry and music in particular, and literature in general; all literary effort was connected with Parnassus—some in the foothills, some at the summit. *To climb Parnassus* means "to write poetry."

parrot.   *Parrots* (their name believed to derive somehow from the French proper name *Perrot*, a diminutive of *Pierre*) reproduce human sounds with great accuracy and have been known to have "vocabularies" of over 100 words, but they of course speak by imitation, without understanding. Parrots have been called Pollys since the early 17th century, when Ben Jonson first recorded the word. Myna birds (from the Hindi *maina*) mimic human speech more precisely than parrots, but have smaller vocabularies. (*See* **chimpanzee; dolphin**.)

parsnip.   *Parsnip* derives from the Latin words *pastinare*, "to dig or trench the ground," and *napus*, "turnip," in reference to the fact that it was thought to be a kind of turnip that the ground had to be trenched for (so that it would grow straight). Incidentally, the Russian word for parsnip is *pasternak*, so the Nobel Prize winning Russian poet's name translates as Boris Parsnip!

Parson Brown orange.   (*See* **orange**.)

Parsons table.   No old parson or any other clergyman invented the durable easy-to-make *Parsons table*. It was an innovation of Manhattan's Parsons School of Design in the early 1930s.

Parthenon.   (*See* **pornography**.)

Parthian shot; Parthian arrow; etc.   (*See* **parting shot**.)

parting shot.   The Parthian soldiers of antiquity were famed as deadly mounted archers. These mail-clad horsemen would ride furiously to the attack, pour a shower of arrows on their enemies and then evade any closer action by rapid flight, withdrawing according to plan and firing their shafts backwards from their horses while galloping away. Such tactics made Parthia, located in what is now northwest Iran, a world power that even defeated the Romans under Mark Antony when he attempted to invade their country in 36 B.C. *Parthian glance*, for a very keen backward glance, became proverbial, as did *Parthian arrow* or *shaft* or *shot*, the last by extension giving us the expression *parting shot*. Thus when you get in the last word in an argument, a *parting shot*, you are shooting a Parthian arrow.

partridge; partridge, always partridge.   Trace the roots of the word *partridge* back to the Greek *perdika*, "a partridge," and you'll find one of the oddest and most expurgated of bird name derivations. For the source for *perdika* is probably *perdesthai*, "to fart," the Greeks most likely naming the game bird for the sound the whirring wings of the rising bird made, which they thought resembled the breaking of wind. *Partridge, always partridge (perdix, toujours perdix)* means "too much of the same thing." It's said that the confessor of a French king admonished him for infidelity, and the King asked him what his favorite dish was. "Partridge," the priest said, and the king ordered him to eat only partridge every day. "How were your meals?" the king asked after a few weeks, and the priest replied, "Very good, but partridge, always partridge." "Ah, yes," said the amorous king, "and one wife is all very well, but not 'partridge, always partridge!'" Of the late brilliant lexicographer and etymologist Eric Partridge, an especially indefatigable worker who took on jobs few others would consider tackling, it was once said, "Partridge is always game."

party crasher.   (*See* **crash**.)

party line.   (*See* **spoils system**.)

party machinery.   (*See* **spoils system**.)

pasquinade.   The first *pasquinades*, witty lampoons or satires, especially those posted in a public place, were hung upon an ancient statue unearthed in Rome in 1501 and reerected at the corner of his palace near the Piazza Navona by Cardinal Caraffa. The mutilated old statue, possibly a likeness of Ajax, Menelaus, or some unknown gladiator, was dubbed Pasquino—either because that had been the name of the Roman gladiator represented or more probably because it stood opposite quarters where a sharp-witted, scandal-loving old man named Pasquino had lived. Pasquino, variously described as a barber, tailor, cobbler, and schoolteacher, had died some years previously. But it became customary on St. Mark's Day to salute and mockingly ask advice from the statue named for the caustic old man, such requests being posted on the statue after a while. These written Latin verses soon took the form of barbed political, religious, and personal satires, often upon the Pope, which were called *pasquinate*; a book of such squibs was published in 1509.

passion flower.   The passion flower was so named in medieval Spain because its parts are said to resemble Christ's instruments of passion, its corona being the crown of thorns, the five sepals and five petals representing the ten apostles (Peter and Judas not counted), etc. A list of these similarities follows:

Leaf—symbolizes the spear
Five anthers—the five wounds
Tendrils—the whips
Column of the ovary—pillar of the cross
Stamens—hammers
Three styles—three nails
Fleshy threads within flowers—crown of thorns
Calyx—the glory or nimbus
White tint—purity
Blue tint—heaven

a passion for anonymity.   Not a man who liked to be up-staged by his staff, Franklin D. Roosevelt announced midway through his first term in office that he was going to appoint several new assistants "with a passion for anonymity." Possibly he was weary of all the newspaper coverage given his "brain trust." Anyway, he did manage to appoint several assistants so self-effacing that nobody remembers them today—and contributed a new phrase to the language as well.

passion killers.   The Wrens (Women's Royal Navy Service) during World War II were issued long, plain, unstylish black knickers, or underwear, that they or other interested parties promptly dubbed *passion killers*, at least getting even with the powers-that-were by way of the King's English.

to pass under the yoke.   After the Romans defeated an enemy they constructed a yoke of three long spears—two upright and one resting horizontally on them—making each vanquished soldier lay down his arms and pass under this archway. From this practice comes the expression *to pass under the yoke*, "to suffer a humility, or defeat, to be disgraced."

pasta fazool.   There is no such Italian dish—not spelled this way. *Pasta fazool* is the Neapolitan-American pronunciation of *pasta e fagioli*, a soup containing beans (*fagioli*), other vegetables, and little *ditalini* pasta.

pasteboards.   (*See* **devil's picture book**.)

pasteurize.   We remember Louis Pasteur for the germ-free *pasteurized* milk that we drink in safety today, but we often forget that his well-known discovery arose out of experiments with France's national beverage—wine. In the 1850s the immortal French chemist first discovered that certain bacteria caused rapid "artificial" fermentation of wine, then that fermentation could be prevented if the wine was exposed to high temperatures—which led to the method whereby milk and other foods could be sterilized by heating and rapid cooling. A mediocre chemistry student, just as Einstein was in math, Pasteur made many brilliant discoveries in his field. This compulsive worker—"I would feel that I had been stealing if I were to spend a single day without working"—proved that the spontaneous generation theory of germs was a myth, his most revolutionary scientific contribution. The *Pasteur treatment* honors his cure for rabies, which has reduced the death rate from hydrophobia to less than 1 percent.

Patagonian.   *Patagonian* generally refers to "a native of Patagonia," but the word was in frequent literary use as a gigantic specimen, a great soul, an immense figure in his field, up until the beginning of the 20th century and is still effectively used that way today. *Patagonia* is a regional name applied to extreme southern South America, specifically the area south of the Colorado River in Argentina, which, incidentally, includes part of the Argentinian province Eva Peron (once La Pampa) named for the wife of the former dictator. The original inhabitants, now virtually extinct, were the *Tehuelches*, whom the Spanish called *the Patagonian giants* when they attempted settlements in southern South America in the 16th century. Early travelers had described these natives as being almost giants and they were named *Patagonians* from the Spanish *patagon*, "a large, clumsy foot."

paternoster.   (*See* **patter**.)

pathos; bathos.   *Pathos*, which derives directly from the Greek word for suffering, is the quality or power in any of the arts to evoke feelings of tender pity, compassion, or sadness, and gives us characters in literature like Ophelia in *Hamlet* or even Dickens's Little Nell. *Bathos* means quite the opposite and was coined by Alexander Pope from the Greek word *bathos*, "depth" (not related to our English word "bath"), to indicate a descent from the sublime to the depths of the ridiculous. Pope and other writers of the early 18th century, including Swift, Gay, and Arbuthnot, made a sport of parodying contemporary writers. Out of this game of wits came Pope's satire "Bathos, the Art of Sinking in Poetry" (1727), in which he invented the word because no similar one existed in English to express the idea.

patience of Job.   (*See* **Job's comforter**.)

patsy.   *Patsy*, American slang for a dupe or sucker since at least 1909, may derive from the Italian *pazzo*, "fool or crazy," brought to America by Italian immigrants. *Pazzo*, in turn, could derive from the Italian expression *uno dei pazzi*, "one of the fools or crazies," which may come from the name of the much ridiculed Pazzi family of 15th-century Florence, who were foolish enough to oppose the powerful Medici and were slaughtered.

patter; paternoster.   Fast talk, often a salesman's or con man's spiel, is called *patter* after *paternoster*, the Lord's Prayer, so named from its first two words (*Pater Noster*, "Our Father") in Latin. When saying the Paternoster, priests recited it rapidly at the start of the prayer, giving us this synonym for rapid talk as early as the 14th century.

Paul Pry.   A meddling idler with no business of his own except everybody else's is called a *Paul Pry*, after the character of that name in British playwright John Pool's comedy *Paul Pry* (1825).

Pawn, Oregon.   (*See* **Pakistan.**)

pawnbroker.   Long before their common name was coined in medieval days, *pawnbrokers* operated under the familiar three golden balls still hanging over many of their shops. It was the Medici family who contributed the symbol of their profession, for Charlemagne made this the family coat of arms long before the Medici family became money-lenders, as a reward to one of their forebears who killed a fearsome giant who attacked him with a weapon made of three golden balls. *Pawnbroker* itself has a more prosaic origin, deriving from *pawn*, "a pledge," and *broker*, "agent," and was first recorded in 1678.

pay dirt.   One authority traces this expression to the Chinese *pei* "to give," used by Chinese miners in California, *pay dirt* thus meaning "dirt that gives gold." However, it more likely derives from the fact that it is dirt containing enough gold dust to pay for working it. The expression is first recorded in 1856.

payoff.   (*See* **high hat.**)

payola.   Entering the American lexicon in 1960, when it was found that disc jockeys in New York, Chicago, and other cities accepted payments from record companies in return for airing their records, the coinage *payola* is a contraction of *pay* and *Victrola*. The word came into the news again in 1974 and 1985 with similar scandals in the record business, but *payola* is also used to mean bribes paid to anyone.

to pay on the nail.   In medieval times a *nail* was a short pillar used as a counter in marketplaces. Accounts were settled at these nails, all money placed on them so that payment was quick and out in the open. This practice led to the expression *to pay on the nail*, for "prompt payment." (*See* **cash on the barrelhead.**)

pay through the nose.   Gamblers in the 17th century coined the expression *to bleed* a victim. "They will purposely lose some small sum at first, that they may engage him more freely to bleed as they call it," a contemporary writer on cardplaying noted. He also observed that these same gamblers would "always fix half a score packs of cards" beforehand whenever they intended to bleed a dupe. Once the "coll" had *paid through the nose*, lost all his blood through the nose, he was "bled white," weak and helpless, until he had nothing left to lose. These last expressions arose later but they clearly derive from the gambling term, which was used to describe extortion or blackmail at about the same time. The bloodletting that physicians and barbers commonly used to treat so many diverse illnesses certainly suggested the expression to the gamblers. Bleeding patients not only made them pale, weak, and helpless but often killed them, as it did Lord Byron.

P.D.Q.   *P.D.Q.* stands for "pretty damn quick," eg., "you'd better get started P.D.Q." Its origin hasn't been established beyond doubt, though it has been attributed to Dan Maguinnis, a Boston comedian appearing about 1867-1889.

pea.   *Pea* comes indirectly from the Latin *pisum*, "pea"; the Early English singular for pea was *pease*, hence *pease porridge hot*, etc. Quite a mania for peas existed in 17th-century France. Madame de Maintenon, Louis XIV's mistress, called it "both a fashion and a madness," and it was at this time that the celebrated *petit pois à la française* was invented. Incidentally, it was proper at the time to lick green peas from their shells after dropping the whole in a sauce, so eating peas off a knife isn't so bad after all! Chinese sugar or snow peas, eaten pod and all, are sometimes properly called *mangetout* ("eat all").

peace at any price.   When British Quaker statesman John Bright (1811-89) opposed the Crimean War he was contemptuously called a *peace-at-any-price man* by Lord Palmerston. He resigned from public life in 1882 when British warships bombarded Egypt.

peaceful coexistence.   Lenin apparently coined the term *peaceful cohabitation* in February 1920, when he referred to "peaceful cohabitation with the workers and peasants of all nations." Two years later a resolution of the Ninth All-Russian Congress of Soviets used the term "peaceful and friendly coexistence [*sosushchestvovaniye*]" between nations. Unfortunately, the term has always been more a propaganda slogan than a sincere policy of any state.

peace in our time. British Prime Minister Neville Chamberlain used this expression after his return from Munich on September 30, 1938, after he had caved in to Hitler. He believed that his actions had averted war, but the Nazis saw them as a sign of weakness, war ensued, and Chamberlain's words became a symbol of the worst kind of appeasement.

the peacemaker. This was the nickname of one of the most famous weapons in American history, the Colt Revolver Model 1873, the name being adopted because it helped lawmen keep the peace in the American West. As an extra benefit, its .44 ammunition could be used in the 1873 Winchester rifle.

peace with honor. The great British statesman Lord Beaconsfield (Disraeli) made this phrase popular in a speech he gave after returning from the Congress of Berlin in 1878, which Bismarck chaired as "the honest broker" (his own phrase). Said Disraeli: "Lord Salisbury [the foreign minister] and myself have brought you back peace—but a peace I hope with honour, which may satisfy our Sovereign and tend to the welfare of the country." Similar words, however, had been used by Shakespeare in *Coriolanus* almost three hundred years earlier.

peach. Peaches were the "persian apples" of the ancient Romans. Their name, *Persicum*, became *pessica* in Late Latin, *pesche* in French, and finally came into English as *peach*. The fruit, luscious to look at, touch, and taste, has described a pretty young girl at least since the ancient Chinese used it as slang for a young bride centuries ago. But the Chinese, and the Arabs, too, also regarded the peach's deep fur-edged cleft as a symbol of the female genitalia and used *peach* in a number of slang expressions referring to sexual love, such as *sharing the peach*, a euphemism for sodomy. In Europe the French have used their word *peche* in similar sexual expressions and *a peach house* was once common in English slang as a house of prostitutes. "Venus owns this tree . . . the fruit provokes lust," English herbalist Nicholas Culpeper wrote in 1652 and language reflects that people around the world shared his opinion. The *Elberta peach*, the most widely sold of American peaches, was probably imported from Shanghai in 1850, but more than one source records a story that shows more imagination. According to this tale, Samuel Rumph of Marshallville, Georgia, received peach-tree buddings from a friend in Delaware, planted them, and eventually harvested a good crop. His wife, Elberta, accidentally dropped a few pits from these peaches in her sewing basket and when their grandson wanted to start an orchard ten years later, she dug them out and asked her husband to plant them. By 1870 trees from the pits were flourishing, and by an accidental cross-pollination a new golden variety resulted, which Rumph named for his spouse. Elbertas, however, aren't conside-

red great eating peaches by those who know their peaches.

peach melba. (*See* **melba toast.**)

to peach on someone. Once common in the jargon of criminals, *to peach on someone* means to inform or "rat" on him. The word is not related to the fruit, deriving instead from an obsolete English word *appeach*, "to accuse." The expression has been used at least since Shakespeare's time.

pea jacket. Not originally a P-jacket (abbreviation of "pilot's jacket"), *pea jacket* derives from the Dutch *pijjekker*, "a short double-breasted coat" very similar to the pea jacket of today that was worn by Dutch sailors as early as the 15th century.

peanut; peanut gallery. Peanuts take their name from their resemblance to peas in a pod. They go by numerous descriptive aliases, including *monkey nuts* and *ground peas* or *nuts*, but their most common synonym, *goober*, is a corruption of *nguba*, a name plantation slaves gave to the peanut and one of the few African words still retained in English. Peanuts are used in hundreds of products. Peanut butter, for example, is an easily-digested, high-protein food that nutritionists say provides an adequate survival diet when combined with a citrus fruit like oranges. Four out of five American homes are said to stock a jar of it in the pantry. Americans aren't as partial to *peanut butter soup*, or to the dish called *Young Monkey Stuffed with Peanuts* invented by futurist chef Jules Maincave during World War I. The *peanut gallery*, usually the cheapest seats in the house, was the gallery, or "second balcony," high up in Gay Nineties theaters, so high up that the crowd seated there were sometimes called the *gallery gods*. Peanuts were the movie snack of the day and the occupants of these cheap seats often rained peanut shells on performers who displeased them.

pear. One of the earliest cultivated fruits, pears are among the few fruits that ripen better after being picked, and the Chinese often ripened them in rooms filled with incense. The fruit, shaped like a Rubens nude, goes incomparably well with cheese desserts, Rabelais writing that: "There is no match you could compare/To Master Cheese and Mistress Pear." The old French *piere*, derived from the Latin *pirum*, gave us our word *pear*. Of the over 3,000 pear species, the *Bartlett* is perhaps the best known in America, representing 70 percent of this country's crop. It is a soft, late-region European-type, as opposed to earlier hard varieties like the *Seckel*, which is named for the Philadelphia farmer who first grew it, during the Revolution. The Bartlett wasn't, in fact, developed by Dorchester, Massachusetts merchant Enoch Bartlett, as is generally believed. Bartlett only promoted the fruit after Captain Thomas Brewer imported the trees from England and grew them in his Roxbury farm. The enterprising Yankee eventually purchased Brewer's farm and distributed the pears under his own name in the early 1800s. They had long been known in Europe as *Williams*, or *William Bon Chretien* pears.

pease porridge. (*See* **pea.**)

pecking order. The famous study made by biologist W.C. Allee in the 1920s establishes that the pecking order among hens has a definite prestige pattern: hens, like many humans, freely peck at other hens below their rank and submit to pecking from those above them. Hens rarely peck at roosters in the barnyard, where the rooster is cock of the walk, but it was widely believed in the 17th century that they often pulled feathers from roosters below them in the pecking order. (*See* **henpecked.**)

Pecksniff. An arch hypocrite who cants moral homilies even while acting immorally, any *Pecksniff* takes his name from Mr. Pecksniff, the hypocritic architect in Charles Dickens's *Martin Chuzzlewitt* (1843-44). (*See* **gamp.**)

pecuniary. *Pecu* is the Latin for cattle, and since cattle were once a common means of barter, the ancients often expressed an estate's value in terms of the number of cattle it was valued at, which gave them the word *pecunia*, for "money or property." *Pecunia*, in turn gave birth to numerous English words, such as *pecuniary*, "pertaining to money"; *impecunious*, "without money"; *peculate*, "to embezzle"; and *peculiar*, "pertaining to that which is one's own," that is, one's own cattle.

peddler. *Peddler* derives from the Old English *ped*, "a pack in which articles were stored to be hawked about the streets." In early America *Yankee peddlers* generally had a bad name, being "proverbial for their dishonesty," according to one early observer, and Northerners probably got the name *damn Yankee*, coined long before the Civil War, from Yankee peddlers who worked the rural South. There are nevertheless many notable exceptions. Among famous Americans who started as peddlers are Parson Weems, the biographer of Washington; Stephen Girard, the Philadelphia banker who helped America finance the War of 1812; Donald Alexander Smith, the Canadian fur trader who later headed the giant Hudson's Bay Company; William Rockefeller, John D.'s father; Abraham Lincoln's father; Bronson Alcott, father of Louisa May; and inventors John Fitch and Thomas Edison. Department stores vehemently oppose peddling today, but, ironically, at least fifteen great department stores were started by former peddlers, including Gimbel's, Rich's, Saks, and Goldwaters. (*See* **Yankee; emporium.**)

pedigree. A wavering three-line symbol used by medieval genealogists in denoting the line of descent of families they were tracing was thought by some observant scholar to resemble the imprint of the bony foot of a crane. In French, the court language in many kingdoms, "foot of the crane" was *pied de grue*, which came to be both the name for the genealogical symbol and the name for the line or genealogical table itself. Introduced into English in the 15th century, *pied de grue* became through distorted spelling *pee de grew*, *petiegrew*, and *peti degree*, among many other versions, before settling down here as *pedigree*.

Peelers. (*See* **bobby.**)

Peeping Tom. According to a later version of the original story, Lady Godiva had but one admirer when she rode nude through the streets of Coventry. The earlier story has everyone in town feasting their eyes on Godiva, but here the plot thickens. Our later version says that a more cunning Lady Godiva issued a proclamation ordering all persons to stay indoors and shutter their windows, so that she could ride naked through Coventry, Lord Leofric would remit the town's oppressive taxes, and she could remain modest as well. But *enter stage left* Peeping Tom, the unfortunate town tailor, or butcher. We say "stage left" because Peeping Tom must have lived on the left-hand side of Hertfors Street—assuming that Lady Godiva rode sidesaddle. At any rate, Peeping Tom peeped, ruined Lady Godiva's plan, and was struck blind for his peeping—cruel and unusual punishment for merely being human and living in a strategic location. (*See* **Lady Godiva.**)

pelican. The pelican is no woodpecker, but in his famous translation of the Bible, St. Jerome, thinking it pecked wood like a woodpecker, named the bird *pelican*, from the Greek word *pelekys*, or "ax beak." This name stuck, as did many legends about the bird, including one that it resurrected its dead young by feeding them its blood, which Shakespeare alludes to in *King Lear*. Wrote Dixon Lanier Merrith in his poem "The Pelican" (1910): *A wonderful bird is the/pelican/His bill will hold more than his/belican./He can take in his beak/Food enough for a week,/But I'm damned if I see how the/helican.*

pell-mell. Pall-mall was an early 16th century British game "wherein a round box ball is struck with a mallet through a high arch of iron, which he that can do it with the fewest blows, or at the number agreed upon, wins." Apparently pall-mall players thrashed about trying to strike the ball and tripping each other up, this resulting in the now obsolete game giving us the word *pell-mell*, meaning "headlong, in reckless confusion."

pemmican. Dried buffalo meat pounded into a powder and sometimes mixed with berries was the staple winter diet of many Indian tribes in the American West. It was called *pemmican,* from the Konestino Indian words *pemis,* "fat," and *egan,* "substance."

P.E.N. *P.E.N.* is the acronym for the International Association of Poets, Playwrights, Editors, Essayists, and Novelists, founded in 1921 by Catherine Dawson Scott and John Galsworthy, who set up a trust fund for the organization in 1932 with his Nobel Prize money. The organization was named P.E.N. when someone pointed out at the first meeting that the initial letters of *poet, essayist,* and *novelist* were the same in most European languages and could serve as the appellation.

pencil pusher; pencil-necked. Both of these are Americanisms. The common *pencil pusher,* usually a contemptuous term for an office worker, is first recorded in 1890. *Pencil-necked* is of very recent origin, and recorded here because I have heard it several times and can find it listed in no dictionary of slang or Standard English. *Pencil-necked* is a contemptuous reference to relatively genteel men made by the boisterous and bullnecked. I heard it last from a huge professional wrestler with bulging muscles in his neck who declared that only "pencil-necked geeks" don't like to watch professional wrestling.

Penelope. Odysseus's wife, Penelope, in Greek mythology cunningly held off a horde of suitors while her husband was absent for ten years. Her name has become synonymous for a faithful wife.

penguin. Though the penguin has a black head, its name derives from Welsh words meaning "white head": *pen,* "head," and *gwyn,* "white." Welsh sailors were responsible for this odd christening when they gave the name *penguin* to the great auk, a flightless bird with white spots on its head that was common on North Atlantic islands in the 16th century. For some unknown reason sailors in other oceans later transferred the name *penguin* to the flightless bird so named today.

Penguinize. In England *Penguinize* means "to publish or republish a book" in paperback. Penguin Books Limited, founded in 1935, specializes in paperbacks, which in days gone forever cost sixpence. No doubt the company hopes that *Penguinize,* or better yet, *penguinize,* will have currency in America, too. *Pocket book* is a term for a paperback book in America, taking its name from the firm Pocket Books, Inc., founded in 1939. There seems to be no verb equivalent to *Penguinize* here, although Penguin publishes books in the U.S. as well. Publishers speak of "bringing it out in paper" or "putting out a paperback edition," etc., but nobody "Pocketbookizes" a book. Here is

one place where the English are clearly outdoing the American love of shortcuts in language. *Penguinize* might yet fill this American language gap, unless someone at Bantam Books comes up with "Bantamize" first.

penis. Most dictionaries derive *penis* from the Latin *cauda,* "tail," and leave it at that, but Partridge's *Origins* tells us that *cauda* superceded the Latin word *penis* as the word for the male sexual organ. The Latin word *penis* probably derives from the Latin *penes,* "within." The word isn't recorded in English until 1693.

the pen is mightier than the sword. It was Edward Bulwer-Lytton who coined *the pen is mightier than the sword,* in his Play *Richelieu* (1839):

> Beneath the rule of men entirely great,
> The pen is mightier than the sword

Long before, in his *Anatomy of Melancholy* (1621), Robert Burton had written: "The pen is worse than the sword." Cervantes, in *Don Quixote* (1605), expressed an entirely different point of view: "Let none presume to tell me that the pen is preferable to the sword." Curiously enough, two great writers, Sophocles and Demosthenes, were the sons of sword makers, the equivalent of munitions makers in our time.

Pennsylvania. *Silvania* is the Latin for woodland, and *Pennsylvania,* formed on the analogy of Transylvania (that home of monsters and werewolves in fiction), means "Penn's woodland." The name does not honor the Quaker William Penn, as is generally believed, but his father, Admiral Sir William Penn (1621-70). Admiral Penn, a naval hero who helped frame the first code of tactics for the British navy, had been imprisoned in the Tower in 1655 for political reasons still unknown, and the author Samuel Pepys speaks bitingly of him in his diary. The crown, however, had become indebted to the admiral, Penn having loaned Charles II 16,000 pounds. On June 24, 1680, the younger Penn petitioned Charles for repayment of this debt, asking for a 300 by 160 mile "tract of land in America. . . ." The tract was to become a colony for Protestant Quakers suffering religious persecution, and Charles repaid his debt with a charter. Penn's account tells us that he suggested the names Sylvania and New Wales. When Charles II added the "Penn" in honor of his father, he strongly objected since Quakers are opposed to such use of personal names.

penny. *Penny* is probably from an Anglo-Saxon word related to the German *pfenning,* though it may derive from the name of Penda, an early Mercian king. Pennies were originally called "coppers" in England, having been made of copper from 1797 to 1860 (before that they were made of silver).

penny ante. *Penny ante* is a poker game in which the *ante*, the money first put in the pot, is limited to a penny. Recorded in 1855 the phrase came to mean anything or anyone cheap or small.

Pentagonese. (*See* **gobbledygook**.)

penthouse. Over the years folk etymology made *penthouse* out of *pentice*, the former word sounding more familiar to English ears even if *pentice* was correct. The *pentice* was a kind of "lean-to" attached to another building, usually a church, the word akin to "appendix." It took several centuries for *penthouse*, first recorded in early 1500s, to become the luxurious separate apartment or dwelling on a roof of a building that it generally is today.

peony. In the guise of Paeon, a physician, the god Apollo tended the wounded on battlefields, according to Greek mythology. His pseudonym became attached to many plants used in healing, especially the flower we still call a *peony*, whose roots and seeds were used in numerous folk remedies and is now the only plant bearing the god's name.

pepper. *Pepper* can be traced back to the Sanskrit *pippali*, for a type of condiment pepper that comes from the dried berries of a climbing shrub. Garden peppers are not related to this shrub, but received the same name when Columbus discovered hot varieties of the garden pepper in the West Indies and wrongly believed they were a new variety of the condiment pepper. Chilli peppers, hot garden varieties, are named after Chile, a country famous for them.

Pepsi generation. The *Pepsi generation* is used, sometimes sarcastically, to mean the now, "with-it" generation. The term comes form the Pepsi-Cola slogan *Come alive, you're in the Pepsi generation*. Recently Pepsi-Cola moved into the Thailand soft drink market and had their slogan translated. It later developed that the Thai translation it was using said: "Pepsi brings back your ancestors from the dead."

period. (*See* **comma**.)

peripeteia. A *peripeteia* is a striking reversal in a play or in life, as Oedipus's discovery of his true identity. The same word with the same meaning was used by the ancient Greeks.

periscope. (*See* **up periscope!**)

Peritas and Bucephala. It is said that Alexander the Great, mourning his dog Peritas, renamed an ancient city Peritas in his honor. The tale isn't unlikely, considering that Alexander did name another city after his horse.

Bucephalus was Alexander's favorite Thracian charger, a spirited stallion that only the conqueror could ride and who would kneel down to let his master mount. Alexander rode Bucephalus in his campaigns to conquer the world and "the bull-headed or bull-courage one" is said to have died of wounds or heart strain at the age of 20, after swimming the flooded Jhelum River and then carrying his master in full armor through a hard day's fighting on a hot June day. The emperor named the ancient city of Bucephala in northern India in his horse's honor, possibly even building it as the fabled charger's mausoleum, its site identified by a mound outside the modern Jhelum.

periwinkle. In Italy the periwinkle is called the *fiore di morto* because it used to be wreathed around dead infants. *Periwinkle* takes its name from the Latin *pervincire*, "to bind around," but whether it was so named because it was used in such burials is unknown.

perk. *Perk* is simply shorthand for *perquisite*, meaning a benefit received by an employee beyond his or her salary and standard fringe benefits. Perks range from a key to the executive washroom to a key to a company car. The expression probably dates from the 1960s.

pernod. Absinthe was generally made from various species of wormwood, *Artemisia absinthium*, the plant so named because it had been dedicated to Artemesia, Greek goddess of the hunt and moon. Long prized for its reputed aphrodisiac powers by the French, the liqueur is 70-80 percent alcohol, but the oil of wormwood in it can cause blindness, insanity, and even death. For this reason absinthe was banned in Switzerland in 1908, in the United States four years later, and outlawed by France in 1915. *Pernod*, a greenish-colored, licorice-flavored liqueur named for its French manufacturer, quickly took its place. *Pernod* does not get a person drunk as quickly as absinthe, being 40-50 percent alcohol, but, except for the anise used to replace the banned oil of wormwood, it contains all the same ingredients.

the perpetual peace. This expression was first used to describe the 1502 peace between England and Scotland, concluded when Henry VII married his daughter to Scotland's James IV. The *perpetual peace* ended two years later at the battle of Flodden Field, in which the British defeated the Scots. Other "perpetual peaces" since then, and "wars to end all wars" (*q.v.*) have ended just the same.

persiflage. "Upon these delicate occasions you must practice the ministerial shrugs and persiflage," Lord Chesterfield wrote in one of his famous *Letters* (1774) to his natural son Philip Stanhope. This is the first recorded use of *persiflage*, "light frivolous talk or banter," which Chesterfield may have coined from the French *persifler*, "to banter."

Persian words in English. Persian words that became English words, usually through other languages, are: *tiger, paradise, pard, scarlet, chess, checkmate, checkers, azure, salamander, taffeta, arsenic, roc, mummy, spinach, jasmine, lilac, seersucker, khaki, scimitar, bazaar, shawl, lemon, divan,* and *van* (from *caravan*).

persimmon. The Powhatan Indian word *putchami* was eventually corrupted into *persimmon* by English settlers. Early colonists in America actually made a beer from persimmons and in the 1860s the expression *walking off with the persimmons* was widely used for "walking off with the prize."

person. The word *person* derives from the Latin *persona*, which was the term for the mask that actors in Greek and Roman dramas wore to portray the various characters. The word came to mean the part anyone played in this world, his or her individuality, coming into English as *person*. In his article "Language Liberated" in *The University Bookman* (Spring 1976), Robert Beum considers some alternatives for sexist "man" terms in the language. Believing, as someone has said, that "the proper study of personkind is person," I've recorded a number of Mr. Baum's tongue-in-cheek suggestions below. Note his advice that "the key rule is that the root 'man,' even when it is derived etymologically from the Latin 'manus' (hand), bears the degrading connotations of sexist tradition and is to be dropped":

personners (manners)
personslaughter (manslaughter)
personhandle (manhandle)
personnuscript (manuscript)

Person overboard! Person the oars!

pestle. (*See* **pistil**.)

Pétain. Henri Philippe Pétain, at a cost of 250,000 dead, halted the German advance at Verdun in World War I under the famous slogan "They shall not pass!" Acclaimed a hero and made commander-in-chief of the French armies, "the savior of Verdun" became associated with extreme rightist political elements in later years. In World War II, when eighty-four, Marshal Pétain was appointed chief of staff of the Vichy government, collaborating with the Nazis and turning France into an authoritarian state. After the war he was found guilty of treason and sentenced to death, but President de Gaulle, his former aide, commuted his sentence to life imprisonment. Pétain, his name long a synonym for traitor, died in 1951, aged ninety-five.

peter boat. Every Peter ever born derives his given name from St. Peter, Peter being the name Christ gave the "Prince of the Apostles," this apparently the first time the name was ever used. Peter was a fisherman of Galilee, who denied knowing Christ three times during His trial, but later repented. Tradition tells us that he was crucified in A.D. 67, head down at his request because he said he was not worthy to suffer the same death as Jesus, and his tomb is under the high altar of St. Peter's in Rome. Many words and expressions derive from Peter's name: Eric Partridge devotes a page or so to them in his *Dictionary of Slang*. The Patron saint of fishermen and many other occupations connected with the sea gives us the Standard English *peterman* for a fisherman and *peter boat* for a fishing boat with stem and stern alike. Stormy petrels also bear Peter's name, because the birds seem to be patting the waves with one foot and then the other in stormy weather, as though they were walking on water. Actually they are flying close to the waves in search of surface-swimming food like small shrimp, but the birds reminded sailors of St. Peter walking upon the Lake of Gennersareth to join Jesus (Matt. 14:29). They were thus named *peterels*, a diminutive of the English Peter, in honor of the apostle and this came to be *petrel* in time. All petrels are regarded as the protectors of sailors and the harbingers of approaching storms. It is considered bad luck to kill one, for the birds were long thought to be the souls of drowned men; whenever one died, sailors believed a crew member would soon die to take its place.

peter out. It seems unlikely that disappointed American miners during the '49 gold rush derived the expression *to peter out*, "to taper off or come to an end," from the French *peter*, "to break wind." This would indeed have been an expression of their disappointment when a mine failed to yield more gold, but there were ample American words available to express the same sentiment. Another guess is that the *peter* here refers to the apostle Peter, who first rushed to Christ's defense in the Garden of Gethsemane, sword in hand, and then before the cock crowed thrice denied that he even knew Him. Most likely the expression springs from the fact that veins of ore in mines frequently *petered out*, or turned to stone. The gunpowder mixture of saltpeter, sulphur, and charcoal, commonly called *peter* by miners, was used as an explosive in mining operations and when a vein of gold was exhausted it was said to have been *petered out*.

Peter Pan. Peter Pan, the boy who refused to grow up, has been familiar to readers and theatergoers for several generations and we now use his name to describe a person who retains in mature years the naturalness of spirit and charm associated with childhood, or one who absolutely refuses to escape from the comfortable irresponsibility of childhood. British dramatist and novelist Sir James M. Barrie introduced his immortal character on the stage in the play *Peter Pan* (1904), although the fantastic world of Peter Pan had previously been presented in his *The Little*

White Bird (1902). *Peter Pan*, a poetical pantomime, as it has been called, charmed audiences from the night it first appeared. Peter has since been played by many great stars, ranging from Maude Adams to Mary Martin, and a statue of him stands in Kensington Gardens, London. Barrie, who described his business as "playing hide and seek with angels," named Peter for one of his nephews, for whom he wrote the story, giving the character his last name from the god Pan, "goat-footed," god of forests, meadows, flocks, and shepherds. Wendy, Peter's girl friend, also borrowed her name from a real person. This was Barrie's own nickname, bestowed upon him by the daughter of his friend, poet W. E. Henley. Little Margaret Henley called him Friendly, then Friendly-wendy, and this ultimately became Wendy, the name he dubbed his character.

the Peter Principle.   Dr. Laurence Peter and Raymond Hull's book *The Peter Principle* (1969) became famous for its premise that "In a hierarchy, every employee tends to rise to the level of his incompetence."

Peter's Pence.   For some 800 years, until Henry VIII abolished the practice in 1534, every English household paid a tax to the pope of a penny a year. The tax was called (Saint) Peter's penny, Peterpenny, and *Peter's Pence*, and several monarchs tried to withhold it from Rome before Henry VIII succeeded, after the Pope refused to sanction his divorce from Catherine of Aragon so that he could marry Anne Boleyn.

Pete's sake!   The *Pete* here is a euphemism for St. Peter, the expression of annoyance (*e.g.* "For Pete's sake, stop fooling around!) probably dating back at least to late 19th-century America.

petit pois.   (*See* **pea**.)

petrel.   (*See* **peter boat**.)

petri dish.   German scientist Julius Richard Petri invented this thin glass or plastic dish with a loose cover commonly used in laboratories today. The shallow dish named for the bacteriologist, who died in 1921, is generally employed in making bacteria cultures. Petri was an assistant of the great German scientist Robert Koch when he devised his dishes in 1887. Koch—the first scientist to introduce a rationalized system of bacteria culturing—had previously grown bacteria in a gel on flat glass slides, his assistant substituting the shallow glass dishes with covers that have been used ever since.

pettifogger.   A real family of financiers may have given its name to the word *pettifogger*, for "an attorney or anyone who argues over petty details with little mean-

ing." The Fugger family, which can be traced back to Bavarian Swabia in the 15th century and who were descended from an Augsburg weaver, made their great fortune lending money to royalty, but became noted, justly or unjustly, for their petty ways. According to one theory, in time a "petty Fugger" became a *pettifogger*, the designation soon applied to people besides the Fuggers.

phaeton.   Rooted in Greek mythology, this light horse-drawn four-wheel carriage takes its name from Zeus's son Phaeton, who took his father's chariot for a ride to the sun one day and drove so wildly that he nearly set the world on fire, before Zeus stopped him with a thunderbolt.

phallus.   (*See* **bull**.)

phantasmagoria.   The word is dictionary defined as "a shifting series of phantasms, illusions, or deceptive appearances, as in a dream or created by the imagination," but it can also mean "a changing scene made up of many elements." It was apparently coined in 1802 by a London showman named Philipstal to describe his magic-lantern exhibition of optical illusions. The word may be based on *phantasm* or *phantom*, but "the inventor of the term probably only wanted a mouth-filling and startling term . . ." and no clear etymology is known.

pharaoh.   Egyptian *pharaohs* took their name from the palaces or big houses, *per-o*, where they resided. The title is first recorded in English in about 843.

pharisee.   (*See* **a thorn in my side**.)

pharos.   *Pharos* has become a synonym for "lighthouse," but it was originally one of the Seven Wonders of the World, a lighthouse built by Ptolemy II on the island of Pharos off Alexandria, Egypt, that was 200 to 600 feet high and could be seen 42 miles away. (*See* **pharaoh**.)

Philadelphia lawyer.   Folklore has it that when Andrew Hamilton successfully defended New York printer John Peter Zenger against libel charges in 1735, establishing the right of freedom of the press in America, observers noted that it took a *Philadelphia lawyer* to get the printer off. But the term is first recorded more than fifty years later, in 1788, in the form of "It would puzzle a Philadelphia lawyer." Another theory claims the words come from the New England saying "any three Philadelphia lawyers are a match for the devil." Philadelphia at the time was the intellectual and literary center of America, and it was only fitting that a very clever lawyer, versed in the fine points of the law, should be named for the city.

philander.   Our word for a male flirt who makes love without serious intentions comes from the name given to lovers in various medieval romances, but certain marsupial animals also bear the name *Philander* and these are named for the Dutch naturalist Kornelius Philader de Bruyn. Philanders, whose males may or may not be philanderers, include the small wallaby (*Macopus brunnii*), first described by de Bruyn in about 1700, the Australian bandicoot (*Perameles lagotes*), and the South American opossum (*Didelphys philander*). Curiously, the name Philander comes from the Greek philandros, "a lover of mankind"—perhaps an ironic reference to the philanderer's lack of discrimination about whom he beds.

philanthropy. *Philanthropy* clearly has its roots in the Greek *philos*, "love," and *anthropos*, "mankind," and means a love for mankind, especially as manifested in donations of money, property, or work to needy persons or socially useful purposes. It is first recorded by Bacon in 1607 and he refers to it as an ancient Greek term.

philippic. Incomparable orator that he was, Demosthenes' eloquent words could not triumph over the military might of Philip of Macedon (382-336 B.C.). Eventually, Philip II, father of Alexander the Great, defeated the Athenians, imposing a very generous peace settlement on them so that he could employ them as allies in his future plans for conquest. But Demosthenes had made such brilliant denunciatory orations against Philip over a period of seven years that these speeches are still known in history as *philippics*. The *philippics* were specifically a series of three passionate invectives against the Macedonian monarch's plan to weld Athens into his kingdom and they comprised a great defense of Athenian liberty, taking their name from the object of their fire.

the Philippines. The Spanish took control of these islands in 1571 and named them for Philip II of Spain.

Philistine. The original *Philistines* made their home in Philistia on the southwest coast of Palestine. These barbarians were Israel's worst enemy, even capturing the sacred ark at one time, until Saul and David, the first Israelite kings, decisively defeated them in battle. They were considered a crude, avaricious people but their name did not come into the language until centuries later, in 1689. At that time a town-and-gown battle in the German university city of Jena had resulted in the death of several people, and a local preacher gave a sermon on the values of education to the ignorant townspeople, choosing as his text "The Philistines be upon thee ..." from Judges 16. The German word for *Philistine* was *Philister* and students began calling ignorant townspeople opposed to education by this name. Almost two centuries later, in 1869, English poet and critic Matthew Arnold used the German slang in his book *Culture and Anarchy*, translating it from *Philister* to *Philistine* and giving the word its present meaning. Wrote Arnold: "The people who

believe most that our greatness and welfare are proved by our being very rich, are just the very people whom we call Philistines." Since then *Philistine* has meant a materialistic, uncultured person.

philodendron. In its tropic homes our common houseplant the *philodendron* is a tree-climbing plant. Noticing this, the first botanists to observe the plant named it after the Greek *philos*, "loving," and *dendron*, "tree."

Philomela. After Procne discovered that her husband, Tereus, had cut out her sister Philomela's tongue and imprisoned her for years, Procne chose a terrible revenge. She killed their infant son Itys and served him to her husband for dinner. Tereus went into shock when told what kind of stew he had eaten, enabling Procne to escape with her sister, but Tereus eventually caught them. He was about to dispatch the sisters when the gods intervened and turned Philomela into a swallow because she had no tongue and swallows cannot really sing, while Procne was turned into a nightingale because the nightingale sings the saddest of songs and Procne was condemned to always sing sadly of the son she had killed so cruelly. Nevertheless, since Roman times poets have confused the Greek myth and made *Philomela* or *Philomel* a universal poetic name for "nightingale," when clearly the word should be *Procne*— though one must admit that *a procne* sounds prosaic at best and asinine at worst. T. S. Eliot is the latest great poet to make this mistake, in *The Waste Land*.

philosopher. The Greek Pythagoras is said to have coined the word *philosopher* from the Greek words for love and wisdom. Up until this time philosophers were called *sophists*, "wise men." Said Pythagoras: "No man, but only God is wise. Call me rather, a *philosopher*, a lover of wisdom."

phlogiston. From the 17th to the 19th century scientists searched for *phlogiston* (from the Greek word for "inflammable"), which was supposed to be the substance within all materials that burned. Great scientific investigators believed in the substance. Joseph Priestley, in fact, named oxygen *dephlogisticated air* when he isolated it in 1774. But by 1800 belief in *phlogiston* was largely abandoned and the word deleted from the lexicon of science, if not fable.

pho. A new word, unrecorded in any dictionary, that entered the language with Vietnamese immigrants to the U.S., pho is a noodle soup with beef that is becoming more popular every year. It is said that along Garden Grove Boulevard in Orange County, California, "it is easier to lunch on pho . . . than on a hamburger."

phoenix. This fabulous bird of great beauty was said to live some 600 years in the Arabian wilderness, then burn itself on a funeral pyre and rise again from its ashes, becoming a symbol of immortality. It was named, indirectly, after the ancient Phoenicians, its color being purple-red, which the Greeks called *phoenix* because the Phoenicians had invented a dye of this color. (*See* **phoenix tree.**)

phoenix tree. *Phoenix dactylifera*, the date palm, is called the *phoenix tree* because of the ancient belief, mentioned in Shakespeare's *The Tempest*, that if it burns down or falls from old age it will spring up fresher than ever from its ruins.

phooey. *Phooey*, as an expression of disgust, is first attested to as recently as 1929 in America and derives from the German-Yiddish *phui*, which seems to be an imitation of the sound of spitting. Most languages have similar throat-clearing sounds for words expressing disgust, these foreign *phooey* synonyms including the Italian *uffa*, the French *pfutt*, or *fi*, and the Spanish *hay*. For some reason the ancient Romans employed *pro*.

photography. (*See* **diorama.**)

Phryne. *Phryne* is a synonym for a prostitute, and a rather complimentary one considering its source. It refers to the Athenian courtesan Phryne, who lived and loved memorably in the fourth century B.C. There was a gold statue of Phryne at Delphi dedicated by her admirers. Her real name was Mnesarite, but the hetaera was commonly called Phryne, "toad," because of her smooth complexion. Born in Boeotia, the country girl made good at her trade in Athens, where her beauty earned her a fortune so great that she once offered to rebuild the walls of Thebes if the words "Destroyed by Alexander, restored by Phryne the courtesan" were inscribed upon them. (There were no takers.) That her body was the most beautiful of her time, or perhaps any other, is illustrated by Praxiteles' statue called *Aphrodite of Cnidus*, which she is said to have posed for. During a festival of Poseidon at Eleusis, Phryne took off her clothes, let down her hair, and in full view of the crowd stepped into the sea, inspiring Apelles to paint his great *Aphrodite Cenadyomene*, for which she modeled. But there is no better story about Phryne than that of her trial for impurity. One of her lovers, the great orator Hyperides, defended her. Just when it seemed that she would lose her case—and her life was at stake—Hyperides pulled the courtroom stunt of all time. Ripping open her robe, he exposed her breasts to the jury, who agreed with him that something so good could not be all bad and let Phryne go free.

Phudnick. (*See* **nudnik.**)

picaresque. A picaresque novel is a novel that deals with rogues and knaves, often satirizing society through their experiences. The word *picaresque*, in fact, derives from the Spanish *picaro*, "rogue." Alain Rene LeSage's *Gil Blas* (1715), Daniel Defoe's *Moll Flanders* (1722), and Thomas Mann's *Confessions of Felix Krull* (1955) are good examples of this type of novel, which is called *Rauberroman* in German.

picayune. In early 18th-century Louisiana both an old French copper coin and the Spanish half-real were called *picayunes*. *Picayune* itself probably derives from the Spanish *pequena*, "little," and the coin influenced the popularity of the contemptuous use of picayune for anything small, mean, or insignificant.

pickle. (*See* **in a pretty pickle.**)

picnic. First recorded in Lord Chesterfield's *Letters* (1748), the word *picnic* comes to us from the French *pique-nique*, which is a century or so older. *Pique-nique* itself is a reduplication on *piquer*, "to pick."

Picts. These ancient people who settled in Ireland and Scotland in about 100 B.C. were so named by the Romans, who called them *Picti*, from the Latin *pictor*, "painter," because they tattooed and painted their bodies.

pidgin English. *Pidgin English*, originally developed by British traders in China, takes its name from the way the Chinese pronounced "business"—"bijin." It combines English and Portuguese, as well as German, Bengali, French, and Malayan. There is even a magazine, *Frend Belong Me* ("*My Friend*"), published in pidgin by the Catholic Mission in New Guinea.

pidgin language. A *pidgin language* has no native speakers, is a *second* language, that is, a language developed as a means of communcation among speakers of various languages. A creole language, on the other hand, does have native speakers. It is simply defined as a pidgin language that has been passed on to succeeding generations as a native tongue. In the U.S. Gullah is an example, as is, of course, the creolized French language of the descendants of the original settlers of Louisiana, which is often called Creole or Cajun. Creole derives from the Portuguese *crioulo*, "native," while *pidgin* is probably from the Chinese pronunciation of "business." (*See* **pidgin English.**)

piece. *Piece*, for "a woman," especially in a sexual sense, has been used since the early 14th century, when it was Standard English. *Grose* defines the word as: "A wench. A damned good or bad piece, a girl who is more or less active and skillful in the amorous congress. Hence the Cambridge toast, 'May we never have a *piece* (peace) that will injure the Constitution.'" The sense of *piece* today is generally "a sexually attractive woman," though the term is considered a sexist one by many. *Hunk* is its male counterpart, this a relatively recent coinage dating back only to the 1940s.

pieces of eight.   Famous as pirate booty, pieces of eight were Spanish silver coins worth about a dollar, though they were frequently cut into *bits* to make smaller coins. Other famous Spanish coins were half doubloons, quarter doubloons (pistols), one-eighth doubloons, and cobs, silver coins of various worth irregularly cut from a silver bar, which were heated and stamped with the royal arms.

piffle; piffling.   *Piffle* is twaddle, nonsense, idle talk. There have been many suggestions concerning the term's origins, including the words *puff*, *pitiful*, and a combination of *piddle* and *trifle*. The word is first recorded in this sense in 1890.

pig.   *Partridge* notes that *pig* was slang for "a British policeman" in 1811, while *Farmer* advises that it was American criminal slang for "a policeman" in 1848. But the designation died out in both England and America by the 20th century. It didn't surface again until American student demonstrations of the 1960s, which suggests a second, independent coinage of the term at that time.

pig and whistle.   All taverns called the *Pig and Whistle* take their name from an old English tavern that originally had the Norse name *Piga Waes Hael*. This name, meaning "Hail to the Virgin" was corrupted in speech to *Pig and Whistle*.

pigeonhole.   In the mid or late 19th century side-by-side compartments in old-fashioned rolltop desks were called *pigeonholes* because of their resemblance to the holes in dovecotes or pigeon houses, which were made to enable pigeons to walk in and out. Since papers were filed in these compartments, *to pigeonhole* became a way of saying "to file away for future reference." But papers filed away in pigeonholes were often ignored because they presented a problem or the prospect of too much work, so the term *to pigeonhole* was humorously extended to mean filing something away with the intention of forgetting about it or doing nothing about it.

piggyback.   The correct word is *pickaback*, but virtually no one calls it that. *Pickaback* dates back at least to the late 16th century, when it is first recorded to mean carrying a person, especially a child, on one's back. The term may have its origins in a *pack* that is *picked* (pitched, thrown) on someone's shoulders, but no one knows for sure. The term wasn't corrupted to *piggyback*, or *pigback*, until the late 18th century.

piggy bank.   Though *piggy bank's* popularity over the years probably has something to do with the relation between hoarding or saving money and the pig's supposed greediness, the main reason the child's bank is called a *piggy bank* is simply because so many of the banks are made in the shape of pigs. They have been made in such shapes since at least 1909, though the first recorded use of the term *piggy bank* is in 1945.

pig latin; hog latin; dog latin.   *Ixnay* ("nix"), *amscray* ("scram"), and several other slang words come to us directly from pig Latin. First known as *dog Latin*, the little language commonly used by schoolchildren can be traced back to at least mid-18th-century England, when there was a *dog Greek* as well as a *dog Latin*. The *dog* in term means the same as it does in *doggerel*, something bad, spurious, bastard, mongrel. *Dog Latin* probably came to be called *pig Latin* and *hog Latin* because its sound resembles the grunting of hogs. The lopped language was at first a combination of Latin and English. Today it is basically formed by taking the first letter of a word, putting it as the rear of the word and adding to it an *ay*. For example, "you can talk pig Latin" is "Ouyay ankay alktay igpay Atinlay." One of the most interesting pig Latin words is *ofay*, a derogatory term among blacks for a white person, which is said to be pig Latin for the word *foe*.

pigtail.   The word *pigtail* did not appear first in English as the name for a twisted plait of hair. *Pigtail* was first used in the 16th century to describe tobacco twisted into a thin string like a pig's tail.

pike.   The *pike* takes its name from its *pike*, or pointed head. After Christ's crucifixion all fishes but the pike were supposed to have dived under the water in terror. Out of curiosity the pike lifted its head from the water and observed the whole scene. Thus parts of the crucifixion are said to be recognizable on a pike's head, especially the cross, three nails, and a sword.

piker.   *Pikers*, or *Pikies*, were settlers who migrated to California from Missouri's Pike County during the 1849 gold rush. Like the "Okies" of the 20th century, the *pikers'* nickname, justly or not, became a synonym for poor, lazy good-for-nothings because they created such an unfavorable impression. Their name seems to have combined with the older English word *piker*, meaning a tramp or vagrant, to give us *piker* in its present sense of cheapskate, which was first recorded in 1901. The English word derives from *turnpike*, because many tramps traveled by foot along turnpikes, toll roads that took their name from the rotating barriers made of pikes, or sharpened rods, at their entrances. (*See* **Pikes Peak or bust**.)

Pikes Peak or bust.   Long a Colorado landmark, Pikes Peak became a guidepost for traders in the early 19th century, and by the time of the California gold rush of 1849 Indians in the area had begun to tell of gold deposits on the mountain. Thousands of people headed West to answer the call "Pikes Peak or Bust." However, gold wasn't found high in the hills until 1860, a year after the height of the Colorado gold rush. The fortunes made from the pockets of gold deposits found in the soft quartz and sandy fillings of what was called *paydirt* (*q.v.*) established Colorado as the successor to California in gold mining, but crime, violence, hardship, and death, proved to be the common lot of the prospector, and most headed back home bitterly disappointed—having experienced elation going up and grim desolation coming down the mountain. In fact, many of the '59ers returned home with the words "Busted, By Gosh!" scrawled on their wagons. *Pikes Peak* was discovered in 1806 by Zebulon Montgomery Pike, who had been chosen to map the northern part of the Louisiana Purchase, but his badly equipped party failed to reach its summit. The explorer and army officer seems to be irrevocably associated with rocks. During the War of 1812, he was killed while leading a charge against the British garrison at York (Toronto), Canada. The retreating British set fire to their powder magazine, which exploded and loosed a piece of rock that fell on his head. (*See* **piker**.)

pilcrow. *Pilcrow* is an old name for a paragraph mark or drawing of a hand pointing, which are printing marks used to attract attention—a paragraph sign in the first case and a direction in the other. The word is apparently a corruption of the word *paragraph*. *Webster's* gives *pilcrow* as an obsolete name for a paragraph mark. But since there are no other names for the two signs above, *pilcrow* ought to be rehired.

to pile Pelion on Ossa. Homer writes in the *Odyssey* of how when the giants Otus and Ephialtes attempted to climb to heaven and overthrow the gods they tried to pile Mount Pelion on Mount Olympus and Mount Ossa on Mount Pelion for a ladder. The giants were destroyed by Zeus, but their plan became synonymous for piling one difficulty on another until a whole plan becomes ridiculous. The two wooded mountains near the coast of Thessaly are now known as Mount Zagora and Mount Kissavo, but no one says "to pile Zagora on Kissavo."

pilgrim. The story of the 102 Pilgrims who founded Plymouth Colony is too well known to bear repeating here, except to say that these Pilgrim Fathers landed on Plymouth Rock instead of in Virginia, as planned, because bad weather had kept them too long at sea and they had run out of beer, among other supplies. Plimoth Plantation in Plymouth, Massachusetts is a re-creation of the second permanent settlement in America as it appeared in 1627, seven years after the Pilgrims landed. The word *pilgrim* means a wanderer, a traveler, a person who journeys a long distance to a sacred place. It has an interesting his-

tory, coming from the Latin *peregrinus*, meaning a stranger. This came into English as *pelegrin* in about 1200, but dissimilation and slothful pronunciation over the years eventually made *pilgrim* out of *pelegrin*. Thus, the Pilgrim Fathers, a proverbially industrious group, take their name from a lazy man's word.

pill. (*See* **a bitter pill to swallow**.)

pillar to post. At first this expression was *from post to pillar*, a figure of speech drawn from the old game of court tennis in the 14th century or earlier. Court tennis, played indoors, differed in many ways from today's lawn tennis, but volleys were even then crucial to the game. One popular volley was from post to pillar, from a post supporting the net or rope to one of the rear pillars supporting the tennis gallery. Apparently players commonly sustained long volleys between these two points, for by the early 15th century Englishmen were regularly using the expression *from post to pillar tossed* outside the game of tennis. In another century the phrase had been reversed to *from pillar to post*, but it still meant the same: "to and fro, hither and thither, from one thing to another without any definite purpose." Modern use of the expression in the sense of going monotonously or fruitlessly from one thing to another is just a logical extension.

pill-pusher. (*See* **bitter pill to swallow**.)

pilot weed. (*See* **compass plant**.)

pimp. Samuel Pepys (pronounced *Peeps*) was the first to record *pimp*, for "a procurer," in his famous *Diary* (1666). The word possibly derives from the French *pimpant*, "seductive," which may come from the Latin *papare*, "to chirp." For the unlikely connection between procuring and chirping, *see* **chippy**.

pinchbeck. Watch and toy maker Christopher Pinchbeck (1670-1732) died the same year that he introduced the *pinchbeck* alloy of 15 percent zinc and 85 percent copper, a gold-colored alloy for the imitation gold watches and jewelry he sold in his shop on London's Fleet Street. Pinchbeck did not live to see pinchbeck become another word for "false or counterfeit, a cheap imitation." The term caught on probably because its first syllable suggests "cheap," which the alloy was, compared to gold, but whatever the reason, the word has survived. Anything spurious but resembling the genuine article is still called *pinchbeck*.

pinch hitters. A pinch hitter in baseball is one who bats "in a pinch," who bats for a weaker hitter when a hit is badly needed. The term is first recorded in 1912.

pineapple. The Spanish conquistadores named this fruit *pina* because of its pine-cone shape and the English translated *pina* to *pineapple*, which they also called the cones of the pine tree.

Pinkerton. When he came to America from Glasgow in 1842, Allan Pinkerton opened a cooper's shop in West Dundee, Illinois, his shop becoming a station in the underground railroad smuggling slaves north. Later he captured a ring of counterfeiters, this leading to his appointment in 1850 as the first city detective on Chicago's police force—a one-man detective squad. In Chicago Pinkerton also organized a detective agency to capture railway thieves, which became Pinkerton's National Detective Agency in 1852. But he achieved national prominence in February 1861, upon foiling a plot to assassinate President-elect Lincoln when his train stopped in Baltimore on the way to his inauguration in Washington. Pinkerton died in 1884, aged sixty-five, but his sons Robert and William continued the agancy. It is from this period on that Pinkerton's was chiefly engaged by industry as spies and strikebreakers, earning the bitter condemnation of labor, especially for its role in suppressing the Homestead Strike in 1892. A *Pinkerton* or *Pinkerton man* came to mean either a private detective or, in the opinion of many working men, something lower than a fink. In 1937 the agency was subjected to Congressional investigation during industrial disputes over the recognition of unions. (*See* **fink; private eye.**)

pink slip. No one knows why *a pink slip* is synonymous for the discharge notice a worker gets when he is fired. The best guess is that the term originated in the late 19th to early 20th century when some unknown company issued pink slips to discharge employees; perhaps the practice then spread to other companies.

pinky, pinkie. *Pinkie* or *pinky*, for the little finger, apparently derives from the Dutch *pink*, meaning the same. It is first recorded in 1808, but was probably used earlier. *Pinkie* had meant "small, diminutive, tiny," mainly among children or adults talking to children, since the 16th century.

pin money. Metal pins, invented in about the 14th century and later manufactured by a monopoly under grants from the British Crown, were so costly and scarce at first that there was a law forbidding their sale except on the first two days of January in every year. About that time of year husbands customarily gave their wives *pin money* to buy all the pins they would need for the months ahead. When pins became less expensive, the expression *pin money* was still used for this annual stipend and came to mean a personal allowance given to a wife by her husband. These were not the pins with solid heads that we know today (which were first called *Poughkeepsie pins* because they were invented in that New York city in 1839), nor safety pins, which were the brainchild of another American ten years later.

pinnace. This little, light, usually two-masted sailing vessel takes its name from the Latin *pinus*, "pine tree," which it was generally made of in days past. The word is recorded as early as 1521.

pipe down. *Pipe down* began life as a dismissal command given a ship's crew to go below decks after a task was completed or a formation had ended. This command was transmitted by the bos'n's pipe or whistle, on which the bos'n could sound notes representing many orders. *Pipe down* came in the late 19th century to mean "shut up," because it got much quieter on deck when the crew obeyed the order to go below and because the phrase *pipe down* itself suggested someone piping down or making less noise.

pipe dream. The opium pipe is the source of this phrase, for "a fantastic notion or story, an illusion." First recorded in Wallace Irvin's *Love Sonnets of a Hoodlum* (1901), the term probably dates back to the 1890s. The expression *pipe*, used by O. Henry, among others, once meant the same.

pipeline. The first pipelines to convey oil were conceived in about 1862 and with them came the obvious word describing them, which has over the years also become slang for a rich source of anything valuable. The best-known oil pipeline of the millions of miles of them in America is The Big Inch, which is actually a 24-inch pipe that conveys oil 1,341 miles from eastern Texas to New Jersey.

pipsqueak. By 1900 American hoboes were contemptuously calling young punk hoboes *pip-squeaks*, perhaps from the little *pips* on playing cards, or the *pips* that were small seeds, + *squeak* for their squeaky adolescent voices. Although these derivations are only guesses, *pipsqueak* did mean a little, worthless, insignificant person in hobo talk, whence it passed into general use. The term passed into British English by 1910, and during World War I, British soldiers called a small, high-velocity German artillery shell a *pipsqueak*. Use of *pipsqueak* for the shell reinforced the earlier meaning, which became a common expression on both sides of "the big pond," as the Atlantic still was called at the time.

piranha. The piranha takes its name from a Tupi Guarani Indian word meaning "tooth fish," and it couldn't be more aptly named. Piranha teeth are formidable indeed—razor sharp, triangular affairs that with each bite can sever a chunk of flesh the size of a quarter as cleanly as a scalpel. In 1976, when 38 Brazilians were skeletonized by a school of piranhas after a bus overturned in the Urubu River, the world knew without a doubt that these vicious little fish were indeed man-eaters. Americans had suspected as much since 1914, when Teddy Roosevelt came home from a hunt with an incredible tale about a man and his mule stripped to bones in moments while fording a Brazilian stream. Ever since that time, the piranha has been featured as the villain in as many jungle films as the crocodile or the boa constrictor.

pirates.   *Pirates*, who have been so called since the 14th century, take their name from the Latin *pirata*, meaning "to attack." They are sea raiders who operate without any authorization except that of their own greed. (*See* **buccaneer; Pittsburgh Pirates; privateer; swashbuckle; walk the plank**.)

pirogue.   The Caribs, a fierce Caribbean tribe, called their dugout canoe *piraguas*, a word that French explorers changed slightly to *piroque* in the 17th century and passed on to the English, who called the canoe a *pirogue*.

piss.   *Piss* is a fine old echoic word, echoing the sound of a bladder being voided, and is similar to several foreign words etymologically unrelated but meaning the same, including the Hungarian *pisalni*. The English word derives from the Latin *pissiare*, "to piss," just as does the Italian *pisciare* and the French *pisser*. "Urinate" derives from the Latin *urinare*, which is what the cultured Romans called the same thing that the common man called *pissiare*.

pissabed.   Dandelions were called *pissabeds* because of the old folk belief that they made people urinate, a belief perhaps associated as much with their golden color as their diuretic property. Gerade recorded the word first, in his 1597 *Herbal*.

pistil.   Apothecaries in ancient times used a club-shaped instrument called the *pistillum* to pound herbs and drugs in their mortars. Eventually, the name of this instrument was abbreviated to pestle, but when botanists named the similar-shaped female organs of flowers after it, they more carefully followed the old Latin name and called the female organs *pistils*.

pistol.   The *pistolet* was originally a 15th century dagger made in Pistoia, Italy, from which it took its name. Later small guns were made in that metalwork and gun-making center and were given the name *pistolet*, too, this subsequently shortened to *pistol*.

pit.   As the term for the stone of stone fruit, *pit* isn't of ancient origin, as one would suppose. It is an Americanism that came into the language midway into the 19th century from the Dutch *pit*, meaning the same, though it may have been in New York State use long before this.

pitch.   Every sales *pitch*, or presentation, harks back to the spiel of a carnival *pitchman* in the early years of this century. The pitchman, in turn, got his name from the pitch, or stand, that he worked from. And *pitch* itself originally meant land selected by a settler in colonial America, the expression recorded as early as 1699. Long before *to make one's pitch* meant to give a sales talk, it meant to settle down on one's land.

pitched battle.   Pitched battles were first carefully planned, even gentlemanly, battles where the battleground was chosen beforehand and tents were pitched near it by the opposing armies at least several days before any fighting took place. They were called such as early as 1549, in contrast to skirmishes or chance encounters, but this term for a planned battle, where complete preparations have been made, came to mean a battle in which the opposing forces are completely and intensely engaged, this latter meaning far more common today.

Pitman.   Sir Isaac Pitman devised his shorthand system in 1837, basing his simpler phonetic shorthand on an earlier method. The former clerk and schoolteacher lived to see almost universal acceptance of his invention, which his brother Benn helped popularize on the other side of the Atlantic when he immigrated to the United States in 1852 and established the Phonographic Institute in Cincinnati. The phonographer died in 1897, aged eighty-four, when the even simpler *Gregg System* (*q.v.*) was replacing *Pitman*.

the pits.   (*See* **it's the pits**.)

pittance.   During medieval times *pittances* were rather large bequests to the church, usually to religious orders, their name deriving ultimately from the Latin *pietas*, "piety." Over the years, however, these traditional bequests became smaller and smaller, a *pittance* finally becoming synonymous with a meager amount.

Pittsburgh, Pa.; Pittsfield, Mass.; Pitt's pictures.   The great English statesman William Pitt, the Elder (1708-1778), is one of the few people to have two U.S. cities named after him. (Pittsburgh, however, was named after Fort Pitt, which had been named in his honor.) Pitt, the Younger (1759-1806), is remembered for the historical *Pitt's pictures*, blind windows that were blocked up because as Prime Minister he augmented England's "window tax" in 1784 and 1797. Rather than pay the tax, people boarded up their windows.

Pittsburgh Pirates.   The baseball team takes its name from the nickname of its first president, J. Palmer "Pirate" O'Neill, who was so called because he signed a player from another club, pirating him away rather unscrupulously. (*See* **pirate**.)

pity the poor sailor on a night like this! A saying *à propos* of a stormy night, this expression dates back to late 19th-century England and is still heard today.

plain brown wrapper. The designation *plain brown wrapper*, often used to describe how sexually explicit material will be sent through the mail, has its origins in the mail-order wars of the 1890s and at first had nothing at all to do with sex. Mail-order companies like Montgomery Ward (the beloved "Monkey Ward" of rural dwellers) and Sears, Roebuck sent their catalogs and goods in unmarked "plain brown wrappers" to protect customers from the wrath of local merchants and their allies, who wanted to see the mail-order firms go out of business from the time Aaron Montgomery Ward founded the first great national mail-order company in 1872.

plain sailing. In technical nautical language *plane sailing* means determining a ship's position on the assumption that the earth is flat and the ship is on a plane; this is a simple, straightforward method of computing distance. But in the 19th century, the words entered general use as an expression meaning "perfectly straightforward action, a course of action that there need be no hesitation about." The word *plane* came to be spelled *plain* and has remained that way ever since.

planet-struck. This medical term for "a tree struck by blight," stems from the old belief that malignant aspects of the planets caused death and suffering on earth. When plants and animals died or fell ill inexplicably they were said to be *planet-struck*. The term is first recorded in 1600.

plaster of Paris. Calcined gypsum has had this name since the 14th century, when English artisans imported what they thought was the best quality gypsum from Montmartre, then outside Paris. Today the name is used no matter where the *plaster of Paris* comes from.

platonic love. Such love, devoid of anything sexual, was first described by Plato in his *Symposium*, where he tells of the pure love of Socrates for young men, a love unusual in its day. Later, in about 1626 in England, the Latin *amor Platonious* was translated and applied to similar love between man and woman, the words often heard today in phrases like, *platonic love*, a *platonic relationship*, and the like. The rare *platonics* is simply talk between *platonic lovers*.

play a hunch. Gamblers once believed that rubbing a hunchback's hump brought good luck. Although the superstition is fortunately all but dead, the expression *to play a hunch*, "to have a lucky notion or premonition," is still frequently heard. The belief that deformed people have special powers or links with the devil is an ancient one. Hunchbacks in particular were believed to share with the devil the ability to see into the future.

to play ball with. From the playgrounds where children entreated others to play baseball with them this expression passed into general and gangster use in the 1930s. In one sense it means to cooperate with or to be fair and honest with. But more commonly its meaning is to be forced to cooperate with someone in order to receive a favor ("You play ball with me and I'll play ball with you"), or under threat of blackmail or violence ("You play ball with us or else!").

to play both ends against the middle. In faro, America's favorite game after poker in the 19th century, *playing both ends against the middle* described the way the dealer provided for a double bet by a player. The phrase came into general use soon after, meaning to use each of two sides for your own purpose.

play fast and loose. This expression for "not being trustworthy or honest, promising one thing and doing another," probably derives from an old con game played by sharpsters at country fairs. In this obsolete game, its exact details long lost, the operator arranged a belt so that a spectator believed he could insert a skewer through its intricate folds and fasten the belt to the table. But the operator had cleverly coiled the belt so that it only appeared to have a loop in its center and he always pulled it loose from the table after the dupe thought he had skewered it. Metaphorical use of the phrase *to play fast and loose* has been traced back to 1547, so the con game was probably being played before the 16th century.

to play hooky. There is no widely accepted explanation for the word *hookey*, or *hooky*. An Americanism that arose in the late 19th century, when compulsory attendance laws became the rule in public schools, *hooky* may be a compression of the older expression *hook it*, "to escape or make off," formed by dropping the *t* in the phrase. Or it could be related to the old slang word *hook*, meaning "to steal": kids stealing a day off from school. *Hooky* has so often been associated with going fishing that it may even owe its life to *getting off the hook* the way a fish can; anyway, school is often as unsufferable as a hook to schoolchildren and many kids squirming in their seats all day look like they are on a hook.

playing for the love of it. There's nothing new about this expression, meaning to play a game without stakes, for the pleasure of playing. It has its origins in Samuel Butler's satire *Hudibras* (1678), which tells of those who "play for love and money, too."

playing the field. *Playing the field* means to have many sweethearts, many dates, with no serious attachment. It was originally a 19th-century British racing term meaning to bet on every horse in a race except the favorite.

playing the market. This expression originated in the Roaring Twenties, or the *Golden Twenties* as they were known on Wall Street. Other expressions that were born in the 1920s include *money bags* for a rich person, *good times*, and finally *Black Thursday*, October 29, 1929, the day of the stock market crash, and the start of the *Great Depression*.

playing to the gallery. Like *playing to the grandstand* (*q.v.*), this saying means "showing off." It is the older phrase, having its origins in the 18th-century English theater, where actors overacted their roles and raised their voices in order to be appreciated by the larger audience up in the gallery beyond the orchestra.

playing to the grandstand; grandstanding. *Playing to the grandstand* is a baseball term first recorded in 1888 and describing a show-off player who tries to make difficult catches, or make easy catches look difficult. Within a few years such players were called *grandstanders*, and the term was soon applied to a show-off in any endeavor.

playing with loaded dice. Play with loaded dice and you have no chance to win. Dice can be loaded with lead or other weights in such a way that a certain number will always or frequently come up. A gambler can then use them to his advantage by slipping them into a game and throwing all sevens, or by weighting them so that another player will shoot "craps" ("snake-eyes": two ones; or "boxcars": two sixes) on each roll. The practice is as old as the game of dice, but the expression seems to be a 20th-century Americanism.

playing without a full deck. This expression, and its variant *playing with half a deck*, dates back to the 1960s, when it was first used to mean someone lacking in intelligence; that is, not having the usual allotment of brains. Besides having the obvious connection with a deck of cards, the phrase owes something to the earlier term *not all there*, for "stupid," or mentally defective, attested to as early as 1821. (*See also* **nobody home.**)

play possum. *Opossum* is one of the earliest of Americanisms. Borrowed from Indian language, it made its first appearance as *appossoun* in 1610, was changed to *opassom* a few years later and within a century was being written as *opossum* and its abbreviated form *possum*. The animal, which Captain John Smith described as having "an head like a swine, a taile like a rat, and is of the bigness of a cat," was known from the earliest days for the way it feigned death when threatened with capture. Trapped possums close their eyes and lay completely limp and no matter how much abuse they are subjected to, will only

become active when thrown into water. Hunters knew this from the earliest days and so although the expression *to play possum*, "to pretend or deceive," was first recorded in 1822 the phrase is probably much older.

to play the fiddle. This is an American expression that apparently arose in the early 19th century, based on the old English expression "to pay the piper," which dates back to 1681: "After all this Dance he has led the Nation, he must at least come to pay the Piper himself"—Thomas Flatman, *Heraclitus ridens*.

play the sedulous ape. Robert Louis Stevenson originated the phrase in a charming essay in which he wrote: "I have played the sedulous ape to Hazlitt, to Lamb, to Wordsworth, to Sir Thomas Browne, to Defoe, to Hawthorne, to Montaigne, to Baudelaire, and to Obermann . . . . That, like it or not, is the way to learn to write." *Sedulous*, from the Latin *sedulus*, "careful," means diligent and persevering in application or attention, so the phrase describes anyone who slavishly imitates somebody.

pleach. An ancient, useful word that lives on mainly to describe a gardening method of pruning and training trees or bushes to make a hedgelike wall. Pleached alleys, rows of pleached (or plashed) trees on each side of a path, are among the most imposing garden features, one of the finest examples being the alley made of pleached London plane trees at Vienna's Schonbrunn Palace. But *pleach*, which means fold or intertwine, was mainly a poetic word in the past, used by Tennyson and Swinburne, among others. Shakespeare wrote in *Antony and Cleopatra*:

Would'st thou be window'd in great Rome and see
Thy master thus with pleach'd arms, bending down . . .

plentiful as blackberries. In England *blackberries*, named for their color of course, are the most common fruit growing in the wild and proverbially came to represent what is plentiful because they outyield all other bramble fruits—one plant can yield up to five gallons of berries. *Plentiful as blackberries* comes to us from Shakespeare, though what he actually wrote was "If reason were as plenty as blackberries, I would give no more reason on compulsion." The English call a cold early May when blackberries are in bloom *a blackberry winter* and in America a *blackberry summer* is a period of fine weather in late September or early October.

Plimsoll mark; plimsolls. The *Plimsoll mark* or *line*, adopted in 1876, was named in honor of maritime reformer Samuel Plimsoll's suggestion that every vessel have a load line, a mark that indicates the limit to which a ship may be loaded. Located amidships on both sides of the vessel, it is a circle with a horizontal line drawn through it showing the water level at maximum permitted loading. This innovation reformed shipping all over the globe, making Plimsoll's name world famous. His name is also remembered by *plimsolls*, rubber-soled cloth shoes or sneakers with the rubber extending about halfway up the shoe, the line between cloth and rubber somewhat resembling a Plimsoll mark.

plug; not worth a plugged nickel.   Since at least 1860 *an old plug*, or simply a *plug*, has meant an inferior horse, one with defects. No one knows whether this expression came from the term *plug* for a counterfeit coin, that is, a coin with defects, or one that had been hollowed out and filled with an inferior metal, which is responsible for the still common saying *not worth a plugged nickel*. In any case, *plug* for a debased coin dates from the late 17th century. *Nickel* itself fits nicely in the phrase from an etymological point of view. Once the chief constituent of the U.S. five-cent piece, nickel was christened by German miners who often found it when mining for more expensive copper. In their disappointment they named nickel after a goblin called Nicholas, whom they blamed for such small mishaps.

plug ugly.   *Plug ugly* describes "a city ruffian or rowdy" or any such disreputable character. First recorded as an Americanism in 1856, the word is of unknown origin, although one early source says "it derived in Baltimore . . . from a short spike fastened in the toe of [such rowdies'] boots, with which they kicked their opponents in a dense crowd, or as they elegantly expressed it, 'plugged them ugly.'"

plum.   The Old English *plume*, derived from the Greek *proumnon* for the fruit, gives us the English word *plum*. *Burbank plums* are probably the most famous in America, and take their name from the noted plant breeder Luther Burbank, who developed some sixty varieties of plums besides the Burbank. The *Damson plum*, another favorite, is named for the place where it originated; according to tradition, Alexander the Great first brought it to Greece from Damascus, Syria; the Romans called it the plum of Damascus, *prunum damas cenum*, which became *damascene plum* and finally *damson plum* in English. The renowned *Greengage plum*, which is actually yellow with a tinge of green, was brought from Italy to France in about 1500, where it was named the *Reine-Claude* after Claudia, *la bonne reine*, queen to Francis I. About 1725, Sir William Gage, an amateur English botanist, imported a number of plum trees from a monastery in France, all of which were labeled except the *Reine-Claude*. A gardener named the unknown variety after his employer, and the *Reine-Claude* has been the *greengage* in England and America ever since. (*See* **political plum**.)

plumb; plumber; plumb crazy; etc.   A carpenter's plumb line is a lead weight on a string used to mark a true perpendicular, so that a house or floor, etc., is not "out of plumb," but corresponds to the perpendicular. *Plumb* (here pronounced "plum") derives from the Latin *plumbun*, "lead," the same word that *plumber* derives from, because a *plumber* works (or used to) with lead pipes. Since a plumb line is completely or absolutely perpendicular, the word *plumb* became an adverb meaning "completely or absolutely" in phrases like *plumb crazy, plumb mad*, and *plumb tired*. Its use is confined to informal or colloquial speech, but the expression is heard frequently.

plumb the depths.   Echo-sounders are now used to determine the depth of water, but in the past a piece of lead on a string (called a *plumb*) was dropped into the water to measure how deep it was. From this practice came the expression *to plumb the depths*, "to sink as low as possible in misfortune or unhappiness." The expression is first recorded in a figurative sense toward the end of the 16th century.

plum pudding dog.   This was once a common name for the Dalmatian, or spotted coach dog, breed. The Dalmatian pointer was called the *plum pudding dog* because of its mottled appearance, its spots being like the plums or raisins in a pudding; the term was first recorded in 1897.

plushed to the scuppers.   A character in Woody Allen's movie *The Purple Rose of Cairo* (1985) gets *plushed to the scuppers*, "drunk," but the expression is recorded in no slang dictionary. It apparently derives from the British slang *plushed*, for "drunk," first recorded in the late 19th century, and *plushed* here coming from *flush* in its sense of "level with, full to the top" (with booze in this case). Perhaps the phrase is a nautical one. *Scupper* is a nautical word for a drain at the edge of the deck that allows accumulated water to drain away into the sea or the bilge. So anyone *plushed to the scuppers* would be drunk to overflowing.

P.M.   (*See* **A.M.**)

P.M.; spiffs.   For many years, perhaps since before 1900, the first term has been common among American retailers, especially in department stores. It means "a reward paid to a salesperson for selling a particular piece of merchandise, usually a slow-moving item." The initials may stand for *particular merchandise*, or *push merchandise*, but no one seems to be sure and no one seems to know exactly where, when, and why the term originated. I would be glad to hear from any reader who can solve one or all of these minor mysteries. *Spiffs*, origin also unknown, means the same.

pocket book.   (See **Penguinize.**)

pocket borough.   (See **to beat the band.**)

pocket veto.   (See **veto.**)

Podsnappery.   Mr. Podsnap in Dickens's *Our Mutual Friend* (1864) is a self-important, self-satisfied man who wears blinders. His name has become a synonym for someone who refuses to admit the existence of a disagreeable situation.

Podunk.   Small backward towns have been called *Podunks* since before 1841, when the term is first recorded. The first Podunk was an Indian place name between what is now Hartford and Windsor, Connecticut, the name deriving from the Mohegan Algonquian word for "neck or corner of land." The humorous sound of *Podunk* led Americans to use it derisively for a little, insignificant place.

poetic license.   John Dryden called *poetic license* "the liberty which poets have assumed to themselves in all ages, of speaking things in verse, which are beyond the severity of prose." Poetic license is the liberty taken by any writer, especially a poet, to fit the language to his needs, to deviate from conventional form, fact, and even logic to create a desired effect. Everything depends on the end justifying the means, that is, whether the poem (or other piece of writing) "works." Luckily, Tennyson presented his poetic license after he wrote the line, "Every moment dies a man/ Every moment one is born." The literal-minded mathematician Charles Babbage had written him that "if this were true, the population of the world would be at a standstill" and urged him to change the line to: "Every moment dies a man/ Every moment 1 1/16 is born."

poet laureate.   In Greek legend Apollo fell in love with and tried to seize Daphne, the daughter of a river, and at her own request she was turned into a bay laurel tree, which became sacred to Apollo. The god ordered that laurel be the prize for poets and victors, this leading to the belief that laurel leaves communicated the spirit of poetry (the ancients put laurel leaves under their pillows to acquire inspiration while they slept) and the tradition of laurel symbolizing excellence in literature. The first *laureates* were university graduates in poetry and rhetoric who were presented laurel wreaths and called "doctors laureate" and "bachelors laureate." Before the title *poet laureate* was conferred upon any poet in England there were a number of court poets: King Henry I (1068-1135) had a Versificator Regis (King's versifier) named Wale. Ben Jonson was granted a pension by James I in 1616 and was a poet laureate in the modern sense, and Chaucer, Skelton, and Spenser had been called laureates

before him; but it wasn't until John Dryden was appointed poet laureate by Charles II in 1668 that the position became official.

poets are born, not made.   True, untrue, or partly true, this is an ancient belief, for it is a translation of the Latin *Poeta nascitur, non fit.* In his "To the Memory of . . . Shakespeare" (1623), in which he gave us the immortal lines "Sweet Swan of Avon!" and "He was not of an age but for all time," Ben Jonson wrote: "For a good poet's made, as well as born."

the Poet's Corner.   Part of the south transept of Westminster Abbey, where many great authors are buried, *the Poet's Corner* was so named by Oliver Goldsmith, later buried there himself; it had been called "the poetical Quarter" before then. In the corner are, among others, the tombs of or monuments to Chaucer, Spenser, Ben Jonson, Shakespeare, Samuel Butler, Drayton, Milton, Davenant, Cowley, Prior, Gay, Addison, Thomson, Goldsmith, Dryden, Dr. Johnson, Sheridan, Burns, Southey, Coleridge, Campbell, Macaulay, Longfellow, Dickens, Thackeray, Tennyson, Browning, and Hardy. In the case of Hardy, his heart is buried in his native Dorset. One of the oddest stories about the Poet's Corner concerns Thackeray's bust there. The novelist's daughter had always "deplored the length of the whiskers on each side of the face of her father's bust," believing that the Italian sculptor Marachetti had made them far too long. Finally, as an old woman, she managed to persuade officials to let another sculptor move the bust into a secluded alcove and chip away at the sideburns until they were the right length. This accomplished, an appropriately bewhiskered Thackeray was restored to his proper niche in the nave.

poinciana.   The tropical *royal poinciana* with its brilliant, long-clawed scarlet or yellow-striped flowers is probably the most striking of all cultivated trees. Popular in Florida and California as well as its native Madagascar, the broadheaded tree grows from twenty to forty feet high and is sometimes called the *Delonix* (Greek for long claw) and the *peacock flower. Poinciana regia*, as well as the entire *Poinciana* genus, containing several showy plants of the pea family, was named by Linnaeus in honor of M. de Poinci, a 17th-century governor of the French West Indies, where the tree is also widely grown and admired. Another, more descriptive name for the tree is *flame-of-the-forest.*

poinsettia.   This bright red flower, a symbol of Yuletide, could not have been named for a more fiery personality. Joel Roberts Poinsett (1779-1851) had much of the Christmas spirit in him, too, at least a great love for the oppressed and a romantic revolutionary desire to better their lives. Poinsett served as a member of the South

Carolina legislature and as a congressman for a number of years, but found himself more in his own element when appointed the first American minister to Mexico in 1825. Here his revolutionary ardor was so excessive that he lasted only four years, his recall demanded first by the regime that he helped overthrow and then by the republican regime that replaced it. By this time Poinsett was a familiar public figure and when he sent specimens of the large, fiery flowers that we know so well back to this country, they were named after him. Poinsett hadn't discovered the plant, of course, and it had even been introduced to the United States before him; his popularity alone accounting for the honor. The ousted ambassador went on to become Van Buren's secretary of war, and a Union leader during the Civil War, despite his Southern origins. The *Poinsettia* genus commemorating him is now considered part of the genus *Euphorbia*, but the gorgeously colored Mexican species, its tapering scarlet bracts so much a part of Christmas, is still called the *poinsettia*. In England it is known as the *Mexican flame-leaf*.

point-blank. A *point-blank* shot made by archers in 16th-century England was one in which the arrow was aimed or pointed directly at the small white, or blank, bull's eye in the center of the target. With the advent of firearms a shot was said to be point-blank when it remained approximately straight over a certain distance. Because close-range *point-blank* firing in gunnery led to brutal destruction, the term became a synonym for direct, uncompromising rejection or blunt, brutal frankness in such terms as *point-blank refusal* and *point-blank denial*.

to point the finger. This expression is first attested to in Shakespeare's *Othello* (1604): "To make me the fixed Figure for the time of Scorne to point his slow, and moving finger at." It came to mean "to single out a guilty person" and ultimately gave us the expression *finger man* for a criminal who singles out a victim for a murder, robbery, or other crime, and *to finger*, the act of singling out a victim for a crime.

to poke fun at; poke. *To poke fun at* has meant to ridicule since at least 1837, when it is first recorded in Barham's *Ingoldsby Legends*: "Poking your fun at us plain-dealing folk." A *poke* in this case isn't a bag (as in *a pig in a poke*), of course, but a thrust or dig with the fingers.

poker; poker face. *Poker* takes its name from the French *poque*, for a similar card game, though the rules of the Persian game *As Nas* (played with five cards) and *poque* (played with three cards) were combined to make America's characteristic gambling game. The game is mentioned as early as 1834 and probably dates back at least ten years earlier. A *poker face*, a face that conceals all emotions, also comes from the card game, in which bluffing is an important tactic.

pokey. Someone going to jail, or the *pokey*, is doubtless often poked along by an officer who pokes him with a nightstick. But while such *pokes* may have influenced the popularity of the word *pokey*, it probably has its roots in the French *poche*, "a small enclosure," or the older *pogy*, "a workhouse or poorhouse."

polar plant. (*See* **compass plant**.)

polecat. The ornery *polecat* is not an invention of the American West. This close relative of the skunk was so-named five centuries ago; the *pole* in its name is a corruption of the French *poule*, "chicken," making it a cat that likes chicken and likes to raid chicken coops to get them.

pole-cat weed. (*See* **skunk cabbage**.)

police action. Though 75,000 U.N. soldiers were killed in it and a quarter of a million wounded, the Korean War cannot officially be called a war because Congress never officially declared it one. It is officially known in history as the Korean Police Action, the Korean Emergency and the Korean Conflict. President Truman approved the coinage *Police Action*, after an anonymous reporter asked him if repelling a raid "by a bunch of bandits," as Truman called the North Koreans, could be termed a "police action." The reporter, however, probably got the term from a speech by Senator William F. Knowland.

political infighting. We have used this term in America since the late 1940s to mean fighting within a political party or any group. The word *infighting* dates back to 1790s England, where it originated as a method of fighting at close quarters, one generally used by lighter boxers to lessen the force of blows from heavier, stronger opponents.

political plum. *Plum* in 17th century British slang meant one thousand pounds, a fortune at the time. This use of the word *plum* probably gave birth to the expression *a political plum*, a political job requiring little work that yields a lot of money, this term an Americanism first recorded in 1887. (*See* **plum**.)

polka; polka dot. At least four dances have been named for the Poles by other countries, and the most popular of them, the *polka*, is not even Polish in origin. *Polka* simply means a Polish woman, just as *Polak*, which gives us the slang derogatory expression *Polock*, means a Polish man. Either the Czechs called the Bohemian dance *pulka* ("half") because of its short half-steps and this word became corrupted to *polka*, or they named it as a tribute to Polish womankind. At any rate, the lively dance—three steps and a hop in double time—took Europe and America by storm after it was introduced about 1830. The polka craze resulted in many fashionable garments and designs being named after the dance, including a close-fitting knitted jacket called the *polka*, and even the American dress fabric with a polka-dot pattern, introduced in 1880 or so. *Polka dot* may have been inspired by the hopping around characteristic of the polka. Its use was originally confined to the uniform, evenly spaced dots in the material, but the words *polka dot* or *polka dotted* are widely applied today.

polliwog. (*See* **tadpole**.)

polo. One of the relatively few Tibetan words in English, *polo* derives from the Tibetan *pulu*, for the name of the ball hit with the mallet used in the game played on horseback. Polo probably originated in Tibet, was adopted by the Indians, and borrowed from them by British soldiers serving in India during the mid-18th century. Other English words whose ultimate ancestry is Tibetan include "panda" and "yak."

polonium. (*See* **curie**.)

poltroon. It was once thought that *poltroon*, for "a coward," was a corruption of the Latin *pollice truncus*, "thumb cut short," referring to the self-maiming of Romans who wanted to avoid military service. This erroneous derivation suggested the falconry term *poltroon*, for a hawk with the talons of its hind toes clipped. It is now thought that *poltroon*, first recorded in 1529, derives from the Italian *poltro*, "lazy good-for-nothing," or the Italian *poltrone*, "colt," after the usual timidity or "cowardice" of young horses.

polyandry. *Polyandry* is that form of polygamy in which a woman has more than one legal husband at a time. It derives from the Greek *polyandros*, "having many husbands," and is first recorded in 1780. Berber Queen Kahena holds the record for polyandry, having had 400 husbands. (*See* **polygyny**.)

polygyny. *Polygyny* is that form of polygamy where a man has more than one legal wife at a time. It derives from the Greek *polygynaios*, "having many wives," and is first recorded in English in 1780. The king of polygyny is Siam's King Mongut of *The King and I* fame, who had 9,000 wives. (*See* **polyandry**.)

pomegranate. Commonly called "Chinese apples" in America, *pomegranates*, "the fruit of the ancients," take their name from the Latin for "many-seeded apple." The thick-skinned red fruit, about the size of an orange, is divided into numerous cells inside, each containing many seeds encased in a crimson, juicy pulp. When the fruit is eaten raw, it is broken open and the red flesh is sucked from the small seeds. Today in the Orient when a newly married couple reaches their new home, pomegranates are broken at the doorway, their crimson-coated seeds signifying both the loss of virginity and an omen that many offspring will come of the marriage. A number of other words derive from the pomegranate with its red skin and seeds. Our *grenade*, a weapon first used in the late 16th century, comes from the French *grenade*, a shortening of French *pomegrenade*, for pomegranate. It was originally filled with grains or "seeds" of powder and thus facetiously named after the many-seeded fruit. Today the word is used in *hand grenade*, which isn't filled with grains of powder anymore, but can create a scene of carnage as bloody as any shattered pomegranate where it explodes. The military *grenadier*, originally a soldier who threw grenades, evolved in much the same way from the French shortening, as did the drink *grenadine* made from the fruit. But the *garnet* stone, its color similar to the flesh of the fruit, was given its name by the Romans, the Latin *granatum* (from *Punic granatum* or Punic apple: the pomegranate) becoming *grenat* in Old French and shifting by methathesis to *garnet* in English over the years.

Pomeranian dog. These little toy balls of hair were produced from many breeds (including big spitz sled dogs) in a northern province of Germany called Pomerania that is now mainly in Poland.

pompadour. Madame de Pompadour, born Jeanne Antoinette Poisson, is probably history's most famous courtesan. In fact, La Pompadour, who became *maîtresse en titre* to Louis XV when twenty-seven years old, had been educated with great expense to be a royal mistress. Raised from an early age by her mother's lover, a wealthy financier who took her from her poor parents, her future had been prophesied when she was only nine by an old fortune-teller, whom Pompadour later pensioned for the accuracy of her prediction. An extremely beautiful girl, she proved to be a kind, generous, and talented woman once she had entrenched herself with the monarch. Surrounding herself with beautiful objects was her passion and she was the undisputed leader of Parisian fashions, causing many styles and costumes to be attributed to her. The most famous, historically, is the *pompadour hairstyle*, which was at first worn in loose rolls around the face but swept upward high above the forehead in the next century and came to be a style worn by men as well as women. The woman's dress called a pompadour, cut square and low in the neck, is also named for her. However, her name is best known as a synonym for mistress. Even on her deathbed she painted her face for the king.

pom-pom girl, pompon girl. *Pom-pom girl* is a synonym for a prostitute, having its origins in the automatic *pom-*

pom guns that Chicago gangsters used in the 1920s. *Pompon girls* or *pom poms* are cheerleaders, so named because they originally waved *pompons*, a variety of chrysanthemums.

poncho. Both the blanket-like coat with the hole in the middle for one's head and *poncho*, the name for it, come from the Chilean Arucan Indians. Mexican *vaqueros* copied the coat from them and Americans adopted it early in the 19th century.

pongo. The legendary *pongo* was "a cross between a tiger and a sea-shark," a huge monster that devastated Sicily before it was slain by the three sons of St. George. For centuries the name was applied not only to the terrible sea monster but also to a gorilla, of all things, probably because by some strange coincidence *pongo* is the name in Bantu dialect for a large ape.

ponticello. Deriving from the Latin *pontis*, "bridge," *ponticello* is an Italian word taken intact into English that means the bridge of a stringed instrument such as a violin. *Ponticello* is also used to describe an adolescent boy's changing voice, which is a little bridge connecting puberty and manhood.

pontoon. The Greek god of the sea, Pontus, gives his name to the *pontoon bridge*, a floating structure, as well as to the *pontoons* on seaplanes and the *pontoon lifeboat*, a lifeboat dependent for buoyancy on a watertight double bottom. *Pontoon* is first recorded in 1591.

pony; Pony Express. The *pony* is related to the young chicken, though only in language. Both words have their roots in the Latin word *pullus*, "a young animal," yielded the French *poulet*, "a young fowl," this becoming the English *pullet* and the French *poulenet*, "a young horse," which became the Scottish *powney* and then the English *pony*. The *Pony Express*, more often called simply the *Pony* at the time, was the common designation for the Central Overland Pony Express Company, which lasted only from April 3, 1860 to October 24, 1861, but is still operating in Western novels and films. It had 190 stations along its route between Missouri and California, riders, including "Buffalo Bill" Cody, changing swift Indian ponies at each station and riding on with the mail—often through bad weather and Indian ambushes. The record for its 2,000-mile run was seven days, seventeen hours, but it couldn't beat the telegraph that connected East and West in 1861, and the Pony Express went out of business that year.

pony up. Since the early 1800s *pony up*, or *poney up*, has been American slang for "to pay up." These words may derive from the German *poniren*, "to pay," but *pony* was British slang for a small amount of money in the early 19th century, probably because a pony is a small horse (not over fourteen hands high), and the term to *pony up* probably derived from this expression. Other uses of *pony* to indicate smallness include the *pony* that is a small glass or bottle of alcoholic beverage and the *pony* meaning a trot or crib—a translation used by students.

poo-bah. A politician who holds several offices, or a pompous self-important person, is called a *poo-bah*. In Gilbert and Sullivan's operetta *The Mikado* (1885) Pooh-Bah is the personal name of the arrogant Lord High Everything Else, this being the source of the word.

poodle. *Poodle*, first recorded in 1825, is short for the German *Puddlehund*. This extremely intelligent dog, bred for over 2,000 years, was widely valued for retrieving, as is shown by the components of its name: *pudeln*, "splash in the water," and *hund*, "hound or dog."

poogye. A usual word for an unusual thing, *poogye*, or *poogyee*, a Hindi term that has come into English unchanged, stands for the Hindu nose flute, "the tubes of which are inserted into a gourd and are blown with the nose instead of the mouth."

pooh-pooh. *Pooh-pooh* is a reduplication of *pooh*, which is probably "a vocal gesture expressing the action of puffing or blowing anything away" and is first recorded in *Hamlet*, as "puh" ("Affection, puh. You speak like a greene girl.") By the early 19th century we find *pooh-pooh* being used to mean "to express contempt or disdain for, to make light of." So common was the interjection *pooh-pooh* in the 19th century that a *pooh-pooh* meant "one addicted to using this expression."

poontang. Thomas Wolfe used this word for the vagina or "a piece" in *Look Homeward, Angel*, and Calder Willingham used it more graphically in *End As a Man*. The black and Southern white expression, first referring to black women and now to both blacks and whites, might be expected to have a diverting story behind it, as unusual as *poontang* sounds. But it probably comes from the French *putain*, "prostitute," by way of New Orleans.

pooped out. Anyone *pooped out* or *all pooped*, feels something like the 19th-century seamen who used the expression *pooped* to indicate what happened when they were caught on the poop or aft deck of a ship when a wave crashed down and washed over them.

poor as a church mouse. This saying, meaning poor indeed, goes back to 17th-century England, but probably was taken from similar German and French expressions that are much older. Church mice in centuries past had lean pickings, if they had any pickings at all. Churches then had no recreational facilities with well-stocked kitchens as do some of their modern-day counterparts. They were used only for religious services and prayer, and a mouse living in one would be hard put to find a crumb.

poor as Job's turkey.   Though the Book of Job doesn't mention his having any turkeys, Job certainly was poor and miserable, which inspired 19th-century Canadian humorist Thomas Haliburton to coin this expression. Haliburton, whose contributions to American English were considerable, wrote in one of his Sam Slick tales about *Job's turkey*, which had but one feather and was so weak with hunger that it had to support itself against the barn when it wanted to gobble.

poor boy sandwich.   (*See* **hero sandwich.**)

poor Joe.   The *poor Joe* or *po' Joe*, as it is called, is another name for the great blue heron, especially in the American South. No "Joe" is honored by the name. It is doubtless from the Vai language of Liberia and Sierra Leone, where *pojo* means "heron," and was introduced to America by Vai-speaking slaves.

poormouthing.   *Poormouthing* describes the talk of a person always pleading poverty or complaining about having no money or material things. This isn't a modern expression or practice—the practice is as old as mankind and the expression, apparently a Scottish one (*to make a poor mouth*), dates back to at least the early 19th century.

Poor Richard's Almanac.   (*See* **almanac.**)

pop.   (*See* **onomatopoeia.**)

popcorn.   Certainly known to the Aztecs, *popcorn* was so named by American settlers on the frontier in the early 19th century. It is a variety of small-eared corn (*Zea mays everta*), the kernels of which pop open when subjected to dry heat and has also been called "parching corn," "popped corn," "pot corn," "cup corn," "dry corn," and "buckshot" over the years. The great quantities of it sold in movie theaters prompted some early movie house corporations to grow thousands of acres of popcorn.

poplin.   This finely corded material is named, indirectly, after the Roman Catholic papacy. Avignon, the French city where it was first made in the 14th century, was a papal city and a seat of the Catholic church, and the cloth was named after the pope.

poppycock.   *Poppycock* means nonsense, the Americanism first recorded in 1865 and deriving from the Dutch *pappekak*, which means "soft dung" and owes its life, in turn, to the Latin *pappa*, "soft food," and *cacare*, "to defecate."

popsicle.   The popsicle might still be an "Epsicle" if Frank W. Epperson (1894-1983) hadn't gone broke in 1929 and sold his patent for his "handled, frozen confection or ice lollipop" to a small company, which changed its name from *Epsicle* to *Popsicle*. Epperson had dubbed his successful product the Epsicle some nineteen years after he accidentally invented it one cold San Francisco night in 1905, when as an eleven-year-old he left a glass of lemonade on his porch and "awoke the next morning to find the drink frozen solid around a spoon that was in it."

porcelain.   Why is *porcelain* named for a pig? The earthenware takes its name from the Latin *porcella*, "little sow," because the Romans believed its finish resembled a cowerie shell, which in turn they thought resembled a sow's vulva.

pork barrel.   Government appropriations used to supply funds for local improvements that are designed to ingratiate congressmen with their constituents have been called *pork barrel* since shortly before the Civil War. Before that the expression simply meant the total contributions to a congressman's campaign fund. In this case *pork* is synonymous with fat, which has always signified abundance or plenty.

pornography; Porneius.   *Pornography* is Greek for "writing of harlots," the term probably deriving from the signs hung outside Greek brothels. Such writing can be divided into *erotica*, which generally centers on "normal" heterosexual love, describing it in detail, and *exotica*, centering on so-called abnormal sex, including sadism, masochism, and fetishism. Pornography can be found in elements of the Old Testament and the plays of Aristophanes and probably goes back far beyond them. The first masterpiece of English pornography is probably John Cleland's *Memoirs of the Life of Fanny Hill* (1749). Pornography has thrived only since the late 18th century, the English word itself first recorded in 1860, and authors of it since have been as varied as de Sade (*see* **sadism**), Swinburne, and Mark Twain. An excellent reference giving details and titles is R. S. Reade's *Register Librorum Eroticorum* (1936). *Porneius* is a character in Greek legend who has been called "fornication personified," a good description, as his name comes from the Greek *porneia*, "fornication." He was the son of Anagnus (inchastity), two of his brothers being Maechus (adultery), and Aselges (lasciviousness). Porneius tried to rape Parthenia (maidenly chastity), after whom the Parthenon (Temple of the Maiden) was named, but the "martial maid" killed him with her spear.

port.   Over 300 years ago *port* began to replace *larboard* as the word for the left-hand side of a ship (probably because *larboard* was too easily confused in speech with *starboard*, the right-hand side). The word *port* here probably derives from port, "a harbor." In the days when the steering gear was on the starboard (that is, steerboard) side, a vessel almost always had to tie up at the dock with her left side toward the port.

porter ale.   (*See* **porterhouse steak.**)

porterhouse steak.   Martin Morrison's Porterhouse in New York City introduced the *porterhouse steak* in about 1814, according to the *Dictionary of Americanisms*. The tender steak taken from the loin next to the *sirloin* is an even more succulent cut than its neighbor, but has a lot of waste. In England, there is generally no distinction between it and sirloin. A *porterhouse* was a tavern serving the dark brown beer or ale called *porter*, once favored by porters and other laborers.

portholes.   Half of a ship's windows are on the starboard side. Yet all windows on a ship are called *portholes*. This is because in early times the only windows on a ship were the *port holes* for guns. When windows were later added for the comfort of sailors sleeping below, on both sides of a ship, they too were called portholes.

Portuguese man-of-war.   This is the common name of *Physalia pelagica*, derisively named the *Portuguese man-of-war* by the English in the 18th century, when the once powerful Portuguese navy had gone into a state of decline. The designation is a strange one, for small as it is, the *Portuguese man-of-war* can be deadly. Actually not an individual animal but a colony of highly specialized polyps, it has tentacles up to fifty feet long that discharge a toxic substance that has painfully stung, paralyzed, and even killed swimmers coming into contact with them.

Portuguese words in English.   Portuguese words that came into English, often through Spanish, include: *apricot, molasses, marmalade, verandah, junk* (via Japanese), and *cuspidor* (possibly through Dutch).

port wine.   This sweet red dessert wine is named *port*, the word first recorded in 1591, because it was first shipped to England from the town of Oporto in northern Portugal. Its types include vintage port, tawny port, ruby port, and white port (made from white grapes).

posey.   (*See* **nosegay.**)

posh.   The old story says that *posh* is an acronym for "*p*ort *o*utward, *s*tarboard *h*ome." British civil servants traveling to India on the Peninsular and Oriental Steam Navigation Company line supposedly liked to have their accommodations on the port side of the ship leaving home and on the starboard side coming back, as these locations were shady and away from the weather. According to the tale, such first-class, or *posh*, staterooms became a syn-

onym for anything elegant or sophisticated. But unfortunately, the famous P & O line has no record of such an expression ever being used. This doesn't prove that the ingenious story isn't true, but the term is just as likely a contraction of "polished" or "polish." *Posh* is first recorded in 1897 as meaning "a dandy" and so may also be a corruption of the slang term *pot* ("big"), a person of importance. A corruption of the Scottish *tosh*, "neat and trim" isn't out of the question, either.

post-haste.   Used in England as early as the 16th century, *post-haste* refers to the post-horse system of delivering mail in those days. Much like the American Pony Express, this earlier system stationed men with fresh horses at intervals along the road, the letters taken relay-fashion at each post and delivered to the next post in haste.

potato.   The white potato is one of the most important vegetables in the world, yet it bears the wrong name. *Potato* derives from the Haitian word *batata*, for "sweet potato," which the Spanish found in the West Indies in 1526 and introduced to Europe. *Batata* was corrupted to *patata* in Spanish, and this altered to *potato* when first used in England. But then the Spaniards discovered the Peruvian white potato, an unrelated plant, and mistook it for just another variety of the West Indian plant. Ignoring the native name for the white potato, *papas*, they gave it the same name as the earlier tuber, and so it too became known as the *potato* in England. The only distinction between the two unrelated vegetables was that one came to be called the *sweet potato* and the other the *Virginia* or *white potato*. The white potato is called "apple of the earth", *pomme de terre* in French, and "earth-apple", *Erdapfel* in German. It acquired the name *Irish potato* when it was first brought to this country in 1719 by a group of Irish Presbyterians and planted in Londonderry, New Hampshire. The colloquial American name *spud* for it derives from the spade-like tool used in digging potatoes. The humorous *Murphy* derives from the wide consumption of potatoes in Ireland—where there are of course many Murphys—at a time when other European countries rarely used the tuber for anything but fodder.

pot-au-feu. (*See* **pot luck.**)

potboiler.   "All men who have to live by their labour have their pot-boilers," Hazlitt wrote, and an obscure English poet lamented: "No far'vring patrons have I got,/But just enough to boil the pot." A *potboiler* is of course a literary work written to make a living, a task performed to keep the pot boiling, or to eat. Financial gain is the only object in writing one, but sometimes genius transcends the immediate object and the result is a work of art. Dr. Johnson's "philosophical romance" *Rasselas* (1759), for example, was written over the nights of one week to meet the cost of his mother's funeral and pay off her debts. Coleridge's *Ancient Mariner* has been called "the most sublime of pot-boilers to be found in all literature," but I suspect there are even greater ones.

pot calling the kettle black.   Dating back to the 17th century, this expression describes someone who faults another for faults conspicuously his own. In ancient times, pots as well as kettles would likely be blackened over the open cooking fires of the day.

Potemkin village.   Russian army officer Gregory Potemkin helped his lover Catherine the Great try to improve the country's economy. He tried to make many reforms in the Ukraine, but corrupt administrators spoiled his plans, and when Catherine wanted to see good results, he decided to trick her. Whether the allegations are true or not, it was said that Potemkin led Catherine on tours to places where conditions were best and even constructed false-front villages, transporting "contented peasants" from one of these sham villages to another just ahead of the Russian empress. As a result *Potemkin village* has become the synonym for something that looks good on the outside but really isn't, or a government plan to fool the people.

pot luck.   No sirloins or barons of beef for peasants in the Middle Ages. Mostly their dinners came from the great iron pots simmering over their fires into which leftovers were tossed from day to day. Often they didn't know exactly what they were having for dinner, so when they asked a visitor to take *pot luck* with them they weren't trying to put him off. It *was* a matter of luck—what was in the pot and whether there would be enough of it to go around. The expression is first recorded in 1592 and came to mean "plain fare," nothing fancy, what we usually have, like the French *pot-au-feu* ("fire pot"), the ordinary family dinner. In Ireland the *pot of hospitality* always hung over the open fire ready to be dipped into by any unexpected visitor. People who offer visitors *pot luck* today, however, often wind up preparing an impromptu banquet for their guests.

pot shot.   A *pot shot* was originally "a shot for the pot," that is, a shot taken at an animal in order to fill the dinner pot, without any regard for rules and from any distance, no matter how close. The earlier *pothunter*, first recorded in 1781, suggested the word, which came to mean, in both military and civilian use, a shot aimed at somebody within easy reach, without giving the person any chance to defend himself, as in an ambush. An abbreviation is *to pot* somebody.

potter's field.   The first cemetery known to be used as a *potter's field*, "a burial place for paupers, criminals and unknown persons," was *Aceldama*, or "field of blood," a barren piece of land near Jerusalem. The Bible tells us that it was originally used by potters and called Aceldama because it was bought with the blood money paid Judas. Believing he had sinned and betrayed the innocent blood, Judas returned the thirty pieces of silver paid him for his treachery and went out and hanged himself, the elder he chose becoming known as the *Judas tree*. When the priests of the temple decided it was unlawful to return Judas's silver to the treasury, since it was "the price of blood," they used it to buy a field to bury strangers in. There are other versions of the origins of the first potter's field. Since the seventh century an area called *Hakked-Dumm*, "price of blood", on a cliff southwest of Siloam, has been regarded as Aceldama, although the absence of clay in the area makes it an unlikely location for a potter's field.

Pott's disease.   (*See* **Bright's disease.**)

pot valor.   *Pot valor* is an older name for *Dutch courage* or "whiskey courage," meaning valor or courage inspired by alcohol. *Pot valor* goes back to at least 1623, while *Dutch courage* dates to the troubles between the Dutch and British in the 17th century. *Whiskey courage* is a fairly recent Americanism.

pound of flesh.   Shylock in Shakespeare's *The Merchant of Venice* (1596) attempts to enforce a contract that allows him to cut a pound of flesh from Antonio, this fictional situation leading to the expression *one's pound of flesh* for the exact amount that is owed someone, no matter what pain it causes the person who must pay him.

pound sterling.   (*See* **sterling.**)

to pour oil on troubled waters.   To soothe or calm a situation by tact and diplomacy is the figurative meaning of the above phrase. The ancients, Pliny and Plutarch among them, believed that oil poured on stormy waters reduced the waves to a calm and allowed a vessel to ride through a storm. The Venerable Bede says in his *Historia Ecclesiastica Gentis Anglorum* (731) that Bishop Aidan, an Irish monk, gave a priest, who was to deliver King Oswy's bride to him, holy oil to pour on the sea if the waves became threatening; his miraculous oil would stop the wind from blowing. A storm did blow up and the priest saved the ship and the future queen by following this advice. Later, Benjamin Franklin mentioned the practice of pouring oil on troubled waters in a letter and it said that the captains of American whaling vessels sometimes ordered oil poured on stormy waters.

powwow.   American Indians called the medicine man a *powwow*, ultimately from an Algonquian word meaning "dreamer." Early settlers used the word in the same way but were soon applying it to a ceremony or meeting where the medicine man performed his magic. It wasn't until the early 19th century that *powwow* was extended to mean any meeting or conference at all.

a pox on you.   Smallpox has been wiped out in the world today thanks to universal vaccination with cowpox virus, a method introduced by Edward Jenner in 1796. But in days past the contagious disease killed thousands every year. *Pox* is an altered spelling of *pocks*, eruptive pustules on the skin that characterize smallpox and other less serious diseases such as chicken pox. *A pox on you!* was often a serious oath in the past, but the expression seems always to have been used humorously, too, as it is today. Shakespeare first recorded it as an exclamation of irritation or impatience in *All's Well That Ends Well* (1601): "A pox on him, he's a Cat [a spiteful backbiter] still."

P.P.C.   Hardly anyone leaves calling cards anymore and fewer still leave calling cards with the initials *P.P.C.* on them. The practice was fairly common once, however, and should you receive one from the two or three people in the world who keep up the practice you'll be glad to know that the letters *don't* stand for "paying private call." They stand for the French *pour prendre conge*, "for taking leave," which means that the party called to say goodbye and found no one home.

practice what you preach.   The King James Version of the Bible translates the idea behind this phrase as "they say and do not" (Matt. 23:3). Over the centuries these words inspired writers to devise poetic improvements upon them and in 1876 or so Rowland Howard came up with *practice what you preach.* The translators of the new Revised Standard Version of the Bible liked this so much that they changed Matt. 23:3 to "they preach but do not practice" and the phrase was in the Bible at last.

pragmatism.   Though William James was the great popularizer of the philosophical doctrine of *pragmatism,* the word was coined in the 1870s by another philosopher, C. S. Pierce, from the Greek *pragma,* "a fact, a deed, a thing done." Stressing the practical as opposed to the theoretical, pragmatism tests the truth and value of something by its utility and workability.

prairie dog.   *Prairie dog* was one of the some 1,528 names given to animals, plants, and places observed on the Lewis and Clark Expedition into the Louisiana Territory in 1803—this said to be a record in vocabulary making. Captain Meriwether Lewis had first called the animal a *barking squirrel,* but this probably more accurate description was changed to *prairie dog* by his friend William Clark.

prairie oysters; mountain oysters.   In a country where the prudish have called the bull "a cow's father," "a cow

creature," "a male cow," "a Jonathan" and "a gentleman cow," it is no wonder that there are so many euphemisms for bull's testicles. In French and Spanish restaurants bull's balls are sometimes called just that on the menus, but in America, when they are offered, they're invariably labeled either "prairie oysters," "mountain oysters," "Rocky Mountain oysters," or "Spanish kidneys." Believed to be an elevating aphrodisiac dish despite their low origins, bull's balls are probably no more than a psychological aphrodisiac. But French neurologist Charles Brown-Dequard, who founded the much disputed "science" of organotherapy in 1889, thought differently. He claimed that both he and his patients had greatly enhanced their sexual prowess by eating bull's testicles. The seventy-year-old scientist went so far as to transplant bull's testicles under the abdominal walls of patients, but it has since been established that testicles cannot store sex hormones such as testosterone and that when transplanted they wither and die.

prairie strawberries.   (*See* **Arizona strawberries.**)

praline.   The Maréchal du Plessis-Praslin, César de Choiseul, got heartburn from eating almonds but couldn't resist them, one story goes. So his servant suggested that he have his chef brown the almonds in boiling sugar to make them more digestible and *voila!*—the *praline.* But another story says that sugar-coated praline candy was named for Praslin when he had his cook prepare something special for King Louis XIV, the field marshal's dinner guest one night. More likely, pralines were invented by Praslin's man as one of the many culinary triumphs that all chefs vied with each other to produce in the 17th century. At first they were called *Praslins* and in time the spelling was altered to *Pralines.* The Comte du Plessis-Praslin, who put down a revolt of the nobles in 1649 and may have served Louis pralines, became Louis XIV's minister of state in 1652 and was later rewarded with the title of duke for which he had politicked so long. He died in 1675, aged seventy-seven, a silver tray of pralines, or praslins, no doubt at his side.

pratfall.   A *pratfall* is old show business slang for a fall on the buttocks taken by a comedian to obtain laughs. *Pratts,* or *prats* is simply rogues' cant for the buttocks. No one knows the origin of the term, which dates back to the 16th century, and there seems to be no connection between it and the older *prat,* for "a trick or prank."

Pravda.   *Pravda,* one of the two most influential Soviet newspapers, means "truth" in Russian, while the other important journal is *Izvestia,* meaning "news." A wry Russian witticism adivises "There's no news in the Truth and no truth in the News."

praying mantis.   The English were calling *Mantis religiosa* the *praying mantis* since at least 1706, when this name for the green or brown predatory insect is first recorded. Also called the *praying locust*, it is so named because of the position in which it holds its forelegs, as if in prayer. It is a beneficial insect in the garden, as it eats many bugs destructive to plants.

precocious.   Trees and fruits that flowered or ripened early were called *precocious* by the English in the early 17th century, the word deriving from the Latin *prae*, "before," and *coquere*, "to cook," which formed *praecoquere*, "to cook beforehand." By the end of the century writers were applying this botanical word to people, especially children who are especially mature or learned for their ages, who are "cooked before their time."

preposition.   Although etymologically the word *preposition* itself means "placed before," prepositions need not always be placed before their objects in a sentence. Most times they are, but in some instances, a preposition must come *after* its object and in others the preposition can be placed either before or after the object. There are governing rules, but it is best to rely on the ear in this matter. For example, "What are you sitting on?" sounds a lot better than "On what are you sitting?" The record for the most prepositions strung together at the end of a sentence is the protest of a child against an Australian bedtime story book: "Mommy, what did you bring that book which I didn't want to be read to out of from about 'Down Under' up for?" Angry at a critic who corrected one of his sentences on the basis of the old bromide that a preposition should not end a sentence, Winston Churchill wrote to him: "This is the kind of nonsense up with which I will not put." British author Joseph Addison liked to end sentences with prepositions—at least he wrote a good many of them that way— and sentences ending with prepositions are therefore said to have *Addisonian terminations*. Interestingly, Richard Hurd, the testy critic who coined that term is heard of no more today, while Joseph Addison, dangling prepositions and all, remains a much-read author.

preposterous.   (*See* **put the cart before the horse.**)

president.   The first Senate of the United States selected "His Highness" as the title of the President of the U.S., the full title decided upon being "His Highness the President of the United States of America and the Protector of the Rights of the Same." However, the House of Representatives voted the title down and the president was referred to as the more democratic *Mr. President*. The first president's wife, however, was called Lady Washington during his terms in office. President Washington himself objected to terms like "Your Majesty." The word *president*, also deriving from the Latin *praesidere*, to preside, govern, was used as the title of the highest officer in an American colony, a practice that

began in Jamestown. William Howard Taft, a president handpicked for the position by his predecessor Theodore Roosevelt, once said that whenever he heard someone say "Mr. President" while he was in office, he looked around for Teddy.

press gangs.   *Impressment* became prominent in American vocabularies before the War of 1812, when British sailors forcibly removed British seamen from American vessels, claiming this was their right, and impressed American seamen into British service at the same time, always explaining later that they took the Americans by mistake. *Press gangs* were the hired thugs who impressed seamen for service aboard British ships during the War of 1812 and had indeed done so since the late 17th century.

pretzel.   There is no proof that *pretzels* are so-twisted to represent "the folded arms of praying children," as is often claimed, and they certainly don't take their name from the Latin *pretiola*, "little reward," because they were given by monks to religiously faithful children. Why they are twisted no one really knows, and the word *pretzel*, first recorded here in 1824, in a reference to pretzels eaten by the Dutch, derives from the German word for "branch", in reference to the branches of a tree that the "arms" of the pretzels resemble.

prevarication.   Roman farmers who ploughed crooked ridges in Rome were called *praevaricors*, their name deriving from the Latin verb for to go zigzag or crooked. The next step was to apply the word to men who deviated from the straight line and gave crooked answers in courts of law, which gave us our word *prevarication*, or lie. (*See also* **delirium.**)

priapus.   A *priapus* is not just any penis or phallus, but a huge penis. It takes its name from the Greek Priapus, who personified the male generative powers and whose mother was so horrified by his monstrous sexual organ that she disowned him! Statues of Priapus's phallus were often placed in gardens and orchards to ensure fertility.

prick song.   In ancient times *prick songs* were songs whose notes were *pricked*, or written down, unlike common songs, which weren't recorded and were preserved by memory. The expression is first recorded in 1463, in the form of *pricked song*.

pride goeth before a fall.   Since the early 16th century the saying has usually been something similar to *pride goeth before a fall* in English. But the biblical proverb (Prov. 16:18) this is based upon uses the words "Pride goeth before destruction, and a haughty spirit before a fall."

primrose; primrose path. *The primrose path* is the path of pleasure, the path strewn with flowers, the lazy, self-indulgent way. The expression is first recorded in *Hamlet:* "Shew me the steepe and thorny way to Heaven; Whilst like a puft and recklesse Libertine Himselfe the Primrose path of dalliance treads." The flower called a primrose is not a rose and not one of the first flowers of spring, as its name implies. It is said to be so named due to "a popular blunder."

Prince Albert coat; Albert chain; etc. Queen Victoria married Albert Francis Charles Augustus Emmanuel, Prince of Saxe-Coburg-Gotha in 1840, despite many objections, loved him deeply, and mourned him in seclusion many years after his untimely death in 1861, aged forty-two. A man of great character and culture, the royal consort was much loved by the British people, one token of their esteem shown by the heavy gold watch chain presented to him by the jewelers of Birmingham in 1849. The prince consort wore this watch chain from one pocket to a button of the waistcoat, setting a fashion named the *Albert chain* or *albert* in his honor. Also named for Albert are *Lake Albert*, or *Lake Albert Nyanza*, in central Africa, discovered by Samuel Baker in 1864, and, oddly enough, the *alberts* or rags that Australian tramps wear in place of socks. The *Prince Albert*, a long double-breasted frock coat, is named for the royal consort's eldest son, Albert Edward, Prince of Wales (1841-1910), who became Edward VII in 1901.

Prince Rupert; Prince Rupert's drops; etc. General of the Royalist armies against Cromwell during the Civil War, and admiral of the British navy in the Dutch Wars, Prince Rupert (1619-82), grandson of England's James I, was a multitalented military man also strongly interested in art and science. One of the earliest mezzotinters, his *Head of St. John the Baptist* is justly famous, and he experimented with guns, shot, and gunpowder. Prince Rupert invented the modified brass called Prince Rupert's metal, the alloy resembling gold and consisting of 60 to 80 percent copper and 15 to 40 percent zinc. *Prince Rupert's drops*, which he also devised, are toys made by dropping molten glass into water, the glass forming small tadpoles which explode into dust if their tails are nipped off. The port of Prince Rupert in British Columbia bears the prince's name also, as does Rupert's Land, once the name for all the land in Canada that drained into Hudson Bay, Prince Rupert having been the first governor of the Hudson Bay Company when it was formed in 1670.

privateer. *Privateers* operate with the consent of a government, usually their own. Privateers were *privately* owned vessels that in England were licensed under Letter of Marque and Reprisal to capture enemy ships in time of war. A captain who had such authorization would not be charged with piracy. Perhaps the most famous privateer in history was the British Sir Francis Drake, who preyed on Spanish shipping in the 16th century as captain of the *Golden Hind*. (*See* **corsair**.)

private eye. Mystery writer Raymond Chandler popularized this term, for "a private investigator," but it has its origins in the "We Never Sleep" motto of the Pinkerton Detective Agency, which was printed over an open eye. (*See* **Pinkerton**.)

Proctophilus winchilli. While they were fishing in the Gulf of Lower California, Nobel Prize winner John Steinbeck and his friend Doc Ricketts noticed a little fish that lived in the cloaca of the sea cucumber and that kept darting in and out of the creature's anus. They named the hitherto unrecorded fish *Proctophilus winchilli*, after gossip columnist Walter Winchell.

prodigy. The Roman word *prodigium* was used to denote an incident of an extraordinary nature to be taken as a prophetic sign, bad or good, by the entire nation. When adopted in English as *prodigy*, the term at first meant the same, but later became applied to an extraordinary person or animal, one with great intelligence or talent, and then to a child possessing these qualities. Since the early 16th century, society has known thousands of child prodigies.

profane. From the Latin *pro*, "before" and *fanum*, "temple." Those within the Roman temple were considered holy, while those outside the temple, *pro fanum*, were unholy, or *profane*.

Promethean. Anyone resembling Prometheus in spirit or action, or anyone creative or boldly inventive can be called *Promethean*. Prometheus of Greek mythology was put to work by Zeus to create men from mud and water. But Prometheus stole Olympian fire for his miserable creations and an angry Zeus chained him to a rock in the Caucasus, exposing him to the fierce vultures there, until Hercules released him.

propaganda. Pope Gregory XVIII organized a *congregatio de propaganda fide*, a congregation for propagating the Christian faith, in 1622, and over the years this organization became the basis for the word *propaganda*, meaning deliberately to spread rumors, lies, or information to harm or help a cause.

proselytize. *Proselytize* means to convert someone to a religion or point of view. The word derives from the Greek *proselutos*, "one who has come to a place or a convert." The first proselytes were apparently Greek converts to Judaism, some of whom accepted the religion wholly and some of whom only agreed to refrain from working on the Sabbath and making sacrifices to heathen gods. *Proselyte* is first recorded by John Wyclif in 1382.

prosit! The German *Prosit!* has been adopted as an English drinking toast. The German word (and the similar Dutch *Proost*) comes from the Latin *prosit*, "may it do good."

prospect. *Prospect*, as a synonym for a salesman's potential customer, is a term that became common only in the past half-century or so. *Prospect* has its roots in the Latin *prospecto*, "to look forward," which in the 15th century was altered to *prospect* and came to mean a landscape viewed from a distance. About 400 years later the word was finally extended to looking forward figuratively when it was applied to a possible customer.

protean. *Protean*, for "something that is constantly changing, or someone who assumes many roles," derives from the name of Proteus, herdsman of Neptune, Greek god of the sea. Wise old Proteus lived in a huge cave tending his herd of sea calves, and no one was able to catch the great prophet because he could rapidly change himself into different shapes.

protest; protestant. (*See* **testify**.)

protoplasm. Czech physiologist Jan Evangelista Purkinje first gave the name *protoplasm* to the living material within the cell, in 1839. He referred specifically to the gelatinous embryonic material in an egg, this first-formed material reminding him of the word *protoplasm* used to describe Adam, the first formed man, in the Bible.

proud as a peacock. During one of his attacks of insanity England's George III insisted on ending every sentence in all of his speeches with the word *peacock*. His ministers cured him of this by telling him that *peacock* was a beautiful word but a royal one, which a king should whisper when speaking before his subjects so they couldn't hear it. As a result the speeches of George III were less absurd. The handsome peacock's strutting gait gave us the term *proud as a peacock* at least as early as the 14th century.

proud as Punch. The Punch and Judy show originated in early 17th-century Italy, where the main character's name was Pulcinello, a vain, pompous character with a shrewish wife, Judy. When the shows came to England Pulcinello's name was corrupted to Punchinello and then shortened to Punch, but his personality remained the same, as is reflected in the old saying *proud as Punch*, being proud over a victory, as Punch was when he bested Judy.

proud as sin. *As proud as sin*, probably originating in the 19th century, can be traced back to similar *proud as . . .* phrases close to five hundred years old. The earliest

appears to be *as proud as Nebuchadnezzar*, recorded in 1526. Since then the *devil*, *Beelzebub*, *Scratch*, *Satan* and even the *Prince of Darkness* have also been used in this phrase equating pride with evil.

Prussian; Prussian blue; prussiate; prussic acid. Since the Franco-Prussian War of 1870, when Prussia's militarism came into full flower, *Prussian* has been a synonym for arrogant, overbearing, cruel, and excessively military. *Prussian blue*, however, has nothing to do with the military, merely having been discovered by the Prussian chemist Diesbach in 1704. It is a color ranging from moderate to deep greenish blue used in painting and fabric printing. A *prussiate* is a ferricyanide or ferrocyanide, which the color was made from, while *prussic acid* (hydrocyanic acid) is made from *Prussian blue*. Prussian blue is sometimes called Berlin blue, after its place of discovery.

P.S. *P.S.*, first recorded in 1757, is an abbreviation always used in place of the Latin *post scriptum* (Latin *post* "after" + *scribere*, "to write"), meaning postscript, an afterthought added after the signature in a letter. One family is said to have named its fourteenth child *Finis*. A problem arose when another child came along, but it was solved by naming the fifteenth *P.S.*

pshaw. Used since the 16th century and called "a natural expression of rejection" by the *O.E.D.*, this exclamation of impatience or contempt is usually pronounced *shaw*, though I often heard it spoken as *shah* when people still employed it. Oscar Wilde once asked George Bernard Shaw what title he'd give to a magazine he proposed starting. "I'd want to impress my own personality on the public," Shaw replied, banging his fist on the table. "I'd call it *Shaw's Magazine*: Shaw-Shaw-Shaw!" "Yes," Wilde said, "and how would you spell it?"

PT boat. PT boats were prompted by Prohibition rather than war. The little boats were originally used by rumrunners because they could outspeed the Coast Guard cutters of the day. Their inventor submitted their design to the Navy during World War II and they were introduced as *Patrol Torpedo* boats, although their size and annoyance to the enemy caused them to be dubbed *mosquito boats* as well.

Ptolemaic system. Before Copernicus scientists believed that the earth was the stationary center of the universe, a philosophy espousing the snug, smug little world where the sun, planets, and stars moved benignly around us. This theory, the *Ptolemaic system*, was essentially that of Ptolemy, an Alexandrine astronomer who lived from about A.D. 100 to 170. Claudius Ptolemaeus took his name from the Ptolemaic dynasty of Egypt, which reigned from the late fourth to the first century

B.C. His famous work the *Almagest*, thirteen books compiling his own and other astronomical findings, set forth the *Ptolemaic theory*. Nothing reliable is known about the great astronomer, geographer, and mathematician aside from his work, which included his famous *Geography*. His *Ptolemaic system* remained virtually unchanged and unchallenged until the heliocentric system advocated by Copernicus and Kepler replaced it in the 16th century. (*See* **Copernican**.)

the public be damned.   In 1882 a reporter asked William Henry Vanderbilt why the New York Central Railroad had continued to run a high-speed train from New York City to Chicago despite the fact that it was losing money. Commodore Vanderbilt told him he did it to compete with a similar Pennsylvania Railroad train. Wouldn't you run it just for the benefit of the public, competition aside, the reporter continued, and Vanderbilt roared the classic reply that has unfortunately become associated with big business ever since: "*The public be damned!* Railroads are not run on sentiment but on business principles."

puckish.   The mischievous or impish are called *puckish* after the sprite in Shakespeare's *A Midsummer Night's Dream*, Shakespeare coining the proper name Puck from *puck*, for "a malicious demon," but creating a character far more merry and attractive. It is Puck who speaks Shakespeare's immortal line: "Lord, what fools these mortals be!"

pudder.   (*See* **gobbledygook**.)

puffery.   In his play *The Critic* (1779) English dramatist Richard Sheridan created a cast of characters including the bogus, verbose critic and author Mr. Puff. Sheridan named Mr. Puff after the English word *puff*, meaning inflated, which is suggestive of the sound made by puffing wind from the mouth and was commonly applied to exaggerated newspaper ads at the time. But Mr. Puff added a new dimension to the word in Sheridan's satire of the malignant literary criticism of the day. Puff talks with the spiteful critics Dangle and Sneer about the absurd, bombastic "tragedy" he has written called *The Spanish Armada*, pushing his play all the while, for he has reduced the art of *puffery* to a science. At one time he even catalogs the puff: "Yes, the puff preliminary, the puff collateral, the puff collusive and the puff oblique, or puff by implication. These all assume, as circumstances require, the various forms of letter to the editor, occasional anecdote, impartial critique, observation from correspondent, or advertisement from the party." So absurdly does Mr. Puff overpraise or blow up his work that his name entered the language in the form of *puffery* as a word for the kind of criticism produced by literary cliques, the mutual back-scratching or logrolling that is usually subtler, but still as common today among the

Sneers and Smears of literature as it was in Sheridan's time. Thanks to Mr. Puff we also have a synonym for a *blurb* (*q.v.*).

Puget Sound.   (*See* **Vancouver**.)

pug-nosed.   People with short snub noses are called pug-nosed because their proboscises resemble those of apes or a breed of dogs. In the 17th century, *pug*, which derives from *puck*, a term of endearment, was a pet name for both apes and a popular type of short-haired dog. Both apes and the pug dog have blunt noses with wide bases that slope upward, which inspired some wag to dub similar human noses pug noses. Students of physiognomy believed that a pug nose was an indication of weakness; even Emerson wrote that "a squint, a pug-nose, mats of hair . . . betray character." In fact, Charles Darwin had a snub nose and Captain Fitzhugh of the *Beagle*, a devotee of the "science," almost didn't hire him as the ship's naturalist because a snub nose was supposed to indicate a lack of energy or determination.

pukka.   Also spelled *pucka*, and rhyming with luck-a, *pukka* derives from the Hindu word *pokka*, meaning "cooked, ripe, mature." The English brought it home from India in the late 17th century and the word has since become a workhorse adjective meaning genuine, good, substantial, permanent, reliable, and conventional.

Pulitzer Prize.   Hungarian-born Joseph Pulitzer was persuaded to immigrate to America by an agent who recruited him for the Union Army in 1864. After serving until his discharge a year later, he settled in St. Louis, where he founded the *St. Louis Post-Dispatch* in 1878. But when his chief editorial aide, Col. John A. Cockerell, shot and killed Col. Alonzo Slayback during a bitter political quarrel, Pulitzer left his paper and moved to New York, where he founded the *New York World* in 1883. He proceeded to become a congressman and make his paper among the best in the world, despite the fact that he went blind at age forty. A liberal, crusading newspaper, the *World* did much to raise the standards of American journalism, employing many of the greatest reporters and columnists of the day. Absorbed by the Scripps-Howard chain in 1931, it was eventually merged out of existence. When Pulitzer died in 1911, aged sixty-four, his will provided a fund to Columbia University, where he had established and endowed the school of journalism, which has been used since 1917 to give annual monetary awards for writing. Prizes in journalism are $1,000 each for local, national, and international reporting; editorial writing; news photography; cartooning; and meritorious public service performed by an individual newspaper. There are also six prizes of $500 for music, first awarded in 1943, and four traveling scholarships.

pull a boner. "Mistah Bones" in American minstrel shows was the end man in the line who rhythmically played a pair of bones, originally polished rib bones from an animal. It is said that "Mistah Interlocutor," the middle man in the line, fired questions at him designed to evoke ridiculous or stupid answers, which became known as *pulling boners.* This is possible, or *to pull a boner* may simply derive from the older American term "a bone-head," a stupid error, slang since about 1860. There is no connection between the Americanism of about sixty years duration and the British expression *a boner,* a sharp blow on the spine that dates back about a century and a half, or *boner,* slang for an erection.

to pull a fast one. *Pull* has been slang for "to engineer a deception" for well over a century, but the expression *to pull a fast one,* "to put over a trick or clever swindle," goes back to only about 1938. Baseball seems the obvious source—a pitcher coming in hard with a fast ball after throwing a lot of "junk." The nod has to go to "fast-bowling at cricket," however, as the expression is first recorded in England.

pullet. (*See* **pony**.)

Pullman car. Abraham Lincoln's assassination made the Pullman sleeping car a reality. George Mortimer Pullman (1831-97), a cabinetmaker, had experimented in building much-needed railway sleeping cars just before the Civil War but couldn't sell his idea, even though he had made a successful test run with two converted coaches. In 1863 he invested $20,000, every penny he had, in a luxurious sleeping car called the Pioneer that he and his friend Ben Field built on the site of the present-day Chicago Union Station. But the Pioneer, unfortunately, was too wide to pass through existing stations and too high to pass under bridges. For two years it lay on a siding, a well-appointed waste, until President Lincoln was assassinated in 1865. Every area through which Lincoln's black-creped funeral train passed brought out it's finest equipment, and Illinois, the Rail Splitter's birthplace, could be no exception. The Pullman Pioneer was the best that the state had, and Illinois spared no expense in promptly cutting down station platforms and raising bridges so that the luxurious car could join the presidential funeral train in its run from Chicago to Springfield. The funeral party traveling in the Pioneer was greatly impressed by the car. As a result, the Michigan Central cleared the line for the big car and other railroads around the country began to follow suit. Pullman soon went into partnership with Andrew Carnegie in the Pullman Palace Car Company and his sleeping cars, or Pullmans, eventually made him a millionaire many times over.

to pull one's leg. (*See* **you're pulling my leg**.)

to pull out all the stops. An organist who pulled out all the stops—levers used to change the sound of the instrument—would be giving his all, the meaning of this phrase. Though the organ, or its rude prototype, originated in Greece, the expression deriving from it dates back to 19th-century England.

to pull strings. This expression was inspired by puppet masters of days past, who manipulated strings or wires on their marionettes from behind a curtain. Unseen, they completely controlled the actions of their puppets, so in the mid-19th century *pulling the strings* or *wires* came to mean controlling the affairs of humans from a distance as if they were puppets.

to pull the wool over his eyes. Most investigations of this expression trace it to the huge wigs that were the fashion in the early 19th century, when *wool* was a joking term for hair. Judges often wore these poor-fitting wigs, which frequently slipped over the eyes, and it may have been that a clever lawyer who tricked a judge bragged about his deception by saying that he *pulled the wool over his eyes.* Or purse-snatchers may have pulled down the wigs of gentlemen to make it easier to snatch their purses while they stumbled about. The actual source is really unknown and although the expression is first recorded in America (1839), it is thought to be of older, English origin.

pull up stakes. These stakes are boundary stakes, not the circus tent stakes that are pulled up when a circus moves to another town. The expression goes back at least to 1640 in America, where settlers who wanted better land than had been given them simply *pulled up their boundary stakes* and moved on to another location, resetting the stakes there.

puma. *Puma* is the Inca name for the American feline *Felix concolor,* also called the cougar, the jaguar, and even, rarely, the South American lion. This word for the big cat was brought back from the Andes by the Spanish conquistador Pizarro in the 1530s.

pumice. *Pumice* is a porous, spongy form of volcanic glass used as an abrasive or polish; there is an entire mountain of it on the island of Lipari. In 1645 one writer reported that "Italians to this day have the habit of pumicing their skin to get off the hair." *Pumice* comes from the Latin *Pumex,* for the substance, while *pounce,* "a fine powder formerly used to blot ink on paper," comes from the same source.

pumpernickel. When in Germany, Napoleon's groom was supposedly offered a slice of coarse, dark rye bread and indignantly refused it, saying that it was fit only for the Emperor's horse, Nickel. "*C'est du pain pour Nickel*," the gourmet groom protested ("It is bread for Nickel"), and *pain pour Nickel* stuck as the name for the bread. But scholars don't appreciate this ingenious story that has the German bread named after a horse, though for once they do offer an interesting tale in exchange. *Webster's* and other authorities derive *pumpernickel* from the German *pumpern* ("to break wind") and *Nickel* ("a goblin or the devil"), inferring that *pumpernickel* is so named because it made people who eat it "break wind like the devil."

pumpkin. The pumpkin didn't get its name because it looks "pumped up" into a balloon shape. *Pumpkin* probably comes from the Greek *pepon*, "a kind of melon," literally "a fruit cooked by the sun." *Pepon* became the Middle French *ponon*, which became the English *pompion*, to which the diminutive suffix *kin* was finally added. Another example of the many words formed from mispronunciations of foreign words.

pumpkin head. (*See* **sap**.)

pumpkinification. Seneca is said to have written a satire on the deification of the Roman emperor Claudius Caesar, which he called *Apocolocyntosis*, coined from the Greek word for pumpkin and meaning "pumpkinification." *Pumpkinification*, suggesting a swollen head the size of a pumpkin and "pumped up" has meant pompous behavior or absurd glorification since at least the mid-19th century, when a British writer called attention to Seneca's satire.

Punch. Legend has it that our beverage *punch* derives from the Hindi *panch*, "five," because it originally had five ingredients: arrack, tea, lemon, sugar, and water. More likely the word comes from the *puncheon*, or large cask, from which *grog* (*q.v.*) was served to sailors in the East India trade. In any event, the Indian beverage was a great favorite with sailors and was brought back to England in the late 1600s.

Punch and Judy. (*See* **proud as Punch**.)

punch drunk. Brain damage in boxers resulting from repeated blows to the head produces many symptoms, the most common being poor coordination, slurred speech, mental deterioration, and a broad-based gait. Old, very impaired fighters suffering this combination of effects were given the name *punch drunk* by Dr. Harrison S. Martland in a 1928 article in the *Journal of the American Medical Association*. However, Dr. Martland probably did not coin the term, as *punch drunk* is recorded in America as early as 1915. In the early 1940s *punchy* began to supplant *punch drunk*.

Punch's advice. *Punch's advice* derives from the most famous joke of the British humor magazine *Punch*. The magazine announced that it would send advice to those about to marry; the advice turned out to be: "Don't."

punchy. (*See* **punch drunk**.)

pupa. The great naturalist Linnaeus coined this technical term for "an insect in the third and usually quiescent state preceding that of the perfect insect." *Pupa* comes from the Latin *pupa*, "little girl or doll." The coinage has been called "a stroke of poetic genius," one writer noting: "If you look at the underside of a moth's pupa [you will] see the shape of its face, eyes and embryonic wings like little arms, all wrapped as if in swaddling clothes which emphasize its likeness to a doll." (*See* **larva**.)

pupil. The smallness of the mirror images seen on the pupil of the eye led to the pupil being named after the Latin *pupilla*, "little girl." Our word *pupil*, for "a student," comes from the Latin *pupulus*, or "little boy," most pupils in days past having been little boys.

purdah. *Purdah* (which derives from the Hindu *pardah*, "curtain") is the Islamic custom of secluding women from the sight of all men except close relatives. It is still practiced by many Muslim women, who conceal themselves completely from onlookers when they go out into the street by wearing the *burqa*, an ankle-length garment with slits for eyes.

puritan. The *Puritans* were originally members of a mid-16th-century Protestant reformation group that wanted to rid the English Church of all traces of Roman Catholicism. Their name means "pure of heart" and a *Puritan* was first defined as "an advanced reformer in the Anglican Church." In time their theology became *Calvinist* (*q.v.*), however, and many of them were driven into exile with the accession of James I in England. Immigrating to America, they composed the bulk of the population of Plymouth Colony, Massachusetts and Connecticut. Noted for industry and intellectual intensity, among other fine qualities, they were even more noticeable for their strict morality and absolute reliance on Scripture. It was these latter qualities, often carried to fantastic extremes, that made *puritan* a synonym for a narrow-minded, excessively religious person blind to the beauty around him.

Purple Heart. George Washington originated the medal called the *Purple Heart* during the Revolutionary War. His order in 1782 explained that "the General, ever desirous to cherish virtuous ambition in his soldiers, as well as to foster and encourage every species of military merit, directs that whenever any singularly meritorious action is performed, the author of it shall be permitted to wear over the left breast, the figure of a heart in purple cloth, or silk, edged with narrow lace or binding." Originally given for "meritorious action," and awarded to three or four Revolutionary War soldiers, it is now granted for battle wounds.

purple prose. This term for ornate, overexaggerated writing has a long history. The Roman poet Horace said that all purple patches (*purpureus pannus*) should be deleted from literary works and should be put away for eight years before being reedited and published—for they could never again be recalled except by time.

pushover. (See **high hat**.)

push (hit) the panic button. Of the many panic buttons that could be the source of this expression, meaning "to act in unnecessary haste or panic," the original appears to be the bell system used for bailouts and ditchings in World War II bombers such as the B-17 and B-24. Often extensive damage to a plane was hard to determine and pilots sometimes pushed the button activating the bell system too soon, causing their crews to bail out unnecessarily when there was only minor damage to the aircraft. The expression is sometimes used today to demand that a job be completed rapidly and well.

puss. Irish immigrants apparently introduced *puss* to America in the early 1880s, the slang word deriving from the Gaelic *pus*, "mouth." Not long after the expression *to make a puss*, "to pout," became part of our vocabulary.

to pussyfoot. Teddy Roosevelt seems to have either coined or popularized *pussyfoot* in about 1905. Meaning crafty, cunning, or moving in a cautious manner, it refers to the way cats can walk stealthily by drawing in their claws and walking on the pads of their feet. It's very unlikely that the redoubtable William Eugene "Pussyfoot" Johnson, a crusading American do-gooder, has anything to do with the expression. Johnson was nicknamed "Pussyfoot" because "of his cat-like policies in pursuing lawbreakers" when he served as chief special officer in the Indian Territory. Later his nickname, in the form of *pussyfooters*, was applied to all advocates of Prohibition. While crusading in England, fresh from his triumph of securing the passing of Prohibition here, Johnson was blinded by a stone thrown by a crusading drunk.

put all your eggs in one basket. (See **egg phrases**.)

to put a sock in it. Seldom heard anymore, this phrase goes back to the days of early phonographs, first invented by Thomas Edison in 1877. The first phonographs had no form of volume control and in order to hold the volume down, teenagers were told to put a sock in the horn to mute the sound. *To put a sock in it* came generally to mean "to stop anyone from talking to much or too loudly."

putative. The fictional author of a work, a character to which the author assigns its authorship, a *putative author* almost always narrates the story and pretends to have written it. *Putative* comes from the Latin for "to think," which suggests that the term arose in the mid-19th century, because the narrator and his readers really think he wrote the book. *Putative marriage*, for an illegal marriage but one made in good faith, is first recorded early in the 19th century.

to put in a good word for someone. To say something favorable about someone, often to help that person obtain a job or some other benefit. *Good word* in this sense is hardly modern slang, dating back to the late 12th century.

to put in one's two cents' worth. The oldest recorded use I can find for this American phrase, which means to interfere or meddle, to butt into a conversation, dates back to only 1945, but it must be much older. The similar British saying, "to put one's oar in another's boat," dates to at least 1500, and the similar but little-known "to come in with one's five eggs" is two or three centuries old.

put one's best foot forward. The *best foot* in the common phrase is the right foot, it having been considered unlucky by the ancients to begin any journey or enterprise with the left foot; many English brides, for example, still put the right foot forward first when they enter the church.

to put (lay) one's finger upon. Sherlock Holmes *seems* to be the first person to have used *to lay one's finger upon*, "to indicate with precision," in Sir Arthur Conan Doyle's *The Memoirs of Sherlock Holmes* (1895): "You lay your finger upon the one point . . ." But a little sleuthing reveals that the expression had been used at least five years earlier as *to put one's finger upon*, in reference to a physician (not Dr. Watson) discovering the cause of an illness.

to put one's foot in it. (See **put your foot in it**.)

to put one's foot in one's mouth. *Every time he opens his mouth he puts his foot in it* is first recorded in the 1770s, when it was said of Dublin politician Sir Boyle Roche, who made remarks in his speeches like: "Half the lies our opponents tell about me are not true!" The expression was probably suggested by the earlier *to put one's foot in it*, possibly suggested by someone stepping in cow flops or something else foul.

to put one's oar in another's boat. (See **to put in one's two cents' worth**.)

put on the spot. The ace of spades is a symbol of death to the superstitious in many lands; in recent times Vietcong soldiers were so afraid of it that American planes "bombed" their strongholds with thousands of the cards to demoralize them. The expression *put on the spot* has its origins in this superstition, which probably derives from the old practice among pirates of sending the ace of spades, which has one printed "spot" in the middle, as a death threat to an informer or coward they intended to kill. Anyone who was sent the ace of spades was *put on the spot*, "in a dangerous position, slated to die." American criminals perpetrated the expression, giving it wide currency, and early in this century it took on a less sinister meaning—though someone *on the spot* is still someone in danger of great failure or embarrassment if he doesn't produce successful results within a short time.

to put the cart before the horse. When Cicero said these words in 61 B.C. they were already proverbial. Actually, their Latin version, literally translated, means "the plow draws the ox in reversed position," but it conveys the same idea, that is, to get things in the reverse order. The Roman proverb was first translated into English in 1279, and over the years the ox became a horse and the plow a cart. The proverb is ancient in French, German, and Italian as well as English. *Preposterous* conveys a similar idea. It is from the Latin *prae*, "before," and *posterus*, "after," and freely translated means "the before coming after," which suggests its meaning of "nonsensical or absurd." By the way, sometimes carts *were* legitimately put before horses, as when horses pushed empty carts into coal mines.

to be put through the mill. Someone *put through the mill* gets rough treatment like the grain that is ground under millstones in a water mill. This is one of numerous old expressions deriving from the milling of grain. Another is the term *to mill about, (q.v.)* Still another is the proverb *much water runs by the mill that the miller knows not of*: many things happen right before us about which we know nothing.

putting on the dog. Lap dogs were all the rage among the new rich in America shortly after the Civil War, especially King Charles and Blenheim spaniels, rather imperious-looking dogs to the common man and certainly very distant relatives sociologically of the average American mutt, who had to work or scrounge for his supper. These snooty dogs being pampered by their snooty owners probably inspired the expression *putting on the dog*, "showing off," which apparently arose in the 1860s as college slang at Yale University. Attempts to derive *put on the dog* from the older *put on side* all seem strained. The reasoning behind the latter is that dogs "show off" by arching out one side while moving their feet in intricate maneuvers.

put to the pale. (*See* **beyond the pale.**)

put up your dukes. *Dukes*, for "fists," probably honors the Duke of York, Frederick Augustus (1763-1820), the second son of England's George III. A total loss as commander-in-chief of the Army, Frederick was nevertheless popular among his subjects. As he had once dueled in public with the future duke of Richmond, his name was associated with fighting, and being an ardent sportsman, he was often seen at the racetrack and prize ring. Possibly this led boxers to nickname their fists *Dukes of York*, the phrase finally shortened to *dukes* and expressions like *put up your dukes*, "let's fight," becoming common. Or else *Duke of Yorks*, Cockney rhyming slang for "forks," was associated with fingers, then hands, and finally fist, or *dukes*—with the Duke of York somewhere in mind. Another even more ingenious explanation has it that noses were called *Dukes* because the Duke of Wellington's nose was big—fists therefore being dubbed *Duke busters*, which ultimately became *dukes*. The Duke may have been immortalized in the language, but he ended his career in disgrace when his mistress admitted to taking bribes with his permission. To save face, he had to pension her off so that she wouldn't publish his love letters.

put your foot in it. The old proverb "The Bishop hath put his foot in it" led to the common expression, *Now you've put your foot in it*. Bishop is, of course, usually an honorific, but the original proverb, used when soup was scorched, may have arisen because of the reputation of a certain bishop or bishops for burning heretics. An alternate explanation is that the saying arose when an anonymous cook stood at the window watching a procession headed by a noted bishop and blamed him for the port soup she burned.

put your shoulder to the wheel. This expression refers to someone literally *putting his shoulder to the wheel* and pushing a cart out of the mud, as was so common on roads everywhere in the days before macadam. The expression goes back at least to Elizabethan times, when it probably was proverbial in the form of *Lay your shoulder to the wheel and push the oxen*.

Pyrrhic victory. After he defeated the Romans at the battle of Asculum in 279 B.C., losing the flower of his army in the action, King Pyrrhus remarked, "One more such victory and we are lost." Other versions of his immortal words are, "One more victory and I am undone," and "Another such victory and I must return to Epirus alone." Pyrrhus had come to Italy with 25,000 troops two years before when Tarentum asked him to help organize resistance against the Romans, but after Asculum and several other battles he returned to the kingdom of

Epirus in northwest Greece with only 8,000 men. The great warrior, a second cousin of Alexander the Great, never did live to revive the Conqueror's empire as he had hoped. He died in 272 B.C, aged forty-six, during a night skirmish in a street in Argos—fatally struck by a tile that fell from a roof—his name only commemorated by the phrase *Pyrrhic victory*, a victory in which the losses are so ruinous that it is no victory at all.

pyrzqxgl. *Pyrzqxgl* plays a rather important role in American fantasy, being the magic word coined by Frank L. Baum in *The Wizard of Oz* (1900).

python. Python derives from the Greek verb meaning "to rot," not a likely source for the name of the largest living snake next to the anaconda. The first python was a huge serpent slain near Delphi by Apollo, and the monster rotted in the sun after it died. The name of the mythological serpent wasn't given to real snakes until 1836, though it had been applied in English to other mythical monsters two centuries before this.

Q

Q. *Q*, developed from Latin, never appears at the end of a word and is almost always followed by *u* in English, though there are transliterated Arabic words offering exceptions: the Arabian sheikdom Qatar, for example, and *qaf*, the twenty-first letter of the Arabic alphabet. Another exception is *Qvoens*, "queens," which early Finns called themselves, leading some ancient European geographers to believe that a race of Amazons lived in northern Europe. Contractions like *Q-boat* (*q.v.*) and abbreviations like *q.v.* don't count. (*See also* **cue**.)

Q-boats. These British warships disguised as merchant ships destroyed many a German U-boat during World War II. "Panic parties," men who abandoned ship when fired upon, were launched by these decoys, tempting the U-boats to come closer so that concealed guns manned by hidden crews could blast them out of the water. They took their name from an abbreviation of the Latin *quaere* "inquire" (which the U-boats did). *Q-boats* were also called *hush-hush* ships and *mystery ships*.

Q.T. A British broadside ballad (1870) contained the line "Whatever I tell you is on the Q.T." This is the first record of *Q.T.* for "on the quiet, in confidence" recorded in English, but no one has established whether the broadside's anonymous author was the first person to use the initials *Q.T.* to stand for quiet. *On the Q.T.* gained more popularity when it appeared in an 1891 minstrel show number called "Ta-ra-ra-boom-de-ay." London "went stark mad over the refrain," which was written by Henry J. Sayers and sung by Lottie Collins. The first stanza follows:

> A sweet Tuxedo girl you see,
> Queen of swell society,
> Fond of fun as fun can be
> When its on the strict Q.T.
> I'm not too young, I'm not too old,
> Not too timid, not too bold,
> Just the kind of sport I'm told—
> Ta-ra-ra-boom-de-ay . . .

If you or your children grew up with "Howdy Doody," you'll notice the similarity between "Ta-ra-ra-boom-de-ay" and Howdy's theme song.

quack. *Quack* is an abbreviation of the 16th-century word *quacksalver*, which meant an ignorant charlatan who peddled nostrums and cure-all medicines in the street, the word deriving from the *quack* sound a duck makes and *salve*, "medicine or ointment." In America quacks were called *medicine men*, after the Indian medicine men, as early as 1830. It might be said that the most famous of American fortunes began with a medicine man, or quack, as John D. Rockefeller's father, William, would be called today. "Dr." Rockefeller was one of the traveling medicine men who put on minstrel shows to sell their wares.

quackgrass. *Agrapyron repens* and the other weedy grasses called *quackgrass* are not so named because ducks like them or because they are used by quacks like medicine men. *Quackgrass*, an Americanism first recorded in 1817, derives from the older British word, *quitchgrass*, *quitch* being an old form of "quick" and *quitchgrass* being a very quick grower and insidious spreader into places where it is not wanted. Other names for *quackgrass* include *quatchgrass*, *twitchgrass*, *couchgrass*, *couch*, and *quitch*.

quadrant. Used in astronomy and navigation since its development centuries ago, the *quadrant* is an instrument properly having the form of a graduated quarter circle that is used for making angular measurements, especially for taking latitudes in navigation. It takes its name from the Latin *quadrant*, "fourth part," or quarter.

quadrille. This five-part square dance for four couples is of French origin, but takes its name from the Spanish *cuadrilla*, "company or troop of soldiers," which is a diminutive of the Latin *quadra*, "square." *Quadrille* was first applied to one of four groups of horsemen taking part in a tournament, but by 1773 was being used to describe the four-couple dance that became so popular in the American South.

quaff. The obsolete German word *quassen*, meaning the same, probably gives us our to *quaff*, "to drink heartily." The word is spelled wrong (*quaff* instead of *quass*) because "the long *s*'s—in print exactly like *f*'s without the cross-stroke—were mistaken for *f*'s" at some unknown date.

quagmired. Hopelessly entangled in a terrible mess, bogged down. A *quagmire*, the word first recorded in 1579, is ground that appears firm but is really jellylike and swallows anyone who steps upon it. The *quag* in the word is a variant of *quake*, "to shake," while *mire* means "muddy land."

Quai d'Orsay. (*See d'Orsay pump.*)

to quail. *To quail,* "to cower, to lose heart in danger or difficulty," is of no relation etymologically to the bird called a quail. Of uncertain origin, it may come from the Middle English *fael,* meaning the same, or from the Latin *coagulau,* "to curdle," which also gives us *coagulate.* *Quail* has been American slang for a sexually attractive girl since the mid-19th century and may derive from the Celtic *caile,* "a girl." However, *quail* meant a harlot or courtesan in the 16th and 17th centuries, because of the bird's supposed "inordinately amorous disposition." The term was used by Shakespeare in *Troilus and Cressida.* The Bard would have liked the alliterative *San Quentin quail*: a U.S. slang term of the 1930s meaning a sexually attractive but underage girl, one who is *jailbait* for any man who consorts with her, who can put a man in San Quentin prison. The bird's name *quail* is probably of Teutonic derivation and imitative origin.

Quaker. The religious Quaker group was founded by George Fox in 1650 as the Society of Friends, but readily accepted the name Quakers derisively bestowed upon them because they bade people to "quake and tremble at the word of the Lord." George Fox claimed that he had spoken these words when being arraigned before Justice Bennet of Derby in 1650 and that the Judge sneeringly called him a *quaker,* but there are earlier references to the term. In one London letter dated October 14, 1647, for example, the writer observes, "I hear of a secte of woemen (they are at Southworke) come from beyond sea, called *Quakers,* and these swell, shiver and shake. . . ." It could well be, then, that the name derives from the trembling of Friends under the stress of religious emotion, which once caused them to "quake, and howl, and foam with their mouths." Despite intense persecution, the beliefs of the Quakers persisted and spread throughout England and America. The Quakers, incidentally, forsook the use of *you* because it was at the time the second-person pronoun employed when addressing superiors. The *thou* they chose in preference to *you* was used in the 17th century to address familiars or inferiors, affirming to them the equality of mankind.

Quaker guns. Fake or dummy guns on ships have long been called *Quaker guns* in allusion to the Quakers' opposition to war and killing. In 1830 an American naval officer wrote: "Our six iron six-pounders and six *quakers* (wooden guns), were, like millennial lion and lamb, lying down together in the hold."

quandary. Etymologists have long been in a quandary about the origins of *quandary,* "a state of perplexity, the difficulty causing it." The word is at least four centuries old. The French phrase *qu'en dirai-je?,* "What shall I say of it?," and Middle English *wandreth* have been con-

sidered as ancestors and rejected by the experts. *Grose* suggests "an Italian word signifying a conjurer's circle," without giving the word. The *O.E.D.* suggests "a corruption of a scholastic Latin phrase," perhaps *quam dare?* or *quando dare?*

quandong tree. *Quandong* is of interest because it is another Australian Aborigine word that has come intact into English, making it one of our most ancient words. The quandong tree is a sandalwood bearing blue berries the size of cherries whose kernel, or "nut," is edible. It is also called the *native peach* (tree).

quantum leap (jump). A *quantum leap,* or *jump,* is a sudden, dramatic change or increase. The term is borrowed from the physicist's field of quantum mechanics, where it refers to an abrupt transition from one energy state to another. *Quantum,* derives from the Latin *quantus,* "how much."

quarantine. People have been quarantined in the United States for every disease from measles to the dread bubonic plague. *Quarantine* itself ultimately derives from the Italian *quaranta,* "forty," in reference to the forty days that travelers from other countries were isolated during the Middle Ages if they had come from a plague-stricken country.

quark. Some scientists believe that quarks, three types of elementary particles, form the basis of all the matter in the universe. The word *quark* was applied to the particles by physicist W. Gell-Man, but he took it from a James Joyce coinage in *Finnegans Wake.* However, unlike Joyce's *quark,* which rhymes with *dark,* Gell-Man's *quark* is pronounced *quork.* There is no argument, as the coiner made this clear in a 1978 letter to the editor of the *O.E.D. Supplement, Volume III.*

quarry. The *quarry* is now the object of any chase—the deer in hunting, the bird flown at in falconry—but it once meant something entirely different. In the Middle Ages the quarry, the word deriving from the Latin *corium,* "skin," was the entrails of the deer placed on the animal's skin as a reward for the hounds after a hunt. Finally it came to mean what the hounds went after. The *quarry* in *stone quarry* derives from the Latin *quadrāia,* "The place where stone is squared," or cut into blocks.

quarter horses. *Quarter horses* are named for their ability to run well in quarter-mile races, not because of their size or lineage. The term is an Americanism, first recorded in 1834, though *quarter races* are mentioned a good fifty years earlier as being very popular in the South. Quarter horses, usually smaller than thoroughbred racehorses, were also called *quarter nags.*

quarter section. The Americanism *quarter section* of land was popularized by the Homestead Act of 1862, which said that any settler could have free 160 acres of public land if he could raise a crop on at least 40 acres of it for five years. The 160 acres equaled a quarter of a square mile and was commonly called a *quarter section* or *quarter*. The former term, however, had been used as early as 1804, and the latter as early as 1640.

quasar. An acronym composed of letters from *"quasi-stellar object" quasar* was coined by scientists in the 1960s to describe any of some 40 million celestial objects, up to ten billion light years distant from earth, which are powerful emitters of radio waves. Quasars are also called *quasi-stellar radio sources*. (*See* **quasar**.)

quassia; quassin. The Negro slave Graman Quassi gives his name to this genus of small trees. Quassi discovered the medicinal value of the bark and heartwood of a group of tropical trees common to the Dutch colony of Surinam in the South American Guianas. Using the drug he extracted to treat his fellow natives, he "came to be almost worshipped by some" and when his discovery was communicated to Linnaeus by C. G. Dahlberg in 1730, the botanist named the genus of trees in the slave's honor. (Quassia's name probably comes from the Ashanti dialect word *Kwasida*.) The drug he discovered is known as *Surinam quassi* today, and is effective against intestinal worms, as a tonic, and as an insecticide. The drug's chief constituent is the bitter *quassin*, which is extracted from the nearly white wood in minute quantities.

The Queen! *The Queen, God Bless her!*, frequently abbreviated to *the Queen*, is the Loyal Toast to Her Majesty's health often made in British naval wardrooms. It is customarily drunk while seated because King William IV, "The Sailor King," is said to have hit his head on a wardroom beam while rising to make the toast.

Queen Anne's lace. According to folklore, the wild carrot (*Daucus carota*) was named for Anne of Bohemia, who married England's Richard II in 1382. A ward of the queen, it seems, chose this herb's delicate flower as a tatting pattern. The little girl came to Anne's attention when she was found innocent of a childish prank and the queen discovered her pattern, which she liked so much that she gave the child permission to name it after her. *Queen Anne's lace* was later transferred to the wild carrot's flower and then to the herb itself. The plant used to be valued as a diuretic and stimulant. Its relative the cultivated carrot is botanically named *Daucus carota sativa*.

Queen Dick; queer as Dick's hatband. Oliver Cromwell's son Richard (1626-1712), who ineffectually ruled England as Protector after his father, had such effeminate ways that he was widely called *Queen Dick*. Whether he was a homosexual isn't known, but homosexuality certainly isn't alluded to in the expression *as queer as Dick's hatband*. This means as *queer*, or "strange," as Dick's *hatband*, or "crown," a crown on the head of such a weak, ineffectual person seeming incongruous or ridiculous to most of his subjects. Though several writers have associated "queer" with homosexual in the phrase, the slang *queer* for homosexual isn't recorded until the 1920s. (*See also* **tight as Dick's hatband**.)

Queen Mary's thistle. The national flower of Scotland was supposedly named for Mary, Queen of Scotts, after attendants presented her a basket of the flowers while she was imprisoned in Fotheringay Castle by England's Queen Elizabeth. Also called the *cotton thistle, Onopordon ancanthium* has a purple top and is covered with little threadlike white hairs.

Queensberry rules. (*See* **below the belt**.)

Queens County, N.Y. (*See* **Kings County**.)

the Queen's (or King's) peace. The *Queen's peace* is the peace or protection of all law-abiding British subjects, though in past times it applied only to those in the royal employ. The term is used in *Blackstone's Commentaries*.

the queen's taste. *To the queen's taste* means completely, thoroughly, utterly. The queen's taste, the most discriminating in the land, would demand the best, something completely or thoroughly done. No one has been able to connect any specific queen with this phrase, which is, oddly, an Americanism and not British in origin, dating back to the late 19th century.

Queen's weather. Queen Victoria was fortunate in having good weather most of the times she appeared in public. Her good luck led to the British expression *Queen's weather*, for "a fine day for a public occasion, an outing, a party, etc." First recorded in 1899, the phrase is probably twenty years or so older.

queer. The German *quer*, "oblique, adverse, perverse, wrongheaded," may be the source of *queer*, but the word is of uncertain origin. *Queer* is first recorded in 1508 with the meaning of strange, odd, or eccentric in appearance or character, taking on many other meanings over the years both in standard English and slang. (*See* **Queen Dick**.)

queer as a three-dollar bill. *Queer* has meant counterfeit money since at least 1810, but *queer as a three-dollar bill* is obviously an Americanism, there never having been an American three-dollar bill. The expression dates back to the 1920s and usually means anything strange, unusual, or suspicious, though it can also mean a homosexual.

queer as Dick's hatband.   (See **Queen Dick**.)

queer plunger.   *Queer plungers* were men who faked drowning in order to be "rescued" by their accomplices, who "carried them to the Humane Society, where they are rewarded by the society with a guinea each." The expression is first recorded in 1758. W. C. Fields did the same as a young man; he was hired by concessionaires to pretend that he was drowning so that crowds would gather and they would sell more food. He called himself a *drowner.*

Queer Street.   The *queer* in this phrase, meaning to be in financial trouble, comes from the word *query*, not from any real city street. The expression arose two centuries ago, when merchants commonly put a query, or question mark next to the names of customers whose financial solvency was dubious.

querencia.   Texans in the 19th century often used *querencia* to mean the places where a Longhorn was born, and there are tales of Longhorns persistently returning to such spots. But *querencia* also meant the place where anyone was born. The word derives from the Spanish *queren*, "to love."

question mark.   The question mark, interrogation mark, or interrogation point, one tradition has it, was formed from the first and last letters of the Latin *quaestio* ("a seeking") which was first contracted to *Q* and finally became *?.* Some authorities claim, however, that it originated as the Greek semicolon—upside down. Another kind of *question mark* is a butterfly (*Polygonia interrogationis*) with two silver spots shaped like a question mark under each wing.

queue up.   People "standing in (or on) line" in America are *queuing up* in Great Britain. The latter term is little heard in the U.S. and derives from the French word *queue*, for "pigtail or tail," which in turn comes from the Latin *cauda*, "tail."

quey calves are dear veal.   A *quey* is a female calf, that is, a valuable calf that will one day give milk. To kill such a calf for veal, or meat, would be foolish, which gives us this old saying similar to *killing the goose that lays the golden egg.*

quibble.   The obsolete English word *quib* probably derived from the Latin *quibus* "who, which," which appeared on many legal documents and came to be associated with odd quirks of the law. In any case, *quib* came to mean an ambiguous or petty argument and may be the source of *quibble*, meaning the same, as well as petty carping criticism. *Quibble* is first recorded in the 17th century.

quiche.   A *quiche* is a pie-like dish made of custard flavored with cheese, onion, bacon, or other ingredients that are baked in an unsweetened pastry shell. The word came into French from the German *Kuche*, "little cake," and seems to have been first recorded in English late in the 19th century.

quick.   *Quick*, spelled *cqicu* or *cwic*, originally meant "the presence of life," or "living" in Old English. Therefore, livestock was once called *quickstock*, "living stock," *quicksilver* was so named because it seemed alive, a *quick fence* was a living hedge of plants, the sensitive flesh under a fingernail was known as the *quick*, and a *quick wine* was a lively, sparkling one. The old use of the word also figures in several common phrases. A woman *quick with child* is carrying a baby that has begun to show signs of life, that is "kicking." *The quick and the dead* just meant the living and the dead before it acquired its present double meaning. As for *stung to the quick*, this simply means that a person is stung deeply in living tissue where it really hurts. Today's use of *quick* as "swift" probably derives from early train conductors telling people to "be quick" or "step lively." (See also **cut to the quick**.)

quick and the dead.   (See **cut to the quick**.)

quick as a wink.   First recorded 1825. Wink = 1/10 sec.

quick as greased lightning.   *Quick as greased lightning* is an Americanism dating from about the 1840s, but is a typical western exaggeration of the British *quick as lightning*, first recorded a hundred years earlier. *Quicker than hell can scorch a feather* is a similar Americanism from the mid-19th century.

quick as (or before) you can say Jack Robinson.   Jackie Robinson, the major leagues first black player, was one of the quickest base runners in baseball history, but he has nothing to do with the old expression *as quick as you can say Jack Robinson*. The phrase goes back to 18th-century England, where there may have been, as Francis *Grose* suggested, in *A Classical Dictionary of the Vulgar Tongue* (1795), a certain Jack Robinson who was in the habit of paying extraordinarily quick visits to his friends—and leaving even before his name could be announced by the butler. *Jack Robinson* was much more likely used in the phrase because it is easy to pronounce and is a very common name in England.

quick-change artist.   Early in this century American theatrical performers who changed costumes frequently during a performance, often because they played multiple roles, were called *quick-change artists*. The expression soon became applied to anyone adept at changing from one thing to another.

quicker than hell can scorch a feather. Davy Crockett is given credit for this Americanism, as well as for *singing psalms to a dead horse, ripsnorter, sockdollager,* and *fine as silk.* He did not of course coin *a Crockett,* for "a violent person," or *a sin to Davy Crockett,* "anything extraordinary."

quicker than you can cook asparagus. Some old-timers still call asparagus *grass,* from the homely expression *sparrow-grass* commonly used as a name for the vegetable over the last three centuries. Asparagus is a Latin word formed from the Greek for sprout or shoot. The Romans cultivated it as early as 200 B.C., growing some stalks at Ravenna that weighed a full three pounds and gathering stems in the Getulia plains of Africa that were actually twelve feet tall. The most flavorful "grass," however, is thin and tender and should be cooked in as little water and as rapidly as possible. Even the Romans knew this, and their Emperor Augustus originated the old saying, *Quicker than you can cook asparagus,* for anything he wanted done within a few moments. Asparagus has been regarded as a phallic symbol since earliest times, but this certainly isn't why perennial patches of it are called *beds,* which is just a common garden term. There is an interesting true story about blanched white asparagus, however. Reported a *New York Times* correspondent at a recent Bonn dinner party: "A certain guest complimented the elegant German hostess and said, 'This white asparagus is as beautiful as an undressed woman,' thereby probably becoming the first asparagus eater to have noted a resemblance between asparagus and the attributes of the *female* sex."

quickie. A *quickie* was originally late 1920s Hollywood slang for a Grade B movie, a film comparatively cheap and quick to produce. By the 1930s the term was being used to mean a quick act of sexual intercourse.

quicksilver. The Romans called this metallic element, mercury, by the name *argentum vivum,* "living silver" because of its liquid mobile form at ordinary temperatures. "Living silver" was translated as *quick silver* (*quick* meaning "living") into a number of languages, coming into English as *cuiceolfor* by about the year 1000.

quick time, march! A familiar U.S. Army command dating from the 19th century. It specifically means marching 120 paces of 30 inches per minute, but has come to mean any fast march in general use.

quick, Watson, the needle. (*See* **Sherlock Holmes**.)

quick with child. (*See* **cut to the quick**.)

quid. British slang today for a one-pound note and formerly meaning a sovereign or a guinea, *quid* is of uncertain origin. First recorded in Thomas Shadevell's *Squire of Alsatia* (1688) it may come from the Latin *quid,* "what," for "the wherewithal."

quiddity. *Quiddity* can mean the "essence of a thing, its essential nature," or be a "trifling subtle distinction in an argument." It was probably first used (though not recorded) in the former sense, deriving ultimately from the Latin *quid,* "what." But scholastics in the 16th century argued so much and so subtly about the *quiddity,* or essence, of things that *quiddity* came to mean a quibble as well.

quidnunc. A *quidnunc* is a busybody, a prying gossip who wants to know everything that's going on. The word is quite appropriately formed from the Latin *quid nunc?,* "what now?"—because such people constantly ask "What now?," "What's the news?," "What's happening?" Steele first records the term in a 1709 issue of the *Tatler.*

a quid of tobacco. Most authorities say that *quid,* for "a plug of tobacco," comes from the Old English *cuidu,* "cud," which makes sense except for the late date when it is first recorded (1727). One old story traces the word to 19th-century Dublin plug manufacturer and tobacconist Lundy Foot, who had the Latin *Quid rides?* ("What are you laughing at?") inscribed on his carriage. Most people who saw the inscription had no Latin and read the "witticism" as English: *Quid rides.* They figured that since Quid was riding, his product might as well be known by his name as well.

quid pro quo. *Quid pro quo,* Latin meaning "something for something," means in English "one thing in return for another, an equivalent, tit for tat, a Roland for an Oliver." Shakespeare used a similar expression in *Henry VI* (1591): "I cry you mercy, 'tis but Quid for Quo."

quietus. *Quietus* derives from the Latin *quietus est,* "he is quiet." The word originally applied only to the discharge of any financial account, or the settlement of obligation. But *quietus* came to apply to the discharge of life itself, as Shakespeare used it in Hamlet:

> Who would fardels [burdens] bear …
> When he himself might his quietus make
> With a bare bodkin [dagger]?

(*See* **bodkin**.)

qui-hy. The Hindi *Koi hai,* meaning "is anyone there?," is a cry used in India to summon a servant. These words, in the form of *qui-hy,* were used by the British when they occupied India to mean an Anglo-Indian, especially one living in Bengal. It also had some British military use in the sense of a summons to a servant.

quillet. A *quillet* is an evasion, the word probably deriving from the Latin *quidlibet*, "anything you choose." Wrote Shakespeare in *Love's Labour's Lost*: Oh, some authority how to proceed;/Some tricks, some quillets, how to cheat the *devil*.

quim. Henry Miller uses *quim* for "the female pudend, a woman's private parts" in several of his books. The term is first recorded in 1785 by *Grose*, who suggests that it may derive from the Spanish *quemar*, "to burn."

Quinapalus. In Shakespeare's *Twelfth Night* the clown invents a character called *Quinapalus* as the authority for a saying of his own. The name can thus be used for an apocryphal source, just as *Ben Trovato* (*q.v.*).

quince. *Quince* may come from the Greek *kydonion* ("melon"), named for Cydonia in Crete. *Kydonion* became *cydoneum* in Latin, this becoming *coin* in Old French, then *quoyne* in Middle English, with *quince* deriving from the plural of the Middle English *quoyne* which is *quine*.

quincunx. An old Roman coin of little value called the *Quincunx* had five dots or dashes on its face (one in each corner and one in the center), indicating that it was worth five-twelfths of an *as*. Any like arrangement of five objects, especially trees in a square or rectangle, is also called a *quincunx*, after the markings on the ancient coin.

quinine. (*See* **Cinchona**.)

quinsy. *Quinsy*, a suppurating (pus-producing) inflammation of the tonsils, or suppurative tonsilitis, comes to us from the Latin *quinancia*, which, in turn, derives from the Greek *kunanche*—which means, simply, "a sore throat." The Greek *kunanche* comes from *kuon anche*, "dog strangulation," because people suffering from the malady "throw open the mouth like dogs, especially mad dogs."

quintessence. Pythagorean alchemists, like everyone before and since, failed in their efforts to find a fifth element other than earth, air, fire, and water. But they *thought* that they had found this *quinta essentia*, or "fifth essence," in the form of ether, which they believed was the rarest and most pervasive of all the elements and formed the substance of the heavenly bodies. Since in a figurative sense fifth essences have been discovered, however, the word *quintessence* (from the Latin *quinta essentia*) means the most essential part or principle of a substance, the present form that can be extracted from it, the rarest distillation of a perfume or an idea.

quip. The best anyone can come up with for the origin of *quip* is that the word is a variant of *quippy*, also meaning a sharp, biting, or clever remark, and that *quippy* may come from the Latin *quippe* meaning "indeed, forsooth (with sarcastic force)." Both words are first attested to early in the 16th century.

the quip modest. Shakespeare seems to have invented this expression, which Touchstone defines in *As You Like It*, as "it was done to please myself." If a person was told that his beard was cut badly and he replied that he cut it to please himself, Touchstone says, this would be *the quip modest*, "six removes from the lie direct."

quirk of fate. A sudden twist or turn of fate, as in "He lost his fortune by a quirk of fate." The word *quirk* is of uncertain origin, but may have originally been an English western dialect word for a sudden flourish or curve in drawing or writing. It also came to mean a peculiarity in action or behavior (Shakespeare used it in this sense), and an evasion or quibble.

quirly. This odd Americanism had some currency into the early 20th century. It was originally a cigarette rolled in a corn shuck instead of paper, but came to be a cowboy word for any cigarette. Its origins are unknown.

quisling; quisle. Of the men and women whose names have become synonyms for traitor only Vidkun Quisling's has shed its capital letter in the dictionaries. A *quisling* is universal for "a traitorous puppet of the enemy" and was one of the most quickly adopted of modern additions to the language, even inspiring the little-used verb *quisle*, which means "to betray one's country." Maj. Vidkun Quisling (1887–1945) earned his rank in the Norwegian army, having served as military attaché in Russia and Finland. An ardent fascist, he formed the National Unity Party shortly after Hitler came to power in 1933, but never attracted more than a minuscule following, most Norwegians considering him mentally unbalanced. Then the Nazis invaded Norway on April 8-9, 1940, and the ridiculous lunatic of the right came into power. Brutally suppressing all opposition, he assumed King Haakon's throne in the palace and drove around in a bulletproof limousine presented to him by Hitler. A megalomaniac who ordered pictures of himself hung everywhere and refused to eat off anything but gold dishes, he was so paranoid that 150 bodyguards accompanied him at all times and every scrap of food he ate was sampled by someone else first. After the war, he was tried for treason, murder and theft, found guilty on all counts, and shot by a firing squad, Norway changing its law against capital punishment for this purpose.

Quisqualis. Like *Mahernia* (*q.v.*), the name of the plant genus *Quisqualis* is another joke played by the pioneer botanist Linnaeus. *Quisqualis*, the genus containing a few woody vines from Malaya and the Philippines, is grown today in southern Florida for its showy pink or red flowers. When Linnaeus examined the plant, he did not know how to classify it or for whom he could name it. He therefore called the genus *Quisqualis*, which in Latin means, literally, "who or what for." Although *Quisqualis* (kwis-kwal-is) is not eponymous, it clearly shows that the naming process is not always so serious a matter; it might even be called an anonymous eponymous word, or a word in want of an eponym. (*See* **mho**.)

quixotic. Don Quixote de la Mancha, the lofty-minded but impractical hero of Cervantes's novel of the same name (1605-15), gives us this adjective embodying his characteristics. One of the great characters of literature, Don Quixote wanders the world with his squire Sancho Panza and his horse Rosinante searching for adventures in which he can be chivalrous. When he tilted with his lance at windmills, imagining them to be enemies, he added still another expression of frustration to the languages of many nations. (*See* **tilt at windmills**.)

quiz. A short test. The tale may be apocryphal, but it's said that in the late 18th century Dublin theatre manager James Daly bet that he could invent and introduce a new meaningless word into the language almost overnight. He proceeded to pay Dublin urchins to chalk the word *quiz* on every wall in town. By morning almost all Dubliners had seen the word, and because no one knew what it meant, the meaningless *quiz* became the word for "a test of knowledge."

quoddy boat. *Quoddy boats*, double-ended keelboats with a gaff mainsail and sometimes a jib set on a detachable bowsprit, take their name from the Pasama*quoddy* Bay between New Brunswick, Canada and Maine, where they first were built. They were long used for lobstering and fishing along the Maine coast.

quonset hut. The *quonset* or *quonset hut* is a prefabricated corrugated metal building shaped like a tunnel that is named for its first place of manufacture, Quonset Point, Rhode Island, during World War II. Virtually the same thing by another name is the Nissen hut, designed by British engineer Lt. Col. Peter Nissen in 1930.

quotidian. Meaning "daily, or everyday, ordinary" *quotidian* is first recorded by John Wycliffe in about 1380. It came into English intact from Latin and can also mean, as a medical term, a certain fever that recurs daily.

R

R. Since Roman times *R* has been thought of as the "dog's letter," or the snarling letter, because its sound resembles the snarling of a dog—*r-r-r-r*. Ben Jonson, in his *English Grammar Made for the Benefit of All Strangers* (1636), put it this way: "R is the dog's letter, and hurreth in the sound; the tongue striking the inner palate, with a trembling about the teeth." Shakespeare has Juliet's nurse in *Romeo and Juliet* call *R* the *dog-name*, when she tells Romeo that his name and rosemary, an herb associated with weddings, both begin with an *R*. In parts of America, especially the Midwest, *R* is still pronounced as the dog letter, while in other regions, particularly parts of New England and the South, it is pronounced as *ah*.

rabbi. Meaning "my lord" or "master" in Hebrew, *rabbi* of course refers to a teacher and scholar of Jewish law who usually heads a synagogue or temple. In police jargon one's *rabbi* is a person who can help further one's career, the person so called because he has influence with higher-ups—just as a *rabbi* has influence with the ultimate higher-up.

rabbiteye blueberry. (*See* **rabbit tobacco.**)

rabbit tobacco; rabbiteye blueberry. *Rabbit tobacco*, or "rabbit terbarker," as Uncle Remus called it, is balsamweed, a plant used as a tobacco substitute by youngsters and others, despite its bad taste. It takes the name "rabbit" because it grows wild, often in fields where rabbits run. The *rabbiteye blueberry* is a blueberry bush native to the southern U.S. and widely grown there. It is so called because to some the berries on the tall (up to 20-foot-high) plants resemble rabbit eyes.

Rabelaisian. (*See* **Gargantua.**)

rachel. Discovered singing for pennies in the streets by the famous voice teacher Alexandre Choron, Élisa Felix, the daughter of poor Parisian peddlers, was trained for the stage and made her debut at the Comedie Francaise just before her seventeenth birthday. Élisa took the stage name Rachel, and her genius as a tragic actress, especially in the plays of Racine and Corneille, was acclaimed throughout Europe. "Rachel the immortal" ranks second only to Sarah Bernhardt among French actresses. While at the height of her fame in such roles as Phèdre in Racine's play of that name, the fawn-colored Rachel face powder, sometimes called *rachel* for short, was named in her

honor by a Parisian cosmetic specialist. On a visit to America Rachel contracted tuberculosis, which led to her death three years later, in 1858. She was only thirty-eight, her tragic last illness and death the theme of a poem by Matthew Arnold.

rack and ruin. A person gone to *rack and ruin*, "to destruction, utter destitution," may feel as though he's being stretched on the infamous rack, but the word *rack* in this centuries-old expression is only a misspelling of the word *wrack*. Even before Elizabethan times *wrack* was a variant form of *wreck*, and since the *w* in it is almost silent, writers took to spelling it *rack*. And so we have the phrase *rack and ruin*, which should really be *wreck and ruin*.

racket; racketeer. English pickpockets, once the best of the breed, invented the ploy of creating disturbances in the streets to distract their victims while they emptied their pockets. This practice was so common that a law was passed in 1697 forbidding the throwing of firecrackers and other devices causing a racket on the city streets. From the common pickpocket ploy the old onomatopoeic English word *racket*, imitative like *crack* or *bang* and meaning a disturbance or loud noise, took on its additional meaning of a scheme, a dodge, and illicit criminal activity. Before 1810, when it first appeared in print, the word had acquired this slang meaning in England, though it was later forgotten and the word *racket* for a criminal activity wasn't used again there until it was reintroduced from America along with the American Prohibition invention from it, *racketeer*. The only other, improbable, explanation given for the word is that it was originally the name of an ancient, crooked dice game.

rack one's brains. This phrase does have its origins in the *rack*, that old instrument of torture introduced into the Tower of London by the Duke of Exeter in 1470 and often called "Exeter's Daughter" at the time. The machine was called the *rack*, or *reck*, from the German *recken*, "to stretch or draw out," and was usually a wooden frame (adapted from those used in leather factories), with rollers at each end. The victim was fastened to the rollers by the wrists and ankles and the joints of his limbs were stretched by their rotation, sometimes until they were torn from their sockets. The rack was abolished in England by 1640, but its memory lived on in many vivid uses of the name. The powerful image of someone racking—stretching or straining—his brains or wits to find the answer to a question is found in the language as far back as 1583, at a time when the real rack was still being used.

radar; laser. These are among the most widely used and lasting of scientific acronyms. *Radar* was coined from *r*adio *d*etecting *a*nd *r*anging during World War II, while *laser* came after the war, from *l*ight *a*mplification by *s*timulated *e*mission of *r*adiation. The English alphabet can produce 456,976 acronyms composed of four letters and hundreds of thousands more if either additional or fewer letters are used. (*See* **quasar.**)

radish. The easy-to-grow *radish* (*Raphanus sativus*) takes its scientific name from its Greek name, *raphanes*, "easily reared." *Radish* itself comes ultimately from the Latin *radix*, "root." The French call the radish by the poetic name *rose of winter*, but the ancient Romans incorporated the word in some earthier phrases—their traditional punishment for sexual offenses such as adultery was the insertion of a large radish in the offender's anus.

Raffles; Raffles Hotel; Rafflesia. Naming the genus *Rafflesia* after English administrator Sir Thomas Stamford Bingley Raffles (1781-1826) could be interpreted as either a compliment or an insult. On the one hand, the species *Rafflesia arnoldi* has the largest single flower known to man—its bloom measuring up to six feet in diameter, three-quarters of an inch thick and attaining a weight of fifteen pounds. On the other hand this same bowl-shaped, mottled orange-brown-and-white flower is commonly called the *stinking corpse lily*. A parasite that grows on the roots of vines in its Malaysian habitat, only the plant's bloom is visible above ground, the rest being a fungus growing beneath it, and its smell of decaying flesh attracts the carrion flies that pollinate it. On balance it seems that Sir Stamford would have been better off if he had only had the world-famous *Raffles Hotel* in Singapore named for him, but since he discovered the plant genus, he really had no one to blame but himself; he should have kept quiet about it. Raffles gained no gratitude from the British powers that were, either. An able colonial administrator in the East Indies, he did much to suppress the slave trade, was conspicuous for his liberal treatment of his subjects, zealously collected much historical and zoological information, and secured the transfer of Singapore to the East India Company in 1819. But he was censured for freeing slaves, and after his death his wife had to pay the costs of his mission to found Singapore. *Raffles* for "a gentleman burglar" comes from the name of a suave character created by Australian writer Ernest W. Hornung in a collection of stories published in 1899.

ragged robin. This is the colorful name for *Lychnis Flos-cuculi*, also called the *cuckooflower*. Tennyson compares the flower to a pretty maid in ragged clothes in *Idylls of the King*. The genus name *Lychnis* comes from the Greek *lychnos*, "a lamp," in reference to the glowing flowers.

raglan sleeve. "I say, bring back my arm—the ring my wife gave me is on the finger!" Lord Raglan is supposed to have said something to this effect immediately after field surgery when surgeons cut off his badly wounded sword arm at the Battle of Waterloo. In any case, Fitzroy James Henry Somerset (1788-1855), first Baron Raglan, was renowned for his courage. Raglan served as aide-de-camp and secretary to the Duke of Wellington, whose niece he married, succeeding him on his death as commander of all British forces. During the Crimean War, Raglan was a familiar figure on the battlefields, dressed in his *raglan* overcoat, a loose-fitting coat with sleeves extending to the neck. The *raglan* had been named for him at about this time, and today the loose *raglan sleeve* is still a popular fashion. He died soon after the siege of Sevastopol, in which 1,500 British troops were lost, and his men blamed him for the rout. Raglan's doctors claimed he died of a broken heart; the official report cited cholera.

to railroad. Americans built railroads in a hurry in the 19th century, and the mountains, rivers, and forests that stood in their way as they crisscrossed the continent were unfortunately regarded as mere obstacles blocking the right of way. The speed with which lines were built and the railroad builders' disregard for anything in the way of "progress" inspired the term *to railroad* by the 1870s. At first it meant to send a person speedily to jail without a fair trial, or by framing him, and then it took on the additional meaning of rushing important legislation through Congress without regard for opposition to it and in disregard of regular procedures.

raining cats and dogs. A literal explanation for *raining cats and dogs* is that during heavy rains in 17th-century England some city streets became raging rivers of filth carrying many dead cats and dogs. The first printed use of the phrase does date to the 17th century, when English playwright Richard Brome wrote in *The City Witt* (1652): "It shall rain dogs and polecats." His use of "polecats" certainly suggests a less literal explanation, but no better theory has been offered. Other conjectures are that the hyperbole comes from a Greek saying, similar in sound, meaning "an unlikely occurrence," and that the phrase derives from a rare French word, *catadoupe* ("a waterfall"), which sounds a little like *cats and dogs*. It could also be that the expression was inspired by the fact that cats and dogs were closely associated with the rain and wind in northern mythology, dogs often being pictured as the attendants of Odin, the storm god, while cats were believed to cause storms. Similar colloquial expressions include *it's raining pitchforks, darning needles, hammer handles,* and *chicken coops*.

raise cain. *Raising cain*, "to cause much trouble or a loud disturbance," is probably a synonym for "to raise the devil," for whom the biblical *Cain* was an early euphemism. The first recorded use of the expression, in a joke printed in the *St. Louis Pennant* in 1840, shows that it was well-known at the time: "Why have we every reason to believe that Adam and Eve were both rowdies? Because . . . they both raised Cain."

to raise hob. *Hob* was the nickname of Robin Goodfellow, the mischievous household spirit of English folklore. *To raise hob* has for centuries meant to act devilishly like him, to be mischievous.

raise Old Ned. (*See* **Old Ned.**)

RAM. (*See* **ROM and RAM.**)

Ramayana. (*See* **Mahabharata.**)

ramshackle. *Ramshackle* is one of the relatively few words Icelandic has contributed to English, if it does come from that language, as some scholars believe. *Ramskakkr*, "very twisted," is the possible Icelandic source for our word meaning "loosely made or held together, rickety, shaky," but there are other suspects, including *ranshacle*, "to wreck or destroy by plundering"—which would make something *ramshackled* "wrecked or destroyed by plundering." The word is first attested to in 1675.

R & R. In World War II, and during the Korean War, R & R meant a *rest* and *recuperation* leave, though in Korea it was extended to rear-echelon units as well as front-line outfits and the initials were generally thought to mean *rest* and *recreation*.

rara avis; rare bird. A rare person or thing, someone out of the ordinary, *rara avis* is the Latin for "a rare bird" and the expression was first used figuratively by the Roman satirist Juvenal. "A bird rarely seen on earth, and very like a black swan," Juvenal called one of his fellow Romans ("*Rara avis in terris nigroque simillima cygne*"). He chose a black swan for his comparison because black swans, native to Australia, were unknown at the time.

rasher of bacon. The *rasher* in this British term, sometimes heard in America, means a slice and probably didn't get its name because it is cooked *rashly* or "quickly." *Rasher* here is more likely a corruption of *rasure*, "a thin slice or shaving."

raspberry. Known to the Romans as the "Red Berry of Mount Ida" (hence the name of the British species *Rubus idaeus*), after Mount Ida in Greece, the *raspberry* probably takes its name from the English *rasp*, "to scrape

roughly," in reference to the thorned canes bearing the berries. First called the *raspis-berry* it has also been called a *brambleberry* and *hindberry*.

ratfink. (*See* **fink.**)

razorbacks. *Razorback hogs*, so named because of their ridged backs, were near-wild animals that weren't native to America and may have been descended from pigs brought here by the Spanish. Texans once held roundups of these slender, speedy animals, the boars of which could be very dangerous when cornered.

read between the lines. Cryptographers commonly used a code whereby the secret message in a letter or other document could be discerned only by reading its alternate lines. This practice, and possibly the use of invisible ink to write messages between the lines of a letter, suggested to *read between the lines*, which by 1865 meant to discern the underlying fact or intention in any document or action.

to read the riot act. If you were actually reading the Riot Act to someone, here's what you'd proclaim: "Our Sovereign Lord the King chargeth and commandeth all persons being assembled immediately to disperse themselves, and peaceably to depart to their habitations or to their lawful business, upon the pains contained in the act made in the first year of King George for preventing tumultuous and riotous assemblies. God save the King." This is the opening section of the Riot Act of 1714, which a justice of the peace or other authorized persons was required by the Riot Act itself to read to rioters. The "pains" or penalty, provided by the act was death, later changed to terms in prison ranging up to life. These were certainly severe penalties, much more severe than those a parent has in mind when threatening a child with punishment if he doesn't cease and desist from a certain activity. But our expression *to read the riot act*, "to severely scold or warn someone," is nonetheless an allusion to the real Riot Act of 1714, designed to control the English middle class and prevent sedition.

ream. Meaning a standard of paper, usually 500 sheets, *ream* comes from the Arabic *risma*, "a bundle of clothes." The explanation for this seemingly odd derivation stems from the fact that the Arabs learned from the Chinese how to make paper out of rags instead of papyrus and passed the technique and the word on to Europe.

Reaumur scale. René Antoine Ferchault de Réaumur (1683–1757) invented the Réaumur thermometer and the thermal scale (0° - 80°) on which it is based. Like the *Celsius scale* (*q.v.*) it was considered by some to be an improvement on Fahrenheit's invention seventeen years earlier, in 1714. Réaumur has been called "the Pliny of the eighteenth century." Both a physicist and naturalist, his versatility involved him in researches ranging from the expansion of fluids and gases to an exhaustive study of insects. The fluid under glass in his thermometer, unlike Fahrenheit's, was four-fifths alcohol and one-fifth water.

rebate.   A merchant who makes a *rebate* gives back part of the buyer's money. But *rebate* has taken a long, circuitous route to the meaning it has today. Once a sporting term, from falconry of all things, *rebate* meant "to bring back a bating hawk," that is, a hawk that has left its perch without being commanded to do so.

rebel yell; Texas yell.   A leading expert believes that the *rebel yell*, or *yalo*, originally used in combat in the Civil War and intended to strike terror into the hearts of the enemy, came from the Creek Indians, loosely combining "the turkey gobbler's cry with a series of yelps." The high-pitched, blood-chilling yell was borrowed by Texans and adopted for their *Texas yell*, but others say the Texans got their yell from the Comanche Indians. In any case, everyone agrees that the "Yah-hoo" or "Yaaaaaheee" of fiction writers sounds nothing like the rebel yell. Several experts believe it is a corruption of the Old English foxhunting cry *tally ho!*

record.   (**See** learn by heart.)

record album.   (*See* **album**.)

the Red Baron.   His name still comes up, in way of comparison, when the exploits of any combat pilot or daring flier are discussed. He was Baron Manfred von Richthofen (1892-1918), the top German ace who shot down 80 Allied planes in World War I until he was killed in combat. He was called *The Red Baron* (and the *Red Knight* and the *Bloody Red Baron*) not because of his red hair, or because he was a bloody killer, but because he flew a bright red Albatross biplane.

red dog.   Linebackers "hound" or "dog" the passer in a football *red dog*, crashing through the line to try to break up a play. When the tactic was invented in the 1960s, "red dog" was the signal if one linebacker was to try cracking the line, "blue dog" if two were to be used, and "green dog" if all three linebackers were to charge. Football fans, however, misused the terms and applied *red dog* to any rush through the offensive line, made by linebackers or linemen, and that is what the term means today. I've also heard it used outside of football for any rush on one person by a group of men.

red-haired villain.   As Rosalind says in *As You Like It*, "His very hair is of the dissembling color." Villains have frequently been depicted in fiction as redheads, perhaps due to the tradition that Judas Iscariot had red hair.

Redheads were once thought to be so deceitful that the fat of dead red-haired men was used as an ingredient in poisons and fish baits. Actually it's hard to think of many murderous, lying, or unreliable real redheads aside from Judas, unless you include Salomé, Lizzie Borden, Nero, Napoleon, Henry VIII, and General Custer. Good old redheads in history include William the Conqueror, Shakespeare, Queen Elizabeth I, American Presidents Washington, Jefferson, and Van Buren (who was, however, called "the Little Magician" and worse), Emily Dickinson, Mark Twain, Sarah Bernhardt, George Bernard Shaw, Winston Churchill, Sinclair Lewis, football great Harold "Red" Grange, Lucille Ball, and Little Red Riding Hood.

the red (bloody) hand of Ulster.   The badge of Ulster, called *the red (or bloody) hand of Ulster*, is a sinister, or left, hand, erect, open and couped at the wrist. According to legend, during an ancient expedition to Ireland it had been decided that he who touched land first would own the land he touched. The future prince O'Neill saw another boat edging ahead of his toward shore and seemed to be beaten. But he hacked off his left hand and threw it up on land ahead of his rival, claiming all of Ulster for his own.

red herring.   Red herring are herring that have been cured and become red in color. Escaping criminals in the 17th century would drag strong-smelling red herring across a trail to make pursuing bloodhounds lose the scent. This practice inspired the popular expression *to drag a red herring across the trail* and the more recent, shortened term *red herring*, which means confusing an issue by dragging in something irrelevant to the matter.

red-letter day.   Holidays, festivals, and saints' days have been marked in red ink on calendars since the 15th century. Red-letter days were memorable and usually happy ones, so the expression *red-letter day* eventually came to mean, more broadly, any pleasantly memorable day, a lucky day more important than most. Incidentally, since purple ink was also used to indicate special days in medieval times, the phrase could just as easily have been "purple-letter day."

Reds; Red Square.   Communists are called Reds because the red flag is the national flag of the Soviet Union and was the banner of international communism before the Russian Revolution. The red flag has been a signal for battle since Roman times, and the color red in national flags usually represents the blood of the people. Before the Communists used it as a symbol of revolution, red was associated with the Jacobins of the French Revolution, the "red republicans" who reportedly dipped their hands in the blood of their royal victims and triumphantly waved them aloft, and with the red-shirted followers of Garibaldi in Italy. *Red Square*, adjoining the Kremlin in Moscow, is *not* named after the Communists, as many people believe. *Red Square* was so named long before the Russian Revolution. Its name may have something to do with the color of buildings formerly in the area, or the fact that Russians believe red to be the most beautiful of colors.

Red Sea. The Romans named the Red Sea (*Mare rubrum*), but they took the designation from an old Semitic name whose meaning is not certain, so no one knows the real reason why the sea is called Red.

red tape. In the early 1900s, when the term arose, lawyers and government officials often tied their papers together with red ribbons. Because excessive formality and time-consuming, rigid adherence to rules and regulations often characterized lawyers and governmental agencies, *red tape* became a synonym for these failings. The words were popularized mainly by Thomas Carlyle, who castigated government officials for *red tapism.*

reformatory. *Reformatory* is an old English word dating back to at least the 16th century, but it wasn't applied to what is in effect a prison for juveniles until the Elmira, New York Reformatory was established early in the 19th century.

refugee. French Protestants called Huguenots, who fled to England in 1685 after the revocation of the Edict of Nantes, were the first people to be called *refugees.* The word derives from the French *refugier,* "to take refuge."

regatta. A *regatta* was initially, back in the 17th century, a race between gondolas on the Grand Canal in Venice. This Venetian dialect word translates as "a strife or contention or struggling for mastery." The first English *regatta,* or yacht race, was held on the River Thames on June 23, 1775.

a regular Trojan. Inhabitants of Troia, or Troy, an ancient city in what is now Turkey that came to be called *Troja* in Medieval Latin, the Trojans were a courageous, industrious people. Legend tells us they labored energetically and cheerfully at even the most arduous tasks. Hence the expressions *to work like a Trojan* and *a regular Trojan,* for hard work done without complaint and a high-spirited industrious worker.

rehash. Englishmen have been using the expression *hash* to mean "old matter served up in a different form" almost as long as they have used *hash* for meat cut up into small pieces, a word that derives from the French word *hache,* "hatchet." In 1672, for instance, Andrew Marvell complained about writers serving "the Reader continual-ly the cold Hashes of plain repitition." It was another two centuries, however, before some wit coined the word *rehash,* meaning the same. More effective, the term suggests a hash made from leftovers that is served once, then warmed over and served at least once again.

rehoboam. (See **jeroboam**.)

reimburse. *Reimburse* someone and you are putting money back into his purse, *reimburse* deriving from the Latin *re,* "back," *im,* "in," and *bursa,* "purse." The word is first recorded in 1611, probably coming into English via the French.

reindeer. *Reindeer* aren't so called because Santa Claus holds their reins on his sleigh. The word comes from the Old Norse *hreinn,* "reindeer" (the reindeer species) + *dyr,* "deer," the word a tautology meaning "reindeer deer."

Reine - Claude plum. (*See* **plum**.)

remacadamized. See *macadam* for the meaning of this word. *Remacadamized* is given here because it is a memorable example of the many languages that have made contributions to English. Even though *macadam* is eponymous in origin, the one word *remacadamized* is composed of Latin, Celtic, Hebrew, Greek, and English elements: *Re* = Latin prefix; *mac* = Celtic "son"; *adam* = Hebrew "man"; *iz* = Greek suffix forming verbs; *ed* = Old English suffix.

remora. In ancient times Roman sailors believed that the little remora (*Remora remora*) fastened itself to their sailing vessels and slowed them down, delaying them, so they named the fish *remora,* or "delayer." In nature the remora attached itself to the undersides of sharks, whales, swordfish, and even tuna by means of its highly efficient suction disk, which is actually a greatly modified first and spiny dorsal fin. Not only does it hitch a free ride, but it also eats pieces of food dropped by the host fish. The remora does do some good, however, by acting as a cleaner fish and removing parasites from its host's hide.

remove (take) the scales from your eyes. Realize the truth, wake up, stop being deceived about someone or something. This ancient expression is from the Bible (Acts 9:18): "And immediately there fell from his eyes as it had been scales; and he [Saul, later St. Paul] received sight forthwith, and was baptized."

requiem shark. Tropical sharks of the family *Carcharhinidae,* especially tiger sharks, are often called *requiem sharks,* their name coming from the French word *requin,* for "shark." The pseudonymous sailor Sinbad explained the derivation of the French word in an

1887 book he wrote about sharks: "The French name for shark is *requin*. This word is probably derived from the Latin *requiem*, and signifies that if a man fall into the sea among sharks, his comrades may repeat for him the usual prayers for the dead. It is seldom, if ever, that a man who is so luckless as to fall amongst sharks appears again; a shriek is heard, a moving mass is seen under the surface and a fin above it; the next wave that breaks against the shipside is crimsoned, and the horror-stricken seamen know that their messmate has gone to that place from which no traveler returns."

retail.   (See **wholesale**.)

retreat, hell.   (See **devil dogs**.)

rhinoceros.   As with *hippopotamus* (q.v.) and many other animals, the Greeks named the *rhinoceros*. They thought the huge horn on its head very formidable and called it *rhinokeros* after the Greek words *rhinos*, "nose," and *keras*, "horn." The rhino's horn, sometimes over four feet long, is an excellent defensive weapon, but it has plagued the animal through the ages, driving it at times to the shores of the Dead Sea of extinction. One old canard had it that a rhino horn used as a goblet could detect the presence of poison; other superstitions claimed that powdered rhino horn could cure many ailments, including epilepsy and bubonic plague, as well as ease the pain of childbirth. Yet what caused the rhino the most trouble was the belief that its horn, similar to the legendary unicorn's, was a sex stimulant. The ancient Chinese, Babylonians, Greeks, and Romans were among many people who believed this. Today at least three species of rhino are becoming extinct because the Chinese value their powdered horn (*hsi chio*) as an aphrodisiac—a large horn brings at least $1,000 in what is definitely a seller's market.

Rhode Island.   One story has Verrazzano, in 1524, observing the island now called Aquidneck in Narragansett Bay and naming it Rhodes Island because it reminded him of the island of Rhodes in the Mediterranean. Later, the island gave its name to the state. Most scholars contend that *Rhode Island* takes its name from the Dutch *Roodt Eylandt*, "red island," for its red clay.

Rhodesia; Rhodes Scholarship.   Poor health, which plagued him all his life, forced empire builder John Rhodes to leave England and Oxford for Africa in 1870. There he joined the rush to the Kimberley diamond fields, and by 1888 he had established De Beers Consolidated Mines, dominating both the diamond mine area and later the Transvaal gold mines. His huge fortune facilitated his entrance into politics, and he served as prime minister of Cape Colony, 1890-96. It was Rhodes's desire from his youth that the British should rule the world. When the British government failed to take action he formed a private company to occupy and develop the terrritory of what became *Rhodesia*, which was named for him five years later, in 1899. (The British protectorate, *Northern Rhodesia*, became the republic of Zambia in 1964, and *Southern Rhodesia* later became Zimbabwe.) The "Empire Builder" had returned to Oxford several times in the course of his brief life—once being sent back to Africa under a virtual death sentence, the doctor noting privately that he had only six months to live. Rhodes finally earned his degree at the university, and his will left an endowment of 6 million pounds for the famed *Rhodes Scholarship* that bears his name.

a rhubarb.   Speculation has been rife for years about how the slang term *rhubarb*, "a heated argument," arose from the name of a popular vegetable. Since the word is often associated with baseball, many writers say it has its origins there. But probably the best explanation, advanced about twenty-five years ago by a veteran actor familiar with theatrical traditions, is that actors simulating angry talk in crowd scenes for "the noise without" gathered backstage and "intoned the sonorous word 'rhubarb.'" The actor-etymologist Alexander McQueen advised that the word produces such an effect "only if two or three work at it," and claimed that this theatrical tradition went back to Shakespearean times, but the slang *rhubarb* for an argument arose only in the late 19th century. It therefore came to mean a "rumpus" or a "row" at about the time baseball was fast becoming America's national pastime. It is easy to see how the stage term could have been applied to an argument on the diamond, especially a mass argument that involved both teams, though there is no solid proof of this. *Rhubarb* itself has an interesting derivation, taking its name from the Latin "rhabarbarum." The Romans called it this because the plant was native to the river Rha (the Volga), a foreign, "barbarian" territory—*rha barbaron*, the plant's name, thus meaning "from the barbarian (foreign) Rha." The first rhubarb planted in America was sent to the great naturalist John Bartram from Siberia in 1770. Americans long called the fruit *pieplant* because it made such delicious pies, especially when combined with strawberries.

rice Christian.   Used as early as 1816 in China and India, *a rice Christian* refers to someone converted to Christianity to improve his economic lot, for material rather than spiritual reasons.

the rich are different from us.   Literary critic Edmund Wilson attributed this remark to American novelist F. Scott Fitzgerald. In his story "The Snows of Kilimanjaro," Ernest Hemingway said he answered Fitzgerald (he called him "Julian" in the story) with the reply: "Yes, they have more money."

rich as a Fugger. The Fuggers were a family of German bankers famous in the 15th and 16th century in Europe for their immense wealth. Their great resources inspired Elizabethan dramatists to coin the phrase *rich as a Fugger*, centuries before "rich as Rockefeller."

rich as Croesus. Croesus, the last king of Lydia (560-546 B.C.), was regarded as the wealthiest man on earth, his name proverbial even while he lived. This very real Midas probably minted the first gold and silver coins, and although he subjugated the Ionian cities of Asia Minor, he was generous to the Greeks, making spectacular offerings to their oracles. A legendary (and chronologically impossible) tale told by Herodotus relates that the Athenian wise man Solon (*q.v.*) once advised Croesus that no man could be deemed happy, despite his riches, until he finished his life happily. Later, after Croesus had been defeated by Cyrus the Great and condemned to be burned alive, he cried out Solon's name three times from the pyre. Cyrus, moved by his explanation and perhaps reflecting on his own fate, spared his captive's life and they became great friends.

rich as Rockefeller. *Rich as Rockefeller* refers to the family fortune amassed by John Davison Rockefeller (1839-1937). The oil refinery that became the Standard Oil Company made Rockefeller a billionaire before it was dissolved by the Supreme Court in 1911. Variations on the phrase above include *he's a regular Rockefeller*, and *Rockefeller* itself is the American equivalent of *Croesus*. John D. may have given only dimes to beggars, but his philanthropies included the founding of the University of Chicago, the Rockefeller Institute for Medical Research (1901) and the Rockefeller Foundation (1913) for worldwide humanitarian purposes in all worth about half a billion dollars. John D. Rockefeller, Jr., built New York's Rockefeller Center, with Radio City completed in 1940.

Richmond, N.Y. (*See* **Kings County**.)

rickey. (*See* **gin rickey**.)

to ride backwards up Holborn Hill. To go to one's own hanging. Up until 1784, the year of the last execution at Tyburn in London, condemned men would go to the gallows riding backwards on a horse all the way up Holborn Hill, which rose steeply from Newgate Prison to the gallows at Tyburn. According to one account, "Some conceive the practice to increase the ignominy, but it is more probably to prevent the condemned from being shocked with a distant view of the gallows, as in amputations surgeons conceal the instruments with which they are going to operate."

to ride roughshod over someone. A roughshod horse had nail-heads projecting from its horseshoes to keep it from slipping, and it's said that similar shoes with projecting points were designed by blacksmiths in the 17th century for use by the cavalry on the battlefield. The gory spectacle of chargers with benailed hooves stomping over men in battle, or even the sight of a roughshod horse accidentally trampling a pedestrian on a city street, suggested the expression *to ride roughshod over someone*, "to treat someone brutally, without the least consideration."

ride out on a rail. (*See* **tarred and feathered**.)

riffraff. *Riffraff* has a complicated history for a little word. It is apparently based on the French phrase *rif et raf*, meaning "one and all." When first used in English *rif and raf* meant just that, but by the 15th century *riffraff* had been compressed from the phrase and meant something entirely different—the dregs of humanity, trash, worthless people. This radical change has been explained in several ways. It may be that another sense of the French phrase *rif et raf*, "a collection of people who steal," is responsible. Or *raf*, may have become confused with the Swedish word *rafs*, meaning rubbish, *riff-raff* coming to mean "refuse and rubbish." Another possibility is that the present meaning derives from the French verbs *rifler*, "to ransack," and *raffler*, "to snatch away," anyone who ransacked or snatched something away being considered *riff-raff*. Or the opposite of the phrase *riff and raff* may have something to do with the coinage. *Riff nor raff* meant "nothing whatsoever" and someone who had *riff nor raff* might have become *riff-raff*, worthless.

rigadoon. There is no Señor Mambo or Mademoiselle Twist, but there apparently once lived a Monsieur Rigadoon—a M. Rigaud, anyway. The rigadoon does sound Scottish, but the lively dance—which resembles the twist in that the two dancers do their pirouetting at a distance from one another—is decidedly Provençal in origin. It is named for Marseilles dancing master Rigaud, who invented it in the late 17th century; the English *rigadoon* is *rigaudon* in French.

Rigg's pyorrhea. (*See* **Bright's disease**.)

rigmarole. Often spelled and pronounced "rig-a-morole," this word means confused, incoherent, foolish or meaningless talk, or any complicated procedure. It derives from a roll of names called the *rageman*, which originated in the 14th century. The name of this roll was altered through mispronunciation to *ragman role* and finally to *rigmarole* in the 18th century. Because the names and addresses on it were often changed or deleted, the rigmarole came to represent any confused or disconnected, incoherent statement.

right; adroit, etc. *Right* is of honorable origin, deriving from the Anglo-Saxon *riht*, "straight, just." As for *adroit*, "cleverly skillful," it is just the French *à droit*, "with the right hand." Similarly, *dextrous*, meaning skillful with the hands, body, or mind, derives from the Latin word *dextrous*, "right-handed"—to call a left-hander *dextrous*, then, is something of a contradiction. *Ambidextrous*, "able to use both hands well," combines the Latin *ambi* "both," with *dextrous*, literally meaning someone who has two right (two good) hands! Unlike *left*, the word *right* usually has the connotation of cleverness and grace in English words and phrases. A *right-hand man* is an invaluable, trusted aide; the *right* side was the place of honor in political assemblies and gave its name to royal or conservative parties of the right; and *right foot foremost* means putting your best foot forward. (*See* **get up on the wrong side of the bed; left-handed compliment.**)

right up my alley. An inside-the-park home run in baseball is often hit *right down the alley*, between two fielders, but I doubt that this is the source of the above phrase, which is sometimes *right down my alley*. The expression, meaning "very familiar and appealing to me," probably has nothing to do with a bowling alley, either. *My alley* here seems to be a synonym for my street, the place where I live and where I'm most at home.

to rile. *Rile*, deriving from the Old French *roiller*, "to roll or flow" (like a stream), was originally an English dialect word common in Norfolk that meant to muddy the water by stirring it up. Riling disturbed the water and suggested *rile's* modern meaning of "to annoy or make angry."

ringer. For a fabled example of a *ringer see* **dark horse.** A *ringer* is a counterfeit, especially a superior horse passed off as an unknown, or a professional athlete posing as an amateur. The word may derive, as *Webster's* says, from the old bell ringer's expression *ring in*, working a certain bell into a performance. But there seems to be very little evidence linking bell ringers with horseracing, sports, and gamblers. Perhaps a better explanation is that *ringer* was once a slang term for "counterfeit," which derived from the sale of brass rings for gold at country fairs. *Dead ringer* has no sinister connotations. It simply means a perfect imitation, a person with an uncanny resemblance to someone else. It derives from *ringer*, with *dead* in this case meaning "absolute," "complete."

ring hollow; ring true. In the past, counterfeit coins could be detected by the dull, flat tone they produced when dropped on stone, in contrast to the clear ring of true coins. The test was called *ringing* or *sounding* a coin, a very old method that one writer dismissed as unreliable in 1796. Nevertheless, the practice was so common that it inspired the saying *to ring true*, to impress one as being genuine or good, as well as its opposite, *to ring false* or *to ring hollow*, the last a phrase that Ben Jonson used. Today real post-1963 U.S. "silver" coins don't give off a clear ring anymore.

ringing the changes. A *change* in the ancient art of bell ringing is the order in which a series of bells are rung. Theoretically it would be possible to ring 479,001,600 changes with twelve church bells without repeating their ringing order—although it would take nearly thirty-eight years to do so. *Ringing the changes* has long been a competitive sport among bell ringers, and the present champions are eight English ringers and their conductor who rang a peal, all the possible changes on a series of bells—on eight bells in 1963. The peal consisted of 40,320 changes and took two minutes short of eighteen hours. Past feats like this inspired the expression to *ring the changes*, to try every possible way of doing something, to state something again and again in different ways, or even to work something to death. The expression is also the name of a con game in which the swindler completely confuses his mark by continually changing money so that the victim loses track of what he gives out.

to ring the bell; to ring a bell. *To ring the bell*, "to succeed at something," is an Americanism that has its origins in either amusement park shooting galleries, where the marksman rings a bell when he hits the target, or in those familiar carnival strength-testing machines, where a person tries to sledgehammer a wooden ball hard and high enough up a board to ring a bell. *Ring the bell* is common in the spiels, or pitches, for both games. *To ring a bell*—"to strike a familiar chord, to evoke a memory"—on the other hand, may refer to memories evoked by ringing church bells or school bells.

riot act. (*See* **to read the riot act.**)

ripsnorter. (*See* **quicker than hell can scorch a feather.**)

ritzy. Cesar Ritz (1850-1918), Swiss restaurateur and hotel manager, built his first Ritz Hotel in Paris in 1898. By hiring the master chef George Auguste Escoffier and adopting such practices as sleeping in every room at least once in order to test the quality of its mattress, this perfectionist made his hotel the greatest of *la belle epoque* and himself the greatest hotelier in the history of the Western World. Ritzes opened in London, New York, and other cities, and *ritzy* or *like the Ritz* quickly became American slang for anything lavish and costly. The word can mean vulgarly ostentatious, too; *putting on the ritz* means *putting on the dog* (*q.v.*) or showing off, and *to ritz* a person means to behave *ritzily* or superciliously toward him.

road. *Road*, for "a rather narrow street or passage," came into English rather late, being first recorded in Shakespeare's *I Henry IV* (1596). It may derive from the Old English word *rode*, for "a journey on horseback," but its origin is obscure.

roadrunner. *Geococcyx californianus* was dubbed the *roadrunner* by American cowboys in the mid-19th century because of its habit of running ahead of horsemen on trails. It is also called the *ground cuckoo, lizard bird, paisano, cock of the desert, snake killer*, and *snake-eater*, among other names. Mexicans used to capture young roadrunners and teach them to kill rats and mice.

roam. No one has proved it, but several etymologists believe that *roam* derives from the city *Rome*, referring to the fact that English pilgrims took a roundabout course to the Eternal City. No better theory has been offered for the word's derivation.

Robert's Rules. *Robert's Rules of Order*, the last word in parliamentary procedure, was originally published as the *Pocket Manual of Rules of Order for Deliberative Assemblies*—a cumbersome title for a little book. Written in 1876, the manual has had surprisingly few revisions. Its author, Brig. Gen. Henry Martyn Robert (1837-1923), was an American military engineer responsible for the defenses of Washington, Philadelphia, and the New England coast.

robin; robin redbreast. There are no true American robins; the bird we call a *robin (Turdus migratorius)* is actually a thrush. Our "robin" takes its name from *robin redbreast*, the British name for another bird species altogether. According to tradition, a robin pulled a thorn from Christ's crown on the way to Calvary, and the blood spurting from the wound dyed the robin's breast red forever.

Robin Hood. Robin Hood, chivalrous defender of the poor and oppressed, may have been based on the Earl of Huntington, Robert Fitz-Ooth, an outlawed 12th century English nobleman (b. ca. 1160) who harassed England's Norman invaders. According to this popular theory, *Fitz* taken away from *Fitz-Ooth* leaves us with *ooth*, the *th* in this changing to *d* and yielding *Robert Ood*—not too far removed from *Robin Hood*. Both the bow and arrow of Robin Hood and the site of his grave are at Kirkless Hall in Yorkshire, where Robert Fitz-Ooth, legend says, was bled to death by a treacherous nun in 1247. But there are abundant theories and places claiming Robin Hood as their own. The legendary outlaw is likely a composite of numerous stories about many early English heroes.

Robin Hood's barn. Places and plants named for Robin Hood abound all over Britain. To *go all around Robin Hood's barn* means to wander in a roundabout way, to arrive at the right conclusion in this manner. Robin Hood, of course, had no barn, living in Sherwood Forest, and trying to get around a barn that wasn't there was an apt description for early travelers lost in the woods.

Robinson Crusoe. Daniel Defoe's novel was based on the true adventures of Alexander Selkirk (1676–1721), a seaman who in 1704 asked to be put ashore on the tiny island of Más a Tierra off South America because he objected to conditions aboard ship. Selkirk spent more than four years alone on the island before being rescued and returning to England, where he became a celebrity. Defoe, a journalist, certainly heard of Selkirk's story and possibly interviewed him. In any case, he wrote the immensely successful *The Life and Strange Adventures of Robinson Crusoe* in 1719, embellishing Selkirk's account and presenting it as a true story. In truth it was the first book to reveal Defoe's genius for vivid fiction and it was written when the author was almost sixty. Selkirk never did go back to the Pacific island, as Defoe had Crusoe do in two sequels, which appeared the same year. His experiences had made him quite eccentric, however, and for a time he lived in a cave near his home in Largo, where it is said he taught alley cats how to do strange dances. *A Robinson Crusoe* is today anyone who lives alone like a hermit for a long time.

robot. In Karel Capek's play *R.U.R.*, first produced in 1921, mechanical men manufactured by the Rossum Universal Robot Corporation revolt and threaten to take over the world. This play marked the first time mechanical men were called *robots*, a word which has since been extended to include people devoid of human feelings who act like mechanical men and any mechanism guided by automatic controls. Capek coined *robot* from the Czech word *robata*, "work," meaning "a slave." The world is saved in the play when the *robots* miraculously become human. The U.S. Census Bureau reported that 5,535 robots were made by American industry in 1984, after its first survey of such machines. The Robatics Industries Association estimates that 16,000 to 17,000 robots are now in use in the U.S. The Census Bureau defines a robot as "a reprogrammable multifunctional manipulator designed to move material, parts, tools, or specialized devices through variable programmed motions for the performance of a variety of tasks." We've all done work like that.

rob Peter to pay Paul. The expression *rob Peter to pay Paul* goes back at least to John Wycliffe's *Select English Works*, written in about 1380. Equally old in French, the saying may derive from a twelfth-century Latin expression referring to the Apostles: "As it were that one would crucify Paul in order to redeem Peter." The words usually mean to take money for one thing and use it for another, especially in paying off debts.

Rockefeller.   (*See* **rich as Rockefeller.**)

rock 'n' roll.   The best guess is that *rock 'n' roll* "reflects a sexual metaphor," as one writer puts it, quoting the lyrics "My baby rocks me with one steady roll." *Rock and roll* music, an outgrowth of black culture in America, of course dates back much earlier than the first recorded use of the term in the early 1950s, deriving from black "rhythm and blues."

Rock of Gibraltar.   (*See* **Gibraltar.**)

rodomontade.   The braggart Moorish king Rodomonte in the Italian epic *Orlando Furioso* (1505-15) gave his name to this word for empty vainglorious boasting, which is sometimes incorrectly spelled *rhodomontade*. Thus Rodomonte's actual bravery has been forgotten in the language.

roentgen ray.   The first Nobel Prize in physics was awarded to German scientist Wilhelm Konrad von Roentgen (Röntgen) in 1901 for his discovery of the X-ray six years earlier. Roentgen called his largely accidental discovery the *X-ray* because he was at first unable to fathom the nature of this shortwave ray; it was an unknown quantity to him and he borrowed the symbol from algebra for it. The physicist, a professor at Munich the last twenty or so years of his life, did much valuable work in thermology, mechanics, and electricity, most of it overshadowed by his great discovery. He died in 1923, aged seventy-eight. X-rays are sometimes called *roentgen rays* in his honor today, and the fluoroscope the *roentgenoscope*. To *roentgenize* is to X-ray someone or something, which is done by *roentgenologists*, who take *roentgenograms*, or photographs made with X-rays. But the use of Roentgen's name does not end here by any means. A *roentgen* is a measurement unit of radiation, and a *roentgenometer* is an instrument used for measuring X-ray intensity.

Roland for an Oliver.   Roland and Oliver were two evenly matched knights of Charlemagne who once engaged in combat that lasted five full days on an island in the Rhine. Every time Roland got in a resounding whack, Oliver replied in kind and the contest to determine who was the better warrior ended in a draw. After the fight, Roland, Charlemagne's nephew, and the intrepid Oliver became devoted friends. Both brave knights were killed by the Arabs in 778 A.D., in an ambush at Roncevaux in the Pyrenees, though one legend tells us that Oliver accidentally killed Roland after himself receiving a fatal wound from the enemy. The long epic poem *Chanson de Roland* of the 11th century tells how Roland and Charlemagne's paladins died and how the king of the Franks avenged them. Many great deeds are credited to the two knights, so many that *a Roland for an Oliver* can mean an exchange of tall tales as well as *blow for blow* or *tit for tat*.

Rolls-Royce.   Regarded by many for many years as the best car in the world, the Rolls-Royce is named for Charles Stewart Rolls and Henry Royce, who first built it in 1904. Royce was the mechanical genius, a manufacturer of dynamos and electric cranes before Rolls, an auto dealer, heard of a new model auto Royce had built and sought him out.

roman à clef; livre à clef.   *Roman à clef* translates from the French as "novel with a key" and is also known as a *livre à clef*, "book with a key," and in German as a *Schlussel-roman*. In such novels thinly disguised portraits of actual well-known persons are presented under fictitious names. When the *roman à clef* originated in 17th-century France "keys" to the real persons involved were often published after the books appeared. Notable instances of "key novels" in England include Thomas Love Peacock's *Nightmare Abbey* (1818), which caricatured Byron, Shelley, and Coleridge; Benjamin Disraeli's *Venetia* (1837); Aldous Huxley's *Point Counter Point* (1928), featuring a disguised D. H. Lawrence, among others; and Somerset Maugham's *Cakes and Ale*, among others of his novels, in which the characters were often hardly disguised at all.

romance.   *Romance* derives from the Latin *Romanice scribere*, "to write in the Roman vernacular," as distinguished from literary Latin. The *Romance languages*, French, Italian, Spanish, etc., are derived from this vernacular Latin. The old French adverb *romany*, for *Romanice*, became a noun meaning a tale told in verse about some hero of chivalry, this becoming *romance* in English.

ROM and RAM.   These are acronyms for forms of computer memory. ROM stands for read-only memory, containing instructions for starting the computer that are permanent and cannot be modified. RAM means random-access memory, containing instructions for the particular task the operator wants the computer to perform; these instructions are temporary, entered from the keyboard or disc and lost when the power is turned off. One wonders if these will become general synonyms for "permanent" and "temporary."

Roman holiday.   A holiday that is obtained at the expense of others, just as the Romans obtained their enjoyment at the expense of the doomed gladiators who fought in the arena. Byron invented the expression in "Childe Harold" when writing of a captured Gaul forced to fight in the arena and "Butcher'd to make a Roman holiday." A Roman holiday is thus also *bread and circuses* (*q.v.*), a public spectacle marked by onlookers pleasuring in the brutal, barbaric display of anything, from an airplane crash to a violent hockey game.

Romeo and Juliet.   Not much is known about Romeo and Juliet, but they were real lovers who lived in Verona, Italy, and died for each other in the year 1303. The Capulets and Montagues were among the inhabitants of the town at that time, and as in Shakespeare's play, Romeo and Juliet were victims of their parents' senseless rivalry. Their story was told in many versions before the Bard of Avon wrote of his "star-crossed lovers." The tale can be traced to Masuccio's *Novelle* (1476) and even before that to *Ephesiaca* by the pseudonymous third- or fourth-century writer Xenophon of Ephesus. Shakespeare found the tale in Arthur Brooke's poem "The Tragical Historye of Romeus and Juliet," containing "a rare example of love constancie . . ."(1562). *Romeo* alone means a male "lover" today and has a derisive ring, but *Romeo and Juliet* still means a pair of youthful, often helpless lovers.

rook.   Farmers in England called this member of the crow tribe (*Corvus fugilegus*) a *hrooc* as early as the eighth century, probably in imitation of its raucous cry. The bird has long been regarded as a pest and was long distinguished from the crow, as this old seed planting rhyme shows: "One for the rook / One for the crow / One for the weather / And one to grow." The chess piece called the *rook* has an entirely different origin, deriving from a Persian word whose original sense is unknown. The thieving bird, however, does give us the word *to rook*, or cheat, which has been used since Shakespeare's time, just as *to gull* (*q.v.*) has been.

rooster and ox story.   This is an Ozarkian euphemism for *cock and bull story*, or *tale* (*q.v.*), a rare triple euphemism, in fact, so constructed because among people in the Ozarks the words *cock*, *bull*, and *tail* (a homophone of "tale") have strong sexual connotations and are taboo.

rope of sand.   Expressing futility, ties that neither bind nor hold, *a rope of sand* is an old English expression that is first recorded in 1624, but may well be proverbial. One early use: ". . . this rope of sand which Tradition is."

Roquefort.   "The King of the blue cheeses," pungent Roquefort is made in France's Roquefort district. Made from sheep's milk, it is marbled with blue-green mold.

Rorschach test.   Popularly known as the ink-blot test, this widely used psychological diagnostic technique was invented in 1921 by Swiss psychiatrist Hermann Rorschach (1884-1922). The *Rorschach test* consists of a series of ten standardized ink-blot designs that the subject observes, relating what he sees by free association to a trained tester. The way the ambiguous colored blots are perceived is thought to reflect the interpreter's personality and emotional conflicts. Though it has been used since 1921, the validity of the Rorschach is not universally accepted.

rosary.   The string of beads used by Roman Catholics to count repetitions of certain prayers is said to be so named because the first ones were made of rosewood, a hard, reddish, black-streaked wood that often has a roselike odor and comes from several tropical trees, including *Dalbergia nigra* and *Pterocarpus erinaceus*, the African rosewood, or molompi. Another theory is that it takes its name from the "Mystical Rose," one of the titles of the Virgin Mary.

Roscian.   Roman actor Quintus Gallus Roscius (ca. 126-62 B.C.) was born a slave but became the greatest performer of his time. Excelling in comedy roles, he was so esteemed that the golden-tongued orator Cicero took lessons from him and became his friend, the two often competing to see who could better express any idea or emotion. Roscius, in fact, wrote a treatise comparing acting and oratory. In an age when actors were held in contempt, his grace and eloquence were praised in poems, Sulla awarded him the gold ring signifying equestrian rank, and he amassed a great fortune, retiring from the stage when still a young man. Over 2,000 years have passed and his name is still a synonym for eminence or perfection in acting. *Roscian* means pertaining to or involving actors, and when we say someone gave a *Roscian performance*, we mean one of outstanding skill. (*See* **thespian.**)

roscoe.   A *roscoe* is underworld slang for "a gun." In his *Dictionary of the Underworld* Eric Partridge suggests that the name derives from either the inventor or manufacturer of a Roscoe revolver. Several major dictionaries tentatively accept this derivation, but it has not been confirmed.

rose-colored glasses.   Some unfortunate people never take their *rose-colored glasses* off, but everybody wears these spectacles occasionally. This attitude of cheerful optimism, of seeing everything in an attractive, pleasant light, has always been with us, while the expression itself goes back to at least 1861, when it is first recorded in *Tom Brown at Oxford*: "Oxford was a sort of Utopia to the Captain . . . He continued to behold towers, and quadrangles, and chapels, through rose-colored spectacles."

a rose is a rose is a rose.   What Gertrude Stein really wrote in her poem "Sacred Emily" was "Rose is a rose is a rose, is a rose," but her words have been misquoted as the above so often that she might as well have written "a rose is a rose is a rose." In her prose Gertrude Stein had no use for nouns: "Things once they are named the name does not go on doing anything to them and so why write in nouns." But in poetry, she felt: "You can love a name and if you love a name then saying that name any number of times only makes you love it more." And poetry is "really loving the name of anything."

rosemary. The homely herb *rosemary* was originally called by the Latin name *ros marinus*, "sea dew," because it was often found on the sea cliffs in southern France. But over the years *ros* sounded more like "rose" to English ears and *marinus* suggested the common name "Mary." The herb was thus dedicated to the Virgin Mary, *rosemary* recorded as early as 1440.

rose of Sharon. There are at least twenty-five species of flowers and shrubs named after the rose, usually because of some physical resemblance. The *rose of Sharon* is one of them, taking its last name not from any woman named Sharon, but from the Hebrew place name Sharon, for the fertile level tract along the coast of Palestine, where the flower mentioned in the Bible was said to grow. The identity of the true rose of Sharon is uncertain and today the name is applied to several plants in America, generally to the showy late shrub *Hibiscus syriacus* (also called *Althea*).

Rotokas. *Rotokas* is a language spoken in the central part of Bougainville Island in the South Pacific. It has the distinction of having the shortest alphabet of any living language, composed of just eleven letters (*a, b, e, g, i, k, o, p, r, t,* and *u*), with six consonants (also the least of any language) and five vowels. The language with the most letters is Cambodian, with 72.

Rotten Row. The London street, originally a royal route, may have originally been called *La Route du Roi*, the Royal Road, with the French expression corrupted into *Rotten Row*. But its name could also derive from *rotteran*, "to muster," for soldiers once mustered there, or from the Anglo-Saxon *rot*, "pleasant, cheerful," or even from *rotten*, referring to the soft material the road was made of. Another of many possibilities is the Norman *Rattan Row*, or "roundabout way," the route over which corpses were carried in olden times to avoid main streets and traffic.

roué. *Roué* was first used to describe the debauched rakes in the duc d'Orlean's crowd toward the beginning of the 18th century. These roués, who weren't really old at all (even though the old cliché makes all roués old), took their name from the French word *rouer*, meaning to torture on the wheel. The reason: the duc and his cronies were so dissolute that many people thought they deserved to be broken on the torture wheel.

rough and ready. This was not only the nickname of General (later President) Zachary Taylor, but the name of a town in California. Applied to a person, *rough and ready* means someone who takes things as they come, who works in a rough but prompt and effective way; referring to things, it means something unelaborate, just good enough to serve the purpose. The term arose at the beginning of the 19th century, some time before the Duke of Wellington could have invented it at Waterloo by instructing a Colonel Rough there, "Rough and ready, colonel!" as the old story goes.

the roughriders. Teddy Roosevelt named his Spanish-American War cavalry unit the Roughriders, after the American cowboy broncobusters called *roughriders*, many of whom were part of his regiment.

Roundheads. Cromwell's soldiers and all Puritans of England's Civil War period were called *roundheads* and *crops* because, in contrast to the Royalists, who had long flowing hair, their hair was "trimmed close to a bowl-dish, placed as a guide on their heads."

round robin. The *round robin* was originally a petition, its signatures arranged in a circular form to disguise the order of signing. Most probably it takes its name from the *ruban rond*, "round ribbon," in 17th-century France, where government officials devised a method of signing their petitions of grievances on ribbons that were attached to the documents in a circular form. In that way no signer could be accused of signing the document first and risk having his head chopped off for instigating trouble. *Ruban rond* later became *round robin* in English and the custom continued in the British navy, where petitions of grievances were signed as if the signatures were spokes of a wheel radiating from its hub. Today a *round robin* usually means a sports tournament where all of the contestants play each other at least once and losing a match doesn't result in immediate elimination.

to rove. In Medieval English the archery term *roven* meant "to shoot randomly." Arrows shot randomly at distant targets, floating through the air, suggested comparison with a person strolling off to distant places, somewhat lazily, randomly, with no apparent purpose, and gave us our expression *to rove*.

rowanberry. The European mountain ash, as the *rowanberry* (*Sorbus ancarparia edulis*) is also called, has an interesting history. It takes the name *rowanberry* from the Danish *rune*, "magic," being so called because it was supposed to have magical powers to ward off evil.

royalties. *Royalties*, in the sense of an agreed portion of the income of a work paid to an author, or a portion of the proceeds paid to the owner of a right (mineral, oil, etc.), is of course connected with the granting of royal rights. *Royalty* in this financial sense seems to have first been used to describe a duty of one shilling a ton on all coal exported from the Tyne for use in England, which England's Charles II granted in 1676 to his illegitimate son the Duke of Richmond as part of a perpetual pension. In the sense of a payment to authors, *royalty* is first recorded in 1880 in *Scribner's Magazine*. But book royalties are of such tenuous value today that one author has suggested a name change to *peasantries*.

Roystonea. It isn't often that someone's entire name, first and last, is taken for a word, but that is just what happened with General Roy Stone, a 19th-century American engineer in Puerto Rico who had the *Roystonea*, or royal palm, named after him. The genus *Roystonea* is well known, including six species of palms. Often used as an ornamental to line avenues in tropical America, its beautiful crest dominates every landscape where it grows, and every portion from its roots to its crown serves some useful purpose. Some of these feather palm species grow to over one hundred feet high and the *Roystonea regia* species is widely planted in southern Florida. Florida's Palm Beach, the wealthy resort where over 25,000 millionaires are said to be resident in season, became a palm-fringed paradise when a cargo of coconuts washed ashore from a shipwreck in 1879, and early residents planted the nuts along the once desolate beach.

rubber. *Rubber* was not even named until 1770, when chemist Joseph Priestley accidentally discovered that the hardened substance could "rub" out pencil marks, and progress in waterproofing did not come until half a century after that. Young James Syme, later to become a famous surgeon, first invented the process for making waterproof fabrics while a student at Edinburgh University in 1823, but the fabric itself was patented a few months later by Scottish chemist Charles Macintosh, who exploited the idea and was really the first person to produce a practical waterproof cloth. Macintosh (1766-1843), a Fellow of the Royal Society, had already invented an effective bleaching powder and improved a number of dyes. Finding that rubber could be dissolved by naphtha, he spread the resulting solution on cotton cloth, cementing another layer of cloth to it. Raincoats made from such double-thick fabrics with a middle layer of rubber won popularity overnight, as did numerous waterproof items that Macintosh manufactured at his plant in Glasgow. But the man who revolutionized outdoor living somehow became associated with his raincoat alone, and even this was spelled wrong from the very beginning. Properly, *mackintosh* or the *mac*, as it is sometimes called, should be *macintosh*, although the incorrect spelling prevails.

rubberneck. "Such a term as a *rubberneck*," H. L. Mencken wrote in *The American Language*, "is almost a complete treatise on American psychology; it reveals the national habit of mind more clearly than any labored inquiry could reveal it." The graphic democratic Americanism is first recorded in 1900, the magazine using it commenting: "Could anything be more eloquently expressive than the phrase 'rubberneck,' to characterize the offensively inquisitive and peering person."

rube. (*See* **clodhopper**.)

Rube Goldberg contraption. Cartoonist Rube Goldberg, as the preposterously "logical" machinery in his comic strips showed, never wanted to disappoint anyone. His complicated diagrammed panels never did, either; the machinery in them performed childishly simple tasks that could have been done far easier by hand. A parody of this mechanized world, these wild and wonderful contraptions made his name synonymous with any complicated, wildly impractical invention or scheme and won him lasting fame as well as exhibitions in the most conservative museums. Goldberg died in 1970, aged eighty-seven, and some of his obituaries failed to mention the fact that he had won two Pulitzer Prizes for his political cartoons.

rub out. To *rub someone out*, "to kill him," isn't gangster talk from the Prohibition era, as is so often assumed. The term dates back to the early 19th-century American Far West and has its origins in Plains Indian sign language, which expresses *to kill* with a rubbing motion. The term is first recorded in George Ruxton's *Life in the Far West* (1848) and it is he who gives the sign language source.

rub the wrong way. An ingenious theory links this expression with the wet-rubbing of unfinished floors in Elizabethan homes. Oak floors that servants mopped against the grain became streaked, such carelessness giving rise to these words for the inept handling of people as well as floors. However, evidence is lacking; the phrase is first recorded in 1862 and must be marked "origin unknown."

Rudbeckia. Under *Adam's apple* we mentioned the Swedish professor who tried to prove that the site of the Garden of Eden was located in the Land of the Midnight Sun. The professor, Olaf Rudbeck (1630-1702), also claimed in his book *Atlantikan* that Sweden had been the locale of Plato's Atlantis. But he was otherwise a fine scientist, discovering the lymphatic system and making various botanical contributions. Linnaeus so admired the Rudbeck family that he named the North American coneflower after both Professor Rudbeck and his son, the junior Professor Rudbeck being a contemporary of

Linnaeus. The *Rudbeckia* genus, some twenty-five species, includes the popular black-eyed Susan and golden glow. Plants in the genus are herbs, usually having yellow rays, and can be annual or perennial.

rudderless.   Since the early 19th century *rudderless*, in reference to the absence of a ship's rudder, has figuratively meant "without guidance or control."

rugby.   *Rugby* is said to have been invented at and named for the Rugby School in Warwickshire, England, where it originated in 1823 when a student picked up the ball and ran with it during a soccer game.

rugger.   (*See* **soccer.**)

rule of thumb.   There are two good choices here. Brewmasters of old often tested the temperature of a batch of beer by dipping a thumb in the brew, their long experience telling them how well the beer was brewing. One theory has it that our expression for a rough, guesswork estimate derives from this practice. More likely it stems from the ancient use of the last joint of the thumb as a measuring device for roughly one inch.

rule the roost.   There's no doubt that this expression is well over four centuries old, but there is controversy about whether it was originally to *rule the roost* or to *rule the roast*. To *rule the roost* would of course refer to the cock who rules the chicken coop and *to rule the roast* refers to the lord of the manor who presided over the carving and dishing out of roast meat at the table and was thus master of the house. Americans still prefer the former expression and the British use the latter. Since early references are found for both versions, the truth will probably never be known. What complicates matters impossibly is that *roost* was formerly pronounced as we now pronounce *roast*, and thus spelled "roast" erroneously, while *roast* was sometimes pronounced *roost* and spelled that way. In any case, the expression means the same—to rule the house or whatever, usually while making a display of power.

rum.   Called *Kill-Devil*, a West Indian name, by early colonists, and the basic liquor made among them (from molasses and sugar), *rum* possibly takes its name from the English *rumbullion*, first recorded in the 1640s, which may have been named for the town of Rambouillet. Another possibility is that it derives from the canting term *rum*, for "good, excellent," which is recorded as early as 1567.

rum, Romanism and rebellion.   This political slogan is usually attributed to the supporters of Herbert Hoover, who used it to defeat Catholic Democratic candidate Al Smith for the presidency in 1928, calling the Democrats

the party of *rum, Romanism and rebellion*. But the words were first used in 1884 by New York Presbyterian minister Samuel D. Burchard, who spoke, in presidential candidate James Blaine's presence, of the Democrats as "the party whose antecedents are rum, Romanism and rebellion," this offending the large Irish Catholic vote in New York, causing Blaine to lose the state by a scant 1,000 votes and thus lose the election to Grover Cleveland. Blaine's political reputation didn't help him either. The Democrat's slogan for that election was "James G. Blaine, James G. Blaine,/ Continental liar from the state of Maine."

rum, sodomy, and the lash.   While Winston Churchill was First Lord of the Admiralty (1911-15), he remarked acidly, in answer to a protest about British naval traditions being violated, that the traditions of the Navy were "rum, sodomy, and the lash."

Rumford stove.   Before Benjamin Thompson, Count Rumford (1753-1814), invented his "kitchen range" most housewives prepared meals over open fireplaces. But the *Rumford stove* was among the least of the count's accomplishments. Rumford led a remarkable life. The Massachusetts-born philanthropist fought for the British during the Revolution, leaving his wife, a wealthy widow fourteen years his senior, and a baby daughter in New Hampshire. After serving as British undersecretary of state and being elected to the Royal Society, he entered the Bavarian civil and military service in 1783. Here he effected numerous reforms, including a reorganization of the army and the education of the poor. It is said that in one day he had 2,600 beggars arrested and sent to a Munich workhouse he had planned, where they were taught to support themselves. It was in this workhouse that the Rumford stove was invented, the wood- or coal-burning range proving so efficient that Rumford was commissioned to build similar cast-iron models for many aristocrats of the day.

rummage sale.   As early as the 14th century the French word *arrumage*, related to our word "arrange," meant "loading a cargo ship." Sometimes cargo from the *arrumage* was damaged during the voyage and warehouses held special sales of these damaged items, sales that were at first called *arrumage* sales and then *rummage* sales. *Rummage* thus came to mean any damaged goods and finally any goods low in quality, including the used clothing and other items sold at charity rummage sales.

to run amok (or amuck).   In 1516 an Englishman translated an Italian work that said of the Javanese, "There are some of them (under the influence of opium) who . . . go out into the streets and kill as many people as they meet. . . . These are called *Amuco*." Within a century, *to run amok* was common in English for "running viciously mad and frenzied for blood." The word *amok* comes ultimately from the Malay *amoq*, meaning attacking desperately, or murdering in a state of frenzy, and was originally applied to an animal in a state of rage.

runcible spoon. A forklike utensil with two broad prongs and one sharp curved prong used for serving hors d'oeuvres. The word was coined in 1871 by English author Edward Lear. The spoon seems to have been invented after Lear described it thusly in "The Owl and the Pussycat":

> They dined on mince and slices of quince
> Which they ate with a runcible spoon.

to run for your life. According to one old tale, a fast runner of the Duke of Monmouth was captured during the Battle of Sedgemoor in 1685 and told that he could run for his life, that is, his life would be spared if he could outrun a horse. The contest was held, the horse losing the long race, and the runner was freed. This is supposed to be the origin of *to run for your life*, though it was probably common long before any such race—if indeed there was one. It is, however, possible for a good runner to beat a horse in a long race like a marathon.

to run hot and cold. There are many traditional stories about the semilegendary fabulist Aesop. He is said to have lived in the middle of the sixth century B.C. and been the black slave of a Thracian named Iadmon. Supposedly deformed and ugly, he won his freedom by telling fables. At any rate, many tales about animals, adapted to moral or satirical ends, circulated under his name, though some of them really date back a thousand years before his birth. One of Aesop's fables is about a satyr who finds a winter traveler blowing on his fingers to keep them warm. When the satyr gives the man a bowl of hot pottage and he blows on that, too, the satyr asks him why. "I am trying to cool it," the man says. The satyr thereupon orders the man out of his cave, declaring "I will have no dealings with one who can blow hot and cold from the same mouth!" Though the traveler wasn't inconsistent—his breath was first warmer and then colder than the object he blew upon—this fable became the basis for the saying *to blow hot and cold*, "to be inconsistent or vacillate." Today the expression is often heard in the form *to run hot and cold*, reinforced in modern times, perhaps, by plumbing that gives us alternately hot water and cold.

to run riot. *The Master of Game*, a hunting manual published in 1410, explains in part that *to run riot* was originally a term describing a hunting dog who lost the scent of the animal he was chasing and began acting unruly and undisciplined—running after other animals instead of the intended quarry. Over the next century the phrase came to be used figuratively for anyone acting without constraint or control.

runt. *Runt*, for "a small, weak person," came into the language as slang in about 1700. It derives from the name of the small breeds of oxen and cattle called "runts" in Wales and the Scottish Highlands as early as the 16th century.

run the gauntlet. The *gauntlet* in this expression was first spelled *gantlope*, deriving from the Swedish word *gattloppe*, from *gat*, "a narrow path," and *loppe*, "run" (akin to our "lope," "elope," and "gallop"), which literally meant "a running of the narrow path." *Gatloppe* was the name of a punishment that originated in the Swedish army. A soldier found guilty of a serious offense was forced to strip naked and run between two rows of his comrades, each of whom struck him with a whip, switch, or even sword as he ran. The length of the rows depended on the severity of his offense. The English observed the use of this punishment by the Germans during the Thirty Years War (1618-1648) and saw American Indians inflict a similar punishment on captives with war clubs. They first called the torture, which often resulted in maiming, *running the gantlope*, nasalizing the Swedish word *gatloppe*, but later further corrupted the key word in the phrase to *gauntlet*, probably because of its resemblance to the English *gauntlet*, for "glove." Today the expression means to encounter trouble on all sides, to be severely attacked or criticized. The confusion between this *gauntlet* and the *gauntlet* that is a glove has led some writers to spell the punishment "gantlet." In any case, both words are pronounced the same way. (*See* **throw down the gauntlet**.)

runway. *Runway*, for "a landing strip at an airport," probably has its origins in the *runway* of burlesque, the narrow ramp extending from the stage into an aisle in theaters or nightclubs, on which women dance within reach of the audience. The Americanism *runway* is, however, recorded as early as 1835 as the path for a deer, and also means the bed or channel of a stream.

Russia. *Russia* derives from the Russian word for the country, *Rossiya*, named after the Vikings who invaded it from the north to establish a kingdom in Russia and who called themselves *rothsmen*, "rowers."

Russian, Polish and Slavic words in English. Russian and Slavic words are the basis for a number of English ones, including: *ruble, czar, kvass, sable, mammoth, knout, cravat, ukase, vodka, droshky, astrakhan, samovar, mazurka, polka, troika, steppe, pogrom, bolshevik, commissar, soviet, intelligentsia, kulak, robot, sputnik, babushka*.

Russian roulette.   Drunken Russian officers of the Czarist courts popularized this "game" in which a revolver loaded with one bullet is held to the head, the barrel spun and the trigger pulled.

rutabaga; Swedish turnip.   Commonly called the *Swedish turnip*, the *rutabaga* derives its name from the Swedish dialect *rotabagge*, for the plant; this relatively new vegetable, first recorded in 1620, is extensively grown in Sweden.

Rx.   The Latin *recipere*, "take this," provides the *R* in the symbol *Rx* used by pharmacists for centuries, while the slant across the *R's* leg is the sign of the Roman god Jupiter, patron of medicine. The symbol looks like *RX* and is pronounced that way.

S

S. Our nineteenth letter can be traced back to the ancient Phoenician and Hebrew alphabets, where it was called *shin*. It did not acquire its present form until it came into Latin.

'S. Oaths like 'Sblood, 'Slife and 'Sdeath are common in the works of Elizabethan writers like Ben Jonson. The 'S is a euphemistic abbreviation of *God's*, always written continuously with the following word.

sabotage. The root of *sabotage* is the French *sabot*, "wooden shoe," but that is as much as anybody really knows about the word, which came into English during World War II from the French *saboter* meaning "to do work badly" or "to destroy machines or a plant in order to win a strike." Why the French made the verb *saboter* out of *sabot*, "shoe," isn't really known, though one persistent old story claims that wooden-shoed peasants trampled down a landowner's crops to win better wages and working conditions. Another story says the term was coined after the great French railway strike of 1912, when "strikers cut the shoes (*sabots*) holding the railway lines." Or it could be that French factory workers threw their shoes into machinery to disable and disrupt a plant.

Sachertorte. History's most famous chocolate cake is named for 19th-century Austrian confectioner Edward Sacher. Sacher, whose cigar-smoking mother served her son's creation to Prince Metternich, actually won a lawsuit from a rival confectioner over who could legally call the cake his own. The cake is made of chocolate torte dough, apricot jam, and chocolate frosting.

sacheverell. Not many preachers or politicians have been put down as properly as Dr. Henry Sacheverell (ca. 1674-1724). "Famous for blowing the coals of dissention," the English clergyman had both "the blower of a stove" and a chamber pot named *sacheverells* after him. The naming was undoubtedly done by Whigs, whom Sacheverell had violently attacked in 1709 in two sermons, especially lashing out against the government's toleration of dissenters. Charged with seditious libel, the fervent Tory was suspended from preaching for three years. But his trial brought about the downfall of the Whigs and he was rewarded with the important rectory of St. Andrew's immediately after his suspension expired. It remained for the dictionaries to take revenge for the Whigs. (*See* **Twiss.**)

the sack. *Sack*, according to legend, was the last word spoken at the Tower of Babel before the world's languages were scrambled, and for this reason it retains a strikingly similar form in over a dozen languages. As for *to get the sack*, here etymologists have outdone themselves, with inventions worthy of Rabelais. By far the best tale is that Turkish sultans who grew tired of a wife or found her troublesome, had her taken from the harem, sewed up in a sack, and dumped into the Bosphorus. As outrageous as the story seems, it could well be the origin of the old expression, which dates back to the Middle Ages, for such "sacking" was widespread among the Turks, and the Romans similarly sewed up condemned criminals in sacks and tossed them in the Tiber. Most authorities, however, seem to accept with some reservations the explanation linking the phrase to the tools of medieval artisans and mechanics. Workmen generally carried their tools in a sack and for convenience's sake left them in a safe place on the job overnight. When an unsatisfactory worker was fired, at the end of his last day on the job, his employer would hand him his pay and the sack containing his tools.

sackcloth and ashes. People used to show grief and sorrow by wearing sackcloth, a coarse material used for making sacks, and throwing ashes on their heads. From this custom came the expression *sackcloth and ashes*, meaning sorrow for something one has done or failed to do (*e.g.*, "He came to me in sackcloth and ashes saying he'd found the book he had insisted I'd taken"). The phrase is an ancient one that is found in the Bible (Matt. 11:21).

sacred cod. (*See* **cod.**)

sacred cow. The Hindu hero Prithu changed himself into a cow to encourage his countrymen to be vegetarians. This and the doctrine of *Ahimsa*, "harmlessness to all living things," preached by Buddha accounts for the fact that cows are still sacred in India, roaming the streets at will. Our fairly recent term *a sacred cow*, "any person or group so highly regarded as to be exempt from even justified criticism," appears to stem from the Hindu belief. It probably came into the language when Mahatma Gandhi's passive resistance movement brought worldwide attention to India. Gandhi himself was a confirmed vegetarian. In his youth he did try eating meat, but gave it up when he had recurring nightmares of animals bleeding in his stomach.

saddler of Bawtry. "Like the saddler of Bawtry, who was hanged for leaving his liquor." This Yorkshire proverb describes someone too much in a hurry. It seems that the real saddler of Bawtry was on his way to the gallows and adamantly refused to stop with his guards for a last drink, as was the custom in York in the 18th century. Passing the tavern by, he hurried to the gallows, where Jack Ketch quickly accommodated him. His pardon from the king arrived only a few minutes later.

sadism. Count Donatien Alphonse François de Sade (1740-1814) seems to have emerged a full-blown "fanatic of vice," the "philosopher of vice," and *professeur de crime* that Michelet and Taine called him. When it happened, how it happened, would stymie a panel composed of Freud, Jung, Job, and the living Buddha. De Sade's upbringing was a factor, as were the licentious times in which he lived, his long years in prison, and perhaps there was even an organic problem. There is simply not enough reliable information available about de Sade—all his voluminous diaries were burned—and to try to make biography from a writer's fiction is fruitless. Sometimes his insights were deep and remarkable, but his was in the main a disordered, deranged mind reflected in his life and licentious work. *Sadism*, the derivation of satisfaction or pleasure from the infliction of pain on others, can be sexual in nature or stem from a variety of motives, including frustration or feelings of inferiority. De Sade's life indicates that many such causes molded his twisted personality. His final testament read in part: "The ground over my grave should be sprinkled with acorns so that all traces of my grave shall disappear so that, as I hope, this reminder of my existence may be wiped from the memory of mankind." (*See* **masochism**.)

sad sack. The term *sad sack*, for "a maladjusted, blundering, unlucky soldier," likable but always in trouble, was widely popularized by George Baker's comic strip "Sad Sack," which appeared in several World War II military publications and later appeared in many newspapers. However, the words were American collegiate slang during the 1930s, their origin unknown.

safari. Safaris are getting back to the original meaning of the word. Once exclusively hunting trips into the African jungle complete with guns, they are now often sight-seeing excursions for camera-toting tourists more in keeping with the Arabic word *safara*, "travel," that is the root of *safari*.

sage (plant). (*See* **salvia**.)

Sahara. *Sahara* has become a synonym for any barren, lifeless place. The desert in northern Africa takes its name from the Arabic *cahra*, "desert," as if that is all that could be said about it.

sahib. (*See* **memsahib**.)

to sail under false colors. Pretending to be something you aren't, to be a hypocrite. These words have their roots in those pirate ships that at the moment of attack lowered their friendly or neutral flag and hoisted the deadly skull and crossbones. The unwritten law of the sea, of course, required that all ships display their true flags or colors so that they could be recognized as friend or foe, but the Jolly Roger was by its nature exempt.

St. Bernard. Men crossed the Alps between Switzerland and Italy centuries before St. Bernard de Menthon (923-1008) founded the shelter now called the Hospice of Great St. Bernard. But the house of refuge he built in 982 made it much easier for travelers to make pilgrimages to Rome through the Mons Jovis Pass, 8,098 feet above sea level and covered with snow ten months of the year. St. Bernard, a wealthy French nobleman who renounced his fortune to become a man of God, was canonized in 1681. Perhaps 200 years before this the monks at this hospice had begun breeding the great dogs that are named after him and training them to track down and rescue travelers lost in blizzards and avalanches. The breed is said to be a cross between a bulldog and a Pyrenean shepherd dog or a Molossian hound, and it once had long hair believed to result from matings with the Newfoundland dog. The long hair was found to be a handicap in the snow, however, and a smooth-haired variety has been developed in relatively recent times. *St. Bernards* are still trained by the monks of the Alpine hospice. Measuring up to about six feet long, they are capable of carrying a man and are bred for intelligence and docility as well as strength. The breed is the world's heaviest dog, one specimen having reached a weight of 246 pounds. Numerous individual dogs have been honored as heroes, including the famous Barry, whose statue is in the St. Bernard Hospice. St. Bernards do not carry little kegs of brandy around their necks; this myth was the result of an early 1900s cartoon.

St. Boniface's cup. Anyone who wants an excuse for an extra drink from time to time might do well to revive the custom of *St. Boniface's cup*. The expression derives from an indulgence granted by Pope Boniface VI or Pope Boniface I to anyone who drank to his good health. A *St. Boniface's cup* was long an excuse for another one of the same. The phrase is not related to *boniface*, for "an innkeeper," which we owe to the convivial landlord of that name in the comedy *The Beaux' Strategem* (1707) by Irish playwright George Farquhar.

St. Elizabeth's flowers. According to tradition, St. Elizabeth of Hungary gave so much food to the poor that her own household didn't eat well. Her husband suspected this and when he saw her leaving the house one day with her apron full of something, he demanded to know what she carried. "Only flowers, my lord," Elizabeth said, and God saved her lie by changing the loaves of bread in her apron to roses.

St. Elmo's fire.   Corposants are luminous discharges of electricity that extend into the atmosphere from projecting objects, their name deriving from the Portuguese *corpo santo*, "holy body." They are better known as *St. Elmo's fire*, and were believed by sailors to be a portent of bad weather. St. Erasmus, the patron saint of Neapolitan sailors, was a fourth-century Italian bishop whose name became corrupted to *St. Elmo*. An Italian legend tells us that he was rescued from drowning by a sailor and as a reward promised to ever after display a warning light for mariners whenever a storm was approaching. St. Elmo's fire does not involve enough discharge of electricity to be considered dangerous. The jets of fire are also seen on wings of aircraft, mountaintops, church steeples, on the horns of cattle, and blades of grass, and even around the heads of people, where it is said that they merely cause a tingling sensation. In ancient times St. Elmo's fire was called *Castor and Pollux*, for the twin sons of Zeus and Leda in Roman mythology, and a single burst of fire was called *a Helen*, for the twins' sister. A Helen was said to be a warning that the worst of a storm was yet to come, while two lights, Castor and Pollux, supposedly meant that the worst had passed. This has given rise to the theory that *St. Elmo* might be a corruption of *Helen* instead of *St. Erasmus*. Still another suggestion is that *St. Elmo* is a corruption of *St. Anselm* of Lucca.

St. Ignatius's bean.   No one knows for which of the seven saints named Ignatius the *Saint Ignatius bean* was named. Neither does anyone know the reason it was so named. The Saint Ignatius bean is the seed of a woody vine called *Strychinos ignatti*, which yields the poison strychnine.

St. Martin's Day; St. Martin's goose; etc.   After he became the patron saint of France, St. Martin's name formed the basis for a number of words. His feast day, *Martinmas* (Nov. 11) replaced the Roman Feast of Bacchus, retaining some of its customs, which probably accounts for the fact that he is regarded as the patron saint of bartenders, drunkards, and reformed drunkards as well. The phrase *Martin drunk*, "very drunk," also comes from St. Martin's association with the old pagan festival of *vinalia*, which noted the time when wines had reached their prime. *St. Martin's goose* was, according to legend, a bothersome goose that the saint ordered to be killed and served for dinner. Because he died while eating the meal, a St. *Martin's bird* was traditionally sacrificed every Martinmas, or *St. Martin's Day. St. Martin's summer*, like *St. Luke's summer* and *All Saints* (or All Hallow's) *summer*, is a European term for our *Indian summer*, the weather around November 11 often providing an un-

seasonable spell of warmth and pleasantness that was called *été de la Saint-Martin* by the French. The halcyon days of St. Martin's summer combine with St. Martin's goose in a strange way to give us the word *gossamer*. Due to its association with both the geese eaten on St. Martin's day and throughout the season, St. Martin's summer came to be called "goose summer" in days past. At this time of the year fine, filmy cobwebs are often found floating lazily in the still air and these delicate "goose-summer webs" are the direct ancestors of *gossamer*, which can either be the webs themselves or fabrics like them.

St. Nicholas.   (*See* **Santa Claus.**)

St. Patrick's cabbage.   Though native to Spain, Saint Patrick's cabbage (*Saxifrage umbrosa*) is found in the mountains of west Ireland as well, for which reason it is named for St. Patrick, Archbishop of Armagh, the Apostle of Ireland. This ornamental with crimson-spotted petals is also known as *London Pride*. St. Patrick is said to be responsible for the shamrock being the Irish national emblem. When captured by a pagan ruler while preaching in the country he plucked a shamrock and explained that its three leaves were distinct and separate on the plant, "just as the Trinity is the union of three distinct persons in One Deity."

St. Peter's cock.   (*See* **John Dory.**)

St. Swithin's Day.

St. Swithin's day if thou doest rain
For forty days it will remain;
St. Swithin's day if thou be fair
For forty days twill rain na mair—

These doggerel lines contain a well-known weather myth popular as early as the 12th century. The legend claims that St. Swithin, or Swithun, a ninth-century bishop of Winchester and counselor to King Egbert, had been buried in the churchyard outside the north wall of Winchester minster, where the "sweet rains of heaven might fall upon him as he wished and he be trodden under foot by those who entered the church." A century after his death it was decided that he should be canonized for miraculous cures he performed and his remains were to be reburied within the cathedral. The day was set, but as a miraculous sign of Bishop Swithin's displeasure, it began to rain on that day and rained for forty days and forty nights, causing the monks to abandon their plans. The date selected for his reinterment was July 15, 971, and July 15 has ever since been generally regarded as *St. Swithin's Day*.

St. Uncumber. St. Wilgefortes, who might be called the patron saint of unhappily married women, is a mythical saint, who, tradition says, prayed to grow a beard so that she could live her life "uncumbered with men." The prayer was granted and the ruse worked well until one of her enraged former lovers had her crucified. According to Sir Thomas More "women [later] changed her name [to St. Uncumber] because they reken that for a pecke of oats she will not faile to uncumber them of their husbondys."

St. Vitus's dance. *St. Vitus's dance*, or chorea, is named for the Roman saint St. Vitus, who became a martyr during the persecution of Christians by the Emperor Diocletian. In the 15th century it became customary for young people to dance frenetic dances around statues of St. Vitus to insure good health for the coming year. Soon, because of the nature of the wild dance, St. Vitus's aid was invoked against the nervous affliction most common among children and adolescents and the disease became popularly known as *St. Vitus's dance.*

salaam. The Arabs use this word, related to the Hebrew "peace," *shalom* (*q.v.*), as a greeting, accompanying it with a low bow with the right palm held on the forehead. Thus in English to *salaam* someone came to mean to pay homage to someone.

salad days. Cleopatra, kidded by Charmian about her old love for Julius Caesar, joked that those were her *salad days* when she was "green in judgement, cold in blood." In other words she loved Caesar unskillfully and without much passion compared to the way she loved Mark Antony. Thus our expression for naive and inexperienced youth comes to us from Shakespeare's *Antony and Cleopatra.* The real Cleopatra was actually a flaming youth, a trained and artful lover before her adolescence, and the *salad days* that Shakespeare has her admit to were distant memories long before she married her brother at seventeen.

salary. (*See* **salt.**)

Salem. The nine or ten places around the world called *Salem*, including Salem, Massachusetts, might be called "Peace," for all take their name, ultimately, from the Hebrew *shalom*, or the Arabic *salaam*, both meaning "peace."

to sally a ship. A ship is sallied, or rolled, by assembling the crew all on one side, then signaling them to rush together to the other side. When the signal is repeated at certain intervals, the ship can be made to roll. In the age of sail, *sally* was also a common expression for the continuous rising and falling or the swinging or bounding motion of a ship at sea. The word derives from the Middle French *saillir*, "to rush forward," which comes from the Latin *salire*, "to leap."

Sally Bee. (*See* **Sarah Bernhardt**.)

Sally Lunn. Sally Lunn used to cry out her wares in the streets of the then fashionable English resort city of Bath toward the end of the 18th century. Her basket was filled with slightly sweetened tea biscuits, which are still called *Sally Lunns*, although a number of cakes and breads also bear the name today. It took an enterprising baker and musician by the name of Dalmer to make Sally Lunn's buns universally known. Dalmer bought her recipe, built some portable ovens mounted on wheelbarrows to deliver Sally Lunns fresh, and even wrote a song about them. The song made the name a catchword that was still popular when nearly a century later a Gilbert and Sullivan character in *The Sorcerer* sang about "the gay Sally Lunn."

Sally Mae. (*See* **Ginnie Mae**.)

salmagundi. The origin of the word is really unknown. A *salmagundi*, "any mixture or miscellany," began as a mishmash of minced veal, chicken, or turkey, anchovies or pickled herring, and onions served with lemon juice and oil. One theory has it that the word comes from *salame condite*, Italian for "pickled meat"; another that it derives from the name of a lady-in-waiting to Marie de Medici, wife of France's Henri IV. Marie is supposed to have invented the eclectic dish, or made it de rigueur at least, and named it after Madame or Mademoiselle Salmagundi, her lady-in-waiting. Later the word was used by Washington Irving for a series of twenty periodical pamphlets that he and two other writers published (1807-08). *Salmagundi; or the Whim-Whams and Opinions of Launcelot Langstaff, Esq. and others*, consisted of satirical essays and poems on New York society and politics, generally satirizing "mobocratic" and "Logocratic" Jeffersonian democracy.

Salmonella. Salmon have no connection with *Salmonella* or *salmonellosis*. The latter is a form of food poisoning that can result in death and is caused by bacteria of the *Salmonella* genus, comprising some 1,500 species. The *Salmonella* genus was first identified by 19th-century American pathologist and veterinarian Daniel Elmer Salmon, who died in 1914. There are often outbreaks of salmonellosis, which is usually caused by infected and insufficiently cooked beef, pork, poultry, and eggs, as well as food, drink, or equipment contaminated by the excreta of infected animals. Nearly all animals are hospitable to the rod-shaped bacteria causing the acute gastroenteritis in humans, and food poisonings caused by them are almost as common as those caused by staphylococci. Incidentally, there is a *salmon disease* dogs and other animals get from eating salmon infested with cysts of flukes, but it has nothing to do with salmonellosis.

salt. In ancient times salt was highly valued, so much so that spilling salt became an unlucky omen among the

Romans. Roman soldiers were in fact paid in salt, (*sal*) at one time, the origin of our word *salary*. Through the centuries a number of expressions reflected the importance of the precious seasoning and preservative. "Not worth his salt" referred to the salary the Romans paid their soldiers; "to eat a man's salt" meant to partake of his hospitality; and "to sit above the salt" was to sit in a place of distinction, above the saler, or saltcellar, at a medieval table. "The salt of the earth" is an even older saying, dating back to biblical times. In Matt. 5:13 the meek, the poor in spirit, the merciful, those persecuted for the sake of righteousness, the peacemakers, the pure of heart are told by Jesus that "Ye are the salt of the earth . . . Ye are the light of the world." The words are still a supreme compliment given to those we most admire as human beings.

saltimbocca. This Italian veal and ham dish looks so delicious that some poetic gastronome several centuries ago named it *saltimbocca*: "leaps into the mouth."

salvia. Some species of salvia have medical properties, causing the Romans to name the genus from the Latin *salveo*, "to save or heal." The flowers are also known as *sage*, which is a corruption of the French word *sauge*, for *salvia*, and *sage tea* has long been thought to have healing powers.

samarskite; samarium. Russian engineer Col. M. von Samarski became one of the few men to have an element named after him, through an unusual set of circumstances. In 1857 a glasslike, velvet-black mineral was discovered in Russia and named *samarskite* in honor of this mine official. Twenty-two years later the scientist Lecoq de Boisbaudran found by means of the spectroscope that samarskite contained a new element. He named this *samarium*, after the mineral in which he discovered it. Thus the little-known engineer was commemorated, indirectly, in a way usually reserved for the famous. Samarium belongs to the rare-earth group and has little commercial importance, though it is used as a catalyst and in the ceramics industry. In about 1901 another element was discovered in samarskite, this called *europium*, after the continent.

sambo. Blacks have probably been vilified with more slur names than any other group in history. All are, of course, disparaging and offensive, and this includes *sambo*. Ironically, the Little Black Sambo of the children's story who helped give the term widespread currency is really an East Indian, but *sambo* was with us long before the boy who melted the tiger to butter. Possibly of American origin, the term was introduced via the slave trade. The word, some believe, derives from the Kongo *nzambu*, "monkey," which became *zambo*, "bowlegged," in Spanish. Alternate choices are the

Foulah *sambo*, "uncle," or the Hausan *sambo*, "second son." It may be that sambo simply comes from the name of a West African tribe called the Samboses, mentioned in European literature as early as 1564.

Sam Browne belt. Born in India, Sir Samuel Browne, V.C. (1824-1901), served most of his military career there with the British army. Awarded the Victoria Cross and knighted for putting down the Indian Mutiny, a rebellion among native troops, he was promoted to general in 1888. Sometime during his long military career Browne invented the belt that bears his name. Designed originally as a sword belt that would support the weight of a sword smartly without sagging from the hips, it consisted of a belt with two auxiliary straps crossing over each shoulder. Later modified to one strap crossing from the left hip over the left shoulder—swords were worn on the left side—the *Sam Browne belt* became compulsory dress for all British officers and was widely adopted by armies throughout the world. It was declared optional in 1939, but is still seen today, especially as part of drill, band, and cadet uniforms.

Sam Hill. If someone could locate any historical record of a Col. Samuel Hill of Guilford, Connecticut, we might find the origin of the phrase *go like Sam Hill* or *run like Sam Hill*. Edwin V. Mitchell makes mention of the man in the *Encyclopedia of American Politics* (1946). It seems that Colonel Hill perpetually ran for office—but no other evidence of his existence can be found. Since no one knows *who in the Sam Hill* he was, Sam Hill must remain "a personified euphemism our Puritan ancestors used for 'hell.'"

Samian letter. (*See* **Y**.)

samoyed. *Samoyeds* are working dogs resembling the chow, but their gentleness and intelligence make them highly valued pets. The dog takes its name from the Samoyed people, a nomadic race of Mongols only 7,000 or so in number living in northwest Siberia and gradually becoming extinct. The strong, heavy-coated *samoyeds*, usually white or cream colored, were developed for pulling sleds, hunting, and herding reindeer. Their masters are an interesting people who domesticate the reindeer and use it for riding as well as milking. The *samoyed husky* happens to be the most widely traveled of all dogs, one having gone along for the space ride in 1957 aboard the Russian *Sputnik II*, which attained an altitude of 1,050 miles. In Russian the breed is called *laika*.

Samson. Just as Delilah's name symbolized treachery, Samson's symbolizes strength. The biblical Samson slew a thousand men with the jawbone of an ass and performed various other prodigious feats as recorded in Judges 13-17. Samson's Achilles' heel was not so much his hair as was his weakness for Philistine women, and he met his match in Delilah, who cut off his long locks, in which his strength or soul resided. After his betrayal by Delilah to the Philistines, Samson's eyes were gouged out and he was brought down to Gaza. *Eyeless in Gaza*, he performed his last heroic deed when the Philistines tried making sport of him; he pulled down the temple of Dagon on his tormentors and himself. Samson's name has been used for weight lifters and strongmen since at least May 28, 1741, when Thomas Topham was called the British Samson.

sand. The old term *sand*, for "grit or courage," probably comes from the expression *sand in his craw*, used by Mark Twain in *Huckleberry Finn* (1884). "Sand in his craw" refers to the belief that a chicken that eats a little sand has more endurance than a chicken that doesn't.

sandlot baseball. Since the early 20th century *sandlot baseball* has meant unorganized baseball games played by youngsters or relatively unorganized leagues of semiprofessional players. The term *sandlot* was made popular by San Francisco's Sand-lot Party of workingmen, who held their meetings in vacant sand lots, in about 1880. *Sandlot* is also used as a synonym for anything amateur, though not so often as *bush league* or *bush* (*q.v.*).

sandwich. At 5 A.M. on August 6, 1762, John Montagu, fourth earl of Sandwich, looked up from the gaming table and decided that he was hungry. The earl, an inveterate gambler in the midst of one of his famous round-the-clock sessions, didn't dare leave his cards for a meal and ordered his man to bring him some cold, thick-sliced roast beef between two pieces of toasted bread. Thus the first *sandwich* was born. The Romans had a similar repast called *offula* before this, and it is said that the refreshment was first invented when in about 100 B.C. Hillel ate bitter herb and unleavened bread as part of the Jewish Passover meal, symbolizing man's triumph over life's ills. But the modern *sandwich*, our convenient quick lunch or snack and an important source of nourishment in this frenetic age, definitely evolves from those mighty gambling sessions, some lasting forty-eight hours and more, in which the dissolute earl passionately participated. Gambling was one of John Montagu's lesser vices, but the earl has as many words honoring him as any politician, another example being the beautiful *Sandwich Islands* (Hawaii) that Captain James Cook named after him because the earl headed the British admiralty during the American Revolution and outfitted the great explorer's ship.

San Jose; San Juan; San Antonio; San Francisco. These, of course, are the names of three cities in the United States and one (San Juan) in Puerto Rico. They also have the distinction of being the four leaders in North and South America among places named after saints: *San Jose* is the name of 429 places, *San Juan* 365, *San Antonio* 337, and *San Francisco* 275. Sometimes these cities aren't named for the same saint, however. One apocryphal story has a construction worker falling from the tenth floor of a building. "San Antonio!" he cries as he passes the seventh floor and, miraculously, he remains suspended in air a few instants. "Which San Antonio?" a sepulchral voice asks. "San Antonio de Padua!" the worker cries. "That's not me," the voice says, and the worker plummets toward the ground below.

Sanka. *Sanka*, a brand of decaffeinated coffee, is a trademark, and must be capitalized. The name of the product, first marketed in 1903, was coined from the French *san*(s) *ca*(ffeine), "without caffeine."

San Marino. Reputedly the world's oldest republic, San Marino, located on the Italian peninsula, is said to have been founded in the fourth century A.D. by Marinus, a Christian stonecutter. Marinus was later canonized as Saint Marinus, or San Marino, and the republic was named after him.

Santa Claus. Yes, Virginia, there was a Santa Claus, a real one—probably. The custom of giving presents at Christmas is based on the legend that St. Nicholas—a bishop of Myra in Asia Minor during the fourth century—gave secret dowries to three sisters who could not have been married otherwise and would have been sold into prostitution if it hadn't been for his generosity. Nicholas, the story goes, was out walking one night when he heard the three sisters crying behind their curtained window. On being told that their poor father could find no husbands for them and had to sell them to a brothel, our Santa Claus dug into his coat and threw three bags of gold to them, disappearing into the night before their father could thank him. A twist on the tale has the bishop turning three brass balls into bags of gold, which is appropriate for the patron saint of pawnbrokers. St. Nicholas is also the patron saint of the Russian Orthodox Church, Greece, Sicily, Aberdeen, scholars, travelers, sailors, thieves, and children, among other groups. Despite the lack of historical facts about him, he is no doubt the basis for our Santa Claus. The eve of his feast day, December 6, is a children's holiday when gifts are given in the Netherlands and elsewhere, the custom calling for someone to dress up as St. Nicholas and present the gifts. The English who settled in New York borrowed both the saint and this custom from the earlier Dutch settlers, moving his day to Christmas, their own gift-giving day, and corrupting his name from the Dutch dialect *Sint Klaas* to *Santa Claus*.

sap. Green, unseasoned wood is often full of sap, and so young, inexperienced foolish people have been called *sapheads* or *sapskulls* since the 17th century. By 1815, its first recorded usage, *sap* had succeeded *saphead* for a *cabbagehead* (1622). *Calabash* (1838), *pumpkin head* (1841) and *chump* (1883) are all similar agriculture-related words for "jingle-brained nincompoops."

Sapphism. (*See* **lesbian**.)

Sarah Bernhardt. "The divine Sarah," as Oscar Wilde called her, is regarded by many as the greatest actress of all time. Born Henriette-Rosine Bernard, the daughter of Jewish parents who converted to Catholicism, she was brought up in a convent until she entered the Paris Conservatoire at thirteen. After making her debut at the Comédie-Française in 1862, she played internationally, winning her great fame in tragic roles largely because of her "voice of gold" and magnetic personality. Probably the tallest, thinnest woman ever to star on the stage (Arthur "Bugs" Baer once wrote, "An empty cab drove up, and Sarah Bernhardt got out"), her nickname *Sally Bee* became the nickname for any tall thin woman, just as her name is a synonym for a great actress.

Sardanapalian; Sardanaplan. The dissolute Assyrian king Ashurbanipal was probably the prototype of Sardanapalus, the semilegendary king of Greek fable whose name has become a synonym for effeminate luxury. King Ashurbanipal lived in the seventh century B.C., the Greeks calling him Sardanapalus because his real name was a difficult one for them to pronounce. It is hard to separate fable from fact concerning Sardanapalus, but he does not deserve the designation "effeminate." Rather he appears to have been a shrewd military strategist and bloodthirsty tyrant who reigned for over forty years, beginning in 658 B.C., and conquered Babylon, parts of Egypt, the Medes and Persians. But as he grew older, Sardanapalus surrounded himself with luxuries, his philosophy, it is said, summed up in a monument he had erected in the city of Anchiale. Its inscription read: "Sardanapalus the king . . . In one day built Anchiale and Tarsus. Eat, drink and love, the rest's not worth this!" The epicure retired to his magnificent palace filled with tempera paintings, woven carpets, and furniture inlaid with gold. Locked up with his wives and concubines, he devoted himself to sensual pleasure. So the legend goes anyway. We only know for certain that the virile king, last of the great Assyrian monarchs, was depicted as effeminately hedonistic by Greek writers under the name Sardanapalus and that he became famous for living in great luxury. Lord Byron helped this misconception along with his poem "Sardanapalus" (1821) in which he wrote: "And femininely meanth furiously. Because all passions in excess are female."

sardonic. A *sardonic* person might be called a dead one, inside and out. The ancient Greeks believed that the *sardone* (*herba Sardonia* in Latin), a poisonous plant native to Sardinia that gave the island its name, was so deadly that anyone unlucky or foolish enough to eat it would immediately succumb to its effects. Victims were said to literally die laughing, going into convulsions, their final contorted expressions after these death throes resembling bitter, scornful grins. The Greeks called their last bitter appearance of laughter *Sardonios gelos*, "Sardinian laughter," *Sardo* being their name for the island. *Sardonios gelos* became the French *rire sardonique*, this resulting in our *sardonic laughter* and *sardonic*, laughter or humor characterized by bitter or scornful derision.

sashimi. Another Japanese word that has recently come intact into the English vocabulary. *Sashimi* means thinly sliced raw fish, which is eaten that way, often with sauces and seasonings.

satan. The Hebrew word *satan*, meaning "adversary," in the Old Testament usually denotes a human adversary, but in places (*e.g.*, Job i, 6-12) it designates an angelic being who torments man with the knowledge or direct authority of Jehovah. *Satan* has been the English proper name of the supreme evil spirit, the devil, since at least the year 900. (*See also* **Old Nick**.)

Saturday. Saturn was the Roman god of time and planting, the Romans naming the seventh day of the week *Saturni dies*, the day of Saturn, after him. This became the Anglo-Saxon *saterdaeg*, and finally our *Saturday*.

satyagraha. Literally meaning "a grasping for truth" in Hindi, this Indian word has come to stand for the nonviolent "passive resistance" of Mohandas Gandhi, which the Mahatma practiced until his assassination in 1948 and which has been emulated by many other great leaders since then.

satyr. Alexander the Great had a dream about this word at the time when he was trying in vain to capture the city of Tyre and was about to abandon his campaign. Alexander dreamed he had captured a satyr. His advisers told him that the word *satyros* (*satyr* in Greek) in his dream was really *Sa Tyros*, "Tyre is his!" and he attacked and captured the city. In any case, our word *satyr* derives from the Greek word for the mythical woodland gods or demons who were the companions of Bacchus. First recorded in English by Chaucer, *satyr* came to mean a lascivious man. *Satyress* is a little-used word for "a female satyr," first recorded in 1840.

sauce mornay. (*See* **Mornay sauce**.)

sauce Robert. This mouth-watering French sauce, which took hours to prepare in its original form, has been credited to Robert Vinot, an early 17th-century sauce maker of whom nothing else is known. But Rabelais described the sauce earlier and it could not have been invented by Vinot, although he may have improved it and given it his name. Still in use today, the ancient sauce is made with white wine, beef gravy, onion, mustard, butter, and salt.

Saudi Arabia. Named for the Arabian Saud family, the political unit dates from the 18th century.

sauterne. This sweet white wine was first recorded in English (1711) as *sauternes*, coming from the Sauternes district near Bordeaux. But since the late 18th century it has commonly been spelled *sauterne* in both England and the U.S.

savage. The Latin *silvaticus* (from *silva*, "forest") or "man of the forest" became the Old French *sauvage*, which came into English as *savage* early in the 14th century.

savarin. (*See* **Brillat-Savarin.**)

save a sailor! According to an 18th-century superstition, when a glass "rings" in a bar or at a table, a sailor will be drowned—unless a finger is placed on the glass to stop the ringing and someone cries out, "save a sailor!"

saving face. (*See* **losing face.**)

savings bank. Although the term *savings bank* is now used to identify a bank that receives primarily the savings of individuals, as opposed to a commercial bank that caters to businesses, the words were first used to describe a child's bank made to save coins. These became popular in the United States after the Civil War, when small coins became popular; before then merchant tokens, certificates, and stamps had been more commonly used. The savings banks were fashioned in many shapes, including the ubiquitous *piggy bank* (*q.v.*).

sawbuck. Our word *sawbuck* for a sawhorse ("in which two supports at each end cross each other and so form a rack for holding that which is sawed") derives from either the Dutch *zaagbok* or the German *sagebock*, both meaning the same. *Sawbuck* is also slang for a ten-dollar bill. First attested in 1850, it is so named because the Roman numeral X for ten resembles the x-shapes on each end of the sawbuck.

saxophone. While working in his father's renowned musical instrument workshop in Brussels, 1840-44, Antoine Joseph Sax invented a series of valved brass wind instruments with a new tone quality. These he named the *sax-horn* (which his father Charles actually invented and he improved upon); the *saxophone*; the *saxtromba*; and the *sax-tuba*. Antoine Joseph, often called Adolphe, left

his ten brothers and sister in Brussels and journeyed to Paris to make his fortune with his inventions. Sax made many influential friends among musicians, including Hector Berlioz, and they helped him to borrow money for a workshop and to promote his innovative instruments. The most lasting of his inventions proved to be the saxophone, although he thought of it as merely a bass instrument, unaware of its true potential. The inventor received many awards in his lifetime, but a poor business sense prevented him from making the fortune he set out to make. He died in 1894, aged eighty, just before the *saxophone*, or *sax*, achieved a major role in modern bands.

say it ain't so, Joe. They said "Shoeless Joe" Jackson, a poor boy from South Carolina, played ball without shoes down home, but he put on spikes when he made the majors and became a great star, his lifetime average of .356 the third highest in the history of baseball. Shoeless Joe never made Cooperstown's Hall of Fame, though, and never will. Jackson was one of the eight Chicago White Sox players who conspired with gamblers to throw the 1919 World Series, after which he was banished from baseball for life. After confessing his role in the affair on September 28, 1920, Jackson walked down the steps of the Cook County Courthouse through a crowd of reporters and a ragged little boy grabbed his sleeve and said "Say it ain't so, Joe." The phrase is still used in reference to any hero who has betrayed his trust.

sayonara. *Sayonara* has become part of America's vocabulary since after World War II, when thousands of G.I.'s were stationed in Japan. But few knew that this is one of the most poignant words for good-bye, its literal translation from the Japanese being "If it must be so."

Say's Law. Says *Say's Law*: In a capitalist economy "the demand for products is equal to the sum of the products." Formulated by the French economist Jean Baptiste Say (1767-1832) in his *Trait d'économie politique* (1803), the theory holds that "a nation always has the means of buying all it produces," and a "general glut" of products on the market is impossible, though there can be overproduction of one or more commodities.

scabiosa. Not a very nice name for a pretty flower, *scabiosa* derives from the Latin word *scabies*, for "itch." The plant was used by the ancients as a cure for certain skin diseases.

scalawag. Undersized, lean, undeveloped cattle that were of little use were called *scalawags* by American ranchers and farmers in the West toward the middle of the 18th century. The term then came to be applied to disreputable people, rogues, scoundrels, rascals, those who refused to work, and had a special use in the South after the Civil War to describe anyone willing to accept Reconstruction. As for *scalawag* itself, the word remains something of a mystery. It may derive from the Gaelic *sgalag*, for "a lowly servant or rustic," but more likely comes from *Scalloway*, one of the Shetland Islands that is known for its dwarf ponies and cattle, which could have been considered worthless. Other suggestions are the Scottish *scurryvaig*, "a vagabond"; the latin *scurra vagas*, "a wandering buffoon"; and the English dialect *scall*, "skin-disease." No one seems to know why the word, with so many possible British derivations, is first recorded in America.

scam. *Scam*, for "a scheme to swindle, rob, or deceive," seems to have originated as carnival talk late in the 19th century. Possibly a variant of "scheme," it may also derive from the British slang *scamp*, meaning to rob a person on the highway, which dates back to the 18th century, or to the British slang *scamp*, meaning a cheat or swindler, recorded in the early 19th century and obsolete by about the time *scam* was born.

Scandinavian words in English. The Vikings, who conquered nearly half of England, the Danelagh, and were later absorbed into the population, contributed thousands of words to the English language—at least 1,500 places in England have Scandinavian names. Words that we owe to their northern Germanic language include: *steak, knife, law, gain, birth, dirt, fellow, guess, leg, loan, seat, sister, slaughter, thrift, trust, want, window, flat, ill, loose, low, odd, tight, weak, call, die, egg, get, lift, rid, same, scare, though, till, both, husband, skin, hit, happy, rotten, ugly, wrong,* and *fell*.

a Scarborough warning. To strike someone first and warn him about his behavior afterward. The expression dates back to 1557, when Thomas Stafford captured Scarborough Castle in Yorkshire and *then* ordered all the inhabitants to leave the town.

scarcer than hen's teeth. Nothing is scarcer because not even Ripley has ever found a hen with even a single tooth. The Americanism, which also means nonexistent, probably goes back to Colonial days, though it was first recorded in 1862.

scarecrow. (*See* crow-herd.)

the scarlet letter. The first mention of people being forced to wear a scarlet capital letter *A* that branded one as an adulterer is reported in the *Plymouth Colonial Records* (1639): "The Bench doth therefore censure the said Mary . . . to wear a badge upon her left sleeve." The letter *I* was used for those found guilty of incest. Any woman "suffering an Indian to have carnal knowledge of her," in John Josselyn's words (*An Account of Two Voyages to New En-*gland, 1674), was made to wear the figure of an Indian cut out of red cloth.

scavenger's daughter. Like the earlier *Exeter's daughter*, this vicious instrument of torture was introduced by an officer of the Tower of London. It consisted of wide iron manacles on which screws were tightened until the victim's head was clamped so tightly to his knees that blood was forced from his nose and ears, and sometimes from his hands and feet. Invented by Sir William Skeffington, lieutenant of the Tower during the reign of Henry VIII, it was first called *Skeffington's gyres*, or *irons*, and came to be called jocularly the *scavenger's daughter*, which both insulted the inventor and was more descriptive.

schedule. The American pronunciation of *schedule*, ("skedule") is probably more British than the British pronunciation ("shedule")—or at least older. The prevailing British pronunciation appears to have been widely adopted only in the second quarter of the 19th century. The word itself derives from the Latin *scedula* and apparently entered the language early in the 15th century.

Schicklgruber. (*See* fuhrer.)

Schick test. While a professor of pediatrics at the University of Vienna in 1913, Dr. Bela Schick devised the famed *Schick test*, a skin test to determine susceptibility to diphtheria. His test consists of injecting diphtheria toxin into a person's skin, the skin becoming red and swollen if the person is not immune. Dr. Schick, born in Hungary, emigrated to the United States in 1923, becoming a naturalized citizen six years later. A pediatrician for many years at New York's Mount Sinai Hospital, he did important work on allergies, wrote several books on child care, and helped found the American Academy of Pediatrics. He died in 1967, aged ninety.

Schillerlocken. *Schillerlocken*, a German fish dish named after the hair of a poet, is curled chips of smoked fish commemorating the curly locks of the poet Johann Christoph Friedrich von Schiller. Schiller (1759-1805) was one of the founders of modern German literature; only Johann von Goethe overshadowed him in his time. Schiller was a great favorite of the German people, and the wide popularity of his works led to the affectionate word made from his surname and *Locken* ("curl").

schlemiehl; schlemihl. Nothing ever turns out right for the awkward and unlucky *schlemiehl*. The word, by now common American slang, comes from the Yiddish *shelumiel*, "one who is worthless," which is said to derive from the name of the first Shelumiel mentioned in the Bible. Shelumiel appears four times in the Book of Numbers as the son of Zurishaddai and the leader of the tribe of Simeon. Nothing is said about him except that he is the leader of 59,300 people and makes an appropriate offering for the dedication of the altar at the Lord's command, but it has been suggested that Shelumiel lost in battle all the time while the other tribal leaders were victorious. Be that as it may, the word *schlemiehl* got a boost from the allegorical tale *Peter Schlemihls Wunderbare Geschichte* (*The Wonderful Story of Peter Schlemihl*), written by the German botanist and poet Adelbert von Chamisso in 1814. In the story the impecunious Peter Schlemihl makes a foolish bargain with the devil, selling his shadow for a never-empty purse and finding himself an outcast from human society because he has no shadow. Through this story, which was translated into many languages and virtually became legend, *schlemihl* came to mean anyone making a foolish bargain, both living a life of its own and reinforcing the meaning of the earlier *schlemiehl*.

schmaltz. In Yiddish *schmaltz*, from the German *smaltz*, is chicken fat, a common, sticky, and greasy substance that gives its name to anything common and stickily sentimental.

schnauzer. Bred for over five centuries in Germany, this breed of dog takes its name from the German word for "growler."

schneider; Schneiderian membrane. The only Schneider I can find whose name became a word is the German C.V. Schneider (1610-80), for whom, as a result of his anatomical researches, the *Schneiderian membrane*, or mucous membrane of the nose is named. But there may be a case for the gin rummy *schneider*: one *schneiders*, or *schneids*, an opponent in gin rummy by winning before one's opponent has scored any points. Did some gin champion named Schneider do this so often that the feat came to be named after him? Or does the word derive from the German *Schneider*, "tailor," as most scholars believe? The term is apparently an Americanism, in use only since about 1940. Perhaps the term derives from "tailor" because tailors cut clothes down and *schneiders* cut down the size of the loser's bankroll!

schooner. "Oh, how she scoons!" an admirer is supposed to have exclaimed when Captain Andrew Robinson of Gloucester, Massachusetts launched the first vessel of this kind back in 1713 as she glided gracefully over the water. Robinson, overhearing the remark, called his ship a *scooner*, which came to be misspelled *schooner* within a year. *Scoon* itself probably derives from the Scottish *scon*, "to skip a flat stone over the water," as in the game ducks and drakes.

schwa. The *schwa* was a Hebrew letter, or masoretic point, expressing an obscure vowel, such as the vowel in the second syllable of the English *linen* or *button*. It became the name of such a vowel in modern languages, as well as the phonetic symbol (ə) for such a vowel.

sciamachy. (*See* **squirrel**.)

scientist. The word *science*, from the Latin *scientia*, "knowledge," is recorded in English as early as 1340, but the word *scientist* didn't make its appearance until five centuries later, in 1840, when it was invented by William Whelwell in his book *The Philosophy of the Inductive Sciences*. Wrote the English scholar: "We need very much a name to describe a cultivator of science in general. I should incline to call him a Scientist."

sciolist. (*See* **Jack of all trades and master of none**.)

the scoots; scootberry. *Scoots* was 19th-century American slang for diarrhea (which sent one scooting to the outhouse), and because the sweetish red berries on the shrub *Streptopus roseus* almost always acted as a physic on youngsters who eagerly ate them, the plant was named the *scootberry*.

scorch; scorched earth policy. The practice of invaded countries retreating before the enemy and burning all the land in his path, leaving nothing for his troops is as old as war itself, but it was first called the *scorched earth policy* at the time when the Japanese invaded China in 1937. It became more familiar when the Nazis invaded Russia in World War II. *Scorch* as a cooking term, by the way, derives from the Old English *scorkle*, which at first meant to skin meat by searing.

score. (*See* **according to Hoyle**.)

scotch. "If a body could just find oot the exac' proper proportion and quantity that ought to be drunk every day, and keep to that, I verily vow that he might leeve forever, without dying at a', and that doctors and kirkyards would go oot of fashion." These were the words of a pioneer sage of Dufftown, Scotland on the benefits of *Scotch* whiskey, which has a base of malted barley and was first made in Scotland. The national name *Scotch* is used to describe many things, often referring to the penuriousness traditionally attributed to the Scottish, *scotch* itself sometimes meaning tight-fisted.

scotch a rumor. The people of Scotland weren't particularly noted for *scotching* or suppressing rumors—no more than anyone else. The expression is actually rooted in the Old French word *escocher*, "to cut."

scot-free. Like *hopscotch*, this term for "absolutely free" has no connection with frugal Scotsmen. A *scot* or *sceot* was a municipal tax in 12th-century England and someone who went *scotfree* was one who succeeded in dodging these taxes. Later the term was given wider currency when *scot* was used to mean the amount that one owed for entertainment, including drinks, in a tavern—anyone who had a drink on the house went *scot-free*. The *scot* in the expression here was reinforced by the fact that all drinks ordered in taverns were *scotched*, or marked on a slate, enabling the landlord to make a reckoning of how much a person owed.

scow. *Scow* is another word born in America; its parent is the Dutch *schouw*, "a large flat-bottomed pole boat or river boat," which, through a mispronunciation, became *scow*. Usually serving as a ferryboat or lighter in the beginning, the scow first entered the language in the mid-17th century and is first recorded in 1669. To *scow* meant to cross a river by scow and America has since known *cattle, dumping, ferry, mud, oyster, snag, sand, steam, stone-trading,* and *garbage scows*.

scram. *Scram*, which gives us the pig Latin *amscray*, meaning the same—*beat it!* (*q.v.*), "get out of here!"—is thought by some semantic Sherlocks to be a shortening of *scramble*, but more likely it comes from the similar German slang *schrammen*. It is first attested to as underworld and circus slang at the turn of the century.

scratch. (*See* **Old Ned.**)

screw. The screw used in woodworking takes its name from a pig, of all things, deriving from the Latin *scrofa*, "sow." The threads on a screw coil resemble a sow's tail; hence the word. Additionally, according to one theory, *screw*, for sexual intercourse, comes from the Latin *scrofa*, which was melded with another Latin word, *scrobis*, meaning "ditch" but also used as Latin slang for the vulva—these two words yielding our word *screw*, for "to copulate." Partridge and others believe that *screw* first recorded in the early 19th century, is associated with the idea of stealing sex from a woman, giving the word's probable ancestor as the earlier British slang *screw*, for "a robbery effected with a skeleton key." Lastly, as underworld slang for a prison guard dating back to the mid-19th century, *screw* was suggested by someone harsh and brutal, one who used thumbscrews on prisoners.

screwball; screw loose. "King Carl" Hubbell's famous screwball, which he introduced in the early 1930s, is probably responsible for this thirties' expression meaning an eccentric person. The New York Giant pitcher used his screwball in winning 24 games in a row, pitching 46 consecutive scoreless innings, and, most amazing of all, striking out in order the greatest concentration of slugging power ever assembled—Babe Ruth, Lou Gehrig, and Jimmy Foxx—in the 1934 All-Star game. Hubbell's erratic pitch obviously got a lot of publicity in the sports pages. Since it corkscrewed crazily as it approached the batter and you never knew how it was going to break, it was inevitably compared with an unpredictable, erratic, eccentric person, helped by the expression *he has a screw loose* ("is a little unhinged"), common since the 1860s.

the screw plot. According to the traditional story, in 1708 conspirators tried to kill England's Queen Anne by removing the screw-bolts from certain huge beams in St. Paul's Cathedral so that the roof would fall in on the Queen and her party and kill them while they worshipped. Apparently, not enough screw-bolts were removed and the roof didn't cave in.

scrimshaw. Up until relatively recent times sailors on long voyages would often spend their spare time carefully carving whalebone, shells, or ivory into decorative and useful objects, ranging from clothespins to elaborate canes and jewelry boxes. This intricate work was called *scrimshaw*, a word whose origins are rather vague. Webster's traces *scrimshaw* to the French *escrimer*, "to fight with a sword," in the sense of "to make flourishes," while other dictionaries suggest *scrimshank*, English military slang for "to evade duty, be a shirker." Just as many authorities believe the word comes from the proper name Scrimshaw, referring to some once-illustrious sailor-carver noted for his craftsmanship. But Scrimshaw, if he did exist, hasn't been identified. *Scrimshaw* work was also called *skrimshander* and today it can mean any good piece of mechanical work.

scrod. Deriving from the Middle Dutch *schrode*, *scrod* means a strip or shred. New England scrod is immature cod or haddock weighing one and a half to two and a half pounds. Sometimes the term is applied to cusk of about the same weight, or to pollack weighing one and a half to four pounds. When fishermen use the word, they are usually referring to gutted small haddock.

scrub team. The English word *scrub*, dating back to at least the 16th century, meant small stunted trees or cattle. In America, by the early 19th century, *scrub* commonly meant "inferior" as well as "dwarf" and by the end of the century was being applied to second-rate college football teams, these *scrub teams* usually "second teams" that couldn't compare with a school's "first teams." *Scrub* for "to wash vigorously" derives from the Middle English *scrobbe* meaning the same.

scuba. *Scuba* is simply an acronym standing for "self-contained underwater breathing apparatus." Popular since World War II, *scuba diving* has enabled millions to see underwater sights previously the province of a few thousand professional divers.

scuttlebutt. Corrupted to *scuttle* in English, the Old French word *escoutilles* first meant the hatch on a ship, then meant the hole or hatchway in the hatch, and finally was used as a verb meaning to open a hole in a ship in order to sink, or *scuttle*, her. The cask, or *butt*, of drinking water on ships was called a *scuttlebutt* because it was a *butt* with a square hole cut in it, and since sailors exchanged gossip when they gathered at the scuttlebutt for a drink of water, *scuttlebutt* became Navy slang for gossip or rumors, in about 1935.

sea. The Old English poets used over thirty words for sea (and 27 for ship), as befits bards of an island nation. *Sea*, however, has lasted in the language. *Sea* is an earlier English word than *ocean* (*q.v.*) and is first recorded in *Beowulf* in the tenth century, its origins doubtful, though it may derive ultimately from the Greek *huei*, "it rains." Today it often represents any large expanse of water more or less enclosed, but it originally had the same meaning as ocean.

Seabees. In World War II special Navy construction battalions built airstrips or runways on many Pacific islands, among other duties. Their name, *Seabees*, is a phonetic acronym from the initials CB, *Construction Battalion*. The *C* was spelled "sea" because they were Navy men.

seacoasts in Bohemia. The expression is used in referring to errors made by authors, deriving from *The Winter's Tale*, where Shakespeare writes of a vessel "driven by a storm on the coast of Bohemia," although Bohemia has no seacoast. Shakespeare made a number of such errors, as have many writers. In *Robinson Crusoe* Defoe has his hero swim naked to a wrecked ship and then put biscuits he finds there into his pockets.

seagoing bellhops. *Seagoing bellhops*, a contemptuous name given to marines by sailors in reference to their colorful uniforms, is an expression still heard among Navy men. It probably originated in England during the late 19th century.

sea horse. The little sea horse, or *Hippocampus*, as it is known scientifically, swims upright and has a head and an arched, very horselike neck. Sea horses are also unusual in their breeding habits. During mating, the female's eggs are fertilized by the male as they are shed, but the female deposits them in the male's abdomen. The male's pelvic fins are converted into a large incubating pouch that holds the eggs and he carries them about until they are ready to hatch, appearing as if *he* were pregnant.

sea lawyer. Back in 1867 one crusty old salt defined a *sea lawyer* as "an idle litigious long-shorer, more given to questioning orders than to obeying them, one of the pests of the navy as well as the mercantile marine." This term for an argumentative seaman or nautical nuisance given to questioning regulations is still used, and the type is still with us for better or worse. A good example is the officer responsible for the mutiny against Captain Queeg in Herman Wouk's *The Caine Mutiny*. Because it is so clever and cunning, the tiger shark is also called the *sea lawyer*, as is the gray, or mangrove, snapper.

seamy side of life. The worst, most degraded side of life. This expression appears to have been suggested by the underside of clothing, where the crude seams, rough edges, and coarseness of the material shows, but another theory holds that the inspiration comes from carpets and tapestries, where the seams or threads of the pattern are visible on the underside. Shakespeare was the first to record the phrase, in *Othello*, where Iago's wife Emilia says that her husband's wit has been turned "the seam side without" by someone who has made him suspect her of adultery with the Moor.

season. *Season* derives ultimately from a Latin word meaning time of sowing, or seedtime. The word was long used for the time of the year when seed was sown, and the division of the year into four separate seasons only dates back to around the 12th century.

Seattle. Seathl, a chief of the Duwamish and Suquamish Indians, is remembered by Seattle, Washington, which was named for him in 1853, two years after it was founded as a lumber settlement.

sea urchin. (See **urchin**.)

Seckel pear. (See **Bartlett pear**.)

second Adam. (See **Adam**.)

second fiddle. This expression arose in the mid-18th century, meaning to occupy a secondary position and alluding to the second violinist of symphony orchestras, who follows the lead of the first violinist.

second rate. (See **first rate**.)

secret; secretary. Advisers who handled confidential matters in medieval Europe were called *secretarii*, their name itself deriving from the Latin *secretum*, "secret." By 1400, we find the word being written as *secretary*, but it is not until Queen Elizabeth I's time that *secretary* was used as a synonym for a minister or cabinet member of the government. *Secretary* first began to be used in its modern sense of a private assistant to an individual in the early 19th century.

securities. Though they sometimes aren't, *securities* should always be safe investments, judging by the derivation of the word from the Latin *se* and *cura*, which literally translate as "without care."

sedulous ape.   Robert Louis Stevenson originated this phrase in a charming essay, confessing that: "I have played the sedulous ape to Hazlitt, to Lamb, to Wordsworth, to Sir Thomas Browne, to Defoe, to Hawthorne, to Montaigne, to Baudelaire, and to Obermann . . . That, like it or not, is the way to learn to write." *Sedulous*, from the Latin *sedulus*, "careful," means diligent and persevering in application or attention, so the phrase describes anyone who slavishly imitates somebody.

seeing eye dog.   Dogs used to guide blind people are called *Seeing Eye dogs*, after the Seeing Eye organization in Morristown, New Jersey, where such dogs have been trained for over half a century.

seeing stars.   This expression was probably used much earlier (there is a 1609 quotation that seems to imply its use), but it is first recorded in the 1891 *Century Dictionary*: "*To see stars*, to have a sensation as of flashes of light, produced by a sudden jarring of the head, as by a direct blow." The phenomenon results from a change in blood flow to the brain. According to neurologist Dr. C. Boyd Campbell: "Blood supplies nerve cells with oxygen, sugar, and other vital nutrients. Any loss of blood to the brain—easily caused by standing up, an action that forces blood away from the head—deprives the nerve cells of these nutrients. This causes a brief, random firing of neurons, which is interpreted by the brain's visual cortex as quick flashes of light, or 'stars.' The phenomenon is also produced by a blow to the head or by stimulating the eye electrically, both of which alter the normal state of nerve cells."

seeing the elephant.   Soldiers in the American Civil War adopted these words to describe their discovery of the savagery of combat, their experience of action for the first time. The phrase came from the language of farmers, who after attending a traveling circus often spoke awesomely of *seeing the elephant*.

to see red.   *To see red*, "to be roused to violent anger," comes from the older saying "to wave a red flag at a bull." The expression became popular in America during this century, deriving of course from the waving of a red cape to rouse the bull in bullfights. No matter that bulls are color blind. The misconception is so widespread and red is so universally associated with violence that the words will be with us long after bullfighting is banned.

seersucker.   No "seer" or "sucker" is behind this one. The Persian *shīr o shakkar*, literally "milk and sugar," is the ultimate source for the name of this crimped linen cotton or rayon fabric that was first made in India, whence the British began to import it in the early 18th century for summer *seersucker suits*. *Shīr o shakkar* became the Hindu *sirsakar*, which was corrupted to *seersucker* in English.

see you later, alligator.   British rhyming slang spread to California in the 1850s, and one result was the word *alligator*, which rhymed with and meant "see you later." Rhyming slang never really caught on in America, and *alligator* in this sense didn't last long, but the full expression *see you later, alligator* remains with us.

seiche.   A *seiche* is a long wave that sloshes rhythmically back and forth as if in a bathtub as it reflects off opposite ends of an enclosed body of water (usually a bay) when it is disturbed by storms, winds, or tsunami. In Los Angeles harbor, one of the few major harbors that have seiching or surging problems, seiches cause big ships to move as much as ten feet, to strain at or snap their mooring lines, and cause damage to piles and to the ships themselves. *Seiche*, a French word, is generally pronounced *saysh*, though people in some regions pronounce it to rhyme with "beach." The term seems to have been coined by a Swiss scientist and is first recorded in English in 1839.

self-help.   British author Thomas Carlyle coined the term *self-help*, "the action or faculty of providing for oneself without assistance from others," in his book *Sartor Resartus* (1833): "In the destitution of the wild desert does our young Ishmael acquire for himself the highest of all possessions, that of Self-help."

to sell like hot cakes.   Hot cakes cooked in bear grease or pork lard were popular from earliest times in America. First made of cornmeal, the griddle cakes or pancakes were of course best when served piping hot and were often sold at church benefits, fairs, and other functions. So popular were they that by the beginning of the 19th century *to sell like hot cakes* was a familiar expression for anything that sold very quickly, effortlessly, and in quantity.

sell the pass.   Irish legend holds that when a regiment of Crotha, Lord of Atha, was holding a pass against the invading army of Trathal, "King of Cael," one of Crotha's soldiers betrayed the pass for money, the invaders were victorious, and Trathal became King of Ireland. This inspired the ancient Irish expression *selling the pass*, "betraying one's own for money or other gain," which became common enough in English, both the expression and the practice.

seltzer.   The German *Wasser selterser*, "water of Selters," gives us the word *seltzer water*, or *seltzer*. Selters, a town in Hesse-Nassau, has long been famous for its effervescent mineral spring.

Semitic. German historian August Ludwig von Schloyer gave this language group its name in 1781, taking it from the name of Shem, a son of Noah described in the Bible as the common ancestor of various ancient peoples who spoke this group of related languages. The principal languages in the group were Hebrew, Aramaean, Arabic, Ethiopic, and ancient Assyrian. Later (ca. 1825) the word was applied to the people who spoke or speak these languages and it has most recently (ca. 1875) been used to refer primarily to Jewish people.

senate. The legislature in ancient Rome consisted of the popular assembly and another group of wise men who were always in their advanced years, because only old men were considered to be truly wise. The latter group was called the *senatus*, or "council of old men," in Latin, this word yielding our word *senate*.

send to Coventry. The historic city of Coventry in England may have been built near and taken its name from *Cofa's tree*, in which case the otherwise anonymous Cofa family name is remembered in at least three words or phrases. The most common of these means boycotting a person by refusing to associate or have dealings with him, which is called *sending him to Coventry*. This phrase is of uncertain origin, arising either because Royalist prisoners were sent to the staunchly Puritan town during the Great Rebellion, or due to the fact that Coventry was at one time so antimilitary that any soldier posted there found himself cut off from all social intercourse, the townspeople even refusing to talk to the troops. *Coventry blue*, is a historical term for a blue thread made at Coventry in the 16th and 17th century which as part of *as true as Coventry blue*, is a proverbial expression dating back several hundred years. The Germans with their devastating bombings laid waste to much of Coventry in World War II, destroying 70,000 homes, all but the great spire of the 14th-century Cathedral of St. Michael, and many other historic sites, which led to the term *to coventrate*—to attempt to bomb a city out of existence.

se'nnight. The Celts, like the Greeks, Babylonians, Persians, and Jews before them, customarily began each day at sunset, this practice giving us the term *se'nnight* for a week, or seven nights. In Genesis, for example, we find the evening coming before the morning in "The evening and the morning were the first day . . ." The same idea gives us *fortnight* (fourteen nights) for two weeks.

sent off with a flea in his ear. To be dismissed peremptorily, with no chance for denial or refusal. Someone so dismissed is distressed and restless—and can do nothing about it—like a dog with a flea in its ear. The expression dates back to the 15th century in England and a century earlier in France.

sent up the river. To be sent to prison. First recorded in the 1930s, this term must be much older. *The river* referred to is the Hudson in New York City and *up* it, at Ossining, is Sing Sing Penitentiary, which was founded in 1830.

separate the sheep from the goats. An old expression that has its origins in the New Testament, Matt. 25:32,33, reading: "And before him shall be gathered all nations; and he shall separate them one from another, as a shepherd divideth his sheep from the goats." It means to divide the good from the bad, the worthy from the unworthy.

sepia. This rich brown color is so named from the cuttlefish, which several centuries ago was widely known as the *sepia* (from the Latin *sepia*, "cuttlefish"). The inky fluid secreted by the sepia was first used to make a dye of this color.

September; October; November; December. When the Romans introduced the *Julian calendar (q.v.)*, they retained several month names from their old Roman calendar, despite the fact that these months no longer had the same position on the calendar. Thus September, once the Roman seventh month of the year, deriving from the Latin *septem*, "seven," remained as the ninth month of the year. The same happened with October, deriving from *octo*, "eight," which became the tenth month; November, deriving from *novem*, "nine," became the eleventh month; and December, deriving from *decem*, "ten," became the twelfth month.

Septuagint. Seventy-two men give their "name" to this word. Tradition has it that Ptolemy II, who reigned from 285 to 247 B.C., had the laws of the Jews translated into Greek by seventy-two scholars, six from each of the twelve Jewish tribes, in a period of seventy-two days on the island of Pharos. The translation became the earliest Greek version of the Old Testament, later erroneously named the *Septuagint* from the Latin *septuaginta*, which means seventy, not seventy-two. Scholars believe that the translation was made in Alexandria at this time, but not at Ptolemy's request, not by seventy-two Jewish scholars, and not in seventy-two days. Nevertheless, the fable about "the seventy" is responsible for the word. The tradition, however, applies only to the Pentateuch; the other books of the Old Testament were translated later. *Septuagint* is often printed as the Roman numeral LXX.

sequin. The Italian gold coin called the *sequin* (based on a Turkish gold coin called a *sequin*, from the Arabic *sikkah*, "coin") had been known in England since at least the early 17th century. Some authorities say that in the late 1870s the word was transferred to the bright spangles on clothes, but others claim that *sequin* in the latter sense has nothing to do with gold coins and derives from "shining artificial flowers invented by a chemist named Sequin in 1802."

sequoia. The largest and tallest living things on earth, the giant *sequoias* of California and Oregon are named for the exalted Indian leader Sequoyah, who invented the Cherokee syllabary, which not only made a whole people literate practically overnight but formed the basis for many Indian languages. Sequoyah (also Sequoya, or Sikwayi) was born about 1770, the son of a white trader named Nathaniel Gist and an Indian woman related to the great King Oconostota. Though he use the name George Guess, he had few contacts with whites, working as a silversmith and trader in Georgia's Cherokee country until a hunting accident left him lame. With more time on his hands, Sequoyah turned his attention to the "talking leaves," or written pages, of the white man and set out to discover this secret for his own people. Over a period of twelve years, ridiculed by family and friends, he listened to the speech of those around him, finally completing a table of characters representing all eighty-six sounds in the Cherokee spoken language. His system, which he devised by taking letters of the alphabet from an English spelling book and making them into a series of symbols, was adopted by the Cherokee council in 1821, one story claiming that Sequoyah's little daughter won over the council chiefs by reading aloud a message that they had secretly instructed her father to write down. Thousands of Indians would learn to read and write thanks to Sequoyah's "catching a wild animal and taming it," in his own words. The redwood tree (*Sequoia sempervirens*) was named for him not long after his death in 1847.

serendipity. A desirable discovery made by accident. English novelist Horace Walpole coined the word in 1754, basing it upon a lucky faculty enjoyed by the three heroes of the old Persian fairy tale "The Three Princes of Serendip." Serendip is an old Arabic name for Ceylon (*Sindhalawipa*, "Lion Island").

a serpent in one's bosom. According to legend, a kind Greek shepherd found a frozen serpent and put it under his shirt. The snake revived but bit its benefactor, which gives us this saying for an ungrateful person.

serpent-licked ears. Anyone with serpent-licked ears is said to have the power of seeing into the future. The ancient Greeks believed that both Cassandra and Helenus had the power of prophecy because serpents licked their ears while they slept in the temple of Apollo.

serviceberry. Another name for the *juneberry* (*amelanchie* species). "The blueberry of the northern plains" was dubbed the *serviceberry* as far back as the 18th century, and the name has a touching story behind it. Since its white blossoms appeared almost as soon as the ground thawed in spring, American pioneer families that had kept a body through winter to bury in workable ground used these first flowers to cover the grave.

set one's cap at. This phrase most likely goes back to the 18th century, a time when ladies wore light muslin caps indoors as well as out. When a suitor came to call, a young woman would naturally put on her best cap and wear it at the most fetching angle in order to impress her man and win a husband. This was called *setting one's cap at* or *for*, a man, an expression still occasionally heard today.

set the Thames on fire. England's Thames River, that cradle of so many far-flung sea expeditions, is usually pronounced to rhyme with *hems*, not *James*. The name is first recorded as *Tamesis*, circa A.D. 893. To *set the Thames on fire* is an old expression, said of the Rhine and other rivers as well, meaning to do something marvelous, to work wonders, to almost set the world on fire. However, one persistent story claims that the *Thames* in the phrase is not the famous river, but a misspelling of *temse*, a word for a corn sieve in the 18th century. According to this theory, a joke about a farm laborer who worked his temse so hard that it caught fire probably led to this expression for "to do something remarkable." As with so many word derivations, the truth will probably never be known.

the Seven Deadly Sins; the seven virtues. *The Seven Deadly* (or *Capital*) *Sins* are pride, wrath, envy, lust, gluttony, avarice, and sloth, while *the seven virtues* are faith, hope, charity, prudence, justice, fortitude, and temperance. The latter expression is recorded in English as early as 1320, the former a hundred years before this.

the Seven Last Words. *The Seven Last Words* are the last utterance of Christ on the cross. This was also the title of a musical composition by Haydn, written in 1785. The words are "My God, why hast thou forsaken me?" (more strictly, "My God, my God, why hast thou forsaken me?"), recorded in Mark 15:34, and Matt. 27:46, which gives the Hebrew as "Eloi, Eloi, lama sabachthani?"

seven names of God. Of the many names the ancient Hebrews had for the deity, *the seven names of God* were those over which their scribes had to take particular care, the names being: El, Elohim, Adonai, YHWH (Jehovah), Ehyeh-Asher-Ehyer, Shaddai, and Zebaot.

seven-sided animal; seven-sided son of a bitch. A one-eyed man or woman: "each having a right side and a left side, a fore side and a back side, an inside and an outside, and a blind side." The expression originated in the late 17th century and lasted until the early 20th. A Western U.S. variant was a *seven-sided son of a bitch*.

seven stages of drunkenness. (See blues.)

Seventh Heaven. The Muhammadan Seventh Heaven, is said to be "beyond the power of description." There each inhabitant is bigger than the whole earth and has 70,000 tongues that speak 70,000 languages—all forever chanting the praises of Allah. In the Islamic graded concept of Heaven, which also prevailed among the Jews, one goes after death to the Heaven he has earned on earth, and the Seventh Heaven, ruled by Abraham, is the ultimate one, a region of pure light lying above the other six, the Heaven of Heavens. Anyone in Seventh Heaven is thus in a state of ineffable bliss, having the greatest pleasure possible.

seventh-inning stretch. These words have become synonymous for a brief break from any long period of sitting. They derive of course from baseball's traditional seventh-inning stretch, which dates back to the late 19th century. One theory credits the ritual to President William Howard Taft, who is said to have stood up to stretch in the seventh inning of a Washington Senator game, prompting the rest of the crowd to follow suit. Better documented is the theory that the tradition originated at a game in 1882 at Manhattan College in New York City. Manhattan College baseball coach Brother Jasper, also the prefect of discipline, instructed restless students in the stands to rise and stretch for a minute in the seventh inning before the game continued. This seventh-inning stretch became a ritual at all Manhattan College games and spread to the major leagues during the 1880s when the college team played exhibition games against the New York Giants in the Polo Grounds.

seven virtues. (See **Seven Deadly Sins**.)

seven-year itch. (See **itch**.)

Seward's folly; Seward's icebox. After having been wounded by John Wilkes Booth's fellow conspirator Lewis Powell at the same time that Abraham Lincoln was assassinated, William Henry Seward recovered and remained in the cabinet of Lincoln's successor Andrew Johnson as Secretary of State. A vigorous opponent of slavery, he had originated the well-known phrases *there is a higher law than our constitution* and *irrepressible conflict*, the last expressing the state of the nation until it became all slave or all free. Seward's most important work in Johnson's administration was the purchase of Alaska from Russia in 1867. Very few had the foresight to appreciate his $7 million acquisition at the time and because Alaska was purchased almost solely due to his determination, although others had made overtures toward buying it before the Civil War, it was widely called *Seward's folly*, or *Seward's icebox*. William Henry Seward died in 1872, aged seventy-one, but the famous nick-

names were used long after his death, even when fortunes were being made in Alaskan gold and fur. *Alaska*, from the Aleut *A-la-as-ka*, "the great country," became the forty-ninth American state in 1959. The Seward Peninsula in West Alaska on the Bering Strait also bears the statesman's name, and Bering Strait and Bering Sea honor Captain Vitus Bering, a Dane who, in exploring for Russia in 1741, is believed to have been the first white man to visit Alaska.

sex for the students, athletics for the alumni, and parking for the faculty. These, according to President Clark Kerr of the University of California, in a speech delivered at another university in 1958, are "the three major administrative problems on U.S. college campuses."

sgnik sdneirf. Early Americans liked to spell backwards things that they detested, as in the case of "o-grab-me" (*q.v.*). This was also the case with the expression *king's friends*, which the Tories called themselves, contemptuous patriots calling them by the derogatory name *sgnik sdneirf*. As for the Loyalists, they called the patriots "rabble."

shack. The Aztec *Xacalli*, "wooden hut," gives us our word for a miserable hut or shanty. *Shack* came into English in the 1870s, in the American southwest, via the Mexican *Xacal*, or *jacal*, which is pronounced as though written "shacal."

shaddock. The ancestor of the grapefruit, the shaddock, or pomelo, reached Europe in about the middle of the 12th century from the Malay archipelago. It was called the *Adam's apple* at first and didn't receive its common name until a Captain Shaddock, a 17th-century English voyager, brought its seed from the East Indies to Barbados, where it was grown extensively. The grapefruit (*Citrus paradisi*) is neither a mutation of the thicker-skinned shaddock (*C. grandis*) nor a cross between the shaddock and sweet orange. It was developed in the West Indies and was given its name because it often grows in clusters like grapes. To further complicate matters, the shaddock is sometimes called the *forbidden fruit* and the grapefruit is called the *pomelo* in different parts of the world. The pink grapefruit was developed in Florida, as was the seedless variety.

shah. (See **kaiser**.)

shake a leg. (See **show a leg**.)

Shakespearean. *Shakespearean* means much more than "pertaining to the work of English author William Shakespeare." The word has come to represent profound universal magistry and vision in writing, among a veritable dictionary of superlatives. Little is really known about the personal life of the world's greatest poet and dramatist. Shakespeare was born in 1564 at Stratford-on-Avon of substantial middle-class parents, his father being an alderman, and received a solid grammar school education, well above the standards for the times. There is evidence that the *Sweet Swan of Avon*, as Ben Jonson called him, left Stratford for London to avoid a charge of poaching. He probably acted in the Earl of Leicester's company and by 1592 had achieved fame as a dramatist and actor. By this time Shakespeare had acquired property and lived like a gentleman with his wife, Anne Hathaway, whom he had married 10 years previously, and with their children, Susanna and the twins Hammet and Judith. Shakespeare was one of the few writers in his day to win fame and wealth. The Bard of Avon died on his own birthday in 1616, aged 52, in Stratford, where he had retired five years before. Countless stories and speculations surround the dramatist's life, ranging from the spelling of his name—the plentiful variations including Shakspeare, Shakspear, and Shakspere—to the alleged infidelity of his wife, the identity of the "dark lady" of the sonnets, and the fantastic theory that Bacon actually wrote his plays. Most of these theories are familiar, but none has been proved.

shako. A military cap in the form of a cylinder or truncated cone, with a visor and a plume or pompom, the *shako* is also worn in a similar version by members of marching bands. It is another of the few words of Hungarian origin in English, deriving from the Hungarian *ozako*, "a peaked cap," the original peak on the cap flattened off over the years.

shalom. *Shalom*, from a Hebrew root meaning "peace," is an Israeli greeting for both hello and good-bye, Leo Rosten noting that Israelis say they use it so "because we have so many problems that half the time we don't know whether we're coming or going." (*See* **Salaam** and **Salem**.)

sham. There is a good story about *sham* that merits repeating. One writer in 1734 claimed that "a Town Lady of Diversion [a prostitute] in Country Maid's Cloaths . . . to further her Disguise, pretends to be so *sham'd*." But her clients discovered after sleeping with her that she wasn't shamed, innocent, or healthy and "it became proverbial, when a maim'd lover [one with veneral disease] was laid up, or looked meagre, to say he had met with a *sham*." It may be true that *sham*, first recorded in the 1670s, derives from the tactics of some prostitute, but there is no absolute proof of it, though the word almost certainly has some connection with the word "shame."

shaman. The medicine man or priest called a *shaman* takes his name in a roundabout way from the Sanskrit *sram*, "to exhaust, fatigue," perhaps in reference to the

exhausting epileptic seizures such medicine men often exhibit when working their magic. The English word *shaman* comes from a Greek modification of the Russian modification of the Tungusic *saman*. *Saman* derives from the Prakrit *samana*, "a Buddhist monk," which comes from the Sanskrit word.

shambles. The Latin *scamellum*, "little bench," became *scamel* in Old English, changing to *shamel* in Middle English and meaning a butcher's block. *Shamel* became *shambles*, for "a slaughterhouse," in the 16th century and soon the word was being used to describe any scene of bloody disorder resembling a slaughterhouse, though in recent times *shambles* has come to mean any scene of disorder, not necessarily a bloody one.

shampoo. The thousands of ads plugging various *shampoo* formulas never mention that the word is one brought back from India, deriving from the Hindi word *champo*, "massage."

shamrock. A word representing the Irish from the Irish language. *Shamrock* simply means "little clover," deriving from the Irish *seamrog*, the diminutive of *seamar*, "clover." The three-leaved plant was used by St. Patrick to illustrate the trinity, which is why *to drown the shamrock* came to mean a drinking celebration on St. Patrick's Day.

to shanghai. The old expression *to ship a man to Shanghai* is the original version of this term. Sailors first used the words to describe how press gangs got them drunk, drugged them, or blackjacked them and forced them in service aboard a ship in need of a crew. Shanghai, a long way from America, was a leading Chinese shipping port, and many a shanghaied sailor did wind up there. *Shanghai* became so common in the 19th century that it was applied to anyone seized or forced to work unwillingly.

Shangri-la. This word, for "a paradise on earth," came into the language in 1933, when English novelist James Hilton published his novel *Lost Horizon*, which described a hidden paradise named *Shangri-la*. The name was used during World War II for the secret base from which U.S. planes flew to bomb Hiroshima and Nagasaki.

shank's mare. (*See* **going by shank's mare**.)

shanty; shantytown. *Shanty*, for "shack or rough cabin," is an Americanism first recorded in 1820 that probably derives from the Gaelic *sean tig*, "old house," though the French Canadian *chantier*, "log hut," is also a strong possibility. *Shantytown*, recorded in 1845, first meant a cluster of shacks near a railyard where railroad construction workers lived. Because many Irish lived in such shantytowns the term soon meant a poor Irish district, *shanty Irish* (1925) coming to mean poor Irish people who lived in such districts.

shark. Sea sharks take their name from land sharks, rather than the other way around. The German *Schurke*, meaning "a greedy parasite," gives us the word *shark*, and German sailors applied this term to the sea creature with the voracious land shark in mind. English sailors brought the word home in 1569, the same year that John Hawkins, the first English mariner engaged in the African slave trade, exhibited a huge shark in London. Quickly adopted to describe the killer fish, the word is first recorded some thirty years earlier in English to describe its human counterpart. (*See also* **shrimp**.)

Sharps rifle. The Sharps rifle "could be fired today and kill tomorrow," said quipsters, in reference to the story that one model could hit a target at five miles. This probably wasn't true, but the rifle—forty different models were made by the Sharps Company between 1840 and 1880—did have remarkable range, power, and accuracy. Hunters called it the "Old Poison Slinger" and it was used extensively in slaughtering the buffalo of America.

shavetail. U.S. Army second lieutenants are called *shavetails* because they are often untrained and untested, like the mules and horses in the old cavalry whose tails were customarily shaven as a warning to handlers and riders.

Shavian wit. George Bernard Shaw contributed his own name to the language in a characteristically clever way. Not liking the way "Shawian" sounded, he Latinized his name to Shavius and coined the adjective *Shavian* from it, leaving us with a sample of his *Shavian wit*. Shaw died in 1950, aged 94, his wit Shavian till the end. However, even he could be bested occasionally. "Isn't it true, my dear, that male judgement is superior to female judgement?" Shaw once asked his wife. "Of course, dear," she replied, pausing briefly. "After all, you married me and I you." (*See also* **superman**.)

shebang. (*See* **whole shebang**.)

sheet anchor. This name for an emergency anchor has confused etymologists for many years. The best bet is that the word *sheet* here derives from *shoot*. According to this theory, the device was first called a *shoot anchor* because when an emergency came, it had to be "shot" out, that is, dropped quickly. In any event, no sheets, or sails, were involved.

she, for a ship. All ships, even a man-of-war, are called *she* in naval parlance. In all Romance languages the word for *ship* is in the feminine gender. Ships were therefore called *she* by sailors when their proper names weren't used. English nouns do not have gender, but this habit of seafaring men from other countries was probably emulated by Englishmen.

shekels. (*See* **gelt**.)

shell out. From the actual "shelling out" of peas and corn—removing the first from their pods and removing corn from the cob—came the figurative use of *to shell out*, "to pay out." Removing a seed from the pod, etc., is like taking money out of a purse or pocket and, furthermore, dried shelled peas and "shelled corn," as it was called in America, were often a medium of exchange in the past. The phrase is first recorded in 1825.

shenango. (*See* **longshoreman**.)

shenanigans. Though now it is always used in the plural, this Americanism for "mischief" or "trickery" was first recorded as *shenanigan* in 1855, in California. There have been several suggestions as to its ancestors, including the Spanish *chanada*, "trick," and the argot German *schinaglen*, meaning the same. More likely it comes from the Irish *sionnachuighim*, "I play the fox," or "I play tricks."

Sheraton style. Only Thomas Chippendale has been more widely acclaimed than Thomas Sheraton (1751-1806) as a furniture designer. Unlike many of his predecessors, Sheraton was not a cabinetmaker and there is no record that he ever had a shop of his own or worked with his own hands building furniture. In fact, only one piece—a glass-fronted bookcase stamped with his initials—is known to have belonged to him. Sheraton's fame comes principally from his *The Cabinet-Maker and Upholsterer's Drawing Book* (1791), which introduced designs noted for simplicity and grace combined with utility. This book, followed by a cabinetmaking dictionary (1802) and an unfinished encyclopedia (1804), was intended for London cabinetmakers and the chairs and other pieces drawn in its pages strongly influenced many designers to adopt the *Sheraton style*, which was based on rectangular shapes, preferring straight lines to curves.

Sherlock Holmes. A. Conan Doyle probably named his detective after sage American author Oliver Wendell Holmes (1809-1894), who was also a professor of anatomy and physiology at Harvard. Sherlock Holmes, however, was modeled in large part on Dr. Joseph Bell (1837-1911), an eminent Edinburgh surgeon under whom Doyle studied medicine and who, like Holmes, often deduced the life and habits of a stranger just by looking at him. Doyle once admitted: "I used and amplified his methods when I tried to build up a scientific detective who solved cases on his own merits." It is said that Dr. John H. Watson, Holmes's Boswell, was intended as a parody of Doyle. In any event, working out of their rooms at 221B Baker Street, Holmes and Watson collaborated on some sixty cases, beginning with *A Study in Scarlet* (1887). In none of these stories did Holmes ever say, "Elementary, my dear Watson," and although he was addicted to cocaine, the great detective never once cried, "Quick, Watson, the needle!" Today the word *Sherlock* has come to mean a detective.

sherry. Via an indirect route, *sherry* is still another word that derives from Caesar's name. Sherry is made in Jerez de la Frontera, Spain, for which it was named, and *Jerez* in turn, commemorates Julius Caesar, having originally been called Xeres, this an adaptation of the Latin *urbs Caesaris*, "the town of Caesar." Sixteenth-century Spaniards pronounced Jerez something like *sherris*, which the English adopted and changed to *sherry* because they believed *sherris* was a plural form. Shakespeare wrote "a good sherris-sack hath a twofold operation in it" in *2 Henry IV*, but today the false singular is always used. It is said that when Sir Francis Drake burned the port of Cadiz in 1587, he seized 2,500 butts of sherry from nearby Jerez. Drake called the wine *sack*, according to the old folk story, but the dockers unloading the barrels noted the letters XERES (for Jerez) on them and became the first to use the word *zherry*, or *sherry*.

shibboleth. Perhaps only racial, religious, and national slurs have killed as many men as this word. *Shibboleth* has been extended to signify a catchphrase, especially one used so often that it has lost its effectiveness. But it still means a "password," which was its original biblical meaning. The word, deriving from the Hebrew *shibboleth*, for "stream in flood" or "ear of corn," is first recorded in Judges 12:1-16, where the Gileadites used it to pick out the sons of Ephraim from the members of other tribes. Jephthah's men slew 42,000 Ephraimites, who couldn't pronounce the *sh* in the password *shibboleth* and had to say "sibboleth."

shill; shillibeer. London's first buses were introduced from Paris by George Shillibeer (1797-1866) on July 4, 1829. His omnibuses, coaches carrying twenty-two passengers and pulled by three horses, immediately caught on in London and were being called "buses" within three years. Apparently, Shillibeer later went into the undertaking business, or at least a combined hearse and mourning coach was named the *shillibeer* after him. The word *shill*, for "a swindler's assistant," a "booster" hired to entice customers, may also derive from his name, especially considering that shills were and are still used to pack tourist buses in order to lure customers aboard. Shillibeer's connection with buses makes him a likely candidate, but there have been other suggestions. One is some notorious shill, probably a circus or carnival em-

ployee, surnamed Shillibeer. Another possibility is the American humorist Benjamin Penhallow Shillaber (1814-90), who printed Mark Twain's first work in his *Carpet Bag*, a weekly important in developing the new school of American humor. In 1847 Shillaber created the character Mrs. Partington, which he used in a number of books, beginning with his *Life and Sayings of Mrs. Partington* (1854). Critics charged Shillaber with lifting his character from English politician and author Sydney Smith. The American admitted that he took the name from Smith's allusion to the legendary Dame Partington, who had tried to sweep the flooding Atlantic Ocean out of her cottage and whom Smith had compared in an 1831 speech with the opposition of the House of Lords to reform. Although Shillaber denied using anything more than the Partington name for his gossiping Yankee Mrs. Malaprop, his own name came into some disrepute and may have become the basis for *shillaber* and then *shill*.

shillelagh. The knobby wooden club, or cudgel, called a *shillelagh* and used as both weapon and walking stick takes its name from the stout oaks of Shillelagh, a town in southwestern Ireland. Once made only of oak or blackthorn, a *shillelagh* can now be any thick knarred stick. The name is first recorded in the 17th century.

shilly-shally. To *shilly-shally*, meaning to hesitate or act in an irresolute way, is a corruption of "Will I, shall I?" or "Shall I, shall I?" The expression dates back to the late 17th century.

shimose. What word did Masashika Shimonose Kogakubachi give us? Masashika Shimonose Kogakubachi got his name into the dictionaries when he invented an explosive made of picric acid. *Shimose powder*, or *shimose*, was used against the Russians in the Russo-Japanese war of 1904-05 and proved highly effective. In France a powder to fill shells was made from it in 1886 and called melenite, while in England experiments in the town of Lydd two years later resulted in the explosive lyddite. All were names for essentially the same explosive, but shimose was the first to be extensively tested in war. Under whatever name you choose to call it, the first modern shell powder—it replaced black powder—has probably caused as much death and destruction internationally as any invention, still being one of the most common military explosives. Perhaps Masashika Shimonose Kogakubachi would rather have had it called by its scientific name of trinitrotoluene.

shindig; shindy. *Shin-dig* is first recorded, in 1859, as a Southernism for "a kick in the shins." It came to mean a loud, lively party within ten years or so and most authorities believe that the party *shindig* derives from the word meaning a kick in the shins. Another possibility is that the party name comes from the Scottish *shinty*, for "a wild form of field hockey played in Scotland" and, later, in America, *shindy* here possibly suggested by players being kicked in the shins. According to this theory, *shinty* (first recorded in 1771) became *shindy* (1821), a sailor's word for "a spree, merrymaking" and *shindy* by mispronunciation later became *shindig*. There was, in fact, a U.S. expression *to kick up a shindy*, "to cause a row or commotion," at about the time *shindig* was born. I would guess that both *shin-dig* and *shindig* derive from *shinty* —*shindy*.

shinplaster.   During the Civil War, beginning in 1862, the North issued paper currency of from 3-cent to 50-cent denominations that were humorously called *shinplasters*. The old story that they were so named because an anonymous soldier plastered his shin wound with them probably isn't true, because paper money had been called shinplasters as early as 1824. More likely they were dubbed shinplasters because such paper money often became valueless and was good for nothing but plastering the shins.

ship.   *Ship* can be traced back to the Old English *scip* or "shape," evidence that the word *ship* arose when a ship was "no more than a trunk of a tree scooped out and *shaped* to enable it to glide safely and smoothly through the water," according to one authority.

ship of fools.   Sebastian Brandt's famous *Narrenschiff*, or *Ship of Fools*, published in 1494, had as its theme the shipping of fools of all kinds from their native land of Swabia to the fictional Land of Fools. The various fools were introduced in the book by classes and reproved for their folly. In fact, in 15th-century Germany there were real *Narrenschiffs*. These most unusual ships were riverboats used to imprison the insane and thus clear city streets of them. Real ships of fools plied up and down the Rhine carrying their cargos of madmen, who were thought to have lost their souls and were supposed to sail back and forth until they became sane again. However, most of them died aboard hell ships, which had no destination save death.

shipping lanes.   In his book *Sailing Directions* (1855) U.S. Navy Lt. Matthew Fontaine Maury recommended "lanes," or "strips," for ships traveling westbound in the Atlantic after the U.S. mail steamer *Arctic* collided with the French steamer *Vesta* in 1854. These lanes became the building blocks for today's complex, internationally approved seasonal routes.

ships that pass in the night.   People who meet by chance and aren't likely to meet again are sometimes compared to *ships that pass in the night*. The expression dates back to the 19th century and seems to have originated in Henry Wadsworth Longfellow's poem *Tales of a Wayside Inn*

(1863): "Ships that pass in the night, and speak to each other in passing . . . "

shirtsleeves to shirtsleeves in three generations.   "There's no' but three generations atween clog and clog," says the old Lancashire proverb that is probably the ancestor of this expression, but American multimillionaire Andrew Carnegie (1835-1919) is credited with the exact words *shirtsleeves to shirtsleeves in three generations*, meaning that family wealth is not long lasting. The words don't apply to the Rockefeller, Du Pont, Rothschild, and Ford families, to name but a few that come quickly to mind.

shit.   From the Indo-European root *skei*, "to divide," comes the Old English *scitan*, "to defecate," that is the ancestor of our word *shit*. *To shit* thus means strictly to divide or cut (wastes) from the body. *Shit*, as slang for nonsense or lies, is an Americanism probably first used by soldiers during the Civil War as a shortening of *bullshit*, another Americanism that probably goes back thirty years or more earlier, though it is first recorded, in the form of its euphemism *bull*, in about 1850.

shit belong-um fire.   This apt bit of pidgin English was used by Lascar seamen employed as stokers on 19th-century British steamers. It means ashes.

shit or get off the pot.   Although *Partridge* gives this as World War II Canadian Army slang "directed at a dice player unable to 'crap out,'" it has been traced to the early 1900s in America, its maiden aunt ancestor probably *fish or cut bait*, "do something now or give up."

"'Shit!' said the Queen" . . .   An old story, unproved one way or the other, has it that those good friends Rudyard Kipling and Mark Twain had a contest between them to see who could write the bawdiest, most offensive story. An effort of Kipling's beginning "'Shit!' said the Queen . . ." was brought to an unamused Queen Victoria's attention, which is why Kipling was never knighted and never became poet laureate.

Shit! The Guard never surrenders!   (See **the Guard dies but never surrenders.**)

shiv.   *Shiv*, for "a dagger or knife," is centuries older than its first mention in 18th-century England. For it was taken into underworld English intact from the Romany *shiv*, meaning the same, long used by the Gypsies.

shiver me timbers!   Although this is a cricket expression referring to the scattering of wickets, for which timber is a slang substitute, it goes back much further. Originally, *timbers!* was an 18th-century nautical slang exclamation with no real meaning to it: "My timbers! what lingo he'd coil and belay." Novelist Capt. Frederick Marryat then embroidered the oath, making it *Shiver my timbers!* in *Jacob Faithful* (1834), an ejaculation you can be sure no one used before this.

shlock.   This Yiddish expression, for "shoddy, cheaply made, defective articles," derives from the German *Schlog,* "a blow" suggesting that the goods have been knocked around and damaged. Pronounced to rhyme with "stock," *shlock* is sometimes spelled *schlock.*

shock.   The French *choc,* a noun of action for "a military encounter," came into English early in the 16th century as *shocke,* with the meaning of the first charge in a battle, or two jousters charging each other and smashing together. By the early 18th century *shock* had come to mean a sudden disturbing impact on the mind as well as the body.

shoddy.   Civil War suppliers cheated the Union Army with a cheap uniform cloth called "shoddy," which literally unraveled on the wearer's back—and added a new adjective to the language.

to shoot down.   *To shoot down* someone's argument or *to shoot it down in flames* means to show that it is wrong or totally worthless, impossible. The expression originated during World War II, when so many planes were shot down and destroyed by the enemy.

to shoot one's bolt.   The *bolt* in this phrase, *he's shot his bolt,* meaning he's finished with his efforts, is not a door bolt, but an arrow—a bolt being an arrow with a bulletlike knob. Among other words and phrases owing their origin to the arrow are *thunderbolt, a bolt from the blue,* "a complete surprise," and *to bolt upright.*

shop.   The word *shop* derives from a Saxon term meaning the porch or lean-to of a house. Such "open rooms or stalls" eventually developed into enclosed stores.

shopping cart.   The first of America's 30 million *shopping carts* were invented and named by Sylman Goldman in 1936 for his Standard Supermarkets in Oklahoma, making him a millionaire in the process.

shopping mall.   In the 16th century the popular Italian game *pallamaglio* (from *palla,* "ball," and *maglio,* "mallet") spread to France, where it became known as *palemail,* which was called *pall mall* when the game was adopted by the English. A large playing area for the game called The Mall in London's St. James Park during the reign of Charles II later became a broad public walk, or promenade, called Pall Mall. It is this public walk where people promenaded that is the basis for our outdoor and indoor *shopping malls* (also called *shopping centers*),

where people promenade along a broad walk lined with shops. *Shopping malls,* or *malls,* as we know them today, are a relatively recent American innovation dating back only to the years after World War II. But rude examples of their kind can be found further back in American history, and they have their deepest roots in many age-old institutions, including the bazaars of Persia, the agoras of ancient Greece, the forums of Rome, and the fairs and marketplaces of medieval Europe. They have been called "the quintessential American place of today," malls being the places where people spend more time than anywhere else except at home or work.

Shoreditch.

I could not get one bit of bread
Whereby my hunger might be fed . . .
So weary of my life at length
I yielded up my vital strength
Within a ditch . . . which since that day
Is Shoreditch called, as writers say—

Shoreditch in London is so named because Jane Shore, Edward IV's cast-off mistress, died there in a ditch, her tale told in the old ballad above.

short fuse.   *He has a short fuse* we say of short-tempered people whose anger explodes at the slightest provocation. The expression originated during World War II, based upon short fuses in bombs and shells.

shorthand.   (*See* **stenography.**)

short hairs.   (*See* **to get by the short hairs.**)

Shortia.   *Shortia* is definitely a "low-growing" genus of evergreen herbs, comprising only two species, but that is not the reason for its name. The genus honors Dr. Charles W. Short (1794-1863), a Kentucky botanist. Native to the mountains of the Carolinas and Japan, the flowers are well adapted for use in a rock garden. The American species is sometimes advertised as *Oconee Bells* and the Japanese, *Nippon Bells.* The plants have beautiful white bell- or heart-shaped flowers, solitary and nodding on long stalks. They are more often called *Shortia,* or coltsfoot, than by their "Bell" names.

short shrift.   So many crimes were punishable by execution in Elizabethan times that condemned persons were often given only a few minutes for last rites on the crowded scaffold. Roman Catholic prisoners were allowed the sacrament of *shriving,* commonly called *shrift,* during which sins were confessed and absolution granted, but their callous executioners frequently permitted only a short version of the customary ceremony. This became known as *to give short shrift,* which from its literal sense has come to mean to cut short, to make quick work of, or to give very little attention to. *Shriving* and *shrift* derive from the Anglo-Saxon *scrifan*, "to make a confession."

shot in the arm. Anything that gives a person renewed vitality, enthusiasm, determination, confidence, or hope. However, if the expression's origins were taken into account it would mean short-lived vitality and false hope, for the words derive not from a shot administered by a doctor but from hypodermic injections of narcotics by drug addicts. Some anonymous drug user coined *a shot in the arm* back in the 1920s, basing it on the medical *shot*, for medicine injected into the body, which had been invented shortly before it. The phrase has nothing whatsoever to do with "Quick, Watson, the needle!," a saying often attributed to Sherlock Holmes. Holmes, in fact, never uttered those words in any of the tales Arthur Conan Doyle wrote about him, just as he never said, "Elementary, my dear Watson."

a shotten herring. Since Shakespeare's time worthless or spiritless persons have been called *shotten herring* because they resemble such fish. Shotten herring are herring that have "shot off," or ejected, their spawn and are weak, tired, and worthless.

shout it from the housetops. Let everybody know. The old expression is from the Bible (Luke 12:3): ". . . and that which ye have spoken in the ear shall be proclaimed upon the housetops."

show a leg; shake a leg. *Show a leg* means to get up from bed, to hurry, or be alert. One version of its birth says that when the bos'n's mate on early 19th-century sailing ships woke up the crew in the morning, he cried, "Show a leg, show a leg or a stocking!" At that time, according to the story, women were allowed to be on board ship, ostensibly as sailors' wives, and a "leg in a stocking put over the side of a hammock indicated that the occupant was a woman, who was allowed to remain until the men had cleared out." A more prosaic and reasonable account says the bos'n cried, "Come on, all you sleepers! Hey! Show a leg and put a stocking on it." *Shake a leg*, meaning "hurry," may derive from this earlier phrase, for both are nautical expressions and no better explanation has been given.

show the white feather. A cock with any white feathers was believed to be poorly bred and too cowardly for cockfighting in days past. This led to the old expression *to show the white feather*, "to exhibit cowardice."

shrapnel. *Shrapnel's shell*, or *shrapnel's shot*, as it was first called, was the brainchild of Henry Shrapnel, a British artillery officer who held the rank of second lieutenant and had only turned twenty-three when he began work on his deadly contrivance in 1783. Shrapnel

had joined the army at the age of eighteen and served in Gibraltar, the West Indies, and Flanders under the Duke of York. He devoted all his spare time and money to developing his invention, the *shrapnel shell*, which consisted of a spherical projectile filled with lead musket balls and a small charge of black powder that was set off by a time fuse, exploding the shell in midair and scattering the shot in an ever-widening circle over a large area. This antipersonnel weapon, which laid low everyone in its path, was finally adopted in 1803 due to Shrapnel's persistent efforts and he was promoted to regimental lieutenant colonel the following year. Although the shell itself wasn't used during World War II, the term *shrapnel* is still applied loosely to shell fragments from any high explosive, whether artillery, bomb, or mine. Henry Shrapnel, who had been promoted to lieutenant general in 1837, died five years later, aged eighty-one. He had never been paid a cent for his important invention and the government refused even to compensate him for the several thousand pounds of his own money that he had spent in developing the weapon.

shrewd. *Shrewd* most likely comes from the name of the shrew, a small, mouselike animal with a long snout, common in England's forests. Extremely truculent animals, shrews will often fight to the death over a bit of food, the victor eating the loser in the bargain. Thus a *shrew* became an evil, vicious person, especially a woman who scolded or nagged, as in Shakespeare's *The Taming of the Shrew*, and the verb *to shrew* formed from this noun gave us the word *shrewd* in its past participle. Over the centuries *shrewd* lost its meaning of evil but retained the qualities of sharpness and cleverness that made the little shrew formidably wicked, so that today shrewd means keen-witted, clever, sharp in practical affairs.

shrimp. Short people are *not* called *shrimps* because they resemble the shellfish in size. As with *sharks* (*q.v.*), it is the other way around. The common little European species *Crago vulgaris* was named *shrimp* from the Middle English word *shrimpe*, which meant a puny person.

shrink. *Shrink*, and *headshrinker*, from which it derives, are Hollywood terms, the latter dating back to the late 1940s and the former coming on the scene some twenty years later. Both, of course, mean a psychiatrist and may be a comparison to the medicine men of primitive tribes who literally shrunk heads to work magic; *headshrink* may refer to the *shrinking*, or lessening, of problems in a patient's head.

shucks. *Shucks* may derive from worthless "shucks" or husks of corn, but the interjection, used to express mild disgust or regret, first recorded in 1847, is thought by some to be simply a euphemism for "shit," as its oldest quotation in the *Dictionary of Americanisms* would seem to indicate: "And Mr. Bagley was there [to shoot] any gentleman who might say 'shucks.'"

shut your face.   Stop talking. This Americanism is first recorded by Upton Sinclair in *King Coal* (1917): "The marshall bade him 'shut his face,' and emphasized the command by a twist at his coat collar."

shyster.   *Shyster*, an American slang term for a shady, disreputable lawyer, is first recorded in 1846. Various authorities list a real New York advocate as a possible source, but this theory has been disproved by Professor Gerald L. Cohen of the University of Missouri-Rolla, whose long paper on the etymology I had the pleasure of reading. Shakespeare's moneylender Shylock has also been suggested, as has a racetrack form of the word *shy*, i.e., to be shy money when betting. Some authorities trace *shyster* to the German *Scheisse*, "excrement," possibly through the word *shicir*, "a worthless person," but there is no absolute proof for any theory.

Siamese twins.   Chang and Eng Bunker were born in Bangesau, Siam (now Thailand) on April 15, 1811, and were discovered at Mekong when they were sixteen. Their bodies were joined by a ligament between the xiphoid cartilages, a short tubular band uniting them at the chest through which their circulatory systems communicated. After P.T. Barnum brought the world-renowned "Chinese Double-Boys" to America, he had considerable trouble with them, claiming that they were the only show business people he couldn't get along with. But then Chang and Eng hated everybody, even each other, Barnum said. At any rate, the two often quarreled with the impresario over his methods and only exhibited when they needed the money. In April 1864 they married two English sisters, Sarah and Adelaide Yates, fathering twenty-two children between them—Chang, ten, and Eng, twelve—according to the records. They finally settled with their families on a farm in New Hampshire, where they died on January 17, 1874, within two or three hours of each other. But the surviving twin did not die of a broken heart, as the story goes; fatal illness in one *Siamese twin* dooms the other unless they can be separated, which was impossible in Chang and Eng's case. The Siamese Twins, as they were billed, gave their name to all others so born after them and the term is also used to describe inseparable friends. Doubles of many kinds are called *Siamese*, such as the *Siamese pipes* with two openings almost at ground level outside some buildings, which fire engines use to pump water into a building for its standpipes and sprinkler system.

sic.   Pronounced "sik," this little word is simply the Latin for "thus, so." It is used in brackets by writers after a word or phrase to indicate that the word or phrase is being reproduced by the writer exactly as it is in the original, even though it is wrong in some way.

Sicilian vespers.   In 1282, the Sicilians massacred their French oppressors throughout the country, the signal to begin the massacres in each city being the bell for evening church services, or vespers. Within a few days Sicilian wits were calling the massacres the *Sicilian Vespers*.

sideburns.   General Ambrose Everett Burnside had a flair for doing the daring, innovative thing in war as well as fashion. Despite his many failures as a general he went on to be elected governor of Rhode Island for three terms, 1866-69, and United States senator for two terms, from 1875 until his death in 1881, at age fifty-seven. From the constant publicity given him, the flamboyant *Burnside hat* that he wore in the field came to be called after the big bluff and hearty general, as were the *burnside whiskers*, or *burnsides*, he affected. Innovative as ever, he had chosen to wear the hair on his face in a new way, shaving his chin smooth below a full mustache and big muttonchops, or sidebar whiskers. Thousands imitated him and his *burnsides*, because they were on only the sides of the face, were soon called *sideburns*, this reversal of Burnside's name having nothing to do with his military reversals, though that might have been appropriate.

sidekick.   American pickpockets once called the side pants pockets *side-kicks*. These are the hardest pockets to pick because they are closest to the hands of a victim and are constantly moving with the motions of the legs. Therefore, any man wise to the ways of pickpockets kept his wallet in his trusty side pocket, or *side-kick*. *Side-kicker* thus became a slang synonym for a faithful buddy, a partner who is always at one's side. O. Henry first recorded the term in one of his stories in 1904 and about ten years later *side-kicker* was shortened to *sidekick*.

sienna.   The Italian city of Siena lends its name to the red color sienna, while Venice gives its own to Venetian red. The colors were apparently invented by artists in those cities. (*See also* **Magenta; Titian**.)

Sierra Leone.   Portuguese sailors off Africa thought they spied a great mountain chain along the west coast and were convinced they heard the roaring of lions coming from those mountains. They thus named the area *Sierra Leone*, "mountain range of the lions," a name that the African country Sierra Leone still bears today, even if the Portuguese seafarers did eventually discover that the "mountain range" they saw were great cumulous clouds in the sky and the roaring they heard was the surf breaking on the beach. (*See also* **Nome; Guinea**.)

Silent League.   A society organized in 1903 (in the U.S. Navy of all places), of men who "solemnly agree to discourage Profanity and Obscenity everywhere so long as they live," in the words of its founder, Chaplain Carroll Q. Wright. As Gary Jennings notes in his delightful *Personalities of Language* (1965): "I know of no sailor today who ever heard of the Silent League, but I know several who are walking evidence that Profanity and Obscenity have outlived it."

silent—like the *p* in swimming.   British in origin and mostly British in use, this punning catchphrase (the obvious pun is on "pee," to urinate) dates back to the early 1900s and, as *Partridge* notes, is sometimes employed jokingly in explaining difficult pronunciations: e.g., "Her name is Fenwick, where the *w* is silent—like the *p* in swimming."

Silent Majority.   U.S. President Richard M. Nixon coined this phrase, in a 1969 speech. He, or his speechwriters, were referring to the majority of people who support the established system of government, morals, etc., but rarely make themselves heard.

silhouette.   Madame de Pompadour had her friend Étienne de Silhouette appointed France's controller general in 1759, but was probably disappointed with the results. Silhouette, then fifty, proceeded to try to get France back on her feet after the bankruptcy brought about by the Seven Years War, not to mention the luxury-loving court where La Pompadour set the style and spent more than anyone else. The new minister started out well enough, raising a 72 million-livres loan, but he soon placed restrictions on the spending of Louis XV himself, proposed a land tax on the estates of nobles, and ordered a cut in government pensions. This naturally angered the nobles, who often found ways to circumvent Silhouette's reforms, and the minister trotted out plans to levy an income tax, triple the poll tax on bachelors, institute a luxury tax, and levy a stringent sales tax. People generally thought such reforms cheap, capricious, and petty, resenting the sacrifices demanded, and when financiers boycotted his treasury operations, Silhouette was forced to resign less than nine months after he took office. In the meantime, his parsimonious regulations had inspired the phrase *à la silhouette*, "according to Silhouette," or "on the cheap." Pants without pockets—and who needed pockets with such confiscatory taxes—were said to be made *à la silhouette*, as were snuffboxes constructed with wood, and coats that were required to be fashioned without folds. The term was also applied to shadow portraits made by tracing the outline of a profile and filling it in with black, or cutting the outline out of black paper. These were called portraits *à la silhouette*, cheap portraits in the fashion of Silhouette, and soon became known simply as *silhouettes*.

Silicon Valley.   Silicon semiconductors and microelectric chips are the backbone of the modern electronics in-

dustry. Their manufacture is the primary industry on the plain between San Francisco and San Jose, California, which is called *Silicon Valley*.

silo drippings.   This synonym for homemade liquor dates back to the late 19th century when it was made on farms in the American Midwest, where Prohibition was often in effect. Silos held corn for the winter feeding of stock and the corn packed in a full silo slowly fermented, forming a potent brew that dripped out of holes drilled in the bottom of the silos and was collected by thirsty farmers.

silver spoon.   The earliest spoons were made of wood, the word *spoon*, in fact, deriving from the Anglo-Saxon *spon*, "a chip of wood." Until the last century most people used pewter spoons, but traditionally, especially among the wealthy, godparents have given the gift of a silver spoon to their godchildren at christening ceremonies. The custom is centuries old throughout Europe and inspired the saying "born with a silver spoon in one's mouth," i.e., born to hereditary wealth that doesn't have to be earned. This expression is not of American origin as the *O.E.D.* implies; the great dictionary only traces the phrase back to 1800 here, but it is much older, for Cervantes used in in *Don Quixote* (1605-1615): "Every man was not born with a silver spoon in his mouth." The Duke of Bedford gave a nice twist to the phrase in the title of his biography, *A Silver-Plated Spoon*. The *silver shoon* in Walter de la Mare's poem "Silver" are "silver shoes," *shoon* being an old plural of *shoe*:

> Slowly, silently, now the moon
> Walks the night in her silver shoon.

Simenon.   A *Simenon* is a serious psychological novel of about fifty thousand words written by author Georges Simenon—and written in a rather unique way. Simenon gets a complete medical examination before he begins one of these critically praised short novels. He then literally locks himself in a room and, working from the barest of notes, allows himself seven days to write each book and three days to revise. *Simenons* are distinct from the author's popular Inspector Maigret stories, which are highly respected in the mystery field. Born in Liege, Belgium on February 13, 1903, the prolific but not prolix Simenon has authored some 500 novels since he began writing at the age of nineteen, many of these admittedly *pot boilers* (*q.v.*) or breadwinners turned out under a score of pseudonyms.

simoleon.   Our slang for "one dollar," common since the late 19th century, may derive from the British slang *simon*, for "sixpence," which can be traced back to about 1700. First the British *simon* became our *simon* for a dollar (ca. 1859 but now obsolete) and then for some reason it became *simoleon*—though this leaves unexplained the shift in accent from the first syllable in *simon* to the second in *simoleon*. *Simon* is said to have been used by the British for "sixpence" because it is alliterative with "six," but Simon Magus (*see* **simony**) has been suggested as an eponym.

Simon Legree.   (*See* **Uncle Tom**.)

simony.   There is a legend that Simon Magus the magician tried to prove his divinity in a dispute with Peter and Paul before the emperor Nero. He attempted to fly up to heaven after jumping out a high window, succeeded in defying the laws of gravity for a few moments, and then found himself cast down to earth by the prayers of the disciples. Simon Magus, who lived in the first century in Samaria, was a skilled magician, his last name, in fact, meaning sorcerer. The story of his conversion to Christianity is told in the Bible (Acts 8:9-24), but the passage instructs us that Simon's conversion was made only so that he could obtain the new powers of sorcery that he thought the apostles possessed. Simon's name, in the form of *simony*, has since been a synonym for traffic in sacred things, such as the buying and selling of church offices, a *simoniac* being one who practices simony. Not much is known of Simon after he was reproached by Peter, but it is believed that he founded a rival religion, a Gnostic sect combining elements of Christianity and paganism, traveling with a former prostitute named Helen and winning a number of disciples called *Simonians*. The traditional belief is that the wily magician died trying to prove his divinity when he attempted to imitate the resurrection of Christ. Simon, it seems, allowed himself to be buried alive, mistakenly believing that he would rise on the third day.

sincere.   According to an old story, *sincere* has its roots in the quarries where Michelangelo worked before he became an immortal sculptor and an accomplished poet. Roman quarrymen often rubbed wax on marble blocks to conceal their imperfections temporarily. Then the Roman Senate decreed that all marble be "without wax," or *sine cera*, this eventually becoming our word *sincere*, "without deception." Most authorities, however, trace *sincere* to the Latin *sincerus*, "clean, pure, sound."

since time immemorial.   We have used this phrase for at least eight centuries, to mean "ancient beyond man's memory or records." But in English law *time immemorial*, according to a 1275 statute, is any time prior to 1189, the year Richard I came to power in England.

sine qua non.   That which is indispensable, an indispensable condition, something essential. Although the words translate as "without which nothing," the original Latin phrase from which they were taken is *Sine qua non potest esse*, "Without which it is not possible to exist." Dating back in English use to the 16th century, the words have their origins in Aristotelian expressions. The term is also used attributively ("Publication is a *sine qua non* condition for the generation of literature"—Thomas De Quincey, *Works*, 1860) and can be used to mean "somebody indispensable." The little-known plural, *sine quibus non*, is not used in the humorous expression for men's trousers—"these indispensables" being called *sine qua nons*.

sing a different tune.   Possibly the wandering minstrels of medieval Europe suggested this expression because they changed the words of their songs from court to court in order to praise the exploits of different lords. They could have, for the phrase is recorded as early as 1390. It now means to act or speak in a different manner, and usually to humble oneself in the process. Generally it's heard in the form of *to make someone sing another tune*, to make him change his behavior or recant what he's said.

Singapore.   Owned originally by the Sultan of Johore, who ceded it to the British in 1824, Singapore is a corruption of the Sultan's name.

to sing for one's supper.   A proverbial phrase, immortalized in the nursery rhyme about little Tommy Tucker, *to sing for one's supper* has its origins in the troubadours who literally sang for their suppers in English taverns.

singing psalms to a dead horse.   (*See* **quicker than hell can scorch a feather**.)

Sinhalese words in English.   Sinhalese, spoken in Sri Lanka, has contributed several words to English, including *beriberi*, and *tourmaline*.

sink one's teeth into.   *To sink one's teeth into something* means to eat it, usually with great enjoyment, or to get into the spirit of anything. The Americanism was first recorded in 1892 as *sink tooth into*: "Only a favored few of the millions of feasters on Thanksgiving Day will sink tooth into genuine wild turkey meat."

si nummi immunis.   *Si nummi immunis* has been called the lawyer's palindrome (reading the same backward as forward). The Latin can be translated as "Pay me your fee and you go scot-free." (*See* **palindrome**.)

Sioux.   These Indians called themselves *Dakotah*, "the allies." However, rival tribes called them the *Nadowessioux*, "little snakes, the enemy," and white explorers in the area mistakenly dubbed them the *Sioux*, from the last syllable of this slur upon them.

sirens.   Represented in mythology as birds with the heads of women, the *Sirens* were the three daughters of the Greek sea god Phorcu (Achelous). Perched on their pleasant island, they lured mariners to death, the sailors enchanted by the Sirens' song and crashing their ships against the rocks. In rare instances they could be defeated, as when Orpheus, the legendary poet, outwitted the Sirens by playing his spellbinding lyre over the sound of their song. The name *siren* is now applied to any sexy, wilful woman.

Sir Galahad.   The prototype of the chivalrous male, the original Sir Galahad may have been added to the Arthurian legends by Welsh author and clergyman Walter Map in about 1200. The son of Lancelot and himself a Knight of the Round Table, he is the hero of the Quest for the Holy Grail. His name is still synonymous for a courteous gentleman, mostly used in the same lighthearted, even humorous ways that it has been for a century or so.

Sir, I have not yet begun to fight!   During the famous battle between the *Bon Homme Richard* and the *Serapis* it seems that some of John Paul Jones's men cried for surrender, but the captain laid one of them low with the side of his pistol, fracturing his skull. Captain Richard Pearson of the *Serapis* then shouted to Jones, asking if he had had enough. Jones uttered the immortal words: "Sir, I have not yet begun to fight!" So Lieutenant Richard Dale later recalled. Jones himself claimed that he answered Pearson's challenge with the far less colorful words "I have not yet thought of it, but am determined to make you strike."

sirloin.   Sirloin, strictly speaking, is meat from the steer's hip, but today it is sold without the prized filet and often goes by the name of shell hip or rump steak. The widely accepted Sir Loin story about its origins shows how highly esteemed in the past was this aristocrat of steaks. The tale is told about numerous British monarchs, including the lusty Henry VIII, James I (on whom Jonathan Swift bestowed credit), and lastly, Charles II, who ruled England from 1660 to 1685. In each case the king in question was supposed to have been so pleased with the succulent slice of pink meat served him that he unsheathed his sword, laid it on the brown-crusted sirloin and knighted it, solemnly declaring, "Hereafter thou shalt be dubbed 'Sir Loin.'" The only bothersome fact is that *sirloin* really derives from an Old English word *surloin* (from *sur*, "above" or "over"), which simply meant the cut above the loin and came to be misspelled *sirloin* in about 1600. This, however, did not prevent writers like Scott from using terms like *the knightly sirloin* and the *noble baron of beef*. The last, practically unheard of today, was a double sirloin, a huge joint weighing up to 100 pounds and comprising both sides of the back.

Sisyphean.   Endless heartbreaking toil is the lot of anyone engaged in *Sisyphean* labors. The term comes to us from the legend of *Sisyphus*, an ancient king of Corinth, who was sent to Hades for crimes against his subjects and condemned forever to roll a huge stone up a steep hill, only to have it roll downhill when he reached the top, so that he must roll it uphill again in an unending cycle.

sit-down strike; sit-in.   *Sit-down strikes*, common in the 1930s, involved workers sitting down at their machines and refusing to let other workers take their places until a strike was settled. *Sit-ins*, a tool of civil-rights and other protest groups in the 1960s, employed the same technique, these passive protests originally being used only against racial segregation.

six of one and a half dozen of another.   Captain Frederick Marryat may have invented this phrase in *The Pirates and the Three Cutters* (1836), or else it was old sea slang that the author recorded. It apparently arose from no specific situation and means "nothing to choose between," "one and the same," simply because "six" and "a half dozen" are identical. *Arcades ambo*, a similar phrase, means two persons having the same tastes or habits in common. It comes from Virgil's seventh eclogue: "*Ambo florentes aetabibus, Arcades ambo*" ("Both in the flower of youth, Arcadians both").

sixes and sevens.   I'm at sixes and sevens, in a state of confusion, trying to explain this expression, which dates back to 1340. One theory is that it comes from the biblical phrase (Job 5:19): "He shall deliver thee in six troubles: yea in seven there shall no evil touch thee." More likely the term evolved from the old dice game of hazard. *Sinque* and *sice* ("five" and "six") were the most risky bets to make in the old game, and anyone who tried to throw these numbers was considered careless and confused. Later, *sinque* and *sice* became "six" and "seven." Perhaps the change simply occurred because the terms looked and sounded somewhat alike. But it is possible that six and seven (an impossible throw in dice and two numbers that add up to the unlucky thirteen) represents a joking shift. Only about a century and a half ago did *set on six and seven* take on its plural forms and become (set) at *sixes and sevens*. The phrase is still widely used today. A similar, older Italian expression, *a tredici*, "at thirteen," may be the source of the phrase.

the $64 question.   On the radio quiz program "Take It or Leave It," which premiered in 1941 and was emceed by Bob Hawk, topics were chosen by contestants from the studio audience and questions on these topics answered by each contestant on seven levels. The easiest question was worth two dollars and the questions progressed in difficulty until the ultimate $64 Question was reached.

The popularity of the show added to the language the expression *the $64 question*, "any question difficult to answer," and inspired a slew of similar quiz shows. A decade later came television's "$64,000 Question" with its plateaus instead of levels, its isolation booth, and its scandals involving prominent contestants who cheated in cahoots with the producers. Then, after a long hiatus, there was the "$128,000 Question," but despite these programs with their inflated prize, *$64 question* retains its place in the national vocabulary.

sizzle (See **onomatopoeia**.)

Sjambok rule. *Sjambok*, for "a rhino-hide whip," is said to come from Malay and ultimately from Urdu. The word, however, is associated with the Boers of South Africa, *sjambok rule* meaning a repressive tyrannical rule of whips and violence. The word is an international one, recorded in the dictionaries of many languages. It seems to have come into English in the first quarter of the 19th century.

to skate on thin ice. The allusion is to skating over ice so thin that it won't bear the skater's weight if he slows down, a form of skating where safety is in speed, as Ralph Waldo Emerson said. The sport was once called *tickledy-bendo* in New England. The metaphor *skating on thin ice* means that someone is taking chances, or is conducting himself in a manner verging on the questionable, dangerous, or indelicate.

skedaddle. *Skedaddle* is often thought of as an Americanism for "to retreat, flee, clear out, depart hurriedly." But the expression probably comes from Scottish and English dialect, possibly deriving from the Greek *skedannunai*, "to split up." First used in America during the 1820s it became popular among Northern troops during the Civil War as a word describing Rebels fleeing the battlefield after a loss.

skeleton at the feast. The Egyptians, according to Herodotus and Plutarch, liked to sit a skeleton or "image of a corpse" at their feasts in order to remind guests of their mortality. Whether this inspired an "eat, drink and be merry, tomorrow you die" atmosphere or assured their hosts that their guests would leave early, isn't known, but the *skeleton at the feast*, now serves as a humorous term for a deadhead, a party pooper, a wet blanket, someone who won't be invited to the next feast.

skeleton in the closet. It took years to find what seemed to be "the perfect lady," one without "a single care or trouble," but, alack and alas, the lady proved to have her dark secret, too. She admitted this and took the investigators to her bedroom closet, where a skeleton hung from the ceiling. After explaining that the skeleton was once her husband's rival, whom he had killed in a duel, she cried: "I try to keep my trouble to myself, but every night my husband forces me to kiss that skeleton!" Certainly this would be one of the most interesting of phrase derivations if the old horror story could be proved. But it can't. No one knows the origin of a *skeleton in the closet*, a shameful secret which a family tries to hide. There have also been attempts to link the words with actual skeletons that doctors hid in their homes or offices when dissection was forbidden by law, none very convincing. We only know that William Makepeace Thackeray first used the expression in print in an 1855 story he contributed to *Punch* and that it was probably in use at least ten years before that.

ski. The noun *ski* derives from the Old Norse *skith*, "snowshoe." Over the centuries *ski* became a verb as well as a noun, so that we now go *skiing* on our *skis*.

skidoo. (See **twenty-three skidoo**.)

to skin alive. *I'll skin you alive*, someone might say to another person in anger, meaning he will severely beat that person. The expression seems to have been recorded first in 1869, in a reference to a shady "skin-em-alive place." But it must be much older and is probably based upon the actual practice of skinning animals alive. According to Edward Hoagland in *The Tugman's Passage* (1982) "the more brutal [American] pioneers" skinned wolves alive "and turned them loose to scare the rest of the pack."

skin game. In the early 1800s *to skin* made its debut as a verb meaning "to strip one of his money." After another fifty years *skin game* was being used for a card game or any other game or scheme in which a person has absolutely no chance to win.

skipper. As *scip* meant *ship* (*q.v.*) in Old English, *scipper* meant a ship's captain. By 1830 the English were pronouncing the latter word *skipper* and using it for the captain of a small merchant vessel, though it now refers to the captain of any ship.

skipper swallows the anchor. This expression originally meant that the captain or skipper of a ship has retired. *The skipper swallows the anchor* dates back to the late 19th-century steamship lines, and is now sometimes used to indicate that death has come as well.

skit. No one really knows the origin of the word *skit*, for "a short comical act in a variety show." A good guess is the Swedish *skjuta*, one of whose meanings is "full of frisks or capers." The word, first recorded in 1820, may also be a back-formation from *skittish*, in its sense of liveliness, levity.

skivvies. *Skivvies*, slang for men's shorts, may derive from the Japanese *sukebei*, "lewdness." In the British navy *skivvy* is a greeting said to have been first encountered as a salutation of Japanese prostitutes, and "Skivvy-skivvy, G.I.?" or "Skibby-skibby, G.I.?" was indeed the way Japanese and Korean street prostitutes and pimps solicited Americans during both Word War II and the Korean Conflict.

skulduggery. *Skulduggery*, for "dishonesty or trickery," has no connection with heads or *skulls*. It does have something to do with adultery. *Skulduggery* is the American variant of the Scottish *skulduddery*, which means illicit sexual intercourse or obscenity, the Scottish word originally coined as a euphemism for *adultery* (*duddery*, "adultery"). Thus the word is doubly euphemistic: *skulduddery* itself and the American *skulduggery* fashioned from it that is first recorded in 1856. In America the word has never suggested any sexual hijinks, usually meaning political trickery.

skull. When the English poet Lord Byron drank from a skull he was hardly being original. Human skulls used as drinking cups have been traced back before 7000 B.C. Herodotus, for example, mentions that the Scythians made drinking vessels out of skulls of their enemies by sawing off the skull below the eyebrows, covering the outside with leather and gilding the inside with silver or gold. He also notes that people near the River Don in southern Russia boiled the flesh of a dead parent with that of sheep and ate it, preserving the parent's skull as a keepsake cup. An old story, "The Lay of Weyland the Smith," tells how the eponymous hero slew his opponent's sons, making golden cups out of their brainpans and gems out of their eyes, which he sent to their mother, and fashioning broaches from their teeth, which he sent to their sisters. Skulls were also used as drinking cups by the Vikings (*See* **Skol!**) and the skulls of saints were used as drinking cups in medieval monasteries. Such customs have led some etymologists to suggest that the word *skull* itself meant a drinking cup before it acquired its present meaning. No proof of the derivation has been established, but there is a strong connection between the Old Norse *skal*, "a bowl," and *skull*. Another possibility is that *skull* derived from the Old Norse *skel*, "a seashell."

skunk. The little striped mammal could squirt his foul yellow spray up to twelve feet so American Indians called him *segankw*, or *segonku*, the Algonquian dialect word meaning simply "he who squirts." Pioneers corrupted the hard-to-pronounce Algonquian word to *skunk*, and it has remained so since. We know the skunk's foul spray as m-butyl mercaptain, or $CH_3C_2CH_2CH_2SH$, but it smells as bad under any name. The skunk was called *enfant du diable*, "child of the devil," by French Canadian trappers, but is also called the *wood polecat* and the *wood*

pussy. The most common species is the striped skunk, *Mephitis, Mephitis* which might be loosely translated as "double stinky," though *mephitis* means a noxious exhalation from the ground.

skunk cabbage. The much-maligned marshland *skunk cabbage* (*Symplocarpus foetidus*) bears little relation or resemblance to the cabbage (*Brassica capitata*). The plant takes its name, an Americanism first recorded in 1751, from its fetid smell and its leaves' supposed resemblance to cabbage leaves. Actually the *skunk cabbage's* large, nearly round leaves are far more handsome and its sheath-like spathe is beautifully colored. But the plant's foul smell has caused it to be called *pole-cat weed* as well as *skunk cabbage*. Other names for it, historically, are *tickleweed* and *dock*. Cheap, poor liquor used to be called *skunk cabbage brandy.*

skyscraper. The world's first *skyscraper* office building was the 10-story Chicago office of the Home Insurance Company built in 1883 by architect William Le Baron Jenney. The fitting name *skyscraper* was given to this first building to employ steel skeleton construction, a building much higher than any other building of its time, but journalists had borrowed the word from the triangular sails that had long been used high on the masts of sailing vessels, scraping against the sky.

slainte! A drinking toast familiar to Irishmen everywhere, *slainte*! (pronounced *s-lawn-cheh*) is simply Gaelic for "cheers!"

slammer. *Slammer* had been slang for "a door" before it became a slang synonym for "prison" in the 1930s. Both terms, of course, refer to the slamming of doors, in the last case the slamming shut of all the metal doors in a cellblock at the same time. (*See also* **hoosegow.**)

slang. The fabled "Dutch General Slangeuberg noted for his abusive and exaggerated epithets when he reproved the men under his command" is *not* the source for the word *slang*. Neither is the Italian *s-lingua—s*, the negative, and *lingua*, "language," equaling *slingua* (slang), or "bad language." No one is sure, but some prominent etymologists, including Ernest Weekley, believe that *slang* may come from the Norwegian *slengjakeften*, "to sling the jaw," "to abuse." The word dates back to the late 18th century.

slapstick. The slapstick used in early low comedies was "a large paddling implement consisting of two boards hinged at one end but loose at the other." Clowns in late 19th-century American variety shows used this slapstick to give other performers laugh-getting light but loud whacks on the rear end. The slapsticks were so widely used that they gave their name to any broad, loud knockabout comedy.

slave; Slav. The word *slave* has nothing to do with Athens in the Periclean Age, when there were twice as many people in bondage as free, or with the "African trade" that created four centuries of suffering. *Slave* came into the language long after the former and long before the latter inhumanity, deriving from the name of a tribe living in what is now Poland and other areas of Eastern Europe. The name of these people meant "noble or illustrious" in their own tongue, but in about 6 A.D. they were conquered by German tribes from the west and forced to serve their conquerors or sold into bondage to the Romans. The Romans called them *Sclavus*, which became the Medieval Latin *sclavus*, "a Slav captive," this term of contempt applied to any bondsman or servile person. *Sclavus* became *esclave* in French and came into English as *sclave*, retaining the *c* until about the 16th century, when *slave* was first used. The word *Slav*, for the race of people in Eastern Europe, comes from the same source, the proud "noble" tribe whose name underwent a complete metamorphosis.

sleazy. *Silesia cloth*, a superior linen fabric that was made in the southernmost province of Prussia (now part of Poland) as early as the 17th century, may give us the word *sleazy*. By this theory *cloth of Silesia* was corrupted over the years to *sleasie*, *sleasy*, and then *sleazy cloth*. The quality of the sleazy cloth deteriorated as fabric makers in other countries tried to imitate it and it finally became a thin cotton fabric used mostly in linings, a cheap thin, flimsy material that easily ripped and gave us the adjective *sleazy*, for "cheap" or "worthless." Another theory, *Partridge* notes in *Name into Word*, traces *sleazy* to the English dialect word *sleaze*, "to part asunder, said of badly woven cloth," which may not have come from *Silesia*. (*See* **shoddy**.)

sleeper. A *sleeper*, for "any unexpected success," dates to the 1930s. One speculation has the word deriving from *sleeper*, for "an unbranded steer," a late 19th-century term that came to mean, in one sense, "something taken for something else." Another vague possibility is *sleeper* for "a bet in faro when the owner has forgotten it, when it becomes public property, anyone having a right to take it." By this reasoning the *sleeper*, or bet, could turn out to be a good one.

sleep like a top. A top spinning at high speed is so still and steady that it hardly seems to move. Writers first compared sound sleepers to spinning tops over 350 years ago, and even though we now know that no one sleeps so soundly the whole night through, the comparison remains a good one—for a spinning top begins to wobble after a while, is rewound, and resumes its still and steady spinning. Some authorities have tried to trace the phrase back beyond its first recorded use in English (1616), to the French word *taupe*, a "mole," the implication being that one sleeps as peacefully as a mole. But the French saying is also to "sleep like a top," *dormir comme un sabot*, not *dormir comme une taupe*, "to sleep like a mole." Tops, like yo-yos, are in fact said to be "sleeping" when they are spinning perfectly. William Congreve played on both meanings when he wrote in his comedy *The Old Bachelor* (1693): "I can ensure his anger dormant, or should be seen to rouse, 'tis but well lashing him and he will sleep like a top." Congreve's play, which brought him sudden fame, has a cast of aptronyms second to few. There is Heartwell, the kind old bachelor; Vainlove, who forsakes his mistress; Fondlewife, the uxorious old banker; and even a cowardly bully named Captain Bluffe.

sleep on a clothesline. The expression "I'm so tired I could sleep on a clothesline," with much more British than American use today, dates back to 18th-century England, when people unable to afford a bed in boardinghouses were charged two pennies to sit on a communal bench through the night, leaning on a clothesline stretched tight in front of them. The taut "two-penny rope" was cut in the morning, the sleepers jolted into reality again.

sleeps. "It was many sleeps away." Among some American Indian tribes a *sleep* was one day, "the measure of time between one sleeping period and the next." The term is recorded as early as 1670 in South Carolina and was adopted by settlers.

slide, Kelly, slide. As Dizzy Dean would have put it, when Kelly "slud," he "slud" hard. Michael Joseph "King" Kelly, who played ball for Chicago and Boston, was a talented hustling player called "the Ten Thousand Dollar Beauty" because he signed for that sum one year, an incredible amount of money for a ballplayer at the time. In 1889 a song was written about Kelly by his friend monologuist John W. Kelly exhorting him to *slide, Kelly, slide*, an expression which has become proverbial. Kelly innovated a number of techniques besides the "hook" or "fadeaway" slide. As a catcher he invented the dirty trick of throwing his mask up the first-base line in order to trip a batter trying to beat out a hit. Kelly played to win. As Boston's manager, he looked up from the bench one day to see a foul ball drifting toward him. At the time, baseball rules specified that substitutions could be made at any point in the game, and seeing that the Boston catcher could not possibly reach the foul, Kelly jumped up off the bench, shouted "Kelly now catching for Boston," and caught the ball for an out. His maneuver led to the rule now on the books that substitutions can only be made when the ball isn't in play.

sliding pond. Is it pronounced "sliding pond" or "sliding pon?" That depends on where you come from in America. Many experts believe that the slides found in most playgrounds were first named *sliding ponds* because they reminded people of how they used to slide on the ice of ponds before playground slides were invented sometime in the 19th century. By this reasoning *sliding pon* is simply a shortening of *sliding pond*. But some *sliding pon* advocates claim that *pon* here is the corruption of any of a number of foreign words that could be applicable. Still another guess is that *sliding pon* comes from "sliding upon." More American terms for *sliding pond* include *sliding board, slide, sliding pot,* and even *chutey-chute* (from the British *chute,* and probably obsolete today). Strangely enough, no major American dictionary lists *sliding pond,* or *sliding pon,* including *The Dictionary of Americanisms* and *The Dictionary of American Slang*—though the terms have been commonly used in some areas since early in this century and must have spread throughout the country by now in both speech and literature.

slipshod. The first *slipshod* people were men in the 16th century who walked the streets in *slipshoes,* a kind of loose slippers. Such men, slopping along shod in their slipshoes, were considered uncouth by respectable people, who soon coined the word *slipshod* for them, *slipshod* ultimately applying to anything done in a slovenly way.

slipslop. "When he gets drunk he gets all . . . erotic," Mrs. Slipslop says in Fielding's *Joseph Andrews* (1742), though the word she is searching for is erratic. She made many similar ludicrous misuses of words and her name in the form of *slipslop* stood for such a blunder until Sheridan's Mrs. Malaprop came along and gave us *malapropism (q.v.).*

slithy. "'Twas brillig and the slithy toves did gyre and gimble in the wabe." Author Lewis Carroll concocted this blend, or portmanteau, word from *lithe* and *slimy* in *Through the Looking Glass* as part of his "Jabberwocky" language.

slogan. All slogans, whether they be catchy advertising phrases or the rallying cries of political parties, are direct descendants of Gaelic battle cries, the word itself deriving from the *sluagh-ghairm* (battle cry) of the Gaels. Gaelic soldiers repeated these cries, usually the name of their clan or clan leader, in unison as they advanced against the enemy. Over the years the word came to describe any catchy phrase inducing people to support a cause (the "Liberty, Equality, Fraternity" of the French Revolution) or a commercial product (the "99 and 44/100ths % Pure" of Ivory Soap). Sometimes *watchword* is used loosely for a slogan, as is *catchword,* though this last is more often employed in a contemptuous sense (as in "advertising catchwords").

slothful. *Sloth,* deriving from the Middle English *slou,* "slow," dates back to at least 1175 as a word for laziness, and the adjective *slothful* is recorded as early as 1390. The arboreal mammal of South America called the *sloth* didn't get its name until the early 19th century. The sloth does virtually nothing for weeks on end, not breathing for long periods, taking at least two weeks to digest its food, and not even springing up if it falls out of its tree. It was named by explorers who observed it, one describing how a sloth took "three or four days at least, in climbing up and down a tree," and another observing that one took "a whole day in going fifty paces."

slow and steady wins the race. When Charles Darwin measured the speed of a Galapagos turtle by walking beside it, he found that it "walked at the rate of sixty yards in ten minutes, that is 360 yards in an hour, or four miles a day—allowing a little time for it to eat on the road." That is certainly slow enough for an expression *slow as a tortoise,* but the creature, unlike the snail, has been noted for his reliability rather than his lack of speed. The expression *slow and steady wins the race* is from the poem "The Hare and the Tortoise" by Robert Lloyd (1733-1764) but can be traced back in all but its exact form to Aesop's fable "The Hare and the Tortoise," in which the hare awakens to see the tortoise crossing the finish line in a race the hare was sure he would win.

slum; slumber. *Slum,* for "a squalid area of a city or town," is a relatively new word first recorded in 1812. The O.E.D. won't venture a guess at its origins, simply labeling it "cant," but it has been suggested that *slum* may derive from *slumber*—perhaps because *slum* first meant the squalid room where a poor person slept, or perhaps because slum areas were erroneously thought to be sleepy, quiet places! *Slumber* comes from the Middle English *slumeren,* "to doze."

slumgullion. By the end of the 19th century *slumgullion* meant a meat and vegetable stew in America, but the word started out meaning "slime." *Slum,* a mispronunciation of slime, had first meant the scummy liquid left over in the tryworks after blubber was processed aboard whaling ships. By mid-century *slum* came to mean a stew. Then miners in the 1849 gold rush borrowed *slum,* for "soup," added *gullion,* an English dialect word meaning "mud," and used *slumgullion* to mean the soupy liquid resulting from sluicing. *Slumgullions,* in turn, seemed to make a funny word for soup to some miners and this became its primary meaning.

slush fund. *Slush fund* originally referred to the surplus fat or grease from fried salt pork, a standard food on 19th-century ships. This slush was usually sold in port, the money raised from it put into a general fund that was used to purchase luxuries for the crew. By 1866 the nautical term had been applied to a contingency fund set aside from an operating budget by Congress, and in later years it took on its current meaning of a secret fund used for bribes or other corrupt practices.

small fry. In her epochal *Uncle Tom's Cabin* Harriet Beecher Stowe introduced *small fry* ("smaller fry") to describe children, but *fry* had been used in this sense as early as 1697. Both expressions refer to the *fry*, "or young, of salmon, herring and other fish." The word derives from the Norse *frae* "seed," meaning the berry or seedlike masses of eggs these fish produce.

smart aleck. If there ever lived a real "smart Aleck," an Alexander so much of an obnoxiously conceited know-it-all that his name became proverbial, no record of him exists. The term can be traced back to about the 1860s and is still frequently used for a wise guy today. The original *smart aleck* may have been at least clever enough to cover up all traces of his identity.

a smart apple. A wise guy or smart aleck is a *smart apple* today, but when it originated in the early 1920s the term meant an intelligent person. An *apple* had simply been a "guy" before this.

smellsmock. Licentious priests were called *smellsmocks* in the early 16th century because people thought their sexual affairs made their smocks smelly and because they knew how to "smell a smock," how to recognize an easy conquest. *Smellsmock* soon came to cover any licentious man, but it survives today only as the popular name of several plants such as the cuckooflower and the woodsorrel.

smellfungus. A discontented person, a grumbler and fault-finder. The first *smellfungus* was British novelist Tobias Smollett (1721-71), who was once imprisoned for libel. Smollett's book *Travels in France and Italy* (1766) was entertaining but ill-tempered and novelist Laurence Sterne parodied the author as "Smellfungus" in his *Sentimental Journey through France and Italy* (1768). Within a short time *smellfungus* was being applied to any ill-tempered grumbler.

to smite someone hip and thigh. *Smite someone hip and thigh* and you smite him all over his body violently. The old phrase is from the Bible, Judges 15:8: "He smote them hip and thigh with a great slaughter . . ."

smithereens. *Smithereens*, as in the expression *blasted to smithereens*, derives from the Irish *smidirin*, "small fragment." It is first recorded in English in the 19th century.

Smithsonian Institution; smithsonite. Despite the fact that he neither had visited nor known anyone living in America, British chemist James Smithson (1765?-1829) left over $508,000, the whole of his estate, "to the United States of America to found at Washington under the name of the Smithsonian Institution an establishment for the increase and diffusion of knowledge among men." The money was actually willed to his nephew with the stipulation that the above condition apply if the nephew died without children—which he did in 1835. Smithson, the illegitimate son of Sir Hugh Smithson and Elizabeth Macie, made many valuable analyses of minerals, and *smithsonite*, an important zinc ore, is also named in his honor. Congress took ten years debating whether or not to accept his bequest, finally accepting largely through the efforts of John Quincy Adams. The museum was founded in 1846.

smoke-filled room. Associated Press reporter Kirke Simpson first recorded the expression *smoke-filled room*, in a newspaper story describing the behind-the-scenes political manipulation used to secure Warren Harding's nomination for president in 1920. However, Harry Daughtery, a friend of Harding, probably coined the phrase.

smooch; smouch. *Smooch*, "to kiss or pet, to make love," may oddly enough be another example of ethnic prejudice in language. Nobody has proved its origins, but it may derive from *smouch*, a favorite word of Mark Twain's, which in its original sense meant to obtain illicitly by cheating or swindling. In all probability it comes from the derogatory Dutch *Smous*, "a German Jew," this word possibly formed from the proper name Moses.

smooth-shaven. English poet John Milton, not a copywriter for razor blades, coined *smooth-shaven*, in about 1635. Milton had as precedents the earlier *smooth-skinned* and *smooth-faced*. (See **lovelorn**.)

snack. *Snacks*, so named, probably, because they are quickly "snatched," have meant "mere bites or morsels of food, as contrasted with regular meals" since the 17th century. Wrote the first writer known to use the word: "When once a man has got a snack . . . he too often retains a hankering . . ."

snail's pace. Since at least 1592 a *snail's pace* has meant "exceedingly slow," but until recently no one knew just how exceedingly slow that was. Recent studies have shown that snails travel at about two feet an hour, or one mile every three months or so.

snake in the grass. *Latet anguis in herbe* ("a snake lurks in the grass") the Roman poet Virgil wrote in the third *Eclogue*, and from this ancient source comes our common expression for a hidden or hypocritical enemy. Proving that times don't change much, the Latin proverb first appears in English as a line in a political song of about

1290: "Though all appears clean, a snake lurks in the grass."

snap beans.   (*See* **string bean**.)

snollygoster.   One very rarely hears this word today, but in the 19th century it was a common Americanism for "a pretentious boaster." The word is probably a fanciful formation coined by some folk poet who liked its appropriate sound; it is first recorded in 1862. A Georgia editor defined a *snollygoster* as a "fellow who wants office regardless of party, platform or principles, and who, whenever he wins, gets there by the sheer force of monumental talknophical assumacy." The type is still common, even if the word isn't.

snood.

> When thou hast heard his name upon
>   The bugles of the cherubim.
> Begin thou softly to unzone
>   Thy girlish bosom unto him
> And softly to undo the snood
>   That is the sign of maidenhood.

One wouldn't think James Joyce wrote this, but it is from his early poem "Bid Adieu to Maidenhood." *Snood* is mostly a crossword puzzle word today; the silk ribbon with which Scottish and Irish maidens tied their hair isn't used much anymore. The headband was worn only by virgins and by custom had to be replaced with another hair covering if a girl married or lost her virginity before marriage. *Snood* is a very old word, dating back to the eighth century and probably derives from Swedish *sno*, "twine, string." In more recent times it has meant a woman's hair net.

snoop.   The verb *snoop* derives from something Americans still do, but which we have no good word for—the Dutch *snoepen*, "to eat sweets secretively." *Snoepen* came to mean the prying and spying that the Dutch in early New York did on their neighbors, and passed into English as *snoop* in the late 18th century.

snorkel.   The *snorkel*, introduced during World War II, was at first only a retractable tube that ventilated a sub cruising slightly below the surface. It took its name from the German *Schnorchel*, "air intake." After the war, *snorkel* became better known as a tube one breathes through while swimming facedown in the water or slightly below the surface.

snow.   The word *snow* is first recorded in about A.D. 825 in the form of *snaw*. Though we have terms like *red snow*, *green snow*, *black snow*, and *golden snow* for snow tinged by algae or foreign substances, we basically make do with the one word *snow* to describe the crystalline white stuff. (The *powder* made for skiers is an exception to

the rule.) On the other hand linguist Benjamin Lee Whorf once reported on an Eskimo tribe that distinguishes 100 different types of snow—and has 100 synonyms (including *tipsiq* and *tuva*) to match them. The walrus also has many synonyms in Eskimo language "In Yupik there are forty-seven words for a walrus, depending on what he's doing," writes Clay Hardy of the U.S. Fish and Wildlife Service. "There is no word for *time*. You tell me who's got the proper values." (*See* **walrus**.)

snowbirds.   Southwesterners use this term today for northerners who come south for the winter, but it originated in the U.S. Army in the late 19th century as a name for men who enlisted for food and quarters during the winter and deserted in the spring.

snuff out.   *Snuff out*, "to kill," is best known as U.S. underworld slang from the 1920s, but it originated in World War I and is British in origin, deriving from the British slang *snuff out*, meaning "to die," which is first attested in 1864 and was probably suggested by the snuffing out of a candle, the flame of the candle compared to the flame of life. Sadistic *snuff movies* of the 1980s and earlier reputedly depict the actual killing of "actors" on the screen.

snug as a bug in a rug.   One would guess that this is a folk saying of untraceable origins, but it apparently is the invention of Benjamin Franklin, who jotted it off in a letter in 1772. It means "the utmost in contentment." Franklin is of course responsible for many maxims that are part of our speech today, including *a word to the wise . . .*, *time is money . . .*, *death and taxes*, *an ounce of prevention . . .*, and *early to bed, early to rise . . .*

soap opera.   *Newsweek* seems to have used *soap opera* first in an 11/13/39 article, putting the expression in quotes as if it were new. Earlier a writer in the *Christian Century* (8/24/39) came very close to coining the term, however: "These fifteen minute tragedies . . . I call the 'soap tragedies' . . . because it is by the grace of soap I am allowed to shed tears for these characters who suffer so much from life." He was referring, of course, to the soap manufacturers who sponsored many of the early radio serials characterized by melodrama and sentimentality that are now called *soap operas*, or simply *soaps* (an abbreviated form that is ten years or so old).

Soapy Sam.   The first *Soapy Sam*, Samuel Wilberforce, Bishop of Oxford and later Winchester, was a noncomformist and controversial clergyman if ever there was one. Wilberforce, son of the great antislavery leader William Wilberforce, tried to steer a middle course between High Church and Low Church factions in England. Although a devout man in his personal life, this position forced him to develop a suave, unctuous manner of speaking, persuasive but versatile and expedient almost to a fault. By 1860 he had earned the nickname *Soapy Sam*, which has since been applied to any slippery, unctuous speaker who can talk his way out of anything. The coining was perhaps given an assist by the initials "S.O.A.P." on the floral decorations above the stall where he preached—these standing for the names Sam Oxon and Alfred Port. Once someone asked him about the nickname and he assured his questioner that he was called *Soapy Sam* "Because I am often in hot water and always come out with clean hands." Bishop Wilberforce died in 1873, aged sixty-eight.

sober as a judge.   In the play *Don Quixote in England* (1734) one of Henry Fielding's characters says: "I am as sober as a judge." Perhaps it was simply Fielding's observation that judges are almost always sober on the bench, but the phrase may have its source in the saying *an appeal from Philip Drunk to Philip Sober* (q.v.). *Sober* is the exact opposite of the Latin word for "in his cups," deriving from *so*, "apart from," and *bria*, "cup."

soccer; rugger.   *Partridge* tells us that *soccer* is a "perversion" of association football, formed in the late 19th century by adding what he calls "the Oxford-*er*" to as*soc*iation football. *Rugger*, a synonym for rugby, was formed in much the same way.

sockdollager.   (*See* **quicker than hell can scorch a feather.**)

sociology.   French philospher Auguste Comte, the father of the discipline of sociology, invented the word *sociologie* for "the science or study of the origin, history and constitution of human society." The word was first anglicized in 1843.

socratic irony; socratic method.   By feigning ignorance, Socrates led his audience into traps, easily defeating them in argument, and this pretended ignorance has since been known as *Socratic irony*. The great Greek philosopher also developed the inductive *Socratic method*, conducting a cross-examination by questions and answers carefully designed to impart knowledge, or to evoke knowledge from those who may have believed they were unknowing. Socrates was born about 470 B.C., the child of a sculptor and a midwife. After receiving a good education and completing a tour of military service in which he was distinguished for his bravery, he devoted his life to the investigation of virtue, justice, and purity. His profound spiritual influence led him to be called the philosopher who "brought down philosophy from the heavens to earth" and he liked to call himself "the midwife of men's thoughts," but he left behind no writings and his work is known primarily through the *Dialogues* of Plato. Condemned to death by the Athenian government in 399 B.C. for neglecting the old gods, introducing new ones,

and corrupting youth, Socrates was forced to commit suicide by drinking hemlock. "The hour of departure has arrived," he said at the last, "and we go our separate ways—I to die, and you to live. Which is the better, God only knows."

soda pop.   At the beginning of the 19th century soda water consisted of nothing but water, a little soda, and sometimes a bit of flavoring. Soon someone thought to force gas into the water and to keep it there under pressure, the soda water sparkling and foaming when the pressure is removed and the gas escapes. The soda was kept under pressure in cylinders that came to be called *soda fountains* and were often quite unsafe, for when dropped the pressure inside them could cause a tremendous explosion, which happened once in a while, according to newspapers of the day. At any rate, the sparkling, popping soda that came out of the fountains probably was responsible for the name *pop*, for "soda," long before soda was bottled. *Soda pop* or *pop*, is not recorded in the language, however, until the early 20th century.

sodomite, sodomy.   Sodom and Gomorrah, the twin sin Cities of the Plain in the Bible, have long represented male and female vice respectively—a *Gomorrhean*, in fact, meaning a lesbian in 16th-century England. A *sodomite* is one who practices *sodomy*, "unnatural intercourse with a human or animal," such practices being attributed to Sodom's male inhabitants. The story of Sodom and Gomorrah is told in Genesis: 18-19. Old Testament scholars believe the story is a mythological attempt to account for the destruction of a city once located near the Dead Sea.

sofa.   The Arabic word *suffah*, "cushion or long bench," gives us our word *sofa*, for "a couch." The word came into English early in the 17th century.

soft soap.   A relatively soft, semiliquid soap containing potash, introduced early in the 19th century, inspired the Americanism to *soft-soap* someone, which dates to about 1830. The soap was oily, as unctuous as a wheedling flatterer.

soldier's breeze or wind.   A sailor's contemptuous regard for landlubbers is reflected in this 19th century term for a wind that is equally forcible going or coming. In other words, when the wind is about abeam going out and coming back, it takes little ability to sail—even a soldier could do it.

solecism.   An error in grammar, or in the use of words, or a breach of etiquette is called a *solecism*. Soli, or Soloi, was an ancient Greek colony in the province of Cilicia, Asia Minor, far removed from Athens. Colonists who settled there developed a dialect of their own that Athenian purists considered barbarous and uncouth, leading them to coin the word *soloikos* as a slang term for ignorant speech. From *soloikos* came the Greek noun *soloikismos*, "speaking incorrectly," like an inhabitant of Soloi, which eventually, through the Latin *soloecismus*, made its entrance into English as *solecism*. In years to come, Yankee colonists would be criticized in much the same way by Englishmen, but the label *Americanism* has always been accepted with pride by Americans. Soli, located in what is now Turkey, was an important, prosperous port in the time of Alexander the Great. When Pompey rebuilt the city after it was destroyed by Tigranes in the Third Mithridatic War, he named it Pompeiopolis. Few of Soli's ruins remain today, but *solecism*, originally slang itself, endures in all modern European languages as a remembrance of the way its citizens "ruined" Greek.

solicitor. In England *solicitors* handle the preliminaries of law cases, while *barristers* alone are members of the *bar* and can take cases to court. Barristers are composed of two classes: junior counsels called barristers and a higher class of king's (or queen's) counsels, who wear silk gowns, as opposed to the formers' gowns of common cloth. In times past a solicitor was "one who solicits in Courts of Equity through counsel," while *attorneys* (from the French *atourner*, to turn over to another) belonged to other courts.

solitary as an oyster. No single Faulknerian sentence could contain all the miseries of the oyster's life, from the *Crepidula fornicata*, or slipper limpet, that multiplies as fast as its Latin name suggests and suffocates whole beds of oysters, to the starfish that grotesquely stick their whole stomachs out of their mouths and into open oyster shells to digest some soft meat. No wonder the oyster tries to keep to itself. No wonder we have the expression *as solitary as an oyster* (first recorded by Dickens in *A Christmas Carol*.)

solitary confinement. *Solitary confinement* in "the hole," a cell removed from all others and often below ground, was a penal punishment originated by the state of Pennsylvania in the late 18th century. Suggested by the Quakers, *solitary* was considered a reform measure at the time, replacing brutal floggings for incorrigible prisoners.

Solomon; Solomon's ring. Solomon, the son of David and Bath-sheba, ruled over Israel for some forty years, and was noted for his wisdom and wealth. The latter and perhaps the former are witnessed by the 700 wives and 300 concubines he kept in great splendor. His wisdom is shown by the tale of the baby he proposed to divide in two. By suggesting this, Solomon determined the child's rightful mother—the false claimant accepting his proposal and the real mother asking that the child be given to her rival rather than be killed. His reign was a great one marked by peace and economic and literary development, Solomon himself having the "Song of Songs" and the books of *Ecclesiastes* and *Proverbs* attributed to him. Yet there was a religious decline and increasing social injustice in the king's time, and the northern tribes revolted upon his death in about 933 B.C. Solomon left Israel saddled with taxes and dissension, but his name remains a synonym for wisdom, the Bible referring to him as "wiser than all men . . . his fame . . . in all nations round about." The wisdom of Solomon is sometimes expressed by the phrase *to have Solomon's ring*, referring to a legendary ring he wore that told him all he wanted to know.

Solomon's seal. Some say that Solomon's seal (*Polygonoatum multiflorum*) is so named because as the flower's stem decays the rootstalk of the plant becomes marked with scars that have some resemblance to official seals such as the seal of Solomon, King of Israel in about 900 B.C. Others hold that the root has medicinal value in sealing up and closing wounds.

solon. "I grow old ever learning many things," wrote the sage Solon in the often quoted line. The wise statesman and lawgiver lived some eighty-two years before he left Athens in about 558 B.C. and died, according to tradition, while wandering somewhere in the East. One of the Seven Sages of Greece, his motto was "Know thyself." Solon initiated many legal and social reforms, including a new constitution for Athens that revived the popular assembly at a time when tension between the rich and poor had reached the breaking point. His love poems and patriotic verse were well known, but the proverbial remark "Call no man happy till he is dead" was probably not his, though attributed to him. Elected archon, officer of the state, in 594 B.C., Solon instituted reforms that laid the foundation for Athenian democracy. His name has come to mean any lawmaker, not necessarily a wise one, *solon* sometimes being used because it takes up less space in headlines and newspaper stories than representative or congressman.

so long! *So long!*, for" good-bye," may not be an Americanism. The *O.E.D.*, gives 1834 as its first recorded date and the source is probably British, since *So long!* isn't recorded in the U.S. until the late 1850s. Other possibilities are that it comes from the Hebrew *sholom*, the German *so lange*, or the Arabic *salaam* (*q.v.*).

sombrero. The great broad-brimmed hat long associated with Mexico takes its name from the shade (in Spanish, *sombra*) that it provides its wearer.

someone stole his rudder. We find this expression, for "a helpless drunk," first recorded in the American West during the 19th century, but it is obviously a borrowing from nautical language, of the sea or the inland waterways of America.

something rotten in Denmark. Hamlet's suspicion about the kingdom of course proved to be well-founded, but what Shakespeare had the prince say was *something is rotten in the state of Denmark*, not the persistent misquotation above.

something up one's sleeve; laugh up one's sleeve. Garments in medieval times had few if any pockets, so men often carried whatever couldn't be hung from their belts in their full sleeves. Probably from this source, rather than from magicians with rabbits up their sleeves, comes our expression for having something in reserve or an alternative plan, although the phrase, in its sense of a scheme or trick, was most likely influenced by magicians concealing in their sleeves the means by which they do a trick. A second expression deriving from the same source is *to laugh up (or on) one's sleeve*, "to ridicule a person secretly." Someone wearing a garment with capacious sleeves was quite literally able to conceal a laugh by hiding his face in his sleeve.

sommobiches. (See **les sommobichors.**)

son of a bitch stew. You use everything but "the hair, horns and holler," according to one recipe for *son of a bitch stew*, commonly made on chuck wagons in the old West. All the innards of a steer, including heart, brains, and kidneys, had to be included in the stew, but the most indispensable ingredient was gut (tripe). This inspired the old saying: "A son of a bitch might not have any brains and no heart, but if he ain't got guts he ain't a son of a bitch."

son of a gun. *Son of a gun* is now a euphemism for the much stronger *son of a bitch*, or even a term of affectionate regard between friends ("You old son of a gun!"), but this expression did not start out that way. It dates back to the early 1800s and was just a little less perjorative than *son of a bitch*, or *son of a whore*, which came into the language at about the same time. In the early 19th century, *son of a gun* meant "a sailor's bastard," but it proceeded to become more innocuous with the passing of time. *The Sailor's Wordbook* (1867), written by British Navy Adm. William Henry Smyth, attempts to explain the expression's origins, but bear in mind that the book was written a long time after the term was born: "An epithet conveying contempt in a slight degree, and originally applied to boys born afloat, when women were permitted to accompany their husbands to sea; one admiral declared he literally was thus cradled, under the breast of a gun-carriage."

son of a sea cook. *Son of a sea cook*, which can mean either a "good guy" or a "mean SOB," depending on the

context, really has little to do with the sea. No sea cook had any hand in it. It seems that the earliest American settlers appropriated the word *s'quenk*, for "skunk," from the Indians around the Massachusetts Bay Colony, pronouncing it *sea-konk*. Thus, a *son of a see-konk* was first a stinking son of a skunk. Because *see-konk* sounded something like "sea cook" it came to be pronounced "sea cook" long after the Indian word was forgotten. The fact that sea cooks were often cantankerous old men probably reinforced the term's present ambivalent meaning.

sophistry; sophomore. The Sophists were not really a school of philosophers but individual teachers who toured the cities of Greece in the mid-fifth century B.C. teaching rhetoric and other subjects. They did, however, share common beliefs. Far less idealistic than the Socratic school, they prepared their pupils for public life, placing little store in truth for truth's sake and accepting money for their teaching, being what might be called pragmatists today. Although their name derived from *sophos*, the Greek word for wise, it was a contemptuous term among their contemporaries. Because they taught the art of persuasion to young men eager for political careers and the methods they taught were often unscrupulous and overingenious, a *sophist* became someone who tries to mislead people with clever arguments, one who tries to "make the worse seem the better reason." *Sophism* is now used to mean a plausible but fallacious argument, and false, specious reasoning is called *sophistry*. The word has thus had almost a complete reversal in meaning since the time when the wise men of Greece were called sophists—before the Sophists came on the scene. The word *sophomore*, a second-year college or high school student, probably comes from *sophom*, an obsolete form of *sophism*, plus the suffix *or*.

SOS. SOS doesn't stand for "Save Our Ship," "Save Our Souls," or "Stop Other Signals." The letters, adopted in 1908 by international agreement, actually mean nothing at all and were chosen only because they are so simple for a wireless operator to remember and transmit in Morse Code—three dits (dots), three dahs (dashes) and three dits (... - - - ...). (See **CQD.**)

Sotadic. (See **palindrome.**)

soubise. Charles de Rohan, Prince de Soubise, may have created the superbly simple sauce that bears his name, but it's more likely that it was created and named in his honor by his majordomo, the great chef Marin. Soubise (1715-87), a famous gourmet who was the grandson of the Princess de Soubise, one of Louis XIV's mistresses, became marshal of France in 1758 through the influence of Madame de Pompadour, Louis XV's mistress. The prince liked to cook as much as he liked making love and war, and his chef Marin was among the greatest of 18th-century culinary artists, his cookbook, *Les Dons* de Comus (Gifts from the Kitchen), appearing in 1739 and intended to brighten the tables of the bourgeoisie, enabling "even third-class persons to dine with grace." A *soubise* is a brown or white sauce containing strained or pureed onions and served with meat; it is made by blending onions simmered tender in butter with a creamy bechamel sauce and rubbing this through a fine sieve.

soul brother; etc. As a term for blacks used by blacks, *soul brothers* has been around since at least the 1950's. Today it is often abbreviated, by blacks, as *the brothers* (or *sisters*) and further shortened to *bro* when used in a greeting. The meaning here is that blacks are alike in the soul, but in earlier combinations *soul* is used in many ways. *Soul driver* and *soul doctor* were terms abolitionists applied to white men who took indentured servants and slaves from place to place in Colonial times to sell them. *Soul sharks* were rapacious preachers, black or white, usually without a pulpit, and *soul butter* was a term for moralizing drivel, black or white, that Mark Twain popularized. *Soul mate* can be someone much loved, or even a mistress, and a *soul kiss* is a long, open-mouthed French kiss. *Soul music* and *soul food* (food like collard greens, black-eyed peas, hog maw, etc., associated with Southern blacks) are also black terms dating back at least to the 1950s.

soul ships. Until the late 19th century, *soul ships* were believed to sail to Brittany's Bay of Souls near Point du Ray and collect recently deceased sailors for the journey to the fabled "Isles of the Blessed" somewhere to the west. *Soul ships* were sighted by many a mariner, just as mermaids and sea serpents were.

sound; sounding. The *sounding* that determines the depth of the water by means of a line and lead is of no relation to the word *sound*, meaning something audible, which derives from the Latin *sonus*. *Sounding* comes from the Old English word *sund*, for "water, sea, or swimming." The *sound* that is an inlet of the sea has the same roots.

soup. Nitroglycerin was dubbed *soup* by safecrackers because the liquid can be obtained by *very very very* gently simmering dynamite in water. The Americanism is first recorded in about 1905.

soup and fish. Dating back to 19th-century America, this term for formal white-tie dinner clothes probably derives from the obsolete American term *soup and fish*, for a lavish dinner of many courses. *Soup and fish* for an elaborate dinner, in turn, is apparently related to the still common expression *from soup to nuts*, but this last term seems to have been first recorded in the 1920s.

soupbone. Baseball pitching great Christy Mathewson appears to have first recorded this term for one's throwing or pitching arm, in his book *Pitching in a Pinch* (1912): "My old soupbone . . . was so weak that I couldn't break a pane of glass at fifty feet."

soup to nuts. (*See* **from soup to nuts.**)

sour grapes. In Aesop's fable "The Fox and the Grapes," a fox spies luscious-looking grapes hanging from a vine. He leaps a number of times trying to get them, failing by a few inches with each leap, and gives up after rationalizing that they are probably sour and inedible anyway. La Fontaine, another great fabulist, later regarded the fox as admirable, remarking that his words were "better than complaining," but the fox's *sour grapes* have come to mean any belittling, envious remark.

sousaphone. "The Stars and Stripes Forever," "The Washington Post," "Semper Fidelis," "Hands Across the Sea," "Liberty Bell," "High School Cadets"—John Philip Sousa composed over one hundred such popular marches, inspiring an English magazine to dub him the March King, a title that remained with the bandmaster throughout his long career. Sousa, the son of Portuguese refugees, began conducting theater orchestras when only nineteen. He became bandmaster of the U.S. Marine Corps band in 1882, his father having played there before him, and formed his famous Sousa's Band ten years later. His band toured the world, bringing him great renown, and he composed numerous comic operas, suites, songs, and orchestral music in addition to his marches. Sousa died in 1932 aged seventy-eight. Besides greatly improving the quality of band music, he invented the *sousaphone*, a large circular tuba standing fifty-two inches high and weighing some twenty-six pounds, with a flaring adjustable bell, adjustable mouthpiece, and a full, rich sonorous tone.

South Carolina. (*See* **North Carolina.**)

South Dakota. (*See* **North Dakota.**)

Southern fried chicken. Originally chicken fried in bacon grease, *Southern fried chicken* has been popular in the American South since before 1711, when the term *fried chicken* is first recorded there. It became popular throughout the country in the 1930s, when it was first widely sold at roadside restaurants.

southpaw. Humorist Finley Peter Dunne, then a sportswriter, coined this word for a left-handed baseball pitcher while covering sports in Chicago in the 1880s. Home plate in the Chicago ball park was then to the west, so that a left-handed pitcher released the ball from the "paw," or hand, on his south side. The word soon came to describe any left-hander.

sowbread. (*See* **cyclamen.**)

sow one's wild oats.   The wild oat (*Avena fatua*) is a common tall plant that looks like its relative the cereal plant oat, but is really a pernicious weed that infests the planting fields of Europe and is difficult to eradicate. About all wild oats, or oat grass, have ever been used for is in making hygrometers, instruments that measure the humidity in the air, the plant's long twisted awn, or beard, readily absorbing moisture. The wild oat's uselessness has been known since ancient times and for almost as long we have had the expression to *sow wild oats*, "to conduct oneself foolishly," to sow weedseed instead of good grain. The expression has been traced back to the Roman comic Plautus in 194 B.C. and was probably used before him. It usually refers to a young man frittering his time away in fruitless dissipation, or to the prolific sexual activities of a young man, and is almost always said indulgently of the young. Rarely, the expression is used in the singular, with a prudish young man who sows "his one wild oat." In the 16th and 17th centuries dissolute or wild young men were called *wild oats*.

sow the wind and reap the whirlwind.   To do something wrong, the results of which are even worse for the perpetrator. The expression is from the Bible, (Hos. 8:7): "For they [Israel] have sown the wind and they shall reap the whirlwind."

soybean.   The ancient Chinese made a sauce called *shi-yu* (*shi*, "salted food," + *yu*, "oil") from this bean, which they apparently named after the sauce; *shi-yu* became *shoyu* and then *shoy* in Japanese, which ultimately became *soy* and *soybean* (soy + bean) in English. The Japanese valued soy sauce so highly that it was part of the salary of Japanese imperial court officers in the fifth century.

spaghetti; macaroni.   Italian for "little strings, strands, or cords," *spaghetti* was brought to Italy by Marco Polo in the early 14th century and so named at that time, though it is apparently not recorded in English until 1888, the editors of the *O.E.D.* much preferring *macaroni* (first recorded by Ben Jonson in 1599), and not including spaghetti until the first supplement to that masterful work. *Macaroni*, an Italian word of obscure origins, has had its derogatory uses. As early as 1764 *macaroni* meant a fop or a dandy (as in the "Yankee Doodle" lyric), referring to London's Macaroni Club, where the members enjoyed foreign foods like macaroni. Then there is *macaroni boats*, a mostly British term for ocean liners carrying Italian immigrants to America in the early 20th century. (*See* **macaronic verse; spic.**)

Spalding; Spaldeen.   Alfred Goodwill Spalding (1850-1915) deserves his place in baseball's Hall of Fame as much as any man. He may not be "the Father of Baseball," but is certainly "Father of the Baseball," and it was only when he came upon the scene with his uniform manufacturing methods that what had been a chaotic minor sport was fashioned into the national pastime. Lively balls were once so rubbery that baseball scores like 201-11 were not uncommon, and others so dead that the phrase "fell with a dull thud" found its way into the language. The former Chicago White Sox manager did not invent the hard ball when he founded his company in 1880, but the rigid manufacturing standards he maintained made it possible for the newly formed National League of Professional Baseball to survive. Such careful preparations over the years have made the *Spalding* trademark synonymous for a baseball. Other sporting equipment manufactured by the firm includes a red rubber ball called the *Spaldeen* (spelled *Spalding*), which has been known by that name to several generations of American youngsters.

spaniel; cocker spaniel.   Shakespeare has Antony speak of the "hearts that spaniel'd me at heels, to whom I have their wishes." *Spaniel* can be a verb or adjective, signifying affectionate humility, as well as a noun. The dog's name simply means "Spanish dog," deriving from the old French *chien espagneul*, which was shortened to *espagnol*, "Spanish", and then *spaniel* in English. Either the spaniel was a breed developed in Spain or the dog reminded Europeans of the Spaniards, who were regarded as submissive and fawning during the Middle Ages. Neither the Spaniards nor the dog is servile, but the breed's silky hair and soft, soulful eyes may have suggested the appearance of the Spaniards. There is no hard evidence for this, however. The cocker spaniel gets its first name either from the way it cocks its long drooping ears or because it was trained to retrieve woodcocks.

Spanish fly.   The blister beetles, *Lytta vesicatoria*, used to make the dangerous reputed aphrodiasiac *Spanish fly* are abundant in Spain. Cantharides, or *Spanish fly*, is medicinally a diuretic and skin irritant.

Spanish words in English.   There are probably five hundred words in American English alone that are borrowed from Spanish. Some of the more common ones include: *cork, cask, anchovy, sherry, spade* (cards), *galleon, grenade, armada, comrade, sombrero, cannibal, Negro, iguana, alligator, armadillo, sassafras, sarsaparilla, mosquito, banana, cargo, desperado, matador, lime, embargo, parade, guitar, siesta, peon, chinchilla, cockroach, vanilla, barracuda, avocado, barbecue, tortilla, plaza, ten-gallon hat, chaps, serape, poncho, adobe, cafeteria, patio, plaza, pueblo, breeze, buckaroo, chaparral, cinch, corral, hacienda, lariat, lasso, machete, ranch, reata, rodeo, stampede, wrangler, alfalfa, marijuana, mesquite, yucca, bronco, buffalo, burro, barracuda, bonito, pompano, coyote, mustang, palomino, pinto, chile con carne, enchilada, frijole,* *jerky, mescal, pinon nuts, taco, tamale, tequilla, calaboose, hoosegow, vigilante, incommunicado, arroyo, canyon, mesa, sierra, couch, coon, creole, junta, mulatto, fiesta, filibuster, hombre, loco, marina, mosey, pronto, rumba, samba, savvy, stevedore, tornado, vamoose.* Some of these are covered in this book.

spencer. This repeating rifle, made by Christopher Spencer's Spencer Repeating Rifle Company, served the Confederates well in the Civil War and went West after that. Said boys in gray of the reliable carbine: "You can load it on Sunday and shoot all week." The rifle was light and ideal for mounted soldiers.

Spencerian. Spencerian refers to the thought of English philosopher Herbert Spencer (1820-1903), especially his attempt to unify all knowledge through the single principle of evolution, his "synthetic philosophy."

Spencerian script. Even as recently as 25 years ago penmanship remained an important subject in American grammar schools, but the increased use of the typewriter and computer has made penmanship exercises almost obsolete. In those days of yesteryear, when a fine hand was a great social asset and absolutely essential in conducting a business, one of the first American styles of calligraphy was that developed by Platt Rogers Spencer (1800-64), a system based on precise slanted strokes marked with flourishes at the end of words. Spencer taught classes in a log cabin on his Geneva, New York farm and lectured at various business schools and academies. His *Spencerian style*, popularized by a series of textbooks he wrote, greatly influenced early 19th century American calligraphy, so much so that today the term *Spencerian script* is used by collectors to describe the handwriting of his period and beyond.

spare the rod and spoil the child. Although you've probably heard someone remark "As the Bible says, 'Spare the rod and spoil the child,'" these words aren't in the Bible. In substance, however, the expression appears six times in the book of Proverbs, especially as: "He that spareth his rod hateth his son: but he that loveth him chasteneth him betimes." *Spare the rod and spoil the child*, in this exact form, was first used by Samuel Butler (1612?-80) in his satiric poem *Hudibras*, Part II (1664):

Love is a boy by poets styl'd;
Then spare the rod and spoil the child.

sparrow. No bird is better known everywhere in Great Britain than the little sparrow, whose name, in the form of the Old English *spearwa*, is first recorded in the seventh century. The small brownish-gray bird of the family *Fringillidae*, also native to the U.S., gives us the term "sparrow-legged," for a person with a big belly and skinny legs. The bird was even used in sparrow-pie, a dish that supposedly made the eater sharp-witted.

sparrow-fart. Toward the beginning of the century British slang for "at dawn" was *at sparrow-fart*, the expression popularized by soldiers in World War I. A polite variant is *at sparrow's cough.*

Spars. (*See* **Wrens.**)

Spartan. "Either come back with it or on it," the proverbial Spartan mother tells her only son when she hands him the shield he is to carry into battle. The inhabitants of ancient Sparta, the Greek city-state noted for its military excellence, were forced to be courageous, frugal, and sternly disciplined almost to a fault. Life there seems to have been equal to one long term of military service without leave from the barracks and battlefields, for women as well as men. Weak children were discarded and the survivors subjected to an ascetic discipline without luxuries or even comforts. Spartan virtues, which can easily become vices, give us the terms *Spartan fare*, "a frugal diet," *Spartan courage*, "that of one who can unflinchingly bear pain or face danger," and *Spartan simplicity*, "the barest necessities of life."

speakeasy. You were supposed to speak softly, or easy, on entering such illegal saloons during the Prohibition era, to avoid attracting the attention of law enforcement agents or informers who might be on the street.

speak softly and carry a big stick. Apparently, this well-known proverb isn't an American invention, but is African in origin. Bartlett's *Familiar Quotations* should note that Theodore Roosevelt's biographer, H.F. Pringle, in his *Theodore Roosevelt* (1931), quotes Teddy as saying in the first recorded use of the expression: "I have always been fond of the West African proverb 'Speak softly and carry a big stick; you will go far.'" Pringle has T.R. saying this in 1900; in the 1901 speech *Bartlett's* quotes, Roosevelt prefaces the proverb with "There is a homely adage that runs . . ."

speculator. The first speculators in the U.S. to be called *speculators* did business during the Revolutionary War boom, though there was no formal stock exchange at the time and wheeling and dealing was done in coffeehouses along Wall Street in downtown Manhattan, or outside. The word *speculator* has its roots in the Latin *speculatus*, observed, watched.

Spencer Jacket; etc. First Lord of the British Admiralty George John, the second Earl of Spencer, who recognized Lord Nelson's potential early, created this short wool jacket. Another Spencer, possibly related, invented the *Spencer sail*, and still another, the cork-filled *Spencer life belt.*

spic.   Before it was applied to Hispanic-Americans this offensive derogatory name was given to Italian-Americans. First recorded in 1915, it is thought to be a shortening of "spaghetti." (*See* **spaghetti; macaronic verse.**)

The Spice Islands.   Punning on the Spice Islands, the Moluccas in Indonesia, this expression was 19th-century slang for a privy or any foul-smelling place.

spiel.   This Americanism, for "sales talk or a line," has been used at least since 1870. It derives from the German *spielen*, "to play a musical instrument." In its American usage the word meant "to talk in a high-flown, grandiloquent manner" before it was used to describe the voluble talk of the carnival barker and then the salesman.

spill the beans.   A fanciful story, widely printed, holds that members of Greek secret societies voted on the admission of new members by dropping beans into jars or helmets. White beans signified an affirmative vote and black beans a negative ballot. Occasionally, the story says, voters would accidentally knock over the jar or helmet, revealing the secret vote, *spilling the beans*. However, the phrase is an American one that entered the language only around the beginning of this century. No one knows how it made its entrance, unless it was on the heels of an older expression, as an extension of *to know one's beans*, "to know what is what."

spinach.   Popeye eating it straight from the can did so much for this vegetable with the young set that spinach growers in one Texas town erected a large statue to the sailor man. Some authorities claim *spinach* comes from the Spanish, tracing it to the Latin *hispanicum olus*, "the Spanish herb." More likely the Persian and Arabian *isfanakh* became the Old Spanish *espinaca*, which eventually changed into the Middle French *espinach* that resulted in our *spinach*. At any rate, the Arabs did introduce the vegetable into Spain, whence it spread to the rest of Europe—Dr. Johnson, for one, enjoying it, Boswell tells us. Napoleon did almost as much for spinach's fame as Popeye by decorating the golden epaulets of his colonels with what looked like gold spinach seeds and were thus referred to as *spinach*—a term that lingers on to this day.

spinet.   Only in this century has *spinet* been used in the United States to describe a small, upright piano. Invented in about 1500 by Venetian musical instrument manufacturer Giovanni Spinetti, the spinet was at first similar to the clavicord. Having one keyboard, one string to each note, and until the middle of the 18th century no attached legs, the small instrument had often been called the *virginal*. In England today *spinet* still designates all small keyboard instruments with one string to a note that

are plucked by a quill or plectrum of leather. The spinet may also be named from the Italian *spina*, "a thorn," in reference to the quill points on the instrument, the naming probably influenced by both *Spinetti* and *spina*. At any rate, the historical information available on the etymology is scanty. In fact, the only reference to the inventor is found in a rare old book entitled *Conclusione nel suona dell'organo, di Adriano Banchieri*, published in Bologna in 1608. Its author states that: "Spinetta [the spinet] was thus named from the inventor of that oblong form, who was one Maestro Giovanni Spinetti, a Venetian; and I have seen one of those instruments . . . within which was the inscription—Joannes Spinetvs Venetvs fecit, A.D. 1503."

spinnaker.   The most probable explanation we have for this word is that back in the 1860s an unknown yacht owner invented a sail rigged at right angles from his racing vessel's side, a sail that extended from masthead to deck and ballooned far out to take advantage of the slightest breeze. The racing vessel was named *Sphinx*, but its crew had difficulty in pronouncing its name, calling it *Spinnicks*. Thus, the new sail was referred to as *Spinnicker's sail* and finally became known as a *spinnaker*.

to spirit away.   Originally, in 17th-century England, this expression refereed to the kidnapping of boys to work on the West Indian plantations. The children were taken as quickly and quietly as possible, to give people the impression that they had been "supernaturally removed."

spit and polish.   Military in origin, this term goes back to Victorian times, probably to the middle of the 19th century, although it isn't recorded before 1895. Meticulous cleaning and smartness of appearance were demanded of sailors in the British navy, which became known as the "Spit and Polish Navy." Enlisted men liked it then no more than they do now and *spit and polish*—the application of one's spittle as a polishing agent and much elbow grease to make an object shine—came to be a perjorative term for finicky, wasteful work in general.

to spitball.   Now outlawed, the *spitball* used to be a perfectly legal pitch in baseball. Many pitchers used it in its heyday and its unpredictable behavior made batters dread the pitch. Though the spitball is outlawed, some modern-day pitchers have been charged with using it—not by actually spitting on the ball anymore, but by more devious methods like moistening the hands and rubbing the ball. The practice, first recorded in baseball in about 1904, has been so common lately that a new slang term has entered the language. *To spitball* means "to speculate" in the stock market and elsewhere because "no one ever knows the way a spitball will break," especially down or up. Schoolboy *spitballs* are of course even older than the baseball variety, the word first recorded in this sense in 1846.

the spittin' image of. The germ of the idea behind this phrase has been traced back to 1400 by *Partridge*, who cites the early example "He's . . . as like these as th' hads't spit him." Similarly, in England and the southern U.S., the expression "he's the very spit of his father" is commonly heard. This may mean "he's as like his father as if he had been spit out of his mouth," but could also be a corruption of "spirit and image." If the last is true, it would explain the use of "and image" in the expression since the middle of the last century. *Spittin' image* would then be derived from "he's the very spirit and image of his father," that is, the child is identical to his parent in both spirit and looks. It's possible that both sources combined to give us our phrase for "exactly alike," which is also written *spit and image, spitting image, spitten image,* and *spit n' image.*

spizorinkum. Born on the American frontier, *spizorinkum* was originally used during the 1850's as the term for "good" hard money, as opposed to greenbacks or paper currency, but soon came to have many diverse meanings, including "tireless energy." It was possibly used so much because people liked the sound of the word! In any case, *spizorinkum* is "an impossible combination" of the Latin *specie* ("kind") and *rectum* ("right"), "the right kind." The word is sometimes spelled with two *zs.*

spliced. This nautical expression, for "the joining together of two pieces of rope," eventually became nautical and then general slang for "to join together in matrimony." It is not modern slang in this sense, dating back to the 18th century, when it is first recorded in Tobias Smollett's *The Adventures of Peregrine Pickle* (1751), which contains characters like the old sea dog Commodore Howser Trunnion and boatswain Tom Pipes.

splice the main brace. There is some doubt as to why *splice the main brace* has come to mean taking a strong, intoxicating drink. The main brace on a ship is the line secured to the main yard, from which the mainsail flies. The implication might be that a good drink braces a body. But one authority says the term derives from the days of sail, when the main brace was the most difficult to splice, being in a highly dangerous position, and that the crew received a double tot of rum after finishing the job on it.

to split hairs. One Englishman has actually split a human hair thirteen times into fourteen parts, the world record, and there are drills so fine today that minute holes can be bored in a single hair. However, when the expression *to split hairs* was coined over three centuries ago (in the original form *to cut a hair*), it was thought to be impossible to really split a hair and the phrase described any

argument making overrefined, caviling distinctions; a *hair-splitter* was one who quibbled over trifles. A politician, Machiavelli, was the first to have the word applied to him.

Spode Ware. "Josiah Spode produced a better porcelain than any that had yet been made in England," wrote Alexandre Brogniart, director of the French plant producing the famous Sèvres ware. "He endeavoured to equal the soft porcelain of Sèvres, which his paste closely resembled. He introduced, or at any rate perfected, the use of calcined bones in the body of the ware." Brogniart was referring to English potter Josiah Spode (1754-1827), who developed his formula of bone ash and feldspar at Stoke-on-Trent in 1799. England's leading chinaware manufacturers all adopted Spode's formula to produce the durable, fine-bone china much esteemed ever since as *Spodeware,* or *Spode.*

spoiled priest. *Spoiled priest* has been used so often in modern literature to mean someone who has failed to live up to the standard expected of him that it probably does mean that by now. But the 19th century term originally meant a priesthood candidate who failed to take his vows.

the spoils of the conquered ocean. When he impulsively decided to become conqueror of Britain in A.D. 40, the mad Roman emperor Caligula, who had made his horse Incitatus a priest and a consul of Rome, started to move his legions across the Channel from Gaul. Then he just as suddenly changed his mind and took his men on a march up and down the beach hunting for seashells! The Roman historian Suetonius says that when Caligula's legions gathered enough shells, the emperor marched them home in self-acclaimed triumph carrying "the spoils of the conquered ocean."

spoils of war. The spoils here are valuable goods, not ruined things, and take their name from the Latin *spolium,* "the hide stripped from an animal." Thus anything stripped or taken from a country after it lost a war became known as "spoils." The word was employed in this sense as far back as 1300 and Dryden used the expression *spoils-of-war* in 1697. *Spoil* in the sense of ruined, useless, takes its meaning from the remains of animal carcasses that have been left to rot after being stripped of their skin.

spoils system. Often attributed to Andrew Jackson, this phrase did arise during his presidency, when the practice of giving appointive offices to loyal members of the party in power was first adopted on a large scale. However, the phrase was suggested by New York Senator William Learned Marcy, who defended Jackson's 1829 policy in a speech a year later. Marcy, a member of the Albany Regency, a political group controlled by "The Little Fox,"

Martin Van Buren, rose in the Senate to defend the appointment of Van Buren as minister to England, his public defense of this political patronage being "the rule that to the victor belong the spoils of war." This remark led to the anonymous coining of *spoils system*, the phrase first recorded in 1838. The political atmosphere of an era can often be seen in the expressions born in that period and during the Jackson and Van Buren administrations we find the following first used in a political sense: *dyed in the wool* (1830), *party line* (1834), *picayune* (1837), *party machinery* (1829), *wirepuller* (1832), and even *expose* (1830), among others. (*See also* **O.K.**)

spondee. The Greeks often made drink-offerings called *sponde* ("libation") to the gods on solemn occasions. A slow meter used in poetry read on such occasions also came to be called *sponde* and it was this word that gave us our word *spondee*, for a "metrical foot of two stressed or long syllables." The *spondee* is often used to slow the rhythm of a line.

spondulix. Where this old American word for money came from is anybody's guess, but *spondulix* is recorded as early as 1856. It's another word that can only be guessed to be of fanciful origin, a funny word that caught on because people liked its sound. Mark Twain used it in *Huckleberry Finn*.

spoof. This word for "a mocking imitation," was coined by British comedian Arthur Roberts, who invented a game called "Spoof" in the late 19th century. What he coined the word from no one knows.

spoonerism. The Reverend William Archibald Spooner, dean and later warden of New College, Oxford, was a learned man, but not spell woken—well spoken, that is. "We all know what it is, to have a half-warmed fish inside us," he once told an audience, meaning to say "half-formed wish." On another occasion he advised his congregation that the next hymn would be "Kingering Congs Their Titles Take," instead of "Conquering Kings Their Titles Take," and he is said to have explained to listeners one time that "the Lord is a shoving leopard." Spooner's slips occurred both in church, where he once remarked to a lady, "Mardon me Padom, this pie is occupewed, allow me to sew you to another sheet," and told a nervous bridegroom that "it is kisstomery to cuss the bride," and in his classes, where he chided one student with, "You hissed my mystery lecture," and dismissed another with, "You have deliberately tasted two worms and can leave Oxford by the town drain!" Nobody knows how many of these *spoonerisms* were really made by Spooner, but they were among the many attributed to him. Spooner was an albino, and his metathetical troubles were probably due to nervousness and poor eyesight resulting from his condition. The scientific name for his speech affliction is metathesis, the accidental transposition of letters or syllables in the words of a sentence, the process known long before Spooner made it so popular that his slips of the tongue and eye were widely imitated. Spooner, who lived to the ripe old age of 86, once called Queen Victoria "our queer old dean" when trying to say "our dear old queen." (*See* **Marrowsky.**)

a spot of tay. When an Irishman says he'll have *a spot of tay* he's being more British than the British. *Tay* is not an ignorant Irish pronunciation of *tea*. The Portuguese introduced the drink we now know as tea into Europe as *cha* and that was the first English name it went by. But as far back as 1650 Englishmen were using the name the Dutch got from the Malayans for Tea, *te*. This was pronounced *tay* in English long before it was pronounced *tea* and was often spelled *tay* to indicate its pronunciation. The pronunciation was common up until the end of the 18th century. In his "Rape of the Lock," for example, Pope spells the word *tea* three times, but rhymes it with "obey," "stay," and "away." (*See* **tea.**)

spring chicken. We find the expression *now past a chicken*, meaning "no longer young," recorded as early as 1711 by Steele in *The Spectator*: "You ought to consider you are now past a chicken; this Humour, which was well enough in a Girl, is insufferable in one of your Motherly Character." *No spring chicken*, an exaggeration of the phrase, is first recorded in America, in 1906.

sprout-kale month. Because cabbages began to sprout in February, the Anglo-Saxons called that month *sprote-Kalemonath*, or *sprout-Kale month*.

spruce. Courtiers in the reign of England's Henry VIII affected the dress of Prussian noblemen, those *hautest* of the *haut* who wore such fashionable attire as broad-brimmed hats with bright feathers, silver chains around their necks, satin cloaks and red velvet doublets. Anything from Prussia had been called *Pruce* during the Middle Ages, but by the 16th century an *s* had somehow been added to the word and courtiers who dressed as elegantly as the Prussian nobleman were said to be appareled in *spruce* fashion. *Spruce* soon meant a smart, neat, or dapper appearance, as is reflected in the phrase *to spruce up*. The neat, trim form of the *spruce tree* may have suggested its name, too, but it more likely derives from the belief that the spruce was first grown in Prussia.

spud. *Spud*, for "a potato," is a Scottish term dating back at least to the 19th century, when a *spud* meant a raw potato and a roasted spud was a *mickey*, cooked jacket and all in the cinders. The word derives from the sharp spade called a *spud* used to dig potatoes, which, in turn, dates back several centuries earlier and is of unknown origin, possibly deriving from the Middle English *spuddle*, a kind of knife. *Spud* definitely is *not* an acronym for the Society for the *Prevention* of *Unwholesome Diets*!

to square the circle.   To attempt something that is impossible, just as it is impossible mathmatically to construct a circle of the same area as a given square. The expression is first recorded by John Donne in 1624.

squaric acid.   (*See* **cubane.**)

squash.   *Asquutasquash*, meaning "that which is eaten raw," was the Narragansett Indian word for a kind of melon. No wonder that early colonists abbreviated the word to *squash*. Later, they somehow transferred the word squash to what we know now as squash, which of course is not usually eaten raw, but which resembles a melon.

the squeaky wheel gets the most grease.   The expression is often heard as above, but what American humorist "Josh Billings" (Henry Wheeler Shaw, 1818-85) said exactly in his poem "The Kicker" was:

The wheel that squeaks the loudest
Is the one that gets the grease.

Josh Billings is also responsible for "It is better to know nothing than to know what ain't so" ("Proverbs", 1874), which, strangely enough, the German philosopher Nietzsche reiterated in *Thus Spake Zarathustra* (1883-1891), though I'm sure Nietzsche never read him: "Better know nothing than half-know many things."

squirrel.   The Greeks were impressed not so much by this bright-eyed rodent's acrobatic performances in trees as by its bushy tail, which they believed the animal wrapped around it like a parasol when the sun was too strong. So they named the animal *skiouros*, "shadowtail," from their words for shade, *skia*, and tail, *oura*, meaning shadytail, the animal that makes shade with its tail. The allusion was pleasant, poetic, but the road to our word *squirrel* proved difficult. *Skiouros* became *sciurus* in Latin and then *escureul* in France before going through nearly a score of English spellings and becoming the *squirrel* that we know today. Another word from the Greek root *skia*, is *sciamachy*, which means a sham fight or shadow boxing, and comes directly from a Greek word meaning "fighting in the shade, fighting with shadows." The term isn't heard in the gym, but political or even CIA *sciamachy* is not unknown.

SS.   SS stands for Schutzstaffel, meaning "protective echelon or elite guard." Growing out of a small group of thugs who were recruited in 1923 to protect Hitler and became the security arm of the Nazi Party, it was expanded under Heinrich Himmler in 1929 and about one million men had passed through its ranks by the end of World War II. The *Waffen* (weapons) *SS* were crack, cruel combat units. The *Totenkopf* (Death Head) *SS* served as guards, executioners, and torturers in concentration camps, taking their name from their black caps and the skull-and-crossbone insignia on their collars.

Stakhanovite.   Soviet authorities reported that coal miner Aleksei Stakhanov vastly increased his production in 1935 by the use of more rational working techniques and teamwork. This voluntary efficiency system, called *Stakhanovism*, or the *Stakhanovite Movement*, in the miner's honor, was strongly encouraged by the Soviet government to speed up completion of the then current five-year plan and it did much to accomplish this national objective. *Stakhanovite workers* were rewarded with higher pay, bonuses, and other incentives, and while the idea behind Stakhanovism was nothing new, its success in the Soviet Union made the word widely known throughout the world. Aleksei Grigorievich Stakhanov, born in 1905, eventually worked for the U.S.S.R. Ministry of Coal Industries, having made the great leap forward from worker to commissar. He won many awards, including the Order of Lenin, before his death in 1977. It is said that the word *Stakhanovite* is now out of fashion in the Soviet Union except as a humorous term for a sycophant.

stalag.   The popular play and movie *Stalag 17* made this word familiar to Americans in the 1950s. A *stalag* is a prisoner-of-war camp, a German shortening of their World War II *Stammlager*, or "group camp."

Stalinism; Stalingrad; etc.   Iosif Vissarionovich Dzhugashvili (1879-1953) took the name Joseph Stalin after joining the Russian revolutionary movement in 1896. Stalin, which means "man of steel," was to become in the form of *Stalinism* a synonym for ruthless dictatorship rarely equaled in any other time or place. There is no doubt that the Soviet leader transformed his country into a great modern military and industrial power after succeeding Lenin. But no nation ever paid a higher price for such "progress." Ten million or more Kulaks, wealthy peasants, were exterminated in order to make Stalin's collective farms a success; another ten million people were eliminated in the Great Purge that lasted from 1934 to 1938; no one knows how many more millions were killed in the continual vengeful, fearful purge that seemed at times to be this paranoid's sole reason for living. *De-Stalinization* began in Russia in 1956 when Nikita Khruschev exposed Stalin's crimes. By 1961 Stalin's body had been removed from the mausoleum in Red Square and every factory, mountain, street and city named after him had been renamed—even the city of *Stalingrad* (now Volgograd), which had been dedicated to him in 1925 because forces under his command drove out the White

Armies during the Revolution. Stalingrad will always be known historically for the great battle that proved to be the turning point in World War II, and Stalin's name is best remembered in *Stalinism*.

The Standing Fishes Bible.   Various editions of the Bible have over the years earned popular names because of printers' errors. In the *Standing Fishes Bible* (1806) Ezekiel, 48:10, reads: "And it shall come to pass that the fishes [instead of "fishers"] shall stand upon it . . ."

to stand pat.   American poker players in the late 19th century invented this expression to indicate that a player was satisfied with the original hand dealt to him and would draw no more cards. Where did the *pat* come from? One theory is that because the word meant "in a manner that fits or agrees with the purpose or occasion" or "incapable of being improved" it was a natural for the poker expression. Another holds that *stand pat* is a corruption of *stand pad*, an older English expression meaning "to sell from a stationary position" and originally referring to peddlers who remained in a fixed location. *To stand pad* was to remain fixed or firm, like a poker player who didn't move to take any more cards. From poker, in any case, the expression passed into general use as a term for taking a firm, fixed position on something.

Stapelia.   Dutch physician J.B. Stapel (d. 1636) is remembered by a carrion flower; the large flowers of the cactuslike *Stapelia* genus, containing some hundred species and having a very unpleasant, fetid odor. Native to South Africa, a few of these curiously marked species—variously colored and sometimes marbled or barred—are grown in the greenhouse for their flowers. There is no record of whether the naming was meant as a compliment or insult.

star.   *Star*, for an actor of exceptional popularity or talent, or both, isn't some press agent's invention as many believe. The term is first recorded in a 1779 book on the theatre in an appraisal of the great English actor David Garrick: "The little stars, who hid their diminished rays in his [Garrick's] presence, began to abuse him." *Star*, as a verb, wasn't used until about 1825. *Stardom* seems to have been coined by O. Henry in a 1911 short story.

starboard; larboard.   Old English ships were steered (*steor*, "steer") by a paddle or board (*bord*) over the right side. This *steorbord* became *starboard* and starboard later became the name for the right side of the ship itself. *Larboard*, the left side of a ship, derives from the earlier *lureboard* (from the Anglo-Saxon *laere*, "empty"), in reference to the fact that the left side was usually empty because the steersman stood on the right, or steering-board (starboard), side.

star chamber proceedings.   A *star chamber* is any committee or tribunal that proceeds by arbitrary or unfair oppressive methods. The term dates to the reigns of British monarchs James I and Charles I when a civil and criminal court called the *star-chamber*, abolished in 1641, notoriously abused its powers and from which there was no appeal. The court, its judges the king's own counselors, was probably so named because it was held in a room, or chamber, in the royal palace at Westminster where the ceiling was decorated with gilt stars. However, Blackstone's *Commentaries* has it that the *star* here derives from the *starra*, or "contracts and obligations of Jews," that were stored in the room.

stark naked.   Although *stark* was a common Middle English word meaning "strong" and is sometimes used to intensify other words, as in *stark raving mad*, it has nothing to do with *stark naked*. The original form of *stark naked* was *start naked*, *start* here being a corruption of the Anglo-Saxon *steort*, meaning "tail or rump." Someone *stark naked* is therefore literally "naked even to the rump."

starling.   This bird, whose name is akin to the Old English for tern, *stearn*, was brought across the Atlantic in 1890 and released in Central Park by literary enthusiasts seeking to introduce to America all the birds mentioned in Shakespeare. It has since become a pest, reminding some gardeners of the Englishman back in 1886 who said, "Few people are aware of how good the starling is to eat." The starling (*Sturnus vulgaris*) constitutes more of the 100 billion birds in the world than any other species, and has long been noted for its ability to speak and whistle.

the stars and stripes; the star-spangled banner.   Though the Continental Congress resolved in 1777 that the U.S. flag be composed of thirteen stripes and thirteen stars, the term *stars and stripes* for the flag isn't recorded until five years later. *Star-spangled banner*, for the flag, was of course inspired by the national anthem, whose lyrics Francis Scott Key wrote in 1814, but the song didn't become our official national anthem until 1931 (though it had for almost a century been called our "national ballad"). (*See* **Old Glory**.)

start from scratch.   Unlike *to come up to scratch*, (*q.v.*), which probably derives from prize-fighting, this was originally a horse-racing expression. A *scratch* in England was the starting line in a horse race and horses started there with no advantage besides their own ability, like anyone who *starts from scratch* in any undertaking. In this sense a *scratch race* is a race without restrictions as to the age, weight, and winnings of the horses entered.

State of Franklin.   (*See* **Tennessee**.)

stateroom.   One persistent old story has the term *stateroom* coined by an early owner of steamboats named Shreve, for whom the city of Shreveport, Louisiana, was named. Shreve, according to this account, named luxurious cabins on his boats after states (*e.g.,* the Texas Room) and they came to be known as *staterooms. Stateroom* is first recorded for the "sleeping apartment on a U.S. passenger steamer" in 1837 by Harriet Martineau, but there is no evidence yet of any Shreve with his finger in the pie. More likely this *stateroom* evolved from the *stateroom* meaning "a captain's or officer's quarters on board ship," which is first recorded in Pepys's *Diary* in 1660.

to stave off.   A *stave* is a stick of wood, the word a back formation from the plural of staff, *staves.* In the early 17th century staves were used in the "sport" of bullbaiting, where dogs were set against bulls. Too often these contests were badly matched, for the bulls frequently had the tips of their horns cut off, and when the dogs got a bull down, the bull's owner often tried to save him for another fight by driving the dogs off with a stave or stick. Because the owner actually "postponed" the bull's death until another day, the expression *to stave off* acquired its present figurative meaning of "to forestall." This is at least a possible explanation for *to stave off,* which we know is associated in some way with beating off dogs.

a Stavin Chain.   A *Stavin Chain* isn't heard much anymore, but since about 1910 it has meant a sexually powerful man very attractive to women, after the hero of a popular American Southwestern folk song.

steak.   *Steak,* an old English word, takes its name from the way such meat was first cooked: on a thin *stake,* from the Old English *staca,* akin to stick. The word is first recorded as *styke* in the early 15th century.

Steak Tartare.   Bloodthirsty about their meals as well as their conquests, the nomadic Tartars liked their meat raw, or almost always so—sometimes they placed a hunk of meat under the saddle and cooked it by friction during hours of riding. At any rate, in medieval times traveling Hamburg merchants learned about a recipe for scraped raw meat seasoned with salt, pepper, and onion juice and named it *Tartar steak* or *steak Tartare* in their honor. This was the first hamburger, (*q.v.*) remaining so until some anonymous Hamburger shaped *steak Tartare* into patties and cooked them. Tartar sauce, a mayonnaise containing diced pickles, onions, olives, capers, and green herbs, takes its name from *Tartar steak,* which was often seasoned with similar ingredients.

to steal a march on someone.   Here the *march* is the distance armed troops can cover in a day. In medieval times enemies could easily figure this distance and, by marching themselves at night, be waiting to surprise their opponents when they arrived at their destination. This was known as *stealing a march* on someone and came to mean "to anticipate someone's moves and thus gain an advantage over him."

steal my thunder.   "Our author, for the advantage of this play, had invented a new species of thunder . . . the very sort that is presently used in the theatre. The tragedy itself was coldly received, notwithstanding such assistance, and was acted but a short time. Some nights after, Mr. Dennis, being in the pit at the representation of *Macbeth,* heard his own thunder made use of; upon which he rose in a violent passion and exclaimed, 'See how the rascals use me! They will not let my play run, and yet they steal my thunder.'" This early account of the origin of the expression *steal my thunder,* from the *Biographia Britannica,* is accurate in all respects, according to most authorities. Restoration playwright John Dennis (1657-1734) had invented a new and more effective way of simulating thunder on the stage (by shaking a sheet of tin) for his play *Appius and Virginia* (1709). The play soon closed, but a rival company stole his thunder, inspiring his outburst and giving us the expression *steal my thunder.*

steamboat.   *Steamboat* is an Americanism dating back to at least 1785, when John Fitch invented the first workable one. Fitch was not able to secure the financial aid necessary to promote his invention after his fourth ship was destroyed, and he died a broken man, leaving a request that he be buried on the banks of the Ohio River so that he might rest "where the song of the boatman would enliven the stillness of my resting place and the music of the steam engine soothe my spirit." His dream became a reality in 1807, nine years after he died, when Robert Fulton's steamboat *Clermont,* which had been called "Fulton's Folly," proved a great success.

steatopygous.   "With many Hottentot women," Darwin wrote, "the posterior part of the body projects in a wonderful manner; they are steatopygous." Darwin clearly appreciated this way that some women extend in his *Descent of Man,* but the word *steatopygous,* when applied to Hottentot Bushmen (especially the Bongos) or anyone else, clearly isn't nearly as complimentary as *callipygian* (*q.v.*) Deriving from the Greek for "fat rumped," its dictionary definition is "a protuberance of the buttocks, due to an abnormal accumulation of fat in and behind the hips and thighs."

steeplechase.   According to one tradition, *steeplechase* originated with a race from church steeple to church steeple in Irish horse country. Another tale credits a group of British riders returning home from a foxhunt with inventing the sport and the word—these foxless riders decided to run a race in a direct line, regardless of obstacles, to the steeple of the village church, the winner the rider "who first touched the stones of the steeple with his whip." In any case, the original horseback races called *steeplechase races* had a church steeple in view as the goal, the riders having to clear all intervening obstacles. The word is first recorded in the British *Sporting Magazine*, in 1805.

steerage. "My grandparents came over in steerage" is often heard in reference to late 19th-century immigrants to America. *Steerage* means passage below decks, near a ship's steering gear. Steerage passage in the late 19th century cost only fifteen dollars, this price, plus twenty-five dollars to prove you weren't a pauper, was all one needed to come to America.

stem to stern. Loosely speaking, the *stem* is the bow of a ship and the *stern* is the rear. Thus *from stem to stern* means "throughout" as in, "We turned the place over *from stem to stern*." The expression is an old one, dating back to at least the early 16th century.

Sten gun. This British light machine gun of World War II is an unusual blend of the first initials of its two inventors' names, Sheppard and Turpin, plus the first two letters of the name of their country, *England*. The *Sten gun*, or *sten*, is not extremely accurate, but is easy to operate, can be fired from the shoulder, weighing only eight pounds, and fires rapidly at the rate of 550 rounds per minute, making it an effective short-range weapon. Mass-produced mainly from stamped parts, the inexpensive *sten* should really be classed as a submachine gun, like the American *Thompson*, or *Tommy gun*, and the German *Schmeisser*, or *burp gun*.

stenography. Though its practice dates back to the ancient Greeks, the word *stenography* is first recorded in the early 17th century. The word derives from the Greek *stenos*, "narrow," and *graphein*, "to write," literally meaning "narrow writing." Other synonyms are the rare *brachygraphy*, "short writing," and *shorthand*, which dates back to 1636 and is the most common term today.

stentorian. Under freak acoustical conditions the human voice has carried over ten miles across water, but its average range is about 200 yards in still air. Stentor, Homer's Grecian herald of the Trojan War, who may have been based on some top sergeant of old, probably had a range far exceeding this. In the *Iliad* Homer tells how the herald faced the enemy to dictate terms in "a voice of bronze . . . as loud as fifty men together." Greek legend claims that Stentor finally met his match in Hermes,

herald of the Gods, dying as the result of a vocal contest with him. But his name lived on as the Greek for loud-voiced and gave us the English word *stentorian*, "extremely loud." A howling monkey, a trumpet-shaped protozoan, an an electric magnifying speaker called the stentorphone also do him homage. (*See* **Hector; Nestor; thersitical**.)

sterling. In medieval England a *starling* was a coin worth about a penny and took its name from the star (*steorra*) embossed upon it. The *pound sterling* began life as one hundred of the smaller *sterlings*, and its value, of course, has risen and fallen over the years.

stet. *Stet* is Latin for "let it stand," the printing term being used as a direction to the printer to reinstate a word or words that had been marked for deletion in a proof or manuscript. The term is a fairly recent one, first recorded in 1821.

Stetson. After poor health forced John Batterson Stetson (1830-1906) to travel west at the time of the Civil War, it occurred to him that no one was manufacturing hats suited to the practical needs of the Western cowboy, and on his return to Philadelphia in 1865 he went into the hat business, specializing in Western-style headgear. The wide-brimmed, ten-gallon felt hats he manufactured immediately became popular with cowboys and have been called *Stetsons*, or *John B's*, ever since.

stevedore. (*See* **longshoreman**.)

stew. Now the synonym for a brothel or a prostitute, a *stew* was in medieval times the town bathhouse. Toward the end of the Middle Ages the town bathhouse became the gathering place for loose men and women, *stew* taking on its present meaning. Our word *stew* for meat and vegetables slowly boiled together comes from the same source, the verb meaning to bathe in a hot bath or *stew*.

stick in one's craw. When you can't swallow something, when it won't go down with you or you are loathe to accept, it *sticks in your craw*. The *craw* is the crop or preliminary stomach of a fowl, where food is predigested. Hunters centuries ago noticed that some birds swallowed bits of stone that were too large to pass through the craw and into the digestive tract. These stones, unlike the sand and pebbles needed by birds to help grind food in the pouch, literally stuck in the craw, couldn't go down any farther. This oddity became part of the language of hunters and the phrase was soon used figuratively.

stickler. The earliest *sticklers* were umpires or moderators at wrestling or fencing matches and tournaments in the 16th century. Within another hundred years the word was being used figuratively, followed by *for*, to describe anybody who unyieldingly insists on something. *Stickler* derives from the Anglo-Saxon *stihtan*, "to arrange or regulate."

the sticks. *The sticks* is an Americanism for the country, or the backwoods. First recorded in 1905, it derives from the use of *sticks* by lumbermen for "timberlands."

to stick to one's guns. It seems sure that this expression was born with some fort or ship being attacked, but though it may be military in origin it is first recorded, as late as 1839, in a popular novel called *Ten Thousand a Year*, the words put in the mouth of a civilian named Mr. Titmouse.

stick your neck out. (*See* **don't stick your neck out**.)

stiff upper lip. Since it is the lower lip that quivers when someone is afraid or on the verge of crying, keeping a stiff upper lip seems to be a rather meaningless expression. Probably there is no logic behind this admonition to be firm in times of trouble, but at least one attempt has been made at an explanation. Young British officers who adopted mustaches tried to keep them trim so that they didn't make their upper lips twitch, such twitching being a sign of lack of control and emotional immaturity to their superiors. The main problem here is that all recorded evidence shows this phrase to be of American origin, from New England in about 1830. Possibly it is just the reverse of the American expression "down in the mouth."

still as a stone. Just as he probably originated *busy as a bee* (*q.v.*), Chaucer probably coined the classic alliterative phrase *still as a stone*, which later became the Shakespearian *stone still*: "I will not struggle; I will stand stone-still"—*King John*. At least both expressions are first recorded in his work.

stink chariot. *Stink chariot* for an automobile was invented by Australian author and editor John Norton, who published a weekly paper called *John Norton's Truth* earlier in this century. It is obsolescent if not obsolete but worth remembering.

stinker; to stink on ice; to stink out loud. *Stinker*, one writer suggests, may derive from the unskilled hands among American buffalo hunters who skinned the freshly killed animals and stank from the blood and intestines that clung to them. *Partridge*, however, states that *stinker* has meant a disgusting contemptible person in British slang since the 17th century. *To stink on ice* and *to stink out loud* are definitely 19th-century Americanisms.

stinkpots. *Stinkpots*, favorite weapons of pirates, were malodorous concoctions made from saltpeter (potassium nitrate), limestone (calcium carbonate), asafetida (a vile-smelling gum resin), and decayed fish that were packed into earthenware jugs, ignited, and hurled onto an enemy ship. Nauseating smoke spread over the deck and through the hold, often discouraging the enemy from fighting, or at least weakening his resistance. Pirates also hung stinkpots from the yardarms and cut them off when they projected over the vessel under attack.

stitch. (*See* **throw into stitches**.)

Stix Nix Hix Pix. (*see* **nix**.)

stocks and bonds; stock market. Both *stocks* and *bonds* have their etymological roots in substantial things. No one knows exactly how the words came to be applied to securities, but *stocks* comes ultimately from the Old English word *stocc*, for "tree trunk," and *bonds* from the early English *band*, meaning "fastening." *Stock market*, and ultimately *stocks*, may come from the name of a London meat and fish market called the Stock Exchange near the site of the Mansion House in the 15th century. An ancient source says this market was so named because it was built on a site where "had stoode a payre of stocks for a punishment of offenders."

stogy. (*See* **Conestoga wagons**.)

stone melons. There are melon-shaped stones on Mount Carmel, said to have fallen there from the cart of a peasant. According to Muhammadan tradition, Elijah saw the peasant carrying melons and asked him for one. The peasant lied that they were stones and Elijah promptly changed them into stones.

stone still. (*See* **still as a stone**.)

stonewall. Confederate Gen. Thomas Jonathan Jackson and his men resisted so hard against Union forces at the Battle of Bull Run during the Civil War that he earned the nickname Stonewall Jackson. His sobriquet gives us the expression *to stonewall*, "to obstruct justice," that became prominent in the language during the Watergate era.

stool pigeon. Fowlers in the past used live decoy birds to lure pigeons and other birds into range of their nets or guns, which helped them to wipe out several species. These live decoys, their eyes sometimes stitched closed, were called *stool pigeons*, *stool-crows*, or the like, probably because they were tied by a long string to small stools that the hunters could move up and down while waiting hidden for their prey (although their name may derive from the Old English word *stale*, meaning "a living bird used to catch others of the same species"). At any rate, in about 1830 the term *stool pigeon* became American slang for a criminal decoy used by the police to catch other criminals, and by the end of the century it meant a police informer. The last meaning was probably influenced by the use of the slang *carrier pigeon* for "an informer" at the time, a carrier pigeon carrying information to the police the way the bird carries messages. *Stoolie*, an abbreviated form of the term, is of relatively recent usage.

stop one's ears. (*See* **to turn a deaf ear**.)

store; stoic. *Store* derives from the roofed colonnades called *stoas* that housed the small shops of merchants in the ancient Athenian agora, that same marketplace where Socrates and his followers gathered, where Solon the wise lawgiver made his fortune as a merchant. In this marketplace the philosopher Zeno taught that "what will be will be," that man must accept his fate calmly in this world. He and his pupils came to be called *stoics* because they met in a *stoa*. Thus the Greek word *stoa*, for "a shop," yielded both the words *store* and *stoic*, this last something many a storekeeper has been forced to be by economic and other calamities over the centuries.

storm door. I had assumed that this term was an Americanism invented in relatively recent times. But lexicographers trace it back to the Dutch *storm deur*, meaning the same, used here in the 17th century, when New York was called New Amsterdam.

stormonter. *Stormonter* is obsolete except in a historical sense and never made the dictionaries, but it tells an amusing story about Benjamin Franklin, who had among his many gifts a genius for coining words. Lord Stormont, the British ambassador in Paris during the Revolution, was the most assiduous spreader of tales about America's defeats at the hands of Great Britain, his aim of course to color the facts and discourage European nations from supporting the American cause. One time a French friend came to Franklin with Stormont's story that six battalions of Americans had laid down their arms. The Frenchman wanted to know if this was true. "Oh, no," Franklin replied gravely, "it is not the truth, it is only a Stormont." Within a day his witticism swept Paris and *stormonter* became a new French synonym for lying. Franklin is also responsible for *harmonica*, the musical instrument he invented in a rude form and named from the Italian *armonica*, "harmonious."

stovaine. The anesthetic *stovaine* was named in an irregular way for its 20th-century French discoverer, Fourneau. The anesthetic has coc*aine* in it, accounting for the last syllable and the "Four" of *Four*neau's name translates into English as *stove*; hence, *stovaine*.

stove. The first *stoves* were saunas, not kitchen appliances. *Stove* comes to us from the Old English *stofa* "a hot air bath," or *sauna*, the hot steam baths brought to England from Scandinavia. *Stofa* didn't change in spelling to *stove* until the 15th century and it wasn't until the 16th century that *stove* was used to mean a furnace.

Stradivarius. Recently the *Lady Blunt Stradivarius* (1721) was auctioned off at Sotheby's in London for $200,000, the highest price ever paid for a musical instrument. Nor is this violin considered to be the finest one made by Antonio Stradivari, that honor usually accorded to the Messiah, or the *Alard Stradivarius*. Amazingly, some 600 of the 1,100 or so violins, violas, and cellos made by Stradivari from 1666 to 1737 still survive today, half of them in the United States—a tribute to the master craftsman's genius. Only the barest essentials are known about the supreme Italian violin maker. Born at Cremona in northern Italy in 1644, he was an apprentice of the distinguished craftsman Nicolo Amati, but he soon developed his own methods, in 1684 opening a shop where his sons Francesco and Omobono worked with him. Stradivari was famous in his own time, his commissions including instruments for England's James II and Spain's Charles III. He died in 1737, aged ninety-three, and to this day his secrets of success have not been discovered.

straight from the horse's mouth. By examining a horse's teeth an expert can make a good estimation of its age; a horse's first permanent teeth, for example, don't appear until it is about two and a half years old. So despite what any crooked horse trader might have wished them to believe, informed horsemen in England stood little chance of being cheated about a horse's age—they had it on good authority, *straight from the horse's mouth*. The expression came into racetrack use in about 1830 and was part of everyday speech by 1900.

straight from the shoulder. The expression means honestly, frankly, and to the point and derives from a boxing term of the mid-19th century. A punch straight from the shoulder was once made by bringing the fist to the shoulder and sending it forward straight and fast. Such undeceptive blows are quick, effective, and often to the point of the chin.

strait; strait-laced. Though used several hundred years earlier, *strait-laced* emerged as a popular figure of speech only in the early 17th century when girdles became fashionable. Wrote one arbiter of taste at the time: "No Maid here's handsome thought, unless she can with her short Palms her straight-lac'd body span." This of course required a lot of tugging on the laces of a bodice or corset, but a woman's body did become very *strait* or "tight and narrow" at the waist. Thus the term *strait-laced* derives not from the word "straight" but from the Middle English *strait*, the same word that gives us the tight and narrow geographical *straits*. *Strait*, in turn, comes from the Latin *strictus,* "to tighten, bind tightly," which also gives us *constriction.* The term *strait-laced* early became related to excessive prudishness because a strait-laced person supposedly drew moral bonds as tight as those on a girdle, while an unlaced, loose, woman was thought to be more voluptuous and less repressed.

strawberry. Several theories have been proposed about the origin of *strawberry,* but none is convincing. Some say the straw mulch often used in its cultivation inspired the name, others that the dried berries were once strung on straw for decorations, still others that the long runners of the mother plant (strawlike when dry) gave the fruit its name. The word was used as early as 100 A.D. in England and doesn't derive from any other language. It may be that the *straw* in *strawberry* is a corruption of the word *strew.* Certainly the mother plant strews, or scatters, new plants all over a patch when it propagates itself by sending out runners. There's always been an air of mystery surrounding the strawberry. The early Greeks, in fact, had a taboo against eating them, as they did against any red food, and pregnant women in the Middle Ages avoided them because they believed their children would be born with *strawberry marks* (small, slightly raised birthmarks resembling strawberries) if they did. A *strawberry roan* is a reddish-coated horse flecked with white hair.

straw boss. A writer discussing hobo lingo in *American Speech* almost half a century ago traced this term to the late 19th century American farm. "The (real) boss attended to the grain going into the thresher," he explained; "the secondman (or straw boss) watched the straw coming out and hence had little to do." Thus the term *straw boss* has come to mean anyone, especially a foreman, who gives orders but has no real authority to enforce them.

strawfoot. Union army slang for a raw rural recruit during the Civil War, *strawfoot* may have been coined by the drill sergeants who taught these men to march. According to one story, many such men didn't know their left foot from their right and the instructors tied hay to their left foot and straw to the right, shouting the marching cadence "Hayfoot! Strawfoot!" rather than "Left foot! Right foot!" But, alas, *strawfoot* is more likely a description of recruits who still had straw from the farm in their shoes.

straw man. (*See* **man of straw.**)

the straw that broke the camel's back; the last straw. Charles Dickens probably invented these expressions in *Dombey and Son,* where he wrote: "As the last straw breaks the laden camel's back." But Dickens got the idea from an old English proverb: *'Tis the last feather that breaks the horse's back.* Both phrases mean someone's limit or breaking point. The strongest camel can carry about 1,200 pounds—a straw more might literally break its back.

stream of consciousness. William James coined this now common term in *Principles of Psychology* (1890) and it has come to mean a literary technique that tries to express the multitude of thoughts and feelings that flow through the mind. James Joyce developed the technique in *Ulysses* (1922), but it had been used long before him by Arestino, Sterne, Diderot, Carlyle, and French novelist Edouard Dujardin, whose work Joyce is believed to have known.

streetwalker. The use of this term, for "a prostitute who works the streets," is an ancient one—older than the use of *streetwalker* for a pedestrian. It is first recorded by Shakespeare's detractor, dramatist Robert Greene, the same Bohemian who died of a surfeit of pickled herrings and Rhenish wine. In a tract on "Conny-catching" written in 1592, in which he describes London's lowlife, Greene wrote of "street walkers . . . in rich garded [attention-getting] gowns." It wasn't until almost three decades later that *streetwalkers* was applied to anyone who walks in the street.

the strenuous life. (*See* **Ananias.**)

strike. Though workers had certainly refused to work on occasion before 1768, the word *strike* is first recorded in that year, when British seamen threatened to strike (take down) the sails on their ships and cease all work until what they called their grievances were settled. This they did, and a new word entered the language.

strike while the iron is hot. A blacksmith has to wield his hammer while the metal on the anvil is red-hot or he loses his opportunity and must heat the iron all over again. Which is the idea behind this phrase meaning to act at the most propitious moment, an expression that goes back at least to Chaucer, who in the *Canterbury Tales* wrote that while the "Iren is hoot men sholden smyte."

to string along with someone. To accept someone's decision or advice, to follow someone as a leader, to go along with someone. In 1799 a political observer speaks of "the sycophantic circle that surrounds the President in stringing to his quarters." *Stringing along* probably comes from the same source as this earlier phrase, which suggests docile pack animals tied together in single file and led by their masters. The phrase isn't recorded until the 1920s.

string bean. *String beans* is an Americanism for green beans, first recorded in 1759 and so named for the string-like fibers along the vegetable sutures. When Burpee & Co. seedsmen developed the Beautiful Burpee, "the stringless string bean," in 1894 the term *string bean* began to take a back seat to *green bean*. It is still heard, however, along with other synonyms like *snap beans* (named for the sound the pods make when broken), *wax beans* (yellow varieties), *kidney beans*, and *haricot*.

stripteaser. (*See* **ecdysiast.**)

strung-out. From its early use as a term for out-of-tune musical instruments—that is, harps or other stringed instruments with their strings removed or relaxed—*strung-out* came to be applied to a human body weakened and unnerved, a *strung-out* person being someone, usually a drug user, one whose nerves and muscles have lost their natural tension and have no tone. The figurative use is an old one, too, dating back to at least the late 17th century.

stubborn as a mule. (*See* **build or set a fire under.**)

stuffed shirt. It may be that the ladies' shirtwaists stuffed with tissue paper displayed in many department store windows at the turn of the century suggested this term for a pompous, pretentious bore who insists on formalities. Though flimsy, the shirtwaists looked imposing and inflated when stuffed with paper. Comparing a man to a lady's shirtwaist would have been an insult in itself, but we only know that the first literary use of the term is by Willa Cather in *O Pioneers!* (1913). Another possibility is that the term simply derived from similar earlier "stuffed" expressions such as *stuffed ballot*, a fraudulent ballot; *stuffed monkey*, a conceited person; and *Stuffed Prophet*, an epithet the *New York Sun* hung on Grover Cleveland when he ran for president in 1892.

stumbling block. William Tyndale apparently coined this expression when he translated Rom. 14:13 into English for his Bible in 1534, the version that fixed the tone and style of the English Bible. In Romans, Paul of Tarsus had written that a good Christian should not put a *skandalon* in his brother's path. Since the *skandalon*, a kind of hunting trap, was unfamiliar to Englishmen of the time, Tyndale changed the word to *stumbling block*, making Paul's phrase "that no man putt a stomblinge blocke . . . in his brother's way." The translator may have invented the term, or it may have been suggested to him by the earlier (1450) phrase *to stumble at a block* (a tree stump), but in any case *stumbling block* quickly became an expression for an obstacle of any kind.

to be stumped. *To be stumped* for "to be baffled" has its origins in the stumps that American settlers had to pull from the earth after felling trees—some stumps were so big and deep-rooted that they perplexed the pioneers. The expression is first recorded in 1812: "John Bull was a little stumped when he saw [Brother] Jonathan's challenge."

Sturm und Drang. The German phrase, pronounced "stoorm and drang," means storm and stress. First applied to the revolutionary literary movement that was awakening Germany under the inspiration of Goethe and Schiller in the late 18th century, the name was suggested by the play *Wirrwarr, oder, Sturm und Drang,* (1776), a romantic drama by Friedrich Maximilian von Klinger. Its adherents, extremely nationalistic, preferred inspiration to reason and were also characterized by opposition to established forms of society. The expression is now often used to mean a time of trouble and stress in the life of a nation or individual.

stymie. *Stymie*, meaning to block or prevent, first recorded in 1902, had been a golfing term meaning to block the hole on the green with your ball (thus stopping an opponent from holing his ball) since at least the mid-19th century. The golfing term, in turn, may derive from the Scottish expression *not to see a styme*, "not to see at all," recorded in the 14th century, or the Dutch *stuit mij*, "it stops."

sub rosa. According to legend, the Greek god of silence, Harpocrates, stumbled upon Venus while she was making love and Cupid, the goddess of love's son, bribed him to keep quiet about the affair by giving him the first rose ever created. This story made the rose the emblem of silence and since the fifth century B.C. a rose carved on the ceilings of dining and drawing rooms where European diplomats gathered enjoined all present to observe secrecy about any matter discussed *sub rosa*, or "under the rose." A similar phrase used at such gatherings was *sub vino sub rosa est*, "What is said under the influence of wine is secret," a reminder that things revealed by tongues made loose with wine weren't to be repeated beyond these walls. The rose was also carved over the Roman Catholic confessional as a symbol of silence and the phrase *sub rosa*, became well known in German as *unter der Rose*, in French as *sous la rose*, and in English as *under the rose* as a term for strict confidence, complete secrecy, absolute privacy. Incidentally, the ancient legend of Harpocrates was inspired by what the Greeks thought was a picture of the Egyptian god of silence, Horus, seated under a rose with a finger at his lips. Actually, the rose in the picture was a lotus and the infant god Horus was merely sucking his finger.

succotash. The first *succotash* was made by American Indians, who cooked corn and beans together in bear grease. Colonists used the word in the early 18th century, if not before then, and it apparently derives from the Narragansett Indian *misickquatash*, meaning "an ear of corn," or the Narragansett *Manusqussedash*, "beans."

succubus. (*See* **nightmare.**)

suck eggs. (*See* **teach your grandmother to suck eggs.**)

sucker. The origin of the word *sucker*, for "a dupe or easily tricked person," is a mystery. One theory holds that the slang word comes from the name of one of the many American freshwater fishes called *suckers* because they have lips that suggest that they feed by suction. Several of these fish are easily caught and might have suggested an easily hooked or hoodwinked person. But the word, first recorded in 1831, could just as well derive from *sucker* in the sense of a not-yet-weaned animal, with the *sucker's* naiveté reminiscent of the innocence of a child still sucking at its mother's breast.

Sudan. Sudan's name translates as "land of the blacks," in reference to the dark-skinned people who live there.

suede. *Gants de Suede*, or "gloves from Sweden," is what the French called the rough-surfaced gloves made in Sweden that were popular in Paris during the 19th century. The English abbreviated the name to *suede* and used it to describe similar leather made anywhere.

suicide gun. Cowboys early in this century called the Colt .32 (and similar guns) a *suicide gun* because it lacked the power to stop an assailant dead in his tracks and thus often led to the death of the man who fired it.

to suit to a "T." (*See* **it suits you to a "T."**)

sulky. The *sulky carriage* takes its name from sulky people. The light, two-wheeled carriage, which is principally used in harness racing today, seats only one person. Those who drove them in the 19th century were presumed to be aloof, and the carriage was named for these "sulky" people who preferred to be alone. The first quote using the word (1756) tells of "a formal female seated in a Sulky, foolishly pleased with having the whole vehicle to herself." The word *sulky* itself may come from the Old Frisian word *sultig* meaning the same, and *sulk* is a backformation of sulky.

Sultan of Swat. Baseball's Babe Ruth, whose name itself is of course a synonym for a great slugger, was called the *Sultan of Swat*—but not only because he swatted the ball. There was a real Sultan of Swat (a small country now part of Pakistan) whose name was well known thanks to a poem by Edward Lear: "Who, or why, or which, or what/ Is the Akhoond [Sultan] of Swat?" The alliterative name probably appealed to some sportswriter in the early 1920s as a natural for the "Bambino" (which Ruth was dubbed when he joined the Boston Red Sox as a pitcher in 1914 when only 19).

Sumerian words in English. (*See* **Hamal.**)

sundae. Wisconsin ice-cream-parlor owner George Giffy probably first called this concoction, which he did not invent, a *Sunday* back in the early 1890s because he regarded it as a special dish only to be sold on Sundays. No one knows exactly why or when *Sunday* was changed to *sundae*.

Sunday. The first day of the week, the *sunnendaeg*, "Sunday," of the Anglo-Saxons, was so called because the day was dedicated to the sun in ancient times.

sunflower. Sunflowers are so named because they resemble the full sun, not because they follow the direction of the sun during the day. *Helianthus* actually turns in every direction whether the sun is out or not. The word sunflower was coined toward the middle of the 17th century.

supercalifragilisticexpialidocious. This word, from a song in the film *Mary Poppins*, may be the longest (34 letters), commonly used word of all time. It means the greatest, the best of all. There are many far, far longer words, but no longer word has been spoken or sung by so many people. In fact, the only rival that comes even close is *antidisestablishmentarianism*, which many people think (falsely) is the longest English word. (*See* **bovine.**)

supercilious. (*See* **highbrow.**)

superman. George Bernard Shaw, not Friedrich Nietzsche, coined *superman*, never expecting a movie to be made of him. The German philosopher's word for a dominant man above good or evil, introduced in *Thus Spake Zarathustra* (1883-91), was *ubermensch*, "overman" or "beyondman." Shaw didn't like the sound of Nietzsche's word and so translated its German prefix *uber* into the Latin *super-* then added to it the English *man*, translated from the German *mensch*. Shaw used the new word for the first time in his play *Man and Superman* (1903). The term was widely popularized by an American comic book character of the same name who made his debut in the 1930s.

supermarket. The world's first supermarket was the A&P, the Great Atlantic and Pacific Tea Co., which was founded by tea merchant George Huntington Hartford in 1859 in New York City and had stores across the country by 1917. But the word *supermarket* didn't come into the language until the early 1920s in California. It was probably first applied to one of the stores in the Piggly-Wiggly self-service chain.

Supreme Example of Allied Confusion. This World War II American and British term, originating with American soldiers and sailors, was a sarcastic play on the initials SEAC, which stood for the South East Asia Command.

sure as eggs is eggs. This 17th-century expression, for "a certainty," almost certainly has no connection with eggs. *Eggs* here is probably a corruption of *X* in a mathematical formula, the expression originally being *as sure as X is X.*

sure as God made little green apples.   Though a very popular song includes this line in its lyrics, the phrase is an Americanism dating back to at least 1909, when it first appeared in print. It means, of course, something positive, a sure thing.

surly.   In medieval times a man who conducted himself admirably, like a knight, was called *sirly,* that is, "like a sir," even if he wasn't strictly speaking a *sir,* a title reserved for knights and baronets. The spelling changed to "surly" over the years and the meaning of *surly* changed from "knightly" to "arrogant" and finally "rude" as knighthood and its emulators faded out of flower and fashion.

surround.   *Surround* derives not from *round,* but from the Latin *unda,* "a wave." *Unda* yielded the Latin *undare,* "to move in waves," which produced *superundare,* "to overflow." *Superundare* yielded the modern French *surrounder,* "to overflow," a word with which English speakers associated the English word *round* and gave it its present meaning.

survival of the fittest.   This term was coined not by Charles Darwin but by British philosopher Herbert Spencer. "This survival of the fittest which I have here sought to express in mechanical terms, is that which Mr. Darwin has called 'natural selection, or the preservation of favored races in the struggle for life,'" Spencer wrote in his *Principles of Biology* (1864-67). Darwin approved of Spencer's coinage in his epochal *On the Origin of the Species by Means of Natural Selection* (1859), which sold out on the day it was printed. Spencer was the founder of evolutionary philosophy, his ideal being the unification of all knowledge on the basis of the single all-providing principle of evolution.

suttee.   *Suttee* is the old Hindu custom of burning the widow on the funeral pyre of her husband, a custom also found in other cultures around the world. The word *suttee* derives from the Sanskrit *sati,* "a virtuous wife." The practice was practically obligatory by custom for 2,000 years but was outlawed in British India in 1829. Its purpose was purportedly to help the soul of both husband and wife in the next world, but its use is not supported by the Vedic texts that its adherents cited to condone the practice.

Svengali.   *Svengali,* a common word unaccountably omitted from many dictionaries, means someone who controls other people and forces them to do as he wishes. The word comes from the assumed name of a Hungarian

musician in George Louis du Maurier's *Trilby* (1894) who hypnotizes the heroine, gaining complete control over her. (*See* **Trilby.**)

swab.   Some 300 years ago a *swab* meant a merchant seaman, probably deriving from the Dutch *swabbe,* "mop," in reference to sailors swabbing or mopping the decks. Before that, as far back as 1592, sailors who cleaned the decks were called *swabbers. Swabbie,* related to both these terms, came into use in the late 19th century.

Swahili.   *Swahili* is not spoken by more Africans than any other language, as is widely believed. This record is held by Hausa, spoken in Nigeria and other parts of West Africa, with some 25 million speakers in all, many of its words borrowed from Arabic. But Swahili, more correctly called *Kiswahili,* with more than 10 million speakers, is the most important language of East Africa, being the official language of Kenya and Tanzania, while spoken fluently in many other countries as a second language. Basically its vocabulary is Bantu but there are many Arabic borrowings. *Swahili* itself derives from an Arabic word meaning coastal, the language having developed in the seventh century among Arabic-speaking settlers of the African coast.

swallow.   (*See* **one swallow does not a summer make.**)

swan song; Swan of Avon; Swan of Meander, etc.   The swan makes no sound other than a hiss when it is angry, but the ancient Greeks thought that the mute bird broke its lifelong silence with one last melodious song just before it died. This *swan song,* according to Socrates, was a happy one, for the dying bird, sacred to Apollo, knew that it would soon be joining its master. The superstition, embraced by poets through the ages, led to the use of swan song to mean a person's last, eloquent words or performance. Shakespeare was called the *Swan of Avon;* Homer was called the *Swan of Meander,* and Virgil the *Mantuan Swan* because Apollo, the god of poetry and song, was fabled to have been changed into a swan and the souls of all poets were at one time thought to pass into the bodies of swans after death. Still other *swans* of literature include: the *Swan of Padua,* Francesco Algarotti; the *Swan of the Thames,* John Taylor; the *Swan of Usk,* Henry Vaughn; and the *Swan of Lichfield,* Anna Vaughan.

A Swartwout.   Samuel Swartwout (1783-1856), collector of the port of New York in Andrew Jackson's administration, stole more than $1 million of public funds and fled to England. Thus a *Swartwout* came to mean an embezzler and *to Swartwout* to embezzle or abscond.

swashbuckler.   Today's swashbucklers are action-packed, romantic films or novels featuring much sword-play. The word, in its oldest sense, means a swaggering show-off and was used this way in Elizabethan times. A *buckler* was a small shield used to catch the sword blows of an opponent and to *swash* meant to dash against. But *swashbucklers* weren't always good swordsmen and often ran when the going got tough. (See **pirate; walk the plank**.)

swear like a trooper. The theatrical profession has been chastised for its vigorous swearing in times past, but this phrase *wasn't* originally *swear like a trouper.* It dates back almost two centuries, to a time when British cavalrymen were noted for their profanity. English soldiers, or troopers, had in fact been famous for their blasphemy since long before Shakespeare's soldier, the fourth of his seven ages of man, "Full of strange oaths and bearded like the bard."

sweatshop. *Sweatshop*, for "clothing factories where people work long hours for little pay," is first recorded in 1892 in America, but the seed of the expression can be found in Henry Mayhew's *London Labour and the London Poor* (1851-61): "I have many a time heard both husband and wife . . . who were sweating for a gorgeous clothes' emporium, say that they had not time to clean."

Sweden. Sweden is named for the Suiones, a native tribe that became dominant in the country by the sixth century A.D.

sweepstakes. *Sweepstake* is recorded as the name of a ship a century before its first mention as a gambling term in 1593, but no one has been able to connect the ship with the word in any way (or even explain the name of the ship!). *Sweepstakes* originally meant "winner take all," as if the winner *swept* all the *stakes* into his pocket after winning a game or race, but later a number of winners in sweepstakes, such as the Irish Sweepstakes have had to divide the stakes among them.

Sweet Adeline. The "Sweet Adeline" in the song of the same name was originally "Sweet Rosalie." Songwriters Richard Gerard and Henry Armstrong wrote "You're the Flower of My Heart, Sweet Rosalie" in 1903, tried to sell it and couldn't. When they decided to name the song's heroine in honor of popular prima donna Adelina Patti and shortened the title to "Sweet Adeline," it sold and eventually became the barbershop quartet hit of all time.

the sweet death. Dating back to the 19th century, this expression refers to death while having sexual intercourse. The first person recorded to die *the sweet death* is Attila the Hun. Attila, said to be a dwarf, died in the arms of a Brunnhildean blonde.

sweeten the kitty. In the game of faro the "tiger" was the bank of house, possibly because the tiger was once used on signs marking the entrance to Chinese gambling houses. Gamblers called the tiger a kitty, and it also became the name for the "pot" in poker and other card games. By the late 19th century *sweeten* or *fatten the kitty* had become a common expression for adding chips to the pot in a poker game or for increasing the payment in any business deal.

sweet Fanny Adams. Fanny Adams was murdered and mutilated in 1812, her body cut into pieces and thrown into the River Wey at Alton in Hampshire. Her murderer, one Fred Baker, was publicly hanged in Winchester. Young Fanny Adams' name, given wide currency, was adopted by sailors to indicate a particularly distasteful meal, since Fanny Adams had been disposed of in a kettle. In fact, when kettles came into use in the British navy they were dubbed *Fannys* as were tins or cans of meat. There is no doubt that Fanny Adams is the basis for the military expression *sweet Fanny Adams*, meaning something worthless or nothing at all.

sweetheart contract. *Sweetheart contracts* are contracts made with favored employers by labor unions in return for similar favors. This term first came into use in about 1900, when it was applied to favoritism by public officials in awarding contracts without open bidding, those who received the contracts making kickbacks and supporting the political machine.

sweetness and light. Jonathan Swift invented this perennial phrase in his *Preface to the Battle of the Books* (1697). Swift took the figure from the beehive when comparing the merits of the bee (the ancients) with the spider (the moderns): "The difference is that instead of dirt and poison, we have chosen to fill our hives with honey and wax, thus furnishing mankind with the two noblest things, which are sweetness and light." Later, Matthew Arnold, in *Culture and Anarchy* (1869), regarded these as the basic contribution of the artist and the basis of culture itself: "He who works for sweetness and light united, works to make reason and the will of God prevail."

sweet talk; sweet mouth. *Sweet talk* is smooth, unctuous flattery designed to win over a person. There is no proof of it, but this Southern Americanism possibly comes from Krio, an English-based Creole of Sierra Leone, specifically from the expression *swit mot*, sweet mouth, for "flattery." To *sweet mouth* someone is the opposite of to *bad-mouth* him.

Swiftian. Merciless, bitter, biting satire is called *Swiftian* after Johathan Swift (1667-1745), British author of *Gulliver's Travels* (1726) and many other trenchant satires.

swindle. *Swindler*, deriving from the German *Schwindler*, "a giddy person," first meant a merchant who took "dizzy risks" that often led to the loss of money. A *swindler* soon came to mean "someone who made money disappear," hence a cheat.

Swiss chard. Chard is a variety of beet that is cultivated for its leaves and stalks. It apparently takes its name from the French *chardon*, "thistle," a word closely related to the Latin word for thistle. *Swiss chard* is the most famous variety.

swive. *Swive* or *swyve*, related to *swerve* and used by Chaucer and many English writers, was an early synonym for sexual congress. There was no shame attached to the expression; in fact, a 17th-century Scottish translation of the Book of Genesis, with all its "begots," was called the *Buke of Swiving*. The *O.E.D.* tells us of an old ballad about Richard of Alemaigne, a legendary king of Germany who "spend al is treasour opon swyving."

sword of Damocles. "Uneasy lies the head that wears a crown." Both Cicero and Horace tell the story of the flatterer Damocles, a fifth-century court follower of Dionysius I (405–367 B.C.), the Elder of Syracuse. Damocles annoyed Dionysius with his constant references to the ruler's great power and consequent happiness. Deciding to teach the sycophant the real perils of power, he invited Damocles to a magnificent banquet, surrounding him with luxuries that only a king could afford. Damocles enjoyed the feast until he happened to glance up and see a sharp sword suspended by a single hair pointing directly at his head, after which he lay there cowering, afraid to eat, speak, or move. The lesson was that there are always threats of danger, fears and worries that prevent the powerful from fully enjoying their power, and the *sword of Damocles* has become a symbol of these fears. The phrase also gives us our expression *to hang by a thin thread*, to be subject to imminent danger.

sybarite. One ancient Sybarite, legend says, complained to his host that he could not sleep at night because there was a rose petal under his body. Inhabitants of the Greek colony of Sybaris on the Gulf of Tarantum in southern Italy, the Sybarites were noted among the Greeks for their love of luxury and sensuousness, and to some extent for their effeminacy and wantonness, all qualities associated with the word *sybarite* today. The fertile land of Sybaris, founded in the sixth century B.C., made luxurious living possible, but too many pleasures weakened the people. The neighboring Crotons, assisting the Troezenians, whom the Greeks had earlier ejected from the city, destroyed Sybaris in 510 B.C., diverting the river Crathis to cover its ruins. It is said that the Sybarites had trained their horses to dance to pipes and that Crotons played pipes as they marched upon them, creating such disorder among their rivals that they easily won the battle. The city of Thurii was later built on or near the site of Sybaris.

syllabus. *Syllabus* began life as a printer's error in a 15th-century edition of Cicero's *Epistles to the Atticans*. In this work Cicero had written *indices . . . quos vos Graeci . . . sittubas appelatis*, meaning "indexes, which were called *sittubas* by the Greeks." The printer misprinted *syllabos* for *sittubas* and *syllabos*, later slightly changed to *syllabus* (instead of *sittubas*), became a synonym for index. Its meaning of index or table of contents was later expanded to mean "an outline or other brief statement of a discourse, the contents of a curriculum, etc."

sycophant. The old story, incapable of proof but widely accepted, is that this word for an *apple-polisher* (*q.v.*) originated in ancient Greece from the Greek *sukophantes* (*sukon*, "fig," and *phainen*, "to show"), which meant an informer on those who exported figs. At one time it was supposedly against the law to export figs from Athens and *sukophantes*, or *sycophants*, often turned in violators of the unpopular law for their own personal gain, these toadies being widely despised.

synagogue. The Hebrew *keneseth*, "assembly," from *kanas*, "to collect or assemble," was translated into Greek in ancient times as *synagoge*, which eventually became the Latin *synagoga*. The Latin yielded the English *synagogue* for "a Jewish house of worship."

syphilis. "Mrs. Grundy's disease" is on the increase in America and throughout the world. Over the ages it has claimed millions, often due to ignorance and superstition, its victims including Herod, Julius Caesar, three popes, Magellan, Columbus, Capt. James Cook, Louis XIV, Henry VIII, Keats, Baudelaire, Schubert, Schumann, Goya, Nietzsche, de Sade, Goethe, Beethoven, Ivan the Terrible, Napoleon, and Lord Randolph Churchill. The disease has gone by many names through history and *wasn't* first contracted among natives in the New World; in fact, it may have been described by Thucydides as far back as 430 B.C. as "the plague of Pireaus." The word *syphilis* itself derives from the name of a character in Girolamo Fracastro's poem *Syphilis sive Morbus Gallicus*, "Syphilis, or the French Disease" (1530). This New World fable tells of the blasphemous shepherd Syphilis who so enraged the Sun God that he struck him with a "new" disease: "He first wore buboes dreadful to the sight,/First felt strange pains and sleepless past the night;/ From him the malady received its name."

T

T. Today's *T* is a modification of the earlier form *X* for the letter. In Hebrew it is called *taw*, and in Greek, *tau*. *T* or *tau* was in ancient times the last letter of the Greek alphabet (as it remains in Hebrew) and thus in medieval times the common expression *alpha to omega*, "including everything," was often rendered as *alpha to Tau*.

tabby cat. Prince Attab, famed in Arab legend, lived in a quarter of old Baghdad named *Attabiya* in his honor. Here a striped silk taffeta material was woven, the streaked fabric called *attabi* by the Arabs after the quarter, *attabi* eventually being transformed to *tabis* in French during the Middle Ages and translated in English as *tabby cloth*. *Tabby* became a verb for "to stripe" soon after, and by 1695 the word was used to describe a brownish dark-striped or brindled *tabby cat* whose markings resembled the material. Old maids were also called *tabbies*, and this may have been because they often kept tabby cats and shared their careful habits, but the word for a spinster is more likely a pet form of Tabitha.

table d'hôte. This French term was borrowed by the English almost four centuries ago. Literally, it means "table of the host" and it originally meant a common table from which guests ate at a hotel. From this it came to mean the complete meal served at a hotel or restaurant.

tabloid. *Tabloid* was originally a trademark for a pill compressing several medicines into one tablet made by Great Britain's Burroughs, Wellcome and Company. The *Westminster Gazette* used the word for the title of a new newspaper it published in 1902 and won a court case in which the pharmaceutical company claimed that the word was private property. Though the first paper called a *tabloid* appeared in 1902, all of the journalistic practices associated with tabloids are much older.

tadpole. *Tade* was an early spelling for "toad," and *pol* meant "head" in 17th-century speech. Therefore, *tadpole* means toad head," an appropriate name for the early stage of a frog when it is little more than a big head with a small tail. The synonym *polliwog* comes from *pol*, "head," and *wiglen*, "to wiggle," meaning "wiggle head."

tail between the legs. (*See* **with tail between legs**.)

Taj Mahal. Shah Jahan built the magnificent *Taj Mahal* to commemorate his favorite wife, Mumtaz Mahall, whose title was Taj Mahal, Crown of the Palace. The mausoleum near Agra, India was begun by the Turkish or Persian architect Ustad Isa three years after Mumtaz died in 1632 and completed by about 1650, nearly twenty years later. The royal lovers are buried in a vault beneath the floor in the octagonal tomb chamber, surrounded by what many consider to be the finest example of romantic architecture in the world. If any structure proves that beauty can be the sole function of a building, it is this spectacular edifice, which is actually more a sculpture than architecture. The great tomb, the luxurious gardens, even the four 133-foot-high minarets at the great tomb's corners, were all built for beauty alone, at a cost of some $15 million.

to take a leaf out of one's book. These words are never used literally for "plagiarism," to my knowledge. *To take a leaf out of one's book* is simply a figurative expression meaning to imitate another person. It is usually highly complimentary to the person aped, for it means he is a model for whatever you wish to do, that he succeeds at it so well that it is best to do it his way. The expression is first recorded in 1809, but the saying it appears to derive from, *to turn over a new leaf*, "to reform," goes all the way back to Holinshed's *Chronicle of England, Scotland and Ireland* (1577). In the earlier phrase the leaves or pages are from a book of lessons or precepts.

take a powder. Nobody agrees about the origins of this slang phrase but there are some wonderful explanations. *To take a powder* means to leave quickly, flee, take off, beat it, dust off, take it on the lam. *Powder* has been used in the sense of "to rush" since the early 17th century, deriving its meaning from the rapid explosiveness of gunpowder ("Cacheus climb'd the Tree: But O how fast . . . he powder'd down agen," 1632). But the phrase seems to date back only to the 1920s, when it was first *take a run-out powder*. One possibility is that it was suggested by the dust (or powder) of a person fleeing down the road, another that "flee" suggested "flea" and thus "flea powder." The most ingenious theory is that the *powder* in the expression represents the "moving" powers of a laxative powder.

take down a peg. A ship's colors in Elizabethan times were raised and lowered by a system of pegs—the higher the peg, the higher the honor. Colors taken down a peg, therefore, reduced the esteem in which the ship was held, even by its crew. This practice probably suggested the expression *to take down a peg*, "to humble someone, lower him in his own or everyone else's eyes," which dates back to about the same time.

take it easy. This expression is an Americanism first recorded in 1927, but it is thought to derive from the British expression *easy does it*, which dates back to the early 17th century.

take lying down. To take a beating or any attack with abject submission. The picture suggested by this expression is so basic to the idea of spineless surrender that you'd think the phrase went back a long way. But it is modern, first recorded in 1888, in an English journal deploring Englishmen who "take lying down any and every inconvenience that the victorious Irish may inflict."

taken to the cleaners. A person defrauded or bilked in a business deal or a confidence game is said to have been *taken to the cleaners*. A relatively recent phrase, probably dating back no further than the 1930s, the words are related to *to be cleaned out*, an early 19th-century saying that sometimes meant "to be duped of all one's money" (usually in a card game), but today always means to lose all one's money.

take one's wife to Paris. This is the German equivalent of "bringing coals to Newcastle," meaning any pointless action, the expression dating back to the late 19th century.

take the bull by the horns. Since the earliest quotation yet found for this expression is 1873, it seems unlikely that it has its roots in bull-running, a brutal English sport popular from the day of King John until it was outlawed in the middle 19th century. Bull-running consisted of a mob with clubs and dogs chasing a bull loosed in the streets and eventually beating it to death, a favorite trick for the braver bull chasers being to grab the poor beast by the horns and wrestle it to the ground. More likely the expression originated in Spain or America. In bullfights Spanish banderilleros plant darts in the neck of the bull and tire him more by waving cloaks in his face and seizing him by the horns, trying to hold his head down. Rawboned early ranchers in the American Southwest also wrestled bulls, or steers, in a popular sport called bulldogging that is still seen in rodeos—the object being to grab the animal's horns and throw him. Either of these practices could have prompted the saying *take the bull by the horns*, "screw up your courage and cope with a dangerous or unpleasant situation decisively, head on."

take the cake; cakewalk. Cakes have been awarded as prizes clear back to classical times, so when slaves on Southern plantations held dance contests to help a needy neighbor, or just for the fun of it, giving a cake to the winning couple was no innovation. But the *cakewalk* inspired by these contests was definitely another black contribution to American culture. Dancers tried to outdo each other with fancy steps, struts, and ways of walking while the fiddler played and chanted, "Make your steps, and show your style!" By 1840 *cakewalk* was recorded as the name of these steps, which became the basis of many top dance routines still seen today. Whether the expression *that takes the cake*, "that wins the highest prize," comes from the cakewalk is another matter. Though the phrase is recorded a century earlier elsewhere, it almost certainly originated with the cakewalk in America. Today it has taken on a different meaning and is said of something (or someone) that is so unusual as to be unbelievable. What we know as *cakes* however, are a comparatively recent innovation. *Fishcakes, pancakes*, and other round baked goods were known long before English cooks began experimenting with the sweet cakes that bear the name today.

take the rag off the bush. (*See* **well, if that don't take the rag off the bush!**)

take the scales from your eyes. (*See* **remove (take) the scales from your eyes**.)

to take the wind out of his sails. This 19th-century expression derives from the nautical practice of sailing to the windward of another ship, thereby robbing its sails of the wind. Through the years the words came to mean to forestall or beat someone by using his own methods or material, to steal his thunder. (*See* **steal my thunder**.)

take to journalism and strong drink. It is said of English author John Mitford (1782-1859) that he "took to journalism and strong drink." Mitford was paid a shilling a day by his Grub Street publisher, "of which he expended tenpence on gin and twopence on bread, cheese and an onion." Rent he had not, as he "lived in a gravel pit, with pen, ink and paper" for the last forty-three days of his life.

take to the hustings. A politician who *takes to the hustings* takes his campaign to the voters. *Hustings* were 18th-century platforms upon which candidates for Parliament made campaign speeches, having taken their name from a similar raised platform called the hustings where officials sat at the Court of Hustings, the supreme court of the city of London. The Court of Hustings, which met at the Guildhall, took its name from the English *husting*, for "a council or court of law," *husting* deriving from the Old Norse *hust-thing* (from the Old Norse *hus*, "royal house," and *thing*, "council"), a royal council, as opposed to a general assembly.

take to the tall timber. Meaning to depart suddenly and unceremoniously, *to take to the tall timber* is a variation on the early 19th century *to break for the high timber*, which meant to escape into the high woods at the edge of civilization in order to make pursuit by the law difficult.

take under one's wing.   A very old expression that was originally in the plural and alludes of course to a hen protecting her chicks under her wings. The source of the phrase is biblical, the famous passage from Matt. 23:37: "O Jerusalem, Jerusalem, thou that killest the prophets, and stonest them which are sent unto thee, how often would I have gathered my children together, even as a hen gathereth her chickens under her wings, and ye would not!"

take with a grain of salt.   Pliny the Elder, who of all ancient historians should most often be taken with a *cellar* of salt, writes that when Pompey seized Mithridates' palace he found the king of Pontus's fabled secret antidote against poisons that had protected him from assassins all his life. It contained 72 ingredients, none of them given by the historian, but the last line of the famous formula supposedly read to "be taken fasting, plus a grain of salt [*addito salis granito*]." The incredulous Pliny isn't known for his subtlety, so it is doubtful that he meant the phrase in any but its literal sense. Nevertheless, the story arose in modern times that Pliny's remark was skeptical and was the origin of the expression *to take with a grain of salt*, "to accept something with reservations, to avoid swallowing it whole." People quoted Pliny's Latin phrase incorrectly and *cum grano salis* was widely accepted as the ancestor of the expression. Actually, the term is little more than three centuries old. Its origin is unknown, and it obviously stems from the idea that salt makes food more palatable and easier to swallow. The Romans knew this, and even sprinkled salt on food they thought might contain poison, but there is no record that they ever used the phrase to indicate skepticism. (*See* **mithridatize**.)

talk a blue streak.   This American expressions refers to lightning bolts and has been traced back to about the middle of the last century, though it is probably much older. Similarly, *a bolt from the blue*, "something unexpected and startling," draws the picture of a lightning bolt striking from a cloudless blue sky, without any warning at all. *Blue streak* refers to a blue streak of lightning flashing through the sky and was used to describe the rapidity of horses and coaches that "left blue streaks behind them" before it became part of the expression *talk a blue streak*, "to talk rapidly and interminably, to talk someone's ear off."

talk through one's hat.   Since the phrase arose at about the time Benjamin Harrison was campaigning for the presidency in his tall handsome beaver hat, it has been suggested that his Democratic opponents coined the expression to help convince voters that Harrison was spouting nonsense in his speeches around the country. There isn't any proof that Harrison's trademark inspired the words, although cartoonists often caricatured him in a big beaver hat. Like another Americanism of about the same time, *keep this under your hat*, "keep it secret or confidential," the origins of the phrase are really unknown. The expression *to eat one's hat*, appears to have been invented by Dickens in *The Pickwick Papers*.

talk turkey.   According to an old story, back in Colonial days a white hunter unevenly divided the spoils of a day's hunt with his Indian companion. Of the four crows and four wild turkeys they had bagged, the hunter handed a crow to the Indian, took a turkey for himself, then handed a second crow to the Indian and put still another turkey in his own bag. All the while he kept saying, "You may take this crow and I will take this turkey," or something similar, but the Indian wasn't as gullible as the hunter thought. When he had finished dividing the kill, the Indian protested: "You talk all turkey for you. You never once talk turkey for me! Now I talk turkey to you." He then proceeded to take his fair share. Most scholars agree that from this probably apocryphal tale, first printed in 1830, comes the expression *let's talk turkey*, "let's get down to real business."

tall, dark, and handsome.   Hollywood publicity men gave us this expression in the 1920s and it may have first been applied to Rudolph Valentino, though he wasn't tall. By 1940 the expression was so well known that it became the title of a movie starring Cesar Romero.

tally.   *Tallies*, or wooden sticks, were used to keep accounts in the British Royal Exchequer in medieval times. To make a tally a notched stick of wood (the number of notches equaling the amount of money owed) was split down the center, each half stick retaining half of the notches—one half being given to the party owed money and the other being retained by the Exchequer. No money would be paid by the Exchequer unless a tally, or match of the sticks, was made. This cumbersome system, often involving notched sticks six feet or more long, wasn't abandoned until 1834, when all the remaining sticks were burned in the furnace of the House of Lords, which overheated the flues and caused the House of Parliament to burn down in the process! But the tallies did contribute the word *tally*, which today means count, to the language. (*See* **just in the nick of time**.)

tam; tam-o'shanter.   The eponymous hero of Robert Burns's poem "Tam o'Shanter's Ride" (1791) wore a cap similar to the traditional woolen cap with the pompon that is worn by the Scots and called a *tam*, or *tam-o'-shanter*.

Tammany; Tweed Ring.   Tammany Hall hasn't the power it once did, but for over 150 years the machine held sway over New York City politics under such bosses as

William Tweed, Richard Croker, and Carmine DeSapio. *Tammany's* unsavory association with machine politics dates back to the late 18th century, but Tammany clubs thrived in this country long before that, mostly as patriotic Revolutionary War organizations that ridiculed Tory groups like the Society of St. George. The clubs were named for Tammanend or Tammenund, a Delaware Indian chief said to have welcomed William Penn and signed with him the Treaty of Shakamaxon calling for friendly relations. Tammanend (sometimes his name is given as *Taminy* or *Tammany*) may have negotiated with Penn for the land that became Pennsylvania and may have been George Washington's friend. The colonists jocularly canonized this friendly Indian chieftain as St. Tammany and adopted his name for their patriotic societies. These gradually died out, but not before one William Mooney had formed a Tammany Society in New York in 1789. By the Jacksonian era the club became one of the strongest Democratic political organizations in America. Thomas Nast created the famous symbol of the Tammany tiger in his cartoons attacking the machine in the 1870s, when the corrupt *Tweed Ring* was fleecing the city of over $100 million.

tandem.   *Tandem* is a humorous coinage, first recorded in 1785. Some anonymous wit took the Latin *tandem*, "at length of time," and punningly applied it to a carriage drawn by two or more horses harnessed not side by side, but one before each other—strung out in a line or at length. *In tandem* has come to mean "in association or partnership" as well as "one following the other."

tank.   The motorized *tank* wasn't invented until World War I. Winston Churchill, who advocated its use, gave it the name *tank* as a "cover name" to help conceal the new weapon from enemy intelligence agents. Before this *tank* had absolutely no connection with war. Possibly deriving from the Indian *tankh*, it had for centuries meant an irrigation pond and then a cistern holding water. The British brought the word back from India, using it exclusively as the term for any large metal container holding any liquid (such as gas and oil tanks) until Churchill appropriated the word.

tantalize.   Tantalus, the son of Zeus in Greek mythology, divulged the secrets of the gods to humans. The Lydian king was punished by being submerged in a pool of water in Hades, a tree laden with fruit above his head. Whenever he attempted to drink the water or eat the fruit they moved just beyond him—the water receding and the fruit tree wind-tossed—causing him agonizing thirst and hunger. This punishment gives us the word *tantalize*.

Tantony pig.   The smallest pig in every litter, one that is traditionally believed to follow its master anywhere, is called a *Tantony pig* after St. Anthony, long the patron saint of swineherds. St. Anthony probably had nothing to do with pigs, other than citing an "unclean demon" as one of the temptations he resisted, but he is often represented in art with a pig by his side. In the Middle Ages, when the pig began to lose its reputation as an unclean demon, it was popularly supposed that the animal was dedicated to the saint. St. Anthony, born about the year 250 in middle Egypt, defeated many "assaults by the devil," including temptations such as "gross and obscene imagings" of beautiful, naked women that Lucifer sent to "harass him night and day."

taper off.   A taper, or candle, gradually diminishes in thickness from the base to the tip. This image suggested the term *to taper off* to Englishmen of the early 19th century. Like the candle growing smaller by degrees, anything becoming gradually less in intensity was said to *taper off*. The words were especially applied to shedding an established habit by degrees, usually to *tapering off* from the habit of hard drinking.

taps.   The military bugle call *taps* may simply derive from the sound of a drum tap, but it could be a corruption of the British drum call *tattoo*, as the recorded first use of the latter word (in 1644) indicates: "If anyone shall be found tiplinge or drinkinge in any Taverne, Inne, or Alehouse after the houre of nyne of the clock at night, when the *tap-too* beates, hee shall pay 2S.6d." In fact, *tap-too* was still being used for *tattoo* in 1833, eleven years after the Americanism *taps* is first recorded. *Tattoo* itself may derive from the Dutch *tap toe*, "to close or turn off the tap," which 17th-century Dutch tavern owners were required to do by military authorities at a certain time every evening, so that soldiers wouldn't be tempted to stay out too late. In any case *taps* was first a drumroll in the American army, meaning "put out the lights and go to bed." The haunting tune we now know as *taps* was written by Union Gen. Daniel Butterfield with the aid of his bugler, Lt. Oliver Wilcox Norton. Now also used at the end of a soldier's burial, its words are: Put out the lights,/ Go to sleep,/ Go to sleep, Go to sleep, Go to sleep./ Put out the lights,/ Go to sleep,/ Go to sleep." (*See* **tattoo.**)

tar.   (*See* **Jack Tar.**)

tarantula   This much-feared, hairy, venomous spider takes its name from the Italian seaport of Taranto, where they were thought to abound in medieval times. From the 15th to the 17th century the bite of tarantulas was believed to cause a dancing mania called *tarantism*, which was actually a hysterical disease epidemic to southern Europe at the time.

ta-ra-ra-boom-de-ay.   (*See* **Q.T.**)

tariff. According to one old tale, the island of Tarifa off the coast of Spain, where the Moors formerly levied taxes upon all who passed, is the source of our word *tariff*. A diverting story, but *tariff* has its ultimate roots in the Arabic *tarif*, "information," which became the Old French *tariffe*, "arithmetic."

tarmac. (*See* **macadam**.)

tarnation. (*See* **darn**.)

tarred and feathered. At Salem, on September 7, 1768, an informer named Robert Wood "was stripped, tarred and feathered and placed on a hogshead under the Tree of Liberty on the Common." This is the first record of the term *tarred and feathered* in America. Tarring and feathering was a cruel punishment where hot pine tar was applied from head to toe on a person and goose feathers were stuck into the tar. The person was then ignited and ridden out of town on a rail (tied to a splintery rail), beaten with sticks and stoned all the while. A man's skin often came off when he removed the tar. It was a common practice to *tar and feather* Tories who refused to join the revolutionary cause, one much associated with the Liberty Boys, but the practice was known here long before the Revolution. In fact, it dates back even before the first English record of tarring and feathering, an 1189 statute made under Richard the Lionhearted directing that any convicted thief voyaging with the Crusaders "shal have his head shorne and boyling pitch powred upon his head, and feathers or downe strewn upon the same, whereby he may be known, and so at the first landing place they shal come to, there to be cast up." Though few have been *tarred and feathered* or ridden out of town on a rail in recent years, the expression remains to describe anyone subjected to indignity and infamy.

tarred with the same brush. Someone who shares the sins or faults of another, though possibly to a lesser degree, is *tarred with the same brush*. The saying may have something to do with *tarred-and-feathered* criminals, but the reference is probably to the tarring of sheep. Owners of a flock of sheep, which can't be branded, used to mark their wool all in the same place with a brush dipped in tar to distinguish them from sheep of another flock. It is said that red ochre was used to make the mark and that brushing sheep with tar served to protect them against ticks.

tart. *Tart* was originally a term of endearment for any woman, chaste or unchaste, the idea of sweetness suggested of course by the pastries. First recorded in the 1860s, the expression came to be applied only to "women of immoral character" or prostitutes by the end of the century.

Tartar sauce. (*See* **steak Tartare**.)

taste. *To taste* meant to touch before it meant to taste. In *Merlin, or the Early History of King Arthur* (ca. 1450) we find the following: "Merlin leide his heed in the damesels lappe, and she began to taste softly till he fell on slepe." *Taste* is recorded in this sense as early as 1290, fifty years or so before the word began to take its present meaning—which may have been suggested by feeling food (tasting it) with the tongue.

tattoo. As far as is known, Capt. James Cook was the first European to record the practice of *tattooing*, when he sailed the *Endeavor* on his historic exploration of the South Seas in 1769. Noting that the Tahitians cut their skin and injected a black dye that left a permanent mark when the wound healed, he called the practice *tattowing* in his diary. This was a fair approximation of the native word *tatau* for the operation. Within a short time the word was being spelled *tattoo*. (*See* **taps**.)

taunt. (*See* **tit for tat**.)

tawdry. Anglo-Saxon Princess Aethelthryth seems to have spent her married life trying to preserve her chastity. Daughter of the king of East Anglia, she protected her virginity through two unwanted marriages that her father had arranged for political reasons, keeping the promise she made as a girl that she would dedicate her life to God. The pious princess carried but one sin on her conscience: in her youth she had loved wearing golden chains and necklaces, and she believed that the cancer of the throat that she died of in 679 had been caused by this worldly vanity. In Norman times Aethelthryth's name was shortened to Audrey and she was finally canonized as St. Audrey. It became the custom to hold fairs on the isle of Ely on St. Audrey's Day, October 17, and the souvenirs sold at these fairs included lace scarves and golden necklaces that were called *St. Audrey's laces*. This merchandise, at first treasured articles, declined in quality until it became known as cheap and showy. Shouted by hucksters as St. Audrey's lace, it was soon clipped in speech to "Sin t'Audrey lace" and eventually to *tawdry lace*. All the gaudy, worthless objects like it were sold as *tawdry*, too, and by the 18th century the word had come to mean anything cheap and tasteless, "showy, tinsel stuff."

taxi. Incensed about the high fares horse cabs were charging in 1907, Harry N. Allen introduced taximeter cabs in Manhattan, naming the 4-cylinder, 16-horsepower cabs he imported from France from the Greek *taxa*, "charge," and the word *cab*, the common short form of the French *cabriolet*. Allen's coinage became shortened to *taxicab* and finally *taxi* long before taxi fares far surpassed those of the horse-driven cabs.

tea. British slang for a cup of *tea* is a *cuppa char. Char* here is a corruption of *cha*, which means tea in England, deriving from the Mandarin *ch'a* for the same. *Tea* comes to us from the Chinese Amoy dialect *t'e.* (See **a spot of tay; teetotal; teabag; tea caddy; tempest in a teapot.**)

tea bag. Tea bags weren't invented until the turn of the century, when an American tea wholesaler named Sullivan began mailing prospective customers one-cup samples of his tea contained in little silk bags. The idea didn't catch on because the cloth changed the flavor of the tea, but during World War II chemists developed a tasteless paper tea bag that became extremely popular and accounts for most of the tea sold in America today.

tea caddy. No relation to the golf *caddy* (*q.v.*), the *tea caddy*, a small box for storing tea, takes its name from the Malayan *kati*, "a weight of about 21 ounces," perhaps because tea used to be packed in 21-ounce boxes. (See **tea.**)

teach your grandmother to suck eggs. Someone who says "Trying to teach him how to swim is like trying to teach your grandmother to suck eggs" is saying that the whole idea is ridiculous because he knew how to swim well long before you were born. Most country grandmothers knew how to suck eggs in days past—poking two small holes in the shell and sucking out the contents through a straw while leaving the shell intact. Today not many grandmothers suck eggs, but people still use the expression, first recorded in the early 18th century.

tearing up the pea patch. Red Barber popularized this Southern U.S. expression for "going on a rampage" when he broadcast Brooklyn Dodger baseball games from 1945-55, using it often to describe fights on the field between players. Barber hails from the South, where the expression is an old one, referring to the prized patch of black-eyed peas, which stray animals sometimes ruined. (See *also* **the catbird seat.**)

teddy bear. Brooklyn candy store owner Morris Michtom fashioned the first teddy bear out of brown plush in 1902 and named it after President Theodore Roosevelt. Michtom's inspiration was a cartoon by Washington Post cartoonist Clifford K. Berryman called "Drawing the Line in Mississippi" that had been reprinted throughout the country. Based on a news story about an expedition Teddy Roosevelt made to hunt bears near the Little Sunflower River in Mississippi, it showed the old Rough Rider with his back turned to a helpless bear cub. Gallant Teddy, it had been reported, refused to kill and even set free the small brown bear that his obliging hosts had stunned and tied to a tree for him to shoot. Apocryphal or not, the story enhanced Roosevelt's reputation as a conservationist and made Michtom rich.

Teddy boys; Teddy girls. London's rebellious *Teddy boys* and *Teddy girls* took their name from the Edwardian styles they preferred, especially the boys' tightly fitted trousers and jackets. *Edwardian* in this case refers to the styles popular in the reign of England's Edward VII, Queen Victoria's son, who ruled from 1901-1910. The opulent styles of the period reflect the self-satisfaction prevalent before World War I and perhaps indicated a rebellious desire on the part of the Teddy boys to return to better days.

teeny-weeny. An Americanism that combines *teeny*, a variant of *tiny*, and *wee*, "small," *teeny-weeny* is first recorded in the 1890s as a word describing someone or something very little. Still used today and immortalized in the popular song "Itsy Bitsy Teenie Weenie Yellow Polka Dot Bikini" (1960), it was helped along by the "Teenie Weenies" comic strip that appeared in many U.S. newspapers from the 1920s up until the 1960s.

teetotal. Meaning total abstinence from intoxicating drink, *teetotal* was invented by English abstainer Robert Turner in an 1833 speech urging everyone else to practice total abstinence, too, to be "tea drinkers totally." (See **tea.**)

telegram. (See **cablegram.**)

telegraph. Simple telegraphic devices have been known since ancient times, but the first to be called a *telegraph* was the one invented by Claude Chappe in 1792. The inventor wanted to call his device the *tachygraphe*, but was advised that this name was inappropriate and should be *telegraphe*, from the Greek words for "afar" and "to write"—"to write from afar." (See **what hath God wrought.**)

telemark. The Telemark region in southern Norway gives its name to the *telemark*, a curving skiing turn made with one ski ahead of the other one. The turn was developed there in the late 19th century and popularized by Sondre Nordheim, the "Father of Ski Jumping."

telephone. *Telephone*, from the Greek roots for "far" and "sound," was a term first used to describe any device for conveying sounds to a distant point. In 1667, for example, Robert Hooke invented a device in which vibrations in a diaphragm caused by voice or sound waves are transmitted mechanically along a string or wire to a similar diaphragm that reproduces the sound. He called this device a *string telephone*. Another inventor, in 1796, called his megaphone a *telephone*, as did the inventor of a speaking tube not much later. Alexander Graham Bell used the old name for his invention as soon as he invented it in 1876. (See **telegraph;** **"Mr. Watson, please come here . . ."**)

telephone Hitler. (*See* **I am going to telephone Hitler.**)

telescope. The great Galileo did not at first use the word *telescope* for the famous instrument that he invented, calling it instead a *perspicillum* and sometimes an *organum*, or *instrumentum*, or *occidale*. In about 1610, a rival and lesser claimant to the discovery, Prince Cesi, head of the Italian Academy, named the instrument the *telescope*, from the Greek word for "far seeing." Only then did Galileo employ the word, and he, in fact, is the first person known to record *telescope*, in a letter of September 1, 1611.

telestitch. (*See* **acrostic.**)

teller. The bank teller takes his or her appellation from the Middle English *tellen* "to count." The term had much wider use in days past, when anyone who counted anything, money or merchandise, was called a *teller. Teller* is recorded in this sense as early as 1480.

tell it to the Marines. Not the U.S. Marine Corps, but the British Royal Marines, formed in the 18th century, are the gullible ones here. The Royal Marines, quartered aboard ships and responsible for discipline, weren't well liked by sailors, who considered them stupid and gullible about the seafaring life and made them the butt of many jokes. Seamen even called empty bottles *marines*. Any tall tale told to a sailor was likely to be met with the response "Tell it to the Marines—sailors won't believe it"; that is, sailors, unlike Marines, were too intelligent to be gulled. The saying soon passed into popular use and was first recorded by Lord Byron in *The Island* (1823), the poet noting that it was an old saying even then.

Tell's apple. (*See* **William Tell's apple.**)

tempest in a teapot. This saying for "making a big fuss over a trifle," was first *a tempest in a teacup*. It has been traced back only to 1857, but is probably older. Similar early English sayings were "storm in a wash basin" and "a storm in a cream bowl" (1678). For that matter Cicero, as far back as 400 B.C., referred to a contemporary who "stirred up waves in a wine ladle," and he indicated that the expression was ancient. (*See* **tea.**)

Temple orange. (*See* **orange.**)

tempura. In Japanese cookery *tempura* is seafood or vegetables dipped in batter and deep-fried. The word, however, is of Portuguese, not Japanese, origin. On Ember Days, which the Portuguese called by the Latin name *Quatuor Tempora*, "the four times of the year," most people in Portugal eschewed meat and ate deep-fried shrimp or other seafood, which came to be called *tempura* after the holy days. By the early 1540s Portuguese sailors had introduced tempura to Japan.

the tenderloin. In New York City, where the expression originated, the *tenderloin* was the area from 23rd to 42nd Street west of Broadway. Gambling and prostitution flourished in this district, giving police officers "luscious opportunities" for graft. In fact, one cop named Williams was so happy to be assigned to the old 29th precinct covering the area in about 1890 that he said he had always eaten chuck steak but from now on he'd "be eating tenderloin." His remark led to the area being dubbed *the tenderloin*, that name eventually transferred to similar places throughout the country.

ten-foot pole. (*See* **wouldn't touch it with a ten-foot pole.**)

1040 form. According to one story, U.S. personal income tax forms are called *1040s* because in 1040 A.D. Lady Godiva rode naked through the streets of Coventry, England, protesting taxes. Another yarn has it that the infamous forms are so named because in 1040 B.C., Samuel, the last of the prophets, gave in to his people's demands that he give them a king, yet warned them that a king would require them to pay taxes. But though these tales are as ingenious as some tax deductions, the I.R.S. says "the mundane truth is that the four-digit number happened to be the next available in the forms numbering system when the *1040* was devised in 1913."

ten-gallon hat. Although the hat's name is usually thought to be an indication of its liquid holding capacity, the Americanism *ten-gallon hat* has its origins in the Spanish word for braid, *galón*. The wide-brimmed hats worn by cowboys were originally decorated with a number of braids at the base of the crown. (*See* **Stetson.**)

Tennessee. Tennessee is nicknamed the *Volunteer State* because over 30,000 Tennessee men volunteered to serve in the Mexican War. Admitted to the Union in 1796 as our 16th state, its name derives from the name of a Cherokee settlement in the area that is of unknown origin. Tennessee had been called *Tenaqui* by the Spanish in the 16th century and went by the name *State of Franklin*, after Ben Franklin, from 1784-88. (*See* **Franklin tree.**)

tennis, anyone? *Tennis, anyone?* began life as *who's for tennis?* in England about eighty years ago, also serving as a conversation opener or an ironic comment on the pastimes of the leisured classes. *Partridge* believes it may have arisen "as a good-natured comment upon lawn tennis as an adjunct of tea parties in the vicarage garden or at country-house weekends," but it has also been suggested that the catchphrase comes from some turn-of-the century English comedy of manners in which "an actor sprang through French windows calling, 'Anyone for tennis?'"

tennis racket. The *tennis racket* owes its name to the Arabic *raqat*, as its alternate spelling *racquet* more clearly shows. *Raqat* in Arabic meant a patch of cloth tied around the palm of the hand. This was the only racket that the ancient Egyptian-Arabic inventors of tennis knew; today's gut racket wasn't invented until the 12th century.

Tennyson bindings. The 19th century expression *Tennyson bindings* is used to indicate affectation of culture. According to Willard Espy, in *O Thou Improper, Thou Uncommon Noun*: "A *nouveau-riche* matron was showing a friend of similar stripe her library, which had been stocked by interior decorators. 'and here,' she said, 'is my Tennyson,' 'No, no, darling,' corrected her friend. 'Those are green. Tennyson is blue.'"

tent. (*See* **tenterhooks**.)

tenterhooks. *Tenters* were frameworks used to stretch woven cloth in the days before modern manufacture (as early as the 15th century) and *tenterhooks* were the pins or hooks that held the cloth in place. Tenterhooks was later applied to the hooks meat is suspended from in butcher shop windows and it is probably from this use of the word that we get the figurative *on tenterhooks*, to be in a state of "painful" or anxious suspense, your curiosity "torturously stretched" to its limits. The dreaded rack, an actual instrument of torture that literally stretched people, was also called the *tenter* and no doubt reinforced the meaning of the phrase, first recorded in the 17th century. *Tenter* probably derives from the same Latin word (*tentus*, "stretched") as *tent*, a tent being stretched canvas.

termagant. Trivegant or Tervagent was a violent, noisy, overbearing character in old morality plays, in which he was erroneously called "a Mohammedan deity." Careless pronunciation changed the name to *termagant*, which became our word for a violent, turbulent, or brawling woman, as well as an adjective for "violence; turbulent; brawling; and shrewish." The term applied to men until about the 17th century, when it was applied to both men and women.

termination with extreme prejudice. This is a CIA euphemism, for assassination, which apparently originated in the 1960s. The CIA reportedly had (maybe still has) a special assassination unit called the Health Alternative Committee.

terrier. (*See* **Airedale terrier**.)

testify; testicles. When a man made a solemn oath in ancient times, he placed one hand over his testicles, his most precious part, the source of his seed, indicating by his action that he believed he would become impotent if he lied. From this custom come our words *testify*, *testimony* and *testicles*, all deriving from the Latin *testis*, "witness." All such *test* words—including *protest*, *protestant*, and *attest*—have this *testicle* connection. Some time ago *Ms.* magazine published a letter stating: "I protest the use of the word 'testimony' when referring to a woman's statements, because its root is 'testes' which has nothing to do with being a female. Why not use 'ovarimony'?"

tetched. *tetched* isn't an American dialect term. This word for "slightly mad, touched" derives from the late Middle English *techyd*, meaning "marked or blemished." *Techyd* was confused in sense with *touched* and also came to mean "a little crazy."

tête à tête. *Tête* is the French word for "head," familiar to us in expressions like *tête à tête*, literally "head to head," which means a private conversation between two people. Interestingly, this important French word came into French from Latin slang. Few people would guess that the French word for head was originally the Latin slang for "pot."

tetragrammaton. (*See* **four-letter word**.)

Texas. Texas takes its name from a Caddo Indian word meaning "friends or allies" (written "texas," "texios," "tejas," "teyas") applied to the Caddos by the Spanish in eastern Tesas, who regarded them as friends and allies against the Apaches. (*See also* **North Dakota**.)

Texas leaguer. A cheap hit that falls between the infield and the outfield in baseball is called a *Texas leaguer* because back in 1886 three players who had been traded up to the majors from a Texas league team enabled Toledo to beat Syracuse by repeatedly getting such hits. After the game, the disgusted Syracuse pitcher described the hits as just "little old dinky Texas leaguers," and the name stuck.

Texas turkey. (*See* **armadillo**.)

Texas yell. (*See* **rebel yell**.)

Thames. (*See* **set the Thames on fire**.)

thank your lucky stars. The idea that the stars sway human destiny is as old as mankind. The phrase *thank your stars* goes back at least to Ben Jonson, who used it in *Every Man Out of His Humour* (1599): "I thanke my Starres for it." *Thank your good stars* is next recorded in 1706, and the variation *thank your lucky stars* is a relatively modern development of the last century or so.

that gets me. *Get one's dander up, get one's Irish up, get one's Indian up*, and even *get one's Ebenezer*

(Ebenezer was a nickname for the devil) *up*, were only a few of the many *get me . . .* terms meaning "to become angry" that were common in 19th-century America. So common were such terms that *that gets me* came to mean "that angers or annoys me."

that rings the bell. That's perfect, just what we wanted. This Americanism, first recorded in 1904, is almost certainly from the carnival game where one tests his strength by driving a weight up a pole with a mallet and wins if he rings the bell at the top.

that's all she wrote. Meaning that's the end of it, it's finished, that's all there is, *that's all she wrote* is first recorded in 1948 as college slang, but probably dates back before World War II. It may have derived from the Dear John letters breaking up a relationship that some soldiers received from wives and sweethearts while away from home. This seems to be indicated by its use in James Jones's novel *From Here to Eternity*, which takes place just before W.W. II: "All she'd have to do, if she got caught with you, would be to holler rape and it would be Dear John, that's all she wrote."

that's life; that's the way it goes; that's the way the ball bounces. *That's life*, meaning "that's fate, that's the fortunes of life, the way things happen," probably dates back at least to the turn of the century. It is thought to be a loan translation of the French *c'est la vie*. The American expression *That's the way the ball bounces*, meaning the same, appears to have originated with U.S. forces in Korea, while the synonymous *that's the way it goes* comes into the language a little later.

that's that! Common in both the U.S. and England for "that's the end of it" or well, *that's that!* probably dates back to World War I, though it isn't recorded until the late 1920s. Variants are *and that's that* and *and that is that!*

theater of the absurd. *The theater of the absurd* is usually associated with the plays of Ionesco, Beckett, and several other writers who emphasize the absurd, illogical, ridiculous aspects of human experience. The term originated in the late 1950s and probably derived from Albert Camus's phrase "the philosophy of the absurd."

Theon's tooth. A bitter, biting critic is sometimes said to have *Theon's tooth*. The expression commemorates the ancient Roman poet Theon, noted for his sharp satires.

therblig. A term used in time and motion study, meaning "any of the basic elements involved in completing a given manual task that can be subjected to analysis," *therblig* is an anagram of the name of American engineer Frank B. Gilbreth (1868-1924) of *Cheaper by the Dozen* fame.

there but for the grace of God go I. On seeing several criminals being led to the scaffold in the 16th century, English Protestant martyr John Bradford remarked: "There, but for the grace of God, goes John Bradford." His words, without his name, are still very common ones today for expressing one's blessings compared to the fate of another. Bradford was later burned at the stake as a heretic.

there's a sucker born every minute. Showman P.T. Barnum lived by this principle, but he probably didn't invent the phrase so often attributed to him. Since there is no recorded instance of Barnum uttering the words, they must be credited to "Anonymous," like another famous American cynicism, *Never give a sucker an even break*, which was the title of a W.C. Fields movie. Terms that Barnum did coin or help popularize include Jumbo (*q.v.*), *bandwagon*, *Siamese twins* (*q.v.*), *the Bearded Lady*, *the Wild Man of Borneo*, *Swedish Nightingale*, *Tom Thumb*, *Three-Ring Circus*, and *the Greatest Show on Earth*.

there were giants in the earth in those days. There seems always to be a feeling, among older people at least, that the present generation is a degeneration of generations past. The notion is an ancient one, the above expression, for example, recorded in the book of Genesis.

thermos. (*See* **Dewar flask**.)

thersitical. Among the loudest, most foulmouthed men of all time was Thersites, an officer in the Greek army at the siege of Troy. The ugly, deformed Thersites, whose name means "the Audacious," liked nothing better than arguing, we are told in the *Iliad*, his mean temper sparing no one, be he humble or great. Greek legend tells us that he reviled even Achilles—laughing at his grief over the death of Penthesilea, the queen of the Amazons—and that Achilles promptly kayoed him permanently with one blow to the jaw. Thanks largely to Shakespeare's treatment of the scurrilous Thersites in *Troilus and Cressida*, we have the adjective *thersitical*, "loudmouthed and foulmouthed." (*See* **Hector; Nestor; stentorian**.)

thespian. A *thespian* is an actor, and as an adjective the word means "pertaining to tragedy or dramatic art." Both words pay tribute to the first professional actor. According to legend, Thespis was a Greek poet of the latter sixth century B.C., who recited his poems at festivals of the gods around the country; he is even said to have invented tragedy and to have created the first dialogue spoken on the stage in the form of exchanges between himself as an actor reading his poems and responses by a chorus. Thespis is probably a semilegendary figure, his name possibly an assumed one. The popular story that he went around Attica in a cart in which his plays were acted is of doubtful authenticity, but may be partly true. (*See* **Roscian.**)

they shall not pass.   This slogan was used by Spanish Republican forces during the Spanish civil war. But *No Pasarán!* had previously been used by the French, as *Ils ne passeront pas*, at the Battle of Verdun in World War I.

thin air.   (*See* **vanish into thin air.**)

thingomabob, thingamajig.   (*See* **dingbat.**)

to think he (she) hung the moon and stars.   Someone who loves somebody madly, and blindly, as if that person were a god. According to Professor Frederick Cassidy, who is in the process of compiling a monumental study of American regionalisms, this expression is a Southernism. It has been around since at least early in this century and by now, deservedly, has spread to other regions of the country.

thinking cap.   This expression seems to have originated in the 17th century as *put on your considering cap*, that is, "take time to think something over." At the time square-cut, tight-fitting caps were worn by scholars, clergymen, and jurists, who were all regarded as intelligent "thinking men" by the masses. Any or all of these professional men could have suggested the phrase, the common man believing that their caps helped them to think. But *considering cap* is most likely a reference to the fact that English judges once put on their caps before passing sentences in all cases, just as they still do before passing the death sentence.

thin red line of heroes.   "The Russians dashed on toward that thin-red line streak tipped with a line of steel," wrote W.H. Russell, the greatest war correspondent of his day, in reporting the Battle of Balaclava for the *London Times.* He was describing the 93rd Highland Infantry which hadn't formed in a defensive square. Rudyard Kipling scoffed at this romantic notion in his poem "Tommy," where his British soldier remarks about a *thin red line of 'eroes* and later adds "We aren't no thin red 'eroes."

third degree.   As a term for "prolonged questioning and rough handling of a person by the police in order to obtain information or a confession of guilt," *to get the third degree* dates back only to about the 1890s in America. The phrase has no connection with "murder in the third degree" or any language of criminal law. The third degree is the highest degree, that of Master Mason, in Freemasonry. Any Mason must undergo very difficult tests of proficiency before he qualifies for the third degree and it is probably from these "tests" that the exhaustive questioning of criminals came to be called the *third*

degree, though there is no brutality, physical or mental, involved in the Masonic exam.

third rate.   (*See* **first rate, etc.**)

this is the sort of nonsense up with which I will not put.   Winston Churchill made the above comment when told that a sentence can never be ended with a preposition.

thistle.   The *thistle* became the heraldic emblem of Scotland in the eighth century or earlier in commemoration of the role it played in an attack by the Danes on Stirling Castle. Barefooted Dane scouts stepped on thistles during that night attack, alarming the Scots and enabling them to defeat the raiders. All thistles are members of the *Compositae*, one of the largest families of plants in the world, including among its relatives such fine garden flowers as marigolds, asters, cosmos, dahlias, and chrysanthemums. But thistles are generally thought of as a prickly weed that is little valued. Abraham Lincoln's lowest estimate of a man was to call him a thistle. The word dates back in English to at least 752 A.D. and its origins are unknown.

a thorn in my side.   The Talmud describes ten classes of Pharisees, members of a strict ascetic Jewish sect arising in the second century whose name in Hebrew means "apart" (from the crowd), "separated" (from the rest of mankind). These classes include the "Immovables," who stood like statues for hours while praying; the "Mortars," who wore mortars, or caps, which covered their eyes so that their meditations wouldn't be disturbed by the sight of passersby; and the "Bleeders," who put thorns in their trousers so that their legs would be pricked as they walked. The Pharisees' tendency to look upon themselves as holier than others gives us our modern definition of a Pharisee as "a self-righteous hypocritical person," and the "Bleeders" among the sect possibly inspired the saying *a thorn in my side.* At least St. Paul may have had them in mind when he described a source of constant irritation or personal vexation as *a thorn in the flesh* in 2 Cor. 12:7. Then again, he may have simply taken the image from native plants like the buckthorn and acadia, whose thorns made travel difficult in the Holy Land. Over the years Paul's biblical phrase was altered to *a thorn in my side*, although the original is still used as well.

a thorn in the flesh.   (*See* **a thorn in my side.**)

thou.   (*See* **Quaker.**)

three-fifths compromise.   Under the U.S. Constitution, slaves were considered property and had no vote, but in order to redress the imbalance of representation between the populous North and the sparsely settled South, the

Southern states were allowed by the Founding Fathers to count each slave as three-fifths of a person for their congressional apportionment. This meant in practice that the more slaves there were, the less power they had and the more power the slaveholders enjoyed.

three-martini lunch.   Lesser variations of this have been a synonym for an expensive, time-consuming, inebriating business lunch for about twenty-five years. Apparently the expression began with President John F. Kennedy who, according to former Senator Eugene McCarthy, "spoke disparagingly of the *martini lunch*." In 1972 Democratic Presidential Candidate George McGovern blasted the *two-martini lunch* and by 1978 President Jimmy Carter, a teetotaling Baptist, was inveighing against the *three-martini lunch*.

three-ring circus.   (*See* **there's a sucker born every minute**.)

three sheets to the wind.   "Sheets" aren't sails in nautical use; neither are they bed coverings. A sheet is the rope or chain attached to the lower corner of a sail that is used for shortening and extending it. When all three sheets on a three-sailed vessel (such as a ketch) are loosened, allowed to run free, the sails flap and flutter in the wind. Thus sailors would say a person slightly drunk had *one sheet to the wind* and that someone who could barely navigate had *three sheets to the wind*. The expression is first recorded in Richard Henry Dana's *Two Years Before the Mast* (1840).

a three-tailed bashaw.   Hardly heard anymore, this old phrase is worth reviving. A *bashaw* is an important Turkish official, now more often called a *pasha*. *Three-tailed* refers to the horse tails attached to this official's standard, three being the most any bashaw boasted. The expression dates back to the 17th century.

threshold.   Farmers originally threshed wheat, separated the grain from the chaff, by trodding on piles of it. According to one theory, this trodding seemed similar to wiping one's feet at the doorway of a house, which took the name *threshold* from such threshing. In any case, the word is first recorded in about 1000 A.D.

Throgmorton Street.   Throgmorton Street is to England what Wall Street is to America—the center of the financial or business world. The Stock Exchange is located on this narrow London Street, which was named for Sir Nicholas Throgmorton (1515-71), who served Queen Elizabeth I as a soldier and ambassador to France and Scotland. The diplomat was given to intrigue, however, and also served two stretches in the Tower, though not stretched on the rack there.

through the mill.   (*See* **to be put through the mill**.)

to throw cold water on (something).   To *cold-pie* or *cold-pig* someone, to wake him up by throwing cold water on him, was a practice well known and despised in Elizabethan times. Perhaps *cold-pigging* suggested the expression to *throw cold water on* (something), "to discourage a plan or practice," for it surely ruined many a good dream. But a lot of guesses are possible here. The expression is at least two hundred years old and could also have been suggested by hydrotherapy, the so-called ocean *cold-water cures* with which many a physical and mental illness was treated by dousing a patient with cold seawater. Anyway, the treatment was said to reduce the "mental heat" of extremely nervous persons and make them apathetic.

throw down the gauntlet.   The English language contains two wholly different words spelled and pronounced *gauntlet*. The *gauntlet* in this expression means glove and derives from the medieval French *gantelet*, "a little glove." Knights of the age of chivalry, though not so noble as they seem in romances, did play by certain rules. When one knight wanted to cross swords with another, he issued a challenge by throwing down his mailed glove, or gauntlet, and his challenge was accepted if the other knight picked up the metal-plated leather glove. This custom gave us the expression *to throw down the gauntlet*, "to make a serious challenge." (*See* **run the gauntlet**.)

throw into stitches.   Here stabbing became a joking matter. The Old English *stice*, from the same Teutonic root that gives us "stick," meant a prick, stab, or puncture inflicted by a pointed object, especially pain caused by acute spasms of the rib muscles after prolonged or violent exercise such as running. These stitches in the side are more painful but similar to pains from excessive laughter, when one "laughs so much that it hurts." Thus anyone who told a funny story that convulsed his audience was said to *throw them into stitches*. Shakespeare seems to have first suggested the expression in *Twelfth Night* (1601) when he wrote, "If you . . . will laugh yourselves into stitches, follow me," but when the exact words were coined is unknown. A *stitch* in sewing comes from the same root word.

to throw the book at.   Sorry, but I can find no record of a judge literally throwing a law book at a convicted criminal. However, during the "Prohibition gangster era "many judges did figuratively throw the *contents* of law books at criminals when sentencing them, imposing every penalty found in books of law for their particular crimes. In underworld argot *the book* came to mean the maximum penalty that could be imposed for a crime, especially life imprisonment. Although its original meaning is still common, the metaphor has come to stand for penalties much less severe as well, sometimes nothing more serious than a parent taking away the car keys from a child as a punishment for coming in too late.

to throw to the dogs.   (*See* **to go to the dogs**.)

to throw to the wolves.   In a grisly Russian folk tale a family pursued by a wolf pack throws infants from their sleigh at intervals to keep the wolves busy until they reach their house. This, or some story like it, may be the origin of the expression *to throw to the wolves*, which means of course to adandon someone or turn someone in in order to benefit oneself.

thug.   An Indian sect of religious fanatics called the *P'hanisigars*, "noose operators," whom the British euphemistically called *Thugs*, from a Sanskrit word (*sthaga*) meaning "rogue or cheater," dated back to at least the 13th century. The thugs supposedly honored Kali the Hindu goddess of destruction with their murders and thievery. They would worm their way into the confidence of travelers, or would follow a wealthy victim for weeks sometimes before finding him in a lonely place and slipping a rope or cloth noose around his neck. The group was as well organized as the Syndicate today, even speaking a secret language, *Ramasi*, and bribing government officials for protection. The British eliminated the Thugs in India in the 1830s when they hanged 412 of them and sentenced another 2,844 to life imprisonment, but the name of the band lives on after them. *Thug*, an ugly word, is still used for ugly criminal types from tough guys to assassins, and *thuggee* is sometimes heard for the crime of strangulation that the Thugs perfected.

thumbs down.   *Habet*! or "he's had it" Roman spectators shouted when they wanted a defeated gladiator to be killed. Their shouts were accompanied by a thumbs-down gesture that is believed to be the ancestor of the one we use today and our expression *thumbs down* for "no!"

Thursday.   Thor was considered the god of thunder in ancient times, and it was thought that it thundered when his great chariot was drawn across the sky. His day was *thuresdaeg* in Anglo-Saxon times, this becoming our *Thursday.*

thyme.   We pronounce the *th* in *thyme* (time) as a *t* because it passed into English from the French with that pronunciation at an early date. Thyme ultimately comes from the Greek *thuo*, "perfume," in reference to the herb's sweet smell.

thyroid.   The *thyroid cartilage*, or *Adam's apple* (*q.v.*), which protects the throat, was named for its resemblance to the shields of Homeric warriors, deriving from the Greek word for "shield" or "shield-shaped." It gave its name to the thyroid gland that straddles the windpipe. The term is first recorded in 1693.

Tiajuana.   The Mexican city doesn't take its name from the Spanish *Tia Juana*, "Aunt Jane," as is sometimes claimed. *Tiajuana* is a corruption of the Amerindian name *tiwana*, meaning roughly "by the sea."

ticker tape.   The tape emanating from the first stock ticker installed in the New York Stock Exchange in 1867 was called *ribbon*. *Ticker tape* didn't come into use until the turn of the century.

tiddly; tiddlywinks.   In British Cockney rhyming slang a *tiddlywink* meant a drink. From this expression comes *tiddly*, for "a little drunk," first recorded in the late 19th century. The game *tiddlywinks* is first recorded in 1870 and may be so named because of the little counters used in playing it, *tiddly* here perhaps being baby talk for "little."

tide.   Though a sea tide is usually thought to be high or low water, anything between ebb and flood, *tide* really means "the fixed time of flood and ebb." *Tide* was originally a synonym for *time*, (as in eventide), so the expression "Time and tide wait for no man" is something of a tautology.

tied to his mother's apron strings.   "Apron-string hold" or "apron-string tenure" was a law about four centuries ago under which a husband could hold title to property passed on to his wife by her family only while his wife lived—provided that she had not divorced him. Many wives therefore controlled the purse strings and made all important family decisions, in which their husbands didn't have much to say. Such men, who often did just as they were told, were said to be *tied to their wives apron strings*, a phrase suggested by "apron-string hold." Because male children in such a family tended to be dominated by their mothers as well, even when they were fully grown, the now more common expression *tied to his mother's apron strings* arose. French writer Gérard de Nerval (1808-1855) actually hanged himself from a lamppost with an apron string. *Apron* is a corruption of *napron*, from the French *naperon*, "a little tablecloth," a *napron* corrupted to *an apron* in English.

to tie the knot.   In ancient times the marriage ceremony in many parts of the world consisted only of a priest or the family patriarch knotting together the garments of the bride and groom to symbolize a permanent union. The practice, still a custom in some countries today, is the basis for the universal saying *to tie the knot*, meaning to get married, for which *tying the knot* has been a symbol in England since at least 1275. The Greeks followed the custom of *untying* a knot to declare a marriage. Brides used the Herculean knot, a representation of the snakes entwined on the rod of Mercury, to fasten their woolen girdles. Only the bridegroom was allowed to untie this knot, praying as he did so that the gods would make his marriage as fruitful as that of Hercules—that is, very fruitful indeed, for Hercules once married the fifty daughters of Thestius, all of whom gave birth to his children on the same night. This last was *not* one of the legendary *twelve labors of Hercules.*

Tiffany glass; etc. Tiffany and Company, the famous jewelry firm in New York City, was founded by Charles Lewis Tiffany (1812-1902). During the Civil War the firm turned out swords and other war supplies, but was noted for its manufacture of gold and silver jewelry, the improvement of silverware design, and the importation of historic gems and jewelry from Europe. Branches were soon opened in London and Geneva, Charles Tiffany winning fame as the inventor of the *Tiffany setting,* as in a ring where prongs hold the stone in place. His son, Louis Comfort Tiffany (1848-1933), became an artist and art patron, remembered chiefly for his invention of *Tiffany glass* in 1890. Trademarked as *Favrile glass,* the iridescent art glass was made by the Tiffany Furnaces, which Louis established at Corona, New York. There glass for mosaics and windows, vases, and Tiffany lampshades were manufactured.

tiggerty-boo. (*See* **everything's all tiggerty-boo.**)

tight as Dick's hatband. This phrase refers to the fact that the crown was too tight or dangerous to be worn by a certain king of England. The particular king's identity is unknown, but one popular theory suggests Oliver Cromwell's son Richard, often called Tumbledown Dick, who was nominated by his father to succeed him but served for only seven months beginning in September, 1658 because he received no support from the army. Another candidate is King Richard III, who assumed the throne in 1483, denouncing the rightful claims of his two young nephews. Long regarded as an evil king who ordered the "accidental deaths" of his nephews, Richard is said to have been uncomfortable wearing a crown bought with blood. He was killed by the earl of Richmond at the Battle of Bosworth Field in 1485. In recent times his historical reputation has improved considerably. (*See also* **Queen Dick.**)

tightwad. *Tightwad,* for a cheapskate who won't part with his money, has its origins in a tightly folded wad of money, *wad* having meant a large roll of money since 1814 or so and *tight* having meant "stingy" since about the same time. *Tightwad* is said to have been invented by Indiana humorist George Ade in his *More Fables* (1900), which first records the term: "Henry was undoubtedly the Tightest Wad in town." (*See* **panhandler; gladhander**)

Tillandsia. Linnaeus gave Spanish moss the scientific name *Tillandsia* because he erroneously believed that it didn't like water—the 18th-century Swedish physician, traveler, and botanist he named it for, Elias Tillands, hated water so much that he once went a thousand miles out of his way to avoid crossing a narrow gulf. *Spanish moss,* incidentally, is a misnomer; the plant is not a tree moss but an epiphyte that takes its nourishment from the air.

till death or distance do us part. The marriage vow among American slaves contained this change in the traditional words *till death do us part* because families were often broken up when slaves were sold down the river.

till the cows come home. Relatively modern amplifications of this one include *Till the cows come home in the morning* and *Till hell freezes over and the cows come skating home over the ice.* The expression has meant "a long, long time" for a long, long time, since about 1600, and the idea behind it is that cows take their own good time about coming home if they aren't driven—often until the next morning, when, with udders painfully swollen, they come home to be milked.

tilt at windmills. Advising his squire Sancho Panza that thirty or forty windmills were "monstrous giants," Don Quixote spurred his steed Rosinante forward, his lance extended to "do good service" and "sweep so evil a breed off the face of the earth." Attacking a windmill, his lance got caught in one of its sails, which lifted the valiant knight into the air and smashed him to the ground, leaving him with nothing but injuries for his effort. This was perhaps the most absurd of the *quixotic* (*q.v.*) adventures of Don Quixote, hero of Cervantes's great satirical novel *Don Quixote* (1605). The book was meant to satirize the age's romantic tales of chivalry that filled its hero's mind, and this particular episode is among its most memorable. Almost as soon as Don Quixote was published it inspired the expression *to fight with* or *tilt at windmills,* "to combat imaginary foes or ward off nonexistent dangers," and the phrase *to have windmills in your head,* "to be full of fanciful notions or visionary schemes."

time is money. (*See* **snug as a bug in a rug.**)

time is of the essence. No eminent philosopher or statesman said this. It was originally a legal term, first recorded in 1873, applied to a contract where time was essential, indeed indispensable to that contract's fulfillment. If, for example, the contract required a manufacturer to deliver goods within three months, he had to deliver them within that time or suffer the consequences.

timothy grass; herd's grass. *Timothy* is another, more popular name for *herd's grass,* both designations referring to meadow cat's-tail grass, *Phleum pratense*, which is native to Eurasia and is widely cultivated for hay in the United States, where it was probably brought by early settlers. Then, in about 1770, one John Herd supposedly found the perennial grass with its spiked or panicled head growing wild near his New Hampshire farm, the grass receiving his name when he began cultivating it shortly thereafter. Timothy Hanson or Hanso gave his prenomen to the same grass when he quit his New York farm in 1720 and moved to Maryland, or possibly Carolina, introducing *Phleum pratense* seed there. *Timothy's seed* became *timothy grass* when it grew and this was finally shortened to timothy.

tin cans (naval destroyers). During World War II American destroyers were called *tin cans* cause they were the smallest, thinnest-armored fleet vessels. Destroyers were also called *rust buckets* at the time, though *rust bucket* more often meant any old ship.

tin ear. A person who has a tin ear is tone deaf and thus doesn't appreciate good music, especially jazz. He can also be deaf to the rhythm of words. The term, dating back to the 1930s, was probably suggested to jazz musicians by the adjective *tinny*, "cheap and poorly made," and the earlier term *tin ear* from boxing, which meant about the same as a *cauliflower ear*.

tingle. (*See* **onomatopoeia**.)

tinhorn gambler. In chuck-a-luck, an ancient dice game very popular during the Gold Rush, gamblers bet against the house that all three dice used would read the same when rolled, or that the sum of all three dice would equal a certain number, or that one of the three dice would turn up a specified number. It is a monotonous game and was looked down upon by players of faro, a more complicated and costly pastime. Faro operators coined the name *tinhorn gamblers* for *chuck-a-luck* players, giving us the expression for any cheap gambler. Pulitzer Prize winner George Williston explained how in his book *Here They Found Gold* (1931): "Chuck-a-luck operators shake their dice in a 'small churn-like affair of metal'—hence the expression 'tinhorn gambler,' for the game is rather looked down upon as one for 'chubbers' (fools) and chuck-a-luck gamblers are never admitted within the aristocratic circles of faro dealers."

tinker. (*See* **not worth a tinker's damn**.)

Tinkers to Evers to Chance. This synonym for a routine double play in baseball should really be *Tinker to Evers to Chance*, referring as it does to the Chicago Cub infield combination of Joe Tinker, shortstop, Johnny Evers at second base, and Frank Chance at first. All three are enshrined in Baseball's Hall of Fame at Cooperstown, New York, but aren't there for the double plays they executed. Actually, the vaunted trio only averaged fourteen twin killings a year from 1906-09, the peak of their career, very low for a double-play combo. Their fame is due principally to a famous Franklin P. Adams poem heralding them.

Tin Lizzie. John Dillinger, the first and only "Public Enemy Number One," once wrote Henry Ford extolling the performance of his car as a getaway vehicle—which shows just how widespread was the Ford's really incalculable influence on society, beneficial or disastrous. Henry Ford's motorcars, though not the first invented, put America and the world on wheels for better or worse; his assembly-line mass-production methods marked the beginning of modern industry, and his *Five-Dollar Day* heralded a new era for labor. Ford (1863-1947), born on a farm near Detroit, Michigan, founded the Ford Motor Company in 1903. First came his two-cylinder Model A and then, in 1909, the immortal Model T, the *Tin Lizzie*, the flivver, America's monument to love, available in any color so long as it was black. *Lizzie* is supposed to have been taken from the common name for a black maid, who like the Model T "worked hard all week and prettied up on Sunday"; but it could also have been a corruption of "limousine."

Tin Pan Alley. The original Tin Pan Alley was and is located between 48th and 52nd Streets on Seventh Avenue in New York City, an area where many music publishers, recording studios, composers, and arrangers have offices. The place was probably named for the tinny-sound of the cheap, much-abused pianos in music publisher's offices there, or for the constant noise emanating from the area, which sounded like the banging of tin pans to some. *Tin Pan Alley*, the term first recorded in 1914, today means any place where popular music is published, and can even stand for popular music itself.

tip. A persistent unsubstantiated story has the word *tip*, for "gratuity," originating with the initials *t. i. p.*, "to insure promptness (or promptitude)," which was supposed to be inscribed on offering boxes in 18th-century English coffeehouses. More likely the word comes from the 16th-century slang *to tip*, meaning "to hand over," which possibly derives from the verb *tip* in its meaning of "to touch lightly." A *tip* as "secret information" probably derives from the same slang source.

Tippecanoe and Tyler too. (*See* **cider**.)

Tironian notes. Marcus Tullius Tiro, the man who invented the ampersand (&), introduced it as part of the first system of shorthand of which there is any record. A learned Roman freedman and amanuensis to Cicero, Tiro invented *Tironian notes* about 63 B.C. in order to take down his friend's fluent dictation. Though a rudimentary system, Tiro's shorthand saw wide use in Europe for almost a thousand years, outlasting the Roman Empire. The ampersand, sometimes called the *Tironian sign* in Tiro's honor, was a symbol for the Latin *et*, or "and." Taught in Roman schools and used to record speeches made in the Senate, Tiro's system was based on the orthographical principle and made abundant use of initials. *Ampersand*, first recorded 1837 by Canadian humorist Thomas Haliburton, is a contraction of *and per se and*.

Titania. (*See* **Uranus**.)

Titanic; titanium. (*See* **uranium**.)

tit for tat. Probably the French phrase *tant pour tant*, "so much for so much," influenced the formation of *tit for tat*, and possibly the Dutch *dit vor dat*, "this for that," helped as well. But the expression derives directly from the six-century-old English phrase *tip for tap*, a "tip" at the time meaning the same as a "tap"—a light blow. As for the idea of tit for tat, a blow for a blow, the Latin *quid pro quo* itself has been around for over four centuries. The French phrase *tant pour tant*, with its sense of paying back, also gave us our word *taunt*, "a sharp or clever rejoinder."

Titian. Tiziano Vecellio, or Vecelli, whose name is anglicized as Titian, began his training as an artist in 1486 when nine years old and did not stop painting until his death of the plague ninety years later, when he was approaching one hundred. The greatest artist of the Venetian school, Titian produced hundreds of paintings during his unusually long and prolific career, including portraits and religious and mythological works, all noted for their magnificent use of color and design rather than for his drawing. In his many paintings the artist often depicted a model with shades of bright golden-auburn hair, and rendered the color so beautifully that the lustrous bronze has since been called *Titian hair*, or simply *Titian*. One tradition claims that Titian's auburn-haired model was his daughter Lavinia, whom he did paint several times.

tittle. *Tittle* is another word for the dot above an *i*, and can also mean an accent, a vowel mark, or any diacritical mark. The word is found in Matt. 5:18: ". . . one jot or one tittle shall in no wise pass from the law, till all be fulfilled." (*See* **I**.)

toady. The *toady* was in the 17th century a *toad-eater*, a conjuror's assistant who would eat a toad (said to be poisonous) so that his master could demonstrate his magic healing powers. Anyone who would eat a toad was considered so low that the word became a contemptible term for a sycophant. By the early 18th century *toad-eater* had been replaced by the shorter *toady*.

Tobit's fish. The principal character in the Book of Tobit, included in the Old Testament Apocrypha, was blinded by the dung of sparrows while he slept in a courtyard. The angel Raphael bid Tobit's son to catch a huge fish in the Tigris and apply its gall to Tobit's eyes, thus curing him of his blindness.

toddy. (*See* **tot**.)

tohu-bohu. I like the sound of this unusual old word, which derives from the Hebrew lamentation *Thohu-wa-bhōhū*. It means emptiness and despair, confusion, formlessness, chaos itself, and unusual as it is, great writers such as Rabelais, Voltaire, Purchas, Browning, and Gladstone have employed it. The original Hebrew words are translated in the Bible in the second verse of the first chapter of Genesis: "And the earth was without form, and void; and darkness was upon the earth." Wrote one 19th-century author: "The world is a *tohu-bohu* of confusion and folly."

toilet. In America, the term refers to what the British call the *water closet*. The word comes from the French *toilette*, which originally meant a "little cloth." This became the British name for the cloth used to cover a dressing table, then meant the table itself, and was finally used for the dressing room in which the dressing table was located. It took over four centuries, but Americans ultimately used *toilet* for the *john* in the room most often used for dressing or making one's toilet. (*See* **John Thomas**.)

toilet paper. *Toilet paper*, or lavatory paper, which Nancy Mitford says is the "U" word for it, isn't recorded until the 1880s. The first commercial toilet paper had been marketed, however, in 1857, when Joseph C. Gayetty of New York City began selling an unbleached, pearl-colored pure manila hemp product at 300 sheets for fifty cents. "Gayetty's Medicated Paper—a perfectly pure article for the toilet and for the prevention of piles" had Gayetty's name watermarked on each sheet. Before this the Ward and Sears's mail-order catalogs were indispensable in the outhouses of America and regretfully, many other books have served this purpose. Wrote Lord Chesterfield to his son in the 18th century: "I know a gentleman who was such a good manager of his time that he would not even lose the small portion of it which the calls of nature obliged him to pass in the necessary-house; but gradually went through all the Latin poets in those moments. He bought, for example, a common edition of Horace, off which he tore gradually a couple of pages, carried them with him to that necessary place, read them first, and then sent them down as a sacrifice to Cloacina: this was so much time fairly gained, and I recommend you to follow his example . . ." It was a *New York Times* critic who related an anecdote about a famous musician's reply to a critic who had panned his performance the night before, the riposte beginning: "As I sit here in the bathroom, your review in hand . . ."

Tokay wine. Produced near Tokay in the Carpathian Mountains near the Russian border, *Tokay* is a long-lasting Hungarian white wine with a strong grape flavor.

Tokyo Rose. *Lord Hawhaw* (q.v.), Axis Sally, and Tokyo Rose were the best known Axis radio propagandists of World War II. Of the triumvirate only Tokyo Rose worked for the Japanese and she was actually a number of women, her name bestowed upon her by American G.I.'s in the Pacific. Iva Togori D'Aquino and Ruth Hayakawa, both Americans of Japanese descent, were mainly responsible for the radio programs beamed from Tokyo. Their sweet, seductive voices and the sentimental music they played were designed to promote homesickness, but more often than not were good for a laugh. Mrs. D'Aquino was sentenced to ten years in prison for treason in 1949 and was paroled in 1956. Mildred E. (Axis Sally) Gillars was convicted of treason by a federal jury the same year and received a ten-to-thirty-year sentence but won a parole in 1961.

Tom and Jerry. The sweet spicy rum drink is named for Tom and Jerry Hawthorne, men-about-town who lived the good life in Pierce Egan the elder's *Life in London* (1821). Egan's books threw light on the manners and slang of London in his day, while his son and sometime collaborator Pierce Egan the younger was known as "a pioneer of cheap literature."

tomato. Those "affected" people who pronounce it "toe-mah-toe" are historically correct. The plant was first called *tomate* in Spain when introduced there from the New World and even in the early 16th century it was pronounced in three syllables. The "o" incidentally has no place at all in "tomato," apparently being there because mid-18th-century Englishmen erroneously believed that it should have this common Spanish ending. *Lycopersicon esculentum* has also been called the *wolf apple*, the *wolf peach*, and the *love apple*. The first two designations arose because most Americans thought that tomatoes were poisonous and didn't eat them until about 1830—the tomato *vine* is, in fact, poisonous, the plant a member of the deadly nightshade family. Why tomatoes were dubbed *love apples* is a matter of some dispute. That they hailed from exotic climes and were a shapely scarlet fruit undoubtedly helped, but the designation owes just as much to semantics as sexuality. All Spaniards at the time of the tomato's introduction into Europe were called Moors and one story has it that an Italian gentleman told a visiting Frenchman that the tomatoes he had been served were *Pomi dei Moro* ("Moors' Apples"), which to his guest sounded like *pommes d'amour*, or "apples of love". However, another version claims that "apples of love" derives

in a similar roundabout way from *pomo d'oro*, "golden apple" (the first tomatoes were gold or yellow), and still another tale has it that courtly Sir Walter Raleigh thought the term up all by himself when he presented a tomato to Queen Elizabeth, coyly advising her that it was an "apple of love." No matter which tale is true, the name stuck and the tomato quickly gained a reputation as a wicked aphrodisiac. In Germany, in fact, its common name is still *liebesapfel* or "love apple."

Tom Collins. Many sources tell us that the *Tom Collins*—that refreshing, tall drink made with gin (or vermouth), lemon (or lime), sugar, and soda water—honors its bartender-creator. Yet no one has been able to establish who Tom Collins was, where he came from, or when he first mixed the drink. Variations on the Tom Collins include the *John Collins* (whiskey) and the *Marimba Collins* (rum). The Tom Collins is claimed by many, but the lack of evidence indicates that its real creator didn't mix well, at least socially. The best prospect is probably John Collins, a 19th-century bartender at London's Limmer Hotel who did not devise but was famous for his gin sling—a tall gin and lemon drink that resembles the Tom Collins.

Tom, Dick and Harry. All of these are very common names, reason enough for them to represent "everybody" or an indiscriminate, unnoteworthy collection of men in the phrase. However, one ingenious theory tried to link the expression with nicknames of the devil. The trouble is that while *Old Harry* and *Dick* (the dickens) or *Nick* have long been nicknames for *Olde Horney*, he has never been known intimately as *Tom*. Also, every *Tom, Dick and Harry* is an American expression of the late 19th century, before the British used *Dick, Tom and Jack* for the same purpose. *Browns, Jones, and Robinson* was used by the British in Victorian times to mean "the vulgar rich."

Tom Fuller. The Choctaw Indians' national dish was a fermented hominy called *tahfula*. To the ears of early settlers in the West this sounded like *Tom Fuller* and by 1848 they had Anglicized the name.

Tommy Atkins. The British army account or record books in the 19th century had a fictitious sample entry in the name of "Private Thomas Atkins" to help soldiers fill in details about themselves. So ubiquitous was Thomas Atkins that he became affectionately known as *Tommy Atkins* and became a nickname for all British soldiers, similar to the American G.I. Joe. British soldiers were frequently referred to simply as *Tommies*.

tommygun. The infamous *chopper* so often hidden in violin cases in gangster movies, takes its name from the patronym of one of its inventors, American army officer John T. Thompson (1860-1940). Thompson and Navy

Comm. John N. Blish invented the .45 caliber portable automatic weapon during World War I and much improved it in later years. Gangsters and reporters popularized the nickname *tommygun* in the Prohibition era along with colorful expressions like *torpedo, triggerman, bathtub gin, hideout, hijacker, to muscle in,* and *to take for a ride.* Although *tommygun* originally identified the *Thompson machine gun,* with its pistol grip and shoulder stock, the term is now used to describe any similar lightweight weapon with a drum-type magazine.

tommyrot. *Partridge* says that the *tommy* in *tommyrot,* "nonsense, bosh," may be a euphemism for the strong British expression *bloody*—British soldiers, called Tommies, once wore scarlet (bloody) uniforms. More likely, as he seems to agree, it comes from the British expression *tommy,* meaning "goods supplied instead of wages" by employers who ran stores on the side something like the more infamous American *company stores* (first recorded in 1872). According to Edwin Radford's *Unusual Words* (1946): "Employees of labour not infrequently owned shops to which the worker had to go to draw money; and there he was compelled to spend a portion of his wages on the purchase of the goods he must consume during the week in order to leave. To the working man, these shops were known as 'Tommy-shops'—the shops where he purchased his 'tommy', or food. The viciousness of this system will be realized when it is stated that the employer could charge pretty well what he liked in the way of high prices for the most inferior food, and the workingman had no chance but to take it, or lose his job." Workers, incensed at the poor stuff bundled onto them at high prices, referred to the goods of the Tommy-shop as "Tommy-rot." The workers' only possible revenge was with words. (*See* **Tommy Atkins.**)

tom-tom. American Indians did not call their drums *tom-toms.* They were so named by the British, who, in the late 17th century, had brought the word *tom-tom* back to England from the East Indies, where such a drum was called a *tam-tam,* this Hindustani word imitative of the sound a drum makes.

tone down. *To tone down,* "to soften or make less emphatic," may be an expression that originated among artists, rather than among musicians as might be suspected. It could have arisen along with the reaction against the varied and vivid colors used by Turner and his school. Many artists in the early 19th century, when the expression is first recorded, did return to the use of more subdued tones in their paintings, and bright canvases at the time were sometimes coated with varnish to soften them.

tongue in cheek. Before Richard Barham invented this phrase in his *The Ingoldsby Legends* (1845) nobody stuck tongue in cheek as a humorous warning that something just said was insincere, so Barham could be credited with inventing the custom as well as the expression. Why he chose *with tongue in cheek* to describe someone engaging in insincerity or irony is a mystery. Especially as anyone actually speaking with tongue in cheek—the tongue tip lodged against the inside of the cheek—wouldn't be understood at all.

tongue oil. In my continuing quest for synonyms for whiskey and other strong drink I've come upon *tongue oil* several times. It's a Western U.S. expression dating back perhaps to the mid-19th century and obviously refers to the way spirits loosen one's tongue.

ton of bricks. (*See* **come down like a ton of bricks on someone.**)

tontine. The *tontine* was an early form of life insurance devised by Italian banker Lorenzo Tonti (1635-1690) and introduced by him into France in 1653. Under the system a number of people subscribe to the tontine, the annuity increasing in value to the survivors as each subscriber dies. Finally, the last surviving member takes all. When the tontine was first introduced, any money from the fund that hadn't been spent by the "winner" reverted to the state after the death of that last subscriber.

too big for one's breeches. Describing someone obsessed with his own importance, *too big for one's breeches* is first recorded in the work of Davy Crockett—born on a mountain top in Tennessee (1786), died at the Alamo (1836)—Congressman and frontier hero, whose life was a tall tale.

too many irons in the fire. "They that have many irons in the fires, some must burne," Captain John Smith wrote in *The General Historie of Virginia, New England and the Summer Isles* (1624), and almost a century before another writer warned, "Put no more so many yrons in the fyre at ones." Then there is the old Scottish proverb "Many Irons in the Fire, some must cool." All of these admonitions illustrate the meaning of the phrase: to be engaged in more activities than one can manage at one time, to bite off more than you can chew. What the allusion is to is another matter. Blacksmiths might be the source; no doubt some blacksmiths weren't skilled enough to handle many pieces of steel in the forge and work over them at the forge in rapid order. But the "cool" in the Scottish proverb suggests that old laundry flatirons, which had to be heated in hot coals, may have been the source. Leave too many laundry irons in the fire at once and those at the edge of the fire might not be hot enough to use.

too old to cut the mustard. (*See* **can't cut the mustard.**)

the toothache tree. American pioneers called the prickly ash (*Zanthophylum americanum*) the *toothache tree* or *toothache bush*, because the white-spined ash-leafed tree's fruit has pungent properties when applied to an aching tooth. The term is first recorded early in the 19th century.

tooth and nail. The Latin equivalent for this ancient phrase was *toto corpore atque omnibus ungulis*, "with all the body and every nail." The French have a similar saying, too: *bec et ongles*, "beak and talons." All mean the same: to fight with tooth and nails, biting and scratching, with weapons, with all the powers at one's command. Figurative use of the expression in England brings us back to the early 16th century, and it was listed as a proverb then.

top banana. A comic or comedian in American burlesque or vaudeville. The expression derives from an old turn-of-the-century burlesque skit that involved the sharing of bananas.

top brass. (*See* brass.)

top dollar. This expression, meaning "full value," probably arose from the game of poker, from the image of the highest stack of poker chips on the table, the pile whose top chip or dollar is higher than all the rest.

topiary. Topiary is the art of clipping or trimming shrubs and bushes into ornamental or fantastic shapes. The word derives from the Latin *topiarius*, "ornamental gardening," and the Romans were indeed expert *topiarists*. Yew, privet, and arborvitae are the best plants to use in this art of leisurely ages, and the animals, people, and geometric shapes made from them must be trained over long periods. Tudor England was a notable age for topiary, which still survives on some large English estates and a few American ones. Excellent examples can be seen in Florence, Rome, and at the Alhambra in Granada.

tor. *Tor* may be one of the first words spoken in England. Generally held to be a Celtic term used in place names, it may be a remnant of the prehistoric language of Bronze Age people on the island. These tribesmen lacked the writing to record their language but may have used *tor* as a place name that the Celts somehow adopted. *Tor* has come to mean "a high rock, a pile of rocks." (*See* **Torpenhow Hill.**)

torpedo. *Torpedo* can mean several things. The electric ray, or torpedo fish, was the first *torpedo*, taking its name from the Latin *torpere*, "to be stiff or numb," in reference to the ray's numbing sting. In World War I, naval men named the self-propelled mines called *torpedoes* after the fish because the mines resembled the actions of the electric ray, stunning all that came into contact with them. Yet torpedo meant a percussion shell before this, in 1786, and described a stationary explosive mine, the kind Admiral Farragut spoke of when he said, "Damn the torpedoes, full speed ahead!" The torpedoes Farragut disdained, were in fact, beer kegs filled with powder.

torpedo juice. Thirsty sailors in World War II sometimes made a potent drink called *torpedo juice* from alcohol drained from Navy torpedoes. This deadly brew soon lent its name to any raw homemade whiskey with killing power.

Torpenhow Hill. *Torpenhow Hill*, a ridge near Plymouth in England, literally means Hillhillhill Hill. The Saxons called it *Tor*, "hill;" the Celts, not knowing the meaning of *tor*, added *pen*, "hill," for the same reason. The Scandinavians added *haug* (how), "hill;" and finally Middle English speakers, not knowing that all the components of the word *Torpenhow* meant hill, added a second word *Hill* to the place name. (*See* **tor.**)

Torquemada. More than 100,000 cases were tried and 1,000 people executed under the administration of Tomas de Torquemada (ca. 1420-98) after the Pope appointed him Spanish Grand Inquisitor in 1483. The harsh rules Torquemada devised and strictly enforced for the Inquisition, including the use of torture as a means of obtaining information, made the inquisitor-general's name a synonym for a cruel persecutor or torturer. Torquemada particularly distrusted the Maranos and Moriscos, Jewish and Moorish converts to Catholicism, many of whom he felt were insincere, and he was partly responsible for the royal decree in 1492 which expelled 200,000 unconverted Jews from Spain. One story, probably exaggerated, says that the hated grand inquisitor never traveled anywhere unless guarded by 250 armed retainers and 50 horsemen.

tortoni. In one story a Signor Tortoni, an Italian restaurateur in Paris during the late 19th century, invented this rich ice cream studded with cherries and almonds or macaroons. Others claim that *tortoni* derives from the Italian *torta*, "tart."

Tory. Dictionary makers were not always nonpartisan. In his great groundbreaking dictionary, Dr. Johnson, committed to the Tory party, defined a *Tory* as: "One who adheres to the ancient constitution of the state, and the apostolic hierarchy of the Church of England—opposed to a Whig." (*Whig* was dealt with as if by the ax-man: "The name of a faction.") *Tory* derives from the Irish *toraidhe*, a pursued person, the term first applied to Irish who were forced from their land by the English and took to the hills, becoming outlaws. It then became the name for Catholics fighting for James II and finally described those who supported the Stuarts as a political party. By the reign of

George III, the party had lost its Stuart bias and vigorously supported the Crown, State, and Church as established by law. Since about 1830 the Tory Party has gradually become known as the Conservative Party and *tory* has become a synonym for "conservative." (*See* **whig**.)

tot.   A relatively recent word, first recorded in 1725, *tot*, for a small child," may go back to the Old Norse *tuttr*, "dwarf," or the Danish *tommeltot*, for "Tom Thumb." It could also derive from *totterer*, or be connected somehow with the Anglo-Saxon *totrida*, "swing." And since *tot* means a small drink, too, the word could come from the earlier *toddy* (rum toddy, etc.), which derives from the Hindi *tari*, "a drink," and is first attested in 1609. A lot of theories for a little word—and no proof for any of them.

tote.   *Tote* is of uncertain origin, but most likely comes from the African Konga and Kikonga language *tota*, meaning "to carry." The word may have passed into English through the Gullah dialect in the Southern U.S.

totem.   A *totem* is an object toward which individuals or groups have a special mystical relationship. Often these people observe totemic taboos, such as the Buffalo people of Ruanda, who will not eat buffalo meat, explaining that they· are descended from the animal for whom they are named. The word *totem*, appropriately, comes from the Algonquian Indian *ototema*, meaning "his relations."

to the manor born; to the manner born.   Some people are *to the manor born*, but Shakespeare, who invented the phrase, has Hamlet say "to the manner born" when he is speaking to Horatio. When Horatio asks what means the flourish of trumpets, roll of drums, and discharge of cannon he hears at midnight, Hamlet replies that the king is having a drinking bout and that each time he drains a flagon he is hailed with this uproar. Horatio wants to know if this is an old Danish custom and Hamlet answers:

> Ay, marry, it is;
> But to my mind, though I am native here
> And to the manner born, it is a custom
> More honored in the breech than the observance.

The phrase therefore refers to a custom, not to aristocracy or high estate, as the word *manor* would imply.

to toe the line (or mark).   Before the Queensberry rules were devised, English prizefights were long and bloody. There was no footwork, no tactics aside from dirty ones. No attempt was made to evade blows from an opponent. Fighters, their bare fists pickled in walnut juice, firmly toed a line officials marked in the center of the ring and slugged it out until one man fell to end the round. The fighters than staggered or were dragged back to their corners for thirty seconds and the match continued until one man couldn't come out to toe the line when the bell

rang for the next round. One of these bouts, the Burke-Byrne fight in 1833, lasted 99 rounds, and poor Byrne, who never gave up, died of the beating he took. The sight of lurching, leaden-armed, broken-handed fighters towing the line for hours at a time, often up to an hour a round, and doing their job of battering each other bloody and senseless with superhuman willpower inspired the saying *to toe the line*, "to do one's job, to live up to what is expected of you or conform with the rules." That the expression was an early one used in track events, meaning that all contestants must place their forward foot on the starting line ("Get ready, get on your mark . . .") also contributed to the popularity of the phrase.

touch and go.   Either coach driving or ship pilotage gave us this term for a narrow escape or a precarious situation in which the outcome is doubtful for a time. Coach drivers used the term *touch and go* for a narrow escape after the wheels of two coaches touched in a near accident, a favorite scene in many costume adventures. The *Sailor's Word Book* (1867) explains the term's possible nautical derivation: "Touch and go—said of anything within an ace of ruin; as in rounding a ship very narrowly to escape rocks, etc., or when, under sail, she rubs against the ground with her keel."

touch-me-not.   The impatiens (from the Latin for impatience) is called *touch-me-not* from the words Christ said to Mary Magdalene after His resurrection (John 20:17). Both terms are appropriate because seed often bursts impatiently from the pods when the plant is touched. The impatiens is called *busy Lizzie* because it blooms so prolifically through the season.

a touch of Caruso.   A great tenor and a lighthearted man of boyish charm, Enrico Caruso (1873-1921) was something of a cutup and once pinched a girl's derrière in a Paris park. Resulting publicity gave rise to the expression *a touch of Caruso* ("Give her a touch of Caruso, chief!"), meaning the turn of a ship's engines astern.

tournedos; Tournedos à la Rossini.   Tournedos are small, round thick pieces of beef, served with a number of sauces and garnished. The Italian composer Gioacchino Antonio Rossini (1792-1868), best known for the *Barber of Seville* (1816), is said to have invented the cut of beef when he conceived *Tournedos à la Rossini* at the height of his popularity. According to the old tale, Rossini was dining at the Cafe Anglais in Paris. Tired of the beef dishes on the menu, he gave instructions for his meat to be prepared in a different way. "Never would I dare to offer such a thing—it is unpresentable!" the *maitre d'hotel* protested. "Well then, arrange not to let it be seen!" the composer countered. Ever after, we are told, *tournedos* were to be served not before the eyes, but behind the diner's back. Hence the name in French: *tourne le dos* ("turn the back"). There is no doubt, anyway, that *Tournedos Rossini* are named in the composer's honor: succulent slices of fried fillet of beef set on fried bread, capped with foie gras, crowned with truffles, and coated with Périgueux sauce. One of the richest, most expensive dishes in the world.

a towering rage; etc.   *Towering* in all such phrases derives from a term in falconry. Castle watchtowers were the tallest structures in the Middle Ages, so high-flying hawks were said "to tower." *Towering ambition* is thus ambition that is beyond ordinary bounds, as high as the towering of a hawk. *Towering rage* or *passion* could both be explained in the same way, rage or passion mounting to its highest point, but there is an added dimension that strengthens the phrases. When a falcon "towers" she hovers at the height of her ascent searching for prey, is ready to swoop down on her victim.

toxic.   (*See* **intoxicated**.)

tradattore, traditore.   *Tradattore, traditore* translates literally from the Italian as "translator, traitor." It is an old Italian saying claiming that a great book or poem can never be translated into another language and retain all its original shades of meaning.

trademarks.   Trademarks—"the name, symbol, figure, letter, word or mark legally adopted and used by a manufacturer or merchant in order to distinguish the goods he manufactures or sells and to distinguish them from those manufactured or sold by others"—must always be capitalized. Trademarks, the term coined toward the end of the 19th century, are also known as brand names or brands, this term deriving from the practice of branding animals to indicate ownership. The U.S. Patent Office began to officially register trademarks in 1870, although they were used several centuries before this. The *Trade Name Dictionary* (1977) lists 106,000 trade names.

trade winds.   These are winds that regularly "blow trade" in one direction or another. In the northern hemisphere they blow from the northeast, and in the southern hemisphere from the southeast. In some places they blow six months of the year in one direction and six months in the opposite direction. *Trade winds* is first recorded in 1626, but the term *to blow trade* is first mentioned in Hakluyt's *Voyages* (1582).

tragedy.   "Goat singer," the Greek *tragodia*, is the earliest ancestor of the word *tragedy*. But we don't know exactly why. R.C. Trench wrote in *On the Study of Words* (1888): "There is no question that tragedy is the song of the goat; but *why* the song of the goat, whether because a goat was the prize for the best performance of that song in which the germs of the future tragedy lay, or because the first actors were dressed, like satyrs, in goatskins, is a question which has stirred abundant discussion, and will remain unsettled to the end."

trailblazer.   A trailblazer isn't someone who blazes new paths by "setting the world on fire." To *blaze a trail* means to indicate a new path by notching trees with an axe or knife. *Blaze* in this sense is the white mark in the notch when the bark is removed. It originally meant the white spot on the forehead of a horse before American pioneers *trailblazed* the new use of the word.

train.   In the mid-19th century, people first gave the name *train* to railway carriages attached to locomotives, obviously because what was most impressive about the locomotive was the fact that it could pull a long train of carriages behind it. *Train*, which comes from the Latin *trahir*, "to drag," had previously been used for anything that trailed behind, but now it took on an entirely new meaning.

travelogue.   *Travelogue*, for "a motion picture or illustrated lecture on travel," usually to exotic places, was apparently coined by American lecturer Burton Holmes, who gave popular illustrated travel lectures at the beginning of the 20th century.

the Treacle Bill.   (*See* **no balm in Gilead**.)

trembling poplar.   (*See* **aspen**.)

triangular trade.   In the triangular trade, ships carried New England rum to the African Gold Coast on the first passage, traded the rum for slaves and transported the shackled slaves to the West Indies on the middle passage, where the slaves were sold for molasses and sugar, which were brought back to New England to make more rum on the final passage. The middle passage was, of course, the worse and most inhuman of the three legs of the journey.

tribulations.   The Roman *tribulum* was a sledge consisting of a wooden block studded with sharp pieces of flint or iron teeth. It was used to bring force and pressure against wheat in grinding out grain. The machine suggested the way trouble grinds people down and oppresses them, *tribulations* becoming another word for troubles and afflictions. The word is first recorded in English in 1330.

trilby hat.   Trilby O'Ferrall, the heroine in British author George Louis Du Maurier's novel *Trilby* (1894), was a beautiful artist's model who fell under the spell of *Svengali* (*q.v.*) and came to a tragic end. Many articles of clothing were named after Trilby while the novel was popular, including the soft felt hat with indented crown that the heroine wore in the stage version of the novel, a hat that remains fashionable today.

trillionaire. It seems impossible that anyone will ever become a British *trillionaire* (a trillion is a million billions in Great Britain; that is 1 followed by 18 zeroes), but some oil-rich Arab might become an American *trillionaire* (a trillion is "only" a thousand billions in the U.S.). Needless to say, there are presently no trillionaires (from the French *trillion*) in the world, but there are a few dozen billionaires, thousands of millionaires, and, as John Jacob Astor 4th said: "A man who has a million dollars is as well off as if he were rich." (*See also* **billionaire; millionaire; multimillionaire**.)

trim his sails. A sailor who *trims his sails*, "adjusts them to take advantage of the prevailing winds," is a good one, but this 19th-century expression is now usually applied to an opportunist in everyday life, one who is skillful in shifting his principles with the prevailing winds, without regard for anyone or anything else.

trip the light fantastic. Milton's poem "L'Allegro" (1632) gives us this expression, meaning "to dance":

Haste the Nymph and bring with thee
Jest and youthful Jollity . . .
Come, and trip it as ye go
On the light fantastick toe.

trivial. Some trivia about the word *trivial*. One theory holds that *trivia* derives from the Roman *trivium*, or "crossroads," where people met to discuss small, insignificant things. Another, less favored, says that during the Middle Ages the seven liberal arts were divided into the *quadrivium* (consisting of arithmetic, geometry, astronomy, and music) and the *trivium* (consisting of rhetoric, logic, and grammar). Since the *trivium* was considered less substantial, its subjects more superficial, the word *trivium* eventually gave us the word *trivial*.

Trojan. (*See* **a regular Trojan**.)

Trojan horse. Ancient Troy is believed to have been located where Hissarlik, Turkey now stands. Here the Greeks waged the Trojan War (about 1200 B.C.) in an effort to claim their Queen Helen, who had been abducted by Paris, the son of the King of Troy. At least so the classical writers claim. The war, probably fought for the control of trade, lasted for some ten years before Troy fell, the last year of the siege recorded by Homer in the *Iliad* and the burning of Troy described by Virgil in the *Aeneid*. Troy finally fell, Virgil writes, when the famous *Trojan horse* was left near the gates of the city overnight. The Trojans believed the giant horse to be a gift to the gods, but its hollow interior was filled with Greek soldiers, who slipped out in the dark and opened Troy's gates to their comrades. Since then the phrase *Trojan horse* has been used for any deceptive scheme.

trolling. The trolls, or dwarfs, of Scandinavian mythology have nothing to do with this word. Meaning in its nautical sense to angle with a running line (which may have originally run on a *troll*, or winch), or to trail a baited line behind a boat, the word *troll* has its beginnings in a hunting term, the Middle French *troller*, which meant "to go in quest of game," or "to ramble."

trompe l'oeil. A painting so realistic that it at first appears three-dimensional is a *trompe l'oeil*. The term is the French for "trick the eye."

trophy. The Greeks and the Romans often collected the arms of a vanquished enemy army after a battle and hung these swords, helmets, and armor on the branches of trees, arranging the display as if the tree were an armed man. This monument was called a *trapaion*, "a turning point," because it was always situated at the place where the turning point of the battle occurred. It is to this monument of victory, the *tropaion*, that our word *trophy* owes its birth.

trouble goin' fall. This old Gullah proverb, once common among slaves on the South Carolina rice plantations, is part of what one scholar calls the slaves' "acceptance strategy of survival." As it was explained by a Gullah speaker: "Trouble made for man. Ain't goin' fall on the ground! Goin' fall on somebody!"

Troy weight. During the 13th century the fairs at Troyes, France, in the province of Champagne, were the most famous in Europe. The weights and measures among merchants there were strictly supervised to ensure honesty and *Troy weight* became a standard of excellence still used today to measure precious metals and drugs.

truck garden. *Truck*, deriving from the Old French *troquer*, "to exchange," was another word for *country pay* (*q.v.*) in earlier times. Since truck most often consisted of vegetables from gardens, the term *truck garden* came to refer to a vegetable garden.

true. In his *Origins*, Partridge traces the adjective *true* to the Old English *treow*, which means both "loyalty" and "tree," a *true* person thus being "as firm and straight as a tree."

true blue. Cloth made at Coventry in England in medieval times was noted for its permanent blue dye, which withstood many washings, not fading at the first washing like so many blue dyes of the day. Its constancy inspired the saying *as true as Coventry blue*, which meant dependable and faithful and was later shortened to *true blue*. The term's meaning was reinforced in the 17th century when the Scotch Presbyterians who fought for their religion called themselves Covenanters and selected blue as the color of their flag. Those unequivocally on their side were referred to as *true blue*.

truffle.   The *diamonds of gastronomy*, as black truffles are called, and the *pearls of the kitchen*, white truffles, are the world's most expensive food (save for a few rare spices), selling recently for over $300 a pound. The underground fungi probably take their name from the Osco-Umbrian *tufer*, which is a variation of the Latin *tuber* ("truffle"). According to this explanation *tufer* changed to the Vulgar latin *fufera*, which became by metathesis (the transposing of letters) the old Provençal *trufa*, this being the basis for the French *truffe* and the English *truffle*. So far, so good—black truffles, after all, are more plentiful in Italy's Umbria region than anywhere in the world. But why the *l* in *truffle*? Some authorities believe that it's there because the English *truffle* derives directly from the Swiss *trufla*, not from the French *truffe*. The Swiss word, they claim, comes from the French *truffe* with the *l* added from another French word, *trufle* ("mockery, cheating"), in allusion to the hard-to-find fungi hiding underground. In any event, there was inevitably confusion between the French *truffe* and *trufle* and it is easy to believe that people accidentally combined the two words, given the truffle's "evasive" qualities. It's interesting to note that the eponymous hero of Molière's famous play *Tartuffe* was named for the Italian word for truffles. Tartuffe appears to have been drawn from the character of a bawdy French abbot of the period, and Molière is thought to have used *tartuffe* to symbolize the sensuous satisfaction displayed by certain religious brethren when contemplating truffles.

Trugen stroke.   Outstanding British amateur swimmer John Arthur Trudgen (1852-1902), introduced the *Trugen stroke* to Europe in 1893, after seeing it used in South America. The stroke, employing a double overarm motion and a scissors kick, is regarded as the first successful above-water arm action used in swimming. Trudgen popularized the idea of minimizing water resistance by bringing both arms out of the water, which paved the way for the reception of the now common *Australian crawl* adopted from South Sea natives. His stroke was sometimes called the *Trudgeon*, another misspelling of the swimmer's name.

tsunami.   *Tsunami* means "storm wave" in Japanese. *Tsunami* (soo-nam-ee) waves have killed tens of thousands. Starting as the result of an undersea volcanic eruption or earthquake, *tsunamis* gather force and can travel at over 400 miles an hour, rising to heights of over one hundred feet before they crash into shore. *Tsunamis* have been traced back almost to the beginning of recorded history, but the word itself did not come into English until the 20th century.

tuba.   A straight war trumpet was called a *tuba* by the ancient Romans, after the Latin word for "arouser or exciter." Over the centuries this word for a war trumpet became attached to an entirely different musical instrument that hadn't even been invented in Roman times.

Tucson bed.   A humorous expression from the Western range that probably dates back to the late 19th century, a *Tucson bed*, after Tucson, Arizona, means "lying on your stomach and covering that with your back." Early cowboys apparently didn't think much of Tucson's accommodations.

Tuesday.   *Tuesday* is named for the Germanic god of war, Tiw, deriving from the Anglo-Saxon *tiewesdaeg*, "the day of Tiw."

tulipomania.   Of all the foolish investment schemes the world has known the 17th-century tulipomania was certainly one of the most reckless. Tulipomania arose in Holland, from where the mania for the purchase of tulip bulbs spread throughout Europe and rose to its height in 1634-37, with investors purchasing bulbs for well over $5,000 each and men losing fortunes on speculations in unusual bulbs. (See **mulberry mania**.)

tuna.   An Americanism first recorded in 1884, *tuna* appears to be an anagram of the Spanish *atun*, for the fish, which had been called the *tunny* (from the Latin *thumis*) in English since at least the 16th century.

tundra.   One of the few words contributed to English by the Laplanders in Europe's far north is the word *tundra*, for the bleak, nearly level barrens these people inhabit. The Lapp *tundra* passed into Russian before being recorded in English during the mid-19th century.

tunnel.   In Medieval English a *tonel* was a net with a wide mouth used to trap birds. From this word derived *tunnell*, for "the shaft of a chimney or any pipe or tube," which gave us the word *tunnel*, for "an underground passage."

tunny.   (See **tuna**.)

tupelo.   The native American *tupelo tree* genus, which includes the black or sour gum tree, means "tree of the swamp" in Creek Indian language. *Tupelo*, recorded in 1730, is a good example of the mess Americans made of some Indian words. It was *ito opilwa* in Creek.

turkey.   The domesticated turkey hardly knows what to eat and has to be attracted to food by colorful marbles placed in its feed; it often catches cold by getting its feet wet and frequently panics and suffocates itself when the flock presses together in fear. For such reasons *turkey* has been slang for any stupid, worthless, useless, unsuitable thing since before 1930. Since the early 1940s *turkey* has often referred to a poorly done theatrical production that fails, sometimes called a *gobble*. The word is also used for a socially incompetent, awkward person, a fake drug capsule, easy money (because turkeys are comparatively easy to catch), an easy task (a *turkey shoot*), a valise, a fifty-cent piece (from the eagle on the coin), and a hobo's suitcase.

Turkish words in English. Turkish words that have enriched the English language include the ancestors of: *turban, tulip, yogurt, caviar, horde, fez* and *vampire*.

to turn a deaf ear. People have been *turning* or *giving deaf ears* to others, "refusing to listen," since at least the 14th century. A similar expression is to close or stop one's ears, the latter used by Shakespeare in *A Winter's Tale*.

turnip. *Turnip* comes from the early English *turnepe*, that word blending the noun *turn* (with reference to the vegetable's neatly round shape) and the earlier English word *nepe*, for turnip.

turn over a new leaf. The leaf turned over is one from a book not a tree. People have been using the expression, for "reforming or amending one's conduct" for almost 500 years and it refers to turning to a blank page in an exercise book where one can begin work afresh, or to a new lesson in a book of precepts. A page of a book is called a *leaf*, however, because the leaves of certain plants were used as manuscript pages before the invention of paper. Many ancient manuscripts written on palm leaves still survive.

turnpike. (*See* **piker**.)

to turn the tables. Collecting antique tables was a fad among wealthy men in ancient Rome, we're told. When these collectors chided their wives about expensive purchases, the women turned them toward these antique tables and reminded their husbands of their own extravagances, "turning the tables on them." A good story, but there is no evidence that it is true. The expression *to turn the tables* doesn't date from Roman times, is only about 400 years old, and possibly derives from the game of backgammon. In backgammon, formerly called "tables" in England, the board is usually divided into two "tables." One rule of the complicated game allows a player to double the stakes in certain situations and literally turn the tables. Another possibility is that the phrase comes from the old custom of reversing the table or board in chess, which enabled a player at a disadvantage to shift the disadvantage to his opponent.

to turn turtle. British sailors in the Caribbean during the 17th century noticed that natives would capture huge sea turtles by turning them over, thereby rendering them helpless, when the creatures came ashore to bury their eggs. Later they used this image when they said that a capsized ship *turned turtle*, and soon the expression came to mean anything upside down.

turpinite. Used in making shells, *turpinite* was for a short time the most powerful explosive in the world, and like the atom bomb inspired the false hope that its terrible effects would end war for all time. The French inventor Turpin concocted *turpinite* about 1894, about six years after he had invented the explosive *lyddite*, which is named for Lydd, England, the town where its preliminary tests were made. Turpinite, said to be tested among sheep with devastating results, inspired fear even among French troops.

turquoise. This blue or green gem was mined in Persia in medieval times and shipped through Turkey to Europe. Europeans, however, believed it to be mined in Turkey and the French called it *la pierre turquoise* ("the Turkish stone"), which soon became simply *turquoise*.

turtledove. No turtles involved here. The mourning dove takes its name from the Latin *turtur*, echoic for the sound that the bird makes, and *dove*, for "a diver." *Turtur* became the Dutch *tortelduyf*, the German *Turteltaube*, and finally the English *turtledove*. The *Song of Solomon's* "The voice of the turtle is heard in the land," refers to the turtledove.

tussie mussie. (*See* **nosegay**.)

tutania. British manufacturer William Tutin, who had a plant in Birmingham in about 1770, may have been as patriotic as the inventors of the *sten gun*, who named their invention from their initials plus the *En* of England. Tutin manufactured a silvery white alloy of tin, antimony, and copper, which he probably named after himself and four letters from Brit*annia*. Possibly someone else fashioned the odd word, however, and the coining of *tutania* was probably influenced by *tutenag*, "a crude zinc."

tuxedo. What do Indians have to do with tuxedos? In 1890, dress requirements at the local country club in Tuxedo Park, New York, forty miles or so from Manhattan, called for men to wear a tailless dinner jacket at most nightly affairs. This was known as a *tuxedo coat* until matching pants were added to the outfit and it became known as a *tuxedo*, which inevitably was shortened to *tux*. The word *Tuxedo* itself derives from the white settlers' pronunciation of the name of the Ptuksit Indians, a subtribe of Delaware Indians who lived in what is now Tuxedo Park. *Ptuksit* meant "roundfoot" or "wolf tribe" in allusion to the wolf, "he of the roundfoot."

tuzzy-muzzy. (*See* **nosegay.**)

Tweedledum and Tweedledee. A 1725 epigram about the relative merits of the composers Handel and Giovanni Battista Bononcini, or Tweedledum and Tweedledee as the poet called them, went as follows:

> Some say compared to Bononcini
> That mynheer Handel's but a ninny;
> Others aver that he to Handel
> Is scarcely fit to hold a candle.
> Strange all this difference should be
> Twixt Tweedledum and Tweedledee.

The epigram, variously attributed to John Byrom, Pope, and Swift, first used the words Tweedledum and Tweedledee, which has since described two people, groups, or things identical in looks, opinions, or certain characteristics. The nicknames, which suggested the contrast between high- and low-pitched musical instruments, were given to German-born English musician George Handel and the musician G.B. Bononcini when a rivalry sprang up between the two while Handel served as director of the Royal Academy of Music. English aristocrats mainly sided with Bononcini, who is little-known today and left no work nearly as popular as Handel's *Messiah*. Tweedledum and Tweedledee were made more famous as the twins in Lewis Carroll's *Through the Looking Glass* (1872).

Tweed Ring. (*See* **Tammany.**)

twelve. Twelve is first recorded in English at about the time the Danish Vikings began invading England in 789 and it may derive from the Old Frisian *twelf*. In any case the victorious Vikings did transmit their duodecimal system to the English. They counted in twelves instead of ten and our 12 inches to a foot, 12 men to a jury and marketing unit of a dozen all evolved from their system.

twenty-one gun salute. Guns were fired as salutes in early times, but a *twenty-one gun salute* is an American expression according to an official U.S. Navy publication: "Guns could not be loaded quickly then, so the act of firing one in a salute indicated that the saluter had disarmed himself in deference to the person being saluted. The larger the number of guns fired, the greater degree of disarmament . . ." Since twenty-one guns was the greatest number found on one side of one of the larger ships of the line, firing all of them became the highest mark of respect, reserved for heads of state. Fewer numbers of guns were fired in salutes to people of lesser importance. But for any salute only odd numbers are used, reflecting the old seagoing superstition against even numbers. This

form of saluting was first recognized in the U.S. in 1875. As commander in chief, the president is accorded the highest salute of twenty-one guns.

twenty-three skiddoo. For well over half a century no one has used this expression seriously, but it is still remembered today—mainly as a phrase representative of the Roaring Twenties, which it is *not*. *Twenty-three skiddoo* is important, too. It goes back to about 1900 and for ten years enjoyed great popularity as America's first national fad expression, paving the way for thousands of other dispensables such as *Yes, we have no bananas, Shoo-fly, Hey, Abbott!, Coming, mother!* and *I dood it!* Twenty-three-skiddoo practically lost its meaning of "scram" or "beat it" and just became the thing to say, anytime. As for its derivation, it is said to have been invented or popularized by that innovative early comic-strip artist "Tad" Dorgan, encountered frequently in these pages under *hot dog, yes man,* and other of his coinages. Regarding its composition, *skiddoo* may be a shortening of the earlier "skedaddle." *Twenty-three* is a mystery. Perhaps it was a code number used by telegraphers. There is even a theory that it "owes its existence to the fact that the most gripping and thrilling word in *A Tale of Two Cities* is twenty-three": Sydney Carton, the twenty-third man to be executed on the twenty-third of the month.

twepping. Homicide was called by the acronym *twep*, "terminate *with* extreme prejudice," in CIA circles during the Vietnam War, and may still be used today. *Twep* was used so frequently that it gave rise to the euphemistic verb *twepping*.

Twiss. Here the Irish had the last word, as is often the case. Author Richard Twiss (1747-1821) may have thought he had put the natives down when he published his uncomplimentary *Tour in Ireland* in 1775, but he hadn't counted on the Irish wit. They promptly began to manufacture a chamber pot called the *Twiss*, but didn't let it go at that. On the bottom of the chamber pot was a portrait of *Richard Twiss*, the picture captioned thus:

> Let everyone ————
> On lying Dick Twiss.

(*See* **crapper; furphy; Oliver's skull; sacheverell; vespasienne.**)

to twist (turn) someone around one's little finger. "[She] had already turned that functionary around her finger," historian John Motely wrote in *The Rise of the Dutch Republic* (1855). This is the first recorded mention of anything like the more embellished expression *to twist someone around one's little finger*, though Motely makes no claim to having coined the phrase.

twitter. (*See* **onomatopoeia**.)

two bits. *Bit* was British slang for money or any small coin (a *threepenny bit*, etc.) as far back as the early 16th century. In U.S. regions bordering on Mexico the term was applied to the Mexican *real*, worth 12 1/2 cents and called a shilling in many Eastern states. By 1730 the expression *two bits*, two Mexican *reales*, or twenty-five cents, was being used in the American Southwest and for many years *quarter* was practically unknown there. *Two bits* became popular throughout the country, as did the expression *not worth two bits*, "practically worthless," but *four-bits* and *six-bits* never caught on nationally.

twofers. *Twofers* has meant two theatre tickets for the price of one in America since about 1948, and is most often used in New York City today for such tickets bought at Duffy Square for Broadway plays. *Twofer*, however, had referred to *two-for-a-nickel* cigars since as early as 1892.

two strings to one's bow. To be prepared for anything, to have an alternate plan. This expression is probably much older than its first recorded use, by Cardinal Wolsey in 1524, having its roots in the archer of ancient times who always carried at least two bowstrings when he went into battle.

two-time loser. In some states a third conviction for a major crime results in an automatic term of life imprisonment for the offender. Thus a criminal who has two such convictions and remains a criminal is a desperate man, *a two-time loser*.

two whoops and a holler. In Western U.S. parlance *two whoops and a holler* means a short distance, not far, "within spitting range." The phrase probably dates back to the late 19th century.

tycoon. *Tycoon* is just an American phonetic spelling of the Japanese *taikun*, for "great prince." The Japanese word, in turn, comes from the Chinese *ta*, "great," and *kiun*, "prince." Americans encountered the *taikun*, whose military title was *shogun*, during Commodore Perry's expedition to Japan of 1852-54 and brought the word home, where it was applied to any powerful man, especially a wealthy businessman.

Tyler grippe. John Tyler (1790-1863) has the dubious honor of being the only U.S. President for whom an epidemic is named. The *Tyler grippe* was a virulent influenza that swept the country at the time he became President in 1841. In fact, Tyler, elected vice-president, assumed office when his running mate, old William Henry Harrison, died a month after being inaugurated as president. Harrison died of pneumonia or the Tyler grippe, or a combination of both.

typewriter. The word *typewriter* was coined by American Christopher Latham Sholes, who patented the first practical commercial typewriter in 1868 (slow, difficult machines, intended primarily for the blind, had been invented as early as 1714). Sholes's "type-writer" had only capital letters. Manufactured by Remington, it was owned by Henry James, Mark Twain, and Sigmund Freud, among other famous early experimenters. Mark Twain, in fact, typed *The Adventures of Tom Sawyer* on Sholes's machine in 1875, this being the first typewritten book manuscript (a fact that Twain kept secret in his lifetime because he didn't want to write testimonials or show the uninitiated how to use the machine).

tyro. A green recruit was called a *tiro* by the Romans, to distinguish him from an experienced ordinary soldier, called a *miles*. In Medieval Latin *tiro* was often spelled *tyro*, which became our term for a novice or greenhorn in any field.

U

U. The letters *U* and *V* (*q.v.*) were at first interchangeable in English, the letters not separated in dictionaries until the early 19th century (*upon*, for example, was often spelled *vpon*). *U* in recent times has become a humorous term for "upper class" or "correct," *non-u* or *un-u* being its opposite.

U-boat. The German *unterseeboot*, "undersea boat," gives us this universal abbreviation, which became popular during World War I.

UFO. *UFO*, as a term, has been in use since the 1950s or earlier, but the first *unidentified flying objects* were reported in America in 1896. UFO's are often called flying saucers, but they have been reported in many different shapes. The first were said to resemble "cigar-shaped airships."

ugh! There is no record of an American Indian ever uttering the sound *ugh!* when he or she meant "yes" or "hello." The term can be traced to dime romances about the American West popular at the turn of the century, its use perpetuated by early American motion pictures. As a sound of contempt and disgust *ugh* is first recorded in 1837 but is probably much older.

ugly as sin. One can't be much uglier than this, even if some sins seem lovely. The expression, though possibly much older, is first recorded in Sir Walter Scott's novel *Kenilworth* (1821) with its many glimpses into the court of Queen Elizabeth.

ugly duckling. Han Christian Andersen's tale "The Ugly Duckling" tells of a sad "ugly duckling" that was actually a cygnet and, to its mother's surprise, grew up into a magnificent swan. Soon after the story was translated into English in 1846 the expression *ugly duckling* became part of the language, usually meaning an unpromising child who grows into an admirable adult.

ukulele. *Ukulele* is the Hawaiian word for "flea." Apparently, it was transferred to the musical instrument that the Portuguese brought to Hawaii in 1879, either because one's fingers hop like fleas from string to string when playing the instrument, or because British army officer Edward Purvis, a member of King Kalakaua's court, nicknamed "the flea" because of his small stature, was a skilled ukulele player who helped make the instrument popular in Hawaii.

ultracrepedarian. (*See* **cobbler should stick to his last.**)

ululate. Meaning to howl or wail, to lament loudly, *ululate* is a word of imitative origin, possibly going back to the Sanskrit *ulukas*, a name for the screech owl.

umber. The color *umber*, dark dusty brown or dark reddish brown, is named for the earth called umber that makes such pigments. *Umber earth* comes from the Italian *terra d'Umbria*, "earth of Umbria," referring to the soil in Umbria, east of Tuscany in northern Italy. Umbria is named for the *Umbri*, a tribe that once inhabited the region. It is a great *truffle* (*q.v.*) producing region.

umbrage. *Umbrage* derives from the Latin *umbra*, "shadow or shade," the same root that gives us *umbrella* (*q.v.*). The expression means to take offense, suggesting someone "shadowed in offended pride, retreating into the darkness of proud indignation." There is a story about the editor of a small newspaper who quickly read a wire service story during World War II stating that the Russians had *taken umbrage* at something, as they often did. Not knowing what the phrase meant, he headlined the story: "Russians Capture Umbrage."

umbrella. The *umbrella* is named for the benefit it provides in hot, sunny countries. It derives from the Latin *umbra* "shade," its diminutive ending making the word mean "a little shade." (*Sombrero* similarly comes from the Spanish *sombra*, "shade.") The umbrella has been known in England since Anglo-Saxon times, but is said to have first been used there as a protection against rain by the world traveler Jonas Hanway in 1760. His innovation caused a riot among sedan chairmen and coachmen, whose vehicles up to then had been the pedestrian's only protection from downpours. (*See* **gamp; umbrage; under the umbrella of.**)

umpire. *Umpire* is a later form of *noumpere*, which meant the same: "one who decides disputes between parties." *Noumpere*, in turn, ultimately derives from the Old French *nonper* (*non*, "not" + *per*, "equal"). Thus, the idea behind the word is that the umpire is not equal to either party in a dispute, is the impartial third person. *Noumpere*, the accepted form up until the 15th century, began to be pronounced *umpire* because people transferred the *n* in the word to the indefinite article: *noumpere* becoming *an oumpere* and finally an *umpire*. In the same way a *napron* became an *apron*, a *nadder* became an *adder*, and an *ewt* became a *newt*.

umpteenth. *Umpteenth* may derive from *M*, or *umpty*, in early Morse Code, which signified a dash. By this theory, *umpty* came to mean "large or many" because *M* (umpty) was associated with the Latin *M*, "a thousand." Adding *teen* for "ten" to a shortened *umpty*, the result was *umpteen*, "many tens," meaning a very large number, and *umpteenth*.

uncial. An *uncial* is a majuscule script, often used in ancient manuscripts, that takes its name from the Latin *uncia*, "inch," because the letters in it are about an inch high.

uncle! *To say* or *cry uncle* has since the beginning of this century meant "to give up, to surrender, to say you've had enough." Apparently it is of schoolboy origin, at least it is most used by schoolboys when fighting, especially when one has another pinned helplessly on the ground. For about thirty years the cry *give!* has been more common in the New York City area, but one still hears the earlier expression. Why *uncle* was chosen by kids is anybody's guess; there probably is no good reason unless a defeated boy originally had to curse his uncle, just as bullies often make their victims curse their mothers and sisters before letting them go. Which is no more than a guess. *Cavy!* a similar expression not heard anymore, is said to date back to Tudor times and be a corruption of the Latin *peccavi*, meaning "I have sinned, I am wrong."

Uncle Remus. Joel Chandler Harris's Uncle Remus tales, collected in *Uncle Remus: His Songs and His Sayings* (1880) and many other books, were among the first and remain the greatest of black folk literature. In the books, Uncle Remus, a former slave, entertains the young son of his employer with traditional "Negro tales" that in St. Augustine's words "spare the lowly and strike down the proud," including the "Tar-Baby" stories and other tales of Brer Rabbit (always the hero), Brer Fox, and Brer Wolf. Harris, born a "poor white" or "red-neck," a piney-woods "Georgia cracker," collected the authentic tales from numerous former slaves. One who helped him a great deal was an old gardener in Forsyth, Georgia called Uncle Remus, and Harris named his narrator after him. The tales, however, probably go back to Africa, where they were born among people who spoke the Bantu language and of course no Uncle Remus is in them. Uncle Remus is considered "a servile groveling 'Uncle Tom'" by some blacks today. Versions of the Brer Rabbit tales without him have been told by Anna Bontemps and Langston Hughes.

Uncle Sam. The original *Uncle Sam* was Samuel Wilson, the nephew of army contractor Elbert Anderson, who owned a store or slaughterhouse in Troy, New York and had a contract to supply the army with salt pork and beef during the War of 1812. Wilson and his uncle Ebenezer, Elbert's brother, worked as army inspectors and frequently inspected the meat Elbert Anderson packed in barrels with the initials "E.A.—U.S." stamped on them. According to a popular version of the story, one soldier asked another what the initials E.A.-U.S. (Elbert Anderson United States) meant and his companion quipped that they stood for "Elbert Anderson's Uncle Sam." Some scholars dispute this story, which was widely accepted during Wilson's lifetime, but no better explanation has been given. The term's first recorded use was in the *Troy Post* of September 7, 1813, which speaks well for the Samuel Wilson theory except that the article only says the words derive from the initials on government wagons. The name *Uncle Sam* caught on quickly as a symbol of the army and then as a national nickname to counteract that of England's John Bull.

Uncle Tom. Everyone knows that *Uncle Tom* comes from the character in Harriet Beecher's Stowe's *Uncle Tom's Cabin* (1852), the immensely popular American antislavery novel that caused President Lincoln to say on meeting Mrs. Stowe, "Is this the little woman whose book made such a great war?" Mrs. Stowe depicted Uncle Tom as simple, easygoing, and servile, willing to put up with anything, though it should be remembered that she intended him as a noble, high-minded, devout Christian and that he is flogged to death by the brutal overseer Simon Legree at the end of the book for bravely refusing to reveal the hiding place of Cassie and Emmaline, two female slaves. Few people know that Mrs. Stowe's model for Uncle Tom was a real-life slave named Josiah Henson, born in Maryland in 1789, who wrote a widely read autobiographical pamphlet. Henson was far from an *Uncle Tom* in the term's recent sense. Like many slaves, he served as the overseer, or manager, of a plantation before he escaped to Canada. Once free, he started a prosperous sawmill, founded a trade school for blacks, whites, and Indians and helped over 100 slaves escape to Canada. When he journeyed to England on business, the Archbishop of Canterbury was so impressed with his speech and learning that he asked him what university he had studied at. "The University of Adversity," Henson replied.

unconditional surrender. "Unconditional Surrender" was the nickname of Union General U. S. (Ulysses Simpson) Grant, who would give "no terms but unconditional surrender" to the Confederates in 1862 when his forces captured Fort Donelson in Tennessee, the first major Union victory of the war. The term has been used in every war since, but got its start with "Old Unconditional."

uncouth. *Couth,* originally meaning "known or familiar," dates back before Chaucer's day. Its antonym *uncouth* is just as old, the word being used in *Beowulf* for "unknown or unfamiliar." The dislike of the unfamiliar, of strangers, foreigners, is probably responsible for the change in the word's meaning over the years to unseemly, awkward, uncultured, etc.

underdog. *Underdog* appears to have originated in a popular 19th century song by David Barker called "The Under-Dog in the Fight," two stanzas of which follow:

> I know that the world, that the great big world
>   Will never a moment stop
> To see which dog may be in the fault,
>   But will shout for the dog on top.
>
> But for me, I shall never pause to ask
>   Which dog may be in the right,
> For my heart will beat, while it beats at all,
>   For the under dog in the fight.

underhanded. We know that four centuries ago card sharks were as proficient at palming cards, holding extra cards under their hands, as sharpsters are today. Such cheating, widespread as it has always been, may have suggested the expression *underhanded*, "in a secret or stealthy manner," though the first writer to use the word in this sense (1545) refers to a plain thief "stealing under hande or craftily."

undertaker. *Undertaker* has been used since at least 1698 for what is in the U.S. euphemistically called a *mortician*. Perhaps the term originated as a joke (for an *undertaker* does *take* someone *under* the ground), but there is no proof of this. *Undertaker* is recorded three centuries earlier in the sense of "one who undertakes a task or enterprise," and an *undertaker* meant "a publisher," and, to be fair, "an author," before it came to mean one who arranged funerals.

under the counter. During World War II dishonest merchants often sold scarce commodities at high prices, keeping the goods out of sight, under the counter, or in a backroom, so that they weren't available to most customers. This practice led to the common term *under the counter.*

under the rose. (See **sub rosa**.)

under the table. (See **aboveboard**.)

under the umbrella of. This phrase means under the protection, dominion, or influence of someone. In various Asian and African countries the umbrella was a symbol of rank or state, an emblem of sovereignty, and the expression may be an allusion to this. As far back as the early 17th century, English writers were commenting on the practice of servants carrying umbrellas to shade sultans from the sun. But the expression could be home-grown, too; just as early, there were figurative references in En-

glish to umbrellas as a means of protection. Perhaps the phrase is simply an extension of the earlier *under the aegis of*, which means the same. The *aegis* was the storm and thundercloud of the Greek god Zeus, who sometimes put it between a favorite and his enemies to protect his favorite. A bright, blazing shield fringed with gold tassels, it had at its center the head of Medusa, a glimpse of which could turn men to stone.

under the weather. Ik Marvel, a pseudonym that resulted from a misprinting of J.K. Marvel, was the pen name of American author Donald Grant Mitchell. In his *Reveries of a Bachelor* (1850) Ik Marvel is the first to record *under the weather*, which has been a synonym for everything from "ill and indisposed" to "financially embarassed" and "drunk," and has even been a synonym for "the discomfort accompanying menstruation."

underworld. Since about 1608, when the term is first recorded, *underworld* had meant hell, or the nether world of the dead beneath the earth. But in the 18th century the word was applied to the world of criminals, who were considered "beneath" proper society. By the 1920s *underworld* was being used in this second sense only to describe organized crime, which the word generally means today.

under your hat. (See **talk through one's hat**.)

undine. An *undine* is a female water spirit, one of the elemental spirits, the spirit of the waters. The word was coined by Paracelsus from the neo-Latin *unda*, "a wave." *Undine*, in the 1814 tale of the same name by German author de la Motte Fouqué, obtains a soul by marrying a mortal and bearing him a child.

unicorn. Medieval writers represented this mythical animal as having "the legs of a buck, the tail of a lion, the head and body of a horse and a single horn—white at the base, black in the middle and red at the tip—its body white, head red, and eyes blue." It takes its name, of course, from the most distinctive of its features, the single horn in the center of its forehead, from the Latin *unum cornu*, "one horn." Described as early as 400 B.C., the mythical beast was thought to be the only animal able to defeat an elephant—by ripping the elephant's belly with its sharp hooves. It could be caught only by "placing a young virgin in its haunts"—the unicorn would lie down placidly at her feet.

Union Jack. *Jack* has meant a small flag used as a mark of distinction on a ship since the early 17th century. It may be that the *Union Jack*, the national flag of Great Britain, takes its last name from this *jack* flown aboard ships. Other possibilities are the French *Jacques*; James, for King James I introduced the Union flag; or a leather surcoat called the *jack* that was often "emblazoned with the cross of St. George."

union suit. Still heard occasionally, as a comic or euphemistic term for men's underwear, the *union suit* was probably so named because top and bottom were "united" in one piece. However, some authorities say the underwear, dating back to the early 19th century, got its name because it was made of a "united" mixture of flax and cotton called "union."

United Nations. Before Winston Churchill suggested the name *United Nations* to President Roosevelt the world body was called the *Associated Powers*. Churchill took the name from a poem by Lord Byron, which he quoted to FDR:

> Millions of tongues record thee, and anew
> Their children's lips shall echo them and say—
> "Here, where the sword united nations drew,
> Our countrymen were warring on that day!"
> And this is much, and all which will not pass away.

United States of America. Thomas Paine, the author of *Common Sense*, a popular tract that attracted many to the side of the American Revolution in 1776, coined the name *United States of America* for his adopted country. The name was first used in the subtitle of the Declaration of Independence: "The Unanimous Declaration of the Thirteen United States of America." However, before the Articles of Confederation was ratified in 1781 the nation was known as *The Congress*. Under the Articles it was called *The United States in Congress Assembled* and under the Constitution was finally called Paine's *United States of America*. It should be added that from as early as 1617 to as late as 1769 the kingdom or republic of Holland was called *the United States*.

Unknown Soldier; Unknown Warrior. The *Unknown Soldier* is the body of an unidentified American soldier killed in France during World War I and buried in the National Cemetery at Arlington, Virginia, his grave a national shrine. The *Unknown Warrior* is his British counterpart, "buried among the kings" in Westminster Abbey. There are similar shrines in Paris and Berlin for French and German unknown soldiers, all from that bloody war.

Upas. According to fable a foul vapor rises from the Javanese *upas tree (Antiaris toxicara)* and "not a tree, nor blade of grass is to be found in the valley or surrounding mountains near it, not a beast or bird, reptile or living thing lives in the vicinity." A Dutch physician noted in 1783 that "on one occasion 1,600 refugees encamped with fourteen miles of it and but 300 died within two months." Such legends inspired the use of the word *upas*, for "a corrupting or evil influence." Legends aside, the milky

juice of the upas contains a virulent poison that is used for tipping arrows.

up Green River. When American mountain men killed a man a century ago they sent him *up Green River*, this referring not directly to Wyoming's Green River but to the common Green River knives used in many a fight. They were called that because they were made at the Green River works and stamped with that designation.

upholsterer. An upholsterer was originally a worker hired by a merchant to "hold up the goods" so that they could be seen by prospective buyers—he was a "holder upper" and was, in fact, first called an *upholder*. Over the years, this same worker came to repair the goods he had held up. By the 17th century he was being called an *upholsterer*, his work consisting of repairing, finishing, or making articles of furniture.

upper crust. "Kutt the upper crust [of the loaf] for your souerayne [sovereign]," an arbiter of good manners wrote in about 1460. He was referring to the old custom, or proper etiquette, of slicing the choice top crust off a loaf of bread and presenting it to the king or the ranking noble at the table. This practice led to the expression *upper crust*, for "rich or important people," those who ate the upper crust, though this meaning isn't recorded until the mid-19th century.

upper hand. A nice story relates this expression to a 15th-century gambling game almost identical to how kids use a bat in choosing up sides for a sandlot baseball game. A stick was thrown to one man, who grabbed it; and the next man placed his hand just above the first man's. The game went on until the winner got the last, or upper, hand on the stick—the upper hand won, if he could throw the stick, which he often barely held by his fingertips, a distance previously agreed upon. The expression *upper hand*, however, is much older than the game, dating back to at least 1200. It derives from the earlier, obsolete *over hand*, which meant the same, the mastery or control "over" a person or thing.

up periscope! Originally used by the English on land to see over hills and bushes, its use recorded as early as 1822, the *periscope* became forever linked with submarines during World War I. At the time, *up periscope!* became a familiar command and "feather" became the word for a periscope's wake. The word *periscope* itself is a learned coinage from the Greek *peri*, "near," and *scope*, "an instrument for observing."

to upset the apple cart. Just as Shakespeare improved the ancient curse *son of a bitch* by making it *son and heir of a mongrel bitch*, some anonymous English wit in the late 18th century transformed an old Roman phrase into *upset the apple cart.* The Roman expression *Perii, plaustrum perculi* ("I am undone, I have upset my cart") meant the same thing, "to ruin carefully laid plans," and might have been changed by some schoolboy who translated the line from Plautus's *Epidicus.* Why the Romans didn't think of using a specific fruit in the expression to make it more graphic is a mystery. They certainly knew all about apples; in fact, the famous French *api* variety apple (our "Red Lady") is named after the legendary Roman gourmet Apicius, who is said to have produced it by grafting.

up the creek, etc.   *Up the creek* means in a bad predicament, on the spot, behind the eight ball. Sometimes the expression is *up Salt Creek,* or even *up Shit Creek*—often *without a paddle.* The expression goes back about a hundred years and was probably first *up Salt Creek,* if we are to judge by the popular 1884 political campaign song "Blaine up Salt Creek." A salt creek is a creek leading through the salt marsh or marshland to the ocean and best explains the phrase, for it is very easy to get stuck in one and, without a paddle, a boatman would have no way to get out. The excremental version conveys the same idea, but makes the situation even worse.

up the river.   (*See* **sent up the river.**)

uptick.   Though it has more complicated technical meanings on Wall Street, *uptick* has come to mean an upsurge or a pickup, especially when referring to the state of the economy. A 1980s term, it of course has its roots in the Street's stock ticker or ticker tape machine.

up to par.   Someone performing or feeling *up to par* is performing or feeling much like he always does. But *par* is a U.S. golf term, from the Latin *par,* "equal," dating to about 1898 and meaning "the score an expert is expected to make on a hole or course, playing without errors, without flukes, under ordinary weather conditions."

uranium; Uranus.   English astronomer Sir William Herschel first named the planet *Uranus Georgium Sidus* after England's absurd King George III, this name later changed, more appropriately, to *Uranus* by German astronomer Johann Bode, so it would be in conformity with other planetary names from classical mythology. *Uranus* is the Latin name of the Greek god of heaven, who was both son and husband of Gaea, god of the earth, whose name gives us *geography, geology,* and other words relating to the earth. The children of Uranus and Gaea, twelve male and female giants called Titans, have their name honored in *titanic,* "anything of great size or force," and the element *titanium,* discovered in 1795. The element *uranium,* so important in today's world, is also in the family, named for Uranus in 1789.

urbi et orbi.   *Urbi et orbi* is the traditional solemn blessing given by popes from the balcony of St. Peter on special occasions such as the election of a pope, though in modern times the custom has fallen into disuse. The words mean "To the city [Rome] and to the world."

urchin.   Englishmen have often been poor at spelling French words and stumbled badly over the synonym for "hedgehog" that the Normans brought to England, spelling *hurcheon* a number of ways before finally settling on *urchin.* They called the hedgehog an *urchin* for a time and also applied the name *urchin* to a mischievous child, because the urchin, or hedgehog, was popularly believed to be a mischievous elf in disguise. People eventually stopped using *urchin* as a synonym for "hedgehog," but not for an impish child. Neither was the name *sea urchin* abandoned. This spiny creature was originally named for its resemblance to the urchin, or hedgehog, and once was called the *sea hedgehog.*

Urginea.   Ben Urgin, not a man but an Arabian tribe in Algeria, gives its name to the genus *Urginea,* comprising about seventy-five species belonging to the lily family and native to the Mediterranean, the East Indies, and South Africa. The bulbs of *U. maritenia,* the only species found in the Mediterranean, are known in medicine as *squills.* Generally gathered for their drug properties, they are used in Sicily for making whiskey. These bulbs often weigh up to four pounds and yield a fluid once considered valuable medically as an expectorant, a diuretic, and for its digitalis-like action on the heart. The first specimen of *Urginea* was found in the territory of the Ben Urgin tribe and named by the German botanist Steinheil.

Uriah Heep.   *Uriah Heep,* the name of the smooth, deceptive law clerk in Dickens' *David Copperfield* (1849), has become over the years a synonym for any "sanctimonious hypocrite, full of sharp practices."

urinate.   (*See* **piss.**)

Uruguay.   Coming from the native Guaraní language, the name of this South American country means "river that makes the sea."

used up.   *Wasted,* for "killed," is a slang of recent times, dating back to about 1955, at least in the sense of "to completely destroy," *to lay waste to.* Far older is *used up,* also meaning "killed," which originated in 1740 at the battle of Cartagena when General John Guise sent a message to his commander-in-chief asking him to send more grenadiers, for those he had were all "used up." All of the 1,200 men Guise had sent to attack the castle of St. Lazar had been killed or badly wounded within a couple of hours.

use him as though you loved him. It's not true that Izaak Walton said of the worm, as bait for fish: "Use him as though you loved him, that is harm him as little as you may possibly, that he may live the longer." He was referring to the frog when he wrote this in his classic *The Compleat Angler, or the Contemplative Man's Recreation* (1653), but his words became misinterpreted over the years, probably because fishermen use worms more than frogs.

The Useless Parliament. A name given to the Parliament convened by Charles I in June 1625, which was dissolved early in August after "having done nothing but offend the king." In the U.S. various Congresses have been given derogatory names; Harry Truman, in an election year, called one Republican-dominated Congress *The Do-nothing Congress.*

U.S. Navy. Britain's American colonies had a *Colonial Navy* until 1631, this replaced by the fifty-three-ship *Continental Navy* in 1776 after the break with Great Britain and when Commodore Esek Hopkins was appointed its commander in chief (the only time a Navy head has held that title, subsequently held only by American presidents). The Continental Navy became the *United States Navy* in 1794.

Utah. Utah takes its name from the fierce proud tribe called the Utes that resided there and whose name meant "hill dwellers." In 1850 the area encompassing present-day Utah was constituted the Utah Territory, the colorful Mormon name for it, *Deseret*, or "honeybee," being rejected by Congress.

utopia. Sir Thomas More's utopia, described in his 1516 book of that name, is probably the most famous of all utopias. More invented the name of his fictional island where everything is perfect, using the Greek for "nowhere" (*ou*, "not," and *topos*, "a place"). His book, translated from English into all the chief European languages, gave us the name for any ideal, visionary place. But "Utopia" is only one of a great many utopias invented by writers over the centuries. Among the first of them was Plato's "Republic," which he described in *The Republic.*

V

V. *V*, along with *j*, is one of the two youngest letters in the English alphabet, not coming into the language until after Shakespeare's time, in about 1630. It previously shared its form with *u*. In the Roman notation it represents 5.

vade mecum. A *vade mecum* is generally a manual or handbook someone carries for ready reference, such as a travel guide, but can be anything a person carries for frequent use. The term, first recorded in 1629 as the title of a book of theological essays, is from the Latin *vade mecum*, "go with me."

vagina. *Vagina*, for "the female sexual organ," the word first recorded in 1682, comes from the Latin *vagina*, "a sheath, a scabbard." Vanilla, the plant that produces the vanilla bean, derives from the same source, being a scientific Latin reshaping of the Spanish *vainilla* (from the Latin *vagina*), meaning "little sheath," in reference to the bean's pod.

valance. Some authorities believe that the short curtain or drapery called a *valance* takes its name from the Old French *avalant*, "hanging down." But the word more likely comes from the Old French town of Valence, once famed for its manufacturers, including curtain makers.

valentine. There were at least two St. Valentines, legend tells us, both Christian martyrs who were put to death on the same day, one an Italian priest and physician and the other the bishop of Terni. Butler's *Lives of the Saints* recounts the priest's story, which is almost identical to the bishop's: "Valentine was a holy priest in Rome, who . . . assisted the martyrs in the persecution under Claudius the Goth. He was apprehended and sent by the emperor to the prefect of Rome who, on finding all his promises to make him renounce his faith ineffectual, commanded him to be beaten with clubs, and afterwards to be beheaded, which was executed on February 14, about the year 270." February 14 had been associated with the mating of birds in ancient times, making St. Valentine's Day, which accidentally fell on this date, an excellent choice for a day for lovers, the day also being fairly close to spring, when as Tennyson wrote, "a young man's fancy lightly turns to thoughts of love." It became the custom to draw lots for sweethearts, or *valentines*, for the ensuing year on *St. Valentine's Day*, this practice probably deriving from a similar Roman custom said to be taken from either the feast of Lupercalia, the feast of Februata, or the day honoring the goddess Juno, all of which fell around *St. Valentine's Day*. By the end of the 18th century, the exchange of gloves and other gifts that accompanied the drawing of lots became the exchange of letters, which were sometimes secret and often humorous or insulting. These letters evolved into the *valentines* that we know today.

Valentino. To say silent screen star Rudolph Valentino was a sex symbol is to put it mildly. Italian born Rodolopho d'Antonguolla came to the United States in 1913, and after working as a gardener, a cabaret dancer-gigolo, and then a bit player in Hollywood, he zoomed to stardom under his stage name in *The Four Horsemen of the Apocalypse* (1921), which was followed by hits like *The Sheik*. Valentino became the embodiment of romance and sex to women all over the world, his name still a synonym for a handsome lover. Yet despite his dark good looks, this star of stars was a timorous lover, a superstitious man who tried to bolster his sexual powers with aphrodisiacs and magic amulets, who always preferred food to women and found his neurotic, clamorous admirers completely undesirable. Valentino died of peritonitis caused by a bleeding ulcer when only thirty-one years old. Over 50,000 people, overwhelmingly women, attended his funeral in New York in 1926, and even today admirers come to mourn at his crypt in the Los Angeles cemetery where he is buried. Some 250 women have claimed publicly that the "Sheik" fathered their love children, many of whom were born years after Valentino's death.

Valhalla. In Norse mythology, the souls of heroes slain in battle spend eternity feasting and rollicking in the celestial hall of Valhalla. *Valhalla* comes from the Old Norse *valholl*, "the hall of the slain," and is sometimes applied to buildings such as Westminster Abbey, where a nation's great men are buried. (*See* **Valkyries**.)

Valkyries. The ancient Norse believed that the twelve nymphs of Valhalla (*q.v.*) rode into battle with them and chose those heroes destined to die, escorting them back to their honored place in Valhalla. These nymphs were called the *Valkyries*, taking their name from the Old Norse for "choosers of the slain." (*See* **Valhalla**.)

vamp. The name of a bookseller in Samuel Foote's play *The Author* (1757) became synonymous for an avaricious publisher, because the character Vamp held that binding was more important than the contents of a book: "Books are like women; to strike they must be well-dressed. Fine feathers make fine birds. A good paper, and elegant type, a handsome motto, and a catching title, have driven many a dull treatise through three editions." *Vamp* was later used as the name of a critic in Thomas Peacock's novel *Melincourt* (1817) and is supposed to be a caricature of the bitter author, editor, and critic William Gifford. Peacock also satirized Gifford, Coleridge (Mr. Mystic), Malthus (Mr. Fox), and Wordsworth (Mr. Paperstamp) in his book. *Vamp* is more commonly used today to mean an unscrupulous woman of seductive charm. Both terms are probably short for *vampire* (*q.v.*).

vampire. Vampire is one of the few English words of Hungarian origin. It comes from the Magyar *vampir* and is infrequently spelled that way, although its ultimate source may be the Turkish *uber*, "witch." This word for a creature of the living dead, "a reanimated corpse" that spends its nights searching for human blood to quaff, is first recorded in English in 1734, and is the same in Russian, Polish, Czechoslovakian, Serbian, and Bulgarian. The term vampire was popularized by Bram Stoker's *Dracula* (1897) and some 47 spinoffs on the novel.

vanadium. The grayish metallic element *vanadium*, used in many alloys, is named for Freya, the fair Scandinavian goddess of love, one of her other names being Vanadis. (*See* **Friday.**)

Van Allen Belt. The *Van Allen Belt*, or *Van Allen Radiation Belt* is "a zone of high intensity radiation surrounding the earth," beginning at altitudes of about 621.4 miles. It was discovered by James A. Van Allen (b. 1915).

Vancouver. Vancouver, the largest city and chief port in British Columbia, Vancouver Island, the largest island off the west coast of North America, and the city of Vancouver, Washington, are all named for English navigator and explorer George Vancouver (1757-1798). Capt. Vancouver, who sailed with Capt. James Cook on his second and third voyages, explored and surveyed the northwest coast of America aboard *Discovery* in 1792. Puget Sound is named for Vancouver's Lt. Peter Puget, who helped the captain's brother finish his book: *A Voyage of Discovery to the North Pacific Ocean and Round the World* (1798).

vandalism. In the year 455 A.D. the Vandals, all 80,000 of them, were led by their King Genseric into Rome, which they captured easily and sacked thoroughly, loading their ships with plunder and sailing off to new conquests. The savage Teutonic tribe finished off the Roman Empire before falling from power almost a century later, after persecuting Christians and extorting their sacred treasures. The Vandals destroyed many precious cultural objects when they sacked Rome and it is probably from their later behavior that the word *vandalism* derives, meaning as it does wanton destruction of property, especially works of art. It is interesting to note that a French churchman first used the word *vandalisme* in this sense at the end of the 18th century. The name Vandal literally means "the wanderers." Before they sacked Rome the tribes had wandered across the Rhine to France, Spain, and Africa, making conquests all the while.

vandyke. When only nineteen, Flemish artist Sir Anthony Van Dyck became Rubens' assistant and pupil. One of twelve children of a wealthy silk merchant, the artist had shown great talent from his early youth and learned much from his Flemish master. Later he went to England where he married a Scotswoman and was knighted by Charles I, becoming one of the most noted portrait and religious painters of his day. Vandyke, as his name was spelled by the English, lived a life of luxury, keeping numerous mistresses, and had to paint prolifically to maintain his life-style. He is known to have done at least 350 portraits in England alone and overwork is often cited as the reason for his early death—he died in 1641, forty-two years old. Vandyke turned out masterpieces on a kind of assembly-line basis. He trained assistants to paint a sitter's clothes, used special models for the hands (in the painting of which he excelled), and would never allot more than an hour at a time to a sitting. Van Dyck depicted noblemen attired in wide collars adorned with V-shaped points forming an edging or border, and his subjects often wore sharp V-shaped beards similar to his own. The large points on the *Vandyke capes* or *collars* were called *Vandykes*, the verb *to vandyke* meaning to adorn a collar with such points, and the characteristic beards were and are still known as *vandykes*.

Vanilla. (*See* **vagina.**)

vanish into thin air. When Shakespeare used this phrase in *The Tempest* to describe ghosts "Melted into air, into thin air," it was already in common use. All air was considered thin at the time, nothing being known about its varying density, and *thin air* was simply employed as an intensive. Other similar phrases of the day were *vanished* (or *melted*) *into smoke*, *wind* and even into *liquid tears*—all meaning the same, "to disappear."

variety is the spice of life. William Cowper's poem "The Task" (1785) is the source of this well-known expression: "Variety is the very spice of life,/ That gives it all its flavors."

varmint. *Varmint* is not an American word, as one would think from scores of westerns. The word for an animal pest or a despicable person is a corruption of *vermin* and of British origin. *Vermin* comes from the Latin *vermis*, "worm."

varnish. (*See* **Coma Berenices**.)

varsity. *Varsity*, for the first-string team of a U.S. college or any school, is simply a shortened form of "university," the *varsity team* initially meaning the university team. In England, where the word is first recorded in 1846, *varsity* (formerly *versity*) means Oxford University or Cambridge University.

vaseline. Among those flocking to America's first oil strike near Titusville, Pennsylvania in 1858, was Robert A. Chesebrough, a Brooklyn chemist, who noticed that workmen with cuts, bruises, and burns used as a soothing ointment, a waxy substance from the pump rods bringing up the oil. Gathering some of the oily residue, Chesebrough took it back to Brooklyn and made a jelly-like product from it. This he patented at once, giving it the trademark *Vaseline*, a word he formed from the German *Wasser* (pronounced "vasser") "water" and the Greek *elaion*, "olive oil."

Vauxhall. It is very rare for an English word to be adopted in Russian as anything more than a slang expression. But that is just what happened with the *Vauxhall* railroad depot in London, which became the Russian *voksal*, their generic word for railroad station. The London depot was named for the Vauxhall district in London, which contained the famous Vauxhall gardens, a popular pleasure resort from 1661 till 1859. The gardens, in turn, took their name from Falkes or Fulkes de Breante, who was lord of a manor called *Falkes Hall* on the site in the early 13th century. Pepys mentions the public gardens, which soon came to be called *Vauxhall*, and Thackeray described them later before the gardens were closed and the site built over. From manor to garden to district to depot to Russian word—many stops along the line, but so it is that the communists, who would not consciously pay homage to royalty, honor an early Norman knight.

vegetable. *Vegetables* have usually been highly prized, right from the beginning, too, the word *vegetable* itself deriving from the Latin *vegetabilis*, which meant animating or life-giving. The Greeks venerated vegetables, making small gold and silver replicas of the most prized ones. The Roman Fabii, who took their name from the *faba*, or bean; the Piso clan, who derived theirs from the *pisa*, or pea; the *Lentuli*, who named themselves after the *lente*, or lentil; and the great house of Cicero, which took its name from the *cicer*, or chickpea—these are only a few noble Roman families whose patronyms honored widely hailed vegetables.

vegetarian. *Vegetarianism* (which is a relatively recent word, used in 1895 by a British health magazine in describing the eating habits of a Chinese sect and modelled after *unitarianism*, etc.) may or may not be the thing for you, though it certainly was for Pythagoras, Aristotle, Epicurus, Diogenes, Cicero, Plato, Socrates, Buddha, Montaigne, Wesley, Pope, Wagner, Swedenborg, Shelley, Tolstoy, Shaw, Gandhi, Mussolini, Hitler and many other famous, infamous, and obscure people who only ate vegetables.

veggies. This "cute" word for vegetables apparently arose in the early 1960s, for it is first recorded in 1966. Obviously a shortening and rearrangement of *vegetables*, it is used by young and old alike.

veil. (*See* **yashmak**.)

vein of my heart. The Gaelic *cushlamochree* gives us this expression, which is the Irish word's literal translation, although *cushlamochree* is used, more simply, for "darling."

vending machine. The term *vending machine* seems to have been introduced either by the Adams' Gum Company (now part of American Chicle) in the 1880s to describe the machine the company used to sell tutti-fruitti gumballs on New York City elevated train platforms, or at about the same time by the Frank H. Fleer Gum Company. At that time Fleer's founder agreed to an experiment proposed by a young vending machine salesman. The salesman argued that vending machines were so great a sales gimmick that people would actually drop a penny in them for nothing. Frank Fleer agreed to buy several machines if the young man's pitch proved true, and the experiment was conducted at New York's Flatiron Building. The salesman set up a vending machine there, with printed instructions to "drop a penny in the slot and listen to the wind blow." He got Fleer's order when hundreds of people contributed their pennies and continued to do so until New York's Finest hauled the machine away.

The venerable monosyllable. *The monosyllable* has been used since about 1715 as slang for the "female pudend," as *Partridge* puts it, or "a woman's commodity," as it is defined in the 1811 edition (called *Lexicon Balatronicum*) of Captain Francis Grose's *Classical Dictionary of the Vulgar Tongue*. *The Venerable Monosyllable*, dating to about 1785, means the same, *Grose* defining it here as "the pudendum muliebre." Both terms are practically obsolete except as encountered in literature.

Venetian blinds. The slatted window shades called *Venetian blinds* are named after the early Venetian traders who introduced them to Europe, but they were invented by the Persians, from whom the Venetians bought them. They are, in fact, called *persiani* by Italians.

Venezuela. Spanish explorers in the area of this country found the inhabitants living along canals that reminded them of Venice, Italy. They accordingly named the area *Venezuela*, "little Venice."

vengeance is mine, saith the Lord. This biblical saying, from Rom. 12:19, doesn't bless or condone human vengeance, as is often thought. This is made abundantly clear by the pertinent passage: "Dearly beloved, avenge not yourselves, but rather give place unto wrath: for it is written, Vengeance is mine; I will repay, saith the Lord." Not only does the whole passage advise against human revenge, it goes on to say: "Therefore if thine enemy hunger, feed him; if he thirst, give him drink: for in so doing thou shalt heap coals of fire on his head. Be not overcome of evil, but overcome evil with good."

veni, vidi, vici. The laconic words of Julius Caesar when he told his friend Amintius of his victory over Pompey's ally Pharnaces at Zela in 47 B.C., the phrase is Latin for "I came, I saw, I conquered." So Plutarch says, but Suetonius doesn't ascribe the words to Caesar, noting only that they were displayed before his title after his victories at Pontus.

venial sin. A *venial sin*, in the Catholic Church, is one that doesn't forfeit grace, a sin that may be pardoned, hence its name from the Latin *venia*, "grace, pardon." It's opposite, a *mortal sin*, is a sin that deserves everlasting punishment, a deadly sin, hence its name from the Latin *mort*, "death."

Venice glass. Long considered to be perfection among glassware, *Venice glass* has been known since the Middle Ages, when it was frequently used for drinking glasses—because poisonings were common at the time and it was widely believed the *Venice glass* was so sensitive that it would break into slivers if poison touched it.

venison. *Venison* comes from the Latin *venatio*, "hunting," and was formerly applied to the flesh of any animal killed in the hunt and used as food. The word is first recorded in the early 14th century and gradually came to mean only the meat of deer. The *venison* mentioned in Genesis is wild goat.

venom. Though it means "poison," *venom* began life as the love potion, *venenum*, that the Roman goddess Venus used to infect human hearts. The Latin *venenum* eventually became the basis of words meaning poison in several languages, our English *venom* being first recorded in 1220 as *venim*.

Venus de Milo; etc. The *Venus de Milo*, now in the Louvre and possibly the finest example of ancient art extant, dates from about 400 B.C., but was discovered in 1820 on the Greek island of Milo, or Milos. Other famous statues of the goddess of love are the Venus de Medici, so

called because it was once kept in Rome's Medici Palace; the Venus Genetrix, a symbol of fecundity, its last name meaning "she that produces"; and the lost nude Venus of Cnidus, purchased from Praxiteles by the Cnidians, an ancient copy of which is in the Vatican. The Venus Callipyge is a late Greek statue standing in the Museo Nazionale at Naples. There is no good reason for connecting this statue with Venus and its last name translates as "beautiful buttocks," to use a euphemism.

Venus mercenaria. Like many seafoods, clams are often regarded as a potent aphrodisiac, especially the common hard-shell clam *Venus mercenaria*. This quahog gets its last name from the Indian wampum beads used in commerce. It probably boasts its suggestive first name because Venus has often been depicted standing in a large seashell. A good example is Sandro Botticelli's famed *The Birth of Venus*, sometimes jocularly called "Venus on the Half Shell."

Venus's-flytrap. This odd plant is said to have been discovered by the governor of North Carolina, Arthur Dobbs, in 1760 and named Fly Trap Sensitive. One of the few plants that wreak revenge on insects, the Venus's-flytrap was officially named *Dionaea muscipula* by English naturalist John Ellis in 1770. This translates as "Aphrodite's mousetrap," indicating sensual love. However, shortly afterward Ellis also coined the common name *Venus's-flytrap* for the plant, this being very similar, as Venus is simply the Roman version of Aphrodite or Dionaea. *Mousetrap* or *flytrap* is understandable, but why was the vegetable animal-eater named after Venus or Aphrodite when it is not particularly beautiful? Though neither etymological nor entymological reference books make any mention of it, John Ellis clearly referred to the similarity of the plant's leaves to the human vagina when he named it for the goddess of love. The *Venus's-flytrap*, a perennial native only to North and South Carolina, is widely grown indoors by gardeners.

Venus's looking-glass; etc. Their strikingly beautiful purple flowers are responsible for all species of the bluebell family (*Specularia*), especially the bellflower, or *Campanula*, being named for Venus, the Roman goddess of beauty. Other plants named after Venus include *Venus basin bath*, the wild teasel; *Venus's-comb*, the shepherd's needle; *Venus's-golden apple* (Atlantia monphylla); *Venus-hair*, the maidenhair; *Venus's-lover*; *Venus-navel*; *Venus's-pear*; *Venus's pride*, Blue Houstonia; and *Venus's-slipper*, the lady slipper.

verbicide. *Verbicide*, "word murder," the act of destroying the sense or value of words, or the perversion of a word from its proper meaning, has been applied in our time to political speechmaking and government gobbledygook or officialese. But the word seems to have been coined by Oliver Wendell Holmes, who patterned it on *homicide*, and applied it to punning in his *The Autocrat of the Breakfast-Table* (1858).

verb. sap. (*See* **a word to the wise.**)

Verdi! Verdi! The Austrians occupying northern Italy in the 19th century couldn't understand why the chant *Vendi! Verdi!* at the end of operas written by Italian composer Giuseppe Verdi frequently inspired anti-Austrian riots. They finally learned that *Verdi* was also an acronym for the name of the man Garibaldi was advocating as head of a united Italy: Vittorio Emanuele, *Re d'Italia* ("Victor Emmanuel, King of Italy"). After the Austrians were expelled in 1857 Victor Emmanuel was crowned king.

verdigris. The greenish patina found on copper, brass, or bronze exposed to the air for long periods of time is called *verdigris*. The word comes from the Old French *vert de Grèce*, "the green of Greece," possibly because of its association with Greek statues. Another word for the patina is *aerugo*, from the Latin word meaning the same.

verme. The *verme* is a legendary fish of the Ganges, which was said to be able to reach up out of the Indian river, seize *elephants* in its jaws and destroy them. The fish was named for the Latin *vermes*, "worm," perhaps by error, perhaps because the fish was thought to be eellike. The word is first recorded in 1572.

vermicelli. Few diners would want to dwell on the etymology of this word for a very thin pasta. For *vermicelli* means "little worms" in Italian, deriving from the Latin *vermis*, "worm, maggot, or crawling insect."

vermilion. Why does this bright red take its name from the Latin *vermis*, for "worm, maggot, or crawling insect." It seems that in days past *vermilion* dye was made from scarlet body fluid of cochineal insects.

vermin. (*See* **varmint.**)

Vermont. *Vermont* had been called *New Connecticut* before being named from the French *vert*, "green," plus *mont*, "mountain." The Green Mountain State was admitted to the Union in 1791 as our 14th state.

vernacular. The *vernacular* is the everyday or native language of a country, as opposed to the formal language of its learned people. The Latin *vernaculus*, "native" or "domestic," is the basis for the word, this in turn deriving from the Latin *verna*, "a native slave, a slave born in a country."

vernier; vernier caliper; etc. A *vernier* is any small, auxiliary movable scale attached to another graduated in-

strument. It is often attached to the transit, sextant, quadrant, and barometer for very accurate measurements. French mathematician Pierre Vernier (1580-1637) invented the scale, describing it in a treatise he wrote in 1631. Vernier was commandant of the castle in his native town of Ornans in Burgundy and later served the king of Spain as a counselor. His invention estimates the nearest tenth of the smallest division on the scale it is attached to. It was originally an improvement on a scale called the *nonius*, invented by the Portuguese scientist Nunez, and proved to be a milestone in the techniques of precise measurement. The *vernier caliper*, the *vernier compass*, both incorporating *verniers*, and the *vernier engine*, a small rocket engine that corrects the heading and velocity of a long-range missile, also bear the French inventor's name.

vernis Martin. (*See* **Coma Berenices.**)

veronica. The classic Spanish bullfighting cape movement called the *veronica* takes its name from St. Veronica, who in ancient legend was the woman who wiped the face of Christ as He carried the cross, her handkerchief retaining an imprint of Christ's face. The cape movement is swung so slowly and near to the face of the bull that it suggested St. Veronica using her handkerchief.

verse. Poems are of course almost always written in straight lines across a page, each line turning at the end into a new line. This suggested the synonym for "poem," *verse*, which comes from the Latin *versus*, a form of the Latin *vertere*, "to turn." *Verse* is recorded in English as far back as 1200 and today often means light pieces of poetry.

very. *Very*, which ultimately derives from the stem of the Latin *verus*, "true," is not one of the ten most frequently used English words (these are *I*, *the*, *and*, *to*, *of*, *in*, *we*, *for*, *you*, and *a*, in that order). But *very*, first recorded ten centuries ago, bears the distinction of being the only foreign (not Anglo-Saxon) word, as well as the only word of more than one syllable, to have any rank at all in the "highest-frequency" category of words used, ranking within the top fifty according to one expert.

vespasienne. Roman Emperor Vespasian (A.D. 9-79) taxed his people inordinately to build public urinals, improving the *pissoirs* even more by selling the urine collected in them to launderers, who used it for bleaching clothing. His obsession with public urinals led the witty French to name them *vespasiennes* after him. (*See* **crapper; furphy; fontage; money doesn't stink; Oliver's skull; sacheverell; Twiss.**)

veterinarian. This word, for "an animal doctor," derives from the Latin *veterinarius*, "belonging or pertaining to beasts of burden," which in turn comes from *veterina animalia*, "beasts of burden" —showing that the veterinarians originally cared exclusively for farm animals. Several rare names for a veterinary used through history are *emplastrist* (for the plasters they used), *unguentarian* (for their ointments), *hippo-jatrist* (hippohorse), and *hippologist* (though this strictly means anyone well versed in the study of horses). Other names that are rarely if ever used anymore are horse doctor and horse leech. In the 17th century *veterinarian* was also the name for a man who rented out horses or mules, like Hobson of *Hobson's choice*. *Vet*, a synonym for *veterinarian* today, has in recent years become a verb meaning to treat or cure as a veterinary does, as, for example, an editor who vets a manuscript.

veto. *Veto*, for "a head of state's power to annul a law passed by a lower body," is the Latin for "I forbid," and was the word used by the Roman tribunes to oppose measures of the Roman Senate. *Pocket veto* is a U.S. term, meaning the veto of a bill by the President or a state's governor in the closing days of a legislative session by retaining it unsigned, by "pocketing" it; it was first employed by Andrew Jackson. France's Louis XVI and Marie Antoinette were called Monsieur and Madame Veto because they vetoed so many decrees of the Constituent Assembly in 1791.

Via Dolorosa. The *Via Dolorosa*, "the Dolorous, or Anguished Way, the Way of the Cross," is the mile-long road in Jerusalem over which Christ carried the cross to Golgotha. It has also come to mean any painful path.

vials of wrath. In the biblical book of Revelations seven angels pour vials full of wrath upon the earth, this being the basis for the expression *vials of wrath*: "vengeance, or wrath upon the wicked."

a Vicar of Bray. A *Vicar of Bray* is someone who holds onto his office or position no matter who is in power and will go to any length to do so. The term refers to a semilegendary Vicar of Bray, Berkshire, in England who became twice a Roman Catholic and twice a Protestant under four different monarchs between 1520 and 1560, in the words of one contemporary writer "being resolved, whoever was king, to die Vicar of Bray."

vicar of hell. Henry VIII playfully gave this title to his "poet laureate," John Skelton, the term being a pun on Skelton being the rector of Diss in Norfolk. *Dis* is a Roman name for Pluto, the mythological ruler of the infernal regions.

Vichy. *Vichy*, or *Vichy water*, is water obtained from springs at the town of Vichy in central France, or any water similar to this water, which has been known in England since the 1850s. The water contains sodium bicarbonate and other alkaline salts and is used in treating digestive disturbances, gout, and other ailments. Not as well known is Vittel water, mineral water which comes from thermal springs in Vittel, France.

Victorian. Myriad things have been named after England's Queen Victoria, who reigned an amazing sixty-three years, from 1837-1901. A plum, a cloth, a large water lily, and a pidgeon all bear the name *victoria*, as does the low carriage for two with a folding top and an elevated driver's seat that was designed in France and named in her honor. Victoria is also the capital of both British Columbia and Hong Kong and a state in Australia; there is a Lake Victoria in East Africa; the Great Victoria Desert in Australia; a Mount Victoria in New Guinea; a Victoria Falls between Zambia and Zimbabwe; a Victoria Island in the Arctic Ocean; and Victoria Land, a region in Antarctica. Then we have Victoria Day, a Canadian national holiday in late May; the Victorian box, a tree; the victorine, a ladies' fur tippet; and the Victoria Cross, a military decoration first awarded "for valor" by Victoria in 1856. And that isn't nearly a complete list. *Victorian* means of, or pertaining to, the queen or the period of her reign and adds a score of terms, such as Victorian sideboard, to the total. *Victorian* alone often refers to the smugness and prudery characteristic of the period, especially concerning sex.

video. *Video*, the Latin for "I see," has been used as a term for television or TV since the 1950s. A more recent coinage, dating to the early 1960s, is the videophone, or picturephone, a telephone with a small TV screen on which callers can see each other. The system has so far proved too expensive to put into general use, but promises to be commonplace in the future.

vie. In the 16th century, *envy* meant to challenge someone to a gambling contest. The word's contraction, *vie*, became popular in gambling houses, meaning to back up one's hand with a bet. One *vied* at cards in this way, that is, "contended or strived against others," and the term later came to mean contending or striving in any sense.

vigorish. Many people have paid usurious rates of interest to loan sharks. The margin of profit in such transactions, 20 percent or more a week, late payment penalties, and other fees, is called *vigorish*, which also means the percentage set by a bookmaker in his own favor. *Vigorish* is one of the few English words with Russian roots, deriving from the Russian *vyigrysh*, "gambling gains or profit," which first passed into Yiddish early in 20th-century America as *vigorish* and was reinforced by its similarity to *vigor*.

viking. These Scandinavian pirates and explorers may derive their name from the Old English *vicing*, "pirate," although this etymology is disputed and some experts hold that Viking comes from the Old English *wic*, "camp," because these Scandinavians set up temporary camps while carrying out raiding expeditions. Today *viking*, with a small *v*, can mean any sea-roving pirate or bandit.

villain. *Villain* derives from the Latin *villanus*, "a serf," and the first *villains*, the word recorded early in the 14th century, were serfs in feudal England. From its meaning of a poor low-born rustic, *villain* within half a century came to mean a base person disposed to criminal acts. The word was first applied to a play's antagonist by Charles Lamb in 1822.

vim. *Vim* is an Americanism first recorded in 1843 and usually regarded as the accusative singular of the Latin *vis*, "strength or energy," though it may possibly be, judging by some of its earliest uses, of imitative or interjectional origin ("He drove his spurs . . .*vim* in the hoss's flank," 1850). The word is usually heard in the alliterative expression *vim and vigor*.

Vincent's infection. (*See* **Bright's disease**.)

a vintage year. *A vintage year* is a year notable for anything. The phrase originated with and still mainly refers to the year in which a good *vintage*, "gathering," of grapes was made into an excellent wine. *Vin ordinaire* is a cheap wine that can be good but is rarely excellent, while *vin de goutte* is an inferior wine made from the last pressing of the grapes.

virago. *Virago* meant a "man-like or heroic woman, a female warrior" when first attested to in about 1000, deriving from the Latin *virago*, meaning the same. Such a woman was likely to be bold and strong-willed, which led to the derogatory use of *virago* for "a bold impudent woman, a shrew, a termagant, a scold," this later use first recorded by Chaucer in 1386.

Virgilian. Virgil (70-19 B.C.), called the *Mantuan Swan* because he was born near Mantua, Italy, is considered the greatest poet of ancient Rome and in medieval times was regarded as the wisest of poets, a magician and enchanter. His name lives on, however, mainly as a synonym for the simple, pastoral beauty described in his poetry, which is *Virgilian*, or has a *Virgilian charm*. (*See* **swan**.)

Virgil's fly; Virgil's gnat. According to an old legend the Roman poet Virgil's (70-19 B.C.) "pet housefly" was given a funeral that cost over $100,000. Musicians, mourners, and eulogists were hired and Virgil's mansion was declared the fly's mausoleum. Later it was discovered that Virgil buried the fly so that he could prevent the state from confiscating his estate and distributing it to war veterans as payment for service—all family cemetery plots and mausoleums being exempt from such confiscations. History confirms that Virgil's property was confiscated and that he got it back, but tells us nothing about his pet housefly. Many medieval legends arose about Virgil, and though this story may be partly true, it probably is an exaggerated version of Virgil's real troubles with his property, plus a tale that he allegedly wrote called the "Culex." Spencer wrote a poem called "Virgil's Gnat," based on the "Culex," in which a sleeping shepherd is stung by a gnat, which has bitten him only to warn him that he is about to be attacked by a serpent. The shepherd kills that gnat and then slays the serpent, but the next night the gnat reproaches him for his cruelty and the remorseful shepherd builds a monument honoring the gnat.

Virginia. That gallant of gallants, Sir Walter Raleigh, suggested that *Virginia* be named after England's Elizabeth I, the Virgin Queen, when in 1584 he founded his colony there, probably on what is now Roanoke Island. (The island, which is in North Carolina, was originally part of the great area from Florida to Newfoundland that Virginia encompassed.) *Virginia*, the Old Dominion state, was the site of the first permanent English settlement, at Jamestown in 1607, and the scene of the British surrender in the American Revolution at Yorktown. Called the *Mother of Presidents*, the state sent Washington, Jefferson, Monroe, Madison, Tyler, William Henry Harrison, Taylor, and Wilson to the White House, and is renowned for many historic shrines. As to the state's exact naming, one writer tells us that "Queen Elizabeth graciously accorded the privileges proposed by Raleigh, giving to this new land a name in honour of her maiden state, and it was called Virginia. Raleigh was knighted for his service and given the title of 'Lord and Governor of Virginia.'"

visa. A *visa* is an endorsement of a person's passport by an agent of another country testifying that his passport has been examined and he is permitted entry into that country. *Visa* is short for the Latin *carta visa*, "the document (has been) examined." It was originally a French term that came into English early in the 19th century.

vitamin. American biochemist Casimir Funk coined the word *vitamin* (or, rather, *vitamine*) in 1912, at which time he was credited with the discovery of the existence of vitamins, organic substances necessary for normal health. Funk constructed the word from the Latin *vita*, "life," and *amine*, from the Greek *ammoniakon*, because he believed that an amino acid was present in vitamins. *Vitamine* was stripped of its *e* when it was found that amino acids were not involved.

vitex. A family of ornamental shrubs and trees often planted to attract bees, *vitex* is named from the Latin *vieo*, "to bind with twigs," in reference to the flexible nature of its twigs. One vitex, *Agnus Castus*, is called the *chaste tree* because the Romans considered it an anaphrodisiac that calmed the body and Athenian maidens who wished to remain chaste often strewed their couches with its leaves.

vixen. Why should a female fox be a *vixen?* The word arose as a corruption in Southern English dialects, with their predilection for *v*, of the Old English *fyxen*, "female fox." First recorded in the early 15th century, it took almost 200 years before the word was applied to an ill-tempered woman or shrew, Shakespeare using it thus in *A Midsummer Night's Dream.*

viz. *Viz*, meaning "namely," represents the Latin word *videlicit*. It needs no period after it. The abbreviation was being used by writers as early as 1540.

vocabulary. *Vocabulary* comes from the Latin *vocabularius*, meaning the same, and is first recorded in the early 16th century. As for the English vocabulary, there are well over a million scientific names for animals, a million for insects, well over 7.4 million for chemical compounds alone; more than 350,000 names are registered as trademarks in the U.S. Patent Office; and one general dictionary lists over 650,000 entries. That alone totals over ten million English words and with scientific words from many other disciplines, jargons of professions and trades, and slang expressions from England and America, the total must come to at least between 15 and 20 million. But of the millions of English words the average person uses only about 2,800 in everyday conversation, the most extensive individual vocabulary being about 60,000 words. Here are some other word counts:

Webster's Second International Dictionary—650,000
  words
Oxford English Dictionary—450,000
Shakespeare's Complete Works—19,000-25,000
New York Times (Sunday edition)—25,000
Chaucer's Works—8,000
Milton's Works—8,000
King James Version of the Bible—6,000

vodka. This alcoholic drink, made from rye, barley, and even potatoes, among other fruits and vegetables, takes its name from the Russian *voda*, meaning "water." The unaged, colorless drink does look something like water, but is so named because such spirits were once thought to be as essential to life as water—*whiskey* and the Scandinavian *aquavit* also derive from words meaning "water." *Vodka* is first recorded in English in 1801, though the drink is of course many centuries older. (*See* **gin; martini; scotch; whiskey.**)

volcano. Deep within Mount Etna in Sicily lived the Roman God of fire, *Vulcan*, making thunderbolts for Jove on his forge. From the Latin form of his name, *vulcanus*, comes our word *volcano*, for "a rent in the earth's crust issuing steam and rocks." *Volcano* is first recorded in English as "Flaming hell" (1613).

Volstead act. Minnesota Congressman Andrew Joseph Volstead drafted and introduced the *Volstead Act* (1919), which provided for the enforcement of the Eighteenth Amendment to the U.S. Constitution forbidding the manufacture, sale, and import or export of liquor. In spite of the strict law, enforcement proved impossible and there followed a period of unparalleled drinking and lawbreaking that some commentators claim marked the beginning of a moral breakdown in society. In 1933 the Twenty-first Amendment, repealing Prohibition, was ratified. Under the *Volstead Act* an intoxicating beverage was defined as one that contains more than .5 percent of alcohol by volume.

volt; voltaic pile. Count Alessandro Giuseppe Antonio Anastasio Volta invented *Volta's pile* or the *voltaic pile* in 1800, this the first electric battery or device for producing a continuous electric current. Volta, the son of an Italian Jesuit priest who left the order to marry, was something of a prodigy as a child. His voltaic pile consisted of zinc and silver plates stacked alternately with moist pads and touched with a conductor to produce an electric force. He also invented an electric condenser and devised the electrochemical series. Before his death in 1827, aged eighty-two, the scientist had reaped honors in almost every country in Europe, had statues erected to him and kings contending for his presence. Napoleon, who once visited his classroom to praise him, made Volta a member of France's National Institute and a count and senator from the Kingdom of Lombardy in 1801. It is said that Bonaparte so admired the great pioneer that he once crossed out the last three letters from the phrase "*Au grand Voltaire*" inscribed on a wall of the National Institute library. Today the unit of electrical force called the *volt* sings electrically of his fame.

volume. Early books consisted of parchment rolled on sticks, just as religious books sometimes are today. Thus the Latin *volumen*, "a coil or roll," from the Latin *volmers*, "to roll," became the French and English *volume*, for "a book."

voodoo. The *Waldensians*, followers of Peter Waldo or Valdo (d. 1217), were accused of sorcery and given the name *Vaudois* by the French. French missionaries later remembered these "heretics" when they encountered the witch doctors who preached black magic in the West Indies. They called the native witch doctors *Vaudois* and the name was soon applied to any witchcraft similar to the magic spells they cast, *Vaudois* eventually being corrupted to *voodoo*. This is the view of Ernest Weekly and some other respected etymologists on the origin of *voodoo*; however, the *Oxford English Dictionary* and a majority of authorities believe the word derives from the African *vodun*, a form of the Ashanti *obosum*, "a guardian spirit or fetish." Today the West African religion is practiced in its best integrated form in the villages of Haiti, voodoo having been brought to the New World by slaves as early as the 1600s.

vote for Boyle, a son of the soil. Hal Boyle, a columnist for the Associated Press, drove into Tunis soon after it fell to the Allies in World War II shouting: "Vote for Boyle, a son of the soil: Honest Hal, the Arab's Pal." Arabs picked up the former part of the phrase, without having any idea what it meant, and kept repeating it as a greeting to puzzled new troops from 1943 through 1944.

A votre santé! *A votre santé* is the most familiar and one of the oldest, of French drinking toasts. Dating back to the 18th century or earlier, it means simply "To your health!"

V-2 rocket. Developed by German scientists and used to bomb England in the last year of World War II, the V-2 liquid fuel rocket proved to be the basis for today's space rockets. The letter *V* stands for the German *Vergeltungswaffe*, "retaliation weapon," while it has a "2" in its name because it was a larger, improved version of the V-1 rocket German scientists had invented before it.

W

W. *W* takes its name from "double *U*." The twenty-third letter of the alphabet is simply two *V*'s (*VV*) joined together. *V* in centuries past was the symbol of both *V* and *U*, being pronounced as a *U* whenever it represented that letter.

wag. *Waghalters* were mischievous young men, merry rogues, who were so-called in medieval times because it was facetiously said that all such jokers would wind up wagging in a halter on the gallows instead of wagging their tongues. The word was shortened to *wagge*, then *wag*, and came to mean "a humorist," most *wags* today being unaware that their name means "a gallows bird."

wailing like a banshee. A *wailing banshee* is in Irish folklore a spirit in the form of a woman—often beautiful, but sometimes an old hag—who appears to or is heard by members of a family as a warning that one of them will soon die. *Banshee* is from the Gaelic *bean sidhe*, "woman of the fairies," and *wailing like a banshee* has come to mean someone, especially a woman, screaming shrilly.

Wales. (*See* **welsh.**)

to walk down the aisle. Americans have been using *to walk down the aisle* as a synonym for "getting married" for almost a century now. A bride who literally "walked down the aisle," however, would be walking along either side of the church and might confuse everyone. The passageway the bride walks "down" to the altar is actually called the nave, though there is no chance that this will alter the expression in the slightest.

walking off with the persimmons. (*See* **eatin' a green 'simmon.**)

to walk like Agag. The biblical King Agag (I Sam. 15:32) was hacked to death by Samuel, but he is remembered mostly by the expression *to walk like Agag*, "to walk softly," because the biblical verse cited says "And Agag came to him [Samuel] softly."

walk softly and carry a big stick. (*See* **Ananias.**)

walk the chalk. As far back as the 17th century it was customary in the American navy for a straight line to be drawn along the deck of a ship as a test for drunkenness. Any sailor who couldn't walk the whole line, placing each foot on it in turn, was adjudged drunk and punished accordingly — often by flogging. Thus, to *walk the chalk*, first recorded in 1823, came to mean to walk a line of sobriety, to obey the rules."

walk the plank. Probably no pirate ever forced anyone to *walk the plank* into the ocean — except in swashbuckling books and movies. The expression most likely originated in the yarn of an old salt or from the pen of a 19th-century magazine writer. Pirates did feed captives to the fishes or told them they were free to "walk home" while far out at sea, but no planks were used. The common practice was to maroon prisoners and pirate offenders on a desert island. The offenders were simply put ashore without clothes or provisions. (*See* **swashbuckler; pirate**.)

wall-eyed. A *wall-eyed person* has an eye or eyes with unusually large white areas, making for defective sight. Shakespeare uses the old term, which dates back to the 14th century and is a corruption of the Icelandic *vald eysthr*, "having a beam in the eye," and has nothing to do with walls, though no one really knows what the "beam" in the Icelandic word means.

wallflower. The prosaic explanation for this word, describing a girl who sits to the side at a dance or party because she is shy or without a partner, is simply that it originated with some poor girl who sat against the wall during a party. But the romantic story is nicer. This holds that such girls are named after the common wallflower of Europe (*Cheiranthus Cheiri*), a sweet-scented, yellow spring flower that grows wild on walls and cliffs. Indeed, the English poet Robert Herrick (1591-1674) claimed that the flower itself is named after such a girl, his delightful derivation telling of a fair damsel who was long kept from her lover and finally tried to escape to him:

> Up she got upon a wall
> 'Tempting down to slide withal;
> But the silken twist untied,
> So she fell, and, bruised, she died.
> Love in pity of the deed,
> And her loving luckless speed
> Turned her to this plant we call
> Now the "Flower of the wall."

the walls have ears. Some walls really did have ears. Dionysius, the Greek tyrant of Syracuse (430-367 B.C.), had a narrow tube inserted from his palace room to the walls of the prison below so that he could overhear the prisoners—and the listening post that he put his ear to in his wall was even shaped like a human ear. In the 16th century Catherine de Medici, the Queen of France's Henry II, is said to have had several rooms in the Louvre constructed similarly, so she could overhear any plots against her. In any event, the expression *the walls have ears*, meaning "you'd better take care, there are spies everywhere," is an old one, first recorded in English in 1620 and probably dating back much further. The *ears have walls* is a recent twist on the old phrase, meaning that some people, especially those in authority, are incapable of listening. It was coined in the late 1960s.

Wall Street.   Wall Street, which is both a street and a term symbolizing the American financial world in general, is located in downtown Manhattan at the southern end of the island and takes its name from the wall that extended along the street in Dutch times. The principal financial institutions of the city have been located there since the early 19th century. *Wall Streeter, Wall Street broker, Wall Street plunger*, and *Wall Street shark* are among words to which the street gave birth. We find *Wall Street broker* first used as early as 1836, and Wall Street being called *The Street* by 1863.

walnut.   (*See* **welsh.**)

walrus.   Walrus comes to us from the Dutch *walrus*, for the animal, which may have been suggested by the Dutch *wolvisch*, "whale." The word is first recorded in about 893. The walrus was often called the *sea horse* and *morse* in ancient times. The Eskimos, closer to nature, have at least six words for *walrus*, ranging from *nutara*, "baby walrus," to *timartik* "large male walrus," and *naktivilik*, "mature walrus." (*See* **snow.**)

Walrussia.   (*See* **Alaska.**)

Walter Mitty.   An ordinary person who has vivid dreams and daydreams of exciting adventures in which he is a hero, like the main character of the short story and film "The Secret Life of Walter Mitty" by American author James Thurber (1894-1961).

wampum.   *Wampumpeak* was a name American Indians in New England gave to shell money. Like most Indian names—including the longer forebears of *squash, hickory*, and *raccoon*—the colonists found *wampumpeak* too long and shortened it to *wampum*, which it remains today. All Indians didn't have the same name for shell money. Virginia Indians called wampum *roanoke*; the Mohave Indians called it *pook*; in northern California it was called *ali-qua-chick*; and in the Northwest it was *hiaqua*. But only *wampum* remains well known today.

wan.   This Chinese family name, whose Chinese character means "ten thousand," has an apocryphal story attached to it. It's said that when soothsayers advised the emperor Ch'in-Shi-Huang-Ti that he would not be able to finish the Great Wall of China until 10,000 more men were buried in it, the tyrannical emperor found a man named Wan, had him buried in the Wall, and went on about his work. *Wan* for sad comes from the Old English *wann*, dark, gloomy.

war; wargame.   Early in the 19th century the Germans developed the idea of simulated military moves made on paper or in field maneuvers as a test for the validity of military theory, the quality of training, and the effectiveness of equipment. They called this testing *kriegspiel*, which was translated as *war games* when the British later adopted the practice. *War* itself is an Old High German word, long used (at least since 1154) instead of the Latin *bellum*. *Kriegspiel* is also the name of a variation of chess. *Bellum* is a poor word for war because of its similarity to *belle*, "beautiful."

war correspondent.   "Since the first gun discharged at Fort Sumter awoke the American world to arms, War Correspondence on this side of the Atlantic has been as much an avocation as practicing law or selling dry goods . . . The War Correspondent is the outgrowth of a very modern civilization." So wrote the first observer to record *war correspondent*, in 1861, when the term, if not the profession, came into being.

ward heeler.   A *ward heeler* is a political hanger-on of a ward boss in American politics, the *heeler*, coming from the comparison of such a man to a dog that "heels" for its master, that is, follows behind submissively in its master's footsteps. The term is first recorded in 1888.

warmonger.   In the Latin dialect spoken by Roman soldiers in western Europe *mangones* were conniving dealers or traders in anything. This word passed into English as *monger* and was used for many compound words, including *fishmonger*. As early as 1590 one who traffics in war (for one reason or another) was called a *warmonger*, by Edmund Spenser in *The Faerie Queene*.

to warm the cockles of one's heart.   The most popular explanation for the *cockles* here says that late 17th-century anatomists noticed the resemblance of the shape of cockleshells, the valves of a scallop-like mollusk, to the ventricles of the heart and referred to the latter as *cockles*. Whether this is the case or not, *cockles* isn't used much anymore except in the expression *to warm the cockles of one's heart*, "to please someone immensely, to evoke a flow of pleasure or a feeling of affection." Behind the expression is the old poetical belief that the heart is the seat of affection.

the War of Jenkins's Ear.   Carrying his left ear back to London in a leather case, master mariner Robert Jenkins claimed that Spanish sailors boarded his brig, the *Rebecca*, which had been peacefully trading in the West Indies, rifled her, and that their commander had lopped off the ear as a further humiliation. Jenkins sent his ear to the king and brought the matter before Parliament, which decided that this was one cutting Spanish insult too many. Jenkins's ear became the major cause of the war between England and Spain that led to the War of the Austrian Succession. The conflict (1739-41) was popularly called *the War of Jenkins's Ear*, which is definitely the oddest name of all wars and surely the only one ever initiated by an ear. Admiral Sir Edward Vernon put down the Spaniards at Portobelo and "One-Eared" Jenkins was given command of another ship in the East India Company's service. He later rose to company supervisor.

the war of the giants.   The War of the Giants was a mythological one in which the giants revolted against Zeus and were put down by the gods with the help of Hercules. The Battle of the Giants took place on September 13, 1515, when the French under Francis I defeated the Swiss mercenaries defending the city of Milan at Mulagnano.

war of the stray dog.   The War of the Stray Dog in 1925, a conflict not much more stupid than most wars, took place when a Greek soldier ran after his dog, which had strayed across the border in Macedonia. A Bulgarian sentry shot the soldier and Greek troops invaded Bulgaria in retaliation. Before the League of Nations intervened over fifty men were killed. Almost as foolish was the Emu War. This took place in 1935 when west Australian farmers, enraged at ostrichlike emus trampling their wheat fields, demanded government help. The government sent troops with machine guns after the birds, which led the soldiers a wild chase through the back country for over a month. Twelve emus were killed and several soldiers injured.

warren.   Just as George Bernard Shaw's play *Mrs. Warren's Profession* resulted in the coining of *comstockery* (*q.v.*), it also gave rise to the word *warren*, for "a prostitute," after the title character in the play. The earlier *warren*, for "a brothel," origin unknown but dating back to the late 17th century, may have reinforced the usage.

the war to end all wars.   World War I. The expression is not from Woodrow Wilson's address to Congress calling for a declaration of war against Germany in 1917, as many people believe. What Wilson said then was *the world must be made safe for democracy. The war to end all wars* was suggested by H.G. Wells's book *The War That Will End War* (1914).

war to make the world safe for democracy.   (*See* **the war to end all wars.**)

warts and all.   The roots of *warts and all* reach way back to a remark Oliver Cromwell (1599-1658) made to an artist painting his portrait: "Mr. Lely, I desire you would use all your skill to paint my picture truely like me, and not flatter me at all; but remark all these roughnesses, pimples, warts, and everything as you see me, otherwise I will never pay a farthing for it." The story may be apocryphal, though it does sound like Cromwell, and historians believe that the Lord Protector, if he did say this, was speaking to Samuel Cooper rather than Sir Peter Lely, who painted less realistic full-length portraits of Cromwell from a miniature Cooper had done.

Washington.   *Washington* is the most popular place name in the United States, recorded in the nation's capital, Washington, D.C., the state of Washington, at least twenty-nine counties, and numerous towns. Washington State, the only state named for an American, was admitted to the union on February 22, 1889, appropriately on George Washington's birthday, which is, of course, a national holiday. Other words honoring the "Father of his country," *first in war, first in peace, first in the hearts of his countrymen*, are *the bird of Washington* (the American eagle), *the American Fabius* (see **Fabian tactics**), *Washingtonia* (a California palm tree), the *Washington thorn*, the *Washington lily*, and *Washington pie*. A *George Washington*, for an honest person, derives from the famous cherry-tree story apparently invented by M.L. (Parson) Weems in his biography of the first president written in about 1800. (*See* **I cannot tell a lie.**)

to wash one's hands of a matter.   Pontius Pilate's washing his hands at the trial of Jesus was a favorite scene in biblical dramas presented by strolling players in medieval times. Pilate was portrayed washing his hands in a basin (although the passage in Matt. 27:24 just says, "He took water and washed his hands") while denying any responsibility for Christ's death sentence. From these dramas and the biblical story of the Crucifixion, *to wash one's hands of a matter* came into popular use as an expression for abandoning something entirely after having been concerned in the matter, for a public disavowal disclaiming all accountability for something, or for disowning all associations with someone.

washout.   Not all word derivations are *cut and dried* (*q.v.*). Sometimes the same expression arises in two or more places from different sources, which may be the case with *washout*, both British and American slang for "a failure." British usage of this term derives from military slang on the rifle range. After one squad had finished shooting at an iron target, the bullet marks in the bull's eye were painted over with black paint and the rest of the target whitewashed to prepare it for practice by the next squad. A shot completely off the target was called a *washout*, because it went off into the air, washed itself out, so to speak, and the military slang for a missed shot, common in about 1850, became slang for a failure some fifty years later during the Boer War. However, before this, probably as early as the 1860s, *wash out* was an American term for the washing away by heavy rains of part of a road or railway. Some writers claim that this term independently suggested American usage of the expression *washout* for a failure, but there are no recorded instances of the figurative usage here until the 1920s. By that time British and American forces had come in close contact during World War I. It seems likely that American soldiers borrowed the term for a failure from British slang without even realizing it, the washout of roads and railways being so familiar to them!

wasp. A disparaging acronym for White Anglo-Saxon Protestant, WASP has been commonly used in America since the early 1960s to describe the nation's "ruling class," who are supposed to be white, of British descent, Protestant, and waspish, too. During World War II, WASP was also an acronym for Women's Auxilliary Service Pilot. (*See* **dago; harp; kiwi; welsh.**)

Wasserman test. Many medical tests, including the Pap test for cancer and the Schick test for diphtheria, are named for the physicians who devised them. The *Wasserman test* was invented in 1906 by August von Wasserman (1866-1925), a German physician and bacteriologist. This laboratory blood test for the diagnosis of syphilis, also known as the cardiolipin test, has been perfected to the point where it is 99 percent effective on normal persons. The test is based on the presence of antibodies in the blood. In most cases a positive *Wasserman* reveals that the patient has syphilis, although vaccination procedures and several diseases, such as leprosy, also produce a positive Wasserman. August von Wasserman, who began his career as a physician in Strasbourg, won international fame for his discovery. He became director of Berlin's Kaiser Wilhelm Institute in 1913.

watercress. Both watercress and land cress are herbs of the mustard group. *Cress* takes its name from the German *kresse*, for the salad green, this word perhaps deriving from an older German word that meant "to creep or crawl" and described the plant's way of growing.

Waterloo. One who *meets his Waterloo* suffers a complete and final defeat, just as Napoleon did in 1815 at the Battle of Waterloo, about nine miles from Brussels in Belgium. The battle was actually fought a few miles south of Waterloo, between Mont-Saint-Jean and Bellenoon.

water of jealousy. Under Mosaic law a woman who had committed adultery was to be stoned to death. But if a husband only suspected his wife of adultery she was given *the water of jealousy* to drink (Deut. 22:22) before the Sanhedrin. The dust from the sanctuary was mixed with the water and the priest said: "If thou hast gone aside may Jehovah make this water bitter to thee, and bring on thee all the curses written in this law." He then wrote down the curses, sprinkled the water on this writing, and gave the woman the rest of *the water of jealousy* to drink.

watt. There is probably no truth in the charming old tale that James Watt watched his mother's teakettle boiling as a child, and later invented the steam engine as a result. Watt, born in Scotland of poor parents, did, however, get off to an early start in his scientific endeavors. In 1765 the inquisitive Scotsman launched into a study of steam when a model of Thomas Neucomen's steam engine was brought to him to repair. He soon invented the first economical steam engine, which was initially used only for pumps in mines but eventually brought steam power to industry on a large scale. Watt devoted his life to perfecting and producing his new engine, manufacturing it with Matthew Boulton of Birmingham. He died in 1819, aged eighty-three. Toward the end of the century the International Electrical Congress named the *watt*, the unit of electrical power—736 *watts* equal to about one horsepower—in the inventor's honor. His name is also remembered by the *kilowatt*, one thousand watts; the *kilowatt hour*, a measurement by which electricity is sold; the *watt-hour meter*, which measures kilowatts; the *watt-meter*, an instrument for measuring a power load; and the *watt-second*, a unit of work. *Wattage* is power measured in watts, and "wattless" is an electrical term meaning without watts or power.

Waves. (*See* **Wrens.**)

to wave the bloody shirt. After members of the Scottish Campbell clan massacred all the MacDonalds they could find one early morning in 1692—after accepting the rival clan's hospitality and staying at their castle for twelve days—the wives of those MacDonalds who were massacred displayed the blood-stained shirts of their husbands to arouse vengeance. Some etymologists believe this to be the origin of the expression *to wave the bloody shirt*, "to deliberately arouse revenge," that is still used today.

we are not amused. It has been said that this reproof often attributed to Queen Victoria is "not in keeping with Queen Victoria's conversation or character" and that she never used the royal "we" save in official proclamations. However, J. A. Fuller-Maitland wrote about an 1884 concert in *A Doorkeeper of Music*: "Alick Yorke sang comic songs, one of them in a flannel petticoat bestowed upon him by the Queen after she had insisted on his giving his famous impersonation of herself in her own presence, as a *douceur* [kindness] after the reproof she felt bound to utter in words that have often been quoted." Another story, one of many more, has the Queen saying "we are not amused" upon seeing an imitation of herself by the

Honorable Alexander Granthan Yorke, her Groom-in-Waiting. Richard the Lion-Hearted, incidentally, was the first king to use the royal *we* in place of *I*.

wearing calluses on his elbows. *Western Words* (1961) by Ramon F. Adams defines *wearing calluses on his elbows* as "spending time in a saloon." Similarly, an *elbow bender*, another term from the Old West, means a "drinking man," because he bends his elbow to convey his glass to his lips.

to wear the willow. An old expression, used but not invented by Shakespeare, *to wear the willow* means to go into mourning, especially for a sweetheart or spouse. The willow, especially the weeping willow, has because of its appearance long been associated with sorrow, regarded as "a sad tree." Robert Herrick wrote: "When once the Lovers Rose is dead . . . Then willow-garlands 'bout the head/ Bedewd with tears, are worne."

weasel words. "Weasel words are words that suck all of the life out of the words next to them just as a weasel sucks an egg and leaves the shell," a writer explained in the June 1900 issue of the *Century Magazine*. The writer then gives an example: "'The public should be protected.' 'Duly protected,' said Gamage, 'that's always a good weasel word.'" The term was applied to politicians in this first recorded use and has often been associated with politicians since then.

weber; Weberian apparatus; Weber's law. The *weber* is the practical unit of magnetic flux, named after German physicist Wilhelm Eduard Weber (1804-91). While a professor at the University of Göttingen, Weber worked with Karl Gauss on terrestrial magnetism, devised an electromagnetic telegraph, and did valuable research on electrical measurements—the *coulomb*, in fact, being once known as the *weber*. A politically committed teacher, he was dismissed from the university for protesting the king's suspension of the constitution. Weber's two brothers were also noted scientists. Wilhelm Eduard collaborated with his younger brother Eduard in 1833 on a study of human locomotion. With his elder brother Ernst he wrote a well-known book on wave motion published in 1825. This same Ernst Heinrich Weber (1795-1878), a physiologist and early psychophysical investigator, is the author of *Weber's law*, a mathematical formulation showing that the increase in stimulus necessary in producing an increased sensation depends on the strength of the preceding stimulus. The *Weberian apparatus*, small bones connecting the inner ear with the air bladder in certain fishes, honors Ernst too.

the web of life. Meaning the destiny of a person from birth to death, *the web of life* is an old expression that alludes to the three Fates of Roman mythology. These Fates are supposed to spin the thread of life, that is, the pattern in which events will occur.

Webster's. Noah Webster's name has become a synonym for a dictionary since he published his *Compendious Dictionary of the English Language* in 1806 and his larger *An American Dictionary of the English Language* twenty-two years later. But the "father of American lexicography" was a man of widespread interests, publishing many diverse books over his long career. These included his famous *Sketches of American Policy* (1785), on history and politics; *Dissertations on the English Language* (1789), advocating spelling reform; and *A Brief History of Epidemic and Pestilential Diseases* (1799). Webster also found time to edit *The American Magazine* and the newspaper *The Minerva*. Beginning in 1806, he lived on the income from his speller—which sold at the rate of over one million copies a year—while he took the twenty-two years needed to complete his monumental dictionary. *Webster's*, as it came to be called (it is now published as *Webster's Dictionary* by Merriam) helped standardize American spelling and pronunciation and recorded many Americanisms.

Wedgwood. (*See* **ode on a Grecian urn**.)

wedlock. (*See* **deadlock**.)

Wednesday. Traditionally a good day for planting crops in ancient times, *Wednesday* is named for Woden, the Old English name of Wotan, the Scandinavian god of agriculture, war, wisdom, and poetry. The Old English *Wodensdaeg*, or *Woden's day*, became our Wednesday.

weed. While a *weed* is really only an uncultivated flower, weeds are generally unwanted pervasive plants that are rooted out from gardens. The word *weed* itself, recorded in one form or another since the ninth century, comes from the Old English *wiod*, a variant of an early Saxon term for "wild."

the Weeping Philosopher. The Greek Heraclitus (d. ca. 475 B.C.) was called *the Weeping Philosopher*, this *agelast* (*q.v.*) so labelled because he grieved at the folly of mankind. His opposite was Democritus of Abdera (fifth century B.C.), called the *Laughing Philosopher* because he laughed contemptuously at mankind's feeble powers.

the Weeping Saint. St. Swithin of *St. Swithin's Day* (*q.v.*) fame is called *the Weeping Saint* because of the tradition of forty days' rain if it rains on his day, July 15th.

weevil. (*See* **boll weevil**.)

we have the receipt of fern seed, we walk invisible. These words, from Shakespeare's *I Henry IV, iv,*

4, were widely believed in medieval times. Because the seed of some fern species was invisible to the naked eye, it was thought to confer invisibility on anyone who carried it.

weigela. The long-popular *Weigela* genus of the honeysuckle family, containing some twelve species, is named for German physician C. E. Weigel (1748-1831). *Weigela*, sometimes spelled *weigelia*, is often grouped with the *Diervilla* genus, the bush honeysuckle, but its bushes have larger, much showier flowers than the latter. *Diervilla* itself is named for a Dr. Dierville, a French surgeon in Canada. Native to Asia, the *weigela* bush is easily cultivated in America and Europe. Its funnel-shaped flowers are usually rose-pink but vary in color from white to dark crimson.

weigh anchor. *Weigh* in this phrase derives from the Old English *wegan*, "to carry or move," which later came to mean "lift" as well. Thus the expression means to lift or haul up the anchor. It is more correct, however, to say *under way* to describe a ship in motion.

welfare. Welfare, in the sense of financial assistance for the poor and needy, goes back only about eighty years. It seems to have first been used in this sense in Dayton, Ohio, in 1904, according to the *Westminster Gazette* (January 28, 1905) and Ernest Weekley's *Something About Words* (1935).

well, back to the old drawing board. Few would suppose that this very common expression for a resigned unruffled reaction to the failure of plans of any kind derives from a cartoon caption. It almost certainly does: from a 1941 Peter Arno cartoon in *The New Yorker* which shows an airplane crash, the plane mangled, rescue squads working frantically, and the plane's designer, plans under his arm, musing aloud, "Well, back to the old drawing board." *Partridge* says it's used "when one has to make an agonizing re-appraisal" and traces it "probably" to World War II aircraft designers.

well, I declare! This expression is hardly used today, but was common among our grandparents, who also used *I declare to goodness!*, which was considered a rather strong term! Both expressions probably date back to 16th-century England, or earlier.

well, if that don't take the rag off the bush! A Southern Americanism originating in the late 19th century, this expression refers to outrageous behavior, as lowdown as stealing the rags or clothes someone in the swimmin' hole has left spread out on a bush.

well-heeled. Before *well-heeled* meant "well provided with money" in American slang, it meant "well provided with weapons." Back in frontier days men who went "heeled" carried a gun, the expression apparently deriving from a cockfighting term meaning to provide a fighting cock with an artificial spur before he went into the pit. *Well-heeled* is recorded in this sense as early as 1867 and it wasn't until over a decade later that it took on the meaning it has today, perhaps because men found that it was easier and safer to protect themselves with money than with guns. In any case, *well-heeled* is not simply the opposite of *down at the heels*, someone so hard pressed for money that his shoes are run down at the heels.

Wellington. Napoleon's greatest adversary fares as well in the dictionaries as he did on the battlefield. Arthur Wellesley, the first duke of Wellington, who began his army career in India and was knighted for his victories there, drove the French from Spain during the Peninsular War and completely crushed Napoleon at Waterloo in 1815. One of England's greatest soldiers, "the Iron Duke" served as prime minister from 1828-30 and in 1842 was made commander in chief of the British armed forces for life. About the only blemish on his record was his aristocratic opposition to parliamentary reform, which caused his ministry to fall. Wellington died in 1852, an idolized old man of eighty-three, and it is said that even death "came to him in its gentlest form." A number of hats, coats, and trousers were named after the great soldier, as were two types of boots: The full Wellington riding boots, which were tight-fitting and came up slightly over the knee, and the half-Wellington, which came halfway up the calf, having a boot made of patent leather and a top of softer material. One apocryphal story has it that Queen Victoria once asked the duke the name of the boots he was wearing. When he replied that they were called *Wellington's*, she remarked, "Impossible! There could not be a *pair* of Wellington's!" The capital of New Zealand is also named for Wellington, as well as the *Wellingtonia*, a New Zealand sequoia. The duke took his title from the town of Wellington in England, where a statue of him stands today. (*See* **beef Stroganoff; beef Wellington.**)

a well-made play. Apparently this expression, for "an entertaining, carefully constructed play with more attention given to plot than characters," is a literal translation of the French *pièce bien faite*, which was applied to the well-made plays of Scribe and Sardou in the 19th century.

welsh. England's native Celts were called *wealhs*, "foreigners"—by the invading Saxons, of all people—and driven off into the western hills. *Wealhs* became Welsh in time and these inhabitants of Wales suffered almost as much abuse at the hands and tongues of the English as did the Scots or Irish. Their traditional enemies used *Welsh* to signify anything poor, such as a *Welsh comb*, the fingers, a *Welsh carpet*, a painted floor, and *Welsh rabbit*, melted seasoned cheese poured over buttered toast. To *welsh*, or renege, on a bet is another contemptuous English reference to the Welsh. The most common explanation is that there were thought to be a great many crooked Welsh bookmakers at the racetracks in the 19th century, *Welshers* or *welshers*, who did not pay when they lost. Names of individual bookmakers, such as a Mr. Bob Welch, have also been suggested, but with no positive proof or identification. *Walnut*, an ancient word, comes from the Anglo-Saxon *wealhhnutu*, meaning "the foreign or Welsh nut." Kinder terms using the Welsh prefix include three breeds of dogs—the *Welsh corgi, springer spaniel*, and *terrier*; the *Welsh poppy*, with its pale yellow flowers; and the small sturdy *Welsh pony*, originally raised in Wales. (*See* **Welsh rabbit**.)

Welsh rabbit. *Welsh rarebit* is entirely wrong as the name for melted seasoned cheese poured over buttered toast. But rather than being an affected, mannered corruption of the correct Welsh rabbit, it is a well-meaning, if misdirected, attempt to remove a slur on Welshmen from the language. The term *Welsh rabbit*, an example of country humor dating back to Shakespeare's time, conveys the idea that only people as poor and stupid as the Welsh would eat cheese and call it *rabbit*, while the much later *Welsh rarebit* of restaurant menus makes the Welsh dish a rare and tasty bit. *Rarebit*, therefore, is an artificial, invented word used in no other connection. (*See* **welsh**.)

we Polked you in '44; we shall Pierce you in '52! This is my favorite of the interesting political slogans interspersed throughout this book. It was the slogan of the Democratic Party in 1852, when dark horse Franklin Pierce did indeed "pierce" the Whigs to become the 14th President of the U.S., just as James Polk had beaten them in 1844.

West Virginia. West Virginia is composed of forty western mountain counties that seceded from Virginia at the outbreak of the Civil War, these counties voting not to secede from the Union and forming their own state government. After rejecting New Virginia, Kanawha, and Alleghany, the new state settled on *West Virginia* for a name, an ironic choice since Virginia extends ninety-five miles farther west than it does. West Virginia had considered seceding from Virginia several times, due to unequal taxation and representation, and the Civil War provided an excellent excuse. Its constitution was amended to abolish slavery and President Lincoln proclaimed *West Virginia* the thirty-fifth state in 1862, justifying his action as a war measure. Called the *Panhandle State*, it has an odd outline, leading to the saying that it's "a good state for the shape it's in." (*See* **Virginia**.)

wet behind the ears. *He's still wet behind the ears* would refer to someone as innocent in the ways of the

world as a newborn baby. The American expression goes back at least a century and refers to the traditional belief, which may be true, that the last place to dry on newborn animals such as calves and colts is the small indentation behind each ear.

wet hen. (*See* **mad as a wet hen**.)

wetting a commission. *Wetting a commission* was an old naval custom, dating back over a century, which consisted of giving a party to a naval officer who had just received his commission. The parchment commission was formed into a cornucopia, filled with champagne, and drunk from as it was passed from hand to hand.

wet your whistle. *Whistle* has been slang for the mouth (because we whistle with it) since Chaucer's time—"So was her jolly whistle wely-wet," he wrote in "Reeve's Tale" (ca. 1386). This explains the phrase *wet your whistle*, "have a drink," very simply, but although the derivation is certain, people keep inventing stories for the expression—all very interesting, all untrue. One old theory makes "wet" a corruption of "whet," while another conjures up an imaginary tankard that whistled for more liquor when it was empty—to *wet your whistle*, according to this yarn, deriving from the pouring of more liquor into the tankard to stop its damn whistling.

we wuz robbed. When Jack Sharkey won a decision over Max Schmeling in 1932 to take the world heavyweight championship, Schmeling's manager Joe Jacobs grabbed the radio fight announcer's mike and shouted "We wuz robbed!" to a million Americans, his words still a comic protest heard from losers in any endeavor. Jacobs's *I should of stood in bed* is even more commonly used in fun. He said it after leaving his sickbed to watch the 1935 World Series in Detroit. According to John Lardner's *Strong Cigars and Lovely Women* (1951), *Bartlett's* is wrong in saying Jacobs made the remark to sportswriters in New York after returning from Detroit, and it had nothing to do with his losing a bet that Detroit would win the Series. Jacobs made the remark, Lardner says, in the press box during the opening game of the Series, when "an icy wind was curdling his blood" at the coldest ballgame anyone could remember.

whaling. Two centuries ago a *whaling*, "a terrible beating," was one given with a whalebone whip. Or possibly, both the whalebone whip and the wales it raised on the skin contributed to the phrase, making it more vivid. Riding whips were commonly made of whalebone in the 18th and 19th centuries and were used to beat more than horses. *Whalebone*, incidentally, is a misnomer: It's not made from the bone of a whale but from a substance found in the whale's upper jaw.

wham bam (thank-ye-ma'am). *Thank-ye-ma'am* is an American courtship term that dates back to the 19th century. Roads at the time had diagonal earthen ridges running across them that channeled off rainwater from the high to the low side and prevented washouts. Rural Casanovas driving their carriages along these rude roads made sure that they hit these ridges hard so that their female companions would bounce up in the air and bump into them. With the head of his sweetheart so close, the gentleman could steal a kiss and usually express his gratitude with a *Thank ye ma'am*, that expression becoming synonymous for a quick kiss or for any hole in the road that caused riders to bump up and down. It wasn't long before some wit took this innocent phrase to bed, or to the side of the road somewhere, and elaborated on it, for in 1895 we find recorded the related expression *wham bam (thank-ye-ma'am)* for quick coitus. As a matter of fact, the first recorded use of both expressions occurs in that year.

what are you, a man or a mouse? There are similar phrases in German and many other languages, and this expression, in a rudimentary form, dates back at least to 1541, when it came from the mouth of a woman, as it often still does today: "Fear not, she saith unto her spouse, a man or a Mouse whether ye be."

what a way to run a railroad! This phrase seems to have first been printed as the caption of a cartoon in a 1932 *Ballyhoo* magazine, wherein an American signalman looks out from his signal box at two trains about to collide and says coolly, "tch, tch, what a way to run a railroad!" But the expression which is now directed at any organized chaos, may date back to the turn of the century, according to the recollections of several word enthusiasts who remember hearing it that far back.

what fools these mortals be. (*See* **puckish.**)

what hath God wrought. These words constitute the first public telegram, sent by Samuel F.B. Morse over an experimental 40-mile line constructed between Washington, D.C. and Baltimore, Maryland on May 24, 1844. There had been telegraphs before Morse's but his was the first electromagnetic telegraph. (*See* **telegraph.**)

what's good for General Motors is good for the country. Former head of General Motors Charles E. Wilson didn't say this when testifying before a Senate committee in 1953 when nominated for Secretary of Defense. The words have become proverbial, but what Wilson said was less arrogant: "I thought that what was good for our country was good for General Motors, and vice versa."

what's new?; what's with you? The greeting *What's new?* has been traced back to 1880s New York. It is

thought to be a translation of the *was ist los?* ("what's the matter?") of German immigrants, as is the similar expression *what's with you?*

what's what. (*See* **to know what's what.**)

what time does the next swan leave? According to the old story, a boat drawn by a swan used in a performance of Wagner's *Lohengrin* was pushed onto the stage before the actor playing Lohengrin could get into it. The perfectly composed tenor quipped: "What time does the next swan leave?" This famous remark has been attributed to a number of famous singers over the years, but it actually goes back to the first tenor to sing the role, over a century ago.

what we gave we have. These wise old words are a loose translation of lines by the Roman poet Martial, which seem to have first appeared as an epitaph on "the good Earl of Courtenay" in the 17th century:

What wee gave, wee have;
What wee spent, wee had;
What wee left, wee lost.

what will be will be. (*See* **store.**)

wheatear. The name of this Old World thrush originally had nothing to do with "wheat" or "ears." First recorded in 1591, *wheatear* comes from the Anglo-Saxon *hwitt,* "white," and *eeres,* "ass," in reference to its white rump. *Wheat* later replaced *hwett* in its name because the bird "came when the wheat was yearly reaped."

wheat germ. (*See* **germ.**)

wheeler dealer. In gaming houses of the 18th-century American West a big wheeler and dealer was a heavy bettor at cards and the roulette wheels. Through this tradition, and the association of a *big wheel* as the man (or wheel) who makes the vehicle (things) run, the expression came to mean a big-time operator by the early 1940's, usually with an unsavory connotation, the *wheeler dealer* being the type who runs over anything in his path with no regard for rules of the road.

when in doubt win the trick. (*See* **according to Hoyle.**)

when in Rome do as the Romans do. This was St. Ambrose's advice to St. Augustine when the latter consulted him as to the proper day of the week to fast. He and his mother were confused because in Rome Italians fasted on Saturday, whereas in Milan they chose another day, and St. Ambrose said: "When I am in Milan, I do as they do in Milan; but when I go to Rome, I do as Rome does!"

when hemp is spun, England's done. Francis Bacon, despite his scientific training, gave the following interpretation of the above prophecy, which he had heard as a child. *Hempe*, he explained, is an acrostic, a word formed from the first letters of the names of five of England's rulers: *Henry*, *Edward*, *Mary* with *Philip*, and *Elizabeth*. When the last one of them, Elizabeth, died in 1603—when Hempe was spun, or finished—England was done, for the new king, James, was not called King of England, but the King of Great Britain and Ireland.

when it hits the fan. This expression "indicative of grave consequences" is of course an expurgated version of *when the shit hits the fan*. Common in the U.S. since about 1930, it is traced by some to the punch line of an old joke. *Partridge*, however says the original reference is to "an agricultural muck-spreader," without further elaboration.

when my ship comes in. *When my ship comes in* dates from several centuries ago, when shipping completely dominated commerce. Many merchants made great profits selling cargo for which they had traded in distant parts of the world and from which they were assured of fortunes if their ships made it back into home port.

when the cat's away the mice will play. (*See* **Chinese language**.)

when the cocqcigrues come. In French legend the *Cocqcigrues* (kok-se-groo) are fantastic creatures unlike animals anybody has ever seen. Thus when the French say *A la venece des Cocqcigrues* ("at the coming of the cocqcigrues") they mean "never." The same meaning is sometimes conveyed in English with *When the Cocqcigrues come*. The word is sometimes spelled *Cocquecigrue*.

where's the fire? "What's your rush?" this phrase inquires when directed at a rather busy person or someone hurrying along. The Americanism is first recorded in the 1920s, but must have been in use before this. *Where's the fire?* may even date back before the invention of the gasoline fire engine in the 1890s, to the days of horse-drawn "fire engines."

whig. England's *Whig* political party, supplanted by the Liberal Party in the late 19th century, was the party opposed to the Tories (*q.v.*), being generally a less conservative group in favor of more democratic government. Its name derives from the obsolete *whiggamore*, a nickname for Scots who drove wagons to Leith to purchase corn, *whiggamore* deriving from *whiggam*, a Scottish expression meaning *Git up*!, addressed to horses. Bishop Burnet explained the origin of the term in *Our Times* (1723): "The south-west counties of Scotland have seldom corn enough to serve them all the year round, and, the northern parts producing more than they used, those in the west went in summer to buy at Leith the stores that came from the north. From the word *whiggam* used in driving their horses, all that drove were called the *whiggamores*, contracted into *whigs*. Now, in the year before the news came down of Duke Hamilton's defeat, the ministers animated their people to rise up and march to Edinburgh; and they came up, marching to the head of their parishes with an unheard of fury, praying and preaching all the way as they came . . . . This was called the 'Whiggamor's Inroad'; and ever after that, all who opposed the court came in contempt to be called *whigs*. From Scotland the word was brought into England, where it is now one of our unhappy terms of dissension." There was also a Whig Party in the U.S. from 1824-54, headed by Henry Clay and Daniel Webster.

whipping boy. Because royalty was considered sacred, or possibly because he was born frail and sickly, the son of England's Henry VIII, the young prince who became King Edward VI when only nine years old, had a whipping boy to take all his punishments for him. Barnaby Fitzpatrick, a sturdy lad, was flogged every time Edward deserved chastisement, whether it be for botching his Greek lessons or insulting an archbishop. Despite this early form of national health insurance, Edward died of consumption in 1553 at the age of sixteen, the commoner Fitzpatrick surviving all his floggings and living to a comparatively old age. Anyway, the practice of princelings employing commoner whipping boys wasn't unusual in Europe four or five centuries ago; Fitzpatrick is only England's first recorded one. When the common practice ceased in more democratic times, it left us with the expression *whipping boy* for a scapegoat, someone punished for mistakes committed by another—especially an official or worker punished for the wrongs of his superior.

whiskey. *Whiskey*, first recorded in 1715, is the spelling used by the Irish, Americans, and French, while the English spell the stuff *whisky*, as do the Germans. Call for whiskey in almost any country in the world and you'll get what you want—a truly universal word that is an Anglicized version of the Gaelic *uisgebeatha*, "water of life." (*See* **gin; martini; scotch; vodka**.)

whiskey courage. (*See* **pot valor**.)

the whiskey is all right but the meat is weak. Computers will never take the place of human translators, as the above illustrates. It is said to have been produced recently by an electronic translator as a translation of *the spirit is willing but the flesh is weak*! (*See* **a blind idiot**.)

white bread. Relatively recent slang, *white-bread* means "bland," or "white middle-class values." It goes back to the 1970s, first recorded in 1977, when *Newsweek* reported that a top black comedian walked off a Las Vegas stage "fed up with doing white bread humor." The expression may have black origins, but this is not certain. It may also be partly a pun of *white-bred*, but it mostly refers to the synthetic white bread of the supermarket, without flavor or character.

white-collar worker; blue-collar worker. *White-collar worker*, dating back to about 1920, means anyone who performs nonmanual labor; it especially indicates salaried office workers and lesser executives who haven't been unionized. His or her opposite in America is the *blue-collar worker*, anyone who works with his or her hands, is usually unionized, and often works for an hourly wage. The *white-collar worker's* counterpart in Britain is called a "black coat." All of these designations were obviously suggested by working attire, just as a "hard-hat," a construction worker, takes his or her name from the protective helmets such workers wear.

whited (painted) sepulchre. Someone who pretends to be morally better than he really is. The expression is from the Bible (Matt. 23:27): "Woe unto you, scribes and Pharisees, hypocrites! for ye are unto whited sepulchres, which indeed appear beautiful outward, but are within full of dead men's bones, and of all uncleanness."

white elephant. The King of Siam, who held the title Lord of the White Elephants, was once considered the owner of all the rare albino elephants in his kingdom, and since they were sacred to him, only he could ride or work one of them. When he wanted to punish a courtier he simply gave a white elephant to him—the beast eating his luckless victim out of house and home. This story is thought to be the source of our expression *a white elephant*—any possession, especially a big house, that is useless, eats up money, and can't be gotten rid of—even though no one has ever found any firm evidence of a King of Siam indulging in any such maleficent munificence.

the White Fleet. In 1907 the United States decided to show the world we were a great naval power by sending 16 battleships and four destroyers on a world cruise. Because all these ships were painted white, they were popularly called the *White Fleet*, or *Great White Fleet*.

White House. Designated the Palace by its architect, the Washington, D.C. residence of U.S. presidents was painted white after being gutted by a fire that darkened its gray Virginia limestone. The designation *White House* is first recorded in 1811, but Teddy Roosevelt made the term an official title by using it on his stationery. Today, of course, it is also a synonym for the Presidency and the U.S. executive branch.

white list. (*See* **blacklist**.)

white-livered. (*See* **lily-livered**.)

white meat. (*See* **dark meat**.)

the White Queen. This designation has nothing to do with Mary Queen of Scots' complexion. She is called *The White Queen* because she wore white mourning clothes after the death of her French husband Francis II.

white rhinoceros. The white rhinoceros of Africa is misnamed, for it is slate gray in color. The white rhino takes its first name from the Dutch *wijd*, "wide," for its wide upper lip and muzzle, this corrupted to *white* over the years. (*See also* **Rhinoceros**.)

whodunit. Two writers for the show business paper *Variety* are usually proposed as the coiners of the word *whodunit*, for "a mystery story": Sime Silverman, in 1936, or Wolfe Kaufman in 1935. But the term wasn't invented by either of them. Daniel Gordon used whodunit in the July 1930 *American News of Books* and probably used it first.

whiz. (*See* **onomatopoeia**.)

whole hog. Probably the expression *to go the whole hog*, or *to go whole hog*, "to go the limit, all the way," has its origins in William Cowper's poem "The Love of the World Reproved; or Hypocricy Detected" (1779). Cowper told a story about pious but hungry Muhammadans who were ordered by Muhammad not to eat a certain unspecified part of the pig. Unable to determine what part, they began to experiment:

> But for one piece they thought it hard
> From the whole hog to be debar'd;
> And set their wit at work to find
> What joint the prophet had in mind . . .
> Thus, conscience freed from every clog,
> Mohometans eat up the hog . . .
> With sophistry their sauce they sweeten,
> Til quite from tail to snout 'tis eaten.

The words *whole hog* and the idea of *going whole hog* are in the poem, but other writers have different ideas about the expression's origins. One links it with the Irish nickname "hog," for a shilling—parsimonious Irishmen in bars were urged to *go the whole hog* (spend the whole shilling) on drink. Another theory says that the *hog* in the phrase was originally a sheep not a hog. Young sheep were called hogs and had to be clipped very carefully because they hadn't been shorn before. Workers were warned not to be careless, to clip the whole animal, or *go the whole hog*, do the job thoroughly.

the whole kit and caboodle. The *caboodle* in this American expression meaning "the whole lot," is the same as the word *boodle*, for "a pile of money," deriving from the Dutch *boedal*, "property." The *whole kit*, of course, means entire outfit. The phrase doesn't read "the whole kit and boodle" because Americans like alliteration in speech and added a "k" sound before boodle in the phrase.

the whole nine yards. For at least thirty years this expression has meant "all of it, everything," as in "Give me the whole nine yards." It did not arise in the garment business but among construction workers, the *nine yards* referring to the maximum capacity a cement-mixer truck can carry—nine cubic yards of cement. I haven't seen this phrase recorded elsewhere.

wholesale; retail. Both of these terms have their origins in the cloth trade. *Wholesale* initially meant to sell whole pieces of cloth, while *retail* derives from a French word meaning to cut up (*tailor*, similarly, means "a cutter"), *retailer* coming to mean anyone who sold anything in small, cut-up lots.

the whole shebang. The earliest recorded use of *shebang* is by Walt Whitman in *Specimen Days* (1862), and Mark Twain used it several times as well. Meaning a poor, temporary dwelling, a shack, this Americanism possibly derives from the Anglo-Irish *shebeen*, "a low illegal drinking establishment," older than it by a century or so. In the expression *the whole shebang*, first recorded in 1879, *shebang* means not just a shack but anything at all, that is, any present concern, thing, business—as in "You can take the whole shebang," you can take all of it.

whoops! Traced only to 1925 by the O.E.D. (Volume IV, Supplement, 1986), *whoops* may be considerably older, though there is no proof of this. It is, of course, an exclamation of dismay or surprise when one stumbles or recognizes a mistake one has made. The expression first appeared in a *New Yorker* cartoon, in the form of *whoops-a-daisy*; it isn't recorded as *whoops* until 1937, in one of Ezra Pound's letters, of all places.

whoosh. *Whoosh*, as an exclamation evocative of a sudden explosive rush of sound (it is used by one television sportscaster presently to indicate a basketball shot going through the hoop), is first recorded in 1899 and is probably older. The term is an Americanism with limited British usage and is an example of *onomatopoeia (q.v.).*

"who reads an American book?" British author Sydney Smith almost set off a full-scale literary war when he asked this famous sardonic rhetorical question in a book review he wrote for the *Edinburgh Review* in 1820. Smith, however, had been reviewing the *Statistical Annals of the United States* by Adam Seybert and was on his way toward making an ironic point that has little to do with literature, as the last paragraph of his essay shows: "In the four

corners of the globe, who reads an American book? or goes to an American play? or looks at an American picture or statue? What does the world yet owe to American physicians or surgeons? What new substances have their chemists discovered? or what old ones have they analyzed? What new constellations have been discovered by the telescopes of Americans? What have they done in mathematics? Who drinks out of American glasses? or eats from American plates? or wears American coats or gowns? or sleeps in American blankets? Finally, under which of the tyrannical governments of Europe is every sixth man a slave, whom his fellow-creatures may buy, and sell, and torture?"

whortleberry. *Whortleberry* originated as the dialect form of *hurtleberry* in southwestern England. *Hurtleberry*, however, remains a mystery etymologically speaking, though there have been attempts to link the *hurt* in the word to the fact that the blue berry could resemble a small black and blue mark or "hurt," on a person's body. Both words refer to the berry *Vaccinium myrtillus* of the blueberry family, and our word *huckleberry* probably derives from *hurtleberry*-which makes Mark Twain's famous character, perhaps aptly, "Hurt" Finn.

who watches the watchdogs? These ancient words take many forms, but derive from the Roman saying *Quis custodiet custodes?*, which means "the shepherd watches over the sheep, but who keeps watch over the shepherds?" The expression is used to indicate doubt about the integrity of someone in a position of trust.

who won't be ruled by the rudder must be ruled by the rock. This saying isn't found in the *Oxford English Dictionary*, *Bartlett's Familiar Quotations*, or any other major collection of quotations. Dating back at least a century, it means "those who won't listen to reason must bear the consequences, like a ship that runs upon a rock if it will not answer the helm."

why should the devil have all the good times? English composer Charles Wesley (1707-88) reputedly said this. The author of over 6,500 hymns, Wesley put the words of them to popular tunes of the day to insure their popular appeal. Many of these hymns, including the famous "Hark! the Herald Angels Sing," and "Christ, the Lord, is Risen Today," are still great church favorites.

wickiup. Indians in Colorado and California sometimes lived in crudely constructed huts called *wickiups*, improvised structures made of brush, saplings, or both. Cowboys often used the word in referring humorously to their own homes.

wide-awakes. *Wide-awakes* were young Republicans, some 400,000 in number throughout the country, who avidly supported Abraham Lincoln for president in 1860.

The group originated in Hartford, Connecticut, and was named for the hat members wore. The hat was made of a fabric that contained no "nap"—hence the pun *wide-awake*.

a wide place in the road.   Truckers popularized this synonym for a very small town. But the phrase was born over a century ago in the American West, where there were many towns so small they were not even on the map.

the Widow.   *The Widow* is often encountered in literature as slang for champagne, the words a corruption of the name of the excellent Veuve Cliquot brand. This usage dates back to Victorian times, when the *widow* was also slang for "the gallows."

widow maker.   Rudyard Kipling is the first writer to record *widow maker* as a synonym for the sea, in *Puck of Pook's Hill* (1906): "What is a woman that you forsake her . . . To go with the old grey Widow-maker?" *Widow maker* was used by Shakespeare for a killer in general, however, and it seems likely that the term was used before Kipling to describe the great elementary force that made widows of so many sailors' wives.

widow's peak.   A point formed by the hair growing down and meeting in the middle of the forehead is called a *widow's peak*. The term, which dates back at least to the 19th century, derives from the earlier *peak*, for "the point of a beard," and possibly from the pointed or peaked hoods that old women sometimes wore. Superstition had it that women with widow's peaks would become widows at an early age.

widow's walk.   A *widow's walk* is an elevated observatory on a dwelling, usually with a railing and affording a good view of the ocean. These watchtowers, often seen on the roofs of old houses, date back to Colonial times and were so named because many women walked in vain on them, waiting for incoming ships that never returned. Taking the form of a cupola, railed-in deck or balcony, they have also been called, less poetically, *the walk, the captain's walk, the observatory,* and *the lookout.*

widow's weeds.   The *weeds* here aren't plants but simply clothing of any kind, deriving from the Anglo-Saxon word for garment—*waede. Widow's weeds,* of course, means mourning garments, the black often worn by widows. The expression contributes the only use of *weeds* for clothing remaining in English, but the word was used by Spenser, Shakespeare, and many other writers for the clothing of both men and women.

wigging.   To be dressed down, reprimanded by a superior. The phrase dates back to the 18th century, when most important people wore wigs. Scoldings from such people were, of course, commonplace.

the wild and woolly West.   Everyone knows that the frontier of the American West was wild, sparsely settled, and lawless, but how did *woolly* get into the expression above. Theories abound: the "woolly," or unshaved, faces of cowboys might have suggested it; or the woolly angora chaps cowboys sometimes wore; or their shaggy sheepskin coats; or perhaps the wool of sheep grazing on the open range. Possibly just the alliteration of the three *w*'s in the phrase is responsible. The first use of the expression, in an 1885 book called *Texas Cow Boy,* has *wild and woolly* referring to a herd of steers.

wildcat.   A wildcat venture, such as a wildcat oil well, is generally a speculative one. The word *wildcat* here comes from the term *wildcat bank,* which originally referred to a Michigan bank that went bankrupt in the 1830s and had on its banknotes a prominent picture of a panther or wildcat.

Wildean.   For the British writer and wit Oscar Wilde (1854-1900). His much publicized affairs and trial made his first name a British slang expression for a homosexual, *to Oscar, Oscarizing,* and *Oscar-Wilding,* in fact, meaning active homosexuality. Wilde is also represented by *Wildean,* referring to his razor-sharp wit. In this respect he was probably even greater than George Bernard Shaw. Once Wilde told a customs inspector that he had nothing to declare but his genius; another time he remarked to some proud chamber of commerce types that Niagara Falls "would be more spectacular if it flowed the other way."

wild-goose chase.   Englishmen in the late 16th century invented a kind of horse race called the wild-goose chase in which the lead horse could go off in any direction and the succeeding horses had to follow accurately the course of the leader at precise intervals, like wild geese following the leader in formation. At first the phrase *wild-goose chase* figuratively meant an erratic course taken by one person and followed by another; Shakespeare used it in this sense. But later the common term's origins were forgotten and a *wild-goose chase* came to mean "a pursuit of anything as unlikely to be caught as a wild goose," any foolish, fruitless, or hopeless quest.

wild man of Borneo.   (*See* **there's a sucker born every minute.**)

wild oats.   (*See* **sow one's wild oats.**)

Williamson.   "The terrible *Williamsons*" have fleeced so many people in recent years that their name has become a generic term for itinerant hustlers. An inbred clan of gyp artists numbering about 2,000, the family descends from Robert Logan Williamson, who emigrated from Scotland to Brooklyn in the 1890s and soon imported his relatives. Today the wandering clan makes its headquarters and major burial grounds in Cincinnati, a crossroads city, or at least they meet there once a year in the spring to bury their dead, exchange notes, and renew friendships. There is not a nonviolent hustler's trick unknown to the Williamsons, from resurfacing a homeowner's driveway with crankcase oil—and departing across the county line with the payment before the next rain washes the "blacktop" away—to an attractive Williamson woman selling her "dead mother's valuable Irish linen" door to door in order to "buy milk" for a baby conveniently bawling in her arms. The family still does well, despite many newspaper and magazine exposés of their cons.

William Tell's apple.   According to fable, William Tell was a famous marksman and the champion of Swiss independence when Switzerland was ruled by Austria in the 13th century. Tell refused to salute the imperial governor and was sentenced to shoot an apple from his son's head. After doing this, another arrow fell from his coat and the governor demanded to know what it had been intended for. "To shoot you with, had I failed in the task imposed upon me," Tell told him and he was cast in prison, from which he was rescued and went on to lead his country to freedom. There are at least ten earlier versions of the tale involving other countries and heroes, the oldest found in the Old Norse *Vilkinia Saga*.

willy-willy; willywaw.   A *willy-willy* is a severe tropical cyclone common to Australia that can be seen approaching in a high column of dust from a great distance. The word is probably an Australian Aboriginal term for the phenomenon, but *Partridge* suggests that *whirlwind* became *whirl*, which became *wil*, which became *willy!* *Willywaw* are squalls in the Straits of Magellan, but light, variable winds elsewhere at sea, the word either deriving from *willy-willy* above or as a corruption of *whirl-whirly*.

wimp.   Weak, unmanly, indecisive men have been called *wimps* since the 1970s and the term is still frequently used. Although the *Popeye* cartoon character Wimpy (of hamburger fame) may have influenced the coinage, it more likely comes from *whimper*.

win, place, and show.   A term for the horses that finish first, second, and third in a race, *win, place, and show* originated at early U.S. racetracks where small boards were used to record the names of the first three finishers of every race. These boards were so small that only the names of the first two finishers were "placed" on the first board, *place* thus becoming the name for the number two horse. A second board was used to "show" the name of the third finisher and *show* became the common term for third place.

Winchester.   The Model 73 Winchester rifle, made in 1873, is the prototype for all the famous *Winchester* models now extensively used for hunting. The first Winchester, however, was made in 1866. Oliver F. Winchester (1810-1880) manufactured the rifle at his plant in New Haven, Connecticut, the weapon based on a number of patents the industrialist had acquired from different inventors. This early repeater became generic for any repeating rifle and was widely used on the frontier. The Winchester, a lever-action rifle with a tubular magazine in the forestock, became the standard repeating rifle mechanism; the Winchester Arms Company, which still operates today, has been a unique eminence in its field for many years.

Winchester geese.   In the 16th century prostitution and geese raising were two major Winchester industries and British prostitutes were called *Winchester geese*, probably because they seemed almost as ubiquitous in the area as the birds. The first part of their name may honor the bishop of Winchester, however, as the brothels in Southwark were under his jurisdiction, and the Church received rent from many establishments based in houses he owned. These revenues, incidentally, helped found and maintain a number of esteemed Oxford colleges. A *Winchester goose* also came to mean a venereal bubo (sore), or anyone infected with venereal disease.

windfall.   Unexpected good fortune has been called a *windfall* since the early 16th century. The expression has its origins in the medieval English law that forbade commoners from cutting down trees but allowed them to keep any trees or branches that the wind blew down.

windjammer.   A *windjammer* meant a "horn player," then came to mean a "talkative person or windbag," and finally, at the end of the 19th century, was the name for any ship with sails. It seems that windy defenders of sailing vessels at the beginning of the age of steamships boasted so much about the superiority of sail that they were called *windjammers* and their name soon became attached to the sailing ships they bragged about.

windmills in one's head.   (*See* tilt at windmills.)

window.   "An eye of the wind" is the meaning of the Old Norse *vindauga* (*vinde*, "wind," plus *auga*, "eye"), which gave us our word *window*. The poetic word appropriately suggests a window's function of letting in both air and light. Shakespeare made *window* a verb in *Antony and Cleopatra* when he had Antony ask: "Wouldn'st thou be windowed [put in a window] in great Rome?" The Old English for *window* was *eyethirl*, "eye hole."

Windy Cap.   Laplanders of yore and many other ancient peoples made a profitable trade in selling favorable winds to mariners, as did individuals like Bessie Millie of the Orkney Islands, who sold winds to sailors for sixpence as late as 1814. These people undoubtedly had knowledge of the weather that others didn't have at the time, but the belief persisted that they could actually influence the winds. It is said that King Eric of Sweden was so familiar with the "evil spirits" that controlled the winds that wherever he turned his cap, the wind would blow. Olaus Magnus, a Swedish historian, says he was commonly known as *Windy Cap.*

wine, women, and song. Despite Thackeray's tongue-in-cheek attribution, this famous phrase, and the couplet of advice to men that it comes from wasn't written by Martin Luther! German poet Johann Heinrich Voss wrote the little poem in about 1775:

Who does not love wine, women and song
Remains a fool his whole life long.

And Byron wrote:

Let us have wine and women
mirth and laughter
sermons and soda-water the day after.

to win hands down. A jockey who wins a race *hands down* is so far ahead of the field that he doesn't have to flick the reins to urge his horse forward and crosses the finish line with his hands down, letting up on the reins. From racetrack slang toward the end of last century the metaphor *to win hands down* passed into general use for any easy, effortless victory, a walkover.

win one for the Gipper. This one is so well known, of course, because President Ronald Reagan played George Gipp, or the Gipper, in a movie about Knute Rockne and his football team at Notre Dame (*Knute Rockne, All American*, 1940). Rockne urged his team to go out and "win this game for the Gipper," who on his deathbed had requested that the team win a game in his honor—and Notre Dame proceeded to do it. Actually, Gipp had made this request of Rockne in 1920 when dying of pneumonia and the coach had used the same appeal several other times before the 1928 game with heavily favored Army that is depicted in the film.

win one's spurs. The allusion here is not to cowboys of the American West but to those days four centuries before when knighthood was in flower and young men dubbed knights by their lords were presented with a gilded pair of spurs. Since then the expression *to win one's spurs* has been extended from the idea of a knight performing a valorous act and winning honor to anyone performing any deed and gaining honor among his peers—from a doctor delivering his first baby to an author publishing his first book.

winter bloom. (*See* **witch hazel**.)

wirepuller. (*See* **spoils system**.)

Wisconsin. Wisconsin takes its name from the Algonquian name for a river within its boundaries that translates as either "place of the beaver" or "grassy place." The Badger State was admitted to the Union in 1848 as our 30th state.

wisdom teeth. (*See* **cut one's eyeteeth**.)

wiseacre. The old story says that Ben Jonson put down a landed aristocrat with "Where you have an acre of land, I have ten acres of it," and that the gentleman retorted by calling him "Mr. Wiseacre." Acreage doesn't figure in this word, however. *Wiseacre* has lost its original meaning, having once been the Dutch *wijssegger*, "a wise-sayer, soothsayer, or prophet," which is apparently an adaption of the Old High German *wizzago*, meaning the same. By the time *wijssegger* passed into English as *wiseacre* in the late 16th century such soothsayers with their know-it-all airs were already regarded as pretentious fools.

the wisest man of Greece. Socrates was declared *the wisest man of Greece* by the Delphic oracle. He said he deserved the honor "because I alone of all the Greeks know that I know nothing." His remark may be the basis of many similar sayings, such as the commonly heard *The longer I live the more I realize how little I know.*

wisteria. A spelling error made by Thomas Nuttal, curator of Harvard's Botanical Garden, led to the accepted misspelling of this beautiful flowering plant—*wisteria* being the common spelling today even though *wistaria* is correct. Nuttal, who named the plant after Dr. Caspar Wistar, had meant to write "wistaria," but his slip of the pen was perpetuated by later writers and *wisteria* has become accepted. All attempts to remedy the situation have failed, even Joshua Logan's play *The Wistaria Trees*, in which the author purposely spelled the word with an *a*. A Philadephia Quaker, Caspar Wistar (1761-1818) taught "anatomy, mid-wifery, and surgery" at what was then the College of Pennsylvania. The son of a noted Colonial glassmaker, Dr. Wistar wrote America's first anatomy textbook, succeeded Jefferson as head of the American Philosophical Society, and his home became the Sunday afternoon meeting place of many notable Philadelphians. Anyone in the vicinity of Sierra Madre, California in the late springtime should see the giant *Chinese wisteria* near the Los Angeles State and County Arboretum. During its five-week blooming period this giant species becomes a vast field filled with over one and a half million blossoms, the largest flowering plant in the world. Planted in 1892 the fabulous vine covers almost an acre, has branches surpassing 500 feet in length, and weighs over 252 tons.

witches weigh less than a Bible. When Jane Wenham was tried as a witch in 1712 she was set free because people at her trial insisted that she be weighed. A true witch always weighed less than a Bible, according to British superstition, and Jane weighed considerably more than the twelve-pound church Bible of the day.

witch hazel. Witch hazel solution is extracted from the leaves and bark of the witch hazel shrub. This plant, in turn, might take its first name from the fact that its branches were often used as divining or dousing rods to locate water. The *O.E.D.* however, believes that the *witch* here comes from the anglo-Saxon *sych*, meaning a tree with pliant branches. Witch hazel (Hamamelis) are not true hazel trees. They are also called winter bloom because they bloom from October to April when their twigs are bare. The *cuckold hazel*, also called the beaked hazel, is a *true hazel* of the genus *Corylus*, and takes its name not because wives betrayed their husbands under it but because of its long hornlike fruits, which someone centuries ago compared to a cuckold's horns.

with a heart and a half. A lovely old Irish expression of thanks, first recorded in 1636. "Once more to you with a heart and a half," wrote the first man to record this expression, in ending a letter to his sweetheart.

with all deliberate speed. Chief Justice Earl Warren used these words in the historic *Brown* v. *Board of Education* decision of May 17, 1954, when the Supreme Court ruled that all public schools be integrated and racial discrimination be ended in them *with all deliberate speed.* Oliver Wendell Holmes, however, recorded the words first, in 1912.

within an ace of. Dice, not cards, gave us this expression for "coming as close as one can get," the "ace" in the phrase referring to the ace, or small point, on a single die. Originally the expression was *within ambsace of,* "ambsace" being a mispronunciation of the Old French for the lowest possible throw in dice—*ambes as* ("both aces"). But by the 17th-century "ambsace" was further corrupted to "an ace" and the phrase became *within an ace of.* *Ambsace* itself was long a figurative term for bad luck. Today *snake eyes* is better known as the lowest throw in dice.

without rhyme or reason. Francis Bacon wrote that Sir Thomas More, chancellor to Henry VIII, once told a friend who had versified a rather poor book he had written: "That's better! It's rhyme now, anyway. Before it was neither rhyme nor reason." But More's witty remark isn't the basis for our expression meaning lacking in sense or any other justification, fit for neither amusement nor instruction. Used in English since the early 16th century, the phrase is simply a translation of the medieval French saying, *na rhyme ne raison.*

with tail between legs. When the expression was figuratively applied no one knows, but it must have been long ago, for as early as 1400 writers have described frightened dogs with their tails between their legs. The attitude of scared, cowardly dogs was transferred to any thoroughly cowed and abased person who stands back *with tail between legs.* The word *coward* is ultimately from the Latin *caudal,* "tail"; it may be an allusion to an animal cowering with its tail between its legs or "turning tail" and running.

witticism. John Dryden coined *witticism* in his play *The State of Innocence, and Fall of Man* (1677), a dramatic version in rhymed couplets of *Paradise Lost* said to be written with Milton's permission, but which was never performed, though the immoderate Dryden considered it "undoubtedly one of the greatest, most noble and most sublime poems which either this age or nation has produced." The first official poet laureate and royal "historiographer" was immoderate in his wit, too—but he did not pen the acid remarks about John Wilmot, the second earl of Rochester, that Wilmot thought Dryden had written in 1679. Thinking he had, however, the furious Wilmot hired a band of masked thugs who severely cudgeled the poet. The prolific Dryden based *witticism* on the earlier *criticism,* writing: "A mighty Wittycism (if you will pardon a new word!) but there is some difference between a Laughter and a Critique."

woe-begone. *Woe-begone* people, those oppressed with misfortune, distress, or sorrow, have been so called since before Chaucer's time. The word is a combination of *woe* (q.v.) and *bigon,* "beat," as is illustrated by the Old English sentence "Me is woe bigon" ("I am beset with woe").

woe is me. *Woe,* first recorded in about 725, has been called "a truly international exclamation of sorrow." The world has always been full of woes, including the Latin *vae* (*vae victus,* "woe unto the conquered!"), the Welsh *gwoe,* the Gothis *wai,* the Armenian *vae,* and the Old Persian *avoi,* among many, many others. The still common expression *woe is me*! is first attested to in 1205 and is probably much older.

wog. Arabs, Indians, and Orientals were called *wogs* by the British during the heyday of their Empire, or at least since about 1930, the derogatory appellation *wog* said to be a word formed from the first letters of *wily* (or *westernized*) *Oriental gentleman.* Another, *O.E.D.* suggestion is *gollywog,* "with reference to frizzy or curly hair," *wog* "indeed being a nursery shortening of *golliwog.*"

a wolf in sheep's clothing. One of the oldest of expressions, still used in many languages, *a wolf in sheep's clothing* dates back to biblical times, being recorded in

Matt. 7:15: "Beware of false prophets, which come to you in sheep's clothing, but inwardly they are ravaging wolves."

wolfsbane. (*See* **aconite.**)

woman. Etymologically, *woman* has no connection with *man*. The word *woman* derives not from *man*, but from the Old English *wif-man*, *wif* meaning "female" and *man* meaning "human being." *Man* derives from the Old English *mannian* meaning the same.

woman of Babylon. (*See* **babble.**)

woman and children first. For more than a century this saying has been part of the unwritten law of the sea—women and children shall be saved before anyone else in the event of a disaster—and in the vast majority of cases, the words have been gallantly honored. The saying seems to have arisen, anonymously, after H.M.S. *Birkenhead* went down off the Cape of Good Hope in 1852 and 491 men were lost while all the women and children aboard were saved and a great tradition was born.

wong. *Wong* here is not a Chinese word, as might be expected, but an old English word meaning meadowland, often used as a commons, that derives from the German *wang*, "mountain slope." First recorded in *Beowulf*, the word's only use today is in British place names and designations of certain fields and common lands.

woodchuck. (*See* **groundhog.**)

wooden nickels. (*See* **don't take any wooden nickels.**)

wooden walls. *Wooden walls* is an old term for England's warships, which protected the country from invasion like a great wooden wall in the water that the enemy could not get by. The term, however, had been used long before the English first recorded it in 1598, for Themistocles called the ships of ancient Athens "wooden walls." *Our watery and wooden walls* was an English variation on the phrase.

woolgathering. In the past, and perhaps even today, people wandered the countryside gathering bits of wool from hedges and bushes that sheep had brushed against. These actual "woolgatherers," often children, went about their work aimlessly, often frolicking in the fields, never able to do their job systematically because the sheep were scattered all over. There wasn't much money to be gained in such an occupation, either. So as far back as the 16th century this literal woolgathering suggested our expression *woolgathering*, meaning unprofitable or trivial employment, absentminded inattention, purposeless thinking, or aimless reverie.

wop. (*See* **dago.**)

word association test. (*See* **Jungian.**)

word for word. As one would expect, this is a very old expression for "exactly" or "precisely," Chaucer first recording it in about 1385: "I could folwe word for word Virgile."

word of honor. One might think that this phrase, for "a solemn promise," goes back to those days when knighthood was in flower. But so far as is known it only dates to 1814, when it is recorded in Donat H. O'Brien's *Narrative Containing an Account of His Shipwreck, Captivity and Escape from France*: "They suspected we were deserters . . . We assured them upon our word of honour, they were very much mistaken."

a word to the wise. So old is this expression that it probably goes back beyond the Latin *verbum sapienti* that it is a translation of. *Verbum sapienti* is so well-known in British university usage that it is commonly rendered as *verb. sap.* there. *A word to the wise (is enough)* is recorded in English as early as the 15th century. An old variant is *a word to the wise suffices*.

workaholic. American pastoral counselor Wayne Oates coined the word *workaholic* for "an uncontrollable need to work incessantly," in 1971, from *work* and *alcoholic*. Himself a workaholic who discovered his sickness only when his "five-year-old son asked for an appointment to see him," Oates published his *Confessions of a Workaholic* in 1972. There have since been many similar but less popular constructions, including *bookaholic* (1977), *wordaholic* (1978), and *hashaholic* (1973), someone who uses a lot of marijuana.

workers of the world, unite! The communist slogan has its counterpart in every language of the world. It comes from the first page of *The Communist Manifesto* (1848) by Karl Marx and Friedrich Engels.

work into a lather. When we tell someone "Don't work yourself into a lather" over something, we mean don't get hot and bothered, don't get angry or worried. *Lather* derives from the Anglo-Saxon word for washing soda or foam and has long been used to describe the flecks of foam on a heavily perspiring horse. From the notion of a horse worked into a hot and bothered state came our expression, probably in the mid-19th century.

to work like a navvy. To work hard at physical labor. The word is *navvy* here, not *navy*, and means laborer. A *navvy* was a man who worked on the many canals that were excavated in England starting in the mid-18th century. These canals were called "navigations" and a laborer working on one was dubbed a "navigator," this soon being shortened to *navvy*.

work like a Trojan. (*See* **a regular Trojan.**)

the world is my oyster. All the pleasures and opportunities of life are open to somone because he is young, rich, handsome, successful, etc. Shakespeare invented or popularized this expression in *The Merry Wives of Windsor* (1600): *Falstaff*: I will not lend thee a penny. *Pistol*: Why, then, the world's mine oyster which I with sword will open.

World War I. No one *knew* that World War I was only the first world war until 1939, when World War II started, but wise men and cynics began using the term even before World War I was over, the phrase being coined in 1918 before the armistice! World War I had another common name: *The War to End All Wars* (*q.v.*). Over 10 million killed and 20 million wounded in *The Great War*, as it was also called, is a conservative estimate, yet this was less than half of those to be killed in World War II. Before the U.S. entered World War I in 1917 it was called *The Great European War*.

wormwood. Since there is nothing wormy about it, why is the herb so named? The best theory is that the "worm" in the word is from the Teutonic *wer*, for "man" and the "wood" from *mod*, the Teutonic for "courage." By this account the word was originally *wermod*, meaning "man's courage," in reference to the herb's supposed aphrodisiacal and healing properties. Absinthium, the classical wormwood, is an ingredient of absinthe, which has probably killed more people than it has sexually inspired. Tarragon is also one of the wormwoods.

to worship the golden calf. One who *worships the golden calf* sacrifices his or her principles for money or personal gain. The expression is biblical in origin, referring to the golden calf made by Aaron that the Israelites worshipped while Moses was absent on Mount Sinai (Exodus, 23), a sin for which they paid dearly.

worth his weight in gold. At present gold prices a person weighing 150 pounds who was literally worth his weight in gold would be worth nearly $1 million. To say someone is *worth his weight in gold* is to say he is an extremely valuable person to the enterprise at hand. The phrase has been traced back to at least 1705, when Joseph Addison, writing about a statue in Italy, said: "It is esteemed worth its weight in gold."

wouldn't touch it with a ten-foot pole. This expression may have been suggested by the ten-foot poles that river boatmen used to pole their boats along in shallow waters. Possibly the expression was first something like *I wouldn't touch that with the ten-foot pole of a riverman* and that this shortened with the passing of pole boats from the American scene. However, the image first appears in the Nantucketism *can't touch him with a ten-foot*, meaning "he is distant, proud, reserved." In the sense of not wanting to get involved in a project or having a strong distaste for something, the words aren't recorded until the late 19th century.

Wreck of the Hesperus. A huge submerged rock off the coast of Gloucester, Massachusetts caused so many shipwrecks in the 18th century that it was called Norman's Woe. Wrote Henry Wadsworth Longfellow in his diary for December 17, 1837: "News of shipwrecks horrible on the coast. 20 bodies washed ashore near Gloucester, one lashed to a piece of wreck. There is a reef called Norman's Woe where many of these took place; among others the schooner *Hesperus* . . . I must write a ballad upon this." The ballad proved to be "The Wreck of the Hesperus," which became so well known that "wreck of the *Hesperus*" also became an expression for any battered or disheveled thing, as in "You look like the wreck of the Hesperus."

Wrens; Waves; Spars. An acronym for the Women's *Royal Naval Service*, *Wrens* was coined in Great Britain during World War I and is the first acronym invented for a woman's naval unit. The *Waves*, Women Accepted for Voluntary Service, seems more labored but worked during World War II. The most ingenious of such inventions is *Spar*, an acronym for the Woman's reserve of the U.S. Coast Guard Reserve (World War II), which was constructed from the Coast Guard motto: *Sempter Paratus, Always Ready.*

wrong side of the bed. (*See* **get up on the wrong side of the bed.**)

wrong side of the tracks. This American expression arose in the 19th century when railroad tracks, which sometimes split a town in two, provided a clear social demarcation—well-to-do people living on the right side of the tracks and the poor living on the wrong side, in the slums or seedy area of town. Today the expression *to be born on the wrong side of the tracks*, "to be born poor and disadvantaged," hangs on despite the fact that the physical distance between rich and poor has increased and that they now tend to live in different towns or counties altogether.

Wrong-Way Corrigan. Douglas "Wrong-Way" Corrigan *may* have gone the wrong way unintentionally. The 31-year-old pilot flew from California to New York in a record time of less than 28 hours and took off the next day in his battered plane to return to California. His plane had no radio, beam finder or safety devices, and had failed safety inspections, which would indicate that he had no plans for a publicity stunt. But even though extra gas tanks blocked his view, it is hard to explain how, after he took off in a westerly direction over Jamaica Bay, near the present Kennedy International Airport in New York, he swung his plane in a wide arc and crossed the Rockaway Peninsula, heading out over the Atlantic Ocean. Presumably, he flew through a thick fog, convinced he was California-bound until the fog lifted that fine morning of July 18, 1938 and he looked down at the grass roofs and cobblestoned streets of Ireland! Corrigan told officials at Dublin's Baldonnel Airport that he had accidentally flown the wrong way and he promptly became known as *Wrong-Way Corrigan*. As a result he became a hero, made close to $100,000, and even played himself in *The Flying Irishman*, a movie based on his "mistake." When asked recently if he had really meant to fly to California, Corrigan replied, "Sure . . . well, at least I've told that story so many times that I believe it myself now."

wuzzy. A good example of how the English have fractured French over the centuries is the London teenage slang *wuzzy*, for "a girl." It was coined in the 1960s from the French word for bird (*bird* being English slang for "girl"), which is *oiseau*.

Wyoming. *Wyoming* comes from the Algonquian *Mache-weaming*, meaning "place of the big flats," actually a west Pennsylvania valley where a pre-Revolutionary Indian massacre had occurred that was celebrated in the popular sentimental poem "Gertrude of Wyoming." It became the name of several U.S. counties and in 1890 that great name-giver Congressman James M. Ashlet bestowed it upon our 44th state ("The Equality State") because it was "a beautiful name," never thinking that "place of the big flats" hardly suited this mountainous western state.

X

X. The twenty-fourth letter in our alphabet represents the fourteenth letter of the Greek alphabet, *ksi*. The Romans used *X* to denote the number ten and *x* in mathematics generally means "an unknown quantity." One theory holds that the *X* stands for a kiss because it originally represented a highly stylized picture of two mouths touching—*x*. Furthermore, in early times illiterates often signed documents with a St. Andrew's cross of *X* and kissed that *X* to show their good faith (as they did with any cross or the Bible), which reinforced the association. But these explanations may be folk etymology, as may the story that mathematically the *X* is a "multiplier"—in this case of love and delight.

Xanthippe. Legend paints Socrates' wife Xanthippe as the classic shrew and her name has become proverbial for a quarrelsome, nagging, shrewish woman. In *The Taming of the Shrew* Shakespeare writes: "Be she as foul as was Florentius' love,/ As old as Sibyl, and as curst and shrewd/ As Socrates' Xanthippe, or a worse,/ She moves me not." The gossips in Athens talked much of Xanthippe's terrible temper and she may have literally driven Socrates out into the open and his marketplace discussions. But then Socrates may have been a difficult husband, and by most accounts is said to have been unusually ugly and uncouth in appearance. Xenophon writes that Xanthippe's sterling qualities were recognized by the philosopher, and various historians, including Zeller in his *Vortrage and Abhandlungen* (1875), argue that she has been much maligned, that Socrates was so unconventional as to tax the patience of any woman, as indeed would any man convinced that he has a religious mission on earth. (*See* **henpecked**.)

Xanthus. In the *Iliad*, Achilles' immortal horse Xanthus, who takes his name from the Greek for "reddish gold," weeps when Achilles' gentle friend Patroclus, who had taken Achilles' place on the battlefield, is killed by Hector while leading the Myrmidons into battle. When Achilles reprimands him for leaving Patroclus on the field of battle, Xanthus reproachfully tells his master that he will soon die, through no fault of his horse but by the decree of inexorable destiny. It is not likely that Xanthus gave his name to the Xanthus River, the ancient name of the Scamander. The river was probably called Xanthus because legend held that it colored the fleece of sheep washed in its waters a reddish gold. (*See* **Bucephalus; Peritas** and **Bucephela**.)

xebec. *Xebec* is a small three-masted vessel once used by pirates on the Mediterranean. Also called *zebec*, or *chebec*, and deriving ultimately from the Arabic word *shabbak*, the vessel is today used to a small extent in commerce.

xeme. The xeme (pronounced "zem") is the fork-tailed arctic gull familiar to maritime explorers and adventurers. It was first observed in Greenland by a British mariner in 1832.

xenia. *Xenia* were the gifts, usually delicacies from the table, that subjects in the Middle Ages presented to their prince when he passed through their estates. The Romans and Greeks had a similar custom, offering xenia to guests and strangers passing by, and the word, in fact, derives from the Greek for "guest or stranger." The singular is *xenium*.

xenophobia. Meaning an unreasonable fear or hatred of anyone or anything foreign or strange, *xenophobia* derives from *xeno*, a learned borrowing from Greek meaning "alien" or "strange," and *phobia*, fear. The word is a relatively new word, first recorded in 1912.

xenotine. When this mineral was discovered it was thought to be a new metal, but that thought proved to be in vain. Thus it was named, a short time later in 1832, from the Greek word for "empty, vain," in reference to the dashed hopes of its discoverer.

Xerox. U.S. inventor Chester Carlson invented the Xerox machine in 1938 and *Xerox* remains a trademark of the company that makes it, its name deriving from *xero*, a learned borrowing from the Greek for "dry," and *graph*, an element from the Greek meaning "drawn, written." Inventor Carlson became a multimillionaire from royalties on his dry copier, the rights to which he sold to what is now the Xerox Corporation in 1947.

Xerxes' tears. The Persian conqueror Xerxes I (Zerksez) was a despot with a great heart, according to one legend. When he was about to invade Greece he is said to have reviewed his huge army and wept at the thought of the slaughter about to take place, saying sadly, "Of all this multitude who knows how many will return?" *Xerxes tears* came to mean a commander's concern for the lives of his troops.

X marks the spot. Now a catchphrase applied to any triviality, *X marks the spot* began life as a common caption under crime photographs in newspapers indicating the exact spot where the murder, etc., occurred. The expression dates back to England early in this century.

Xmas. *Xmas* is neither an abbreviation nor a "vulgar commercial invention" of recent vintage. *X* has been used to symbolize the syllable "Christ" in English since at least 1100, when it was recorded in *Xianity,* for "Christianity." The Old English word for Christian recorded in the 12th-century *Anglo-Saxon Chronicle* begins with an *X,* and the word *Xmas* itself was used as early as 1551. The Greek word that gives us the English word Christ begins with the letter *chi,* or *X,* leading some writers to believe that the *X* in *Xmas* symbolized the cross.

x-rated. In 1968 the Motion Picture Association of America began to rate films as a guide for moviegoers. Their system ranged from *G,* "general, all ages permitted," to *X,* "restricted, no one under 17 admitted." The *X* rating referred to explicit sex and violence in a movie and became so common that *x-rated* almost immediately became a term for anything pornographic or sexy, from a film to a book or even a person!

x-ray. (*See* **roentgen ray**.)

XX. *XX* was slang for a twenty-dollar bill back in the 19th century. The term seems to have originated in about 1850, a variation on it being the *double X.*

XXX. Bottles marked with *X*s, for "booze in cartoons," have their basis in reality. Nineteenth-century British breweries marked bottles *X, XX,* or *XXX* to indicate alcoholic content—the more *X*s, the more kick. (*See* **X** for *XXX*s used for kisses.)

xylophage. Any *xylophage,* which takes its name from the Greek *xylo,* "wood," and *phagein,* "to eat," is a wood-eating insect, such as a termite. The adjective *xylophagous* means "feeding on wood" and usually refers to the teredo worm and other crustaceans, mollusks, and fungi that perforate or destroy timber.

xylophone. An *xylophone,* the word first recorded in 1866, is composed of the Greek *xylo,* "wooden," + *phone,* "voice or sound," the "wood," of course, referring to its flat wooden bars, which are played by a small mallet. When tubular resonators are attached to these bars the instrument is called a marimba.

XYZ Affair. In 1797 President John Adams sent three representatives to France to negotiate a maritime treaty that would prevent French pirates from attacking American ships. But three of Talleyrand's agents (identified only as X, Y, and Z) intercepted them and demanded a $1-million "loan" for France before they would be received by the French government. The agents refused to negotiate on these terms and returned home. One of them, Charles Cotesworth Pinckney, allegedly uttered the slogan "Millions for defense, sir, but not one cent for tribute." Pinckney, however, always claimed he only said: "No, no, no! Not a single sixpence!"

Y

Y. Our letter *y* can be traced back to the Greek alphabet, the Greeks having added it to the Phoenician alphabet. It is called *the Samian letter* after Pythagoras (the Samian Sage, born at Samos in the sixth century B.C.) because the Greek philosopher employed the letter (also called the *Letter of Pythagoras*) as his emblem of the straight and narrow of virtue, "which is one, but, if once deviated from, the farther the lines are extended the wider becomes the breach."

yacht. *Yachts* were originally pirate ships. This pleasure craft takes its name from a type of speedy German pirate ship of the 16th century called the *jacht* that was common on the North Sea. British royalty found that this type of vessel made excellent pleasure boats a century later, spelling the German word *yaught*, which finally became *yacht.*

yackety-yak; ya-ta-ta. *Yackety-yak*, "idle pointless talk," and *ya-ta-ta*, "chatter or empty conversation," both mean about the same thing and are both probably imitative of the sound of such talking, though possibly influenced by *yap* (*q.v.*) *Yack*, for such talk, is first recorded in about 1870, while *ya-ta-ta* probably originated in the 1930s. *Yackety yack* also means laughter and a *yack* has been American slang for a laugh since the late 19th century.

yahoo. Bestial or brutish people are called *yahoos*, after the Yahoos in Jonathan Swift's satire *Gulliver's Travels*, nauseating hateful beasts in human form who prefer "nastiness and dirt." Eric Partridge suggested that Swift may have coined the word after *yah!* and *who?* —"*yah!* being typical of coarse ignorance and brutality, and *who?* of defiance." Other possibilities are (1) the name of "the Cariban tribe the Yahos, on the coast near the borderline of Brazil and French Guiana"; (2) "the name of a degraded East African tribe often mentioned by early travelers"; and (3) "a learned pun by Swift on a Greek word sounding like *yahoo* that meant sleepy, or "dopey."

yak. (*See* **polo**.)

Yale blue; Yale lock. *Yale blue*, a reddish blue, takes its name from the Yale University colors. It is the royal blue of the Egyptian Rameses dynasty, also called Rameses. *Yale lock* has no connection with the school. American inventor Linnus Yale (1821-68) invented numerous locks,

including the trademarked key type with a revolving barrel that bears his name. Linnus founded a company to manufacture locks at Stamford, Connecticut the same year that he died.

Yale University. *Yale University*, ranking after Harvard and William and Mary as the third oldest institution of higher education in the United States, is named for English merchant Elihu Yale (1649-1721). Founded in 1701 as the Collegiate School of Saybrook, Connecticut, the school was named Yale College at its 1718 Commencement, held in the first college building at New Haven. It became a university in 1887. Yale might have been called Mather University, for Cotton Mather suggested naming it so in return for his financial support, but Elihu Yale won out when he donated a cargo of gifts, books, and various goods that brought about 562 pounds when sold. Yale had been born in Boston in 1649, but returned with his family to England three years later. He served with the British East India Company, and as governor of Fort St. George in India until scandals in his administration led to his removal in 1692.

y'all. The American Southernism *y'all*, "you all," has been explained as a *calque* ("a filling in of an African structure with English material") from the West African second person plural *unu*, which is also used in the American black Gullah dialect. This interesting theory is advanced in a study by Jay Edwards in Hancock and Decamp's *Pidgins and Creoles . . .* (1972): "In the white plantation English of Louisiana, the form *y'all* functioned precisely as did the *unu* of the slaves. The use of *y'all* (semantically *unu*) was probably learned by white children from black mammies and children in familiar domestic situations."

yam. *Yam* can be traced back to the Senegal *nyami*, meaning "to eat," and was introduced to America via the Gullah dialect *njam*, meaning the same, in 1676. The word, however, had come into European use long before this. (*See* **Dioscorea**.)

yank. *Yank*, to pull abruptly or vigorously, is of uncertain origin. A U.S. invention, probably originating in New England early in the 19th century and much used since then, it has nothing to do with the word *Yankee* (*q.v.*), for a New Englander. It may be akin to the English dialect word *yerk*, a variant of *jerk*, but there is no proof of this.

Yankee. The most popular of dozens of theories holds that *Yankee* comes from *Jan Kee* ("little John"), a Dutch expression the English used to signify "John Cheese" and contemptuously applied to Dutch seamen in the New World and then to New England sailors. From a pejorative nickname for New England sailors, the term *Jan Kee*, corrupted to *Yankee*, was applied to all New Englanders and then to all Americans during the Revolution; the most notable example of this is found in the derisive song "Yankee Doodle." Nowadays, the British and Southerners use it for Northerners, and Northerners use it for New Englanders, who are usually proud of the designation.

yap. *Yap* is an echoic word that first meant only the barking of a small dog. The word is first recorded in this sense in 1603, and it apparently took over two centuries before *yapping* was applied to a person who *yaps* as well as a dog that *yaps*. In the process *yap* also became American slang for the mouth, as in *shut your yap*, recorded in about 1900, and American slang for a stupid person. The Yap Islands in the West Pacific, noted for the stone money long used by the Micronesians there, are not named from the English *yap*, taking their name instead from a native language.

Yarborough. Little is known about Charles Anderson Worsley, the second earl of Yarborough, aside from the fact that he was a knowledgeable card player and made himself a small fortune, giving 1,000 to 1 odds that his bridge-playing companions held no cards higher than a nine. The odds were with the English lord, for the chances of drawing such a thirteen-card hand are actually 1,827 to 1 against. Yarborough, born in the early 19th century, died in 1897, an old and probably rich man. Since his wagers, a *Yarborough* has been any hand in whist or bridge with no card higher than a nine, although the term also means a hand in which there are no trumps.

yardarm. A ship's *yard* (from the Anglo-Saxon *givid*) is a long, thin spar hung crosswise to the mast to support a square sail. The *yardarm* is simply one *arm* or part of this *yard*.

Yare. *Yare* (pronounced *yar*, which usually rhymes with far) has been around since the late 14th century as an expression for an easily manageable fine ship that answers readily to the helm. "Our ship is tyte and yare," Shakespeare wrote in *The Tempest*. Another famous literary use of the word occurs in Justin H. McCarthy's *A Ballad of Dead Ladies: After Villon, Envoy*:

Ou sont les neiges d'antan?
Alas for lovers! Pair by pair
  The wind has blown them all away;
The young and yare, the fond and fair;
  Where are the snows of yesterday?

In the poem *yare* is pronounced to rhyme with *fair*, as it sometimes is.

yarmulke. *Yarmulke*, the skullcap worn by Jewish males, is said by most dictionaries to be a Yiddish word that derives from a Tartar word, which in turn comes from the Polish word for skullcap. However, in an article published in the *Hebrew Union College Annual* (V.26, 1955) Dr. W. Gunther Plaut concludes that *yarmulke* derives ultimately "from the Latin *almucia* or *armucella*, the amice (vestment) worn by the priest." The theory that *yarmulke* derives from a Hebrew word meaning "awe of the king" is a nice story but only folklore. The skullcap is worn, of course, as a sign of respect before God, this a custom not only among Jews but practiced by many people of the East.

yarn. To *spin a yarn* was originally naval slang dating back to the early 19th century for "to tell a long, often incredible story." Its obvious source is the yarn lofts ashore where yarn was spun to supply ships with rope, work that took a long time and in which the threads of a rope were interwoven like the elements of a good story. Eventually *yarn* became a synonym for a story or tale itself.

yashmak. In case you've been looking for the word for the white or black double veil used to cover the whole face of Muslim women in public, or to hang just below their eyes, this is that word. *Yashmak*, from the Arabic *yashmaq*, for the same, isn't attested to in English until 1844. The first English writer to record the word noted that "the yashmak . . . is not a mere semi-transparent veil, but rather a good substantial petticoat applied to the face." *Veil*, first recorded in 1276, comes ultimately from the Latin *velum* for "covering."

yclept. *Yclept* is the only survivor, and a weary one at that, of many words formed with the prefix y—in Middle English. *Y* was simply used to make past participles, and so *yclest* was blessed, *yclad* was clothed, etc. *Yclept*, the last of these irregular English verb forms is just *y* attached to the old verb *clepe*, "call" and means "called (so-and-so), named, styled." It is abundant in the works of many Elizabethan poets and is occasionally still used humorously, when the writer knows he is affecting a literary archaism. John Taylor the Water Poet has a poem on birds *yclept*—"Wheat ears":

The name of Wheat ears on them is yclep'd
Because they come when wheat is yearly reaped.
  —1653

ye; ye olde gift shoppe. *Ye* served in the past as both the plural of "you" and as a mark of respect when talking to a single person, but has never meant "your" in English.

The "Ye's" on those signs adorning half-timbered Tudor-style establishments that read *Ye Olde Gifte Shoppe, Ye Olde Hot Dogge House*, etc., should actually be pronounced "the," not "ye," for that was what they meant in Ye Olde Englishe times. The letter *Y* in "ye" really is not a *Y* but a "thorn," the Anglo-Saxon symbol for "th." This Anglo-Saxon diphthong was originally written something like a *P*, but careless writers and sign painters in later years left it partially open at the side so that it came to resemble a *Y*, and early printers printed it as such. The "ye" in old manuscripts and signs was never pronounced as anything but "the" until modern times.

yeah.   *Yeah* is not a modern corruption of "yes" as many people believe. It is an old form of the affirmative still used in England's East Anglia dialect.

yegg.   *Yegg* can mean a safecracker, an itinerant burglar, a thief, or an insignificant criminal. The most common explanation has the word deriving from the surname of John Yegg, a late 19th-century American safe-blower whose life remains a blank. The word first appeared in print as *yeggmen*, "tramps," in 1901. Other suggestions for its source are the German *jager*, meaning "hunter"; *yekk*, a Chinese dialect word once used in San Francisco's Chinatown that means beggar; and the Scottish and English dialect *yark* or *yek*, "to break."

yellowbacks.   (*See* **greenbacks**.)

yellow-dog contract.   The yellow dog, generally considered to be a cowardly common cur or mongrel, has long been a symbol of utter worthlessness in America. The term *yellow dog* has been used in expressions of contempt since at least 1833, when it is first so recorded, and toward the late 19th century it began to be heard in the term *yellow-dog contract*, a contract in which company employees do not or cannot join the union. Though outlawed by the Wagner Act in 1935, yellow-dog contracts still persist.

yellowhammer.   This bird is named not for any hammer but from the earlier *yellow-ham* (Old English *geolu*, "yellow" + *hama* "covering"), in reference to its bright yellow markings. The European yellow bunting, as it is also called, was once believed to be cursed because it fluttered about the Cross and was stained by Christ's blood, which colored its plumage and marked its eggs with red forever after. In times past children were encouraged to destroy its "cursed eggs."

yellow journalism.   *Yellow* has been used to describe sensational books and newspapers in the U.S. since 1846, the "yellow" referring to the cheap yellow covers some sensational books were wrapped in. *Yellow journalism* was first used in 1898, when the phrase was applied to the sensational stories that appeared in Hearst's *New York Journal* and Pulitzer's *New York World* about Spanish atrocities in Cuba.

yellow pages.   The classified ad sections in telephone books which are printed on yellow paper in contrast to the white pages of the rest of the phone book, have been so called since 1906 when the Michigan State Telephone Company of Detroit first included such pages in its directory. *Yellow pages* has led to such recent coinages as the *Silver Pages*, telephone numbers of particular interest to older people or "senior citizens."

Yellow Peril.   Late in the 19th century fears arose in Germany that China and Japan would vastly increase in populaton within a few decades and would invade nations all over the globe, massacring the inhabitants. These irrational fears spread throughout Europe and America during the 1890s under the name of *the Yellow Peril*.

Yellowstone National Park.   The *Yellowstone* here is an anglicization of the French *roche jaune*, "yellow rock," which was probably a translation of the Minnataree Indian name *Mitsiadazi*, meaning the same.

Yemen.   This republic in southwest Arabia takes its name from the Arabic for "to the right," that is, to the right of the Mecca, the holy city in Arabia that is the birthplace of Muhammad. In ancient times it was called *Arabia Felix*, due to a mistranslation of *Yemen* by Ptolemy.

yen.   The *yen*, meaning an intense craving, and the *yen* that is a Japanese monetary unit could both derive from Chinese words. The *yen*, for a craving, possibly comes from the Pekinese *yen*, "opium" (though it may be an alteration of the noun *yearn* or *yearning*), and is first recorded in America toward the beginning of the 20th century. The *yen* that has been the Japanese monetary unit since 1875 derives from the Chinese *yuan*, "a circle or round object," hence a coin.

yenta.   Yiddish for a gossipy woman who talks too much, who talks nonstop relentlessly and can't keep a secret, *yenta* may derive from the name of some unknown blabbermouth called Yenta. The proper name Yenta for a woman probably derives from the Italian *gentile*. A talkative character named Yenta Talabenta in a play by Sholom Aleichem popularized this term.

yes-man.   In a 1913 cartoon the great sports cartoonist T. A. Dorgan depicted a newspaper editor and his assistants looking over sheets fresh from the press. The assistants, all praising the edition, are labeled *yes-men*, leading many authorities to credit TAD with the coinage. The expression quickly became a name for assistant directors in Hollywood (Wilson Mizner's "land where nobody noes"), *Variety* labeling one unfortunate director "super-yes-man," and was well known enough in general speech for *Yes-Man's Land* to be used as the title for a book in 1929. Another theory is that *yes-man* may be of German origin, a translation of *Jaherr*, "a compliant person, one unable to say no," which was used by a German author who wrote about America in 1877. In any case, Dorgan certainly popularized the expression.

yggdrasil. In Scandinavian mythology the *yggdrasil* is the *world tree*, an ash whose roots and branches bind together in heaven, hell and earth. Sitting in this fabulous tree from which honey drips, are an eagle, a squirrel and four stags; at its base is a fountain of wonders.

Yiddish words in English. Among the Yiddish words that have become part of American English are the common *kosher, kibitzer, chutzpah, schlemiel, schnook, schmuck, pastrami, matzo, lox, borscht, bagel, blintz, knish, nosh, gelt, mavin, mazeltov, mazuma, megillah, mensch, meshuga, nebbish, schlock, schmaltz, schnozzola, shamus, shekel, yenta, zaftig* and many, many more, some of which are treated at length in these pages. (*See* **Hebrew.**)

yoked. *Yoked* is today a synonym for "mugged." It arose with 19th-century "Jumper Jacks," or muggers, who preyed on seamen, who *yoked* a sailor by grabbing him from behind by the yoke of his tight collar and twisting his neckerchief.

yokel. The English green woodpecker was named the *yokel* because its call sounds like "yo-KEL, yo-KEL." Toward the beginning of the 19th century, people in England began calling country bumpkins *yokels* because they lived where the yokels sang.

York. New York (*q.v.*) is named for a Duke of York who ruled over York in England. The name *York* itself comes from the Celtic *Eburacon*, "the place of the yew trees." This became the Latin *Eburacus*, but to the Anglo-Saxons who ruled England after the Romans *Eburacus* sounded like *Eoforwic*, their "boar town," and to the Vikings who invaded after them *Eoforwic* sounded like *Iorwik*. Over the years *Iorwik* was shortened to *Iork*, which was finally transliterated into *York*.

Yorkshire pudding. Not a dessert pudding, but an unsweetened baked batter made of flower, salt, eggs, and milk that is often put under roasting meat to catch its drippings. *Yorkshire pudding* honors the county in northern England where it was invented or perfected, its name being first recorded in a 1747 cookbook.

you. (*See* **Quaker.**)

you bet! you betcha!, etc. *You bet!* means "surely, without a doubt, certainly" and has been a popular American expression of affirmation since the mid-19th century, the variants *you betcha!*, *bet your sweet ass!* and *you bet your sweet life!* being not much younger. The expression arose with the gambling-pioneering spirit in 19th-century America. *You bet your bippy!* is a comical play on the expression dating back to the 1960s, with the nonsense word "bippy" probably a euphemism for "ass." I believe the expression was invented for, or popularized by, Rowan and Martin's *Laugh In*—a television comedy show.

you can bet your bottom dollar. Originating out West about 1857, these words, meaning to bet one's last dollar or money, referred originally to the last silver dollar in a stack or hoard of coins and came eventually to mean the last of one's resources.

you can't cheat an honest man. W. C. Fields is responsible for this by now proverbial expression, not P. T. Barnum, as is sometimes reported. Fields, who once worked as a professional *drowner* (he faked drowning so that the concessionaires who hired him could sell refreshments to the crowds that gathered), did manage to cheat an honest man once in a while.

you can't con me. (*See* **con.**)

you can't make an omelet without breaking eggs. First recorded in 1859, this expression for "nothing can be accomplished without sacrificing something valuable," is a translation of the old French saying *on ne saurait faire une omelette sans caser des oeufs*. The word *omelet* is from the French *omelette*, which meant "a thin plate, the blade of a sword," the *omelet* named for its thin flat shape.

you can't make a silk purse out of a sow's ear. By painstakingly using both silk fibers and the skin or hair of a sow's ear, a man actually did make a silk purse out of a sow's ear a few years back. But the expression means you can't make something good out of something naturally inferior in quality. George Herbert was the first to record an approximation of the old saying in his *Jacula Predentum or Outlandish Proverbs* (1633), but Jonathan Swift first recorded it fully in *Polite Conversations* (1768).

you can whistle for it. These words, or *Go whistle for it*, mean "you won't get what you want from me, you might as well whistle for it and see if that does you any good." An old superstition among sailors held that a wind could be raised to aid a becalmed ship by whistling for it, making a sound like the wind. *Whistle for it* possibly arose from that practice.

you don't know the tune. Mark Twain's wife constantly tried to cure him of cursing. When he cut himself shaving one day, he launched into a tirade that included every four-letter word in his vocabulary and Mrs. Clemens tried shocking him by repeating every word he said. Mark Twain ended all such efforts by calmly saying, "You have the words, dear, but you don't know the tune."

youngberry. The *youngberry* is generally considered to be a hybrid variety of dewberry, which, in turn, is simply an early ripening prostrate form of blackberry. The large, dark purple sweet fruit has the high aroma and flavor of the *loganberry* (*q.v.*) and native blackberry. The youngberry was developed by Louisiana horticulturist B.M. Young about 1900 by crossing a southern dewberrry and trailing blackberry, or several varieties of blackberries. Its long, trailing canes are generally trained on wires. Popular in the home garden, the berry is extensively planted in the American Southwest, South, Pacific Northwest, and California.

young in (at) heart. This expression, meaning those emotionally and spiritually youthful, only dates back to the 1920s and is probably American in origin, but no more is known about it. A movie so entitled popularized the phrase in 1939.

Young Turk. A *Young Turk* is an insurgent within any group, such as a political party, supporting progressive policies. The latter phrase derives from the Turkish reform party that dominated Turkish politics from 1908-18. Many modern European methods were introduced by these Young Turks, who succeeded in making Turkey a republic.

you pays your money and you takes your choice. You might as well rely upon luck in a situation where there are similar alternatives. Most Americans would guess that the term is associated with carny talk or minstrel shows, but it is British in origin. Still much used humorously, this Cockney phrase has been traced to a short poem published in *Punch* in 1846:

What every please my little dears:
You pays your money and takes your choice
You pays your money and what you sees is
A cow or a donkey as you pleases.

you're not the only pebble on the beach. You're not the only woman or man available. This 19th-century expression became a common one with Harry Braistel's 1896 song of the same title.

you're pulling my leg. Early English hangmen were so inept that friends or relatives were permitted to pull on a victim's dangling body to end his suffering. This gruesome practice was once thought to be the origin of the humorous phrase *you're pulling my leg*, meaning you're fooling me, making fun of me, putting me on. Several word detectives worked overtime to establish the roundabout explanation for this, to no avail in the end, for it turned out that the phrase didn't go back to the days of blundering English hangmen at all; that misconception had been fostered by the misdating of the first quotation using the phrase, which appears now to have originated no earlier than the mid-19th century. Instead of being real gallows humor, the phrase seems to be connected somehow with tripping a person up. One theory is that British footpads or muggers worked in pairs, including a specialist known as a "tripper up." Using a cane with a curved handle or piece of wire, this tripper up would trip his victim so that his accomplice could pounce on him and relieve him of his wallet. Since this was a ruse and a leg was actually being pulled, it gave rise to the expression *you're pulling my leg*. This, too, is only a theory, however. The most we can say is that the phrase probably has some relation to somebody being tripped up or fooled.

Your Majesty. All English kings and queens are called *Your Majesty*, but the custom did not begin until the reign of Henry VIII. Previously, titles such as *His Grace, His Excellent Grace, His Highness*, and *High and Mighty Prince* had been used.

you-uns. *You-uns* and *you-all* (*see* **y'all**) are collective second-person pronouns found originally in southern U.S. dialect and nowhere else. The closest that has been found to them is the collective second person *you-together* that is sometimes heard in English East Anglia dialect today.

yo-yo. *Yo-yo*, for the child's toy that spins up and down on a string, was once a trademark. This was true in 1929 when a Chicago toymaker patented the toy and was granted the trademark *Yo-Yo*. The manufacturer had noticed a Filipino youth playing with such a toy on the streets of San Francisco and purchased it from him. In his application for the trademark he claimed that he had coined the word *Yo-Yo* after noticing that children often shout "You! You!" to each other when playing some games. All he had done was to strike the *u* from these words, he explained. In any case, the novelty sold millions, until a competitor marketed the same product under the same name. The Chicago manufacturer quickly brought suit for infringement of his trademark, but after hearing the evidence the court ruled against him. It seems that his competitor offered incontrovertible proof that he had been raised in the Philippines and as a boy had often played with a toy called a *yo-yo*. There was no doubt that the toy was of ancient Oriental origin and that it was long called by the Philippine name *yo-yo*. The court ruled that the trademark should never have been issued and today any manufacturer can use the term *yo-yo*.

Yttria.   (*See* **gadolinite**.)

Yucatan.   Though not proven, *Yucatan*, meaning "I don't understand you," is supposed to be the answer the Spanish explorer Francisco Fernandez de Cordoba received and recorded as a place name in 1517 when he asked a native the name of the area we know today as Yucatan. (*See* **indri; kangaroo; llama; Luzon; Nome**.)

yule.   *Yule*, which is akin to *jolly*, meant December or January in English before it meant Christmas, the word first recorded in 1726. In this sense it derives from an Old Norse word meaning one of the winter months. As a word for Christmas it probably derives from the Old Norse *jol*, the name of a heathen festival at the winter solstice.

yuppie.   *Yuppie* is a recent coinage of the last five or so years which apparently originated in the New York City area but already is nationally used. It means and is constructed from "*y*oung *u*rban *p*rofessional."

Z

Z. Z has been called *izzard, zed,* and *zee* in English. It has been considered useless by many writers, including Shakespeare, who wrote: "Thou whoreson Zed! Thou unnecessary letter!" It was the last letter in the Roman as well as the English alphabet.

zaluzania, Zaluzianskya. Polish physician Adam Zaluziansky von Zaluzian probably never dreamed that his long tongue twister of a name would be given to anything, yet it became the scientific designation for not one but two plant genera. *Zaluzianskya* (often spelled with an "ie" ending) is the beautifully fragrant night-blooming phlox, the genus embracing about forty South African species. While all such nocturnal flowers may bloom in the daytime, on overcast days, or toward evening, their finest flowering and greatest fragrance comes long after sunset. The Prague doctor, who published an important herbal, *Methodus Herbariae* (1602) has his last name honored by the genus *Zaluzania,* comprising about seven species of small shrubs with white or yellow flowers that are mainly grown in the greenhouse outside their native Mexico. Strangely enough, despite their long, scientific designations, neither genus seems to be known by any popular common name.

Zamzummin. *Zamzummin* is a synonym for giant ignored by American dictionaries, though the word has been used allusively and figuratively by writers like Sir Thomas More and Richard Burton for centuries. The original Zamzummins were a race of giants, "a people great, and many, and tall" mentioned in Deuteronomy.

zany. *Zanni* in Italian is the pet form of the proper name Giovanni (John). As early as the 16th century *zanni* meant a silly fool in Italian, perhaps for some Giovanni no longer remembered. In any case, the word *zanni* came into English, corrupted to *zany,* and became our word for the same and for anything ludicrously or whimsically funny.

zap. Appropriately enough, Buck Rogers' "paralysis gun" first made the sound *zap* back in 1929, when the character created by Philip Francis Nowlan made his appearance in comic strips. Coined by Nowlan, the onomatopoeic word soon became a verb meaning to kill or shoot someone. Since then it has taken on the added meanings of "to move quickly" and has become a noun meaning a blow, an argument, and even energy or power ("He's lost some of his zap").

za vasheh! This Russian drinking toast has some currency in the U.S. and England. *Za vasheh!* translates as "To yours."

zealot. The Jewish sect called the Zealots fiercely resisted the Romans until the fall of Jerusalem in *A.D.* 70. Their name thus came to describe a fanatical person who immoderately pursues his goals with great passion, the word *zealot* recorded in this sense as early as 1638. *Zealot* is ultimately from the Greek *zeloun,* to be zealous.

zebra. The African cross between a horse and ass could be named for the wind god *Zephyrus,* because of the animal's swiftness, but *zebra* most likely comes from the Abyssinian word *zebra,* for "the striped beast."

zenadia bird. (*See* **Bonaparte's gull.**)

zenith. In some obscure way unknown to scholars the Arabic *samt* in the term *samt ar-rar,* "way or path over the head," became the Greek *zenith,* which ultimately became the English term for the point of sky directly overhead, or, figuratively, "the highest point, the acme, the culmination or climax." The word is first recorded in 1387.

zephyr. A *Zephyr* is a soft, gentle breeze, taking its name from Zephyrus, the Greek god of the west wind. Shakespeare makes the first recorded mention of the word in this sense in 1611: "They are as gentle as zephires blowing below the violet, / Not wagging his sweet head."

zeppelin. After a career as a soldier that included a volunteer stint with the Union army during the Civil War, the intrepid German adventurer Count Ferdinand von Zeppelin retired from the German army with the rank of general and devoted himself to the development of dirigible airships. Zeppelin, inspired by a balloon ascent he made in St. Paul, Minnesota, built and flew his first rigid airship in 1900 when sixty-two years old, the initial flight lasting twenty minutes. But he had to build and test four Luftschiff Zeppelins in all before convincing the German government that his invention was militarily sound. *Zeppelins* came to be used extensively by the Germans in World War I, some eighty-eight of them constructed by their inventor at his factory in Friedrichshafen. Nevertheless, they didn't work out. Although they attained speeds of up to thirty-six miles per hour and were used to bomb Paris and London, the airships ultimately proved too unwieldly in combat. Count Zeppelin died in 1917, aged seventy-nine, the term *zeppelin* being used by then to mean any dirigible.

zero.   *Zero* derives from the Arabic *cifr*, meaning the same, which passed into Italian as *zefiro*, finally becoming *zero* in French and English. The word wasn't used in English for the arithmetical figure *o* until the early 17th century. The Arabic *cifr*, in turn, came from a Sanskrit word meaning "empty, nothing." Our word *cipher*, which meant "zero" before it meant a code, also derives from *cifr*.

zest.   In the 17th century the French called a piece of lemon or orange peel added to a drink to give it flavor a *zest*, a term that may have derived from the Latin *scistus*, "cut." *Zest* passed into English and came to mean anything agreeable or piquant in flavor and, finally, hearty enjoyment or gusto.

zeugma.   *Zeugma* is the Greek word for "yoking" or "joining" and in English means a figure of speech in which a verb is used with two subjects or two objects, or an adjective is used to modify two nouns—although the verb or adjective is appropriate to only one noun. *Zeugma* is often unintentional, as in "She caught a cold and a husband" but it is a common satrical device. An example often quoted is Dickens's phrase in the *Pickwick Papers*: "Miss Bobo . . . went straight home, in a flood of tears, and a sedan chair."

Z-gram.   Chief of U.S. Naval Operations, Admiral Elmo Zumwalt, issued terse, direct memos that were models of conciseness and clarity. These were dubbed *Z-grams* in the 1960s and became naval slang for such model memos, a thing rare in the armed services.

zhlub.   *Zhlub* has during the past fifteen years or so been slang for an insensitive, boorish person. It derives from the Yiddish *zhlub*, meaning the same, which, in turn, comes from a Slavic word. A variation is *zhlob*.

zigzag.   To *zigzag*, to make frequent sharp turns from side to side, probably comes from the German *Zickzack*, which is an echoic word possibly formed of the elements *ziche*, "to dodge about" and *zacke*, "a serrated edge." The word came into English, from the French *zigzag*, in the early 18th century.

zigzag course.   This term probably arose during World War I. A *zigzag course* is a ship's course first to the right of the base course and then to the left. It was originally used in avoiding enemy submarines, but the term is now applied to any devious action.

zilch.   *Zilch*, "nothing," is an Americanism that has been traced back to the 1920s when a *Joe Zilch* meant a good for nothing college boy. Other sources, however, trace the expression to a character called Mr. Zilch in a *Ballyhoo* magazine cartoon series of the 1930s, in which Mr. Zilch was never seen but scantily clad, wide-eyed girls, reacting to things he had obviously done, cried "Oh, Mr. Zilch!" Since Mr Zilch wasn't depicted, according to this theory, he came to represent nothing, or *zilch*.

zillionaire.   *Zillionaire*, for someone with wealth of mythical proportions, is an Americanism that appears to date back only to the late 1940s or early 1950s. (*See* **millionaire**.)

zinc.   The German *Zinc* is the direct ancestor of our metal *zinc*, first attested to in 1651, but the origin of the German word is obscure—though it may be linked with the German *Zin*, for "tin."

zinnia.   *Youth and old age*, the *zinnia* species *elegans* is called and anyone who has seen how profusely the annual flower blooms and how quickly it succumbs to the first frost will appreciate the folk name. The same applies to all the zinnia genus, which Linnaeus named for Johann Gottfried Zinn, whose life was as bright and brief as his namesake's. Zinn, a German botanist and physician who was a professor of medicine at Gottingen, died in 1759 when barely thirty-two. In 1753 he had published what is said to be the first book of the anatomy of the eye. There are about fifteen species of the *zinnia*, which is the state flower of Indiana. Most modern tall forms, with flowers in many colors, come from the Mexican *Zinnia elegans* introduced in 1886 and growing to heights of about three feet. Another explanation for *elegans'* youth-and-old-age nickname may be the stiff hairs on the stem or the coarse plant itself, in contrast to the soft flowers, or the plant's tendency to develop the powdery mildew disease when poorly cultivated. But the spring frost analogy is nicer.

zip code; zip.   The *zip* in *zip-code* is an acronym for zone improvement *p*lan, an acronym that was invented to convey the idea of speed—zip! The system and name for it were introduced by the U.S. Post Office in 1963. A *zip*, for "a person of low intelligence" is also an acronym, deriving from the zero *i*ntelligence *p*otential of psychological jargon.

zipper.   According to one etymologist: "In 1921 B.F. Goodrich Company thought that overshoes equipped with slide fasteners would create a sensation and in 1923 hit upon the word 'zipper' as the trademark for the new galoshes." Other experts, however, trace the word back to the 1890s. The confusion probably lies in the fact that the zipper was *invented* in 1893, by one Whitman L. Judson, who called it the Universal Fastener and patented it as the "clasp locker or unlocker for [highbutton] shoes." His invention went through various name changes—including the *C-Curity* (the first zipper for men's flies), and the *hookless fastener*—before an anonymous executive at Goodrich came up with *zipper*. In any case, Goodrich did not protect its trademark and anyone can make and sell zippers today.

zizzer. Since at least 1930, *zizz* has meant "to sleep" in the British navy because the word is suggestive of snoring. From this came the naval slang *zizzer*, for "bed," mainly confined to British English.

zodiac. Many people know the signs of the *zodiac*: Taurus, the bull; Pisces, the fishes, etc. But few know the origin of the word *zodiac* itself. *Zodiac* derives from the Greek *zoon*, "animal," being so named, of course, because most of the signs were named for animals.

zombie. Zombie was originally the snake god worshipped in West Indian voodoo ceremonies based upon the worship of the python god in West Africa. Since dead people were said to be brought to life in these ceremonies, such imagined corpses shuffling along half dead and half alive were called *zombies*. By the 1920s this word naturally became applied to any oafish "dummy" without much intelligence or spirit. It is also the name of a cocktail that makes one feel like a zombie.

Zonta Club. *Zonta Club* is one of many service clubs composed of businesswomen. Its members are devoted to promoting world peace and fellowship. The club, founded in 1919, takes its name from the American Sioux Indian word *zonta*, meaning "to be trusted."

zoom. (*See* **onomatopoeia**.)

zoopraxiscope. One of the earliest motion picture projectors, the *zoopraxiscope* was built by photographer Eadweard Muybridge in about 1880 to project sequential pictures he had taken a few years earlier of a running horse—the pictures taken for railroad tycoon Leland Stanford, who had bet (correctly) $25,000 that a running horse sometimes had all four feet off the ground at the same time. Muybridge coined the word from the Greek elements *zoi*, "living" + praxis, "action" + *skopein*, "viewing instrument." He seems to have first called the instrument the *zoogyroscope*.

Zoysia grass. For some odd reason none of the major dictionaries include *Zoysia grass*, which is commonly planted today, especially for play areas and for lawns in the deep South. The popular grass, generally planted by bits of rootstock called Zoysia plugs, is named for Austrian botanist Karl von Zois. There are only four species of the creeping grass. Zoysia takes a lot of wear and tear, forming a dense, tough turf, but has one major drawback—it turns a haylike color in the late fall and is among the slowest of grasses to green up again in the spring. Some zealous Zoysia lawn keepers give nature a tender, loving hand by painting their grass with green latex and other preparations in the off-seasons. Yet another reason why anyone reincarnated in suburbia wouldn't do badly if he came back as a lawn.

z's. *Z's* is American slang for sleep. Originating within the last twenty-five years or so, the term probably derives from the *Z's* indicating snoring in comic strip and cartoon captions, which themselves represent the sound of snoring.

zwieback. Zwieback is a hard dry toast popular with adults and even made specifically for babies. The word, first recorded here in 1894, is a German one meaning "twice baked."

Zwinglian. Pertaining to Huldreich Zwingli or his doctrines. Huldreich or Ulrich Zwingli (1484-1531), a Swiss Protestant reformer, served as chaplain and standard bearer to troops fighting against Catholic sections of Switzerland that did not accept the official recognition of the Reformation. He was killed at the battle of Kappel. Zwingli's views were close to Martin Luther's, except for his purely symbolic interpretation of the Lord's Supper, which estranged the two men and made a united Protestantism impossible.

zyzzyva. Often destructive to plants, the *zyzzyva* (pronounced ziz-ih-vuh) weevil is a leaf-hopping insect of tropical America that provides one of the best examples of onomatopoeia at work in the creation of words. Although most dictionaries give its origin as "obscure," if they give it at all, the word probably derives from the Spanish *ziz, zas!*, which is "echoic of the impact of a blow," the reference being, of course, to the noise made by these cicada-like insects.

ZZZ. ZZZ has been used by cartoonists to represent the sound of snoring for fifty years or so. In any case, the last possible word with which to end an alphabetically arranged word book is ZZZ, unless there is somewhere an unrecorded ZZZZ . . .